McDONALD INSTITUTE MONOGRAPHS

Changing materialities at Çatalhöyük:
reports from the 1995–99 seasons

By Members of the Çatalhöyük teams

Edited by
Ian Hodder

Çatalhöyük Research Project Volume 5

BRITISH INSTITUTE AT ANKARA
BIAA Monograph No. 39

Çatalhöyük publications in this series:

Volume 1 *On the surface: Çatalhöyük 1993–95,*
edited by Ian Hodder (ISBN 0-9519420-3-4)
Volume 2 *Towards reflexive method in archaeology: the example at Çatalhöyük,*
edited by Ian Hodder (ISBN 1-902937-02-3)
Volume 3 *Excavating Çatalhöyük: South, North and KOPAL Area reports from the 1995–99 seasons,*
edited by Ian Hodder (ISBN 1-902937-27-9)
Volume 4 *Inhabiting Çatalhöyük: reports from the 1995–99 seasons,*
edited by Ian Hodder (ISBN 1-902937-22-8)
Volume 5 *Changing materialities at Çatalhöyük: reports from the 1995–99 seasons,*
edited by Ian Hodder (ISBN 1-902937-28-7)
Volume 6 *Çatalhöyük perspectives: themes from the 1995–99 seasons,*
edited by Ian Hodder (ISBN 1-902937-29-5)

Published jointly by:

McDonald Institute for Archaeological Research
University of Cambridge
Downing Street
Cambridge, UK
CB2 3ER
(0)(1223) 339336
(0)(1223) 333538 (General Office)
(0)(1223) 333536 (FAX)
dak12@cam.ac.uk
www.mcdonald.cam.ac.uk

British Institute at Ankara
10 Carlton House Terrace
London, UK
SW1Y 5AH
(0)(20) 7969 5204
(0)(20) 7969 5401 (FAX)
biaa@britac.ac.uk
www.biaa.ac.uk

Distributed by Oxbow Books
United Kingdom: Oxbow Books, Park End Place, Oxford, OX1 1HN, UK.
Tel: (0)(1865) 241249; Fax: (0)(1865) 794449; www.oxbowbooks.com
USA: The David Brown Book Company, P.O. Box 511, Oakville, CT 06779, USA.
Tel: 860-945-9329; Fax: 860-945-9468

ISBN: 1-902937-28-7
ISSN: 1363-1349 (McDonald Institute)
0969-9007 (BIAA)

Edited for the Institute by Chris Scarre (*Series Editor*) and Dora A. Kemp (*Production Editor*).

Cover illustration: *Beads in child burial from Building 6 in the South Area of Çatalhöyük.*

Printed and bound by Short Run Press, Bittern Rd, Sowton Industrial Estate, Exeter, EX2 7LW, UK.

CONTENTS

Contributors

Erhan Akça	University of Çukurova, Adana
K. Göze Akoğlu	Department of Physics / Archaeometry, Middle East Technical University
Sonya Atalay	Department of Anthropology, University of California, Berkeley
Adnan Baysal	Department of Archaeology, University of Liverpool
Petya Blumbach	School of Geography and the Environment, Oxford University
Céline Bressy	UMR 6636 of CNRS-ESEP, Institut Dolomieu, France
Tristan Carter	Department of Cultural and Social Anthropology, Stanford University
Craig Cessford	Cambridge Archaeological Unit, Cambridge
Kate Clark	School of Chemistry, University of Bristol
James Conolly	Institute of Archaeology, University College London
Mark Copley	School of Chemistry, University of Bristol
Sarah Cross May	English Heritage
Richard Evershed	School of Chemistry, University of Bristol
M. Cemal Göncüoğlu	Department of Geological Engineering, Middle East Technical University
Naomi Hamilton	Department of Archaeology, University of Edinburgh
Thomas Higham	Oxford Radiocarbon Accelerator Unit, Oxford University
Ian Hodder	Department of Cultural and Social Anthropology, Stanford University
Brian Jackson	National Museums of Scotland
Selim Kapur	University of Çukurova, Adana
Asena Kizilarslanoğlu	University of Çukurova, Adana
Peter I. Kuniholm	Wiener Laboratory, Cornell University
Jonathan Last	English Heritage
Sturt W. Manning	Department of Archaeology, Reading University
Slobodan Mitrović	Çatalhöyük Research Project
Maryanne W. Newton	Wiener Laboratory, Cornell University
Mustafa Özbakan	Department of Physics / Archaeometry, Middle East Technical University
Serap Özdöl	University of Ege, İzmir
Ay Melek Özer	Department of Physics / Archaeometry, Middle East Technical University
Nicholas J.G. Pearce	Institute of Geography and Earth Sciences, University of Wales, Aberystwyth
Gérard Poupeau	Centre de Recherche en Physique Appliquée à l'Archéologie, Institut de Recherche sur les Archéomatériaux, Pessac, France
Nerissa Russell	Department of Anthropology, Cornell University
Musa Serdem	University of Çukurova, Adana
Ana Spasojević	Department of Cultural and Social Anthropology, Stanford University
John G.H. Swogger	Çatalhöyük Research Project
Vedat Toprak	Department of Geological Engineering, Middle East Technical University
Burcu Tung	Department of Anthropology, University of California, Berkeley
Ali Umut Türkcan	Department of Archaeology, University of Anadolu, Eskisehir
Asuman G. Türkmenoğlu	Department of Geological Engineering, Middle East Technical University
James F. Vedder	Los Altos Hills, California
Willeke Wendrich	Cotsen Institute of Archaeology, UCLA
Katherine I. Wright	Institute of Archaeology, University College London

Figures

Tables

Acknowledgements

This publication of four volumes (Volumes 3, 4, 5 and 6 in the British Institute at Ankara / McDonald Institute Monograph Series), would not have been possible without the help of a large number of individuals, institutions and sponsors. We have attempted to list everyone who assisted the Çatalhöyük Research Project during the period of excavation (1995–99) and post-excavation work (2000–03) covered in these volumes and apologies are extended to anyone who has been inadvertently overlooked.

Funding for the field research was provided by a wide variety of corporate and academic bodies. Academic bodies include the British Academy / Arts and Humanities Research Board, the British Institute at Ankara, the Turkish Ministry of Culture and Tourism, the Newton Trust, the McDonald Institute for Archaeological Research, the European Union, the National Geographic Society, Kress Foundation, the Heber-Percy Trust, Lloyd Cotsen, Dayton Foundation, the Flora Family Foundation, Stanford University, National Science Foundation and the Polish Academy of Sciences.

Corporate sponsorship without which the Çatalhöyük Research Project would be impossible has included generous contributions from Koçbank, Boeing, Koçsistem, Visa International, Fiat, Merko, Glaxo-Wellcome, British Airways, Thames Water and Shell. Other support has been provided by IBM, Pepsi, Eczacıbaşı, Arup, Meptur and the Turkish Friends of Çatalhöyük, especially Reşit Ergener. Substantial personal donations have been made by Mr John Coker, and other donations were made by Mrs Dorothy Cameron and Mary Settegast.

The main institutional partners of the Çatalhöyük Research Project have been Cambridge University, Stanford University, University of California at Berkeley, University College London, Liverpool University, Middle East Technical University, Poznań University, and the University of Thessaloniki. Many other institutions have supported or contributed to the project in some way. In particular, I would like to mention the Science Museum of Minnesota, Museum of London, Museum of London Archaeology Service, University of Pennsylvania, University of Sheffield, University of Wales at Cardiff, the Museum of Natural History, Selcuk University, Istanbul University and Karlsruhe Media-Technology Institute.

The project also wishes to thank Ömer Koç for his continued support of the project in many ways.

The project works in Turkey with a permit from the Ministry of Culture and Tourism, General-Directorate of Cultural Heritage and Museums. Over the period covered by these publications much support and advice was given by the department and I would particularly like to thank the Director Generals M. Akif Işık, Engin Özgen, Kenan Yurttagül, Ender Varinlioğlu, Dr Alpay Pasinli, Nadir Avcı and the Assistant Director Generals Ömer Yiğit Sayılgan, Necati Ayaz, M. Aykut Özet, Abdülkadir Karaoğlu, Kenan Yurttagül and İlhan Kaymaz.

The project works under the auspices of the British Institute at Ankara. We would like to thank Sir Timothy Daunt and the directors David French, acting director David Shankland, Roger Matthews and Hugh Elton as well as the administrators Gülgün Girdivan (formerly Kazan), Yaprak Eran in Ankara and Gina Coulthard in London. Additionally we are grateful for the support of the BIAA committee members for continued support, the Ambassadors Özdem Sanberk, Korkmaz Haktanir, Akın Alptuna and staff at the Turkish Embassy and consulate in London and the Ambassadors Kieran Prendergast, David Logan and Peter Westmacott, and staff at the British Embassy in Ankara. The patrons of the project are Professor Lord Renfrew of Kaimsthorn and Sir David Attenborough. Board members have included Sir Mark Russell, George Warren, John Curtis, Nicholas Postgate, Lady Diana Daunt, Andrew Sherratt, Trevor Watkins, Malcolm Wagstaff, Christopher Stevenson, Charly French, Martin Jones, Chris Scarre and Sevket Sabancı.

Special thanks must be made to the government temsilci (representatives) who were Ali Önder (1995), Baykal Aydınbek and Osman Ermişler (1996), İlhame Öztürk and Gülcan Küçükkaraaşlan (1997), Edip Özgür (1998), Osman Ermişler, Recep Okçu, Edip Özgür, Candan Nalbantoğlu, (1999), Vahap Kaya and Enver Akgün (2000), Dursun Çağlar and Nejat Atar (2001), Rahmi Asal and Yaşar Yilmaz (2002) and Belma Kulaçoğlu (2003). The Museum of Anatolian Civilisations at Ankara, especially the director Ilhan Temiszoy have also been consistently helpful. We are indebted and ever grateful to Erdoğan Erol the director of the Konya Museums Services and his staff, in particular

Kazim Mertek who is curator of the Çatalhöyük artefacts stored in the Archaeological Museum.

In Konya help and support was provided at many levels. The Vali Ahmet Kayhan, the Cultural Directors Osman Siviloğlu and Necip Mutlu, the Director of the Koruma Korulu Ayhan Alp, the DSI (Turkish Water Authority), officers at the Emniyet, our bank managers Aydın Kimyonşen and Arif Kutluca, our accountant Ahmet İçyer. In the local town of Çumra we are much appreciative of the help of the Kaymakams Bülent Savur, Abdullah Aslan, İbrahim Öğüz, Adem Yilmaz, Osman Bilgen, Osman Taşkan and the Belediye Başkans Recip Konuk, the late Abidin Ünal and Zeki Türker. We would also like to extend our thanks to İbrahim Gökce from the local fire brigade who provided water on 'dry days', our local doctor Ömer Yıldırım, health officer Abdullah Akpınar and the Jandarma commitants. At our local store Abdullah Yetiş has always been on hand to help and metal workers Ayhan and Musa Veziroğlu and carpenters Sami Güdül and sons have produced some of our more challenging constructions on site.

We are also grateful for the support of Pelin Ulusoy Tepret amd Yilmaz Ulusoy, all the members of Atolye Mimarlık — Ridvan Övünç, Ceren Balkir, Sinan Omacan and Didem Teksoz. The Hilton Hotel in Konya, in particular Emrullah Akçakaya. The Büyük Londra Hotel in Istanbul, Roget Short and Asim Kaplan from Karavan.

From the local village of Küçükköy we would like to thank the people and their muhtar Huseyin Ceviz. The work would be impossible without the local men and women who work with us at the site. The excavations were ably assisted by Ismail Yaşli who was our site foreman from 1995–99 and Arif Arslan, Ridvan Büyüktemiz, Riza Büyüktemiz, Mehmet Çağlar, Kemal Fati, Ahmet Kayserlı, Hakan Kılıçarslan, Mehmet Kuşçuoğlu, Taner Kuşçuoğlu, Marem Köse, Galip Kiraz, Halil Nurkoyuncu, Osman Özdil, Mehmet Salmancı, Metin Yilmaz, Mevlut Sivas, Mustafa Sivas, Mustafa Yaş, Gazi Yaşlı, Hülusi Yaşlı, Hasan Yaşlı, Hüseyin Yaşlı, Hüseyin Veli Yaşlı, Mustafa Veli Yaşlı, Osman Yaşlı, Paşa Yaşlı, Veli Yaşlı, Tamer Yiğit, Mustafa Zetin. A team of women have the laborious task of sorting through heavy-residue samples which they do with amazing enthusiasm, Dane Gökdağ, Nesrin Günaşık, Ayfer Kiraz, Hafize Sarıkaya, Saliha Sivas, Gülcan Tüfekçi, Fadimana Yaşlı, Fatima Yaşlı, Hatice Yaşlı, Hülya Yaşlı, Rabiya Yaşlı, Saliha Yaşlı, Şenay Yaşlı and Suna Yaşlı.

The teams at the site have been fed and watered by our cook Ismail Salmancı and kept in comfort by our house staff who have been Rükiye Salmancı, Nevriye Şener, Necati and Nazmiye Terzioğlu and their daughter Nefise, Mavili Tokyağsun and Teslime Tüfekçi. Our camp managers who undertook momentous bureaucratic procedures as well as many thankless tasks for the smooth running of the camp and project. They were Özgür Özdilsiz, Özkan Köse, Murat Ufuk Kara, Cinar Dirim, Tolga Pekperdahçı, Melih Pekperdahçı and Hüsnü Tayanç. The site has been ably protected by the local guards Mustafa and Hasan Tokyağsun, Sedrettin Dural, Sadet Kuşçuoğlu, and Ibrahim Eken.

During the period in question the project was ably administered by Amanda Cox, Josephine Stubbs, Becky Coombs, Christina Clements, Jackie Ouchikh and Katerina Johnson with support from Colin Lomas of the McDonald Institute. Anja Wolle provided invaluable computer support. The site directors were Roger Matthews (1993–96) and Shahina Farid (1997– to present), to whom I and the entire project are deeply indebted.

A special thanks is owed to all those who worked at the site in the period covered by this volume 1995–99. Their names include the following: Meltem Ağcabey, Engin Akdeniz, Göze Akoğlu, Ali Akin Akyol, Mary Alexander, Peter Andrews, Steve Archer, Başak Arda, Michael Ashley-Lopez, Eleni Asouti, Sonya Atalay (Suponcic), Meral Atasağun, Banu Aydinoğluğil, Douglas Baird, Michael Balter, Jason Bass, Adnan Baysal, Harriet Beaubien, Åsa Berggren, Zeynep Beykont, Nurhayat Bilge, Hatice Bilgiç, Ömer Bilgin, Catherine Bonner, Dušan Borić, Peter Boyer, Başak Boz, Mehmet Bozdemir, Keith Bradflaad, Jenny Bredenberg, Dorothée Brill, Jasmina Brinkhuizen, Deniz Bulak, Ann Butler, Ivan Butorac, Ayfer Bartu Candan, Can Candan, Tristan Carter, Thomas Cawdron, Dagmar Cee, Serdar Cengiz, Craig Cessford, Adrian Chadwick, Adam Cohen, James Conolly, Anwen Cooper, Bruno Coppola, Chris Cumberpatch, Aylin Çavdar, Predrag Dakic, Daniela Delfs, Meltem Delibaşı, Burghard Detzler, Jo Deverenski, Clark Dobbs, Linda Donley-Reid, Louise Doughty, Miriam Doutriaux, Warren Eastwood, Makbule Ekici, Martin Emele, Aylan Erkal, Amanda Erwin, Arturo Escobar, Freja Evans-Swogger, Andrew Fairbairn, Lindsay Falck, Shahina Farid, Lu'chen Foster, Sheelagh Frame, Alexander Gagnon, Duncan Garrow, Adriana Garza, Robert Geiger, Soultana Geroussi, Catriona Gibson, Caitlin Gordon, Atakan Güven, Lori Hager, Carolyn Hamilton, Charlotte Hamilton, Naomi Hamilton, Christine Hastorf, Stamatis Hatzitoulousis, Margaret Hauselt, Lucy Hawkes, Emily Hayes, Chris Hills, Ayşe Hortacsu, Liz Hunt, Vladimir Ilic, Ioannis Imamidis, Brian Jackson, Emma Jenkins, Don Johnson, Azize Kadayifci, Elif Kavas, Nurcan Kayacan, Amanda Kennedy, Kathryn Killackey, the late Heinrich Klotz,

Mark Knight, Afriditi Konstantinidou, Evan Kopelson, Kostas Kotsakis, Perihan Kösem, Esin Kuleli, Aslı Kutsal, Emine Küçük, Evangelia Kyriatzi, Despina Lahandiou, Paul Lapinski, Jonathan Last, Su Leaver, Leola Leblanc, Nessa Leibhammer, Sara Leuke,Tonya Van Leuvan-Smith, Claudia Lopez, Gavin Lucas, the late Maria Magkafa, Tona Majo, Harpreet Malhi, Louise Martin, Daniéle Martinoli, Sabrina Maras, Frank Matero, Roger Matthews, Wendy Matthews, Stephanie Meece, David Meiggs, Sinan Mellaart, Jamie Merrick, Boris Michalski, William Middleton, Arlene Miller Rosen, Dragana Milosevic, Slobodan Mitrović, Theya Molleson, Caitlin Moore, Peter Moore, Joseph Mora, Rachel Moritz, Elizabeth Moss, Cassie Myers, Julie Near, Charlie Newman, Aglaia Nitsou, Vladimir Novaković, Aylin Orbaşlı, Emin Murat Özdemir, Serap Özdöl, Latif Özen, Jessica Pearson, Paolo Pelegatti, Don Pohlman, Tom Pollard, Dietmar Puttman, Tiffany Raszick, Tim Ready, David Reese, Roddy Regan, Michael Richards, Tim Ritchey, Neil Roberts, Celia Rothmund, Natalie Rusk, Nerissa Russell, Andy Schoenhofer, Joshua Seaver, Kent Severson, Orrin Shane, David Shankland, Julia Shaw, Colin Shell, Connie Silver, David Small, Lothar Spree, Laura Steele, Mirjana Stevanović, John-Gordon Swogger, Robert Symmons, Jez Taylor, Jo Taylor, Vuk Trifković, Ruth Tringham, Sybilla Tringham, Burcu Tunc, Richard Turnbull, Catherine Turton, Ali Türkcan, Mustafa Türker, Asuman Türkmenoğlu, Katheryn Twiss, Mehmet Uluceviz, Heidi Underbjerg, Anne Marie Vandendriesch, James Vedder, Dimitrios Vlachos, Margarete Vöhringer, Thomas Vollherbst, Barbara Voss, Trevor Watkins, Sharon Webb, Willeke Wendrich, Fabian Winkler, Anja Wolle, Michelle Wollestonecroft, Martin Wrede, Nurcan Yalman, Lisa Yeomans, Çiçek Yildu and Levent Zoroğlu.

Team members who worked on publication material off-site included: Erhan Akça, Alexander Bentley, Wendy Birch, Petya Blumbach, Céline Bressy, Ian Bull, Kate Clark, Mark Copley, Sarah Cross May, Şahinde Demirci, Mohammed Elhmmali, Begumşen Ergenekon, Richard Evershed, Cemal Göncüoğlu, Thomas Higham, Huw Griffiths, Elizabeth Hadly, John Hather, Gordon Hillman, David Jenkins, Selim Kapur, Asena Kızılarslanoğlu, Peter Kuniholm, Ripan Malhi, Sturt Manning, Kevin McGowan, Joanna Mountain, Maryanne Newton, Mustafa Özbakan, Aymelek Özer, Nicholas Pearce, Vincent Perret, Gérard Poupeau, Douglas Price, David Roberts, Claire Scudder, Musa Serdem, Jane Sidell, Wim van Neer, Marcel van Tuinen, Vedat Toprak, Asuman Türkmenoğlu, John Williams and Katherine Wright.

Volumes 3–6 in this series would not have been produced without the work of Craig Cessford. The project, and I particularly, owe him an enormous debt in pulling the reports and work together into these volumes. Assistance has also been given by Louise Doughty, Shahina Farid, Katerina Johnson and Anja Wolle. Many illustrations in these volumes are a team effort but final figures have been produced by Craig Cessford, Helen Jones, Dora Kemp, Sophie Lamb, Duncan Lees, Margaret Matthews and Anja Wolle. Reconstructions are the work of John Swogger and photographic images were taken by project members unless cited. We also wish to thank the anonymous reviewers for their comments and suggestions.

Finally we are very grateful to Dora Kemp, Production Editor for the McDonald Institute Monograph Series whose hard work and dedication to high-quality publication standards has reproduced our work to its best advantage.

As always it is a special pleasure to acknowledge the continuing input of James and Arlette Mellaart and their son Alan. The continued work at the site would not have been possible without their understanding and kindness. It cannot have been easy to hand over such a remarkable site to a new team. I am deeply grateful to them for continuing to support our work and for having the generosity of spirit to remain as advisors and mentors for us. It was a particular pleasure to have James and Arlette's grandson Sinan Mellaart work with us at the site in 2001.

Chapter 1

Changing Entanglements and Temporalities

Ian Hodder

This volume (Volume 5 in the sequence of McDonald Institute/British Institute of Archaeology at Ankara monographs publishing the work of the Çatalhöyük Research Project) discusses interpretation of the material obtained during excavation of the site from 1995 to 1999. Earlier work (on the surface of the mound in 1993–95) is published in Volume 1 in the same series (Hodder 1996), and the methodology is described in full in its own volume, Volume 2 (Hodder 2000). The excavation and the interpretation of contexts and buildings excavated in 1995–99 are described in Volume 3.

Volume 4 deals with various aspects of the inhabiting of Çatalhöyük. It discusses the relationship between the site and its environment, using a wide range of evidence from faunal and charred archaeobotanical remains to phytoliths, shells and charcoal. It looks at the evidence from human remains which inform us about diet and lifeways. It explores the ways in which houses and open spaces in the settlement were lived in. In all these ways, a picture is built up of the way in which people moved through and lived in the natural and cultural environment of Çatalhöyük.

Volume 5 deals with other aspects of the material culture excavated in the 1995–99 period. In particular it discusses the changing materiality of life at the site over its approximately 1100 years of occupation. It includes discussion of ceramics and other fired clay material, as well as chipped stone, ground stone, worked bone and basketry. As well as looking at typological and comparative issues in relation to these materials, the chapters explore themes such as the specialization and scale of production, the engagement in systems of exchange, and consumption, use and deposition. A central question concerns change through time, and the degree and speed of change. The occupants of the site increasingly get caught up in relations with material objects that start to act back upon them.

Volume 6 is also based on the 1995–99 excavations but its aim is synthetic, drawing on material from Volumes 3 to 5 to deal with broad themes. Data from architecture and excavation contexts are linked into broader discussion of topics such as seasonality, art and social memory.

Background and method

with contributions from Shahina Farid, Craig Cessford and the Çatalhöyük teams

Çatalhöyük (Fig. 1.1) was first excavated by James Mellaart in 1961–65 (Mellaart 1962; 1963; 1964a; 1966a,b; 1967). His work focused on the southwest area of the East Mound where over 160 buildings were excavated in 14 levels numbered from 0, I, II to XII. Level VI was subdivided into VIA and VIB. These excavations established the importance of the site as a large and densely-packed Neolithic 'town'. No further work was conducted at the site until the present project began in 1993. The first years of the project were spent in surface survey, and excavation began in earnest in 1995.

This volume is concerned with presenting the results of specialist analysis of material from three areas at Çatalhöyük, known as South, North and KOPAL (The KOnya Plain PALaeoenvironmental Project directed by Neil Roberts) (Fig. 1.2), excavated between 1995 and 1999. The excavations in the South Area between 1995 and 1999 were focused upon a 20 × 20 m area in the southwest part of the mound, which was investigated by James Mellaart in the 1960s. The main aim of our work in this area was to investigate the earlier phases at the site and to determine if waterlogged remains survived. To this end a range of buildings and external areas corresponding to his Levels VIB to XII, although Level VIII is the latest level where significant amounts have been investigated, plus earlier deposits designated Level Pre XII.A–E, were excavated. Located some 200 m to the northeast, the aims in the North Area, which was excavated between 1995 and 1998, were to investigate an entire structure on a part of the mound that had not been previously excavated. The KOPAL excavations consisted of a long trench across the northern flank of the mound to inves-

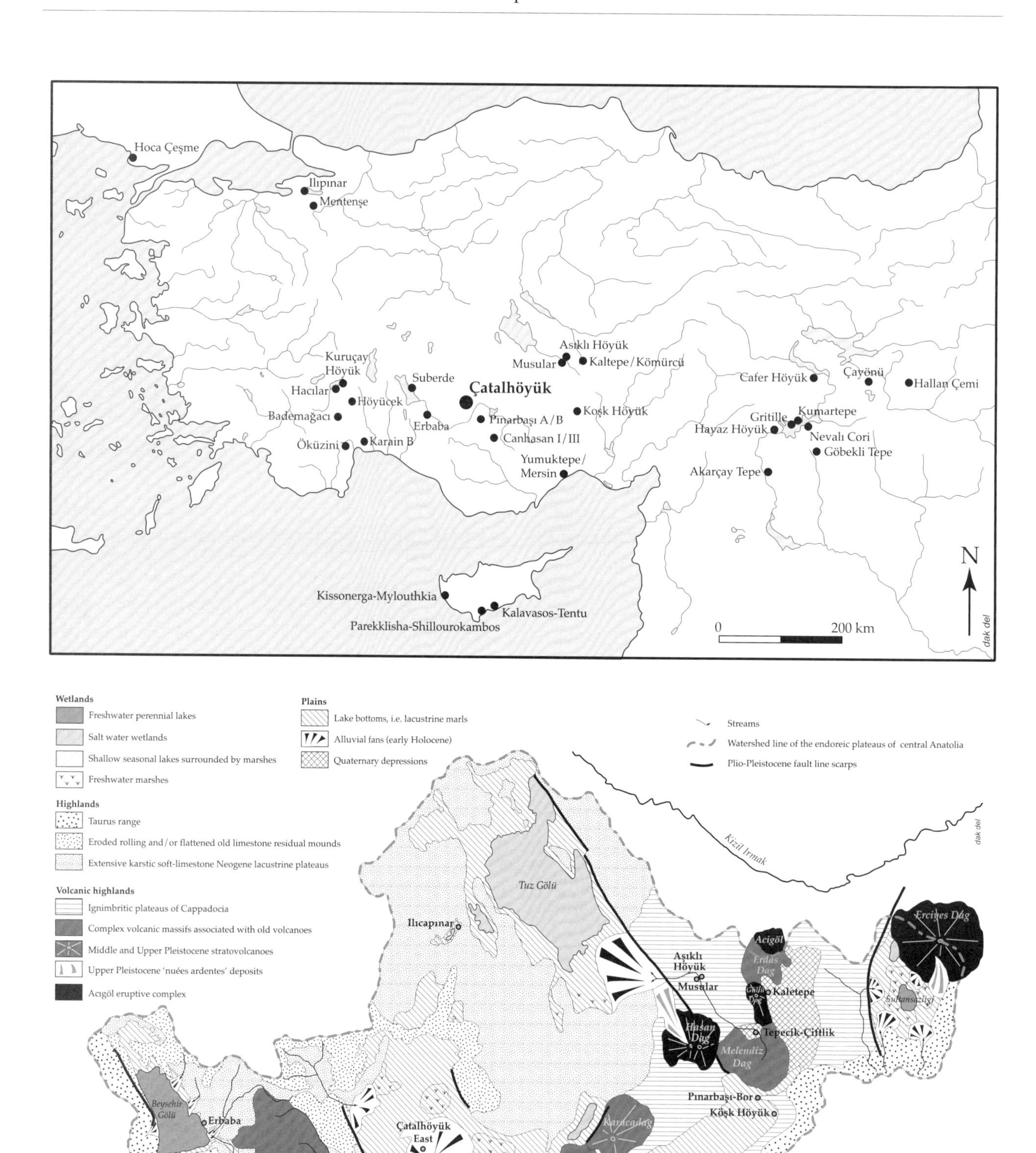

Figure 1.1. *Neolithic Anatolia and central Anatolia. Upper: Çatalhöyük in the context of contemporary sites in Anatolia and adjacent regions. Lower: the geomorphology of central Anatolia. (Redrawn from Kuzucuoğlu 2002, figs. 2–7.)*

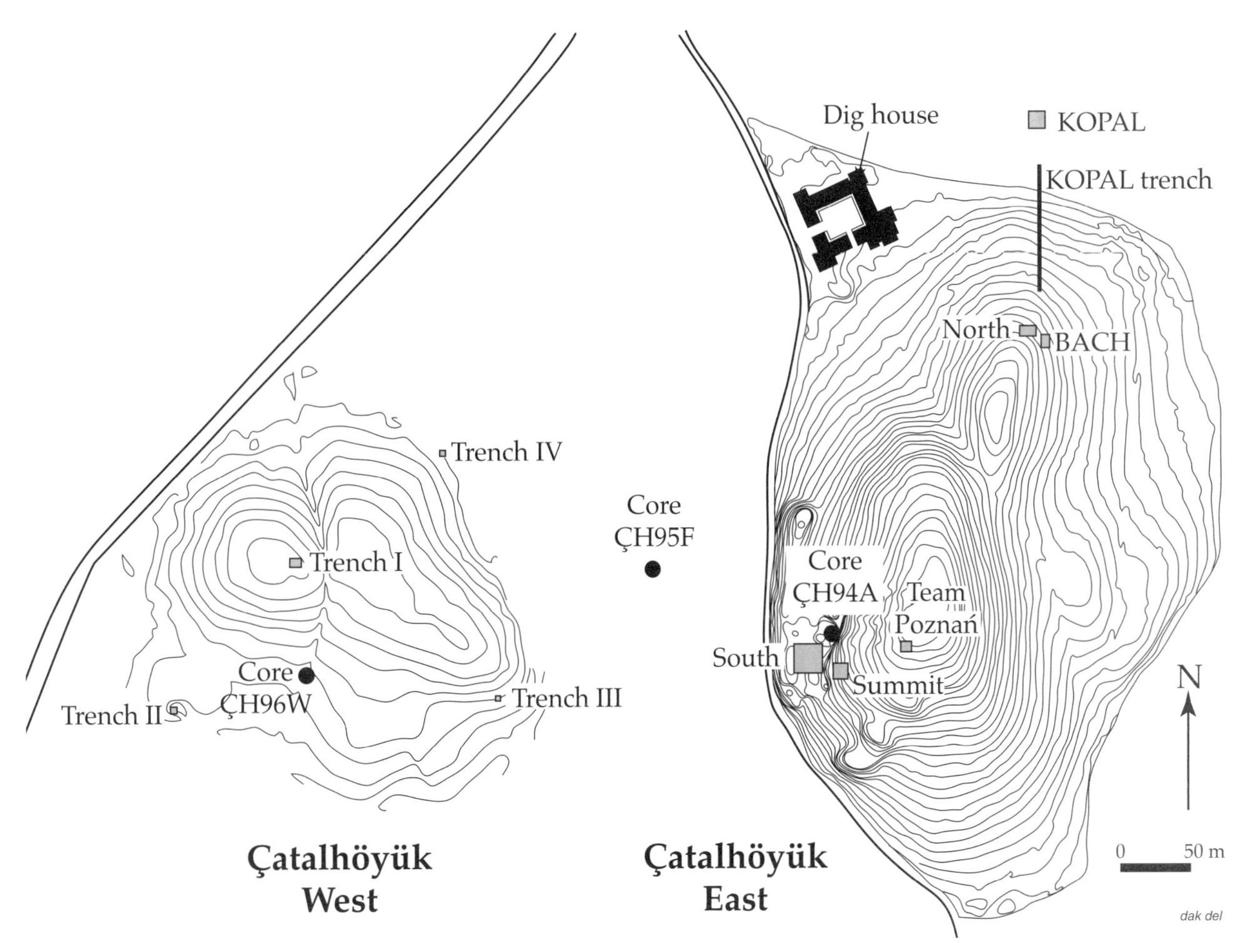

Figure 1.2. *Plan of Çatalhöyük East and West.*

tigate site-formation processes (1996–97) and an off-site area to the north of this to determine what natural and cultural deposits were present (1997 & 1999). At the same time excavation took place in a number of areas of the mound (BACH, Summit & Team Poznań) and on the adjacent Chalcolithic mound, Çatalhöyük West. Detailed results from these other areas will be presented in future volumes but where appropriate are discussed here. The results of the excavations in the South, North and KOPAL Areas are presented in Volume 3 (Parts 2, 3 & 4) and greater background information is given in the introduction in the same volume (Part 1). The aim of the following section is simply to present the information that is necessary to contextualize the reports in this volume. For further information Volume 3 Part 1 should be consulted.

A modified form of single-context (unit in the Çatalhöyük Research Project terminology) excavation and recording was employed, combined with an intensive and extensive sampling regime, including both wet and dry sieving. The unit (referred to as a four-figure number in brackets, such as (4279)) forms the basic element of a nested hierarchical system that includes features (groups of related units referred to as F. 27), space (spatially-bounded entities generally defined by the walls of buildings and referred to as space 203), buildings (groups of spaces forming a structural entity), areas (spatially-discrete location where excavation has occurred) and mounds. Chronological grouping is provided by phases / subphases (temporal divisions within a particular space or building, usually reflecting identified changes in the spatial organization or arrangement of a space of building) and levels (broadly contemporary groups of spaces and buildings based upon the system devised by James Mellaart in the 1960s).

Units are divided into five general categories. Layer describes construction / make-up / packing layers, deposits related to the construction of buildings and / or features, or a floor which is any deposit inside or outside a structure that forms a surface upon which activities of any sustained duration occur. Middens are described as layers which are deposits primarily related to the deliberate disposal of cultural material, again

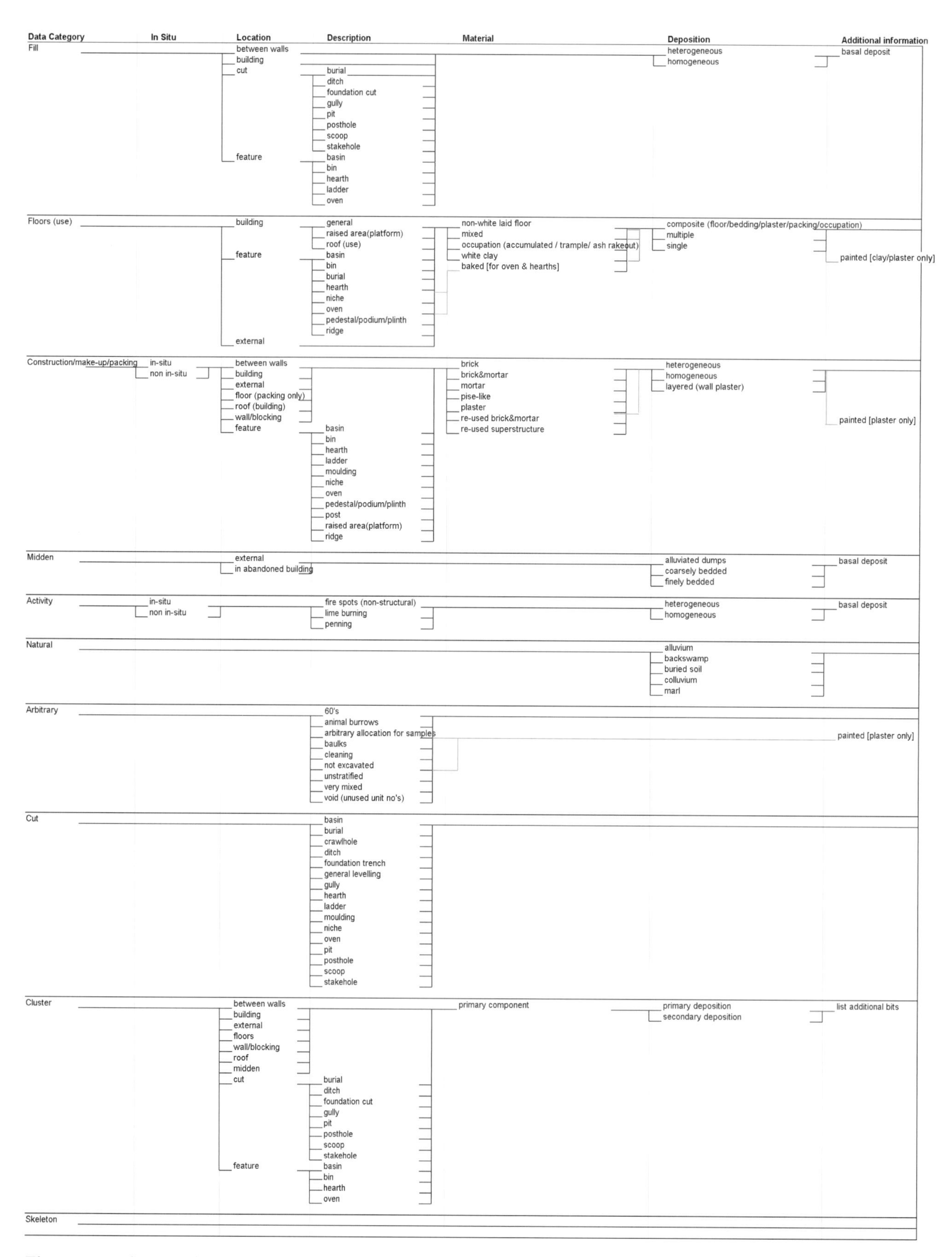

Figure 1.3. *The nested data category system.*

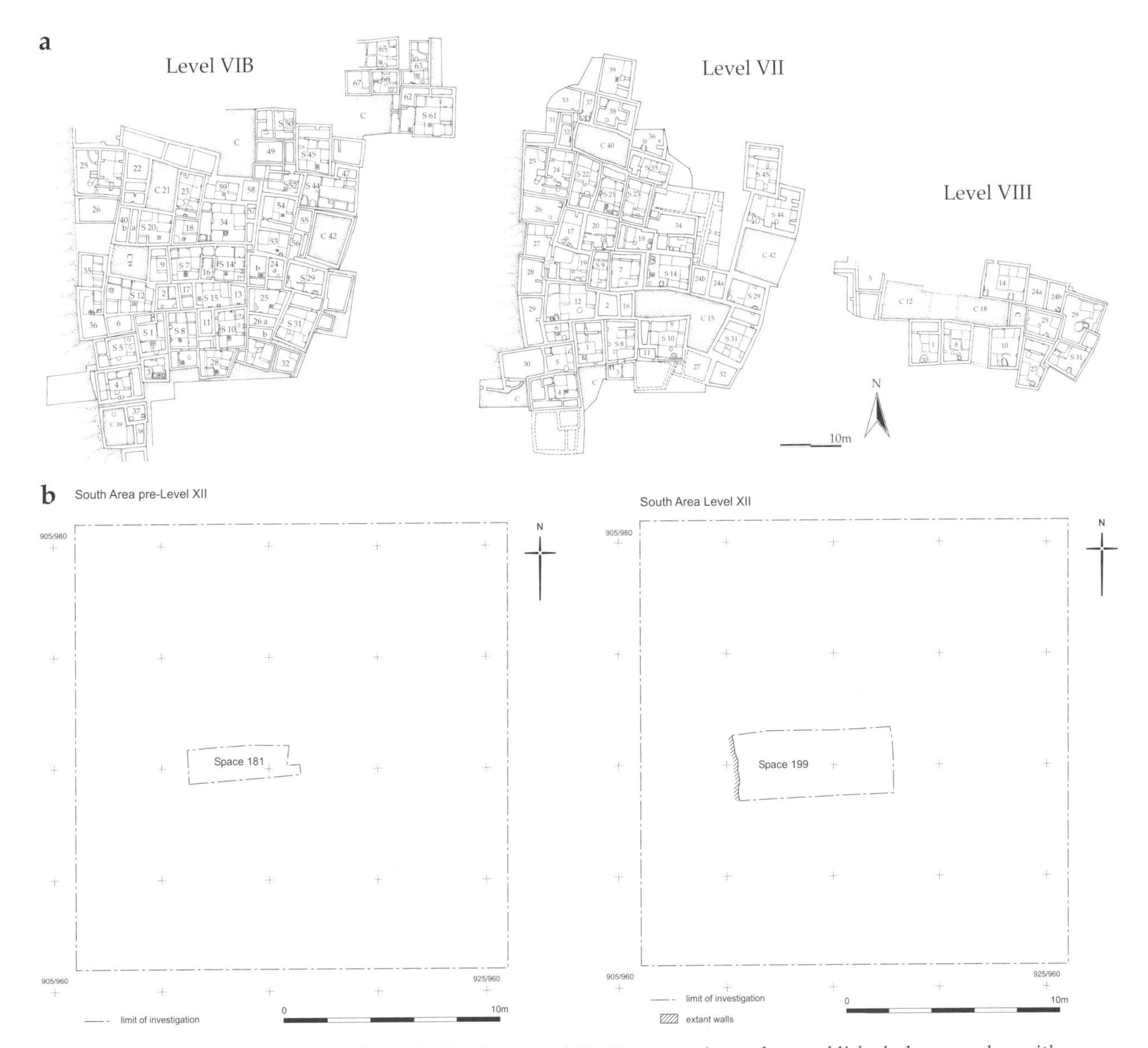

Figure 1.4. *Plans of excavated levels in the South Area: a) 1960s excavations where published plans overlap with recent excavations; b) recent excavations; c) location of South Area excavation in relation to 1960s excavation Level VII (building terms used by Mellaart are shown in italics).*

either outside or inside a structure. Fills are also layers that have been deposited in any form of negative space, be that a cut, the limits of an upstanding feature or a whole space or building. An arbitrary layer is a subdivision of a layer or a grouping of layers carried out for practical reasons during excavation. Clusters are discrete deposits of primarily material inclusions such as obsidian, bone, botanical material or a combination thereof, representing possible depositional significance. Skeletons describe human remains only and a cut is any recognizable event that led to the removal of another deposit. These general categories are further divided at post-excavation stage using fixed terminology to enable data search, into ten primary data categories of fill, floor, construction, midden, activity, natural, arbitrary, cut, cluster and skeleton (Fig. 1.3). Activity deposits relate to a heterogeneous range of activities that produce distinctive remains including fire spots, lime burning and penning, while natural refers to any deposit whose formation was primarily, but not necessarily exclusively, due to natural rather than cultural forces. These nested data categories then provide information on whether they are *in situ*, their location, their basic description, the material of which they are composed, the nature of their deposition, and whether they are a basal deposit.

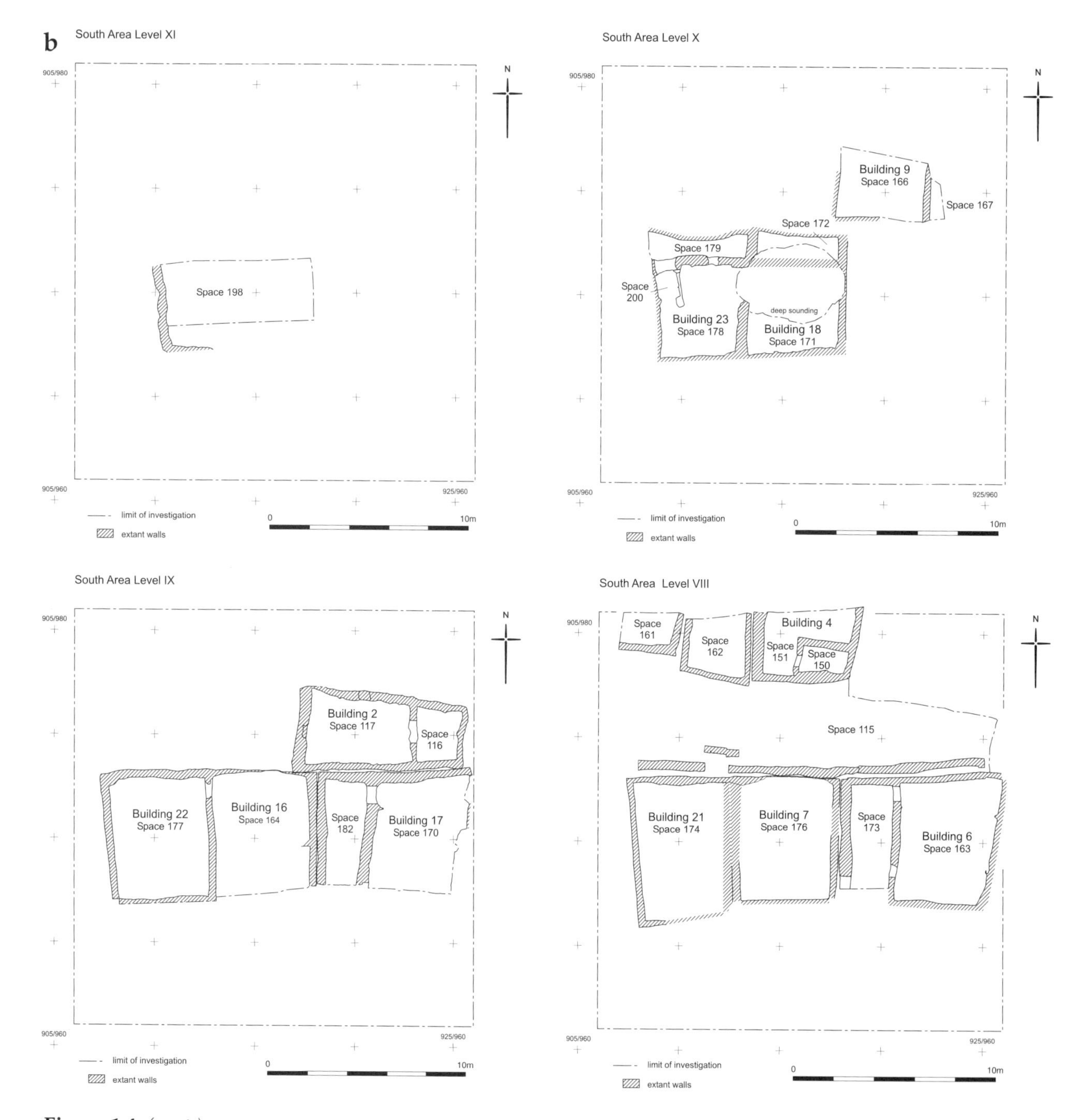

Figure 1.4. *(cont.)*

During excavation selected units were prioritized for study based on discussions between the excavators and laboratory specialists. This formed the basis for a group of 355 units that was studied by as many specialists as possible, representing around 10 to 20 per cent of the deposits excavated depending how this value is calculated. Statistical analysis (Chapter 2) suggests that they are a relatively good representation of the excavated data categories and levels (Figs. 2.1 & 2.2).

Bayesian analysis of all reliable radiocarbon determinations from Çatalhöyük using BCal (Buck *et al.* 1999) indicates that the main occupational sequence at Çatalhöyük revealed so far probably lasted around 950–1150 years, beginning at 7400–7100 cal BC and ending between 6200–5900 cal BC (Figs. 1.4 & 4.3). Of the various excavation areas with which the reports in this volume are concerned (see Figs. 1.4 & 1.5), the South Area (Levels Pre-XII.D to VIB) covers the earlier part of this sequence beginning between

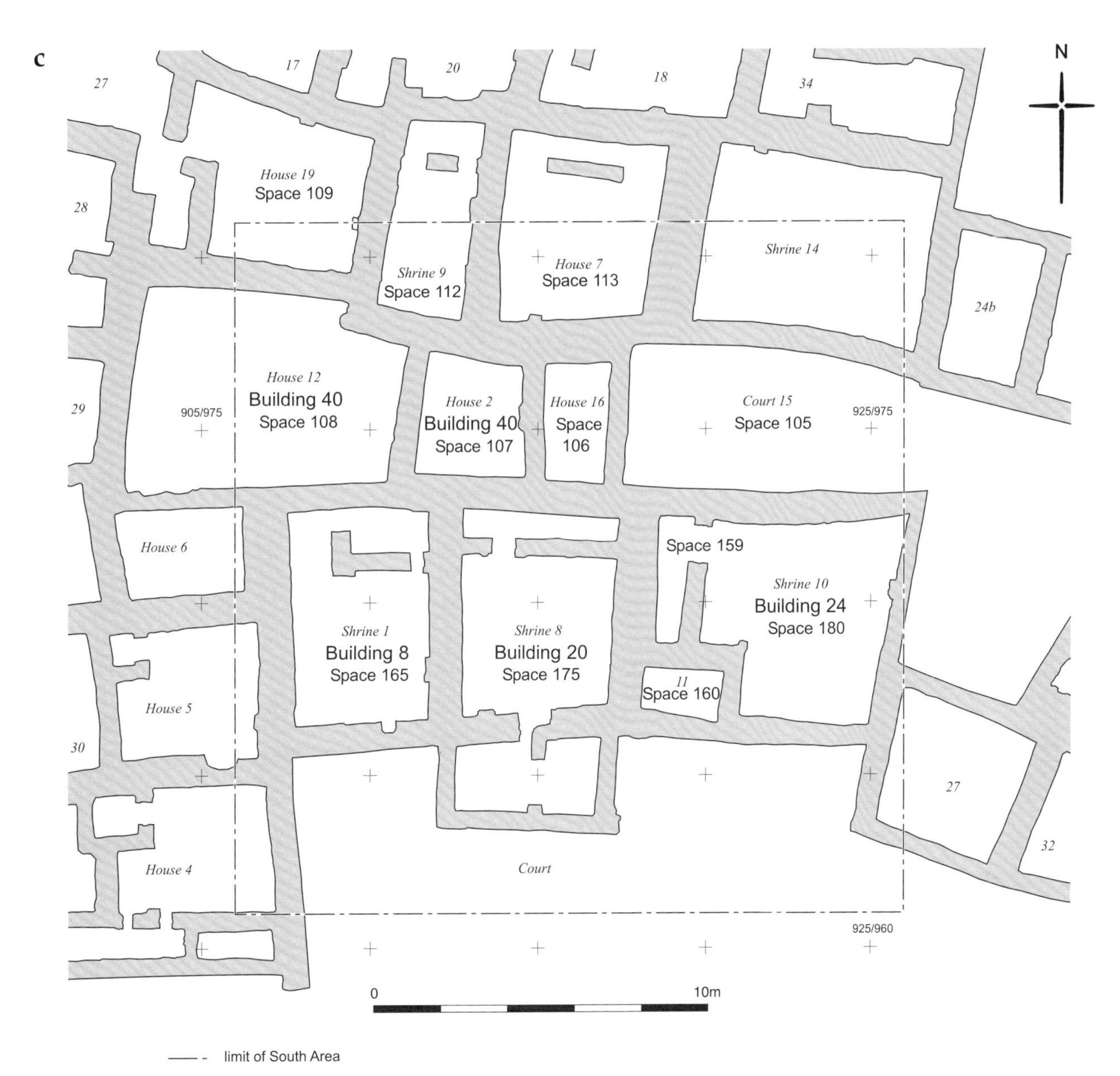

Figure 1.4. *(cont.)*

7400 and 7100 cal BC and ending between 6500 and 6300 cal BC. The pottery evidence suggests that the North Area deposits correspond to Levels VII and VI (Chapter 5), which is broadly supported by other artefactual evidence. Absolute dating would place the North Area deposits slightly earlier in Levels VIII and VII. The discrepancy is not great given various methodological issues discussed in Chapter 4 and the North Area excavations broadly overlap with the latest levels investigated between 1995 and 1999 in the South Area. The earliest activity in the off-site KOPAL Area has not been successfully radiocarbon dated, but the quarry pits and other possible related activities probably fall within the period of Level Pre-XII.B to IX and earlier activity there probably corresponds to Level Pre-XII.D to Pre-XII.B. The next phase of renewed natural backswamp clay formation can be equated to Levels XI to IX. Finally, the later buried soil horizons and land surfaces with some evidence of *in situ* cultural activity are either contemporary with or more probably slightly later than the end of occupation at Çatalhöyük East.

For comparative purposes with other central Anatolian sites Çatalhöyük is later than Aşıklı Höyük and Pınarbaşı A, while Canhasan III, Suberde and Musular overlap with parts of the Çatalhöyük sequence. Erbaba and Pınarbaşı B probably overlap with the later levels at Çatalhöyük, while Çatalhöyük West and Canhasan I are later than Çatalhöyük East. Further afield the occupation of Çatalhöyük overlaps with that of

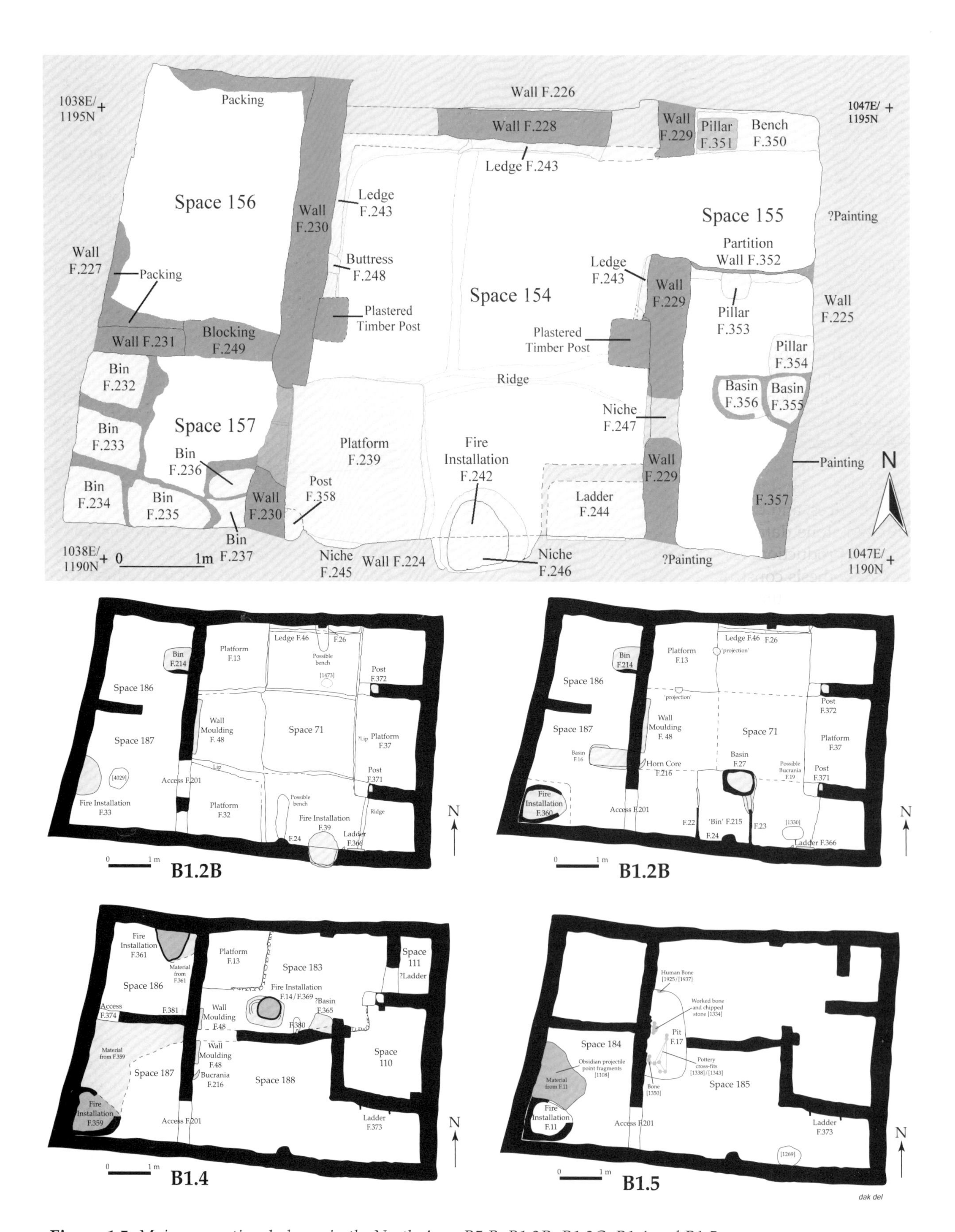

Figure 1.5. *Main occupational phases in the North Area, B5.B, B1.2B, B1.2C, B1.4 and B1.5.*

Bademağacı, Hacılar, Höyücek and Kuruçay Höyük in the Lake District, Karain B, Öküzini and Yumuktepe/Mersin on the Mediterranean coast, Akarçay Tepe, Cafer Höyük, Çayönü, Gritille, Hayaz Höyük and Kumartepe in southeast Anatolia and Hoca Çeşme, Ilıpınar and Mentense in northwest Anatolia.

Synopsis and integration

One of the most fascinating aspects of being involved in a project with large numbers of different types of scientific specialist is the integration of different types of data. In this chapter an attempt is made to select some of the results of the different specialists and to weave them together in terms of an overall synopsis of material entanglement and temporality at Çatalhöyük. What is remarkable is that often the different types of data coincide so that a stronger argument can be built. There are many examples below. For example, ceramic data fit with clay-ball data to document a shift in cooking practices, and bead data fit with worked-bone or chipped-stone data to suggest a primarily domestic mode of production. These fits do not constitute a 'test' of a hypothesis constructed on the basis of one type of data, though they are normally construed in such a way in archaeology. Rather, the process is a hermeneutic one. As more and more data seem to fit together, the argument is strengthened — but future data, or changes in perspective may lead to revisions.

The notion of 'materiality' has become of widespread interest in archaeology in recent years (e.g. Chapman 2000; Meskell forthcoming; Tilley 1999; and see articles in the *Journal of Material Culture*). These new interests in material culture have a complex heritage. They partly derive from structural Marxism and the importance of objective conditions (Friedman & Rowlands 1977), and from anthropological studies of material culture (Miller 1987; 1998), but they also come from practice theories (Bourdieu 1977), and from attempts to break down mind/body, subject/object oppositions in the phenomenological tradition (Thomas 1996). A similar emphasis on breaking down mind/object distinctions is found in the cognitive development and evolutionary psychology perspectives that have been championed by cognitive-processual archaeology (Donald 1991; DeMarrais *et al.* 1996; Mithen 1996). Another important contribution is from the French emphasis on technologies (e.g. Dobres 2000; Lemonnier 1993).

An approach which is of special relevance to Çatalhöyük has been proposed by Renfrew in a series of papers about shifts in materialization at the start of the Neolithic (1998b; 2001; 2003). Renfrew has identified a phase in cognitive development to add to the stages described by Donald (1991). Renfrew's phase of symbolic material culture has two subphases. The first is associated with sedentism and early farming. Here external symbolic storage in monuments and other material culture creates collective memory and socially-cohesive groups and ranks. The second is associated with the early use of metals. Gold, copper and bronze help to create notions of value and commodity on which wealth, prestige and further social ranking become based. It is especially the first subphase which is relevant to Çatalhöyük, although it could be argued that the exchange of beads and obsidian created value and prestige at the site.

In both subphases, the point emphasized by Renfrew is that the material objects do not just express social facts. Rather they constitute social concepts and relations. Thus they have an active role. Renfrew wishes to escape from mind/matter dichotomies, and to argue, in a tradition that extends back and across to Cartesian critics (Gell 1998; Heidegger 1927; Latour 1996; Merleau-Ponty 1962), that mind and object are mutually constitutive. Thus, the notion of a system of weights depends on the experience of heavy things. Renfrew talks of a hypostatic approach which transcends the mind/matter dichotomy and which can be termed 'substantialization' (2001, 129) or material 'engagement' (2001, 128; 2003). While arguing that these are general processes associated with humans, he is also arguing that they gear up at the transition to farming and in the Bronze Age. For a long period after the appearance of *Homo sapiens sapiens*, there was little change. But then, in his two subphases, material engagement became more marked and social complexity increased.

Certainly I endorse the view put forward by Renfrew that the material symbol precedes or is inseparable from the concept, and I would presume that this was a general characteristic of humans (and probably other animals). The view is for me related to the foundational claim by Merleau-Ponty (1962) that consciousness is always 'consciousness of' something. Similarly, the links made by Renfrew between things, value, commodity and exchange seem to be very general. The notion that an object becomes a gift through presentation, and thus comes to have value in further exchange seems at the basis of all exchange and must have been in play in the Upper Palaeolithic at the very least. According to Renfrew (2001, 127) it was only with the Neolithic that materials took on a symbolic power so that the process of engagement led to social and economic change. But in the Upper Palaeolithic and earlier, objects certainly had symbolic power. So the problem becomes — what changes in material engagement occurred at the transition to

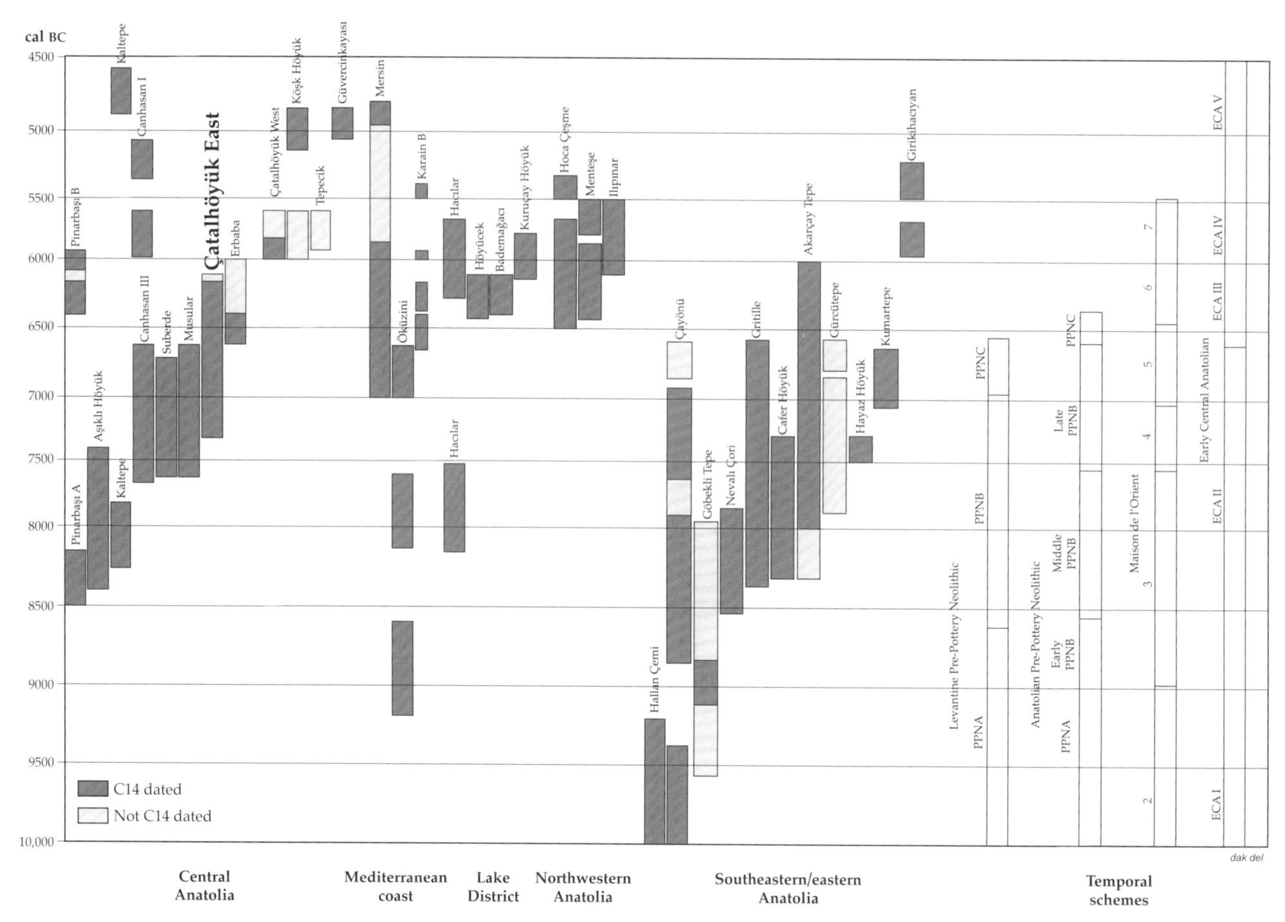

Figure 1.6. *Dated Neolithic sites in Anatolia and the Çatalhöyük sequence (partially based upon Thissen 2002a).*

farming, sedentism and the use of bronze? Can we take Renfrew's insight that something significant happened at this juncture in human development and understand something of the changes that occurred? How did materiality shift?

Material entanglement

One thing that happened was that there just became a lot more of it — a lot more things made by people. This is a point well made by Renfrew, that 'human culture became more substantive, more material' (2001, 128). He recognizes that this is related to sedentism. Those following a mobile existence are limited in terms of the accumulation of materials. But once people have settled, the potential for surrounding oneself with material things increases. This is not just a set of symbolic relations with things — it is also a material entanglement (generalizing from Thomas 1991). Humans get increasingly caught up in society through their involvement with objects.

Çatalhöyük occurs many millennia after the emergence of sedentism in the Near East and Anatolia (Belfer-Cohen & Bar Yosef 2000; Özdoğan 2002). But as a fully-sedentary society (Volume 4, Chapter 1), it provides a good example of the degree of entanglement that had occurred in large settlements by the seventh millennium cal BC. As one of many instances at the site, we can look at the decision made by the inhabitants to live in mudbrick houses. Having made that decision, they then decided, at least by Level XII to plaster the floors and walls with a fine mud plaster, rich in lime. At least one of the reasons for plastering floors may have been to limit infestation from mice. We have found many examples of mice bones and mice activity in the houses (Volume 4, Chapter 4), and they must have constituted a nuisance resulting from the dense packing of houses. Whatever the reasons, it was decided to plaster the floors and walls. But where to get the lime-rich muds from? Around the edges of the site we have found marl extraction pits. These were dug down through alluvium in order to get to the Pleistocene lake marls which were fine and lime-rich and could easily be processed to make the plaster for the walls and floors. So it was necessary to get the tools to dig the holes, and the containers to carry the mud. And there had to be agreement about who could dig where off the edge of the mound; and about which time of the year would be best for plastering. And there would be the social effort of getting enough plaster collected; and also different types of plaster. It turned out that the fine plasters themselves did not stick well on the walls so that rougher foundation layers needed to be put on first with more organic temper. So now people had to be organized to get different types of clay, and to collect and prepare the temper. In order to get a group of people together for all the digging and carrying of different types of clay and temper and water, all at the right moment, it is likely that some sort of exchange would be offered — say a small feast. So that meant getting an animal killed and prepared. And a plastering tool was needed. Cattle scapulae may well have been used in this way (Chapter 16), but that meant the group of people plastering had to have access to a cow, or to someone that had a scapula.

And so on. My point here is simply that one material act (plastering a floor) involves a network of entanglements — with the properties of materials, but also with a web of social relations. There were also beliefs and symbols involved — perhaps cattle scapulae had some special significance (Chapter 16). Certainly they are deposited in very distinctive ways in relation to hearths during house abandonment (Volume 3, Parts 2 & 3). So the entanglements extend into a network which is material, social and conceptual.

Imagine the same analysis extended over a wide range of things that emerge in the Neolithic — making pots, polishing stone axes (and mirrors at Çatalhöyük), making bricks, storing grains, looking after the herds. The degree of entanglement implied by all this is massive. This shift is perhaps just a matter of degree in relation to earlier entanglements, but I want to argue that the degree of entanglement gradually increases through time throughout the occupation of Çatalhöyük.

Another good example of this increasing entanglement is provided by the pottery–clay balls nexus. Last (Chapter 5) sees the introduction of pottery at Çatalhöyük in Levels XI or XII (see also Volume 3, Part 2) as part of a wider first use of vegetable tempered pottery in the Near East around 7000 cal BC (Aurenche *et al.* 2001; Moore 1995; Vandiver 1987). This is then followed at Çatalhöyük by a series of changes around Level VII which involve more pottery, more controlled firing and better pastes, mineral temper, and thinner walls. Then there is a further change around Level IV in the use of a wider range of shapes, and gradually increasing decoration into the Chalcolithic.

Last relates the major Level VII shift to the increased use of pottery in cooking, alongside a contemporary decline in clay balls which had been used for cooking in the earlier levels of the site (Chapter 6). It is of interest that in the early Neolithic of Greece, Vitelli (1995; also Perlès 2001) also argues that initially pottery is not used for cooking and storage — but for social display. The shift to the use of pottery in cooking at Çatalhöyük has many implications for the cooking process itself. Cooking could become more varied, complex, controlled. It also became dependent on the technology of pot production. The shift involved a more elaborate and longer, or more intensive pottery productive process — ageing the clay etc. Also, the clay now used from Level VII onwards had to be obtained from farther away. So, through time, people became more and more involved in a complex nexus, both material and social, surrounding cooking and clay production and exchange.

In these examples, people at Çatalhöyük became increasingly involved in a seamless web of material–social interactions. They became entangled in the social relations necessary to obtain material goods, and material goods were necessary to provide the materials and media for increasingly complex social interactions. The examples given so far show how material entanglements lead into social entanglements. But equally, social structures are needed for the material engagements to be possible. A good example is provided by the introduction of pottery itself. The reasons may, as in Greece, have been largely social (see below, and Chapter 5) but whatever the reasons it is clear there was a delay. People clearly had the technology to make fired clay figurines and to fire lime plaster well before they fired pots. Why the delay? I suggest that the primary reason was that people were not yet socially 'ready'. By this I mean that they were not sufficiently 'entangled' in long-term social/material relations. They were not yet sufficiently networked into a web of specialized entanglements to sustain the production and use of pottery. They were not sufficiently involved in long-term durations, to maintain the long-term involvements and entanglements involved in rights to dig clay, knowledge to find temper, time and tools to form clay, and time and social relations to obtain fuel to fire pottery.

Exchange and accumulation

So materiality is an essential part of the construction of more complex social relations in the Neolithic. There are two aspects of things made by humans — their duration and specificity — that seem to be especially important in creating social relationships. I want to call these two aspects of crafted things their 'thingness'. A key area in which thingness creates society is exchange. Exchange of food can be seen as involving immediate obtaining and sharing in certain hunter-gatherer societies, so that long-term relationships are not set up (Woodburn 1980). But in many societies, the thingness of crafted material things — their duration and specificity — creates longer-term debts and dependencies. Weiner (1992) describes how objects may be given, but they have histories that create links between people well beyond the act of exchange itself. The reciprocity is 'stretched out' and relations of indebtedness and dominance are extended.

The faunal data discussed in Volume 4, Chapter 2, provide evidence of feasting. This may have been carried out at various scales, but at least in some cases sufficient quantities of meat seem to have been consumed for several houses to be involved. Presumably prestige would have been gained from such feasting events (Bender 1978; Dietler & Hayden 2001; Hayden 1990). But the materialization of the feasting would have extended its social efficacy through time. Some of the feasting seems associated with the foundation and abandonment of houses, in which case the houses themselves commemorate the feasting largesse. It may also be the case that the wild bulls that were particularly associated with feasting (Volume 4, Chapter 2), were commemorated in quadruped figurines or in the bucrania placed in houses. But there were also artefacts used in feasting that could have extended the social effects of the events in material form. For example, Spasojević (Chapter 11) notes that the obsidian associated with a possible feasting deposit in Space 105 has a large ratio of used and retouched pieces, while a number of the bones show cut marks. Some of the obsidian used in such events may have been retained and caused the events to be 'stretched out' over time.

Evidence that exchange was used to set up specific sets of relationships over the social landscape is provided by the obsidian-sourcing results (Chapter 12). Carter notes that the two Cappadocian sources, Göllü Dağ-East and Nenezi Dağ, used for the Çatalhöyük obsidian are the same distance away, and the obsidian has equivalent technical qualities. So the preference through time for Nenezi Dağ obsidian must be partly cultural-social, and is perhaps linked to specific networks of people, places, exchange, workshops and quarries. Very specific exchange networks have been noted in relation to the use of the Cappadocian quarries by the inhabitants of Aşıklı Höyük (Binder 2002).

So as crafted material objects are exchanged, their 'thingness' has social effects. The objects endure, and they are associated with specific memories. Thus objects create extensions of events and become involved in longer-term social dependencies. This may be one way of understanding the early introduction of pottery. In the extreme case where I give you a piece of meat in exchange for a handful of gruel or berries, there is an immediacy to the exchange. There may be memories and associations of the event, but the event can be relatively transient. But if I give you the meat in a pot, then the gift is 'stretched out' over time. If I keep the fat of sheep and goats in a pot (see Chapter 7), the processing of the animals is 'remembered' in the pot and its contents — the products stretch out over time. The pot can re-instantiate the memories, exchanges and events as it is kept and re-used.

As people become more and more entangled, they need to mobilize more resources in enabling longer-term and larger-scale social relations. In the examples that I have given so far, they need to accumulate in order to give feasts that are part of building houses and plastering walls. They need to store fuel to make lime plaster or to make pots. They need to store fat in pots in order to make a social exchange. Entanglement in material things seems to involve accumulation and storage as a necessary part of the mobilization of resources. Storing and hoarding in relation to individual houses occur from very early on in the Levant and Anatolia. Storage occurs already in the Khiamian and Natufian (Cauvin 1994). Ritual feasting occurs at Jerf el Ahmar and Mureybet in open areas in the PPNA (Cauvin 1994; Stordeur *et al.* 2000). And Ohalo II, at 20,000 years ago beside the Sea of Galilee has brushwood huts, burials within the settlement, and storage pits (Watkins 2003). There are claims for very early communal storage, for example at Jericho (Naveh 2003), but in many cases early storage occurs in or in relation to houses, and this is certainly true of Çatalhöyük. So for societies structured around communal sharing and reciprocity, or for societies engaged primarily in immediate exchanges, what can justify 'private' (house-based) storage? What happens when people start to keep and not give?

The clearest example of accumulation at Çatalhöyük is the hoarding of obsidian below floors. In every house there is at least one shallow scoop, somewhere near the oven / hearth and ladder entry. In these scoops are found up to 77 pieces of obsidian. As shown by Conolly (1996; 2003) and Carter *et al.* (Chapter 11), these obsidian pieces are blanks or pre-forms for making a variety of tools. Associated with these caches there is evidence of *in situ* obsidian working, and in one case at least, the flakes can be refitted onto a pre-form that is like those found in the caches. Some scoops are empty or have only a few pieces in. It seems clear that obsidian was brought directly as pre-forms from the sources in Cappadocia (170 km away) and taken into the house where it was buried. People then dug down and excavated pieces when they needed them and worked them nearby inside the house.

This all seems straightforward — except the burying. Why bother to bury the pre-forms? Why not just keep them in a bag or a niche or in the rafters or in a basket or a wooden box? We know all these containers existed. So why bury the obsidian, when it would then have to be dug up when needed? Perhaps these valued objects needed to be hidden to prevent theft, but there are other ways of hiding. Part of the answer may be suggested by one of the hoards — the one in Building 1 (Volume 3, Part 3). In this scoop there were twelve blades (probably blanks for projectile points), six positives and six negatives from opposed platform cores. But the pieces do not fit together. They are very regular and must have been chosen from a variety of different cores. In this case too, a basin was soon built over the cache, suggesting it was not intended to be retrieved. Together with the symmetry of the blades, this suggests that this deposition was a ritualized event. The same parts of the floors, near the ovens and the house entrance, were also where neonates and very young people were buried (other people are buried away from the ovens, usually in the more northerly parts of houses). Is it possible that the caching of obsidian beneath the floors was connected in some way with the web of meanings associated with the burial of neonates in oven and entry areas?

If such indeed was the case, the obsidian when it returned from its cache would have had added aura. The removal and distancing of things often creates aura (Benjamin 1969), and the crossing of people and things into liminal or ritualized space (Turner 1969) can allow a renewal or rebirth. So when the obsidian returned it may have had special meanings, which may have added to the authority of those that hid and revealed it. The gifts of projectile points or other tools made from the cached obsidian would have had special memories and associations and would thus have created longer-term relationships and indebtedness.

The same process is not found for other artefact types. For example, some of the beads are made of exotic stones (and shells) — such as apatite and maybe carnelian. The so-called lead beads of Çatalhöyük in reality consist of galena, lead sulphide (Sperl 1988). This material was very well suited for producing grey shining beads that can be combined with other coloured stones like carnelian, copper, limestones etc. There are also copper beads. Most of the beads are from marble and other stones available in the 40-km radius near the site (Chapter 18). It could be argued that the beads were 'stored' as necklaces — mainly on children and female adults found in graves, but there is no evidence that the beads in graves were ever retrieved. As a further example, the basalt and andesite materials that were used to make a majority of the ground-stone tools come from volcanic outcrops 40 km or so away (Chapter 17). But there is no evidence that these were hoarded. An example indicating the special status of obsidian is provided by the flint. In comparison with the obsidian, it too came from long distances. But it is very rare in hoards (Chapter 11). A particular set of meanings was created for obsidian. As well as the links to the neonates below the floors, an aspect of this suite of meanings may be a link to hunting. Carter (Chapter 11) suggests that obsidian was made into hunting or killing points, whereas flint was not. In many small-scale societies, there are strong taboos surrounding hunting points and spears (Testart 1982). Perhaps the obsidian (like the neonates) had to be buried because it was seen as 'dangerous' — because it was a material used to kill animals. Perhaps the location of the hoarding near fire and entry/exit areas can also be made sense of in this way.

Long-term dependencies in exchange, the idea of keeping while giving, can be created by marking or stamping objects in distinctive ways. The stamp seals found at Çatalhöyük may have had something to do with ownership (Chapter 8). They occur mainly in the upper levels of the site — from Levels VII to II, but with a concentration in Levels VI to II. There may, then, be more of a concern with ownership and property in upper levels of the site, although this argument is perhaps undermined by the two cases of inscribed designs on obsidian in the Pre-XII levels (Chapter 11). There is also depositional evidence (Chapter 8) that the stamp seals are closely associated with houses. They again emphasize the domestic scale of keeping while giving. But also they begin to do something else. They extend the designs seen in the art in the houses out onto other, more moveable objects and perhaps bodies. Through time, things may become involved in a shift away from the centrality of the house to the importance of exchange between houses. As one moves into the Late Neolithic and Chalcolithic at sites such as Çatalhöyük West and Hacılar, the designs that had been found on walls and in houses at Çatalhöyük East are now found on pottery (Hodder 1990). With the seals, and the objects stamped, these things can be moved around and exchanged between houses. The designs used in the art shift from being inward and house-focused to being about outward interaction between houses.

Specialization of production

Another aspect of the appropriation of thingness in order to construct social relations concerns production. In the production of material things, the specific histories, associations and memories of objects are crafted in the interests of the producing group. The social group involved in production becomes entangled in and invests in its own materiality and specific long-term durations are set up. Rather than involving short-term dependencies, there is an engagement in types of artefact that necessitate long-term provisions and technologies — rather than exchanging a piece of wild meat that has involved limited productive engagement, there is exchange of objects that involved longer-term labour and a wider web of social dependencies. At Çatalhöyük, most of the longer-term links that are set up through production are small-scale and house-based.

The small-scale and often house-based scale of production is shown in a number of types of data. The lime burning in Level Pre-XII.B in Space 181 seems to have been small-scale, perhaps at the household level, despite the fact that large amounts of lime-rich material would have been needed to make one of the hard lime floors in the earliest levels (Volume 3, Part 2). Baysal & Wright (Chapter 13) conclude that the activities associated with ground stone, food processing or ochre grinding etc., were done at a small scale given the size of the artefacts. The existence of ovens in all houses, and the faunal evidence for intensive bone processing in houses suggest a domestic scale of food preparation. The same can be said for the storage of food on the basis of the provision in all houses of facilities for grain and other storage (bins and baskets). As regards the clay balls (Chapter 6), petrographic analysis conducted on a small number of balls, mini balls, and objects illustrates that there actually is not one recipe for clay balls, but instead, ball fabric can vary considerably within buildings and from level to level. Atalay attributes this variability to the choices in mineral inclusions made by individual clay ball crafters during production, and to variability in clay sources and the use of different sources by different crafters. The impression gained from the variability of brick production (Chapter 10) is of dispersed local house-based production. But, given that different clay fabrics and tempers were used for different types of object (balls, figurines, pots, bricks, plasters) even within the same house, Atalay (Chapter 6) argues for a small-scale part-time craft specialization.

A similar claim can be made for the beads (Chapter 14). These were made at the domestic scale, probably near the hearth or oven (as in Buildings 17 & 18). It is of interest that evidence of bead production in Building 18 occurs through several phases. Different houses focused on different types of object and this specialization was passed on through time. Thus while Building 18 had a focus on beads, Mellaart (1967) noted that his Shrine VI.A.10 had fourteen stone figurines and VI.A.44, the 'Leopard Shrine', had eight stone ones. Baysal & Wright (Chapter 13) interpret the VI.A.10 example as including unfinished objects, and thus *in situ* production. Another example is Shrine A.III.2, which 'produced a large number of stone tools as well as raw material and might have been a stoneworker's shop' (Mellaart 1962, 55). Mellaart found nine figurines in AII.1, five of these were very similar to each other and were found around the hearth. Hamilton (Chapter 9) suggests domestic production or house-based traditions in figurine production because of their diversity and the sometimes clustering of groups and types in buildings. The concentration of stone figurines in particular buildings could suggest some house-based part-time specialization of production, although in some cases we may be dealing with house-based preferences in use or discard habits.

The presence of substantial amounts of pre-forms and waste from bone tool manufacture in the South Area is noted in Chapter 16. The distribution of this manufacturing debris suggests household-level rather than specialized production. There are some indications, however, that there may have been limited, part-time specialization in bone-tool production. People who were particularly skilled at such a craft may have supplied their neighbours. It might have been thought that the obsidian mirrors involved a high degree of specialized knowledge and skill, but Vedder's experiments (Chapter 19) show that the total amount of time involved is limited (three to four hours of fine polishing) and that the work could have been carried out part-time between other tasks.

There may have been an element of specialization in crop-seed storage, given the exclusive use of bins in Building 1 for lentils, and the predominance of einkorn-wheat storage in E.VI.17. Given that we do not find such concentrations in the charred seeds around ovens, and given that Building 5 probably has a variety of stores (Volume 3, Part 3), this pattern is unclear and may be the result of preservation problems. It remains possible, however, that exchange between house units produced the mixing of seed types (Volume 6, Chapter 6; Volume 4, Chapter 8).

There may also have been some larger-scale centralization of production. Several of the examples mentioned above as having evidence of some degree of specialized production are more elaborate buildings (e.g. Mellaart's Shrine 10), and Conolly (1996) and Hamilton (1996) have argued that more elaborate buildings were associated with obsidian cores and figurine production. Specialization of production may have increased through time. For example, large ovens in open areas that could have served several houses were found by Mellaart (1967, 63) in Levels IV and V. Thus some houses may have become dominant over others partly through an ability to provide more food, or through the production of valued objects. However, the evidence for this larger-scale of production remains slim.

Temporality

As already noted, the most distinctive aspects of things are that they endure and that they are specific. They outlive the momentary engagements and interactions of social life. They outlive human lives. They create connections and histories. Take again the example of plastering a Çatalhöyük house. The feasting and coming together and working disappear, but the social process is fixed in the plaster walls and in the memories surrounding them. The social immediacy has been made to endure. The social relations have been objectified and can be evidenced (in the plaster), and can be called upon again. This shift in the nature of thingness is parallel to the important distinction made by Woodburn (1980) between immediate and delayed return societies. Complex hunter-gatherers and early farmers only receive a return for their joint labour after some delay. Woodburn argues that delayed return societies need institutions to hold them together between the investment of labour and its return. But this 'holding together' is in part created by entanglement in thingness. Indeed, it can be argued that the institutions (ancestors, kinship, etc.) come about through such entanglements.

Material things that endure are associated with memories and histories. Categories of things are usually related in some way to categories of people, and may help to constitute the roles of people. I have been very struck by the numbers of different categories of containers which people lived with at Çatalhöyük. In fact, there are different pot types, and although they are not highly diverse (Chapter 5), it seems they were involved in categorical distinctions: they were used for storing animal fats (see Chapter 7 on residue analysis of potsherds). There are several different basket types (Chapter 15) and we know that different types of basket were used for young and old people in burial (Volume 4, Chapter 9). Mellaart also discovered a wide range of wooden containers (1967, 215–16). In some buildings we have pots *in situ* on floors (a complete pot was found set into the floor by an oven in a building excavated in the South Area in 2002). We also have the traces of where the baskets were placed in the southern and western parts of buildings (Volume 3, Part 3). So as you walked around a building at Çatalhöyük, you would have walked through a social map laid out on the floor. This map was made up of baskets, pots, wooden containers, all in their places and associated with different categories of people, or different individuals. They are associated with different foods produced and prepared by different people. The social order is here sedimented in the material world.

The pace of cultural, economic and social change in the Upper Palaeolithic is extremely slow. In the early tell sites in Anatolia and the Near East, there is remarkable continuity, with house built on house over centuries, even the hearths staying in the same place in the deep sounding at Aşıklı Höyük (Esin & Harmankaya 1999). In PPNA Jericho, there are 32 occupation horizons associated with the monumental tower (Kenyon 1957). Even in the eighth and seventh millennia at Çatalhöyük, there is remarkable continuity. One component of this slow pace of change may have been that social structures were embedded within the material world. As people were socialized at Çatalhöyük, they learnt social rules in the practices of daily life, moving around houses and stepping between pots, baskets and wooden containers (Hodder & Cessford 2004).

This emphasis on continuity is seen in house rebuilding, and in the repetition of what is done where in the houses. The codification of internal space into 'clean' and 'dirty' areas inside Çatalhöyük houses is discussed at length in Volumes 3 and 4. Although a rather different perspective is presented by Baysal & Wright (Chapter 13), the overall evidence for the codification of construction, use and discard activities in different parts of the houses is strong. Codification is also seen in relation to lithic projectile points. These were predominantly made of obsidian and rarely of flint; on the other hand, the two daggers that have been found with carved bone handles were both made of flint (Mellaart 1967, 213 & pl. XIV; 1997 archive report). Another example of codification is provided by the bone tools. These were mainly made on distal ends of metapodials of sheep/goat, rather than on hunted wild animals (Chapter 16). All these codified and practical rules may have inhibited change.

An overall lack of change is seen in subsistence. There is great stability in plant use during the excavated phases as shown by the archaeobotanical data (Volume 4, Chapter 8) and few major shifts in the faunal data (Volume 4, Chapter 2). There are no dramatic changes in the bone-tool assemblage through time in the levels considered here (Chapter 16). Baysal & Wright (Chapter 13) do not see any clear variations in materials or types of ground-stone artefacts from the early levels to later ones. The same is also seen in stamp seals (Chapter 8). There is a continuation of some favoured seal designs throughout the levels. This is especially true of two patterns (pseudo-meander and composite design type 4). This is another example of real continuity — despite being only in the upper levels.

But there is also change. Detailed anatomies of the buildings at Çatalhöyük show an endless cycle of movement and reorganization. In particular, the ovens and hearths and bins keep moving around the building, shifting from one side to the other along the south wall, or being blocked up and shifted into side rooms, and then back into the main rooms (Volume 3). There is an endless restlessness through the sequence of around 18 levels as pottery comes in, obsidian becomes more specialized, stamp seals are introduced, figurines change in style, social differentiation becomes more marked and houses become more independent. The objectification of the social order in constructed material culture also provides a potential for change. By moving an oven one can confront social status or gender relations.

The rate of change as measured by Cessford (Chapter 4) shows a speeding up in the upper levels. The overall length of occupation of the East Mound in all likelihood was 950 to 1150 years. There are probably 18 levels overall although the definition of levels is somewhat arbitrary, and some levels are better defined than others (Volume 3). The overall length of level is 50 to 80 years, but they are longer earlier and shorter later (Chapter 4). This decrease in length of level through time also was noted by Mellaart in that he found more replasterings of walls in earlier levels (1964a, 116–17; 1967, 50). The increased rate of change in the upper levels is related by Cessford & Near (Volume 6, Chapter 11) to the fact that burning of houses on abandonment seems to occur mainly in Level VII and later.

Rates of change may have been very complex. One possible glimpse of this is that there is a discrepancy with the dating of the North Area in relation to the South sequence of levels. The pottery suggests Building 5 and 1 date to VII to VI or V; but the radiocarbon determinations suggest Levels IX to VII. The period of Levels VIII to VI is when the main pottery changes occur. Is it possible that the North Area was more innovative than the South Area, at least in terms of pottery styles?

There are many examples of material change that in various ways must have confronted highly-codified practices. For example, between Levels XII and VIII pottery changed hardly at all; between VI and II most stylistic elements changed (see Last 1996), though without further technological 'ruptures' like the Level VII transition. On the one hand, the new technology and the greater levels of skill that were demanded probably produced more scope for innovation; on the other hand, broader social factors may have also influenced potters, if we accept the argument that the construction and use of houses, for instance, became more dynamic in the upper levels of the site (Düring 2001).

While the bone-tool industry (Chapter 16) is quite stable through the occupation of the site, there seem to be some minor changes around Level IX. These include the use of a somewhat wider range of taxa and elements and a slight decline in splitting in the points; a change from cut to drilled perforations in the needles; and the appearance of worked boar's tusk and some minor tool types, many of them associated with woodworking.

There is also change in obsidian. During the Pre-XII levels, there is a decline in the use of obsidian industry 2 (microblade technology) as well as industries 4 and 6 (Chapter 11). For example, inscribed obsidian points only occur in Pre-XII levels (Chapter 11). Göllü Dağ-East source of obsidian had a long use from at least Level IX, whereas Nenezi Dağ comes in in a major way only in Levels VII–VI. The latter is associated with a specific technology — unipolar pressure-flaked blade technology (obsidian industry 5) which becomes the mainstay industry at Çatalhöyük. The pattern of an increase in Nenezi Dağ in Levels VII–VI, and its association with industry 5 needs further confirmation, but it is interesting in the context of the shift earlier recognized by Conolly (1999b) in Levels VI.A–B — he saw a shift from flake- to blade-based assemblages, and from percussion to pressure-flaking technologies. Also production became more restricted or specialized. We can now see that this shift is related to shifts in sources (Chapter 12). As another example of change in obsidian, burials with mirrors occur in Levels VI.B, V and IV (Chapter 19).

Constructing histories

So, in the most general of terms, the entanglement of people in thingness may have contributed to a lack of change, but on the other hand, the materiality of social life also allowed that life to be contested and re-crafted. Made objects were caught up in tensions between continuity and change. As already noted, one of the characteristics of things is that they endure and can create links through moments of time. There is much evidence of how things 'stretch' between times at Çatalhöyük. For example, in Chapter 4, Cessford estimates that about 50 per cent of the dates obtained on large structural timbers are too early. Looking at the AMS dates obtained from plant materials in Building 1 and 5, overall it appears statistically likely that between 25 and 50 per cent of the plant material dated was residual to some degree.

The point is not just that there was lots of 'old stuff' lying around, although that in itself is a major difference from mobile hunter-gatherers. Rather, the point is that this 'stretchness' was used to create duration and links with the past. In Chapter 4, Cessford notes that a cattle skull and horn cores (1400) which were deposited at the same time as the lentils in Building 1 had a 51 per cent probability of being earlier than them by up to 150 (95 per cent probability) or 80 (68 per cent probability) years. Horns, skulls and teeth of wild animals are found curated in houses, and there is evidence that sculpture from earlier houses is retrieved and reused. The retrieval and reuse of human skulls also suggests a use of 'documents' of past events in new contexts through time (Volume 4, Chapter 1; Hodder & Cessford 2004). All this suggests the construction of histories and durations using material objects.

Ground-stone artefacts show much evidence of re-use and re-working, as a result of the lack of locally-available raw materials. A long use-life for ground-stone artefacts is found in many village societies as discussed by Baysal & Wright (Chapter 13). As well as the practical issues involved, social factors such as inheritance can play a role in the history of such artefacts. For example, in a number of village societies, daughters inherit milling tools from their mothers (Chapter 13). Matrilineal inheritance of stone milling tools can be documented in Akkadian documents from second-millennium Mesopotamia (Wright 2000). In third-millennium Mesopotamia, legal texts used the expression 'to transfer the pestle' (in this case made of wood) to indicate the transfer of property (land, gardens, slaves) from person A to person B (Chapter 13). Whilst these examples are not directly relevant to Çatalhöyük, the ethnographic literature does suggest that we should be aware of the cultural as well as practical elements of artefact life-histories.

Many seals display signs of long and probably heavy use (Chapter 8), and the same can be said for some of the figurines (Chapter 9). Their long use might suggest that they were kept for longer than an individual human life span. Bone tools also sometimes show traces of heavy wear, and there are examples of repair of bone ornaments (Chapter 16). These items are not found in burials and it is possible that they were handed down across generations, as part of the transfer of property that often constitutes an important component of house-based societies (Joyce 2000).

In the upper levels of the site there seems to be more change and the rate of replacement of houses increases. One important set of shifts involves a move of decoration and symbolic elaboration from the house to objects such as stamp seals and pottery. The histories that were constructed with objects became less house-based. In the lower levels, animal head installations occur but these are not found in the upper levels (well-documented examples are limited to Levels VI and VII) (Volume 6, Chapter 18), whereas it is in the upper levels that the elaborate narrative scenes of animal baiting occur. One aspect of this shift is from permanent to transient art forms. So again, it seems that while the house is a central social unit throughout the occupation of the site, it begins to be challenged by a new set of materialities towards the top of the sequence. These new materialities seem to be more about interactions between people rather than with the pasts of individual houses. To explore this change further we need to consider other aspects of social change.

Social change through time

One aspect of the engagement or entanglement with material culture in the earliest levels of the site concerns whether there was use of local versus non-local resources. In Volume 4, there is discussion of a possible shift from the use of local to more non-local resources. In the charcoal data (Volume 4, Chapter 10), in Level Pre-XII.A to VII there is more oak and then an increase in juniper in Levels IX–VII. Through time there is also more intensive exploitation of firewood. Asouti sees the increase in oak in Level Pre-XII.A indicating people going further away for timber and firewood, as a result of clearance and degradation of nearby wetland vegetation.

Similarly, sheep and goat stable isotopes are tightly clustered in Pre-XII.C–D, but are much wider in Pre-XII.A–B, and are even more widely spread in levels above XII (Pearson pers. comm.). This suggests a shift towards multiple feeding grounds, and parallels the charcoal evidence of a shift from local to extra-local fuel use. The evidence of on-site penning is also in the lower levels, so the notion of a local to a wider grazing of animals is strengthened.

The faunal data (Volume 4, Chapter 2) show that after Level Pre-XII.B only heads and hides of pigs and deer are brought onto the site. This could again be because people had to go farther and wider for resources. Perhaps the local drying out after the earliest levels is linked to this shift. But it should also be noted that many of these temporal trends could be explained as spatial differences. This is because our evidence for the earliest levels comes from contexts that are off the edge of the site, or close to it (Volume 3, Part 1). Nevertheless, at present temporal change seems the most likely explanation.

Certainly, the changes continue through time. The faunal data suggest (Volume 4, Chapter 2) that there is an increase in the presence of female and subadult cattle in Levels VI–V which the faunal team suggests could be related to smaller individual units exploiting wild cattle, or it may be that cattle become scarcer on the plain after Level VI.

After the introduction of pottery in Level XII, it seems that many of the materials could have come from local sources. The analysis of the sourcing of clays (Chapter 5 on CD) suggests that a lot of the constituent materials could have come from local sources, though the increased use of gritted fabrics after Level VII could suggest the use of colluvial hill deposits, and a few sherds may come from farther afield.

Oak and juniper were the main construction timbers — the use of structural timbers declines, according to Mellaart, at the top of the site in Level II (1967, 64). This could result from deforestation of the environment through extensive use, but there could be other factors involved such as changes in exchange patterns. There may also be a link to the sedimentological evidence for a drying out of the local soils right at the end of the occupancy of the East Mound (see above).

This evidence for a shift from local to wider resources may be linked to environmental changes. The charcoal evidence (Volume 4, Chapter 10) shows a changing relationship with the environment during the early occupation of the site. In particular a major change separates Levels Pre-XII.B–D from Pre-XII.A to VII. In the lowest levels there are more riverine taxa (willow / poplar, elm) and hackberry. Asouti (Volume 4, Chapter 10) sees a gradual decline in precipitation after *c.* 7000 cal BC as the juniper increases. It is of interest, therefore, that data from the microfaunal study (Volume 4, Chapter 4) show a greater representation of amphibians in the lowest levels of the site. Micromorphological evidence (Volume 4, Chapter 19) suggests that there is a major change in the selection of mudbrick building materials from the predominant use of grayish backswamp-related deposits in Levels XII to VIII, to oxidized orange or brown sediments in later levels. In the KOPAL Area to the north of the East Mound, there are a series of Late Neolithic and Chalcolithic buried soil horizons above the early backswamp clay. These indicate a significant drying out towards the end of the occupation of the East Mound (Volume 3, Part 4).

But there are also possible social reasons for the shift. Initially, Çatalhöyük seems to have sucked in population from the surrounding landscape (Baird 2002). We have not excavated houses from the Pre-XII levels, and so it is difficult to assess the degree of house-based variation. But a primary concern may initially have been social-group cohesion and internal exchanges. There may have been more of an emphasis on communitas and on caring for the resources of the group as a whole. There was a smaller population that may have emphasized the sharing of local resources. But through time, as population increased into Levels VII and VI, there is evidence of increased, if still small-scale, specialization. This is seen in the more complex ceramic and obsidian production, if not also in figurine manufacture. It is possible that this internal specialization led to a need to exploit a wider diversity of environments, and to compete more extensively for resources. As a result there was a shift from local to non-local resources, as noted above. On the other hand, the picture is complex and non-subsistence resources may have been used in different ways. For example, Carter suggests (Chapter 11) that in terms of flint procurement and chipped-stone styles, cultural interactions may have been broader before Level Pre-XII.C, reducing in scale after that time, even though distant sources such as the obsidian sources in Cappadocia and flint sources probably in southeastern Anatolia continued to be exploited throughout the occupation of the site.

A possible example of the increased importance of the house after the earliest levels is provided by the use of lime plaster. Fired lime-plaster floors occur at the site up to Levels XII and XI. The early hard lime plasters produce floors of a single, or very few, layers. The practices of making and using them were very different from the later levels. Although the firing of lime does not seem to have been on a very large scale (Volume 3, Part 2), it still involved a longer process of preparation and wider collection of resources such as dung for fuel than the later use of mud plasters. During use there was not the frequent need to replaster as was found in the later levels. Thus, in the early use of lime-plaster floors, major construction events were followed by painting of the floors and then less repetitive remakings. The later, endless process of replastering may have been less easy to control (for example through ritual) because so frequent and so dispersed. Perhaps we see here an example of a shift of emphasis from the collective to the individual house.

One of the aspects of the house at Çatalhöyük which is so distinctive is the burial of large numbers of people below the floors. Again, we do not know how people were buried in the Pre-XII levels, but burial is less common beneath house floors at earlier sites such as Aşıklı Höyük, and it would have been more difficult to dig burial pits through the hard lime-plaster floors in the earliest levels. Certainly, the levels in which houses have been excavated show that the largest numbers of burials occur in houses in Levels VI and VII, in both the South and North Areas. This evidence supports the notion that the house became increasingly important into the middle of the sequence. I have noted above that there is some degree of specialization of production based in the house, and some slim evidence for some larger-scale specialization. In fact, the best evidence for some houses becoming dominant over others in the middle levels is provided by the burial data. It seems clear that some houses became preferential places of burial, perhaps for groups of houses (Volume 4, Chapter 1).

After Level VI, the settlement begins to shrink. The northern eminence is abandoned, and although there is some occupation of the eastern slope to produce a small eastern eminence (Hodder 1996), the overall area of occupation becomes small in the uppermost levels (although the West Mound may have been occupied by this time (Cessford pers. comm.) based on ongoing dating program). In the uppermost levels there is more evidence of increased focus on interactions between houses, and the duration of 'levels' decreases. There may be less continuity between houses (Düring 2001; though see Volume 6, Chapter 11 by Cutting for a rather different view), slightly more division of houses into separate rooms (Volume 6, Chapter 11), and perhaps more separation of houses (Düring 2001). As already noted there is evidence of larger-scale food preparation in the form of large ovens. Streets occur in the plans of Levels II, III and possibly IV. Overall, the impression is gained of a slight shift to greater functional differentiation between independent units, and more focus on material interactions rather than material continuities. The shifts are slight, and we need much more evidence of the lower and upper levels before they can be substantiated with any certainty. But some form of three-fold sequence seems possible — in crude and over-simplified terms from community to house to functional differentiation and interaction.

There may be related shifts in gender relations. Age and gender organization at the site are discussed in Volume 4, Chapter 1. Here I wish to point only to possible evidence of a change in gender through time. Hamilton (Volume 4, Chapter 13) notes a *slight* increase in numbers of female burials in houses in upper levels — and there is also a greater emphasis on female figurines in the upper levels (Chapter 9), and there are clusters of the famous seated female figurines around hearths and in buildings. This increased representation of women may be partly linked to the craft specialization and 'industrialization' of food preparation (outside large ovens). It is often the case that as craft specialization increases, women become more clearly identified with domestic production and men focus on other spheres of production and exchange (e.g. Silverblatt 1988). It is also possible at Çatalhöyük that as the focus of power shifted away from domestic production and control of ritual, so it became possible for the house to be represented by women — not only because women became increasingly associated with the house, but also because male interests had partly shifted elsewhere. Thus perhaps in the upper levels, females and female figurines could be more clearly linked to the house and hearth, or female figurines could be used to represent the house. However, until houses in the uppermost levels of the site have been excavated by the current project it is difficult to explore these initial ideas further.

Human and material agency

It is clear that the materialization of social structure at Çatalhöyük did not lead to fixity and lack of change. The opposite seems truer, that material entanglement produced an objectification of the social structure so that it could be contested and changed. The rate of change seems to increase through the sequence. There is much emphasis on constructing continuities through time, and links to ancestors were a central part of claims to membership of 'houses'. But at the same time, there were moves to transform traditional modes of life. There is a continual tension between continuity and change, with the latter beginning to get the upper hand in the upper levels of the site.

The inverse of objectification is greater awareness of the self (Winnicott 1958). More specifically for the post-Pleistocene, by creating greater possibilities for crafting change through crafting material worlds, the human as agent becomes more apparent. Human representations do occur of course throughout the Upper Palaeolithic, but active humans, running and hunting and interacting with animals become especially common in early Holocene art and symbolism. In Anatolia and the Near East, it often seems as if, while human representations occur early on, they come to have a clearer and more central role through time. The Natufian has an animal rather than a human art (although female representations occur already in the Khiamian) (Cauvin 1994). There are human representations at Göbekli Tepe, and they are prevalent as statues slightly later at Nevali Çori. At Çatalhöyük, despite some recent finds in the lower levels, there seems to be an increase of the large rounded seated female figurines in the upper levels — and all of clay (Chapter 9). In Greece, Perlès (2001) notes that in EN1 in Thessaly figurines are indistinctly human, and highly schematic. In EN2 and EN3 figurines are more clearly human and sexual features are more clearly marked.

The picture is complex, but in the most general of terms I think it is possible to see an increase in the representation of humans, especially active humans, gradually emerging in the Holocene. Helms (2003) argues that a shift from animal gods, to ancestors, to human gods may accompany the development of farming and settled village life. I would argue that this shift towards a centring of human agency comes about as the inverse of the entanglement process. As people become more invested in a web of material relations they have constructed, the 'artifice' of social, ritual and mythic life becomes clearer. The ability to change and re-craft by changing material culture becomes more marked, and humans become more clearly agents.

Unfortunately we do not know what the mirrors found at Çatalhöyük were used for (Chapter 19), but it is tempting to suggest that, whatever their specific function, they were the prime indicators of a greater awareness of self image as a product of the objectification of the social structure. There emerges a new technology of the body seen in a set of equipment related to bodily decoration (grinding stones used to grind ochre, and shells containing ochre associated with a small spatula in graves, although we cannot be sure these were used for body painting, and they often occur in graves with children so they may have had more of an apotropaic function: see below).

The increased emphasis on human agency seems closely linked to the idea that materials too have agency (Gell 1998). As Hamilton notes in Chapter 9, and as Voigt (2000) has also argued, many of the humanoid figurines at Çatalhöyük seem to be quickly made, and then broken and discarded, and some are placed in walls and between houses as votives. Hamilton notes that some of the small clay horns that are found in wall plasters and oven walls may have got their accidentally, and certainly, the inclusion of artefacts in plasters and clays as background noise is discussed by Cessford (Chapter 3). In some cases the horns and figurines seemed so out of place in an otherwise clean deposit that a votive or protective role seemed more likely to the excavators (see Volume 3, Part 1 & Volume 4, Chapter 1).

The stabbing of quadruped figurines (Chapter 9) also seems a clear instance of material agency in that presumably the stabbing of the clay material was thought to have effects in the world. Another possible example of material agency with regard to figurines is deposit (4321) which contains five figurines, three of uncertain type. Occurring at the interface of Spaces 159 and 173, this may have been a foundation deposit (Chapter 9). Conolly (Chapter 11) argues that there are cases of intentional depositions of obsidian. For example, (1387) and (1388) in Building 1, part of F.364, are deposits of obsidian placed at the base of a moulded wall feature.

The concentration of beads on juveniles and infants may indicate an apotropaic function (Chapter 14), as may the occurrence of shells with ochre and spatulae in childrens' graves. A similar protective or apotropaic function can be argued in relation to decoration around burial platforms in Building 1 (Volume 3, Part 1). Carter (Chapter 11) argues that there are cases of individual obsidian pieces being placed in special locations as part of construction events. For example, a large sharp obsidian flake was placed behind oven F.473 in Building 18. In addition a flint perforator was placed in bin F.515 with red ochre as part of the abandonment of Building 18. There are also examples from Buildings 1, 2, 5, 17 and 23 of obsidian projectiles being placed in retrieval pits in the centre of the west walls as part of abandonment practices. These obsidian examples may involve placing objects with a special value or aura in contexts where they may have had a protective role, or may have been given as gifts or sacrifices or offerings to the spirits or deities.

Conclusion

So, at the broadest of scales Renfrew was right to point to important changes in human engagement with materiality in the Neolithic. But this was not so much a shift in symbolic power, as a shift in the degree to which people became so entangled with material objects that these objects came to have greater impact or agency in their lives. In making things, humans made themselves in the way that we have come to know them (Childe 1939).

Overall, the 'thingness' of things — that is their duration and specificity — seem to be involved in the social processes of Çatalhöyük in two contradictory ways. There is a continual tension at the site between continuity and change. On the one hand, the increased materiality of life leads to a greater potential for constructing continuities, especially based in the house as it is reused and rebuilt over centuries. There is repeated replastering, there is burial beneath floors, there are installations of animal heads and sculpture on walls that last through the occupation of houses and may be taken for reuse in later buildings. On the other hand, the increased materiality of life allows that life to be endlessly re-crafted by shifting an oven here, by changing foodways, pot and obsidian types there, and by beginning to accumulate beyond the domestic sphere.

The process of accumulation seems initially to have been very house-based, but even here the move beyond reciprocal relations, and the keeping instead of giving, may have been made possible by wider changes in material entanglement. For example, obsidian may have been cached as part of material/symbolic 'protection', and wild bulls may have been used in feasting and giving but the heads could be kept and curated as markers of the largesse. In these ways reciprocal exchange turned into the long-term display of status and prestige. As this process continued through time, specialization and differentiation increased. At least in terms of control of the ancestors, some 'dominant' houses may have emerged, and spheres of accumulation extending beyond the house became more important.

To conclude at the most general of levels, it is possible to situate the shifts at Çatalhöyük within a larger context of change in the Neolithic of Anatolia and the Near East. The recent finds of large elaborate ritual centres such as Göbekli Tepe (Schmidt 2001), and the strong emphasis on ritual buildings at other PPNA and early Aceramic sites such as Jerf el Ahmar and Çayönü (Özdoğan 1999; Stordeur *et al.* 2000) have very much altered narratives of the development of village life. It is clear that many sites in the tenth to eighth millennia cal BC were centred around communal rituals — it is even possible that one route to settled village life was the participation in ritual events and feasting. The investment in public works, as at Jericho, is sometimes remarkable (Kenyon 1957; Naveh 2003). Houses, on the other hand, are initially often relatively unelaborated with few internal divisions. House complexity increases through time. In the central Anatolian region one can see this shift very clearly. At Aşıklı Höyük in the late ninth and early eighth millennia cal BC, there are ceremonial buildings, but houses are much less elaborate than at Çatalhöyük in the ensuing millennia. At Çatalhöyük a wide range of functions from burial, ritual, art to storage, manufacture and production are more clearly drawn into the house. We have seen this emphasis on the house increase through time at Çatalhöyük until in the uppermost levels other areas of exchange and production become increasingly important.

In conceptualizing this overall set of changes, it may be helpful to return to Durkheim's (1893) distinctions between mechanical and organic solidarity. By mechanical solidarity Durkheim meant social cohesion based upon the likeness and similarities among individuals in society, and largely dependent on common rituals and routines. By organic solidarity he meant social cohesion based upon the dependence between individuals performing different tasks and with different values and interests. There is a greater division of labour.

It is not clear that all sites in Anatolia and the Near East in the tenth to seventh millennia cal BC can be placed into this neat scheme, and there are dangers in suggesting an evolutionary sequence. But new excavations in the area have certainly opened the possibility that village communities emerged within a primarily mechanical form of social cohesion, whereas through time individual houses become more important and there is more specialization and perhaps more organic solidarity emerges. Certainly at Çatalhöyük, there are intimations of both forms of solidarity throughout the sequence. On the one hand, there are repetitive practices in houses which all seem very similar. This looks very much like mechanical solidarity despite the absence of common ceremonial buildings. On the other hand, there is evidence of functional differentiation as some houses focus on bead production, and others on figurine production, and others on ritual links to the ancestors. This looks much like organic solidarity. Through time in the sequence, there are intimations that it is the organic form of solidarity that increases as specialization increases and interactions between houses become more important.

While it may be helpful to look at Çatalhöyük though the perspectives of evolutionary change from less to more complex, or from communal to differentiated, or from mechanical to organic solidarity, I have preferred in this chapter to focus on the lived materiality of daily life. I have argued that we can see an evolutionary change, but that it is extremely slow, and based on an increased entanglement between humans and crafted material things. This increased entanglement may have produced the stadial shifts from communal to differentiated or from mechanical to organic, but the primary process was long in gestation, extending well back into the Palaeolithic, and it was complex and highly-distributed. In other words, there were no simple or single causes. In a highly-distributed process, people became more dependent on things, which meant more dependence on people and on social relations, which meant more need for the accumulation of things, which meant more possibilities for social agency, and so on in a complex cycle. The greater materialization involved shifts in temporalities, as change became faster and more contested. There were changes in technologies and in exchange and in relations with the spirits and gods. In a seamless web, everything changed in relation to everything else. In small incremental events, people found they could move an oven here, change a pot type there, start eating in new ways, put more emphasis on human rather than animal gods. These small events all involved a greater web of material/social interactions. But they also involved perhaps the most fundamental change of all — the greater objectification of human agency. In the end, it was the tinkering with things, and the accumulation and keeping of things, that led to the interventions which, in areas of the world that had suitable plants and animals, we call domestication and the agricultural revolution.

The smallest of actions, such as the decision to plaster the house floors with fine muds, or the decision to keep obsidian pre-forms below the floors, had as much impact as the first planting of a seed or the first tethering of a cow. This is because the small decisions involved changes in material–human relations that also changed the ways people interacted with each other and with the spirit world. In other words, they contributed to changes in discourse and practice that were part of and necessary for the longer-term delayed return systems that underpin settled village life and farming.

Chapter 2

Statistical Integration of Contextual Data

Sarah Cross May

The statistical integration of excavation data with finds data was based on determining contextual similarities and differences within and between data sets. Much of the effort involved in this centred on relating finds information collected for internal analysis, to excavation data collected as a framework for understanding. While there were some methodological difficulties, the results were rewarding. Analysis involving more than one data set was more powerful than analysis involving only one data set regardless of how many variables are studied within one data set.

The strongest source of variability is the distinction between data category (e.g. midden, fill, floor). There is little variability based on 'levels' or phasing, or area of the site (North, South & KOPAL Area). There is some distinction between these groupings but it is mostly relating to different proportions of data categories being present at different times and places on the mound.

The composition of middens is more tightly defined than the composition of other data categories. This runs counter to the impression of middens being a very broad category. Similarly, the density of material recovered from floor units is often higher than similar material recovered from fill or middens. Some distinctions within data categories such as inside vs outside fills, coarsely-bedded vs finely-bedded middens and laid vs packed floors were examined and differences were noted for some data sets but not others.

Methodology

Data

Data sets

Data on the following 11 groups of material were analyzed: excavation records, faunal material, charred botanical material, shell, lithics, ground stone, clay objects, beads, figurines, phytoliths and ceramics.

Data bases

A separate data base was established to hold and manipulate all of the available data. The excavation data base provided the main core of this data base and other data sets were linked to the appropriate tables through the unit number. Because different specialist teams were working to different levels of analysis there are variable numbers of tables for each data set. For example, the single table holding the data from clay-object analysis has one entry for each excavation unit. In contrast there are three tables for lithics, one with an entry for each unit, one with an entry for each bag of lithics studied, and one with an entry for each piece of stone studied in greater detail.

Data quality

Clearly any analysis is based on the assumption that our data are 'clean' — that the original measurements were accurate, that data entry was coherent and complete. For most data sets I have used little information beyond density. I took time at the beginning of the analysis to check calculated fields (such as the weight fields in the botanical data base) and hunt down values for key fields (such as volume). This was part of the establishment of the analysis data base and was important for clarifying the status of the data.

The analytical priorities sample

While 3662 units were excavated, detailed analysis in this chapter and much of the volume could only be carried out for analytical priorities. While some material has been studied for many more units (e.g. lithics) most of the analysis discussed here is based on the analytical priorities sample, known as 'the 355'. These units were chosen through a combination of site priority tours, negotiation between specialists, and a plan to represent levels and unit types well. The sample is in no sense random but, chosen during and after the excavation, it has been designed to represent the site and our interest in it. This does not invalidate statistical analysis but we do need to be aware of the influence of our choices on patterning in the material. (For example, our perception of what middens 'ought' to be will have influenced the middens that became priorities). There is no absolute method of checking

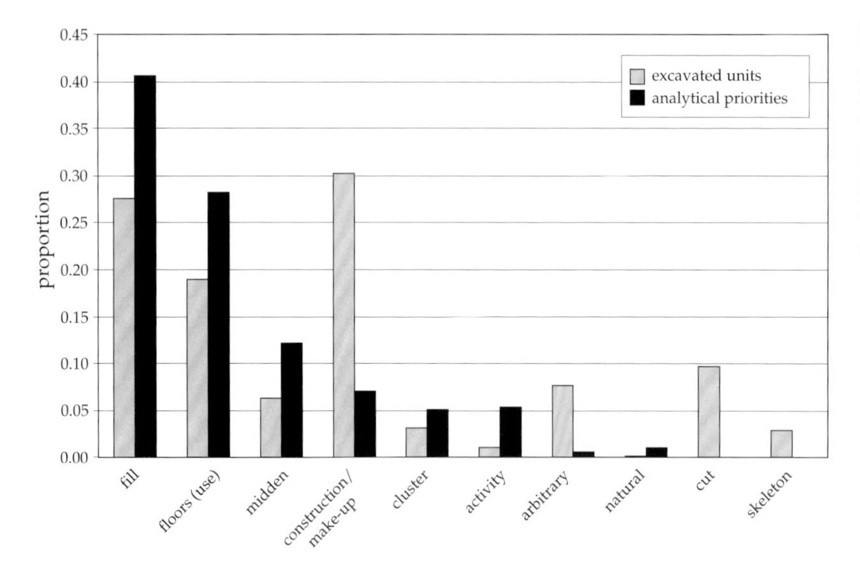

Figure 2.1. *Number of units studied as proportion of sample by data category.*

Table 2.1. *Distribution of analytical priorities by excavation area.*

Area	Excavated units	Analytical priorities
KOPAL	90	10
North	1049	132
South	2517	213

whether we have chosen particularly 'clean' floors or complex middens, though heavy residue may be useful if we want to pursue this. We can, however, check whether we achieved the aims of representing the variation present on site and facilitating the crossovers between specialists.

Representing variation

The analytical priority data set seems to be a surprisingly good reflection of the overall sample given the long history behind its selection. The representation of different data categories shows some difficulties but the major categories are well represented (Fig. 2.1). Arbitrary units are under-represented, which is clearly a positive choice. Similarly, while cut features are important stratigraphically, they should not contain information for further analysis. The low representation of skeletons in the sample is because the skeletons were given separate unit numbers and therefore contain little information for other specialists. Nonetheless the activity of burial remains under-represented in the analytical priority sample. There were 174 burial fills excavated but only 7 are in the priority sample. The construction/make-up category is severely under-represented as well. This seems to be for two reasons: 1) the composition of construction material is seen to relate to off-site conditions and less culturally-interesting choices; 2) there is perceived to be little variation in the composition of this material.

The remaining data categories (activity, cluster, fills floors and middens) are over-represented since they represent the main focus of interest at the site. Looking at these as a sub-sample, they show a fairly reasonable distribution, with a slight over-emphasis on middens and activity areas, owing to particular interest in these types of units.

The analytical priority sample is a good reflection of the kinds of material on site which are of interest to the research. The under-representation of construction materials is deliberate. The under-representation of burial impedes integrated study. Within the data categories of interest, the units are surprisingly well distributed in relation to overall proportion. The representation of the different excavation areas on site is also well balanced (Table 2.1). The slight over-representation of the KOPAL Area was necessary if any statistical work could be considered. The over-representation of the North Area is explained by two factors: 1) excavations in the North Area required the splitting of one context into many units, so more units may not represent more depositional events; 2) the focus on one building allowed questions which required more units within the layer (the coherence of the phasing encouraged spatial questions and the multiple samples which go with them).

Considering the representation of different 'levels' of the site is complicated by unease with the terminology of levels which is a legacy from the Mellaart excavations. The excavators emphasize that the level of a building (how many buildings from the notional top it is) should not be confused with a 'level' of the site. Each building is built individually and comparing two buildings with the same level number is not the same as comparing two contemporary buildings. Also, since level relates to building, not all units have levels. Some cannot be assigned to a building level because of lost information, others form part of a sequence separate from building levels (e.g. KOPAL Area and Level Pre-XII material, but also some unstratified 'external' deposits within the mound). This conceptual unease is reflected in the complex naming of levels. For example, levels of the units from the North Area have been prefixed with North or 'N' to deter people from comparing Level VII–VI material in the North Area with Level VII material in the South

Area, or from making simple sequential statements.

Taking this into account, there are five levels where the analytical priority sample differs substantially from the excavation sample. There are no unstratified units in the analytical priorities for obvious reasons. Level Pre-XII units are over-represented, both because the excavation was so focused here and because the foundation of the mound was of particular research interest. Levels IX and VII are under-represented. This is because the Mellaart excavation of this material left a substantial number of units that had been partially excavated and were therefore less suitable for detailed study. Level VIII largely represents the material reached after removal of the partly-excavated material and so is better represented. North Level VI–V is the material from Building 1 and is over-represented both because it is the most complete building that has been excavated and because it was excavated early in this excavation cycle (so the material was available for analysis earlier). All of the other levels seem to be in reasonable proportion (Fig. 2.2).

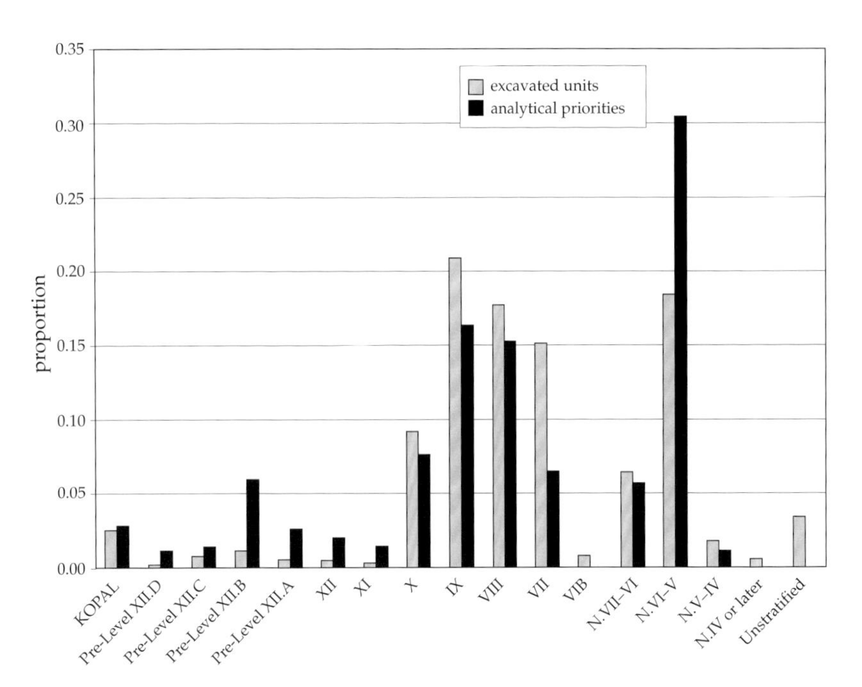

Figure 2.2. *Number of units studied as proportion of sample by level.*

Facilitating cross-comparison

The overlap in units studied for different data sets is strong (Table 2.2). Indeed this was a prime reason for selecting 355 units that could be studied by as many specialists as possible. Both faunal and botanical analysis is available for almost all of the analytical priority units. Shell and lithic information is also available for the vast majority. The smaller number of units with information on clay objects, beads, figurines and ceramics all reflect restricted distributions on site. The strong base in the faunal and botanical studies allows for a broad range of comparisons. Generally, the amount of overlap is unsurprisingly controlled by the data set with the smallest number of units studied (e.g. there are 337 units with faunal analysis, of which 317 can be compared with one of the 327 units with botanical analysis.). The cross comparison works well with multiple data sets as well (Table 2.3). There are more units with all nine data sets considered than there are with only one.

Table 2.2. *Cross-tabulation: number of units studied by data set.*

	Faunal	Botanical	Shell	Lithics	Clay obj	Beads	Ground stone	Figurine	Ceramics
Faunal	337	317	282	261	174	147	100	73	76
Botanical		327	269	251	165	138	92	65	69
Shell			285	232	162	137	99	69	71
Lithics				269	158	132	89	66	68
Clay obj					177	103	78	54	55
Beads						149	57	62	56
Ground stone							101	45	41
Figurine								73	29
Ceramics									76

Heavy residue as a proxy measure

Although specialist analysis focused on the analytical priority sample, there was a comprehensive program of flotation sampling. Samples were taken from 2499 units. Although the primary purpose of flotation was to collect charred botanical remains the heavy residue from the flotation was sorted into material and size classes and these classes were weighed providing a basic quantification of material for a very much

Table 2.3. *Number of units studied by number of data sets.*

Number of data sets	1	2	3	4	5	6	7	8	9
Number of units	11	21	51	70	54	58	43	34	13

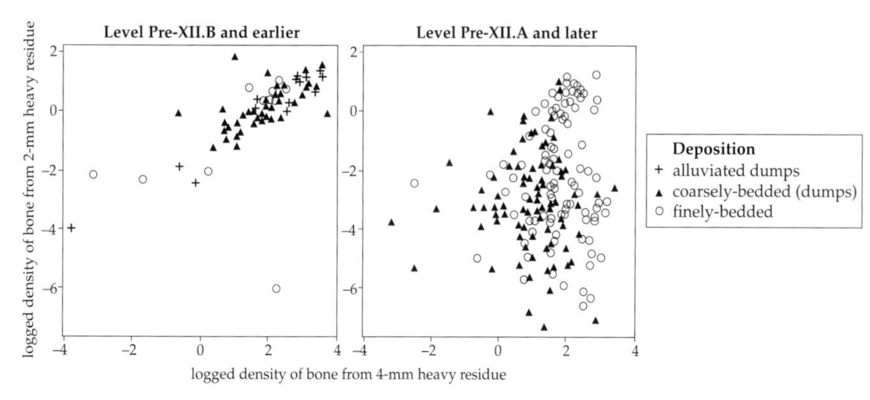

Figure 2.3. *Heavy-residue bone from middens by level group and deposition.*

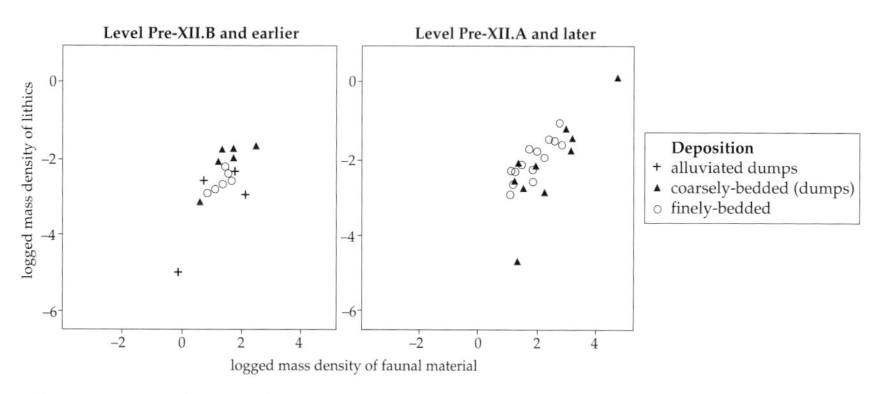

Figure 2.4. *Lithics vs faunal material from middens (analytical priorities).*

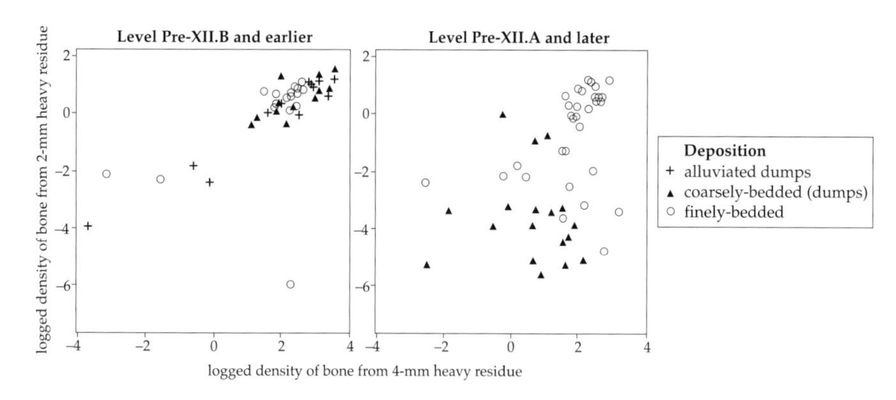

Figure 2.5. *Heavy-residue bone from middens (analytical priorities only).*

broader base of units. This material has been assessed separately (see Chapter 3) in order to provide the kind of primary analysis which had been provided for other data classes. That analysis has focused on tabulation and plotting and has pointed to some interesting but complex patterns. The only variable available for any material class is density but the larger sample makes this material quite attractive for further analysis.

Generally speaking densities from heavy residue corresponded well with densities from more detailed analysis for faunal and lithic material (for further discussion see Chapter 11 & Volume 4, Chapters 2 & 23), but there are still some problems with using heavy residue as a measure for lithic and faunal density. Looking at a scatter plot of faunal density from the 2-mm fraction vs the 4-mm fraction there is a striking pattern. There appears to be a distinction between coarsely-bedded middens and finely-bedded middens. Using a T-test to compare the means of the 4-mm fraction the difference between the two is significant at the .001 level (Fig. 2.3). In addition there is a striking cluster of units with high density, which could indicate a different pattern in the lower levels. The densities from the faunal data base, however, do not show this distinction (Fig. 2.4). This could be because the larger heavy-residue sample was picking up a pattern selected against by the analytical priorities, but the same pattern (though less dramatic) is present if we only look at the heavy residue from analytical priority units (Fig. 2.5). These kinds of methodological problems mean that both the heavy residue and the analytical priority results need careful consideration before interpretations can be made.

Selection of variables

The selection of variables was governed by availability of data. There are many variables that could be used to work within a single data set, but which cannot be extended for comparison. The most obvious example is internal classifications such as species, but this also extends to more comparable aspects such as fragmentation (see below). Some of this is due to intrinsic differences between different types of data, some is simply to do with approach.

The main variable used in the analysis for quantifying finds data is density. Internal classifications were examined for botanical, faunal and lithic analysis. The main variables for classifying excavation units are data category and level. Other variables such as colour, assessment of burning, inclusions and spatial positioning were examined for particular issues.

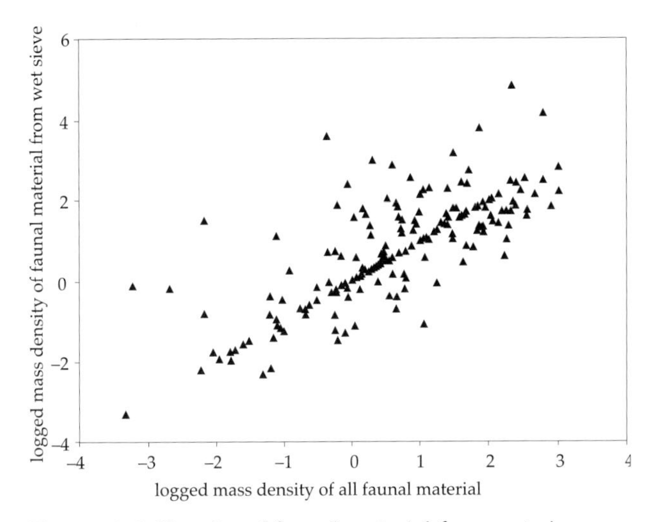

Figure 2.6. *Density of faunal material from wet sieve vs overall faunal density.*

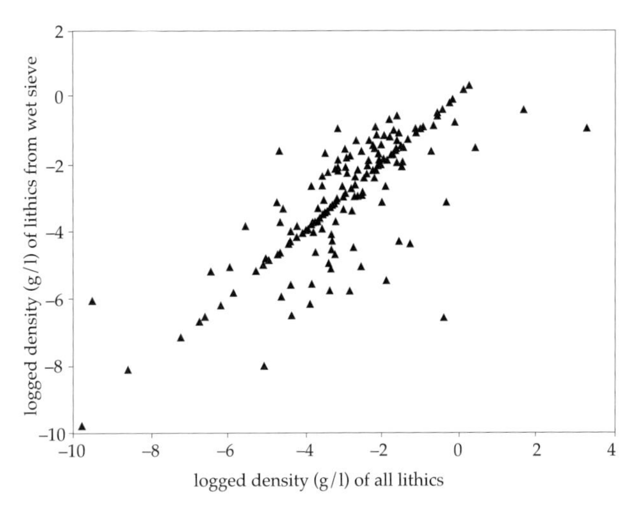

Figure 2.7. *Density of lithics from wet sieve vs overall lithics density.*

Issues with density as a variable

Although density is a good variable because it can be used to describe most data sets there are some issues in using it for the core of the analysis. It focused attention on variation in quantity of material, rather than in the composition, taphonomy, or diversity of assemblages. It may be sensitive to internal scale issues. While scale is an interesting subject of study in its own right, certain data sets have structural issues relating to scale (e.g. density of phytoliths is not the same conceptual category as density of faunal material since the packing is at a different scale). It also glosses over issues of intentionality (e.g. placed material and residual material are counted together). These issues need to be kept in mind when discussing the results. There are two other issues which are more practical but no more tractable. The first is whether to calculate density on counts or weights. The second is a methodological problem concerning volume measurement.

The issue of weights vs counts is essentially internal to each data set. Some types of material are better represented by weight, because fragmentation is not of particular interest, others are better represented by count, an obvious example being beads. For particular questions it could be useful to examine the count vs weight.

The concern about volume concerns the measurement of dry-sieve volume and the completeness of recovery from the dry sieve. Density is used rather than raw weights or counts to get away from correlations due to size masking other patterns. But volume is measured differently for large units than small, small units are often completely wet sieved so the volume is measured at that stage, while large units have been dry sieved and measured in the field in graduated buckets. This should not create a substantial difference, but there is some concern that the counting of buckets on unit sheets is not easily checked. The situation is complicated by the issue that wet sieving has a higher recovery rate than dry sieving. This particularly effects density based on count because wet sieving picks up more small material. Figure 2.6 plots densities based on material recovered from wet sieve only vs density based on all material in the data base. While the relationship approaches one to one in most cases, there are a substantial number of units where the density of material from flotation is higher. There are also some units with lower 'wet' densities. The same pattern is evident for lithics (Fig. 2.7).

Log-normality in the distributions

The specific choices for analysis have been partly governed by the deeply-unbalanced nature of the distributions. If the densities clustered around a centre point we could simply quote means and standard deviations and know immediately whether a value was high, low, or expectable. But they do not. So we need to look at the shape of the distributions as well as the centre point. This can be done with medians and quartiles. Means and standard deviations are difficult to use unless the distribution approaches normal. But frequency histograms, boxplots and inferential statistics are more informative.

Sadly, the distributions have really high frequencies for low values and also some infrequent very high values, which means that a straight histogram is very difficult to read. We can look at the bottom end (say, values under .5 g/l) but then we will not see what is going on with higher-density samples, which can be important. Also because both of the axes need to be

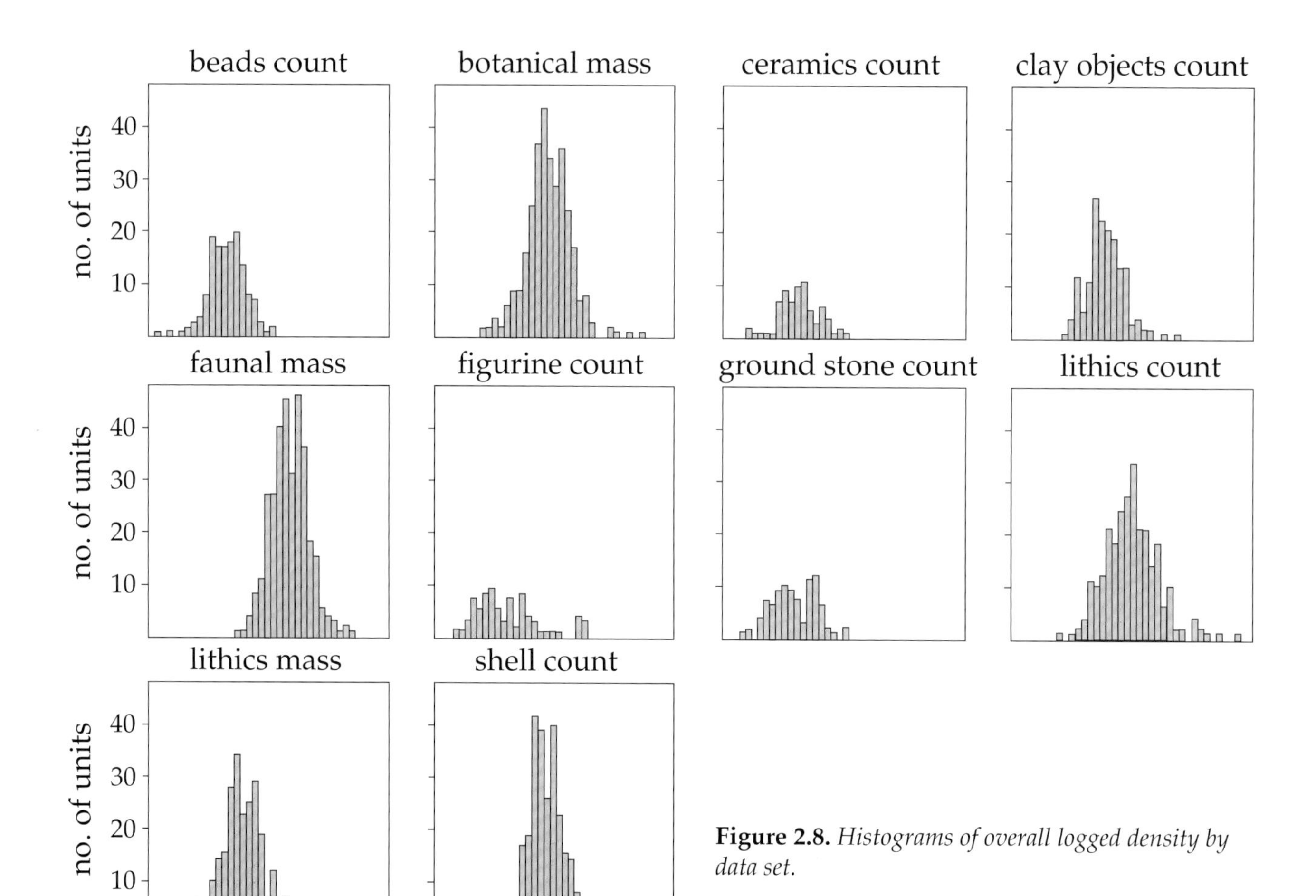

Figure 2.8. *Histograms of overall logged density by data set.*

very large, variation in the mid-range of the distribution, where multiple distributions could overlap, is masked. A way out of this problem is to transform the data by changing the measurement scale to a logarithmic scale. This is no different than multiplying centimetre measurements by 2.5 to produce a scale in inches. The kind of frequency distribution found at Çatalhöyük is very common, particularly in archaeology and is referred to as a 'lognormal' distribution.

Selection of analytical techniques

The general approach of the analysis has been exploratory. 'Such an approach ... seems to reflect a deeply ingrained tendency amongst archaeologists to prefer to interpret patterns rather than develop and test hypotheses' (Shennan 1988, 244). This is intended as criticism, but really shows that 'ordination' methods are exactly what we are looking for in this project, a method of getting at the structure of patterns so that we can interpret them, rather than a method to 'prove' our interpretations.

I have also generally tried to use techniques that lead to graphic output. This is partly because pattern recognition and interpretation are usually easier from graphic display, but also because it takes the emphasis off the absolute values of different data sets. While these may be important within analysis of individual data sets they can be distracting in comparing between data sets because of issues of scale.

Other than graphic and tabular presentation of the data, grouped in various ways, the main techniques used in this analysis have been non-parametric correlation, principal components analysis and inferential tests for particular questions.

Plots of the density of material in floor units were produced in order to examine spatial patterning within buildings. Since there are only 92 floor units in the analytical priorities this analysis is of limited use and the results will not be discussed here. Plots were produced for Building 1 Phase 2 and Building 17 Phase B, because these are the only buildings and phases with sufficiently good analytical priority coverage of floor units to make the plots worthwhile. The heavy residue offered a better chance to examine spatial patterning in excavated material, particularly since the main variable of interest was density (see

Chapter 3). One of the main results of that work is to suggest that floor variation relates mainly to preparation rather than use.

After transformation of the data by applying a logarithmic scale then many of our distributions approach normal (Fig. 2.8). While the shape of some of these histograms still indicates the multiple factors which affect these distributions, none of them are strong enough to base classifications on. The approach used here has been to apply classifications based on field assessment and other analysis to the distributions in order to see which of these classifications produces significant patterning within the overall distributions.

The first stage in analysis is to identify the pattern of presence and absence within units, to look at the basic composition of the sample. This can highlight important patterns in the rarer material such as ceramics and figurines. After this density is considered. There are two ways in which density distributions can be characterized; by central tendency and by variance. For some of our comparisons the central tendency is fairly constant but the variance is markedly different; in others the variance is fairly constant while the central tendency moves. The first suggests one set in which the variable is controlled for in deposition and another where either many rules or no rule applies. The second suggests that both sets are part of the same set of rules, taking different positions within the same structure of deposition.

The main classifications used are the data categories, which are also considered in terms of differences between levels. The distributions are also considered split according to whether the units are 'inside' or 'outside'. All of these classifications cross cut one another and some of the analysis consists of exploring how these relationships interact.

Table 2.4. *Density distribution of all studied material.*

	N	Minimum	25	50	75	Maximum
Shell (count/l)	279	0.0000	0.0826	0.1791	0.4600	16.0000
Bead (count/l)	520	0.0001	0.0092	0.0286	0.0675	8.0000
Figurine (count/l)	316	0.0000	0.0000	0.0029	0.0248	4.0000
Clay obj (count/l)	171	0.0022	0.0230	0.0479	0.1111	7.3333
Ceramics (sherds/l)	351	0.0003	0.0062	0.0146	0.0385	8.0000
Worked stone (count/l)	143	0.0001	0.0031	0.0078	0.0357	0.6667
Lithics (grams/l)	1620	0.0001	0.0095	0.0337	0.1180	2503.0290
Faunal (grams/l)	331	0.0370	0.7619	1.7500	4.8000	193.4333
Botanical (grams/l)	319	0.0020	0.0820	0.1913	0.6058	181.4565

Analysis

Overall distributions

Univariate analysis

Because the distributions are markedly non-normal, quartiles are the most useful method for summarizing them. While density figures for other sites are not currently available, these summaries are included here (Table 2.4) in the hope that it may be possible to compare between sites in the future. The N refers to the number of units in the sample, units with zero values for a data set were not included. The other columns show the densities for the minimum, the 25th percentile, the 50th percentile, the 75th percentile and the maximum. The median (50th percentile) is probably the best single measure but all of the figures are useful for comparison.

The logged values of these figures have been plotted as histograms in Figure 2.8. The greatest differences between these graphs stem from the number of units with the data set present (discussed above, Tables 2.2–2.3). The data sets in few units, beads, ceramics, figurines and ground stone are also found in low densities within those units. The more common data sets, shell, lithics, clay objects, and botanical material share a similar range of densities in the middle of the overall range. The highest densities are associated with faunal material. Most of the distributions approach normality when logged, but there are indications of more complex distributions relating to the classifications discussed below.

Correlations

Spearman's Rho was used to test correlation's between untransformed densities. This test was chosen because of the log-normal distributions involved. Spearman's Rho is based on rank order and so is less sensitive to heteroscedasic distributions than other correlation tests.

For densities based on counts the vast majority of material is positively correlated to a significance level of .001 (Table 2.5). There are no negative correlations, so there are no data sets which 'avoid' each other. There is a low number of correlations with ceramics, but this is probably partly because of the restricted chronological range for this material. Indeed if correlation is based only on levels with ceramics present, then ceramics are also positively correlated with faunal material at the .001 significance level and lithics to the .05 level, though there remains no correlation between ceramics and either shell or botanical material. Lithics, however, are stubbornly uncorrelated with ground stone as well as ceramics.

The positive correlation of densities based on weights is even stronger (Table 2.6). All data sets are

Table 2.5. *Correlations between data sets based on Spearman's Rho for densities (count/l) for 328 units.*

	Lithic	Shell	Beads	Figurine	Clay obj	Ceramics	Grounds tone	
Lithics	1	0.365	0.223	0.191	0.413	0.084	0.006	Correlation Coefficient
	.	0.000	0.000	0.001	0.000	0.128	0.912	Sig. (2-tailed)
Shell		1	0.229	0.388	0.270	0.022	0.159	Correlation Coefficient
		.	0.000	0.000	0.000	0.686	0.004	Sig. (2-tailed)
Beads			1	0.194	0.247	0.175	0.133	Correlation Coefficient
			.	0.000	0.000	0.001	0.016	Sig. (2-tailed)
Figurine				1	0.103	0.169	0.185	Correlation Coefficient
				.	0.063	0.002	0.001	Sig. (2-tailed)
Clay obj					1	0.244	0.273	Correlation Coefficient
					.	0.000	0.000	Sig. (2-tailed)
Ceramics						1	0.269	Correlation Coefficient
						.	0.000	Sig. (2-tailed)
Ground stone							1	Correlation Coefficient
							.	Sig. (2-tailed)

Table 2.6. *Correlations between data sets based on Spearman's Rho for densities (grams/l) for 347 units.*

	Lithics	Faunal	Botanical	Clay obj	Ceramics	Ground stone	
Lithics	1	0.332	0.235	0.318	0.147	0.125	Correlation Coefficient
	.	0.000	0.000	0.000	0.006	0.020	Sig. (2-tailed)
Faunal		1	0.483	0.396	0.287	0.347	Correlation Coefficient
		.	0.000	0.000	0.000	0.000	Sig. (2-tailed)
Botanical			1	0.166	0.170	0.178	Correlation Coefficient
			.	0.002	0.001	0.001	Sig. (2-tailed)
Clay obj				1	0.259	0.323	Correlation Coefficient
				.	0.000	0.000	Sig. (2-tailed)
Ceramics					1	0.278	Correlation Coefficient
					.	0.000	Sig. (2-tailed)
Ground stone						1	Correlation Coefficient
						.	Sig. (2-tailed)

Table 2.7. *Component matrix for principal component analysis based on standardized count densities of primary data sets.*

Variable	**Component**	
	1	**2**
Lithics	0.5133	0.6527
Shell	0.5900	0.6111
Beads	0.6989	–0.3499
Figurine	0.6492	–0.4947
Clay obj	0.7333	–0.2433
Ceramics	0.6112	0.0795

Table 2.8. *Component matrix for principal component analysis based on logged mass densities of primary data sets.*

Variable	**Rescaled Component**	
	1	**2**
Lithics	0.76842	–0.43787
Faunal	0.70499	0.15833
Botanical	0.72707	–0.33683
Clay obj	0.6503	0.73045

positively correlated at the .05 significance level and the vast majority are positively correlated at the .001 significance level. The lithics have less significant correlations with both ceramics and worked stone. This is the same relationship shown in the count density correlations and may indicate a pattern worth considering further.

Principal components analysis

Principal components analysis uses matrix algebra to determine common underlying components or factors, which explain a proportion of the variance in all of the factors considered together. Its primary purpose is data reduction because rather than plotting data on six or seven axes you can plot the important patterning on two axes (see Baxter 1994). So it fits quite nicely with the overall strategy of exploratory and graphic analysis adopted here. It can also be used to consider the relationship between variables by looking at the component co-efficients associated with them used to produce the factors.

Tables 2.7 and 2.8 show the component co-efficients for analyses based on count and mass densities respectively. Because not all data sets can be described by either mass or count the position of lithics and clay objects is crucial to understanding the relationships between groupings. In both analyses the first factor is relatively well balanced between all the variables. The second factor shows two groupings. Lithics and clay objects are in separate groups for both analyses. In the count-based analysis clay objects are grouped with beads and figurines, while in the mass-based analysis they are linked to faunal material. Lithics are grouped with shell in the analysis by count and with botanical material in the analysis based on mass.

Data categories and levels

Each data category represents different types of activity and has different issues in terms of analysis. The entire mound is made up of cultural material, but some of it is more amenable to analysis and/or has been modified more in the past (compare mudbrick and clay objects). Midden is residue from life collected in one place. Fill is more episodic bringing together of material with the specific intention of filling a space. Both fill and midden contribute substantially to the growth of the mound but there is a shift with midden providing the bulk in the lower levels and fill in the upper levels. Floors are of interest because we hoped to get at primary discard, but many of the patterns here are related to construction. Construction units are interesting for variation between walls and features and for the relationship with the other data categories.

Presence–absence analysis

Data categories in levels

Much of the difference between levels is expressed by changes in the balance of data categories. Similarly some data categories (such as middens) are particularly connected with some phases in the development of the mound. There is no data category that is found in all levels (Table 2.9). In the KOPAL Area all of the priority units are either fill or natural. The natural units have anthropogenic material and there is some overlap between this data category and the alluviated dump group within middens in the Level Pre-XII phases. Middens are persistently present in the South Area levels, with the exception of Levels XI and X, which are dominated by penning deposits. These are 'activity' in terms of data category. There are no middens from the North Area since the excavation focussed so tightly on the buildings themselves. Floors are absent before Level X except for a group from Level Pre-XII.B. In the deep sounding this relates to the restricted range of excavation but in Levels XI and XII this is because of the previous excavation of the area. Fills are present in most levels, which is partly a product of the broad range of fills that there are (filling, buildings, features, spaces between walls, cuts). Although most of the fills are from North Area Levels VI–V (representing Building 1) as a proportion of the units from that level it is not a particularly important data category. Construction material (including make-

Table 2.9. *Number of units in priority sample by level and data category.*

Level	Activity	Arbitrary	Cluster	Construction	Fill	Floors	Midden	Natural	Total
KOPAL	-	-	-	-	6	-	-	4	10
Pre-XII.D	-	-	-	-	-	-	4	-	4
Pre-XII.C	1	-	-	-	-	-	4	-	5
Pre-XII.B	6	-	-	-	3	4	8	-	21
Pre-XII.A	2	-	-	-	1	-	6	-	9
XII	5	-	-	1	-	-	1	-	7
XI	4	-	-	-	1	-	-	-	5
X	-	-	6	-	7	14	-	-	27
IX	1	1	4	3	17	25	7	-	58
VIII	-	-	3	1	20	17	13	-	54
VII	-	-	2	2	18	1	-	-	23
N.VII–VI	-	-	-	7	6	7	-	-	20
N.VI–V	-	1	2	11	65	29	-	-	108
N.V–IV	-	-	1	-	-	3	-	-	4
Total	**19**	**2**	**18**	**25**	**144**	**100**	**43**	**4**	**355**

Table 2.10. *Number of units in analytical priority sample by level and data set.*

Level	Lithics	Faunal	Shell	Bead	Figurine	Clay obj	Ceramic	Botanical	Ground stone	Total
KOPAL	9	10	9	1	2	8	-	10	6	10
Pre-XII.D	4	4	4	4	1	4	-	4	4	4
Pre-XII.C	5	5	5	5	4	5	-	4	4	5
Pre-XII.B	21	21	20	14	9	19	-	20	10	21
Pre-XII.A	9	9	9	9	8	9	1	8	7	9
XII	7	7	6	5	2	5	-	6	2	7
XI	5	5	5	4	1	5	1	5	1	5
X	27	22	20	12	2	15	7	21	2	27
IX	48	52	41	21	11	29	16	53	17	58
VIII	46	51	45	26	15	41	19	49	14	54
VII	17	23	20	7	4	17	11	21	9	23
N.VII–VI	4	17	13	3	1	4	1	19	2	20
N.VI–V	63	107	85	38	13	15	19	103	22	108
N.V–IV	4	4	2	-	-	1	1	4	1	4
Total	**269**	**337**	**284**	**149**	**73**	**177**	**76**	**327**	**101**	**355**

Table 2.11. *Number of units in analytical priorities by data set and data category.*

	Lithics	Faunal	Shell	Bead	Figurine	Clay obj	Ceramic	Botanical	Ground stone	Total
Fill	106	141	117	55	21	65	36	138	37	144
Floor	76	92	74	40	11	37	12	93	14	100
Midden	42	43	43	35	29	43	20	40	34	43
Construction	10	24	19	4	3	6	-	25	4	25
Cluster	11	12	8	2	2	6	3	9	3	18
Activity	18	19	17	12	5	15	1	16	4	19
Arbitrary	2	2	2	1	-	1	-	2	1	2
Natural	4	4	4	-	2	4	-	4	4	4
Total	**269**	**337**	**284**	**149**	**73**	**177**	**76**	**327**	**101**	**355**

Table 2.12. *Significance of differences between three categorizations, Kruskal Wallis test.*

Variable	Data category	Level	Inside:outside
mass density lithics	0.116	0.000	0.138
mass density faunal	0.000	0.000	0.000
mass density botanical	0.000	0.012	0.002
mass density clay obj	0.388	0.000	0.209
mass density ceramics	0.002	0.022	0.073
mass density ground stone	0.000	0.000	0.000
count density lithics	0.000	0.089	0.697
count density shell	0.065	0.000	0.626
count density beads	0.000	0.013	0.000
count density figurine	0.000	0.007	0.000
count density clay obj	0.000	0.026	0.000
count density ceramics	0.000	0.001	0.369
count density ground stone	0.000	0.000	0.000

up and packing deposits) is concentrated in the upper levels.

Data sets in levels

Most data sets are found in similar proportions in all levels (Table 2.10). The non-appearance of ceramics in the lower levels is likely to be a genuine chronological difference rather than a difference stemming from the different data categories under investigation. Lithics are under-represented in the upper levels, but this may be methodological since not all the material from heavy residue was available for analysis when this material was being analyzed. On the other hand there is a generally low value for non-biological material from these levels, particularly for North Area Level VII–VI, the level of Building 5. Of the artefact types, beads are the most commonly present. If this difference relates to varying data categories then it is interesting to consider that it is the non-biological material which is most affected by the sample not including middens.

Data sets in data categories

Looking at the presence of data sets in data categories most data sets are represented in reasonably proportionate amounts (Table 2.11). The interesting exception is that the artefacts are disproportionately present in middens, confirming the pattern described above. Shell and botanical material are both slightly under-represented in clusters. This is particularly interesting for botanical material since some clusters were defined for the presence of charred botanical remains. Of the 18 clusters, 8 were defined for obsidian, 5 for faunal material 2 for charred botanical remains, 2 for clay objects and 1 for owl pellets. So most data sets were present in clusters that were defined for other substances.

Univariate density analysis

By contrast with the presence–absence analysis, the density of material in different data categories shows significant differences for all data sets except shell and clay objects and lithics measured by mass (Table 2.12). This different behaviour for shell is in keeping with a number of other patterns discussed below and may indicate that shell represents more than one type of behaviour. The clay objects and lithics are the only two common data sets that can be measured clearly by both mass and count and their difference in pattern is interesting in this light.

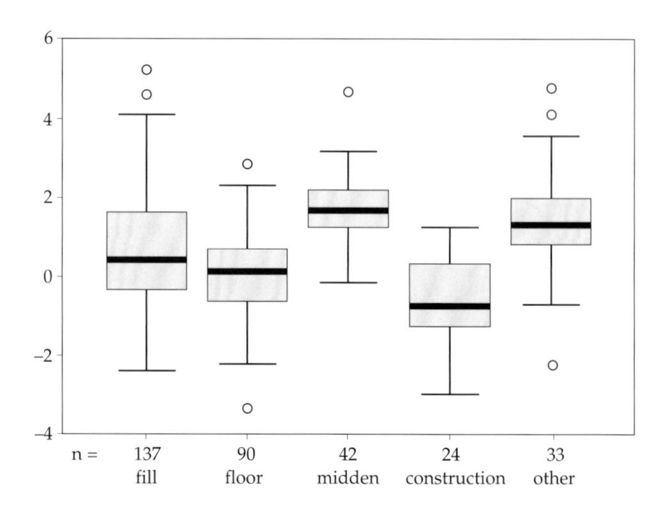

Figure 2.9. *Logged density (g/l) of faunal material by data category.*

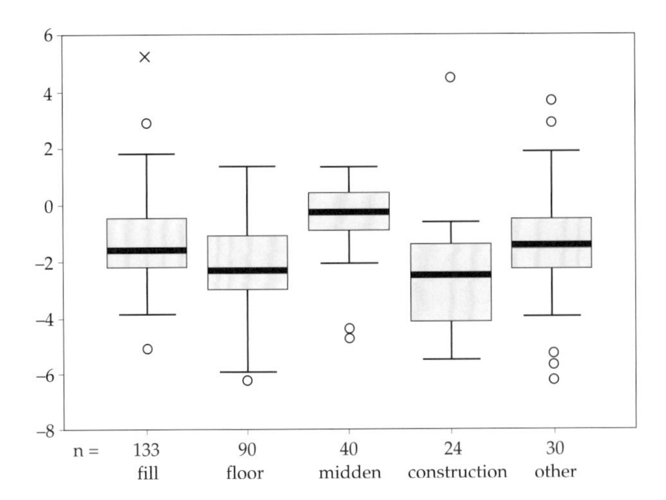

Figure 2.10. *Logged density (g/l) of botanical material by data category.*

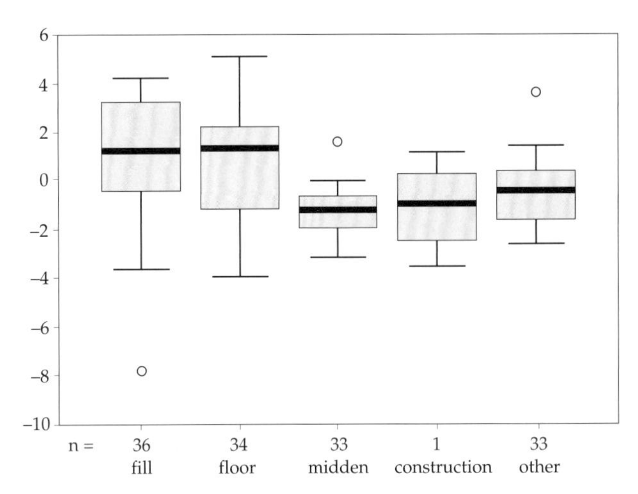

Figure 2.11. *Logged density (g/l) of ground stone by data category.*

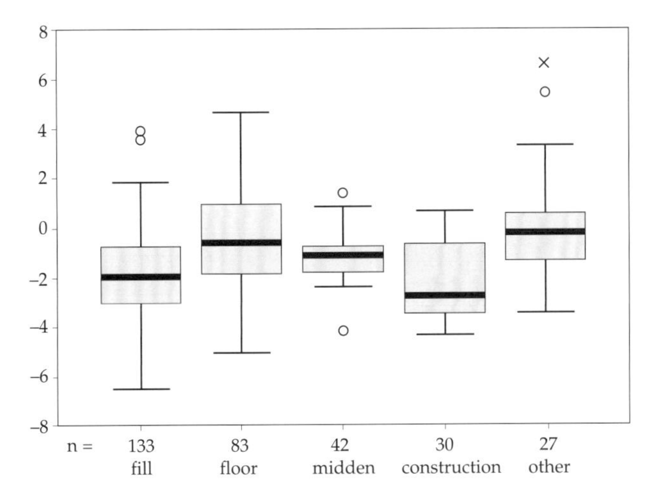

Figure 2.12. *Logged density (count/l) of lithics by data category.*

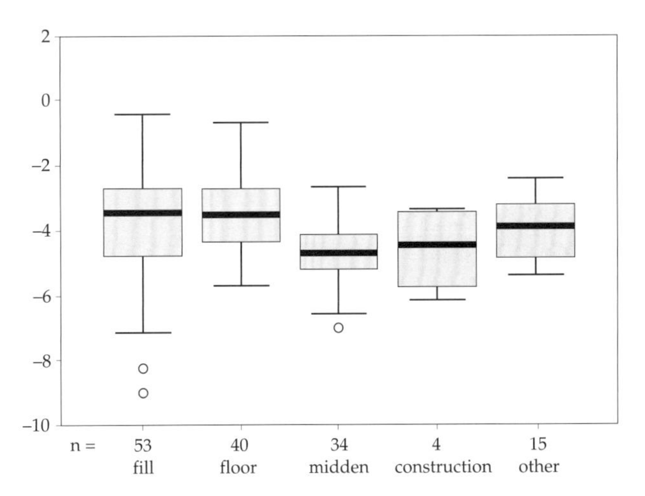

Figure 2.13. *Logged density (count/l) of beads by data category.*

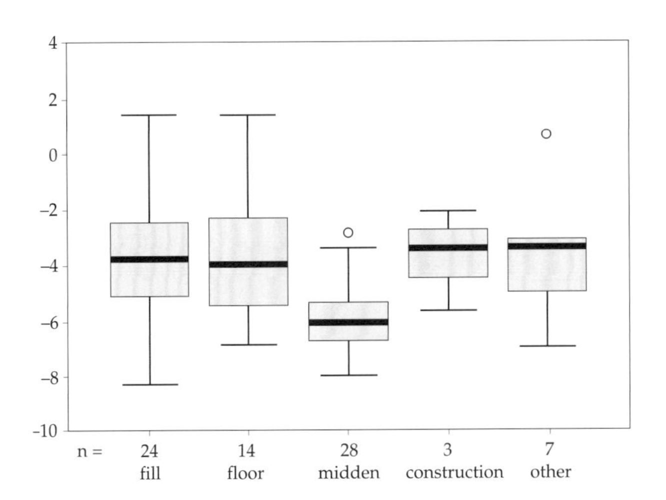

Figure 2.14. *Logged density (count/l) of figurines by data category.*

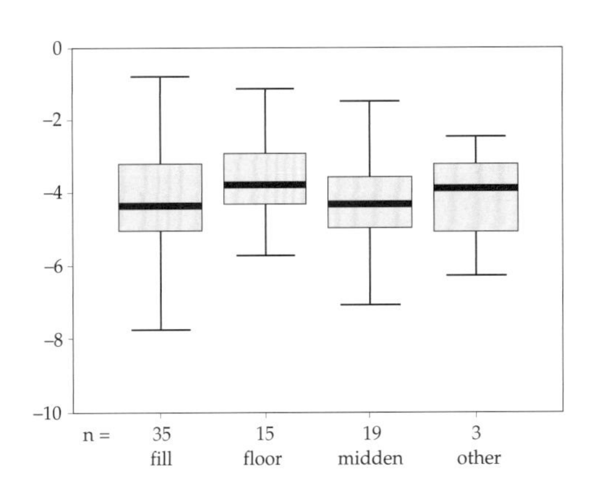

Figure 2.15. *Logged density (count/l) of ceramics by data category.*

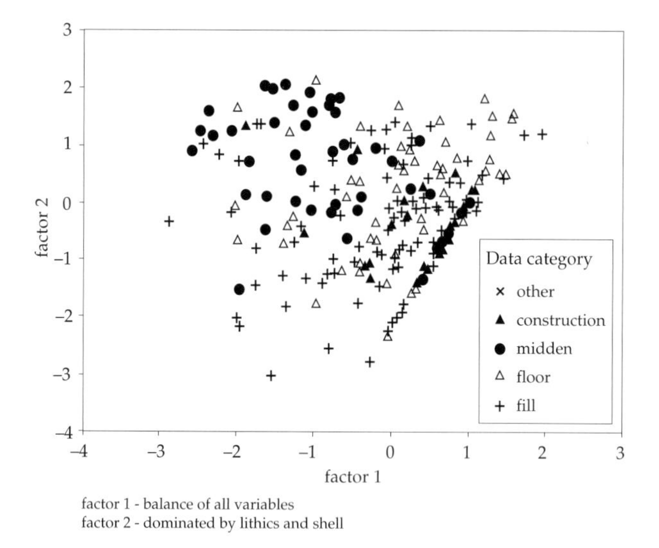

Figure 2.16. *Scatterplot of principal components analysis on standardized count densities.*

Most data sets show substantial and significant differences between data categories, both in terms of presence–absence and in the distribution of density. Figures 2.9–2.15 show boxplots of the logged densities of the data sets that show differences between data categories. The significant difference in the ceramic count density is due to the absence of ceramics from construction units. All of the other data categories show quite similar distributions. For all of the other data sets middens have markedly smaller variance than the other data categories. For faunal and botanical material this small variance is coupled with a higher mean density. For ground stone, beads and figurines, however, middens have a substantially lower mean density than fills and floors. This highlights the difficulty of using density to measure rare material. A single sherd of ceramics in a small unit registers as a higher density than a single sherd in a large unit. While this reflects the rarity of the material it masks the importance of middens, in which these material types are found most commonly. The number of units along the category axis should be taken into account when reading these graphs.

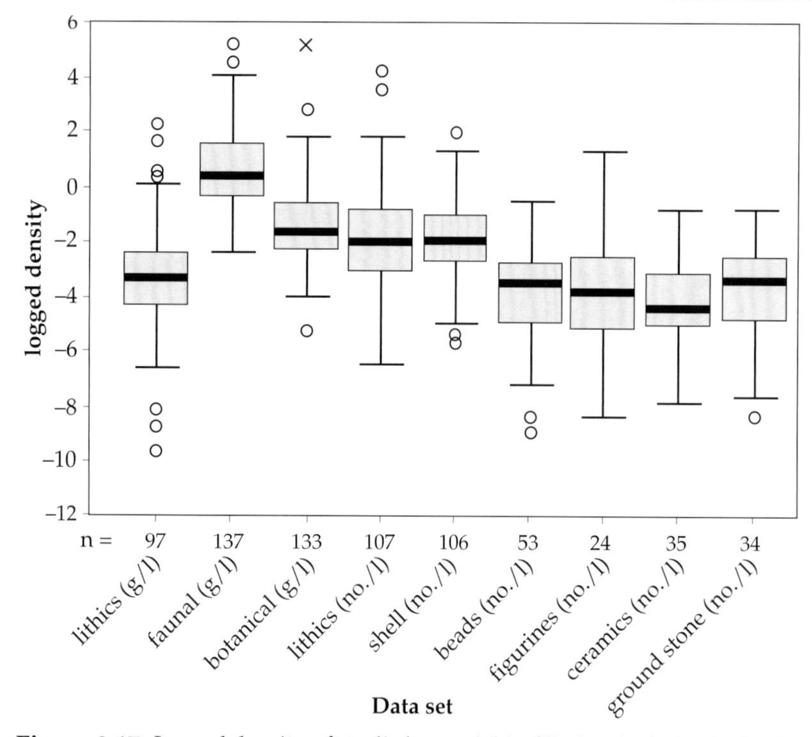

Figure 2.17. *Logged density of studied material in fills (analytical priorities).*

Table 2.13. *Density distribution of all studied material in fills.*

	N	Minimum	25	50	75	Maximum
Shell (count/l)	114	0.0000	0.0609	0.1404	0.3813	8.0000
Bead (count/l)	203	0.0001	0.0077	0.0286	0.0588	1.6000
Figurine (count/l)	133	0.0000	0.0000	0.0020	0.0139	4.0000
Clay obj (count/l)	64	0.0022	0.0193	0.0498	0.1587	7.3333
Ceramics (sherds/l)	166	0.0003	0.0046	0.0120	0.0287	0.5000
Worked stone (count/l)	58	0.0001	0.0033	0.0114	0.0658	0.5000
Lithics (grams/l)	561	0.0001	0.0097	0.0290	0.0944	97.0300
Faunal (grams/l)	139	0.0968	0.7430	1.5528	5.2143	193.4333
Botanical (grams/l)	133	0.0057	0.1060	0.2067	0.6166	181.4565

Principal components analysis

Figure 2.16 shows a scatterplot of the two factors from the analysis detailed in Table 2.7 based on count densities. Generally speaking the distribution remains fairly clumped and mixed but there is a slight separation of midden units, which suggests that they are more distinctive than other data categories. This backs up the picture from the univariate analysis of density, which showed smaller variance for middens for most data sets.

Fills

Fills are the most common data category on site. The 949 fills excavated comprise over 50 per cent of the total excavated volume. The 144 priority units make up just under 40 per cent of the volume of the sample. This discrepancy is because middens are over-represented in the analytical priority sample. Fills are concentrated in the upper levels of the site because they are associated with buildings. Much of their matrix appears to be construction material, but they all have substantial amounts of other cultural material as well. Filling empty space prior to construction is the essential feature of tell formation and the composition of these fills will reflect abandonment and construction practices which are at the heart of the community.

Figure 2.17 is a boxplot for all data sets within fill units (Table 2.13). As with the overall picture, data sets which occur less frequently also occur in lower densities. That being said, the density distributions are remarkably similar across data sets, particularly for beads, figurines, ceramics, and ground stone. Faunal material is the dominant material analyzed from the data category with both high frequencies and high densities.

The data category has been divided on the basis of what space is being filled. Most deposits fill buildings prior to reconstruction. The next largest group fills cuts of various types. The majority of these are also part of the reconstruction process filling the pits created by the retrieval of posts and other features which were reused in other buildings. Only burials, scoops, stakeholes, and some postholes were filled during the use of the building. Features were filled as a stage in the closing of a building. While there could be variation based on the type of feature, it is unlikely to be a product of use. Although there are five different categories of feature that can be filled, only bins are represented well in the priority sample. The last group of fills, between walls, differs from the others because it can include very slow processes of deposition as well as the faster profiles represented by the other groups. This group may have more similarities with middens.

There are three groupings for the distribution of material in these different categories (Table 2.14). Shell, botanical and faunal material are ubiquitous. Beads, although rarer, belong in this group because they are evenly distributed between the fill classes. Clay objects, ceramics, figurines and ground stone are over-represented between walls and under-represented in building fills. Lithics show the opposite pattern being under-represented between walls and in features.

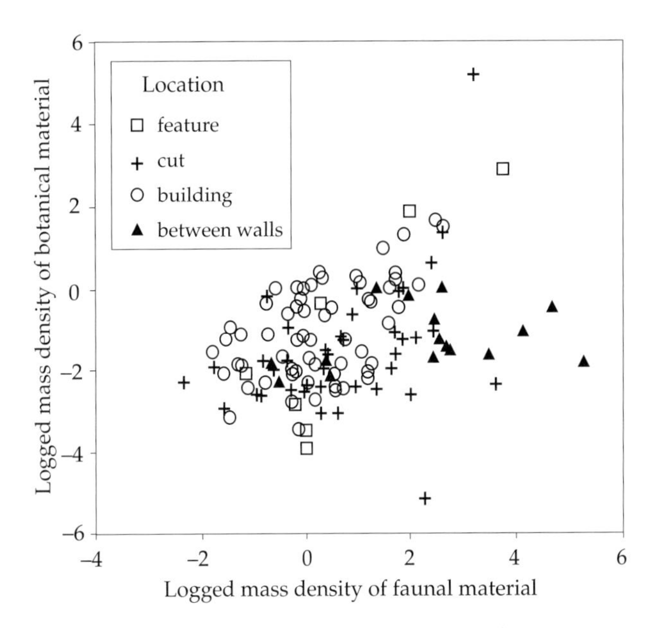

Figure 2.18. *Faunal vs botancial densities (g/l) for fills by location.*

Between wall fills also stand out when considered in terms of density. Figure 2.18 is a scatterplot of the logged mass densities of faunal vs botanical material marked by different fill locations. While there is generally a strong correlation between the two data sets, this breaks down for fills between walls. These fills have high values for faunal material but show no correlation with botanical material for which they have only middle range densities.

Building fills: Building fills represent the closure of a building in advance of the construction of a new building. Since buildings were filled individually, each building could have had a different signature reflecting available fill material at the time. However, as the differences between spaces within one building are often greater than the difference between buildings, it seems that the variation reflects a more complex practice. Since fills link two buildings in time their

Table 2.14. *Presence of material in fills by location.*

Location	Total	Botanical	Faunal	Shell	Lithics	Beads	Clay obj	Ceramics	Figurine	Ground stone
Building	68	65	68	57	55	26	22	20	6	16
Cut	47	47	46	37	34	19	27	7	7	11
Feature	15	14	13	11	9	4	6	2	2	2
Between walls	14	12	14	12	8	6	10	7	6	8

Table 2.15. *Presence of material in building fills based on the presence of fire installations in the space.*

Fire installation	Total	Lithics	Botanical	Faunal	Figurine	Beads	Ceramics	Clay obj	Shell	Ground stone
Present	36	29	35	36	1	15	7	8	31	7
Absent	12	8	12	12	0	3	4	1	9	2
Unknown	18	16	16	18	4	7	8	12	16	6

Table 2.16. *Presence of material in building fills based on the presence of burials in the space.*

Burial	Total	Lithics	Botanical	Faunal	Figurine	Beads	Ceramics	Clay obj	Shell	Ground stone
Present	23	23	22	23	2	10	5	10	19	5
Absent	29	19	28	29	1	12	9	1	24	6
Unknown	14	11	13	14	2	3	5	10	13	4

Table 2.17. *Presence of material in building fills based on the type of floor in the space.*

Floor type	Total	Lithics	Botanical	Faunal	Figurine	Beads	Ceramics	Clay obj	Shell	Ground stone
Laid	13	11	12	13	1	3	3	3	9	2
Occupation	22	16	21	22	1	11	6	1	19	4
Mixed	18	17	17	18	2	8	4	12	17	6
Unknown	13	9	13	13	1	3	6	5	11	3

Table 2.18. *Presence of material in building fills based on room status of the space.*

Room status	Total	Lithics	Botanical	Faunal	Figurine	Beads	Ceramics	Clay obj	Shell	Ground stone
Main room	31	26	30	31	1	11	7	12	26	8
Side (features)	21	15	21	21	1	9	5	0	18	3
Side (no features)	3	3	3	3	2	2	2	3	3	2
Unknown	11	9	9	11	1	3	5	6	9	2

cultural composition might reflect perceptions of the continuing importance of the space being filled.

I have divided spaces on four different criteria: the presence of a fire installation, the presence of one or more burials, the nature of the floor and an overall assessment of the room in the building plan (Tables 2.15–2.18). A range of measures was used to assess the composition of the infill of these spaces. Although each division picks up some variation the floor was the best discriminant, followed by the presence of burials. It is surprising that the overall assessment was not more powerful, since it takes a number of elements into account. This pattern is not a direct result of use since it relates to the fill deposited after the space is abandoned (often after an episode of scouring). It is a detail in the process of abandonment and reconstruction which is responsive to the original use of a space.

Beginning with the presence of material, some groupings between data sets are apparent. Clay objects and lithics respond in the same way as each other. They are under-represented in fills of spaces without burial, with only occupation floors, without fire installations and in spaces classified as side rooms. The pattern is stronger for clay objects than it is for lithics.

Ceramics and beads could form a contrasting group, potentially joined by figurines, though the numbers of units with figurines are so low that they should really be discounted. The pattern is not as consistent as that shown by the clay objects and lithics. Ceramics are under-represented in the fills of main rooms, and of spaces with fire installations. Beads are under-represented in spaces with laid floors and with mixed floors. They are also slightly under-represented in the fills of spaces with fire installations.

These patterns also show some relationship between the classification criteria. Spaces without burials, fire installations, or any laid floors show similar patterns of infill to spaces classified as side rooms. The side rooms with features are the spaces avoided for the deposition of clay object in the fill. Interestingly, there are clay objects in 5 of the 20 non-fill units studied from these types of spaces — so the fill is not simply mirroring established deposition patterns. This may also be reflected in the fact that most data sets are best represented in the fills of spaces with mixed floors.

Density: The grouping of data sets based on presence–absence is indicative that not all data sets respond in the same way to the character of the space, which will also complicate the question of what kinds of divisions are important. Table 2.19 shows the significance of differences between the density distributions for building fills classified on the basis of these criteria. The greatest number of significant differences is connected with the classification by underlying floor type.

Density analysis is helpful for exploring this further, especially for those fairly ubiquitous data sets such as faunal and botanical material and shell. Faunal and botanical material tend to react strongly to the presence of fire installations and burials. They have higher densities for the former and lower densities for the latter. Figure 2.19 shows that fills over occupation floors have higher densities of both botanical and faunal material than fills over other types of floors. Shell shows a similar pattern (Fig. 2.20). Lithics on the other hand show the highest densities for fills over spaces with mixed floors (Fig. 2.21). Spaces with laid floors also have lower variance than those with other types of floor. The presence of fire installations appears to have less effect, though it is possible that there is greater variance in spaces with fire installations than those without them.

Floors

The data category 'floors' incorporates all use surfaces, those deliberately laid and consolidated with plaster and those resulting from use (Table 2.20). The initial hope for analysis was that they may show patterns relating to use. The closure of buildings and preparation for re-

Table 2.19. *Significance of differences between building fills of spaces with varying characters, Kruskal Wallis test.*

Variable	Burial	Floor	Room status	Fire
Mass density lithics	0.025	0.012	0.359	0.367
Mass density faunal	0.000	0.000	0.020	0.002
Mass density botanical	0.001	0.000	0.000	0.545
Mass density clay obj	0.045	0.032	0.004	0.009
Mass density ceramics	0.326	0.848	0.135	0.100
Mass density ground stone	0.049	0.342	0.031	0.078
Count density lithics	0.044	0.001	0.034	0.034
Count density shell	0.005	0.016	0.283	0.068
Count density beads	0.367	0.449	0.409	0.696
Count density figurine	0.262	0.676	0.003	0.005
Count density clay obj	0.000	0.000	0.000	0.000
Count density ceramics	0.432	0.387	0.101	0.070
Count density ground stone	0.447	0.333	0.087	0.194
Mass density heavy residue	0.011	0.000	0.000	0.002
Diversity of heavy residue	0.000	0.000	0.000	0.003

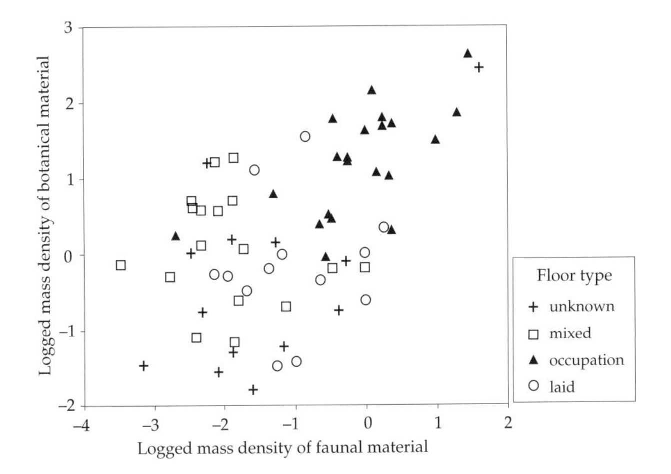

Figure 2.19. *Faunal vs botanical densities for building fills by underlying floor type.*

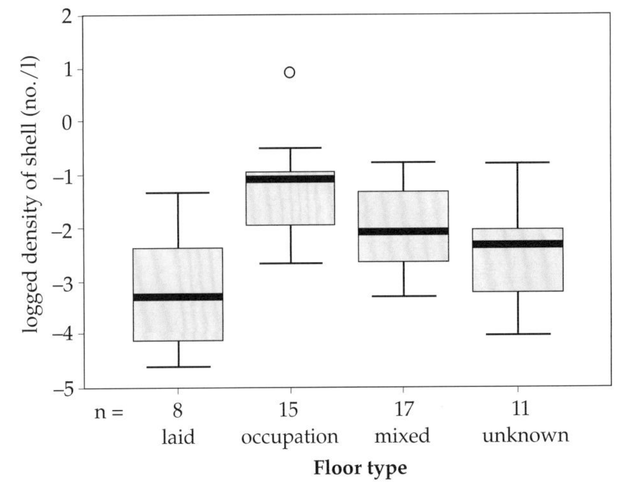

Figure 2.20. *Logged density of shell (count/l) in building fills by underlying floor type.*

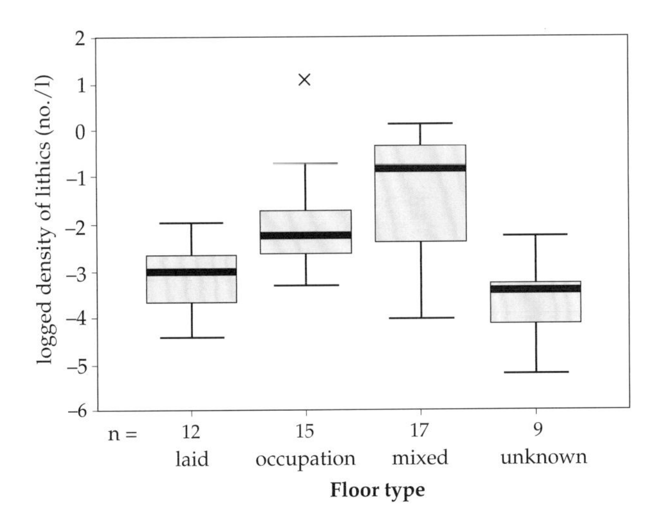

Figure 2.21. *Logged density of lithics (count/l) in building fills by underlying floor type.*

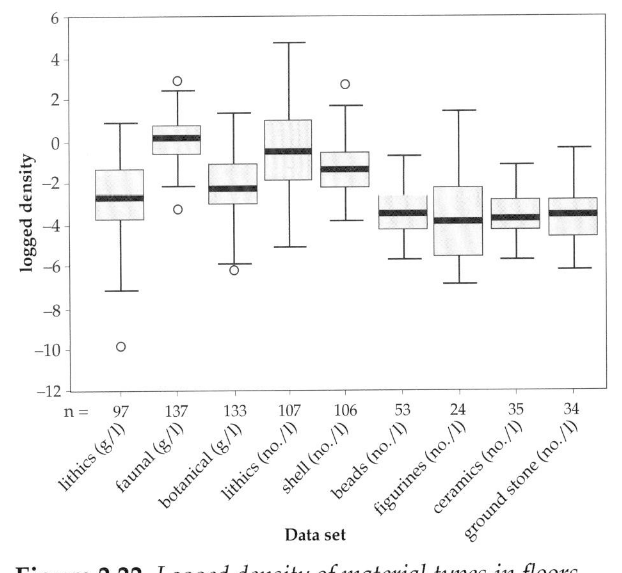

Figure 2.22. *Logged density of material types in floors (analytical priorities).*

Table 2.20. *Density distribution of all studied material in floors.*

	N	Minimum	25	50	75	Maximum
Shell (count/l)	74	0.0200	0.0970	0.2514	0.5611	14.4737
Bead (count/l)	100	0.0005	0.0225	0.0597	0.1955	8.0000
Figurine (count/l)	62	0.0000	0.0000	0.0039	0.0728	4.0000
Clay obj (count/l)	36	0.0061	0.0247	0.0784	0.1868	1.3231
Ceramics (sherds/l)	33	0.0010	0.0138	0.0289	0.0870	1.0000
Worked stone (count/l)	15	0.0020	0.0100	0.0256	0.0556	0.6667
Lithics (grams/l)	348	0.0001	0.0148	0.0400	0.1599	8.5300
Faunal (grams/l)	92	0.0370	0.5571	1.1667	2.0523	17.6159
Botanical (grams/l)	91	0.0020	0.0456	0.0949	0.3400	3.9637

construction however appear to have scoured most traces of use. The results of the analysis mostly point to differences in the preparation of the surface. The possible exception is the distribution of lithics in 'occupation' floors, which may reflect use.

Figure 2.22 is a boxplot showing the density distributions for all data sets from floors. As with the distributions for fills (see Fig. 2.17) there is a tendency for rare data sets to have low densities. An interesting departure from the pattern for fills is the high densities for lithics when measured by count while the mass densities remain similar. This may relate to a larger proportion of micro-debitage which could result from *in situ* preservation of knapping debris. This would be a rare example of information concerning use recovered from floors.

Floors can be divided on the basis of the extent of preparation (Table 2.21). Laid floors (including baked, white clay and non-white laid floors) and occupation, there are also a small number of mixed floors. While most of the cultural material in floors appears to derive from the preparation (see Chapter 3) some of the material may relate to use. Comparing the presence of different data sets in the different types of floors it is clear that there are similar numbers of floor units with faunal material and botanical material in both classes. On the other hand, there are more units with lithics, beads, clay objects and shell in the occupation category than in the laid category. The numbers are small for ceramics figurines and ground stone but it seems that ceramics and figurines are more likely to be found in occupation floors while ground stone has an even chance.

This suggests one of two things. It is possible that the material that occupation floors were prepared from more often contained these data classes, or it could be that the material is there as residue of activity. Density analysis may help distinguish between these two options, since if more 'midden' material was used in the preparation we should expect higher densities of material overall. That being said, field records suggest that 'occupation' floors are formed through use which would be borne out by the second option. Further, if occupation floors have rougher surfaces they would be more difficult to sweep after use and would therefore be more like to preserve evidence of use. Ground stone is often quite large, and may reflect abandonment behaviour rather than preparation or use.

The pattern is less clear cut for location. Floors have been classified as external, the floor of a building or the floor of a feature (Table 2.22). Although there are more units with all classes of material from building floors, this is largely because more of these units were studied. The distribution of material in proportion to the total number of units is even. The only exceptions are ceramics beads and figurines, which are found in a substantially smaller proportion of feature floors than building floors. The small number of external floor units prevents useful comparison. Relationships between inside and outside are considered more generally below.

Density: The overall low density of material from floor units, even occupation floors means that the differences in density between the different categories are rarely significant (Table 2.23). There are far fewer

Table 2.21. *Presence of data sets in floors based on material composition.*

Material	Total	Botanical	Faunal	Lithics	Beads	Clay obj	Shell	Ceramics	Figurine	Ground stone
Laid	45	43	41	30	15	11	30	3	3	6
Occupation	47	43	45	40	22	23	39	10	8	8
Mixed	8	7	6	6	3	3	5	3	0	0

Table 2.22. *Presence of material based on location of floors.*

Location	Total	Botanical	Faunal	Shell	Lithics	Beads	Clay obj	Ceramics	Figurine	Ground stone
Building	71	67	65	54	51	33	25	14	9	8
External	4	4	4	4	4	2	3		1	2
Feature	25	22	23	16	21	5	9	2	1	4

Table 2.23. *Significance of differences between floors with varying characteristics, Kruskal Wallis test.*

Variable	Material	Location	Building
Mass density lithics	0.253	0.007	0.212
Mass density faunal	0.000	0.048	0.208
Mass density botanical	0.000	0.957	0.010
Mass density clay obj	0.053	0.247	0.000
Mass density ceramics	0.058	0.361	0.242
Mass density ground stone	0.756	0.177	0.982
Count density lithics	0.000	0.078	0.000
Count density shell	0.012	0.208	0.001
Count density beads	0.853	0.023	0.444
Count density figurine	0.453	0.218	0.574
Count density clay obj	0.139	0.411	0.075
Count density ceramics	0.065	0.077	0.269
Count density ground stone	0.486	0.659	0.670

significant differences between the different classifications of floors than there are between fills. Even the distinction between occupation floors and laid floors (under the material classification) has far fewer significant differences than the fills which cover those same floors. The results for the location variable, picking up the distinction between feature floors (bins, hearths, ovens etc.) and building floors (all others), show only three significant differences between these classes and none of them to the .001 level. Faunal and lithics are found in slightly higher densities in building floors.

In those circumstances where there is a significant difference between different classifications the relationships between the variables are quite strong. Figure 2.23 is a scatterplot of the lithic and faunal densities for floors marked by their material composition. The distinction between laid floors and occupation floors is very striking.

Principal components analysis: Since floors were a data category with a substantial spread in the overall plots by data category it is useful to break the category down and examine it in more detail. Figure 2.24 is a plot of the principal components representing the count density of lithics, faunal, beads, figurines, clay, ceramic botanical and ground stone within floor units in the analytical priority marked by material. The components only account for 47 per cent of the variance in the overall matrix, so fine tuning which data sets to consider would probably produce more a powerful plot. Nonetheless there is interesting pattern. The component matrix shows that most of the artefact classes are grouped together (factor 1), but lithics is grouped with the biological data sets (factor 2). The plot of these components marked by floor material shows a striking grouping (Fig. 2.24). White clay and non-white laid floors occupy a similar position on the graph, suggesting that the distinction in material is not necessarily related to colour, at least in regard to the finds composition. They have lower values for both factors, perhaps suggesting that less of their variance is accounted for by this analysis than occupation floors, the bulk of which have higher values. The floors labelled as mixed fall in between these two groupings in a satisfying fashion.

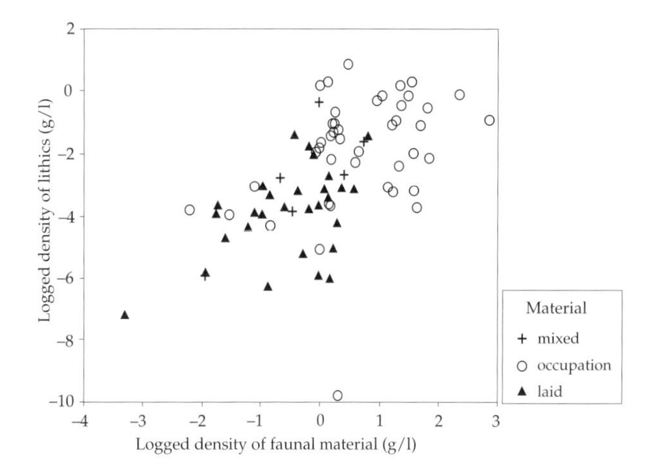

Figure 2.23. *Lithic vs faunal densities for floors by material composition.*

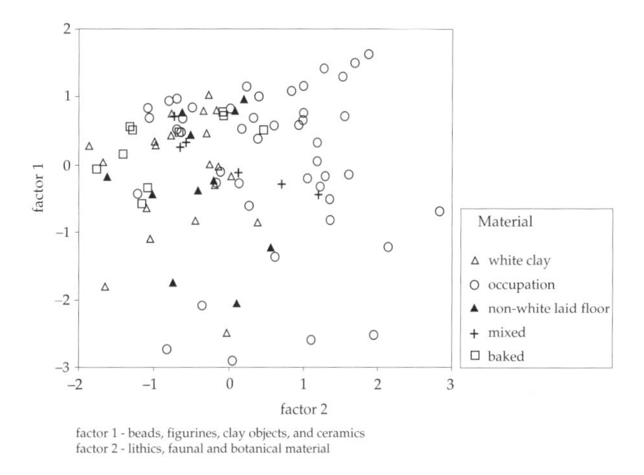

Figure 2.24. *Scatterplot of principal components analysis based on count density for floors marked by floor material.*

Middens

Figure 2.25 shows boxplots for all data sets within middens (Table 2.24). This graph shows much greater variation than the other data categories which have been discussed so far (Figs. 2.17 & 2.22). All of the distributions have quite small variances and there is a large difference between the high-density faunal material and the low-density figurines. This underlines the picture which has already emerged that middens are a tightly-defined category. They are the place for the deposition of closely-defined categories of mate-

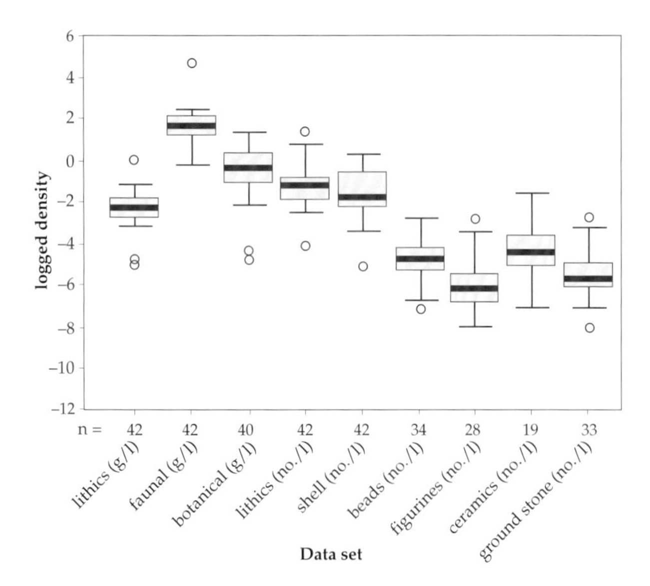

Figure 2.25. *Logged density of material from middens (analytical priorities).*

rial and not a general dumping ground as might be thought.

Middens are an important data category because of their high proportion of cultural material. Even though they are slightly over-represented there are still only 43 in the priority sample. They can be broken into alluviated dumps, coarsely-bedded dumps and finely-bedded deposits (Table 2.25). It is also useful to consider the middens in Level Pre-XII.B and earlier vs those higher in the sequence (Table 2.26) because they represent the difference between middens at the edge of the built area and middens in the middle of the built area.

Since middens are so rich, most data classes are ubiquitous in terms of the first division (Table 2.25). An interesting exception is ceramics. While its absence from the alluviated dumps is probably temporal the under-representation in the finely-bedded middens is interesting. While some of this may be related to the absence of ceramics in lower levels, the difference is clear in the upper levels as well. Ceramics is the only data set to show a difference in the number of units between lower levels and upper levels.

Density: The density distributions for material within middens indicate that neither level nor bedding produce the kind of significant differences between groupings that have been shown above for subsets of fill and floors (see Table 2.27). This is probably partly due to the very small variances in the distributions in general but it may also indicate a similarity in depositional practice. It is interesting to note the large number of significant differences if middens are classified according to the space number that they occupy. This suggests that particular places had the same kinds of material deposited in them over time.

The relationship between middens and floors is explored in Figure 2.26. The high densities that were shown for occupation floors made it worthwhile considering if middens were composed of sweeping from the other floors. Comparing this figure with Figure 2.23 it is clear that while there is definitely an overlap in the distribution of faunal densities, the lithics densities of floors are consistently higher creating a strong separation between the data categories in Figure 2.26. While the middens may be composed of material created, or consumed within buildings, this material has a different composition from that left on occupation floors.

Table 2.24. *Density distribution of all studied material in middens.*

	N	Minimum	25	50	75	Maximum
Shell (count/l)	42	0.0050	0.1178	0.1920	0.6418	1.4117
Bead (count/l)	102	0.0003	0.0055	0.0121	0.0257	0.1818
Figurine (count/l)	70	0.0003	0.0015	0.0039	0.0125	0.4444
Clay obj (count/l)	42	0.0066	0.0217	0.0430	0.0982	0.2573
Ceramics (sherds/l)	84	0.0008	0.0066	0.0148	0.0377	8.0000
Worked stone (count/l)	49	0.0001	0.0020	0.0037	0.0080	0.0678
Lithics (grams/l)	176	0.0021	0.0542	0.0997	0.2068	2.0382
Faunal (grams/l)	42	0.8883	3.5171	5.4770	9.1331	112.5294
Botanical (grams/l)	40	0.0093	0.3881	0.7532	1.5468	3.9509

Table 2.25. *Presence of material in middens by deposition type.*

Deposition	Total	Lithics	Botanical	Faunal	Figurine	Beads	Ceramics	Clay obj	Shell	Ground stone
Alluviated dumps	4	4	4	4	1	4	0	4	4	4
Coarsely bedded (dumps)	18	17	16	18	12	12	12	18	18	16
Finely bedded	21	21	20	21	16	19	8	21	21	14

Table 2.26. *Presence of material in middens by level.*

Level	Total	Lithics	Botanical	Faunal	Figurine	Beads	Ceramics	Clay obj	Shell	Ground stone
Pre-XII.B and earlier	16	16	15	16	10	15	0	16	16	13
Pre-XII.A and later	27	26	25	27	19	20	20	27	27	21

Table 2.27. *Significance of differences between middens with varying characteristics, Kruskall Wallis Test.*

Variable	Level	Bedding	Space
Mass density lithics	0.042	1.000	0.054
Mass density faunal	0.017	0.846	0.028
Mass density botanical	0.000	0.771	0.043
Mass density clay objects	0.138	0.000	0.001
Mass density ceramics	0.001	0.862	0.000
Mass density ground stone	0.426	0.874	0.035
Count density lithics	0.078	0.122	0.785
Count density shell	0.214	0.068	0.017
Count density beads	0.269	0.391	0.175
Count density figurine	0.654	0.293	0.595
Count density clay objects	0.126	0.001	0.004
Count density ceramics	0.000	0.518	0.000
Count density ground stone	0.621	0.677	0.011

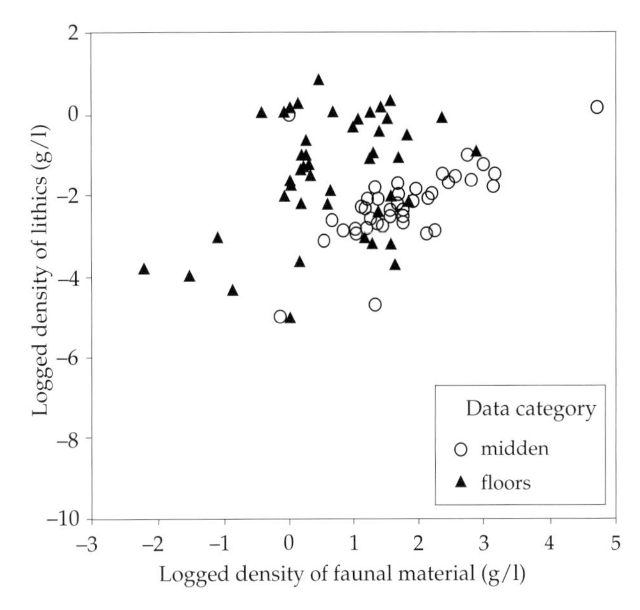

Figure 2.26. *Lithic vs faunal densities for middens and floors.*

Inside outside

Definition and distribution: To discuss the difference between inside space and outside space we need to define the terms. For the purpose of the initial analysis inside space was defined as any space surrounded by four bonded walls. There are certainly spaces which fit this definition which appear to be treated like outside spaces (such as the later phases of Building 2) and other spaces which could in fact be inside but the walls have not been reached (such as Level Pre-XII.A). Where these circumstances show up as anomalies in the analysis it will refine our sense of what the terms mean. I suspect that (as with everything else) an inside space is defined by the behaviour which takes place within it — but the definition is an attempt to step into the circle at a defined point.

Because the units needed to be considered individually we have only identified 'inside/outside' for analytical priority units. There are 92 units in the sample that are outside by this definition. A first look at the whole data set suggests that the proportion is the same for all the 3600 units (about 1000 outside). While this creates a difficulty in comparisons because the sample sizes are not equal, the proportion in itself is information about the use of space on site. Looked at in terms of volume the situation is more balanced. Outside units make up 45,287 cubic metres of the priority sample while inside units comprise 41,062 cubic metres. Although there are more than twice as many inside units as outside, the outside units are often much larger.

Some of this is due to excavation methodology since inside spaces were more likely to be dug in grids and spits and outside (especially midden) units tended to be dug as single entities. It is also because inside space includes small units such as oven fills. Looking at the distribution of data categories (Fig. 2.27) it is clear that many of the distinctions that we see between data categories may relate to the inside–outside distinction since the two are nearly mutually exclusive. The volume of 'internal' middens, while small, confirms that construction form does not completely determine the inside–outside distinction. The 'activity' category is almost completely outside because it is a category used to describe activities where there is little or no structural evidence.

At first glance it looks that construction deposits are under represented in inside spaces with nearly 70 per cent by volume outside. On closer examination, this figure represents only two units, and almost all the volume comes from one unit. This unit (4518) comes from the deep sounding and is described as 'general midden/dump equivalent to (4824)/(4836). Quite a lot of cleanish building-type material, could represent a solid 'raft' for wall to west' (Unit Sheet 4518, CC, 19.07.99). The excavator also says that the unit was mixed because of the speed of excavation (CC pers. comm.).

The inside–outside distinction is well picked up by the data-category classification. The existence of some cross-classified units shows that this is not because of circular definitions (e.g. midden is not just an outside fill). The connection between chronological and spatial distinctions has been discussed a good deal in 1999 and 2001. The Pre-XII levels may well be outside the contemporary enclosed area, and certainly enclosing walls have not been found. The KOPAL Area is definitely 'off site'. Only two levels have comparable volumes of inside and outside material: Level VIII and North Level VI–V.

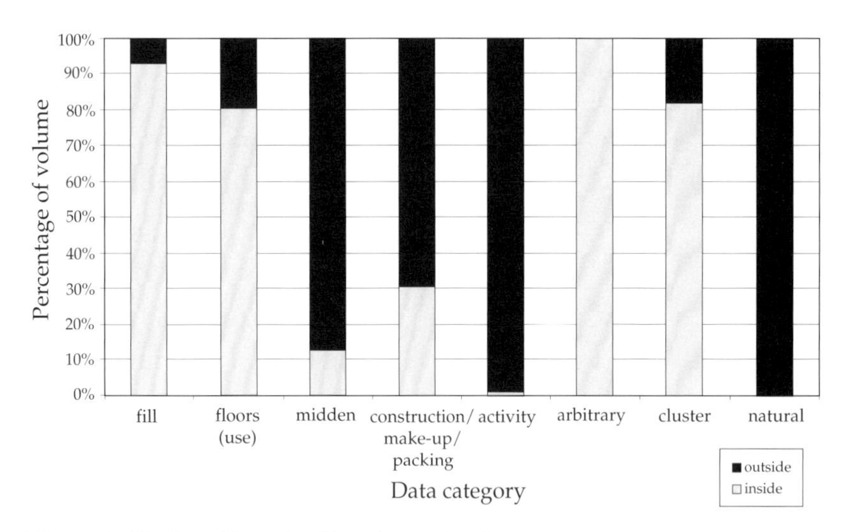

Figure 2.27. *Outside vs inside volumes by data category.*

Table 2.28. *Overall excavated volume and count of units inside and outside by level.*

Level	Outside volume (l)	Outside count	Inside volume (l)	Inside count
KOPAL	6436.0	10	0.000	0
Pre-XII.D	3831.0	4	0.000	0
Pre-XII.C	1682.0	5	0.000	0
Pre-XII.B	12,146.5	21	0.000	0
Pre-XII.A	6101.0	9	0.000	0
XII	4548.0	7	0.000	0
XI	1748.0	5	0.000	0
X	0.0	0	4164.925	27
IX	0.0	0	18,184.730	58
VIII	7927.0	15	5165.800	39
VII	651.0	7	5176.200	16
N.VII–VI	0.0	0	891.850	20
N.VI–V	216.6	9	7295.500	99

Table 2.29. *Overall presence of data classes inside vs outside.*

	Outside	Inside
Figurine	44	29
Ground stone	50	51
Clay objects	80	97
Beads	59	90
Ceramics	21	55
Lithics	81	188
Botanical	84	243
Shell	85	199
Stone	88	176
Faunal	92	245
Total	**92**	**263**

Table 2.30. *Level VIII presence of data classes, inside vs outside.*

	Outside	Inside
Figurine	10	5
Ground stone	8	6
Clay objects	15	26
Beads	11	15
Ceramics	12	7
Lithics	13	33
Botanical	14	35
Shell	14	31
Stone	14	31
Faunal	15	36
Total	**15**	**39**

Table 2.31. *North Level VI–V presence of data classes, inside vs outside.*

	Outside	Inside
Figurine	4	9
Ground stone	3	18
Clay objects	4	11
Beads	4	35
Ceramics	1	18
Lithics	3	60
Botanical	7	96
Shell	6	79
Stone	7	41
Faunal	9	98
Total	**9**	**99**

Presence—absence (Table 2.29): There is a greater proportion of units with the more restricted data sets such as clay objects, ground stone, and ceramics occurring in outside fills than in inside fills. This is particularly striking for figurines and ground stone. The more ubiquitous data sets, however, are fully present in both locations. The figures from Level VIII (Table 2.30) show the same distribution which confirms that the pattern is not simply related to temporal or on-site/off-site considerations. In fact the preferential deposition of ceramics in outside units is stronger considered for Level VIII than for the site as a whole, which is striking considering the complete absence of ceramics from the lower levels. The figures from North Level VI–V (Table 2.31) are more difficult to interpret because the disparity in the number of units is so high. It is possible that stone, lithics and ceramics have a different pattern of deposition in this level than the earlier one. If so, it would correspond with recognized changes in the technology of at least ceramics and lithics. Since the volume of these categories is more equal than numbers of units, it is worth considering the same material in terms of overall density.

Density: Tables 2.32–2.35 show count density of data classes taking into account all outside and inside spaces within the priority sample including the units with zero values for particular materials. This gives an overall impression of the abundance of material, as opposed to specific values for separate depositional events. The impression from this set of tables is different to the presence–absence picture, but should not be taken as more accurate. Densities can mask depositional differences because they essentially take a mean

Table 2.32. *Total analytical priority count density based on all units, inside vs outside.*

	Outside	Inside	Outside:inside
Bead	0.008	0.004	2.01
Ceramic	0.002	0.005	0.42
Clay objects	0.042	0.038	1.11
Faunal	4.803	1.961	2.45
Figurine	0.003	0.001	3.50
Lithic	0.269	0.257	1.05
Shell	0.375	0.090	4.16
Stone	0.004	0.004	1.19

Table 2.33. *Level VIII count density based on all units, inside vs outside.*

	Outside	Inside	Outside:inside
Bead	0.002	0.004	0.51
Ceramic	0.010	0.004	2.61
Clay objects	0.046	0.091	0.51
Faunal	3.720	1.345	2.77
Figurine	0.003	0.001	2.87
Lithic	0.299	0.294	1.02
Shell	0.092	0.111	0.82
Stone	0.006	0.002	3.26

Table 2.34. *Level VII count density based on all units, inside vs outside.*

	Outside	Inside	Outside:inside
Bead	0.006	0.001	7.95
Ceramic	0.017	0.005	3.24
Clay objects	0.124	0.087	1.42
Faunal	11.888	4.055	2.93
Figurine	0.017	0.001	14.58
Lithic	0.459	0.179	2.56
Shell	0.238	0.062	3.86
Stone	0.011	0.008	1.36

Table 2.35. *North Level VI–V count density based on all units, inside vs outside.*

	Outside	Inside	Outside:inside
Bead	0.046	0.008	6.12
Ceramic	0.032	0.008	4.00
Clay objects	0.083	0.004	23.32
Faunal	8.818	1.589	5.55
Figurine	0.129	0.001	104.79
Lithic	0.074	0.038	1.93
Shell	0.185	0.089	2.07
Stone	0.134	0.008	17.44

for the whole volume. Presence–absence may pick up outliers better, which is important when dealing with small discrete data sets such as ceramics and figurines. This is particularly important where the data set relies on flotation samples for recovery since lower proportions of large units are floated than small units.

Table 2.32 shows the overall figures. Only ceramics have a higher density inside than outside and this is probably accounted for by the large volume of outside units in the Pre-XII levels, as discussed above. Clay objects, lithics and unworked stone are found in roughly equal densities outside and inside. Beads, faunal material, figurines and shell have substantially higher density values outside. This pattern is constant for faunal material and figurines but varies for shell and bead. The first level to have both inside and outside units in the analytical priority sample is Level VIII (Table 2.33), which has the large midden in Space 115 surrounded by a series of buildings. Mellaart originally excavated the buildings to the south. So, while the area of the inside space is larger than the outside, the volume of internal priority units is only slightly larger than that of outside priority units. Also included in the outside units are smaller between wall fills, some of which have a distinctive pattern discussed below. In this level there are a number of data classes which have a higher internal density than external density including shell and beads, which demonstrates that other factors may be influencing the pattern from the site as a whole. The ceramics also reverse the pattern for the site as a whole, and this much higher external density is pattern for the other levels as well. It is interesting that lithics retain a similar ratio of densities in this level as the site as a whole. Middens are often perceived to be lithic rich but the internal fills are comparable for this level.

Level VII (Table 2.34) was more heavily affected by Mellaart's excavations than Level VIII. Most of the external units in this level are between wall fills, though there are some in Space 106 as well. The volume of the external units in the analytical priority sample is nearly one tenth of the volume of the internal units so small variations will create larger effects than for Level VIII. All of the data classes show higher external densities in this level, though the very high ratios for figurines and beads should be offset by their low densities in both locations. The faunal and ceramic ratios remain consistent from Level VIII but all of the other data classes show shifts to higher external densities, both in relation to external units from the earlier level and to contemporary internal units.

The North Area excavations (Table 2.35) focused around a single building and the external spaces were excavated largely as an adjunct to the building. Two of the external spaces continue beyond the edge of excavation and none of them were excavated to their bottoms. The volume of the external analytical priority units is the smallest in relation to the internal units of any of the levels discussed, less than five per cent. The generally low densities for all data classes in both locations should temper the remarkably high ratios. The exceptions to this are the faunal material and the figurines. The faunal material is continuing its pattern from the other levels. The figurines show a substantially higher density in these external units than they do in any other context on site. This relates to a single deposition in Space 153, which is being considered as a special deposit potentially related to a feasting event.

Taking this broad discussion of density of material as a whole it is clear that the nature of external space is different for different levels and the deposition patterns reflect this variability. That being said both faunal material and figurines have consistently higher densities outside and ceramics have higher densities outside in levels where they exist at all. The only indication of preferential deposition inside comes from Level VIII where beads, clay objects, and shell all have lower densities outside. A more detailed analysis of the distribution of densities is provided in the accompanying CD. (The CD also contains analysis of the internal variation within the faunal and lithic data sets.)

Conclusions

The statistical approach to contextual integration described here has produced promising results. The priority sample offers a useful representation of variation on site and the framework of data categories allows a clear framework for investigating that variation. The large number of data sets with information on densities has provided a base from which analysis can build. Once the density data are log-transformed they are quite amenable to a range of exploratory analyses and presentations. There is more detail available for the density analysis, which has not been discussed here but supports the same kinds of patterns (see CD for some additional analyses). Other variables are more difficult to define, especially in a manner that is comparable across data sets.

Archaeologically the clearest result is that the field interpretation of units, and their separation into data classes is a powerful description of context. It illuminates variation in composition better than other classifications. Because it responds to a number of variables at once, it provides an intuitive version of the multivariate approach which has been conducted statistically here.

Contextual variation is greater between data categories than it is between levels. In terms of the quantifiable variation in composition there is more activity-based difference than there is chronological difference. Within this certain data categories are more broadly defined than others. Notably fill, and more surprisingly floors have a range of compositional profile which is greater than may have been expected. Middens in contrast appear to be a tightly-defined category for particular types of deposits including some of the rarer material on site. This supports the existing understanding within the project, that 'rubbish' is no less culturally significant than other 'cleaner' types of deposition.

Chapter 3

Heavy-residue Analysis

Craig Cessford
with contributions by Slobodan Mitrović

Heavy residue (henceforth HR) consists of the material recovered from flotation samples, which sinks during the flotation process (for descriptions of the methodology see accompanying CD and Volume 4, Chapter 7). The general conclusion from an analysis of the methodology is that a potentially substantial margin of error exists in certain respects so minor differences cannot be assumed to be meaningful. As such this study is similar to micro-artefactual material studied on many sites, with the distinction that both macro (>4 mm) and micro (<4 mm) artefacts are studied together. For this reason the term HR has been used in order to distinguish wet-sieved material from dry-sieved and hand-picked material discussed in Chapter 2. There is some overlap between the material discussed in this and the previous chapter, in that >4-mm material from the flotation/wet-sieve process was included with dry-sieve and hand-picked counts and weights by the specialist teams. However, the >4-mm densities used in this chapter were calculated solely from the material recovered by wet-sieving. The HR data from three areas, North, South and KOPAL, excavated between 1995 and 1999 have been analyzed. Analysis undertaken has varied between the three areas, and within individual areas. In general analysis has focused upon:

- general comparison between different types of deposit;
- spatial and temporal variation across floor deposits;
- specific inter-unit comparison prompted by particular archaeological issues.

Most previous analysis of micro-artefactual material has concentrated upon a restricted range of depositional contexts, generally those believed to relate directly to *in situ* occupational activities. The strategy at Çatalhöyük involved sampling all deposit types for flotation and treating the material from all deposits as similarly as practical. This provides a much wider sampling population and allows the HR data to be used to address a wider range of issues with regard to the patterning of material. It also allows floor deposits to be more richly contextualized. This is particularly important given the complex site-formation processes on highly-stratified and densely-occupied tell sites. Such processes mean that it is often uncertain if material is residual or intrusive and whether it is in primary, secondary or tertiary contexts, a topic of considerable importance for interpreting the material.

Once floated, the heavy and light fractions are treated separately and the light residue is not included in this analysis. As it was impractical to sort all the light fractions these have been excluded as this would bias the results. The material is sorted into three size ranges; greater than 4 mm (henceforth 4 mm), between 4 mm and 2 mm (henceforth 2 mm), and between 2 mm and 1 mm (henceforth 1 mm). From the inception of HR analysis in the Çatalhöyük Research Project it was anticipated that one of the main applications of analysis of densities of material from HR would be to examine patterning within floor deposits to attempt to identify activities. This was perceived as being 'needed because the floors were carefully swept clean in antiquity' (Hodder 1999a, 159) and 'these tiny fragments probably reflect some of the actual activities that took place on the floors, such as food preparation, cooking and obsidian working' (Martin & Russell 2000, 61–3). As such this work fits well with the normal analysis of micro-artefacts (see Courty *et al.* 1993; Dunnell & Stein 1989; Fladmark 1982; Hassan 1978; Miller-Rosen 1989; 1993; Rainville 2000; Sherwood & Osley 1995; Sherwood & Osley 1995; Sherwood *et al.* 1995; Stein & Telset 1989). A focus on micro-artefact patterning is based primarily upon the belief that micro-artefacts are more likely to represent traces of *in situ* activity than larger macro-artefacts. The perception is that micro-artefacts will be swept into corners, trampled into floors, buried when floors were muddy or occur in accumulations of dust

Table 3.1. *North, South and KOPAL Area flotation samples.*

Unit type	North Area all		North Area correctly sorted		South Area all		South Area correctly sorted		KOPAL Area all/ correctly sorted	
Activity	0	0.0%	0	0.0%	74	3.3%	70	3.3%	0	0.0%
Arbitrary	16	1.6%	12	1.4%	31	1.4%	30	1.4%	0	0.0%
Cluster	4	0.4%	4	0.5%	18	0.8%	18	0.8%	0	0.0%
Construction/make-up	219	21.3%	197	22.3%	708	31.1%	660	30.7%	0	0.0%
Fill (+ cut + skeleton)	537	52.1%	493	55.9%	505	22.2%	482	22.4%	24	48%
Floors	254	24.7%	176	20.0%	610	26.8%	576	26.8%	0	0.0%
Midden	0	0.0%	0	0.0%	326	14.3%	312	14.5%	0	0.0%
Natural	0	0.0%	0	0.0%	1	<0.1%	1	<0.1%	26	52%
All Units	1030	100%	882	100%	2275	100%	2149	100%	50	100%

and ash. They are thus perceived as becoming almost incidentally incorporated into floor deposits rather than being moved around, or even totally removed, in a more intentional manner as macro-artefacts might be. Essentially it is postulated that micro-artefact 'depositional sets' as recovered in the archaeological record are more directly related to 'activity sets and areas' which occurred in the past (Carr 1984, 114) than macro-level material. Additionally this micro level may counteract 'stereotypical designations for room function' and allow for multifunctionality and changeability (Özbal 2000). There is no agreed methodology with regard to appropriate overall sample size, what size constitutes the upper or lower range of micro-artefacts and which material types to look at (see Dunnell & Stein 1989; LaMotla & Schiffer 1999; Lass 1994; Miller-Rosen 1989; Özbal 2000; Rainville 2000; Sherwood *et al.* 1995; Sherwood & Osley 1995; Stein & Telset 1989). This is largely because different conditions, both in terms of materials present in the archaeological deposits and pragmatic issues relating to time and resources, necessitate different strategies. The flotation samples included in this study (Table 3.1) consist of 1030 samples from the North Area, 2275 from the South Area and 50 from the KOPAL Area amounting to just under 60,000 litres of material.

North and South Areas

Given the broadly comparable nature of the deposits in the North and South Areas these are considered together. This study will focus mainly upon a general comparison between different types of deposit. Several types of analysis were undertaken; ubiquity, presence, diversity and density. What constitutes a meaningful difference in any of these types of analysis has not been rigorously defined or statistically tested, given the limitations of the data a minimum value of around ten per cent has been adopted as a heuristic device. Analysis of various deposit types was undertaken on an *ad hoc* basis between 1996 and 1999 and the results presented. Analysis focused upon the presence and absence of different material types within deposits and the density of certain material types. Additionally it was decided to analyze the different size ranges into which the material was sorted separately. The basic framework was determined by the data category system. Where appropriate, spatial and temporal patterning was also considered. In general it was decided only to consider differences between types of deposit where there were more than fifty samples of each type, although in certain instances this rule was ignored when a particular issue was considered to be important enough to warrant special treatment.

Ubiquity

In all, after some combination to allow for variation in terminology, 56 categories of material were recovered from flotation samples in the both excavation areas. Fifteen material types were recovered in five or more samples in both areas (Tables 3.2–3.3). Previous analysis had focused specifically on three of these categories; plant, bone and chipped stone as these were judged to be the most informative. All three of these types of material occur in the majority of the flotation samples and can be characterized as relatively ubiquitous inclusions, as they occur in over 50 per cent of samples at any given fraction sizes and in over 80 per cent of samples overall. The HR data for these materials was compared to the more detailed results of specialist analysis, using the Wilcoxon signed rank test. This indicated that while bone and chipped stone from HR can be taken as reliable indicators of these types of material, plant cannot. This appears to be because the initial HR sorting classified a lot of non-botanical material as plant. The only other materials to occur in anything approaching these percentages of sample were building material, plaster, mollusc, eggshell and stone. Building material and plaster were not sorted consistently in different years. Mollusc and eggshell were omitted due to problems with the data, as they had initially not been sorted separately and combining the two categories appeared to be *a priori* nonsensical. Stone was not included, as it

Table 3.2. *Occurrence of material types in North Area samples.*

Material	4-mm occurrence		2-mm occurrence		1-mm occurrence		Occurrence at all sizes in reliable samples		Occurrence at all sizes in all samples	
Beads	43	4.9%	71	8.0%	39	4.4%	138	15.6%	146	14.2%
Bone	825	93.5%	790	89.6%	796	90.4%	855	96.9%	992	96.3%
Chipped stone	599	67.7%	626	71.0%	492	55.8%	764	86.6%	856	83.1%
Clay balls / objects	85	9.6%	0	0.0%	0	0.0%	85	9.6%	86	8.3%
Clay	23	2.6%	3	0.3%	0	0.0%	26	2.9%	27	2.6%
Dung	3	0.3%	3	0.3%	2	0.2%	6	0.7%	6	0.6%
Eggshell	186	21.1%	403	45.7%	373	42.3%	513	58.2%	563	54.7%
Figurines	31	3.5%	2	0.2%	1	0.1%	34	3.9%	38	3.7%
Mollusc	640	72.6%	779	88.3%	771	87.4%	841	95.4%	972	94.4%
Ochre	1	0.1%	4	0.5%	0	0.0%	5	0.5%	5	0.5%
Plant	576	65.3%	725	82.2%	691	78.3%	811	92.0%	884	85.8%
Pottery	34	3.9%	1	0.1%	0	0.0%	35	4.0%	38	3.7%
Stone	654	74.1%	N/A	N/A	N/A	N/A	N/A	N/A	N/A	N/A
Worked bone	8	0.9%	0	0.0%	0	0.0%	8	0.9%	9	0.9%
Worked stone	7	0.8%	0	0.0%	0	0.0%	7	0.8%	8	0.8%

Table 3.3. *Occurrence of material types in South Area samples.*

Material	4-mm occurrence		2-mm occurrence		1-mm occurrence		Occurrence at all sizes in reliable samples		Occurrence at all sizes in all samples	
Beads	120	5.6%	302	14.1%	243	11.3%	505	23.5%	516	22.7%
Bone	2030	94.5%	2023	94.1%	2051	95.4%	2136	99.4%	2252	99.0%
Chipped stone	1427	66.4%	1604	74.6%	1371	63.8%	1864	86.7%	1951	85.8%
Clay balls / objects	649	30.2%	7	0.3%	1	<0.1%	652	30.3%	666	29.3%
Clay	21	1.0%	0	0.0%	0	0.0%	21	1.0%	23	1.0%
Dung	8	0.4%	2	0.1%	1	<0.1%	11	0.5%	11	0.5%
Eggshell	443	20.6%	1133	52.7%	1226	57.0%	1498	69.7%	1515	66.6%
Figurines	98	4.6%	8	0.4%	0	0.0%	104	4.8%	106	4.7%
Mollusc	1603	74.6%	1978	92.0%	2020	94.0%	2109	98.1%	2126	93.5%
Ochre	8	0.4%	2	0.1%	1	<0.1%	9	0.4%	10	0.4%
Plant	1222	56.9%	1815	84.5%	1929	89.8%	2049	95.3%	2130	93.6%
Pottery	138	6.4%	0	0.0%	1	<0.1%	138	6.4%	143	6.3%
Stone	1835	85.4%	N/A	N/A	N/A	N/A	N/A	N/A	N/A	N/A
Worked bone	25	1.2%	1	<0.1%	0	0.0%	25	1.2%	26	1.1%
Worked stone	13	0.6%	1	<0.1%	2	0.1%	16	0.7%	16	0.7%

was not generally sorted at the 2-mm and 1-mm fraction sizes. No other material type was present in over 50 per cent of the samples and most types were represented in fewer than ten samples. Beads occur in around 15 per cent of North Area samples and 20 per cent of South Area samples and might be classified as moderate inclusions. Pottery, figurines and clay balls / objects occur in between 3 and 10 per cent in both areas with the exception of clay balls / objects, which occur in around 30 per cent of South Area samples. These might be classified as occasional inclusions. All other material types represent rare inclusions. Examples found in less than five samples include copper, coprolite, fish scales, slag and textile. These frequencies of occurrence lead to an intuitive hierarchy of material from flotation samples (Table 3.4). As plant, stone, mollusc, eggshell, building material and plaster were deemed unsuitable for analysis this hierarchy supports, the on-site selection of bone and chipped stone as the most suitable materials for detailed analysis.

Table 3.4. *Ubiquity of material types.*

	Occurrence	Material
Ubiquitous	Over 80% of all samples	Plant, bone, chipped stone, mollusc, stone (also probably building material)
Very frequent	50–80% of all samples	Eggshell (also probably plaster)
Moderate	10–50% of all samples	Beads, Clay balls / objects (South Area)
Occasional	3–10% of all samples	Clay balls / objects (North Area), clay, figurines, pottery
Rare	Less than 3% of all samples	Worked bone, worked stone, insect, metal, ochre, dung, slag, textile

There is some apparent patterning in terms of scalarity, with certain materials being more common at the smaller fraction sizes, although often with little difference between 2-mm and 1-mm, and others being much less common in the two smaller fraction sizes. In the first instance this probably relates to objects such

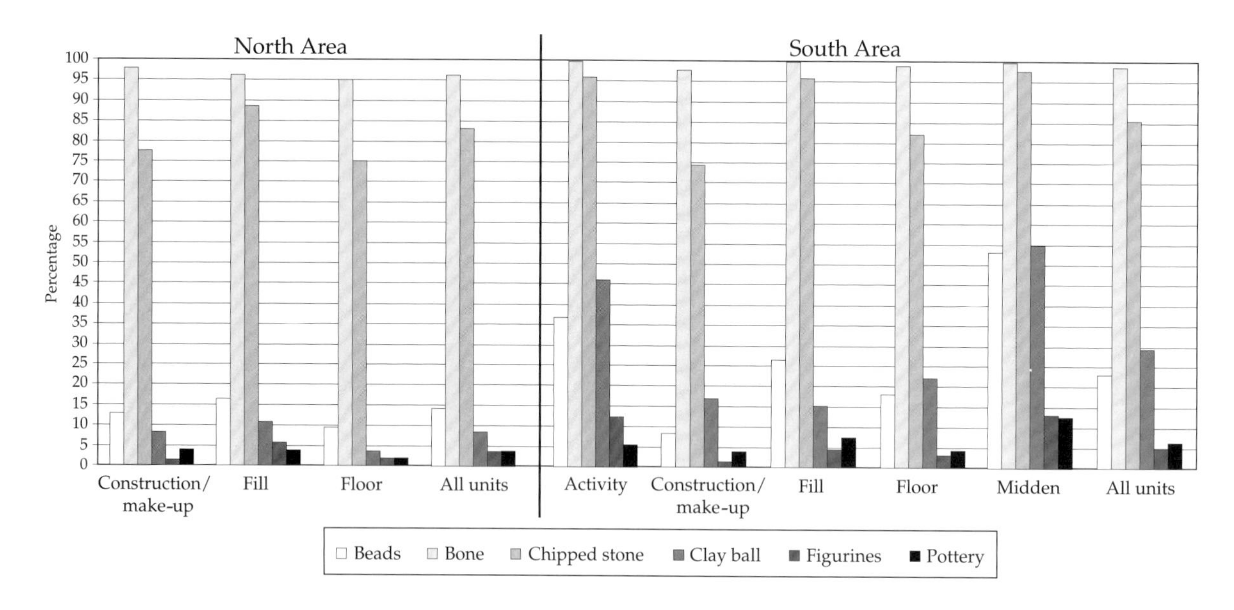

Figure 3.1. *Presence of material types in different types of deposit in the North and South Areas.*

Table 3.5. *Presence of material types in major North Area deposit types.*

	Construction/make-up (219 samples)		Fill (537 samples)		Floor (254 samples)		All units (1030 samples)	
Beads	28	12.8%	89	16.6%	24	9.5%	146	14.2%
Bone	214	97.7%	517	96.3%	241	94.9%	992	96.3%
Chipped stone	170	77.6%	476	88.6%	191	75.2%	856	83.1%
Clay balls/objects	18	8.2%	59	11.0%	9	3.5%	86	8.3%
Figurines	3	1.4%	29	5.6%	5	2.0%	38	3.7%
Pottery	9	4.1%	20	3.7%	5	2.0%	38	3.7%

as beads which are usually smaller than 4 mm, or fragile and unlikely to survive in large fragments, such as mollusc and eggshell. Where objects are rarely found at the smaller fraction sizes, such as pottery and clay balls/objects, this appears to relate primarily to issues of identification, as it is impossible to visually distinguish some artefact classes in the smaller fraction sizes. The one apparent exception to this is chipped stone which is easily identifiable and does appear to relate to some form of genuine scalarity of deposition. Although largely due to taphonomic and recovery processes, this variation is important as it shows that different types of artefact, at least as identified and studied, do relate to different scales of deposition. The clearest difference between the two areas is clay balls/objects, which occur three times as frequently and in 20 per cent more of the total samples in the South Area. This appears to reflect a genuine temporal change in material culture (Chapter 5). Eggshell and stone are both around 10 per cent more common in South Area samples and this is primarily due to differences in unit types between the two areas.

Presence

Presence analysis involves a simple consideration of whether or not a type of material is found in each sample regardless of fraction size; as such it involves all samples. There appears to be some relationship between sample size and diversity but it does not appear to be an over-riding factor.

General

The presence and absence of materials can be analyzed for different types of deposit. It only appears worthwhile to consider material types found in more than thirty samples in both excavation areas (Fig. 3.1; Tables 3.5–3.6). In the North Area bone is present in roughly the same percentage in fills, floors and construction/make-up deposits, but chipped stone is more commonly present in fill than the other two deposit types. This is probably due to differences in sample volume, which appears to be a major factor in presence, with small samples being more likely to have material absent. Beads, pottery, clay balls/objects and figurines are less likely to be present in floors than in fills or construction/make-up deposits. With the exception of pottery the materials are less likely to be present in construction/make-up deposits than fills. Figurines occur noticeably less frequently in construction/make-up deposits than fills in comparison to the other types of material.

In the South Area, activity deposits are more likely to contain all the material categories, with the exception of pottery whose absence is due to temporal

Table 3.6. *Presence of material types in major South Area deposit types.*

	Activity (74 samples)		Construction/make-up (708 samples)		Fill (506 samples)		Floor (610 samples)		Midden (326 samples)		All units (2275 samples)	
Beads	27	36.5%	61	8.6%	134	26.5%	110	18.0%	172	52.8%	516	22.7%
Bone	74	100%	694	98.0%	506	100%	603	98.9%	325	99.7%	2252	99.0%
Chipped stone	71	95.9%	527	74.4%	486	96.0%	502	82.3%	319	97.9%	1951	85.8%
Clay balls/objects	34	45.9%	121	17.1%	178	15.4%	133	21.8%	179	54.9%	666	29.3%
Figurines	9	12.2%	12	1.7%	23	4.5%	18	3.0%	43	13.2%	106	4.7%
Pottery	4	5.4%	27	3.8%	37	7.3%	25	4.1%	40	12.3%	143	6.3%

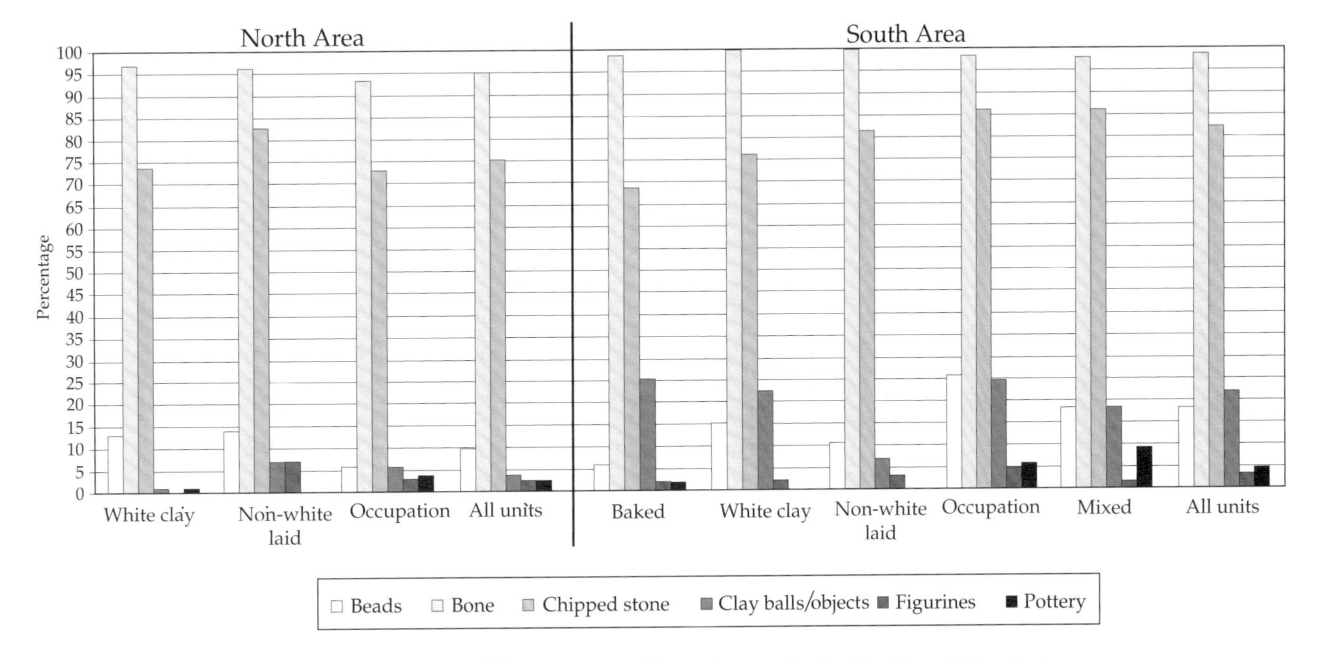

Figure 3.2. *Presence of material types in different types of floor deposit in the North and South Areas.*

factors. Construction/make-up deposits have the lowest presence for all material types, with the exception of clay balls/objects. Fill deposits are more likely to contain the material categories, with the exception of clay balls/objects and figurines and the value for clay balls/objects is particularly low. Floors are less likely to contain all the material categories. Middens are more likely to contain all the material types and have the highest presence for all material types.

Differences between the two areas are that beads are more common in South Area floors and especially fills, chipped stone is more common in South Area fills and clay balls/objects is more common in all South Area deposit types, but particularly in floors.

Floors

Floors can be divided by compositional material type into five main types, Only three of these occur frequently enough in the North Area for consideration (Fig. 3.2; Tables 3.29–3.30 on CD). In terms of presence of material there is relatively little difference between the various floor types in the North Area, but the South Area shows more differentiation. Occupation floors are more likely to have material present and chipped stone and beads are less likely to be present in baked floors and clay balls/objects are less likely to be in non-white laid floors. In terms of comparison between the two areas, marked differences are the higher presence of clay balls/objects in white clay and occupation floors in the South Area and beads and chipped stone in occupation floors in the South Area. The greater frequency of beads is at least partially due to bead manufacturing in Building 18 and the chipped stone values may also relate to patterns of working, with evidence for *in situ* knapping in several South Area buildings particularly Building 23. Clay balls/objects have similar values for non-white laid floors in both areas but markedly higher values in the South Area for occupation floors and particularly white clay floors. The patterning of figurines appears to vary with occupation having a higher value than non-white laid floors in the South Area, but this situation is reversed in the North Area.

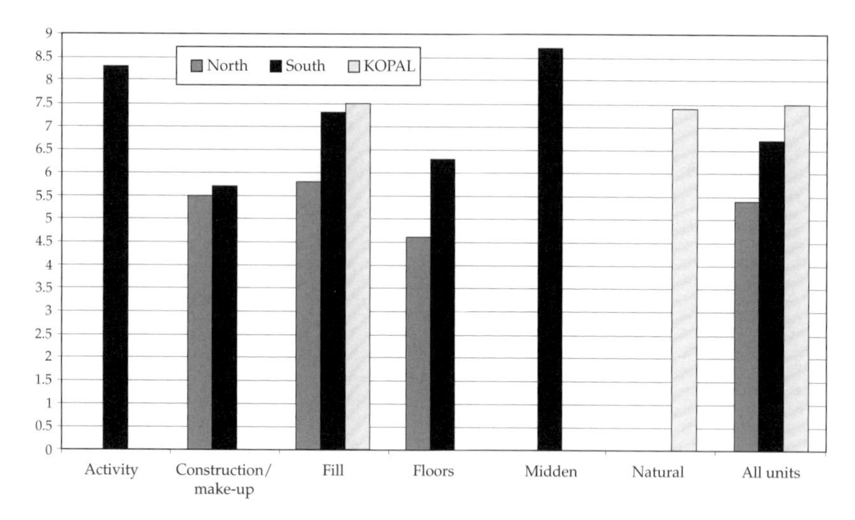

Figure 3.3. *Diversity in different types of deposit in North, South and KOPAL Areas.*

Fills

With fills it appeared worthwhile to consider several types of fill (Tables 3.31–3.32 on CD). In the North Area chipped stone, clay balls/objects and figurines are less likely to be found in burial fills than in fills in general. In the South Area there appears to be some variation of beads, clay balls/objects and figurines between different types of fill, although this may relate mainly to variations in sample volume. Chipped stone is more common in burial fills in the South Area than the North Area. This probably reflects the fact that in the North Area burials are concentrated in the northern part of the building, where chipped stone is less common, whereas in the South Area burials are spread more evenly across buildings. Figurines are more common in North Area inter-building fills than in fills in general, but this is not the case in the South Area.

Activity

Activity covers three disparate types of deposit so it seems worth attempting to divide these despite the low number of samples (Table 3.33 on CD). The high presence of beads in activity deposits is mainly due to fire spots and lime burning, as penning has levels of beads similar to those for deposits in general. The high levels of clay balls/objects are also primarily due to these two types of deposit, although penning also has higher levels than deposits in general. The high level of figurines in fire spots is intriguing, but it is unclear how meaningful this is.

Middens

Middens can be divided into three categories on the basis of the nature of their deposition (Table 3.34 on CD). In general finely-bedded middens appear to be marginally more likely to contain most material types than coarsely-bedded middens. Alluviated dumps appear to be more likely to contain beads and less likely to contain figurines than other types of midden, but this is based on a low number of samples. The presence of pottery in alluviated dump deposits must be due to misidentifications and highlights the potential impact of this when there are a relatively low number of samples.

Middens can also be considered by space (Table 3.35 on CD). This appears to show that beads and clay balls/objects are more commonly present in earlier midden deposits and that pottery is less common. Indeed it is absent from dry-sieved and hand-picked samples in the earliest levels and the presence here is probably due to misidentifications during sorting. It appears that the Spaces 116 and 117 are less likely to have beads and clay balls/objects present and also possibly chipped stone and figurines, especially in contrast to Space 115, suggesting that this is not due to temporal factors.

Construction/make-up

There are three main types of construction/make-up deposit, only *in situ* examples of these have been considered (Table 3.36 on CD). This appears to show that floor construction/make-up deposits are more likely to contain chipped stone, beads and clay balls/objects fragments than construction/make-up deposits in general and feature construction/make-up deposits are less likely to contain chipped stone. With feature construction/make-up deposits (Table 3.37 on CD) it appears that chipped stone and clay balls/objects are less likely to occur in bin/basin construction/make-up deposits than in hearth/oven construction/make-up deposits. With wall/blocking (Table 3.38 on CD) mortar is more likely than brick to contain chipped stone, beads and clay balls/objects, but less likely to contain pottery.

Diversity

Diversity analysis involves a simple count of the total number of material types found in each sample regardless of fraction size; as such it involves all samples with certain categories excluded. This measure of diversity is not the same as the measure of variability discussed in Chapter 2.

General
There are broadly similar levels of diversity in the major unit types (Fig. 3.3; Table 3.39 on CD), with the exception of South Area, activity and midden deposits, which have higher levels, and floors in the North Area, which have a somewhat lower diversity. Fill and floor have lower diversities in the North Area than the South Area, although construction/make-up is similar. The greatest level of diversity identified in the North Area was 13, high levels of diversity came from a range of unit types particularly building fills. In the South Area the highest level of diversity was 15, found in middens, a floor and the fill of a scoop. Most of these form a tightly-defined stratigraphic group in Space 181 Level Pre-XII.B. Other high levels of diversity were found mainly in middens and fire spots.

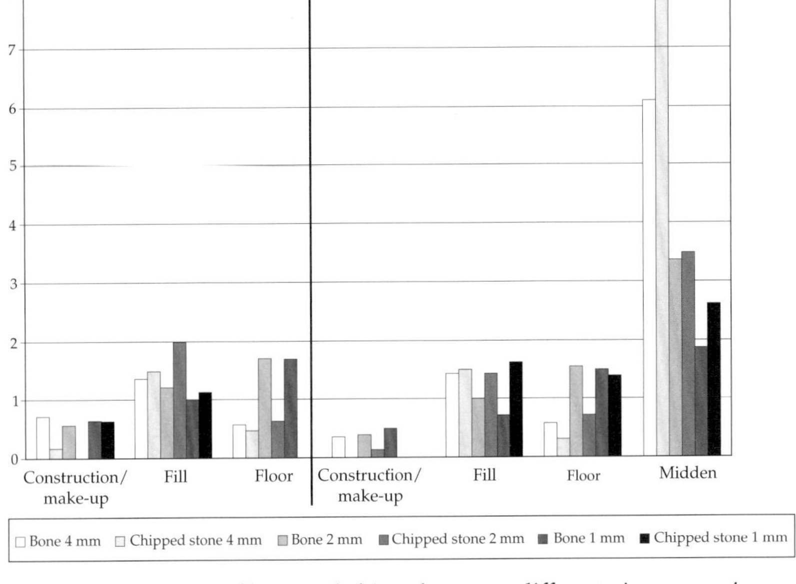

Figure 3.4. *Density of bone and chipped stone at different size ranges in different types of deposit in the North and South Areas.*

Floors
Floors can be divided by compositional material type (Table 3.40 on CD). In the North Area non-white laid floors show the highest level of diversity followed by white clay floors with occupation floors having the lowest, the differences do not appear to be particularly marked. In the South Area occupation floors show the highest diversity followed by mixed and then non-white laid floors, with baked and white clay floors having the lowest diversity. The difference between the North and South Areas appears to be particularly distinct for occupation floors.

Fills
Fill deposits can be divided into those that occur inside a building and those found outside (Table 3.41 on CD). Neither excavation area demonstrates a marked difference in diversity between inside and outside fills, the minor difference is reversed between the two areas.

Activity
Activity has a generally high level of diversity, within this the highest diversity is lime burning (10.4) followed by fire spots (8.7) with penning (7.5) being the lowest, although even this is a relatively high diversity. Many of these deposits are stratigraphically closely associated with midden deposits that have higher levels of diversity and it is unclear if the high diversity values for activity deposits are due primarily to those actual activities or material from nearby midden deposits becoming incorporated into them.

Midden
Middens have a generally high level of diversity, within this the highest diversity is in alluviated dumps (10.2), followed by finely-bedded (8.9) with coarsely-bedded the lowest (8.3). If we consider middens by space (Table 3.42 on CD) this shows that the earlier middens have higher diversities than the later ones, the high diversity for alluviated dumps is actually relatively low given their temporal context. This is

Table 3.7. *Density of bone and chipped stone in North Area in major deposit types.*

	Construction/make-up (197 samples)			Fill (493 samples)			Floor (176 samples)			All units (882 samples)	
Bone 4 mm	0.366667	0.72	Mod. Low	0.695152	1.37	Mod. High	0.287152	0.57	Mod. Low	0.507407	1.00
Chipped stone 4 mm	0.001667	0.16	Low	0.015384	1.49	Mod. High	0.004833	0.47	Low	0.010345	1.00
Bone 2 mm	0.013333	0.57	Mod. Low	0.028571	1.21	Typical	0.040000	1.70	High	0.023529	1.00
Chipped stone 2 mm	0.001481	0.30	Low	0.010000	2.00	High	0.003200	0.64	Mod. Low	0.005000	1.00
Bone 1 mm	0.006452	0.65	Mod. Low	0.010000	1.00	Typical	0.016852	1.69	High	0.010000	1.00
Chipped stone 1 mm	0.000784	0.65	Mod. Low	0.001379	1.14	Typical	0.000000	0.00	Low	0.001212	1.00

Table 3.8. *Density of bone and chipped stone in South Area in major deposit types.*

	Construction/make-up (660 samples)			Fill (482 samples)			Floor (576 samples)			Midden (312 samples)			All units (2149 samples)	
Bone 4 mm	0.342500	0.35	Low	1.390230	1.43	Mod. High	0.570000	0.59	Mod. Low	5.916000	6.09	High	0.971429	1.00
Chipped stone 4 mm	0.000000	0.00	Low	0.030227	1.51	High	0.006111	0.31	Low	0.155778	7.79	High	0.020000	1.00
Bone 2 mm	0.033333	0.39	Low	0.085714	1.00	Typical	0.132667	1.55	High	0.289306	3.38	High	0.085600	1.00
Chipped stone 2 mm	0.001429	0.14	Low	0.014343	1.43	Mod. High	0.007179	0.72	Mod. Low	0.034891	3.49	High	0.010000	1.00
Bone 1 mm	0.020000	0.50	Low	0.028286	0.71	Mod. Low	0.060000	1.50	High	0.073905	1.85	High	0.040000	1.00
Chipped stone 1 mm	0.000000	0.00	Low	0.002963	1.63	High	0.002500	1.38	Mod. High	0.004753	2.61	High	0.001818	1.00

Table 3.9. *Density of bone and chipped stone in floor types in the North Area.*

	Building floor (148 samples)		Feature floor (28 samples)		All floors (176 samples)	
Bone 4 mm	0.250000	0.87	0.407727	1.42	0.287152	1.00
Chipped stone 4 mm	0.004379	0.91	0.031900	6.60	0.004833	1.00
Bone 2 mm	0.037037	0.93	0.049545	1.24	0.040000	1.00
Chipped stone 2 mm	0.003333	1.04	0.001394	0.44	0.003200	1.00
Bone 1 mm	0.015238	0.90	0.021818	1.29	0.016852	1.00
Chipped stone 1 mm	0.000196	N/A	0.000000	N/A	0.000000	1.00

Table 3.10. *Density of bone and chipped stone in floor types in the South Area.*

	Building floor (424 samples)		Feature floor (141 samples)		All floors (576 samples)	
Bone 4 mm	0.660000	1.16	0.31125000	0.55	0.570000	1.00
Chipped stone 4 mm	0.010000	1.64	0.00000000	0.00	0.006111	1.00
Bone 2 mm	0.150000	1.13	0.07027000	0.53	0.132667	1.00
Chipped stone 2 mm	0.010000	1.39	0.00214300	0.30	0.007179	1.00
Bone 1 mm	0.067083	1.12	0.02594595	0.43	0.060000	1.00
Chipped stone 1 mm	0.003333	1.33	0.00021600	0.09	0.002500	1.00

Table 3.11. *Density of bone and chipped stone in feature floor types in the North Area.*

	Bin/basin floor (9 samples)		Hearth/oven floor (19 samples)		All floors (176 samples)	
Bone 4 mm	0.405455	1.41	0.520339	1.81	0.287152	1.00
Chipped stone 4 mm	0.031250	6.47	0.033333	6.90	0.004833	1.00
Bone 2 mm	0.081818	2.05	0.040678	1.02	0.040000	1.00
Chipped stone 2 mm	0.027273	8.52	0.000000	0.00	0.003200	1.00
Bone 1 mm	0.023636	1.40	0.020000	1.19	0.016852	1.00
Chipped stone 1 mm	0.000833	N/A	0.000000	N/A	0.000000	N/A

mainly due to some samples from the later spaces having low values, rather than examples from earlier levels having particularly high values.

Density

Density analysis was undertaken for bone and chipped stone at all three fraction sizes and calculated as grams of material per litre of original sample size. There is a relationship between density and sample size, with high densities more likely to occur in small samples, but it is a weak relationship. The broadly log-normal distribution of densities indicated that median values are a more reliable indicator than mean values. For ease of comparison the overall median value for all units can be expressed as a nominal value of 1.00 and the median values for specific types of units can be expressed as a second figure based on this. Results can be summarized as: low (0.00 to 0.50), moderately low (0.50 to 0.75), typical (0.75 to 1.25), moderately high (1.25 to 1.50) and high (1.50+).

General

In the North Area (Fig. 3.4; Table 3.7) construction/make-up has uniformly lower than overall median values for both material types at all size ranges. Fill has typical or higher than overall median values for both material types at all size ranges. Floors have lower than overall median values for both material types at 4 mm and for chipped stone at all sizes, but higher than overall median values for bone at 2 mm and 1 mm. In the South Area (Fig. 3.4; Table 3.8) construction/make-up is uniformly low, especially for chipped stone, and middens are uniformly high, especially at 4 mm and for chipped stone. Fill has a mixed pattern for bone with levels declining as the fraction size decreases and high chipped-stone values while floors have mixed patterns although the values generally increase as the fraction size decreases. In general the North and South Area results fall in the same broad category or vary by only one. Exceptions to this are the 1-mm chipped stone for fill and floors where the South Area values are considerably higher.

As well as considering median density values the HR data were examined to determine if exceptionally high or low density values were meaningful. The majority of examples were found to come from samples of relatively small size, typically less than five litres and often less than one litre. In many cases it appears that the level of precision in measuring sample volume and in weighing materials may have produced unrealistic density values for such small samples, by over or underestimating their densities. Additionally some of the high densities come from specifically-targeted small samples relating to visually-identified concentrations of material within a deposit and therefore can not be taken as typical of the deposit as a whole. In some instances exceptionally high density values do appear to represent genuine patterning and these have been integrated at the appropriate place. In general, however, exceptional results are frequently misleading as examination on a case by case demonstrates that the majority are due to errors. The degree of errors detected was not, however, enough to seriously effect the general analysis of densities.

Construction/make-up

Comparison of densities between multiple samples of different types of brick and mortar in Building 1 indicated that although some differences existed, variation within a single type of brick or mortar was frequently quite pronounced and could be greater than the distinction between different types of brick or mortar.

Floors

Floors can be divided into general building floors and those located within a feature. In the North Area (Table 3.9) feature floors have higher median values for both materials at 4 mm and bone at all sizes, but lower values for chipped stone at the two lower size ranges. The pattern is rather different for the South Area (Table 3.10) where feature floors have lower median values than building floors; this is more pronounced for chipped stone than bone. For feature floors in the North Area (Table 3.11) both bin/basin and hearth/oven floors have

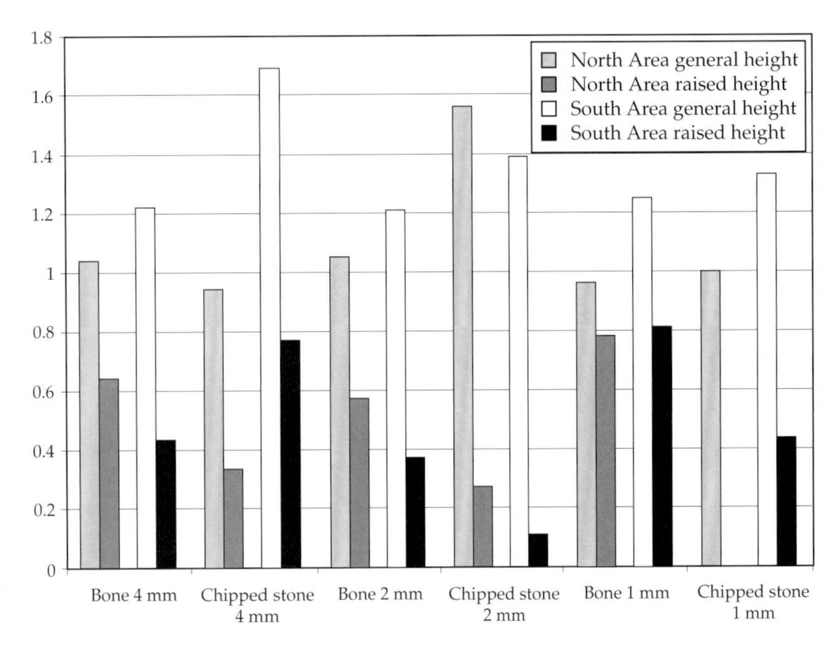

Figure 3.5. *Density of bone and chipped stone at different size ranges in general height and raised height floors in the North and South Areas.*

Table 3.12. *Density of bone and chipped stone in feature floor types in the South Area.*

	Bin/basin floor (20 samples)		Hearth/oven floor (118 samples)		All floors (576 samples)	
Bone 4 mm	0.858099	1.51	0.257857	0.45	0.570000	1.00
Chipped stone 4 mm	0.002083	0.34	0.000000	0.00	0.006111	1.00
Bone 2 mm	0.265000	2.00	0.049000	0.37	0.132667	1.00
Chipped stone 2 mm	0.006667	0.93	0.001922	0.27	0.007179	1.00
Bone 1 mm	0.135429	2.26	0.019677	0.33	0.060000	1.00
Chipped stone 1 mm	0.000400	0.16	0.000189	0.08	0.002500	1.00

Table 3.13. *Density of bone and chipped stone in different height floor types in the North Area.*

	General height floor (110 samples)		Raised height floor (38 samples)		All floors (176 samples)	
Bone 4 mm	0.297560	1.04	0.182519	0.64	0.287152	1.00
Chipped stone 4 mm	0.004556	0.94	0.001591	0.33	0.004833	1.00
Bone 2 mm	0.041834	1.05	0.022979	0.57	0.040000	1.00
Chipped stone 2 mm	0.005000	1.56	0.000851	0.27	0.003200	1.00
Bone 1 mm	0.016190	0.96	0.013182	0.78	0.016852	1.00
Chipped stone 1 mm	0.000774	N/A	0.000000	N/A	0.000000	N/A

Table 3.14. *Density of bone and chipped stone in different height floor types in the South Area.*

	General height floors (404 samples)		Raised height floors (20 samples)		All floors (576 samples)	
Bone 4 mm	0.695455	1.22	0.242784	0.43	0.570000	1.00
Chipped stone 4 mm	0.010312	1.69	0.004688	0.77	0.006111	1.00
Bone 2 mm	0.160556	1.21	0.048438	0.37	0.132667	1.00
Chipped stone 2 mm	0.010000	1.39	0.000767	0.11	0.007179	1.00
Bone 1 mm	0.075200	1.25	0.048472	0.81	0.060000	1.00
Chipped stone 1 mm	0.003333	1.33	0.001111	0.44	0.002500	1.00

Table 3.15. *Density of bone and chipped stone in general floors of different material types in the North Area.*

	White clay floor (48 samples)		Non-white laid floor (20 samples)		Occupation floor (42 samples)		All floors (176 samples)	
Bone 4 mm	0.210667	0.73	0.241111	0.84	0.653909	2.28	0.287152	1.00
Chipped stone 4 mm	0.001176	0.24	0.006667	1.38	0.004915	1.02	0.004833	1.00
Bone 2 mm	0.026136	0.65	0.059952	1.50	0.053000	1.32	0.040000	1.00
Chipped stone 2 mm	0.002083	0.65	0.008333	2.60	0.005227	1.63	0.003200	1.00
Bone 1 mm	0.016771	1.00	0.013810	0.82	0.020275	1.20	0.016852	1.00
Chipped stone 1 mm	0.000000	N/A	0.000833	N/A	0.001278	N/A	0.000000	N/A

Table 3.16. *Density of bone and chipped stone in general floors of different material types in the South Area.*

	Baked floor (71 samples)		White clay floor (34 samples)		Non-white laid floor (97 samples)		Occupation floor (188 samples)		Mixed floor (85 samples)		All floors (576 samples)	
Bone 4 mm	0.186667	0.33	0.261520	0.46	0.500000	0.88	1.062333	1.86	0.415000	0.73	0.570000	1.00
Chipped stone 4 mm	0.000000	0.00	0.000000	0.00	0.000000	0.00	0.035667	5.84	0.025000	4.09	0.006111	1.00
Bone 2 mm	0.040000	0.30	0.038333	0.29	0.193750	1.46	0.290500	2.19	0.080000	0.60	0.132667	1.00
Chipped stone 2 mm	0.000000	0.00	0.003286	0.46	0.002083	0.29	0.020714	2.89	0.010000	1.39	0.007179	1.00
Bone 1 mm	0.011250	0.19	0.010556	0.18	0.070000	1.17	0.140000	2.33	0.040000	0.67	0.060000	1.00
Chipped stone 1 mm	0.000000	0.00	0.000477	0.19	0.002000	0.80	0.005189	2.08	0.005000	2.00	0.002500	1.00

Table 3.17. *Density of bone and chipped stone in occupation floors in different buildings.*

	Building 2 (45 samples)		Building 4 (16 samples)		Building 6 (22 samples)		Building 17 (83 samples)		Building 18 (26 samples)		Building 23 (29 samples)		All occupation floors (251 samples)	
Bone 4 mm	1.048000	1.00	0.733333	0.70	0.940694	0.90	1.047750	1.00	1.449784	1.39	0.721667	0.69	1.045000	1.00
Chipped stone 4 mm	0.021739	0.65	0.033333	1.00	0.050611	1.52	0.011667	0.35	0.171510	5.15	0.044167	1.33	0.033333	1.00
Bone 2 mm	0.010000	0.03	0.005833	0.02	0.315789	1.04	0.530000	1.74	0.37375	1.23	0.336667	1.10	0.305000	1.00
Chipped stone 2 mm	0.010000	0.50	0.013810	0.69	0.026714	1.34	0.012174	0.61	0.048918	2.45	0.005833	0.29	0.020000	1.00
Bone 1 mm	0.010000	0.07	0.005833	0.04	0.238012	1.72	0.288000	2.08	0.206154	1.49	0.180323	1.30	0.138667	1.00
Chipped stone 1 mm	0.001623	0.30	0.003500	0.66	0.006222	1.17	0.005000	0.94	0.017307	3.25	0.014167	2.66	0.005333	1.00

broadly similar median densities of both material types at 4 mm, but at 2 mm and 1 mm bins/basins have higher median densities than hearths/ovens. In the South Area (Table 3.12) bin/basin floors have higher median values than hearth/oven floors, particularly for bone. This suggests that the distinction between feature floors and building floors for chipped stone is a general one, but that for bone it is based on hearth/oven floors only, as bin/basin floors actually have higher median densities of bone than building floors.

General floors can be divided between those covering raised areas and those at the general floor height (Fig. 3.5; Tables 3.13–3.14). In both areas raised floors have consistently lower median densities for both material types at all sizes, particularly for chipped stone. The general height floors can be divided into material types. This indicates that in the North Area (Table 3.15) white clay floors have lower densities for both material types, particularly for chipped stone, with the exception of bone 1 mm which is the same as the overall median. Non-white laid floors show a mixed pattern for bone but uniformly higher than median values for chipped stone. Occupation deposits have higher than median densities of bone, particularly at 4 mm, and higher than median densities of chipped stone at the two smaller fraction sizes. In the South Area (Table 3.16) baked floors and white clay floors have low median values for both material types at all fraction sizes and occupation floors have high median values for both material types at all fraction sizes. Mixed floors have high values for chipped stone, but low values for bone. Non-white laid floors have low values for chipped stone, although this becomes less pronounced as the fraction size decreases, and a mixed pattern for bone.

Attempts to look at densities on a building by building basis are hindered by the relatively low numbers of samples of different floor types from individual structures (Table 3.17). Building 2 has low chipped stone and bone at the two smaller fraction sizes, Building 4 has low bone at the two smaller fraction sizes, Building 17 has high bone at two lower fraction sizes and Building 18 has high chipped stone at all fraction sizes.

Floor deposits and in situ *activities*

Traditionally one of the most common applications of micro-artefactual studies has been to study spatial and temporal variation of densities of material in floor deposits as a means of identifying *in situ* activities. Initially this approach was also adopted by the Çatalhöyük Research Project, until it was realized that there were a number of problems with it (Cessford 2003). The fundamental underlying assumption of such analysis is that micro-artefacts in floor deposits entered that deposit during its use as a floor and were not already present either incidentally or deliberately in the material used to create the floor. The first indication that the link between micro-artefacts and *in situ* activities needed to be critiqued was the realization that such material is present in almost all samples and in particular in wall plaster. The white plaster floors found at Çatalhöyük are visually similar to white plasters found on walls and micromorphological examination indicates both are composed of similar white calcareous clay sediments (Matthews *et al.* 1996, 304). Given that micro-artefacts in wall plasters are unlikely to relate to *in situ* activities taking place on vertical surfaces, a comparison of these two deposit types should prove useful. In the North Area (Fig. 3.6; Table 3.18) there is a rather mixed picture, with both material types having higher median densities at 4 mm in wall plaster than in white clay floors but lower median densities in most of the lower fraction sizes. In the South Area (Fig. 3.6; Table 3.19) the results appear to indicate a difference in the median density of chipped stone, with wall plaster having much lower values. The picture of bone is less clear with lower values in the two larger fraction sizes, although these are still around half the value for white clay floors, and a higher value in the lowest fraction sizes. Given that the material in wall plaster is unlikely to relate to *in situ* activities this suggests that some of the material in white clay floors, and by extension other floor types as well, may not relate to *in situ* activities. Most of the chipped stone may relate to *in situ* activities and some of the bone at higher fraction sizes. Given the higher number of wall-plaster samples from the South Area these are perhaps more likely to be reliable. This suggests that perhaps half of the bone in white clay floors could be related to activity, but that there is no such clear relationship for chipped stone.

This conclusion is supported by more detailed specialist analysis of material. The faunal material from wall plasters revealed that they generally have low densities of material and the fragments are usually small. Beyond this general pattern there is a good deal of variation and the profiles of the different wall

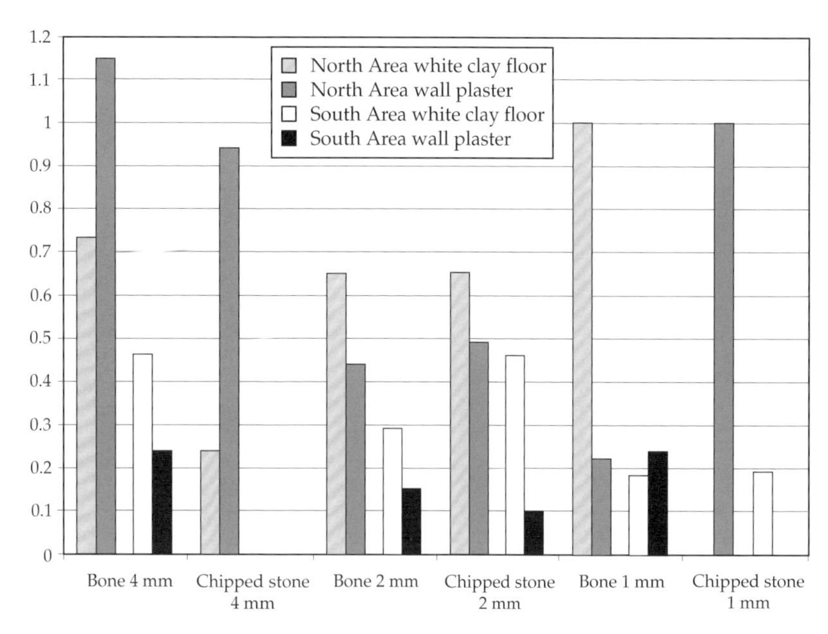

Figure 3.6. *Density of bone and chipped stone at different size ranges in white clay floors and wall plaster in the North and South Areas.*

Table 3.18. *Density of bone and chipped stone in white clay floors and wall plaster in the North Area.*

	White clay floor (48 samples)		Wall plaster (12 samples)		All floors (176 samples)	
Bone 4 mm	0.210667	0.73	0.329060	1.15	0.287152	1.00
Chipped stone 4 mm	0.001176	0.24	0.004537	0.94	0.004833	1.00
Bone 2 mm	0.026136	0.65	0.017500	0.44	0.040000	1.00
Chipped stone 2 mm	0.002083	0.65	0.001574	0.49	0.003200	1.00
Bone 1 mm	0.016771	1.00	0.003750	0.22	0.016852	1.00
Chipped stone 1 mm	0.000000	N/A	0.001250	N/A	0.000000	N/A

Table 3.19. *Density of bone and chipped stone in white clay floors and wall plaster in the South Area.*

	White clay floor (34 samples)		Wall plaster (40 samples)		All floors (576 samples)	
Bone 4 mm	0.261520	0.46	0.137582	0.24	0.570000	1.00
Chipped stone 4 mm	0.000000	0.00	0.000000	0.00	0.006111	1.00
Bone 2 mm	0.038333	0.29	0.020000	0.15	0.132667	1.00
Chipped stone 2 mm	0.003286	0.46	0.000697	0.10	0.007179	1.00
Bone 1 mm	0.010556	0.18	0.014667	0.24	0.060000	1.00
Chipped stone 1 mm	0.000477	0.19	0.000000	0.00	0.002500	1.00

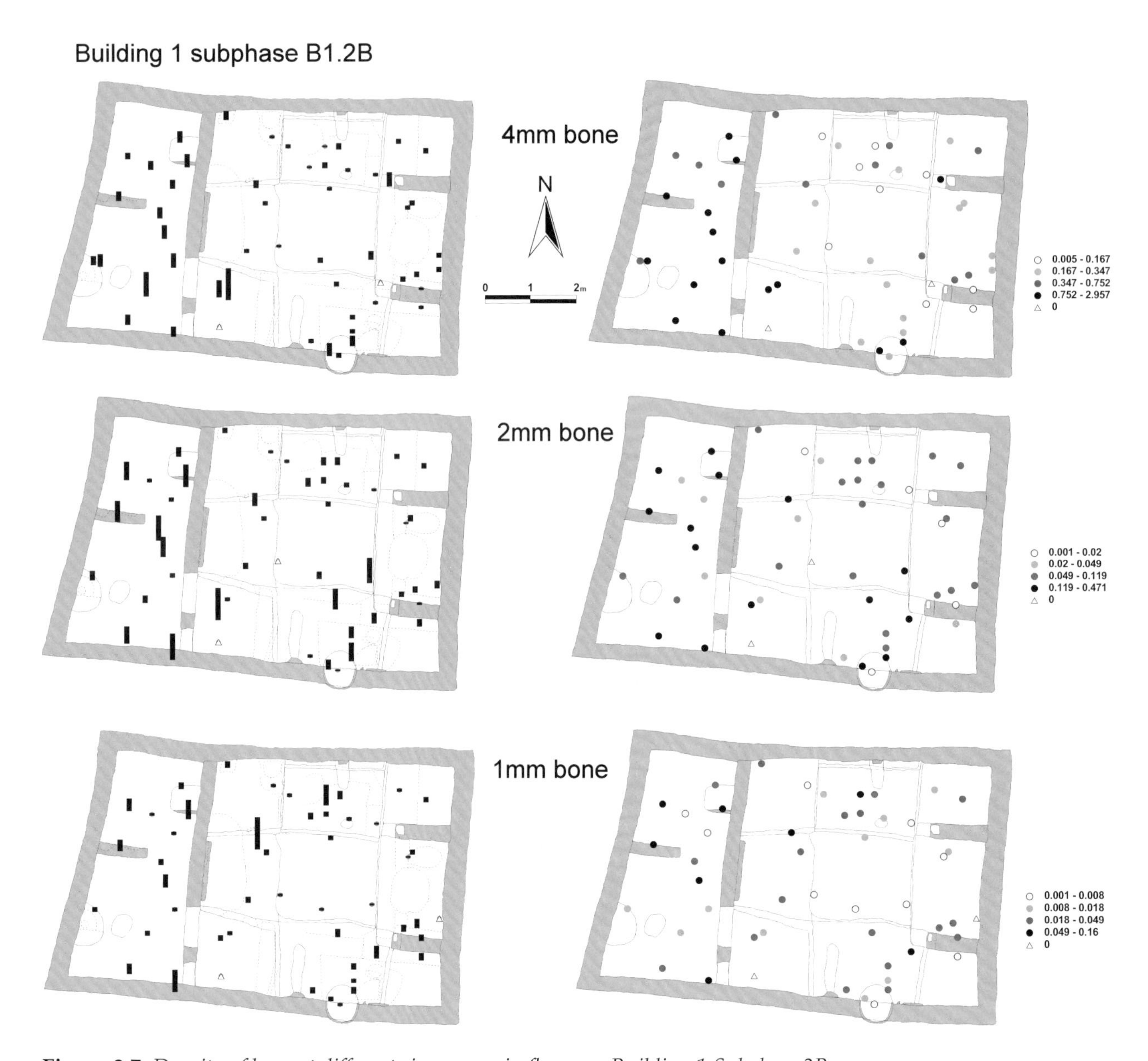

Figure 3.7. *Density of bone at different size ranges in floors on Building 1 Subphase 2B.*

plasters variously resemble assemblages from 'clean' floors, 'dirty' floors, 'low-traffic' floors, and 'empty' fills. They are not very different from what is found in other kinds of constructional material such as brick, mortar and packing, except that some of these non-floor deposits sometimes have higher densities or larger pieces. Analysis of the composition of the archaeobotanical assemblages indicates that over fifty per cent of the samples from the North Area can be said to fit into one of two 'standard sample profiles' for relative material composition. The first 'standard sample profile' is interpreted as representative of tertiary or very mixed deposits and can be thought of as 'background noise'. The second 'standard sample profile' contains a much more limited range of materials and probably represents material from less fully mixed deposits. The two 'standard sample profiles' are found in a wide range of contexts, including constructional materials, fills and floor deposits. Floor deposits that conform to the two 'standard sample profiles' are therefore highly unlikely to relate to *in situ* activities. The impression is that in general 'floor assemblages' are largely already present in the constructional material.

The idea that some micro-artefactual material was already present in the constructional material receives support from a detailed programme of accelerator mass spectrometry (AMS) dating in the North Area. Consideration of the determination, including Bayesian statistical analysis (Buck *et al.* 1999),

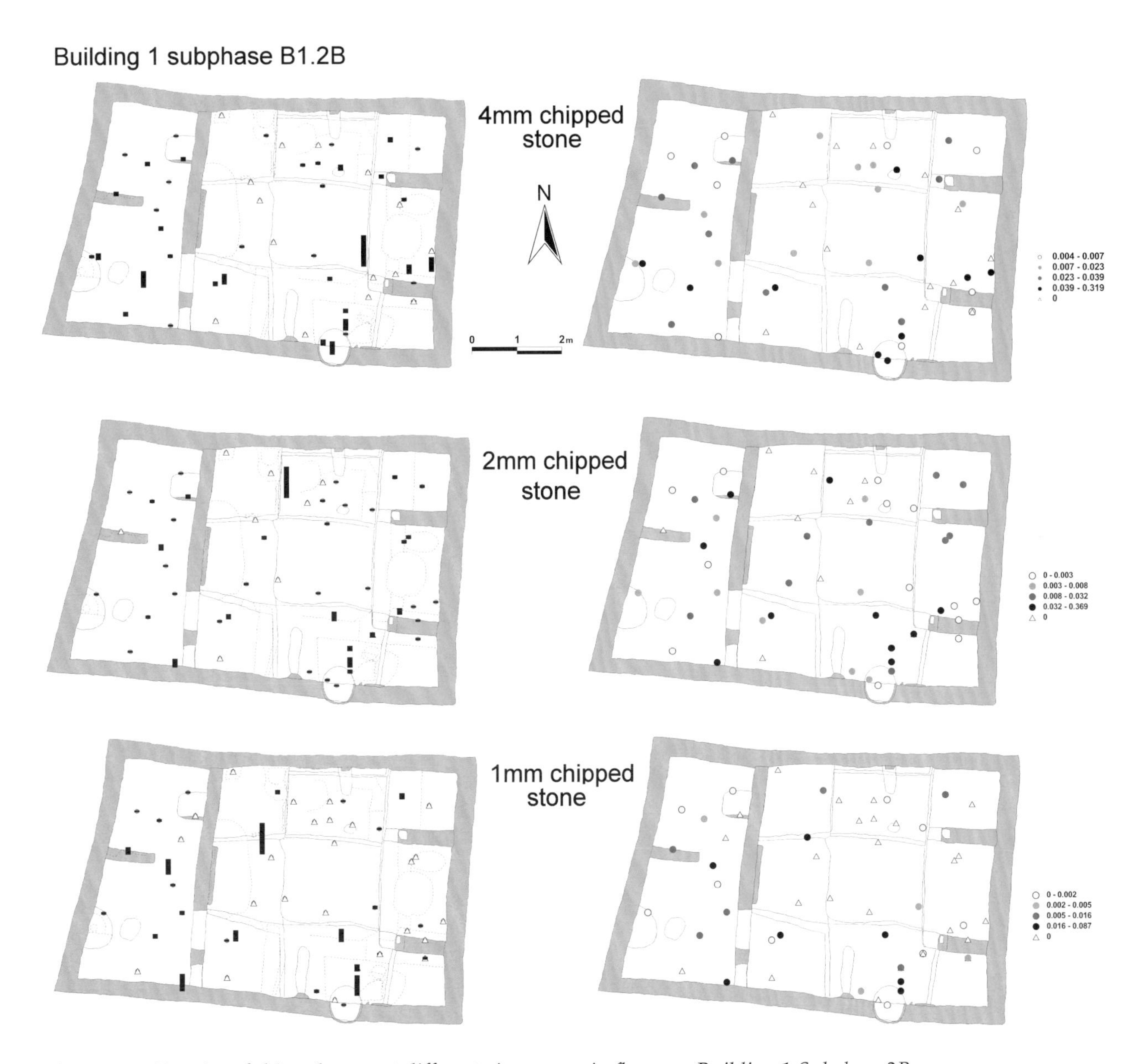

Figure 3.8. *Density of chipped stone at different size ranges in floors on Building 1 Subphase 2B.*

indicated that some of the archaeobotanical material in floors was broadly contemporary with their use as floors. This need not demonstrate a link between archaeobotanical material and *in situ* activities, but does show it is at least possible. The majority of the determinations were, however, probably older than the floor deposits in which they were found by decades and in occasional instances centuries. Similarly faunal material also proved to be probably older than the floor deposits and is likely, probably by centuries. Although there are possible complications with the determinations on animal bone this suggests that the archaeobotanical and faunal material in deposits are not from the same source and neither relates to *in situ* activities.

This demonstrates that at least some of the micro-artefactual material in floor deposits was either accidentally or deliberately incorporated in the deposits prior to their use. A separate complicating factor is the variation in duration of different floor deposits. Buildings at Çatalhöyük were probably occupied for between fifty and a hundred years. Within this period, which is likely to vary between buildings, the length of time represented by different floor deposits varies. Some floor deposits might survive for the entire occupation of a structure, whereas others are of shorter duration lasting for only a specific phase or less. Floors in different areas of a structure were replaced at different points in time; this means that different sets of floor deposits do not represent the same lengths

Table 3.20. *Density of bone and chipped stone in inside and outside fills in the North Area.*

	Inside fill (445 samples)		Outside fill (48 samples)		All fills (493 samples)	
Bone 4 mm	0.610172	0.89	2.477315	3.60	0.688636	1.00
Chipped stone 4 mm	0.014907	0.97	0.021328	1.39	0.015385	1.00
Bone 2 mm	0.025985	0.91	0.048077	1.68	0.028571	1.00
Chipped stone 2 mm	0.010000	1.00	0.013594	1.36	0.010000	1.00
Bone 1 mm	0.010000	1.00	0.011667	1.17	0.010000	1.00
Chipped stone 1 mm	0.001379	1.00	0.001429	1.04	0.001379	1.00

Table 3.21. *Density of bone and chipped stone in inside and outside fills in the South Area.*

	Inside fill (442 samples)		Outside fill (40 samples)		All fills (482 samples)	
Bone 4 mm	1.332316	0.96	2.253855	1.62	1.390230	1.00
Chipped stone 4 mm	0.030606	1.01	0.026043	0.86	0.030227	1.00
Bone 2 mm	0.088095	1.03	0.072500	0.85	0.085714	1.00
Chipped stone 2 mm	0.015000	1.05	0.00925	0.65	0.014343	1.00
Bone 1 mm	0.028571	1.01	0.025000	0.88	0.028286	1.00
Chipped stone 1 mm	0.002963	1.00	0.002288	0.77	0.002963	1.00

Table 3.22. *Density of bone and chipped stone in burial and non-burial inside fills in the North Area.*

	Non-burial inside fill (379 samples)		Burial fill (66 samples)		All inside fills (445 samples)	
Bone 4 mm	0.586538	0.96	0.840000	1.38	0.610172	1.00
Chipped stone 4 mm	0.014815	0.99	0.015000	1.01	0.014907	1.00
Bone 2 mm	0.024545	0.86	0.036923	1.29	0.028571	1.00
Chipped stone 2 mm	0.008889	0.89	0.014815	1.48	0.010000	1.00
Bone 1 mm	0.008667	0.87	0.024242	2.42	0.010000	1.00
Chipped stone 1 mm	0.001333	0.97	0.002000	1.45	0.001379	1.00

Table 3.23. *Density of bone and chipped stone in burial and non-burial inside fills in the South Area.*

	Non-burial inside fill (392 samples)		Burial fill (48 samples)		All inside fills (442 samples)	
Bone 4 mm	1.272944	0.96	1.730000	1.30	1.332316	1.00
Chipped stone 4 mm	0.030455	1.00	0.031250	1.02	0.030606	1.00
Bone 2 mm	0.070588	0.80	0.464348	5.27	0.088095	1.00
Chipped stone 2 mm	0.014286	0.95	0.020000	1.33	0.015000	1.00
Bone 1 mm	0.024348	0.85	0.162857	5.70	0.028571	1.00
Chipped stone 1 mm	0.002963	1.00	0.002540	0.86	0.002963	1.00

of time. Simply comparing densities of material in different floor deposits is therefore flawed as higher densities could simply represent floors of longer temporal duration. Given the apparent impossibility of precisely estimating the temporal duration of different floor deposits, this severely compromises approaches based upon density. Other problems include the possible effects of differences in floor hardness and coverings on the incorporation of micro-artefacts into floor deposits.

It is clear that the link between micro-artefact density and *in situ* activities on floor is a problematical one at Çatalhöyük, but this does not mean that none of the material relates to such activities. Densities of material appear to represent a rather blunt instrument for approaching this question, although they may be more applicable on simpler sites. The focus upon quantity of material, whereby relatively disparate categories of material are treated as single entities, rather than the composition, taphonomy, or diversity of assemblages may not be the most useful approach to the detection of activities. It could be argued that if the existence of a level of 'background noise' of material already present in the material that floors are created from is accepted then it is the differences in density, particularly higher densities, that relate to *in situ* activities. Such an approach assumes that 'background noise' is a spatially- and temporally-constant factor that can be 'filtered' out, by assuming that the lowest density observed equates to the level of 'background noise'. Such an assumption is not supported at Çatalhöyük where it appears that floors in different parts of a building were composed of different materials and that the sources of such material vary through time. Results from attempts to plot spatial variation of micro-artefact in floor deposits are included in Figures 3.7–3.8 and on accompanying CD. It does appear that in some instances such plots do reveal patterning related to *in situ* activities, but these are in the minority and may relate to buildings where specific activities were focused.

Occupation floors in particular have high densities of material, whose composition often proves to be distinctive when studied, and micromorphological study of floors has detected the presence of distinct thin bands of organic material that probably relate to activities. The inability of HR analysis to detect traces of activities on floors is not necessarily because these do not exist but because this is a rather blunt instrument for detecting subtle patterning.

Fills

Fills can be analyzed using a basic inside versus outside division. In the North Area (Table 3.20) outside fills have higher median densities, particularly of bone, and the distinction declines as the fraction size decreases. A comparison between the different external spaces showed some distinctions; in particular Spaces 69 and 73 which are quite similar in terms of location and width had more in common than Space 153 which is probably rather different. In the South Area (Table 3.21) outside fills have lower median densities, particularly of chipped stone, with the exception of bone at the largest fraction size.

In the North Area (Table 3.22) burial fills have higher median densities of bone at all three fraction sizes than other inside fills and higher chipped-stone densities at the lower two fraction sizes. The higher median densities of bone may be due to the presence of small fragments of human skeletal material from disturbed burials. There is no obvious explanation for the pattern of chipped stone. In the South Area (Table 3.23) burial fills have higher median densities of bone at all three fraction sizes than other inside fills, but that there is no consistent relationship for chipped stone. A comparison of different phases of general infilling in the North Area revealed a wide pattern of variation, apparently linked to the sources of material being utilized for the process.

Middens

When middens are considered by depositional type (Fig. 3.9; Table 3.24), finely-bedded middens have higher densities of both bone and chipped stone at all fraction sizes and clay balls/objects at 4 mm than coarsely-bedded middens. Alluviated dumps

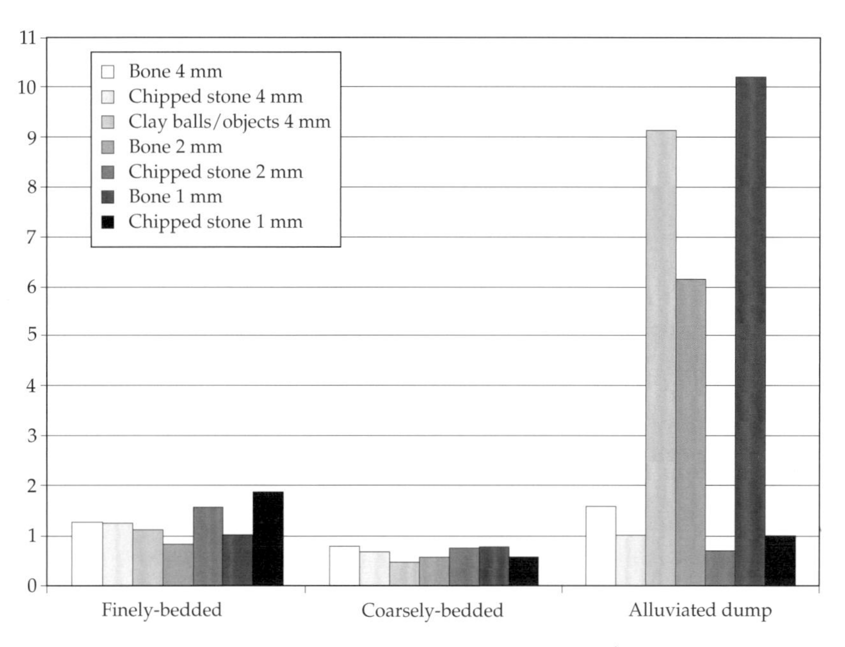

Figure 3.9. *Density of bone, chipped stone and clay balls/objects at different size ranges in different types of midden by depositional type.*

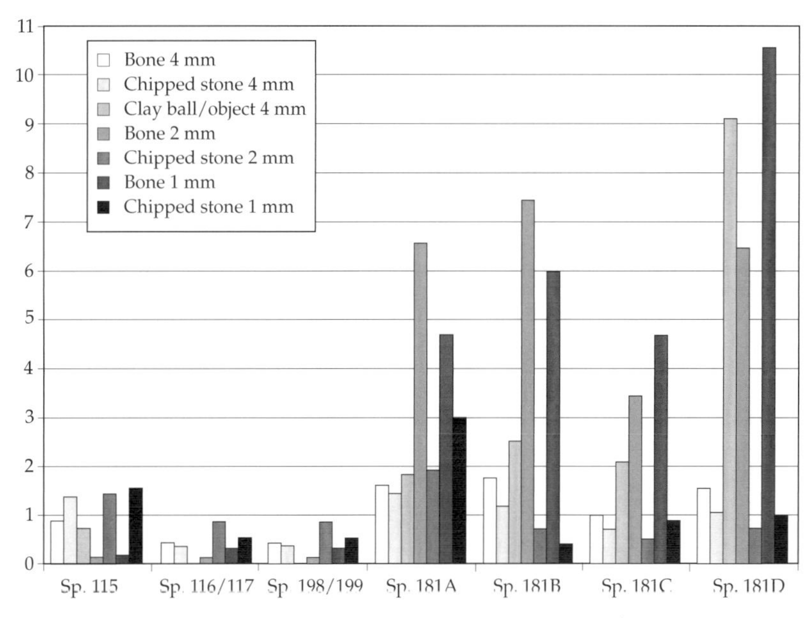

Figure 3.10. *Density of bone, chipped stone and clay balls/objects at different size ranges in different types of midden by space.*

Table 3.24. *Density of bone and chipped stone in different types of midden by deposition in the South Area.*

	Finely-bedded midden (139 samples)		Coarsely-bedded midden (152 samples)		Alluviated dump midden (21 samples)		All middens (312 samples)	
Bone 4 mm	7.314286	1.24	4.629642	0.78	9.147059	1.55	5.916000	1.00
Chipped stone 4 mm	0.194545	1.25	0.101293	0.65	0.158947	1.02	0.155778	1.00
Clay ball/object 4 mm	0.337778	1.14	0.137732	0.46	2.706470	9.13	0.296335	1.00
Bone 2 mm	0.230556	0.80	0.158824	0.55	1.783448	6.16	0.289306	1.00
Chipped stone 2 mm	0.054360	1.56	0.025000	0.72	0.024000	0.69	0.034891	1.00
Bone 1 mm	0.073905	1.00	0.055625	0.75	0.754074	10.2	0.073905	1.00
Chipped stone 1 mm	0.008900	1.87	0.002500	0.53	0.004571	0.96	0.004753	1.00

have a mixed pattern for chipped stone and high median densities of bone, which increases as the sample size decreases. Part of this may be due to the sticky nature of the alluviated dumps that could mean that some of the weight is sediment rather than bone, but it appears unlikely that this is the entire cause. When middens are considered by space (Fig. 3.10; Table 3.25) there appears to be a pattern with the later middens in Spaces 115 and 116/117 having low median densities of bone in comparison to the earlier middens, particularly at the two smaller fraction sizes. Space 115 and Level Pre-XII.A Space 181 appear to have high densities of chipped stone.

Activity

The limited number of samples makes the use of figures for the density of materials rather unreliable but some general patterns do seem to be apparent. With regard to lime-burning deposits the median values for all materials at all fraction sizes are markedly lower than those for the Level Pre-XII.B middens they are associated with are. It appears possible that some of this material relates to accidental incorporation of midden material in these deposits and was not deliberately included. For penning deposits those from Level XI Space 198 and XII Space 199 have markedly higher levels of both bone and chipped stone at all fraction sizes than the deposits from Level IX Space 117. This is similar to the pattern for density in midden deposits, which appear to be lower in Spaces 116/117 than in other middens.

Quantifying deposition

The extensive and intensive HR sampling regime at Çatalhöyük, with its standardized recovery techniques and explicit sampling procedures, means that it is possible to attempt to consider broadly how much

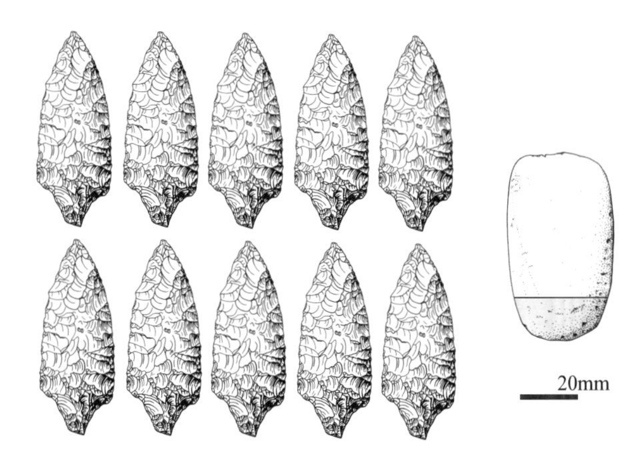

Figure 3.11. *Comparison of obsidian projectile point and greenstone and gabbro axe interaction per building per year.*

Table 3.25. *Density of bone and chipped stone in different types of midden by space in the South Area.*

	Sp.115 Level VIII (112 samples)		Sp.116/117 Level IX (53 samples)		Sp.198/199 Levels XI–XII (6 samples)		Sp.181.A Level Pre-XII.A (31 samples)		Sp.181.B Level PreXII.B (46 samples)		Sp.181.C Level Pre-XII.C (43 samples)		Sp.181.D Level Pre-XII.D (17 samples)		All middens (314 samples)	
Bone 4 mm	5.205517	0.88	2.538710	0.43	5.415849	0.92	9.535714	1.62	10.495740	1.77	5.939394	1.00	9.200000	1.56	5.916000	1.00
Chipped stone 4 mm	0.213573	1.37	0.058000	0.37	0.066514	0.43	0.226333	1.45	0.184740	1.19	0.111351	0.71	0.163333	1.05	0.155778	1.00
Clay balls/objects 4 mm	0.220556	0.74	0.000000	0.00	1.210129	4.08	0.544400	1.84	0.745483	2.52	0.619394	2.09	2.706470	9.13	0.296335	1.00
Bone 2 mm	0.044444	0.15	0.041562	0.14	0.816068	2.82	1.900000	6.57	2.157222	7.46	0.996571	3.44	1.875294	6.48	0.289306	1.00
Chipped stone 2 mm	0.050968	1.46	0.030385	0.87	0.017407	0.50	0.067143	1.92	0.025200	0.72	0.017778	0.51	0.025882	0.74	0.034891	1.00
Bone 1 mm	0.014286	0.19	0.025403	0.34	0.255129	3.45	0.347692	4.70	0.443258	5.99	0.345455	4.67	0.782000	10.58	0.073905	1.00
Chipped stone 1 mm	0.007368	1.55	0.002583	0.54	0.009662	2.03	0.014286	3.01	0.001973	0.42	0.004211	0.89	0.004706	0.99	0.004753	1.00

of certain types of material was deposited at the site. The HR data can be combined with the topographical modelling of the site (Pollard *et al.* 1996), which allows the volume of the mound to be accurately calculated, to provide values for how much material was deposited. The absolute dating sequence for the site (Cessford 2001; Chapter 4) then allows the calculation of annual values. This of course only deals with the amount of material deposited at the site and does not include material that may have once been present at Çatalhöyük, but was then exported to another site or deposited away from the site for any reason. It can therefore only be considered as providing minimum atemporal values.

If we take the values for obsidian, where the archaeological density is probably a reliable proxy value for the density of Neolithic deposition, then it appears that around 130,000 kg of material was deposited at Çatalhöyük (Cessford & Carter forthcoming). This results in figures of 132–240 kg of obsidian per year. As this material originated some 190 km away from the site at the sources of Göllü Dağ-east and Nenezi Dağ (Chapters 11–12) the transportational effort can be expressed as 25,800–45,600 kg / km per year. Based on current population estimates (Volume 4, Chapter 16) this equates to 16.5–68.6 g of obsidian per person per year, or 146.7–266.7 g per occupied building per year. Obsidian was transported to Çatalhöyük in pieces weighing around 60 g, or one piece every one to four years per individual or two to four pieces per year per occupied building. Artefacts such as projectile points and scrapers typically weigh around 10–15 g, equating to between one and seven artefacts per person per year or ten to twenty-seven per occupied building. These calculations are of course highly simplistic but do perhaps begin to help us contextualize the scale of 'interaction' between people and obsidian at Çatalhöyük somewhat.

Similar approaches can be adopted for other materials. It appears that in total around 300,000 kg of andesite and basalt from Karadağ utilized mainly for querns and handstones, 17,700 kg of greenstone and gabbro probably from between Çumra and Karaman used mainly from axes (Chapters 13 & 17) were deposited at the site. There was also apparently around 1130 kg of marine shell primarily from the Mediterranean (Volume 4, Chapter 6). Although the origins of these materials are less precisely defined than for obsidian, the transportational efforts per year for the various materials are approximately 15,050–27,350 kg / km for basal and andesite, 748–1364 kg / km for greenstone and gabbro and 209–399 kg / km for the overland element of marine shell. The figures translate to around 40–160 g of andesite and basalt and 2–10 g of greenstone and gabbro per person per year. As an andesite or basalt quern weighs 1000–1500 g and a greenstone

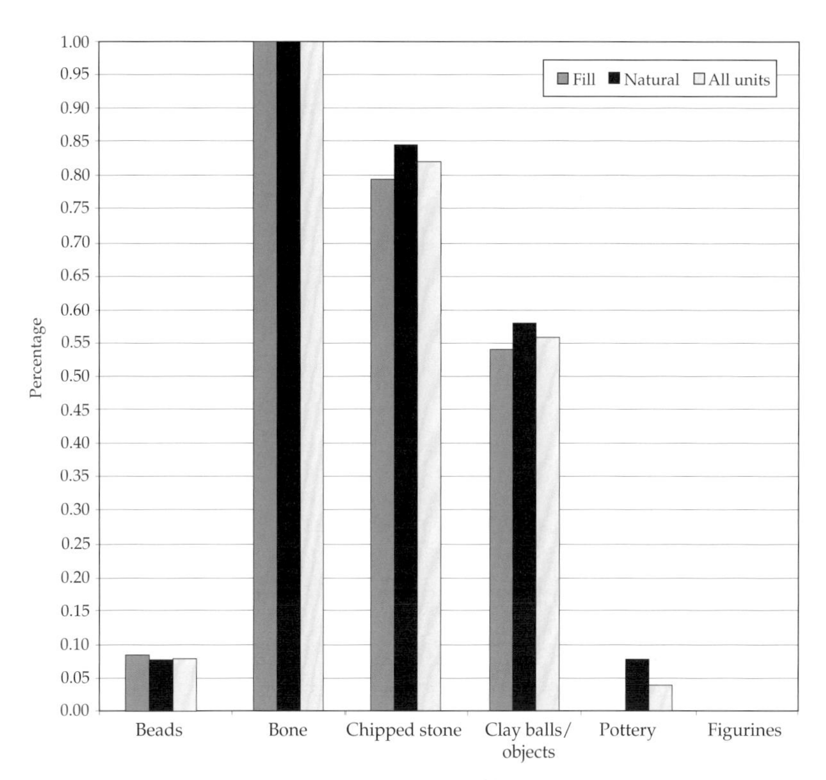

Figure 3.12. *Presence of material types in different types of deposit in the KOPAL Area.*

Table 3.26. *Occurrence of material types in KOPAL Area samples.*

Material	4-mm occurrence		2-mm occurrence		1-mm occurrence		Occurrence at all sizes in all samples	
Beads	0	0%	1	2%	3	6%	4	8%
Bone	50	100%	50	100%	50	100%	50	100%
Chipped stone	21	42%	35	70%	23	46%	41	82%
Clay balls/objects	28	56%	0	0%	0	0%	30	56%
Dung	0	0%	1	2%	0	0%	1	2%
Eggshell	8	16%	39	78%	48	96%	49	98%
Mollusc	45	90%	50	100%	49	98%	50	100%
Plant	25	50%	47	94%	46	46%	50	100%
Pottery	2	4%	0	0%	0	0%	2	4%
Stone	50	100%	N/A	N/A	N/A	N/A	N/A	N/A
Worked stone	2	4%	0	0%	0	0%	2	4%

Table 3.27. *Occurrence of material types in major deposit types in KOPAL Area.*

Material	Feature fill (24 samples)		'Natural' layer (26 samples)		All units (50 samples)	
Beads	2	8.3%	2	7.7%	4	8.0%
Bone	24	100%	26	100%	50	100%
Chipped stone	19	79.2%	22	84.6%	41	82.0%
Clay balls/objects	13	54.2%	15	57.7%	28	56.0%
Pottery	0	0%	2	7.7%	2	4.0%
Figurines	0	0%	0	0.0%	0	0.0%

Table 3.28. *Density of bone, chipped stone and clay balls/objects in major deposit types in KOPAL Area.*

	Feature fill (24 samples)		'Natural' layer (26 samples)		All units (50 samples)	
Bone 4 mm	0.584448	0.97	1.014446	1.68	0.604167	1.00
Chipped stone 4 mm	0.000000	N/A	0.000000	N/A	0.000000	N/A
Clay balls/objects 4 mm	0.141655	2.12	0.050263	0.75	0.066833	1.00
Bone 2 mm	0.181154	1.05	0.164000	0.95	0.173333	1.00
Chipped stone 2 mm	0.001792	0.77	0.003000	1.29	0.002333	1.00
Bone 1 mm	0.072951	0.84	0.105000	1.20	0.086957	1.00
Chipped stone 1 mm	0.000000	N/A	0.000000	N/A	0.000000	N/A

or gabbro axe around 90 g this suggests that less than one quern or axe was deposited at the site per person per year. Whilst such figures contain a degree of uncertainty they are methodologically comparable and provide a fresh perspective for the comparison of different types of artefact. Comparison of the minimum values per year per occupied building suggests that we have ten obsidian projectile points and 0.23 greenstone and gabbro axes (Fig. 3.11). When there are issues that suggest that the archaeological density of material is not a reliable proxy for the original Neolithic density of material this technique obviously becomes much less reliable but is still potentially broadly useful. In the case of animal bone (Volume 4, Chapter 2) taphonomic factors mean that the archaeological density is likely to substantially underrepresent the amount of Neolithic deposition. Nevertheless it does allow us to suggest that the number of sheep and goats killed and consumed each year was in the hundreds or low thousands and that the total population from which these were derived was in the thousands.

All of the values thus calculated ignore material that was once present at Çatalhöyük, but was not deposited at the site. They therefore only provide minimum values and additionally are atemporal, ignoring probable fluctuations. Despite these caveats they provide at least some insight and can be considered as minimum values, which can potentially aid an understanding of economic and social aspects of the site. There are also a number of assumptions and potential inaccuracies in the calculations. These mean that the precise results are not particularly reliable but they do indicate orders of magnitude.

KOPAL Area

There is a relatively small number of samples from the KOPAL Area and these are generally larger than those from the North and South Areas. The material types that were common in the other areas were all also common in the KOPAL Area (Fig. 3.12; Table 3.26). Clay ball/object occurs much more frequently in the KOPAL Area, especially in comparison to the North Area but also to the South Area. There is a restricted range of context types in the KOPAL Area. The main distinction is between the fills of features, primarily pits, and general layers of largely naturally-deposited material with a cultural component, termed alluvium or backswamp clay. At a basic presence level there appears to be no obvious distinction between fills and general layers (Table 3.27). In terms of diversity (Fig. 3.3) both fills (7.5) and general layers (7.4) score similarly. These results are close to those for fills in the South Area, but higher than those for the North Area and are lower than South Area middens.

In terms of density of bone and chipped stone there is little apparent difference between fills and general layers (Table 3.28), with the exception of 4-mm bone, which has a higher median density in general layers. 4-mm clay balls/objects have a higher median density in feature fills. In comparison with the other excavation areas the 4-mm median density for clay balls/objects is markedly higher in the KOPAL Area. The median densities for bone are higher than the North and South Areas at the two smaller fraction sizes and intermediate for the higher fraction size. The median densities for chipped stone in the KOPAL Area are consistently notably lower than the North and South Areas; in particular they are not comparable to midden deposits.

Conclusions

The results of HR analysis, whilst complex, do indicate that the technique is useful in identifying patterning of deposition of material. It is clear that the processing of large numbers of samples from a range of deposit types produces HR data that reveal meaningful patterning. The different types of analysis undertaken such as ubiquity, presence, diversity and density all revealed different types of patterning and all appear to be valid and useful methods and are not simply different ways of examining the same phenomena. Similarly, different scales and different material types reveal different depositional phenomena; in particular 4 mm is often distinct from 2 mm and 1 mm, which are frequently quite similar. Although the fraction sizes adopted are relatively arbitrary they do strongly indicate that the deposition of material is a scalar phenomenon. There is little simple patterning, which is perhaps unsurprising given the complex nature of depositional practices on highly-stratified tell sites. It appears that much of the material deposited at the site occurs as a form of 'background noise', indicative of residuality in a densely-occupied site where the raw material for creating most deposits was obtained from sources which already contained cultural material. There therefore appears to be only a low level of agency or intentionality associated with the deposition of at least some micro-artefacts. In essence there is a form of negative choice or deliberate unintentionality in that it is acceptable for most deposit types to contain most forms of material. This conclusion, whilst important in itself as it serves to challenge the implicit assumption in most previous work that micro-artefacts can be simplistically linked to *in situ* activities, is largely a negative one. It does appear that some of the material represents a higher level of intentionality and that by considering a large number of samples from a range of contexts it is possible to identify this. Some material was deliberately placed in particular deposits and represents the traces of *in situ* activity or abandonment. At a gross density-based form of analysis it is probably impractical to go further than this as more detailed considerations of assemblage composition and variation are probably required. Results that appear to represent genuine patterning and are important are:

- Middens contain a more diverse range of materials and higher densities of material than other deposit types. It is important to note that the macro-artefacts in Chapter 2 clearly indicated lower variance in midden densities within particular artefact sets.
- Alluviated dump middens contain the highest density and diversity of material followed by finely-bedded middens. Coarsely-bedded middens have the lowest densities.
- Construction / make-up deposits have low densities of material.
- Floors at a raised height, usually referred to as platforms, have a lower density of material than general height floors.
- Different floor types contain different densities of material, with white clay floors containing the least and occupation floors the most.
- The off-site KOPAL Area displays a markedly different pattern from the other areas, particularly with regard to chipped stone.

HR analysis clearly forms an important methodological tool. In particular the large quantity and diverse sources of samples makes it highly useful, especially when not all material types are studied from all excavated contexts. The analysis undertaken so far has been relatively superficial and it is hoped that with the generation of a larger set of data more specific analysis will become possible and that work of a greater statistical complexity may also be undertaken in future.

Acknowledgements

The work on HR would be impossible without the efforts of all those who so diligently took and processed all the samples involved. Special thanks are due to Sarah Cross May and Anja Wolle for their general assistance and to Nerissa Russell, Julie Near and Tristan Carter for information on faunal, archaeobotanical and chipped-stone material.

Chapter 4

Absolute Dating at Çatalhöyük

Craig Cessford
with contributions by Petya Blumbach, K. Göze Akoğlu, Thomas Higham, Peter I. Kuniholm, Sturt W. Manning, Maryanne W. Newton, Mustafa Özbakan & Ay Melek Özer

A number of absolute-dating techniques have been applied at Çatalhöyük with varying degrees of success; various dating programs have been run at different times with different specific aims and to different standards. They have shared the broad aims of establishing the commencement, floruit and end of Neolithic occupation at Çatalhöyük and within this sequence to date the various phases or 'levels' at the site. It should be noted that for dating purposes the concept of 'levels' as defined by Mellaart in the 1960s is rather problematic. 'Levels' are not necessarily discrete unified rebuilding, occupational and abandonment events but do represent relatively contemporaneous building deposits (see Matthews & Farid 1996 and Volume 3, Part 2). Beyond the site itself the dating evidence is also used to place Çatalhöyük in various spatial and temporal contexts, particularly the central Anatolian Neolithic (for recent discussions of the Near East generally see Aurenche *et al.* 2001 and van der Plicht & Bruins 2001) (Fig. 1.1). The overall success and accuracy of scientific dating techniques is reliant upon several factors:

- the quality of care in sampling and how the samples relate to the events being dated;
- the quality and care in taking and handling the samples;
- the quality of the laboratory processing and analysis;
- the clarity with which the aims of the dating program are defined and implemented (Bowman 1990; Buck *et al.* 1994b, 252).

Certain of these factors mean that some of the dating evidence from Çatalhöyük is problematic in terms of the construction of an overall intra-site chronology. Some determinations, particularly from the 1960s, are unlikely to have a close temporal relationship to the archaeological events that they are associated with.

The major elements of the corpus of the dating evidence for the site are:

- conventional radiocarbon determinations on material from the 1960s excavations;
- AMS (accelerator mass spectrometry) radiocarbon determinations on material from the 1990s excavations;
- dendrochronological analysis on material from the 1960s and 1990s excavations;
- optically-stimulated luminescence determinations from the 1990s excavations.

The lack of a local Anatolian dendrochronological sequence stretching back to the Neolithic means that in terms of absolute dating this technique is still reliant upon radiocarbon dating and the large standard deviations for optically-stimulated luminescence limit the usefulness of this technique. Archaeomagnetic intensity dating undertaken in the 1960s (Bucha & Mellaart 1967) has not contributed any useable results. Additionally there are a number of radiocarbon and OSL determinations from sediments near the site (Roberts *et al.* 1999), which will be considered where they can be related to the archaeological sequence.

In general terms the approach adopted has been to assess each of the sets of dating evidence independently, focusing initially on the South Area where the various sets are considered and an overall sequence constructed. Discussions of the North Area, inhaled particulate carbon, mineralized hackberry, the KOPAL Area and some general discussion follow this. Unless otherwise stated all dates are quoted to two standard deviations.

Bayesian methodology

The stratified nature of the deposits at Çatalhöyük and the division of the site into phases make it suitable for the application of Bayesian statistical techniques. These are of 'wide applicability to radiocarbon determinations from sites where good information exists about the relationship between the events being dated' (Buck *et al.* 1991, 819; see also Buck *et al.* 1992; 1994a,b; 1999). Bayesian techniques require the clear definition of the problems to be addressed and utilize prior archaeological knowledge, which is explicitly stated and incorporated into a probability model. The underlying concept of Bayesian statistics can be broadly summarized as prior belief plus data equals posterior belief. The incorporation of such *a priori* knowledge can be viewed as corresponding well to the tenets of a postprocessual interpretative archaeology and it is important to consider such techniques in terms of changing theoretical perspectives, rather than just methodological progress (cf. Lucas 1997, 11–12). In the interests of clarity several definitions based upon the BCal terminology will be adopted (see CD for details). The advent of accurate calibration techniques means that we must begin to think of dating in terms of real calendar years and are in a position to consider the actual duration of defined archaeological cultures, sites and phases within sites (see Evin 1995). The creation of an overall model for the dating of Çatalhöyük combined with Bayesian statistics should go some way to achieving this.

Calibration

All determinations were calibrated using the OxCal program (v.3.5) (Bronk Ramsey 2000) using atmospheric data from Stuiver *et al.* (1998). Where two replicate determinations were produced from a single sample these were pooled using the R Combine function of OxCal.

South Area sequence
by Craig Cessford

Excavations in the South Area during the 1960s and 1990s revealed an archaeological sequence from the earliest to the latest phases currently known at Çatalhöyük. In contrast all other areas that have been investigated have only been concerned with parts of this sequence. This means that the dating evidence from the South Area constitutes the core dating sequence for the site as a whole.

1960s determinations
During the 1960s two series of radiocarbon determinations were undertaken at the University of Pennsylvania. The first series, from excavations up to 1963, was published by Mellaart (1964a, 114–19; 1967, 49–53). He noted the problem of determinations from timbers, where there might be a considerable time lag between felling and final deposition owing to reuse, and suggested that some of the material dated may have been intrusive. This first series was also published in the journal *Radiocarbon* (Stuckenrath & Ralph 1965), as was a second series that included material excavated in 1965 (Stuckenrath & Lawn 1969). The determinations have subsequently been republished and discussed by a number of authors (Aurenche *et al.* 1987, 705–6; Bordaz 1973; Mellaart 1989; Newton & Kuniholm 1999; Todd 1976, 98–107; 1980, 149; Waterbolk 1987, 43–5; Yakar 1991, 30–31 & 218). These determinations possess only a limited amount of contextual information. The original *Radiocarbon* lists make comments regarding the reliability and problems of certain determinations. It is unclear if these comments pre- or post-date the sample results and may represent retrospective attempts to account for perceived inconsistencies. Todd noted that 'anomalies occur throughout the sequence, and it is surprising that greater consistency is not displayed by the dates from the various levels' (1976, 106–7). The Level X determinations 'cover an unreasonably long period of 255 years, and several of them are later than Mellaart's original estimate for the duration of the level' (Todd 1976, 107). Todd concluded that 'while the chronology of the site as a whole can be established within reasonable limits, precise dating of individual levels remains uncertain' (Todd 1976, 107). Waterbolk noted the possible impact of timber reuse, that 1960s standards of pre-treatment and other procedures were not uniform and that there was a lack of inter-laboratory comparison (1987, 43–5). Having said this Pennsylvania can fairly be viewed as one of the leading radiocarbon laboratories of the time and the number of determinations undertaken is quite impressive for the 1960s, as might be anticipated given Mellaart's existing interest in radiocarbon dating (e.g. Mellaart 1960).

Mellaart has subsequently mentioned a number of other radiocarbon determinations. When discussing his 1963 deep sounding he describes a layer

> eventually dated by carbon 14 but without much conviction (and hence unpublished). A date of 9666±110 BP, calibrated to *c.* 8500 BC gave rise to disbelief in the 1960s, at least in Anatolia ... A series of carbon 14 dates from the surrounding levels on what at the time of discovery were regarded as inappropriate substances for radiocarbon dating, i.e. bone, wood, shell, vegetable matter, gave dates in the range of 13,200±400 to 9600±110 BP, but were regarded as unreliable and thus ignored (Mellaart 1998, 39–41).

No laboratory numbers or other references for these dates are given. In earlier reports Mellaart states that these deposits were not sampled for radiocarbon analysis in 1963 (1964a, 118) and the state of the deep sounding in 1965 (Mellaart 1966a, 166) suggests that it was unlikely that they were sampled then. The results quoted are at variance to more recent determinations from the same sequence and have not been incorporated in this study.

Given the complexity of the archaeology and the large number of buildings and levels which Mellaart excavated the number of radiocarbon determinations obtained is by modern standards quite small, with less than 10 per cent of structures being dated. The excavation records do not allow any of the samples to be assigned to a precise archaeological context, and the criteria for collecting and selecting material for dating purposes would also not meet standards now deemed acceptable. The material dated is not precisely identified, although in some instances this can be retrospectively rectified. More recent excavations have greatly improved our understanding of the complex constructional, occupational and abandonment histories of buildings, which has implications for the 1960s determinations. It has also become apparent that levels as defined by Mellaart are complex phenomena. Additionally it can be seen from the 1960s reports that in some instances Mellaart later alters the levels to which individual buildings were assigned and indicates that there are still unresolved stratigraphic issues. This means that the 1960s levels cannot be treated as a simple stratigraphic sequence.

The ideal solution would be to reject any determinations from problematic contexts and undertake a new dating program on carefully-selected material to provide a full chronological sequence for the site. This is especially true, as studies have shown that a high proportion of older radiocarbon determinations can be problematic (Baillie 1990; Bruins & van der Plicht 1998). Unfortunately this is impractical for a number of reasons. If totally rigorous criteria were applied then almost all of the 1960s determinations, including subsequent determinations based upon material excavated in the 1960s, would be rejected. Whilst determinations have been obtained from the more recent excavations these do not cover the full sequence excavated by Mellaart. Additionally, given the site's stratigraphic complexities and the total excavation of buildings in the 1960s these determinations remain the only evidence for particular structures. Instead an alternative approach has been adopted of selecting a subset of 1960s determinations that are considered more 'reliable' by excluding all examples with clearly identified problems. This does not simply mean accepting those that support existing preconceptions and rejecting those that do not, but developing criteria that can be applied. Reliability in this context refers solely to the relationship between the sample and the event being dated. It also needs to be remembered that statistically five per cent of determinations should fall outside the period covered by two standard deviations even if there are no problems.

The 1960s determinations were obtained from five different sources, all of which can now be seen to be problematic in different respects.

- *Charcoal from structural timbers:* These come from either *in situ* posts or from material in the fill of buildings, interpreted as collapsed roofbeams. These formed the major source for 1960s determinations, but are inherently highly problematic as they suffer from two major sources of error. The charcoal dated may represent 'old wood' if the heartwood was selected. Work at Jericho has shown that on average determinations on charcoal are 150–300 earlier than those on short-lived material (Bruins & van der Plicht 1998), but this probably varies on a site-by-site basis. The amounts of materials required for conventional dating in the 1960s mean that it was impossible not to include material from multiple tree rings spanning wide periods in a single determination. This is a particular problem as many of the dated samples were from juniper or oak, which can be long-lived and have relatively narrow growth rings, but is less of a problem for elm. Additionally the recent excavations have demonstrated that the majority of structural timbers were removed from buildings prior to abandonment, presumably for reuse in later structures. This appears to be confirmed by dendrochronological analysis (see below) and charcoal studies (Volume 4, Chapter 10), which indicate that some timbers had been reused.
- *Charcoal from hearths:* Whilst apparently more 'reliable' than structural timbers the charcoal in hearths is potentially problematic as it could have been used previously as structural timbers. This is especially true if the charcoal is juniper or oak, which were primarily imported for use as timbers. This hypothesis is supported by an apparent strong correlation between the occurrence of broad-ringed oak stem wood and the presence of signs of fungal decay, suggesting that old structural timbers were reused as firewood (Volume 4, Chapter 10). Such material may also suffer from the 'old wood' problem.
- *Deposits of charred grain seeds:* Grain deposits were found in a number of contexts including storage bins, associated with hearths and in piles on floors (e.g. Mellaart 1963, 45–6). As grain is short-lived and such deposits are likely to be in their primary

context they should provide good dating evidence.
- *Human brain material:* This should provide good dating evidence, but bodies were sometimes subject to post-depositional disturbance and movement.
- *Charcoal in building fills:* Recent excavations have demonstrated that the material used to fill abandoned buildings varies considerably and came from a variety of possible sources; in some cases it may incorporate residual material. It appears that to get enough material for a single sample numerous pieces of charcoal, including material from different contexts, were combined. Such samples are inherently less reliable than those based on 'single entities' (Ashmore 1999).

On this basis determinations from structural timbers and building fills can be viewed as highly problematic, charcoal from hearths as potentially problematic and *in situ* grain deposits and human skeletal remains as the most 'reliable' material.

1990s determinations

During the 1990s AMS determinations have been produced by a number of laboratories. The first of these studies was undertaken on samples taken in 1997 at the Purdue and Arizona laboratories (Göktürk *et al.* 2002). Following the 1999 season a further series of determinations took place at Oxford (Cessford 2001; 2002). The majority of these AMS determinations have been undertaken on charred plant remains, although charcoal has also been utilized and there has been some experimental dating of mineralized plant material, which is discussed by Higham and Blumbach (see below). In general the AMS determinations from the 1990s excavations have fewer concerns regarding their reliability than those from the 1960s, although residuality is a potential issue in some instances and the determinations on charcoal are problematic owing to the potential 'old-wood' effect. None of the material dated has a demonstrable functional relationship to the deposits they occur in so there is only a reasonable probability that the material is associated with the archaeological events being dated (Aitken 1990, 90–91). The use of seeds means that the time difference between the samples and the deposits is likely to be negligible and the fact that they come from prolonged systematic excavations increases their reliability (Aitken 1990, 90–91). With regard to the series from the Oxford laboratory the species selected were typical of the source contexts and the samples were so rich in botanical remains that any contamination is likely to be insignificant. Selection criteria for the material dated at Purdue and Arizona were less rigorously defined.

Overall sequence

The archaeological sequence in the South Area at Çatalhöyük spans fifteen building 'levels', with XIII the earliest and 0 the latest and Level VI subdivided into VIA and VIB. Additionally some deposits excavated in 1999 that are earlier than Level XII cannot be securely assigned 'levels' and have been subdivided into phases Level Pre-XII.D to Level Pre-XII.A of Space 181. The radiocarbon determinations from this sequence will be discussed in order from the earliest to latest (Table 4.1; Figs. 4.1–4.2). When attempting to decide which determinations provide the most accurate dating evidence the main factors that will be taken into account are the type of material dated, the context from which it was recovered and its relationship to any other determinations with which it enjoys a direct stratigraphic relationship.

Level Pre-XII.D represents the earliest deposits that have been dated. Although (5329) (OxA-9893) is physically below OxA-9778 (5324) these alluviated dumping deposits were not well stratified and probably represent a mixture of materials from different sources. The results indicate dates in the range 7330 to 7050 and 7480 to 7080 cal BC. Prior to this there was some quarrying activity in this area known as Level Pre-XII.E. As there is unlikely to have been a substantial time lag between Level Pre-XII.E and Level Pre-XII.D the two phases probably fall within the same date range. The possibility of a phase of activity prior to Level Pre-XII.E that has been entirely removed cannot be discounted; in any case it is unlikely that the trench excavated located the earliest deposits of the site as a whole.

Two determinations PL-980525A and AA-27982 were taken from charcoal fragments in a clay silt matrix at the base of core ÇH94A (Roberts *et al.* 1996, 25, figs. 2.2–2.3), producing results of 7600 to 7180 and 7480 to 7050 cal BC. Determinations from cores have less stratigraphical control than those from excavation and there is the possibility that the charcoal represents 'old wood' or residual material, especially as it was not precisely identified; there is, however, no inherent reason that the determinations should not be reliable. This core was also dated by OSL, which produced determinations of 11,136±2219 BP for the upper part of the marl and 8886±1664 BP for the alluvial clay (Roberts *et al.* 1996, 25 & table 2.2; Roberts *et al.* 1999, table 3), both underlying the radiocarbon determinations. Although they have large standard deviations they are compatible with the radiocarbon determinations. The determination on the marl probably relates to 're-bleaching' of the sediments caused by some form of reworking or disturbance of the top of the marl (Roberts *et al.* 1999, 624), which could either

Table 4.1. *Radiocarbon determinations from the South Area.*

Lab. no.	Unit	Level	Building/ Space	Context	Material dated	Reliability	Age (uncal BP)	SD	δ13C	Age (cal BC) to 1 S.D.	Age (cal BC) to 2 S.D.
P-796	N/A	II	A.II.1	Bin or hearth	Grain	High	7521	77	Unk	6440–6250	6480–6220
P-774	N/A	III	A.III.1	Unknown	Charcoal	Low	7531	91	Unk	6460–6250	6570–6210
A-18104	N/A	IV	E.IV.1	Post	Charcoal, juniper	Low	8065	50	–23.5%	7140–6830	7300–6750
A-18105	N/A	IV	E.IV.1	Post	Charcoal, juniper	Low	7710	100	–23.9%	6650–6450	7050–6250
A-19344	N/A	IV	E.IV.1	Post	Charcoal, juniper	Low	7620	50	–22.3%	6500–6415	6590–6380
A-19345	N/A	IV	E.IV.1	Post	Charcoal, juniper	Low	7626	52	–23.0%	6505–6420	6600–6380
A-19346	N/A	IV	E.IV.1	Post	Charcoal, juniper	Low	7670	50	–23.1%	6590–6440	6640–6420
A-19347	N/A	IV	E.IV.1	Post	Charcoal, juniper	Low	7998	54	–23.7%	7060–6820	7070–6690
A-19348	N/A	IV	E.IV.1	Post	Charcoal, juniper	Low	7982	52	–23.2%	7060–6770	7060–6690
A-19349	N/A	IV	E.IV.1	Post	Charcoal, juniper	Low	7944	65	–23.1%	7040–6690	7060–6650
A-19350	N/A	IV	E.IV.1	Post	Charcoal, juniper	Low	7918	54	–23.2%	7030–6680	7040–6640
A-19351	N/A	IV	E.IV.1	Post	Charcoal, juniper	Low	7747	65	–23.9%	6640–6480	6690–6440
P-775	N/A	IV	E.IV.1	Post	Charcoal, juniper	Low	8037	96	Unk	7120–6710	7350–6650
P-776	N/A	V	E.V.4	Post	Charcoal, juniper	Low	7640	91	Unk	6600–6400	6650–6250
P-1361	N/A	V	F.V.1	Hearth	Charcoal, juniper	Medium	7499	93	Unk	6440–6240	6500–6090
P-769	N/A	VIA	E.VI.A.25	Unknown, probably storage bin	Grain	High	7505	93	Unk	6440–6250	6510–6090
P-1365	N/A	VIA	E.VI.A.70	Ladder	Charcoal, juniper	Low	7729	80	Unk	6640–6460	6770–6410
P-1362	N/A	VIB	E.VI.B.27	Post	Charcoal, elm	Low	7904	111	Unk	7040–6640	7100–6500
P-797	N/A	VIB	E.VI.B.28	Post	Charcoal, juniper	Low	7629	90	Unk	6590–6390	6650–6250
P-777	N/A	VIB	E.VI.B.10	Post	Charcoal, juniper	Low	7704	91	Unk	6640–6450	6850–6350
P-1364	N/A	VIB	E.VI.B.70	Post	Charcoal, elm	Low	7936	98	Unk	7040–6690	7100–6500
P-827	N/A	VI	E.VI.1	Burial	Charred human brain	High	7579	89	Unk	6510–6260	6600–6230
P-781	N/A	VI	A.VI.1	Roofbeam	Charcoal, oak	Low	7524	90	Unk	6450–6250	6510–6100
P-770	N/A	VI	A.VI.1	Roofbeam	Charcoal, juniper/oak	Low	7912	94	Unk	7030–6650	7100–6500
P-772	N/A	VI	E.VI.1	Post	Charcoal, oak	Low	7572	91	Unk	6500–6250	6600–6220
P-1375	N/A	VI	E.VI.25	Post	Charcoal, elm	Low	7661	99	Unk	6640–6420	6700–6240
P-1363	N/A	VI	E.VI.49	Beam	Charcoal	Low	7911	103	Unk	7040–6650	7100–6500
PL-972431A	1091	VII	Space 105	Fill of wall cut	Charred seeds, Cerealae	Medium to low	7810	80	–22.7%	6760–6480	7050–6450
AA-27980	1091	VII	Space 105	Fill of wall cut	Charred seeds, Cerealae	Medium to low	7790	60	–24.4%	6680–6500	6900–6450
PL-972431A & AA-27980 combined	1091	VII	Space 105	Fill of wall cut	Charred seeds, Cerealae	Medium to low	7797	48	N/A	6680–6500	6750–6470
PL-9800565A	1532	VII	Space 107	Construction	Charred seeds, Cerealae	Medium to low	8050	70	–22.6%	7140–6820	7300–6650
PL-980561A	1084	VII	Space 108	Floors	Charred seeds, Cerealae	Medium to low	7850	80	–22.3%	6990–6530	7050–6450
PL-9800507B	2701	VII	Space 109	Oven construction	Charred seeds, Cerealae	Medium to low	7850	90	–24.1%	7030–6530	7050–6450
PL-9800563A	1888	VII	Space 112	Hearth base	Charred seeds, Cerealae	Medium to low	7760	90	–22.4%	6660–6460	7050–6400
PL-9800570A	2730	VII	Space 112	Fill of scoop	Charred seeds, Cerealae	Medium to low	7800	90	–23.3%	6750–6470	7050–6450
PL-980520A	2704	VII	Space 112	Hearth base	Charred seeds, Cerealae	Medium to low	7780	80	–25.0%	6690–6470	7050–6400
PL-980519A	2703	VII	Space 112	Hearth lining	Charred seeds, Cerealae	Medium to low	7760	80	–22.5%	6650–6470	6900–6400
PL-980518A	2310	VII	Space 113	Floors	Charred seeds, Cerealae	Medium to low	7840	80	–24.0%	6980–6510	7050–6450
P-778	N/A	VII	E.VII.24	Unknown, probably storage bin	Grain	High	7538	89	Unk	6460–6250	6570–6210
P-1366	N/A	VII	E.VIII.45	Building fill	Charcoal	Low	7684	90	Unk	6640–6440	6700–6260
PL-980513A	2732	VIII	Space 115	Finely-bedded midden	Charred seeds	Medium	7850	100	–22.2%	7050–6500	7050–6450

Table 4.1. *(cont.)*.

Lab. no.	Unit	Level	Building/ Space	Context	Material dated	Reliability	Age (uncal BP)	SD	δ13C	Age (cal BC) to 1 S.D.	Age (cal BC) to 2 S.D.
PL-9800566A	1579	VIII	Space 115	Coarsely-bedded midden	Charred seeds	Medium	7820	90	–22.9‰	6820–6500	7050–6450
PL-980560A	1587	VIII	Space 115	Finely-bedded midden	Charred seeds, Cerealae	Medium	7910	80	–22.3‰	7030–6650	7060–6590
PL-980511A	1883	VIII	Building 4, Space 151	Building fill	Charred seeds, Cerealae	Medium	7800	100	–22.9‰	6800–6460	7050–6400
PL-980512A	2348	VIII	Building 4, Space 151	Building fill	Charred seeds, Cerealae	Medium	7860	100	–19.9‰	7030–6590	7050–6500
P-1367	N/A	VIII	E.VIII.45	Hearth	Charcoal, elm/oak	Medium	7853	97	Unk	7030–6530	7050–6450
PL-980410A,B	2328	IX	Building 2, Space 117	Dump	Charcoal	Medium	7815	60	–24.4‰, –24.5‰	6730–6500	7050–6450
PL-9800568A	1889	IX	Building 2, Space 117	Bin fill	Charred seeds, Cerealae	Medium	7880	90	–21.9‰	7030–6610	7100–6500
P-779	N/A	IX	E.IX.8	Floor and fill	Charcoal	Low	8190	99	Unk	7450–7060	7550–6800
P-1369	N/A	X	E.X.29	Midden	Charcoal	Medium	7937	109	Unk	7040–6680	7150–6500
P-1371	N/A	X	E.X.29	Midden	Charcoal	Medium	7844	102	Unk	7050–6500	7050–6450
P-1372	N/A	X	E.X.29	Midden	Charcoal, elm	Medium	7915	85	Unk	7030–6650	7060–6590
P-1370	N/A	X	E.X.28	Hearth	Charcoal, elm	Medium	8036	104	Unk	7140–6700	7350–6600
P-782	N/A	X	E.X.1	Hearth	Charcoal	Medium	8092	98	Unk	7310–6820	7450–6650
OxA-9774	4715	XI	Space 198	Penning deposit	Charred seeds, *Scirpus*	High	7935	50	–23.2‰	7030–6690	7050–6650
OxA-9946	4715	XI	Space 198	Penning deposit	Charred seeds, *Scirpus*	High	7980	55	–23.3‰	7050–6770	7060–6690
OxA-9774 & OxA-9946 combined	4715	XI	Space 198	Penning deposit	Charred seeds, *Scirpus*	High	7955	37	N/A	7040–6710	7050–6690
P-1374	N/A	XII	E.XII.29	Building fill	Charcoal, elm	Low	7757	92	Unk	6660–6460	7050–6400
OxA-9947	4822	XII	Space 199	Penning deposit	Charred seeds, *Triticum*/*Hordeum*/*Scirpus*	High	7985	50	–22.4‰	7060–6820	7060–6690
OxA-9775	4826	XII	Space 199	Burning event	Charred seeds, *Triticum*/*Scirpus*	High	8090	55	–20.5‰	7290–6860	7320–6820
OxA-9948	4826	XII	Space 199	Burning event	Charred seeds, *Triticum*/*Scirpus*	High	8090	50	–20.7‰	7290–6860	7310–6820
OxA-9775 & OxA-9948 combined	4826	XII	Space 199	Burning event	Charred seeds, *Triticum*/*Scirpus*	High	8090	37	N/A	7180–7040	7300–6860
OxA-9949	4848	Pre XII.A	Space 181	Burning event	Charred seeds, *Pisum*	High	8050	50	–21.7‰	7080–6820	7300–6700
OxA-9950	5276	Pre XII.B	Space 181	Lime burning	Charred seeds, *Triticum*/*Pisum*	High	8030	50	–21.4‰	7080–6820	7090–6700
OxA-9776	5292	Pre XII.B	Space 181	Fill of scoop	Charred seeds, *Scirpus*	High	7985	55	–23.5‰	7060–6770	7060–6690
OxA-9892	5317	Pre XII.C	Space 181	Burning event	Charred seeds, *Lens*	High	8150	50	–23.7‰	7300–7060	7330–7050
OxA-9777	5323	Pre XII.C	Space 181	Coarsely-bedded midden	Charred seeds, *Lens*	High	8160	50	–23.9‰	7300–7070	7330–7050
OxA-11267	5323	Pre XII.C	Space 181	Coarsely-bedded midden	Silicified/Calcified seeds, *Celtis*	High	8050	60	–10.1‰	7120–6820	7300–6700
OxA-9778	5324	Pre XII.D	Space 181	Alluviated dump	Charred seeds, *Triticum*/*Pisum*	High	8240	55	–21.4‰	7450–7080	7480–7080
OxA-9893	5329	Pre XII.D	Space 181	Alluviated dump	Charred seeds, *Triticum*/*Scirpus*/Cerealae	High	8155	50	–22.0‰	7300–7070	7330–7050
PL-980525A	N/A	?Pre XII.D	Core ÇH94A	Unknown	Charcoal	Medium	8390	90	–24.0‰	7580–7330	7600–7180
AA-27982	N/A	?Pre XII.D	Core ÇH94A	Unknown	Charcoal	Medium	8195	80	–24.0‰	7320–7070	7480–7050
PL-980525A & AA-27982 combined	N/A	?Pre XII.D	Core ÇH94A	Unknown	Charcoal	Medium	8283	60	N/A	7480–7180	7520–7080

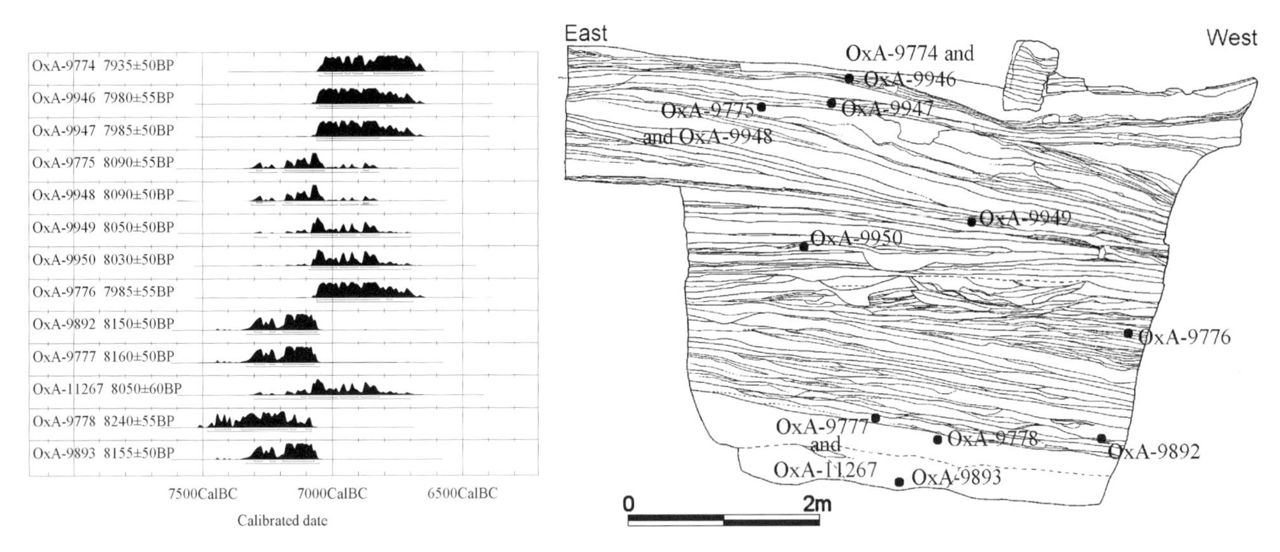

Figure 4.1. *Section and plot of Spaces 181, 198 and 199 showing radiocarbon determinations.*

be natural or relate to some form of human activity. The description of the deposits dated by radiocarbon suggests they are broadly similar to Level Pre-XII.D and the determinations are broadly compatible with these. Other determinations from cores have not been considered because the two dates from core ÇH94D are problematic as the results are the reverse of their stratigraphic locations, while core ÇH95E is from between the East and West mounds and the date of the cultural deposits it is below is uncertain (see Roberts *et al.* 1996; 1999).

Level Pre-XII.C begins with a distinctive layer (5323) sealing the Level Pre-XII.D deposits; this was dated to 7330 to 7050 cal BC (OxA-9777). An identical result was achieved from a burnt deposit (5317) (OxA-9892), lying stratigraphically slightly above this. Taken in conjunction these results suggest that there was no significant time lag between phases Level Pre-XII.D and Level Pre-XII.C. This indicates that the material dated from Level Pre-XII.D was not residual, as was initially believed to be possible. (5323) was also dated by a determination on mineralized hackberry (OxA-11267), the results of this were compatible with those from the charred material.

Level Pre-XII.B was dated by determinations from two deposits. Although stratigraphically (5292) is later than (5276) the results are practically indistinguishable at 7060 to 6690 (OxA-9776) and 7090 to 6700 (OxA-9950) cal BC respectively. These results are discernibly later than those of Level Pre-XII.D and Level Pre-XII.C, suggesting that the layers between (5317) and (5292)/(5276) took some time to accumulate. Overall Level Pre-XII.B probably dates to between 7120 to 6940 cal BC.

Level Pre-XII.A is dated by a single determination from (4848) (OxA-9949), a distinctive *in situ* burning episode that is the earliest deposit of this phase. It is dated to 7300 to 6700 cal BC and is not readily distinguishable from the Level Pre-XII.B determinations, suggesting that there was no significant time lag.

Level XII is dated by determinations from the 1960s and the 1990s. The transition to Level XII Space 199, stratigraphically directly above Space 181, is marked by a burning event (4826); this was dated by two determinations (OxA-9948 & OxA-9775) to 7300 to 6860 cal BC. A determination on a stratigraphically-later deposit (4822), believed to be associated with the penning of sheep/goats, produced a date of 7060 to 6690 cal BC (OxA-9947). Level XII is also dated by determination of elm charcoal from the fill of Building E.XII.29 (P-1374), corresponding to 7050 to 6400 cal BC. Doubt has been cast on this sample, as the 'fill may derive from some other context' (Stuckenrath & Lawn 1969, 154); it appears that it derives from the fill of the underlying Level XIII building and was described as 'not truly representative of Level XII' (Todd 1976, 99). Comparison with the Level X building directly above it suggests that this determination is unreliable as there is only a 10 to 15 per cent chance that this determination is earlier than the Level X determination.

Level XI is dated by two determinations from Space 198, stratigraphically directly above Space 199. These come from (4715), another set of deposits believed to be associated with the penning of sheep/goats, and produced results of 7050 to 6650 (OxA-9774) and 7060 to 6690 (OxA-9946) cal BC, suggesting a date of 7050 to 6690 cal BC.

Level X is dated by determinations from Buildings E.X.1, E.X.28 and external area E.X.29. Building E.X1 was dated from charcoal in a hearth (P-782) expected to date final occupation of Level X (Stuckenrath

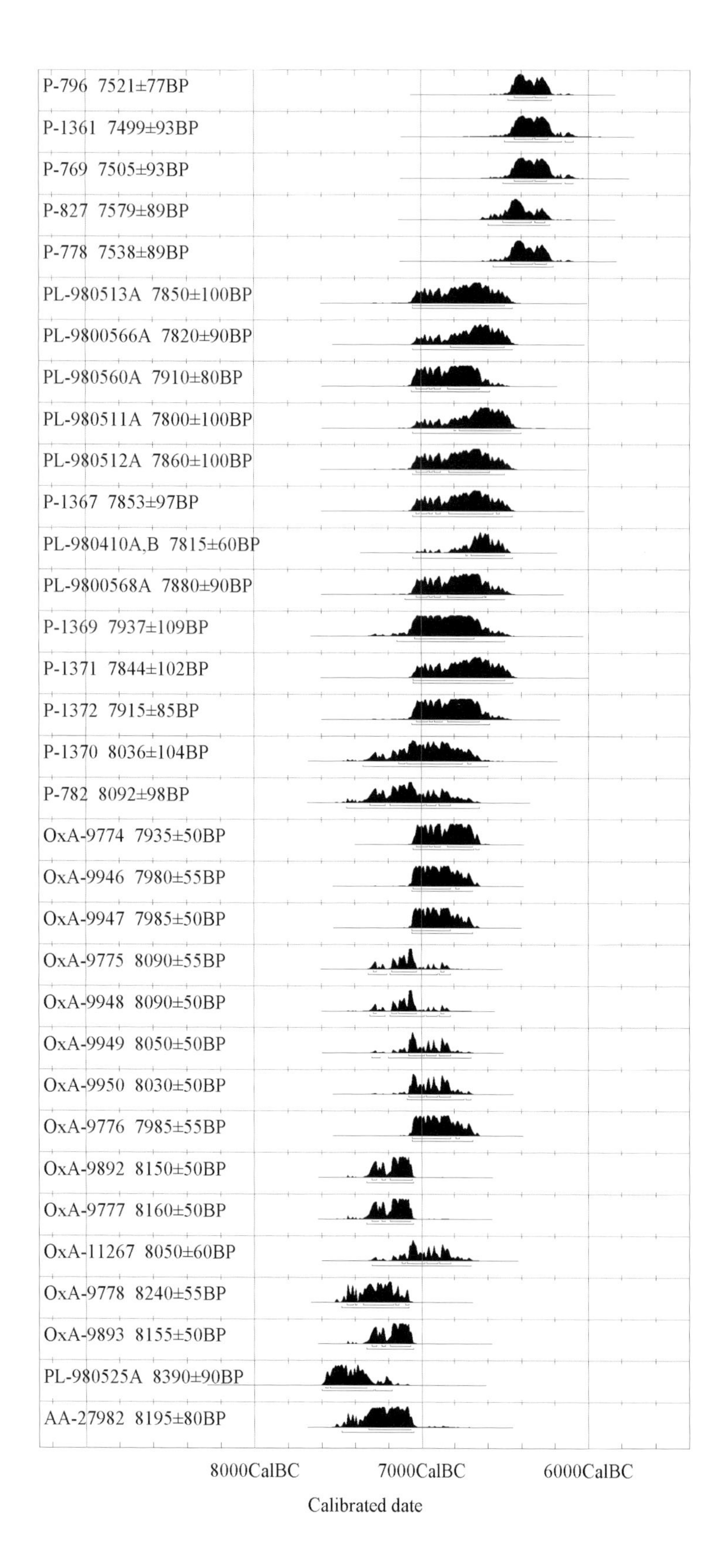

Figure 4.2. *Plot of South Area radiocarbon determinations classified as 'high' or 'medium' reliability.*

& Ralph 1965, 191). The building was re-excavated as Building 23 (Volume 3, Part 2). Although badly damaged from exposure the building had a complex structural history and numerous hearths and ovens were identified. It is likely that the material dated came from one of several hearths or ovens of Building 23 (Volume 3, Part 2). There is a 22 to 24 per cent probability that this determination is later than the Level XI dates, which it directly overlies and it produces a result of 7450 to 6650 cal BC. The determination from Building E.X.28 (P-1370) comes from elm charcoal from a hearth in the lowest floor deposits (Stuckenrath & Lawn 1969, 155) and produced a result of 7350 to 6600 cal BC. The midden area E.X.29 has three determinations (P-1369, P-1371 & P-1372) (Stuckenrath & Lawn 1969, 155) from 'thick bands of charcoal, which produce several radiocarbon dates' (Mellaart 1966b, 6). The determinations may be ordered, with P-1369 being below P-1371, which is in turn below P-1372 (Stuckenrath & Lawn 1969, 155). These produce dates in the range 7150 to 6450 cal BC; if combined they would give a determination of 7900±56 or 7040 to 6640 cal BC. All Level X determinations come from charcoal, most of which is unidentified, and may therefore be problematic.

Level IX is dated by determinations from both the 1960s excavations and those of the 1990s. The 1960s determination comes from Building E.IX.8 (P-779), on specks of charcoal from its floor and fill, and was expected to date final occupation of Level IX or the fill immediately following (Stuckenrath & Ralph 1965, 191). This determination corresponds to 7550 to 6800 cal BC and Todd suggests that the determination is probably too early, but gives no reason (Todd 1976, 104). The sample was not given the same pre-treatment as the rest of the samples (Stuckenrath & Ralph 1965, 191). The description indicates a mixed origin sample with an early outlier probability. This structure was re-excavated in 1999 and numbered Building 16 (Volume 3, Part 2). The floors in the southern part of Building 16 contained numerous fragments of charcoal while the fill was relatively sterile with regard to inclusions. It is not certain where the infilling material was derived from and how old some of the inclusions may have been at the time of deposition. Building E.IX.8 is later than Building E.X.1 and the Level XI Space 198. There is only a six or seven per cent likelihood that it is later than the Level XI determinations. The mixed origins of this sample and the fact that the species of charcoal is unknown means that it is quite likely that the material dated incorporated older charcoal, either through 'old wood' or residuality.

The two determinations from the 1990s excavations come from Space 117 of Building 2. The earlier determination (PL-9800568A) is on charred seeds from (1889), a heterogeneous filling in bin F.257 and corresponds to 7100 to 6500 cal BC. This deposit occurs at the end of the phase 5 occupation of Building 2 and is one of the last deposits prior to the abandonment of the building. It is unclear where exactly the material that composes this deposit was derived from. The later determination (PL-980410A,B) is on charcoal from (2328), a coarsely-bedded midden in niche F.593. It occurs during the phase 7 infilling of Building 2, after the occupation in the building has ended and as such occurs at the transition of Level IX to Level VIII. The result quoted is the weighted average of two runs and corresponds to 7050 to 6450 cal BC.

Level VIII is dated by determinations from both the 1960s excavations and those of the 1990s. The 1960s determinations both come from Building E.VIII.45, on elm and oak charcoal from a hearth (P-1367) and charcoal from the building fill (P-1366) (Stuckenrath & Lawn 1969, 155). These correspond to 7050 to 6450 and 6700 to 6260 cal BC respectively; if combined they would produce a result of 7764±66 or 6760 to 6440 cal BC. It appears that Level VIII falls within the period 6790 to 6460 cal BC and although both these determinations are mixed and could incorporate older material they are in good agreement.

The 1990s excavations are dated by determinations from the external midden area Space 115 and Space 151 of Building 4. There are three determinations on charred seeds from Space 115; from coarsely-bedded midden (1579) (PL-9800566A), finely-bedded midden (1587) (PL-980560A) and finely-bedded midden (2732) (PL-980513A). These correspond to 7050 to 6450, 7060 to 6590 and 7050 to 6450 cal BC respectively. Space 151 is dated by two determinations from the same general homogeneous building fill. The determination from (2348) (PL-980512A) corresponds to 7050 to 6500 cal BC, while the determination from (1883) (PL-980511A) corresponds to 7050 to 6400 cal BC.

Level VII is dated by determinations from both the 1960s excavations and those of the 1990s. The 1960s determination is on grain from Building E.VIII.24 (P-778). This was expected to date the destruction of the building, but it was suggested that it could be intrusive and come from Level VIA (Mellaart 1964a, 116–17; Mellaart 1975, 285; Stuckenrath & Ralph 1965, 191). It corresponds to 6570 to 6210 cal BC. Determinations from 1990s excavations come from charred plant material from Spaces 105, 107, 107, 108, 109, 112 and 113. Space 105 is dated by two determinations from (1091), the homogeneous fill of the foundation cut for wall F.56 (PL-972431A & AA-27980). This deposit marks the transition from Level VIII to VII and could relate to either level. The determinations correspond to 7050 to 6450 and 6900 to 6450 cal BC; if combined they give a result of 6750 to 6470 cal BC. Space 107 is dated by a determination from (1532), a homogeneous constructional material (PL-9800565A), which corresponds to 7300 to 6650 cal BC. A set of floors in a niche in Space 108 (1084) was dated by a determination (PL-980561A) to 7050 to 6450 cal BC. Space 109 is dated by a determination from a homogeneous constructional deposit (2701), part of oven F.82 (PL-9800507B), dated to 7050 to 6450 cal BC. Space 112 is dated by four determinations. Three come from phase 2; (2703) the lining of hearth F.96 (PL980519A), (2704) the base of hearth F.96 (PL980520A) and (2730) the homogeneous fill of a scoop (PL-9800570A). These date to 6900 to 6400, 7050 to 6400 and 7050 to 6450 cal BC respectively. Space 112 is also dated by a determination from (1888) the base of a phase four hearth (PL-9800563A), which corresponds to 7050 to 6400 cal BC. Space 113 is dated by a single determination from floors (2310) (PL-980518A), which corresponds to 7050 to 6450 cal BC.

Additionally there are two dendrochronology sequences from timbers recovered from section cleaning of the fill of a building east of structure VII.32 (see Matthews & Farid 1996, fig. 14.6). 'The outer wall of this building has partly eroded to expose well-plastered floors, and room fill which comprises steeply-sloping layers of burnt and unburnt materials' (Matthews & Farid 1996, 280). The structure shows a pattern of localized burning and the fill included 'large beams of juniper wood more than 20 cm in diameter' (Matthews & Farid 1996, 296). CTL-17 is described as coming from a roofbeam and the end of this timber has been dated to 6576+30/–66 BC, corresponding to 6636 to 6444 cal BC. CTL-16&20 is from an untrimmed post with the terminal growth ring probably still present. The end of this timber has been dated to 6623+30/–66 BC, corresponding to 6683 to 6491 cal BC. The overall dendrochronological sequence (see below and Newton & Kuniholm 1999) suggests that CTL-17 was probably in its primary context and had not been reused. The sequence for CTL-16&20 ends 46 years earlier than

CTL-17. There are a number of possible reasons for this. CTL-16&20 may have been reused, CTL-17 could relate to a rebuild of the structure or CTL-16&20 was simply felled earlier. CTL-17 is a 'roofbeam' in the sense used by Mellaart of timbers in the fill of burnt structures. It has been suggested that CTL-16&20 is an *in situ* vertical structural timber or 'post', but there is no primary documentary evidence in the archive to substantiate this so it should be provisionally classified as non *in situ* material.

Level VI covers two levels, VIB and VIA of which VIB is the earlier. These were only distinguished during the 1962 season (Mellaart 1963, 40) and some determinations can only be assigned to Level VI. Mellaart records that there was particularly violent fire at the end of Level VIB, which he generally refers to as a 'conflagration', and after this each level ends in a fire (1964a, 115). This meant that large structural timbers were frequently preserved *in situ* and these were used for dating. These timbers may suffer from the 'old wood' problem; the outer layers may have been removed by shaping and in some instances timbers may have been reused in successive structures. As buildings in earlier levels had not been burnt so frequently this suggests that reuse of timbers from earlier buildings may have been particularly common in Level VIB. All these factors mean that there is a strong possibility that the determinations from them may be older than the context they were found in. Level VIB is dated by determinations from Buildings E.VIB.10, E.VIB.27, E.VIB.28 and E.VIB.70. E.VIB.10 is dated by a determination (P-777) on juniper charcoal from a post in the west wall behind bulls' heads, expected to date the construction of VIB (Stuckenrath & Ralph 1965, 191). There was a triple bucranium against the western wall. Although it was 'considered unlikely' that this post was renewed in Level VIA (Stuckenrath & Ralph 1965, 191) Mellaart states that the ceiling of the 'central part of the building must have been raised' (1967, 125). This casts some doubt upon whether the post was installed in Level VIB or VIA. This determination corresponds to 6850 to 6350 cal BC. Building E.VIB.27 was dated by a determination (P-1362) on elm charcoal from a post (Stuckenrath & Lawn 1969, 155); this corresponds to 7100 to 6500 cal BC. Building E.VIB.28 was dated by a determination (P-797) on juniper charcoal from a corner post (Stuckenrath & Ralph 1965, 192), probably in the southwest corner of the building (Mellaart 1964a, fig. 2). This corresponds to 6650 to 6250 cal BC. Building E.VIB.70 was dated by a determination (P-1364) on elm charcoal from a post (Stuckenrath & Lawn 1969, 155), and this corresponds to 7100 to 6500 cal BC.

Level VIA is dated by determinations from Buildings E.VIA.25 and E.VIA.70. Building E.VIA.25 was date by a determination (P-769) on grain expected to date fire at the end of Level VIA (Stuckenrath & Ralph 1965, 192). This corresponds to 6510 to 6090 cal BC. Building E.VIA.70 was dated by a determination (P-1365) on juniper charcoal from ladder fragments. It is unclear if ladders were constructed from a single piece of timber or were composite structures so this sample could be mixed. Mellaart refers to 'part of the wooden ladder, carbonised, but still *in situ*' (1966a, 174). This determination corresponds to 6770 to 6410 cal BC, which is rather later than P-1364 from E.VIB.70.

Determinations that can only be broadly assigned to Level VI come from Buildings A.VI.1, E.VI.1, E.VI.25 and E.VI.49. Building A.VI.1 is dated by two determinations. One is from oak and juniper charcoal from a roofbeam in the main space of building (P-770), expected to date construction of VIB unless reused (Stuckenrath & Ralph 1965, 192), but may represent reuse of a Level VII timber (Mellaart 1964a, 117). Mellaart states that 'the building was destroyed by fire and two large roof beams, running east to west, were found in the debris. The wood has been identified as oak (*Quercus* sp.) and Juniper (*Junipericus* sp.)' (1963, 52). This determination corresponds to 7100 to 6500 cal BC. This piece of timber was studied for dendrochronology as sample CTL-6 (see Newton *et al.* below); bark was present on the timber and it was felled in 6491+30/–66 cal BC, or 6551 to 6359 cal BC. This makes it highly likely that the 1960s radiocarbon determination is too old, either because it was not taken from the outer part of the timber or because of the oak that was also dated. The other determination from Building A.VI.1 is on oak charcoal from a roofbeam of an L-shaped storeroom (P-781) (Stuckenrath & Ralph 1965, 192). This has been assigned to either Level VIB (Stuckenrath & Ralph 1965, 192) or VIA (Mellaart 1975, 285) and corresponds to 6510 to 6100 cal BC, but must be earlier than the determination from Building A.II.1. Building E.VI.I is dated by two determinations; one on human brain material from skeleton 3 buried under the central platform (P-827) is probably from Level VIB or early VIA (Stuckenrath & Ralph 1965, 192). The other is on oak charcoal from a post in the main room (P-772) (Stuckenrath & Ralph 1965, 192). P-827 corresponds to 6600 to 6230 cal BC while P-772 corresponds to 6600 to 6220 cal BC. Building E.VI.25 is dated by a determination on elm charcoal from a post (P-1375) (Stuckenrath & Lawn 1969, 155) and corresponds to 6700 to 6240 cal BC. This is broadly in agreement with P-769 from E.VIA.25. Building E.VI.49 was dated by a determination on charcoal from a beam in a storeroom (P-1363); the results were taken to suggest reused Level VII material (Stuckenrath & Lawn 1969, 156; also Breunig 1987, 60). It corresponds to 7100 to 6500 cal BC.

Although Levels VIB and VIA were dated by a relatively large number of determinations in the 1960s many of these are problematic as already noted. Mellaart believed that there was a particularly violent fire at the end of Level VIB. When the excavation area was extended in 1965 it became clear that these fires were limited and did not cover the whole site (1966a, 172). Nevertheless Mellaart's interpretation of the fire at the end of Level VIB suggests that this is a single event and that all the Level VIB buildings were abandoned at the same point in time. This stands in contrast to earlier levels, where recent work has shown that individual buildings were built, occupied and abandoned at different points in time and levels can only be viewed as broadly contemporary. The most reliable dating evidence for Level VI comes from determinations from materials other than structural timbers such as P-769 on grain of Level VIA and P-827 on human brain from Level VIB or early VIA. These correspond to 6510 to 6090 and 6600 to 6230 cal BC. The dendrochronological results from timber CTL-6 of Level VI, which corresponds to 6551 to 6359 cal BC, are also likely to be accurate unless the timber was reused. When the other determinations from structural timbers are considered some of them are almost certainly too early (P-770, P-1362, P-1363 & P-1364) and others are also probably too early, although some overlap does exist (P-777 & P-1365). The remainder are broadly accurate (P-772, P-781, P-797 & P-1375). In general terms it appears that there is around a 50 per cent likelihood of a 1960s determination from a structural timber having a good relationship with the date of the archaeological context in which it was found.

Level V is dated by determinations from Buildings E.V.4 and F.V.1. Building E.V.4 is dated by a determination on juniper charcoal from a post (P-776) (Stuckenrath & Ralph 1965, 192), corresponding to 6650 to 6250 cal BC. Structural timber implies potential early outlier probability. Building F.V.1 is dated by a determination on juniper charcoal from a hearth (P-1361) (Stuckenrath & Lawn 1969, 156), corresponding to 6500 to 6090 cal BC.

Level IV was dated by a determination (P-775) from juniper charcoal of a post in Building E.IV.1 (Stuckenrath & Ralph 1965, 192). This determination corresponds to 7350 to 6650 cal BC and it was stated that the original sample was taken from centre of large beam and could be reused (Mellaart 1964a, 116; Mellaart 1967, 51; Stuckenrath & Ralph 1965, 192). This timber was redacted to allow dendrochronological wiggle matching with ten determinations (A-18104, A-18105, A-19344, A-19345, A-19346, A-19347, A-19348, A-19349, A-19350 & A-19351) (see below and Newton & Kuniholm 1999). The dendrochronological sequence CTL-1/1EG ends in 6484+30/–66 cal BC, correlating to 6544 to 6352 cal BC, but bark is not present so this is not the felling date.

Level III is dated by one determination from Building A.III.1 (P-774). This determination was published by Mellaart (1964a, 116), but does not occur in the *Radiocarbon* list (Stuckenrath & Ralph 1965), so there is no contextual information. It corresponds to 6570 to 6210 cal BC, but must be earlier than the determination from A.II.1.

Level II is dated by a determination on two types of grain from Building A.II.1 (P-796) and was expected to date the destruction of Level II (Stuckenrath & Ralph 1965, 192). Mellaart refers to 'remains of grain, which had evidently been burnt on the ceremonial hearth' plus storeroom with 'two plaster bins for grain' and a 'grain bin in the south storeroom' (1963, 45–6). He also states that 'scattered all over the floor of the main storeroom as well as in the storerooms along the west side of the building were at least seven small deposits of grain, and legumes' (1963, 46). The hearth, 'a fine rectangular structure about 1 m square, was provided with a raised kerb and with a low bench and platform west of it and had been coated carefully with red painted plaster, renewed not less than three times' (Mellaart 1963, 45). It is clear that there are a wide range of possible contexts which could be the origin of sample P-796 and the statement that two types of grain were dated might suggest that the sample was a mixture of two of them. Helbaek states that in 1962 he identified einkorn, emmer and naked barley from Level II (1964a, 121). This determination corresponds to 6480 to 6220 cal BC.

Levels I and O have not been dated.

The 1960s and 1990s excavations in the South Area have provided a set of radiocarbon determinations spanning Level Pre-XII.D to Level II. It is probable that there are earlier phases of activity at Çatalhöyük and the latest Levels I and O plus any that have been entirely removed by erosion have not been dated. Few of the determinations from the South Area have full or high certainty of association with the archaeological events they were recovered from (Waterbolk 1971, 15–16). Many may also have a substantial time difference of decades or centuries between the C14 being dated and the depositional context (Waterbolk 1971, 16–17). The dominant approach in archaeology is to adopt a 'pick-and-mix' approach, selecting those determinations that produce a consistent pattern and rejecting those that do not. A more rigorous approach is to select determinations on an explicit set of criteria and rank determinations as being of 'low', 'medium' and 'high' reliability. In the case of the determinations

Table 4.2. *Proposed overall date ranges for levels at Çatalhöyük.*

Level	Earliest beginning at 95% probability expressed decadally	Latest end at 95% probability expressed decadally	Earliest beginning at 68% probability expressed decadally	Latest end at 68% probability expressed decadally
0	Later than end of Level II	No data	Later than end of Level II	No data
I	Later than end of Level III	No data	Later than end of Level III	No data
II	6370	6090	6310	6220
III	6410	6230	6370	6270
IV	Later than end of Level VI	Earlier than start of Level II	Later than end of Level VI	Earlier than start of Level II
V	6440	6090	6370	6220
VIA/B	6550	6350	6520	6330
VII	6690	6460	6660	6500
VIII	6790	6460	6710	6520
IX	Later than end of Level XI	Earlier than start of Level VII	Later than end of Level XI	Earlier than start of Level VII
X	7010	6730	6950	6770
XI	7050	6800	7040	6850
XII	7070	6840	7060	6860
Pre-XII.A	7080	6870	7080	6950
Pre-XII.B	7120	6940	7080	7030
Pre-XII.C	7200	7050	7140	7070
Pre-XII.D	7460	7090	7320	7150
?Pre-XII.D (from core ÇH94A)	7600	7050	7580	7070
Pre-XII.E	No data	Earlier than end of PreXIID	No data	Earlier than end of PreXIID
Alluvium (from core ÇH94A)	12,220	5550	10,550	7220
Marl (from core ÇH94A)	15,580	6690	13,360	8910

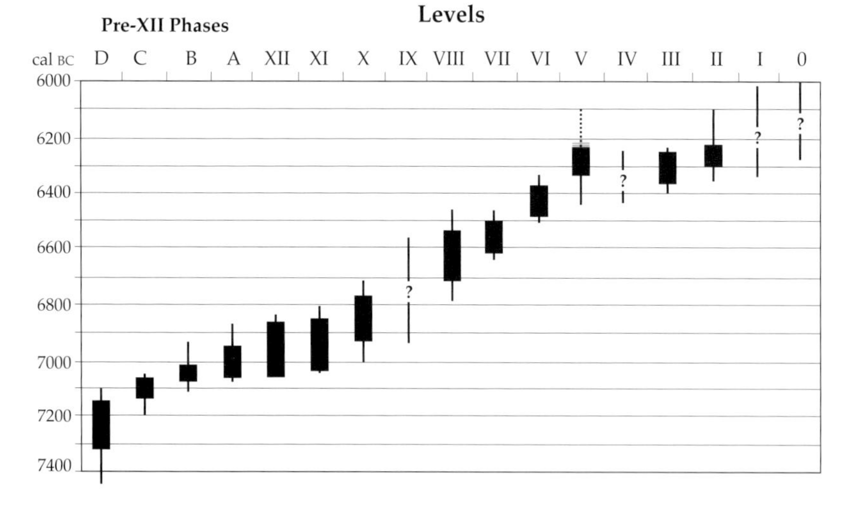

Figure 4.3. *Dates of Çatalhöyük levels from new sequence.*

from Çatalhöyük those that are derived from structural timbers are of 'low' reliability', as these suffer severely from issues of 'old wood'. An exception is made for those where there are dendrochronological sequences. Additionally where there is a direct stratigraphic relationship between determinations that contradicts the relationship between the ages of the two determinations this has been used to identify determinations of 'low' reliability. These criteria do not address issues such as residuality that are a major factor at Çatalhöyük. 'High' reliability applies to determinations where there is a consistently dated stratigraphic sequence or where there is short lived material from a context with a low probability of residuality. Determinations other than those that meet the criteria for 'low' or 'high' reliability have been classified as 'medium' reliability.

On the basis of this an overall sequence can be created. The determinations can be grouped by level by quoting the cumulative outermost dates; dates can also be inferred for some levels without evidence by assuming an absolute temporal relationship for levels separated by an intervening level (Table 4.2; Fig. 4.3). An alternative approach is to look at the boundaries as defined by BCal for the beginning and end of particular levels where these can be reasonably defined (Table 4.3), effectively what is being calculated is the range of dates between which a level is likely to begin or end. These do not work well for the beginning and the end of the dated sequence.

Table 4.3. *Proposed date ranges for BCal-generated level boundaries.*

Level	Earliest beginning at 95% probability expressed decadally	Latest end at 95% probability expressed decadally	Earliest beginning at 68% probability expressed decadally	Latest end at 68% probability expressed decadally
0	Later than end of Level II	No data	Later than end of Level II	No data
I	Later than end of Level III	No data	Later than end of Level III	No data
II	6410–6200	6380–????	6350–6240	6350–????
III	6430–6250	6410-6200	6400–6300	6350–6240
IV	Later than end of Level VI	Earlier than start of Level II	Later than end of Level VI	Earlier than start of Level II
V	Later than end of Level VII	Earlier than start of Level III	Later than end of Level VII	Earlier than start of Level III
VI A/B	6510–6350	6460–6300	6470–6400	6440–6260
VII	Later than end of Level IX	Earlier than start of Level V	Later than end of Level IX	Earlier than start of Level V
VIII	6830–6500	6660–6420	6740–6570	6590–6460
IX	Later than end of Level XI	Earlier than start of Level VII	Later than end of Level XI	Earlier than start of Level VII
X	7040–6770	6970–6680	6960–6820	6890–6740
XI	7060–6830	7030–6760	7060–6850	6960–6800
XII	7080–6860	7060–6830	7070–6920	7060–6850
Pre-XII.A	7080–6810	7080–6860	7080–7010	7070–6920
Pre-XII.B	7160–7000	7080–6810	7100–7040	7080–7010
Pre-XII.C	7280–7070	7160–7000	7200–7080	7100–7040
Pre-XII.D	????–7080	7280–7070	????–7150	7200–7080

Length of occupation

In terms of how long Çatalhöyük was occupied, the elapsed time between the earliest determination OxA-9778 and the latest determination P-796 is in the range 890 to 1080 years (68 per cent probability) or 830 to 1220 years (95 per cent probability). As Levels I and 0 are not included it seems reasonable to suggest that the main occupational sequence at Çatalhöyük probably falls within the range 900 to 1300 years and in all likelihood was 950–1150 years. The earliest evidence for occupation at Çatalhöyük dates to the period around 7400 to 7100 cal BC and when allowance is made for various factors the end of Neolithic occupation probably occurred 6200 to 5900 cal BC.

Although neither the start nor end of occupation at Çatalhöyük is precisely defined, in broad terms the site falls mainly into *Masion de l'Orient periode* 4/5, but the latest levels from V onwards probably fall into *periode* 6 (Aurenche *et al.* 2001, 1196–8; Cauvin 2000, xvii–xviii; Evin 1995, table 2). No generally-agreed system of terminology exists for the Neolithic of central Anatolia. One recently proposed system (Özbaşaran & Buitenhuis 2002) would place the Çatalhöyük sequence in periods ECA (Early (Holocene) central Anatolia) II (*c.* 9000 to 7000 cal BC) and III (*c.* 7000–6000 cal BC). The early levels up to Level Pre-XII.B or Level X can be placed in ECA II and the later levels from XII or IX in ECA III. The transition from ECA II to III or IIIA to B is based primarily upon the appearance of pottery, which is mainly documented at Çatalhöyük. ECA III is divided into subphases A and B, relating to changes in ceramic and lithic technology, again mainly documented at Çatalhöyük around Level VI.

Length of levels

The earliest levels can be sequenced relatively closely as the determinations come from a single well-understood stratigraphic sequence (Tables 4.4–4.5). For the later levels there have been a number of attempts to estimate how long particular levels and buildings were occupied. Mellaart suggested that buildings were replastered once a year and this could be used as a relative dating technique, but recognized that this was not certain (Mellaart 1964a, 117; 1967, 50). This use of plaster counts has continued to be utilized and it has been suggested that the evidence of the dendrochronological sequence (Newton & Kuniholm 1999) supports this. More recent work has shown that plastering is more complex with considerable spatial variation within buildings. Some annual cycle may still be involved and the maximum number of replasterings in any building may give an indication of the length of its occupation and it seems reasonable to use these as a 'general guide' (Todd 1976, 107). If as seems likely occupation varies from building to building then Mellaart's failure to provide replastering figures for individual structures is unfortunate and limits analysis. He quotes the following figures: Level II *c.* 50 to 60 maximum, Level III *c.* 40 maximum, Level IV *c.* 40 or less, Level V *c.* 50, Level VIA *c.* 60+, Level VIB *c.* 100 to 120 or *c.* 100 maximum, Level VII *c.* 120 maximum, with a general conclusion that Levels O to VIA have thin layers of plaster showing shorter periods of occupation and Levels VIB to X have thick layers of plaster showing prolonged occupation (Mellaart 1964a, 116–17; 1967, 50). It appears that Mellaart focused upon the building in a particular level with

Table 4.4. *Elapsed time between determinations in Level Pre-XII.D to XI.*

Earlier event	Later event	Time elapsed in years to 1 S.D.	Time elapsed in years to 2 S.D.
Level Pre-XII.D (OxA-9778)	Start of Level Pre-XII.C (OxA-9777)	10 to 150	0 to 280
Level Pre-XII.D (OxA-9778)	Start of Level Pre-XII.B (OxA-9776)	120 to 290	60 to 410
Level Pre-XII.D (OxA-9778)	Start of Level Pre-XII.A (OxA-9949)	170 to 360	80 to 490
Level Pre-XII.D (OxA-9778)	Start of level XII (OxA-9948 and OxA-9775)	210 to 430	120 to 520 or 120 to 530
Level Pre-XII.D (OxA-9778)	Level XII (OxA-9947)	210 to 420	120 to 530
Level Pre-XII.D (OxA-9778)	Level XI (OxA-9946 and OxA-9774)	300 to 500 or 320 to 520	190 to 630 or 190 to 640

Table 4.5. *Elapsed time between boundaries in Level Pre-XII.D to XI.*

Period	Earlier event	Later event	Time elapsed in years to 1 S.D.	Time elapsed in years to 2 S.D.
Duration of Level Pre-XII.C	Start of Level Pre-XII.C	End of Level Pre-XII.C	Up to 120 years	Up to 220 years
Duration of Level Pre-XII.B	Start of Level Pre-XII.B	End of Level Pre-XII.B	Up to 50 years	Up to 160 years
Duration of Level Pre-XII.A	Start of Level Pre-XII.A	End of Level Pre-XII.A	Up to 40 years	Up to 130 years
Duration of level XII	Start of Level XII	End of Level XII	Up to 40 years	Up to 110 years
Duration of Level XI	Start of Level XI	End of Level XI	Up to 100 years	Up to 190 years
Duration of all Level Pre-XII phases	Earliest Level Pre-XII.D date	End of Level Pre-XII.A	140 to 330 years	70 to 470 years
Duration of all phases until end of Level XI	Earliest Level Pre-XII.D date	End of Level XI	240 to 480 years	160 to 590 years

Table 4.6. *Elapsed time between determinations in later levels.*

Earlier event	Later event	Time elapsed in years to 1 S.D.	Duration of individual levels	Time elapsed in years to 2 S.D.	Duration of individual levels
Start of Level XII	End of Level III	640 to 800	*c.* 55–75	520 to 840	*c.* 45–80
Start of Level XII	Determination from Level II	660 to 830	*c.* 55–70	570 to 950	*c.* 45–80
Start of Level X	End of Level III	510 to 690	*c.* 55–80	430 to 780	*c.* 45–90
Start of Level X	Determination from Level II	550 to 730	*c.* 50–75	460 to 830	*c.* 45–85
Start of Level XII	Start of Level VI	510 to 650	*c.* 85–110	410 to 680	*c.* 70–115
Start of Level X	Start of Level VI	370 to 540	*c.* 90–135	310 to 620	*c.* 75–155
End of Level VI	End of Level III	20 to 139	*c.* 5–45	0 to 190	*c.* 5–65
End of Level VI	Determination from Level II	60 to 170	*c.* 15–45	20 to 260	*c.* 5–65

the greatest number of replasterings. This suggests that if they did occur annually there would be a tendency to overemphasize the length of levels and occupation. On the basis of the radiocarbon determinations Mellaart suggests that Level X to II cover an eight-hundred-year span with perhaps another one hundred years represented by Levels I and O (1964a, 118; 1967, 53; also Todd 1976, 104). In fact Levels X to II probably cover 490–700 years (68 per cent probability) or 420–780 years (95 per cent probability), significantly less than Mellaart estimated. Mellaart also suggested that Levels X to VIA cover 600 to 700 years and that V to O only lasted around 300 years (1964a, 117).

It is possible to estimate the length of levels using BCal. Such estimates are generally more useful over longer spans, but cannot include the start and end of the overall sequence. The time elapsed over a number of levels and the average number of years per level was measured in a number of different ways (Table 4.6). This shows a reasonable level of agreement, with all results falling in the range of 50 to 80 (68 per cent probability) or 45 to 90 (95 per cent probability) years per level. This shows that the levels cover a rather shorter time span than Mellaart believed. These results are broadly comparable with ethnoarchaeological observations that mudbrick buildings in semi-arid climates tend to last 50 to 100 years (Horne 1994, 180; Kramer 1982, 264; Watson 1979). Mellaart suggested a change in the length of levels between Levels VIB and VIA, arguing that between Levels X to VIA individual levels lasted around 100 to 120 years while in later Levels V to O they only lasted around 50 years (Mellaart 1964a, 117). Whilst Mellaart's estimates are rather high the general pattern he identified appears correct (Table 4.6). If we take the dendrochronological sequences CTL-17 and CTL-6 these could be taken to imply that the length of Level VII was 86 years. If CTL-16&20 replace CTL-17 the figure is 132 years. Both of these figures appear to fall within the acceptable range, although CTL-17 is probably the more reliable. This compares to Mellaart's plaster count of 120 for this level.

These figures can be compared with the length of time in Level Pre-XII deposits. If we compare with the postulated average length per level for the whole site we achieve an estimate of around 2.5 to 8.5 (68 per cent probability) or 1.0 to 11.5 (95 per cent probability) levels. If we use the figures for the earlier levels then the estimate is rather shorter at 1.5 to 5.0 (68 per cent probability) or 1.0 to 7.5 (95 per cent probability) levels. Evidence from excavation and cores suggests that, prior to later truncations, the natural ground surface at Çatalhöyük may have been in the region of 1001 m (Roberts *et al.* 1996). The Level XII deposits excavated begin at around 1002.8 m, indicating a build up of *c.* 1.8 m prior to Level XII that relates to putative earlier building phases. Buildings were generally demolished to a height of around 0.5 to 1.5 m; in general those in the earlier levels were demolished to a lower surviving height than those in later levels. These figures suggest that there may be between one and four building levels prior to Level XII, with three or four being the most probable. Although this is only a rough estimate it agrees with the dating evidence, suggesting there are around 17 or 18 levels at Çatalhöyük.

Dendrochronology: the wiggle-matched sequence
by Maryanne W. Newton, Peter I. Kuniholm & Sturt W. Manning

Dendrochronology at Çatalhöyük has previously been discussed in Kuniholm & Newton (1996) and Newton & Kuniholm (1999). The dates reported here differ from those published in 1999 due to the discovery of a previously unmeasured ring in relative year 1180, and use of the revised calibration curve INTCAL98. A 577-year tree-ring chronology, built from the sequences of eleven long-lived juniper trees excavated from Çatalhöyük in the 1960s, has been radiocarbon wiggle-matched, providing calendrical dates spanning the years 7060 to 6483 +30/−66 cal BC. To the dendrochronological sequence reported in 1996 has been added a 126 year sequence compiled from the scattered charcoal remains of a single juniper tree excavated from the Summit Area.

Radiocarbon dating, the wiggle-matched sequence
The wiggle-matched dendrochronology sequence is based on the analysis of seven radiocarbon dated decadal samples taken from the longest-lived single tree sample in the Çatalhöyük master tree-ring chronology (CTL-1), plus three samples from a shorter lived sample CTL-1EG (Table 4.7). The latter may have been a branch fragment of the main stem (its parent tree) CTL-1. Most of the lots are not strictly

Table 4.7. *Wiggle-matched series radiocarbon dates. For further details see Table 4.1.*

Dendro ID	Rel. Years	Lab. No.
CTL-1 Lot A	1006–1016	A-18104
CTL-1 Lot F	1026–1036	A-19347
CTL-1 Lot G	1036–1046	A-19348
CTL-1 Lot H	1076–1086	A-19349
CTL-1 Lot I	1116–1126	A-19350
CTL-1 Lot J	1497–1506	A-19351
CTL-1EG Lot C	1503–1508	A-19344
CTL-1 Lots C&J, Averaged	1497–1508	N/A
CTL-1 Lot B	1527–1536	A-18105
CTL-1EG Lot D	1550–1558	A-19345
CTL-1EG Lot E	1560–1566	A-19346

10 year samples, due to the difficulty in cutting out precise decades of very small rings. The cut decades were trimmed and recorded to reflect the dated end products, even though they do not precisely match the intended model. Any additional error is offset by the already large errors inherent by the potential of decadal mismatching. The dates for Lots C and J overlap in absolute time (dendrochronologically), but differ in radiocarbon years. They are combined, pre-calibration, in this model (the dates may be combined within a 95 per cent confidence level according to a χ^2 test: test statistic of $2.4 \leq \chi^2_{1;0.05} = 3.84$).

The dates are calibrated against the INTCAL98 curve, which for the eighth and seventh millennia BC is based on dendrochronologically-dated wood from South Germany and Ireland. A 41-year gap in the German oak chronology in the fifth millennium BC was discovered and corrected in 1996, thus shifting up (earlier) all calibrated dates that predate that gap. The dates reported here thus supersede, as well as supplement, those reported in Kuniholm and Newton (1996) and Newton & Kuniholm (1999). Figure 4.4 is a composite probability plot of the posterior distribution of the radiocarbon dated decades calculated according to the wiggle-matched model. It illustrates how a model in which the number of calendar years between samples is known precisely (reflected here as 'gaps' between the dendrochronologically-dated decades) substantially reduces the large error margins associated with any single radiocarbon date in isolation. The unshaded (hollow) background histograms show the total dating probability for each sample in isolation, whereas the much more tightly-constrained double-humped shaded (solid) black histograms show the total dating probability for each sample as part of the wiggle-match (note how this area is the same for every decade in the wiggle-match, essentially a graphic representation of the error associated with the wiggle-match). The upper and lower lines beneath the shaded histograms indicate the wiggle-match date

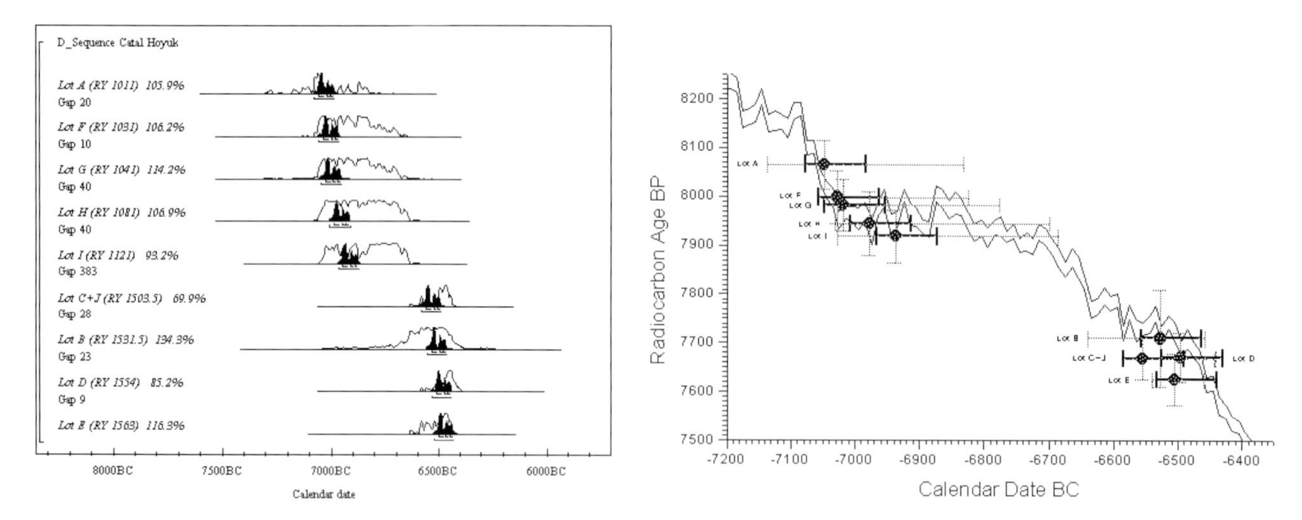

Figure 4.4. *The Çatalhöyük wiggle-match, plotted as modelled and the wiggle-match plotted against the INTCAL98 calibration curve.*

ranges for each sample at respectively 1σ (68.4 per cent) and 2σ (95.4 per cent) confidence.

The specific best fit based on the minimum of the sum of squares of differences for the wiggle-match sequence, expressed in terms of the mid-point of the first dated sample (Lot A, Relative Year 1011), is calculated as *c.* 7048 BC. The basic combined error on the wiggle-match in radiocarbon terms at 1σ confidence is ±19 radiocarbon years. Translated into calendar years, the margins become about +9/–57 calendar years. The much narrower upper limit is due especially to the constraints of the calibration curve between *c.* 7085 and 7015 BC. This is illustrated in Figure 4.4, which plots the wiggle-match against the calibration curve, and with it the error margins at 1σ and 2σ confidence. However, it is appropriate to allow for additional uncertainties in the wiggle-match for: i) the potential laboratory offset between Arizona radiocarbon measurements (these data) and those at Seattle, Belfast, Heidelberg, and Pretoria/Groningen (the calibration data) which we estimate as of the order of ≤25 carbon 14 years; ii) the potential mismatch between CTL dated samples and the decades dated for the calibration curves which we estimate as ≤15 carbon 14 years; and iii) a possible small error factor associated with time dependent regional differences in atmospheric radiocarbon which we estimate as ≤15 carbon 14 years. The allowance for possible inter-laboratory offsets is arbitrary, but defensible based on recent inter-laboratory comparison data. The estimate for a possible decadal mismatching effect is based on analysis of single year radiocarbon data versus decadal data sets. For approximately decadal growth samples the factor used is a generous allowance. Minor regional differences in contemporary radiocarbon levels have been claimed in a few cases. Recent research shows detectable regional/latitude differences in $^{14}CO_2$ levels as measured in the carbon 14 concentrations in tree rings from low-mid latitudes during periods of significant solar driven carbon 14 change episodes (Kromer *et al.* 2001; Manning *et al.* 2001). There are currently no comparable data indicating such an episode during the time covered by the Çatalhöyük dendrochronology. So barring that, and in the absence of major altitude differences or major ocean input, all available data indicate an at most very small possible difference covered by the ≤15 carbon 14 year allowance used here. Incorporation of these factors in fact makes no difference to the wiggle-match fit range at 1σ confidence; it remains at +9/–57 calendar years. Taking a conservative position, however, we cite the CTL wiggle-match total error at 2σ confidence as +30/–66 calendar years. The radiocarbon dates, performed by AMS by the NSF Arizona AMS Facility at the University of Arizona in 1996, are not high precision. Even given conservative estimates of added error, the user should be wary of placing too literal an emphasis on the calendar year equivalents reported here.

Dendrochronology, the tree-ring sequences

Table 4.8 lists the dated samples in the Çatalhöyük dendrochronology; it includes the newly-dated juniper sample (CTL-37-44) from (2662) in the Summit Area. The synchronization of the curve from this sample with the master chronology is illustrated (Fig. 4.5). Of concern when interpreting the dates is the kind of chronological information they convey. Only one sample (CTL-6), preserves bark, and so its last growth ring provides the only date that can be pinned to an activity or event in the lives of the inhabitants of Çatalhöyük, i.e. the cutting of a tree for incorporation into a building. But this does not preclude the possibility that the final deposition of the sample, as a roof timber in a structure in Mellaart's Level VIB, was not its initial point of use. Dendrochronological analysis does, so far, indicate one possible example of wood reuse in the dates for samples CTL-16&20 and CTL-17, depending on whether the last preserved ring on CTL-16&20 is the waney edge (terminal growth ring). These timbers were part of the same building, which was exposed in section and is contiguous to Mellaart's House E.VII.32 (Matthews & Farid 1996, 296 & fig. 14.6). If CTL-16&20 was reused, then it was at least 46 years older than CTL-17 when the structure was built. Alternatively CTL-16&20 was part of the original construction, and CTL-17 was a roof timber added in a remodelling at least 46 years after initial construction. Such distinctions between the dates of interior construction components and roofing matter are noted in material from the early Iron Age levels at Gordion, though in that case it is roofing thatch material that is dated later than the interior beams (de Vries *et al.* 2003). An estimation of the condition of the exterior of this sample was made in the field (it was an untrimmed post). While we believe the last preserved ring in the sequence is at or close to the terminal growth ring, with the absence of bark and with such small growth rate (average annual ring growth of 0.39 mm), the potential for a certain number of rings missing at the end cannot be discounted.

Table 4.8. *Calendar dates for components of Çatalhöyük dendrochronology (p = pith, +1 = 1 ring counted, but not measured, vv = unknown number of rings missing at end, B = bark, W = waney edge).*

Dendro ID	Relative Years	Level	Wiggle-matched BC Years
CTL-1	1+1000–1544vv	IV	7059–6516 BC+30/–66 (t.p.q.)
CTL-1EG	1+1483–1576vv	IV	6577–6484 BC+30/–66 (t.p.q.)
CTL-37-44	1+1273–1399vv	est. IV/V	6787–6661 BC+30/–66 (t.p.q.)
CTL-3	p+1+1299–1479+1vv	V	6761–6581 BC+30/–66 (t.p.q.)
CTL-9	1271–1416vv	VIA	6789–6644 BC+30/–66 (t.p.q.)
CTL-13&14	1276–1478vv	VIB	6784–6582 BC+30/–66 (t.p.q.)
CTL-4	P+1357–1478vv	VIB	6703–6582 BC+30/–66 (t.p.q.)
CTL-6	P+1322–1569B	VIB	6738–6491 BC+30/–66 (bark/felling date)
CTL-12	1339–1486vv	Unknown	6721–6574 BC+30/–66 (t.p.q.)
CTL-17	p+1121–1483+1vv	est. VII	6939–6576 BC+30/–66 (t.p.q.)
CTL-16&20	p+1224p–1437W?	est. VII	6836–6623 BC+30/–66 (waney edge?)

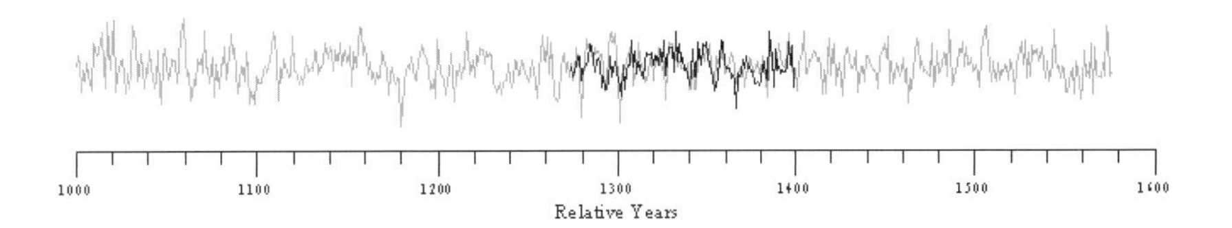

Figure 4.5. *Synchronization of the dendrochronological curve from the Summit Area with the Çatalhöyük master dendrochronology. Curves normalized to an exponential curve with twenty-year running mean.*

The dated tree ring sequences (Table 4.8) offer, at minimum, firm *termini post quo*. To apply these results to questions of intra-site chronology in the absence of robust sets of tree ring data, then, will require integrating radiocarbon data. Ideally, this will include dates on short-lived material from contexts explicating the life histories of individual buildings, i.e. roofing material such as reeds, final occupation floor deposits including grain and/or grasses; and, where good organic samples are available, laminated deposits from wall and floor plasterings. For one attempt to integrate the dendrochronological data with the radiocarbon data from the earlier excavations, we refer the reader to Newton & Kuniholm (1999). In that report, the authors proposed that the dated tree-ring series as *termini post quo* are not inconsistent with radiocarbon dates from stratified deposits in the Mellaart excavations, nor with the theory offered by Mellaart that plaster counts be conceived as quasi-annual records. Admittedly, the data are not high precision, and the model fits only at wider confidence intervals. Given indications from the current excavations of wood reuse (in the removal of timbers from abandoned buildings presumably for reuse) (Volume 3, Parts 2 & 3) and its possible bearing on the interpretation of dendrochronological results, we hope new high precision radiocarbon data from high-quality contexts will enhance the picture now available. The potential of rings lost at the end of any of the dated sequences must also be emphasized. CTL37&44 from the Summit Area illustrates this point. It was compiled from six charcoal fragments collected as (2662), though there are still undated fragments from this unit (ring counts of 95, 64, and 46 respectively), which may extend the sequence on either end. Without the fragments to bridge gaps, however, and in the absence of significant individual cross-dates against the master chronology, the full sequence of the collected timber cannot be determined.

Optically-stimulated luminescence dating of mud brick

by Mustafa Özbakan, Ay Melek Özer & K. Göze Akoûlu

Luminescence dating techniques, i.e. thermoluminescence (TL) and optically-stimulated luminescence (OSL) have been extensively used for dating a wide range of materials such as ceramics, hearths, flints and sediments. In both techniques, luminescence emitted by constituent mineral grains, which is the dating signal, is measured by a highly-sensitive photomultiplier tube system. In TL the dating signal is obtained by heating the sample, while for OSL dating the signal is obtained by shining a beam of light onto it (Aitken 1998). The basic principle of the OSL technique is to compare the dating signal with the signals obtained from portions to which known doses of nuclear radiation have been administered by a radioisotope source with a known activity. This comparison allows the evaluation of the laboratory dose of nuclear radiation needed to induce luminescence equal to that acquired subsequent to the most recent bleaching event, palaeodose (Aitken 1998). In principle the age is then calculated from the equation: Age = Palaeodose / Annual Dose. The annual dose represents the dose rate at which energy is absorbed from the flux of nuclear radiation emitted by the radioactive impurities of thorium, uranium and potassium-40 in the material, as well as by cosmic rays and by rubidium-87 to a minor extent. The annual dose is evaluated by assessment of the radioactivity of the sediment carried out both in the laboratory and on-site. The OSL technique has been introduced to mud-brick samples since they were found to contain quite enough feldspar and quartz minerals. In this study, the dates refer to the last time that the constituent grains of material were exposed to daylight. Luminescence dating has previously been applied at Çatalhöyük by Parish (1996), who obtained determinations from Levels XII and IV / III.

Methodology and results

Five mud-brick samples were collected from walls of buildings of Levels IX, VII and VII / VI by the excavation team and sent to METU, Archaeometry Department in 1999. The mineral compositions of samples were determined by XRD (X-ray Diffraction) and FTIR (Fourier Transform Infrared) analyses and feldspar and quartz minerals were identified. In the meantime, the calibration of the Optical Dating System and Low Level Alpha Counting System was carried out.

The samples were prepared by following standard TL dating procedures as described by Aitken (1985). The surfaces of the bricks, which may have been exposed to the light during their collection, were carefully scraped off. Then the remaining samples were treated with hydrochloric acid (HCl, 10 per cent) and hydrogen peroxide (H_2O_2, 38 per cent) to remove any organics, and thoroughly rinsed with distilled water, then with acetone in order to remove all traces of chemicals from the previous treatments. Samples were subdivided into coarse grains (>90 mm) and fine grains (<90 mm). To displace the samples on discs, a silicon spray was used. The spray has been checked for radiation and heating stability before it is used and found that radiation or heating has no effect on the spray. Samples were measured in ELSEC 9010 Dating System. The stimulation source for quartz samples was the 514 nm green light. An array of the infrared diodes was used for the polymineral fine grains (Spooner *et al.* 1990) resulting in a signal only from feldspars. Scattering from discs was normalized by applying short shines between 0.5 and 1 seconds. The palaeodose (or Equivalent Dose, ED) was determined by the additive dose technique, where the laboratory doses are added to portions of the natural sample and the growth is extrapolated to zero luminescence signal to give the ED (Rees-Jones & Tite 1997). Samples were irradiated by an Sr90 (strontium-90) source delivering 0.0308Gy / sec. In order to remove electrons from traps that are filled during the laboratory irradiation, preheating was used. All quartz samples were preheated at

Table 4.9. *OSL determinations.*

Sample	Unit	Wall	Level	Age in ka (uncal BP)	SD in ka	1 SD (BC)	2 SD (BC except where stated)
Parish 1996	N / A	N / A	XII	9.50	1.50	9100–6000	11,000–4500
S.5206a	5206	F.554	IX	7.77	0.62	6500–5100	7100–4500
S.5206b	5206	F.554	IX	7.14	0.57	5800–4600	6400–4000
S.5206a+b combined	5206	F.554	IX	7.43	0.42	5900–5050	6400–4600
S.4240a	4240	F.74	VII	3.07	0.23	1360–880	1600–650
S.4240b	4240	F.74	VII	5.68	0.92	4700–2800	5600–1800
S.2817a	2817	F.52	VII	8.54	0.62	7300–5900	7900–5300
S.2817b	2817	F.52	VII	8.45	0.73	7300–5700	8000–5000
S.2817a+b combined	2817	F.52	VII	8.50	0.47	7050–6050	7500–5600
S.3707a	3707	F.253	VII	2.37	0.23	660–180	900–AD 50
S.3707b	3707	F.253	VII	2.80	0.28	1150–550	1500–200
S.3010a	3010	F.4/6	VII / VI	2.79	0.27	1150–550	1400–200
S.3010b	3010	F.4/6	VII / VI	6.34	0.57	5000–3800	5600–3200
Parish 1996	N / A	N / A	IV / III	8.00	1.75	7800–4300	10,000–2500

220°C for five minutes while the polymineral samples were at 160°C for two hours. The annual dose determination was done by low level alpha counting (ELSEC Low Level Alpha Counter 7286) system to determine uranium and thorium contribution to annual dose rate and atomic absorption spectrometry (AAS) to determine K_2O per cent content. For the cosmic ray component of annual dose rate, TL dosimeter discs (Al_2O_3:C) were placed and kept for eight months in the site where samples were taken. The samples were:

- (5206) from F.554 the western wall of Space 182, the narrow western room of Building 18, assigned to Level IX;
- (2817) from the northern wall F.52 of Spaces107 and 108, assigned to Level VII;
- (3707) from F.253 the eastern wall Space 112 Level to Level VII;
- (4240) from the northern wall F.74 of Space 159, the narrow western room of Building 24, assigned to Level VII and partially excavated in the 1960s as shrine 10 of Level VII. Building 24 lies directly above Building 18, with a direct stratigraphic relationship via the intervening Level VIII Building 6;
- (3010) is from wall F.4/6 on southern side of Building 1 which is broadly approximate to Levels VII/VI.

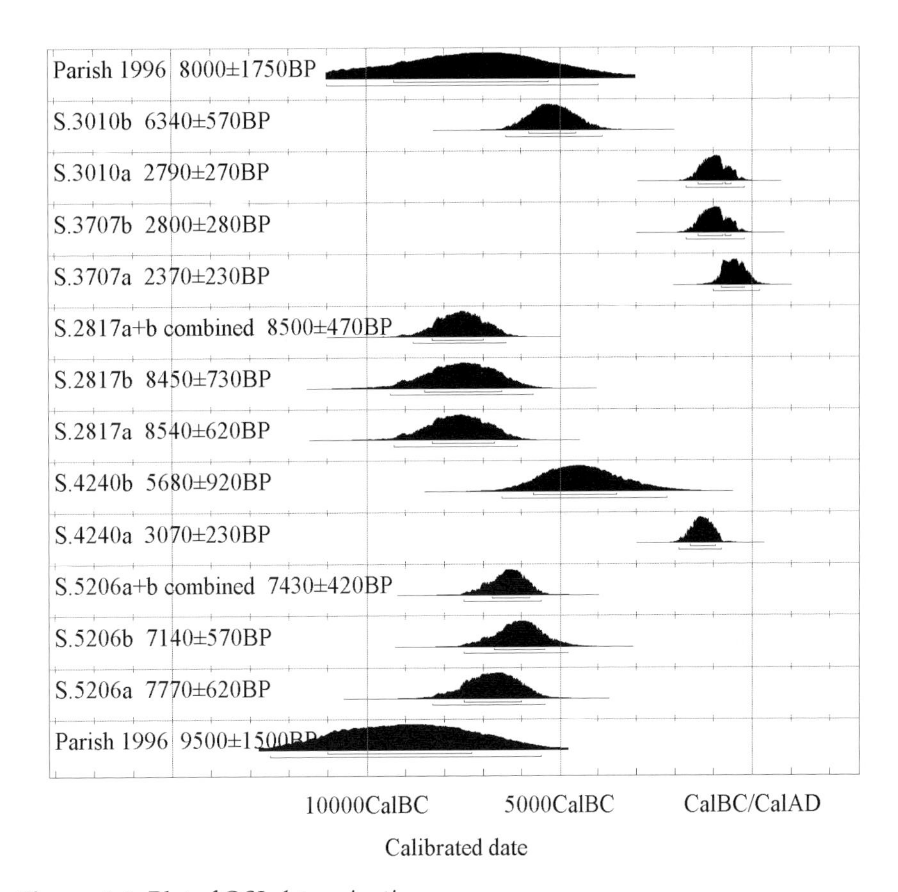

Figure 4.6. *Plot of OSL determinations.*

The results are shown in Table 4.9 and Figure 4.6, where a and b represent the ages done by IRSL (Infra Red Stimulated Luminescence) and GLSL (Green Light Stimulated Luminescence), respectively. In several instances the IRSL and GLSL determinations are not in good agreement and failed the OxCal3.5 X-test for combination at 5 per cent. The cause of this difference may be due to the partial bleaching of the samples during burial (Godfrey-Smith *et al.* 1988). When the samples where the IRSL and GLSL determinations are in good agreement are compared with the overall absolute dating sequence derived from radiocarbon and dendrochronology S.5206 appears to be slightly too young, although the IRSL determination on its own is compatible. Both the IRSL and GLSL for S.2817 are perfectly compatible with the radiocarbon sequence. In order to be certain, the OSL dating studies for the same and different levels of the same site must be repeated for a large numbers of samples.

Conclusion

It can be concluded that the optical-dating technique might have the potential to provide a new routine dating method. Furthermore, the problems encountered in optical-dating technique such as insufficient bleaching, fading and saturation of the signal can be minimized by repeating the dating measurements for a large number of samples from the same site. Thus, for Çatalhöyük, to establish a chronology for the site based on direct dating of buildings, the OSL technique may have a considerable importance.

Radiocarbon determinations from the North Area

by Craig Cessford

The North Area is located on the northern eminence of the mound some two hundred metres away from the area investigated by Mellaart. Work here focused on a single structure Building 1, which was excavated in its entirety, but also included adjacent external areas and the later phases of the preceding structure

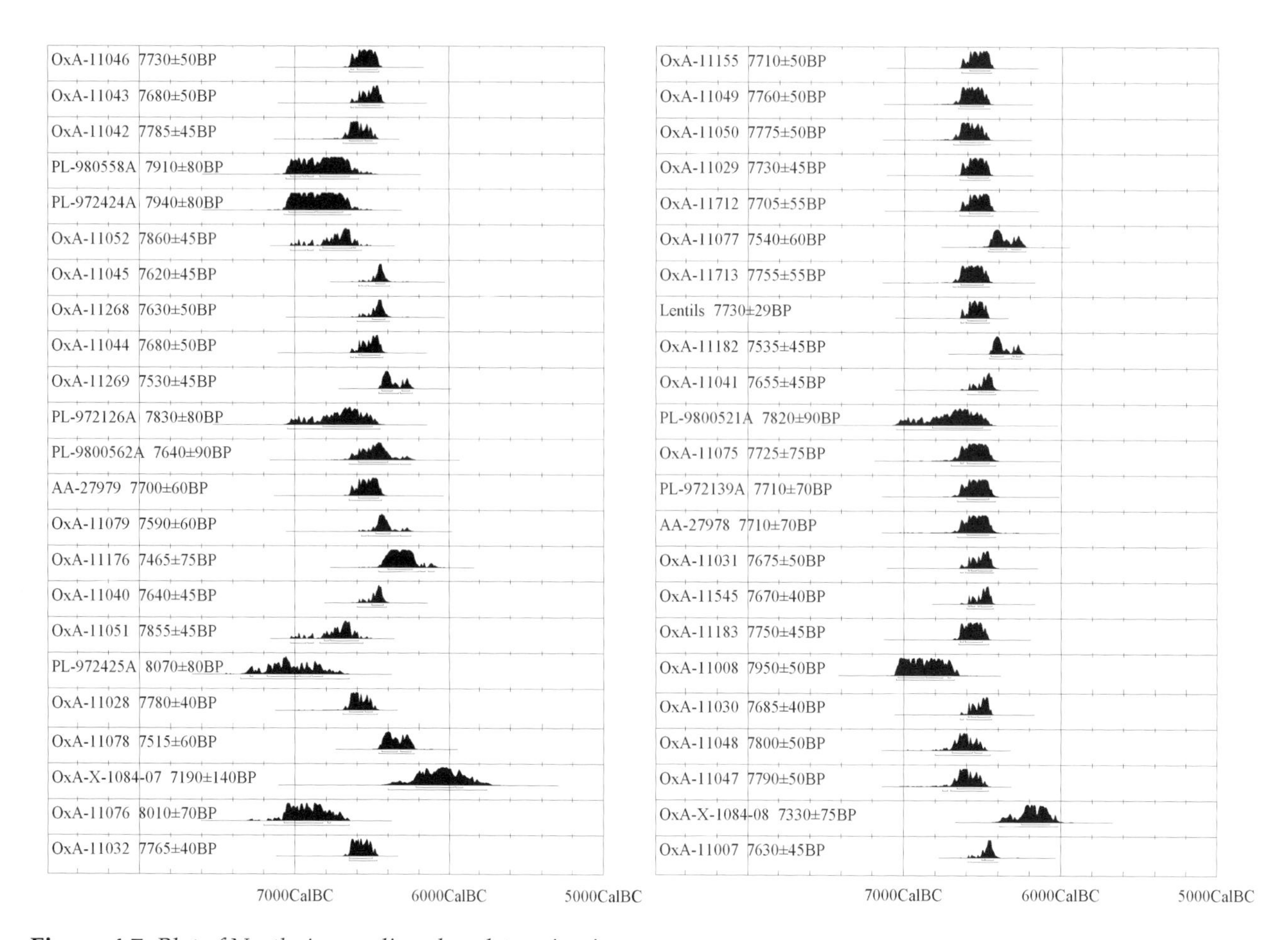

Figure 4.7. *Plot of North Area radiocarbon determinations.*

Building 5 (Volume 3, Part 3). Although the overall absolute dating sequence of Çatalhöyük is now relatively well understood (Cessford 2001), the lack of direct stratigraphic relationships between different excavation areas means that these require independent absolute dating. The key to successful absolute dating of archaeological sites is understanding the nature of the relationship between the material being dated and the events that are being dated. This is particularly important on sites such as Çatalhöyük occupied for long periods with complex depositional processes where the likelihood that deposits can incorporate either residual material of earlier date or intrusive material of later date is an ever-present problem. For this reason it was decided to date a range of different types of material from a variety of types of depositional contexts. The material selected came from assemblages subject to detailed specialist analysis and had the twin aims of trying to date the North Area phases precisely and to determine which types of material and / or context provide good dating evidence. An initial series of AMS determinations was undertaken on samples taken in 1997 at the Purdue and Arizona laboratories by Hale Göktürk (Göktürk *et al.* 2002). A more recent series took place at Oxford Radiocarbon Accelerator Unit of the Research Laboratory for Archaeology and the History of Art in 2001–02 (Table 4.10 & Fig. 4.7).

North Area sequence

The earliest deposits dated relate to the occupation (Phase B5.B) of Building 5. This structure was then systematically abandoned and filled with material. Construction work then began on Building 1 whilst infilling continued (Subphase B1.1B). Construction work on Building 1 was then completed (Subphase B1.2A) and occupation began (Subphase B1.2B). After a period some of the internal features were modified and occupation continued (Subphase B1.2C). This was followed by extensive modifications to the structure (Phase B1.3) after which the building was reoccupied (Phase B1.4). Eventually Building 1 was abandoned, although some later activity did take place in the area (Subphase B1.5B). A number of adjacent external areas were also excavated (Phase B1.E); stratigraphically it appears that these correspond to subphases B1.1B and

Table 4.10. *Radiocarbon determinations from the North Area.*

Lab. no.	Unit	Phase/ subphase	Context	Material dated	Reliability	Age	SD (uncal BP)	δ13C	Age (cal BC) to 1 S.D.	Age (cal BC) to 2 S.D.	Probability later than lentils	Elapsed time from lentils to 2 s.d.	Elapsed time from lentils to 1 s.d
OxA-11046	3810	B5.B	Packing against wall	Charred seeds, *Triticum dicoccum*	Medium	7730	50	–21.3	6640–6470	6650–6460	48.6%	–140 to +130	–70 to +70
OxA-11043	2166	B1.1B	General fill	Charred seeds, *Triticum dicoccum*	Low	7680	50	–22.8	6590–6450	6640–6430	65.9%	–110 to +160	–40 to +110
OxA-11042	2165	B1.1B	General fill	Charred seeds, *Triticum/Hordeum*	Low	7785	45	–23.1	6650–6500	6690–6470	28.7%	–180 to +100	–120 to +30
PL-980558A	2181	B1.1B	General fill	Charcoal	Low	7910	80	–23.2	7030–6650	7060–6590	8.3%	–250 to +40	–190 to –60
PL-972424A	2198	B1.1B	General fill	Charred seeds, Cerealae	Low	7940	80	–24.0	7040–6690	7070–6640	5.2%	–260 to +20	–210 to –80
OxA-11052	2529	B1.1B	Skeleton	Human bone, old man	High	7860	45	–18.3	6820–6610	7030–6570	7.8%	–220 to +30	–170 to –60
OxA-11045	3036	B1.E	External fill	Charred seeds, *Lens*	Medium	7620	45	–21.0	6480–6420	6590–6390	90.9%	–30 to +210	+30 to +150
OxA-11268	3036	B1.E	External fill	Calcified seeds, *Celtis*	Medium	7630	50	–9.4	6500–6420	6600–6390	86.0%	–60 to +200	+10 to +150
OxA-11044	3030	B1.E	External fill	Charred seeds, *Lens*	Medium	7680	50	–21.0	6590–6450	6640–6430	66.1%	–110 to +160	–40 to +100
OxA-11269	3030	B1.E	External fill	Calcified seeds, *Celtis*	Medium	7530	45	–11.4	6440–6260	6460–6240	99.9%	+40 to +240	+80 to +180
PL-972126A	1442	B1.2A	Fill of basin	Charred seeds, Cerealae	Medium	7830	80	–22.4	6820–6450	7050–6450	22.1%	–220 to +100	–150 to 0
PL-9800562A	1416	B1.2	Floor sequence	Charred seeds, Cerealae	Medium	7640	90	–22.7	6590–6400	6650–6250	69.6%	–120 to +200	–30 to +130
AA-27979	1416	B1.2	Floor sequence	Charred seeds, Cerealae	Medium	7700	60	–23.5	6590–6460	6650–6440	56.8%	–130 to +150	–60 to +90
OxA-11079	1429	B1.2B	Floor sequence	Charred seeds, Cerealae	Medium	7590	60	–22.6	6480–6385	6570–6250	93.2%	–30 to +230	+40 to +170
OxA-11176	1417	B1.2B	Floor sequence	Charred seeds, Cerealae	Medium	7465	75	–21.6	6400–6240	6460–6100	99.6%	+40 to +270	+90 to +200
OxA-11040	1459	B1.2B	Floor sequence	Charred seeds, Cerealae	Medium	7640	45	–21.7	6505–6430	6600–6410	83.9%	–70 to +190	+10 to +140
OxA-11051	2115	B1.2B	Skeleton	Human bone, old woman	High	7855	45	–18.5	6810–6590	7030–6560	8.7%	–220 to +40	–170 to –40
PL-972425A	2124	B1.2B	Grave fill	Charcoal	Low	8070	80	–24.3	7290–6820	7350–6650	0.7%	–260 to -40	–210 to –100
OxA-11028	1226	B1.2B	Fill of scoop	Charred seeds, Cerealae	Medium	7780	40	–22.6	6650–6500	6690–6470	30.6%	–160 to +100	–110 to +30
OxA-11078	1415	B1.2C	Floor sequence	Charred seeds, Cerealae	Medium	7515	60	–22.2	6440–6250	6460–6230	99.6%	+40 to +250	+80 to +190
OxA-X-1084-07	1424	B1.2B	Skeleton	Inhaled particulate carbon	Low	7190	140	–23.0	6220–5910	6400–5750	99.3%	+50 to +280	+90 to +220
OxA-X-1045-13	1456	B1.2C	Floor sequence	Animal bone, sheep- and cattle-sized fragments	Medium	7850	110	–18.9	7050–6500	7050–6450	30.0%	–240 to +130	–90 to +50
OxA-11032	1456	B1.2C	Floor sequence	Charred seeds, Cerealae	Medium	7765	40	–22.0	6650–6500	6650–6470	36.2%	–160 to +110	–100 to +40
OxA-11155	1454	B1.2C	Floor sequence	Charred seeds, Cerealae	Medium	7710	50	–21.6	6590–6460	6640–6450	54.9%	–120 to +140	–60 to +80
OxA-11049	1959	B1.2C	Skeleton	Human bone, juvenile	High	7760	50	–19.4	6650–6500	6660–6460	38.8%	–160 to +110	–100 to +50
OxA-11050	1960	B1.2C	Skeleton	Human bone, juvenile	High	7775	50	–19.3	6650–6500	6690–6460	33.7%	–170 to +110	–100 to +40
OxA-11049 & 11050 combined	1959/ 1960	B1.2C	Skeletons	Human bone, juveniles	High	7768	35	N/A	6650–6500	6650–6470	34.0%	–150 to +100	–100 to +40
OxA-11029	1332	B1.3	Storage	Charred seeds, *Lens*	High	7730	45	–24.1	6600–6470	6650–6460	48.6%	–130 to +130	–70 to +70
OxA-11712	1332	B1.3	Storage	Charred seeds, *Lens*	High	7705	55	–23.0	6590–6460	6650–6440	55.8%	–120 to +150	–60 to +90
OxA-11077	1344	B1.3	Storage	Charred seeds, *Lens*	Low	7540	60	–23.3	6460–6260	6470–6230	98.9%	+20 to +250	+70 to +190
OxA-11713	1344	B1.3	Storage	Charred seeds, *Lens*	High	7755	55	–23.5	6640–6500	6690–6460	40.7%	–160 to +110	–90 to +50
OxA-11029, OxA-11712 & OxA-11713 combined	1332/ 1344	B1.3	Storage	Charred seeds, *Lens*	High	7730	29	N/A	6600–6480	6640–6460	N/A	N/A	N/A
OxA-11182	1344	B1.3	Storage	Animal bone, wild goat horn core 1344.X4	Medium	7535	45	–15.5	6450–6260	6460–6250	99.9%	+40 to +240	+70 to +190

Table 4.10. *(cont.)*

Lab. no.	Unit	Phase/ subphase	Context	Material dated	Reliability	Age	SD (uncal BP)	δ13C	Age (cal BC) to 1 S.D.	Age (cal BC) to 2 S.D.	Probability later than lentils	Elapsed time from lentils to 2 s.d.	Elapsed time from lentils to 1 s.d
OxA-11041	2142	B1.3	Fill of posthole	Charred seeds, *Hordeum vulgare* var.	Medium	7655	45	–22.6	6530–6430	6600–6420	77.7%	–80 to +180	–10 to +120
PL-9800521A	2142	B1.3	Fill of posthole	Charred seeds, Cerealae	Medium	7820	90	–22.9	6820–6500	7050–6450	26.4%	–220 to +110	–150 to +10
OxA-11075	1400	B1.3	General fill	Animal bone, cattle skull with horncores 1400.X3	Medium	7725	75	–17.9	6640–6460	6700–6420	49.0%	–150 to +140	–80 to +80
PL-972139A	1349	B1.3	Fill of basin	Charred seeds, Cerealae	Medium	7710	70	–23.0	6600–6460	6660–6420	52.7%	–140 to +150	–70 to +80
AA-27978	1349	B1.3	Fill of basin	Charred seeds, Cerealae	Medium	7710	70	–22.1	6600–6460	6660–6420	52.6%	–140 to +150	–70 to +80
PL-972139A & AA-27978 combined	1349	B1.3	Fill of basin	Charred seeds, Cerealae	Medium	7710	49	N/A	6590–6460	6640–6450	55.0%	–130 to +150	–60 to +80
OxA-11031	1390	B1.4	Stakehole	Charred seeds, Cerealae	Medium	7675	50	–23.2	6590–6440	6640–6430	67.8%	–110 to +170	–40 to +110
OxA-11545	1391	B1.4	Stakehole	Charred seeds, pulses	Medium	7670	40	–22.8	6590–6440	6600–6430	73.0%	–90 to +170	–20 to +110
OxA-11183	1366	B1.4	Base of hearth	Charred seeds, Cerealae	Medium	7750	45	–21.6	6640–6500	6650–6460	41.8%	–140 to +110	–90 to +50
OxA-X-1042-22	1358	B1.4	Floor sequence	Animal bone, sheep-sized fragments	Medium	7870	60	–17.8	6990–6640	7050–6500	19.6%	–280 to +60	–130 to +30
OxA-11030	1358	B1.4	Floor sequence	Charred seeds, *Triticum dicoccum*	Medium	7685	40	–23.5	6590–6450	6640–6440	66.4%	–100 to +160	–30 to +100
OxA-11048	1466	B1.4	Skeleton	Human bone, adult man	High	7800	50	–17.7	6690–6500	6800–6450	25.8%	–80 to +90	–130 to +20
OxA-11047	1378	B1.4	Skeleton	Human bone, old man	High	7790	50	–17.9	6660–6500	6750–6460	29.0%	–170 to +100	–120 to +30
OxA-X-1084-08	1378	B1.4	Skeleton	Inhaled particulate carbon	Low	7330	75	–24.7	6250–6070	6390–6020	100.0%	+70 to +270	+100 to +220
OxA-11007	1334	B1.5B	Pit fill	Animal bone, worked point 1334.X14, sheep/goat metacarpal	Medium	7630	45	–18.4	6500–6420	6590–6400	87.9%	–50 to +200	+30 to +150

B1.2A inside the structure. The dated sequence spans the later part of Building 5 and the complete occupational sequence of Building 1.

Lentil deposit

The development of AMS dating has meant that charred short-lived plant material such as seeds have tended to replace the longer-lived wood charcoal as the main source of material for radiocarbon dating. Although this undoubtedly represents a major advance it has been recognized that great care needs to be taken in the selection of such material for dating purposes (Larting & van der Plicht 1994, 4; Prendergast 2000; van der Plicht & Bruins 2001, 1160). The potential for the presence of residual earlier material or intrusive later material within assemblages cannot be entirely avoided, although careful analysis and selection can minimize it. Archaeobotanical analysis at Çatalhöyük suggests that with a few specific exceptions the majority of assemblages are relatively mixed and derive from a number of sources rather than relating to single specific activities. To paraphrase Archimedes *On the Lever* 'Give me a firm enough place to stand, and I will move the earth'. Dating material about which there is no taphonomic doubt provides an analytical fulcrum that is the basis for rigorous comparison.

The only deposit from the North Area that undoubtedly relates to a single contemporary event is storage context (1332)/(1344), a deliberately-placed deposit of lentils which represents a single year's harvest of a short-lived species that was purposefully burnt as part of phase B1.3. Unfortunately the first pair of determinations obtained from this deposit (OxA-11029 & OxA-11077) were not compatible, failing the Chi-Squared test for combining at five per cent. To clarify the situation two more determinations from this deposit were undertaken (OxA-11712 & OxA-11713). Three of the four determinations are in good agreement (OxA-11029, OxA-11712 & OxA-11713) and when combined give a date of 7730±29 BP. The aberrant determination (OxA-11077) has a 98.9 per cent likelihood of being later than the combined result from the other three determinations, by 20 to 250 years (95 per cent probability) or 70 to 90 years (68 per cent probability). There are no obvious reasons for this and it is likely that this is an apposite reminder that even at two standard deviations around one in twenty determinations will produce misleading results.

Other plant material
The majority of determinations from charred plant material in the North Area appear to be acceptable when their relationship to the dating of the lentil deposit is compared to the relevant stratigraphic relationships and the likely duration of intervening phases. There are also a number of determinations that are stratigraphically earlier than the lentil deposit but are later than it. OxA-11079 and OxA-11040 are too late at the 68 per cent probability level, whilst OxA-11176 and OxA-11078 are too late at the 95 per cent probability level. There are no obvious reasons for this, although a number of these determinations are clustered spatially. Additionally determination OxA-11045, whose stratigraphic relationship to the lentil deposit is less certain, also appears to be too late at the 68 per cent probability level. This determination comes from the external deposits (Phase B1.E). When considered in conjunction with the other determinations from this area this raises the possibility that either these deposits are later than is believed or that they contain intrusive material, something that is possible given the nature of the deposits in question.

It was felt on various archaeological and taphonomic grounds that material from a scoop (1226) (OxA-11028), posthole (2142) (OxA-11041) and stakeholes (1390) (OxA-11031) and (1391) (OxA-11545) might also relate to nearby activities within Building 1 that resulted in the rapid deposition of botanical material. In all cases the determinations support this conclusion. Consideration of the rest of the charred-seed determinations, which were not expected to have a direct relationship with the contexts in which they were found, shows that they form a relatively coherent group and may be broadly contemporary with the deposits in which they occur. It is, however, statistically probable that some of the material in question is in fact residual, although this can only be clearly demonstrated in a few instances. One determination PL-972424A is too early at 68 per cent probability, suggesting that it represents residual material. The clearest example is posthole fill (2142) where there is an 87.9 per cent probability that the determination on the general cereals present is earlier than the barley, which it is believed may have been deliberately placed. Overall it appears statistically likely that between 25 and 50 per cent of the plant material dated was residual to some degree. Determinations on mineralized plant remains were in good agreement with those from charred plant remains.

Charcoal
Charcoal is a problematic dating material at Çatalhöyük and was only included in the earlier set of dates undertaken at Purdue. These determinations are potentially not closely related to the archaeological events in question as the contexts probably contain residual material and the species of tree was not identified. PL-972425A in particular is much earlier than the context in which it was found. Although PL-980558A is broadly the same age as some of the determinations on charred seeds from the same set of deposits it is also likely to be residual.

Human bone
The main archaeologically-attested burial rite at Çatalhöyük is inhumation within buildings. The body is placed in a hole and it can be stratigraphically demonstrated that in most instances this was cut during the occupation of the structure. In the case of Building 1 just over 60 individuals were interred immediately prior to or during the occupation of the structure. Whilst there is evidence for the disturbance and redeposition of earlier burials and some delayed burial the material selected was from skeletons that can be identified as the primary burial of undisturbed individuals. As such this should prove ideal material for dating purposes, although it must be remembered that determinations on bone relate not to the time of death, but the lifetime of the individual. Other potential problems include a freshwater reservoir effect (Cook *et al.* 2002; also Larting & van der Plicht 1998). Freshwater fish are likely to have been only a minor dietary component at Çatalhöyük and any impact is likely to have been correspondingly minor. Small amounts of contamination from the surrounding matrix are also possible (cf. Larting & van der Plicht 1994, 5), although the relatively good survival of collagen argues against this. Overall the determinations on human bone are in agreement with the stratigraphic sequence and the determinations from the lentils, forming an internally-consistent sequence once the effects of the different ages at death of the individuals are taken into account. Determinations on inhaled particulate carbon from the ribs of skeletons produced determinations that were too young.

Animal bone
Animal bone from two main types of context was dated; these were floor contexts and relatively large

pieces of faunal material that appeared to have been deliberately placed. The determinations from floors were composite rather than single entities, which it could be argued renders them less useful as dating evidence (Ashmore 1999). Initial results suggested that this material was substantially earlier than the botanical material from the same deposits and the lentils. Unfortunately it transpired that these determinations (OxA-11008 & OxA-11032) were subject to contamination in the laboratory ultra-filtration process. The results were corrected and reissued (OxA-X-1045-13 & OxA-X-1042-22). These determinations are still probably earlier than the charred seeds from the same deposits (62.9 per cent & 83.8 per cent probability) by up to 300 (95 per cent probability) or 130 (68 per cent probability) years. Given the problematic nature of these determinations, however, it would be unwise to place too much weight on these results.

The determination from a wild goat horn core (1344), one of a group of thirteen placed over the lentils, has a 99.9 per cent likelihood of being later than the determinations from the lentil deposit. As this is impossible it appears likely that the highly-burnt nature of this material has somehow affected the determination. A cattle skull and horn cores (1400) which were deposited at the same time as the lentils has a 51 per cent probability of being earlier than them by up to 150 (95 per cent probability) or 80 (68 per cent probability) years. As they cannot be later than the lentils this leaves a 49 per cent probability that they are contemporary; this actually underestimates the likelihood given that determinations on bone relate to the lifetime of the animal rather than its death.

A worked bone point (1334), one of a group of deliberately-placed bone and chipped-stone items found in a later pit, has an 87.9 per cent likelihood of being later than the lentils. It could be between 50 years older to 200 years younger (95 per cent probability) or 30 to 150 years younger (68 per cent probability). This generally confirms that this pit was dug and the items placed relatively soon after the building was abandoned.

The levels of the North Area

It is impossible to precisely calculate how the determinations from the North Area fit into the overall site sequence, but statistical probabilities can be calculated. Stratigraphically the earliest determination comes from phase B5.B and this is most likely to correspond with Levels IX (18.9 per cent probability), VIII (41.0 per cent probability) or VII (31.1 per cent probability). The most reliable set of determinations from the phase B1.3 lentil deposit probably also come from Levels IX (16.5 per cent probability), VIII (43.4 per cent probability) or VII (34.9 per cent probability). The latest determination from Subphase B1.5B probably comes from Levels VIII (18.6 per cent probability), VII (45.5 per cent probability) or VI (26.4 per cent probability). Artefact typologies suggest that Building 1 corresponds to Level VI (mainly Chapter 5, but see also Chapters 9 & 11). Given that levels are no longer considered to represent single absolutely contemporary site wide events the discrepancy between the AMS and artefact typologies is probably not significant.

Conclusion

The AMS determinations from the North Area allow Building 1 to be assigned to Levels VIII or VII in the general site sequence. The large number of determinations from a relatively short but well-understood stratigraphic sequence provide a useful analytical 'lever' given the existence of a stable dating 'fulcrum' in the form of the lentil deposit. Although it is generally only possible to discuss material in terms of statistical probability this work has clearly revealed that a larger number of determinations are unacceptable than might have been anticipated and that some of the charred seeds and animal bones dated are clearly residual.

AMS dating of inhaled particulate carbon

by Craig Cessford & Tom Higham

Black granular deposits identified during excavation adhering to the ribs of skeletons of old individuals were identified by quantitative x-ray diffraction and x-ray spectroscopy as a mixture of carbon and clay inhaled through prolonged environmental contact (Molleson *et al.* forthcoming). This was interpreted as being inhaled from fires in poorly-ventilated buildings and indicates respiratory disease, specifically anthracosis, and similar results have been reported from mummified skeletons (Volume 4, Chapter 25). A mixture of animal dung, mainly from sheep and goats, and wood, from a variety of tree species, was used as fuel (Asouti & Fairbairn forthcoming; Fairbairn *et al.* 2002). Although this material is of mixed origin rather than representing a 'single entity' (cf. Ashmore 1999) its context means that it is potentially an important source of material for absolute dating. Two samples from ribs that had black carbon staining from Building 1 were pre-treated and AMS dated (Table 4.10). These determinations can be contextualized by considering the radiocarbon ages of other materials nearby, and specifically the age of one of the skeletons that has also been AMS dated. They have been given OxA-X-*nnnn-nn* numbers because of their non-routine chemistry and novel/experimental nature.

Methodology

The bones were cleaned using an inert gas to remove any adhering non-autochthonous material or dust. The carbon staining material was scraped from the surface of the bone using a scalpel. In the case of OxA-X-1084-07, 11.15 mg was obtained for pre-treatment, whilst OxA-X-1084-08 produced 22.8 mg of material. Both samples were treated using 1 M HCl at 80°C for one hour and then rinsed in Milli Q water. They were then treated with 0.1–0.4 M NaOH gradually increasing in temperature from room temperature to 80°C. The samples were then rinsed again and reacidified with 1 M HCl at 80°C for one hour, then rinsed with Milli Q water. The samples were dried in an oven at 80°C and weighed before AMS dating. The yields of material after this pre-treatment protocol was applied were <50 per cent of the start weight. OxA-X-1084-07 produced a yield of 24 per cent. Percentage C yields after combustion were also low; OxA-1084-07 yielded 5.5 per cent C and OxA-1084-08 4.8 per cent C. For charcoal, percentage C averages *c.* 55–65 per cent. The yield data suggest that this material is not as pure as charcoal derived carbon ought to be. The sample isolated after pre-treatment probably consists of small amounts of carbon derived from lung inhalation products as well as low-carbon bearing sediment and particles from the immediate depositional environment. This mirrors the results from x-ray diffraction and x-ray spectroscopy that identified this material as a mixture of carbon and clay.

If the carbon material on the ribs is derived only from inhaled smoke particulate matter then we ought to expect a $\delta^{13}C$ value within the range of the values for the wood and plant material being used as fuel. Radiocarbon derived $\delta^{13}C$ data are available for charred seeds of *Scirpus* (average: –23.2 per mil, n = 3), Lens (–23.3, n = 7) and *Triticum* (–21.7, n = 33) and for Juniper charcoal (–23.4, n = 10) and unidentified charcoal (–24.1, n = 10). The $\delta^{13}C$ value for OxA-X-1084-08 is slightly depleted in comparison to other stable isotope data of charcoal, but the date is closer to the age expected than OxA-X-1084-07. Generally speaking, the $\delta^{13}C$ values are reasonably close to the value expected.

Results

Both individuals from whom inhaled particulate carbon was dated were buried under the floors of Building 1 during its occupation (Volume 3, Part 3). The material dated came from skeletons (1378) and (1424). The earliest of these was (1424), also known as burial F.30, the tightly-flexed burial of the articulated skeleton of an old woman lying on her left side with her head to the south in a crouched position interred during subphase B1.2B of the occupation of Building 1. (1378), also known as burial F.28, was the tightly-flexed crouched burial of complete articulated skeleton of an old man lying on his left side with his head to the west who was interred during phase B1.4 of the occupation of Building 1. Building 1 has also been dated by a number of other AMS determinations. For comparative purposes the most important of these are a determination from the ribs of skeleton (1378) and the series of determinations from the deposit of lentils (1332)/(1344). Of the four determinations obtained three are in good agreement and when combined produce a result of 7730+/–29 BP.

When the determination on inhaled particulate carbon from skeleton (1424) is compared to the combined determination from the lentils it is shown to be 50 to 280 (95 per cent probability) or 90 to 220 (68 per cent probability) years younger. A similar comparison for the inhaled particulate carbon from skeleton (1378) shows it to be 70 to 270 (95 per cent probability) or 100 to 220 (68 per cent probability) years younger. A comparison with the determination from the ribs of skeleton (1378) shows that the particulate carbon is 90 to 320 (95 per cent probability) or 150 to 280 (68 per cent probability) years younger. These results show that the two determinations from inhaled particulate carbon both underestimated the age of the material being dated. There is a 40.0 per cent probability that the determination on particulate carbon from (1424) is earlier than that from (1378), which means that the results are potentially compatible with the stratigraphic sequence. The material from (1424) is likely to be between 90 years earlier and 60 years later than (1378) (95 per cent probability) or between 40 years earlier and 30 years later (68 per cent probability). On various grounds it is likely that the period between the two interments was between 10 and 40 years, which agrees well with the results of the determinations from inhaled particulate carbon.

The low percentage C value and small sample size after pre-treatment, coupled with the fact that the radiocarbon results are younger than expected, suggest that there is a contamination issue to consider. Assuming there is a background level of contamination in the archaeological context caused, for example, by factors such as movement of particulate matter in rainfall solution down through the site profile or from fluctuations in the water table, intrusion of rootlets, or bioturbation from small organisms, then larger samples ought to be less affected than very small ones. As the sample size decreases the influence of a contaminant increases in its effect, and the offset from 'true' age increases. In the case of the inhaled particulate carbon, the sample size is small and the percentage C yield is low, therefore it is possible that a carbon contaminant of a more modern age has influenced the results. A modern carbon contaminant contributing around five to seven per cent by weight would result in a shift of around 500 years in a modern direction at this age.

Discussion
Although the AMS determinations on inhaled particulate carbon from skeletons at Çatalhöyük underestimated the age of this material the results are not wildly inaccurate and the relationship between the two determinations themselves is acceptable. This suggests that dating of such material may be useful, especially if larger quantities can be obtained.

AMS dating of hackberry
by Thomas Higham & Petya Blumbach

Celtis sp., or hackberry, is a deciduous tree or shrub of the elm family (Ulmaceae). Remains of its mineralized endocarp (seed casings) are sometimes found in archaeological contexts and they appear to survive well. We investigated whether *Celtis* sp. would furnish reliable AMS dates by testing a small number of endocarps. *Celtis* sp. is a radiocarbon sample type yet to be investigated in the Near East. We saw potential in testing and evaluating this novel material at Çatalhöyük because contexts with *Celtis* sp. seeds had already been dated by numerous AMS determinations on organic seeds in association with excavated *Celtis* sp. seeds. We wanted to determine whether these seeds would produce radiocarbon ages that were similar to reliable materials from identical stratigraphic horizons.

Background
There are about seventy species of hackberry worldwide (Preston 1976) including North America, the Near East, eastern Europe (Jahren *et al.* 1998), and the Pacific Rim (see also O'Connor *et al.* in press). *Celtis* sp. endocarps are common amongst the botanical remains at Çatalhöyük and findings have been reported throughout the excavations (Volume 4, Chapter 8). Overall abundances of endocarps in some areas of the site may indicate that they were fruit-processing areas (Volume 4, Chapter 10). *Celtis* sp. endocarps are unusual because they are predominantly composed of calcium carbonate (*c.* 70 per cent weight in modern samples) rather than organic carbon, which means they are well-preserved in the archaeological and fossil record (Cowan *et al.* 1996; Wang *et al.* 1997; Jahren *et al.* 1998). Hackberry endocarps have in fact been recovered from contexts dating to millions of years old, so they potentially provide a useful archaeological as well as palaeoenvironmental dating substrate in a range of different areas and over long time periods (Jahren *et al.* 2001). According to Fairburn *et al.* (Volume 4, Chapter 10), *Celtis* species from central Anatolia cannot be confidently identified on the basis of the preserved endocarps, but it is likely that *Celtis tournefortii* is the species present at Çatalhöyük, because it is the dominant variety in central Anatolia and the Konya plain. Whilst it is unlikely that hackberries were cultivated in Neolithic times, they were probably extensively collected in prehistory for consumption (van Zeist & de Roller 1995; Woldring & Cappers 2001).

Single hackberry endocarps hold potential for reducing errors in AMS dating archaeological contexts, because they are 'single entity' samples (Ashmore 1999). A 'single entity' is a sample whose inbuilt age can be assigned to a single calendar year. Amongst the advantages of dating 'single entity' samples is the avoidance of potentially 'averaged' dates through using mixed samples that may have a significant inbuilt age. Other scholars have investigated the potential for *Celtis* sp. to yield reliable radiocarbon ages and the results appear promising, particularly when modern control samples are considered. Wang *et al.* (1997), for instance, obtained *Celtis* endocarps collected historically between 1993 and AD 1850 and found that they yielded carbon 14 measurements indistinguishable from the carbon 14 levels in the contemporary atmosphere. They suggested that provided the crystallinity of the dated endocarps could be shown to be unaltered from their original aragonite, one could expect reliable radiocarbon determinations from older samples (Wang *et al.* 1997). They also radiocarbon-dated hackberry endocarps from natural and archaeological contexts that were in association which other materials considered reliable for dating. Some results were at odds with that expected, but in most of these instances this was considered to be due to a taphonomic reason. In general, the authors considered that *Celtis* ought to produce reliable determinations if the context of the material could be confidently ascribed. To determine with confidence whether *Celtis* sp. is reliable for AMS radiocarbon dating for archaeological sites one clearly requires samples that come from a secure context within a site. We therefore obtained six endocarp samples from contexts at Çatalhöyük to test the reliability of *Celtis* sp. for dating this site, and potentially other sites in Anatolia and the Near East.

The endocarps were physically pretreated by air-blasting using aluminium oxide powder, they were then crushed using a pestle and mortar. Part of each sample was analyzed using powder X-Ray Diffractometry (XRD) at the Geology Department at Oxford Brookes University to determine whether there was any exogenous carbonate present. One potential source of error in radiocarbon dating of carbonates is that they may be prone to recrystallization and exchange (Higham 1994). Recrystallization occurs when bicarbonate in the depositional matrix precipitates onto the carbonate of the material that is to be dated. Much depends on whether the sample to be dated is within an open or closed system. If the former, then exchanged carbon may contain carbon 14 of an older or younger age. If the latter, there ought to be no age shift associated with the reprecipitated carbonate. All endocarps were predominantly aragonitic, with the exception of the sample from (5323), which showed a small calcite peak. While it is difficult to quantify the precise proportions of calcite on the basis of these spectra we estimate the sample comprised approximately five per cent exogenous calcite. The other hackberry samples were solely aragonitic.

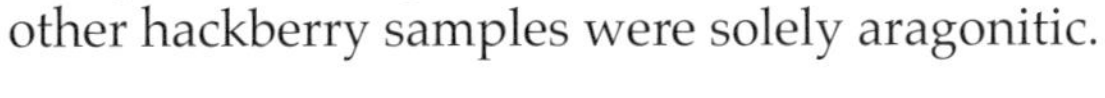

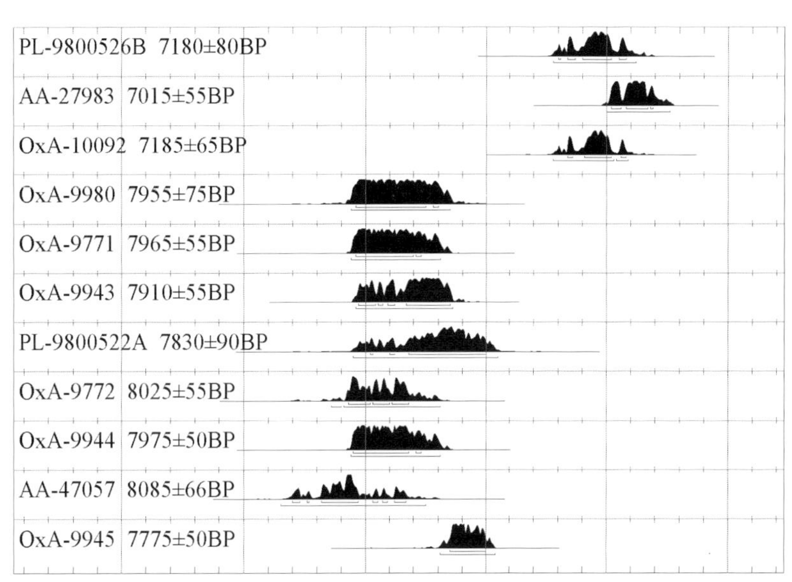

Figure 4.8. *Plot of KOPAL Area radiocarbon determinations.*

Results

Four hackberry samples were selected for AMS dating at the Oxford Radiocarbon Accelerator Unit (Bronk Ramsey & Hedges 1999; Bronk Ramsey *et al.* 2000). Results and associated calibrated ages BC are shown alongside previously-dated charred seeds from the same contexts (Figs. 4.1 & 4.7; Tables 4.1 & 4.10). Jahren *et al.* (2001) obtained $\delta^{13}C$ values for hackberries which mostly fell between –9.0 and –15.0 per mile from various sites in the western USA. These values are comparable with our values, which span –7.9 to –11.4 per mile. One sample from context (4715) was failed due to a problem with the loading of the graphite into the target, despite the fact that it produced a result within one standard deviation of two paired charred-seed determinations from identical contexts. As a precaution this sample is being reanalyzed and the result will be published in future elsewhere. Samples in contexts (3036) and (5323) were statistically indistinguishable at one standard deviation implying that they ceased metabolizing carbon 14 at the same time in prehistory. The samples from context (3030) were statistically indistinguishable at two standard deviations. In all cases the calibrated age ranges disclose significant overlap between paired samples.

The *Celtis* sp. endocarps were composed of *c.* 100 per cent carbonate. In contrast, Wang *et al.* (1997) found that the endocarp carbonate content ranged from 41 to 70 per cent weight. This could be a product of differing composition due to different species, or it could be due increasingly decayed organics in the older samples. One would expect the percentage of carbonate in modern endocarps to be lower, because organic materials would still be present.

Conclusion

Our comparison of *Celtis* sp. carbonate AMS determinations with results obtained previously from Çatalhöyük shows an acceptable level of agreement. The preliminary results therefore imply that AMS radiocarbon dating of *Celtis* sp. endocarps from this site is reliable. Further radiocarbon dating is required to show this unequivocally and we are currently involved in analysing more material.

Radiocarbon determinations from the KOPAL Area

by Craig Cessford

The off-site KOPAL Area was investigated in 1997 and 1999 (Volume 3, Part 4). After the 1997 season two layers were dated with three determinations; after the 1999 season six deposits were dated with eight determinations (Fig. 4.8; Table 4.11). These can be related to the determinations obtained from work in 1997 as (2410) is equivalent to (6020), specifically the upper subdivision of it identified as (6086) whilst (2412) is equivalent to (6010) (Volume 3, Part 4).

Table 4.11. *Radiocarbon determinations from the KOPAL Area.*

Lab. no.	Unit	Phase	Material dated	Age (uncal BP)	SD	δ13C	Age (cal BC) to 1 S.D.	Age (cal BC) to 2 S.D.
PL-9800526B	2410 =6020/ 6086	Buried soil horizons and land surfaces	Charcoal	7180	80	23.0%	6200–5920	6220–5880
AA-27983	2410 =6020/ 6086	Buried soil horizons and land surfaces	Charcoal	7015	55	–23.2%	5980–5810	6000-5740
PL-9800526B & AA-27983 combined	2410 =6020/ 6086	Buried soil horizons and land surfaces	Charcoal	7069	45	N/A	6000–5840	6020–5810
OxA-10092	6020 =6086	Buried soil horizons and land surfaces	Charred seeds, *Triticum*	7185	65	–22.2%	6160–5920	6220–5910
OxA-9980	6020 =6089	Buried soil horizons and land surfaces	Charred seeds, *Triticum*	7955	75	–19.4%	7040–6700	7060–6650
OxA-9980 & OxA-10092 combined (X-Test fails at 5%)	6020	Buried soil horizons and land surfaces	Charred seeds, *Triticum*	7543	49	N/A	6460–6260	6470–6240
OxA-9771	6013	Renewed natural backswamp clay formation	Charred seeds, *Triticum*	7965	55	–21.8%	7040–6770	7060–6690
OxA-9943	6013	Renewed natural backswamp clay formation	Charred seeds *Triticum*	7910	55	–22.1%	7030–6650	7040–6640
OxA-9771 & OxA-9943 combined	6013	Renewed natural backswamp clay formation	Charred seeds, *Triticum*	7938	39	N/A	7030–6700	7040–6680
PL-9800522A	2412 =6010	Quarry pits and related activities	Charred seeds, Cerealae	7830	90	–22.4%	6980–6500	7050–6450
OxA-9772	6075	Quarry pits and related activities	Charred seeds, *Triticum*	8025	55	–21.0%	7070–6820	7140–6690
OxA-9944	6075	Quarry pits and related activities	Charred seeds, *Triticum*	7975	50	–20.9%	7050–6770	7060–6690
OxA-9772 & OxA-9944 combined	6075	Quarry pits and related activities	Charred seeds, *Triticum*	7998	37	N/A	7060–6820	7060–6700
AA-47057	6025	Quarry pits and related activities	Animal bone, cattle phalanx	8085	66	–18.2%	7300–6830	7350–6750
OxA-9945	6079	Unknown	Charred seeds, *Scirpus*	7775	50	–23.0%	6650–6500	6690–6460

Discussion

Stratigraphic definition was relatively poor in the KOPAL Area and there was a lower density of archaeobotanical material. This means that the determinations are inherently more problematic and their stratigraphic relationships less reliable. OxA-9945 is problematic as it was anticipated that this would be the earliest determination from the KOPAL Area, but its results do not agree with the rest of the sequence. This suggests that the feature from which it was obtained is a later intrusion. On the basis of the other determinations it appears likely that this feature is later than (6025) and (6075) and could be later than (6010) and (6013) as well. Determinations OxA-9980 and OxA-10092 that were obtained from the same sample are not in good agreement with each other, failing the Chi-Squared at five per cent of the OxCal R Combine function. Roberts *et al.* (Volume 3, Part 4) have dismissed OxA-9980 as 'too old'. In fact there is evidence that the layer in question is a mixed deposit containing material of different ages. It appears that it is a composite deposit consisting of alluvial material and buried soils. If OxA-9980 relates to an early stage of these processes such as (6089), or even to material from the preceding phase, and OxA-10092 to a later stage such as (6086) these determinations make sense.

The earliest-dated phase in the KOPAL Area is the quarry pits and other possible related activities, dated by four secure determinations. These probably fall within the period of Level Pre-XII.B to IX; these are the levels with more than a 10 per cent likelihood with the highest probability around Level XI. Given

Table 4.12. *KOPAL Area phases.*

KOPAL Area phase	Environment	Dates (cal BC)	Equivalent to main archaeological sequence
Natural lake marl	Permanent lake	Dated elsewhere to *c.* 21,000 to 15,000	Natural lake marl
Organic clay silt (not present in KOPAL Area)	Relatively wet environment	7940 7180 (1 SD) or 8200–7080 (2 SD)	Either earlier than any activity or up to Level Pre-XII.C
Natural backswamp clay formation, part of Lower Alluvium	Wet with seasonal, if not permanent, flooding of KOPAL Area	Dates elsewhere show that this begins around 7550–7050	Earlier than any activity or up to Level Pre-XII.D or later
Quarry pits for clay, marl and deltaic sands; infilled with alluvium and cultural material; possibly other activities	Dry enough for activity, at least seasonally, in KOPAL Area; fills indicate spring flooding	7070–6500 (1 SD) or 7140–6450 (2 SD)	Levels Pre-XII.B to IX
Renewed natural backswamp clay formation, cultural material probably colluvially derived	More permanently flooded landscape	7040–6650 (1 SD) or 7060–6640 (2 SD)	Levels XI to IX
Buried soil horizons and land surfaces; some evidence of *in situ* cultural activity	Significantly drier environment, stable enough for soil development; reduced flooding frequency	6200–5810 (1 SD) or 6220–5740 (2 SD)	Latest levels of Çatalhöyük East (II or later) to early levels of Çatalhöyük West
Upper Alluvium	Wetter again indicating at least seasonal and possibly permanent flooding of KOPAL Area	Dates elsewhere show onset at *c.* 2450	Intermittent use of East mound for burial and other purposes

that the earliest events in the KOPAL sequence are not dated they may be contemporary with earlier phases and there are a number of similarities of material culture that suggest an overlap with Level Pre-XII.D to Pre-XII.B in particular. It appears likely that the quarry pits and other events were a relatively short-lived phenomenon. By comparing the determinations it appears to have lasted between half a century and 500 years; the likelihood is that it spans one or two centuries. The next phase of renewed natural backswamp clay formation is dated by two secure determinations; it appears that this can be equated to Levels XI to IX, with a possibility that they could belong to Level Pre-XII.B to VIII. The latest directly dated phase in the KOPAL Area is the buried soil horizons and land surfaces with some evidence of *in situ* cultural activity. This phase is dated by three secure determinations that are 90 to 300, 270 to 420 and 150 to 300 (68 per cent probability) or 10 to 390, 190 to 510 and 10 to 410 (95 per cent probability) years later than the Level II determination from the mound (P-796). Allowing for the lack of determinations from the latest levels on Çatalhöyük East, plus later erosion, it appears that the formation of the buried soil horizons and land surfaces is either contemporary with or more probably slightly later than the end of occupation at Çatalhöyük East.

One phase of sedimentary activity known from elsewhere in the Çarsamba Fan that was not present in the KOPAL Area, either because it never formed or was later entirely removed, is an organic silty clay deposit. This predates the Lower Alluvium and has been dated by sections and cores at the sites of Kizil Höyük I and Avranthi Höyük (Baird 1996, fig. 3.1) to around 7940 to 7180 cal BC (Roberts *et al.* 1999, 624–5 & table 1) (Table 4.14). If we take the latest determination for the organic silt (Beta-90021) and compare it with the earliest determination from Level Pre-XII.D (OxA-9778) there is a 75.2 per cent probability that the determination from the silt is earlier. The likelihood is that the earliest determination from Space 181 is 200 years earlier to 390 years later (95 per cent probability) or 20 to 90 years later (68 per cent probability). If we compare the same determination from the organic silt to the first well-defined phase, Level Pre-XII.C there is an 89.3 per cent probability that it is earlier and an 8.8 per cent change that it is contained in this phase. This suggests that the earliest occupation at Çatalhöyük is likely to be contemporary with or just later than the organic silt phase and occurs at around the start of the Lower Alluvium. Based on these comparisons the KOPAL Area can be placed in its overall archaeological and sedimentary contexts (Table 4.12).

Table 4.13. *Radiocarbon determinations from the BACH Area and cores.*

Lab. ref.	Area	Unit	Context	Material dated	Age (uncal BP)	SD	δ13C	Age (cal BC) to 1 S.D.	Age (cal BC) to 2 S.D.
PL-980514A	BACH	2215	Building fill	Charred seed	7810	100	–24.7	6810–6470	7050–6450
PL-980559A	BACH	2255	Building fill/midden	Charcoal	7730	80	–24.4	6640–6460	6770–6410
AA-27976	BACH	2255	Building fill/midden	Charcoal	7780	55	–24.6	6650–6500	6750–6460
PL-980559A & AA-27976 combined	BACH	2255	Building fill/midden	Charcoal	7764	45	N/A	6650-6500	6660-6460
PL-980515A	BACH	2256	Building fill	Charred seeds	7620	100	–23.6	6600–6270	6650–6230
PL-980524A	Core ÇH96W	N/A	Unknown	Charcoal	6940	80	–24.4%	5890–5720	5990–5660
AA-27981	Core ÇH96W	N/A	Unknown	Charcoal	7040	40	–24.8%	5990–5840	6000–5800
PL-980524A & AA-27981 combined	Core ÇH96W	N/A	Unknown	Charcoal	7024	37	N/A	5980-5840	5990-5800
Beta-90022	Core ÇH95F	N/A	Unknown	Organic matter	6760	80	–24.2%	5730–5560	5800–5510

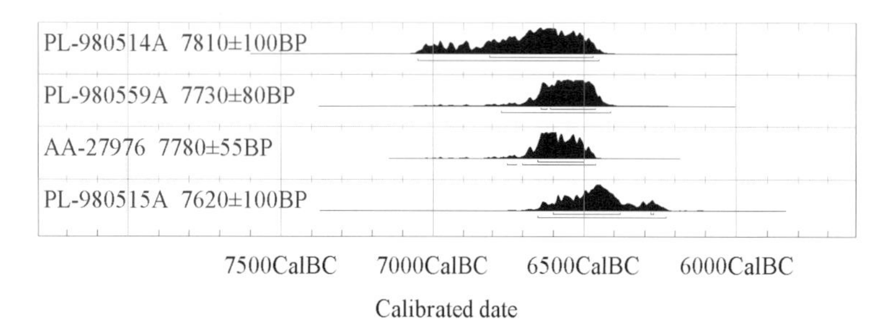

Figure 4.9. *Plot of BACH Area radiocarbon determinations.*

Conclusion

by Craig Cessford

An overall sequence for the absolute intra-site chronology of Çatalhöyük has been constructed. This is mainly based on the South Area sequence, which has been compared to the results from the North and KOPAL Areas. Çatalhöyük was occupied from around 7400 to 7100 cal BC until 6200 to 5900 cal BC for a period of 900 to 1300 years. Buildings were typically occupied for around 45 to 90 years. There is evidence that the length of occupation was longer during the earlier levels and decreased around Level VIA, when it appears that the construction and use of buildings became more dynamic (Düring 2001).

Other areas of Çatalhöyük East

One other excavated area at Çatalhöyük East has been radiocarbon dated, the BACH Area located on the northern eminence close to the North Area (Table 4.13 & Fig. 4.9). Although analysis of this area is ongoing the determinations can be compared to the North Area and the general sequence. Four determinations from this area relate to a period after the latest excavated building in this area had ceased to be occupied. The determinations were initially equated to Levels VI or V and interpreted as later than those available from Building 1 in the North Area (Stevanović & Tringham 1998). The relatively small number of determinations, the use of unidentified charcoal and potential residuality hinder such comparisons. The BACH Area determinations are broadly contemporary with those determinations from the North Area that accurately date the occupation of Building 1, supporting the evidence of artefact typologies, particularly pottery, which suggest that the BACH Area and Building 1 are contemporary at around Levels VIII or VII.

No radiocarbon determinations have been produced for the Summit Area, located next to the South Area, but there is a dendrochronological sequence. This comes from (2662), an ashy burnt fill with a possible fallen or destroyed wooden feature. Stratigraphically the Summit Area can be linked to the main sequence established in the 1960s and equated to Levels V and IV. The end of the dendrochronological sequence falls around Level VII, suggesting either the absence of a large number of tree rings from the recovered charcoal fragments or reuse of the wood.

Çatalhöyük West

Çatalhöyük West has been dated by two determinations on charcoal from the base of core ÇH96W (Göktürk *et al.* 2002) (Table 4.13 & Fig. 4.10). The core encountered *c.* 6.5 m of archaeological deposits overlying *c.* 0.8 m of alluvium. The dated material came from 6.1 to 6.24 m below the mound surface at a height of 999.46 to 999.32 m. The determinations are 340 to 530 or 280 to 430 (68 per cent probability) and 250 to 610 or 200 to 510 (95 per cent probability) years later than the Level II determination from the East Mound. As Levels I and O on the East mound have not been dated and the core may not relate to the earliest occupation of Çatalhöyük West it is probable that there was only a relatively brief interval between the occupation of the two sites, or possibly no interval at all. The determinations from Çatalhöyük West are either just earlier, by up to 70 (68 per cent probability) or 160 (95 per cent probability) years, or more probably slightly later, by up to 290 (68 per cent probability) or 400 years (95 per cent probability), than those from the buried soil horizon and land surface formation in the KOPAL Area. Given the nature of these deposits it is highly probable that the commencement of occupation at Çatalhöyük West is contemporary with the formation of soil horizons and land surfaces in the KOPAL Area.

There is also a determination from a core ÇH95F taken between Çatalhöyük East and West (Roberts *et al.* 1999, table 2; Volume 3, Part 4) (Table 4.13). This is considerably later than Level II of Çatalhöyük East and 70 to 380 or 160 to 330 years later (68 per cent probability) or 20 years earlier to 380 years later or 80 to 420 years later (95 per cent probability) than the basal determinations for Çatalhöyük West. The determination is from an area of permanent standing water into which waste material was dumped and can be assigned to the Early Chalcolithic. This is above an OSL determination of 6496±1777 BP and below one of 5400±1019 BP.

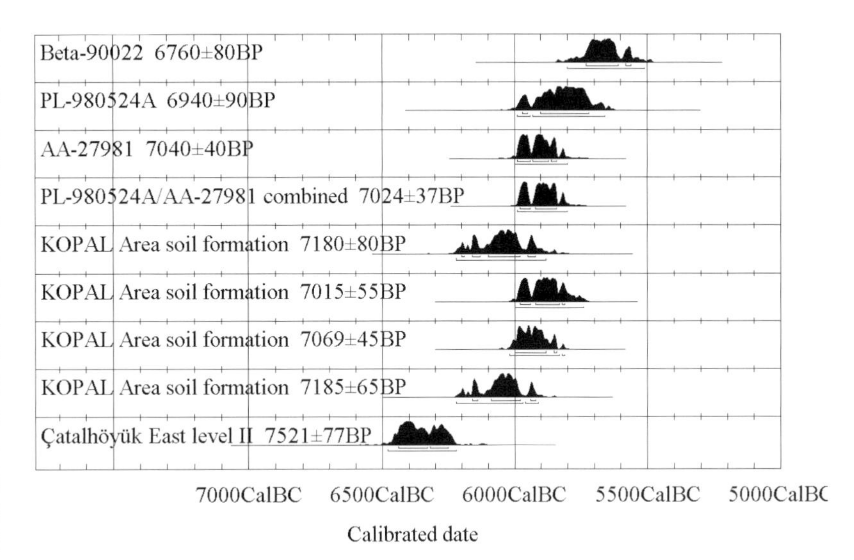

Figure 4.10. *Plot of Çatalhöyük West radiocarbon determinations and other determinations for comparative purposes.*

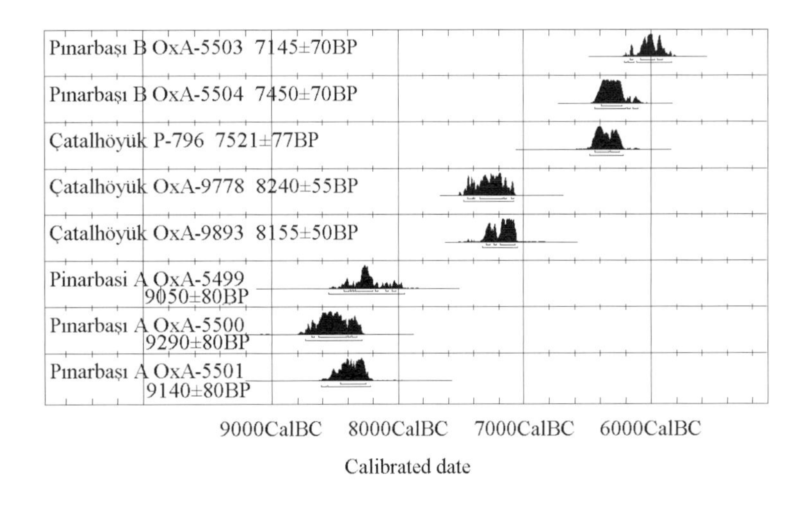

Figure 4.11. *Plot of determinations from Pınarbaşı A and B and earliest plus latest determinations from Çatalhöyük.*

Other central Anatolian sites

Relatively few other central Anatolian Neolithic sites have been radiocarbon dated and in many instances the determinations that exist are problematic, due to lack of precise contextual information and issues relating to the material dated (for a recent discussion see Thissen 2002a,b and Kuniholm & Newton 2002). Unless otherwise stated all comparisons in this and the next section are based on determinations published by Thissen (2002b). For general summaries of sites see Özdoğan & Başgelen (1999) and Yakar (1991) and (1994). It must be remembered that it is the relationship between radiocarbon determinations that are being compared, not the relationships between sites. As the determinations do not necessarily relate to a site's latest or earliest deposits this means that the relationships between sites may be rather different. The main comparison has been with the earliest (OxA-9778, Level Pre-XII.D) and latest (P-796, Level II) secure determinations from the Çatalhöyük sequence. Early sites that can be compared are Canhasan III and Pınarbaşı A on the Konya plain, Aşıklı Höyük, Musular and Kaltepe/Kömürcü in Cappadocia and Suberde.

The earliest determinations from Canhasan III are earlier than Çatalhöyük, but the later determinations overlap with the sequence up to approximately Level XI. Pınarbaşı A (Watkins 1996, 53–5) (Fig. 4.11) is the closest dated site to Çatalhöyük, and analysis shows that the determinations from it are earlier than

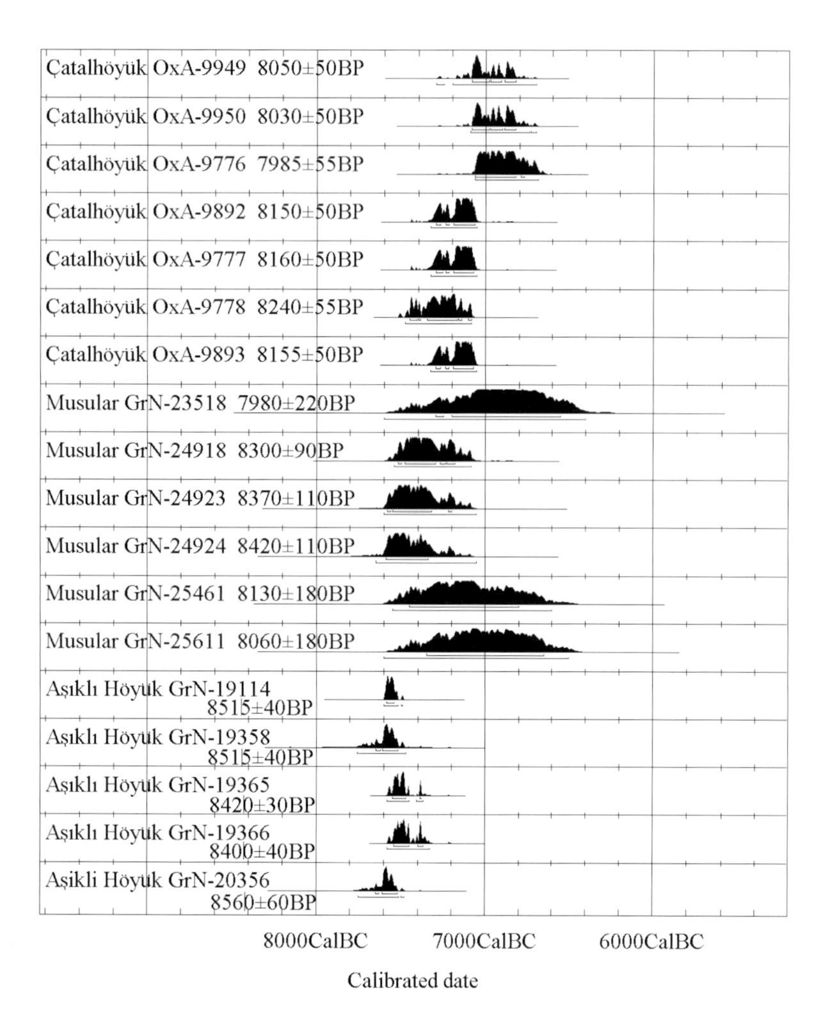

Figure 4.12. *Plot of latest radiocarbon determinations from Aşıklı Höyük, all determinations from Musular and earliest determinations from Çatalhöyük.*

Table 4.14. *Determinations from geomorphological organic silt phase on Çarsamba Fan.*

Site	Lab. ref.	Material dated	Age (uncal BP)	SD	Age (cal BC) to 1 S.D.	Age (cal BC) to 2 S.D.
Kizil Höyük I	Beta-90021	TOM	8330	120	7530–7180	7580–7080
Avranthi Höyük	Beta-90019	TOM	8700	100	7940–7590	8200–7500

Table 4.15. *Time elapsed between latest determinations at Asıklı Höyük and earliest determination from Çatalhöyük.*

Aşıklı Höyük determination	Area of Aşıklı Höyük	Time elapsed to OxA- 9778 [68% probability]	Time elapsed to OxA- 9778 [95% probability]
GrN-20356	East of wall	250 to 440	120 to 530
GrN-19366	SW quadrant	140 to 340	0 to 400
GrN-19365	SW quadrant	160 to 350	30 to 410
GrN-19114	North quadrant	230 to 400	120 to 450
GrN-19358	Deep Sounding	240 to 450	100 to 550

those from Çatalhöyük by 750 to 1300 (95 per cent probability) or 900 to 1200 (68 per cent probability) years.

At Aşıklı Höyük the latest activity at the site is represented by Phases 2C–2A, which covers a wide area on the summit of the mound (Fig. 4.12). Comparison with the latest determinations from each of the excavation areas (GrN-20356, GrN-19366, GrN-19365, GrN-19114 & GrN-19358) indicates that they are all likely to be earlier than Level Pre-XII.D at Çatalhöyük and are certainly no later than this (Table 4.15). Analysis suggests that Aşıklı Höyük was abandoned 100 to 400 years prior to the earliest known occupation at Çatalhöyük. The determinations from Musular (Fig. 4.12), located close to Aşıklı Höyük, suggest that the occupation may predate the earliest deposits at Çatalhöyük, but could overlap with Level Pre-XII.D and possibly Level Pre-XII.C. At the quarry site of Kaltepe/Kömürcü the single determination from the basal deposits is 400 to 1020 (95 per cent probability) or 560 to 890 (68 per cent probability) years earlier than Çatalhöyük. The earliest determination from the upper deposits is 1200 to 1660 (95 per cent probability) or 1330 to 1550 (68 per cent probability) years later than Çatalhöyük. There is a substantial gap between the basal determination and the earliest determination from the upper deposits, of 2800 to 3480 (95 per cent probability) or 3000 to 3330 (68 per cent probability) years. Sourcing indicates that the quarry at Kaltepe/Kömürcü was not a source of obsidian for Çatalhöyük, but it is unclear whether or not it was being exploited contemporary with Çatalhöyük, as exploitation need not have been continuous.

The earliest determinations from Suberde (Bordaz 1973; Duru 1999, 171–2; Yakar 1991, 172–5) may predate the earliest deposits at Çatalhöyük, but could overlap with phase Level Pre-XII.D and conceivably Level Pre-XII.C. The later determinations could reasonably be contemporary with deposits as early as Level Pre-XII.B and might be as late as Level X.

Later sites that can be compared are Canhasan I and Pınarbaşı B on the Konya plain and Erbaba and Kösk Höyük. The earliest determination from Canhasan is likely to be later than Çatalhöyük, although they could conceivably overlap. When comparing it to the Level II determination it is likely to be between 70 years earlier and 510 years later (95 per cent probability) or 100 to 400 years later (68 per cent probability). This sequence is confirmed by recent wiggle-matched dendrochronological sequences for Level 2B, which end at 6484+116/–34 and 5954+116/–34 cal BC (Kuniholm & Newton 2002). Pınarbaşı B (Watkins 1996, 51-3) (Fig. 4.11) is likely to overlap with or be just later than the latest levels at Çatalhöyük. The earliest determination could be as early as Level VI, but is likely to be somewhat later, probably falling in the range of Levels IV to O. When compared to the determination for Level II it is between 160 years earlier and 220 years later (95 per cent probability) or 40 years earlier to 140 years later (68 per cent probability).

Most of the determinations from Erbaba (Duru 1999, 172; Yakar 1991, 148–51) have such wide standard deviations that comparisons are meaningless. The one determination with reasonable standard deviations could fall between Levels XI and VI at Çatalhöyük, with the highest likelihood being towards the middle of this range. The only published date from Kösk Höyük is a wiggle-matched dendrochronological sequence, which belongs to Level 1 and ends at 4911+102/–58 cal BC (Kuniholm & Newton 2002), much later than the Çatalhöyük sequence.

Sites outside central Anatolia

Further afield there are a number of other sites whose determinations can be compared with those from Çatalhöyük. All sites located within three hundred kilometres were compared and sites from outside this were looked at if there were specific reasons. Sites within three hundred kilometres fall into three main groups; the Lake District, the Mediterranean coastal zone and Cyprus. Outside this zone comparisons were made with important groups of sites in southeastern/eastern Anatolia and northwestern Anatolia. It was reluctantly decided not to include comparisons with the northern Levant; this was due to the large number of important sites with radiocarbon determinations in this area, which would have massively expanded the scope of the analysis.

Lake District

Dated sites in the Lake District include Bademağacı, Hacılar, Höyücek and Kuruçay Höyük. The dating of sites in this area by Duru (1999) has recently been challenged by Schoop (2002), who has proposed a shorter chronology that generally agrees with the published determinations. Bademağacı is believed to be contemporaneous with Çatalhöyük. The earliest level dated is 4, with other determinations from Levels 3 and 1. Level 4 overlaps with the later parts of the Çatalhöyük sequence, possibly as early as Level VI, or is later by up to 220 (95 per cent probability) or 110 years (68 per cent probability). Level 3, which has been compared to Çatalhöyük Levels VIII to II on the basis of the obsidian typology (Duru 1999, 182), has a similar possible range to Level 4. Level 1 may overlap with Çatalhöyük Level II, but is more likely to be later by up to 220 (95 per cent probability) or 160 years (68 per cent probability). The Hacılar determinations are rather problematic; some individual determinations appear to be unreliable and the large standard deviations render precise comparisons impossible. The 'aceramic' site, which may in fact possess pottery (Duru 1989), is dated by a single determination, 100 to 970 (95 per cent probability) or 280 to 700 years (68 per cent probability) earlier than the Çatalhöyük sequence. Ceramic Hacılar has more determinations, but the stratigraphically earliest from Level IX (P-314) appears to be too late and the description of the sample processing gives cause for concern (Stuckenrath & Ralph 1965, 145). The determinations from Levels VII and VI appear to be more reliable. The determination from Level VII probably falls between Levels XI and VII at Çatalhöyük, although it could potentially be as early as Level Pre-XII.C. The determination from a Level VI post could be as early as Çatalhöyük Level IX, but could post-date the Çatalhöyük sequence by up to 450 (95 per cent probability) or 260 years (68 per cent probability). A more recent wiggle-matched dendrochronological sequence from this post that ends at 6211+126/–44 cal BC (Kuniholm & Newton 2002) significantly improves our understanding of the dating of this level. The latest conventional radiocarbon determination from this post (A-41604) is unlikely to be earlier than Çatalhöyük Level IV and is likely to be later than the Çatalhöyük sequence by up to 230 (95 per cent probability) or 180 years (68 per cent probability). The determination from a hearth of this level (P-313 & P-313A combined) is likely to be later than the Çatalhöyük sequence, although it could fall in Level II, and could be later by up to 270 (95 per cent probability) or 200 years (68 per cent probability). At Höyücek the Shrine Phase has been dated by six determinations; it lies beneath the undated Sanctuary Phase and over the undated Early Settlements Phase. The earliest determination from the Shrine Phase is likely to fall between Levels VII and II in the Çatalhöyük sequence. The latest determination is likely to be comparable with Çatalhöyük Level III or later and could post date the Çatalhöyük sequence by up to

220 (95 per cent probability) or 180 years (68 per cent probability). This suggests that the Shrine Phase is contemporary with the later levels at Çatalhöyük, the Sanctuary Phase is later than the Çatalhöyük sequence and the Early Settlements Phase may be contemporary with the earlier parts of the Çatalhöyük sequence. The earliest determination from Kuruçay Höyük is likely to be later than the Çatalhöyük sequence, although it could correspond to Level II, and could be up to 270 (95 per cent probability) or 210 years later (68 per cent probability).

The Mediterranean coast

Dated sites on the Mediterranean coast include Karain B, Öküzini and Yumuktepe / Mersin. At Karain B *Archäologischer Horizonte* 13 is probably contemporary with Levels IX to VI at Çatalhöyük. *Archäologischer Horizont* 12 is likely to be contemporary or just later than the latest dated levels at Catalhoyuk, centering around Level II, but could be as early as Level IV whilst *Archäologischer Horizont* 9 to 11 are all likely to be later than Çatalhöyük. At Öküzini the majority of the determinations are much earlier than Çatalhöyük, with only one determination that overlaps with the Çatalhöyük sequence, probably falling within Level Pre-XII.B to VIII. At Yumuktepe / Mersin the determinations from the Early Neolithic Levels XXXIII, XXX and XXIX overlap with the later part of the Çatalhöyük sequence. Level XXXIII at Yumuktepe / Mersin is likely to fall within Levels X to VII at Çatalhöyük and Level XXIX is likely to overlap with Levels VII to II at Çatalhöyük. The earliest determination from the Middle Neolithic Level XXVI could be as early as Level VI in the Çatalhöyük sequence but might postdate the Çatalhöyük sequence. This suggests that the Early Neolithic sequence at Yumuktepe / Mersin spans the middle and later levels at Çatalhöyük and that the middle Neolithic may overlap with the later levels at Çatalhöyük or post date them.

Cyprus

Sites in Cyprus that appear to be contemporary with the early part of the Çatalhöyük sequence include Kalavasos-Tentu, Kissonerga-Mylouthkia and Parekklisha-Shillourokambos (Peltenburg *et al.* 2001b, 38–42 & fig. 3). The earliest Kalavasos-Tentu determinations are earlier than Çatalhöyük, but it is likely that the latest determinations overlap with the earlier part of the Çatalhöyük sequence, possibly as late as Level IX although it is probable that they are earlier than this. Kissonerga-Mylouthkia is likely to overlap with the earlier part of the Çatalhöyük sequence up to Level X. The other determination is unlikely to be later than Level Pre-XII.B. Parekklisha-Shillourokambos could be earlier than the Çatalhöyük sequence, but is likely to overlap with the earlier part of the sequence up to Level XII.

Southeastern/eastern Anatolia

Dated sites in southeastern / eastern Anatolia include Akarçay Tepe, Cafer Höyük, Çayönü, Gritille, Göbekli Tepe, Hallan Çemi, Hayaz Höyük, Kumartepe and Nevalı Çori (see Bıçakçı 1998). Each of the five levels at Akarçay Tepe is dated by a single determination. The earliest Level V is earlier than the Çatalhöyük sequence by 270 to 780 (95 per cent probability) or 400 to 640 years (68 per cent probability). The Level IV determination could be as late as Level Pre-XII.C, but is more likely to be earlier than the Çatalhöyük sequence by up to 420 (95 per cent probability) or 310 years (68 per cent probability). The Level III determination overlaps with the Çatalhöyük sequence between Level Pre-XII.B and VIII. The Level II determination either overlaps with the later part of the Çatalhöyük sequence from Level VII onwards or is later by up to 110 (95 per cent probability) or 20 years (68 per cent probability). The Level I determination could overlap with Level II of the Çatalhöyük sequence, but is likely to be later by up to 270 (95 per cent probability) or 200 years (68 per cent probability). The majority of dates from Cafer Höyük predate the Çatalhöyük sequence, but the latest determinations partially overlap with it. The latest determination from Level III could be earlier than the Çatalhöyük sequence, but is more likely to overlap with it and might be as late as Level IX.

The three latest Neolithic phases at Çayönü are the Cell Building subphase, Cell Building-Large Room Building transition phase and the Large Room Building subphase. The Cell Building subphase is likely to be earlier than the Çatalhöyük sequence, by up 340 (95 per cent probability) or 250 years (68 per cent probability), but could be contemporary with Level Pre-XII.D. The Cell Building-Large Room Building transition phase could begin earlier than the Çatalhöyük sequence, but is more likely to overlap with it between Level Pre-XII.D to IX. The Large Room Building subphase could be as early as Çatalhöyük Level Pre-XII.B and as late as Level VI. There are two determinations from the fill of the *Schlangenpfeilergebäude* (Snake Pillar Building) at Göbekli Tepe. These are 1410 to 1970 or 1260 to 1920 (95 per cent probability) or 1540 to 1840 or 1360 to 1810 years (68 per cent probability) earlier than the Çatalhöyük sequence.

Gritille is dated by a series of determinations from Levels E to B. The determinations from the earliest phases is likely to be 340 to 1030 (95 per cent probability) or 510 to 880 (68 per cent probability) years earlier than the Çatalhöyük sequence. Both of the determinations from Level C are likely to be earlier than the Çatalhöyük sequence, although the later of the two could reasonably be as late as Level Pre-XII.C. The earlier determination is likely to be 80 to 550 (95 per cent probability) or 220 to 460 (68 per cent probability) years earlier than the Çatalhöyük sequence, while the later determination could be up to 440 (95 per cent probability) or 320 (68 per cent probability) years earlier. The Level B determinations suggest that this phase probably overlaps with Level Pre-XII.A to VII of the Çatalhöyük sequence.

The latest determination at Hallan Çemi (Beta-66850) is likely to be 1070 to 2040 (95 per cent probability) or 1380 to 1890 (68 per cent probability) years earlier than the Çatalhöyük sequence. Period 4 at Hayaz Höyük is dated by two determinations, the earlier of these is probably earlier than the Çatalhöyük sequence by up to 330 (95 per cent probability) or 230 years (68 per cent probability), but could be as late as Level Pre-XII.C. The later might also be earlier than the Çatalhöyük sequence, but could be as late as Level IX. Kumartepe is dated by a single determination, which probably falls within Level Pre-XII.A to IX of the Çatalhöyük sequence. There are a number of determinations for Nevalı Çori Levels I/II; the latest is 930 to 1420 (95 per cent probability) or 1060 to 1290 (68 per cent probability) years earlier than the Çatalhöyük sequence. The latest determination from burial 72 at Nevali Çori from Levels III/V is 180 to 690 (95 per cent probability) or 300 to 540 (68 per cent probability) years earlier than the Çatalhöyük sequence.

Northwestern Anatolia

Dated sites in northwestern Anatolia include Hoca Çeşme, Ilıpınar and Menteşe. At Hoca Çeşme there are four determinations from Phase IV. The earliest is likely to fall within Çatalhöyük Levels VIII to VI while the latest could be as early as Level IV, but is likely to be later than the Çatalhöyük sequence by up to 410 (95 per cent probability) or 220 years (68 per cent probability). Phases from II onwards produce determinations later than the Çatalhöyük sequence. Ilıpınar is generally later than Çatalhöyük; the earliest determination is between 20 years earlier and 390 years later (95 per cent probability) or 130 to 290 (68 per cent probability) years later than the Level II determination from Çatalhöyük. The beginning of the Menteşe sequence could fall as earlier as Levels VIII to VI in the Çatalhöyük sequence and it certainly continues after the end of the Çatalhöyük sequence. The earliest published determination (Thissen 2002b, 323) is 10 to 370 (95 per cent probability) or 90 to 280 (68 per cent probability) years later than the Level II determination from Çatalhöyük.

Conclusions

The production of an intra-site chronological sequence for Çatalhöyük based upon a rigorous consideration of all the relevant available evidence has provided a much firmer basis for placing the site in a temporal framework. The sequence produced is still capable of much refinement and development and given the nature and pace of the current fieldwork it is likely that the South Area will remain the key to this framework for the foreseeable future. There are major lacunae in the framework, particularly the lack of determinations from the latest Levels I and O. Given the stratigraphic complexity of the site the provision of more determinations from all levels at the site would be advantageous. More dendrochronological determinations and the linking of the Çatalhöyük dendrochronological sequence to later Anatolian sequences could make an important contribution to the dating of the site.

Acknowledgements

Craig Cessford would like to thank Caitlin Buck for generous assistance with BCal and James Connolly, Hale Göktürk, Danièle Martinoli and especially Laurens Thissen for supplying information on determinations. All the staff of the Oxford Radiocarbon Accelerator Unit have been helpful, particularly Tom Higham, and Anja Wolle provided much support. Many of the determinations were funded by a number of Natural Environment Research Council grants. Christine Hastorf, Julie Near and Andy Fairbairn (archaeobotanical team), Louise Martin and Nerissa Russell (faunal team) and Basak Boz and Theya Molleson (human remains team) facilitated selection of material for dating. Ian Hodder, Shahina Farid, Tristan Carter, Jonathan Last, Naomi Hamilton, Sonya Atalay, Willem Van Neer and Eleni Asouti also provided useful input.

For the dendrochronology results the Malcolm and Carolyn Wiener Laboratory for Aegean and Near Eastern Dendrochronology is supported by the National Science Foundation, the Malcolm H. Wiener Foundation, and individual patrons of the Aegean Dendrochronology Project. We thank the NSF-Arizona AMS Facility and Dr Douglas Donohue at the University of Arizona for running the dates and for their help with their interpretation. We thank Dr Bernd Kromer for his help with the wiggle-match, Carol Griggs, Christine Groneman, Ken Harris and Mary Jaye Bruce for their help in the dendrochronology laboratory and Craig Cessford and Wendy Matthews for their comments.

Chapter 5

Pottery from the East Mound

Jonathan Last

This chapter discusses the pottery recovered during five seasons of excavation (1995–99) on and around the Neolithic East Mound at Çatalhöyük, in three areas: North, South and KOPAL (off-site trench). The report is based almost entirely on visual observations of the pottery (using 4×, 8× and 15× hand lenses); separate reports discuss ceramic petrology and organic residues. For comparative purposes briefer references are made to the pottery from other excavation areas at Çatalhöyük; the BACH Area, which lies adjacent to the North Area and has a directly comparable assemblage, the Summit, which belongs to a later Neolithic level and the Chalcolithic West Mound, material from which is currently being analyzed. The report summarizes the quantitative and metrical data for the North and South assemblages in terms of both typology and deposition / post-depositional processes, discusses general trends across time and space, and suggests interpretive approaches to the Çatalhöyük pottery from the perspectives of function, technology and tradition.

In one sense the existence of this chapter represents a failure because it perpetuates the traditional archaeological division of labour by dealing with a single category of material. While the inhabitants of Çatalhöyük may well have had a concept of 'pottery' as a material category and 'pot-making' as a distinctive practice, the mode of that conceptualization was quite possibly very different from our own. Although I suggest below that other clay technologies at the site (e.g. clay balls, figurines, mud bricks) had little in common with pottery in terms of techniques and recipes, there may have been conceptual links that the discussion here fails to acknowledge. Alternatively, who is to say that pots were not categorized in terms of their appropriate contents or locations (cf. Miller 1985, 180–81), information that currently largely escapes us, as explained below? These issues are raised, if not answered, at points in the text below. Noticing these, I urge the reader to follow them and break away into other chapters, whether in this volume or the synthetic discussions of Volume 6. If I am sure of one thing, it is that any inhabitant of Neolithic Çatalhöyük would say 'Your story treats these objects as if they meant something in their own right. Let me tell you a better one ...'.

Quantification and methodology

Pottery was not abundant in the excavations. The data base for the North and South areas includes 1245 items recovered from stratified contexts but the definitely Neolithic assemblage comprises a total of 1216 potsherds, excluding intrusive later pieces and fragments subsequently judged to be from clay balls or other forms of fired clay. The 1216 catalogued sherds have a mean weight of 17.3 g, giving a total of *c.* 21 kg. The assemblage is divided among the two areas as shown (Table 5.1), with the figures for BACH (up to the 2001 season) and KOPAL Areas included for comparison. This shows that the South Area produced most of the pottery (though from a much greater volume of soil) and had the larger mean sherd weight, reasons for which are discussed below. The North and BACH Areas have assemblages of similar size, but the North area sherds are larger on average. The smaller KOPAL assemblage contains relatively large sherds, which implies this off-site material is not substantially reworked (see Volume 3, Part 4).

Table 5.1. *Quantification by area. * Vessel 6003.S1 counted as one sherd.*

Area	Sherds	Mean wt (g)	Rim EVE	Priority units	Priority units with pottery	Sherd from priority units
South	989 (62.4%)	18.5	11.9	213 (60.0%)	57 (26.8%)	233 (23.6%)
North	227 (14.3%)	11.0	2.4	132 (37.2)	19 (14.4%)	65 (28.6%)
KOPAL	161 (10.2*)*	17.9	(not assessed)	10 (2.8)	0	-
BACH	209 (13.2%)	7.5	1.8		-	-

Of the 355 priority units considered in detail in Volume 3, 76 (20 per cent) produced pottery, totalling 298 sherds (24.5 per cent of the total assemblage). Table 5.1 also shows their distribution among the two areas. The South area priority units were more likely to include pottery but a larger proportion of the North assemblage came from priority units. None of the KOPAL material was associated with the priority units towards the base of the trench. The total rim EVE (Estimated Vessel Equivalent) is approximately 14.3 (assuming sherds for which a diameter could not be measured fit the mean measurement of *c.* 144 mm). This figure implies that the combined North and South Area assemblages represent the physical equivalent of just 14 complete pots (although it in fact comprises small parts of hundreds of vessels). Only in five cases were near-complete vessels (including a full profile) recovered: three from the South Area, one from the KOPAL Area and one from the North Area (see below, Vessels 1–5). Because of the small quantities of pottery involved, every sherd could be analyzed individually in terms of the following variables (those marked * not recorded for KOPAL):

- Fabric: inclusion type, size, sorting, and density hardness;
- Firing: exterior, interior, and core colour firing flaws;
- Form and manufacture: wall thickness, surface treatment, evidence for manufacturing technique (e.g. coil, slab breaks), vessel shape, rim or base shape, profile and diameter, lug presence, form and size;
- Use: presence of sooting, use-wear;
- Breakage, deposition & formation processes: sherd size & weight, *rim & base percentages, *abrasion, joins.

Sequence and dating

South and North Areas

The small number of sherds and their distribution across numerous spaces and phases means there is little opportunity to study patterning and variability within individual assemblages. However, the vertical coverage of the excavations (Levels VI to XII and Levels Pre-XII) allows an overview of the introduction and development of ceramic technology through time. The key features, which indicate an essentially simple and conservative tradition of potting followed by a more developed technology, can be summarized as follows:

- a conservatism of form, the entire assemblage comprising simple bowl and jar shapes, with an absence or scarcity of plastic elements such as lugs, handles and feet (the relatively high number of lugs in Mellaart's Level VI assemblage (see Last 1996) is not paralleled in the North Area finds).
- an absence of decoration, with surface treatments restricted to smoothing, burnishing and possibly slips — though some of the burnishes are rather fine and careful.
- developments in technology over time, with improvements visible in manufacture (perhaps related to a change in clay sources) and firing. These seem to be related to changes in the use and quantity of pottery on the site, principally occurring between Levels VIII and VI (Level VII forming a transitional assemblage).
- chronological trends in fabrics, with vegetable (straw) tempering succeeded by mineral tempering, also during Level VII and no doubt related to the other technological developments. Small quantities of non-vegetable fabric types in the early levels may show a limited degree of experimentation before this time.

The relative dating of the sequence has been constructed in different ways for the different areas. The various spaces in the South Area are tied stratigraphically into Mellaart's building levels. In contrast, the levels assigned to spaces in the North (and BACH) Areas are derived from the pottery typology itself. The unfortunately small quantities from Building 5 (North Area) correspond best with Level VII assemblages in the South Area, which implies that Building 1 (North Area) and the very similar Building 3 (BACH Area) belong to Level VI (they could, on their own, equally well be Level V). The system of levels devised by Mellaart must be treated with some caution when applied to other areas of the site, since it represents stratigraphic abstractions from a continuous process of ceramic and occupational development, and does not imply a precise synchronization between different areas and spaces. Nevertheless, one might imagine that trends in one area of the site were contemporary (at least in archaeological terms) with trends in another. According to Cessford (Chapter 4), the most likely conclusion from the radiocarbon dates is that Buildings 5 and 1 broadly correspond to Levels IX to VII. This is slightly earlier than the pottery suggests, but the discrepancy is not major given the inherent difficulties.

Table 5.2 shows that nearly half the total assemblage belongs to Level VIII (Midden Space 115 and infill of Spaces 116 and 117). Less than 10 per cent belongs to the early levels below Level VIII, although a higher proportion of these came from priority units and therefore have full contextual data available.

KOPAL Area

The finds from the upper levels of the mound and the succeeding period, represented in this report by the KOPAL Area assemblage, but also including the earlier (Level IV–III) Summit Area assemblage, suggest the later tradition was more innovative and dynamic, with developments over time in vessel shapes and sizes, handle and base forms, surface treatment and decoration, all presaging features of Early Chalcolithic (West Mound) assemblages, though clearly derivative of the Level VI tradition. The KOPAL Area material also suggests there was a greater variety of fabrics at the end of the Neolithic.

Table 5.2. *Quantification by level (North, South and KOPAL). * Vessel 6003.S1 counted as one sherd.*

Level	Sherds	Mean wt (g)	Rim EVE	Priority units with pottery	Sherd from priority units
KOPAL	161* (11.9%)	17.9	(not assessed)	-	-
I–V	-	-	-	-	-
VI	239 (17.6%)	10.1	3.1	18 (24.3%)	64 (26.8%)
VII	169 (12.4%)	11.9	1.7	11 (14.9%)	36 (21.3%)
VIII	672 (49.5%)	19.3	7.6	26 (35.1%)	144 (21.4%)
IX	80 (5.9%)	28.0	1.6	10 (13.5%)	34 (42.5%)
X	32 (2.4%)	10.5	0.2	7 (9.5%)	15 (46.9%)
XI	3 (0.2%)	20.8	-	1 (1.4%)	2 (66.7%)
XII & Pre-XII	2 (0.1%)	1.8	-	1 (1.4%)	1 (50.0%)

The KOPAL Area assemblage is dated to the end of the Neolithic/transitional Chalcolithic by the radiocarbon dates from this area (later than any dates from the East Mound) (Chapter 4). The majority of the pottery is associated with a buried land surface which has been dated *c.* 6200 to 5700 cal BC, about 1000 years later than the earliest pottery from the South Area. The main features of the assemblage are necked jars and S-profile bowl forms typical of the later Neolithic (Level IV and above) or Early Chalcolithic, a proportion of red-slipped surfaces and the presence of vegetable inclusions in some cases (about 30 per cent of the large assemblage from (6020)). While the first two features suggest an assemblage contemporary with the upper levels on the East Mound, the third is more problematic, since these fabrics, with a mixture of mineral and vegetable temper (see below) are not consistently represented in any stratified assemblages from the site. The radiocarbon dates also suggest the assemblage dates to the period when the East Mound was abandoned, since Level II ended *c.* 6200 to 6100 cal BC (Chapter 4). However, none of the painted wares associated with the Early Chalcolithic West Mound were found; samples from cores possibly contemporary with the base of the West Mound occupation are dated around 6000 to 5800 cal BC, but we do not yet know anything of the material culture of these levels.

Ceramic technology

Fabrics

A pottery assemblage is usually divided into wares distinguished by a suite of shared characteristics relating to clay sources, temper, manufacture, forms, surface treatments and firing. In prehistoric societies with a household level of production, however, it is rare to find canonical wares or normative categories (cf. Baird 1991; Peltenburg 1991). Instead we should imagine that potters drew selectively on the total knowledge base available within the community, influenced by family traditions, what they were taught and personal preferences. This selective application and transmission of tradition and knowledge is perhaps best captured by Bourdieu's (1990) concept of habitus.

At Çatalhöyük there is great uniformity in many of these characteristics, both over time and between different parts of the site. Traditions of forming, decorating and firing pots were stable and long-lived although, as mentioned, an important transformation occurs around Level VII. The primary means of differentiation, both within and between an assemblage, is based on fabrics and the primary (visual) definition of fabric is by inclusions or temper. Three broad fabric groups have been identified, which can sometimes be broken down into sub-groups or fabrics (though these often appear to represent abstractions from a continuum of variability). In general, petrographic analysis confirms these groups, although not the attribution of every individual sherd, principally because a number of 'uniques' were identified (for details see CD). The correlation between my fabric groups and the thin-section results (sample of 50) is shown in Table 5.3.

South Area

Group 1

The earliest pottery on the site (Pre-Level VII) is predominantly vegetable-tempered. The density of organics, which survive mainly as elongated voids within the fabric (occasionally as charcoal or phytoliths), was recorded as well as their mean and maximum size, and any additional mineral inclusions, principally quartz, calcite and what looks like mica, which probably reflect natural components of the clay (see CD). Descriptive

Table 5.3. *Correlation between visual and petrographic fabric groups.*

	Petrographic group			
	I	II	III	Unique
Visual group				
1	24	-	-	5
2	1	6	-	1
3	-	2	8	3

Table 5.4. *Organic-tempered fabrics (Group 1), South Area. *Sherds taken for residue analysis and not examined in detail.*

Fabric	Sherds	Mean weight (g)	Mean thickness (mm)
1a	461 (62.7%)	18.6	10.0
1b	64 (8.7)	19.2	10.2
1c	192 (26.1)	17.8	9.7
1d	12 (1.6)	46.7	9.8
1e	6 (0.8)	84.1	13.2
1*	13	17.8	9.6
Total	**748**	**19.5**	**10.0**

categories follow PCRG (1995). Typically in assemblages of this period, chaff or straw represents 5 to 25 per cent of the volume, with a good deal of variation (Vandiver 1987, 17). Although it proved difficult to isolate distinct fabrics, it was possible to see — within a general continuum — differences in the density of vegetable and mineral inclusions and in fabric colour (though the latter may largely reflect firing conditions and can vary across a vessel or even a sherd).

The major fabric (1a) has dark grey cores, common organics, usually in the size range *c.* 1–5 mm, and sparse fine mineral. Sometimes the sherd has a sandy feel, suggesting a higher mineral content at a microscopic scale. A second fabric (1b) has greater densities of visible mineral, sometimes slightly coarser. A third (1c) has lighter coloured (greyish-brown, brown or buff) cores, sometimes with lower densities of organics than 1a. Minor fabrics include a few sherds with unusually coarse mineral grits (1d) or vegetable matter (1e). The relative proportions of these fabrics within the assemblage are shown in Table 5.4. They show little difference in terms of mean weights or thickness, although the combined figures for 1b, 1d and 1e (weight: 29.5 g; thickness: 10.4 mm) suggest sherds with coarser inclusions tend to come from larger and/or thicker-walled vessels. A further issue is whether the different fabrics have chronological significance. Dividing the assemblage broadly by level (Fig. 5.1) we see that proportionately more of the 1b and 1d assemblages come from the earlier Levels XI to IX, compared with the 'standard' fabric 1a. While recipes were generally conservative and stable, there is some evidence for slightly more variability in the

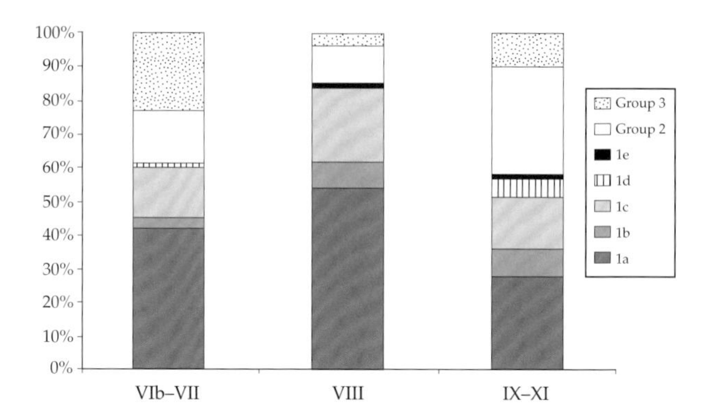

Figure 5.1. *Fabric proportions by level, South Area (partially-complete vessels counted as one sherd).*

lower levels; this also fits with the relatively high proportion of non-Group 1 fabrics in these levels (see below), compared with the benchmark of the large Level VIII assemblage. This pattern may indicate an early period of experimentation before a standard fabric became predominant. Then in Level VII, with the rise of a new type of mineral-gritted pottery, there is a relative decline in the grittier organic-tempered fabric 1b.

The organic matter within the pottery is generally poorly sorted but relatively fine, varying in size from <1 mm to 5 mm on average (particle sizes of 10 mm or more were noted in 28 cases, with a maximum of 25 mm). It appears to be chopped grass (monocotyledon stems) and the inclusion of carbonized seeds of wheat and barley in at least 11 sherds suggests the temper may be cereal straw (Volume 4, Chapter 8). Rye (1981, 34) suggests that use of this type of temper may be more common where pottery making is a seasonal activity, coinciding with the end of harvesting, but it also has specific technological characteristics that might have been deliberately selected (see below). The Group 1 fabrics also occasionally contain other inclusions that may provide information about the nature of the added material, including rodent bones (2 cases) and several small snail shells (27 cases). While these suggest the temper was stored in such a manner that small fauna occasionally got into the material, shells were also found in another eleven sherds of different groups (a similar proportion of *c.* four per cent), not all of which contained organic matter. They may therefore have been present in the clay or water, rather than the temper.

Group 2

The thick-walled vessels of the early levels are not all primarily organic-tempered. A number of sherds contain predominantly fine mineral inclusions (sand), sometimes mixed with a little vegetable matter

(Group 2). These sherds are generally grey-brown or light brown in fabric colour (just 19 per cent are described as dark grey throughout), which may reflect the sparse/absent organic matter rather than a different clay source. Petrographic analysis suggests these differ from Group 1 mainly by the absence of straw. Two subgroups are distinguished: fabric 2a has sparse organic matter, while 2b has rare or no organics. In general the Group 2 fabrics resemble those of the clay balls, suggesting some overlap in the two clay technologies, although the latter never contain organic temper.

Although wall thickness is generally comparable to Group 1 there is a trend towards thinner walls in some of the Group 2 sherds, shown by the slightly lower mean weights and thicknesses for the less organic 2b (Table 5.5). The figures for mean sherd weight for fabric 2a are slightly inflated by the inclusion of large sherds from a near-complete vessel found in Space 182 (Vessel 3), but even without this pot the mean sherd weight is *c.* 21.4 g and thickness 11.4 mm, still larger than for Group 1. The distribution of these sherds through the South area indicates this Group is a relatively consistent minor presence in the assemblage. Figure 5.2 shows a slight increase in the proportion of Group 2 sherds from Levels VIII to VII, although the highest number, proportionately, comes from the small, pre-Level VIII assemblage. This suggests the Group 2 assemblage does not simply represent a transition towards the mineral-tempered fabrics of Level VI and above. However, the slightly raised proportion of 2b in Level VII compared to Level VIII may indicate that some of the sherds assigned to this fabric in the later level are actually part of the new ceramic types (Group 3; see below). Although the inclusions are generally fine and mixed, occasionally specific minerals are found which may be deliberately selected. In particular, Vessel 3 contains rare but consistently present, very coarse, rounded calcareous inclusions (see below).

Table 5.5. *Sand-tempered fabrics (Group 2), South Area.*

Fabric	Sherds	Mean weight (g)	Mean thickness (mm)
2a	53	30.6	11.1
2b	88	16.1	8.6
Total	141	21.5	9.5

Table 5.6. *Mineral-tempered fabrics (Group 3), South Area. *Probably all same vessel.*

Fabric	Total	Description
b	13 (23.6%)	Common fine/medium white/buff, reddish and quartz grits
f	9 (16.4%)	Moderate fine to coarse mainly quartz grits
n	8* (14.5%)	Common medium/coarse clear, white and red grits
l	6 (10.9%)	Dense grey fabric with sparse/moderate fine white grits
k	5 (9.1%)	Common medium/fine whitish grits
j	4 (7.3%)	Moderate fine to coarse white/buff grits
o	4 (7.3%)	Moderate fine/medium white/buff, reddish and quartz grits
d	3 (5.5%)	Sparse fine/medium mainly white grits
a	1 (1.8%)	Moderate fine mainly white mineral grits
c	1 (1.8%)	Sparse/moderate medium/coarse white and quartz grits
m	1 (1.8%)	Moderate medium/coarse white and red-brown grits

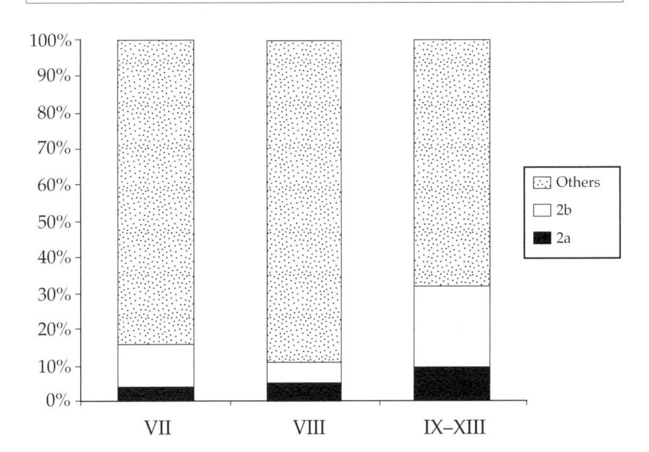

Figure 5.2. *Sand-tempered fabrics (Group 2), South Area (partially-complete vessels counted as one sherd).*

Group 3

Thin-walled, dark-faced, mineral-gritted fabrics are characteristic of the upper levels on the mound (especially Levels VI–V). However, they are also found earlier and 96 sherds of this type were recovered from the South Area. These include a group of 22 refitting sherds (Vessel 1) from Space 160, the only space of Level VIB in this area. The Group 3 sherds are distinguished from fabric 2b by the predominance of coarser (medium/coarse) grits, on average, as well as by thickness and colour. The mean thickness is 5.9 mm and mean sherd weight 9.0 g, lower values than for both Groups 1 and 2. Fabric colours are predominantly dark or reddish (58 per cent of sherds fall into these groups).

The Group 3 sherds can be divided into a number of fabrics based on inclusion size, density and type (Table 5.6; not including Vessel 1 and other joining sherds). Quartz seems to be the main mineral represented in the (visible) temper, but petrographic analysis has shown the presence of volcanic minerals, such as feldspars, amphiboles and hornblendes (see CD). In many cases differences between the fabrics identified visually are relatively minor, so they probably once again represent a continuum of variation. However, the main fabric (3b) stands out as particularly 'gritty' while fabrics 3l and 3n are also distinctive. The last of

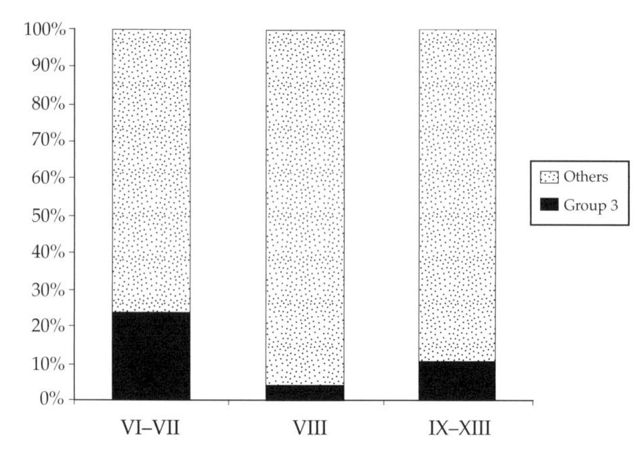

Figure 5.3. *Mineral-tempered fabrics (Group 3), South Area (counting Vessel 1 as one sherd).*

these comprises a group of eight sherds, some refitting, from Space 182 of Level IX; they include abundant, well-sorted, relatively coarse mixed grits. The sherds appear to form the rounded base junction of a vessel probably of simple bowl form, with some possible sooting on the interior surface. With the calcareous-tempered vessel mentioned above (Vessel 3) also from this space, there are signs of experimentation in fabrics (or even importing of pots) in the early levels of the site. Trading of fineware pots is indeed attested in Neolithic contexts in the northern Levant (Moore 1995) and the unusual Group 3n vessel is the best candidate from the early levels at Çatalhöyük.

The distribution of the Group 3 sherds through the different levels is shown (Fig. 5.3). Unlike Group 2 these fabrics show a very low presence prior to Level VII (less than four per cent if we exclude the vessel from Space 182), followed by a sudden increase in that level. Nearly all of the Level VIII Group 3 sherds (87 per cent) come from the midden Space 115, which may have accumulated over a lengthy period. While the general trend over time is clear, however, details of the distribution suggest the proportions of Group 3 fabrics are not simply related to chronology: within Space 115, for instance, they represent a higher proportion of the earlier phase B assemblage than the later phase A.

Group 4

A single sherd from Space 160 (Level VIB) was tempered predominantly with grog. The presence of grog has previously been noted in petrographic thin sections from the North Area (see CD).

North Area

Through Level VII changes occur in many aspects of the pottery, not only in terms of fabrics but also manufacturing techniques (seen in e.g. vessel wall thickness), firing (fabric and surface colours) and forms. I suggest below that these changes relate to technological advances opening a new range of possible functions for pottery at Çatalhöyük. Level VI and VII assemblages were encountered in both North and South Areas, but the larger Level VI assemblage comes from the North Area.

Table 5.7. *Organic-tempered (Group 1) and sand-tempered (Group 2) fabrics, North Area.*

	Group 1	Group 2
Mean weight (g)	14.8	15.8
Mean thickness (mm)	9.3	7.6

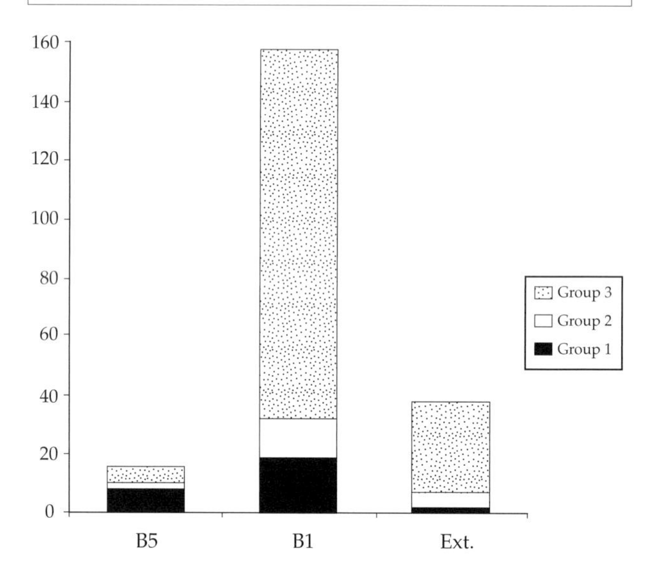

Figure 5.4. *Organic and sand-tempered sherds (Groups 1–2), North Area.*

Groups 1 and 2

Group 1 material from the North Area comprises 28 sherds (12 per cent of the total), with another 21 sherds (9 per cent) assigned to Group 2. The Group 1 and 2 material is distributed between the three main assemblages (Building 5, Building 1 and external spaces) as follows (Table 5.7; Fig. 5.4). The proportion of Group 1 sherds in the small Building 5 assemblage is similar to that in the Level VII assemblage from the South Area (see Fig. 5.1), suggesting that the North sequence is broadly equivalent to Levels VII–VI. It is unclear whether the numerically larger (but proportionately much smaller) assemblage in Building 1 (nearly all from Phase B1.1) can be considered residual, or whether Group 1 material was still in use in Level VI. Building 3 in the BACH area has produced a similar proportion of Group 1 sherds (8.4 per cent). However, mean sherd weight in Building 1 is low compared to the South Area (although thickness is also somewhat lower) and abrasion is significantly higher (4.6 to 4.8

for Building 1 against 3.5 to 3.7 for the South Area — see below for explanation of abrasion 'scoring'), which might suggest they are residual.

Group 3

Regardless of the significance of the Group 1–2 sherds, it is Group 3, mineral-gritted sherds which predominate in Building 1 and the external spaces. These are broken down by fabric in Table 5.8. Compared to the South Area we see a greater proportion of the more sparsely tempered, primarily quartz-gritted fabrics 3c, 3e and especially 3f, but a lower proportion of 3b, 3j and 3k; fabrics 3l and 3n are not found in the North Area while 3d and 3o retain similar proportions. The rise of 3f and decline of 3b in particular suggest that the average Group 3 sherd in the later levels is less gritty with a mineral component more focused on quartz. This table does not include 20 sherds found in Building 1 forming a large part of a pot (Vessel 4) whose fabric resembles 3f but also includes a little vegetable matter. Organics may occur as sparse or accidental inclusions in Group 3 material: they are found in nine South Area sherds (nine per cent) and two other North area sherds (one per cent), the trend therefore being as one might expect.

Table 5.8. *Mineral-tempered fabrics (Group 3), North Area.*

Fabric	Total	Description
f	54 (40.6%)	moderate fine to coarse mainly quartz grits
e	16 (12.0%)	sparse fine to coarse mainly quartz grits
c	13 (9.8%)	sparse/moderate medium/coarse white and quartz grits
o	13 (9.8%)	moderate fine/medium white/buff, reddish and quartz grits
d	11 (8.3%)	sparse fine/medium mainly white grits
b	10 (7.5%)	common fine/medium white/buff, reddish and quartz grits
a	5 (3.8%)	moderate fine mainly white mineral grits
j	4 (3.0%)	moderate fine to coarse white/buff grits
g	2 (1.5%)	sparse/moderate fine to coarse quartz and reddish grits
h	2 (1.5%)	common fine white angular quartz
i	1 (0.8%)	moderate fine to coarse mainly quartz grits with sparse fine to coarse calcareous grits
k	1 (0.8%)	common medium/fine whitish grits
p	1 (0.8%)	sparse/moderate very fine grits only

KOPAL Area

Above Level VI there is little sign of substantial changes in inclusions, although no detailed analysis has been undertaken. The basic recipe, once accepted, appears to have been relatively stable. The pottery from the Summit Area is generally tempered with relatively sparse and fine mineral grits like groups 3e–f. However, there is a trend from grey fabric colours and dark surfaces to buff fabrics and buff/brown/red surfaces, which may partly reflect changes in firing technology but probably also relates to the use of different clay sources, containing varying amounts of iron and organic inclusions. Future petrographic investigations may provide more detail about sources and inclusion types. The principle of two tempering traditions at the site, with a relatively rapid transition around Level VII, seems clear, however.

It is only at the end of the Neolithic and in the Early Chalcolithic that things once again change substantially. On the West Mound we see a greater variety of recipes and an emphasis on iron-rich calcareous fabrics, which fire pink and contain fine white inclusions. Prior to that, the poorly-understood transition between the two mounds at Çatalhöyük may be enlightened by the assemblage from upper deposits within the KOPAL Area. For the purposes of this discussion all the ceramic material from KOPAL Area deposits not containing Classical pottery are treated as if a single phase. The KOPAL Area sherds are still predominantly quartz-tempered with a similar mix of other mineral inclusions to the North Area. Whereas the majority of the North Area sherds (*c.* 65 per cent) contain some coarse or very coarse inclusions, among the KOPAL Area sherds that falls to 47 per cent. On the other hand, a few sherds contain much coarser material than the North Area norm, with grits up to 5 mm in size. There are also a few more specialized fabrics, such as a group containing primarily conglomerate-type grains. This all suggests that a greater variety of recipes was in use, and perhaps reflects a broader range of vessel sizes and/or functions. Supporting this is a greater mean vessel wall thickness in the KOPAL Area (7.8 mm) and the presence of part of a very large pot (Fig. 5.26:3). Miniature vessels are also well represented in the later levels of the East Mound, but not among this group.

The most significant feature of the KOPAL Area fabrics, however, is the reappearance of organic inclusions, which are found in greater or lesser amounts in 47 per cent of the sherds (they are often rare but in 28 per cent they appear in sparse/moderate quantities and in five sherds seem to be the predominant inclusion). However, the fabrics do not generally resemble those from the South Area, which contain dense organic matter and little mineral. Moreover, mean thickness for these sherds is 8.0 mm, little more than the KOPAL Area average and a lot less than the Group 1 South Area mean of *c.* 10 mm (Table 5.4). This is not a reappearance/survival of an old technology, but signs of experimentation and diversification, with recipes that can perhaps be understood in technological terms (see below).

Table 5.9. *Body sherd thickness in mm by level.*

	Level						
Thickness	**VI**	**VII**	**VIII**	**VIII–IX**	**IX**	**X–XII**	**Overall**
Mean	5.7	8.1	10.1	9.8	9.3	8.4	8.4
Minimum	1.5	3.0	3.0	2.5	4.0	2.0	1.5
Maximum	18.5	18.0	26.0	20.5	19.0	15.5	26.0

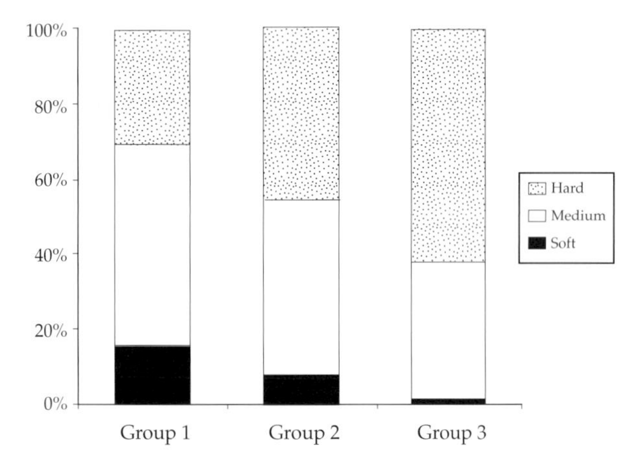

Figure 5.5. *Ceramic hardness by fabric group.*

Forming techniques

All the Neolithic pottery at Çatalhöyük is handmade. Direct evidence for manufacturing techniques is rare, but occasional breaks along joints are evident on the Group 1 sherds, both at the junction of base and wall (e.g. Figs. 5.20:2–3) and just below the rim (e.g. Figs. 5.22:4, 5.17:4,6). While coil-building is probably the most common means of producing handmade vessels world-wide it has been suggested that Neolithic communities in the Near East used a method termed 'sequential slab construction' for making chaff- or vegetable-tempered wares (Vandiver 1987). The nearest site to Çatalhöyük with evidence for this technique is Mersin (Vandiver 1987, 20). The method of examination used to find these slabs was xeroradiography, which has not been attempted here. Although the use of slabs cannot be ruled out at Çatalhöyük, the breaks seen among the South Area assemblage (and Mellaart's finds) are consistent with coil-building. Moreover, Vandiver's suggestion that heavily fibre-tempered clay cannot be coiled may be contradicted from current evidence in the area around Çatalhöyük, where straw-tempered tandir ovens are made from coils (though of course these are very large in diameter). There are also occasional examples of small pinch-pots (Fig. 5.17:5) and pots other than vessels, such as a pedestal-like object (Fig. 5.17:7).

The most obvious trend over time in the North and South Areas in terms of forming pots is towards thinner walls, as shown below (Table 5.9). The point of transition is once again Level VII, coincident with the changes in forms and temper. More variety may be apparent again in the early levels, which seem to show a gradual increase in wall thickness, but this is hampered by a small sample size (30 sherds of Levels X to XII). The implication of the suite of technological and typological changes is discussed as a whole below, but it may be that the Level VI pots were thinned out using a technique like paddle and anvil, which would not have been necessary (or possible?) with the earlier vessels. In the KOPAL assemblage, as mentioned, there may be a greater variety of vessel sizes accounting for a rise in mean wall thickness. There is also some evidence for further technological advance, with two examples of mat-impressed bases, suggesting the vessel could have been turned on a surface during the manufacturing process.

Firing technology

The majority of vessels throughout the early levels at Çatalhöyük (pre-Level VII) appear to have been fired in relatively uncontrolled conditions and at low temperatures; petrographic analysis of mineral changes confirms the non-uniform nature of firing, but also shows that temperatures sometimes reached as high as 1100°C (see CD). About 70 per cent of South Area Group 1 sherds have dark grey cores (where the organics have not been completely burnt out) indicative of a short firing time and about 28 per cent have fire-clouding or severe mottling on exterior surfaces. Both features are associated with open firing (Gibson & Woods 1990, figs. 28–9). If we take only larger fragments, above *c.* 50 mm in length, over 40 per cent of Group 1 sherds show variation in exterior surface colour, compared with just 20 per cent of Group 3.

The more even firing of the later Group 3 pottery reflects the suite of technological changes occurring around Level VII. The reduction in mottling suggests a greater control of air flow during the firing process and perhaps a switch from open or bonfire firing to closed ovens or even purpose-made kilns; Todd (1976, 79) suggests that Mellaart found two kilns in houses of Level VI. Some mottled colours remain, however, including Vessel 4 from Building 1. The later pottery is also more highly fired, best shown by the general hardness of the fabric (since the lower quantities of organic matter would anyway reduce the number of dark cores), as represented in Figure 5.5. The categories reflect in general terms the resistance to scratching by fingernail of the fabric (not the surfaces which, if burnished, are often much harder): soft fabrics scratch with minimal pressure, medium with some pressure and hard with firm pressure or not at all. The graph shows a clear trend towards harder fabrics in Group 3, although a substantial number of Group 1 sherds are 'hard' and with the addition of a surface burnish would have been fairly robust.

Surface colour is, like fabric colour, a reflection of firing conditions and clay types, here perhaps sometimes complicated by the addition of a slip (see below). Surface colours also show a trend over time with a change around Level VII. The early pottery is generally rather light-faced (buff, mid-brown or light to mid-grey). Later on, the post-Level VII pottery is overwhelmingly dark-faced (dark grey, dark brown or grey-brown). Strongly oxidized surfaces (red, pink or orange) are rare and when they do occur may reflect refiring of sherds (e.g. a group in Space 187 of Building 1). After Level V in the sequence, however, lighter colours become more common again, especially buff and mid-brown. Also in the later Neolithic deposits, including the KOPAL Area assemblage, red surfaces were deliberately achieved by the addition of a slip.

A more detailed analysis of surface colours (exterior and interior) for the South Area shows some variation between fabrics (Fig. 5.6). Since surface colours can vary greatly across a single vessel, as mentioned, more detailed analysis (e.g. by Munsell shades) would probably be inappropriate. Here 'dark' means dark grey or very dark brown, 'medium' mid- to dark brown, and 'light' buff, yellowish or light brown. The graph shows that compared with the predominant medium/light colours of Group 1, the Group 2 sherds show a divergence with roughly even numbers of dark and light surfaces. The later Group 3 wares then show a greater emphasis on dark surfaces combined with a significant number of reddish-brown shades. The material from the Level VIII midden (Space 115) and the North Area Level VI house (Building 1) were compared in more detail, breaking down exterior and interior values (Fig. 5.7). The figures show that while many shades are equally represented in both assemblages there are far more dark brown surfaces in Building 1 at the expense of previously prominent light-brown colours. Reddish surfaces are also more common, as in the Group 3 material in the South Area. Mixed and mottled colours account for 30 per cent of the earlier exteriors, but less than 20 per cent in Building 1 (the difference is less marked for the interiors). In general interior surfaces are more likely to be dark grey (in both assemblages) and less likely to be mixed/mottled.

The KOPAL Area assemblage once again shows a different pattern (Fig. 5.8). As with other aspects of the assemblage, a greater variability is the key factor, with an even distribution of surface colours among which are a relatively high proportion of reds (both slipped and unslipped) and oranges — the former more common on exteriors and the latter on interiors. Compared with the earlier assemblages both dark grey interiors and mottled/uneven firing are much reduced.

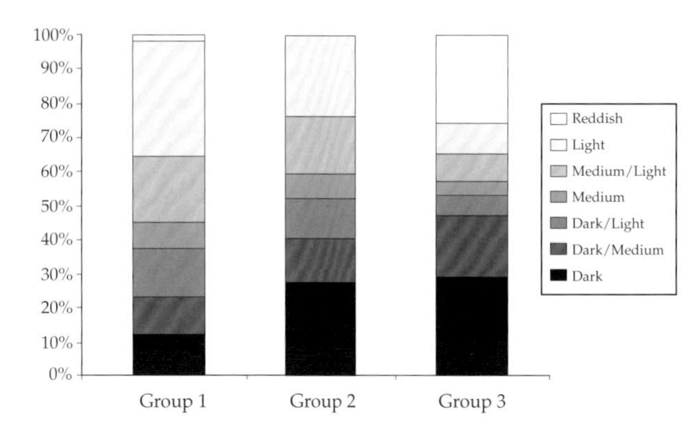

Figure 5.6. *Surface colours (exterior and interior combined), South Area.*

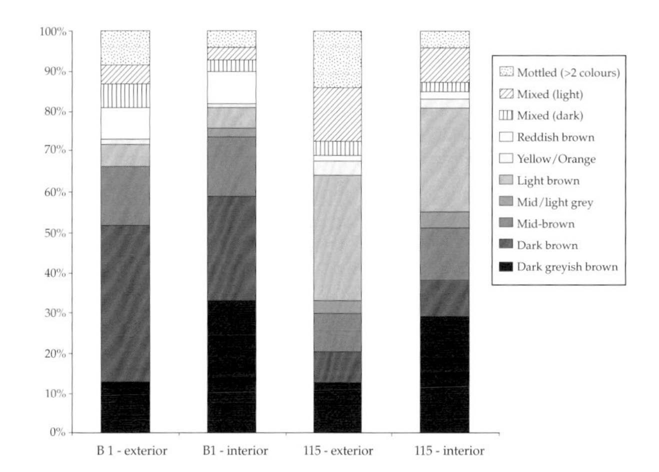

Figure 5.7. *Surface colours, Building 1 and Space 115.*

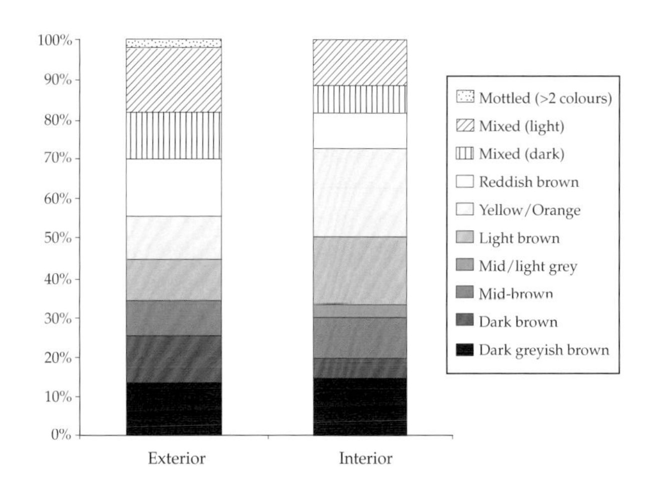

Figure 5.8. *Surface colours, KOPAL Area.*

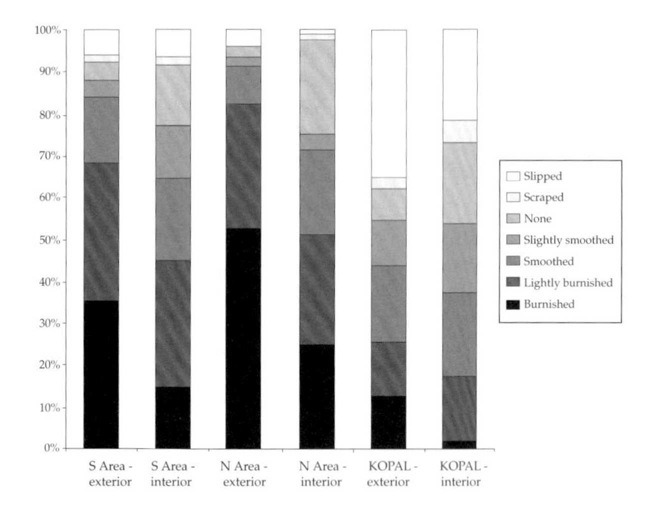

Figure 5.9. *Surface treatment, all areas.*

Surface finish and decoration

Surface finish on the South and North Area pottery is largely restricted to burnishing or smoothing (the difference essentially being the presence of a visible lustre); highly-polished pieces are rare, as are rough, untreated surfaces. In a few cases interior surfaces were finely scraped, presumably to thin the vessel wall (this is a common surface treatment in the Early Chalcolithic). Formal decoration (incision, painting, plastic) is entirely absent in both areas. However, it may be inappropriate to relegate the burnishing to a mere 'surface treatment': it is both time-consuming and difficult, as well as potentially decorative in terms of the reflective qualities of the burnished surface (see below).

The South Area assemblage shows that almost 70 per cent of sherds are burnished to some degree on the exterior and almost half on the interior (most of them less highly); conversely more interiors show just a slight smoothing or no treatment (Fig. 5.9). Scraped and apparently slipped surfaces comprise just some two per cent and six per cent respectively in both cases. The recognition of a slip is problematic, since it is hard to distinguish from a fine burnish except microscopically (Vitelli 1984). For this study a possible slip has been recorded where there is a sharp differentiation between surface and fabric colour and/or the surface is flaking off as a separate layer. This might be an underestimate as it does not include cases where the surfaces show less vegetable matter than is apparent within the paste, which may indicate the application of a temper-free (self-)slip. However, petrographic analysis (see CD) seems to confirm that true slips were rare. In the North Area burnished exteriors rise to over 80 per cent while only about 50 per cent of interiors are burnished; a higher proportion (*c.* 20 per cent) have no discernible treatment. The greater difference between interiors and exteriors in the later assemblages might be explained in terms of an increased emphasis on the outward appearance of the vessel (seen in the predominance of dark external surfaces) and the greater number of closed (holemouth) forms whose interiors might not usually be visible to the user or easily reachable for the potter (see below). Scraped and ?slipped surfaces are if anything less common. The KOPAL Area is different again, once more indicative of a greater divergence or variability in pottery manufacture, suggesting that a greater range of vessels of different type/function were in use. This is shown by an increase in the number of surfaces with both little treatment (smoothing) and slips (many of which are also carefully burnished).

The burnishes (and slips?) applied to the surfaces of most early, South Area pots may have served to make these porous, often poorly-fired vessels more durable. While the uneven firing in the early levels does not give the impression of a decorative attention to surfaces, unlike the glossier slips and burnishes of the later levels, when firing — and therefore colour — was better controlled, the greater number of burnished exteriors compared to interiors suggests appearance (shininess?) may have been important. The Group 2 sherds are also relevant here: a high proportion of these (50 per cent) have a full burnish on their exterior, and they also comprise over 40 per cent of the small group of sherds identified as having an 'exceptional' burnish, despite representing just 16 per cent of the total assemblage. Hence we might see these fabrics as a distinct class of early 'fineware'.

How the burnish was applied is uncertain but in general, especially for the mineral-gritted pots of later levels, the visible burnish lines suggest a hard tool (stone, bone or ceramic) rather than a soft cloth. The consistent presence of deliberately rounded potdiscs (up to four per cent of the assemblage) might indicate one type of burnishing tool (e.g. Figs. 5.22:9–10). However, the lack of uneven wear on most of these pieces does not suggest they were used intensively as burnishers. Sometimes the visible burnishing lines show the direction in which the potter worked. There is little other evidence for potters' 'motor actions' at the site, so these directions were recorded where the orientation of the sherd could also be determined (usually rims). In the South Area 50 per cent were burnished horizontally, 35 per cent vertically and 15 per cent diagonally. In the North Area a very sample suggests a slightly greater amount of vertical burnishing (50 per cent), which might reflect the larger number of relatively tall jars (see below).

Other surface treatments are rare. Unusually, two sherds from close to the base of different vessels within (2029) (Level VIII; Building 2, building fill) had a hard yellowish deposit on the interior surface; it is not clear what this represents but could perhaps be a resin aimed at waterproofing the pots.

Along with other developments in technological sophistication, it is the Early Chalcolithic that sees the appearance of painted decoration, suggesting that an expansion in the functional role of pottery is intimately linked to their ability to convey information about the identity of their maker / users. Moreover the rise in decoration of pots coincides with the disappearance of painted decoration from the walls of houses. This argument will be developed further elsewhere (see also Last 1998) but suggests that pots, as decorative and potentially symbolic items, should not be considered independently from other aspects of the household.

Vessel forms and typology

The Neolithic pottery from Çatalhöyük has a very limited range of forms up to Level VII, principally comprising tub-shaped bowls with broad, flat bases, rounded base junctions and upright walls, often slightly inturned at the rim (e.g. Figs. 5.21:1, 5.15:5). Almost no vessels show carinations, changes of angle or points of inflexion, suggesting the shape was conceived of and manufactured as a unit, like an organic container, rather than divided into elements such as neck / body / foot, etc. From Level VI the 'classic' dark-faced holemouth jars predominate, although forms remain simple and lenticular (Fig. 5.23:1). Only from Level IV onwards are more complex profiles visible, including (slightly) necked jars and S-shaped bowls (e.g. Fig. 5.25:1), while it is not until the Early Chalcolithic that a full range of forms and sizes are made. A typology of rim, base and lug forms was devised for the (post-Level VII) surface assemblage published previously (Last 1996) and is used here with slight modifications (see below).

Rims

Because complete or near-complete profiles are rare it is often hard to tell whether simple rim forms belong to jars or bowls (as defined metrically by proportions of waist diameter to height). The few available profiles suggest that inturned (closed) rims are generally from holemouth jars rather than globular bowls, while upright (open or neutral) rims belong to shorter (bowls) rather than taller vessels (jars). However, there are exceptions — a number of Group 1 bowls have slightly inturned rims while Vessel 4 (see below) is a jar with a neutral rim angle.

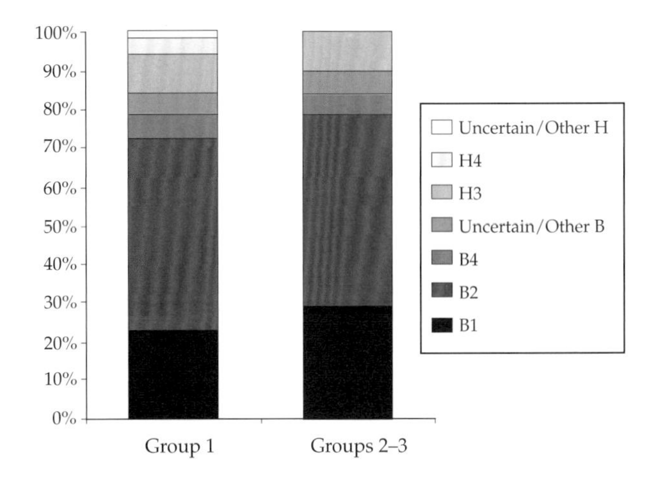

Figure 5.10. *Rim forms by fabric group, South Area.*

Table 5.10. *Rim forms by fabric group, South Area. *Larger angles indicate more open forms.*

	Group 1	Group 2	Group 3
Number (form uncertain)	163 (9)	16 (3)	5 (0)
Mean rim thickness (mm)	6.2	5.8	3.8
Mean diameter (mm)	141	143	235
Mean angle	85°	83°	90°

Open or neutral vessel rims ('bowls') are divided into four basic types:

B1 *with upright wall and slightly inturned rim* (Figs. 5.15:1, 5.15:5, 5.22:1, 5.23:1);
B2 *with upright wall and straight rim* (Figs. 5.16:1–2, 5.17:1, 5.17:4, 5.18:1–2, 5.19:4, 5.21:2, 5.22:2, 5.23:4) (B1/2 - Figs. 5.17:2–3, 5.18:3, 5.19:2–3);
B3 *with upright or S-profiled wall and everted rim* (Figs. 5.25:1–2, 5.26:2);
B4 *open bowl or dish* (Fig. 5.16:4).

Closed vessels ('holemouths') are also divided into four types, though H1 (developed neck) and H2 (incipient neck) are amalgamated here, since necked forms are so scarce:

H1/2 *with incipient neck/everted rim* (Figs. 5.26:1, 5.26:3);
H3 *with straight wall and neck* (Figs. 5.22:3, 5.23:2–3);
H4 *with inturned rim* (Figs. 5.16:3, 5.23:5–6).

In the South Area over two-thirds of the measurable rim sherds in Fabric Groups 1 and 2 fall in the 'tub-shaped' category (B1/B2), with a much smaller number (*c.* ten per cent) of closed forms (mainly H3; Table 5.10; Fig. 5.10). Although many 'holemouth' forms in the upper levels are tall jars, the few complete profiles from the South Area are all bowls (diameter greater than height), whether or not the rim is slightly inturned. The five Group 3 rims are also all neutral forms (e.g. Figs. 5.22:.1, 5.22:5), in contrast to the North

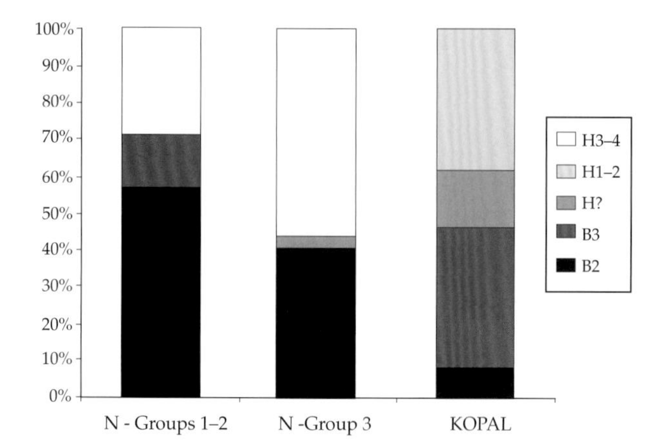

Figure 5.11. *Rim forms by fabric group, North and KOPAL Areas.*

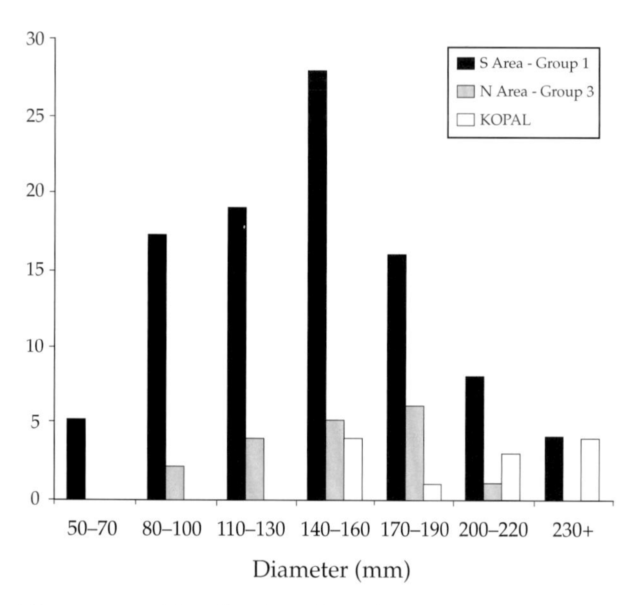

Figure 5.12. *Distribution of rim diameters.*

Table 5.11. *Rim forms by fabric group, North and KOPAL Areas.*

	North Area		KOPAL
	Groups 1–2	Group 3	
Number (form uncertain)	7 (0)	26 (1)	15 (2)
Mean rim thickness (mm)	6.2	4.7	5.7
Mean diameter (mm)	169	143	199
Mean angle	82°	76°	88°

Area (see below), perhaps suggesting that fabrics began to change in Level VII before the introduction of a new range of forms in Level VI.

The number of measurable rims in the North Area is much less but one difference is apparent, with over half of the Group 3 rims being holemouth forms, as well as a couple of those in Groups 1–2 (Table 5.11; Fig. 5.11). This documents the second major aspect of the transition from Levels VIII–VI, along with the change in fabrics: the replacement of open or neutral by closed forms (seen also in the lower figure for mean rim angle). Finally, the KOPAL assemblage (13 measurable rims) shows the development of more complex necked and everted-rim forms (B3 and H1/2: Figs. 5.25:1–2, 5.26:1–3). Vessel size has been assessed by measurement of rim diameter in the relatively few cases where enough of the rim survived for reasonable accuracy (handmade rims are generally irregular). The mean diameter for the different fabrics in the South Area is generally comparable — around 140 mm (Table 5.10); that for Fabric 3 in the North Area is similar (Table 5.11) but the few Group 1/2 rims there are generally rather large (the disparity can probably be ascribed to small sample size). Mean thicknesses at the rim tend to be rather less than lower down on the body, but the general trend for Groups 1 and 2 to be considerably thicker than Group 3 is still seen. Meanwhile, the higher mean thickness (compared to Group 3) and diameter for the KOPAL Area assemblage seems to indicate the production of larger vessels, while the neutral mean angle masks a distinction between closed holemouths and bowls with more open, everted rims.

Comparing Fabric Groups 1 and 3 in their main areas we see that the detail of the rim diameter distribution shows a normal-type distribution around the mean figure (Fig. 5.12). There are fewer large and small vessels in the North Area, but the small sample size shows that only one more vessel would be needed in these groups to make the distributions very similar. There is no sign of a bimodal distribution that would show the deliberate production of different size classes, and even the largest pots here are relatively small (but see Fig. 5.18:4). However, such a distribution is evident in the KOPAL Area with a group of medium-sized bowls and one of larger jars (we know from other evidence that miniature/small vessels were also being produced).

Height and detailed shape information is available in only the few cases where complete profiles are preserved (Vessels 1–5 and two small pots with parts of the rim and base present):

Vessel 1: Space 160 (Level VI), 22 sherds ((3343) & (3344)); Fig. 5.22:1
Bowl form B1; rim diameter 160 mm; base diameter 80 mm; height 120 mm; Fabric 3.
The sherds comprise about half of a thin-walled, medium-sized, open bowl with a slightly inturned rim, simple flat base with rounded junction, and dark brown or grey-brown burnished surfaces.

Vessel 2: Space 163 (Level VIII), 16 sherds ((4273) & (3999)); Fig. 5.21:1
Bowl form B2/1; rim diameter 140 mm; base diameter

130 mm; height 100 mm; Fabric 1a.
The sherds form the majority of a typical, thick-walled, Group 1 tub-shaped bowl. Some pieces of this vessel came from 'Mellaart backfill' (3999), suggesting that either the backfill was overdug or the top of *in situ* deposits had been disturbed since the 1960s.

Vessel 3: Space 182 (Level IX), 7 sherds ((5226), (5231) & (5240); Fig. 5.15:5
Bowl form B1; rim diameter 135 mm; base diameter 100 mm; height 100 mm; Fabric 2a.
This tub-shaped bowl of slightly globular profile had a somewhat unusual fabric with rather sparse vegetable matter augmented by occasional, very coarse fragments of calcareous matter. The vessel had mottled surfaces with some dark ?fire-clouding on the interior of the rim.

Vessel 4: Space 188 (Level VI), 20 sherds ((1289), (1302), (1318) & (1400)); Fig. 5.23:1
Jar form B1; rim diam. 122 mm; base diam. 70 mm; height 135 mm; Fabric Group 3.
This vessel was found in three major pieces lying over an area of about one square metre. Although it came from Level VI, overall the vessel has a number of slightly 'archaic' attributes: its neutral (rather than closed) shape, the presence of some straw in the paste and the uneven firing. Its wall thickness (6 mm), however, is typical of Level VI.

Vessel 5: KOPAL Area, (6003); Fig. 5.25:1
Bowl form B3; rim diameter 220 mm; base diameter 140 mm; height 140 mm; coarse mineral temper.
This vessel is typical of the latest levels on the East Mound, having an S-profile body shape with upright rim, a developed base (see below) and a reddish-brown slip. The best parallels come from surface scraping and collection in Area 11 (eastern plateau) of the East Mound (Last 1996) and some material from pit F.101 in the Summit Area (c.Level III). The interior of the base has an extensive blackened area suggesting the pot was used for cooking.

4624.S1: Space 170; Fig. 5.15:2
Bowl form B2/4; rim diameter 100 mm; base diameter 90 mm; height 65 mm; Fabric 2b.

4905.S1-X2: Space 173; Fig. 5.15:1
Bowl form B1; rim diameter 140 mm; base diameter 120 mm; height 65 mm; Fabric 1a.

The restricted range of vessel shapes and sizes in the South and North Areas is mirrored in the details of rim forms. Rim profiles are characterized as pointed,

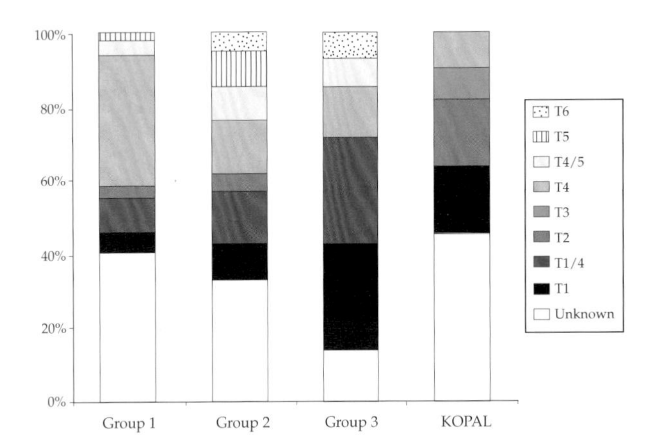

Figure 5.13. *Base forms by fabric group/area.*

Table 5.12. *Base forms by fabric group/area. *Larger angles indicate more upright forms.*

	Group 1	Group 2	Group 3	KOPAL
Number	132	21	14	11
Mean thickness (mm)	11.4	10.1	4.5	8.2
Mean diameter (mm)	132	96	68	112
Mean angle*	61°	53°	41°	33°

flattened or rounded, but this can vary around the lip of a single vessel and potters may not have been too concerned with the exact shape. What is clear is that more elaborate forms, such as bevelled, expanded or everted rims are rare or absent, and there was no decorative emphasis on the rim. There is a little elaboration in the KOPAL Area to the extent that everted forms are found, but in profile they remain simple. It is only in the Chalcolithic that a few more elaborate forms, such as lid seats or anti-splash rims, are found.

Bases

Bases at Çatalhöyük are divided into six (T) types:

1. *simple, angular junction* (Figs. 5.15:4, 5.18:5, 5.22:7, 5.23:1, 5.24:1);
2. *'developed' or 'footed' base* (Figs. 5.20:4, 5.21:3, 5.26:4–5);
3. *ring-base*
4. *simple, rounded junction* (Figs. 5.15:2, 5.22:1);
5. *rounded base (no defined junction)* (Figs. 5.21:4, 5.22:8);
6. *pushed-up or omphalos base* (Figs. 5.15:3, 5.24:2).

In the present assemblage, however, they are — like the rims — restricted in form, nearly all broad and flat with simple junctions; Group 1 sherds tend to have more rounded junctions (T4) while Group 3 are more angular (T1; *Graph 13*). There is no sign in the North or South Areas of pinched-out feet or applied ring-bases or feet; the only example of a ring-base (T3) is from the KOPAL Area — though these do occur in

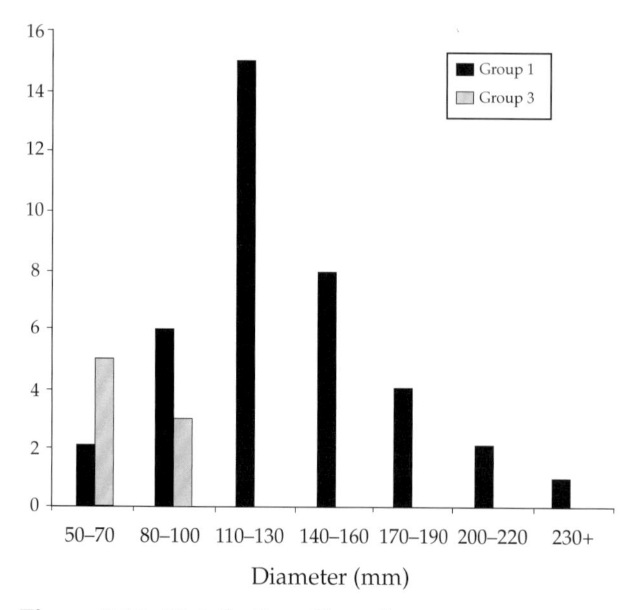

Figure 5.14. *Distribution of base diameters.*

the upper levels of the East Mound, including the Summit Area. While we can note the presence of some 'footed' bases (T2) in the South Area (e.g. Figs. 5.20:4, 5.21:3, 5.22:6) they are not part of the same tradition as those from the Summit or KOPAL Areas (e.g. Vessel 5; Fig. 5.25:1).

Another difference between Groups 1 and 3, as with the rims and bodies, is in mean thickness (cf. Figs. 5.21:4 & 5.24:3). Also, while Group 1 bases have diameters very similar to rims and a steep base/wall angle (the typical tub shape), Group 3 vessels have much smaller bases (Table 5.12; see also Fig. 5.14) and shallower angles, typical of hemibowl or globular shapes. This is also shown by the lower number of base sherds, proportionately, in the Group 3 assemblage: only 3.5 per cent were identified as bases, compared with 16.6 per cent of the Group 1 sherds. The KOPAL Area mean base diameter again masks greater variation between large and small vessels.

Lugs and handles

Lugs are extremely rare in the earliest levels and show a wide range of forms, suggestive of occasional experimentation but no fixed tradition. Hence the lug typology devised for the surface assemblage is not useful here. In the South Area there are three examples, all in Fabric Group 1: a roughly-made, small, unperforated lug from Space 106, a unique, rather finely-made, open bowl rim with a small perforated lug emerging from the top of the rim in Space 117 (Fig. 5.20:1), and another unique piece, a large conical lug from Space 163 (Fig. 5.21:5). The ratio of lugs to rims is 3:178 (2 per cent), compared with a figure of 15 to 25 per cent for Mellaart's assemblage from Level VI and above (Last 1996).

Despite the increasing frequency documented elsewhere, the small North Area assemblage only includes three lugs, and again none of them are of the standard 'Mellaart' type. The examples, all found in Building 1, include a small, unperforated lug from Space 186, broken off from the vessel (Fig. 5.24:4), a perforated lug emerging straight off the rim (in this case horizontally rather than vertically) from Space 187, and a basket handle, probably the earliest known example of such a form at Çatalhöyük, from Space 188 (Fig. 5.24:5); a very similar example was found by Mellaart in Level IV. The first and third examples are in mineral-tempered fabrics, while that from 187 is straw-tempered and may therefore be residual.

The main 'era' of lug handles probably spans Levels VI–IV and is poorly represented in the present assemblage. By the time of the KOPAL Area assemblage, lugs are again relatively rare and becoming decorative features in the form of small, 'vestigial' knobs, such as Figure 5.26:6. However, a partially reconstructable vessel from the hearth area of surface (6003), similar in form to Vessel 5 although with an everted rim, darker surfaces and a finer fabric, had two low horseshoe-shaped lugs positioned just above the point of inflexion on the belly of the pot (Fig. 5.25:2). These appear to be unique in terms of known Neolithic forms, though they show a vague resemblance to the smaller lugs found on some Early Chalcolithic pots. Hence this vessel supports the idea that the KOPAL Area assemblage can be seen as a transitional Neolithic/Chalcolithic group. As with vessel forms and sizes, the West Mound excavations have produced a much wider range of lug types, including loop and basket handles, horseshoe shapes, vertically-set perforated lugs and various 'vestigial' examples.

The lugs on the middle and upper bodies of Mellaart's Level V holemouth jars are usually perforated, suggesting the pots could be suspended, either when stored or being carried. Only two perforations are present in the current assemblage, however (see above), and there are no signs of either pre- or post-firing suspension holes.

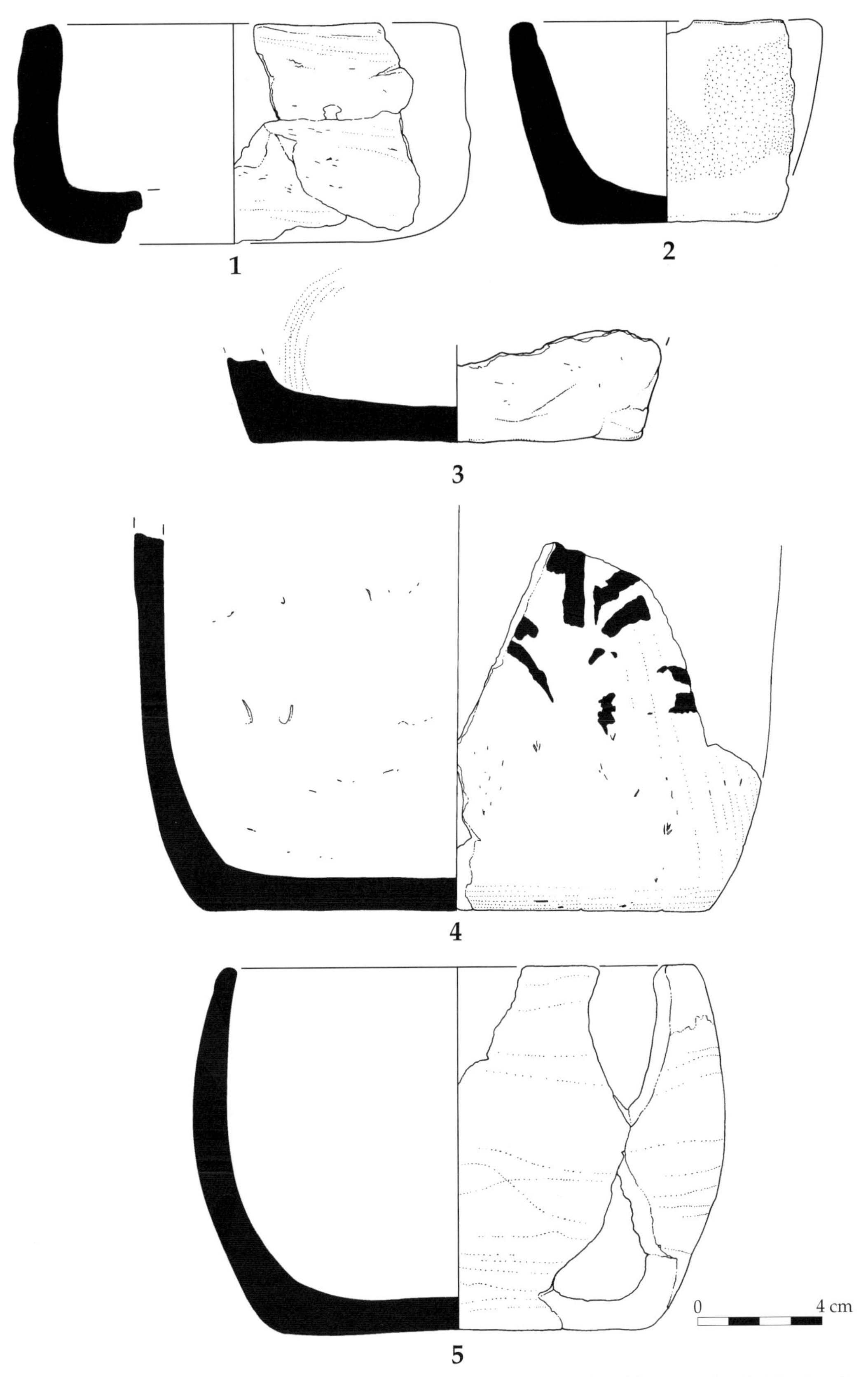

Figure 5.15. *Pottery from the South Area Level IX: 1) 4905.X2-S1, bowl profile, fabric 1a; 2) 4624.S1, bowl profile, fabric 2b; 3) 5242.X1, ?omphalos base, fabric 1a; 4) 4359.X1 etc, simple base, fabric 1a; 5) 5226.X1 etc., bowl profile, fabric 2a (by John Swogger).*

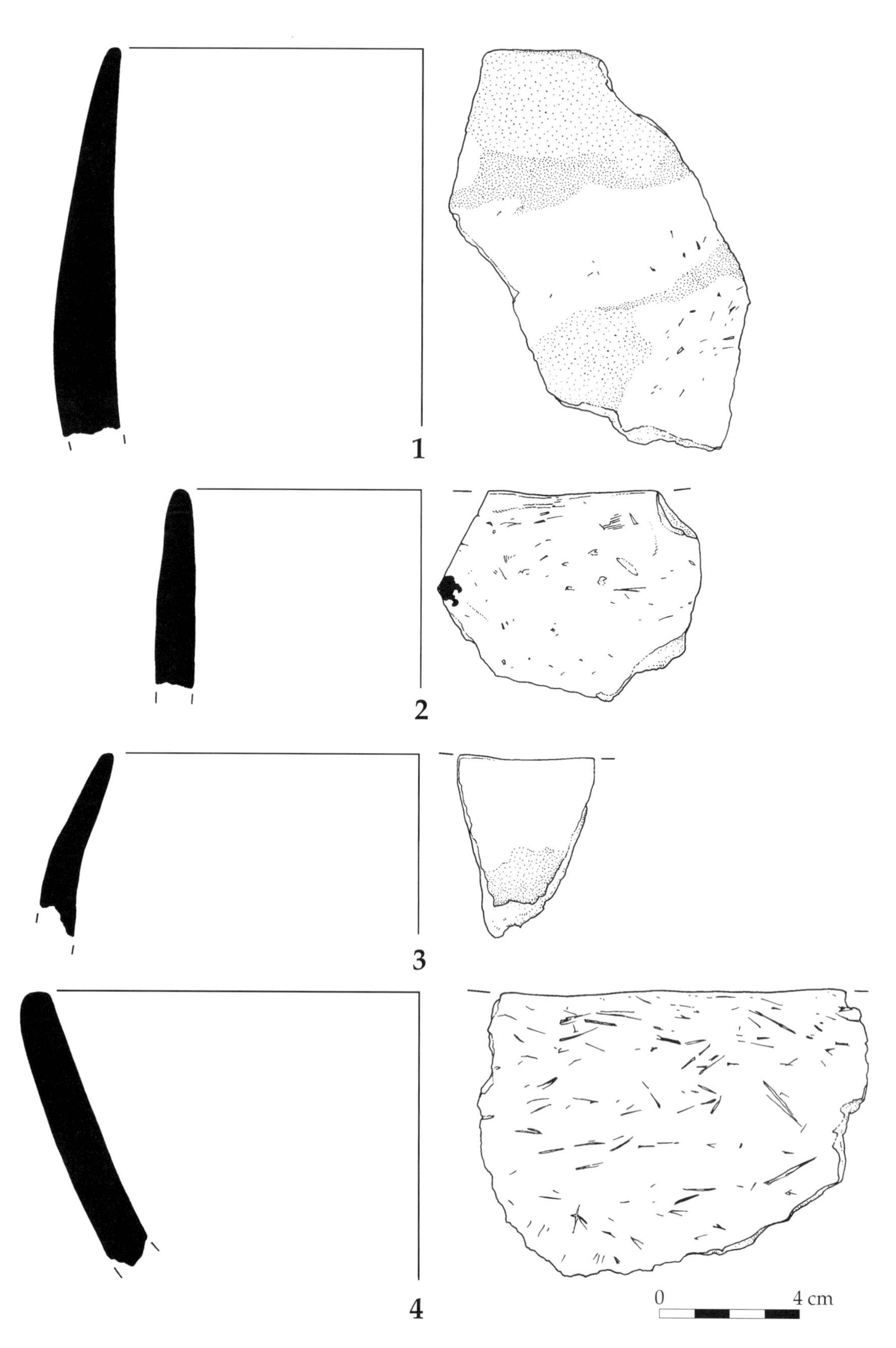

Figure 5.16. *Pottery from South Area Level VIII, Space 115: 1) 1037.S1, bowl rim, fabric 1a; 2) 3773.S2, bowl rim, fabric 2a; 3) 2340.S3, holemouth rim, fabric 1a; 4) 4491.S1, bowl rim, fabric 1e (by John Swogger).*

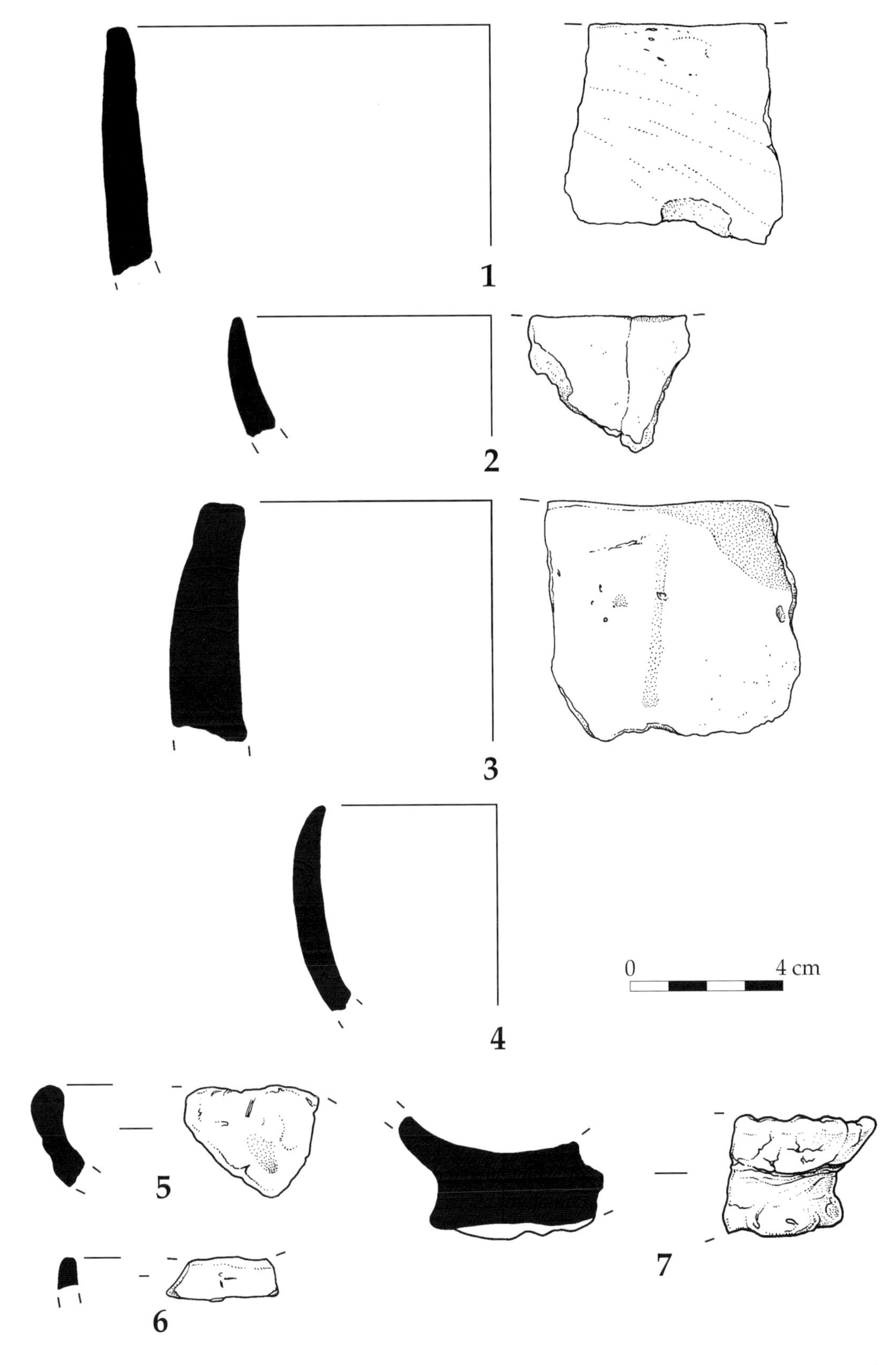

Figure 5.17. *Pottery from South Area Level VIII, Space 115: 1) 4491.S2, bowl rim, fabric 1a; 2) 4121.S25, bowl rim, fabric 1a; 3) 4121.S67, bowl rim, fabric 2a; 4) 1037.S5, bowl rim, fabric 1a; 5) 3713.S1, irregular rim, fabric 1a; 6) 1505.S1, rim (with coil break), fabric 1a; 7) 3740.X5, object, fabric 2a (by John Swogger).*

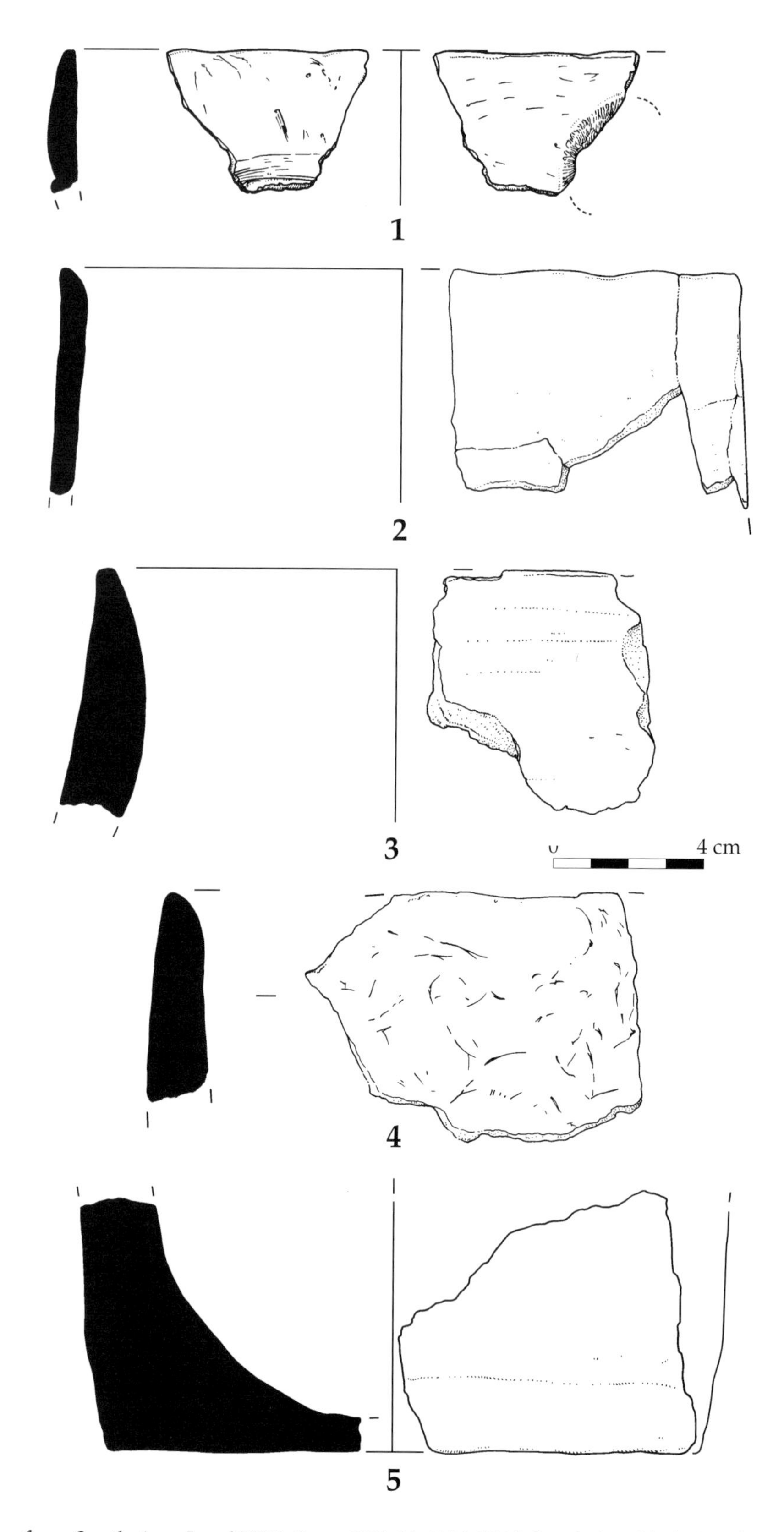

Figure 5.18. *Pottery from South Area Level VIII, Space 115: 1) 4121.S115, bowl rim, fabric 1a; 2) 3740.S1+S21+4121.S164, bowl rim, fabric 1a; 3) 4121.S68, bowl rim, fabric 1a; 4) 4121.S113, bowl rim, fabric 1c; 5) 4121.S161, simple base, fabric 1a (by John Swogger).*

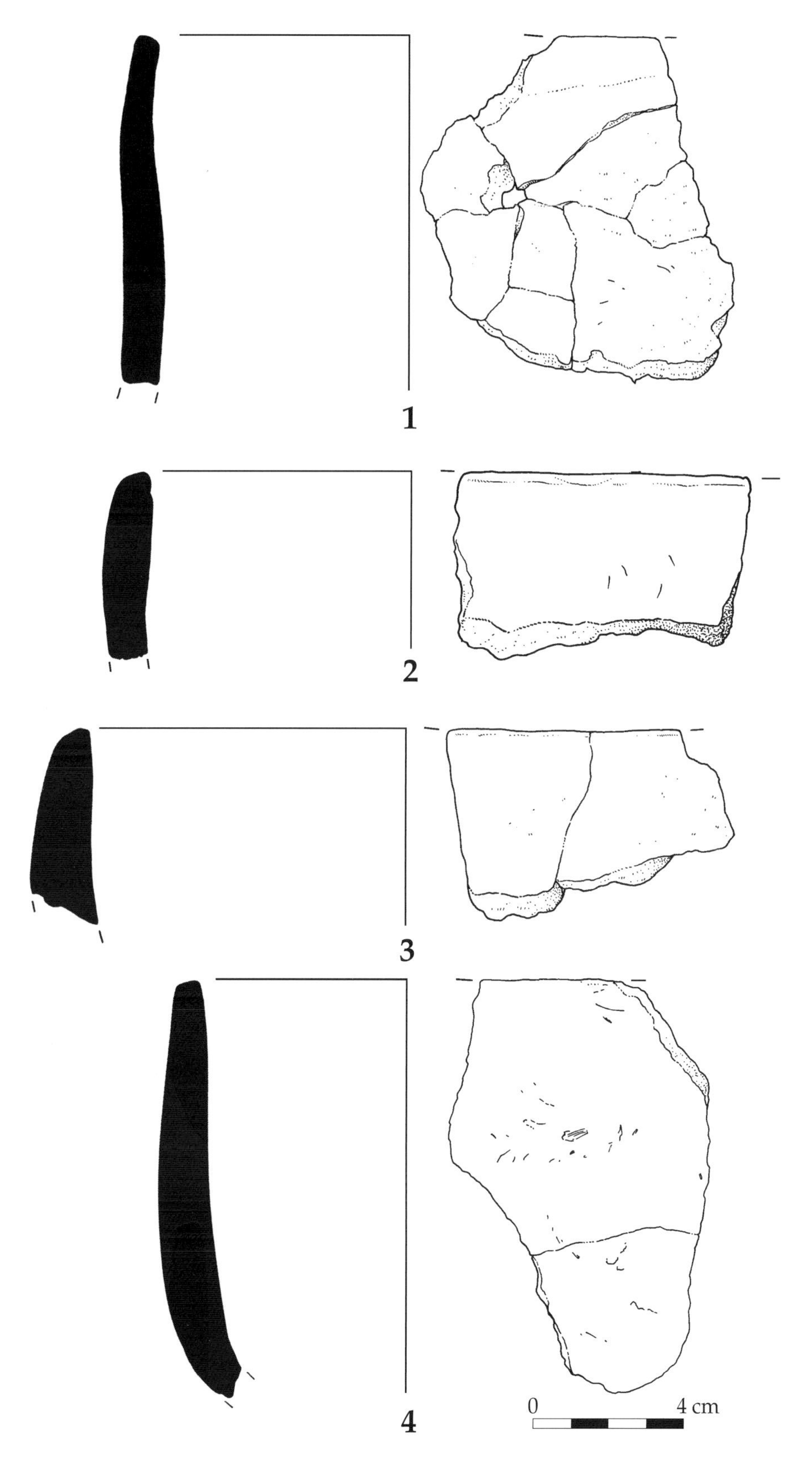

Figure 5.19. *Pottery from South Area Level VIII, Building 2: 1) 2329.S2, bowl rim, fabric 1a; 2) 1868.S1, bowl rim, fabric 1a; 3) 1816.S1+S3, bowl rim, fabric 1a; 4) 1584.S5, bowl rim, fabric 1b (by John Swogger).*

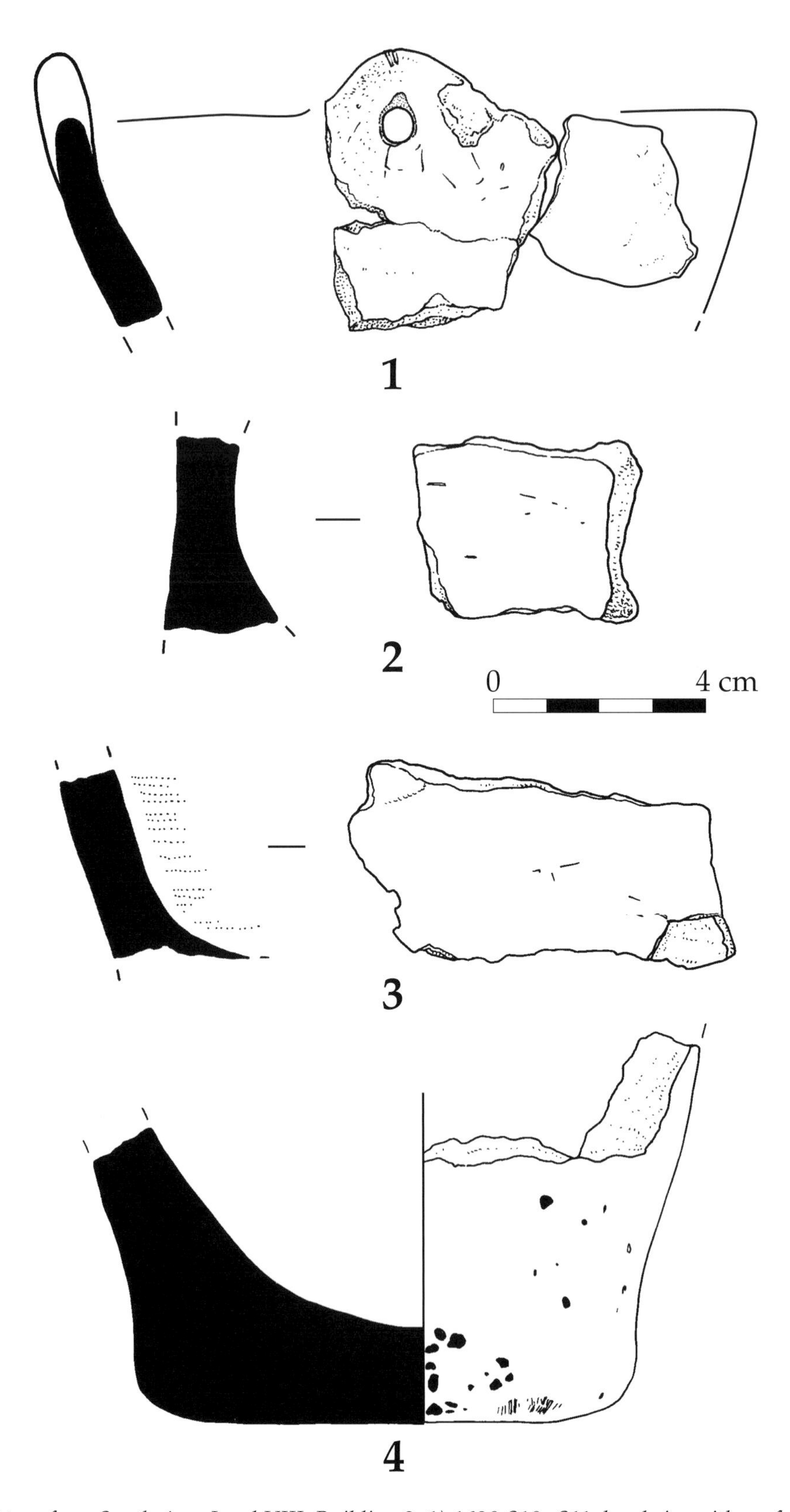

Figure 5.20. *Pottery from South Area Level VIII, Building 2: 1) 1620.S10+S11, bowl rim with perforated lug, fabric 1a; 2) 2029.S1, base (with coil break), fabric 1a; 3) 2308.S1, base (with coil break), fabric 1c; 4) 1612.X1, footed base, fabric 1a (by John Swogger).*

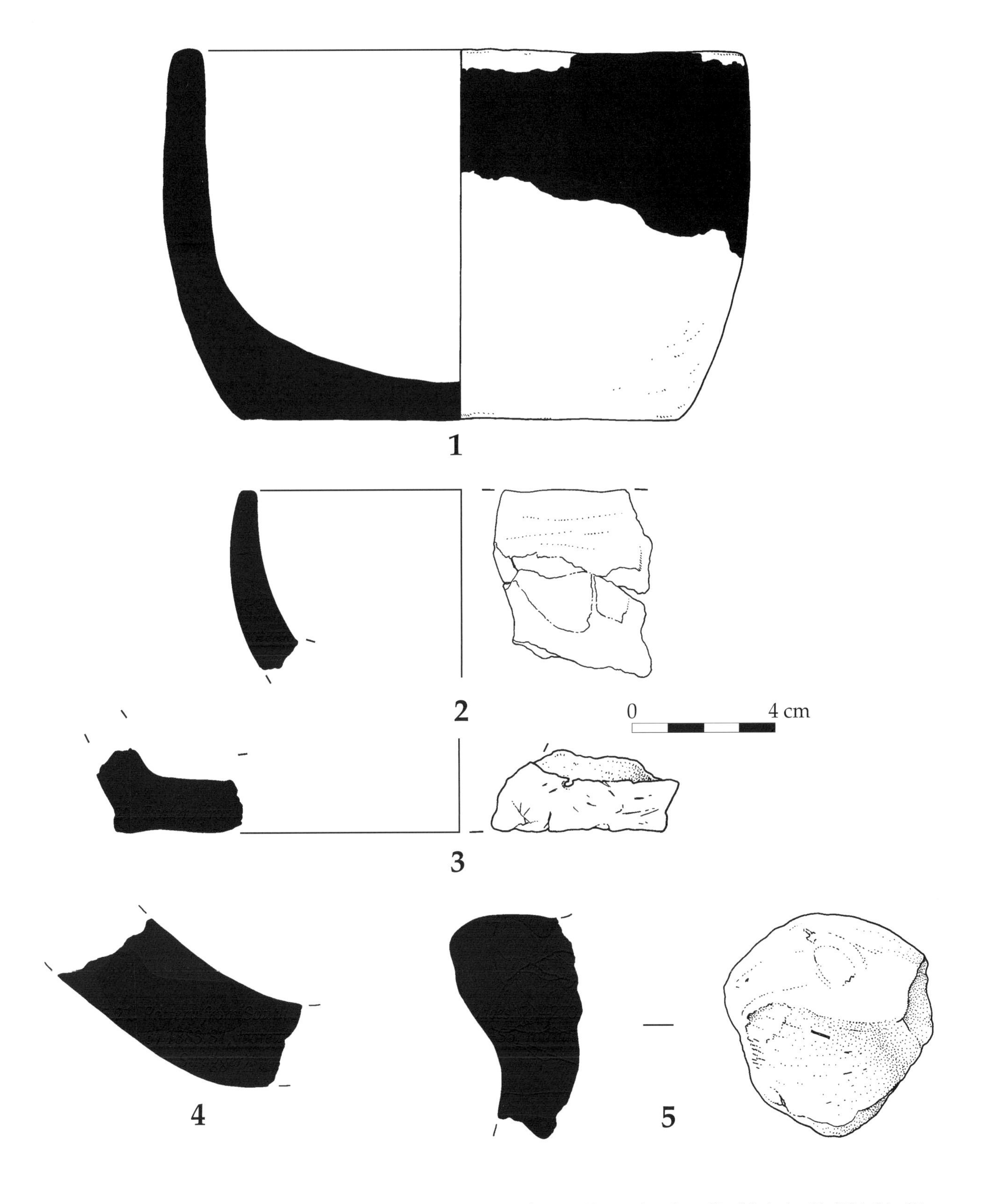

Figure 5.21. *Pottery from South Area Level VIII, other spaces: 1) 4273.X1 etc, bowl profile, fabric 1a; 2) 4321.S4+S7, rim fabric 1c; 3) 1883.S1, footed base, fabric 1a; 4) 4290.S1+S5, rounded base, fabric 1a; 5) 4291.S3, unperforated lug?, fabric 1b (by John Swogger).*

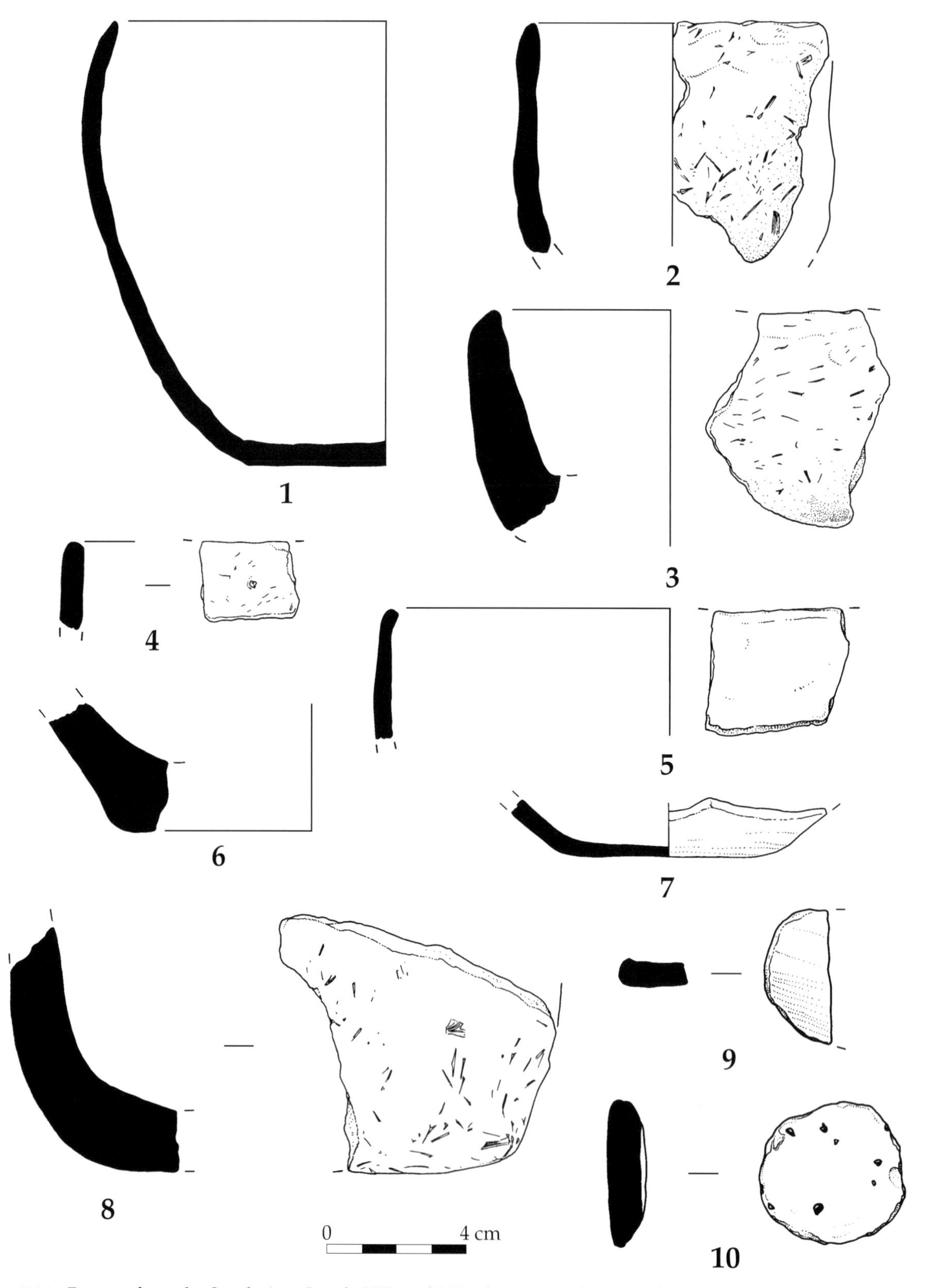

Figure 5.22. *Pottery from the South Area Levels VIB and VII: 1) 3343.X1, bowl profile, fabric 3e; 2) 3736.S1, bowl rim, fabric 1a; 3) 1091.S1, bowl rim, fabric 1a; 4) 1071.S2, bowl rim (with coil break), fabric 1a; 5) 4261.S1, bowl rim, fabric 3f; 6) 1567.S1, footed base, fabric 1a; 7) 1065.S2, simple base, fabric 3b; 8) 3126.S5, rounded base, fabric 1e; 9) 1544.X1, potdisc fragment, fabric 1b; 10) 1073.S5, potdisc, fabric 1c (by John Swogger).*

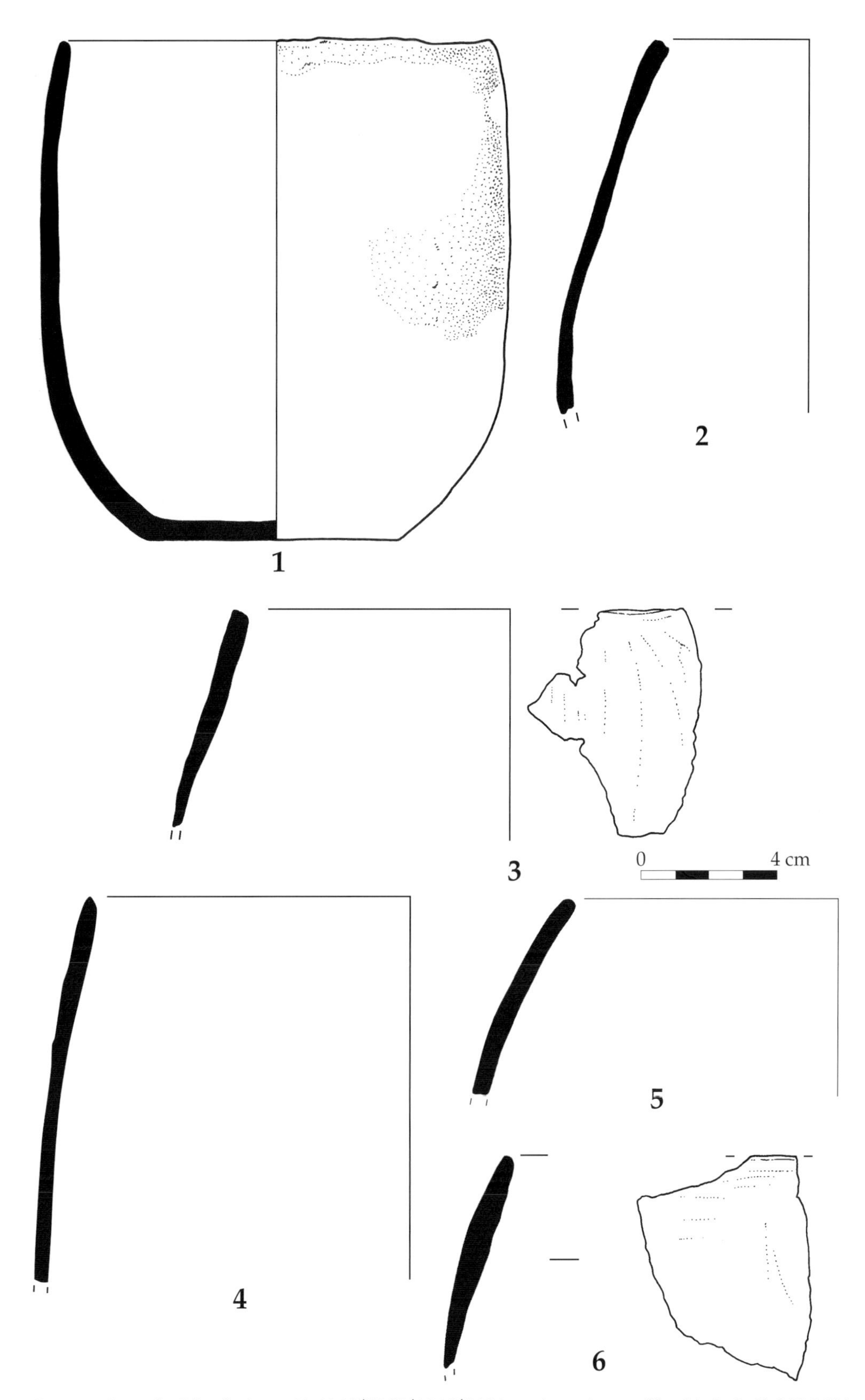

Figure 5.23. *Pottery from the North Area: 1) 1289/1302/1318/1400 various, jar profile, fabric 3; 2) 3021.X1+S1, holemouth rim, fabric 3f; 3) 1130.S1, holemouth rim, fabric 3f; 4) 3042.S1-S3, holemouth rim, fabric 3f; 5) 1333.X4, holemouth rim, fabric 3f; 6) 1154.X1, holemouth rim, fabric 3f (by John Swogger).*

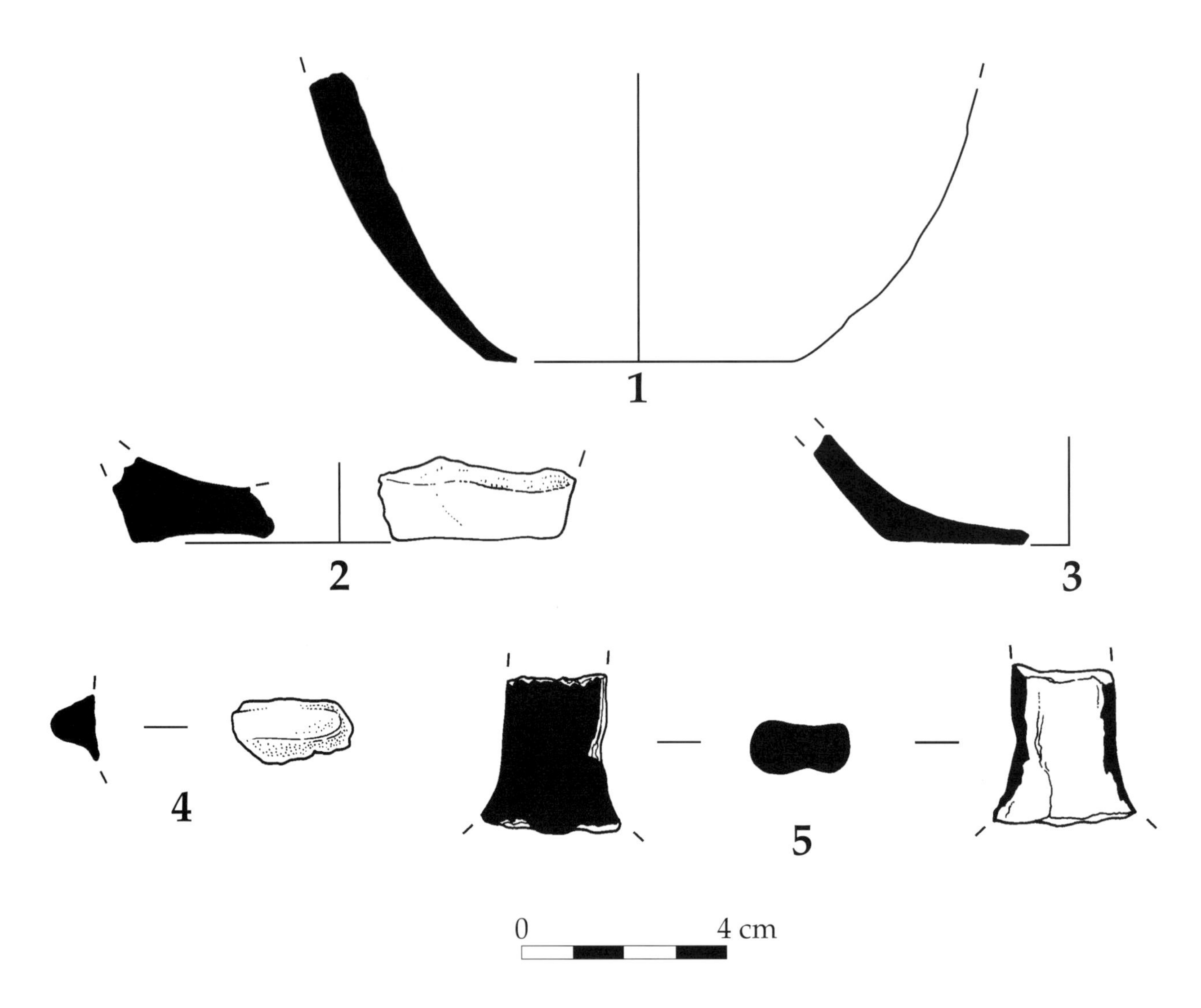

Figure 5.24. *Pottery from the North Area: 1) 1427.X1+X3+X4, simple base, fabric 3f; 2) 2570.S1, ?omphalos base, fabric 2a; 3) 2165.S3, simple base, fabric 3f; 4) 1110.S1, unperforated lug, fabric 3f; 5) 1333.X5, basket handle, fabric 3c (by John Swogger).*

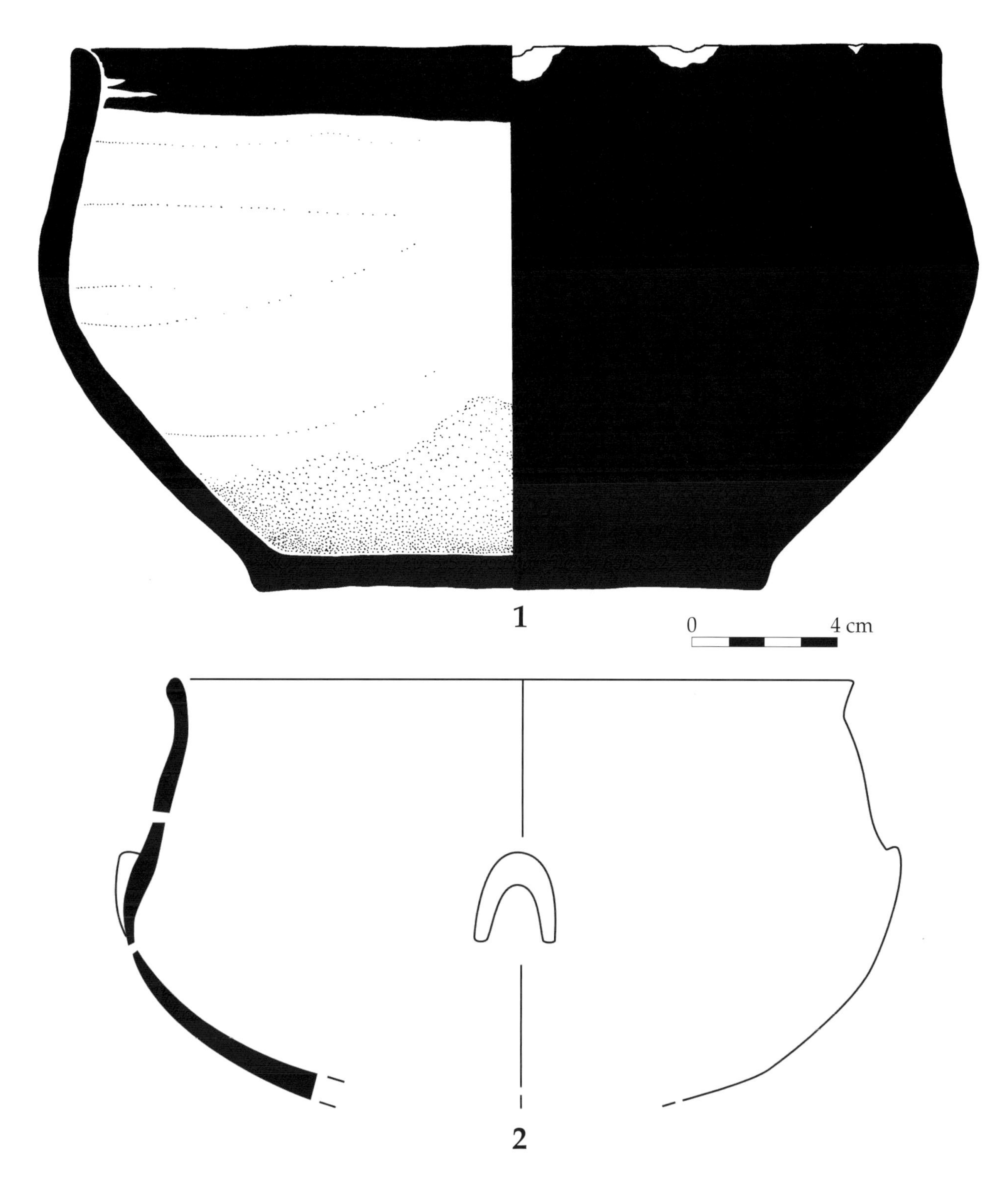

Figure 5.25. *Pottery from the KOPAL Area: 1) 6003.S1, bowl profile; 2) 6003.S2, lugged bowl profile (reconstructed) (by John Swogger and Jonathan Last).*

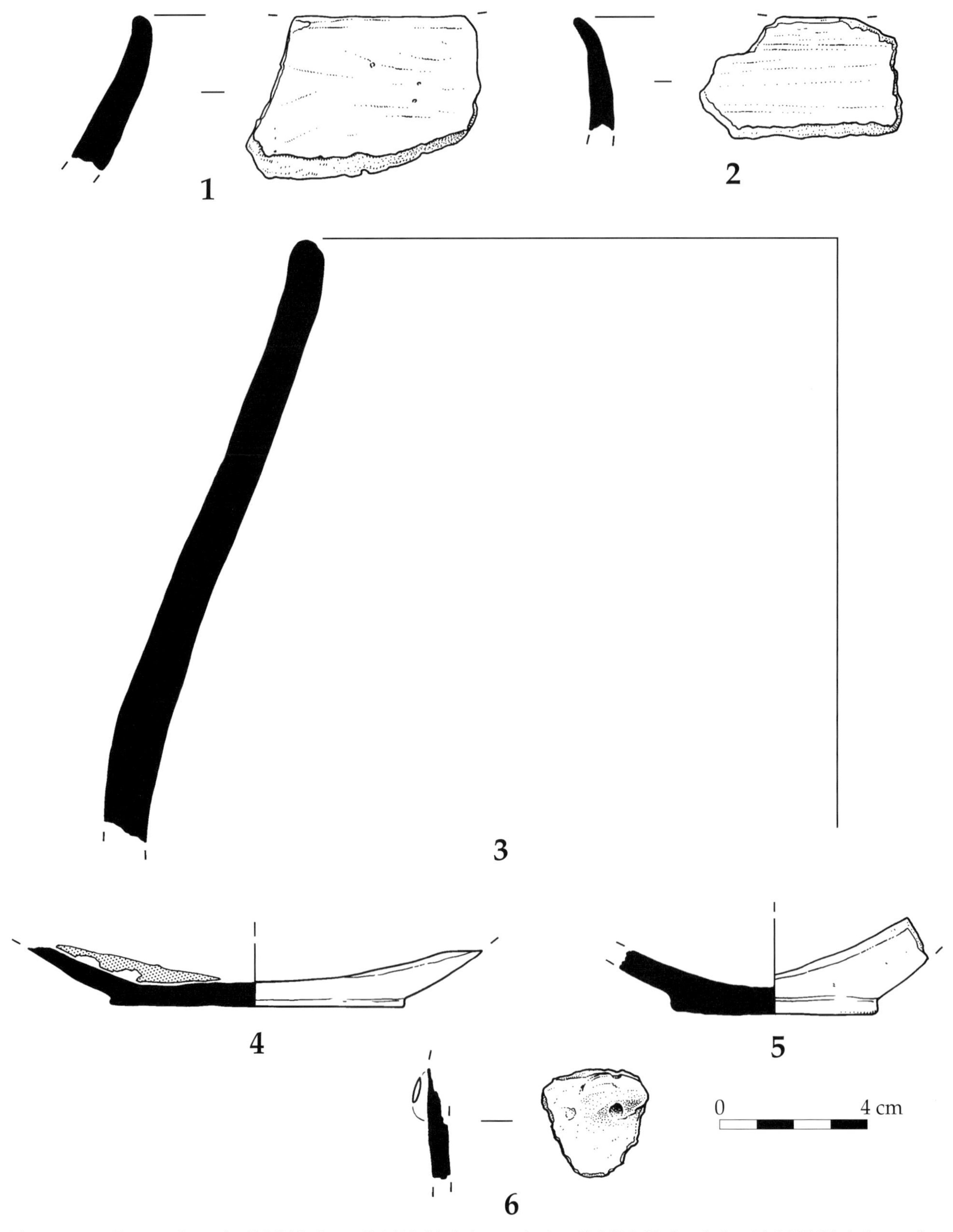

Figure 5.26. *Pottery from the KOPAL Area: 1) 2405.S1, holemouth rim; 2) 2405.S2, bowl rim; 3) 2407.S1, holemouth rim; 4) 2400, footed base; 5) 2405.S6, footed base; 6) 2410, perforated lug (by John Swogger).*

Interpretation: technology and tradition

The Near Eastern context

The pottery from the South Area at Çatalhöyük is among the earliest in the whole of western Asia. Moore (1995) has identified a more or less contemporaneous horizon of early pottery from the Mediterranean to the Zagros, which he dates to the late ninth/early eighth millennia BP (around 7000 cal BC or a little later). The revised dating for Çatalhöyük puts it in this range, with Level XII, the earliest known to have pottery (from Mellaart's excavations) producing a radiocarbon determination of 7985±50 BP (OxA-9947); this level is dated within the broader sequence to *c.* 7000 to 6900 cal BC. No pottery has been found in deposits dated to Level Pre-XII (Space 181) but since these are apparently off site (or at least not built-up), there is a question of whether they are the type of deposit in which pottery would be expected. On the other hand, since Level Pre-XII.A at the top of this space looks like the typical within-settlement 'midden' deposits, which in later levels do contain pottery, it seems reasonable to assume that the whole of Space 181 is indeed aceramic (see below).

The question of the origins of pottery technology is complicated at Çatalhöyük by a wide variety of clay and plaster technologies found in Level XII and below. These include sun-baked mud brick and clay figurines, oven walls and linings, plaster on walls and floors, and, most interestingly, a series of fired clay objects with coarse mineral inclusions, in a variety of shapes (the 'balloids': see Chapter 6). Elsewhere it has been suggested that early pottery technology represents a combination of forming processes used for plaster bowls (not found at Çatalhöyük) and compositional features of mud brick (Vandiver 1987). Vandiver asks us to consider the various technologies of 'earthy pastes' or 'soft stones' together. These established craft traditions are seen as a model for the development of a forming technique based on a heavily vegetable-tempered paste and sequential slab construction — though there is some evidence for different forming techniques at Çatalhöyük (see above). Figurines and the cooking of food are considered by Vandiver not to be implicated in the origins of ceramic technology, but the clay objects from the KOPAL Area may refute the latter. They seem to be predecessors of the clay balls, which could have been used for boiling water or heating food within ovens (see below).

It is suggested that in vessel forms (Moore 1995) and manufacturing techniques (Vandiver 1987), as well as chronology, there is a great homogeneity to this early Near Eastern ceramic horizon. The potential technological antecedents have just been outlined, but the cultural 'reasons' for the adoption of ceramic vessels are less clear. In general the transition from pre-pottery to pottery-using Neolithic cultures in the Near East is associated with settlement dislocation and discontinuity, but there is no sign of widespread changes in aspects of the plant or animal economy that might have required new methods of processing or storing these resources.

At Çatalhöyük, as elsewhere, there did eventually (from Level VII) come a shift to using mineral temper, and perhaps better clays, allowing or necessitating the adoption of new manufacturing techniques. However, tradition ensured that many features of the pottery, such as forms and surface treatments, actually changed very little. Although the quantity of pottery in use, and presumably therefore the range of functions, increased (see below), ceramic typology across this boundary depends primarily on wall thickness, surface colour (which relates to improved control of firing conditions) and paste inclusions. There is some development in vessel form (see above) but, in general, shapes remained simple and the absence of decoration persists. Only in the upper Neolithic levels (Level IV and above) and in the Early Chalcolithic is there a significant increase in the complexity of pottery forms (e.g. carinated, footed and miniature vessels) and decorative techniques (slips and incision, then painted motifs). Vandiver suggests the change to grit temper occurred in the Near East from around 7500 BP (*c.* 6400 to 6300 cal BC). At Çatalhöyük Level VII is dated to *c.* 6600 cal BC, perhaps a little earlier than the general date for this transition, though it is noted that grit-tempered pottery is found relatively early at Mersin (Vandiver 1987).

This is one narrative about the origins and development of ceramic technology. It has a broad scale and a *structural* quality. It assumes a common interaction sphere and cultural transmission across the whole of western Asia, without ever explaining the basis of that interaction, and therefore the context(s) in which pottery use and manufacture were adopted. Despite this cross-fertilization, which surely occurred at the level of ideas and language, the narrative also emphasizes tradition over innovation, and the mundane or practical over the symbolic or meaningful (cf. Vitelli (1995) on the 'magical' context of early Neolithic pottery in Greece).

Technology and performance

Another level of analysis focuses on the details of pottery recipes to establish the uses and functions to which it was suited. It largely follows the experimental work of Michael Schiffer and his students on the performance characteristics of different tempers and

Table 5.13. *Advantages/disadvantages of South Area pottery. ✓ = positive effect, x = negative effect, ? = uncertain effect, - = no effect. Larger/bold type shows significant effect.*

	Organic temper	Thick walls	Low firing	Burnishing
Impact strength	-	✓	**x**	?
Portability	**✓**	**x**	-	-
Abrasion resistance	**x**	✓	**x**	✓
Cooling effectiveness	-	x	?	**x**
Heating effectiveness	**x**	**x**	?	✓
Thermal shock resistance	-	**x**	**✓**	?
Open firing possible	**✓**	?	**✓**	-
Drying effectiveness	**x**	**x**	-	-
Ease of manufacture	**✓**	✓	-	**x**

surface treatments (Schiffer 1990; Skibo *et al.* 1989; 1997). In particular, a study of organic-tempered pottery (Skibo *et al.* 1989) has shown the advantages and disadvantages of this type of paste. These can usefully be tabulated in relation to the specific characteristics of the Group 1 material from the South Area (Table 5.13). The first group of characteristics can be characterized as related to 'durability'. The advantages and disadvantages are roughly equal. Because organic tempered fabrics are lighter and less susceptible to breakage than mineral-gritted ones they are considered to be useful for mobile groups, and there is indeed some correlation between pottery fabrics and lifestyle in the Americas. We might therefore suggest that this style of pottery was adopted in the Konya plain while the ancestors of the Çatalhöyük people were still mobile foragers and/or herders, the type of lifestyle implied by the finds from Pınarbaşı A near Kara Dağ (though this site is apparently aceramic) (Watkins 1996). A more radical suggestion is that Çatalhöyük itself, at least in the lower levels, represents only a seasonal occupation and people, with their pots, were dispersing to other sites at different times of year. On the other hand, the early pottery at Çatalhöyük is so thick-walled that it is not particularly light, so the mobility hypothesis may be inappropriate. Thick walls, along with burnishing of surfaces, may well have increased impact strength and abrasion resistance to some extent, so the early pottery may represent a trade-off between portability and strength. However, the low firing temperatures would have produced a soft fabric with little innate strength.

The second group of characteristics relate to 'function', especially in relation to cooking. Here the negatives of organic-tempered fabrics seem to outweigh the positives and the suggestion made here is that the early pottery was not used for cooking, certainly there is little evidence for use-related sooting or burning on pots (see below). Organic-tempered wares are particularly poor for heating water and it is striking that experimentally Skibo *et al.* (1989, 131) were unable to get water to boil in organic-tempered pots. The thick walls would also have decreased both heating and cooling (i.e. evaporation) effectiveness. While burnishing might alleviate the former, it is more effective on interiors, which are less commonly or finely burnished at Çatalhöyük. The burnished exteriors might have hindered evaporation by closing off many of the pores in the fabric. The low firing temperatures would have produced pottery with greater resistance to the stresses and strains of repeated heating and cooling (thermal shock) but the thick bases might have been more prone to cracking and spalling. It seems more likely that heated clay balls were used as 'pot-boilers', though perhaps in containers of other material, such as skin bags.

This scenario receives partial confirmation from the organic residue evidence (see Chapter 7). The much greater proportion of sherds producing lipid residues from the Summit Area than the North Area and especially the South Area does indeed suggest an increasing use of pots for cooking over time (assuming lipids are more likely to be taken up by the vessel when heated). However, the absence of residues on clay balls too is slightly puzzling, and may indicate preservational differences between the upper and lower layers of the mound.

The final group of characteristics relates to manufacture, and it is here that the positives of organic-tempered fabrics seem to outweigh the negatives. Organic temper serves to increase effective firing temperatures and vessel strength under poorly-controlled firing conditions and makes wet clay workable and stronger for slab building (it may hinder coil formation, however: Vandiver 1987). Certainly poor control of firing is evidenced by the mottled surface coloration of most vessels from the South Area. It is possible also either that poor-quality clay from local alluvial sources necessitated the addition of water and vegetable matter to increase plasticity to the point where vessel forming was possible (this might also reflect the prevalence of simple forms built up from a thick base), or that clay was being quarried wet and adding mineral would have been far less effective at making it workable without prolonged drying than organic temper. In fact a major component of the local clay is montmorillonite (see CD), which has good plasticity but high shrinkage during drying; coarse temper would have been required to reduce the danger of cracking. A different approach was clearly taken with the clay balls, either in terms of the drying process, or because they were easier to form with wet clay than vessels, or because a higher failure rate was tolerated during their firing and use.

The eventual technological shift to mineral-tempered pottery was associated, as mentioned, with thinner walls and a more controlled firing environment. In terms of manufacture this would have required ageing of the clay to achieve workable plasticity (Vandiver 1987), but reduced drying time and making the drying process more even. While the manufacturing process and its associated routines would have altered, therefore, it seems likely that these developments had much to do with heating / cooking performance. Firstly, there was a particular emphasis on thin bases (often thinner than the walls) and therefore on the transmission of heat and thermal shock resistance rather than vessel durability. Secondly, the mineral (quartz) grits are often relatively coarse: in comparison to the fine sand in the clay balls this would have enhanced both shock resistance and the transmission of heat through the body of the vessel. Thirdly, the quantity of pottery in use appears to increase, implying new types of function which may well have included cooking, while the number of clay balls found appears to decline at the same time, suggesting some of their functions had been replaced.

These developments may have been dependent on new clay and / or temper sources, providing a more easily-worked paste as well as one with better heating properties. Thin-section analysis of a small number of Level VI sherds from the North Area (Building 1) by David Jenkins and John Williams (pers. comm.) suggests that most of these vessels were manufactured 'from a colluvial 'clay' deposit that did not require additional tempering and was 'the product of a recent, fresh volcanic terrain'. The larger petrographic analysis by Özdöl *et al.* (see CD) also suggests a shift from local clays (deriving from lake environments) to a colluvial source. Whatever the precise source of this material, presumably the limestone terraces or volcanic 'bajadas' to the south of the site, it suggests that the Çatalhöyük potters may have become more prepared to travel or trade over some distance to acquire a workable clay. Most likely it was clay rather than finished vessels which was imported, since the presence in one sherd of micritic accretions similar to that identified in sediments local to the site suggests that the manufacturing process took place at Çatalhöyük.

This second narrative is therefore broadly *functional*. Technology provides a range of possibilities, and Schiffer's 'behavioural' paradigm assumes that technical choices will seek to optimize the performance of objects in specific material conditions. However, we have already suggested that traditions can be remarkably stable. Questions of technological change and stability can only be addressed by a contextual study of material culture as a product of culturally-situated human practices. Every potter and therefore every pot carries a habitus (*sensu* Bourdieu 1990) which comprises far more than a merely technical understanding of ceramic manufacturing processes.

Tradition and meaning

All the broader social issues touched on in these two narratives were crucial to pottery manufacture, as to all other human activities at Çatalhöyük. The homogeneity of early Near Eastern ceramics suggests potting was a conservative tradition, relatively resistant to change across space and time. However, this needs to be explained in the context of each individual site. At Çatalhöyük one might note the conservatism of other clay technologies. For instance, the general size and shape of the mud bricks (long and thin) used in house construction hardly change between the base of the South Area and the top of the West Mound, perhaps a millennium and a half later. This may relate to the likelihood that the significance of the house (seen in wall decorations and burial practices, etc.) made architecture a highly-ritualized practice (Last 1998).

Similarly, it has been suggested that the emergence of pottery might have been associated with certain ritual practices, such as feasting (Hayden 1995) or shamanism (Vitelli 1995). However, at Çatalhöyük there is no clear association between pots and the feasting deposits identified in the animal-bone assemblage, nor are pots ever found in graves. On the other hand, if cereal straw was indeed being used to temper the early pots we can suggest the incorporation of the agricultural product within the body of the vessel could have served to make a symbolic statement. It links pots with specific times of the year, when straw was available, and specific domestic activities and locales, including fire installations and storage bins. The later recipes, in contrast, imply a knowledge of particular clay sources in the wider landscape and bring parts of that landscape into the house, more analogous with other exotic materials like obsidian. The developments in ceramic technology may have had clear functional benefits but we should not lose sight of the possible conceptual shift which they necessitated.

The mechanics of the change between the two potting traditions has to be understood in human and generational terms. The discussion above has stressed the difference between the Level VIII and Level VI assemblages without addressing how the transition occurred. This gives the impression of a sudden revolution, and in archaeological terms it may be so, occurring in the space of one building level (Level VII). But in human terms Level VII might easily have encompassed two or three generations and we should rather envisage a piecemeal development, with different individuals (both among the potters and the users of pottery) learning, adopting or resisting the new ideas; different generations making and using different types of pottery simultaneously; and technological change ultimately dependent on the old generation dying out. The contingent nature of these changes may be seen in the varying proportions of fabric types in the different Level VII assemblages, although it is not clear whether these differences might relate to differential adoption of the new pottery types by individual households, or perhaps to the initial use of the new types for certain functions only, which were not evenly distributed across the site.

Another interesting question concerns the continuing innovation within the new potting tradition. Between Levels XII (looking at Mellaart's assemblage) and VIII pottery changed hardly at all; between VI and II most stylistic elements changed (see Last 1996), though without further technological 'ruptures' like the Level VII transition. On one hand, the new technology and the greater levels of skill that demanded probably produced more scope for innovation; on the other hand, broader social factors may have also influenced potters, if we accept the argument that the construction and use of houses, for instance, became more dynamic in the upper levels of the site (Düring 2001).

The recognition that long-term structural and functional narratives are inadequate to understand the social context of pottery at Çatalhöyük brings in new interpretive strands linked to other material assemblages and architectural contexts. These issues are considered further in some of the themed discussions (Volume 6). But one possible example of social/traditional factors is the role of burnishing. It may have been necessary to provide a degree of waterproofing and/or abrasion resistance to the porous early fabrics. In the later phases, when these requirements were reduced, burnishing was retained and even became finer, in the context of a firing technology which allowed a much greater control of surface colour. In the later levels the problem of distinguishing between a fine burnish and an applied slip shows the decorative significance of the treatment. It continued as a component of ceramic tradition at Çatalhöyük into the Chalcolithic, with the painted pottery from the West Mound usually still burnished, to a higher degree than many of the equivalent wares from Canhasan I, for instance.

Neolithic pottery was not painted with designs equivalent to those found on architectural features, but perhaps the retention and enhancement of burnishing as the main feature of Level VI and later pottery almost literally 'reflected' its significance. If pots were primarily used in the vicinity of hearths and ovens, as anecdotal evidence suggests (Mellaart pers. comm.; but see below), their reflective surfaces would have enhanced their visibility, a kind of mnemonic for the particular networks of meaning in which they were bound up (Last 1998). Otherwise, their plainness does not necessarily denote insignificance. As Miller (1985) has shown, pots can serve as marginal, background 'frames' for ritual action, their significance shown by the fact they are noticed only when inappropriate or absent.

Use and deposition of pottery

Pottery typologies, in so far as they are not simply imposed by the archaeologist, represent an accommodation between the available technology and the *habitus* of the potter. However, they only deal with the production of an object. Although pots were most likely produced with a particular function or range of functions in mind, the intentions of the potter do not determine the way a pot is subsequently used and ultimately disposed of. It is unfortunate that pottery analysis rarely pays as much attention to issues of consumption and deposition as to production and typology.

Use and origins

One difficulty with interpreting the Çatalhöyük pottery is that evidence for its use is rarely as obvious as that for its manufacture. I outlined above a possible narrative of technological change in pottery manufacture which is in part related to vessel function, but finding direct evidence for the way these pots were used is difficult. Visible carbonized deposits suggestive of cooking were noticed on eight sherds only (four from the South Area, four from the North). The suggestion made above was that the early, Group 1 pots were not suitable for direct heating and it may be significant that only two such sherds (one from Space 105, one from Space 115) had evidence for burnt deposits. Sooting was, however, noticed on the unusual mineral-gritted vessel from Space 182 (see above). On the other hand, with so few examples overall it is hard to make a positive case for the use of any pots from the North or South Areas in cooking (and the organic-residue analysis does not counter this impression). Other types of use-related visible residues on sherds are equally rare; although the yellow resin-like(?) deposits mentioned above may fall into this category.

Another possible approach to understanding the use of these pots is to consider the contexts in which they were found. Here the problem is that so little of the assemblage was found *in situ* as *de facto* or primary refuse (to use Schiffer's (1976) terms). As noted above, Mellaart suggests that pots tended to be associated with hearths in his excavations and that these usually lie in the southern part of the building (e.g. Mellaart 1962, 57). Vessel 4 indeed comes from the southern end of Building 1, close to the location of a fire installation; however, that belongs to an earlier phase. In the early levels such an association is even less clear: the few (near-) complete vessels in the South Area come from two ancillary spaces (Spaces 160 & 182), areas not usually associated with ovens and hearths, and the northwestern quarter of a main room (Space 163). Only in the off-site KOPAL Area, ironically (since there is no clear evidence for structures), does there appear to be a clear association between hearths and pots.

Understanding the amount of pottery in use at any one time may provide a clue to its function(s) but this point remains moot in the absence of more extensive excavations in the North Area (e.g. of midden deposits), and of information on other types of container (e.g. baskets, skins, wooden boxes). Analysis of Mellaart's assemblage (Last 1996) suggests a large increase in the quantity of pottery associated with the technological and formal changes around Level VII, as does the fact that he originally considered the early levels to be aceramic (e.g. Mellaart 1963, 44 & 102; 1964a, 82). However, the present work has only produced a small assemblage from the Level VI spaces in the North and BACH Areas and it is unclear whether this reflects a continued low level of pottery use at this time or simply that comparable deposits have not been excavated: most of the South Area assemblage derived from an external midden (Space 115), while the North finds all came from within buildings or narrow between-wall spaces.

One instructive comparison is between Level VI Building 1 and Level IX Building 2, the most completely-understood building in the South Area (Table 5.14). At first glance the counts suggest, in contrast to Mellaart, that the quantity of pottery in use did not alter greatly between these levels. On the other hand, the formation processes of the two structures are very different — Building 1 contained no deposits classed as midden, the most common source of pottery finds, while over three quarters of the pottery from Building 2 derived from midden. Taking these out of the equation, we see that B1 has almost five times as much pottery from fill, floor and make-up units. To better compare like with like, only building fill contexts were selected for both areas. Although they produced similar total quantities, about three times as much fill was excavated in the South Area (counting only those units that contained pottery) so densities are significantly lower. On this basis we can suggest that some 3 to 5 times as much pottery was in use in the North Area than in the South Area. If we allow for differences in mean vessel size by counting rim sherds only, the figures would reduce slightly, perhaps a difference of 2.5 to 4 times. Nevertheless, the greater quantity of material suggests a greater range of functions for pottery over time.

At a more basic level, however, the most obvious point about the pottery from the site is how little there is overall. This is made most clear by contrasting the number of sherds from the North and South Areas with those from Early Chalcolithic Building 25 on the West Mound, where excavations in 2000 produced over 5000 sherds (not including many thousands more from disturbed contexts over the building). There is an order of magnitude difference between the quantity of pottery in use in the lower and middle levels of the East Mound and that in use 1000 years later on the West Mound; there is also a huge difference in the range of vessel forms and sizes. The material from the Summit and KOPAL Areas lies somewhere between these two extremes, in terms of both quantity and variety.

This progressive expansion in the use of pottery over time is what one might expect with a new technology. However, it returns us to the question of exactly what was the context of use into which the early tub-shaped pots from the South Area of the East Mound were introduced. Neither spatial analysis nor organic-residue analysis have provided many clues about vessel function, in both cases due to insufficient data at present. The little information there is (small sizes, low quantities, peripheral locations) might suggest a role in storing or preparing some substance kept or used only in small quantities. Yet there is no contextual evidence that the early pottery was either a prestigious material or ritually significant; it does not occur in burials or feasting deposits, for instance. On the other hand, seeking a single, functional explana-

Table 5.14. *Comparison of selected North and South Area assemblages.*

	Sherds	No. of rims	Total weight (kg)	Sherds from midden
Building 1	182	30 (16.5%)	1.8	-
Building 2	179	37 (20.7)	3.3	141 (78.8%)
			Density (sherds/100L)	
Fill (North)	124	24 (19.4%)	0.6	
Fill (South)	130	28 (21.5)	0.2	

tion for the introduction of pottery is not necessarily the most useful approach; all technologies are embedded in social relations and there could equally well have been symbolic or political reasons for certain individuals or groups to adopt the use or production of fired-clay vessels, whether to supplement or replace other types of material. We need to interpret the pottery contextually, looking for changes in other areas of technology or society (e.g. lithic production/procurement, subsistence strategies, etc.) happening at the same time.

Re-use and deposition

Despite their brittleness pots are rather durable items, as ethnographic studies of use-lives show. However, small- to medium-sized vessels, which predominate in the assemblages from the North and South Areas, are more susceptible to breakage than large storage vessels simply because they are more often moved around. In many cultures cracked, chipped or even substantially-broken pots remain in use; archaeologically this is often seen in the presence of features such as mendholes, so it seems significant that these are not found at Çatalhöyük. Their absence either shows that a relatively low value was ascribed to pots or that cracked pots were no longer functional (e.g. if pots were used solely to hold liquids).

Once broken beyond repair pots are still frequently a source of useful material, a point often overlooked by archaeologists who see sherds simply as rubbish. Potsherds may indeed have use-lives of their own, and both ethnographic and historical accounts record numerous uses for them. At Çatalhöyük, as mentioned, a number of rounded 'potdiscs' were found (Figs. 5.22:9–10). Their function is hard to assess, however, since they seem not to show the uneven wear one might expect on burnishers, are too small to have been lids or stoppers, given the known mouth diameters of vessels, and are never perforated to suggest a use as spindle whorls. Other possibilities include gaming pieces, counters and tokens, but although they represent a relatively high proportion of the sherd assemblage, their overall quantities do not indicate they were particularly common objects.

At some point the fragments of broken pots were discarded, mostly in spaces removed from living areas. While depositional patterns are likely to primarily reflect discard and maintenance practices, rather than use, it is important to recall that these strategies form part of the routines of everyday life and are just as likely to be embedded in broader social practices and to realize symbolic structures as any other type of activity.

Depositional practices and post-depositional processes for different deposits containing pottery at Çatalhöyük can be compared by considering indices such as sherd size, abrasion, joins and density per unit volume. Only abrasion needs further clarification: sherds were 'scored' on a scale from 1 to 7 depending on the degree of rounding or wear seen on both edges and corners. Visual 'scores' for abrasion essentially represent an ordinal scale of measurement, and not a ratio scale. Nevertheless a numerical value was necessary in order to allow the calculation of summary statistics (primarily means) for all sherds in a context. It must be borne in mind that a higher mean sherd wear value in one context compared to another implies no more than that: tests of correlation and statistical significance would be inappropriate. This being said, the difference between a worn and a fresh assemblage should be ascertainable. The recording of abrasion is designed to provide a gauge of the low-energy weathering processes undergone by the sherd, which may include exposure to the elements, kicking or trampling on a soft matrix. In contrast, sherd size will reflect higher-energy impact events, caused by the initial breakage of the pot and subsequently by actions like trampling on a hard matrix. Both sherd size and weight are strongly correlated with vessel thickness ($r = 0.77$ & $r = 0.64$ respectively), so overall differences between mean sherd size for the South (39.7 mm) and North Areas (35.6) can be explained largely in terms of the greater thickness of the Group 1 sherds.

The statistics for the South Area, broken down by deposit type, are as follows (Table 5.15). They show that pottery is most common in midden deposits, then in building fills, floors, fills of restricted areas (features, between walls), and construction make-up (of walls or features). The tendency for sherds to occur most frequently in external midden contexts, while the few complete pots come from within buildings, suggests fairly intensive maintenance strategies by which the surfaces where pots were used and kept were generally cleared of artefacts, either as regular housekeeping or prior to replastering or abandonment events. Building fills have a considerably lower density than other context types so do not appear to derive from e.g. midden deposits (note that, as previously, the soil volumes only include units in which some pottery was found). The 'other fill', floor and midden sherds are larger on average than those from building fills and walls, perhaps indicative that they are closer to their primary depositional context (the greater mean size of the 'other' fill category is somewhat tempered by the much greater thickness). Abrasion is fairly even, but the building fills, perhaps surprisingly, have the lowest wear; this may indicate that they were rapidly buried in this type of deposit and therefore more protected from the elements than sherds in midden, etc. Sherds

Table 5.15. *Sherd statistics for South Area deposit types. * Sherds/100L of soil, not including contexts with no pottery. ** Number of sherds joining other pieces within or without that group. *** Building fill includes foundation fill.*

Deposit type	Sherds	Soil vol. (litres)	Dens.*	% Grp 1	% Rims	**% Joins	Size (mm)	Wt (g)	Thick. (mm)	Abr.
Midden	561 (56.7%)	64,033	0.9	87.5	18.7	13.5	40.4	19.3	9.6	3.6
Building fill	189 (19.1%)	73,100	0.3	65.6	20.6	11.1	36.8	14.8	9.2	3.2
Floor	88 (8.9%)	8630	1.0	34.1	12.5	40.9	39.5	23.1	9.5	3.5
Other fill	67 (6.8%)	1192	5.6	74.6	22.4	29.9	46.1	24.1	11.6	3.7
Wall or feature	49 (5.0%)	4710	1.0	65.3	6.1	12.2	37.5	11.8	8.4	3.6

from walls are not noticeably smaller or more abraded than other deposits; however, they do have a low proportion of feature sherds and joins (all the joins relate to one large base assigned to wall 447 in Space 164). For whatever reason floors also have relatively few rims but there is a large number of joins (influenced by the presence of occasional reconstructable vessels).

In the North Area, as mentioned, information on extra-mural deposits equivalent to Space 115 is lacking but if we take the 'between-walls' units as the best approximation to midden, we see the following (Table 5.16). Most densities are slightly higher than the equivalents in the South Area (which support the suggestion that pottery was generally more common). Again, building fill contexts have the lowest density. Size is lowest in 'other fills' (not including fill between walls in this case) and wall deposits, and this time the wall sherds do have higher abrasion scores. Note that the abrasion figures are generally lower for Group 3 sherds than the softer Group 1; it is clear that they are to a large extent determined by the greater hardness of the mineral-gritted sherds, the coefficient of correlation between the percentage of mineral-tempered sherds and degree of wear is $r = -0.63$. The 'other' group and walls have a low proportion of rims and the latter assemblage lacked joins. Tables 5.15–5.16 show that difference in sherd size between North and South Areas is much less than difference in weight, indicative of the varying thicknesses of Group 1 and Group 3 sherds. One might expect the thicker Group 1 vessels to produce larger sherds when broken; that they do not (or not by much) can probably be ascribed to their softer condition (because they are lower-fired, more porous and overall less well burnished). The difference in abrasion statistics has a similar cause.

Contextual analysis

Further information on use and depositional practices, as well as on broader issues of formation processes, comes from contextual analysis of the assemblage. Since much of this is incorporated into the detailed stratigraphic narratives of Volume 3, here I consider general differences between spaces and phases in the different areas.

North Area

Statistics for the North Area are hampered by small sample sizes. The Volume 3 narratives consider the deposits primarily by phase (Volume 3, Part 3), but it is also illuminating to summarize the differences between spaces across all phases (Table 5.17). The constant feature in the division of space within Building 1 is wall F3, separating the main eastern spaces (Spaces 71, 110, 111, 183, 185 & 188) from the ancillary western rooms (Spaces 184, 186 & 187). The third assemblage to consider is that from the extramural areas (Spaces 69, 73 & 153). While this large-scale comparison suggests some broad differences, including spatial variations in fabrics, joins and sherd size, they can mainly be explained by the peculiarities of individual spaces, e.g. the presence of a largely complete pot (Vessel 4) in Space 188 (eastern region), and a high proportion of Group 1 sherds in Space 71 (eastern region). Overall, there is greater variability within each group than between them, so there is no real sign of continuity in deposition over different phases.

More productive is to break the assemblages down by phase. The main groups of interest are shown in Table 5.18. Building 5 proper (Spaces 154 to 157) produced just five potsherds, which represent a mere two per cent of the North Area assemblage. No sherd joins have been recognized and only two pieces (3845.X1 & 4014.X2) are associated with the occupation phases B5.B and B5.C. However, the fill units assigned to B1.1A have a high proportion (60 per cent) of Group 1 fabrics, suggesting that whatever the source of these deposits, the assemblage is unrelated to the occupation of Building 1 (Level VI). B1.1B also has a large number of sherds (47 per cent) belonging to Groups 1 or 2, which overall still looks more typical of Level VII.

The extra-mural contexts in the North Area are divided into two main phases. Cessford (Volume 3, Part 3) states there is good stratigraphic evidence that the majority of the deposits in the external spaces correspond to internal subphases B1.1B and B1.2A. While Phase B1.E1 only produced six sherds, the two largest pieces being in 'archaic' fabric Groups 1 and 2 (a similar ratio to phase 1B), the larger assemblage from phase B1.E2, again evenly distributed across the

Table 5.16. *North Area deposit types.*

Deposit type	Sherds	Soil vol. (L)	Dens.	% Rims	% Joins	Size (mm)	Wt (g)	Thick. (mm)	Abr.
Between walls	34 (15.5%)	1741	2.0	20.6	32.4	37.3	12.3	5.7	2.3
Building fill	123 (55.9%)	14718	0.8	21.1	28.5	37.6	12.7	6.1	2.6
Other fill	28 (12.7%)	1124	2.5	7.1	21.4	28.4	5.7	5.3	2.6
Floor	24 (10.9%)	1832	1.3	12.5	25.0	37.1	10.4	6.1	2.7
Wall	11 (5.0%)	331	3.3	9.1	-	29.1	7.0	6.2	2.9

Table 5.17. *North Area by 'Region'.*

Space	No.	% Grp 1	% Rims	% Joins	Size (mm)	Wt (g)	Thick. (mm)	Abr.
Building 1 Eastern	98	11.2	13.9	34.7	38.4	12.1	5.9	2.6
Building 1 Western	53	5.7	18.9	15.1	30.3	7.4	5.2	2.4
External	36	5.6	19.4	30.6	36.9	11.9	5.6	2.3

Table 5.18. *North Area by space and phase (selected groups).*

Contexts	No.	% Grp 1	% Rims	% Joins	Size (mm)	Wt (g)	Thick. (mm)	Abr.
B5/B1.1A	16	56.3	-	-	33.6	15.9	8.3	3.7
B1.1B (not walls)	36	38.9	33.3	22.2	34.3	10.9	7.6	3.7
B1.E2	29	3.4	18.2	37.9	40.7	13.8	5.6	2.3
B1.2	18	5.6	-	33.3	38.6	9.7	5.7	2.8
B1.3 (Spaces 186/187)	22	-	9.1	9.1	20.7	2.7	5.0	2.5
B1.3 (Space 188)	37	2.7	16.7	54.1	49.6	19.1	5.4	2.1
B1.5A (Spaces 186/187)	20	-	25.0	30.0	34.8	9.7	4.7	1.8
B1.5B (Pit F.17)	16	-	18.2	37.5	30.9	6.2	4.4	2.3

three main extra-mural spaces, is a fresh assemblage (with several joins and a fairly large mean sherd size) of typical Level VI type. This suggests either that the external material has more to do with the occupation of Building 1 than its construction, or that the phase B1.1 assemblages are largely residual material, redeposited in the building make-up. The abrasion scores for the latter seem relatively high compared to the South Area, which may support the latter scenario.

Subphase B1.2B is the first major occupation phase in Building 1 and shows clear differences from the previous phases. Of 13 sherds only one is primarily vegetable-tempered and this is a small fragment in a burial fill (1956), so is presumably residual. All the occupation and abandonment phases of Building 1 are associated with Group 3 sherds typical of Level VI (a few Group 1 sherds can be interpreted as residual). In phase B1.3 the distinction between Spaces 186/187 in the west and Space 188 in the east has much to do with the presence of Vessel 4, as mentioned, but the low number of joins and small mean sherd size of the former group stands out across the different phases and suggests some unusual formation processes in the ancillary spaces. This might have something to do with a burning event which led to 45 per cent of sherds from Space 187 having red surfaces indicative of refiring (the overall figure for the North Area is just 14 per cent). In abandonment subphase B1.5A there is still a clear division between the eastern spaces and the west, though the nature of that difference changes. In this phase all but five sherds derive from Spaces 186 and 187 and there is a high number of sherd joins across units, showing the essential unitary nature of deposition. Sherd size and abrasion also show a clear difference from the preceding phase B1.3. Finally the latest group, from subphase B1.5B pit F.17, comprises a number of sherds many of which may derive from the same vessel. Although there is the suggestion of a deliberate deposit (Volume 3, Part 3) it is interesting that sherd size is smaller and abrasion higher than for subphase B1.5A.

For the North Area we are also able to correlate overall sherd densities (across all contexts, not just those with pottery) with phases in the construction–occupation–abandonment sequence of the buildings. Table 5.19 shows that the highest densities belong to the infill phases contemporary with or post-dating the use of Building 1 (B1.3, B1.5, B1.E2). The occupation phases have moderate densities (B1.2, B1.4, B1.E1) while the construction phases have low to moderate densities (B1.1). This difference between the construction make-up/infill and the post-occupation infill is striking and suggests they may have been conceptually distinct processes; however, it may in part reflect changes in the use of pottery associated with the transition from Level VII to VI (Building 5 occupation has a lower density than Building 1), and therefore needs to be 'tested' with buildings of other levels.

Table 5.19. *North Area sherd densities by activity type.*

Phase	Total (L)	% Floated	Sherds	Density	Interpretation
B5	3664	45.1	5	0.14	Occupation / Abandonment
B1.1A	34,027	7.8	11	0.03	Construction / Infill
B1.1B	30,204	10.6	44	0.15	Construction / Infill
B1.2A	(2390)	(66.0)	-	-	Construction / Occupation
B1.2B	3523	72.2	13	0.37	Occupation
B1.2C	2598	76.6	5	0.19	Occupation
B1.3	5874	43.1	61	1.04	Remodelling / Infill
B1.4	2116	56.1	4	0.19	Occupation
B1.5A	5604	42.8	25	0.45	Abandonment / Infill
B1.5B–C	2167	48.3	23	1.06	Post-abandonment
B1.E1	2169	9.9	6	0.28	Extra-mural (Activity?)
B1.E2	3025	37.4	29	0.96	Extra-mural (Infill)
Overall	94,971	21.6	226	0.24	

South Area

The South Area has more spaces with a reasonable sample size but only three (Spaces 105, 115 & 117 phase 7) produced more than 50 sherds and many assemblages are again very small. Several of the larger ones also have lower finds densities than the North Area spaces because of the greater volume of soil excavated.

Level VII

The different spaces of Level VII show a great variation in the proportion of 'archaic' Group 1 fabrics, from less than 50 per cent in Space 106 to more than 80 per cent in Space 107. This may reflect fine-scale chronological variation or functional differences and is discussed in more detail in Volume 3. This variation presumably accounts for most of the differences in the other statistics, such as abrasion scores, though it is interesting that there is relatively little difference in mean thickness (which seems to be largely due to the fact that the late Group 1 fabrics are rather thin: 9.1 mm average). Densities and absolute quantities are higher for Spaces 105–107 than for 109, 112 and 113, while there are a low number of joins throughout.

Space 105 produced the largest Level VII assemblage, mostly from 'foundation fills' (Table 5.20). Compared with Building 5/Building 1 Phase 1, the only comparable assemblage from the North Area, the sherds are relatively large and unabraded, but the overall figure disguises some important differences. If the fills (both 'foundation' and 'between walls') are divided into 'heterogeneous' and 'homogeneous' deposits (information from excavation data base) the latter have considerably larger but more abraded sherds; this difference can be largely ascribed to the predominance of Group 1 sherds in the 'homogeneous' fills and Group 3 in the 'heterogeneous' deposits. The implication is that the latter group of fills is chronologically later, functionally distinct and/or contains residual material. The remaining sherds of Space 105 derive from walls and, typically, are much smaller and more abraded than those from other context types.

The material from Space 106 largely comprises finds from building fill. Compared with the material from Space 105 (overall) the sherds are smaller, but the assemblages are otherwise similar. It is not possible to divide the assemblage into 'Group 1' and 'Group 3' contexts as with Space 105. However, there is a high proportion of Group 2 sherds (30 per cent — compared with an average of 16 per cent across Level VII).

The smaller assemblage from Space 107 has a similar proportion of Group 1 sherds to the 'homogeneous' fills of Space 105; however, they are smaller and also rather thin-walled. Little pottery came from the other spaces of Level VII (21 sherds), but these include the only finds from floor contexts (in Spaces 108 & 112). Outside the designated spaces, those sherds from between-wall fills are relatively large, particularly in comparison to those from the walls themselves.

Level VIII

Level VIII is dominated numerically by Spaces 115 and 117 (Phase 7), assemblages which have average values for most attributes. These represent middens in an open space and abandoned building respectively and do not indicate a great difference in the formation processes involved. In contrast, Spaces 163 and 173 of Building 6 have a greater integrity (more joins) and slightly larger (but considerably thicker) sherds. Internal differences within Building 6 are marked by differences in abrasion (lower in Space 173) and fabric (a high number of Group 2 sherds in Space 163).

Approximately one half of the total pottery assemblage from the South Area came from external deposits in Space 115. The earlier Phase Sp.115.B has slightly larger but more abraded sherds on average, though all the midden sherds are larger (and more worn) than the few sherds from foundation fills. Phase Sp.115.B also has fewer rims proportionately than Sp.115.A (larger vessels?) and considerably fewer joins. The midden can alternatively be divided into 'fine' and 'coarse' deposits. This resembles the phase division because 99 per cent of Sp.115.B sherds come from coarse midden and 80 per cent of Sp.115.A from fine. One striking difference is in the number of Group 3 sherds. There are none in Sp.115.A fine midden contexts but they comprise 17 (seven per cent) of the Sp.115.B coarse assemblage. If this were a chronological feature, there would be more in the later Sp.115.A,

Table 5.20. *South Area by space and level (selected groups).*

Context	No.	% Grp 1	% Rims	% Joins	Size	Wt	Thick.	Abr.
Level VII								
Space 105 heterogeneous foundation fills	22	31.8	18.2	-	30.4	6.9	6.8	2.5
Space 105 homogeneous foundation fills	26	73.1	15.4	11.5	41.2	18.2	9.1	3.5
Space 106 building fill	25	48.0	16.0	4.0	32.3	10.3	7.7	3.0
Space 107 all contexts	16	81.3	18.7	18.7	35.6	12.5	7.5	3.6
Fills between walls (all spaces)	12	58.3	41.7	-	40.7	14.1	7.9	3.2
Walls (all spaces)	22	54.5	9.1	-	29.9	8.0	8.0	3.9
Level VIII								
Space 115 midden Phase A	155	85.8	22.6	19.4	38.6	15.6	9.0	3.5
Space 115 midden Phase B	249	87.1	16.1	8.8	43.0	22.9	10.1	3.7
Space 115 foundation fill	10	90.0	10.0	-	30.9	7.6	9.0	3.5
Space 116 Phase 7	23	91.3	21.7	8.7	39.7	25.0	9.4	3.7
Space 117 Phase 7	125	91.2	20.8	17.6	39.4	16.9	9.9	3.6
Building 6 Phase 2 (except Vessel 2)	22	50.0	18.2	22.7	43.2	27.8	15.6	4.0
Building Phase 5	14	92.9	7.1	28.6	45.1	22.3	12.1	3.5
Spaces 151, 161 and 162 building fill	22	77.3	13.6	-	32.0	11.1	9.1	3.7
Level IX–X								
Spaces 116 and 117 Phases 1 to 6	29	89.7	20.7	17.2	42.8	21.0	9.3	3.8
Space 170 Phase A	14	50.0	42.9	35.7	39.8	19.2	9.4	3.1
Building 18 occupation	13	30.8	15.4	-	25.8	10.0	10.4	3.4

so the sequence hints at the complexity of technological change at the site. Another way of assessing variability within Space 115 is in terms of densities of material. The small Sp.115.A coarse assemblage, for instance, has a relatively high density overall (2.4/100 L) but a great variation between contexts (r = –0.27). Sp.115.A fine has a lower density (1.1) but a stronger correlation (r = 0.62), while Sp.115.B coarse is similar (1.2; r = 0.98 or 0.77 excluding the large unit (4121)).

The material from the infill of Building 2 (phase 7) is assigned to Level VIII in contrast to the building itself, which is Level IX. In part this shows the artificiality of Mellaart's division into building levels, especially given the connections between Phases B2.6 and B2.7 (see Volume 3, Part 2) and the similarity of the statistics, though the sherds from the infill are slightly smaller. Within Phase B2.7, there is little difference between the two spaces, which suggests a single filling event. Space 117 has more joins proportionately, while Space 116 has a greater mean sherd weight, which is mainly due to one extremely large base sherd.

The majority of the Phase B2.7 sherds (accounting for 89 per cent of the assemblage) come from deposits classified as coarse midden. Within these, although a minority in terms of absolute numbers, the density of material is considerably higher in Space 116 (1.7 sherds/100 L) than 117 (0.4). One point to consider in assessing this, as with Space 115 above, is whether material is evenly distributed across the midden contexts or clustered in particular units. Assuming recovery rates are equal, there does seem to be a reasonable correlation (r = 0.75) for 14 contexts in Space 117, excluding the very large unit (1692), which has an extremely low density (0.1 sherds/100 L compared to 0.7 for the remaining contexts). In the small assemblage from Space 116, in contrast, there is no correlation between sherd counts and unit volumes. In fact 43 per cent of the sherds came from two contexts representing just eight per cent of the total volume, (1612) and (1629).

Building 6 provides a rare, more-or-less complete view of a structure from the South Area, comprising main room Space 163 and ancillary room Space 173. However, the total assemblage (64 sherds) is barely one-third that of Building 1 in terms of sherd count, and it is spread across a number of phases, meaning there are few coherent assemblages of any size. The pottery of occupation Phase B6.2 divides into two groups: feature fills (pits, graves and postholes) and floors/occupation deposits. Overall in this phase there is a high proportion of Group 2 sherds (45.5 per cent compared with the Level VIII average of 11.1 per cent); including four of the five from floor/occupation contexts. The scanty floor assemblage also comprises slightly smaller but less abraded sherds than those from the feature fills. In contrast, all the sherds of B6.5 derive from Space 173 and all but one from building fill (4321). Overall the sherds from the building fill are less abraded and less broken, allowing for the lower mean thickness, than those from Phase B6.2; there are also a higher proportion of Group 1 fabrics, and fewer rims.

Other spaces are somewhat different: although Spaces 151, 161 and 162 produced only small quantities of pottery, and have rather different assemblages, as a combined group they have considerably smaller sherds than the fill of Building 6 (though they are also thinner).

Levels IX–X

In Level IX there is greater variation again in the proportion of Group 1 fabrics between different spaces (also reflected in the abrasion statistics), and a high overall number of joins and mean sherd size compared to Level VIII. It is notable that the earlier phases of Space 117 resemble the Level VIII midden directly above more than the other Level IX buildings. Meanwhile, the two spaces of Building 17 (Spaces 170 & 182) differ in most respects, in part related to reconstructable vessels in the latter. The assemblage from Building 17 is almost twice as big as that from the Building 2 occupation, but it largely comprises material from infill. The assemblage from Space 170 has a high proportion of Group 2 material (43 per cent), including a complete profile of a small bowl (see above). The Space 182 assemblage was, as mentioned, an unusual one because of the group of sherds of fabric 3n (see above).

The assemblage from Building 18 of Level X derives from a small number of Phase 2 contexts, mainly floor or occupation deposits. Like some other small assemblages, there is a high proportion of Group 2 sherds. The sherds are small overall, suggesting a well-trampled floor, but abrasion is moderate, perhaps implying they were not long left exposed to weather (cf. the large but worn sherds in B6.2).

Pre-Level X

Only four sherds came from contexts assigned to pre-Level X deposits and just two of these are secure. Both came from Space 198 of Level XI (penning context (4850)), and comprise joining fragments of a Group 2 vessel with a finely-burnished (and slipped?) exterior. This is the earliest securely-stratified pottery from the South Area and it would be interesting to compare any absolute dates with the spaces of Mellaart's Level XII, which produced rather more finds.

No pottery at all was recovered from the pre-building layers of Level Pre-XII.A to E in Space 181. None of the fired-clay objects recovered from lower down in Space 181 (and from the lower deposits in the KOPAL Area) can be reconstructed as vessels, and they are completely different in fabric from the Level XI to VIII pottery. The absence of pottery from the base of the mound may indicate either a genuine 'aceramic' site (albeit one with a certain level of fired-clay technology) or simply that pottery was not being discarded in these deposits, perhaps because they lay some way from contemporary houses. Elsewhere on the site Mellaart excavated a sounding as far down as Level XII and recovered pottery from every layer, including a Level XII building. This may support the latter idea, but perhaps more likely implies that the 'Level XII' deposits in these two areas are not in fact contemporary. If the Space 181 units look like a 'normal' midden in terms of other types of material this would provide a strong case for the earliest occupation at Çatalhöyük indeed being aceramic.

Regional comparisons

It is hard to find material directly comparable with the Neolithic pottery from Çatalhöyük elsewhere in central Anatolia, where most excavated sites are either aceramic (e.g. Aşıklı Höyük, Canhasan III) or later Neolithic/early Chalcolithic (e.g. Hacılar, Canhasan I). Esin (1999) pointed out that in central Anatolia we have no evidence of how the transition from the Aceramic to Ceramic Neolithic took place (clearly that evidence may be forthcoming from Çatalhöyük in the future). Moreover, as Özdoğan (1999, 11) has stated, compared to the Levant (or Europe) excavated Turkish sites are a long way apart so 'we are still trying to interpret over distances that represent hundreds of kilometres'.

Given this chronological and spatial coarseness, due to the small number of excavated sites, comparisons for the Çatalhöyük pottery are necessarily rather general. Traditionally they have been drawn with finds from Suberde, 80 km to the southwest, where thick-walled, vegetable-tempered pots with simple forms, pinkish-buff surfaces and dark cores were discovered (Bordaz 1968), and Erbaba (see below), where a gritty, burnished monochrome ware in simple holemouth and bowl forms with characteristic horizontal, perforated lugs seems to resemble the pottery of Çatalhöyük Level VI (Bordaz & Bordaz 1976). Radiocarbon dates indeed suggest that the Suberde finds may be comparable with the earliest pottery at Çatalhöyük, while Erbaba, though poorly dated, is probably somewhat later (see Chapter 4).

These sites have, however, only seen limited investigations. One with a much better stratigraphic sequence lies to the southeast, across the Taurus, at Yumuktepe (Mersin). Recent work at this site has added something to the evidence from the 1950s, but the basic picture is unchanged, with the seventh-millennium levels producing small fragments of dark-faced burnished fine wares (DFBW) and some impressed decoration (Caneva 1999; Garstang 1953, 20–21). At Tarsus, similar DFBW was accompanied by light, gritty, coarse wares (Mellink, in Goldman 1956). Although burnishing is common at Çatalhöyük, there are few close comparisons with the early DFBW from Mersin, which has a much higher polish. However, the deep sounding at Mersin has produced some thick-walled, light-faced pottery that resembles the Group 2 fabrics (there is no straw temper) from Çatalhöyük (F. Balossi pers. comm.).

Further north, some of the sites surveyed in the Nigde region, east of the Konya plain, by Ian Todd (1980) may also overlap with Çatalhöyük, although the assemblages from e.g. Pınarbaşı-Bor and Kösk Pinar seem to have more in common with the later levels of the East Mound, despite the fabrics frequently containing straw temper. More recently, excavations at the site of Musular, close to Aşıklı Höyük in the Aksaray region, have revealed one multi-roomed building of the Ceramic Neolithic period (Özbaşaran 2000). The pottery from this site is plain, poorly fired, slipped and burnished with straw and grit temper, but the red slips and range of shapes, including cups and flaring bowls, again suggest a later Neolithic date.

The largest assemblages of roughly-contemporary ceramics, however, have come from the Lake District, west of the Konya plain, around Burdur. Erbaba, on the east side of Beysehir Gölü, has been mentioned and pottery resembling that of Çatalhöyük Level VI and above has also been found at Alan Höyük, on the south side of the lake (see http://tayproject.eies.itu.edu.tr). But it is the more recent excavations further west at Kuruçay, Höyücek and Bademağaci which have produced greater quantities and longer sequences of material, spanning the Neolithic and Chalcolithic periods (Duru 1999). Duru's chronological scheme, which sees Höyücek and Bademağacı starting before 7000 cal BC (i.e. contemporary with pre-Level XII layers at Çatalhöyük) and a few early seventh-millennium finds from Kuruçay and Hacılar, has recently been challenged by Schoop (2002), who suggests none of these pre-date 6500 cal BC. As shall be seen, this 'short chronology' makes more sense in terms of ceramic comparisons.

The pottery from Kuruçay Level 13 and the so-called Early Settlements Phase (EYD) at Höyücek includes mottled, burnished S-profile bowls and globular jars (Duru 1995). In the latter case this material pre-dates a phase with more elaborate pottery which is dated around 6300 cal BC, probably contemporary with the upper levels of the East Mound, suggesting the EYD may be approximately equivalent to Levels VI–V at Çatalhöyük. However, close attention to the pottery forms shows there are few typological parallels between the assemblages. The pottery from the early levels at Höyücek (and Bademağacı) includes vertically-pierced cylindrical lugs and basket handles, features which are extremely rare at Çatalhöyük, and do not predate Level VI. These typological differences, as well as the later discrepancies between e.g. Kuruçay and Çatalhöyük West, support Duru's (1999) statement that there are no close ties between the Lake District, except perhaps its western edge, and the Konya plain. Vessels of Çatalhöyük type are not generally among the Early Neolithic repertory of this area.

Moreover, just as most of the ceramic assemblages excavated elsewhere in Anatolia post-date Çatalhöyük Level VI, the South Area levels also appear to be older than most if not all of the Lake District settlements, especially if we follow Schoop's (2002) alternative chronology. The earliest material from Duru's excavations is probably that from Level 6 at Bademağacı, which was excavated in 1998 and does not so far have associated radiocarbon dates. The pottery is described as a pale greyish beige fabric with thick walls, a self-slip and light burnishing; the temper is mineral, including mica; and forms are primarily hemibowls with thick, flat bases and flattened or flaring rims (the flattened form is seen as an imitation of woodworking). The typical Lake District bell-shaped and cylindrical vessels with cylindrical lugs then appear in the succeeding Levels 5 and 4. Duru (1999) suggests Level 6 could date as early as the late eighth millennium BC, but Schoop's redating to the mid-seventh millennium seems more plausible.

In short, the Level VI and later pottery from Çatalhöyük has generic similarities (relatively simple forms, the use of burnishing) with a range of assemblages from sites both east and west of the Konya plain. Pottery contemporary with that from Level VII and below is much harder to find, but *may* be present at Suberde, Mersin and Bademağacı. Although there may have been a simple, generic pottery tradition at the beginning of these sequences, it is clear that in terms of forms and fabrics local or regional potting traditions were established at a relatively early stage. Nevertheless, continuing contact between different groups is likely, given the movement of obsidian from Cappadocia, and it is plausible that other forms of technology were passed on in the contexts of these wide-ranging exchange networks. However, with little published information about spatial distributions and vessel functions at these sites, much further research is needed in order to understand the social contexts and networks within which ceramic technology was introduced to Anatolia and subsequently developed.

Chapter 6

Domesticating Clay: the Role of Clay Balls, Mini Balls and Geometric Objects in Daily Life at Çatalhöyük

Sonya Atalay

This chapter focuses on clay balls, geometric objects, and mini balls excavated since 1995. The clay balls found during James Mellaart's 1960s excavations were not systematically recorded or analyzed, although he does mention them in a discussion of crafts and trade at Çatalhöyük. 'Clay balls, baked in ovens ... were common and some of the balls bear incised decoration. Baked clay was also used for the production of beads, and pendants, slingstones, stamp-seals and statuettes' (Mellaart 1967, 217). It is not clear what Mellaart was referring to in this description of clay balls and slingstones made of clay. In other places (Mellaart 1967, 78), he uses the term 'clay ball' synonymously with 'sling ammunition'. There is one additional mention of clay balls from another source (Mellaart 1966a, 188), where Mellaart postulates that balls were put inside skins or bags and lashed to a stick to form a 'cheap macehead'; although he admits this would have little effect in hunting wild cattle, boar, or deer. A report based on a selection of clay balls recovered during the 1993 to 1995 surface collection and surface scraping has also been published (Hamilton 1996, 229–33) and more generally such items were discussed by Denise Schmandt-Besserat (1977). This report provides a general description and overall distribution of clay-ball fragments found on the surface, and offers two preliminary functional interpretations of the balls (most likely as pot stands or possibly as potboilers). Previous publications were not based on detailed analysis of the materials, but did offer a preliminary overview of the clay balls and ideas for their use.

In 1997 I developed a systematic recording method for the clay balls and began recording all excavated material. The goal of this chapter is to report on the specific recording and analysis data of the clay ball materials uncovered since the excavation began in 1995, and to put forth my current interpretations for these data. These interpretations are more detailed than previously-published archive reports (Atalay 2000; Suponcic 1998; 1999), yet are still preliminary because they are based only on fully-analyzed materials, which is less than a quarter of what has been excavated thus far.

Recording method: phase 1 and phase 2

Since its inception in 1997, the clay-ball recording system I originally designed has been updated, adjusted, and improved (Atalay 2000). As a result, clay-ball materials were recorded using one of two methods: phase 1 or phase 2. In phase 1, unit counts and brief descriptions for the following attributes were recorded: shape, size, mass, fragmentation, level and type of wear or weathering, surface texture and evenness, surface and core colour, surface features (burning or residue), surface elaboration, heat treatment, size and type of matrix inclusions (using a 10× hand lens), presence and percentage of interior pitting, fabric type, and interior notes. An overall impression of the unit was also recorded. After using this recording method for several field seasons, I decided that recording each attribute individually was more productive and informative. Examining each pieces' individual attributes was necessary to produce the overall unit count, and the added time of recording these attributes individually seemed relatively minimal. Units analyzed before the individual piece recording system of phase 2 was established were not re-recorded. Therefore, units analyzed using the phase 1 system include only summary unit counts for each of the attributes mentioned above.

Classification method

The clay balls, objects and minis are all human-made objects in a variety of geometric shapes formed using clay. Shape and size were the preliminary attributes used to classify pieces by type. Below is a description of the way shape and size were used for classification, followed by a description of the types created thus far.

Shape
Clay-ball materials excavated prior to the 1999 field season are predominantly spherical, but include a small number of pieces (termed balloids at the time) that seem to have been squashed or flattened. They appear to have had a spherical form originally, but seem to have been unintentionally deformed before firing. Prior to 1999, in addition to spherically- and near-spherically-shaped pieces, a relatively small number of geometrically-shaped clay objects (88 pieces), mostly fragments (63 of the 88), including cylindrical, conical, flat rounded, and rectangular pieces were excavated. Since the geometrically-shaped pieces occurred in such limited numbers, were often excavated along with groups of clay balls or in similar contexts with clay balls, and have a clay fabric consistent with that of the clay balls, they were grouped and recorded along with the balls, but were noted as having a non-typical shape. All materials (balls, balloids, and geometric objects) at that point were classified into 1 of 2 groups, Balls or Mini Balls, depending on their size. During the 1999 field season, when large quantities of non-spherical geometric objects were excavated in both the South and KOPAL Areas (Suponcic 1999), I presumed the balls and objects were related in some way, and that the difference in shape represented a temporal change from objects, in early levels, to balls, in later levels. At that time, I revised the classification system and began categorizing and recording geometric solids as a third group called Clay Objects. The 88 geometric objects from the 1996 to 1998 field seasons were re-examined and reclassified as Clay Objects, and appear as such in this report. Balloids were also re-examined and are now categorized as either balls or objects, depending on my observations of their shape and sphericity.

Table 6.1. *Number and percentage of clay balls within set range.*

Diameter range (cm)	**4.0–4.9**	**5.0–5.9**	**6.0–6.9**	**7.0–7.9**	**8.0–8.9**	**9.0–9.9**
No. of balls	17	151	233	89	8	1
Per cent of total	3	30	47	18	2	0

Diameter
Early observations of clay-ball materials indicated a distinct group of balls with much smaller diameter. Additionally the colour, texture, and lack of durability of these smaller balls, which crumble easily and nearly disintegrate when wet, demonstrate that they were not fired, or at least not as highly fired, as the larger clay balls and objects. Examination with a 10× hand lens showed the smaller spheres to have a clay matrix quite different from the typical ball matrix; marked predominantly by having far fewer inclusions. Owing to the substantial difference in size, heat treatment, and clay fabric, these small balls are classified as a third type called Mini Balls.

Description of type-groups

Using the criteria of shape, diameter, and paste as described above, I created the tripartite classification of Balls, Mini Balls, and Clay Objects. Further preliminary classification of the Clay Objects was done according to object shape. Little has been previously published in relation to developing a typology of this artefact class, with the exception of Schmandt-Besserat's (1992) excellent analysis of clay tokens from various sites throughout the Near East, and the Poverty Point clay cooking objects (Poverty Point Objects or PPO's) from a late Archaic Native American site in Louisiana (Ford & Webb 1956). Using some of the terminology and shape categories of these systems, I developed a classification and typology system specifically for the Çatalhöyük clay-ball materials. Below is a brief description of these types, and some of the general attributes of each; including size, weight, fragmentation, and surface appearance.

Figure 6.1. *Balls, mini balls, and objects from various units to demonstrate size range. One ball has an incised 'X' and several others have visible residue and fire clouding.*

Type 1: clay balls

Ball size

From the 355 units (priority units) reported here, clay balls occurred in 140 units, with a total of 2188 pieces. Diameters were recorded for all pieces with full diameter intact. The distribution of diameters can be seen in Table 6.1. In early excavation, clay balls seemed to cluster into size categories. Closer examination indicates that they actually do not cluster into size 'groups', but rather have diameters ranging steadily from 4.0 to 9.0 cm, with a mean diameter of 6.3 cm. Most units excavated thus far have balls with a range of diameters. In Figure 6.1 several whole balls from various units are shown with mini balls for comparative size scale. It is clear that units with a greater number of pieces with measurable diameter also have balls with a greater range of diameters, indicating there was no standard size for the balls. Considering units with 20 or more measured ball diameters, there is a significant amount of variety in the diameter range, also indicating that no standard ball-size categories existed. Furthermore, no significant size patterning is apparent for balls within each building, or for the site as a whole. More material from a greater number of units, further comparisons of ball-diameter range between various contexts, within, and between spaces and buildings, combined with analysis of ball mass and interior fabric will certainly prove interesting and informative for thinking about crafters' decisions during production, as well as questions related to the possible use of clay balls as standardized measuring devices. However, based on the current data, clay balls do not have a standard size or weight, and were not used as standardized weight or measurement devices.

Ball mass

In the units studied thus far there are 108 whole clay balls ranging from 58 g to 614 g. In Figure 6.2 the diameter of whole balls is plotted against their mass, showing that mass varies directly with diameter. As with ball diameter, there is no clustering of these balls by weight, but rather they follow a steady continuum.

Ball fragmentation

Of the 2188 clay-ball pieces included in this report, 77.6 per cent (1678) are fragments smaller than a quarter of a ball. There are 108 whole balls (4.9 per cent), 10 balls with three-quarter-ball fragmentation (0.5 per cent), 89 half-balls (4.1 per cent), and 302 quarter-balls (13.8 per cent). Balls have predominantly angular breaks and tend to break into roughly quarter-sphere segments and conical-shaped fragments as illustrated by several fragmented pieces in Figure 6.3. I have not yet conducted any substantial work on refitting pieces, so it is difficult to determine how much non-faced interior might have been lost during breakage. In the 355 units examined thus far, all pieces had a definite exterior surface that was clearly a portion of a rounded exterior. However, I suspect that clay balls are recognized and categorized as 'clay balls' precisely because they have a rounded, spherical, exterior surface. It certainly seems possible that a ball breaking in antiquity resulted in large pieces, and/or conical-shaped fragments, all with easily recognizable rounded exterior surfaces; but also would have

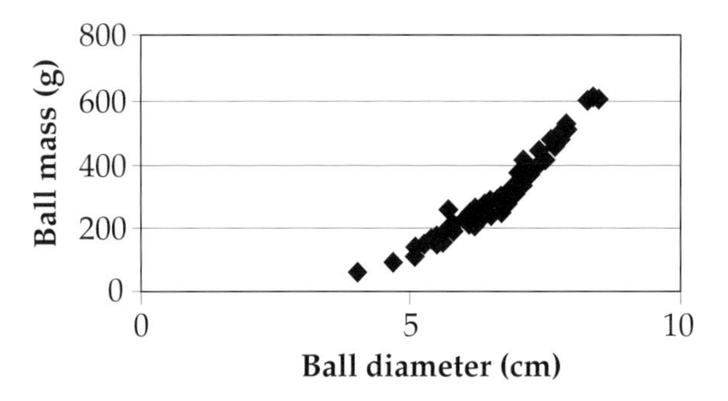

Figure 6.2. *Clay-ball mass plotted against diameter.*

Figure 6.3. *Whole and fragmented balls and objects illustrating typical fragmentation.*

Figure 6.4. *Examples of residues and fire clouding on whole balls.*

produced a number of non-faced, non-spherical fragments of clay-ball interior. Such interior pieces might have easily been overlooked or mistaken for burned building material and thus become 'non-artefacts' or artefacts of a different category (i.e. burned building material, daub, brick, fired clay etc.). Future experimental work combined with refitting of pieces within and across contexts will help to clarify this point and other issues of ball fragmentation.

Ball surfaces

The balls studied thus far have a variety of surface features; some seemingly intentional elaborations and others likely accidental. Figure 6.4 illustrates some of the variety of surface features. Intentional elaborations include incised lines, holes, circles, and fingernail designs. There are also numerous basket and matting impressions (Chapter 15), cordage impressions, plant or seed impressions, palm/handprints, fingerprints and finger-impressed areas. While these markings on a ball's surface could have occurred while the crafter was forming and shaping the ball and/or during the drying process, I believe many balls were intentionally elaborated using basket, matting, plant and/or hand and finger impressions.

The evidence for this is the high occurrence of multiple types of markings on a single ball, as well as the depth into the surface which some of these markings display. A large amount of pressure was necessary to make many of the deep impressions visible on the balls. Even if crafters stacked wet or leather-hard balls on top of each other for transport or drying in baskets or on matting, it seems very unlikely they would move and re-stack the balls multiple times, onto a variety of different surfaces, while they were still soft enough to take such an impression. This is not to say that clay balls were not dried in baskets or on matted areas. In fact, they most likely were dried in precisely such ways. I only wish to point out that people crafting the balls may have also actively used the drying surface, other nearby woven materials, plants, grasses, seeds, their fingers, palms, or other devices, to intentionally elaborate the surface of the balls they made.

Another surface feature present on some balls is fire clouding, in large or small areas (Figs. 6.1 & 6.4). Fire clouds may be the unintentional result of firing, or may be an elaboration method chosen by clay-ball crafters to enhance the beauty of the objects (Pedley 1993, 34) or to give a ball their own touch or signature. Fire clouding does need not to be viewed as a mistake, or as incompetence on the part of the crafters' firing and pyro-technology skills. The intentionality of the balls' fire clouding is unclear, but it is noteworthy that the majority of the balls have no fire clouding on their surface and their interiors have been oxidized completely through to the core. This indicates a high level of pyro-technology and firing knowledge, at least on the part of some crafters.

A number of balls have a residue on their surface (Figs. 6.1 & 6.4). The residue is reddish-black to dark black and occurs as drops, speckles, or in built-up layers that seem to have trickled, in a once-liquid form, down the surface of the ball. Ethnographic information from local villages indicates residues very similar in colour and patterning are common on the base of clay ovens from the dripping fat and grease produced during grilling and roasting meat (Küçükköy Seminar 06.08.01). I believe at least some of the visible residues are plant or animal food remains resulting from the balls' and objects' use in cooking.

Organic-residue analysis is underway on a number of samples in order to determine the precise nature of the residue. A small pilot study (Chapter 7) of nine ball fragments produced no evidence of organic residue. However, none of the ball fragments in this preliminary study had visible residues on their surface. Further analysis of balls and objects with visible residue is necessary to understand its origin. Experimental work with modern-made clay balls and objects used for grilling, boiling, roasting, and parching, must also be submitted for organic-residue analysis to better

Table 6.2. *Count and percentage of mini-ball diameters within a set range.*

Diameter range (cm)	0.5–0.9	1.00–1.49	1.5–1.9	2.0–2.49	2.5–2.9
No. of mini balls	3	38	49	3	1
Perc ent of total	3	40	53	3	1

understand the expected residue absorption into these dense, non-porous clay ball materials. These balls and objects have a much lower porosity than the pottery from Çatalhöyük which yielded degraded animal fats in GC / MS analysis (Chapter 7). This issue is addressed in further detail in the interpretation section below (see also Atalay 2003).

Type II: mini balls

Diameter

Mini balls were found in 40 of the 355 units studied and totalled 135 pieces. The diameter range is 0.9 to 2.6 cm, with a mean diameter of 1.5 cm. Table 6.2 shows counts within a set range for all minis with a measurable diameter. The majority (53 per cent) of the minis fall within the 1.5 to 1.9 cm range, and 93 per cent of all minis are 1.0 to 1.9 cm in diameter. In comparison with the smallest clay ball diameter of 4.0 cm, the mini balls are distinctly smaller and are easily identifiable by size alone. Figure 6.1 clearly illustrates the difference in size between several typical-sized clay balls and mini balls.

Mass and density

As with clay balls, mini-ball mass increases with diameter. One noticeable difference between the balls and the minis is that minis have a lower density than the larger-sized balls. This is due to the difference between the fabric used for minis and that used for clay balls.

Interior fabric

Using a 10× hand lens, I viewed and recorded all visible mini-ball interiors, and compared them with clay-ball interior fabrics. The minis are lacking the mineral inclusions that were used as temper in the clay balls. This is not to say that mini balls have no mineral inclusions; in fact very small minerals are visible in most mini balls. However, the visible minerals in mini balls are much smaller and less abundant than those within clay balls. Petrographic analysis of clay balls, mini balls, and objects confirms the clay-ball / mini-ball distinction. This difference in fabric is either related to crafters' choices of source material or to their decisions about the preparation of clays for making balls and minis. It seems that the mini balls were made from clay in its natural state, while the balls and objects were

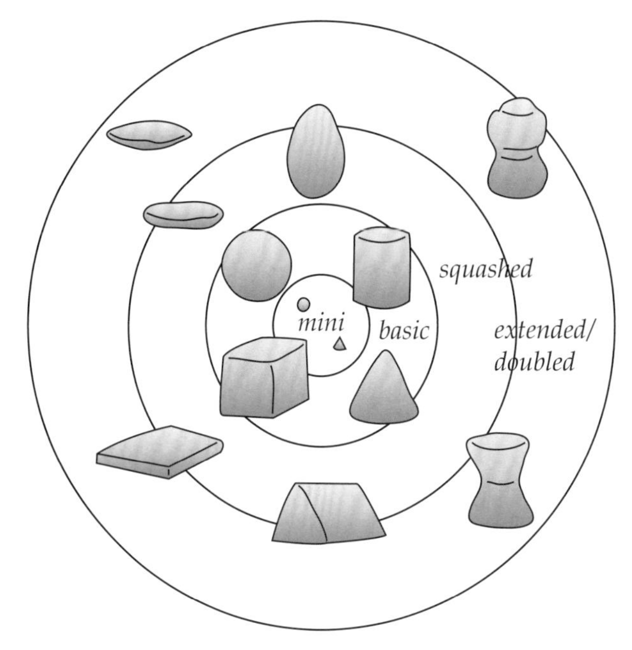

Figure 6.5. *The range of clay-object shapes. (by John Swogger).*

made using clays with large amounts of mineral (and sometimes organic) temper added to them.

Heat treatment

Another clear distinction between minis and clay balls is the minis' lack of firing. Minis are generally not hard fired; they were most likely sun-dried, resulting in a crumbly dusty surface that will easily dissolve after excavation when washed or soaked in water. While there are examples of mini balls that have been fired, these are usually completely, although sometimes partially, reduced; indicating that they were covered or buried during heat exposure, and were probably unintentionally fired.

Surface treatment

Mini balls have very little surface elaboration. The incisions and impressions found on clay balls are nearly completely absent on mini-ball material. The few exceptions to this are the organic voids that run into the interiors of some minis. One unique example of mini-ball surface elaboration is 1803.X1 from the South Area, Space 116, Building 2. This mini ball has incised lines filled with a white plaster or marl-like material spiralling around its surface. Aside from 1803.X1, mini balls lack surface elaboration; including the fire clouding and residue seen on larger balls and objects. Minis have a range of surface evenness and textures. Some are smooth, even, and appear to have a high amount of care put into smoothing the surface; while others have an uneven rough or silty surface.

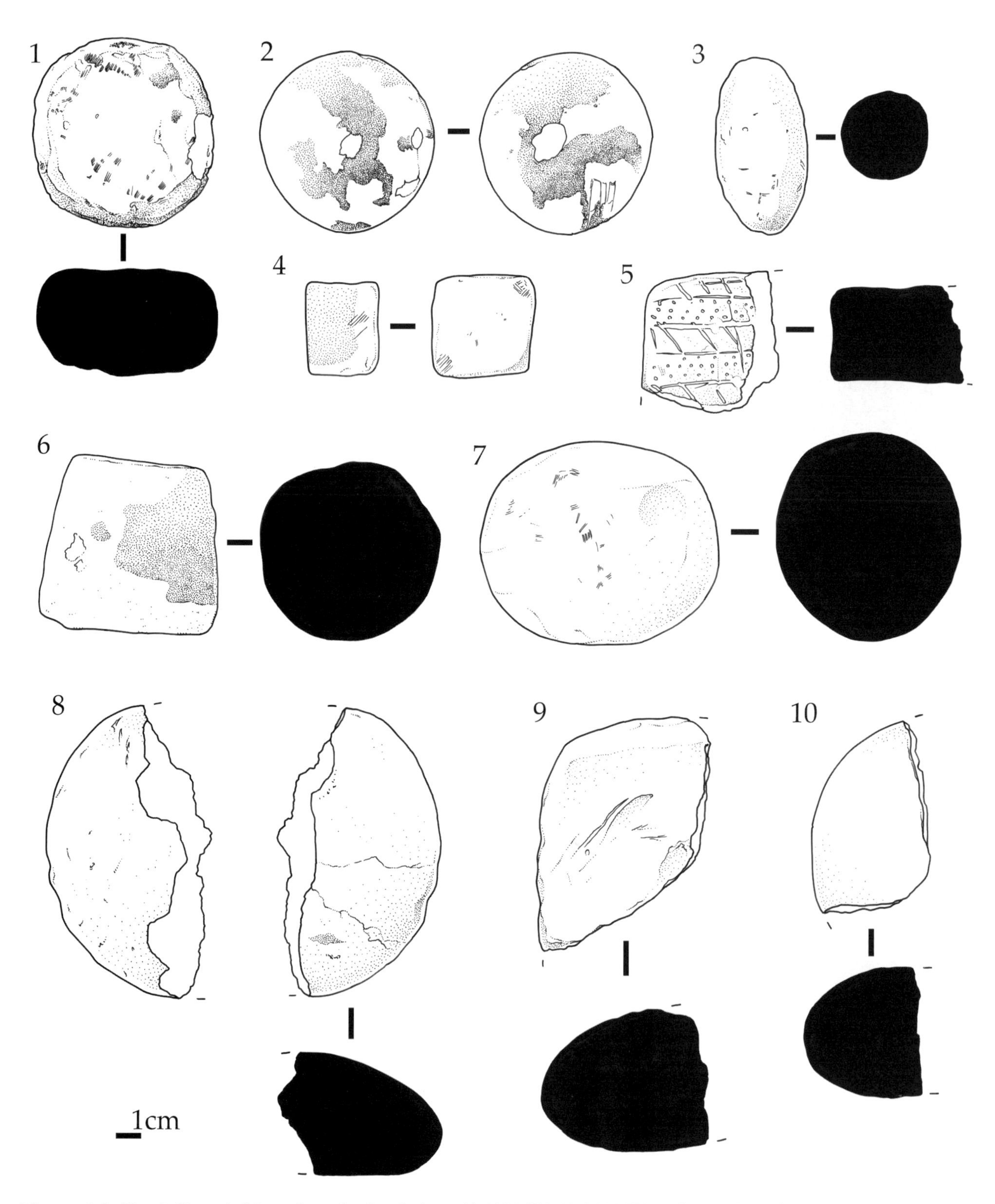

Figure 6.6. *Clay balls and objects from the South Area: 1) 1889.X6; 2) 1889.X94; 3) 3979.D1; 4) 4548.X1; 5) 5329.M1; 6) 5154.X8; 7) 5154.X3; 8) 5326.M1; 9) 5328.M2; 10) 5329.M3 (by John Swogger).*

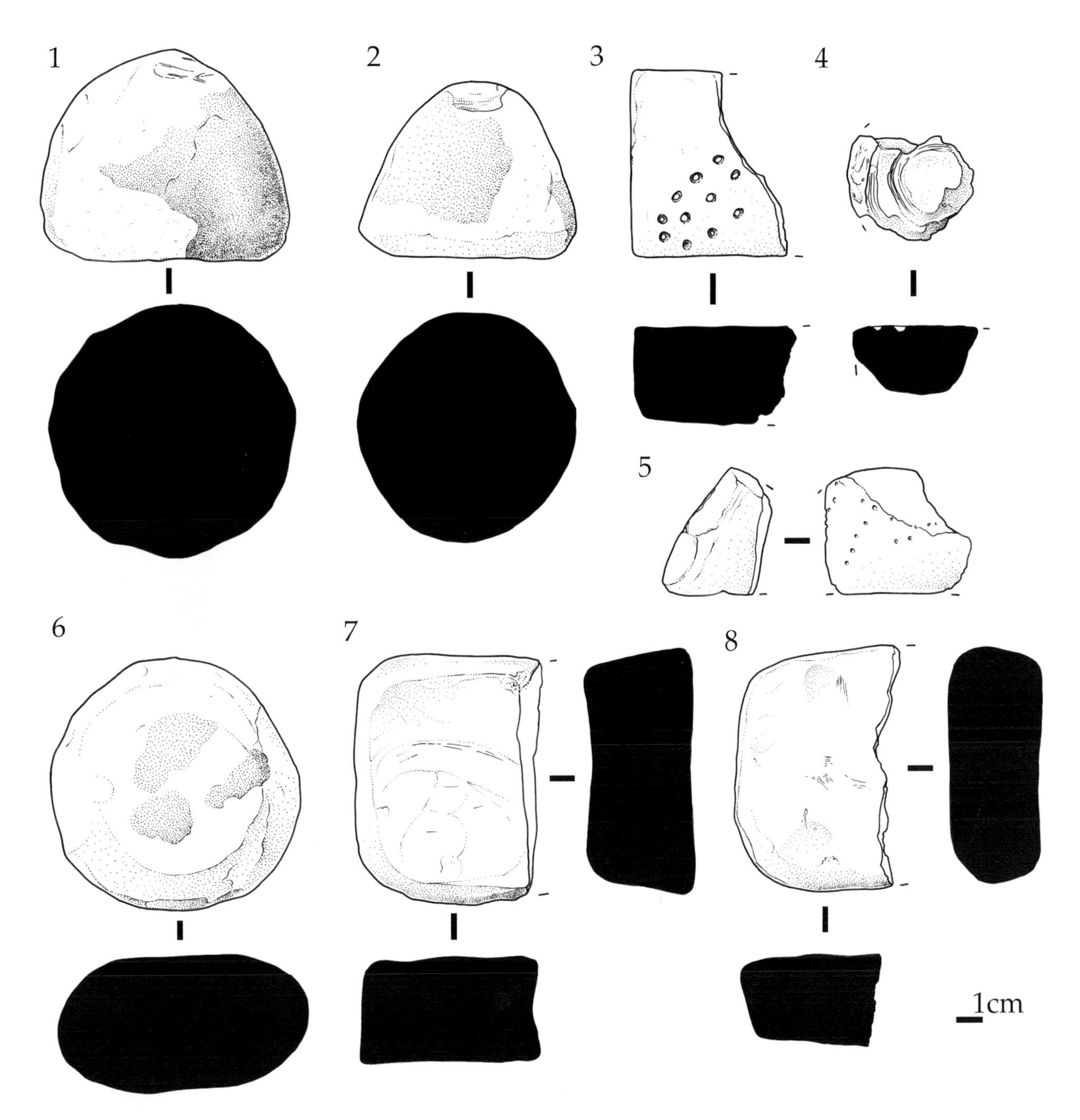

Figure 6.7. *Clay balls and objects from the KOPAL Area: 1) 6025.D; 2) 6025.D1; 3) 6025.M3; 4) 6025.M5; 5) 6079.M4; 6) 6039.D1; 7) 6079.M1; 8) 6079.M2 (by John Swogger).*

Type III: geometric clay objects

Shape

The most distinct feature of the clay objects is their shape in comparison with the clay balls. Figure 6.5 shows the range of shapes recorded thus far (see also Figs. 6.6–6.7). Currently there are six object subtypes: rectangular, cubical, conical, cylindrical, and both flat-based and convex-based rounded shapes. Whenever possible, each piece has been categorized into a subtype. Pieces with indeterminate subtype were classified more generally as rectangular or rounded. Of the 355 units studied, 65 units have objects, for a total of 1083 pieces. 96 per cent (1039 pieces) of the objects studied are fragment-size pieces; many of those were non-diagnostic and difficult to categorize into a subtype. Many fragments can only be categorized as rectangular or rounded subtypes. There are also pieces that could not be classified with certainty as rectangular or rounded; these were labelled as non-diagnostic objects.

Table 6.3. *Dimensions and mass of all whole geometric objects.*

Area	Unit	Shape	Mass (g)	Dimensions (cm)
KOPAL	6025	Conical	341	8.1W × 6.2H
KOPAL	6025	Conical	622	8.9DW × 7.7H
KOPAL	6079	Rectangular	625	10.6L × 9.1W × 3.6H
South	1091	Conical	317	7.6W × 6.2H
South	1092	Spherical (non-symmetrical spheresque)	289	7.3D
South	1092	Spherical (flat sphere)	222	6.7W × 5.3H
South	1668	Spherical (flat sphere)	193	6.8L × 5.5H
South	1873	Spherical (flat sphere)	236	6.4D
South	1889	Conical	120	5.6W × 4.5H
South	1889	Conical	320	5.9W × 5.9H
South	1889	Cylindrical	158	4.9W × 5.8L
South	1889	Cylindrical	250	7L × 4.7H × 6.1W
South	1889	Double sphere	244	6.0 D × 7.2H
South	1889	Flat-based convex top	230	6.2W × 5.4H
South	1889	Flat-based convex top	248	6.7W × 4.5H
South	1889	Flat-based convex top	248	7.1W × 4.1H
South	1889	Spherical (flat sphere)	128	5.1D
South	1889	Ovoid	185	7.0L × 5.6W × 4.9H
South	3314	Cylindrical	112	6.2L × 4.0D
South	3740	Double conical	67	4.9W × 4.3H
South	4225	Object	166	6.6D × 3.5H
South	4465	Elliptical (potato-shaped)	240	7.8 cm L
South	4530	Spherical (with flat bottom)	122	8.1W
South	4548	Cube	66	3.8L × 3.7W × 2.9H
South	5292	Conical	287	7.5W × 5.7H

Size and mass

Unlike spherical balls which have a diameter that is both easy to measure and compare, the diversity of object subtypes makes it more difficult to make comparisons of shape and size. Table 6.3 shows the basic dimensions and mass of all whole objects and illustrates the size diversity that exits, even within one subtype. As more objects are excavated, recorded, and studied it will be possible to make a more thorough comparison of object size and weight; but at this point it is only possible to note the variety of sizes and weights within each subtype. As with the clay balls, the range of size and shape indicates that the objects were not used as a standard weight-measurement device, although their use in terms of symbolic measurement is possible.

Fragmentation

One interesting aspect of clay-object fragmentation is that few pieces retain a quarter or more of their original size. 96 per cent of the objects are fragments, and another 2.4 per cent (25 pieces) are whole objects. There are no three-quarter size pieces and the half and quarter pieces together only comprise 1.5 per cent of the total (16 pieces). This may, in part, be due to the difficulty of determining the original shape of the objects, since labelling a piece as a half or quarter requires knowledge of the original complete shape. Fragment pieces can be quite large, but are often not large enough to determine what fraction of the whole object is represented.

Surface

Objects have surface markings similar to the clay balls in type and amount. Fire clouding on objects is most often visible on the flat surface, indicating that firing or repeated heating of those objects occurred with the flat surface on the ground, where there was a limited oxygen supply. Residue similar to that found on the clay balls is also present on a number of objects. Like the residue on the balls, object residues appear to have dripped in liquid form down the side of the objects, and are sometimes visible in areas where they rolled onto the bottom of objects as well. The organic-residue pilot study reported in this volume (Chapter 7) did not include any clay objects, although analysis is currently underway on a number of objects with visible surface residues. In terms of object elaborations, there are far fewer basket and matting impressions on the objects than on the clay balls, and fewer seed and plant impressions. Elaborations on objects are predominantly finger and palm prints, fingertip and finger-nail indentations, and incised lines and holes.

Distribution by area

Impressionistically, it seemed evident since excavations began in 1995 that clay balls were more abundant in the South Area than in the North and BACH Areas. Similarly, the high density of clay objects found in the KOPAL Area appeared comparable to that from the South Area. The density calculations, by both count and weight, for studied clay-ball materials confirm that the South and KOPAL Areas do indeed have similar densities, and that both had much higher densities than the North Area. Comparative density figures for Building 3 in the BACH Area, which neighbours the North Area, are not presented here, but are similar to the North Area density. Table 6.4 lists the weight and count density for all clay-ball materials (including balls, minis, and objects) from the North, South, and KOPAL Areas. The KOPAL and South Areas are similar in mass density (1.918 and 1.813 g/l respectively), but both are more than ten times higher than the North Area (0.178 g/l).

When comparing the count density of all three areas, the North Area (0.006 pieces/L) is roughly eight times less dense than either the South or KOPAL

Areas. These figures illustrate the low density of clay-ball material in the North Area; however, it is not accurate to directly compare North and South Areas without taking into consideration the context from which these materials were retrieved. The material from the North Area came predominantly from fill and occupation materials within two buildings (Buildings 1 and 5), while in the South Area material came from both within and outside seven buildings (Buildings 2, 4, 6, 16, 17, 18 & 23).

Table 6.4. *Mass and count densities for all balls, mini balls and objects.*

Area	Mass (g)	No. of pieces	Soil volume (litres)	Mass density (g/litre)	Count density
KOPAL	12,342	340	6436	1.918	0.053
North	1515	55	8511	0.178	0.006
South	121,924	3014	67,255	1.813	0.045

Table 6.5. *Mass and count density with external/internal division.*

Area	External vs internal	Mass (g)	No. of pieces	Soil volume (litres)	Mass density (g/litre)	Count density (pieces/litre)
KOPAL	external	12,342	340	6436	1.918	0.053
South	external	64,439	1995	48,403	1.331	0.041
North	external	802	22	1459.1	0.550	0.015
South	internal	57,485	1019	20,852.86	2.757	0.049
North	internal	713	33	7051.85	0.101	0.005

Originally I suspected the higher density of clay-ball materials in the South Area was the result of the increased amount of exterior contexts excavated there; and that clay balls were generally in higher concentrations in exterior areas site-wide. However this turned out to be completely unfounded. As Table 6.5 illustrates, the density difference between North and South Areas is even more pronounced when the material is divided into internal and external contexts; but, contrary to what I had suspected, the predominant difference between the two areas is the result of the high variance between interior, not exterior, building contexts. The mass density of material from within buildings is ten times higher in the South Area than in the North Area, while the comparison for external areas is considerably less, with the South Area having slightly less than three times greater density than the North Area.

Clay-ball materials, including balls, minis and objects, were certainly used differently, were imbued with diverse symbolic meanings, and played variable roles in daily life; all of which varied by person, family, clan(?), generation, and temporally throughout the entire occupation of this site. A pronounced difference in material culture, such as the disparity of clay-ball material from building interiors between the North and South Areas, is exciting in that it signals a shift in what Bourdieu refers to as habitus (1977).

Working to interpret this signal is, of course, much more complicated, and requires a larger sample size as well as the integration of data from other segments of material culture. At this stage, with the data available from these 355 units, the issue of changing habitus must be termed in the form of many more questions to be considered: Who changed their daily patterns of activity, and in what way(s) did they change? Is this the result of changing ideas of what belongs inside a building? Do the balls play a similar role in people's daily life but are being disposed of differently in the North Area? Were the balls made / used differently, in different contexts, and / or less frequently in the North Area? Is this pattern of changing habitus visible in other areas of material culture?

From the evidence available thus far, my current interpretation of this patterning is that it is closely related to a shift in pottery production, which begins in Level VII, and is complete by Level VI. This shift in pottery, which occurs between Buildings 5 and 1 in the North Area, includes a move from organic-tempered, thick-walled, un-sooted vessels to mineral-tempered thin-walled vessels that show evidence of heating over a fire (see Chapter 5). As I have described elsewhere (Atalay 2000; 2003; Suponcic 1999), and will discuss further below, my interpretation of the clay balls and objects is that they were part of domestic practice and were used as heat-transfer devices in cooking and food preparation. I view the dramatic drop in clay-ball density in the North Area, along with the shift in pottery to a type that is more conducive to cooking rather than storage, as the result of changes in food production and preparation patterns.

The density of clay-ball materials decreases dramatically in Level VII and above (later in time). Further evidence to support this idea comes from the BACH Area, which, on the basis of its pottery, is thought to be contemporary with the Building 1 from the North Area (see Chapter 5). The BACH Area includes material from within Building 3, as well as from several spaces on the exterior of the building. While I have not yet completed a detailed analysis of all BACH Area material, it is clear that it also has a very low density of clay-ball material, similar to that of the North Area. The difference in the density of clay-ball materials between North and South Areas may be the result of a shift from cooking with balls to cooking in pots. If so, it appears the change was not accompanied by a shift in the types of foods prepared, since neither the faunal nor botanical data indicate dramatic shifts. Another interpretation of the difference between North and South Areas ball density, although less likely, is that the two areas represent different 'neighbourhoods' with diverse populations who practised different cooking methods. It is difficult at this point to conclude anything more about this correlation between pottery and clay balls until further excavation takes place in both exterior and interior Level VI–VIII contexts in the North, South, BACH and other excavation areas. But similar shifts in cooking practices from indirect cooking using stones or clay objects to direct heating using pottery are well documented in numerous archaeological cases (Crown & Wills 1995; Oyuela-Caycedo 1995; Sassaman 1995). In each of these examples a shift in pottery technology — from organic-tempered to mineral-tempered thinner-walled vessels — also accompanied the transition.

There is a distinct difference in the density of clay-ball materials found in the South Area compared to both the North and BACH Areas. The sampling system employed in this analysis has not provided enough data on occupational contexts to produce comparable density figures for each of the areas of excavation. However, observations of the primary contexts in each of the three occupation areas (North, BACH & South) demonstrate clearly that clay balls are much more common in occupation contexts of the South Area than in both the North and BACH Areas.

Beginning with Level VII South, which is likely the closest in time to Buildings 1, 3, and 5 in the North and BACH Areas, there were three occupation contexts that contained clay balls in *in situ* contexts. Two of these were from between-wall contexts (between Spaces 165 & 168 and between Spaces 113 & 107) in which whole balls and a rich collection of faunal material appear to have been deliberately deposited in a single dumping event, from the roof of a nearby building into the inter-building space. Space 112 contained oven feature F.96, which contained a series of half clay balls placed face up to form the base of the oven. In this case, the balls were found *in situ* in an occupational context, although the balls were all broken and had been re-used in association with this oven.

Level VIII South included two excavated buildings (Buildings 4 & 6), and the southern most 2/3 of Building 4. The portion of Building 4 that was excavated contained no *in-situ* or primary-use clay-ball contexts. However, in Building 6 there were five occupation contexts that contained clay balls. The floor of oven F.433 was lined with numerous clay balls. In addition, there was a clay-ball pit filled with a number of whole clay balls in Space 163, and three clay-ball pits filled with whole and fragmented balls in various phases of Space 173 of the same building. Although not in an occupation context, the open area of Space 115, which was filled with dump deposits infilling the earlier building from Level IX (Building 2), also had a very high clay-ball density.

Level IX South had three buildings that were excavated (Buildings 2, 16 & 17), and in each of these clay balls were found in occupation or use contexts. Building 2 contained the clay-ball bin (1889), which was filled with nearly 100 whole balls and objects, and appeared to have been covered quickly, and contained large sections of faunal bone, worked bone and an unusual charcoal assemblage (Volume 3, Part 2). There was also a between-wall context that had a number of whole clay balls, was rich in faunal bone, and appeared to be a single depositional event. Furthermore, every unit from this building that was included in the sampling strategy and had clay-ball materials was very high in ball density. The infill units from this building were particularly high in ball density in comparison to other infill units.

From this same Level IX Building 16 contained several whole balls *in situ* inside oven F.438, and inside oven F.439. Excavators believed each of these contexts to be the result of the primary use of these ovens and not related to later infill. Building 17 also contained clay balls and objects (unit (5154)) in association with an F.555. Unit (5154) contained whole clay balls and objects inside a cut behind oven F.555.

In Level X South, where two buildings were excavated (Buildings 18 & 23), clay balls and objects occurred in domestic-use contexts in both buildings. Both buildings had been excavated by Mellaart in the 1960s, and a large number of whole clay balls from these buildings were collected during those excavations. However, because Mellaart did not record the specific locations from which these balls came, it is impossible to know if, in fact, these are from primary use or *in situ* contexts or from building infill. From the features remaining in these buildings after the 1960s excavations, which the Cambridge team excavated during the 1999 field season, there were clay balls and objects found in association with ovens in each building. In Building 18 whole balls were found in rake-out contexts in association with the use of oven F.473. In Building 23 balls were found in the base of oven F.539. This building also contained oven rake-outs that had high a density of clay-ball materials.

Levels XI, XII, and Pre-XII in the South Area differ from these earlier levels in that they did not contain a similar type of domestic architecture. Level XI contained stabling contexts and pit fills, Level XII was primarily penning deposits, and Pre-XII Levels were off site. While these levels do contain clay balls and objects, they are not comparable to the later South levels or to the domestic architectural structures found in the North and BACH Areas of the site.

Turning to the two buildings in the North Area (Buildings 1 & 5), as I have pointed out previously, the amount and density of clay-ball materials from North Area buildings is low, and there is a striking lack of interior features which contain clay balls and objects in occupational or use related contexts. This stands in stark contrast to the situation described above for the South Area. There was only one primary use-related *in situ* clay-ball context excavated thus far in the North Area. Space 156 of Building 5 contained one whole clay ball that was placed between a wild goat horn core, along with other items, under the packing deposits north of the wall in that space. This context is very different from those found in the South Area, where clay balls in occupational or use contexts are most often found in association with ovens, ashy rake-out near ovens, or with food remains deposited in between-wall contexts, as described above.

In the BACH Area the pattern of clay-ball distribution was very different from that found in the South Area. In the BACH Area, clay balls and objects were not found in primary or use contexts. The balls and objects found in this area (Building 3) were predominantly from building-fill contexts, and from brick and mortar contexts, in which they were used as building material. However, it does seem that clay balls were in use to some extent after the occupation of Building 3, since they occur in midden contexts that infill the building. However, in that midden they are present in lower density than in similar contexts from the South area. The mini-ball feature F.758 described above is similar to South Area ball contexts in that it was associated with an oven. However, unlike the clay balls associated with ovens in the South Area, the mini balls in this feature were not fired, and as such do not seem to have been part of the functional use of the abutting oven, but had a symbolic relationship to it.

Noteworthy clay-ball contexts

The most informed understanding of the clay balls must include consideration of the contexts in which the materials were found. In the case of the clay balls, the most fundamental contextual division seems to be into occupation and non-occupation intra-building contexts. Addressing site-formation processes is crucial for any intra-site or household-level research (Cameron & Tomka 1993; Deal 1985; LaMotla & Schiffer 1999; Schiffer 1987), but is particularly important in an analysis of clay-ball materials because of the lack of understanding surrounding their use and role in daily life.

More common or familiar groups of material culture have a history of knowledge and assumptions relating to their use. Although there are exceptions, it is often taken as a secure starting point that lithics were used as tools, pottery was used for storage and cooking, faunal remains result from human consumption and tool use, floral remains result from human and animal food and medicinal use and as building material, and so on … for any number of other pieces of material culture. For these items of material culture, although their functional uses are clearly understood a contextual approach is still required to gain an understanding of their meanings and the symbolic capital they held and reflected during daily use. The clay balls, minis, and objects are different from the above mentioned categories of material culture because, in addition to trying to understand the meanings and symbolism they may have carried, I am also striving to understand their functional role(s).

It is not common to find large numbers of artefacts or other pieces of material culture in primary use context within the buildings of Çatalhöyük. Buildings have very little remaining on the floors (Volume 3, Parts 2 & 3; Mellaart 1962; 1963; 1964a; 1966a; 1967), and were likely emptied or cleaned out before they were destroyed, filled in, and/or built upon. Despite this general pattern, in a number of contexts in the South Area, clusters of clay balls and geometric objects were not removed before new features were constructed, or building infilling took place. It is interesting to ask why these clusters of whole balls and objects were constructed over or left behind when the building went into disuse; and furthermore, what this tells us about the role of clay balls in daily life.

It is useful to examine these contexts to gain a glimpse into the multiple ways that balls were used before these buildings were infilled and built over. The few examples of clay balls in primary occupational contexts come from the South Area Levels X VIII, including contexts from inside Buildings 2, 6, 17, and 23 (Fig. 6.8).

Mellaart mentioned several cases of finding 'clay boxes filled with … sling ammunition', but does not mention the precise context in which they were found, or even which building they were found within (1967, 63). I have examined and recorded all of the clay balls collected by Mellaart. These were labelled by 'house' or 'shrine' number, and it is clear that several groups of whole balls were recovered from a number of 'houses' and 'shrines', most likely filling bins — from just such occupational contexts as he described in the quote above. Because of the lack of contextual data

Figure 6.8. *Clay balls and objects in the South Area. Upper left - clay ball and stone oven base F.539. Upper right - clay-ball bin fill (1873) during excavation. Lower right - clay-ball pit F.440. Lower left - clay balls (5154) stored at head of oven F.555.*

from the 1960s excavations it is impossible to know if these were similar to the clay-ball bin and pit fills discussed below, although it seems likely, from the large number of whole pieces found, that they were together in clusters of some sort. Unfortunately none of the buildings from which clay balls were collected by Mellaart are comparable to the Level VI–VII buildings in the North Area. Thus even in using Mellaart's material there is nothing to provide a direct comparison in South Area clay ball contexts for those from the same level and time period in the North Area in order to address the question of the major discrepancies in site-wide ball distribution. It is interesting to note though that although four buildings in the South Area contained clusters of clay balls in various contexts, and other buildings had a high density of balls and objects in fill and midden areas, there are no clay-ball clusters or contexts of high ball density from either of the buildings excavated in the North Area.

Bin and cut fills

Building 2, Space 117 from Level IX had a bin F.257 over a large oven in the southwest corner (Volume 3, Part 2). The bin was filled with a number of whole clay balls (47) and geometric objects (12), as well as several fragments of clay ball (72). Covering these balls was an interesting mix of faunal material and several bone tools. One very distinctive feature of this unit is the calcareous ashy deposits covering nearly all ball pieces in a thin powdery layer, or in clumps, along with charcoal or hard grey ashy pieces adhering to the surface of the balls and objects. I believe this ashy material clung to the balls as a result of their being placed into the bin while hot, and possibly with wet or moist materials. Another important feature of the clay-ball materials from this unit is the high percentage and wide variety of elaboration on the pieces. A high number of pieces also have dark residues from liquid that rolled down their surface. All of these features seem to indicate that the materials were deposited in some purposeful way, possibly during feasting or celebration, which was beyond everyday use in heating and cooking.

It may be that bin F.257 was the usual storage place for both whole and broken balls, creating a convenient storage area for their frequent use in the oven F.268 below. It is unlikely that the balls would have received enough heat while sitting in either the above oven or bins to be useful for cooking; rather the balls were most likely only stored in the bin(s), where they would have been easily reachable for heating in the oven. During daily practice, while hot, the balls could have been used for boiling water, foods, or bones and nuts for grease extraction in baskets or skins. They would have also been useful for grilling or roasting meat and/or for parching grains, or breads, while hot in the base of an oven. They were probably used in one or several of these ways on the day they were deposited into this bin, the only difference from usual daily practice being that they were deposited while hot and with ashy and calcareous marl or plaster, and possibly with water or wet organic materials (food?), and were then covered with the other materials found over them (faunal, stone, charcoal, pottery, and botanical materials).

The difference in firing patterns of the material from this bin, together with the excavator's notes make it clear that these materials were not burned, heated, or fired *in situ*. The balls and objects had been exposed to various amounts of heating and use in life, prior to collection and deposition in this bin. The question of why so many whole balls were covered with such an unusual mix of materials and then left in this bin remains unclear. One idea is that a number of households used this space and stored their clay cooking balls here, or a number of households brought their favourite or best clay balls to this building and participated together in a final feast or celebration of some sort, after which they deposited and covered the balls. It seems most likely that the final use of these balls and their deposition in the bin was associated with the infilling (whole or partial) of Building 2 since there is a high density of clay-ball materials that also have calcium carbonate/ashy deposits on their surface in the building's basal fill.

Another example of a cluster of balls and objects, also from Level IX, is Unit (5154) from Building 17,

Space 170. A cut next to oven F.555 in the northeast of the space was filled with whole balls (11) and objects (4), and several broken ball pieces (7). The balls and objects are not particularly smooth or well made and, unlike many of those from (1889) described above, have no surface elaborations. They also do not have the calcareous and ashy deposits found on the majority of balls from (1889). These balls were likely in their usual storage space for use in conjunction with oven F.555, and were not used immediately prior to deposition. Many of the balls from this unit are similar in size (diameter range 6.4 to 8.4 cm) and colour (light greyish-brown). My interpretation of this feature is that balls and objects were stored in this cut for convenient use in cooking with oven F.555, and when a new oven F.548 was built the balls were left in place and covered in order to provide a strong (and heat retaining) base for the new oven. However this does not explain why whole and usable balls were used as fill material rather than re-used mound clay.

Clay-ball pits

In addition to the above-described cut and bin filled with clay balls, there are also a number of pits which were found containing whole clay balls. F.440 (containing (4290) & (4291)) from Building 6, Space 163, contained 272 clay ball pieces including 17 whole balls. The 17 whole balls are very similar in size (diameters range from 5.7 to 8.4 cm) and surface texture. However, the pieces show varying degrees of oxidation and reduction, and balls similar in size have very different core patterns, indicating differential levels of heat treatment. These balls also had different amounts of wear — some had very sharp, angular edges, while the broken edges of others were rounded. There was also a varying amount of residue visible on the ball surfaces. All of this information indicates that the balls had different production and use histories, and were being stored in this pit for future use. The proximity of the pit to two fire installations also indicates that the balls were likely used in conjunction with cooking and/or food preparation activities related to the nearby hearths.

A similar but smaller pit filled with clay balls was found in the same building in the adjoining Space 173. (4941) contained only five pieces of clay ball (two half balls and three fragments); two of these have a hard surface but are unfired. The two unfired pieces appear to have been only sun-baked. All five pieces have angular edges with low weathering. It is unlikely that these pieces were in the pit drying prior to firing because I was unable to find any refits to indicate that the pieces were part of the same ball. The fragments most likely came from two different balls, which were broken, and then deposited and covered without receiving much exposure. These may have been used as building material of a sort in order to fill the empty pit space before building over it. In this case, it is unclear if the pit had been used to store the balls, or if the ball pieces were added as construction material to strengthen the floor before rebuilding. Another two pits filled with clay balls were found in Building 6, Space 173 ((4915) & (4918)). One of these (4918) may be a post retrieval pit that was filled with clay balls after the post was removed. With the exception of this possible post retrieval pit, all four of the clay ball pits found in this building were located next to fire installations.

Oven bases

In several cases, broken clay ball and geometric object pieces were used in oven construction, either directly as the base of the oven, or as an insulation layer in oven floor construction. Although these are re-use contexts, they do help to understand the way balls were used after breaking, while providing further examples of the association of balls and geometric objects with fire installations.

In the southern part of Space 112, 42 pieces of clay ball formed the base of oven F.96. These balls were all broken into hemispheres and placed with the rounded side up. Although when originally placed the balls were fragmented into halves, cracking (probably from repeated heating) caused many of the half balls to break *in situ* into smaller pieces. All pieces have a large amount of residue and some areas of dark fire clouding on the top (rounded area) of each ball which occurred in situ and is likely from food residues that came in contact with the balls during grilling or roasting. Some of the residues have also dripped to the interior of each ball through cracks and salt deposits that follow the lines of the residue. The fire clouding, residue, and salt patterns all indicate that the balls formed the floor of the oven and the daub like material found covering them during excavation was part of the oven superstructure.

In Building 23, Space 178, another group of clay ball pieces (5004) were used, along with stone fragments, to form the floor of a fire installation F.539. This feature contained 93 clay ball pieces (all quarter balls and fragments), which all have low wear. These balls were predominantly placed rounded edge up, probably to form an even or flat base. Unlike the broken half balls used in the oven discussed above (F.96), this oven had a floor covering the broken ball (and stone) fragments, indicating that the balls did not come into contact with meat or plant foodstuffs but were used for their heat retention properties. These, and other similar examples, illustrate the clay balls' re-use as general building material. They also indicate that during re-use balls retain their spatial, and likely symbolic, association with heat, fire, food preparation, and cooking.

Building 6, Space 163 had several Units (4174), (4176) and (4177) associated with F.416, an oven covering the clay-ball pit F.440, that contained balls, objects, and minis. All of the ball materials associated with this feature have a heat exposure pattern, which indicates that they were fired in an oxygen-weak environment. These ball fragments were probably broken in household use, stored for varying amounts of time, and later used for construction and rebuilding of this oven, in order to hold in the oven's heat.

Clay-object distribution

Another significant point apparent in the clay-ball and object data is the distribution of geometric objects across the site. While only 10 per cent of the total of all ball / mini / object materials came from the KOPAL Area, KOPAL Area units contained a remarkably larger percentage (30 per cent, 329 pieces) of the total geometric objects studied thus far. Prior to 1999, a small number of geometric objects were found in the South Area from a variety of contexts, but the 1999 excavation season was the first to uncover these objects in high density, in units with few or no clay balls or mini balls (Suponcic 1999). Two distinct areas had a high density of geometric objects, the KOPAL Area and Space 181 in the South Area.

The density of objects in the KOPAL Area is 1.89 g / L and 0.05 pieces / L and, although slightly lower than that of KOPAL Area, Space 181 also has a relatively high density of clay objects with 0.59 g / L and 0.02 pieces / L. Both the North Area (0.03 g / L and .0007 pieces / L) and the South Area outside of Space 181 (0.22 g / L and 0.003 pieces / L) have much lower densities, between 2 to 70 times lower than those of KOPAL Area or Space 181. Although these two areas have a high geometric object density, no primary contexts of clay balls or objects were found in either area. This, coupled with the high fragmentation of pieces, may suggest that the objects were disposed of into the off-site areas of KOPAL Area and Space 181 after use.

Space 181 is thought to have been located away from the area of occupation during the Neolithic (Volume 3, Part 2). KOPAL is an off-mound area, likely used during the Neolithic for various activities that may include marl 'quarrying' (Volume 3, Part 4). It is unclear at this point if geometric objects occur in these two areas because of each area's association with some sort of off-site activity, or if this pattern is related to a temporal similarity between the areas. The lower-most units from Space 181 were rich with clay objects, and represent the deepest area of excavation reached thus far. According to the most recent carbon 14 and dendrochronology dates (Chapter 4), the KOPAL Area may date to as late as Level XI and as early as Level Pre-XII.B, indicating that KOPAL Area and Space 181 material may be contemporary. It is unclear if the high concentrations of clay objects in both these areas is linked to a temporal relationship between the KOPAL Area and Space 181, or a pattern related to differential use, meaning, and associations of balls and objects. A third option, one which combines these two interpretations, is also possible — people may have used geometric objects for certain off-site activities, such as to grill large cuts of meat, or for preparing certain types of food on special occasions, possibly for feasting. These off-site activities themselves might have then changed in frequency, type, or location through time.

Although most contexts apart from the KOPAL Area and Space 181 have a low density of geometric objects, there are several with a relatively high object density. These features and units themselves are discussed in more detail elsewhere (Volume 3, Part 2; Atalay 2003), but are worth mentioning briefly here because of their high density and the primary nature of the contexts in which they were found. (1889) (also discussed above) is the fill of a bin F.257. This bin is helpful for understanding the connection and similarity of clay balls with geometric clay objects because it contained 102 balls (47 whole) together with 12 geometric objects (10 whole). The geometric objects from this feature have a variety of shapes, many that are common in the lower levels of Space 181 and in the KOPAL Area; these include cones, a flat-based short cylinder with rounded top, a double cone, an ovaloid, and a cylinder. Although the shapes are comparable to material found in the KOPAL Area and Space 181, their fabric is similar to the clay balls found inside the bin with them. This fabric is unlike that from the objects found in the KOPAL Area and Space 181, but is consistent with the overall clay ball fabrics found in Building 2 and other Level IX–VIII buildings. The material from (5154), the fill of a cut behind oven F.555 described in further detail above, is another example of balls and objects occurring together in high density in a primary context. The 11 objects from this unit include a cone, a cylinder, an ovaloid, and a discoidal-shaped piece and, as with (1889), these objects have similar shapes to those found in the KOPAL Area and Space 181, yet the fabric is similar to the ball materials with which they were found.

Another context category in which objects have been found in high density is between-wall spaces. The balls and objects from (4225) and (4465), both between-wall units, were either dumped off or rolled off the roof and, although in secondary context, seem to have been relatively undisturbed since deposition. In addition to having a high object count and weight density, these units also both contained several whole objects. This is particularly interesting since the entire volume of Space 181 did not contain any whole objects, and the KOPAL Area units studied thus far contained only three whole pieces in total. These two between-wall contexts, although much smaller by volume, have a much higher density of whole pieces. (4225) has one whole object with five whole balls, and (4465) has one whole object with two whole balls; both had numerous non-whole pieces as well. As with the bin and cut units found filled with clay balls and objects near ovens, these contexts indicate that balls and objects were used together in conjunction with daily activities.

One final context with high geometric-object density is the oven F.416 in the southern part of Space 163 in Building 6. This oven covered a pit filled with clay balls, and broken ball and object fragments were used to form part of several oven floors in (4176) and (4174) (Volume 3, Part 2). The balls and objects appear to have been used in the creation of this oven, and as with the other similar examples, were probably used because of their heat-retaining properties, and possibly due to their associations and links to food and food preparation. Although several examples of similar oven construction using clay balls exist from other South Area buildings, this is the only example which contains a high density of geometric objects found together with clay balls.

There are a number of questions related to the patterning of the geometric objects that are unanswerable at this point. Any convincing explanation must take into account the presence of a high density of clay objects in two distinct areas (South Area Space 181 and the KOPAL Area), both of which are off site and have very small amounts of clay balls. Additionally, the on-site locations discussed above, and their association with ovens and / or food remains, must be taken into account. The relationship of balls to objects is interesting and is one of the main questions I plan to investigate when further excavations provide more data. More generally, the use and meaning of the geometric objects, and how these changed through time and across space requires further investigation before anything more definitive can be said in terms of the relation of geometric objects to clay balls and to other groups of material culture on site.

Variability in fabric

A number of the geometric objects found in both the KOPAL Area and Space 181 have a fabric different from that of most clay balls. Petrographic analysis conducted on a small number of balls, mini balls, and objects illustrates that there actually is not one recipe for clay balls, but instead, ball fabric can vary quite a bit within buildings and from level to level. I attribute this variability to the choices in mineral inclusions made by individual clay-ball crafters during production. It is also likely due, in part, to variability in clay sources and the use of different sources by different crafters. For the most part, these types of small-scale production differences in clay-ball fabric are difficult to discern with the bare eye, or even with a 10× hand lens. Fabrics that appear to be quite similar in macro view often have quite different fabric matrixes in thin section.

A comparison of three clay-ball samples illustrates this point. The three samples (2588.M1, 2502.M1, 2261.M1), which exhibited only slight variations in colour and texture when examined on a macro level, displayed quite distinctive fabrics when examined petrographically. Examination of these three ball fragments with a hand lens (10×) showed very similar fabrics consisting of well- to moderately-sorted mineral temper (quartz and mica) with very few organic voids. However, after thin sections were made and examined using a polarizing petrographic microscope, differences in their fabrics, based on the size, sorting, and variety of mineral and organic inclusions, became clear. 2588.M1 has a large amount (75 per cent) of inclusions with very little clay fabric. This dramatically contrasts with the 20 to 30 per cent and 10 to 20 per cent inclusions seen in 2502.M1 and 2261.M1, respectively. The differences between the inclusions in these samples was not limited to their amount, but also extended to the sorting and size of these inclusions. 2588.M1 inclusions were poorly sorted with minerals ranging from 50–800 μm, while 2502.M1 had moderate- to poorly-sorted inclusions from 75–500 μm. At the other end of the spectrum, sample 2261.M1 had well-sorted inclusions with a smaller size range (only 50–350 μm).

Moving beyond the size and amount of the mineral inclusions, I would like to address the types of inclusions present and their relative abundance. All samples had similar mineral inclusions, including quartz, feldspar, biotite mica, hornblende, and basalt. The relative percentages of these minerals were also fairly similar — in 2261.M1 and 2502.M1, quartz content was 50 per cent of all inclusions, and in sample 2588.M1, the quartz content was only slightly higher, at 67 per cent. Feldspar content ranged from 7 per cent to 17 per cent (highest in 2502.M1). In 2502.M1 and 2588.M1 hornblende and biotite mica content was relatively low, at 3 per cent each in both samples. However, in 2261.M1 these minerals were found in much higher amounts as each made up 17 per cent of total inclusions.

In terms of sphericity and roundness, the samples seemed to be relatively similar with nearly all inclusions being angular or sub-angular. There was only one case in which the inclusions were sub-rounded — the basalt and calcareous rock inclusions in 2588.M1. Sorting, however, varied greatly between samples. 2261.M1 was the most well sorted, with all inclusions being well sorted (with the exception of quartz which was moderately sorted). Inclusions in 2502.M1 ranged from poorly to well sorted while 2588.M1 was predominantly poorly or moderately sorted.

The analysis of the surrounding clay matrix of the three samples also provided an interesting comparison. Colour was very different in all three samples, ranging from light yellow-brown (2261.M1) in PPL to dark brown-black (2588.M1), and in XPL the colours ranged from golden brown (2261.M1) to dark brown (2588.M1). It also seems important to note that, of all three samples, one had a very low birefringence in XPL (2588.M1). In two samples (2588.M1 & 2261.M1) the inclusions nearest the surface of the clay balls were much more closely compacted. There were also areas in 2261.M1 and 2502.M1 with 'inclusion-free' clay aggregates. These clay aggregates are composed of fine material well below the 50 μm coarse/fine ratio. One additional important observation is that rounded vesicular voids were present in two of the samples (2502.M1 & 2261.M1).

These results clearly illustrate the diversity of fabrics found in clay balls, and inform us about the production of the balls as well as about the level of craft specialization and the social organization of production (Atalay 2003). This study illustrates the variation in the amount of inclusions, as well as the similarity in mineral types used — all strong indicators that individual crafters used different and distinct recipes for producing clay balls. Moreover, the relative size and shape of the inclusions also lend support to the idea that individual producers were involved, to greater or lesser extents, in working the raw materials used in clay-ball production prior to mixing temper with clay.

In the scenario described above, individual crafters may have travelled to an area with a sandy tempering source to obtain materials to be used as inclusions. Tempering materials may have also been derived from the remnants or small pieces of stone-grinding debitage. Crafters may have further processed some of the tempering materials by crushing them (more so in some cases, and less so in others), resulting in greater angularity. Whether from sandy river-sides or crushed ground-stone debitage, these tempering agents would have been mixed with fine-grained wet clay, resulting in the vesicular voids characteristic of very wet-clay production seen in some thin sections (noted in samples 2502.M1 and 2261.M1 above). Evidence of mixing clay with the tempering agents can be seen in these same two samples, and in numerous others, which have visible clay aggregates that contain no tempering materials. It is most likely that crafters used a fine-grain clay source to which they added both processed and unprocessed tempering agents, sometimes without completely incorporating these inclusions into the overall clay-ball fabric.

One final note should be made about the crafting of clay balls, based on the close packing of clay and inclusions toward the surface of several thin sections. Such packing is likely the result of pressure created after the initial forming of the clay balls, possibly during the semi-dry or leather-hard stage. This observation may indicate that the tempered clay mixture was formed into spherical shape while in a very wet state, as postulated above. These balls would have then been left to dry for some time, and later smoothed by hand-pounding before firing. An alternative idea is that the very wet slurry-state clay and tempering agents were mixed, and sometime later, after drying, hand-sized lumps of this mixture were pulled apart and formed into spheres. The spheres would have become compacted on the surface by the action of hand beating during shaping and smoothing. Both of these explanations can account for the compaction of materials visible on the surface of the balls in thin section, while also explaining the vesicular voids remaining on their interior.

Object fabric

In 1999, when large quantities of geometric objects were found in Space 181 and the KOPAL Area, it was obvious upon visual inspection with a 10× hand lens that many objects had a fabric markedly different from clay-ball pieces from the South and North Areas. Rather than the fine, well-sorted mineral temper common for balls in the South, North, and BACH Areas (as described in the three samples above), these objects have a more coarse, poorly-sorted mineral temper which includes a wider variety of minerals (beyond the previously seen quartz, mica and feldspars). The objects also contain a larger amount of organic voids, seemingly produced by the use of plant materials as temper.

As discussed above, not all geometric objects are from the off-site areas of Space 181 and the KOPAL Area. Geometric objects are also present in on-site contexts, sometimes in high density along side clay balls; most notably, as discussed above, in bins near ovens ((1889) & (5154)), in between-wall contexts ((4225) & (4465)), and forming the base of ovens ((4174) & (4176)). However, the objects from these contexts do not have the coarse, poorly-sorted mineral and organic-tempered fabric common in objects from the KOPAL Area and Space 181, but rather have a fabric similar to the fine, well-sorted mineral matrix found in clay balls.

While it is clear that there are differences in clay ball and object fabrics, it is not as apparent why this diversity exists. Were the larger tempered objects from Space 181 and the KOPAL Area made using a different clay source, which had more naturally-occurring inclusions? Or are the larger inclusions the result of crafters' decisions about the appropriate and necessary amount of mineral material to add to the raw clay? Do the differences in fabric indicate that one set of crafters made the objects, and another the balls? In his analysis of Jordanian ceramics Kalsbeek (1969) suggests that temper size affects the clay's workability and helps the crafter to produce cohesive forms and Rice (1987) provides many ethnographic accounts of potters' preferences for adding temper to increase the clay's workability. It may be the case for the early clay objects that larger amounts of inclusions helped to improve the clay's workability and made it easier to form geometric shapes. In time crafters may have found that objects made with fewer mineral inclusions worked as well, or better, than those with a large percentage of inclusions. The lower percentage of inclusions certainly would have made the ball and object surfaces much smoother and less crumbly and gritty after firing. Were these highly mineral-gritted objects made in a different season, possibly when better clay sources were not available? Or could the difference in fabric be related to the functional role of the objects, and how might this have changed the meaning of those objects? It may be that objects played a different role in daily life, one that required them to have more tempering material, possibly for greater heat transference. If the balls were used for boiling and parching, and the objects for grilling, would a greater amount of mineral inclusions have been beneficial in objects? Or is this fabric difference simply the result of experimentation and technological improvement through time, and a further indication of the temporal relationship between the off-site areas of Space 181 and the KOPAL Area? If this is the case, when and why did the shift in fabric type occur, and why did a shift from objects to balls take place? And finally, what is the relationship of the changing ball and object fabrics to the shift in pottery fabric during Levels VII–VI, from organic-tempered pieces to more grit-tempered wares? Although these, and many other questions, remain unanswered for now, it is certain that those living at Çatalhöyük had a strong interest and ability to work clay, and to transform it as necessary for their desired outcome. The intricacies of how and why these changes in transformation took place are part of my ongoing and future research goals, and require further excavation and analysis.

Interpretations of functions and meanings

The most central concern I have had in working with the clay balls is how to best interpret the data in order to better understand daily life at Çatalhöyük. After first seeing the clay balls in 1997, I had a number of working hypotheses about how they were used. My early hypotheses were related to the function or use of the clay balls, and were focused on answering questions such as 'What were they for?' or 'How were they used?' Through ethnographic research, literature reviews, and public education presentations I compiled a group of hypotheses related to the role of clay balls in daily life. These include balls used as hunting slings, stone boilers, cooking stones, counters or tokens, gaming pieces, standardized weights, digestive devices, grinders, mace heads, or weapons (see Atalay 2003 for a more comprehensive list).

Archaeological literature abounds with the necessity of moving beyond functional interpretations and the importance of symbolism in material culture in general and ceramic materials in particular (Hodder 1982; Tilley 1996; Vitelli 1993). In terms of clay balls, I felt that the symbolic aspects of the balls were important and should certainly form part of my analysis. The symbolic role of the balls, and the associations, meanings, and messages they held for those who used and made them were on my mind, but the challenges of addressing issues of ideation archaeologically in a prehistoric context led me to (unconsciously, I think) give this area second priority. As my research progressed, the importance of giving equal footing to both the clay balls' symbolic meaning(s) and their function(s), and the impossibility of making explicit distinctions between these two realms, became clear.

One hypothesis offered by a nine-year-old girl during a classroom outreach visit reminded me that for the people engaging with the balls as part of everyday life ball function and meaning were not separate conceptual entities. Therefore, an examination of the use and symbolism of the balls, minis, and objects

Figure 6.9. *Julia Parker (Yosemite Miwok/Paiute) preparing nuppa (acorn mush) using a traditional stone-boiling technique: 1) stones heating in fire; 2) using wooden tongs to place hot stones into cooking basket after water rinse; 3) stirring hot stones in boiling acorn mixture; 4) nuppa boiling after 3–5 minutes of stirring; 5) using wooden stirrer to remove stones; 6) thanking the fire for its role in cooking the nuppa (photos by Raye Santos).*

must be considered together in the context of daily Neolithic experience. Her hypothesis states that clay balls were census-taking devices, in which ball size and elaboration indicated a person's age group and status ranking. According to her model, a mini ball would have been produced for every newborn, and, with each rite of passage to the next level of knowledge or age group, a larger clay ball would have been crafted and given, and the smaller ball broken. She further posited that balls with markings or elaborations might indicate a special status or knowledge on the part of the owner. My reason for including this anecdote is not because I find it to be the strongest hypothesis related to the balls, but because this experience with a nine year-old's sophisticated ideas about the ways that clay balls may have 'functioned' to communicate meaning, status, knowledge, and belonging was a powerful reminder of the multiple and changing meanings and messages that humans attribute to material culture, even from a very early age.

The actions and activities surrounding the clay balls were filled with significance, and the balls certainly carried messages and were encoded with meanings related to those actions that moved beyond a purely functional role. To those who crafted and used the clay balls the realm of function and meaning were expressed simultaneously; one cannot be understood without a consideration of the other. With this in mind, in discussing the role of clay balls at Çatalhöyük I find it is difficult to work within the linear format that a written publication requires. In linear text it is much more difficult to integrate ideas of function and meaning, since one idea / discussion must come first, and may therefore take primacy. I prefer to have two columns with clay ball meanings discussed in one, and clay-ball functions discussed in a second vertically parallel column, or alternatively, to have paragraph / sections related to each topic italicized or in a different font inner-woven with each other. However both of those seemed difficult and burdensome for the reader, and I have decided to present the two concepts separately, while noting that they are both interrelated and equally important.

Keeping in mind the importance of both clay-ball function and meaning, I have chosen to begin with a discussion of the function of the clay balls, because that was how I, myself, first began to approach the material. My major working hypothesis for the clay balls is that they were used in cooking; for boiling, grilling, parching, and roasting as stones and clay objects are / were used for cooking in many areas around the world as witnessed in both the ethnographic and archaeological record. Ethnographic and archaeological examples from a range of cultural groups around the globe provide details on how stones (and / or clay objects) are used for cooking. My own conceptions of how hot stones and clay objects can be utilized as heat transfer devices for cooking without the use of pottery come primarily from ethnographic examples from such diverse locations as North America (Driver & Massey 1957; Ortiz 1991), Canada (Teit 1930), Mexico (Pennington 1963), Africa (Marshall 1976; Tanaka 1980), and Papau New Guinea (Fitz-Patrick & Kimbuna 1983), where a majority of the cooking was done using rounded cobbles or flat stones.

Ethnographic and ethnohistoric examples from California (Hudson & Blackburn 1982; Ortiz 1991) (see Fig. 6.9) and other areas of North America (see Driver & Massey 1957 for an excellent comparative overview) describe cooking methods in which stones are heated in a fire and placed into a basket or skin that is filled with food or water. The stones are stirred until the food is cooked or until the water boils. As stones cool they are removed and replaced with another group of heated stones. Using this method results in boiled grains or meats or boiling hot water in a matter of minutes, without the use of pottery.

In Papau New Guinea (FitzPatrick & Kimbuna 1983), North America (Wandsnider 1997), and a range of other locations around the globe heated stones are also used for pit cooking (roasting) — stones are placed in a pit with food items, covered with moist branches, and sealed with mounded soil. The food-filled pit is left untouched to roast overnight, or at least for eight or more hours, and upon opening yields cooked, warm food. Archaeological examples of this type of cooking have also been found — most notably at the site of Poverty Point in Louisiana (Ford & Webb 1956) where archaeologists have documented this method of cooking using geometric-shaped clay objects rather than stone. This site has yielded hundreds of tons of clay balls and fragments from both midden and pit-oven contexts. It is believed that clay was shaped into geometric forms and used for pit cooking and stone boiling because of the natural resources available in the area. The site lies on an aeolian plain that is abundant with clay, but lacking in stone.

Although not as frequently present in the ethnographic literature, heated stones can also be used to line the base of an oven or hearth for parching grains (Hudson & Blackburn 1982; Sassaman 1995), and this may have been the method used for cooking at the pre-pottery Neolithic site of Aşıklı Höyük (Özbaşaran 1998). Parching can also be done using clay lumps rather than heated stone. Clay parching is practised today in some rural areas of Turkey, where grains such as barley are stirred with heated lumps of white clay (ak toprak) to prepare a dish called kavurga. In preparing kavurga the heated clay lumps are used not only to impart warmth to the barley, but also because of the sweet taste which they add to the food (Erkal pers. comm. 1999). Parching methods using stone or clay are used either to render foods edible, or to prolong their storage capabilities for longer-term use. Furthermore, as in the kavurga example, parching with clay can have the added advantage of enhancing the food's taste.

While there is evidence to indicate that clay balls were used for cooking, I believe their use was not specifically limited to various forms of food preparation and cooking. The balls likely had multiple purposes within the domestic sphere — heating rooms is one example of the way the heat-retaining properties of the balls might have been used for transferring heat in a non-cooking context. Although clearly seen as being useful for transferring heat, the functions and meanings of the balls were not static, and certainly varied from person to person, and changed through time, during the life cycle of a ball itself, and depending on the context of use.

There is a wealth of data to support the heat-transfer/cooking theory. The clay-ball primary contexts found thus far all occur within houses; filling a basin (Building 2, (1889)), filling a cut behind an oven (Building 17, (5154)), filling several pits (Building 6, (4290), (4915), (4918) & (4942)), lining the base of several ovens (Space 112, (2704), Building 6, (4174), (4176) & (4177) and Building 23, (5004)). These contexts are all in close proximity to ovens or hearths. This association of clay balls with ovens also occurs in southeast Europe, where clay balls have been found inside ovens (Tringham & Stevanović 1990), and in Greece (Perlès 2001), where clay objects have been found near hearths. It may seem that the close proximity of balls to fire installations is indicative of their production environment rather than evidence of their use in association with ovens/hearths for cooking or heating in daily life. However, the balls found at Çatalhöyük in these contexts have been fired to different degrees, and in different firing environments. The variation in their heat treatment indicates that they were produced independent of each other, and brought together near the oven for use, not as part of the production process. Additionally, the presence of whole balls along with broken fragments, many from different firing environments, near a fire installation is not consistent with the idea of a drying/firing stage of production, which would result in newly-made whole (or broken refit) balls with a similar firing pattern. Furthermore, several re-use contexts, where balls were found lining the base of a fire installation, indicate associations of the balls with ovens/hearths and/or an understanding of the heat retaining properties of the clay balls.

Differences between clay-ball and object fabric on the one hand and early (pre-Level VI) pottery, figurines, and mini balls on the other, are consistent with the idea that balls and objects were created with repeated heating/reheating in mind. The balls and objects have a variety of quartz and other mineral-tempering materials that would have improved their heat-transfer capacity (Kingery 1960; Skibo *et al.* 1989). The fabric composition of mineral-tempered balls and objects are quite different from the organic-tempered pottery, and the minimally-tempered mini balls and figurines. The addition of mineral temper, sometimes in large percentages as in the objects from the KOPAL Area and Space 181, is especially significant because of the site's location on an alluvial plain, where stone was not abundant.

Obtaining stone raw materials and processing them for inclusion as mineral temper would have required significant time and effort (Arnold 1985). The organic-tempered pottery and figurines found on-site illustrate that people held the pyro-technological and technical skills necessary to make clay balls without mineral temper. Considering the extreme time and effort necessary to produce and process the mineral temper for clay balls and objects, such tempering material was likely a crucial part of a balls' construction, and was probably related to their role in daily life. The inclusion of mineral temper into clay ball and object fabric strengthens the heat-transfer theory and adds to a clearer understanding of how the balls were used and what they may have meant to those who made and used them.

Further indication that the clay balls and objects were associated with cooking and food preparation is the correlation found in pre-Level VII areas of low pottery density (pottery types which are organic-tempered and lack fire-sooting) with high clay-ball density, combined with the very low clay-ball density and increased pottery density (pottery types which are grit-tempered and more often fire-sooted) that occurs in later levels (Level VII and above). The shift in pottery fabric begins in Level VII and continues through Level VI and later (Chapter 5). These shifts may be indicative of a connection between the balls/objects and the pottery, one that I believe is related to changing food-preparation (cooking) practices. In this scenario, balls and objects would have been used for boiling, grilling, roasting, and parching, but would have slowly been replaced by cooking in grit-tempered pottery. The shift in Level VII–VI pottery fabric from organic to mineral temper would have given the pottery greater thermal-shock resistance, making it possible to use in cooking food directly over a fire. The exterior sooting on pottery in Level VII and later also supports this interpretation of a shift toward cooking with pottery (Chapter 5).

This heat-transfer/cooking theory is the strongest tenable hypothesis about the role of the balls at Çatalhöyük, but there are also several other hypotheses. As stated above, I compiled a list of ideas and possibilities, and used the most probable of these as a series of multiple working hypotheses to guide my research questions and design. During the course of research I addressed each of these, but found the strongest evidence from multiple sources supports the idea of balls and objects used in heating, cooking, and food preparation; and mini balls used as mnemonic or counting devices.

One of James Mellaart's interpretations of the clay balls is that they were used as sling projectiles for hunting birds (1967). Korfmann's research on the use of the sling as a weapon in the prehistoric Near East includes the use of stone balls used as sling projectiles (1972). One problem with this idea for the Çatalhöyük clay balls is the weight of the balls and the difficulty a hunter would have carrying these any significant distance for off-site hunting. It is the mineral inclusions that give the balls their weight, and if the primary purpose of the balls was for hunting it would be counter-productive to add mineral temper rather than organic inclusions, which would decrease their weight dramatically making them easier to transport. Furthermore, a hunting scenario does not adequately explain the high density of broken ball fragments found on site, in middens, and reused in building materials. Although not impossible, it seems unlikely that a hunter would carry a skin or bag filled with heavy balls off site to hunt and locate, retrieve, and transport the broken fragments home for midden disposal or reuse in other contexts. Russell & McGowan (Volume 4, Chapter 3), in their report on bird hunting and procurement also find the idea of using balls for hunting birds at Çatalhöyük highly unlikely.

Counting and record keeping is the most likely explanation for the mini balls, but does not adequately explain the larger geometric objects and balls. Schmandt-Besserat's work (1992) on the small geometric clay objects (tokens) found at sites throughout the Near East refers to objects much smaller in size than the clay balls and objects from Çatalhöyük. It seems most likely that the mini balls and the limited number of mini geometric objects found at Çatalhöyük were used in a way consistent with Schmandt-Besserat's counting theory. The Çatalhöyük balls and objects, however, are generally much larger in size than the largest of Schmandt-Besserat's examples (which she lists as 3 to 5 cm). Balls and objects from Çatalhöyük have also undergone a different heat-treatment pattern than the smaller mini balls, and include large quantities of mineral temper that is not common in the mini balls found on site. I have not examined the tokens from Schmandt-Besserat's study so it is difficult to make a more complete comparison of their fabric composition or level of heat treatment with the mini balls from Çatalhöyük. I certainly agree that balls and objects had definite and clear symbolic meaning for those who made and used them. However I believe that balls and objects obtained their meaning(s) from the associations of clay as a raw material and through their daily use as transformers of raw-food materials to cooked/edible food, not as symbolic markers of counted materials. The mini balls however do seem likely to have carried such symbolism, and I believe they were used in this way.

Another hypothesis on the use of the balls and objects is that they were toys or gaming pieces. From the material I have recorded at Çatalhöyük there is no strong evidence to support the use of balls and objects as toys and / or for use in games. Evidence to support this gaming theory, such as marks or areas of impact on ball surfaces, are not apparent on these materials. Broken fragments and refit pieces show no indication of exterior impact or chipping which would indicate their use as toys. Furthermore, breakage patterns are consistent with interior cracks and heat-stress breaks, not chipping or contact scars resulting from impact, as would be expected from use in ball games.

Similarly, the balls do not indicate signs of use in grinding or as imitation grinding stones. The pieces I have examined thus far have relatively smooth surfaces with minimal abrasions, and do not have signs of long-term scraping or grinding use. There are, however, examples of reworked fragments of broken balls that have wear patterns indicating their use in grinding. One of these appears to have been used in grinding red pigment of some sort since its broken and evenly-ground interior surface was covered in red pigment.

The idea that balls were wrapped inside a skin and attached to a handle for use as 'cheap mace heads' (Mellaart 1966a, 188) is not supported by the clay-ball data. As discussed above for grinding, the balls have little exterior pock markings or chipping to indicate repeated impact. Additionally, the primary contexts in which balls with different heat treatments were found — filling bins, pits, or cuts — does not make sense in terms of mace head use since it would indicate that the balls were produced at different times, possibly by different crafters, and were then stored near an oven or hearth. If these were mace-head performs a more logical storage location might have been outside the building. It seems unlikely that the balls were stored in mass quantities outside buildings and were only placed inside ovens and pits as fill / construction material to provide a strong basal floor for the next building because clay, soil, and / or recycled mound clay were the materials of choice for packing and construction purposes.

While visiting Cappadocia in central Anatolia I witnessed a woman weaving who used large rounded stones wrapped in fabric as loom weights (pers. observ., September 1999). It is possible that clay balls were used in a similar way, as loom weights, but no evidence has been found to indicate that any type of loom weaving existed or that loom weights of any sort were used. Remains of basketry and matting have been found at Catalhoyuk both in phytolith form and impressed on the surfaces of clay balls (Chapter 15), and woven textiles have been found. But, unlike in the ethnographic case which used stone, in producing a loom weight from clay it would have been less labour intensive, more economical in terms of raw material resources, and easier to use a loom weight with a hole in its centre.

Balls similar to those found at Çatalhöyük have been excavated at the southeast European site of Selevac (Tringham & Stevanović 1990). In the Selevac case, balls were also found inside ovens, sometimes in groups of three. The hypothesis given for these balls was also one associated with cooking — balls were interpreted as part of combustion equipment used to determine oven temperature. Following the assumption that similar clays with similar temper and firing conditions will become a certain colour at a distinct temperature, Tringham & Stevanović hypothesize that the ball's colour while inside a heating oven would have signalled to the cook that the oven was hot enough for use. This explains the balls' association with ovens / hearths and the mineral tempering of the balls for repeated heating. I agree with Tringham & Stevanović that the balls would have been well suited for this task and it is feasible that this was one of the multiple uses of the balls and geometric objects at Çatalhöyük. However, this would require only a small number of balls and, even taking into account frequent breakage due to thermal fatigue after repeated heating, the balls produced on site at Çatalhöyük and found stored in pits and bins near ovens are probably too abundant to have served solely in this capacity.

Re-use and recycling

Not only were these balls / objects multifunctional when whole, they were also saved and stored after breaking for re-use in a variety of ways. In some of the re-use contexts, balls maintained their proximity to ovens / hearths and probably retained their association with food and cooking. This is particularly true for oven F.96 in Space 112, where broken half-ball pieces were placed round side up to form the oven's base. This feature may have been used for grilling, to keep meat or bread from touching the hot ashes. It may have also been used for parching nuts and / or grains between the gaps of the heated ball hemispheres. This oven is a clear illustration of the people's understanding of the clay balls' ability to hold and transfer heat effectively.

Several clay-ball pieces were reworked into rounded pieces with unclear meaning / function(s). Some hypotheses regarding these pieces include their use as gaming pieces, grinding tools, pottery-making (burnishing) tools, and / or bottle stoppers (Last pers.

comm. 2001). Unlike the oven example, in this type of reworking and re-use the ball fragments may have lost their association with heating, food, and / or cooking, and effectively become new artefacts, carrying a completely new set of meanings for those who used such reworked pieces.

Many ball and object pieces were saved and re-used later as construction material. Building fill contexts have a high percentage of large pieces, indicating that they were specifically chosen as construction material because of their bulk. Bricks and mortars also contain a considerable amount of clay-ball, object, and mini-ball material. This is particularly true in the North Area, where the brick and mortar contexts are among the highest clay-ball and mini-ball densities. This is noticeable partly because North Area clay-ball and object densities are generally much lower than those in the South and KOPAL Areas, but also particularly so because North Area brick and mortar contexts simply have higher count and weight densities of clay-ball materials than similar contexts in the South Area. This is likely the result of builders using mound clay (i.e. from older abandoned buildings and midden areas), which held high densities of clay balls in the construction of Buildings 1 and 5 in the North Area; while in the construction of the earlier South Area buildings fresh off-mound clay sources may have been utilized.

As Schiffer (1987) and others (Deal 1985; LaMotla & Schiffer 1999) discuss, large pieces of usable materials referred to as provisional discard are often stored within a house in an out-of-the-way place. The few primary clay-ball contexts found at Çatalhöyük are pits and bins filled with numerous whole and fragmented clay balls and objects. These fragments typically have variable amounts of wear on their broken edges, perhaps indicating that they had been stored for different amounts of time. Provisional discard is a common contemporary practice in the local village near the site (Küçükköy). According to Yaşlı *et al.* (Küçükköy Seminar 06.08.01), large and / or bulky pieces of broken items are stored out of the way and used later for filling in holes or pits, or in a variety of other contexts. Items that are too small or not beneficial for re-use are placed in a kulluk, or ash pile, for discard into the local fields.

One depositional pattern of clay balls and objects appears to be provisional discard in which broken ball and object fragments were stored and then later re-used as construction material in building fill, packing, bricks, and mortar. Through their reuse, balls were transformed into a different artefactual category. I agree with Hodder (1999b, 84) that, 'theory constructs objects'. As archaeologists, we have begun to think more critically about the power that human action in the past and present has to transform an object's function and meaning in fundamental ways. These shifts have relevant and important implications; both in the past, for those engaging with the material culture, and for us, as archaeologists in the present who create artefact categories in our organization of materials. For example, clay-ball fragments found within bricks and mortar or used as building materials are washed, labelled, and sent to me for recording, and further analysis. They are not !abelled as building material, but once again are transformed (or maybe re-formed?), this time by archaeologists' actions, back into clay balls. At the same time, the remainder of the human-made bricks, mortar, fill, and packing are transformed / re-formed into dirt or clay, the raw material from which they were originally made, and left sitting on the back dirt pile.

While I believe it is important to think carefully about the human transformative action in the past which converted the clay balls to building material and the implications of this in social actors' perceptions of their material world, I do not believe this transformative process was an all or nothing prospect, where clay balls completely lost their 'original' meaning and, in the mind of the builder, become nothing more than raw materials needed for making a house, wall, or sturdy floor. Rather, it seems feasible that while clay balls were considered by those building the house as useful construction materials, the balls may have also simultaneously retained certain aspects of their former meanings, such as certain associations of warmth, prosperity, and their own transformative abilities associated with wild and domestic, raw and cooked, etc. Furthermore, when used in construction, on some level they may have been seen as providing or transferring these positive qualities to the newly-built house and its inhabitants.

Another area to address in relation to the functions and meanings of clay-ball materials is the relationship of clay balls to geometric objects. As I have presented elsewhere (Suponcic 1999), prior to the 1999 study season, few clay geometric objects had been excavated, and those uncovered were categorized as odd-shaped clay balls or balloids. When large numbers of geometric objects were excavated during the 1999 field season in the off-site areas of KOPAL and the lower levels of Space 181 in the South Area, these were classified as a third type of clay-ball material (geometric objects). Based on my analysis, although similar in spherical shape and clay material, clay balls and mini balls had very different uses and meanings. However clay balls and geometric objects had similar functions and shared certain similarities in meaning. Similarities in ball and object fabric and heat treatment support the idea that they were related in daily practice. Although we have no examples of geometric objects from South Space 181 or the KOPAL Area found in primary context, a bin (1889) and pit (5154) in the South Area outside Space 181 were filled with clay balls and objects, both in occupation contexts. The proximity of geometric objects to clay balls in these contexts, along with their similarity in fabric and heat treatment indicates that both had related functions and / or meanings.

Although balls and objects appear to be related, differences remain between the two types. In looking at the proportion of balls to objects in various areas and contexts a marked difference in quantity, as measured in count and weight density, is evident. As discussed above, the balls and objects have an inversely proportional relationship in terms of density, which can be explained by a temporal shift from objects (early in time) to balls (later in time), a difference in activities associated with balls (on-site activities) and objects (off-site activities), or some combination of these temporal and spatial differences. If, as the evidence thus far indicates, both balls and objects were used to transfer heat for the preparation and cooking of food, then the high density of clay objects (and low density of clay balls) in both the KOPAL Area and Space 181 may indicate that in the early settlement geometric objects were used more frequently in cooking activities; and with time balls became the shape of choice.

Alternatively, if objects were used predominantly for one certain type of food-preparation activity — for example grilling meat — then the difference in object density in the KOPAL Area and Space 181 may indicate high levels of grilling during early settlement, followed by a decrease in that activity during later levels of occupation. In this scenario, when grilling activities (using objects) decreased; parching, boiling or other activities that utilized balls would have increased. Such a shift in people's food-preparation and cooking choices would have also been related to the kinds of foods they were consuming (wild or domestic, plant or animal etc.). It may be that objects and the grilling activities associated with them are predominantly for use with wild-meat preparation, while balls are mostly used for parching grains or boiling domestic plants. However, at this point the faunal and flora data do not indicate that any substantial temporal changes occurred.

Mini balls

Mini balls offer an interesting example of how archaeologists classify material culture. With their spherical shape formed from clay the clear choice for their artefact categorization was into the realm of 'clay balls'. As a person interested in clay use, technology, and manufacture, I was thrilled in my early analysis of clay balls to see such a range of sizes. And, as the Çatalhöyük finds person in 1997 and 1998, I myself had originally categorized the mini balls as a small version of the larger clay balls. However, after spending time recording and analyzing the mini balls, it is clear that although similar in shape and material, they are not simply mini versions of larger clay balls. They are quite different in both their fabric and the heat treatment they received, and likely had very different uses and meanings from the clay balls and objects. One possibility is that they are the products of children who were imitating their mother's and / or father's production of larger clay balls. The problem with this interpretation is that the mini balls have not undergone the same surface or heat treatment as the larger balls, and the clay fabric of the mini balls is lacking the mineral temper found in larger balls and objects. The lack of mineral inclusions may be explained as children playing with bits of clay in its raw form, before it was mixed with mineral temper. However, it seems that children playing with clay and mimicking their parents' behaviour would have done so while clay balls were being crafted using the same mineral-tempered clay used for clay balls. Also, it seems that if mini balls were being created by children in an educational or training effort, then more of them would have ended up fired or with some sort of heat treatment. The mini balls would not have taken much space in a firing pit / area, and children engaged in mimicking behaviour as a learning endeavour would have certainly benefited from also learning the effects of heat on their products. This indicates that the mini balls were not training or practising tools for children.

Another interpretation of the mini balls, also potentially related to children, is that the mini balls were toys used as gaming pieces of some sort, for children and / or adult entertainment. This idea is supported by the occurrence of groups of mini balls found together in several contexts — one feature had ~800 mini balls and the next largest group had 13 minis clustered together. There are no cases of mini-ball clusters found together with other objects, which might be considered gaming pieces (i.e. reworked pottery sherds or clay-ball pieces, sheep / goat knuckle bones, coloured stones etc.). Furthermore, one BACH Area mini-ball feature (discussed in greater detail below) which held over 800 minis contained mini balls that were clearly still wet when placed into the fresh, wet plaster tray that held them. While the role if this feature remains unclear, it does not support the interpretation of mini balls as toys or gaming pieces.

Denise Schmandt-Besserat (1992) has recorded and studied a number of pieces that resemble the mini balls found at Çatalhöyük from sites throughout the Near East. Although her study does not include any Çatalhöyük materials, the mini balls closely resemble the plain sphere type she describes from other Near Eastern Neolithic sites. Schmandt-Besserat interprets these mini balls and geometric clay shapes as tokens used for counting and record keeping. She argues that tokens were early forms of record keeping that eventually evolved into early writing systems. My interpretation of the mini balls is that they were used in a similar way, as a form of record keeping. However, I would like to expand the interpretation to one of memory devices, which were not necessarily used bureaucratically in keeping track of food stores or supplies, but rather on a household and personal level for a family or group to keep track of materials and to commemorate or represent other items — such as numbers of people, days, or particular events.

Of the many forms and types of tokens presented by Schmandt-Besserat, only a very limited number of these types have been found at Çatalhöyük. All of the mini pieces from the 355 units chosen for analysis and presentation in this volume were spherical in shape, as were the nearly 800 pieces found together in one feature in the BACH Area (discussed below). Furthermore, in all the mini balls and token-like pieces that I have recorded or studied thus far at Çatalhöyük, only six are non-spherical in form. Using Schmandt-Besserat's approach, Çatalhöyük's mini balls fall into the 'small and large sphere plain token' type, which she postulates signified a form of grain measurement. She states,

> it should be assumed, however, that during prehistory, cones, spheres, and disks represented non-standardized measurements of grain. They referred probably to containers in which the goods were traditionally handled, such as a 'small basket', a 'large basket', or a 'granary' (Schmandt-Besserat 1992, 151).

The presence of large quantities of mini balls with a wide range of sizes, yet very few non-spherical shapes indicates that, at least in the case of Çatalhöyük, the mini balls do not signify any one type of commodity or staple (such as an amount of grain). These mini balls are very simple to produce without any type of specialized knowledge — one would need access to only a small amount of clay to produce them. Their variation in size, colour, and surface treatment indicates that they had a number of different producers, and were not intended as a standard form of measurement or currency. This implies personal use, rather than larger-scale interaction. In this kind of small-scale production one person's 'small' sphere would not be same size as another's. The lack of distinctive 'small' or 'large' mini balls and the overall variation in size range found within one building indicates that at Çatalhöyük mini balls from the same household would not have been effective for tracking small and large baskets of grain. The evidence from Çatalhöyük points to mini balls' use as a general counting tool and personal memory device, rather than a more formalized representation of a distinct quantity of a particular commodity. It seems most likely that mini balls were used for counting and signification, as Schmandt-Besserat suggests, but of a wider variety of items; including non-food items such as people or events, and in a way that was not related to a pre-specified quantity.

While this volume deals specifically with the materials from the South, KOPAL and North Areas, I would like to briefly discuss a very interesting mini clay-ball feature from the BACH Area that was excavated during the 2001 field season. A more in depth discussion of this feature exists elsewhere (Atalay 2001; 2003) so I will keep my comments brief. F.758 consists of over 800 unfired mini balls found packed into the wet plaster of a tray-like feature on the floor of Building 3, abutting and immediately to the south of a fire installation. The impressions in the base of the plaster tray-like feature indicate that the mini balls were placed there while the plaster base was wet. The balls themselves were not fired, and the deformation pattern of some indicates they were not even fully dried when put into place. Sometime after placement, the balls were covered over with white plaster that matched the tray base. Although abutting a fire installation, none of these mini balls appear to have been heat affected to any large degree. I have put forth a preliminary interpretation of this feature as the remains of an event that marked the initial habitation of this building and/or a feast associated with its initial construction and habitation (Atalay 2001).

It seems significant that these mini balls were placed next to the fire installation. In her analysis of hearths and ovens at the Aceramic Neolithic site of Aşıklı Höyük, Özbaşaran (1998) points to the importance of the hearth ethnographically and the numerous associations of hearths with 'life' and as 'the heart of a house'. This unique mini-ball feature, with such a large number of freshly made minis formed from clay and placed onto a freshly-laid white-plaster surface next to the building's 'heart' led me to envision some form of community event. In my imaginings, a selection of community members — including children, adults, and elders — each formed and placed a ball to commemorate some event, possibly the construction or renovation of the house or possibly a relative's burial in the platform to the north. This may have been done with the hope of imbuing the building, family, house, or home with their collective good wishes — in a form of Neolithic 'house-warming' feast. This interpretation is, of course, purely speculative, but I believe any interpretation of this feature must consider its placement next to the hearth as important and meaningful. It also illustrates the way in which the minis may have been used to both count people and to remember or commemorate a specific community or family event.

Integrating meanings

An inquiry into the roles of balls, minis, and objects in daily life must not only address functional interpretations but must also include the meanings which these important pieces of domestic life held for social actors who produced, used, and re-used them. Attempting to gain an interpretive understanding of any piece of material culture is difficult in studies of both past and contemporary cultural groups. This difficulty is compounded for materials such as the clay balls because their role in daily life is not clearly defined nor easily understood using an archaeological gaze, which is automatically distanced by time, space, and cultural understanding. Although I resist the temptation to place primary importance in this clay-ball research into interpretations of clay-ball function, it does seem beneficial to begin an inquiry into the meaning of a collection of material culture with reference to its function and use. From the position of a researcher using an archaeological perspective it seems that meaning is often more easily approached from the standpoint of an informed functional understanding of an object. However, our own daily practice and interactions with material culture illustrate that meaning and function are not so easily disentangled. As we have each experienced in our own lives in reference to common everyday objects as well as items we hold near and dear, the pure function of a piece of material culture does not always hold primacy in the eyes of a human actor. With this in mind, it is not only possible to theorize about the meanings of clay balls, minis, and objects, but rather it seems critical to think about their meanings in order to build better hypotheses and interpretations of their functions.

The lack of clear understanding of clay-ball function has the advantage of calling their use into question; forcing us, as contemporary peoples with no clear cultural equivalent to the clay balls, to think critically about their use. With the use of the clay balls in question there is a lower risk of making unexamined assumptions. However, we must also be careful not to immediately relegate the balls to the category of the unknown (and assumed unknowable) realm of the spiritual or ritual aspect of culture, as can be all too easy when dealing with materials that are not clearly understood using contemporary western models of knowledge common in scientific inquiry. Within these ways of knowing, the spiritual realm itself is unfortunately often reduced to playing a functional role in people's daily lives.

A dialectical approach seems appropriate in which ideas about clay-ball functions and meanings are intermingled, and each area of inquiry is used to inform the other in order to move closer to an interpretive understanding of the materials. For those engaged with these materials as part of their daily practice, there was probably not only one function for the balls. The balls and objects seem to have had multiple uses — one's experiences, understanding and/or knowledge of their use was likely dependant upon one's status and role in society. Some useful questions to ask toward understanding both balls and objects include: Were clay ball crafters also clay-ball users? If so, did the meaning of the balls vary from crafter to crafter? Did each crafter intend to use the balls in precisely the same way? If there was not a complete overlap between clay-ball crafters and users, would we not expect that the meaning of the balls would differ between crafters and users, as well as within each of these groups?

The role of the balls for those who dug, mixed, and formed the clay into shapes and fired the objects was probably dramatically different from those who had no connection to these activities and experienced the clay balls through a very different set of practices, such as those involved in day-to-day heating and cooking with the balls. Similarly, the meaning and use of the clay balls themselves changed throughout their use life — as they moved from whole pieces used as heating or cooking utensils to broken fragments used in oven building material; from stored pieces in the bottom of a house pit or the corner of a room, to room packing or building material for bricks or mortar. The meaning and use of the balls were certainly flexible and they changed depending on the person interacting with the materials and the life of the object itself. While it seems impossible to thoroughly understand the full complexity and myriad meanings and uses of the balls, objects, and minis, it is possible to begin constructing some facets of meaning that may have existed.

Domestication of clay

I approach the clay balls, mini balls, and geometric objects by first thinking of the raw material from which they were made — clay. Clay was a crucial raw material for the inhabitants of Çatalhöyük. They lived in houses made of clay, slept on platforms moulded from clay, used it regularly to coat their walls, and to form the hearths and ovens that provided warmth and were used to cook their food. Stevanović's (1997) description of the Neolithic in southeastern Europe as the 'Age of Clay' can equally be used to describe this period at Çatalhöyük. In such an environment, clay would probably have held a number of powerful meanings and associations, and the items made from it would have held the potential of carrying a certain amount of symbolic capital. Clay is a soft and malleable material which crafters, builders, and others were able to form into shapes as they saw fit. Knowledge of the locations of this important resource would certainly have been valued. The value and quality of clay sources were probably based on a variety of details that combined practical, functional, and ideological factors such as the clay's workability, amount and type of inclusions, colour, vicinity to sacred landmarks, and position in the spiritual and cultural landscape.

We must not underestimate the effect this material must have had, in varying degrees, for those living at, visiting, or even first settling at Çatalhöyük. Although the events and processes of first settlement are not clearly understood, it is reasonable to consider that clay played some role in this process. Members of a society who travel across the landscape, outside of their settlements, to locate or procure important raw materials such as clay may be seen as having tremendous knowledge and power because of their understanding of the outside world and their knowledge of clay resources (see Rice 1987, 115–24 for several ethnographic examples). It is logical that after travelling they return home with a different worldview, and may gain leadership or respect for such knowledge. For those travelling and moving around the landscape before the site of Çatalhöyük was settled, the abundant presence of the valuable clay material created in massive amounts by the action of the Çarsamba River was a great, although not completely rare, find. Clay was not the only abundant material in this Neolithic alluvial plain, it was present in combination with other earth-derived materials, such as the marl used for floors and plasters to cover platforms and bins and to model bulls heads and sculptural building features. It is not difficult to envision that clay, marl, and other material resources found in conjunction with these raw-earth materials had strong importance and significance.

Economically-important resources, such as agricultural land, wild-plant and animal-food supplies, and a good water source, are often the first to come to mind when considering important factors for site choice and settlement. But the ethnographic record reminds us that migrating groups do not always choose settlement locations based on factors that are purely economic. One example that I am most connected and familiar with is that of my own tribe's migration across parts of North America long before European arrival. In this case, the Anishinabeg people were told by the Great Spirit to follow the trail of a tiny shell that is still sacred for our people. Elders were told in a dream that wherever the megis (cowrie) shell was found would be a good place for the Anishinabeg people to settle and live. These shells were not eaten and had no trade or economic value, but they were, in fact still are, a crucial part of our spiritual beliefs and practices. While this is one example from the Ojibwe oral tradition that I know first hand, there are certainly many other examples of migration and settlement choice based on, or at least including, resources that do not hold economic significance. While I do not wish to overstate the significance of clay and earth-derived materials, the importance of assets such as these must be considered when asking why Çatalhöyük was originally chosen for settlement.

Beyond its possible significance in early site choice and settlement, as a crucial raw material clay played a vital role in people's daily lives. I argue that human interaction with clay be likened to the controlling and manipulating processes surrounding plant and animal domestication. Like these living organisms, clay was also domesticated. Human access, manipulation, control, experimentation, and overall interactions with clay followed a slow process of domestication. Earth in its raw, wild form was located and gathered, transported onto the occupation site, and, through human manipulation in the form of added minerals and tangible mixing and forming, was transformed into a human-made product with the qualities desired by its makers and users.

As Hodder describes for the process of domestication on a much larger scale for the Near East and Europe, there was a simultaneous 'celebration and control of the wild' (1990, 10). This certainly seems to have been as true for clay as it was for plants and animals. Crafters were involved in a complex series of changing technological processes and experimentation, including travel across the landscape for locating, extracting, and transporting the necessary raw materials. This was followed with mixing, forming, and firing — each a skill that involved a strong knowledge base — some newly-acquired through experimentation, others passed down through oral tradition and learned experience. In each of these activities human actors were involved in the slow process of taming the natural environment of which they were a part.

In the case of clay, they literally moulded the outside world and its resources into the forms they desired, and solidified those forms through their knowledge and control of other earth elements such as stone, air, and fire.

Through this process of domestication clay's importance and meaning would not have been experienced equally by all members of society, but rather a range of social meanings and significance surrounded clay as it was understood and experienced by different people, to a greater or lesser degree. Furthermore, not all actors at Çatalhöyük played an equal role in clay's domestication. One's knowledge of clay sources, uses, crafting technology, pyro-technology, and one's level of interaction with materials made from clay would have influenced a person's level of participation as well as their understanding of, and the attention paid to, any of the symbolic messages surrounding clay. At Çatalhöyük, the potential messages held by clay likely went beyond the value of the material itself and the use of the objects made from the clay and were even more heightened by the power imbued in the items by the crafters making them. As Vitteli (1993) argues in her work in Neolithic Greece at Franchthi Cave, those crafters who held the power to form, and thus transform, clay from its natural soft state to a solid state, using fire, may have acquired a great deal of social value and power. They may have even been seen as having shamanistic power.

Adding to this would have been the transformative and regenerative power of fire used to produce and/or heat the balls and objects. Hodder (1990), in his discussion of Neolithic Scandinavia, has discussed the potential of fire as a powerful force for prehistoric cultures. These archaeological cases are also supported by ethnographic examples which illustrate that fire can be highly valued and respected as a regenerative, life giving, and powerful force (Boyd 1999; Colomeda & Anne 1999; Wilkinson 1999). It is particularly useful in agricultural societies which utilize fire as part of crop- and land-management strategies. In fact, burning fallow fields before planting is common practice in the villages surrounding Çatalhöyük and in other agricultural villages in central Anatolia (pers. observ. 1999).

Clay-ball crafters combined clay, an important raw material filled with associations and symbolic messages, with mineral inclusions that were quite limited in supply, adding the power of fire to transform the soft malleable mixture to hard objects that held their shape permanently. Through this process, knowledgeable crafters brought together two powerful forces — clay and fire. The earth was used for growing crops, if not immediately on site, then nearby. In a way similar to the practices in contemporary nearby villages, fire may have been used for land clearing and crop control by burning overgrown vegetation in the preparation for planting gardens or crops, adding nutrients to the soil in the process. Using the power of fire to transform clay into a hard, lasting piece of material culture would have been a powerful skill, and the balls produced through firing likely held multiple meanings to those who made them, including associations of both earth and fire. If producers and users were not one in the same, then it is reasonable to assume that balls held a separate (although possibly overlapping) but equally powerful set of meanings and associations for those who used them.

If production was at the household scale and clay-ball crafters were producing material for their own use, these meanings and associations, whatever they might have been, need not have remained constant throughout the life of the objects. It is possible to envision the ball crafters holding certain associations in mind while obtaining raw materials, forming, and firing the balls, and then later having a very different set of ideas and associations in mind while using the balls in daily practice. And again after breaking, during reuse, the ball fragments may have conjured up a number of yet other associations.

Meanings in balls and objects

Beyond the abstract meanings and symbolism of clay balls and objects, they also have the potential to carry meaning and messages as individual pieces of material culture through their surface elaborations. Such elaborations, which include incised lines, patterned fingernail incisions, fingertip indentations, finger and palm prints, plant and seed impressions, and woven basket and matting impressions, may have been used to mark ownership or craftsmanship. Crafters may have used these marks to give individual style or signature to the items they made. From the view of the user, in communal cooking or feasting exterior markings would help to indicate which balls or objects belonged to whom. In a more abstract sense, plant and seed impressions on ball surfaces may further indicate an association of these items with plant foods. Features such as the clay ball bin in Building 2, (1889) may indicate that these items, although made of a common material and embroiled in daily household practice, may have also played a role in small and large scale ritual(s), in this case possibly involving feasting and/or the final 'closing' of this building.

Clay balls, objects, and minis need not only have been used in large-scale occasional ritual, but, as their importance in domestic daily life suggests, they were also probably involved in day-to-day smaller household scale ritual involving cooking, food preparation, or fire keeping and heating. A beautiful example and powerful reminder of the importance of such small-scale daily ritual activity is from a contemporary example of stone use for cooking amongst the Yosemite Miwok / Paiute of California. Figure 6.9 (p. 156) shows Julia F. Parker transferring hot rounded river cobbles first to water to rinse off the ash, and then to a basket filled with pounded acorn meal. Once the stones are in the basket, Ms Parker stirs the stones with a wooden looped stirrer for several minutes, removing the cooled stone and adding newly-heated cobbles. After the acorn has been cooked in this way, Ms Parker offers a small amount of the acorn preparation to the fire. What are the archaeological traces of this small-scale ritual action? There are none. This practice exists and is reproduced as knowledge learned through daily practice (habitus), passed down from generation to generation.

Clay balls and objects may have also held messages and meaning by their very presence and use in a household. If we assume for now that objects and balls were associated with cooking and food preparation in some way, and the KOPAL and South Areas material represents a shift in food-preparation practices from using objects early in time and clay balls later, then the objects may have carried some association connected with concepts of traditional, maybe even 'old-fashioned', ways of life. Similarly, the difference in ball density between the North and BACH Areas on the one hand and the South Area on the other, may represent another shift in cooking practices, from parching, grilling, and / or boiling foods to heating foods over a fire in ceramic containers. If such a shift did occur we might envision people associating the balls with the past, or a more traditional way of life; while pottery may have represented a more 'progressive' way of cooking. If these types of shifts in cooking technology did occur, it is unlikely that change would have been immediate, and both methods would have been in practice simultaneously. We would expect variation in household cooking assemblages with a variety of combinations of balls and pots, until balls eventually go out of use completely and pottery becomes ubiquitous. However, during the transition period, both balls and pots would have been charged with meaning and could have even served as identity markers, where people who continued to use the older methods of ball cooking where seen as more traditional and other families, clans(?), groups, neighbourhoods, etc. who began using pottery were viewed as being more progressive.

I do not believe such changes need have occurred in a passive way; in fact I envision people actively using their food and method of preparing it as a self-marking tool, or as a way of identifying their beliefs and ideology to their neighbours. Additionally, we need not make the assumed connections of pottery = new = technologically superior = more desired / better, and clay balls / objects = out-dated / old-fashioned = inferior = unwanted. It may be that there was some opposition to the new technology, even active resistance; in which case both pots and balls would have been highly charged with meaning. The act of cooking itself, particularly in open areas, such as on roofs, would have served to mark part of one's identity. Alternatively, the difference in clay-ball density between North and BACH Areas and the South Area may not be a temporal difference, but rather a spatial difference, where distinct groups of people or neighbourhoods existed who had different methods of cooking their food, differences in diet, or a combination of both. Further excavation in the North and BACH Areas that reveal Levels VII and below are needed to properly address this possibility.

These speculations are only some of the multi-levelled meanings of balls and objects and their links both to clay as a raw material and to balls as crafted objects, with multiple associations linked to food, earth, regeneration, transformation, and identity. The balls can also aid us in gaining broader cultural understands of the people who lived at Çatalhöyük. From this analysis of the clay balls and objects it is clear that those crafting these items had a high degree of pyro-technological skill. Even in some of the early levels, where pottery was not found at all, there were 9-cm diameter objects, which had oxidized completely through the core. Producing a fully-oxidized core on a clay object of such thickness is difficult and would have required tremendous pyrotechnological skill. Further evidence to support the level of clay crafting knowledge and skill present on site is the high degree of surface smoothness and evenness present, both in texture and colour, on the majority of clay balls and objects.

Through my own experimental work using clay and mineral resources available during the site's occupation, I found that mixing clays, shaping balls and objects, and firing them to such an even colour and surface texture was quite difficult, even for an experienced potter. Although it seems that rolling a piece of clay into a sphere between one's palms would be quite simple, in fact it was difficult to obtain a well-rounded sphere, and even more difficult to form an evenly and symmetrically-shaped cone or rectangular shape. Firing these pieces in an open air firing pit also proved challenging for obtaining balls and objects with even surfaces and no fire clouding or surface markings. Reaching the proper mixture of mineral temper to keep the balls and objects from cracking or exploding through even one initial heating/firing was also a complicated process. Producing balls up to 9 cm in diameter with even surface colour tone, oxidized completely through the core, and a highly-smooth yet unburnished surface texture required an incredible amount of control in the firing environment and indicates incredible experience in pyrotechnology and clay crafting. This is particularly interesting considering it was a time when fired-pottery was produced and used in very small quantities. Further indication of these people's pyro-technology skill is found in several lime-burning contexts and in the use of lime plaster, which would have required a high heating temperature for extended periods of time (Volume 3, Part 2).

Analysis of clay balls, objects, mini balls, bricks/mortars, figurines, and pottery indicates that a variety of people (or groups of people) used clay in their daily production and crafting practices. Petrographic evidence of a selection of pottery, clay-ball, and object pieces, combined with a more comprehensive analysis of ball, object, pottery, figurine, and brick fabrics on a macro level and with a 10× hand lens indicates a wide diversity of recipes and production techniques used for each of these groups of material. Of course we would not expect all items made from clay to be made using the same recipe or technique. Each played such a different role in daily life, and each would have followed a recipe appropriate for its functional requirements, and in both aesthetic and symbolic terms. Furthermore, differences in manufacturing techniques and fabrics illustrate the distinctiveness of actions and daily practices associated with the production of each category of clay material. It seems unlikely that the same person held the knowledge, time, or ability to craft all of these materials on a regular basis; rather a small-scale form of craft specialization fits the clay material data more closely.

In terms of the clay balls, large-scale changes do seem to have occurred during the site's occupation. Early levels indicate more variety and experimentation resulting in fabrics with a wider range of mineral types and sizes; while ball materials from later levels show less variability in fabric type. However, all variability in clay-ball materials is not simply due to experimentation and/or technological change over time. Macro- and micro-level inspection, including petrographic results, indicate that clay-ball materials from the same level were crafted using a range of recipes. This variability indicates there was not a single clay-ball crafter, but that numerous people were involved in their production. Whether this indicates a strictly household level of production by members of one household for use in that household is not clear. When considering the range of pyrotechnology and clay-working skills apparent from a comparison of pottery with clay balls, some level of craft specialization does seem most likely. More comprehensive inter- and intra-household comparative analysis is necessary to provide a more in-depth understanding of the scale and organization of clay-ball crafting at Çatalhöyük. Additionally, ongoing and future analyses of clay, and materials made from clay, will certainly help to clarify broader concerns of clay crafting and production.

Concluding summary

While uncertainties and questions surrounding clay-ball use can be frustrating, it is also refreshing to study a group of material that is not bounded by preconceived notions of function, and which must be addressed critically from the starting point. As with all pieces of material culture, the balls can be used to address many topics at many levels related to daily life at Çatalhöyük. I have attempted to put forth and discuss a number of possibilities for the multiple uses and meanings of the clay-ball materials and after analyzing an admittedly limited amount of material thus far I feel the strongest argument converged upon from multiple lines of evidence is that balls, mini balls and geometric objects had multiple uses; they held and were held within a complex web of meanings. These meanings occur on many levels, including the symbolism of the clay itself, the stone and fire used to craft the pieces, their association with earth and food, and their power as objects which have been transformed and are themselves transformers. In its transformation from a wild raw material into shaped products of material culture clay itself was domesticated, as were plants and animals at this site. Clay was brought onto the site from the outside environment in its natural state, and through crafters' mixing of mineral and organic tempers the raw clay was controlled, formed, and then transformed into a variety of shapes with a range of uses.

The evidence indicates that balls and objects were used primarily to transfer heat to food and possibly rooms. Balls and objects maybe have been utilized for boiling in pits or baskets, for parching nuts or grains, for rendering plant and animal fat, in roasting food inside pits, and for grilling or baking. A number of changes occurred in the production of clay balls and objects through time and across the site, and in the latest levels (Level VI and above) clay-ball and object density decreases dramatically. This involved changes in the habitus of people's daily activities and may indicate a shift in cooking technology from indirect heating using balls and objects to direct heating with pottery.

Mini balls, although similar in material and shape to larger clay balls, have a different clay matrix and appear to have had a different role in daily life, most probably as memory devices used for remembering people or events and for counting food items or animals. Balls, minis, and objects also offer a window into other areas of cultural understanding including the advanced level of pyro-technology skill held by those living at the site, the importance of re-use and recycling of material culture, and the small-scale yet specialized level of organized craft production.

Chapter 7

Organic-residue Analysis of Pottery Vessels and Clay Balls

Mark Copley, Katherine Clark & Richard Evershed

The porous nature of unglazed pottery vessels ensures that during the processing of food (e.g. cooking) lipids are absorbed into the vessel wall. In this state animal fats, plant oils and plant waxes are known to survive burial for several thousand years (Evershed *et al.* 1999). Following excavation, these lipids can be analyzed using a suite of modern analytical techniques, including high-temperature gas chromatography (HTGC) and HTGC/mass spectrometry (HTGC/MS; Evershed *et al.* 1990), to derive quantitative information and to identify the compounds present in the sherds. Characterization of lipid extracts to commodity type has only been possible through detailed knowledge of diagnostic compounds and their associated degradation products that are likely to occur during vessel use or burial. For example, triacylglycerols (TAGs) are found in abundance in modern animal fats and plant oils, however they are largely degraded to diacylglycerols (DAGs), monoacylglycerols (MAGs) and free fatty acids during burial/vessel use. Analyses of numerous pottery vessels have shown that free fatty acids tend to predominate, and this has been verified through laboratory-simulated degradation experiments (e.g. Charters *et al.* 1997; Dudd *et al.* 1998).

Identifications of commodities processed in pottery vessels rest on comparisons between the structures and distribution of lipids present in residues with those of reference materials, taking account of changes induced by degradation during use and/or burial. By adopting the above approaches it has been possible to detect the processing of animal fats (e.g. Evershed *et al.* 1992), marine animal fats (Hansel *et al.* 2004), leafy vegetables (Evershed *et al.* 1991; 1994), maize (Reber *et al.* 2004), specific plant oils (Evershed *et al.* 1999; Copley *et al.* 2005a), palm fruit (Copley *et al.* 2001) and bee products (Evershed *et al.* 1997b; 2003). The chemical structures of some commonly-detected lipids from archaeological organic residues are shown in Figure 7.1. Compound-specific stable carbon isotope measurements provide a further means of defining the origins of organic residues. To this end GC-combustion-isotope ratio mass spectrometry (GC-C-IRMS) is employed, which allows the carbon stable-isotope ($\delta^{13}C$) values of individual compounds (within a mixture) to be determined. It has been found that the $\delta^{13}C$ values for the principal fatty acids ($C_{16:0}$ and $C_{18:0}$) are crucial in the ability to distinguish between different animal fats, e.g. ruminant and non-ruminant adipose fats and dairy fats (Evershed *et al.* 1997a; Dudd & Evershed 1998; Mottram *et al.* 1999), as well as in the identification of the mixing of commodities (Evershed *et al.* 1999; Copley *et al.* 2001). For an overview of the use of compound specific stable isotopes in archaeology see Evershed *et al.* (1999).

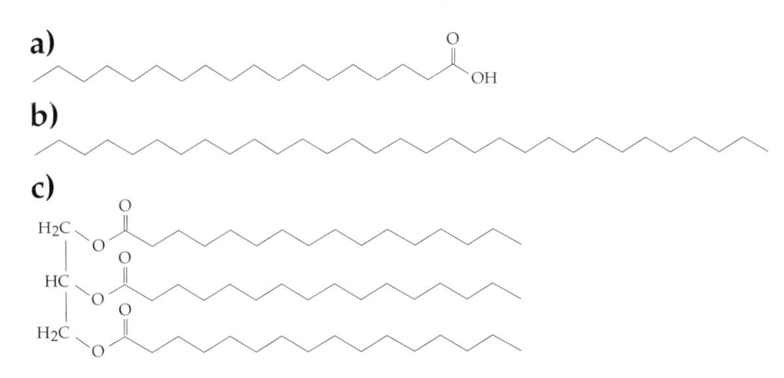

Figure 7.1. *Some commonly-occurring lipids: a) n-octadecanoic acid ($C_{18:0}$ fatty acid); b) n-nonacosane (C_{29} alkane); c) tripalmitin (C_{48} triacylglycerol).*

Investigations performed to date have shown lipids to survive in archaeological pottery from sites representing a wide geographical range, e.g. Europe to southern Egypt. Up to now, the oldest pottery in which lipids have been detected are from early Neolithic vessels from southern Britain dated to *c.* 4300 cal BC (Stott *et al.* 2002). The lipids residues present in these latter vessels are derived predominantly from animal fats (Copley *et al.* 2003; 2005b).

Table 7.1. *The pottery samples from Çatalhöyük. FA are free fatty acids ($C_{16:0}$ and $C_{18:0}$); MAG are monoacylglycerols; DAG are diacylglycerols and TAG are triacylglycerols; tr are trace abundances; n/d not detected.*

Sample no.	Context	Sample/ x-find	Area	Space, Level	Lipid components detected and assignment based on lipid distributions
CH1	1033	98	South	115, VIII	n/d
CH2	1821		South	117, IX	n/d
CH3	1668		South	115, VIII	n/d
CH4	1692	S.3	South	117, IX	n/d
CH5	1741	S.1	Summit	101, IV/V	n/d
CH6	1816		South	117, IX	n/d
CH7	1668	S.6	South	115, VIII	n/d
CH8	4121	S.22	South	115, VIII	FA; MAG; DAG; TAG Degraded animal fat
CH9	1822		South	117, IX	n/d
CH10	1660		South	117, IX	n/d
CH11	1889	S.3	South	117, IX	n/d
CH12	1765	S.2	Summit	IV/V	FA Highly-degraded animal fat
CH13	2022	S.3	South	112, VII	n/d
CH14	2623–2666		Summit	IV/V	FA; MAG; DAG; TAG Degraded animal fat
CH15	2652	S.3	Summit	IV/V	FA; TAG (tr) Highly-degraded animal fat
CH16	1163	S.15, X.2	North	183, VII/VI	n/d
CH17	1128	S.10	North	183, VII/VI	FA; MAG; DAG; TAG Degraded animal fat
CH18	1037	S.33	South	115, VIII	n/d
CH19	1427	X.3	North	71, VII/VI	n/d
CH20	1590	S.3	South	115, VIII	n/d
CH21	1596	S.4	South	117, IX	n/d
CH22	1620	S.4	South	117, IX	n/d
CH23	1620	S.5	South	117, IX	n/d
CH24	1620	S.8	South	117, IX	n/d
CH25	1652		South	115, VIII	n/d
CH26	1657	B	South	115, VIII	n/d
CH27	1657	A	South	115, VIII	n/d
CH28	1302	X.2	North	188, VII/VI	n/d

Table 7.2. *The 'clay balls' from Çatalhöyük (n/d = not detectable).*

Sample no.	Context	Sample/ x-find	Area	Space, Level	Lipid components detected
CHCB1	1674		South	105/159, VII	n/d
CHCB2	1873		South	117, IX	n/d
CHCB3	3650	S.3	South	117, IX	n/d
CHCB4	1889		South	117, IX	n/d
CHCB5	1506	S.4	South	105, VII	n/d
CHCB6	2704	S.4	South	112, VII	n/d
CHCB7	1668	S.5	South	115, VIII	n/d
CHCB8	3609	S.3	South	116, IX	n/d
CHCB9	1595	S.3	South	115, VIII	n/d

Materials and methods

Lipid analyses were performed using our established protocols that are described in detail in earlier publications (e.g. Evershed *et al.* 1990; 1999). Briefly, analyses proceeded as follows:

Solvent extraction of lipid residues

Approximately 2 g samples were taken and their surfaces cleaned using a modelling drill to remove any exogenous lipids (e.g. soil or finger lipids due to handling). The samples were then ground to a fine powder, accurately weighed and a known amount (20 μg) of internal standard (*n*-tetratriacontane) added. The lipids were extracted with a mixture of chloroform and methanol (2:1 v/v). Following separation from the ground potsherd, the solvent was evaporated under a gentle stream of nitrogen to obtain the total lipid extract (TLE). Portions (generally ⅕ aliquots) of the extracts were then trimethylsilylated and submitted directly to analysis by GC. Where necessary, combined GC/MS analyses were also performed on trimethylsilylated aliquots of the lipid extracts enabling the elucidation of structures of components not identifiable on the basis of GC retention time alone.

Preparation of trimethylsilyl derivatives

Portions of the total lipid extracts were derivatized using *N,O*-bis(trimethylsilyl) trifluoroacetamide (20 μl; 70°C; 20 min; Sigma-Aldrich Company Ltd, Gillingham, UK) and analyzed by GC and GC/MS.

Saponification of total lipid extracts

Methanolic sodium hydroxide (5 per cent v/v) was added to the TLE and heated at 70°C for 1 h. Following neutralization, lipids were extracted into hexane and the solvent evaporated under a gentle stream of nitrogen.

Preparation of fatty acid methyl ester (FAME) derivatives

FAMEs were prepared by reaction with BF_3-methanol (14% w/v; 2 ml; Sigma-Aldrich, Gillingham, UK) at 70°C for 1 h. The methyl ester derivatives were extracted with chloroform and the solvent removed

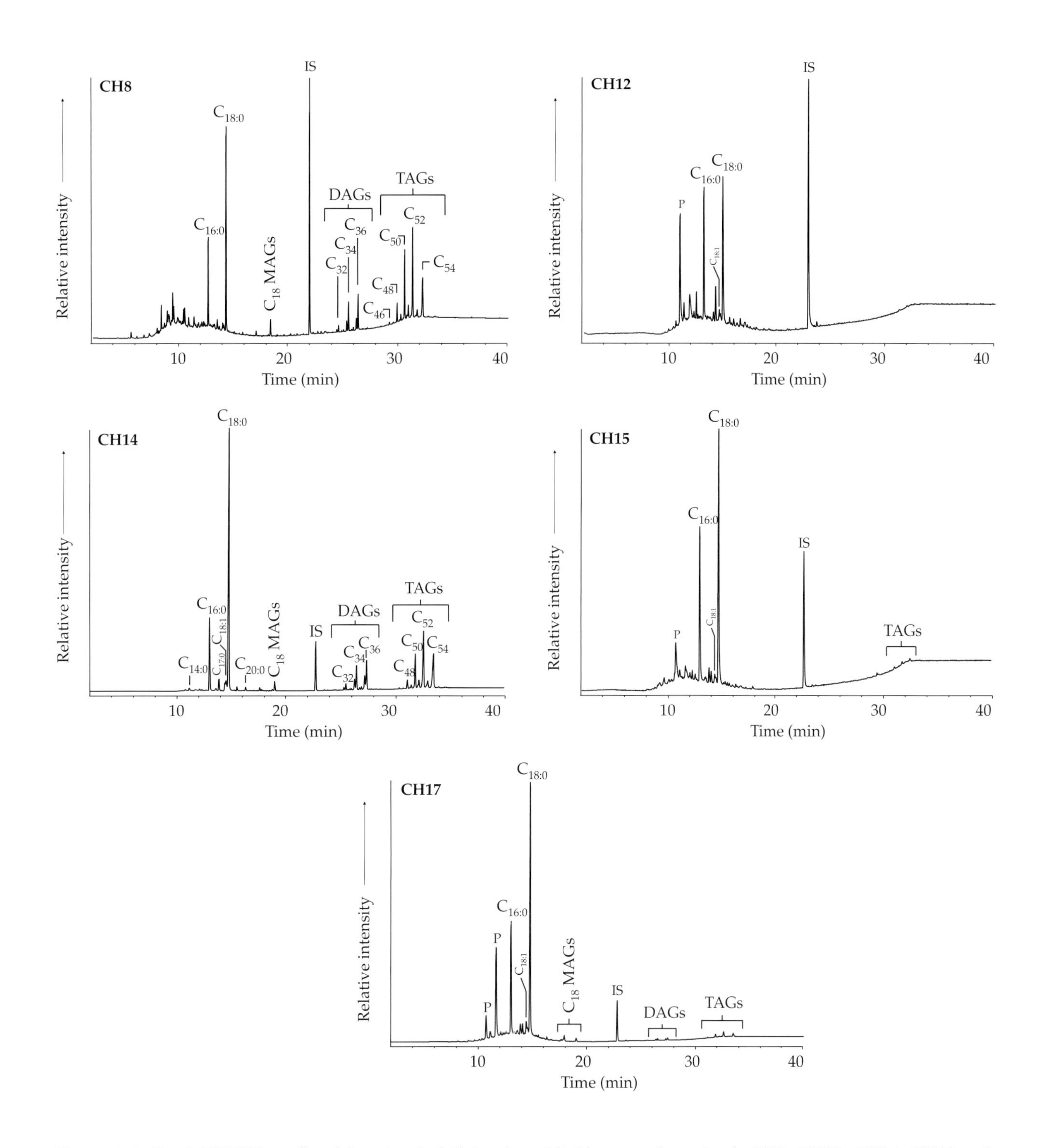

Figure 7.2. *Partial HTGC profile of the trimethylsilylated total lipid extract from sherds CH8, CH12, CH14, CH15 and CH17 containing lipid components characteristic of degraded animal fats. FAx:y are free fatty acids of carbon length x, and degree of unsaturation y. C_x MAGs are monoacylglycerols of carbon length x, DAGs are diacylglycerols, and C_x TAG are triacylglycerols of carbon length x. IS is the internal standard (C_{34} n-alkane). P is a plasticizer contaminant originating from plastic bags in which the sherds were stored.*

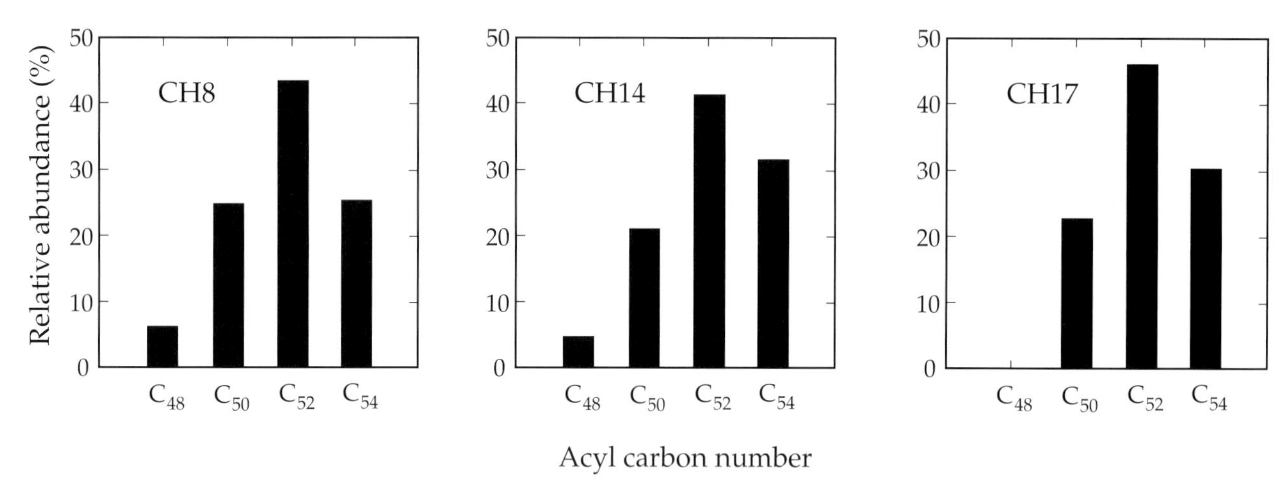

Figure 7.3. *The triacylglycerol distributions of the Çatalhöyük pottery samples. The distributions are indicative of degraded animal fats.*

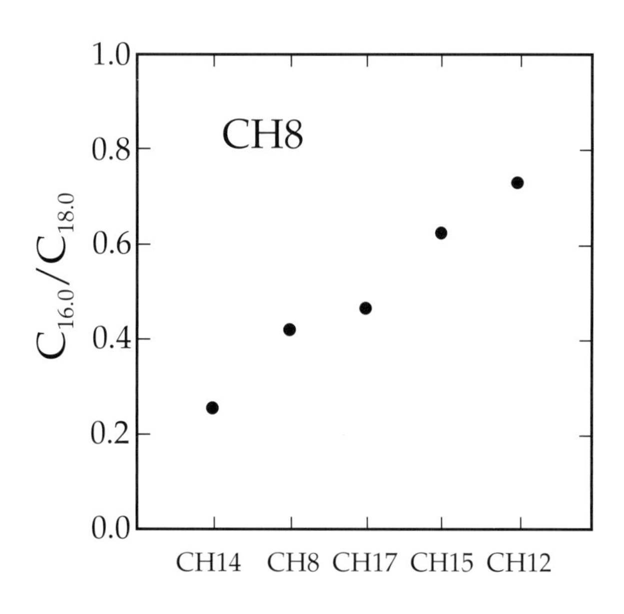

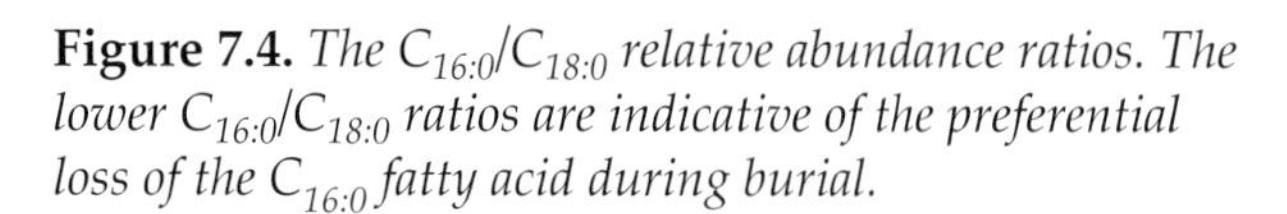

Figure 7.4. *The $C_{16:0}/C_{18:0}$ relative abundance ratios. The lower $C_{16:0}/C_{18:0}$ ratios are indicative of the preferential loss of the $C_{16:0}$ fatty acid during burial.*

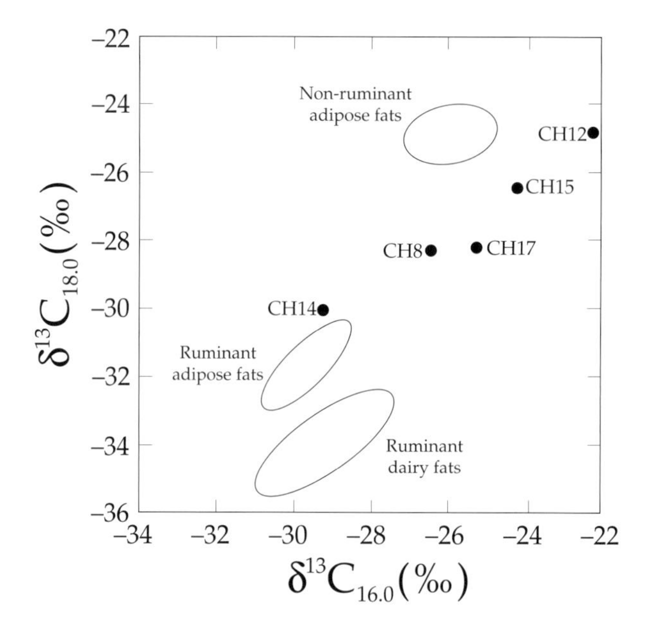

Figure 7.5. *$\delta^{13}C_{18:0}$ plotted against $\delta^{13}C_{16:0}$ values. The reference ellipses (1 s.d.) are constructed from the $\delta^{13}C$ values of the fatty acids obtained from modern C_3 fed domesticated animals. Points between the fields represent the mixing of the respective commodities in the pottery vessels in antiquity (either contemporaneously or through vessel re-use). However, this graph cannot be solely used to classify fats originating from animals fed on a mixed C_3/C_4 diet (cf. Fig. 7.6).*

under nitrogen. FAMEs were re-dissolved into hexane for analysis by GC and GC-C-IRMS.

Samples

A total of 28 sherds and 9 'clay balls' were submitted for organic-residue analysis; Tables 7.1–7.2 list the sample details.

Results and discussion

The GC and GC/MS analyses served to quantify and identify compounds in the lipid extract, such that it is possible to determine the presence of: i) an animal fat or plant oil; and/or ii) plant epicuticular waxes; and/or iii) beeswax; and/or iv) mid-chain ketones that indicate that the vessel has been strongly heated (Evershed *et al.* 1995; Raven *et al.* 1997). Furthermore, GC-C-IRMS analyses can distinguish between ruminant and non-ruminant adipose fats and dairy fats by investigating the $\delta^{13}C_{16:0}$, $\delta^{13}C_{18:0}$ and $\Delta^{13}C_{18:0-16:0}$ values.

Potsherds

GC analyses were performed on the solvent extracts of a sub-sample of each potsherd. Table 7.1 lists the sherds, their provenance and the lipids detected. A total of five of the 28 potsherds (18 per cent) yielded significant abundances of lipid. Figure 7.2 shows partial gas chromatograms of the sherds that contained absorbed lipid residues, indicating the compounds detected. In all five of the sherds degraded animal fat residues were present. These are characterized by the distribution of free fatty acids, mono-, di- and triacylglycerols referred to in the introduction. The TAG distributions for the three sherds that contained these components are shown in Figure 7.3, and are all typical of degraded animal fats, rather than plant oils. The TAG distributions seen in degraded fresh milk fat are characteristically wide, due to the inclusion of lower molecular weight (minor) TAGs (C_{40} to C_{44}). None of the sherds contained these lower molecular weight TAGs.

The $C_{16:0}/C_{18:0}$ fatty acid relative abundance ratios are shown in Figure 7.4. Fresh fats from animals typically display ratios in the region of 1.0 to 2.0, whereas in plant oils this ratio is typically significantly greater than 3.0, owing to characteristically low abundance of $C_{18:0}$ in plant oils. It is notable that all of the $C_{16:0}/C_{18:0}$ relative abundance ratios from the Çatalhöyük sherds are significantly lower than 1.0, with values that are rarely seen in nature. Although lipids generally are regarded as hydrophobic and thus insoluble in water, the presence of the carboxyl group in fatty acids does mean that they are sparingly soluble in water, with their solubility increasing with decreasing carbon number, thus the $C_{16:0}$ fatty acid is relatively more water soluble than the $C_{18:0}$ fatty acid (Bell 1973). This phenomenon was first detected in prehistoric pottery from northern European sites, and we would anticipate the effect to become even more exaggerated at sites of greater age, such as Çatalhöyük. Hence, this would explain the unusual fatty acid distributions seen in the vessels subject of this analysis, as represented by the ratios plotted in Figure 7.4. Thus, while the high abundance of $C_{18:0}$ strongly suggests an animal origin, in view of this leaching phenomenon, classification of the origin of the fats to species level cannot be accomplished on the basis of fatty acid distributions alone, except at exceptionally arid sites (Copley *et al.* 2001; Copley 2002).

The $\delta^{13}C_{18:0}$ and $\delta^{13}C_{16:0}$ values of the principal fatty acid components are plotted in Figure 7.5. The ellipses are generated from the $\delta^{13}C$ values of the fatty

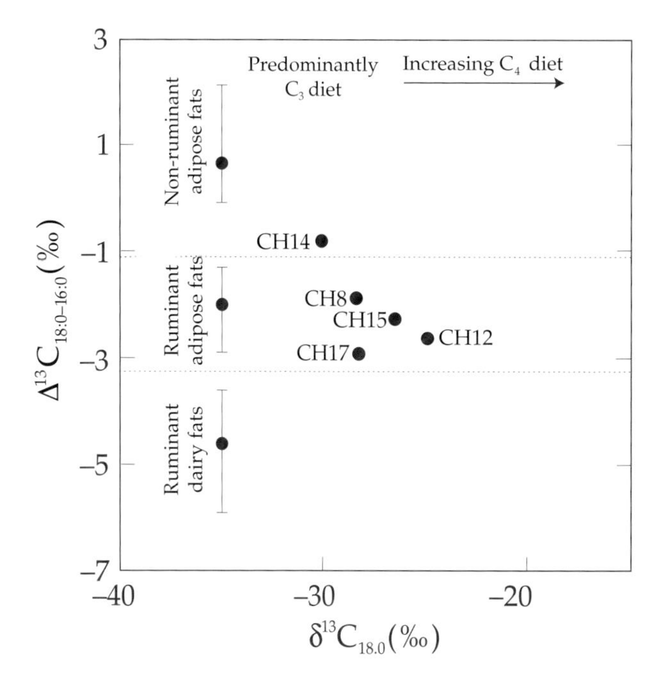

Figure 7.6. *Plot of $\Delta^{13}C_{18:0-16:0}$ against $\delta^{13}C_{18:0}$ values. The $\Delta^{13}C_{18:0-16:0}$ values of the reference fats shown in Figure 7.5 are plotted to the left of the diagram (mean values and ranges are illustrated).*

acids obtained from modern animals reared on strictly C_3 diets. Where C_4 plants, such as *Chenopodiacceae* and *Cyperaceae*, are not found (e.g. prehistoric Britain), these ellipses serve to classify the potsherd extracts to commodity type. From this graph it appears that CH14 is the only sherd that contained ruminant adipose fats, and that the remaining sherds are all of mixed ruminant/non-ruminant origin. C_4 plants do appear to have played a role in the diets of domesticated animals (see Volume 4, Chapter 15). Therefore, the $\Delta^{13}C$ values are calculated ($= \delta^{13}C_{18:0} - \delta^{13}C_{16:0}$) which have previously proven to be useful in distinguishing the fats of animals reared on mixed C_3/C_4 (or highly-varied C_3) diets (Copley 2002).

The $\Delta^{13}C_{18:0-16:0}$ and $\delta^{13}C_{18:0}$ values of the sherds are plotted in Figure 7.6, allowing their classification to be undertaken whilst simultaneously illustrating the relative contribution of C_3/C_4 plants to the animals' diet. The majority of the sherds plot in the region of the graph indicative of predominantly ruminant adipose fats, and although CH14 displays $\delta^{13}C$ values indicative of a non-ruminant fat, it is likely that this sherd too has a significant ruminant adipose fat contribution. The $\delta^{13}C_{18:0}$ values obtained from the majority of the sherds are indicative of a predominantly (but varied) C_3 diet, possibly with some contribution from C_4 plants as well. Only CH14 exhibited fatty acids with $\delta^{13}C$ values indicative of a solely C_3 origin. Of particular interest is the fact that none of the sherds plot within the dairy fat region of the graph.

Clay balls
A total of nine 'clay balls' were submitted to organic-residue analysis. The samples are listed in Table 7.2. No lipid residues were detected in any of the 'clay ball' samples.

Discussion

In summary, 5 of the 28 sherds (18 per cent) contained absorbed lipid residues. The proportion of sherds containing organic residues from Çatalhöyük is similar to that observed at other sites in the region of similar date. For example, pilot studies have shown that 44 per cent of sherds from Tell Bouqras and 11 per cent from Tell Sabi Abyad, Syria (which are dated to the sixth millennium BC) contained absorbed organic residues. Given the antiquity of these three sites, it is not unexpected that these percentages are lower than the 50 to 60 per cent that we routinely detect from British Neolithic pottery.

Fatty acids in living organisms are predominantly found in the form of TAGs. However, during vessel use/burial, these TAGs are degraded to DAGs, MAGs and free fatty acids. These lipid components were detected in 60 per cent (3/5) of the sherds containing organic residues, illustrating the remarkable level of survival of these compounds in some of the oldest archaeological pottery ever submitted to organic residue analysis.

None of the 'clay balls' yielded lipids suggesting that it is very unlikely that they were in contact with liquefied lipid-rich organic materials for any period of time during their use. Thus, while these negative data do not support the use of the clay balls in pot boiling, this suggestion of their use cannot be completely ruled out, especially in view of the fact that such a high proportion of the sherds lacked detectable lipid residues.

The low concentration of $C_{18:1}$ in the sherd extracts is consistent with its oxidative degradation during the period of burial, and is compelling evidence that the lipids are not modern contaminants. No plant lipids (e.g. *n*-alkanes, wax esters) were detected in any of the sherds, although given a larger sample size it might be expected that these components will be observed in some sherds.

The $\Delta^{13}C_{18:0-16:0}$ and $\delta^{13}C_{18:0}$ values of the fatty acids from the sherds indicate that four of them (80 per cent) are of a predominantly ruminant adipose fat origin, and that a further sherd is indicative of the mixing of ruminant adipose fats and non-ruminant fats. Based on the faunal remains at Çatalhöyük it is likely that these ruminant fats derive primarily from sheep/goats, while the non-ruminant fats probably derive mainly from equids (see Volume 4, Chapter 2). It is possible that some C_4 plants were consumed as forages/fodders by the animals whose products were processed in at least four of the vessels. None of the sherds contained dairy fats, and further work is currently being undertaken in this laboratory to determine the extent and antiquity of dairying in the region. To our knowledge these are the earliest residues from pottery vessels for which detailed biomolecular and isotopic analyses have been undertaken.

Acknowledgements

We would like to thank Jim Carter and Ian Bull for technical assistance.

Chapter 8

Some Remarks on Çatalhöyük Stamp Seals

Ali Umut Türkcan

This chapter will present the first stamp seals of Anatolia recovered at the early Neolithic settlement of Çatalhöyük during James Mellaart's excavations between 1961 and 1965 and during the excavation period since 1993. The Çatalhöyük stamp seals constitute the largest and earliest assemblage in early Neolithic Anatolia with 31 examples. Most of them (27) were recovered by Mellaart. The more recent excavations have revealed four more seals, three of which are broken. All of the stamp seals are made of clay and are generally well baked.

The stamp seals were recovered in Mellaart's so-called 'shrines' or in houses and in adjacent middens between these buildings, from Levels II–VII. They had a rich variety of shapes and patterns when compared to stamp repertoires at other sites in the early Neolithic in Anatolia. The main aim of this chapter is to make a detailed typological analysis of patterns and forms of Çatalhöyük stamp seals in relation to levels and contexts. In addition, functions and analogies with other seal assemblages will be discussed in the light of recent evidence.

The contextual data

The majority of the assemblage has already been published by Mellaart. However, no scale or any dimensional information was provided in the publications (1962, 56. pl. VIIc; 1964a, 97. figs. 41 & 42; 1967, 219–20, pl. 12. fig. 56). Re-examination of the assemblage concluded that the published examples are not all the artefacts found in 1960s excavations. Other unpublished examples were found stored in the Anatolian Civilizations Museum in Ankara. Study of the examples in the museum in 1997 showed that there were 27 stamps, including 6 unpublished examples (Figs. 8.1–8.2). Only two seals from 1965 (Nos. 11 & 12), the last season of Mellaart's former excavation, were illustrated in publication (Mellaart 1967, pl. 121).

The contextual information of the seals is varied. The distribution of the seals was not restricted to a particular context or building group. There are seven examples from Level II, three from Level III, eleven from Level IV, two from Level VI and one from Level VII (see Table 8.1 and Catalogue on CD). The absence of any seal dated to Level V is perhaps merely a matter of coincidence. Nine of the seals do not have any contextual information or location. With regard to the previous excavation records, one is assigned as a surface find and one is assigned as belonging to the excavation but without context. Three seals have neither a level, nor a context assigned. Observing their spatial contexts, the seals have been recovered in a variety of localities such as houses, more elaborate houses termed 'shrines' by Mellaart, and open midden areas, which Mellaart designated as courtyards (Fig. 8.3).

The contextual can now be divided as the following context categories:

'Shrines'

Seven seals have been recovered in the spaces that Mellaart preferred to call 'shrine'. They are recorded in three different shrines between Levels II, III and IV. They have been recovered in shrines II.A.I (Nos. 3, 4, 5, 6), III.A.I (No. 10) and IV.E.I (Nos. 18, 19). It is notable that Shrine II.A.1 contained four stamp seals that are valuable in regard to their precise context. They were recovered as scattered all over the floor of the main room of the shrine with other assemblages (Nos. 3, 4, 5 & 6). As Mellaart states (1962, 46),

> four stamp seals of baked clay with incised designs and about a dozen pottery vessels together with much obsidian, some chert and flint and several hundred palettes, pounders, querns and polishers (mainly from the north store) completed the inventory.

It is unfortunate that the contextual integration of the data is not more precise for the rest of the seals.

Houses

Twelve of the stamp seals were recovered in structures considered by Mellaart to be houses. Three houses of Level II contained a seal each (B.1, B.2, B.3). In Level III, three examples occur as single pieces in houses (A.2, A.4, B.2) while two occur together in another (E.3). In

Figure 8.1. *Stamp seals 1–16.*

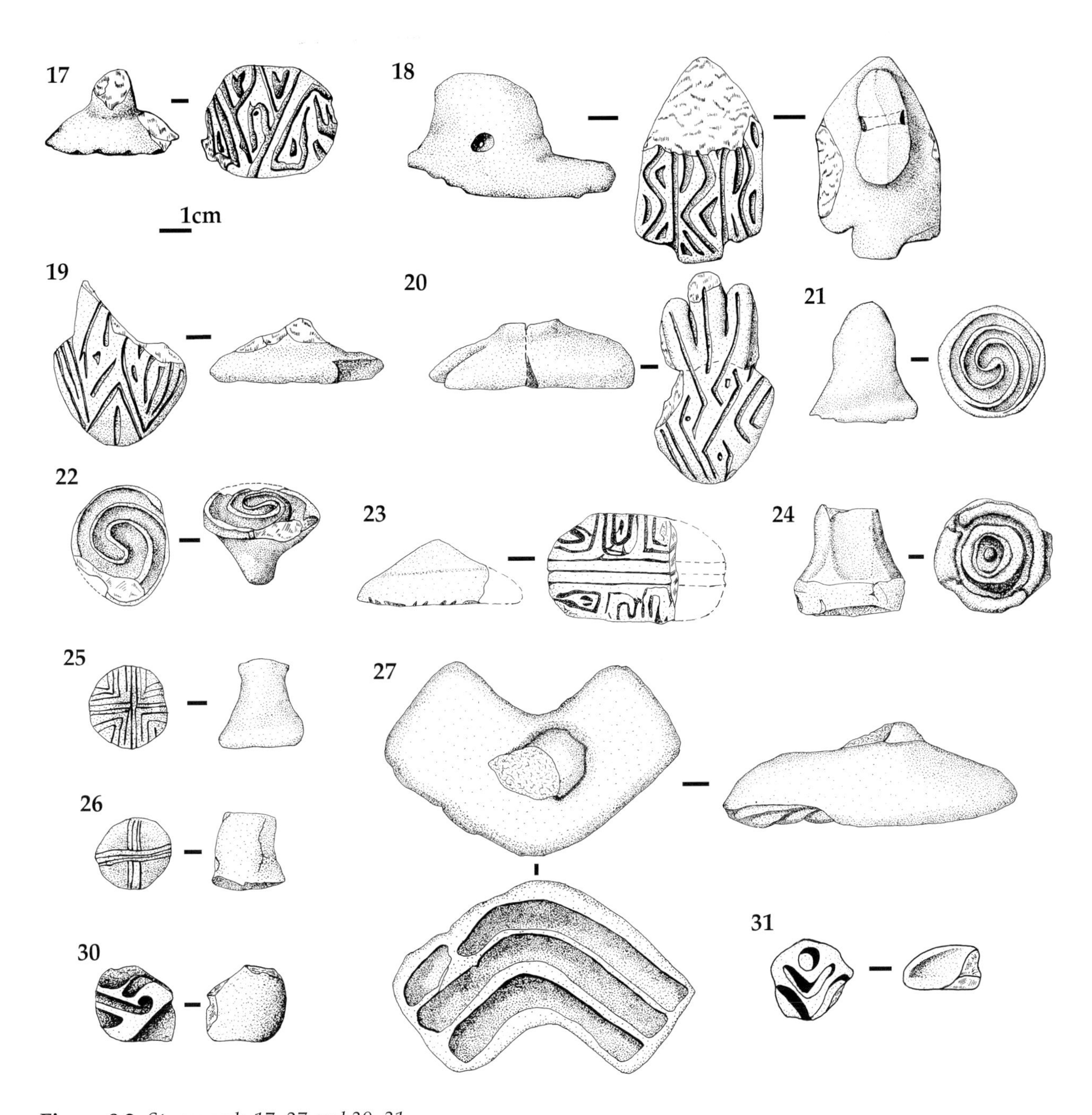

Figure 8.2. *Stamp seals 17–27 and 30–31.*

Level VI, one seal has been recovered in House A.1 house and the earliest clay stamp seal, which belongs to Level VII, has been recovered in House E.15.

Middens/Burials

Five seals have been recovered in places that Mellaart described as 'courtyards'. Three examples were recovered together in a courtyard in Area F dated to Level IV (Nos. 11, 12, 13). Two examples were recovered in the same courtyard area which is located in Area E dated to Level IV (No. 16) and Level VI (No. 23). These last two examples were both found with burials, although the sex of the skeletons could not be determined (Mellaart 1964a, 95, fig. 41.6 & 41.10; 1967, 209).

The general dispersal from the contexts shows that seals are most commonly found in houses (12) followed by 'shrines' (7) while others came from middens (5). From the more recent excavations, it is unfortunate that only four unstratified stamp seals have been found as surface finds. All of these seals are fragmentary. Two of them were already published by Hamilton (1996, 240; figs. 12.6.4–5). In addition, there are three unstratified stamps from Mellaart's assemblage (Nos. 25, 26 & 27)

Most of the material (90 per cent) derives from Mellaart's contexts from the 1961–65 excavations. However, the inadequate documentation and lack of fixed co-ordinates limit the conclusions that can be drawn about the contexts of seals. The excavation areas, such as A, B or F are mentioned without giving precise locations. Furthermore, building numbers are frequently changed within the A, B, F or E areas. Although the seals in 'shrines' have been mentioned, it should be noted that the distinction between 'shrines' and houses is being reconsidered by the present project.

Table 8.1. *Stamp seals.*

Catalogue no.	Excavation no.	Dimensions (in cm)	Level	Context	Year recovered
1	239	H: 3.5, L:3.4	II	House B.1	1962
2	5	H:3.5, L:6.0, W:5.4	II	House B.3	1961
3	241	H:3.2, L:6.2, W:4,3	II	Shrine A.1	1962
4	242	H:2.0, L:5.8; W:4.7	II	Shrine A.1	1962
5	243	H:2.9, L:6.2, W:4.3	II	Shrine A.1	1962
6	240	H:2.6, L:4.2, W:2.2	II	Shrine A.1	1962
7	238	H2.5, L:6.2, W:6.0	II	House B.2	1962
8	28	H:2.2, L:5.0, W:4.6	III	House A.2	1961
9	12	H:3.0, L:7.5, W:3.5	III	House A.4	1961
10	4	H:3.0, R:5.7	III	Shrine A.1	1961
11	601	H:2.0, L:4.8, W:2.1	IV	Courtyard in Area F	1965
12	608	H:3.5, L:5.5, W:4.2	IV	Courtyard in Area F	1965
13	577	H:1.8, L:3.6; W:3.1	IV	Courtyard in Area F	1965
14	237	H:1.6, R:2.9	IV	House E.A.1	1962
15	235	H:2.0, R:4.5	IV	House E.?8	1962
16	431	H:2.9, L:4.8, W:4.2	IV	Burial in courtyard in Area E	1963
17	14	H:1.8, L:3.8, W:3.5	IV	House E.2	1961
18	236	H:2.9, L:5.9, W:3.6	IV	Shrine E.1	1962
19	72	H:1.6; L:4.8, W:4.0	IV	Shrine E.1	1961
20	20	H:2.2, L:5.9, W:3.9	IV	House E.3	1961
21	13	H:3.6, R:3.2	IV	House E.3	1961
22	282	H:2.3, R:3.0	VI	House E,A.1	1962
23	433	H:3.6, L:3.6, W:3.1	VI	Burial in courtyard in Area E	1963
24	679	H:2.8, R:3.0	VII	House E.15	1965
25	44	H:2.5, R:2.2	Unknown	Unknown	1961
26	62	H:2.0, R:2.0	Unknown	Unknown	1961
27	15	H:3.1, L:9.2, W:4.3	Unknown	Unknown	1961
28	30	H:1.6, L:2.6, W.2	Surface find	Surface find	1994
29	2	H:2.0, L:3.0, W:3.0	Surface find	Surface find	1993
30	?	H:1.9, L:2.4, W:2.2	Surface find	Surface find	1996
31	47	H:1.3, L:2.4, W:2.1	Surface find	Surface find	1996

Typology

The Çatalhöyük baked-clay seals bear incised ornaments with many different shapes. The dominant form is flat-faced, with a round (or elliptical) or rounded rectangular base with conical or rounded handles of which some are perforated (three examples, Nos. 2, 15, 18). Some examples have unique forms that make them distinctive which are not seen in other Early Neolithic period assemblages. Furthermore, these unique forms raise questions about their stamping functions. The typology used is based primarily on forms and patterns. In forming the typology, the rears that are generally handles and the face sides that bear the designs, have been examined separately.

Forms

Handle forms

The handle forms are divided into four groups (Fig. 8.4) and are recognized particularly with regard to their profile.

1. *Conical*: This is the most common handle type among the stamp seals. They have a generally conical shape with a pointed apex in some examples. This type

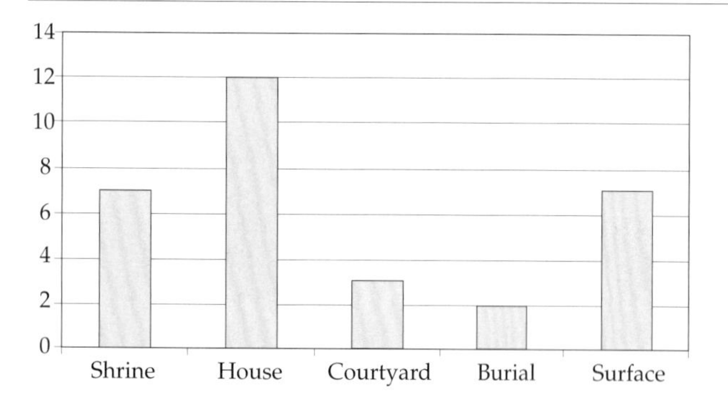

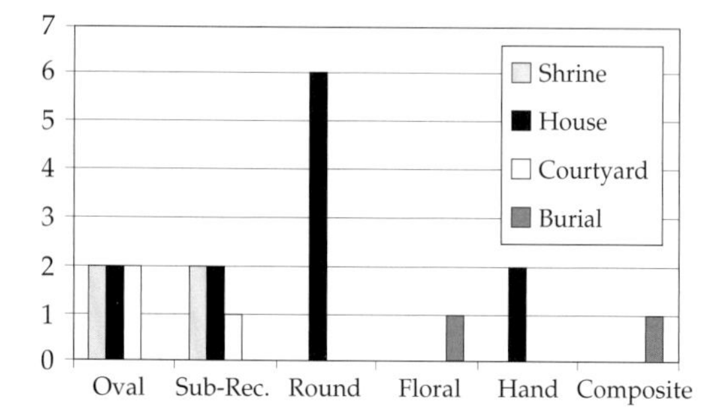

Figure 8.3. *Context distribution of stamp seals.*

of handle is seen on 13 stamp seals in every level (Nos. 4, 9, 10, 11, 12, 14, 15, 16, 17, 21, 22, 23 & 29).

2. *Cylindrical*: These are the handles that have a cylindrical shape, with the base of the cylinder being the seal face. This type of handle is seen in Nos. 24 (Level VII) and 25 and 26 (unstratified).

3. *Sub-rectangular*: These handle forms have rectangular shapes but rounded corners. This type of handle is seen in Nos. 3 and 6 (Level II) and 18 (Level IV).

4. *Flattened oval*: These handle forms are oval-shaped in profile but flattened on both sides. This type of handle is seen in Nos. 2 and 5 (Level II).

Apart from these handle types there are also seven unidentified and non-categorized handles that are in a very fragmentary condition of which either the tips or the whole handles are broken off (Nos. 19, 20, 27, 28, 30 & 31). Only three handles have evidence of having been perforated for suspension (Nos. 2, 15 & 18). Besides that, one handle (No. 5) has finger impressions on both sides of its handle. The handle has been flattened and impressed, perhaps so that it can be held firmly.

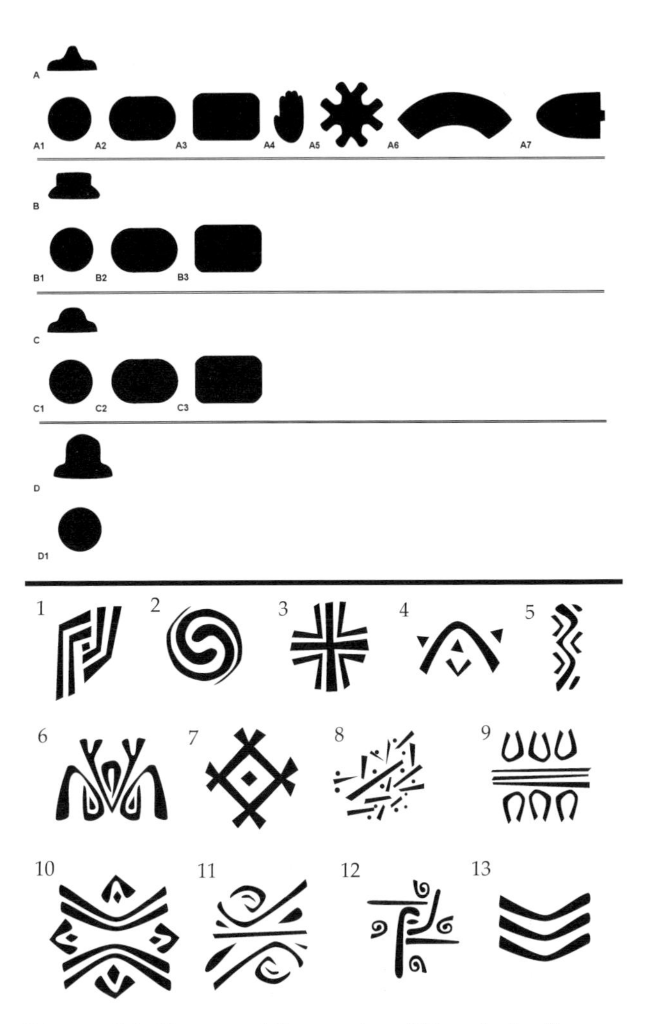

Figure 8.4. *Stamp seal form and motif typologies (by John Swogger).*

Base forms

For the base forms, it may be said that they are enormously variable. Within that variety, there are seven identifiable types (Figs. 8.4–8.5). Their typological description and distribution in relation to the levels are as follows:

1. *Round forms*: This is the only base form that is seen in all levels. Two examples are from Level II (Nos. 1 & 4), one is from Level III (No. 10), two are from Level IV (Nos. 14 & 21), one is from Level VI (No.22) and one is from Level VII (No. 24). However, two examples do not have any contextual data (Nos. 25 & 26).

2. *Oval forms*: This is seen in Level II where there are four examples (Nos. 2, 3, 4 & 5), three examples are from Level IV (Nos. 11, 12 & 17) and one example is from Level VI (No. 23).

3. *Sub-rectangular forms*: This type is seen in Level II where there are two examples (Nos. 6 & 7) and there is one example from Level III (No. 8). Two examples are unstratified (Nos. 28 & 29).

4. *Hand-shaped forms*: Two examples of this base type from Level IV (No. 19) and Level VI (No. 20). The hand shaped forms are a subject of great interest. According to Mellaart, they form a link between the paintings of hands in the cave art of Europe, the wall paintings of Çatalhöyük Levels VII and VI.B (VII.8, VI.B.8, VI.B.10 & VI.B.15) (Mellaart 1967, pls. 41 & 43) as well as the hands painted on the pottery from Hacılar Levels V–II and early Chalcolithic IIB (Mellaart 1970, 45, 48 & 74).

5. *Floral-base form*: This type has been recovered in Level VI (No. 16). The form with four leaf panels (quatrefoil) recalls a floral design, which is also seen on many wall paintings in Çatalhöyük from the east wall of Shrine VI.B.I and in Shrine A.III.8 (Mellaart 1967, pls. 29, 31, 33 & 34). The same patterns are also seen on the Early Chalcolithic Hacılar Level II B and I bowls (Mellaart 1970, 44.12, 58, 60–63 & 65–6).

6. *Composite form with rectangular three bands*: This form is seen on one seal (No. 18). The overall seal face is divided into three panels. The band in the centre is slightly projecting.

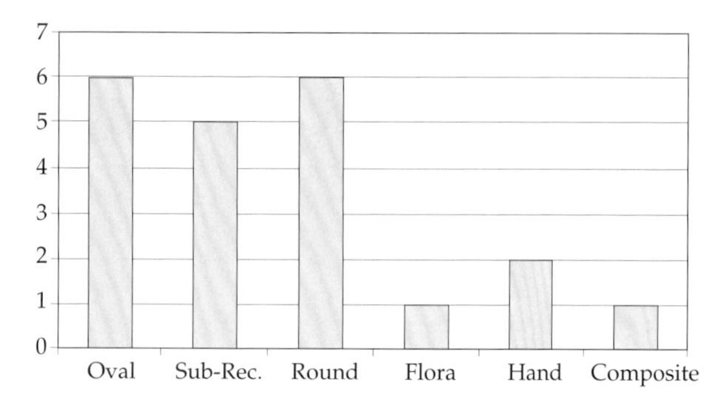

Figure 8.5. *Stamp seal forms.*

7. *Boomerang-shaped form*: This is seen in one unstratified seal (No. 27). It is an outstanding form that recalls the boomerang, with the two short sides curving.

8. *Handleless groove forms*: These stamps are extraordinary with a deep groove on the face side. The form of these stamps is unparalleled among Near Eastern stamp seals. The common features of these variable forms are deep grooves right at the centre and flat rears without handles. The main grooved forms are seen on four stamps (Nos. 1, 7, 8 &13). Three of them have the same form and seem to have been deliberately broken through the centre. Two of them (Nos. 7 & 8) have sub-rectangular face sides with a deep groove and have been incised with pseudo-meander patterns. A third (No. 1) has a face side that is flat but slightly rounded at the sides with a deep groove in the centre. Its rear is flat and does not have any handle. Although the shapes are reminiscent of stone polishers, their clay material and ornamented faces prevent us from thinking of them as polishers. My suggestion is that the grooves right in the centre functioned with a knot of one or more ropes tied across the centre so as to hold firmly and/or make an impression.

A rather different form (No. 13, Level VI) is irregular when compared to other grooved forms. Actually, this form does not seem to be a stamp seal with its much rounded form and face side on which grid patterns are incised smoothly. It is definitely not suitable for stamping and its function remains enigmatic. However, its grooved centre and the overall form, which is broken off (deliberately?), suggest a close relation with the other extraordinary forms (Nos. 1, 7 & 8) with regard to their doubtful seal function.

Remarkably, some baked-clay objects (termed 'Tonkisser') from Tell Karanovo (Hiller 2001, fig. 1.B1–5; Hiller & Nikolov 1997, fig. 5.4) have close parallels with the two sub-rectangular grooved examples from Çatalhöyük (Nos. 7 & 8). These 'Tonkisser' which are dated to Karanovo IV (Late Neolithic) have flat-faced sides that have been incised. Although grooves cannot be recognized, the objects are very similar to the rectangular examples Nos. 7 and 8. In addition, one example (Hiller 2001, 1.B2) has been ornamented with a very similar meandroid pattern to that seen on Nos. 7 and 8. Furthermore, Hiller stresses that the favoured patterns on the Karanovo examples are typical combinations for Early Neolithic Balkan 'pintaderas' such as meandroid, spiraloid and diagonal hatchings (2001, 4).

Patterns

A typological analysis of the pattern groups will allow comparison with similar patterns either in Çatalhöyük (i.e. wall paintings and figurines) or in the iconography of neighbouring cultural regions (Aceramic Northern Levant, Early Neolithic and Early Chalcolithic Pisidia and Early and Late Neolithic southeastern Europe). The patterns on stamp bases that are termed seal faces in the descriptions, are divided into 13 pattern groups. Their schematic illustrations are shown in Figure 8.4:

1. *Pseudo-meander*: This pattern is the most common (eight seals) (Nos. 4, 6, 7, 8, 9, 10, 11 & 20). The pattern is composed of pairs of interlocking lines that step across at a 45° angle. Every point at which pairs of interlocking lines meet is filled with a dot. These rotating pairs of distorted meanders give an impression of basket or reed basket weaving. No. 6 is noteworthy with its two curving figures facing each other. The pattern seems likely to be the main symbol or concept behind the pseudo-meander patterns of Çatalhöyük.

2. *Spirals*: The pattern is seen on two seal faces (Nos. 21 & 22). The seal face has a deep and wide engraved channel of a simple clockwise spiral. These patterns which are very common in Early Neolithic Balkan seals, display close parallels with the seals from Early Neolithic Nea Nikomedia in Greece, and Karanovo I–II sites such as Azmaska and Kirdzali in Bulgaria (Makkay 1984, 81). The deep carved ones from Nea Nikomedia are especially noteworthy.

3. *Criss-cross*: The pattern is composed of simple crosses on the seal face. They are seen in Levels IV to VI (Nos. 14, 25 & 26).

4. *Composite of diamond motif surrounded by triangles*: The pattern is seen on two seals of different levels; Nos. 5 (Level II) and 12 (Level IV). In the centre are an elongated ellipsoid and a curving motif that recalls the bucranium. This central combination of motifs is enclosed by three sets of diagonal lines, each of which meets above the central motif. At either side are three

roundels that are separated by encircling lines. In the No. 5 example, the central motifs are much more emphasized, the curving line at the bottom forms into a clear bucranium symbol, and the oval pattern becomes a diamond.

5. *Wave motifs set into three panels*: This is seen on one seal from Level IV (No. 8). Every panel is engraved with curving (or meandering) lines with small decorating patterns around it. The curving lines run across the panels and give an impression of rotation. The space between the carvings of the main line is filled by small motifs.

6. *Symmetrically-arranged curving motifs*: This is seen on one seal from Level IV (No. 17). The pattern on the face is mainly composed of lines that coil up on either side. In the centre are two pairs of diagonal lines that make a triangle. There are also small triangles inside the space. The small triangles are filled by heart shaped motifs. On either side of the base, there are curving motifs that are hard to identify.

7. *Floral*: Only one example presents itself in Level VI (No. 16). The pattern is identical with its form. It is composed of four leaf panels (quatrefoil) with a diamond motif in the centre. The pattern resembles a floral design that is also seen on wall paintings such as the east walls of shrine VIB.I and of shrine A.III.8 (Mellaart 1967, 29, 31, 33 & 34). The same pattern can also be seen in Late Neolithic Hacılar bowls (Mellaart 1970, 58, 61 & 65).

8. *Line and dot*: This pattern is represented by the examples in Levels II and IV (Nos. 1 & 19). The pattern scheme is composed of irregularly spaced dots and lines. However, No. 19 shows a more regular arrangement with curving and bent lines.

9. *Wavy lines in three parallel longitudinal bands*: This is seen on one seal from Level VI (No. 23). The pattern is composed of longitudinal lines and curving patterns. Two oscillating lines are separated from each other by three parallel longitudinal lines so as to give a symmetrical affect. The curving patterns stand perpendicular to horizontal parallel lines in the centre.

10. *Triangle and V motifs in symmetrical arrangement*. This is seen in Level II (No. 3). The pattern is composed of two curving parallel lines that almost meet in the centre with oval motifs at each side. There are two projecting lines and triangles which are seen on the short sides. On each short side, the pattern between projecting lines is elongated and becomes a drop motif.

11. *Coiled motifs divided by parallel lines in the centre*: The pattern is seen on one seal from Level II (No. 2), and is composed of coiling designs that are encircled by rounded lines. Coiling motifs are set diagonally between the lines dividing the face into two panels.

12. *Diamond motif encircled by spirals*: This is seen in Level VI (No. 15). The motif arrangement shows a rotational symmetry. Deep carved spirals at the edges of the stamp run around the central combination in a clockwise manner. Two curving lines encircle the drop motif in the central area. Apart from these curving lines, there are two straight lines dividing the seal face into three zones.

13. *Three curving parallel lines*: This is seen on one unstratified seal (No. 27). The pattern is composed of three parallel curving lines. The form of the seal is identical with the outer contours of the pattern.

Combining the evidence, two important results emerge. First, there is a striking preference in a majority of the seals for symmetrical composite designs instead of single basic motifs. This could suggest a style narrative of some form. Second, there is a continuation of some favoured designs throughout the levels. This is especially true of two patterns (pseudo-meander and composite design type 4). The most repeated and favoured pattern is the so-called pseudo-meander. The meaning behind this repetitive design, which occurs in wall paintings and on later pottery, may be investigated within the context of abstract, symbolic Neolithic art. 'Infinite' meander patterns are often regarded as the earliest examples of abstract art. Similar repeating patterns are first seen in the Upper Palaeolithic settlement of Mezin in Ukraine. Chikalenko (1953, 534) regards these patterns as the beginnings of the real symbolist expression in art with the harmony of rhythm and symmetry. Furthermore, Marshack suggests (1972) that a 'zigzag iconography', multiple serpentine bands and meandering abstract patterns are found in much of the very earliest art in the Upper Palaeolithic. Marshack (1985) argues that there is only a limited number of logical ways of depicting the cyclical time that is observed in the sun and moon; these patterns may be mainly meanders, spirals, concentric circles, and zigzags, all of which are seen in the seal pattern repertoire. However, use or transformations of similar symbols over millennia do not imply a continuity of meaning. The meanings may have changed or may have been alienated while the symbol itself remained the same.

The meander patterns are also widely found in following periods. They can be traced into the

Figure 8.6. *Reconstruction of stamp seals being used on textiles (by John Swogger).*

Early Chalcolithic period in Anatolia and into Early Neolithic Balkan cultures. In Chalcolithic Anatolia, the same pseudo-meander (regular meanders with dots in the centre) reappears in a wall painting from Canhasan I (French 1962, fig. 9.4, pl. II) and pottery. In Hacılar, Chalcolithic seals of level II B, dated to 5480–5250 BC (Mellaart 1975), show the continuity of this tradition right from Çatalhöyük until the end of the fifth millennium. In the opinion of Mellaart, Early Chalcolithic pottery with bold curvilinear ornaments in fantastic style owes its origins to the meandroid patterns of the Çatalhöyük seals (1975, 100).

Another continuity in the patterns of seals can be observed for an outstanding pattern (type 4) which is seen on seals from different levels; Nos. 5 (Level IV) and 12 (Level II). The general impression is that this design may have been developed during Level IV at the same time that pseudo-meander patterns became mature. The central diamond (or oval-shaped) motif is surrounded by triangles above. On either side a roundel is seen with inclining lines. In Level II, the pattern is executed in the same arrangement but in a more stylized way.

Function

When the stamp seals of Çatalhöyük are examined (see Typology above), a wide variety of forms and patterns are encountered, including some outstanding forms. Naturally, these combinations give rise to the impression that some 'stamp-seals' might have served a function involving more than just sealing. However, no impressions left by these seals on clay have so far been recovered in either Çatalhöyük or in any other contemporary Anatolian Neolithic and Early Chalcolithic site. It has been suggested that they were used on perishable materials such as textiles or skins or even for the decoration of the human body as in the case of the so-called 'pintaderas' (Bray & Trump 1982, 190; Mellaart 1964a, 97). Thus I am fully aware that the word 'seal' may not be appropriate for the all artefacts discussed in this study. The term has been retained in order to be in accordance with the terminology previously used and to avoid terminological confusion.

The flat-based stamps may also have been applied on textile fabrics since these are known from Çatalhöyük (Mellaart 1964a, pl. XXIV a–b). The following question then arises: did the inhabitants of Çatalhöyük decorate these textiles with vegetable dyes? Unfortunately, vegetable dyes do not preserve well. Although some white or black spots can be distinguished on some seals (Nos. 7 & 12), it is hard to decide whether they are paint remains or post-depositional features such as salts without analysis using spectroscopy.

As regards to how the Çatalhöyük seals were used, Mellaart points out that 'such stamp seals become extremely common in Level II, from which no wall paintings have so far been recovered. Did stamped cloth hangings take the place of textile paintings in the earlier shrines?' (1964a, 97). However, when the number of the seals is examined, it is found that the majority of seals come from Level IV where wall paintings are seen in five different buildings (Mellaart 1967, 81, fig. 13).

As for using the stamps to decorate the body, the frequent use of ochre in burials (Mellaart 1964a, 93), and a seated woman figurine which was painted with crosses recalling floral patterns (Mellaart 1963, fig. 28), seem to suggest that the bodies could have been ornamented with stamped designs. Taking this evidence into account, it is possible that the stamps may have been used as so called pintaderas. Both stamp and roller pintaderas occur in many native American cultures (Bray & Trump 1982, 190).

As already noted, the four stamp seals from 'shrine' A1 in Level II are valuable with regard to their precise context. They were recovered scattered all over the floor of the main room with other material including several hundred palettes, pounders, querns and polishers, mainly from the north store of the building (Mellaart 1963, 46). This remarkable association with several palettes, pounders and querns, suggests the possibility that the stamps were linked to a paint preparing process. This contextual evidence strengthens the notion that the stamps functioned as pintaderas (von Wickede 1990, 63). If we accept that they had been used on textiles, we can also presume that they could also have been used on textile sacks for recording or indicating ownership.

On the other hand, many seals display signs of long and probably heavy use. Their long use might suggest that they were kept for longer than an individual human life span as a precious object. There seems to be a possibility that many seals were handed down or used over many generations in Çatalhöyük, probably throughout many levels of habitation as portable individual objects that could have been kept. It is of interest that there is still limited evidence of deposition in burials, except for two non-building examples.

As regards some of the other forms, some small cylindrical examples (Nos. 25 & 26) could not have been used as stamps, due to their smooth patterns which would not leave a recognizable mark or trace even on clay. They have a rather different size and the patterns were made roughly. My suggestion is that they could have been so called tokens or 'calculi', counting devices. The mini clay balls can be considered within this 'calculi' system as well (Chapter 6); wider argument has been made by Schmandt-Besserat (1977; 1997).

Above all, if the function of the clay stamps was to seal or identify a particular elite group or individual, one would expect the production and variety of stamps to have increased with the increase in population and in its institutions. As the society grew in size and complexity there would have been greater demand for stamps, each with a particular mark. Therefore, it is not surprising that the clay stamps occur at Çatalhöyük where we see a large and dense settlement.

As mentioned above, most of the patterns strongly resemble each other and tend to continue through many levels. Pattern varieties and their groups seem to have been made intentionally alike to display similar authority or emphasize social affiliation. From this point of view, they may be related to identity and social status. However, there is little evidence for a link to social status, or to age or gender given that only two examples (Nos. 16 & 23) come from burials.

Discussion

The next step is to see what can be combined from the distribution patterns of these seals in terms of chronology and origins. The earliest stamps and stamped impressions (on plaster plaques) are known from the Pre-Pottery Neolithic period in the Levant. They first occur in Aceramic levels at Ras-Shamra (Level VC). The Ras Shamra stamps, which are made of steatite, have been radiocarbon dated to between 7550 and 6450 cal BC, broadly contemporary with the Çatalhöyük stamps (Contenson 1992, 197). There is also evidence for use of stamps on gypsum plaster in Tell El-Kowm, just west of the Euphrates (von Wickede 1990, 55–70; Stordeur 1982b). From that time onwards, stamp seals are recovered in small numbers at many Neolithic sites. These first stamp seals of the Aceramic Levant are generally made of stone and ornamented with basic linear and zig-zag motifs.

As mentioned above, the seals that were recovered in Çatalhöyük, constitute the largest and earliest stamp-seal assemblage in Early Neolithic Anatolia with 31 examples. A stone object from (5212) in Space 182, Building 17 of Level IX (Fig. 8.7) has an incised design and is similar in size to the clay seals. This is a flat gabbro stone of which one side is carved with line and dot patterns similar to the type 8 pattern (seen on Nos. 1 & 19). It could be either a handleless stone stamp or a decorated stone plaque. If it is a seal it would be earlier than the clay examples from the site, but as its status is uncertain it has been excluded from the catalogue pending further discoveries.

The next thing that should be noted is the scarcity of stamp seals in Anatolian Aceramic sites in comparison to the Levant. Stamp seals are totally absent in Aceramic assemblages in central Anatolia and make their first appearance in the early Neolithic period at Çatalhöyük (Özdoğan 1999, 216). This phenomenon might be related with the sudden increase of ceramic Neolithic sites around the middle of the seventh millennium cal BC beyond the Taurus range in central Anatolia; over a hundred pottery Neolithic sites are known from central Anatolia. Özdoğan (1997, 15) suggests that 'this is also the time when the earliest Neolithic sites make their appearance in the Aegean and in the Balkans'. This possible population shift and the 'Neolithization' process of western Anatolia and southeastern Europe seem to be linked to the spread of stamp seals. However, the origins of the Çatalhöyük stamp seals are still open to debate given the lack of evidence for an earlier tradition in Aceramic central Anatolia and given the contextually isolated analogies with northern Levant. It is evident that, as Makkay (1984, 75) states, neither the earliest Anatolian, nor

Figure 8.7. *Stone object 5212.X2.*

the early European Neolithic stamp seals indicate any substantial affinities with the currently known earliest stamp seals of northern Levant and the Near East.

As a conclusion of prime importance, available evidence seems to indicate two stamp-seal traditions in two different areas that evolved at different rates. One of them belongs to the northern Levant where the earliest examples have been recovered. Levant stamp seals in later periods are a subsequent development from the same tradition. The other tradition, which is in our scope of interest here, is Anatolian, leading on to the early Neolithic southeastern European stamp-seal assemblages. The different material, forms and decoration of early Neolithic Anatolian seals — mostly the Çatalhöyük seals — suggest an independent development from the earlier Aceramic Levantine seals, especially with regard to their iconography. The Anatolian/southeastern European seals constitute a different assemblage with unique forms and patterns when compared to the Levantine (late PPNB) and Mesopotamian clay stamps. On the other hand, the Çatalhöyük stamp-seal assemblage with its unique design features can be seen as occupying an intermediary position between the Near Eastern and more remote southeast European seals on the basis of present evidence (Makkay 1984, 72, 78; von Wickede 1990, 55–70).

The distribution and similarity of stamp seals have always been regarded, together with painted pottery and ceramic figurines, as evidence for cultural affiliations between Anatolia and early Neolithic cultures in southeastern Europe. Many researchers have the opinion that typological and chronological evidence gives a clear indication of Anatolian influences in the introduction of the earliest stamp seals of Greece (Thessalian) and Balkans (Nea-Nikomedeia, Karanovo I–II, Starčevo-Körös examples) during the Early Neolithic in the Balkans (Onassoglou 1996, 163; Makkay 1984, 72–5; Perlès 2001, 54; Rodden 1964, 565). The stamp seals are likely to have been introduced into the Balkans and Greece with the use of contemporary pottery technologies.

These two groups of stamp seals seem to share the same traits in their pattern repertoires (Makkay 1984; Onassoglou 1996, 163; Perlès 2001, 54). In a detailed typological analysis, Makkay points to six similar pattern traits between Çatalhöyük and Neolithic Balkan stamp seals (1984, 73–4). Based on these comparative results, spirals (including also concentric circles) and varieties of complex meander patterns seem to be the most common traits linking these two groups. These two traits also link Çatalhöyük and Pisidian examples, including early Chalcolithic Hacılar IIB seals (see below for detailed discussion).

What Mellaart (1964a, 97) called the 'pseudo-meander' pattern is intriguing in many ways. The pattern is frequently executed on Çatalhöyük seals (nine seals) but is not seen in contemporary Levant and Mesopotamian glyptics. On the other hand, the pseudo-pattern and its schematized varieties are widely seen in early Neolithic Balkan seal and pottery assemblages in Early Neolithic Karanovo I–II, and Thessalian contexts. Another parallel is the use of clay material. Manufacture in clay is observed mainly for Nea Nikomedeia, Starčevo and Karanovo I–II stamp seals. The Thessalian specimens are somewhat different in their preference for stone and composite labyrinthine patterns which are absent from the Çatalhöyük seals. This latter pattern is also familiar on Starčevo and Nea Nikomedeia stamp seals (Makkay 1984, 73; Onassoglou 1996, 163). Besides the fact that all 18 seals from Nea Nikomedeia are manufactured in clay, the early Neolithic Nea Nikomedeia and Çatalhöyük stamp seals have many similarities in their forms and decoration and manufacturing techniques, as seen in the use of deeply-cut incised lines (Rodden 1964, 565; Makkay 1984, 73).

Moreover, similar stamp seals have been reported from other early Neolithic and early Chalcolithic sites in the Pisidian Region (Lake District), the region adjacent to the central Anatolian plateau, but not in the quantities and variation that occur at Çatalhöyük. There are similar baked-clay stamp seals, some of which display the same decoration patterns (e.g. pseudo-meander patterns), in early Chalcolithic Hacılar IIB (Mellaart 1970, 164, fig. 187.8–10 & pl. CXIX), early Neolithic Bademağacı (Duru 1998, pls. 18/5–6 & 23/4–5; Umurtak 2000, 1–3 & fig. 3.1) and Höyücek (Duru 1992, 561 & pls. 20, 22; Umurtak 2000, 1–3 & figs. 3.8–9).

There seem to be two pattern groups linking the Çatalhöyük and Pisidian stamp seals. First is the concentric circle on a seal from Bademağacı EN3 (Umurtak 2000, 3.1 & pl. 5.1) that is similar to seal No. 24 (Level VII) and to the two spiral patterned stamp seals Nos.

21 and 22. It should be noted that these examples also share the same conical handle forms. The second link is the meandroid or sub-meander pattern. The pattern is seen on two early Neolithic examples from Höyücek KAD level (Duru 1992, 561 & pls. 20 & 22; Umurtak 2000, 1–3 & figs. 3.8–9). They can be compared with the seals of pattern group 1 or pseudo-meander (see Nos. 4, 6, 7, 8, 9, 10, 11 & 20). In addition, early Chalcolithic examples have similar pseudo-meander patterns. Although they display stylization, they have similarities with the pseudo-meander composition at Çatalhöyük. According to Makkay, the patterns on certain Hacılar II seals may be regarded as simplified versions of earlier Çatalhöyük pieces (1984, 79).

As regards shape comparisons, the Pisidian and Çatalhöyük forms are very similar on both sides and as regards the handles. Common features are conical or rectangular (mostly trapezoidal) rears and sub-rectangular, oval and round face sides. All handles, except conical and fragmented ones (Umurtak 2000, figs. 3.1–2 & 3.7), are perforated in contrast to the few perforated examples found at Çatalhöyük (Nos. 2, 15 & 18). Early Neolithic Höyücek KAD (Sanctuaries Phase) and later early Chalcolithic Hacılar IIB examples are almost identical to each other in relation to the perforated, low handles.

Apart from the Çatalhöyük and early Neolithic/Early Chalcolithic Pisidian examples, stamp seals have also been recovered at Köşk Höyük, which is another central Anatolian Late Neolithic settlement (Özkan 2001). In contrast to the Çatalhöyük and Pisidian stamp-seal iconography, the Köşk Höyük iconography generally shares its decorative patterns with the early Halaf glyptic of Upper Mesopotamia. Evidently, the iconography belongs to a different tradition under strong southern Halaf influence (Özkan 2001, 19). Thus clear differences are observable between the western Pisidian (Lakes District) area and the eastern Cappadocian area (with late Neolithic Köşk Höyük) in central Anatolia.

Conclusion

As mentioned before, the Çatalhöyük stamp seals provide us with information about the earliest such objects in Neolithic Anatolia, as far as one can tell from present evidence. Therefore, stamp seals or so called 'pintaderas' deserve greater consideration than they have so far been accorded. Unfortunately, the absence of sealings restricts interpretations that can be made at present of their function and use. At this stage, it is not possible to demonstrate fully that these stamps are true stamp seals used for stamping commodities. However, when new finds in precise contexts increase in number through the ongoing excavations, more light will be shed on their functions as well as other more or less contemporary seals from the secure contexts of Early Neolithic and following period settlements.

Figure 8.8. *Stamp seals 1, 19, 8 and 4.*

As Oates (1996, 65) suggests,

> this prehistoric information system, the first such in human history, involved the use of simple seals carved with patterns that were impressed on plaster and clay. It was to form the basis of accounting procedures followed widely not only throughout the Near East but elsewhere in the ancient world.

Although the real function is not so certain, the identification of these objects as stampers appears firm. They are not probably absolute evidence of private property but may be the earliest step toward writing in the Near East. Therefore, Çatalhöyük which lies in the heart of Anatolia seems to be one of the first precursors of 'this prehistoric information system' with its use of stamp seals in the early seventh millennium cal BC.

Acknowledgements

This research resulted from my MA study at Hacettepe Üniversitesi (Ankara) under the supervision of Armağan Erkanal. I would like to thank Armağan Erkanal, Tuba Ökse for their comments during my research. This paper also benefited very much from constructive criticisms and comments from Ian Hodder, Colin Renfrew, Joan Oates and Marie Henriette Gates when I was at McDonald Institute for Archaeological Research in Cambridge for research (granted by the British Council in Ankara) in 1998. I am very grateful to all for their valuable help. Any remaining errors are my own.

Chapter 9

The Figurines

Naomi Hamilton

Pieces of approximately 526 figurines have been found during the current excavations. Of these 183 can be identified with considerable certainty as non-animal and as recognizable parts of human or humanoid figures, 229 as animals, and the remainder are unidentifiable parts or cannot be assigned with certainty to one group. They occur in a range of contexts, both internal and external to buildings, and display varied characteristics. Most are fragmentary but a number are complete or almost complete. The excavations in the BACH and Summit Areas are to be published separately. Owing to the small size and varied nature of the figurine assemblage I shall include the BACH and Summit Area figurines in the general discussions about form, use, etc. but a contextual analysis of that material will be left for inclusion in later publications. Without these assemblages, the number of figurines is reduced to 384, of which 146 are anthropomorphic, 146 zoomorphic, and the remainder unclear. Some of these are unstratified or come from contexts that are in some way dubious; the totals quoted are occasionally not consistent as such examples had to be excluded from some quantifications. In some of the discussions, where relevant or necessary, I shall refer to the figurines found by Mellaart, 254 of which I have recorded in some way (Table 9.5 on CD), although I have already treated that material in some depth (Hamilton 1996, 215–27). However, this chapter mainly deals with figurines found by in the recent excavations. In 1996 I also dealt with the surface finds from our present work (Hamilton 1996, 227–9), but they will be included in this study where relevant.

Table 9.1. *Figurine typology and number of each figurine type from recent excavations.*

Type	Description	Clay	Stone	Total
1	Humanoid, whole, with divided legs	13	0	13
2	Humanoid, whole, with undivided conical base	12	0	12
3	Humanoid head only	21	0	21
4	Humanoid, headless, with divided legs	36	0	36
5	Humanoid, headless, with undivided conical base	8	0	0
6	'Fat female', whole, seated	0	0	0
7	'Fat female', headless, seated	0	0	0
8	Human head	9	1	10
9	Human male	0	0	0
10	Human female and animal	0	0	0
11	Human male and animal	0	0	0
12	Human, whole, standing	1	0	1
13	Quadruped standing	16	0	16
14	Animal other/unsure	0	0	0
15	Unclear if human or animal	22	0	22
16	Human, headless, standing	1	0	1
17	Human limb only	1	0	1
18	Animal head only	9	0	9
19	Animal horn only	118	0	118
20	Uncertain part	65	1	66
21	Human, whole, seated	1	0	1
22	Animal, seated	1	0	1
23	Animal, lying	2	0	2
24	Animal, stance unclear	0	0	0
25	Multiple humans	0	0	0
26	'Fat female', headless, standing	0	0	0
27	'Fat female', whole, standing	0	0	0
28	?Female, seated, lower part only	3	0	3
29	Concretion	0	3	3
30	Humanoid limb/lower part	24	0	24
31	Human body, no head/legs	2	0	2
32	Humanoid body, no head/legs	6	0	6
33	Human base only	3	0	3
34	Phallic	1	1	2
35	Modified pebble	0	0	0
36	Human upper body	1	0	1
37	Human female, headless, seated	0	0	0
-	Total humanoid	120	0	120
-	Total human	22	1	23
-	Total animal	146	0	146
-	Total other	88	5	93

I will be using contextual and visual analyses to consider possible uses and meanings of figurines, particularly as they relate to understanding social structures at Çatalhöyük. The typology I use (Table 9.1) was developed while recording Mellaart's material in 1995, and utilizes both form and fragmentation. It has been added to as new forms, or generally fragments, have been recovered during excavation, and has proved to

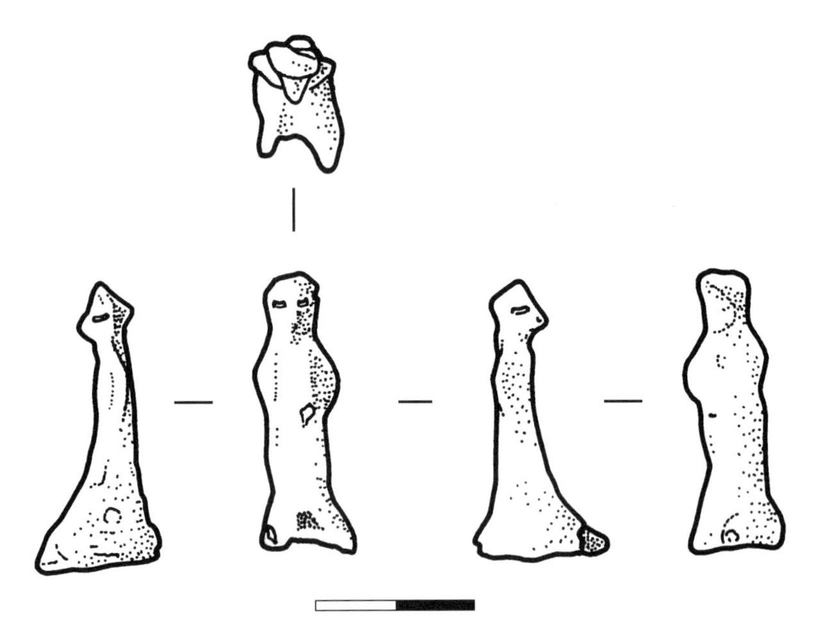

Figure 9.1. *Humanoid figurine 4121.D5.*

with or without divided 'legs/feet' and extending into a neck surmounted by a schematic head (e.g. Fig. 9.1). The heads vary in their detail from a basic triangular form with a pinched nose to those with headscarves, hats, puncture holes for the attachment of hair or headgear, and facial features. A number of atypical figures which cross the humanoid/human boundary are mentioned below (see Fig. 9.1). Although there is a considerable difference in size between the smallest and largest, most are approximately the same in size and form suggesting that they have the same use and meaning. Of the 22 humanoids from the recent excavations whose complete height is known, the smallest is 10.0 mm high and the largest 36.5 mm, and 50 per cent fall within the range of 20 to 30 mm. Mellaart had some larger examples, with a range from 15.9 to 57.8 mm. The level in which they were found seems to have no bearing on size. They are all made of clay.

be flexible and useful in contextual analyses. It is clear that a far more detailed typology could be made using this system, as more or less subtle differences could be recognized. I make no claims that the typology is anything other than a pragmatic tool that I have found adequate for my purposes.

Figurine types

The figurines at Çatalhöyük come in a variety of forms. Indeed, the variety is so great that a simple classification cannot encompass the range; yet for my purposes I believe a simple classification is sufficient. I divide the anthropomorphic representations into three main groups: human, humanoid and schematic. There are also a few natural rocks that approximate to a human form but have not been altered or have been altered only in very minor ways. Within each group there are several types in my overall typology, but this major tripartite division is almost certainly relevant to function as well as form, while my detailed typology takes into account fragmentation. Zoomorphic figures form a separate group. In the data base, humanoid figurines are represented by types 1, 2, 3, 4, 5, 30 and 32; human figures are recorded as types 6, 7, 8, 9, 10, 11, 12, 16, 17, 21, 25, 26, 27, 28, 31, 33, 36 and 37; schematic figures occur as types 34 and 35, while type 29 is concretions or 'natural' stones with human aspects; and zoomorphic figurines are types 13, 14, 18, 19, 22, 23 and 24.

Humanoid figurines

The humanoid figures have fairly simple and undifferentiated bodies consisting of a roughly conical base

Perhaps the most important observation to make about the humanoid figurines is that they are all sexless in form. They represent generalized humans, sometimes with specific features which might well indicate more about their sex, age or other status but which cannot now be recognized or understood. The lack of physical indications of sex might be because they are clothed, as suggested by the fact that some wear scarves or hats. This headgear might tell us something about social differentiation, but without other representations to guide us we cannot read it. There is a well-known figurine from Mellaart's assemblage wearing a leopard-skin hat, but although it is generally regarded as male, sex is not shown explicitly (Mellaart 1963, fig. 20, pl. XXIc).

Mellaart found these figurines stuck in building walls and between houses, and regarded them as votives. My term 'humanoid' is intended to avoid a functional interpretation, but it is likely that Mellaart was substantially right, at least in some instances. However, many humanoids found in the current work were in open areas among deposits suggesting domestic refuse or building fill. These might well fit Broman's (1983; Broman-Morales 1990) suggestion of 'wish vehicles' for those she examined at Jarmo — crude or schematized representations that were used for the moment, then abandoned. The making of the figurine might itself represent a wish or prayer of some kind, the fulfilment of which might or might not involve the retention of the item for some time. The large percentage of damaged humanoids (only 8 out of 120 are complete, although a number of others have just minor damage which could be accidental) could indicate a requirement to stop the action of the wish or prayer at some point by breaking the figure before abandonment. However, the majority of undamaged figurines are humanoid, and therefore it is clear that destruction was not always necessary. The evidence points to a range of uses and meanings.

Human figurines

Human figures are more difficult to describe, as they encompass a broader range of types and, being generally found in a severely-fragmented state, it is not always clear what form they took originally. To some extent, human figurines are defined by their difference from humanoid figures, owing to the considerable standardization of the latter. The human figurines found by Mellaart include a group of seated females with large breasts and placid faces, often with their legs crossed or to one side and arms across the chest, and these are widely thought to be typical of the figurines from the site. However, they were a minority; others were standing, and a few were shown with animals. Many of the heads found during the current excavations are regarded as belonging to human figures because of the attention to facial features and hair, and the difference in form from the triangular heads with pinched nose so common on humanoids. Unfortunately, it is not possible to be sure what type of body they were attached to, and it is certainly possible that the human group ought to be subdivided if only we knew more clearly what they looked like when whole. They are made of clay or stone.

Many of the famous human figures found by Mellaart were discovered inside buildings, which has assisted in their interpretation as religious images and the interpretation of the buildings as shrines. However, 25 of the 62 probable humans found by Mellaart or two fifths of the total, have no building attribution on their records and were presumably found in open areas. The distinction between human and schematic figures is extremely difficult to make as there is some degree of stylization in most human figures and some human element in all schematic ones. Therefore any count is fairly rough, and each investigator would probably draw the lines slightly differently. All but two of the human figures found during the current work were in external areas or in building fill (see below).

Humanoid/human figurines

The distinction between human and humanoid figurines is not always simple. This is because a number of apparent humanoids have features normally found in human figures and absent from the vast majority of humanoids, so that there seems to be a continuum of representation although it affects only a tiny number of figurines. In fact, it is only when complete figures are found that this issue becomes apparent, as most

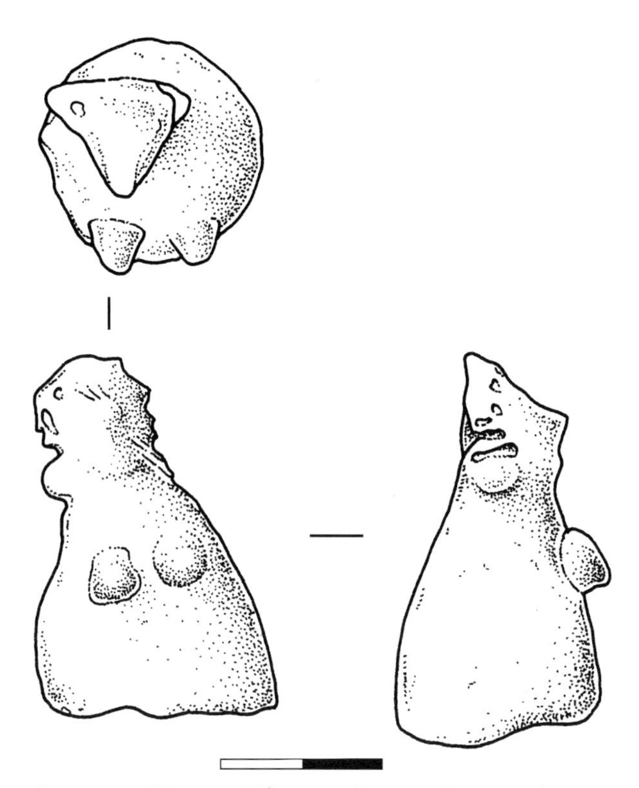

Figure 9.2. *Humanoid/human figurine CHC 686/2.*

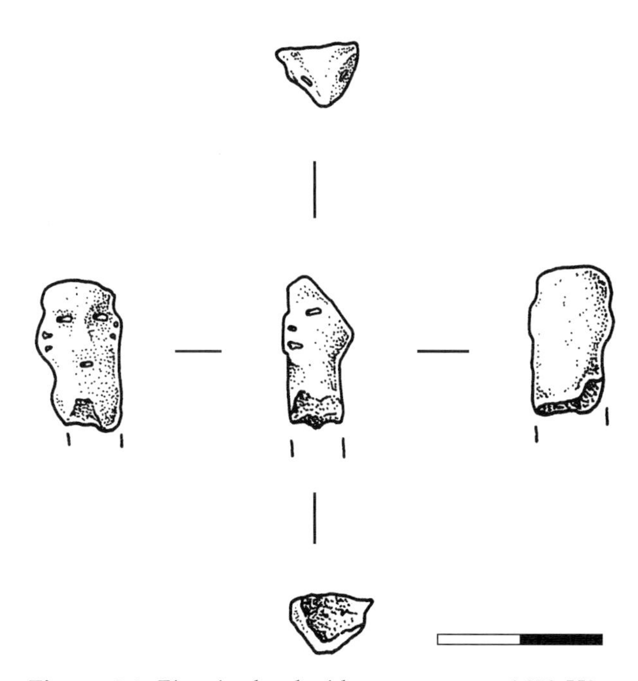

Figure 9.3. *Figurine head with ear punctures 1652.H2.*

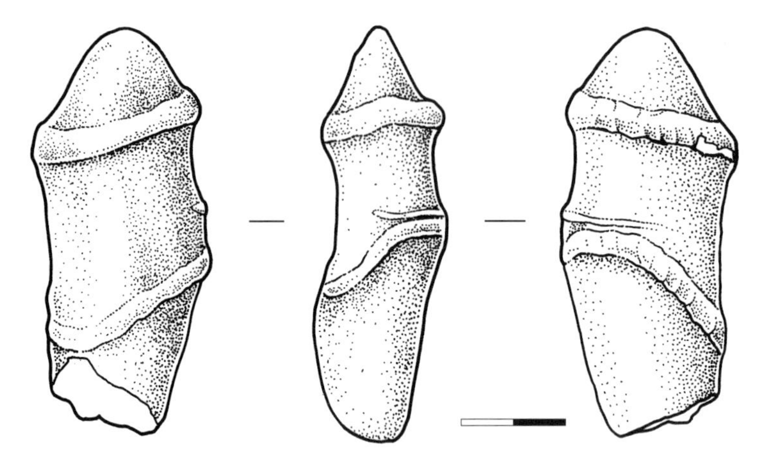

Figure 9.4. *Schematic stone figurine 1505.X1.*

would have been placed in one category or the other if the heads had either been missing or were the only part present. Thus there is at least one example among the Mellaart assemblage of an apparent humanoid with breasts (Fig. 9.2). This could be seen as exceptional, as an unusual emphasis on sex in a context in which sex is irrelevant because the humanoid figures represent generalized humans. Or it could be an atypical representation of a female in a group known to all users to represent males; finally, it could be an unnecessary emphasis in a group known by all users to represent females. On the other hand, it could be seen as an unusually schematized human figure, in which the normal details of the body are ignored and only the breasts retained for emphasis. A similar problem arises in the treatment of several heads. While humanoid heads are normally fairly standardized as triangular blobs with pinched noses, occasionally sporting headgear or hair, a couple have been found with punctures for the attachment of other materials for hair or a headdress, or for earrings (Fig. 9.3). This treatment is known on a number of human figures, and isolated heads with this feature have been recorded as human but the discovery of such heads attached to humanoid bodies shows again the continuum of representation, and the difficulty of classification within our modern categories. A final area of crossover is painted details. One of Mellaart's humanoids has what seems to be a cloak painted in black down the back of the body with a strap around the neck. Another has red streaks emanating from the nostrils. With such low numbers, interpretation is particularly difficult.

Schematic figurines

The schematic figures are a tiny group of those from the current excavations, although Mellaart found a larger number of figurines that, while having human aspects, had not been adapted sufficiently to the human form to be regarded as truly human. Most were made of stone, and came from the early levels. This group also includes items such as phallic stones (e.g. Fig. 9.4). The boundary between this group and the 'natural' group is blurred. For an investigation of gender, the first two groups are most important, but clearly phallic stones may be extremely relevant.

Zoomorphic figurines

All the representations of animals found in the current work are quadrupeds. Some seem to give indications of particular species, particularly cattle or goats; others are basic quadrupeds. A number of them have been stabbed during manufacture, and this is probably relevant to understanding use and purpose. As many figurines are broken, the original size is not always easy to estimate, but size varies greatly as with the anthropomorphic figures. Horns broken from heads are by far the most common fragment, with 118 found so far. No figures showing humans and animals together have been found in the recent excavations.

Material

The vast majority of figurines found during current work are made of clay; some unfired, some sun dried, most baked lightly, a few well fired. The clay tends to be very fine, with few inclusions. Inclusions may be mineral or vegetable. A very small number of figurines are made from marl or plaster, which is extremely fine with no inclusions. Rather more are made of stone, although the recent excavations have found only a handful and they tend not to be detailed representations. However, Mellaart found a considerable number of stone figurines with elaborate detail.

It might be expected that the material in use would affect the type of representation due to the plasticity of clay as a medium, yet it is not quite that simple. When I reassessed Mellaart's material in 1995, it seemed that only after Level VI did figurines depicting full-breasted large-hipped female forms occur, and these were all made of clay, a material which seemed to be used first for human figures in Level VI and became the most common material after that time. So one could assume that the type of representation had been hampered by the material in use (stone) and that this factor explains the low emphasis on sexed figurines before Level VI. However, clay was used for humanoid and animal figurines prior to Level VI, and very elaborate stone figures of humans that do not emphasize sex were made during and before

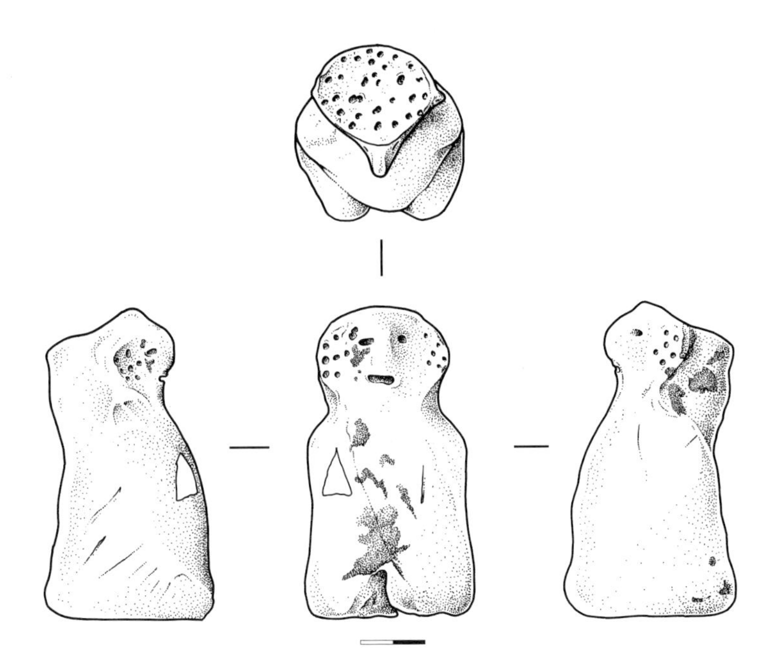

Figure 9.5. *Figurine 5043.X1.*

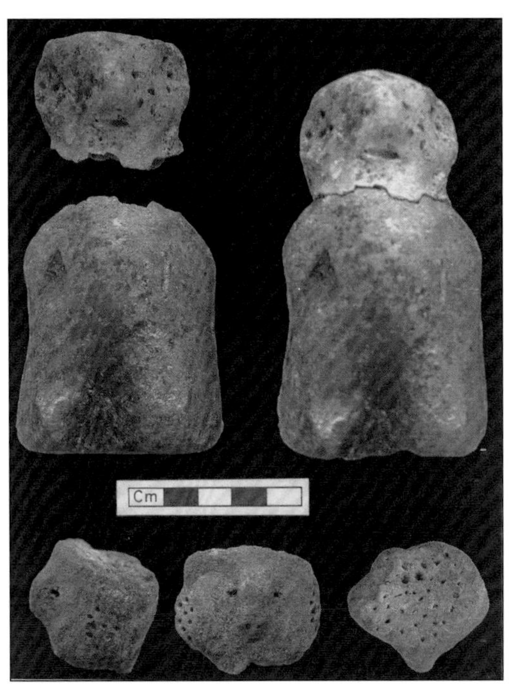

Figure 9.6. *Figurine 5043.X1 (above) and head 5021.D1 (below).*

Level VI. If complicated representation was possible in stone, presumably it would have been feasible to make full-breasted large-hipped figurines of stone if that had been the required imagery, although it would have been a more skilled job. Thus I suggested (Hamilton 1996, 225–6) that changing gender relations might have led to an emphasis on the mature female form which was most easily portrayed in clay, therefore leading to a change in the dominant material for figurines. I would add now that this change in material might be related to a greater use of figurines and a wider range of people making them, so that the lower skill level needed to produce figurines from clay rather than stone could also have influenced the change in material. However, it must be noted that nearly all the figurines found in the lower levels of the site in the recent excavations are of clay (see Table 9.2) and recent work has produced a few fragments of full-breasted large-hipped clay figurines from below Level VI, mainly from Level VII contexts. Therefore my suggestion that altered representation reflects a changing social ideology around Level VI may have been premature. Only a larger assemblage drawn from the full range of levels at the site will answer the question of whether a changing ideology was mainly responsible for this, or whether different ideologies were being represented by different makers and/or users of figurines throughout the life of the site. Most of Mellaart's stone figurines were found in only two buildings, VIA.10 which contained 14 and VIA.44, the 'Leopard Shrine' which contained eight human figurines, and therefore the distributions are very skewed. It is worth noting that a large unsexed clay figurine has been found by the current excavations in Level IX (Figs. 9.5 & 9.6), on which sex certainly could have been portrayed if desired.

Table 9.2. *Figurines by level and material.*

Level	Clay figurines	Stone figurines	Total
N.V–IV	17	0	17
N.VI–V	70	1	71
N.VII–VI	17	0	17
VI.B	2	0	2
VII	49	0	49
VIII	95	1	96
IX	40	2	42
X	16	0	16
XI	1	0	1
XII	11	0	11
Pre-XII.A	21	1	22
Pre-XII.B	43	0	43
Pre-XII.C	15	0	15
Pre-XII.D	2	0	2
KOPAL	2	0	2

Table 9.3. *Numbers of figurines by general context.*

Context	Anthropomorphic	Zoomorphic	Total
Buildings	56	56	112
Spaces between buildings	21	13	34
Midden-like building fill	23	8	31
Open areas	29	65	94
Foundation cuts	6	0	6

Context of deposition

Figurines have been found in a wide range of contexts (Table 9.3). They occur both within buildings and in open areas, as well as between buildings and in the walls themselves. The vast majority of those from within buildings actually come from the infill, rather than being on floors. A consideration of the soil matrix and other finds suggests that the infilling material may often derive from open areas (although in some cases it is almost sterile and may represent carefully broken down and cleansed mud brick). The place of origin of those found in open areas is, of course, unknown. In very few cases can the find context be regarded as the use context, thus the context of deposition may bear very little relation to the context of use, and may give no information of relevance to the meanings attached to figurines. This is completely at odds with the previous interpretations of Çatalhöyük figurines, most of which regard them as religious items found *in situ* in shrines. This is largely because Mellaart found a number of figurines in burnt buildings, some of which he viewed as shrines. However, although those figurines received a lot of attention in publications, many others were found in different contexts, some unfortunately not recorded on their labels and therefore no longer known. Moreover, Mellaart did not sieve all deposits, and therefore had a very different retrieval rate in comparison to the recent excavations, in particular where small fragments are concerned.

A more detailed examination of the context of deposition must be broken down in several ways: by building; by space; and by type of deposit. However, context has broader meanings too, thus fragmentation is an aspect of the context of deposition, as is the type of figurine in question. It is only when all these have been taken into consideration that we might be able to understand something of the meanings and uses of figurines at the site.

Numbers by context

It is clear that since most figurines are found in secondary depositional contexts, largely in 'midden' or in post-occupation room fill, the number per building is probably irrelevant. The only times when the number per space may be relevant is in external contexts such as inter-building slots and open areas, and the rare occasions when figurines have been found *in situ*, or probably *in situ*, inside buildings. Of the 146 anthropomorphic figurines found during the recent excavations, 21 were in spaces between buildings, 23 were in midden-like fill of abandoned buildings, 29 were found in open areas (including 2 in scoops, 1 in a fire spot, and 1 in a penning area), 6 were from foundation cuts and the rest were from buildings. Of those from buildings, 3 came from walls/blocking, 20 were from deliberate room fill deposits, 3 from construction/make-up, 1 from a foundation cut, 2 from fill of pits, 1 from the fill of a bin, 1 from a basin, 2 from postholes, 1 from an oven floor and 8 from occupation deposits on floors. Three of these were from oven rake-out.

Of the 146 zoomorphic figurines from the recent excavations, 13 were in spaces between buildings, 8 were in midden-like fill of abandoned buildings, 65 were found in open areas (generally midden, with 1 found on an early floor, 1 in a bone cluster and 3 from fire spots) and the rest were from buildings. Of those from buildings, 17 were from deliberate room fill deposits, 1 from a foundation cut, 6 from walls/blocking, 2 from pit fill, 1 from the fill of a bin, 1 from a basin construction, 2 from postholes, 2 from oven floors, 2 from burial fills, 1 from a niche, 1 from a moulding, 2 from floor make-up and 17 from occupation deposits on floors, of which 12 were from oven rake-out.

Of these contexts, only the figurines found on floors, in oven rake-out, in pits, burials, niches, mouldings, basins and bins might be *in situ* as concerns use rather than discard, and might therefore yield some information relevant to purpose and meaning. That leaves only 11 anthropomorphic and 25 zoomorphic figurines from buildings that might give meaningful contextual information. Foundation cuts in external areas might also be contexts of deliberate deposition, and the small number of figurines found in these will also be discussed.

Floors

Of the five anthropomorphic figurines found in occupation deposits on floors (other than rake-outs) 1416.H1 is a humanoid missing its head and right leg, from floors beneath oven F.11 in Space 187, Building 1; 2801.H1 is four non-joining fragments of a humanoid from floors in Space 109; 5020.H1 is part of a humanoid head missing the face, found in a mixture of floors and floor packing/make-up in Space 170, Building 17; 4011.H1 is a complete humanoid (except for a small chip on the base), recovered from a small area of accumulation or make-up on a floor in Space 155, Building 5, while 5043.X1 (Figs. 9.5 & 9.6) is a large human figure broken deliberately into two parts, both of which were present, and deposited in a depression in the floor overlying an oven in the southeast corner of Space 170. This belongs to a demolition phase and, considering the deliberate damage to the figurine immediately prior to deposition, it must be regarded as an *in situ* figurine with possible uses linked either to demolition or closure. The other pieces may have been deliberately placed in make-up etc. but all could have arrived in buildings accidentally as part of the imported materials used for constructing floors. The good condition of 4011.H1 suggests that it may be roughly in a position of use but it could have been swept aside with debris and lost.

All six zoomorphic fragments found on floors are animal horns. 2801.H1 found in multiple floor remains in Space 109, 1422.H2 from a floor in Space 71 and 5291.H1 found on an external surface in Space 181, are under 1 cm long, the first two fragments, the last complete. 1410.H2 comes from between floor packing, and is 1.5 cm long. 5087.H1 comes from multiple clean floors in Space 178 and is nearly 2 cm long, while 3343.H1 was found in multiple floor remains in Space 160 and is just over 3 cm long. Clearly all are small enough to be accidental inclusions, even 3343.H1, although they could have been placed deliberately into floor make-up.

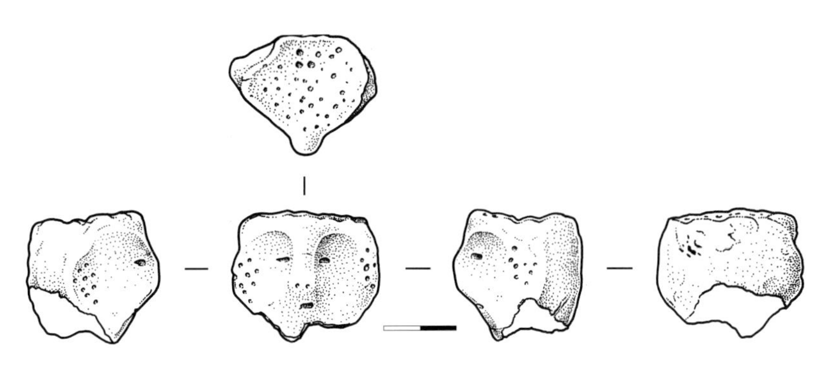

Figure 9.7. *Figurine 5021.D1*

Oven rake-out/occupation floors

Three anthropomorphic figurines were found in ashy deposits interpreted as oven rake-out or occupation floors, and this is a very interesting context in which to find figurines. This may well be a context of discard rather than use, although claims are made elsewhere in these volumes for *in situ* obsidian knapping and bead manufacture in such areas (this volume Chapter 14 & Volume 3, Part 2). 4318.H1 is the partial head of a humanoid, with the face missing, found in ashy spreads probably associated with fire installation F.438 in Space 164, Building 16; 5021.D1 (Figs. 9.6 & 9.7) is a large, elaborate human-type head found in layered rake-out or occupation related to fire installation F.538 in Space 170, Building 17; and 4139.H1 is the lower body of a tiny seated human figure, only 13 mm high to the waist, from occupation or rake-out in Space 117, Building 2. There is a clear difference between the heavily abraded state of the first of these, and the excellent condition of the other two. The large head 5021.D1 (Fig. 9.7) is broken fairly cleanly from its body, which might yet remain in the deposits which were left to support the adjacent wall which was leaning badly. The head was found during flotation rather than recognized *in situ*, so that its precise location is unknown. It is closely related to 5043.X1 (Fig. 9.5), discussed below. Similarly the break through the waist of 4139.H1 is fairly fresh. The state of 5021.D1 (Fig. 9.7) and 4139.H1 suggest they may have been placed deliberately in the rake-out/occupation floors, or were associated with fire installations in use rather than just in discard. The size of 5021.D1, 4 cm wide and over 3 cm high, makes it unlikely that it arrived in the deposits accidentally, or at least without being noticed.

12 zoomorphic figurines were found in occupation deposits, all of them just horns. They cluster in Space 171, Building 18, with 4539.H1, H2, H4, H5, H6 and H7 associated with oven F.477 in a deposit that has evidence of bead manufacture; 4533.H1, H2 and H3 associated with the later oven F.473 in the same area, also in a deposit with evidence of bead manufacture, and 4530.H1 in the final rake-out event of that oven, again with a large number of beads (Chapter 14). They range in size from 4 to 20 mm in length. Of the two remaining pieces 4316.H2 was found in Space 164, Building 16, and 4136.H1 in Space 117, Building 2. At 11 mm and 13 mm long respectively, they are also small. Clearly all these fragments are small enough to have ended up in rake-out or occupation deposits accidentally, but the large cluster in Space 171 in deposits with evidence of bead manufacture indicates either that figurines were also being made here and broken pieces abandoned in the rake-out, or that they had some significance, either in relation to manufacturing processes or to fire. The fact that all the fragments are animal horns, and no other parts of animals are represented, makes it unlikely that they are debris from figurine production although this is the part most likely to break during manufacture. However, although these have been catalogued primarily as animal horns, several display unusual curves or cross-sections which led me to wonder if they were body jewellery made of clay, probably earrings but perhaps nose or lip studs, and they have received this second classification in the notes. Anthropomorphic figurines are sometimes shown with multiple ear piercings, yet no obvious earrings have ever been found at the site. As with the possibility that clay beads were far more common than is apparent, but were not fired and have therefore not been preserved (Chapter 14), it may be that clay body jewellery was widely used but has not

survived in a recognizable form. The presence just of 'horns' and no other body parts would make much more sense if these are in fact clay earrings or even finger rings which were being manufactured in the same area as stone beads, and found their way into the rake-out, perhaps because they were broken, perhaps because they were being dried in the heat of the oven and either cracked or got lost. If so, this is important evidence of household production, joining other evidence from the same room.

Oven floors

Three figurines were found built into oven floors. 5117.H1 is anthropomorphic, the lower part of a small seated human, less than 1 cm high. Post-depositional burning has penetrated the base deeply. It was found in the remnant of an oven base full of clay balls in Space 200, Building 23. Two zoomorphic fragments were found in the floor of oven F.11 in Space 187, Building 1. Both are animal horns: 1184.H1 is just over 1 cm and 1444.X1 less than 2 cm in length. All three are so small they could be accidental inclusions caught up in constructional material.

Walls and plaster

Two anthropomorphic figurines were found in walls. 1518.H1 is a crude humanoid neck fragment from the wall dividing Spaces 107 and 108, and 3632.H3 is a miniature humanoid head and upper body from a wall in Space 112. In both cases brick and mortar were undifferentiated. Five zoomorphic figures were found: three are horns: 3632.H1 from Space 112, 4492.H1 from brick in Space 115, and 1686.H1 from mixed brick and mortar in Space 105. 2575.H2 is the rear end of an animal found in mortar in Space 71/152/186, Building 1, and 4389.X1 is a complete quadruped (though all extremities are damaged) that was stabbed twice during manufacture. It is crude in style and was made carelessly, and has post-depositional burning on the left side. Measuring 45 mm long and 31 mm high it is by far the largest of these pieces, and was found in mortar in Space 165, Building 8. Two points stand out here: two fragments were found in a single deposit (one anthropomorphic, the other zoomorphic); and all but the last are small fragments. Overall there is no evidence to suggest they were found in a context of use or deliberate deposition, with the possible exception of 4389.X1.

In addition to figurines found in walls themselves, a few were found in plaster. 4140.H1 is a damaged humanoid head 9 mm high found among wall plaster fallen through post-1960s excavation erosion from wall F.410 in Space 163, Building 6. 4357.H1 is a curved animal horn, or possibly an earring, found in wall plaster on the east face of wall F.447 in Space 164, Building 16. It is 14 mm long. 2131.H1 is a substantial curved animal horn 43 mm long made of plaster and found in the plaster moulding around a timber support in Space 71, Building 1. Thus while the first two of these fragments are small and should probably be seen as accidental inclusions, the last may have been placed deliberately in the plaster during construction.

Fill of cuts

Several figurines were found in the fills of pits, postholes and foundation cuts. 1630.X1 is a humanoid missing its head and feet, found in a mixed rubble fill of a pit in the southeast corner of Space 106. 1905.H1 is a complete humanoid 26 mm high with burning on one side, found in the burnt rubble fill of a plaster-lined pit F.43 cut into platform F.32 in Space 71, Building 1. Despite its excellent condition, the burning suggests it found its way into the pit with the burnt rubble rather than being deposited deliberately, although if the rubble were thrown in while hot the burning could have occurred *in situ*. Two zoomorphic figurines were also found in pits, both horn fragments. 1200.H4 comes from the fill of a late pit cutting the corner of the northwest platform in Building 1, thought to be cut for the retrieval of an object from the adjacent wall. 3856.H2 is a roughly-modelled and burnt fragment from a pit in Space 154, Building 5. Both of these could be accidental inclusions.

1591.H1 is a beautifully-made but damaged and worn humanoid body fragment from a clayey fill with charcoal patches found in a wall foundation cut in Space 107. 4339.H1 is a tiny, neat humanoid damaged on its upper and lower surfaces but otherwise complete, found in an ashy deposit along with pieces of clay ball, pottery and stone in a posthole in the southern part of Space 163, Building 6. 4656.H1 is a tiny, complete humanoid-like figure 10 mm high found in the clay-silt fill of a post-retrieval pit in Space 170, Building 17. Two animal horn fragments were also found in postholes: a small piece 3190.H1 in Space 112, and much larger 1561.H1 in Space 106/107, 35 mm long.

Of these nine figurines, three are obviously much better preserved than the others, but it is not clear whether they were placed in these cuts/pits deliberately, or owe their good preservation to their tiny size. Nevertheless, the position of 1905.H1 in a plaster-lined pit, and of 4339.H1 and 4656.H1 in postholes are all more indicative of deliberate deposition than the contexts of the other figures, which seem to be mixed backfill of cuts, but the two zoomorphic fragments in postholes do not have the same quality of preservation.

Probably two anthropomorphic figurines were retrieved from the fill of a bin or basin. 4793.H1 is a human head found in a deposit of building rubble, the upper fill of basin F.488 in Space 173, Building 6. It has an unusually flat shape and has punctures surrounding the face area; the face itself is missing, as is the body. 1889.H1 is 6 fragments of what seems to be a single humanoid, but all are so eroded that no pieces can be joined accurately. They were found in the fill of bin F.256 in Space 117, in a deposit of 'domestic rubbish', mainly clay balls along with ash and animal bone. One animal horn fragment, 2789.H1, was found in the same bin. The severely-damaged state of all three figurines shows that even being found in bins and basins is not a clear indication that they are *in situ*, as these all seem to be accidental inclusions in contexts of at least secondary discard.

Two fragments were found in burial fills in Space 163, Building 6. Both are small animal horns and could be regarded as accidental inclusions. 4464.H1 was in the fill between the skeleton and overlying wooden plank in burial F.492, and 4397.H6 came from the fill of burial F.460. There is nothing in their condition, size or position to suggest deliberate inclusion.

An animal horn fragment was found in the lowest fill of niche F.217 in Space 154/155, Building 5. It is fairly large, 19.3 mm long, but broken at both ends. The notes suggest this fill may have been used to raise the level of the base of the niche, but the horn could be an accidental inclusion.

Finally, 4965.X1 is a quadruped missing its head, found in the plaster surface of basin F.521 in Space 200, Building 23. At 37 mm long and 28 mm high it is unlikely this was not seen during the plastering process.

External foundation cuts

Although the above discussion has been concerned with figurines found inside buildings, as being most likely to offer information regarding use, the presence of figurines in foundation cuts in external areas may also be relevant to use. Seven have been found, all in Space 105. Only one is zoomorphic, 1051.X1 a quadruped of unclear stance owing to severe damage that has removed all legs and the underside of the body. The six anthropomorphic figures are 1051.H4, a rather worn humanoid 23 mm high without its head; 1067.X1, also missing its head and of similar size; 1073.H1, a sturdy humanoid 26 mm high without its head; 1073.X3, a large humanoid head 30 mm high; 1073.H2, a human head and neck; and 1073.X1, a whole humanoid of unusual shape with possible arms or breasts. A further fragment, 1073.H3, is unclassifiable, possibly a large humanoid leg, but I mention it because of the density of figurines in this context. The damaged condition of all but one of these figurines mitigates against the view that they were placed deliberately in a foundation cut for protective or magical purposes, but such a number of figurines in one place is extremely unusual, even when (1073) had 720 litres of dry-sieved soil. The excavators comment on the presence of discrete deposits of material within this unit, in the form of 'domestic rubbish' such as bones or clay balls. It is possible therefore that this cluster of figurines was removed as one such discrete deposit from its place of use and put in this cut either as rubbish disposal or in a deliberate way.

Discussion

This brief consideration of the type and condition of figurines found in different contexts within buildings shows that there is little evidence to support the idea that the find context of most figurines, anthropomorphic or zoomorphic, has any relevance to their context of use or of initial discard. Most are in secondary depositional contexts which also contain a range of 'domestic' refuse, such as animal bones, knapped stone debris, clay balls, stone beads, bone tools and botanical remains, and only a tiny number are in contexts of deliberate disposal. The context that seems most relevant is ash, and to a lesser extent charcoal and burning, which may occur in occupation or rake-out deposits or in pit fills as well as in external midden areas and between walls. Altogether 69 figurines occur in deposits which are described as being dominated by ash, charcoal or burning (and another 30 indeterminate fragments of types 15 and 20). This indicates that, generally, figurines have been discarded in a rubbish area where oven/fire debris is stored rather than being placed deliberately. There are a few potential exceptions, 5043.X1 (Fig. 9.5), was certainly put deliberately where it was found, but this may not have been a context of use. The presence of figurines in postholes and foundation cuts may be deliberate, but as the soil matrices in which they occur are generally ashy this may be the medium through which they were deposited in these places rather than through intention. Overall, there is little information concerning use that can be gained from this study of close context of deposition.

Types by context

Humanoids

The vast majority of humanoid figurines found in the current excavations were discovered in external midden-type or dump deposits (64), or in room fill and foundation layers (19). That is, they were not in use contexts, and they were generally found amongst

Table 9.4. *Anthropomorphic types by context.*

Context	Humanoids	Humans	Other anthropomorphic	Total
External midden/dump	64	12	2	78
Room fill/foundation	19	5	1	25
External cuts	0	2	1	3
Natural	0	1	0	1
Buildings (use)	13	5	1	19
Floor deposits	4	2	0	6
Bin/basin fill	2	1	0	3
Postholes	2	0	0	2
Occupation/rake-out	1	2	0	3
Foundation cut	2	0	0	2
Plaster	2	0	0	2

deposits, materials and artefacts regarded as rubbish or in soil imported for constructional purposes (Table 9.4). Only 13 out of 120 were found in buildings in the contexts discussed above, all of which are almost certainly contexts of discard or accidental deposition. Four are in floor deposits, three in floor construction, two in bin/basin fill, two in postholes, one in an occupation or rake-out deposit, two in foundation cuts and two in plaster.

A small number of humanoids are complete or only slightly damaged: seven figurines are complete, while a further seven have only minor damage such as chips missing from extremities. Of the complete ones, three come from unstratified contexts, one from a basin (1905.H1), one from a posthole (4656.H1), one from building fill (2553.H1) and one from an external foundation cut (1073.X1). Of those with minor chips, three come from between building fill (4465.H3–5), two from building fill (4256.H1, 4325.H1), one from ashy fill in a posthole (4339.H1) and one from occupation deposits on a floor (4011.H1). None of these appears to have been deposited deliberately, although the 4465 group is unusual in forming a stylistic group as well (see below). Although it is a very small proportion of the assemblage, it shows that figurines were discarded in a range of contexts, including open areas (which were, of course, the recipients of quantities of ashy rake-out material as well as the source of much building fill), when complete and still 'usable'. Of the remaining humanoids, condition ranges from nearly complete to small fragments, and is as variable as context.

Humans

25 figurines found during the current excavations have been classified as human, although this category is much more varied than the humanoid group. Again, they come from a range of contexts (Table 9.4): midden (11), external cuts (2), between building dumps (1), natural (1), unstratified (1), building infill (3), floor construction (1), floor use (2), bin fill (1), occupation or oven rake-out (2). The only one that appears to have been deposited deliberately is 5043.X1 (Fig. 9.5), discussed above. 5043.X1 was broken into two before deposition, with the head lying alongside the body in a position not possible if the figure had simply fallen over. It was placed in a pit overlying an oven, in what the excavator regarded as a closure event during restructuring of the building. 5021.D1(Fig. 9.7), has a less clear context, but its great similarity to 5043.X1, and its proximity, suggest that it may also have been deposited deliberately. 5043.X1 is complete, though broken in two (the break being as fresh as possible given that it has been buried for some nine thousand years) and is the only complete human figure found so far. As with the humanoids, there does not seem to be much evidence of find context relating to use context. However, the recovery of the majority of human figures from midden and external dumps as opposed to within buildings certainly mitigates against the suggestion that they are sacred items in the common usage of that term. Fragmentation is discussed below.

Other anthropomorphic figures

A small number of figurines remains: two are concretions, three are probably phallic. Only one is from inside a building, and may have been *in situ*. 1187.H1, a triangular concretion with a rough affinity to a human female form, was found in the lower burnt fill of Space 187 and might conceivably have been in use there when the building was burned. Unfortunately, however, it was only found in flotation, so it is not clear whether or not it was on a floor. The other four come from a mixture of external contexts but probably all from secondary ones. One probably phallic (unfortunately broken) figurine (5292.H2) came from the burnt fill of a cut in Space 181 Level Pre-XII.B. It is made of clay and covered with a slip, an extremely unusual feature for figurines but more common among geometric clay objects from this level. 4868.H1 is also from Space 181, from Level Pre-XII.A. A natural stone that may have been used as a figurine, it was found in a burning event but this is not likely to have been a context of use. 3053.X1 is another clay phallic figure, found in between building fill in Space 153, and 1505.X1 (Fig. 9.4) is a natural fossil very penile in form, found in midden in Space 115. There are too few figurines in this category to draw strong conclusions, but most are clearly in contexts of secondary deposition.

Animals

The internal contexts of zoomorphic figurines have been discussed above. The most striking aspect was the number of pieces in occupation or rake-out deposits, all of one type and mainly in one room. As with other types, most zoomorphic figures were found in external areas with a number in room fill.

One aspect of zoomorphic figures that could relate to context of deposition is stabbing. Five stabbed figures have been found, and two more may have been stabbed, their fragmentary condition makes it difficult to be sure. However, their find contexts are so varied that it is unlikely to be significant in terms of use. 4389.X1 is a carelessly-made standing quadruped with slight damage to horns, ears and tail, that was stabbed twice in the left side. It was found in mortar in a wall in Space 165, Building 8. 4518.D1 is one of a group of five zoomorphic figures found in this unit, two roughly complete, one head and two horns, found in midden or dump in Space 199. The front legs are broken and horn/ears and tail missing. It was stabbed in the belly and possibly in the broken left side. 1612.X3 was found in midden roomfill in Space 116. A sturdy, chunky quadruped missing a rear leg, it was probably stabbed in the front left leg. 1055.H2 is a sturdy standing hornless quadruped with minor damage to face and tail, found in 1960s backfill in Space 108 and therefore unstratified. It had been stabbed in the right side and the mouth. 3037.H1 is a large standing quadruped 36 mm long without its head and neck, and was found in a bone cluster in a dump between buildings in Space 153. It was stabbed through both left legs. Its context, among large bones that could be the remains of a special meal, is suggestive of the common interpretation of stabbing in animals, hunting magic. However, this is the only one of the five discussed so far to have such a context. 2508.H3 is a quadruped shown lying down, a rare pose. It is missing its rear legs and base, earns/horns and nose, and may have been stabbed through the ear although its damaged state makes this uncertain. The pose could relate to stabbing if hunting magic were involved, but its context in foundation infill in Space 71, Building 1, gives no information to support this. 5072.X1 is the large head and neck of an animal, 33 mm long in this state, with a probable stab showing in the break through the neck. The hole is so large that it may well have contributed to the breakage at that point. It was found in rubble used for floor construction in Space 170.

The variety of contexts of the stabbed figures gives no help in understanding use or meaning. Only one was found in any meaningful context, a bone cluster, and while this is strongly suggestive, a far larger sample is needed. However, only 18 type 13 figures have been found so far, and five of those have evidence of stabbing, a substantial proportion. As most figurines are too fragmentary for stabbing to show, the vast majority (118 of 146) surviving only as horns, it may be that is was far more common than is apparent at present from the archaeological record, and that future work will uncover more in contexts that give indications of use and purpose.

Numbers by type

Humanoids

It is clear that, in contrast to the general impression that human figurines are common at the site, the majority of figurines are humanoids, although the demarcation between the two groups is not simple, a fact which underlines the human aspects of the humanoids. (Humanoids have sometimes been viewed as animals, a number of those from the old excavations are inventoried as animals and some of the current team members have believed that humanoids are animals or birds.) Of the 146 non-animal figurines found during the current excavations, 120 are humanoid (Table 9.1). It is not clear whether there is any significance in the two types of humanoid: with divided legs (types 1 & 4) or conical bases (types 2 & 5). 46 have divided legs and 17 are conical, and the remainder are unclear because they survive only as heads (18) or body fragments (28). The extent to which other details of humanoids should lead to further subdivision of this category is also unclear, as it is not possible to read the information they contain. Twelve humanoids have, or had, headscarves and one other seems to wear a hat or cap, while another may have hair depicted. In addition, one has eyes incised and another may have one eye (the BACH Area assemblage includes another two with incised eyes and two with just one eye) and two others have no faces, just a hollowed area from which the face appears to have been removed. These details could relate to age, sex, gender, or status of some sort that cannot be understood from the level of data currently available, or may relate to the meaning or purpose of the figurines. Therefore it may be relevant to assess numbers of each type, but this is fairly meaningless without any interpretative framework within which to understand them. Perhaps these are the wrong elements to consider anyway, maybe size is a more important variable, and indeed size does vary greatly (although most fall within a fairly narrow range).

Of the ten possible figurines found during the surface survey three and possibly four are humanoid. One of these, ÇH 94.1, is faceless, with a flattened area where the face should be, and has a headscarf,

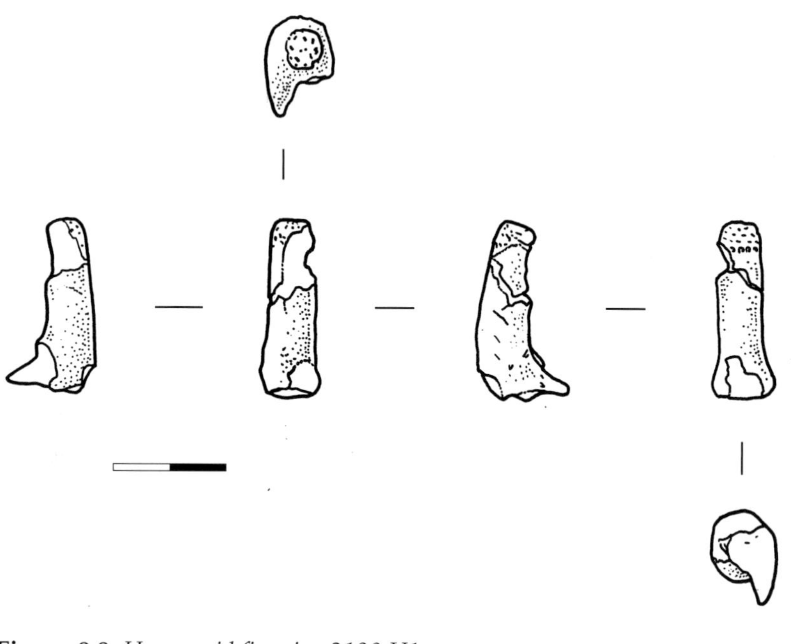

Figure 9.8. *Humanoid figurine 2198.H1.*

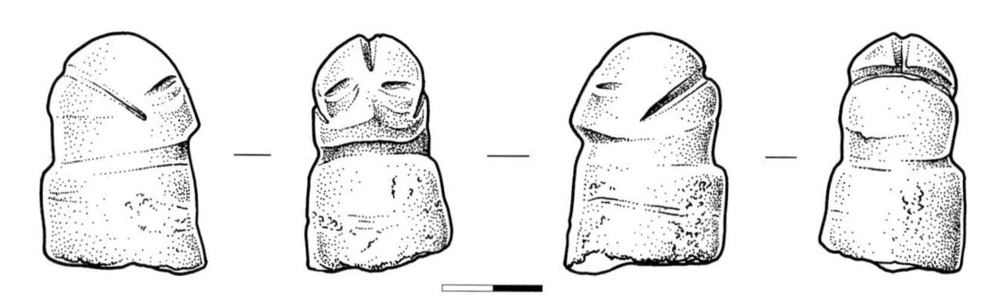

Figure 9.9. *Phallic white marble head 4116.D1.*

hat or hair sticking out behind the head (Hamilton 1996, 234). The three definite humanoids are all from sub-surface units, so that although their precise contexts are not known they are likely to be substantially in their original area of deposition (Hamilton 1996, 228).

Discussion

The incidence of headgear/hair indications, of occasional facial features other than a nose, or of just one eye on a number of humanoids could all have special meaning, but this cannot be understood at present. The existence of three faceless examples, all with scarves and two with a concave area where the face should be is intriguing, but again there is currently no contextual data which can help explain them. Mellaart found a stone human head, the face of which had been deliberately omitted or excised (Mellaart 1962, pl. IXd), so clearly this treatment was not restricted to humanoids but it is rare, and presumably significant.

Humans

The human figurines found during the current excavations show great variety (Table 9.1). The largest single type is heads, with twelve examples, but these are themselves very varied and there is no way of knowing to what type of body they were attached. In general, heads are classified as human if they show more detail than is common on humanoids or schematic figures or are in a different style, they tend to have features delineated, and many have punctures for the attachment of hair or headdress. However, the existence of a humanoid figurine (2198.H1, Fig. 9.8) whose atypically-shaped head is covered in holes executed in neat rows around the back and sides and more randomly on top, and one among Mellaart's material whose typically humanoid-shaped head has punctures for hair/headdress and earrings(?) does bring into question the assignment of all complex heads to human rather than humanoid figures. Again, this demonstrates the human features of humanoids and the lack of a clear division between the two groups. As the face is missing on 2198.H1 it is not known whether it also had more complex facial details than is normal on humanoids, which would blur the dividing lines even further. Indeed, the atypical shape of its head means it would not have been counted as a humanoid if the head had been found alone, and perhaps it should be regarded as human. The twelve heads consist of a phallic white marble head and shoulders with incised eyes and mouth/chin (4116.D1 Fig. 9.9); three rounded clay heads with no facial features other than a nose (1056.H1, 1073.H2 & 4121.H6); two large clay heads with punctures in the top for attachment of hair/headdress and facial features indicated by punctures or incisions (5021.D1, basically identical to the head of complete figurine 5043.X1 Figs. 9.5–7, and 2739.H2); one medium head missing its face with punctures surrounding the face area (4793.H1); two medium heads with punctured ears, incised features and red pigment added (in one case to indicate a beard?), both broken in half vertically (4921.H1 & 4839.H2); and one small head with incised facial features, punctured ears, and a flat back (1652.H2 Fig. 9.3). The head and shoulders of two crude schematic figures were also found (4102.D1 & 4102.D2). The combination of great variety within the group and strong similarity between certain heads indicates that there might have been a number of specific and well-known types which were represented in this form for certain purposes, while some are generalized humans. In particular the strong similarities between the two half heads (4921.H1 & 4839.H2), one from Building 6 in Level VIII and the other from Space 181 in Level Pre-XII, suggest a long lived 'ideal type' rather than accident. The similarities between 5021.D1 and 5043.X1 (Figs. 9.5–9.7), can be attributed to manufacture by and / or for the same person / people, as both came from the same building.

The remaining twelve human figurines include seated forms, four similar figures apparently female lower bodies of the 'fat-woman' style known from Mellaart's excavations (4261.H1, 5117.H1, 1664.X2 (Fig. 9.10) & 1653.H3) and one sexless seated figure 4139.H1; two sexless standing figures, one large and complete (5043.X1: Fig. 9.5), one small and headless (1620.X3); four bases of standing figures (5226.H2, 5290.H3, 5292.H1 & 6025.H1, the last from the KOPAL Area, off the mound itself); and a detailed miniature upper body and head with punctured decoration (1664.X4: Fig. 9.11). This variety of form and pose is similar to the range of human head types mentioned above. While some are like those found by Mellaart, several are completely new to us.

Five to seven human figurines were found during the surface survey (see Hamilton 1996, 227–9). These consisted of a stone head with incised facial features; three standing figures, two clearly female, the third surviving only as a base but identical to one of the female ones; the torso of a possibly cloaked figure, sexless; and two further possible torso fragments, also sexless.

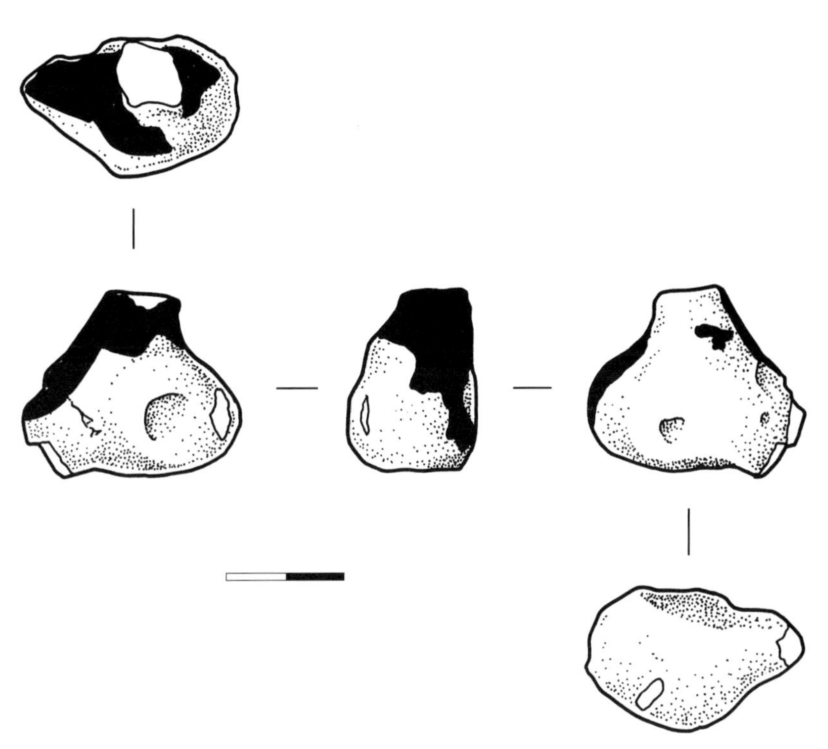

Figure 9.10. *Figurine 1664.X2.*

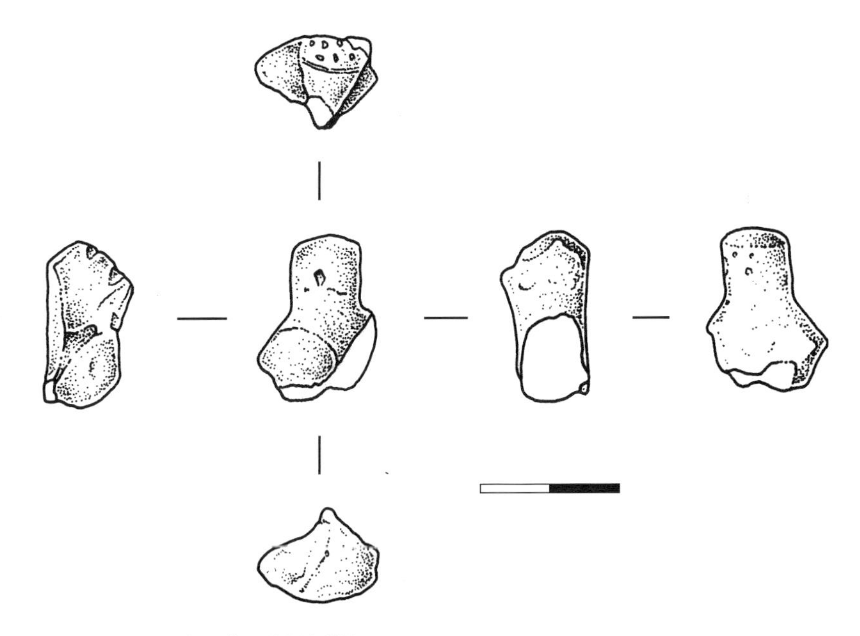

Figure 9.11. *Figurine 1664.X4.*

Discussion

It is clear that anthropomorphic figurines come in such a range of types and exhibit such variety both in broad imagery and in detail that counting specific types is not only too problematic to be worthwhile, but is unlikely to offer any insights into the uses, meanings and purposes of figurines at Çatalhöyük. While there are some obvious general types among the material, unless there is some way of understanding which features might be the more relevant to note, subdividing these types into specific groups will lead to a fragmentation of the data group beyond any useful level. It is interesting when figurines that are clearly related to one another in some way are found in the same building, as with 5021.D1 and 5043.X1 (Figs. 9.5–9.7). While such cases may shed some light on use and meaning, it is only when a large number of figurines of one type is found that numbers seem to be relevant, leading for instance to the separation of humanoid from human figurines in this work even though it is clear that there is some overlap between the two groups.

Animals

The vast majority of zoomorphic figurines that are complete enough for form to be recognized show standing quadrupeds. However, a handful of examples seem to be either lying down or seated. Only in one case does this coincide with the animal being stabbed, as might have been expected, and may rather be related to issues such as domestication. If species are being depicted with some realism, cattle seem to be the most commonly shown, but some look more like sheep and goats, while one or two are more canine, and one very equine. Among Mellaart's assemblage there are clear representations of boar and leopards, but none has been found in the current work.

However, animal horns make up 78 per cent of the zoomorphic assemblage (if they are all horns, and not clay jewellery such as earrings, finger rings and nose studs, as suggested above). They exhibit great variety in both shape and size, some are straight, others strongly curved, or twisting, some large and others tiny. The majority seem to be cattle horns, but several appear to be goat horns. Whether or not species should be recognized in this was is unclear, as it is rare for a complete quadruped to survive with its horns intact, and therefore it is not possible to assess whether cattle are shown with specifically cattle horns or whether just horns sufficed.

Similarities by context

There are several different contexts within which figurines can be examined for information relating to use and meaning: the excavation unit, feature, space, building, and broad level from which they come. These will offer different types of information, but all are potentially useful. Here I will look at similarities of style, unusual material, or peculiar features between figurines found within the same context, in search of clues as to meaning and deliberation behind deposition.

The excavation unit

The excavation unit is the smallest context of analysis used at the site, and ideally represents a single depositional event. As figurines are rare, the great majority of units contain none, yet a few units contain multiple figurines and this must be relevant in some way. On the whole, variation appears to relate to disposal rather than use. Altogether 54 units contain more than one figurine, of which 44 have more than one identifiable part (excluding (4116) and (4709), which are groups of unstratified objects which do not necessarily originate from the same deposit). An examination of these shows that only a handful contain figurines that are clearly related either in form or in unusual features such as atypical materials.

Starting with internal deposits, (4321) (building infill, at the horizontal interface of Spaces 159 and 173) contains five figurines, three of uncertain type. All are atypical, two seem to resemble each other strongly as far as can be understood from their fragmentary state, but are unlike any other figures and may be human or humanoid. One is unintelligible and may be part of a human figure or something else completely and two are heads, one fairly normal humanoid, the other surprisingly large and animal-like while having humanoid features. The wide variety perhaps argues against them being a deliberate group, while the similarity of 4321.H1 and 4321.H4 to each other and difference from the other figures suggests these two were made together and deposited deliberately.

Turning to units from external areas, (4465) (Space 117/159 between building fill) has three unusually shapeless humanoids which are roughly made and bear a stronger resemblance to each other than to most other humanoids, and a fourth possibly human base which is rather similar. All four are made of the same fine marl/plaster and form a group, and the similarity of both form and material is striking, suggesting that they were made as a 'job lot' and perhaps deposited together deliberately.

(1073) in Space 105 has five figurines (discussed above). Not particularly similar in form, but it is worth noting that they are all humanoids, and occur within a foundation cut.

From the large open area Space 115, (4102) (block of midden left in 1998) produced two figurines with strong resemblance to each other, an unusually shapeless humanoid and a large featureless human or humanoid head. This unit is clearly part of another one or more excavated in 1998. (4121) has 15 figurines, 13 of them humanoids of various shapes, sizes and styles. Most are standard humanoids, yet there are strong resemblances between the three that still have heads (4121.D1–3), while with one exception the bases are all in the same style as 4121.D2. Three are atypical: one complete, with incised eyes and indication of arms, a feature which would normally move it from the humanoid to human category and perhaps should do in this case, although it is an indication rather than proper arms (4121.D5 Fig. 9.1); the other two heads, one very rounded and perhaps human rather than humanoid (4121.H6), one peculiarly flattened (4121.H4). These atypical figurines do not resemble each other. In many ways most of the other humanoids do form a stylistic group. Unfortunately, (4121) is not a normal unit, rather it is the midden remaining after the 1998 season, removed as a single large unit (11,385 litres of dry sieve) at the start of the 1999 season for reasons of speed rather than archaeological accuracy, and therefore it contains an unspecified number of separate depositional events and should not be treated as a single unit for analytical purposes.

(3021) Space 153 (between building fill) contained 21 figurine fragments. Of these, eight were of unclear type, eight were humanoids, and six were animal horns. The humanoids and horns show great variety in shape and size, and with the exception of one humanoid and one large horn they are crudely made. It is this crudeness, and the fact that they were not baked deliberately and have been preserved due to contact with heat related to the burning of Building 1, that unifies them. Although stylistically they are not uniform, they appear to have been made at one go, along with a group of clay beads, and either thrown, or dropped accidentally, from the roof of one of the buildings surrounding this space. The implication is of transient objects, made for the moment, perhaps for a game or a ritual, and then abandoned. This is clearly of importance to the question of use and purpose.

In Space 181 (4518) has nine figurines, two of them humanoids, two fairly complete quadrupeds, an animal head and three horns (plus one unclear) but there are no unifying factors, rather there is great variety within the group. (5290) has 22 figurines, four probably parts of humans, six humanoids all different from each other, and twelve animal horns of various shapes, sizes and degrees of fragmentation and abrasion. This is the largest group of figurines from a single unit, but there are no reasons to see them as unified in any way. Rather, unlike (3021), it is a very large unit (2325 litres of dry sieved soil) of midden-type deposit, and this accounts for the large number of figurines found within it.

Discussion

Of the 44 units with multiple figurines, eight have been discussed above because of unusual features or large size of assemblage. Of these, only four contain figurines which have unusual features within the whole assemblage yet are similar to each other, suggesting that they were made at the same time or for the same purpose and were deliberately deposited together. However, (4121) is not a unit in the normal usage of the term, although the figurines could potentially all have come from a single deposit within it. A fifth (3021) contains figurines that were clearly deposited roughly together, although they show no particular similarities, but again excavation difficulties make it impossible to be sure they really were a single group. Only one of these five units occurs within a building, and this is in a context of apparently secondary deposition. This raises the possibility that the infill of buildings was not entirely random but that specific deposition of items was carried out during the backfilling operation and that these items could carry ritual significance of some kind.

Spaces/rooms

No patterning was identified in the variation of figurines by feature. The space is the next level of grouping used for units, and it is possible that figurines from within the same space will demonstrate similarities suggesting manufacture by the same person(s) or for the same purpose. As spaces are either internal or external, it is also possible that there will be a substantial difference in the type of figurine found in different kinds of space, as well as the condition and number. I shall consider the internal spaces first, then the external spaces, discussing any which contain figurines that are linked stylistically or through other elements. Mellaart's figurines can also be considered when it is known which room they came from. Spaces linked by openings in the walls, or vertically, are grouped together.

Internal spaces/rooms

Space 163 contained two humanoids (4339.H1 & 4256.H1) that are distinctive and similar miniatures of roughly the same style, dimensions, colour, fabric (extremely lightweight and full of voids) and quality. (4339) and (4256) are spatially close to each other and both are ashy deposits suggesting that the similarities between the figurines found in them are not accidental. However, (4339) is a posthole fill, whereas (4256) is building fill noted to have a higher incidence of charcoal than the surrounding soil and perhaps representing rake-out, or the uppermost fill of the underlying building. The almost identical nature of these two figurines should influence the final understanding of these deposits.

Space 170 had ten figurines. Two of them (5021.D1 and 5043.X1 Figs. 9.5–9.7, discussed above) are almost identical and unlike any others found so far at the site, although the use of punctures to create facial features and ?hair attachment is found on several other figures. The other pieces bear no resemblance to these two: one is a unique humanoid-type (4656.H1), one a faceless humanoid (4624.H1).

Mellaart's AII.1 had seven human figurines in its main room, five of them clearly very similar in style (although with minor differences) and apparently found grouped around the hearth, which reinforces the idea that they were made as a single unit, overriding the differences in stance and size which are apparent. The other two figures were completely different (Mellaart 1963, pls. xxiii & xxiv).

13 figurines were apparently found in the main room of EVI.10 (Mellaart 1963, pl. xix–xxi). Two are very similar, showing people standing behind leopards. Two more are often grouped with them because of their association with leopards, one riding a leopard, one with a leopard skin hat. However, these are not related stylistically, on simple iconographic grounds one could link the person riding a leopard with another showing a bearded person riding another animal. Two other figurines, both schematic and one with considerable human detail, are phallic, although they are very different from each other. Two more schematic ones are standing figures with hands clasped in front of the body, which could link them. The remainder are all different. Similarities can, therefore, take a range of forms: style, imagery, shape and material. All the figurines from VI.10 are made of stone, which may be relevant to the variety of shape.

Discussion

It is clear that, where the anthropomorphic figures are concerned, in a few instances there are striking unities of style which contrast strongly with the main figurine complement. Occasionally there are other aspects that could be seen as unifying factors such as topic or material, but in most cases no links can be found between the figurines found within the same space. Several reasons for this variability can be suggested, in particular the different depositional processes leading to the figures being found in the same space; stylistic changes over time; and the use of broad types which occur in many contexts. Thus the general similarity of most humanoid figurines to each other, which is the basis of their identification, will also lead to a similarity between many humanoids found within spaces. However, major differences from the main assemblage do occur albeit rarely, suggesting that clusters of atypical figurines may have been made by the occupants of the buildings in which they were found. This likelihood is much stronger when they occur in similar contexts within the space or in close proximity to each other.

External spaces

Two humanoids, 1051.H4 from Space 105, and 1057.H1 from Space 115, the eastern end of which underlies Space 105, have a similar peculiar shape and pattern of breakage, although they are slightly different sizes. As (1051) is an arbitrary layer and neither piece was recognised in the field, their findspots are not known so there is no information about whether they could be connected. 1057.H1 was originally assigned to Space 105, the re-evaluation taking place during post-excavation, and it may be that these two figures were deposited either in close proximity or at a similar time to each other, as a result of manufacture and / or destruction by one person or for a single or particular purpose.

Between Space 117 and Space 159, the group of three atypical humanoids from (4465) discussed above and indeed the fourth figurine from this unit, which is a possible human base made from the same unusual fabric (marl / plaster) but is much larger than the others, show specific similarities suggesting unity of manufacture and / or use.

Space 73 contained 11 figurine fragments, two of them very curved humanoids which could be similar to each other but whose fragmentary state makes this unclear. They come from deposits of building rubble, one lot very burnt (1315), the other with burnt material in it (3061). 3061.H1 is very burnt on one side, suggesting that either it was within the burnt material or else the burnt material was added to the deposit when still hot. A hunched humanoid from the same space, 3044.H1, also resembles them in some ways. This curved form is rarely seen, but from adjacent Space 153 3021.H1 displays it strongly, and 3030.H2 may be similar. Thus some similarities may be seen between figurines within and across these two spaces, which may not be surprising as the material in these spaces seems to have derived from the roofs of surrounding buildings. Given the similarity of figures in these spaces on the south and east sides of Building 1, it is plausible that they came from the roof of Building 1 rather than from a neighbouring, so far unexcavated, building.

Discussion

The anthropomorphic figurines from external areas seem to have fewer similarities between those found within the same units than those from internal areas. This would suggest that the external areas are places of discard possibly used by a range of people, whereas there is some suggestion of more structured and deliberate deposition in internal areas. However, the data for internal spaces is heavily dependent on Mellaart's data, and similar information for external spaces is not available due to excavation and retrieval techniques used in the 1960s.

Buildings
Buildings are sometimes single roomed, but are generally made up of two or more spaces. It is therefore worth considering whether the figurine complement of a building shows any peculiarities that suggest a specific purpose, or manufacture by a single person or for a particular occasion.

Building 6 has 12 figurines from the current excavations, which dealt only with below floor remains. Striking similarities in Space 163 have been dealt with above; there is no link at all between those found in Space 163 and those from Space 173, which are completely dissimilar. None of the figurines excavated by Mellaart have been attributed to this building.

Building 17 has 14 figurines. The extraordinary similarity between two of them from Space 170 has been discussed above, but the others are completely different both from these two and from each other.

Striking similarities are apparent among certain figurines found by Mellaart within specific buildings. Thus a group of four figurines with leopard imagery was found in VIA.10. However, as discussed above, while two of these are very similar in form, the others are linked purely through imagery rather than form and one, the 'boy on a leopard', could with equal ease be linked instead to other figures riding animals. This group has no clear relationship to the other ten figurines found in the building, nor were they found in one of the buildings with leopard sculptures on the walls, as might have been expected. The nine figurines found in AII.1 have been discussed above.

During the surface survey, two almost identical anthropomorphic figurines were found in adjacent scrape squares (CH93.30 & CH94.32: see Hamilton 1996, 233–4). They have no strong similarities in form to any other figurines from the site, and I suggest that they were made by the same person and were probably deposited in the same building. However, due to the nature of the work we were carrying out, and the fact that one of these figures was kicked up by a mattock and its place of deposition is therefore not known, it is impossible to be certain about this.

Discussion
There is enormous variability in the number of figurines found in each building, and very few buildings have collections of figurines that appear to form a coherent group in terms of form or iconography. Although there are striking similarities on occasion, they are a tiny minority.

Links/similarities across unconnected spaces

In a few instances, strikingly similar figurines have been found in deposits distant from each other in space or time. Humanoid/human head 3049.H1 from Space 154, Building 5 is unusual but similar to a much larger one from Space 115 (4102.D2). 4921.H1 from Space 182, Building 17, Level IX, and 4893.H2 from Space 181, Level Pre-XII.A, are not identical but resemble each other in form, punctured features, and the fact that each has been broken in half vertically through the thickest part of the face. Each survivor is the right hand side of the head. Three faceless humanoids have been found, 4624.H1 from Space 170, Building 17, Level IX, the much larger 5323.H1 from Space 181 Level Pre-XII.C, and sub-surface find 818.H1/CH94.1, likely to belong to Level VII or VI. Finally head 1652.H2 (Fig. 9.3), from Space 115, Level VIII, is almost identical to 6260.X1 from BACH, which also has the upper body. This piece is unstratified, being found in an animal hole, but is likely to be post-Level V. The existence of such closely-similar figurines, which themselves stand out as unusual in the total assemblage, in very different parts and levels of the site suggests the existence of formal and long-lived types. Their rarity may indicate that they were made and used by specific groups such as lineages.

Levels

The term 'level' was used by Mellaart, and although the present excavations have shown that the site's stratigraphy is more complicated than suggested by Mellaart's terminology, it has been found useful as a general way of relating our excavations to his. This makes it possible to look at broad trends in material culture within the two sets of data knowing which items are roughly contemporary, and this is likely to be an important way of considering style, use and meaning of figurines. The recent excavations have carried out work on Levels Pre-XII.E to approximately Level VI (Table 9.2).

Level Pre-XII.D
This is the earliest level from which figurines have been recovered. Only two have been found, a humanoid body and an animal horn.

Level Pre-XII.C
15 fragments have been found, a clay faceless humanoid with headscarf (5323.H1), 10 animal horns (or ear-studs?) and 2 uncertain pieces. This humanoid is particularly large, the head itself being 21 mm wide

and approximately 19 mm high (with a small bit of neck remaining). It was heavily burnt, although no burning is noted in the deposit description, suggesting that it was burnt prior to deposition in the midden.

Level Pre-XII.B

This group of 43 fragments contains three humanoids of a standard style; two rather large unusual humans, showing that considerable variety existed at this early date: 5292.H1, the base of a figure that is probably standing but possibly seated (52 mm high extant, 35 mm wide), is fired and has a slip, an extremely rare occurrence among figurines although both these features are common among the geometric clay objects found at this level; 5290.H3 is the base of a composite figurine (38 mm high extant, 42 mm wide), with part of the lower body moulded around a core, another rare feature found in only two or three other figurines so far. (Although not very large, these are bigger than most human figures found by the current excavations. Mellaart found a number of large figures.) There was also one possibly phallic item unfortunately very damaged (5393.H2); two animal heads; nineteen animal horns; and six unclear.

Level Pre-XII.A

21 fragments were found, including two pieces of humanoids, and the earliest elaborate human head, with pierced ears and traces of paint or possibly a slip (4839.H2). This is extremely well made. The earliest stone figure also dates to this level, what appears to be the base of a standing human figure although its fragmentary state makes it impossible to be sure what type it belonged to, if it really is part of a figurine (4868.H1). Nine animal horns and six unclear pieces complete the group.

Level XII

Eleven figurines have been found in this level. Of the three quadrupeds, two are beautifully-made small 'farmyard toy' animals with wear polish on them, while the third is crudely made and stabbed. This different quality of manufacture may relate to purpose. Three animal horns, an animal head, two humanoid fragments and one unclear were also found. No humans were found, although it is a small assemblage.

Level XI

The recent excavations have discovered just one figurine in this level, the lower part of a humanoid.

Level X

Sixteen figurines come from this level, of which one, and possibly two, are humanoid limbs and the remainder animal horns (or ear studs?) of varied form.

Level IX

We have found 42 figurines in Level IX, of which 13 are humanoids in a range of styles, including a miniature non-self-supporting T-shaped one (4656.H1), and a second 'faceless' one with headscarf (4624.H1) similar to, but far smaller than, the one found in Level Pre-XII.C (this one also has the neck, but the head itself is 11 mm wide and approximately 10 mm high). There are also eight human forms including the first 'fat female' types for which the site is famous, one buttock with patches of red pigment (1664.X2: Fig. 9.10), part of a composite figure; a tiny stylised human with stub arms and head punctures (1664.X4: Fig. 9.11), and the two almost identical large figurines, 5021.D1 and 5043.X1, discussed above (Figs. 9.5–9.7) with multiple head and face punctures. Nineteen animal horns and one head were found, plus seven unclear.

Level VIII

96 figurines have been recovered from this level, which has been excavated more extensively than the earlier ones. At least 33 are humanoids in a range of styles and sizes, including one with an outsize head (4321.D2), one with incised eyes and stub arms (4121.D5: Fig. 9.1), one with what seems to be details of stitching on a hat although it could merely depict a hairstyle (2899.D1), and some schematic humanoids. A number of the 24 uncertain pieces are probably fragments of humanoids. There are six human heads, three with punctures for attachment of hair, material or earrings: a large unbaked one cut from its body which has facial features incised (2739.H2); one missing its face (4973.H1) and a miniature highly-stylized one (1652.H2: Fig 9.3). The other three are crude and featureless. The rest of the assemblage consists of a seated human base, a phallic fossil (1505.X1: Fig. 9.4), a quadruped lying down (1093.H1), five other quadrupeds, two animal heads, and nineteen animal horns in a range of sizes and styles. It is clear that humanoids dominate this group and humans are rare.

Level VII

49 figurines have been found in Level VII, far fewer than in Level VIII. However, although a similar area has been excavated in each, much of the Level VII trench was remnants of Mellaart's excavation and therefore a great deal less archaeological deposit has been removed in the recent excavations. Very few humans have been found at this level, just two small rounded heads with no features other than a pinched nose. There are 22 humanoids in a range of shapes

and sizes, some large, some tiny, and some hunched styles. Four are extremely crudely made. Two roughly-complete animals were found, both of them stabbed, and a further eight fragments were recovered, six of them horns.

Level VI

Because the new excavations started work in Mellaart's old trench at Level VII, and only carried out small amounts of work in adjacent VIB contexts, only two uncertain fragments have been assigned to this level from the South Area. Some figurines from the surface survey appear stylistically to belong to this period and stylistic elements do suggest this (Hamilton 1996, 223–9).

North Area

Owing to the difficulty of matching up levels between the South and North Areas, the material from Buildings 1 and 5 cannot be assigned with certainty to any one level. A study of the ceramic and knapped stone assemblages has led to the conclusion that Building 5 approximates to Levels VII or VI. Seventeen figurines have been found in and around Building 5 during excavation. Of these four are humanoid, one is a quadruped, six are animal horns and five are uncertain parts. None has any special features.

Building 1 seems to equate roughly with Level VI on the basis of analysis of the lithics and ceramics, while AMS dating suggests VIII or VII (see Chapter 4). None of the 71 figurines found in and around this building are human, although one typically humanoid in shape had punctures covering the head and should be counted as a human/humanoid cross-over (2198.H1: Fig. 9.8). One natural stone approximating to the 'fat female' form was also found (1187.H1), as well as one possibly phallic clay item (3053.H1). Nineteen humanoids were found, two of them complete, two with lumps of clay between the legs that might possibly indicate maleness (1416.H1, 3030.H1) although it could be simply very crude manufacture (indications of sex are extremely rare on humanoids but a couple have breasts, see above). The quality of humanoid manufacture and completeness is very variable. 21 animal horns of varying size and condition were recovered, including a large plaster one from a wall moulding (2131.H1), as well as four quadrupeds, one of them stabbed (3037.H1). A large number of these figurines are of unbaked clay, and seem to have been preserved accidentally through contact with burning when the south part of Building 1 was destroyed by fire. This includes both humanoid and zoomorphic figures. A further seventeen figurines were found in deposits post dating Building 1.

Discussion

This brief overview of figurine styles and materials by level does show some element of change over time. The number of figurines found in each level shows a lot of variation, from one in Level XI to 96 in Level VIII. This cannot be accounted for purely by the amount of excavation carried out in each level, nor the type of deposit being excavated as is clear from the range within Space 181. Human figures are very rare with only 23 being found altogether as well as a concretion in female form and a human/humanoid cross-over. The earliest human figures are from Level Pre-XII.B (just two, one covered atypically in slip), and the latest from Level VII with most from IX (eight) and VIII (seven). Standing figures seem to pre-date seated ones; although a possible seated figure was found in Level Pre-XII.B, the first definite one is from Level IX. Elaborate human-style heads with punctures, incised features, and use of pigments occur first in Level Pre-XII.A and run through the sequence. They vary enormously in size, ranging from *c.* 10 mm to 50 mm high, and have widely-differing elements indicated and emphasized. Some are fairly naturalistic, while others are extremely stylized.

If Mellaart's assemblage is added to the discussion the picture changes. Humans become common in Level VI, and dominate in Level V, after which humanoids seem to cease. The form shows great variety: even the 'classic' 'fat female' seated figures come in a range of styles, with legs crossed, to the side, stretched forward, or bent underneath; with hands at breasts or on knees; with or without a fixed head (some have holes for attachment of a head); with or without breasts (although the majority have breasts), occasionally with decoration. Many others are standing, and of these some are slim, others have large bulging stomachs. A few humans are shown with animals, mainly in Level VI, the earliest is from VII, and a possible one in III is the latest by far. Just two or three show more than one person, and these occur in Level VI. Male figurines are rare, and biological sex is never shown. Rather, identification depends on hair, beards and shape of torso, not very safe indicators (see Hamilton 2000). The earliest male figure comes from Level VII and the latest from VI, suggesting that this is a short-lived motif, although it may relate more to the needs or ideology of specific groupings (households, lineages, clans, etc.) since they were found in a very restricted number of contexts coming from buildings VII.21 (1), VI.A.44 (2), VI.25 (1), VI.A.10 (4).

In the assemblage from the recent excavations humanoids occur throughout the levels with 120 altogether, the majority in the middle levels of the site: VIII (33) VII (22), VI/V (19) and IX (13). The earliest is much larger than most later ones, and is faceless, again as with the humans, atypical. Humanoids exhibit a range of form, a few being very detailed and many fairly schematic, with a number of very crude examples. There is a great range of humanoid styles, but the level of fragmentation precludes any statistical assessment of the frequency of each style or of change over time. According to Mellaart's data humanoids end in Level V but in the absence of recent excavations of buildings later than Level VI–V, this cannot be explored further at present. The humanoid/human cross-over figures come from Levels VIII to V, and each is rather different from the others. These figures are apparently rare, although they can only be identified clearly when they survive complete or nearly complete. There is a good chance that a number of heads treated as human, and bodies regarded as humanoid, actually belonged to cross-over figurines but this cannot be ascertained unless both parts are found and can be shown to join convincingly.

Phallic imagery, which has not previously been recognized at this site, does exist but again is rare. One possible phallic object of clay was found in Level Pre-XII.B (unfortunately too damaged for certainty), a natural phallic stone in Level VIII, and one phallic figurine in Level VI–V. An unstratified phallic figurine also probably belongs to Level VII (4116.D1: Fig. 9.9). At least three and possibly four of Mellaart's Level VI figurines are phallic, though two of them are equally strongly female, demonstrating mixed sex symbolism.

149 zoomorphic figurines have been found, 125 of them just horns, a number of which could actually be clay jewellery.

By far the most common material for figurines is clay, and this is used for humanoid, human, human–humanoid cross, phallic and zoomorphic figures. Stone is fairly rare, and is used for human, schematic and phallic figures but not for humanoids. The recent excavations have found hardly any stone figures. So far only six stone figurines have been found by the current excavations, and of these three are natural concretions, fossils or pebbles which have been selected for their resemblance to the human form and sometimes possibly slightly adapted to reinforce the human aspects. Because of this, it is difficult to be sure at times whether stone items are figurines or natural occurrences. The earliest stone figurine comes from Level Pre-XII.A but among Mellaart's assemblage they dominate the human representations and make up half of all Level VI figurines. Altogether Mellaart found 39 stone figurines out of an assemblage of 116 human, roughly one third of the group. Almost all stone ones are human or human with animal. As with male images, this may relate to specific makers or users, since most of Mellaart's Level VI figurines came from just three buildings. Other materials are rare: a head found by Mellaart has obsidian eyes; a slip has been found on a couple of figurines; pigment is used occasionally, sometimes just a patch of colour as in the earliest occurrence, on a Level IX figure; sometimes in a painted design, first seen in Level VI. Red, presumed to be ochre, is the most common pigment; black is also used.

Fragmentation

The vast majority of anthropomorphic figurines found in the new excavations are broken, as are many found by Mellaart. The extraordinarily low incidence of complete human figures in the recent excavations contrasts strongly with the Mellaart data, but much of the difference may be accounted for by the materials used, as most of the Mellaart examples were made of stone. The fact that many of them came from buildings could also have protected them and/or skewed the data. The humanoids are rather different, for while Mellaart did find many complete or only slightly-damaged ones, his retrieval systems did not allow for the recovery of small fragments, many of which would not have been recognizable as figurines anyway without careful study, whereas the current excavation not only sieves all deposits, but floats part of each, and the majority of figurines have reached me via these routes, frequently as discouragingly small and damaged pieces. As has been seen in the discussions of context (above), the overwhelming majority of figurines found by the current excavations were in secondary depositional contexts, either in midden or in room fill, and this almost certainly relates to the high level of fragmentation, some of which may well have been exacerbated by their depositional context (especially those in room fill which derived from midden). Nevertheless, as discussed in my previous reanalysis of Mellaart's material (Hamilton 1996, 219–21) it is clear that broken figurines were found in buildings alongside complete ones, suggesting continued importance and curation.

Only seven undamaged anthropomorphic figurines have been found in the new excavations, although a number of others have very minor damage. It is worth looking briefly at the information about these undamaged figures. Three are stone: a concretion found in heavily-burnt building fill (1187.H1); a phallic fossil found in a Level VIII midden (1505.X1:Fig. 9.4), and a phallic 'bust' that is unstratified (4116.D1: Fig. 9.9). It is likely that their condition owes more to their material (stone) than to their place of deposition. Of the remaining four, three are humanoids found within buildings (2553.H1 in foundation fill; 1905.H1 in a pit or basin let into the floor; and 4011.H1, which has a small chip of damage, was in a floor use deposit), while the other was in an external area (humanoid 1073.X1 from a foundation cut containing domestic refuse). It is clear that neither place nor broader context of deposition can be the main factor in the preservation of these figurines, since even those from within buildings have a range of context. Four of these figurines are humanoids, whereas it would generally be expected that greater care would be taken of human images (especially if they represented deities as is frequently suggested).

No whole human figure has been found, but one further figurine should be considered here. 5043.X1 (Fig. 9.5), a large human figurine, was deliberately broken prior to deposition (the break on each piece was fresh, that is clean with just slight traces of soil and plaster clinging in some places, and absolutely no sign of abrasion or of exposure in its broken state) and the head was placed alongside the body in a basin dug into the floor above an oven in what appears to be ritual closure activity during remodelling of Building 17. Thus in some ways this should be counted as a complete, but not whole, figurine. It is feasible that the damage was not deliberate at all, but that the figurine got broken at the time of the restructuring work and was therefore deposited in the pit rather than remaining in use. However, the damage was not severe. The figurine was broken into two large pieces that could easily have been stuck together again. The fact that the break was at the neck may simply be because this is the most fragile area, but could also relate to the common separation of head and body found in the assemblage, including the modelling of separate heads and bodies with peg holes for attachment, and the retention of body-less heads as well as the mending of broken figurines, for instance, Mellaart found a large head in VI.44 alongside elaborate figurines, one of which (a human with leopard) had been broken and mended in antiquity. The discovery of an almost identical head nearby, also broken from its body (which was not found) raises questions about meaning and purpose, but also about fragmentation. To break one figurine could be a misfortune, to break two looks like purposefulness. 5021.D1 (Fig. 9.7), also has a fresh break, indicating purposeful and possibly protected deposition rather than dumping, which tends to lead to abrasion and wear of broken surfaces.

The lack of a second body may relate to excavation methodology rather than deposition, which leaves part of the issue unanswerable at present (see above), but the condition of the break suggests similar depositional practice to that for 5043.X1 (Fig. 9.5).

Not one zoomorphic figurine was found undamaged, although a couple had only minor damage. Most are represented only by horns, and many of those that survive as larger pieces are still badly broken.

The extent of damage to figurines of all kinds is extremely variable. Some humanoids are missing a 'foot' or have a broken headscarf, while many are broken through the neck and only either the body or the head is found, while some of the larger ones have damage at several points. Human figures are commonly found badly fractured, perhaps just a limb or the base of a body survives, and a number of the heads are broken in half. Although some of this damage was probably accidental and even post-depositional, in particular loss of headscarves and ends of limbs, some seems to have been much more deliberate. For instance, to break a head fairly precisely in half suggests purposeful action rather than accident, particularly as this tends to involve breakage through the thickest part. The discovery of broken figurines in Franchthi Cave led Lauren Talalay to suggest that they may have been used as contracts, and that each party to the contract took part of the figurine away with them as evidence (Talalay 1987). I am not suggesting a similar purpose here, but the breaking in half of figurine heads might reflect a sharing of important cultural property. Such an idea cannot be proved on the current evidence, but it is a possibility that can be borne in mind for future interpretation should relevant data be found during future excavation.

As with the complete figurines, the level of fragmentation seems to have little relevance to the find context, although the smallest fragments tend to be found either in external dumps or in building fill. This suggests that these are secondary depositional contexts or that the deposits have been reworked or subject to activity or weathering which might have increased damage to figurine fragments beyond its original level. Animal horns are particularly frequent in midden and in ashy rake-out or occupation deposits.

Discussion

Almost all figurines found by the current excavations are broken, as are many found by Mellaart. This includes apparently '*in situ*' figurines found in buildings, some of which seem to have been broken purposefully immediately prior to deposition while others appear to have been retained in use despite their damaged state. On the other hand, some complete figurines have been found in external areas, although the vast majority of figurines from external areas are fragmentary. Because of the different quality of the Mellaart and recent data, the two groups are not directly comparable in terms of context, and even using the recent assemblage alone it is not yet clear what influenced fragmentation. However, it can be said that depositional context does not have a primary causative role in either protecting or damaging figurines. Rather, a number of factors may have been involved in the different levels of completeness found, and these probably relate to the uses and meanings of figurines.

Use and meaning

The traditional interpretation of anthropomorphic figurines at Çatalhöyük is that they represent a goddess or a suite of deities, and this was Mellaart's view at least where the human figures were concerned (Mellaart 1962, 57; 1963, 82–95; 1964a, 73–81; 1967; 1990). (For further discussion of this, of major contributions to figurine theory including Ucko 1968, and further references see Hamilton 2001, chap. 4). Voigt (2000) is the latest to support this approach, based largely upon Mellaart's data and the discovery of apparent 'cult buildings' containing sculptures at two rather earlier sites in eastern Anatolia, Nevali Çori (Hauptmann 1988; 1993) and Göbekli Tepe (Türe 1999). However, in my view there is little basis for such an interpretation (again, discussed in detail in Hamilton 2001, chap. 4). Moreover, a 'deity' interpretation addresses neither issues of use nor of meaning beyond the most general view of them as involved in religious ritual. My interest is in using figurines to understand social behaviour and even if I believed they did represent deities, this would take us no closer to understanding this. Before moving on to possible uses and meanings that *can* be recognized, I shall set out briefly the problems with the 'deity' interpretation.

Any assumption that the figurines represent deities involves a belief not only in some form of organized religion, but also in the presence of shrines, the evidence for which is very unclear (Hamilton 2001, 20–22). Not only were figurines not found in most buildings regarded as 'shrines', but they were found in a number of buildings regarded as domestic dwellings. Moreover, many were found in external areas among 'rubbish'. Second, although many of the human figurines found in buildings in the 1960s were undamaged, some were broken, as were many of those found outside buildings by the Mellaart and current excavations. Religious material is not generally treated in such a cavalier fashion, but tends to be either curated or disposed of in an organized and protective manner. Third, the representations range from natural stones through seriously schematic images and generalized humanoid figures to elaborate and highly-developed human forms. Thus there is little likelihood that they represent a clearly-defined group of deities.

One of the difficulties in interpreting this assemblage is the lack of many helpful parallels. A number of sites in eastern Anatolia and beyond have figurines similar to the humanoids (for some of the nearest geographically see Voigt 2000 for Hajji Firuz Tepe and Gritille) but there are few comparisons for the human figures. Kosk Höyük (Silistreli 1984; 1986; 1988), slightly later than Çatalhöyük, has a number of very interesting human figurines as well as relief mouldings on pottery, but the corpus is small and we are awaiting full publication. Animal figurines are known from the earlier site of Aşıklı Höyük, but no humans or humanoids are mentioned (Esin & Harmankaya 1999, 128 & fig. 21). The 'shrine phase' at Höyücek in the lake district, which is broadly contemporary with the later levels at Catalhöyük, has produced a considerable assemblage of 'mother goddess figurines and idols of baked clay' (Duru 1999, 178–9 & figs. 22-4). These were mainly found in three buildings interpreted as 'sanctuaries' and it appears that different types were used in different 'sanctuaries'. This is a highly-significant assemblage and is much richer than the finds reported from other sites in the Lake District, such as the anthropomorphic examples from Erbaba (Yakar 1991, 149) or the zoomorphic examples from Suberde (Yakar 1991, 175). so far there seems little that can help in direct comparison, but as another fascinating assemblage its interpretation might assist in understanding our own material in new ways in the future.

The topics dealt with in this chapter give some idea of possible approaches to use and meaning. It is clear that there are several different broad types of figurine, although there is some level of continuum between them. This suggests that there were probably several different uses and meanings attached to the varied forms, and these might also have overlapped to some extent. Although different materials could account for some of these differences, overall there is no reason to believe that the use of stone rather than clay was behind the variation in imagery, although the natural and schematic figures are of stone and all humanoids are made of clay. Rather, the choice of material is likely to relate to use and meaning rather than simply, or at all, to form. Some of the most detailed and elaborate figurines are made of stone, and therefore the use of stone did not restrict the imagery that was possible. On the other hand, most of the 'voluptuous' or 'fat female' figurines are made of clay, which is plastic and therefore far better suited to this form. The majority of these figures are also from the later levels, and this may also be relevant.

Context has to be regarded as one of the most important pointers to use and meaning, and the extensive discussions above have demonstrated that the vast majority of figurines found in the recent excavations have been in secondary depositional contexts which give little insight into the original context of use. Mellaart found far more figurines within buildings in apparently '*in situ*' contexts, but without the detailed excavation and recording procedures in use by the current team it is difficult to be certain of this in many cases, and impossible to correlate the contexts of 1960s finds with 1990s finds. Even those figures which may have been *in situ* do not appear to have been deposited in contexts of use. Rather, humanoid 1905.H1 in the pit/basin in the floor of Building 1, and human 5043.X1 (Fig. 9.5), in the basin in the floor of Building 17, both seem to be in positions of discard. In the case of 5043.X1 the discard is certainly deliberate, with 1905.H1 less obviously so, but contexts of discard nevertheless. The most useful aspect of contextual deposition has been the occurrence of two almost identical human figurines, 5043.X1 and 5021.D1 (Figs. 9.5–9.7), in one building in close proximity to each other, and the discovery of two basically identical figurines from a similar area in the surface survey. These indicate the probability of household, personalized or localized production and use, and may relate to meaning. The presence of so many figurines in external areas or in building fill indicates a great deal of unstructured disposal, although there are cases of groups of unusual figurines that suggest deliberate deposition. These also seem to have a lower than normal rate of damage, which could relate to purposeful deposition and therefore to use and meaning.

A combination of material and fragmentation may be relevant to understanding use and meaning. Breakage may have been an essential part of use. For instance if the making of the figures was the important part and was related to magic or wishes of some kind (as suggested for the Jarmo figurines: Broman 1958; 1983), breaking them might also have been important for ending the magical action or wish. This might explain why most, but not all, humanoids, which are mainly generalized representations of people although a few have specific features which might relate to particular individuals, are broken. Presumably there were cases in which the action of the magic or wish was intended to continue, or the time to end it had not arrived when it was buried. It might also explain why the humanoid figures were made exclusively of clay. To make them of stone would have created much greater difficulty in destroying the images.

Other plausible interpretations of the humanoid figures are protective images, or personal items relating to aspects of life. These could have been used in various rites of passage, or given at birth, and might have been destroyed for a range of reasons within this usage, for instance at the change from one life role to another. Again, such explanations would allow for a number of humanoids to survive intact, if certain roles or activities were never undertaken or entered upon. The use of humanoids as votives, suggested by Mellaart, is covered by Broman's idea of wish vehicles (above). A use in sympathetic magic, suggested for stabbed animal figures, is also possible, perhaps related to the birth of children or the health of any individual. Again, these could involve the eventual destruction of the image, although this is not necessarily required. The existence of three humanoids without faces, from which the faces appear to have been excised during manufacture, certainly suggests a magical meaning, although it could also reflect an extreme form of generalization, the opposite of the high level of detail found on a handful of humanoid figures.

Finally, some archaeologists have regarded the humanoid figures as part bird, because of the long beak-like nose. Personally I find this unlikely, since we are dealing with small figures with the main facial feature being a simple pinched nose, and there is little scope for making it less beak-like at that scale. However, it is feasible that some level of totemic representation is involved here, given the occasional occurrence of large birds at the site in both figurine and painted form. Now that it is clear that excarnation of burials did not normally take place, the old explanation of vulture imagery is no longer relevant, and this makes a 'bird-man' interpretation of humanoids even less credible.

Some of the interpretations suggested here for humanoid figurines could also be offered for the human images. However, the use of recurrent forms, particularly in Level VI (for instance, males riding animals, or groups with leopards or leopard skin clothing), suggests that these might either represent ancestors or totems of families, lineages or clans. This seems the most likely explanation for the two almost identical figurines found in Building 17, although why they should have been abandoned during remodelling of the structure is unknown. Certainly this is more reasonable than to suggest they were deities which were abandoned. It also makes sense of the fact that both sexes seem to have been represented although many images (including 5043.X1: Fig. 9.5), are not sexed and a few appear to combine both sexes. The humanoids, on the other hand, are not sexed so far as can be ascertained at this time. The puncture holes in some human heads might have been for the attachment of hair, but they could also hold feathers or other materials that might also be related to totemic aspects, perhaps from the animal world.

The occurrence of almost identical figurines across a huge time span (see above) suggests the existence either of ideal types or of site wide imagery, although it could be lineage or clan based, or relate to ancestors. Examples of this are the faceless humanoids, which occur in Levels XII and IX as well as one from the surface (probably Level VI or V); and head 1652.H2 (Fig. 9.3), from Level VIII and the head on bust 6260.X1 from Building 3 but unfortunately unstratified. Moreover, although humanoids exhibit great variety and represent a very generalized human form, similar versions can be found throughout the life of the site, rather than there being any clear development of form taking place over time. Alongside these similarities and continuities is great variation in form of both human and humanoid figurines, suggesting household rather than specialized production and probably a lineage or clan-based imagery rather than a unified Çatalhöyük imagery based on deities.

A final point is that Çatalhöyük anthropomorphic figurines are never shown doing anything, other than riding an animal, unlike some elsewhere (for instance, a few Hacılar figurines are shown holding babies (Mellaart 1970); and rather later a considerable number in Cyprus are depicted carrying out a range of activities including making things and giving birth (Karageorghis 1977; 1990; Morris 1985). This offers us few clues about use and meaning, other than to suggest that activity is not what they are about. In particular, the paucity of birth scenes makes it unlikely that they were primarily concerned with childbirth and human fertility. A single figurine from Çatalhöyük is said to depict birth. This is the most famous of all, the female supported by two felines, found in a grain bin in building AII.1. This interpretation is not accepted by all scholars, but even if it is correct, it is just one figurine and belongs to the late period of the site when imagery seems to be changing, as does the demography (see Angel 1971). The lack of activity argues in favour of an ancestor or totem interpretation.

The uses of zoomorphic figurines are generally seen as magical, often related to hunting. Clearly stabbing animal figures during manufacture could be related to this, as could posture such as lying down, but so far very few figurines displaying these features have been found. This has been discussed in detail above. Other elements such as deliberate breakage could indicate use and purpose, but is less easy to identify. Figurines of animals could also have been related to domestication, again animals sitting or lying down could be relevant, but the numbers are too small and contexts too variable at present to help. They could also have been toys. Several small well made figurines could have been children's toys, and have evidence of use wear on their surfaces, suggestive of use over a period of time rather than being made for almost immediate disposal as in hunting magic. Several anthropomorphic figurines could also have been toys or, more likely gaming pieces or counters.

Discussion

The use and meaning of figurines at Çatalhöyük are uncertain, but there is little doubt that more than one use and meaning was involved. A careful examination of context, material, fragmentation and imagery leads to a number of possible interpretations, but these do not include their use in organized religion. Rather, the anthropomorphic figures are likely to have represented ancestors or totems (human figures), and been used for magical, non religious ritual (e.g. rites of passage etc.) and / or votive purposes (humanoid figures) and discarded once they were no longer of relevance or to put an end to their magical action. Zoomorphic figures were probably used in magic, for games and for teaching purposes.

Sex and gender

Given the interpretations of anthropomorphic figurines offered above, what can we learn of sex, gender and social structure from a study of figurines? The most important point concerning sex that has become apparent to me whilst examining figurines from Çatalhöyük is that many are sexless. The majority of the assemblage, from both Mellaart's and the recent excavations, consists of humanoid figurines, and these do not show sex in an obvious way (although as mentioned above, it is possible that aspects such as whether or not divided legs are shown, and the style of head, including use of scarf or hat, do in fact carry information about sex or status of some sort). This needs to be emphasized because it is widely believed that the figurines from Çatalhöyük, and from many prehistoric sites, depict female bodies exclusively or almost exclusively. That is simply not the case. Even when just the human figures are considered, sex is not always shown, or is under rather than over stated. This topic has already been addressed for the Mellaart assemblage (Hamilton 1996, 225–6), from which it seemed that the overt sexing of figurines began in Level VI on rare occasions only, but that after Level VI not only were no male figures found but emphatically female figures made up at least half the data set. Of the 26 figurines found by Mellaart in Levels V to II, 10 are 'typical' seated 'fat females'; three are standing 'fat females', two standing figures have bulging stomachs but small breasts, three seated figures have emphasized hips or stomach but small or no breasts. Of the remainder, one is a standing slim figure, two are heads only, two are unfinished and unclear, two are humanoid / human cross-overs, and one is a schematic stone figure. Of Mellaart's 36 Level VI figurines, only six are 'fat females' while another six are regarded as male and four are phallic. Several others are female but without the large hips / buttocks and / or breasts seen so commonly in the later levels, and some are sexless. Thus there is certainly a change of emphasis around Levels VI and V. However, the 1990s data set includes a few 'fat female' figurines from before Level VI: one from Level VIII, two from Level IX, and a possible one from Level Pre-XII.B. This demonstrates that the type was in existence before Level VI, although perhaps only occurring rarely. On the other hand, the *in situ* large figurine from Building 17 is sexless, as are several large figures from the early levels found by the current excavations.

Voigt has attempted to address the issue of sex / gender, but again using only Mellaart's data (Voigt 2000, 283–7). Although she notes some similarities and differences in male and female stance and associations, the re-use of limited and long-available data takes us little further, especially as new data are now available. Her conclusion, that 'during the seventh millennium, the spirit world of sedentary communities in Anatolia was gender balanced' (2000, 290) may be correct but requires a stronger evidence base and clearer explanation of the statement than she offers at present. This is particularly so since she regards the humanoids as instruments of magic, owing to their similarity with figurines from Hajji Firuz Tepe and Gritille (but using Mellaart's published data for their depositional context, which is not in full agreement with unpublished information), thus apparently excluding them from the sex / gender discussion.

It may be that all our data, Mellaart's and the current excavations, are skewed by very localized production, with imagery based at a household level, so that a single building can contain figurines which appear to contradict or overthrow broad themes. However, in general it can be said that strongly-sexed figurines are in a minority, particularly in the early levels, and that they become far more common in the latest levels of the site. Moreover, all the strongly-sexed figurines are female, and the male and phallic figures all occur in Levels VII and VI. This situation suggests to me that there is a change in sex / gender ideology during the lifetime of the site, and that the change is centred on Level VI although aspects of it started earlier. This change may relate to other developments at the settlement at that time (see Conolly 1996; Düring 2001; Hamilton 1996; Last 1996), such as greater specialization of production. Such major economic shifts would have had profound repercussions in both the social and ideological spheres, which may be reflected in the figurine imagery among other things. The move from sexless and lightly-sexed figures (i.e. females with small breasts and / or hips, or males marked by shape of torso or indication of a beard) to strongly-sexed female figures, and the loss of male and phallic figures after Level VI, indicate that an ideology related to sex / gender and possibly concerned with the role of women (but perhaps concerned just as much with the role of men) was altering, and that figurines were utilized to portray this ideology and perhaps to broker it. What this ideological change consisted of is difficult to understand. The 'fat-female' figurines depict confident, mature women, in poses that suggest elders (particularly when found 'gathered in council' as in A.II.1) rather than women groaning under the weight of pregnancy. The lack of images of babies also argues against the pregnancy suggestion. It is sometimes argued that generalized human figures might represent babies, and therefore some people might think that the humanoid figurines are candidates for this role. However, the degree of elaboration found on some of these images, and the types of clothing indicated, mitigate against this suggestion and there is no question in my mind that these cannot be regarded as 'baby wishes'.

Any consideration of the increasing depiction of female bodies and growing emphasis on the sexing of these bodies during the lifetime of the settlement must go hand in hand with a consideration of the representation of males, for which I am largely dependent on Mellaart's data. As I have said above, there are no male or phallic figurines known from levels later than VI, although there is obviously the possibility that this is a result of skewed data at present. Most of the male and phallic images come from Level VI, and they deserve proper attention. Male figures are never shown with primary sex characteristics. Rather, they have been identified on the basis of apparent beards, curly hairstyles, lack of breasts, slim hips with broad shoulders, and pose. Specifically, several are shown riding animals, which tend to be regarded as bulls (one is identified as a leopard, on the basis of drilled spots and body form) although they have no horns, a peculiar oversight given the frequency of cattle horns as symbolic features within buildings, so that perhaps they are generalized animals, or sheep. Sheep certainly do not carry the same glamorous associations as bulls to the Western mind, but we now know that sheep / goat makes up the mainstay of the meat diet, not cattle as originally reported (Volume 4, Chapter 2). Moreover, the association of males with bulls in Western ideology need have no application to prehistory in general and Çatalhöyük in particular; it has merely been naturalised as part of our gender ideology and iconography.

If these images are accepted as males, which seems reasonable in the context of the low level of sexing on the female figurines they are found with, the significance of the association with animals is of interest. The loss of male imagery is not complete, since the two 'hunting shrines' covered in wall paintings showing wild animals and humans, most of whom are identified as male, date to Levels V and III.

The phallic images are more complex but just as important. Although there are very few, they are extremely varied in form, ranging from a fossil that looks like a penis and has not been modified to carry any other human imagery (1505.X1: Fig. 9.4), through phallic, sexless 'bust' 4116.D1 (Fig. 9.9), to complex figures depicting both sexes, one phallic figure carved to show drooping breasts (ÇHÇ 167; Mellaart 1963, fig. 19) and a schematic triangular apparently female figurine which is nevertheless phallic when viewed from the back (ÇHÇ 465; Mellaart 1964a, pl. XVIb) and is reminiscent of the well known two sex figurines from Sotira in Cyprus (Swiny & Swiny 1983) and Tepe Yahya in Iran (Lamberg-Karlovsky & Meadows 1970). This mixed imagery suggests that sex was not as dichotomized during the early levels of the site as it became after Level VI. Had it occurred alongside the overtly female figures of the later period, it would seem anomalous, but within the context of lightly-sexed figurines it fits well.

The fact that most figurines are sexless must be relevant to any understanding of sex and gender at Çatalhöyük. It is reasonable, perhaps essential, to separate the humanoid figures from the rest, since they are a fairly unified group that clearly represents generalized humans and seems to have had a different function or role within society, although what that function or role consisted of is not clear. It is possible that they are sexed but in ways that cannot now be understood, but even if other indicators were being used, this in itself suggests that sex was not the most important aspect of the figures. While it could be argued that the lack of femaleness is indicative of maleness, such a line of reasoning not only works from negative evidence, but suggests that maleness would have been regarded as a negative characteristic, that males are non females. This, of course, is in line with Cucchiari's postulated origin of the sex / gender system (1981; for a discussion of this paper see Hamilton 2001, 96–9). Given the existence of both male and phallic imagery alongside humanoids, including the possibility of a phallic figurine in Level Pre-XII.B, it seems unlikely that this is a correct reading of the Çatalhöyük iconography. However, humanoids occur from the earliest levels of the site until Level V, and it is probably not a coincidence that they seem to disappear at the same time as the male and phallic figures. Indeed, the 'humanoid with breasts and arms' is from Level V, and may represent an attempt to continue the humanoid tradition within an altered sex / gender ideology. Turning to the human figures, there is a clear move away from ambiguously- or lightly-sexed figurines towards strongly-sexed female figures. Although lightly-sexed figurines occur occasionally from Level V onwards, this is really an absence of breasts on figurines which have large hips and stomach.

Discussion

Overall, the evidence from each group of figurines combines to suggest a major change in sex / gender ideology at around the middle of the existence of the settlement, specifically between Levels VIII and V, with the strongest evidence coming from Levels VI and V. This change may well reflect much broader shifts in a range of industries at Çatalhöyük.

Conclusions

An exhaustive study of the contextual information available for the figurines indicates that the majority were not found in their place of use, and that many were probably in secondary depositional contexts rather than even in primary contexts of discard. Therefore there are only rare instances in which find context can indicate use or meaning, although it is possible that some discard practices were related to building closure. An examination of fragmentation suggests that damage may be related to use and meaning as much as to the accident of post-depositional processes.

However, as one would expect, it is a study of form and iconography that offers the most information relevant to society and usage. This paper includes an examination of similarities by context that suggests that, where human figurines are concerned, production was on a household / lineage / clan basis and involved specific, rather than site wide, imagery possibly referring to ancestors or totems. The humanoids appear to be a more unified group, but they also show great variation and this may also relate to the unit of production, but the low rate of discovery '*in situ*' within buildings makes it more difficult to assess whether differences and similarities have a household basis. There is no doubt that the different broad categories of human and humanoid reflect different uses and meanings, and each group may itself contain figurines made for a variety of purposes.

There is clear evidence of a growing emphasis on the 'fat-female' figure, and a loss of non-female imagery after Level VI. Far from supporting the belief that the figurines represent goddesses within a matriarchal society, the shifts in the iconography both in terms of the representation of the female body and the abandonment in the later period of non-female images indicate that this may be a matter of social and economic change (suggested by changes in other aspects of material culture such as the pottery and knapped stone), rather than religious ideology.

The zoomorphic figurines are even more fragmented than the anthropomorphic ones, surviving largely as horns. Five, or perhaps seven, were stabbed during manufacture, which may relate to hunting magic, but beyond this there is little to assist with understanding their use. Teaching aids, toys and magical figures related to hunting and domestication are all reasonable options, but context has not enabled me to give more weight to any one of these rather than another.

Chapter 10

A Preliminary Investigation of Mud Brick at Çatalhöyük

Burcu Tung

Mud brick is one of the most commonly-used building materials in the world today, and has been since the sixth millennium BC. This is not to say that it was not used before, for Çatalhöyük itself is a wonderful example of this type of architecture. Despite its frequency in architecture, mud brick has been taken for granted by many archaeologists. This report is an introduction to the investigation of this building material at Çatalhöyük. Through the analyses of mud brick, one can learn how people exploited their surrounding resources.

In modern architectural studies, there has been little analysis and study of mud brick. From the 1970s onward, modern 'adobe' houses became a popular focus of study in many areas across the USA. Mud brick is no longer seen as a primitive building material, and today there are many who work on it, from conserving traditional buildings to the production of sturdier mud bricks (for good examples see Dithier 1982; McHenry 1984).

This is not surprising, for there are many advantages of mud brick; it is cheap, it is produced from earth itself, it has incredible insulation properties, and it can be shaped into many different forms giving the builder a chance to be aesthetically creative and innovative (Norton 1997; Oates 1990, 389). Almost all types of soil and sediment can be used in the making of mud brick, though some need more modification than others. When the sediment used is too clayey, the tempering of sand as well as chaff is common (Norton 1997); when an expanding type of clay is used, tempering with chaff is common (Norton 1997); in some parts of the world even dung tempering is used (Bourgeois *et al.* 1989, 55). Yet there is one major deficiency mud brick contains, which hinders its usage throughout the world: its weakness to rain. Thus mud-brick architecture is seen mostly in arid and semi-arid environments, where a short annual maintenance is usually enough to make the house ready for the coming year.

The investigation of ancient mud brick is in some cases related to conservation studies where there is literature on producing the mixes that will endure unfavourable weather conditions. In a study of this type, Eriç (1980, 81) notes that to make good mud bricks, 40 per cent of the soil used should be sieved through a 60 μm mesh and that there should be no aggregates that have a width larger than three centimetres within the mixture. An earlier study conducted by Torraca *et al.* (1972) of the preservation of mud bricks in five different archaeological sites located in the Near East (Samarra, Ur, Coche, Aqar Quf, and Tell Umar) it was shown that the mud bricks produced in these sites contained more sand than the levee sediments. The authors came to the conclusion that the intentional addition of sand to clayey deposits must have been a common practice in ancient Mesopotamia. Another interesting study was conducted by the US Department of Interior, National Park Service, on old but 'successful' mud-brick structures located throughout the United States (McHenry 1984). The particle size analyses of the samples showed that on average they contained 23 per cent of sand and / or coarse aggregate, 30 per cent of sand and/or fine sand, 32 per cent of silt, and 15 per cent of clay; while x-ray diffraction analysis showed that except for a few cases, the bricks contained large or medium amounts of mica (McHenry 1984, 51–2).

Other studies of mud brick involve geoarchaeological investigations of tell formation processes (Courty *et al.* 1989; Goldberg 1979; Rosen 1986). In most archaeological sites in the Near East, and definitely for Çatalhöyük, mud brick is the primary material in tell formation. In her study of mud brick from different settlements in the Near East, Rosen (1986, 4) notes that the most durable mud brick contains a relatively high clay content of 25 to 45 per cent of the composition, and emphasizes that this type of resource is the hardest to attain and process, thus the producers have to face a choice between their labour time and the durability of the structure. In his analyses of second-millennium BC ancient Egyptian mud brick, Kemp (2000) states that the bricks used in Karnak

Table 10.1. *List of mudbrick samples analyzed.*

Sample no.	Level	Building
Mudbrick 63	III	Building 2
Mudbrick 48	V/VI	Building 1
Mudbrick 49	V/VI	Building 1
Mudbrick 58	VI B	East of building 31
Mudbrick 01	VI B–A	Shrine 61
Mudbrick 51	VII	Building 4
Mudbrick 52	VII	Shrine 10
Mudbrick 95	VII	East of building 32
Mudbrick 54	VIII	Shrine 25
Mudbrick 55	VIII	Building 10
Mudbrick 53	XII	Building 25

Table 10.2. *List of sediment samples analyzed from backswamp clay.*

Sediment sample	Location on section 95PC1
1	100–105 cm
2	120–125 cm
3	151–156 cm
4	190–195 cm
5	230–235 cm
6	250–255 cm
7	270–275 cm

show very little to zero percentage of clay, with varied silt content; while Amarna mud bricks show six to ten per cent clay. He concludes that sand has a regular appearance as a temper in the mud bricks and that the absence of clay does not necessarily hinder their production (2000, 81). Micromorphological studies related to mud brick can be seen in site reports where there are brief descriptions of how mud brick looks in thin section (i.e. Matthews *et al.* 1996; Goodman 1999). Micromorphology has also been used to illustrate the variety of locally-available resources for construction (Courty *et al.* 1989, 235; Goldberg 1979).

Methodology

I carried out a preliminary investigation of mud-brick samples collected in the 1995 summer field season. The sediments analyzed in this also come from an exposed section studied during the same season. Thus the quantitative data presented in this pilot study do not reflect the variation at Çatalhöyük, and further research needs to be conducted to attain larger and more representative sample sizes. It is also important to note that most of the samples analyzed may not be representative of the entire bricks from which they came, simply because very small amounts of soil (*c.* 2 g) were used for most of the analyses.

In total, samples of 11 mud bricks from 10 different buildings belonging to the different levels of the mound, and seven sediment samples from an exposed section of the Çarşamba palaeochannel 95PC1 (see Roberts *et al.* 1996) have been analyzed (Tables 10.1–10.2) using a suite of different analytical techniques that include particle-size analysis, loss on ignition, magnetic susceptibility, x-ray diffraction and micromorphology. The analyses of particle size, loss on ignition, and magnetic susceptibility were conducted in the Department of Geography, University of Cambridge under the supervision of Dr Steve Boreham. The x-ray diffraction analysis was carried out in the Department of Earth Sciences, University of Cambridge, by Dr Christopher Jeans and myself, following the methodology of Griffin (1971). Thin sections for micromorphological investigation of the mud bricks were prepared in the McBurney Geoarchaeology Laboratory of the Department of Archaeology, University of Cambridge by myself under the supervision of Karen Milek, and analyzed using optical polarizing microscopes following Bullock *et al.* (1984). Dr Wendy Matthews kindly let me use her own thin sections of the related sediments for analysis.

I conducted particle-size analysis only on the mud-brick samples because I received the sediment samples already processed, after they had been sieved through a 250 μm mesh. This analysis was very important in understanding the ratio of clay to silt to sand, which gives an insight into both the composition of the mud bricks, and into the possible type of depositional system the sediments used were related to. Loss on ignition analyses were carried out both on the mud-brick and sediment samples to assess their content of organic matter and calcium carbonate. Magnetic susceptibility was again conducted on all samples, to gain some degree of information on the possible mineralogy of the samples. However, it was the x-ray diffraction analyses conducted on the clay, silt and sand fractions of both the mud-brick and sediment samples that finalized the determination of the mineralogy, for provenance-related studies. Micromorphological studies were key in determining the full range of inclusions within the mud brick, in identifying the processes the bricks have gone through during and after their production, and provenance.

Results of analyses

The mud-brick samples were macroscopically analyzed before they were processed for further examination. The samples ranged from greyish-brown to yellowish-brown in colour, and from sandy silt loam to clay loam in texture. All of the samples were massive in structure, having a moderately strong to rigid consistency. They all had carbonized plant remains within their matrix, but not exceeding two per cent of content. Two samples, coming from Building 1, had fine root remains as post-depositional features. This was not surprising considering that the building is located very near the surface of the mound. The results are very similar to those that have been recorded in unit sheets by excavators themselves, as well as by Matthews & Farid (1996).

The results of the particle-size analysis show in general that the mud bricks, if we assume they were not artificially mixed, come from an alluvial depositional system, but each from different energy flows (Steve Boreham pers. comm.). The percentage distributions of the clay to silt to sand can be seen in Figure 10.1, where the high clay content (44 to 27 per cent) is evident. The loss on ignition analysis of the mud-brick and sediment samples can be seen in Figure 10.2. The organic matter in the mud-brick samples is higher than in the sediment samples, but this is not surprising since direct visual observation shows that the mud bricks contain more organic matter. The magnetic susceptibility results are not provided in this paper because they did not pertain to any questions that were relevant for this investigation.

Though x-ray diffraction was conducted on the sand, silt, and clay fractions of all the samples, only the clay mineralogy will be discussed in this paper. The results can be seen in Figure 10.3 where there is a large difference between the clay composition of the mud bricks and the sediments. The main clays that have been identified in the samples are kandite and chlorite, mica, and smectite. The mud-brick samples show a lesser amount of kandite and chlorite (roughly 8 to 10 per cent) compared to the sediment samples (roughly 12 to 17 per cent), while the amount of mica is much higher than the levels observed in the

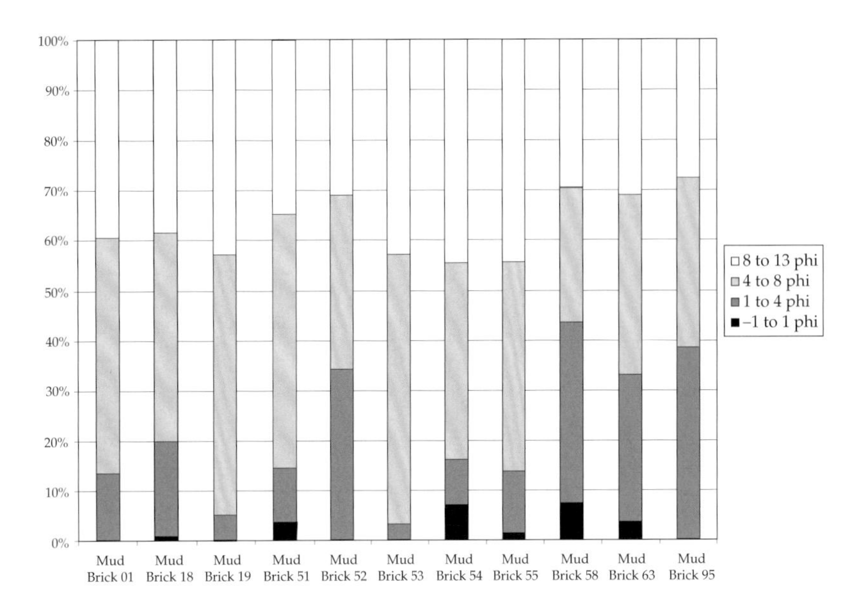

Figure 10.1. *Particle-size distributions of the mud-brick samples. –1 to 1 phi is coarse sand, 1 to 4 phi is medium/fine sand, 4 to 8 phi is silt, and 8 to 13 phi is clay.*

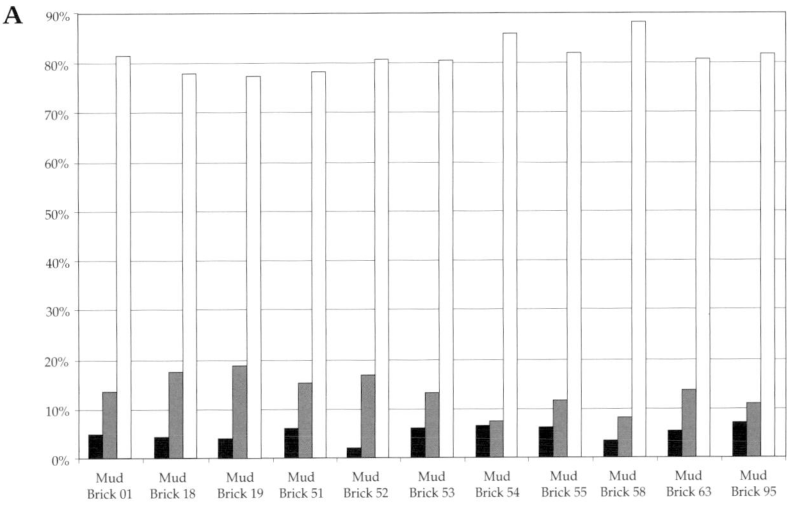

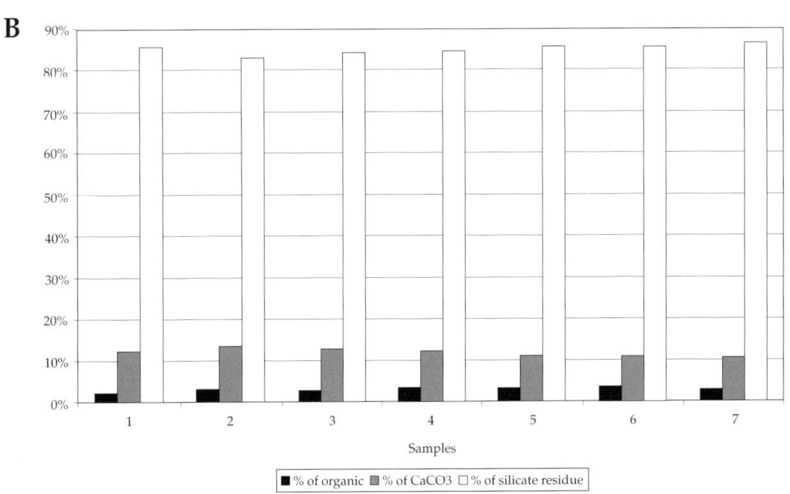

Figure 10.2. *Loss on ignition results: a) mud-brick samples; b) sediment samples.*

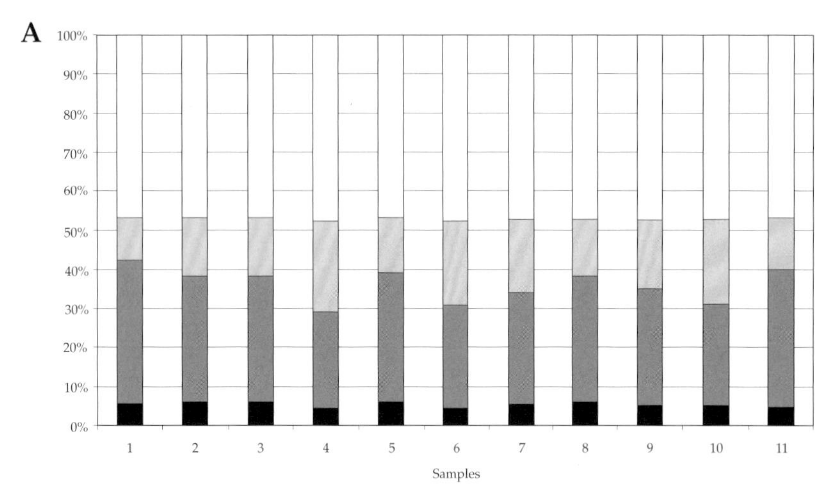

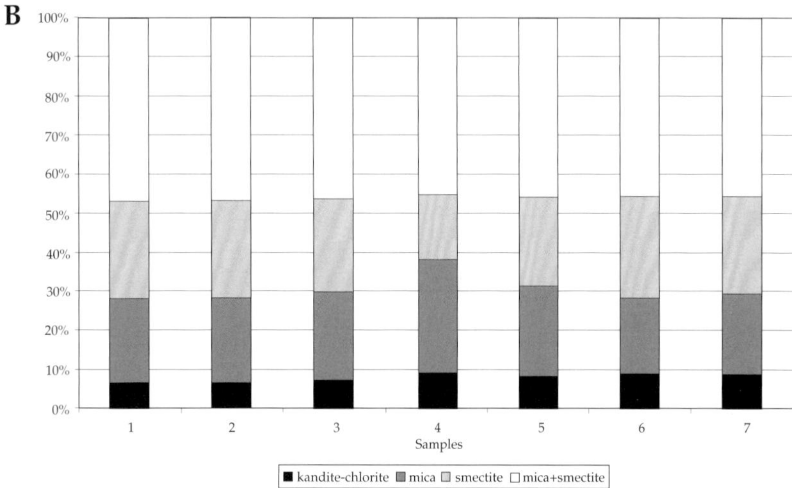

Figure 10.3. *Clay mineralogy of samples analyzed: a) mud-brick samples; b) sediment samples.*

lic b-fabric is produced by abundant calcium carbonate formations in the groundmass. In some cases under high magnification (×400) individual calcite crystals can be seen. Calcium carbonate is an easily soluble salt that can easily pass and move through soils with water (Courty *et al.* 1989, 169). When water evaporates from the soil, precipitation of calcium carbonate may occur, resulting in neoformations in the soil (Courty *et al.* 1989, 169). The coarse mineral component in all the mud-brick examples displays the same mineralogy. In summary, the sand grains are dominated by quartz and feldspar. Calcite and chert are common while hornblende and volcanic materials are few. The morphology of the sand grains changes in every example from being angular to sub-rounded. The thin section of the related sediment shows the same mineralogy in its sand, but the amount and size of the sand grains are very different when compared with the mud brick.

All of the examples have bone, shell, phytoliths, and spherulites within them, even though there are slight (<2 per cent) variations in the relative amount of each component. The samples also show similarities in the amount of organic matter with a few examples exhibiting higher percentages (the maximum difference is *c.* four per cent). Every mud-brick sample has weakly to strongly impregnated or pure iron nodules within the groundmass. Almost all examples have formations of gypsum infillings within the voids, and some examples have gypsum crystals within the groundmass.

sediment samples (roughly 48 to 69 per cent compared to roughly 35 to 51 per cent). The implications of this will be dealt with in the following sections.

The micromorphological investigations of the 11 mud-brick thin sections and related sediment gave interesting results. The mud bricks have certain similarities with one another, but they have important differences as well. Although the general composition (as in clay, silt, sand, bone, shell etc.) in the mud bricks is similar, there are significant differences in particle-size distributions and in the colour of the groundmass.

All the mud-brick and related sediment samples have a crystallic b-fabric, characterized by a birefringence caused by the presence of joining or overlapping crystallites (e.g. calcite) or very small mineral fragments (Stoops 1999, 72). As a result of the crystal formations within the matrix, it is impossible to see any orientation in the clay component that might indicate specific processes, such as puddling or moulding. In the mud-brick samples, the crystal-

Discussion

Differences of colour between the mud-brick samples from the start through to macroscopic analysis suggest different sources in their production. The samples come in a variety of colours that do not appear to show any systematic patterning through the stratigraphic layers of the mound. However, the sample size is small, and Matthews & Farid note a general change in colour of the mud brick from Level VIII to VII from grey to pale brown (1996, 282–7). All the samples show variation in their particle-size classes, indicating that the samples have been made from different sediments and/or mixtures from sediments from slightly different origins and parts of the floodplain complex. Again, the particle-size analysis of the mud-brick samples shows that they come from an alluvial depositional system, but from different energy flow areas. This difference suggests household production, rather than centralized production, and this result correlates with other indicators of the organization of production that have been discussed in this and other volumes. Another rather interesting result of this analysis is that the clay percentages of the samples correlate with what Rosen describes as sturdy mud bricks.

The micromorphology analyses show that all the mud brick and the related sediment samples, the latter deriving from a backswamp clay (see Volume 3, Part 4), contain the same mineralogy. This suggests that the sediments that were used to make the bricks came from the same alluvial environment, but not necessarily the same sediment. This correlates with the particle-size class difference, seen through micromorphology, between the backswamp clay and mud bricks showing that the mud brick could not have originated from the backswamp clays. This is further proven through the x-ray diffraction results, which show that while the mud bricks are rich in mica, the sediments are rich in smectite. Smectite would not have been a good type of clay to use for mud-brick production because of its expansion qualities. This leads to a very interesting point: the people of Çatalhöyük must have known the properties of different clays, and they were certainly choosing specific clay resources for producing their mud bricks.

As for production techniques, the first hints come from macroscopic analysis in the field. The bricks change in size, throughout levels, within each level and even within the same building. As Matthews & Farid point out (1996, 289), this fits with evidence that the bricks were moulded *in situ* on the walls, but further experimental work is needed. The samples analyzed for this study have a massive structure (like all the bricks seen in the mound) that is most likely caused by puddling processes in their manufacture. All samples contain the organic voids from chaff temper, that can be see by the unaided eye, though some seem to have more chaff than others, and this is most likely related to the particle-size distribution of the mud brick, though a specific study of this has not yet been carried out.

Interesting hints about production come from micromorphological analysis. The presence of spherulites in nearly all samples is a strong indicator that sheep and/or goat dung was purposely added in the composition. This is a practice seen in other parts of the world, and it has been noted that when the dung dries, although it does not smell it keeps insects away (Bourgeois *et al.* 1989, 55). Medium-sized iron nodules and gypsum fillings inside some voids of the mud-brick samples were possibly caused by a slow drying process, but these types of formations can also be produced by post-depositional processes. Experimental work and comparative studies would be helpful for the further understanding of the production techniques.

Conclusions

This study has shown that the making of mud brick and building houses is a complex process, and it is not possible to gain production information solely with the types of analyses conducted here. Experimental archaeology holds great promise for the further understanding of the production of mud bricks and the steps involved in building a house. Further geomorphological studies conducted in the near vicinity of the site may have the potential to reveal locations of the resources used to produce the mud bricks. As regards micromorphology, examining thin sections form which the calcium carbonate content has been removed may open a new window into the groundmass, revealing formation processes more clearly. I would also like to emphasize that though the study of mud brick does have potential for revealing some of the sociocultural behaviour of these ancient settlers, it should not be studied alone for this purpose, but rather integrated with all the other materials used in constructing the houses, especially the mortar and the plaster.

Acknowledgements

I would like to thank Ian Hodder for his kind support, starting from my first days in the project when I was still an undergraduate. I would not have been able to conduct this research without the help and advice of Charly French, Christopher Jeans, Steve Boreham, Neil Roberts, and Wendy Matthews. I am in debt to Shahina Farid, Karen Milek, Julie Miller, and everyone in Cambridge during those hectic days. And finally, I would like to thank Sonya Atalay for going over the first version of this paper and giving valuable insight on many things.

Chapter 11

The Chipped Stone

Tristan Carter, James Conolly & Ana Spasojević

Introduction

Tristan Carter

This chapter presents a detailed report on the chipped stone from the 1995–99 excavations at Çatalhöyük, documenting the material recovered from the North and South Areas, from approximately Level VI down to the mound's basal deposits (Level Pre-XII.D) and the off-site KOPAL Area. We present a 'traditional' technological and typological analysis of the chipped stone, detailing through time the various industries and raw materials employed and relating these modes of consumption (*chaînes opératoires*) to contemporary activity at other sites in central Anatolia and beyond. The issues of how a raw material was introduced to the site, how it circulated within the community, where and how it was worked, where and how the implements were used and at what point and location the material was discarded / deposited, has already been broached in part in the integrated reports of the various levels, spaces and buildings in Volume 3 (Parts 2 to 4). This chapter offers a fuller discussion of the material, plus a diachronic and synchronic perspective on the variant *chaînes opératoires* documented at the site. In turn, our data and interpretations will be located in the longer-term discussion of chipped-stone technology and its socio-economic context and significance at Çatalhöyük, i.e. developing upon, updating and critically commenting on those who have gone before us, namely the work of Bialor (1962), Mellaart (1964a, 103–13; 1967, 213–14), Balkan-Atlı (1994a) and Conolly (1996; 1999a,b) amongst others.

During 1995–2001 the material under consideration was sub-divided for study into three sections. The chipped stone from Levels IV / V–VI / VII in the North Area is discussed by James Conolly, the South Area material from Levels VII–VIII is reported on by Ana Spasojević, while Levels IX–Pre-XII.D in the South Area and the 1999 KOPAL Area assemblages are presented by Tristan Carter. All remaining sections, unless otherwise stated, are written by Carter.

Structure of the report

It is intended to present our discussion of the new chipped-stone assemblages from Çatalhöyük in chronological order from the 'bottom up', i.e. to commence with the material from the Level Pre-XII.D basal deposits of Space 181, and then to work our way up through the South Area sequence to Level VII, then to move across to Buildings 1 and 5 of the North Area (Levels IV / V–VI / VII). The report detailing the chipped stone from the off-site 1999 KOPAL Area, the dating of which is a key issue is presented last of all, though chronologically it probably falls within the upper part of the Level Pre-XII sequence investigated in the South Area (*c.* Level Pre-XII.B). Chapter 19 (on CD) is a report dedicated to the recent analysis of the renowned obsidian mirrors from Çatalhöyük. These objects were discovered in the 1960s excavations, but were studied during the course of the new project, in combination with an experimental programme and an associated project to represent the process of reconstruction and re-presentation.

Background to the analysis and methodology

The practical issues pertaining to the sampling strategy implemented for the publication of the archaeology investigated at Çatalhöyük during the 1995–99 seasons have been documented elsewhere (Volume 3, Part 1, with a summary in Chapter 1 of this volume). Of the 355 priority units chosen by the Çatalhöyük Research Project for team-wide analysis, 158 fell within the remit of Carter, Spasojević studied 77, while Conolly discusses 120. In most instances however, the authors were able to look at and comment upon many more assemblages than their allotted priority units.

The analysis focused on deconstructing each level's assemblage by technology, or 'industry', and then by raw material: obsidian and flint. The term 'industry' is derived from a French tradition of lithic analysis and has no ramifications with regard to

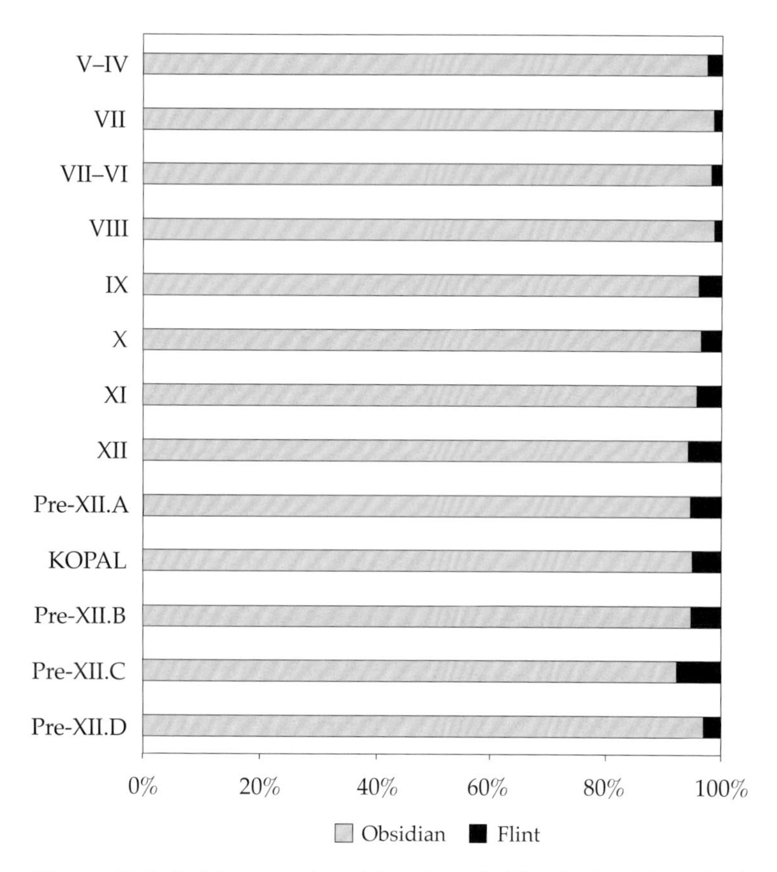

Figure 11.1. *Relative density of dry-sieve obsidian by level (number/litre).*

the quantity of material; it refers to a distinct knapping tradition as defined through the modes and mechanisms of production (cf. Newcomer 1975). For many of our industries we have only a small segment of the reduction sequence represented; in some instances only the end products. The latter cases usually compare minority components of an assemblage, typically finely-made implements (prismatic blades, naviform blades, biface performs and large scrapers, for example) that are considered ready-made imports. With these industries there may also have been some 'lumping together' of distinct traditions because our samples are so small. This is particularly pertinent with regard to our non-local prismatic blade industries (obsidian and flint), where it was difficult to ascertain whether subtle differences within a sample were the result of to-be-expected variability in a single industry, or a reflection of distinct technologies. In due course these issues should be resolved through access to larger samples. This leads us to stress the point that our work is ongoing. We offer detailed description, discussion, interpretation and conclusions throughout the chapter, which not only shed light on the chipped stone from the new Çatalhöyük excavations, but also act as points of departure for future debates and research topics. We have no doubt that by the time the next set of publications is prepared some of our conclusions and theories will have been challenged, if not refuted. However, it is also further envisaged that a proportion of these critiques will be levelled by ourselves.

Throughout the report there is a generic distinction between obsidian and 'flint' (Fig. 11.1). The latter term was placed within inverted commas to indicate that it is being employed as shorthand for a variety of siliceous materials, most commonly a variety of different-coloured limnoquartzites, plus lesser amounts of red and green radiolarite, chert, jasper and genuine flint. The term 'obsidian' is, to an extent, equally reductionist, as trace-elemental analysis of a large sample of obsidian from the site has indicated that the early Neolithic community was consuming at least two different sources at any one time (see Chapter 12). However, the ability to visually discriminate between products of these various sources is limited. Thus we continue to use the term obsidian. We trust that the reader will remember that each 'obsidian' assemblage may include more than one raw material, while the 'flint' often comprises a variety of resources. All references to use-wear are based on macroscopic inspection alone.

The chipped stone from the 1995–99 excavations

As noted above, the structure of this report commences with the earliest deposits, working through the sequence of the South Area (Level Pre-XII.D–VII), via the North Area, to the material generated by the 1999 KOPAL Area.

Pre-XII levels

The Level Pre-XII sequence of Space 181 comprises the lowest section of the trench sunk in the South Area in 1999 (see Volume 3, Part 2), a series of deposits approximately 4 m in depth down to the base of the mound. The absence of any architectural features in this Level Pre-XII sequence meant that it was impossible to phase the earliest deposits in the normal manner. The *sondage* was subdivided stratigraphically into Phases A to E, with Level Pre-XII.A being the uppermost, while Level Pre-XII.E was the modified natural marl surface. The excavation of this trench was the first time that the base of the mound, albeit in an area apparently off site, had been reached. Mellaart had sunk his own *sondage* in the vicinity in 1963 but had failed to reach natural because of technical difficulties (Mellaart 1964a, 73; 1998, 39–41). By extension, the lowest levels of Space 181 have produced the earliest chipped-stone assemblages from Çatalhöyük, including material that technologically and typologically find exact parallels with material from a number of Aceramic Neolithic sites in central Anatolia, including Aşıklı Höyük, Musular, Canhasan III and Suberde. In turn, certain components of the Level Pre-XII.C–D can be seen to relate to modes of production and consumption that have much more widespread currency in the second half of the eighth millennium BC, i.e. relating to the later PPNB 'interaction sphere' of southeast Anatolia, the Levant and Cyprus.

The detailed descriptions of the obsidian and flint industries in each level are provided on the attached CD. Summary descriptions of each industry are provided here.

Obsidian industry 1: The dominant obsidian industry at Çatalhöyük from its basal levels (Level Pre-XII.D), up to at least Level VI.B, was the manufacture of small, unstandardized blades and blade-like flakes from opposed platform cores, a relatively low-skilled percussive technique that was performed locally.

Obsidian industry 2: Level Pre-XII.B–D (Aceramic Neolithic) produced evidence for on-site manufacture of distinctive regular prismatic microblades / microliths, the tail end of a Mediterranean Epi-Palaeolithic tradition (see below).

Obsidian industry 3: This industry involved the flaking of long blade-like burin spalls from the margins of non-local scrapers and projectiles; referred to as 'edge blades'.

Obsidian industry 4: Bipolar prismatic blades of non-local manufacture. This 'industry' subsumes a number of different knapping traditions through time; the lack of associated cores / production debris makes it difficult to offer further subdivisions.

Obsidian industry 5: Unipolar prismatic blades whose manufacture is almost certainly non-local up to Level VI.A. This 'industry' again includes a number of different techniques.

Obsidian industry 6: The Aceramic Neolithic levels (Pre-XII.A–D) produced a series of large, flat flakes used to make scrapers. These pieces may derive from a distinct reduction sequence, or could be by-products from a large bipolar blade industry; none were sampled.

Obsidian industry 7: Throughout the Neolithic the bulk of Çatalhöyük's obsidian was procured in the form of thick part-worked flakes that were probably knapped at the quarries; most complete examples come from hoard. These 'quarry flakes' again embody more than one *chaîne opératoire*, with some representing biface preforms, while others become the cores for industry 1.

Flint industry 1: A microblade prismatic industry analogous to obsidian industry 2 that is similarly retricted to Levels Pre-XII.B–D.

Flint industry 2: A large bipolar blade tradition analogous to obsidian industry 4.

Flint industry 3: A unipolar large prismatic blade tradition analogous to obsidian industry 5.

Flint industry 4: It is tentatively suggested that there might be a fourth flint-working tradition, namely a rather low-skilled flake industry.

Flint industry 5: The manufacture of small, unstandardized blades and blade-like flakes from opposed platform cores, a relatively low-skilled percussive technique analogous to obsidian industry 1.

Flint industry 6: The flaking of long blade-like burin spalls from the margins of non-local scrapers and projectiles ('edge blades') analogous to obsidian industry 3.

Level Pre-XII.E

Level Pre-XII.E represents the base of Space 181, the natural surface under the mound into which a series of pits had been dug for marl extraction. No anthropomorphic material was associated with (5331) the single unit associated with this phase, hence its interpretation as natural.

Level Pre-XII.D

Level Pre-XII.D is the earliest archaeology of the Space 181 sequence, a series of seven alluviated, midden/dump layers overlaying the marl quarrying features of Level Pre-XII.E. Each of the seven units produced chipped stone, with a total of 888 pieces (Table 11.1 & Figs. 11.2–11.3). The assemblage comprised 867 pieces of obsidian (97.1 per cent) and 26 of flint (2.9 per cent), weighing 233.35 g and 49.49 g respectively (Fig. 11.1. & Table 11.2). The data display marked discrepancies with regard to the obsidian and flint assemblages in terms of their recovery and mean weights (Tables 11.3–11.4), with only 11.1 per cent of the obsidian com-

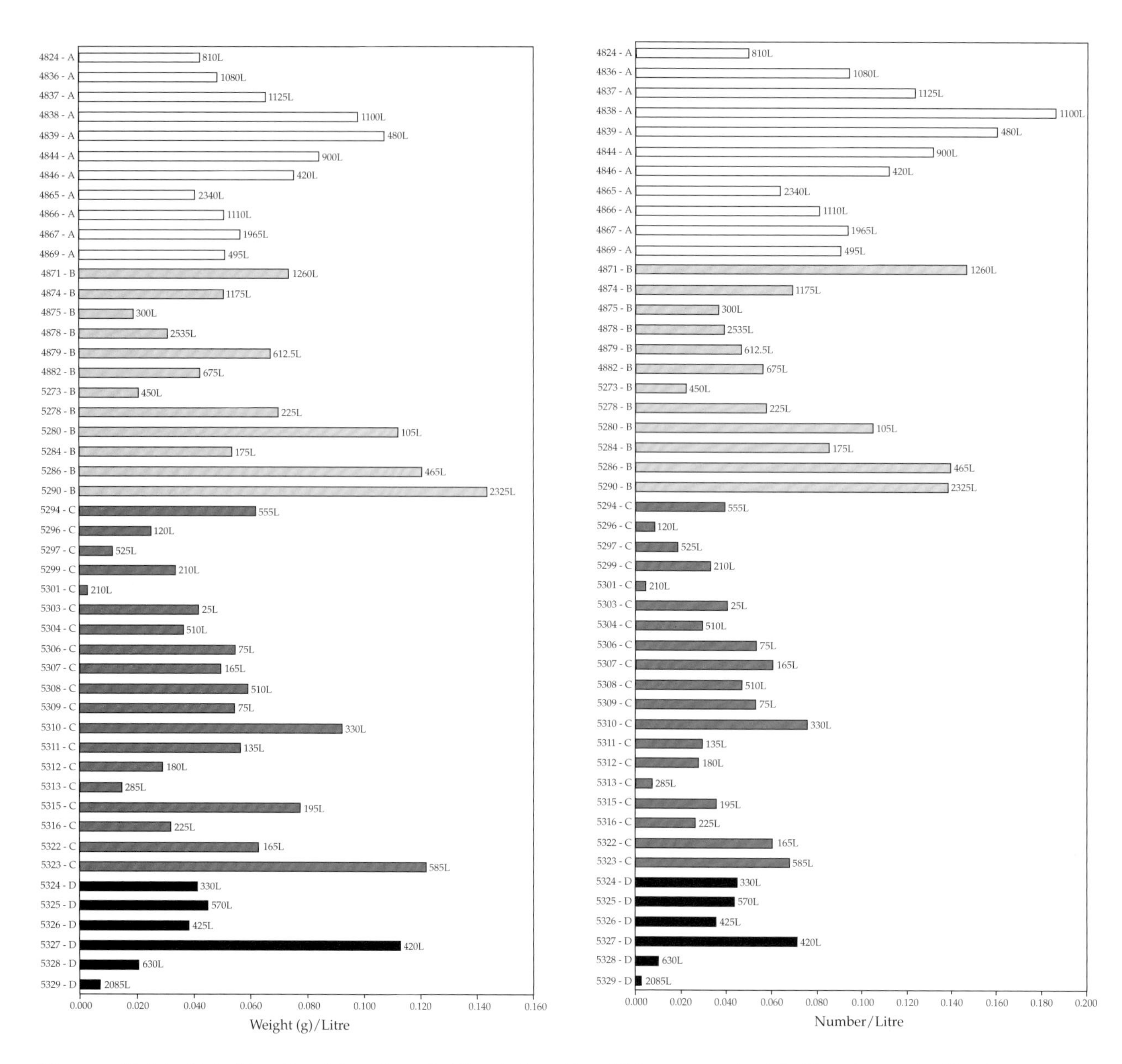

Figures 11.2 & 11.3. *Density of dry-sieve obsidian in Level Pre-XII sequence (weight/litre & number/litre).*

ing from the dry sieve, compared to 50.0 per cent of the flint. In turn, the mean weight of a piece of obsidian from Level Pre-XII.D was only 0.27 g, compared to 2.36 g for flint; furthermore, 91.0 per cent of the flint (by weight) came from the dry sieve. In part these figures reflect the larger than usual number of flotation samples that were taken from these early contexts, a process that concomitantly reduced the relative quantity of obsidian from the dry sieve. However, on a more general level, it was noted that most of the flint was present in the form of finished implements, while in contrast the obsidian assemblage was dominated by small flakes and shatter, the residue from knapping activities, albeit in secondary context. This pattern sets the tone for what we find at Çatalhöyük throughout the Neolithic sequence, i.e. that flint was consumed at the site primarily in the form of ready-made blanks, whereas certain obsidian industries were located 'in house', generating not inconsiderable quantities of knapping debris.

With the Level Pre-XII.D chipped stone coming from midden/dump deposits, i.e. secondary contexts, this report is necessarily limited with regard to what can be said concerning the specifics of production and consumption. Instead it focuses on the technological and typological aspects of the assemblages, plus their chrono-cultural relationships in a central Anatolian and wider context. The first point to stress is that the early material, both Level Pre-XII.D and Pre-XII.C, is characterized by its technical variety, embodying a great many contemporary industries and products, with evidence for at least five distinct obsidian blade industries. In turn, a significant component of the assemblages from both levels finds direct parallels in central Anatolian Aceramic Neolithic sites, and a minority relates ultimately to late PPNB traditions of southeast Anatolia, Cyprus and the Levant.

The obsidian (Fig. 11.4a–4c upper on CD)
The descriptions of obsidian industries on the accompanying CD are based on a study of the obsidian from the dry sieve and >4-mm heavy-residue sample from each unit excavated in Level Pre-XII.D, i.e. not only those prioritized. The material from the >2-mm and >1-mm heavy-residue samples were also scanned for diagnostic pieces; a few microliths came from the former and are discussed in the text.

The flint (Fig. 11.4c lower on CD)
As with the discussion of the obsidian from Level Pre-XII.D, the account of the flint industries on the CD draws upon all dry sieve and >4-mm material from each of the units excavated, with the addition of a few diagnostic pieces from the >2-mm heavy-residue sample. The flint component from Level Pre-XII.D comprised 26 pieces, 2.9 per cent of the total chipped stone (Fig. 11.1), albeit 17.5 per cent by weight due to it being made up almost entirely of end-products. Indeed, there was a near complete absence of knapping debris, with only one piece of flint from the >1-mm heavy-residue sample, the remainder coming from >4-mm and dry sieve (Tables 11.1–11.2). In further contrast to the obsidian assemblage, over a third of the flint blanks could be classified as tools on the basis of macroscopically-visible use wear (n = 10, 38.5 per cent), while over a quarter had been retouched (n = 7, 26.9 per cent). Three pieces, a non-cortical flake (5327.A25) and two prismatic blades (5325.A29, 5324.A9), had been burnt prior to their discard into the midden/dump.

Table 11.1. *Relative proportion of raw materials in chipped-stone assemblages from the levels investigated by the 1995–99 excavations by count.*

Level	Total chipped stone	Obsidian	Percentage of total	'Flint'	Percentage of total
Pre-XII.D	893	867	97.09	26	2.91
Pre-XII.C	1487	1373	92.33	114	7.67
Pre-XII.B	4809	4566	94.95	243	5.05
Pre-XII.A	5648	5355	94.81	293	5.19
XII	972	924	94.38	55	5.62
XI	248	238	95.97	10	4.03
X	6110	5907	96.68	203	3.32
IX	11,476	11,070	96.46	406	3.54
VIII	25,142	24,835	98.80	307	1.20
VII	5870	5793	98.70	77	1.30
North VII–VI	1543	1517	98.30	26	1.70
North V–IV	113	110	97.35	3	2.65
KOPAL	306	291	95.10	15	4.90

Table 11.2. *Relative proportion of raw materials in chipped-stone assemblages from the levels investigated by the 1995–99 excavations by weight.*

Level	Chipped stone (g)	Obsidian (g)	Percentage of total	'Flint' (g)	Percentage of total
Pre-XII.D	893.000	867.000	97.09	26.000	2.91
Pre-XII.D	282.840	233.350	82.50	49.490	17.50
Pre-XII.C	644.405	511.705	79.41	132.700	20.59
Pre-XII.B	1177.044	1160.488	78.57	316.556	21.43
Pre-XII.A	1348.949	1109.050	82.22	239.899	17.78
XII	143.649	112.209	78.11	31.440	21.89
XI	35.956	27.737	77.14	8.219	22.86
X	1153.387	1083.060	93.90	70.327	6.10
IX	5342.862	5056.199	94.63	286.663	5.37
VIII	5029.000	4843.300	97.40	185.700	3.80
VII	780.000	727.000	93.20	53.000	6.80
North VII–VI	102.800	-	-	-	-
North V–IV	1735.300	-	-	-	-
KOPAL	222.165	131.435	59.16	90.730	40.84

Table 11.3. *Mean weight of obsidian and 'flint' by level.*

Level	Obsidian number	Obsidian weight (g)	Obsidian mean weight (g)	'Flint' number	'Flint' weight (g)	'Flint' mean weight (g)
Pre-XII.D	867	233.350	0.27	26	49.490	2.36
Pre-XII.C	1373	511.705	0.37	114	132.700	1.16
Pre-XII.B	4566	1160.488	0.26	243	316.556	1.47
Pre-XII.A	5355	1109.050	0.21	293	239.899	0.82
XII	924	112.209	0.12	55	31.440	0.57
XI	238	27.737	0.12	10	8.219	0.82
X	5907	1083.060	0.18	203	70.327	0.35
IX	11,070	5056.199	0.46	406	286.663	0.71
VIII	24,835	4843.300	0.20	307	185.700	0.62
VII	5793	727.000	0.18	77	53.000	0.73
North VII–VI	1517	-	-	26	-	-
North V–IV	110	-	-	3	-	-
KOPAL	291	131.435	0.45	15	90.730	8.25

Table 11.4. *Obsidian count and weight by recovery method by level (Pre-XII.D–Level IX & KOPAL).*

	Dry sieve count	Dry sieve count %	Flotation count	Flotation count %	Dry-sieve weight (g)	Dry-sieve weight %	Flotation weight (g)	Flotation weight %
Pre-XII.D	96	11.07	771	88.93	129.810	55.63	103.540	44.37
Pre-XII.C	240	17.48	1133	82.52	314.410	61.44	197.295	38.56
Pre-XII.B	977	21.40	3589	78.60	1477.244	77.24	358.098	22.76
Pre-XII.A	1275	23.81	4080	73.19	775.670	69.91	333.380	21.09
XII	134	14.50	790	85.50	84.810	75.58	27.399	24.42
XI	7	2.90	231	91.10	7.590	27.40	20.147	72.60
X	506	8.57	5401	91.43	882.840	77.58	255.173	22.42
IX	959	17.81	4427	82.19	3245.390	91.98	283.130	8.02
KOPAL	88	30.24	203	69.76	125.120	95.20	6.315	4.80

Raw materials

The Pre-XII.D flint assemblage was dominated by varying coloured limnoquartzites (n = 23), followed by single blades of green radiolarite and dark-orange chert, and a part-cortical flake of black-brown flint (5328.A11: Fig. 11.4c:12 on CD). The limnoquartzites are relatively fine-grained and included light-brown (n = 6), brown (n = 3), grey-brown (n = 3) and tan (n = 5), though there is a distinct possibility that these four variants may in fact be differing hues in the same raw material. There were also individual pieces of orange, white with macroscopic black plant inclusions ('white planty'), white-yellow, white-grey and pink-grey.

Technology

Over half the flint assemblage was comprised of blade and blade-like flake end-products (n = 15, 57.7 per cent), most of which could be categorized as regular and prismatic in form, i.e. with primarily parallel dorsal ridges and margins. The majority of these pieces had been used and a significant proportion had been modified (Table 11.7). With only such a small data set, plus the fact that the flint material is largely disassociated from its manufacturing debris, it is much more difficult to assign the assemblage to distinct traditions. Three industries can be discerned with some confidence, each of which replicates one of the Level Pre-XII.D obsidian traditions, with flint industry 1 a microblade prismatic industry (cf. obsidian industry 2), flint industry 2 an opposed platform/naviform large blade industry (cf. obsidian industry 4), and flint industry 3 a large prismatic blade industry from unipolar cores (cf. obsidian industry 5). Notably, there is nothing in the flint assemblage akin to obsidian industry 1's small percussive blades/blade-like flakes, or their opposed platform cores/*pièces esquillées*.

The consumption of chipped stone in Level Pre-XII.D

The detailed description of how the chipped stone was consumed at Çatalhöyük, on a level-by-level basis, is dealt largely with in Volume 3; a brief resume is offered here. Each of the seven midden-dump layer units excavated as Level Pre-XII.D produced quantities of chipped stone; the assemblages were all quite similar, in terms of structure and their technological and typological diversity, particularly with reference to the obsidian component. Some discrepancy could be noted, however, with regard to the amount of chipped stone in each unit, with a quite striking decrease in the relative quantity as one approached the base of the mound (Figs. 11.2–11.3).

In most cases one can argue that none of the assemblages represent *in situ* deposits, owing to their variety, the lack of concentration of any one industry (or tool type), and the material's predominantly fragmentary state. The chipped stone is thus considered to be in a secondary context. The material's freshness argues against it being exposed for any great length of time prior to it being covered by the next midden deposit. Three pieces of flint had been burnt before their introduction into the midden/dump, from (5324), (5325) and (5327).

Level Pre-XII.C

Contextually, typologically and technologically there is a great deal of continuity to be witnessed between the assemblages of Levels Pre-XII.D and Pre-XII.C. The chipped stone from Level Pre-XII.C essentially represents a larger sample of those industries documented in Level Pre-XII.D, whereby there would be good reason in the future to discuss the two sets together as the earliest material from the site. The archaeology of Level Pre-XII.C is much the same as its predecessor, in that aside from a fire spot (5317) it consisted entirely of midden/dumps, excavated as 29 units. These deposits were slightly richer in chipped stone than those of Pre-XII.D (Fig. 11.2–11.3).

Each of the 29 units excavated in Level Pre-XII.C produced chipped stone, a total of 1487 pieces, with 1373 of obsidian (92.3 per cent) and 114 of flint (7.7 per cent), weighing 511.705 g and 132.7 g respectively (Tables 11.1–11.2). The Level Pre-XII.C assemblages thus generated a significantly larger proportion of flint than Level Pre-XII.D, both by number and weight, though

Table 11.7. *Relative quantity of utilized and modified pieces in 'flint' assemblages by generic type (flakes and blades), from Pre-XII.D–Level IX & KOPAL (below the backswamp clay assemblage).*

Level	No. of flakes	Flakes used	Flakes retouched	No. of blades	Blades used	Blades retouched
Pre-XII.D	11	2 (18.2%)	1 (9.1%)	15	8 (53.3%)	6 (40%)
Pre-XII.C	57	5 (8.8%)	9 (15.8%)	57	26 (45.6%)	29 (50.9%)
Pre-XII.B	66	14 (21.2%)	7 (10.6%)	98	70 (71.4%)	52 (53.1%)
Pre-XII.A	207	15 (7.2%)	7 (3.4%)	75	45 (60%)	27 (36%)
XII	40	0	0	12	8 (75%)	1 (8.3%)
XI	8	0	0	2	1 (50%)	0
X	163	3 (1.8%)	2 (1.2%)	28	13 (46.4%)	9 (32.1%)
IX	207	2 (0.97%)	2 (0.97%)	36	22 (61.11%)	20 (55.56%)
KOPAL	3	2 (66.7%)	1 (33.3%)	11	6 (54.5%)	3 (27.3%)

the mean weight of each piece of obsidian was slightly higher in Level Pre-XII.C and that of the flint over a gram less (Tables 11.2–11.3; Figs. 11.2–11.3). Compared to Level Pre-XII.D, a slightly higher proportion of the Level Pre-XII.C material came from the dry sieve, no doubt a reflection of the intensive flotation sampling strategy employed in the lowest phase of Space 181 (Table 11.4). In contrast, more flint from the heavy residue is noted, part of the overall increase in this phase's flint component.

The obsidian (Fig. 11.5a–e on CD)
The study of the Level Pre-XII.C obsidian is based on an analysis of the dry sieve and >4-mm material from each unit excavated, i.e. not only those prioritized. The >2-mm and >1-mm heavy-residue samples were also scanned for diagnostics; a few microliths came from the former and are discussed in the text. The industries are described on the CD.

The flint (Fig. 11.5f–g on CD)
As with the discussion of the obsidian from Level Pre-XII.C, the study of the flint industries on the accompanying CD draws upon all dry sieve and >4-mm material from each of the units excavated, with the addition of a few diagnostic pieces from the >2-mm heavy-residue sample. Level Pre-XII.C generated 114 pieces of flint, some 7.7 per cent of the chipped stone from this phase, and 20.5 per cent of the assemblage by weight; compared to Level Pre-XII.D, this represents almost a five per cent increase by number and three per cent by weight (Tables 11.1–11.3). While much of the flint continued to be recovered in the form of end products, a far higher proportion than before came from heavy residue in the form of microdebitage and shatter (72.8 per cent compared to 50.0 per cent in Pre-XII.D). This provides evidence that some of these raw materials were being worked on site at this time (Table 11.8).

Alongside the increased proportion of knapping debris, there was an attendant decrease in the relative quantity of tools; it remains the case however that over a quarter had been used (n = 31, 27.2 per cent), while nearly a third had been retouched (n = 26, 31.6 per cent). In contrast to the Level Pre-XII.D material, only one piece had been burnt prior to deposition, an end-scraper on a non-cortical flake (Fig. 11.5d:11 on CD).

Raw materials
As with the preceding phase, the Level Pre-XII.C flint assemblage was dominated by limnoquartzites of varying colours (n = 102, 89.5 per cent), mainly tan, brown, grey-brown, grey and light grey (n = 89, 78.1 per cent), conceivably different hues of a single raw material. The other colours included orange red (n = 6), orange white, red brown (n = 5), red green, white (n = 2), buff white, 'white planty', 'yellow-grey planty', yellow brown and blue grey. It remains quite possible that a petrographic analysis would lump much of this material together. Limnoquartzites were represented in each of the four industries defined below.

The remaining eleven pieces of the flint component comprised three green radiolarite microliths, three pieces of red radiolarite (blades and blade-like flakes), a blade-like flake of red brown chert, two retouched pieces of grey brown flint (flake and blade-like flake) and two pieces of brown flint, one a sickle on a blade-like flake (Fig.11.5f:11 on CD) and the second a patinated (residual) prismatic blade. The final piece was another 'kick-up', a Levallois flake of heavily patinated white quartzite, of Palaeolithic date (5318.A15).

Technology
Half the flint assemblage could be classified as blades or blade-like flakes from varying traditions (n = 57, 50.0 per cent: Table 11.7), precisely the same ratio as witnessed in Level Pre-XII.D. Technologically most of the flake material probably also relates to blade industries, with three rejuvenation pieces and a variety of less diagnostic manufacturing debris. Unsurprisingly it was the blade material that dominated the 31 pieces

Table 11.8. *Relative quantity of non-obsidian component ('flint') by recovery procedure (Pre-XII.D–Level IX & KOPAL below the backswamp clay).*

Level	Total	Dry sieve	>4 mm	>2 mm	>1 mm
Pre-XII.D	26	13 (50%)	12 (46.2%)	0	1 (3.8%)
Pre-XII.C	114	31 (27.2%)	76 (66.7%)	6 (5.2%)	1 (0.9%)
Pre-XII.B	243	119 (49%)	83 (34.2%)	37 (15.2%)	4 (1.6%)
Pre-XII.A	293	100 (34.13%)	86 (29.4%)	85 (29%)	22 (7.5%)
XII	55	15 (27.3)	37 (67.3%)	1 (1.8%)	2 (3.6%)
XI	10	3 (30%)	5 (50%)	2 (20%)	0
X	202	10 (5%)	69 (34.1%)	104 (51.5%)	19 (9.4%)
IX	406	28 (6.9%)	151 (37.2%)	178 (43.8%)	49 (12.1%)
KOPAL	14	12 (85.8%)	1 (7.1%)	1 (7.1%)	0

classified as implements on the basis of use-wear (n = 26, 83.9 per cent) and the 36 designated as tools due to their intentional modification (n = 29, 80.6 per cent: Table 11.7). As with the obsidian from Level Pre-XII.C, the flint from this phase essentially represents a technical continuity of what was documented in the Pre-XII.D deposits.

The consumption of chipped stone in Level Pre-XII.C

Each of the midden/dump assemblages showed broad similarities with those from Level Pre-XII.D, embodying a wide range of knapping traditions and tool types. In no instance did the state, freshness, or form of any of the Level Pre-XII.C material suggest that it was in primary context. However, it is possible to discern differences between unit assemblages that may not be entirely fortuitous, suggesting that these midden/dump deposits represent the accumulation of material from a variety of primary contexts and/or that in certain instances particular implements were being deposited deliberately in these off-site spaces. For example, (5304) produced three of the seven flint sickles from Level Pre-XII.C while (5316) generated two. (5323) is interesting because it contained a greater proportion of larger, non-local pieces; this material seems to have come from a 'different sort of place', as it included lots of projectiles, plus piercing and scraping tools, i.e. a suite of implements related to the varied modes of consuming wild animals.

Level Pre-XII.B

Level Pre-XII.B is the longest subdivision of the Space 181 sequence, excavated as 41 units. It also comprised a more complex archaeology than the preceding subphases, for amongst the numerous layers of midden/dump, were also fire spots, a pit, plus various features related to lime burning and the production of plaster (Volume 3, Part 2). A total of 4809 pieces of chipped stone came from Level Pre-XII.B, with 4566 pieces of obsidian (94.9 per cent) and 243 of flint (5.1 per cent), weighing 1160.488 g and 316.556 g respectively (Tables 11.1–11.2).

As with the preceding phases, the data display discrepancies with regard to the obsidian and flint assemblages in terms of their recovery and mean weights (Table 11.4), with only 21.4 per cent of the obsidian coming from the dry sieve, compared to 49.0 per cent of the flint. In turn one notes that the mean weight of a piece of obsidian from Level Pre-XII.B was only 0.26 g, compared to 1.47 g for flint (Table 11.3). In turn while numerically the flint assemblage was split roughly half-and-half between the two different recovery processes, by weight the majority came from the dry sieve, while the opposite was true for the obsidian (Table 11.4). Thus we again have a situation where the obsidian assemblage contains a large quantity of small flakes and shatter (knapping debris), while the flint assemblage was dominated by end products with only a small amount of material relating to manufacture and modification. In the context of the new Çatalhöyük excavations, the Level Pre-XII.B flint assemblage is also the most varied with regard to raw materials.

The obsidian (Fig. 11.6a–b on CD)

The study of the Level Pre-XII.B obsidian industries on the CD is based on an analysis of the dry-sieve and >4-mm material from each unit excavated, i.e. not only those prioritized. The >2-mm and >1-mm heavy-residue samples were also scanned for diagnostics; a few microliths came from the former and are discussed in the text.

The flint (Fig. 11.6c–e on CD)

As with the discussion of the Level Pre-XII.B obsidian, the following discussion of the flint draws upon all dry-sieve and >4-mm material from each of the units excavated, with the addition of a few diagnostic pieces from the >2-mm heavy-residue sample. Level Pre-XII.B generated 243 pieces of flint, 5.1 per cent of the chipped stone from this phase (numerically). The relative proportion of the flint component fluctuated amongst the different units, comprising 7.3 per cent of the (5290) assemblage (n = 70) and 12.4 per cent of its dry-sieved material (n = 49). Indeed, over a quarter of the flint from Level Pre-XII.B came from (5290) (28.8 per cent). Just under half of the flint came from Level Pre-XII.B's dry-sieve sample (49 per cent), a notable increase compared to Level Pre-XII.C's 27.2 per cent (Table 11.8). However, there was also a parallel increase in the amount of material from the >2-mm heavy-residue sample (n = 37), indicating that not all the flint was entering Çatalhöyük as ready-made

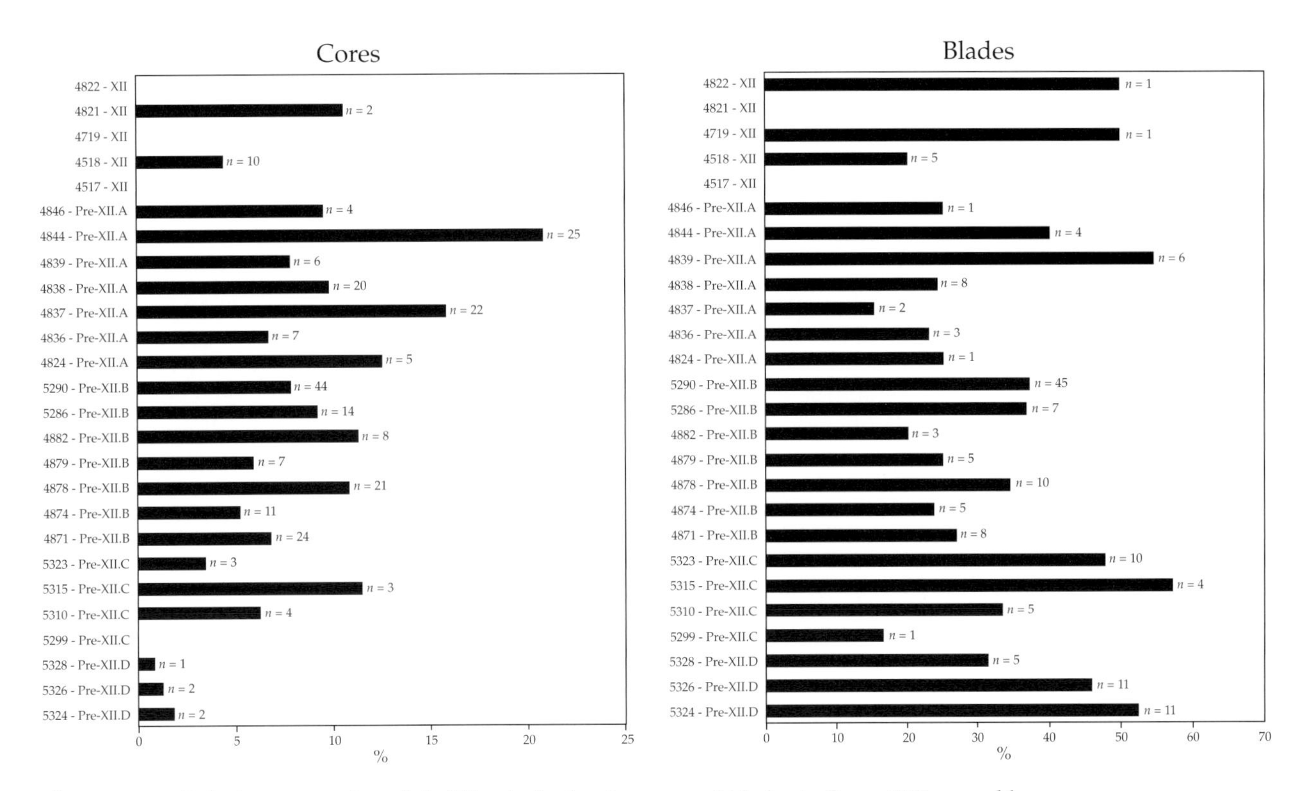

Figure 11.7. *Relative proportion of obsidian industry 1 cores and blades in Space 181 assemblages.*

implements, but that a certain amount of on-site knapping was occurring, if only in the form of retouch and other forms of modification (see below). Based on a sub-sample of the dry sieve and >4-mm material (n = 171), just under a half could be classified as tools on the basis of use wear (n = 84, 49.1 per cent), a slight increase from Pre-XII.C, while over a third had been retouched (n = 59, 34.5 per cent), a similar figure to that from the preceding phase. As with Pre-XII.D, a small number of the pieces of flint from this phase had been burnt (n = 11), coming from four units, mainly at the base of the sequence. The fact that only part of any one assemblage showed traces of burning suggests that their exposure to fire occurred prior to their inclusion in the Space 181 midden and that these deposits are made up of material from different loci.

Raw materials

As with the Level Pre-XII.C–D material, the flint component of Level Pre-XII.B was dominated by various coloured limnoquartzites (119 pieces from the sub-sample of 171, 69.6 per cent), of which the tan/brown/grey-brown/grey/orange-brown 'types' were the most common. There were also small amounts of the 'white planty' variant (n = 2), plus others of white, yellow and rose. The next best-represented raw material was a very distinctive red radiolarite, with 40 pieces (23.4 per cent), a notable increase from Pre-XII.C (n = 3: Fig. 11.36). In turn, there were eight pieces of blue-grey flint, including a part-cortical chunk from a tabular nodule (Fig. 11.6e:10 on CD), plus two pieces of green radiolarite, one piece of possible red chert and a prismatic blade of good-quality mahogany-coloured radiolarite (4871.A22). The latter raw material possibly comes from the north Levant, with not dissimilar material known from the Syrian-Iraqi border (H. Wright pers. comm.).

With regard to these raw materials' consumption in Level Pre-XII.B, the limnoquartzites were present throughout the sequence, exploited for the manufacture of microblades (flint industry 1), plus large prismatic blades from opposed platform and unipolar cores (flint industries 2 & 3). Compared to other raw materials, a far higher proportion of the limnoquartzite 'assemblage' can be described as knapping debris and shatter (all of the flint from the >1-mm and >2-mm heavy-residue samples was tan, grey-brown and grey limnoquartzite), suggesting strongly that this material was being worked on site. Moreover, a far smaller proportion of the limnoquartzite blanks display use-wear (n = 55, 46.2 per cent), or modification (n = 39, 32.8 per cent). There were also six exhausted/near-exhausted limnoquartzite cores. None were related to the manufacture of large prismatic blades, though some are probably associated with microblade production; unfortunately few are diagnostic due to their intensive reduction. One piece was classifiable as a *pièce esquillée* (4871.A15), almost certainly from bipolar reduction (rather than use) and forms part of the evidence for flint industry 5, discussed below.

The red radiolarite was similarly represented throughout Level Pre-XII.B, albeit with a concentration in the earlier part of the sequence, with over half of the sample coming from a single unit, (5290) (n = 24, 60.0 per cent). The material was consumed primarily in the manufacture of prismatic blades (n = 24, 60.0 per cent), at least some of which came from opposed platform cores (flint industry 2); the remaining material comprised non-cortical flakes (n = 11), blade-like flakes (n = 4) and one cortical flake. Exactly half of this material displayed use-wear (n = 20), while eleven pieces had been modified (27.5 per cent), including five glossed pieces (sickles), two borers, a notched piece, a side-/end-scraper and two blades with simple edge modification (see below for details). With only one cortical flake and no cores, it seems clear that these red radiolarite blades were imported, the majority being from the *plein débitage*, or 'centre blades' (Fig. 11.6c:1, 5–7, 9 on CD), plus six secondary series blades, two with remnant cortex and four with remnant cresting scars (Fig. 11.6d:5 on CD). Red radiolarite was not employed for the manufacture of microblades/microliths (flint industry 1), further suggesting its non-local reduction.

The small amount of blue-grey flint (n = 8) was also comprised mainly of prismatic blades that we can assume were procured as finished items (n = 6); none are recorded as having come from opposed platform cores, thus they may all relate to flint industry 3. Aside from one tiny piece from heavy residue, every blank had been both used and retouched, with three sickles, three end-scrapers and a blade with simple edge modification (Figs. 11.6c:8 & 11.6e:10 on CD). The green radiolarite is known in very small amounts from both Level Pre-XII.C–D deposits where it was represented primarily in the form of microblades, including modified microliths (cf. Fig. 11.5g:6–7 on CD). It is thus significant that one of the two pieces from Level Pre-XII.B was a perfect microblade core (Fig. 11.6e:7 on CD). Finally, the single pieces of red chert, and the aforementioned mahogany radiolarite, were both present as prismatic blades, both used, with the latter retouched (4871.A22).

Technology

Of the 171 sub-sample of dry sieve and >4-mm heavy-residue material, over half was made up of blades and blade-like flakes (n = 98, 57.3 per cent: Table 11.7), most of which could be classified as regular prismatic types (n = 88). Typically, a significant proportion of this material had been used (71.4 per cent), while over half had been modified (53.1 per cent: Table 11.7). The remainder of the assemblage was made up of 66 flakes (only six being cortical), of which less than a quarter had use-wear, while only 10 per cent had been retouched (Table 11.7). Finally, there were seven cores, the first flint nuclei to be documented in this chapter, after the one flake-core from Level Pre-XII.C. The cores embodied more than one reduction strategy, including what appeared to be exhausted pieces from an industry technologically analogous to obsidian industry 1, plus a flake core (5291.A12) and a fine microblade core of green radiolarite (Fig.11.6e:7 on CD). Thus the Level Pre-XII.B flint assemblage is technically more varied than those from earlier levels, in contrast to what appears to be a decrease in the number of industries in the Level Pre-XII.B obsidian.

The consumption of chipped stone in Level Pre-XII.B

As with the earlier deposits in Space 181 the form and structure of the Level Pre-XII.B chipped-stone assemblages provide little evidence to suggest that any of the material was *in situ* (with the possible exception of clay surface (5291)), though perhaps other media (e.g. animal bone) might provide more conclusive data regarding such matters. As mentioned previously, Level Pre-XII.B comprises a more complex archaeology than the other subphases of Space 181. However, none of the fire-spots ((4873), (4877) & (4881)), lime burning ((4872), (4876) & (5274)), accumulations ((5272) & (5275)), the gully-fill (4884) or post-pad (4883), produced anything that was not documented in the midden/dump deposits. Indeed, they were material-poor by comparison, aside from (5277) a scorching event that was far more productive, with not insignificant quantities of obsidian from the heavy-residue samples (Figs. 11.2–11.3).

Turning to the midden/dump deposits, while they are on average richer than those from Levels Pre-XII.C–D (Figs. 11.2–11.3), they also display a great deal of variability within the sequence. They also contain roughly the same range of material, with regard to technology, typology and raw materials. The Level Pre-XII.B chipped-stone assemblages also show a number of technological and typological changes that have important chrono-cultural ramifications, specifically the demise in the upper part of the sequence of those industries most strongly associated with a central Anatolian Aceramic Neolithic tradition, namely the microblades/microliths (obsidian industry 2), the 'big-blade' component of the opposed platform material (obsidian industry 4) and the large circular scrapers (obsidian industry 6). The Level Pre-XIIB assemblages are also the most varied from the new Çatalhöyük excavations with regard to the range of different 'flints' represented, with a variety of different coloured limnoquartzites, plus small amounts of red and green radiolarites, blue-grey flint, one piece of possible red chert and a prismatic blade of good-quality mahogany-coloured radiolarite that may have come from as far as the Iraqi-Syrian border. One of the most common media for the consumption of these exotic stones is that of the glossed blade, or sickle. This tool type embodies a range of raw materials (tan / grey / grey-brown / orange-brown / pink-red / grey-white limnoquartzites, red / green radiolarites and grey-brown / blue-grey flints), made on various blades (flint industries 3 and 4), and ranging from 2.13 to 5.25 cm long. Undoubtedly these implements are the products of various raw-material sources, whose manufacture was performed by different knappers employing various traditions, to produce implements that were intended for hand-held use, or insertion into a haft with others as composite tools. One wonders how these blades' different modes of handling, their variant colours and place of origin, related to / structured their modes of consumption (cf. Taçon 1991). Did their differences embody and / or signal their appropriateness for certain tasks and taboos for others? Might they have related to different types of plant procurement? Who may have used them?

Level Pre-XII.A

Level Pre-XII.A is the uppermost sub-phase in Space 181, excavated as 21 units (with 17 producing chipped stone), ten of which were prioritized for team study. The archaeology of Level Pre-XII.A was slightly less varied than that of Level Pre-XII.B, being dominated by a series of midden / dump layers, interspersed with three fire spots, a pit and a surface. A total of 5648 pieces of chipped stone came from Level Pre-XII.A, with 5355 pieces of obsidian (94.8 per cent) and 293 of flint (5.2 per cent), weighing 1109.05 g and 239.899 g respectively; these figures are eminently comparable to those for Level Pre-XII.B (Tables 11.1–11.2).

The data display discrepancies with regard to the obsidian and flint assemblages in terms of their recovery and mean weights (Table 11.4) showing both continuity and change from the preceding level (Table 11.4). Once again heavy residue generated the most obsidian (the dry sieve produced the bulk by weight), a reflection of the large quantities of knapping debris from local consumption. However, we also note a much-increased proportion of the flint coming from heavy residue and a related drop in the mean average weight of flint blanks (Table 11.4). This indicates that while the flint component still includes a significant number of finished implements, usually prismatic blades, on-site reduction of these variant siliceous resources was becoming more common

Chipped stone came from each of the ten prioritized units, with seven midden / dumps ((4824), (4836), (4837), (4838), (4839), (4844) & (4846)), two fire spots ((4845) & (4848)) and a pit fill (4842). The following discussion of the Level Pre-XII.A obsidian is based on the study of the dry-sieve material from each of these ten prioritized units, representing a sub-sample of 1041 pieces from the total assemblage.

The obsidian (Figs. 11.8a–11.8b upper on CD)

The obsidian assemblages from Level Pre-XII.A described on the attached CD contain evidence for both continuity and discontinuity from the preceding phases. The 'in-house' blade and blade-like flake obsidian industry 1 remains the mainstay mode of consumption, with the 'edge blade' (obsidian industry 3) and two long prismatic blade traditions (obsidian industries 4 & 5) continuing to be attested as minority components, albeit with some differences with regard to how these blanks were subsequently modified. Conversely, with only a single microblade, it is apparent that the demise of obsidian industry 2 documented in the early stages of Level Pre-XII.B is now complete, while the large flat flake scrapers of obsidian industry 6 are completely absent.

The flint (Fig. 11.8b lower on CD)

In contrast to the study of the obsidian from Level Pre-XII.A, the following discussion of the flint is based on an analysis of the entire assemblage of 293 pieces, i.e. each unit excavated from this phase, and all samples (dry-sieve, >4-mm, >2-mm and >1-mm heavy residue). The Level Pre-XII.A assemblage produced a total of 293 pieces of flint, 5.2 per cent of the total chipped stone from this phase by number, and 17.8 per cent by weight (Tables 11.2–11.3), comparable figures to those from the preceding phase. Just over a third of the flint came from the dry-sieve sample, a slight decrease from Level Pre-XII.B (Table 11.4). Conversely, Level Pre-XII.A has the greatest (relative) quantity of flint recovered as tiny flakes and shatter from the >1-mm and >2-mm heavy-residue samples (Table 11.8), indicating a continuing increase in local knapping and modification of these exotic resources. Unlike the obsidian, the following analyses are based on the complete assemblage of 293 pieces.

Compared to Level Pre-XII.B, a notably smaller proportion of the assemblage could be classified as implements on the basis of use wear (60/293, 20.5 per cent). Even when focusing on the >4-mm and dry-sieve sample, less than a third had been used (60/193, 31.1 per cent), in contrast to the 49.1 per cent for Level Pre-XII.B and 34.5 per cent for Level Pre-XII.C (Table 11.7). There was also a major decrease in the relative proportion of modified pieces, with only 17.6 per cent of the >4-mm and dry-sieve sample having been retouched (*n* = 34), compared to 34.5 per cent of the Level Pre-XII.B material, i.e. half as many. Once again, a quantity of flint from Level Pre-XII.A had been burnt, a total of 20 pieces (Level Pre-XII.B had 11). Interestingly the *in situ* burning horizon (4845) did not produce a significant quantity of burnt flint, indeed it generated less than the midden/dump (4866): (4866) (*n* = 8), (4865) (*n* = 4), (4838), (4845), (4867) (*n* = 2), (4839), (4869). This indicates that as with the previous levels the burnt pieces had been exposed to fire in other contexts, unless one countenances the possibility that the implements themselves were deliberately burned prior to their off-site discard, as some form of cleansing ritual.

Raw materials

As with the preceding phases in Space 181, the Level Pre-XII.A flint component was dominated by various coloured limnoquartzites (*n* = 270, 92.2 per cent). The tan, brown, grey-brown and grey variants comprised the lion's share (*n* = 249), the remainder including small amounts of white (*n* = 6), orange, pink, cream and translucent 'planty' types. The next best-represented raw material was red radiolarite (*n* = 15, 5.1 per cent), followed by grey-blue flint (*n* = 5, 1.7 per cent), green radiolarite (*n* = 2, 0.7 per cent) and a single blade-like flake of red jasper.

Of the 270 pieces of limnoquartzite, the majority were in the form of flakes and shatter (*n* = 186), of which four were part-cortical; only six had been used (one a *pièce esquillée*) and two modified (one an end-scraper 4866.A7). The material should thus be considered predominantly knapping debris, probably associated with the manufacture of small blades and blade-like flakes (flint industry 5), for which we have seven cores and two chunks. Limnoquartzites also continued to be exploited for the manufacture of large prismatic blades from both opposed platform and unipolar cores (flint industries 2 & 3), though microblade production (flint industry 1) is no longer attested in Level Pre-XII.A, mirroring the tradition's disappearance in obsidian (see above).

Just over a third of the red radiolarite was in the form of prismatic blades (*n* = 6), from opposed platform and unipolar cores (flint industries 2 & 3), the remainder being a single blade-like flake and eight tiny unused non-cortical flakes. This knapping debris is probably to be associated with the modification of the prismatic blades (each had been retouched and used). Indeed, while the assemblage included a crested and secondary series (part-cortical) blade, the complete absence of cores, or diagnostic preparatory and rejuvenation material argues against the industry being a local one. The five pieces of grey-blue flint included two non-local prismatic blades (flint industry 2) and two small blade/blade-like flake cores (flint industry 5), while the two pieces of green radiolarite were in the form of a non-cortical flake and a unipolar prismatic blade (flint industry 2). The single piece of red jasper was a small, unused blade-like flake of indeterminate technology.

Technology

Over two-thirds of the flint from Level Pre-XII.A was in the form of small flakes and shatter (*n* = 207, 70.7 per cent), in marked contrast to the blade-dominated assemblages of Level Pre-XII.B–D. Only a tiny amount of this material had either been used or retouched (Table 11.7). Blades continued to form a significant minority, with 75 examples (25.6 per cent), most of which could be classified as regular prismatic types (*n* = 61) from flint industries 2 and 3. As with the material from Levels Pre-XII.B–D, a large proportion of the blades were both utilized and modified (Table 11.7). Finally, there were nine cores pertaining to flint industry 5. The Level Pre-XII.A flint assemblage is therefore directly comparable to that of Level Pre-XII.B, albeit with the complete cessation of the microblade tradition (flint industry 1).

The consumption of chipped stone in Level Pre-XII.A

The archaeology of Level Pre-XII.A was dominated by a series of midden/dump layers, interspersed with three fire spots, a pit and a surface. The chipped-stone assemblages from the midden/dump deposits were, for the most part, quite similar in terms of their relative density and the structure, form and life histories of their component parts. The exceptions relate to intensity of implement consumption, as for example with (4839) where over half its blades from obsidian industry 1 had been used, a notably higher proportion than other midden/dump deposits (Fig. 11.10). However, it is a burning horizon (4845) that provides us with some of the clearest evidence yet for structured deposits in Space 181 and the use of this off-site area as an area for staged activities, above and beyond its use as a midden/dump. (4845) was an *in situ* burnt surface between two midden/dump layers ((4844) & (4846)), that generated a not insignificant quantity of chipped stone. Most of the material was akin to that from preceding deposits, but it also included two complete bifacially-modified obsidian points found lying together, unbroken but with impact damage from use (Fig. 11.8:5 on CD). Only one of the thirteen other projectiles from Level Pre-XII.A was recovered whole (Fig. 11.8:6 on CD), suggesting strongly that these points had been deliberately placed on the ground before the fire was lit. Moreover, another deposit was made some 40 cm away, on the same surface, involving the placement of an obsidian blade-core (possibly a much reduced large prismatic blade) and a pointed implement of grey-brown limnoquartzite (Figs. 11.8a:11 & 11.8b:15). The latter piece might be considered another projectile, in which case it is in itself of note, owing to the extreme rarity of flint points.

Projectiles are a significant component of the Level Pre-XII.A obsidian assemblages, not only with regard to their number, but also the variety of shapes and their life histories. While the Level Pre-XII.A projectiles have variable form and embody different *chaînes opératoires*, one can note an element of commonality in that most of them had been used prior to their deposition in Space 181. Eight of the thirteen points from our sample had impact damage on their tips; the five other pieces were all distal and medial sections, i.e. missing their tip. This intensive use of projectiles has been witnessed throughout the Level Pre-XII sequence and will continue to be seen in later phases. The fact that these implements, made on non-local blades, were brought back to the site after the hunt, suggests strongly that these were valued objects; the range of types is also considered most significant.

Finally, one other piece of obsidian from Level Pre-XII.A is worthy of further discussion, a possible fragment of our second inscribed Canhasan point (Fig. 11.8b:1 on CD), the first having been recorded from a midden/dump deposit in Level Pre-XII.C (Fig. 11.5b:12 on CD). As recovered it could be categorized as the medial section of a blade-like flake, with retouch along one margin of the dorsal surface. This modification had been truncated however, with a flake initiated from the distal end of the piece removing most of its surface; it is thought that originally the dorsal face was covered by retouch. The phenomenon of reducing modified obsidian implements has been discussed above (obsidian industry 3) and the Level Pre-XII.A assemblage has produced numerous examples of this practice, including a flake with covering retouch that had been knapped from the face of a projectile of some form (Fig. 11.8:10 on CD). Returning to the alleged Canhasan point, it is the ventral surface that is of the greatest significance, with a triangle containing a vertical line inscribed in the centre. The triangle is a common design element on the Canhasan inscribed points and there are a few pieces that offer parallels for the Çatalhöyük example. One has the remnant apex of a triangle with a single vertical line inside it (Ataman 1988, fig. 87, 49E018W), while another had a triangle with its base at the distal end and vertical lines inscribed within it (Ataman 1988, fig. 86, bottom centre, see also fig. 87, T.6 and 49FO61W).

Level XII

In the new Çatalhöyük excavations Level XII is represented solely in the South Area, specifically Space 199, located beneath Level XI (Space 198) and above the Level Pre-XII.A deposits of Space 181. The distinction between the two levels is that Level XII lies within the settlement, while the deep Level Pre-XII.A–D series of midden/dumps were deposited outside of the site. A neonate burial F.525 at the base of Level XII may mark the transition in the place and use of this part of the site, while a wall F.551 indicates the existence of buildings immediately adjacent. The archaeology of Space 199 itself relates to an interior open area. Aside from the burial, there was a fire spot (4826) and at the top of the Level XII sequence, a series of deposits interpreted as the residue from the open penning of animals, excavated as three units in the eastern half of Space 199 ((4719), (4821) & (4822)) and one in the west (4517).

Level XII produced a total of 979 pieces of chipped stone, with 924 pieces of obsidian (94.4 per cent) and 55 of flint (5.6 per cent), weighing 112.209 g and 31.44 g respectively; the relative proportions of the raw materials are comparable to those from the preceding phase, Level Pre-XII.A (Table 11.4). Conversely, Level XII produced on average less dry-sieve material (Table 11.4). When this evidence is taken into consideration with other data, it can be suggested that these open spaces saw little primary (or deliberate) consumption of chipped stone and that much of what was collected from Space 199 probably derived from nearby structures (see below).

Level XII was excavated as fifteen units, nine of which generated chipped stone; six were chosen as priorities: three of the penning deposits ((4719), (4821) & (4822)), plus (4820) a hearth located within the penning sequence, the fire spot (4826) and the wall foundation (4518). Chipped stone came from each of these priority units.

The obsidian (Fig. 11.9a–11.9b upper on CD)

The study of the Level XII obsidian is based on an analysis of the dry sieve and >4-mm material from each of the nine units that produced chipped stone, i.e. not only the six prioritized. The >2-mm and >1-mm heavy-residue samples were also scanned for diagnostics. The obsidian from Level XII is largely comparable to that of Level Pre-XII.A in that it was dominated by the 'in-house' small blade/blade-like flake tradition (obsidian industry 1), complemented by the usual minority component of non-local prismatic blades, predominantly unipolar (obsidian industry 5). In contrast, the 'edge-blade' tradition (obsidian industry 3) appears to be dying out. Level XII also produced a large part-worked flake that seems to be a preform for a projectile (Fig. 11.9b:2 on CD). These distinctive pieces are common in building hoards from Çatalhöyük's later levels (Conolly 2003); they also represent a distinct *chaîne opératoire* and have thus been labelled obsidian industry 7. The description of the obsidian industries on the accompanying CD is based on an analysis of 307 pieces of obsidian from the dry-sieve and >4-mm heavy-residue sample.

The flint (Fig. 11.9b lower on CD)
As with the obsidian, the discussion of the Level XII flint is based on a study of the dry sieve and >4-mm material from each of the nine units that produced chipped stone, i.e. not only the six prioritized. The >2-mm and >1-mm heavy-residue samples were also scanned for diagnostics. Level XII generated 48 pieces of flint, 4.9 per cent of the chipped stone from this phase (15.4 per cent by weight: Tables 11.1 & 11.4), a comparable proportion of the assemblage compared to that of Level Pre-XII.A. Just over a quarter of the flint came from the dry sieve, a decrease from the preceding phase, yet we also witness a significant decrease in the amount of shatter from the >1-mm and >2-mm samples (Table 11.8). These data further suggest that the Level XII open spaces were not being employed to work chipped stone, either obsidian, or flint. Based on a sample of 52 of the 55 pieces, only a small proportion of the assemblage displayed traces of use ($n = 7$, 13.5 per cent), while only one piece was modified, a complete denticulated sickle blade (Fig. 11.10b:4 on CD). These figures are far lower than witnessed in Level Pre-XII.A.

Raw materials
The flint component of Level XII is notably less varied than those from the Level Pre-XII sequence, for aside from a single piece of knapped limestone, the assemblage was comprised entirely of limnoquartzites, with the light-brown/tan/brown-grey variants dominant. There was no green, or red radiolarite, nor any of the blue-grey flint.

Technology
The flint assemblage is made up primarily of unused non-cortical flakes (40/52, 76.9 per cent), i.e. very similar to that of Level Pre-XII.A and in contrast to the blade-dominated assemblages of Levels Pre-XII. B–D. There were nine non-local prismatic blades (flint industries 2 and 3), six of which were used and one retouched, plus three blade-like flakes (flint industry 5), two of which were used and one retouched (Table 11.7). Technologically the assemblage is not dissimilar to that from Level Pre-XII.A, albeit less varied in terms of modified material and with an absence of cores.

The consumption of chipped stone in Level XII
The largest assemblage from Level XII came from its basal deposit, (4518) a wall-foundation layer. The material was technologically and typologically comparable to that from the Space 181 midden/dump assemblages that immediately preceded it. Above (4518) were a series of penning deposits that produced much lower densities of chipped stone (Figs. 11.10 & 11.11). These assemblages were also far less varied than that from the wall foundation, in terms of reduction sequences and implements represented, quantities of used material and modified pieces. Small non-cortical flakes dominated the penning deposits, with the occasional blade and/or core from obsidian industry 1. Little of this Space 199 chipped stone relates to manufacture and use and is thought to have come from surrounding buildings, perhaps in the form of material swept off roofs. A single complete sickle blade 4719.A1 might be *in situ*, perhaps employed to cut the plant material used for the animals kept here, though it actually bears no gloss suggesting that it had yet to have been used. Its classification as a sickle is due to its denticulated profile and similarity to other glossy pieces (cf. Ataman 1988, 63).

The other notable features from Space 199 were a fire spot (4826) that produced only one tiny obsidian flake, plus the neonate burial F.525 ((4827) & (4830)). The latter context generated an insignificant quantity of chipped stone, material that almost certainly came from the soil dug to fill the feature, rather than having been added deliberately as part of the burial rites.

The Level XII assemblages were remarkably similar in that where they produced diagnostic material it only ever related to obsidian industry 1. In only two instances, (4517) and (4518) was there evidence for the consumption of debitage manufactured by different techniques, with a number of prismatic blades from obsidian industries 4 and 5 ($n = 19$).

Level XI
As with the preceding phase, Level XI is represented only in the South Area, excavated as Space 198, the uppermost part of the 1999 *sondage* underneath the Level X structures Buildings 18 and 23. The archaeology of Level XI was dominated by a series of deposits from a penning area inside the settlement, as it had been in Level XII. The deposits were excavated as three layers in the eastern part of Space 198 ((4710), (4715) & (4716))

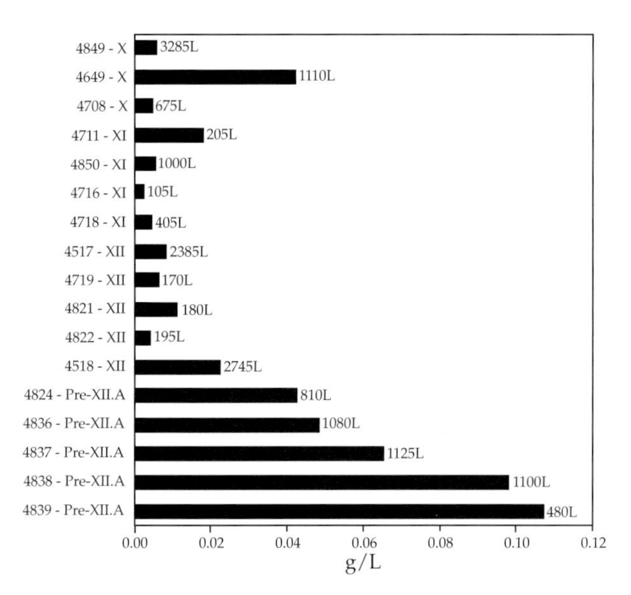

Figure 11.10. *Comparing the Level X basal infill/ foundation with preceding Level XI penning deposits and the uppermost midden/dump sequence of Space 181 (Level Pre-XII.A) — dry-sieve obsidian, weight/litre.*

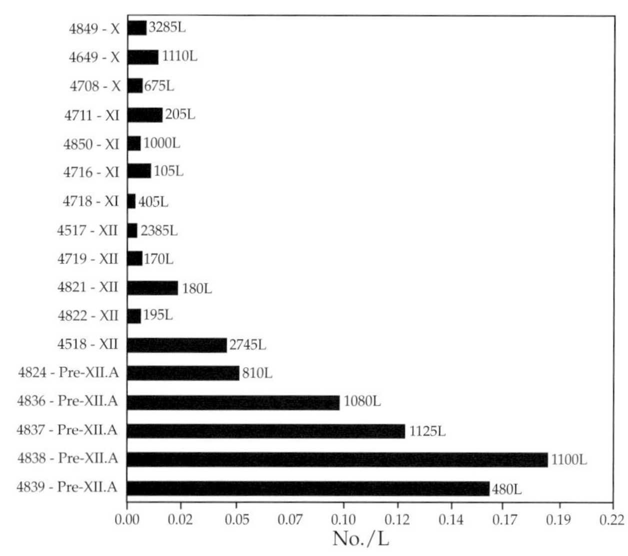

Figure 11.11. *Comparing the Level X basal infill/ foundation with preceding Level XI penning deposits and the uppermost midden/dump sequence of Space 181 (Level Pre-XII.A) — dry-sieve obsidian, number/litre.*

while the western half, under Building 23, was dug as a single unit (4849). These layers overlay a basal midden/dump (4718), while at the top of the sequence was a pit. Of the ten units dug in Level XI, five were chosen as priorities, namely the four aforementioned penning deposits, plus (4711) the pit fill.

Of the ten units that comprised Level XI, six produced chipped stone, with a total of 248 pieces (Table 11.1), comprising 238 pieces of obsidian (96.0 per cent) and 10 of flint, weighing 27.737 g and 8.219 g respectively (Tables 11.1 & 11.4). The following discussion is based on an analysis of all dry-sieve and >4-mm material, i.e. not only the material from the priority units; none of the Level XI material was illustrated.

The obsidian

The Level XI deposits generated only a small amount of chipped stone. The assemblages overwhelmingly comprised small, broken non-cortical flakes, of which only one was used. The few diagnostic pieces relate almost entirely to the 'local' small percussive blade industry (obsidian industry 1); other traditions are poorly represented, with two modified prismatic blades from obsidian industry 5. The comments regarding the obsidian industries on the attached CD are based on a study of 93 pieces of obsidian from the dry sieve and >4-mm heavy-residue sample.

The flint

Ten pieces of flint came from Level XI, 4.0 per cent of the chipped-stone assemblage from this phase (22.9 per cent by weight, Tables 11.1 & 11.4), figures not entirely dissimilar to those from Level XII. Only two pieces came from the >2-mm sample and none from the >1-mm, suggesting that as with Level XII, the open penning spaces of Space 198 were not used for working chipped stone.

Raw materials

Each of the ten pieces were limnoquartzite, mainly tan/light-brown, aside from one white flake; the absence of other raw materials mirrors what was seen in Level XII.

Technology

Eight of the pieces were small, unused, non-cortical flakes; the two diagnostic pieces were a medial section of an prismatic blade from a unipolar core (flint industry 3), plus a complete and utilized blade-like flake (flint industry 5).

The consumption of chipped stone in Level XI

The nature of the chipped stone from the Level XI penning deposits is directly comparable in structure, technology, typology and life history to that from the Level XII penning deposits. The only concentrations of material came from a small pit (4711) and the midden/dump level at the base of the Level XI sequence (4718), though neither were particularly rich assemblages (Figs. 11.10–11.11).

Figure 11.13. *Hoard (4209) during excavation plus 4209.X1 and 4209.X4.*

Level X

Level X is represented in the South Area by the archaeology of Buildings 9, 18 and 23. Building 9 remains largely unexcavated, with only two units investigated in Space 166, its western half, and one in Space 167 to the east. The central portion of Building 18 was missing due to the 1963 deep sounding, while Building 23 had been excavated partially as Shrine X.1 in the 1960s. Some undisturbed deposits remained in Building 18 either side of the *sondage*, a sequence of fire installations with related 'dirty area' to the south (Space 171), and a series of finely-laminated clean floors and two bin complexes to the north (Space 172). Underneath the structure, there was also part of a substantial foundation deposit (4708). Building 23 comprised three spaces, the largest room in the south (Space 178), with a narrow side-room to the west (Space 200) and to the north a narrow room aligned east–west (Space 179). Space 178 contained a number of undisturbed features including fire installations and two sets of obsidian clusters, one stratified above the other. These are *in situ* deposits of knapping debris related to the working of 'quarry flakes' that had been retrieved from hoards sunk into the floor of the 'dirty area'.

The combined assemblages from Buildings 9, 18 and 23 produced a total of 6110 pieces of chipped stone, 5907 of obsidian (96.7 per cent) and 203 of flint (3.3 per cent), weighing 1083.06 g and 70.327 g respectively (Tables 11.1 & 11.4). The notable increase in the relative proportion of obsidian in Level IX appears to be a reflection of the different kinds of context that we are now dealing with (inside buildings, as opposed to exterior spaces) and the impact of the obsidian-rich clusters of Building 23.

The obsidian (Fig. 11.12a–11.12c left on CD)

The discussion of the Level X obsidian industries on the attached CD is based on the analysis of all dry-sieve and >4-mm heavy-residue obsidian from Buildings 18 and 23, i.e. not only those units chosen as priorities. The sample represents a total of 1107 pieces, 604 from Building 18 and 503 from Building 23. Given its far larger size, it is perhaps not surprising that the Level X obsidian assemblage is more varied than that from Level XI. Moreover, it has to borne in mind that we are also now dealing with chipped stone from the inside of buildings, i.e. from quite different contexts to those discussed previously. The Level X obsidian, from both buildings, continued to be dominated by the 'in-house' manufacture of small blades knapped from opposed platform cores using a percussive technology (obsidian industry 1). Indeed, two groups of material from Building 23 provide us with *in situ* debris from this tradition, including cores and blades that refit. There were also a few 'edge blades' (obsidian industry 3) a tradition that has been poorly represented since Level Pre-XII.A, plus the usual small quantities of non-local fine prismatic blades (obsidian industries 4 & 5). Finally, both structures produced large 'quarry flakes' (obsidian industry 7), pre-forms for both projectiles and the manufacture of the small blades/blade-like flakes of obsidian industry 1. The following comments are based on an analysis of 1107 pieces of obsidian from the >4-mm heavy-esidue sample and dry sieve, 604 from Building 18 and 503 from Building 23. Due to time constraints, it was only possible to produce line drawings of material from Building 18; a subsequent publication on the Building 23 knapping deposits will rectify this situation.

The flint (Fig. 11.12c right on CD)

Of the 203 pieces of flint from Level X, the analyses are based on a sub-sample of 194 pieces, i.e. all dry-sieve, >4-mm and >2-mm material generated in this phase (and some of the >1-mm heavy-residue sample), not only that material produced by priority units. A total of 203 pieces of flint came from Level X, 2.9 per cent of the chipped stone from this phase (1.8 per cent by weight), a decrease compared to the relative proportion of raw materials witnessed in preceding levels, particularly with reference to the weight (Tables 11.1 & 11.4). We also witness a significant change in the assemblage's structure, with a notable decrease in the dry-sieve component and a concomitant increase in material from the >1-mm and >2-mm heavy-residue samples (Table 11.8), most of which came from Building 23 (see below). Almost certainly the reason for such a structural difference between the Level X and Level XI flint assemblages is that we are comparing different contexts, i.e. the inside of buildings, versus external spaces and middens. Of the 203 pieces of flint from Level X, the following analyses are based on a sub-sample of 194 pieces.

Table 11.9. *Chipped stone from Level X by building, number and weight by raw material.*

Building	Total chipped stone	Obsidian count	Obsidian weight (g)	Flint count	Flint weight (g)
18	2519	2430	383.289	89	43.803
23	3543	3430	718.544	113	26.515

Table 11.10. *Obsidian from Level X by building, number, weight and mean weight.*

Building	Obsidian	% of total	Weight (g)	% of total	Mean weight (g)
18	2430	41.47	383.289	34.79	0.16
23	3430	58.53	718.544	65.21	0.21

Raw materials

The Level X flint was dominated by limnoquartzites, 97.4 per cent of the total assemblage ($n = 189$), of which the tan / brown / grey-brown / grey type was the most popular, with at least 166 pieces (85.1 per cent), the others including small numbers of pink, red-brown, orange and white variants. The remaining material comprised five pieces of red radiolarite (two from Buildings 18 and 23, one from Building 9) and single pieces of honey-coloured flint and grey limestone. All of this material has been seen before in earlier levels, aside from the honey flint, present in the form of a fine prismatic blade with gloss (5095.A1). This sickle came from the fill of a small circular pit in Building 23, a feature that originally had almost certainly contained an obsidian hoard.

Technology

As with the Level Pre-XII.A to Level XI assemblages, the flint from Level X was dominated by unused flakes (84.0 per cent: Table 11.7), of which only three were cortical. The remainder of the material included two cores, a chunk and 28 blades and blade-like flakes. The latter material included two unmodified microblades (flint industry 1), twelve non-local prismatic blades (flint industries 2 & 3), thirteen blades and blade-like flakes (flint industry 5) and an 'edge blade' (flint industry 6). Typically, a far higher proportion of the blade assemblage had been both used and modified (Table 11.7). Technologically the Level X assemblage is similar to that preceding it, albeit with an additional three pieces that warrant the re-inclusion of flint industry 1 and the definition anew of flint industry 6.

The consumption of chipped stone in Level X

Before we consider the chipped stone from inside the Level X structures, a few brief comments can be made about the level's earliest material, from the soil raft underlying Buildings 9, 18 and 23, the deposit that terminated the area's prior use as an open-space midden. The first point to make is that there is little difference between the Level X foundation and the Level XI midden that preceded it (Figs. 11.10 & 11.11), with regard to the relative density of material, the variety of industries represented, the types of blanks, their state and history of use. The assemblages were both dominated by non-cortical and unused flakes, debitage from obsidian industry 1 and a few broken non-local prismatic blades (mainly obsidian industry 5). There was also the occasional 'quarry flake' (obsidian industry 7), mainly in the form of knapped chunks, aside from a broken biface from under Building 23 (5125.X6), and a single complete example from beneath Building 18 (Fig. 11.12c:2). The flint component from these fills was small and largely nondescript, aside from a small side-scraper and a blade-like flake (4689.A1–2).

Consumption inside the buildings

That Building 23 produced the larger quantity of chipped stone of the two Level X structures (Tables 11.9–11.13) is perhaps not surprising given the degree to which Building 18 had been truncated by the 1960s excavations. Despite the numerical imbalance, one can view clear parallels with regard to the consumption of chipped stone in these buildings. In both instances most of their obsidian and flint came from the southern half of the structure's main room, in proximity to fire installations, Space 171 in Building 18 and the south-east part of Space 178 in Building 23 (Tables 11.11 & 11.13). These material rich ashy rake-out and trampled floor deposits by the hearths and ovens have come to be termed the 'dirty areas' of these structures.

The 'dirty' areas

In Building 18 each of the analyzed surfaces, rake-outs and tramples associated with the ovens along the structure's southern wall were highly productive ((4530), (4539), (4540), (4557), (4548), (4578) & (4587)), certainly far more so than the floors at the northern end of the building (4686), indicating that this area was a focus of chipped-stone production, consumption or discard. In Building 23 we have much the same picture (Figs. 11.14 & 11.15), with by far the greatest quantity of material coming from the structure's

Table 11.11. *Relative quantity of obsidian from Level X spaces by recovery procedure.*

Building	Space	Total	Dry-sieve	>4-mm	>2-mm	>1-mm
18	171	2251	67 (3%)	560 (24.9%)	821 (36.5%)	803 (35.6%)
18	172	179	15 (8.4%)	83 (46.4%)	42 (23.5%)	39 (21.7%)
23	178	3214	371 (11.6%)	297 (9.3%)	1340 (41.8%)	1198 (37.3%)
23	179	44	21 (47.7%)	4 (9%)	7 (15.9%)	2 (4.4%)
23	200	172	6 (3.5%)	76 (44.2%)	60 (34.9%)	30 (17.4%)

Table 11.12. *'Flint' from Level X by building, number, weight and mean weight.*

Building	'Flint' count	% of total	Weight (g)	% of total	Mean weight (g)
18	89	44.06	43.803	62.29	0.49
23	113	55.94	26.515	37.71	0.23

Table 11.13. *Relative quantity of 'flint' from Level X spaces by recovery procedure.*

Building	Space	Total	Dry-sieve	>4-mm	>2-mm	>1-mm
18	171	85	2 (2.3%)	43 (50.6%)	31 (36.5%)	9 (10.6%)
18	172	4	2 (50%)	0	2 (50%)	0
23	178	105	2 (1.9%)	24 (22.8%)	70 (66.7%)	9 (8.6%)
23	179	4	4 (100%)	0	0	0
23	200	4	0	2 (50%)	1 (25%)	1 (25%)

southern 'dirty' area, the southeast corner in particular ((4780) & (4783)), in marked contrast to the amount of chipped stone from the compound floor layers in the northern part of Space 178 ((4504) & (4779)). The form and structure of these 'dirty-area' assemblages again indicates clearly that obsidian was worked in this part of the building.

Turning to the composition of these 'dirty area' assemblages, obsidian comprises the vast majority of the material. For example, the combined total of chipped stone from (4530), (4533), (4539), (4540), (4548), (4553) and (4557) in Building 18/Space 171, was 1574 pieces, of which only 59 were flint (3.9 per cent). The assemblages were also dominated by small, unused and fresh non-cortical flakes, i.e. material that relates to episodes of production and transformation rather than use. Given the material's freshness and the fact that most of the flakes were recovered complete, it seems that the debris became a part of these ashy rake-outs only a short while after it had been knapped, somewhere in the immediate vicinity.

Technologically, the material from Building 18 and 23's 'dirty areas' is dominated by knapping debris from the 'in-house' obsidian industry 1. The absence of cortical material indicates that production of blades/blade-like flakes did not commence with the reduction of raw nodules. Instead the raw material that represented the point of departure for this industry was in the form of largely decorticated 'quarry flakes', i.e. the material that forms the primary component of hoards (see below). The category of 'quarry flakes' encompasses three main type of blank. There are large, flat and decorticated flakes with discontinuous irregular bifacial removals, large flat flakes with one or more edges retouched into scrapers (Fig. 11.12c:2 on CD), or true 'bifaces', i.e. a large flake that has received a greater amount of dorsal and ventral modification, whereby it is recognizable as a projectile preform (Figs. 11.12b:3 & 11.12c:1 on CD). It is important to note that these are not the only types of object from obsidian hoards, they less commonly include large blades from obsidian industries 4 & 5. Nor are hoards the sole context within which one can find whole 'quarry flakes' (cf. Fig. 11.12c:2 on CD), though they are certainly the most common.

It is the roughly-worked 'quarry flake' and the large flake scrapers that constitute the cores for the manufacture of obsidian industry 1 blades/blade-like flakes. The clearest evidence we have for this is provided by a group of material from the southeast 'dirty' corner of Building 23 ((4987), (4989) & (4990)). These assemblages are probably the most informative groups of chipped stone from Level X, three clusters of obsidian located next to a small, shallow, circular hole (4996). It is believed that the pit may originally have contained an obsidian hoard, on the basis of its location, comparanda from other buildings and the association of the flaking debris. The hoard itself had obviously been retrieved, with a proportion of the obsidian then knapped in the immediate vicinity. The material included remnants of thick, non-cortical flakes, of exactly the form recovered from other hoards, including two fragmentary examples of the large side-scrapers (with use-wear) which had been reduced as cores in the tradition of obsidian industry 1.

(4989) comprised 80 pieces of obsidian, most of which were individually plotted on a 1:1 plan and recorded as X-finds. It was not possible to undertake a full refitting programme in order to ascertain exactly how many 'quarry flakes' the knapping debris represented. It was, however, possible to find four sets of conjoining flakes, blades and blade-like flakes, including a small fine blade that was refitted to a core. Furthermore, the debris was all very fresh, much of it was recovered complete and very few pieces showed any signs of use or modification, indicating clearly that this assemblage represents an *in situ* hoard retrieval and knapping deposit. To the author's knowledge,

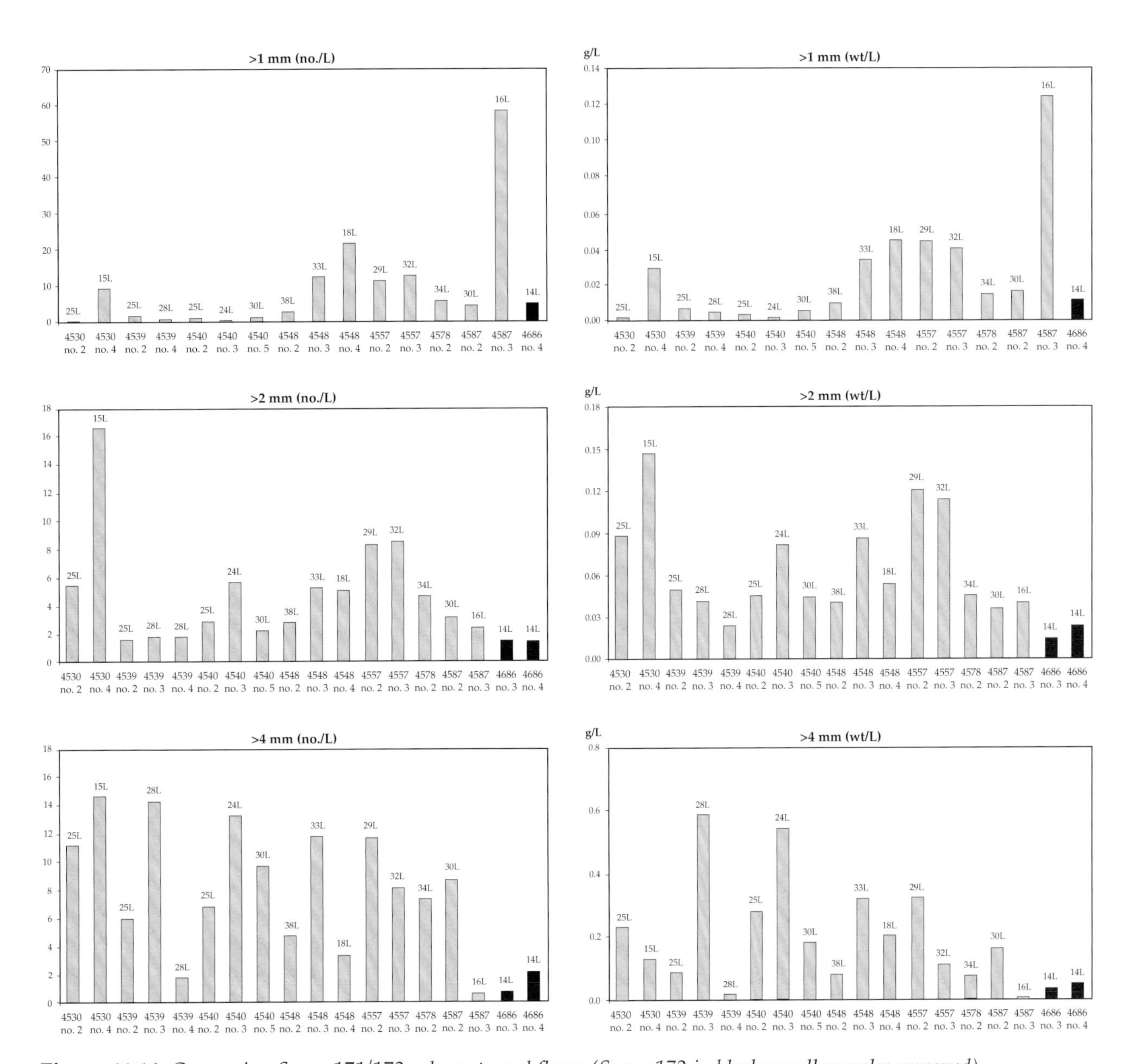

Figure 11.14. *Comparing Space 171/172 rake-outs and floors (Space 172 in black; small samples removed).*

this is the first time a knapping event has ever been found in a primary context at Çatalhöyük. In much the same place, but at a lower stratigraphic level, was another group of obsidian clusters ((5005), (5096) & (5103)) in conjunction with a small, circular pit (5111). From the assemblages' context and form, this appears to be an earlier episode of hoard retrieval and *in situ* knapping.

Aside from these 'dirty-area' clusters containing debitage relating to obsidian industry 1 (blades/ blade-like flakes, cores with minimal platform preparation and relatively high incidences of opposed platform reduction), the lower assemblage(s) also included a large biface made on a thick non-cortical flake. The latter represents a preform for projectile manufacture, indicating that more than one lithic tradition was being performed here in tandem. Preliminary results from recent characterization studies undertaken on a number of pieces of obsidian from these clusters further suggests that more than one source is represented amongst this material (O. Yavuz Ataman pers. comm.), further indicating the convergence of multiple *chaînes opératoires* in these loci. Moreover, if the focus of attention is expanded away from obsidian specifically, to chipped stone in general it is notable that the (4987) assemblage contained a lot of flint. While the heavy residue sample from this unit generated 511 pieces of obsidian (26.89 per litre), it also included 65 pieces of tan/brown/grey limnoquartzite; in both instances the >2-mm sample was the richest ($n = 341$ and $n = 60$). The material was dominated by small, unused, non-cortical flakes; none of this material was technologically diagnostic and the assemblage lacked both cores and end products. With most of the material being so small and regular, one might consider that it represents the tiny waste flakes generated by retouching and modification of larger blanks, perhaps the transformation of prismatic blades into sickles, or perforators. A directly comparable group of material comes from the 'dirty area' of Level IX's Building 17 (5121), Space 170). It should be stressed, however, that in the context of Level X, only in the case of (4987) does one of these 'dirty-area' assemblages contain both obsidian and flint in significant quantities together.

In sum, the southeast part of Building 23 has produced evidence for a range of lithic resources being transformed in the same space, at the same time, with different obsidians plus limnoquartzites. This is interesting, if only to show that in this instance our archaeological category of 'chipped stone' and the grouping of siliceous materials with conchoidal fracture habits as conceptually interrelated material culture (and thus a relevant field of study), does appear to be somewhat borne out by the Neolithic data. Moreover, one can note how this zone of transformative processes represents the intersection of numerous *chaînes opératoires*.

While Building 23 produced good evidence that it originally had at least two obsidian hoards buried in its southeast 'dirty area' (with its associated clusters and pits), Building 18 seems to have lacked such features. It did, however, contain two 'quarry flakes' in the form of individual finds. The first, a large and complete part-cortical flake with heavy use-wear and retouch came from the building's foundation fill (Fig. 11.12c:2 on CD). One might countenance the possibility that it represents the remnants of a hoard, and that the cut of the pit was missed during excavation, however the excavator assures me that this was not the case (C. Cessford pers. comm.). Moreover, the flake is located in the northern part of the Building's fill in Space 172, whereas the hoards are usually found in association with that part of the building with fire installations, which in this instance is the southern Space 171. The second large 'quarry flake', a biface/projectile preform, came from the abandonment infill, again from Building 18's northern end in Space 172 (Fig. 11.12c:1 on CD). One of the Building 18 rake-out units did contain part of a large flake scraper that had been much reduced (Fig. 11.12b:6 on CD), amongst a mass of small non-cortical debris.

While these 'dirty-area' assemblages are clearly dominated by debris relating to the transformation of 'quarry flakes' (obsidian industry 7) and the associated manufacture of small 'in-house' blades/blade-like flakes (obsidian industry 1), they also include small quantities of material that relate to other traditions and other knapping activities. For example, rake-out (4540) in Building 18 also produced an 'edge blade' (obsidian industry 3), and two prismatic blades (obsidian industries 4 or 5) that can be classified as point preforms, one complete (Fig. 11.12b:3 on CD), the other only a tip (Fig. 11.12b:1 on CD). These preforms required further shaping and thinning, processes that would have further contributed to the generation of the tiny non-cortical flakes that give the 'dirty areas' their material-rich texture. Unfortunately it is impossible to clearly delineate and quantify the material relating to these other traditions due to the fact that much of the tiny flake material and shatter is simply undiagnostic.

The 'dirty-area' assemblages also contain implements for which we have no associated manufacturing debris, specifically the larger and more regular prismatic blades (obsidian industries 4 & 5). No doubt these products were introduced from outside (as tools, rather than as performs for further modification), enjoying most of their use-life within the building, until ultimately being included amongst the accumulations of chipped stone and other objects that constituted these material-rich deposits. For example, we have four broken perforators in the Building 18 rake-outs, implements that were probably used in the in-house manufacture of bone and stone beads (Chapters 14 & 17) prior to their discard. Three were obsidian (4540.A3, 4548.A4 & 4557.A3 (Fig. 11.13a:14–15 on CD) and one was tan limnoquartzite (4557.A4).

The argument has been forwarded, and will be developed further in this chapter, that one pattern regarding the consumption of chipped stone in buildings at Çatalhöyük, is the heightened deposition of knapping debris and small quantities of used material close to fire installations. Arguably the relationship might not be with fire *per se*, but with a nexus of transformative processes, not least cooking, plus a range of other activities that one might loosely classify as 'craftwork' (e.g. bead manufacture in Building 18). One can note further patterns within these rich chipped-stone deposits, above and beyond their recurrent location/context, specifically that while evidence suggests that obsidian industry 1 was primarily responsible for the generation of their contents, we find few end products. Naturally the relative proportion of blades and blade-like flakes to 'waste' material will favour heavily the latter, however it remains the case that a significant proportion of the implements generated by this industry were evidently used and deposited elsewhere.

Another significant feature of these assemblages is that not only are the end products poorly represented, or completely absent, but also there appears to have been a deliberate attempt to remove larger pieces in general from these deposits. This is particularly true with regard to the non-cortical knapping debris, in that one rarely recovers pieces over 1.5 cm^2, with all the chunks and larger flakes having been carefully winnowed out; as an aside, the largest remaining flakes are invariably used. One might view this process of extraction as being underwritten by functional considerations, i.e. the removal of material that could either be further reduced / used as an implement, or practical ones, namely that one would not want large, angular and sharp pieces of obsidian left laying around on surfaces where adults and / or children sat to undertake cooking, crafts or other activities. Another, not necessarily mutually-exclusive interpretation, might relate to the highly-structured practices that occurred within these buildings and the underlying attitudes regarding 'dirt' and 'cleanliness', as further witnessed through the re-plastering of walls and surfaces, the cleaning (scraping) of floors and the removal of virtually all mobiliary items (and some fixed) from the building during the process of its abandonment.

While highlighting the contextual and structural similarities of these 'dirty-area' assemblages, it is also important to stress that distinctions can be made between them, both at an intra- and inter-building level. For example, the obsidian assemblages from (4539) and (4578) (Space 171, Building 18) were restricted with regard to the range of traditions represented, containing only debitage and shatter from obsidian industry 1. In turn, while some assemblages were dominated by tiny non-cortical flakes and shatter ((4539) & (4540)), others included larger chunks of material ((4533) & (4548)), indicating that the process of 'winnowing out' the 'macro' material was more / less meticulous in some instances than others. Finally, we also have suggestions that the clusters and rake-outs from the southeast corner of Building 23 included obsidian from different Cappadocian sources (O. Yavuz Ataman pers. comm.). In sum, these differences indicate that subtly variant *chaînes opératoires*, events and associated narratives were embodied in the construction of these assemblages and their depositional events.

A final comment can be made on the small flint component from these 'dirty areas'. Flint was poorly represented in Building 18 as a whole, but in the rake-outs and trample it was restricted almost entirely to limnoquartzites (mainly tan / light brown / brown-grey) in the form of undiagnostic non-cortical flakes (an occasional larger piece having use-wear), plus a few blades and blade-like flakes from flint industry 5. The handful of exceptions included the aforementioned perforator made on a prismatic blade of tan limnoquartzite (4557.A4), a scraper made on a part-cortical flake of 'white planty' limnoquartzite (4530.X4) and four other broken prismatic blades (flint industry 3). The assemblage, such as it is, is might indicate a limited and sporadic production of limnoquartzite blades and blade-like flakes and perhaps some transformation (through retouch and re-sharpening) of non-local prismatic blades. With regard to the locus of activity and the techniques wielded, the consumption of flint in Building 18 mimics that of the 'obsidian', but it occurs far less frequently and in some episodes was not represented at all, as in the case of rake-out (4533).

In the southeast corner of Space 178 in Building 23 there is a different pattern of consumption to that witnessed in Building 18, with a significant quantity of flint accompanying one of the obsidian-rich 'dirty-area' assemblages (4987). The unit produced 65 pieces of limnoquartzite, predominantly brown, and exclusively in the form of fine non-cortical flakes under 1 cm^2 (60 pieces from the >2-mm sample). We here have an instance where both 'obsidian' and flint are being worked and deposited in tandem. The exact mode of transformation is uncertain, for the debris is so regular in form, but at the same time technically undiagnostic. It is tempting to view the material as perhaps relating to the modification of larger blanks, such as the denticulation of blades into sickle elements, or the manufacture of perforators, the implements subsequently removed for use elsewhere. Only one other assemblage amongst the obsidian clusters provided a notable quantity of flint, with (5087) producing thirteen small flakes of the same raw material and form as described above. However, Building 23 generated a not inconsiderable amount of flint, albeit in the form of tiny flakes and shatter, whereas the Building 18 assemblage comprised less individual pieces but weighed almost twice as much (Table 11.12). Simply stated, in Building 23 they made flint implements as well as procuring them from outside, while the inhabitants of Building 18 employed tools that were made elsewhere.

Outside the 'zones of transformative processes'

Beyond the 'dirty areas' there is a rapid fall-off in the consumption of chipped stone in Buildings 18 and 23, i.e. the floor surfaces of Space 172 and Space 178 north of ridge F.528. In Building 18, heavy-residue samples from the remnant northern strip of floor in Space 172 (4686) indicated that small amounts of obsidian were in circulation in this part of the structure, but no flint. The same could be noted with respect to

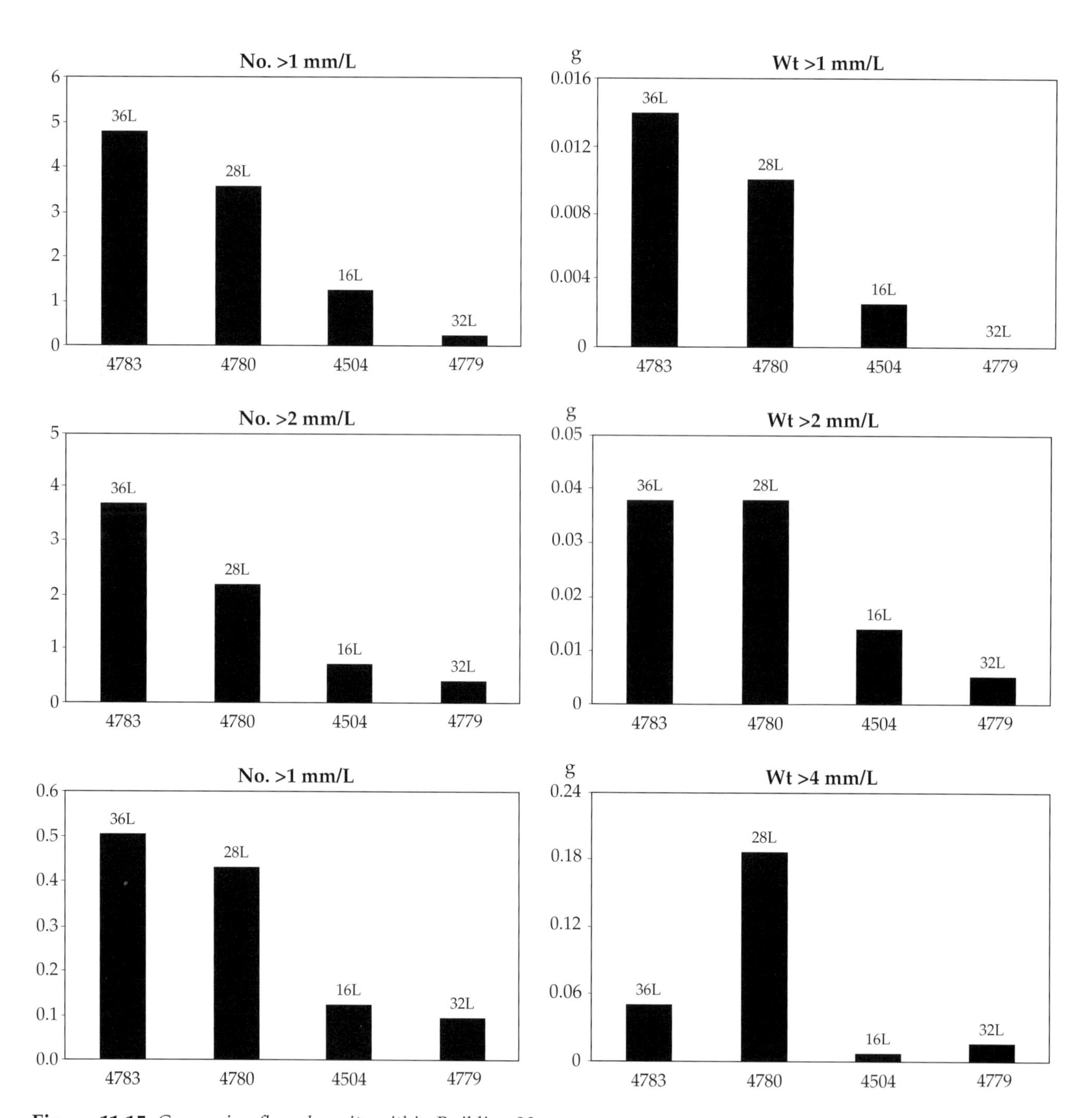

Figure 11.15. *Comparing floor deposits within Building 23.*

Building 23, with floor surfaces (4779) and (4504) producing notably less material than from the 'dirty-area' floor, with the former unit the least productive of all (Fig. 11.15). The material from these contexts is usually a combination of small non-cortical flakes, shatter and limited quantities of debitage from obsidian industry 1; flint is very poorly represented at the 'micro' level in these areas.

While chipped-stone consumption has a strong association with fire installations (and/or the 'zones of transformative processes'), one can conversely note a negative relationship between chipped stone and other constructed features, bins in particular. Little obsidian came from the fills and structural debris associated with these features in Building 18 ((4664) & (4669)–(4673)), certainly much less than was recovered from (4686), the related floor in Space 172. Only in one instance was it possible to suggest an intentional relationship between chipped stone and these features, with an ochre-stained finely-worked perforator made from a prismatic blade of striped brown/white limnoquartzite placed into the northwestern bin F.515 (Fig.

11.12c:3 on CD). One might consider this a structured deposit, with the tool possibly related to the bead manufacture that occurred in the other ('dirty') end of the building, the piece interred deliberately in the process of abandoning the structure, with an ochre layer subsequently deposited in bins F.515 and F.516.

Beyond the 'dirty areas', much of the chipped stone within these buildings seems to be present in the form of a low 'background noise', the residue of occasional tool use and modification, shatter and spray from the knapping activities of the 'dirty area', or perhaps in some instances introduced accidentally as part of the plaster laid on floor and wall. There are exceptions, albeit in the form of significant individual finds, usually relatively large in size, of non-local production and almost all from Building 18. This material can be viewed as relating to two main themes: deposits relating to construction and those relating to destruction and abandonment.

Instances of make-up and construction

There are sufficient distinct deposits of 'interesting' groups of chipped stone associated with instances of make-up and construction to warrant the claim that obsidian and flint, in certain forms, enjoyed an important role in the events surrounding the building of a structure at Çatalhöyük and the creation of certain features within it. For example, in Building 18 a large, sharp obsidian flake was found behind oven F.473, covered by a layer of plaster on the northern face of the southern wall of Space 171 (wall F.470). The flake is highly distinctive in form (it looks like a pair of obsidian trousers), and appears to be a rejuvenation piece from the base of a naviform blade core (obsidian industry 4), bifacially retouched and heavily used (Fig. 11.13b:5 on CD). Technically and typologically it is a unique piece in our Level X assemblage; interestingly, a grooved antler sickle-handle (4677.X1) had been built into the wall of bin F.516 in Space 172, diagonally opposite oven F.473, arguably an analogous act of consumption.

Building 18 also produced a small but interesting group of material from (4574), the make-up deposit between ovens F.499 and F.472 in Space 171. The five pieces of obsidian comprised three non-cortical flakes, one notched (Fig. 11.12a:18 on CD) and another used (4574.A2), the medial section of a fine, narrow regular prismatic blade (4574.A3), plus a more distinctive prismatic blade, 4.6-cm-long part-cortical, heavily used and backed (Fig. 11.12a:1 on CD). In turn, the base of oven F.501 produced three pieces of chipped stone, two of which were flint, including part of a small brown limnoquartzite blade, plus a larger used, non-local prismatic blade of red radiolarite (4589.A2). Another make-up layer, (4579), included a chunk of a much reduced 'quarry flake' (Fig. 11.12b:9 on CD), but given that it was not found alone, but with another twelve pieces of obsidian from the >1-mm and >2-mm heavy-residue samples, it may represent 'background noise' in the 'dirty area', rather than a piece that had been deliberately placed as part of the acts surrounding the making a new floor surface.

Instances of destruction, demolition and abandonment

The other type of context where one notes the deliberate addition/deposition of 'interesting' pieces of chipped stone relate to instances of destruction, demolition and abandonment, such as the aforementioned placement of a limnoquartzite perforator in bin F.515 (Fig. 11.12c:3 on CD). Significantly, another perforator, of translucent 'planty-yellow' limnoquartzite was recovered from the infill of oven F.499 (4575.A1), an analogous act both with regard to the type of implement and its consumption in the act of demolition and abandonment of a built feature. A third perforator/ borer from Building 18, made on a prismatic blade of grey-blue and red-striped radiolarite, came from the infill deposit associated with the structure's abandonment (Fig. 11.12c on CD). While this implement was one of a number of pieces of chipped stone from this unit (i.e. it is not a unique deposit akin to the examples from bin F.515 or oven F.499), perforators seem to be a recurrent and highly-emblematic form of material culture in Building 18. This suggests that the inclusion of the radiolarite piece into the abandonment infill was both deliberate and meaningful.

Infill (4355) also produced one of the complete 'quarry flakes' (a biface) discussed above (Fig 11.12c:1 on CD), while the other individual 'quarry flake' came from (4689), Building 18's foundation fill (Fig 11.12c:2 on CD), though one could argue that this layer could equally be perceived as the termination of the area's previous use, as much as it represents the construction of something new. Thus perhaps one might see all of these structured deposits as marking events of transformation, signalling and embodying liminal spaces and times between 'what was' and 'what would be', acts of commemoration and change.

Building 18 also produced a used bifacially-retouched tanged point from (4668) (Fig. 11.12a:4 on CD), a thick plaster layer related to the destruction of a plastered feature during the structure's demolition and abandonment. In turn, a small, complete and unused bifacial point came from the fill of a post-pit in the western part of Building 23 (Space 200), deposited there after the post had been retrieved (5129.X1). These are significant pieces because they form part of a general pattern of placing obsidian projectiles in post-retrieval pits as part of an abandonment ritual, specifically the post-pit in the centre of the western wall, having also been recorded in Buildings 2 and 17 (Level IX), plus Building 1 (see below).

Finally one can comment on the negative evidence, i.e. what we do not find amongst these contexts of destruction, demolition and abandonment. For instance, despite the recovery of an alleged sickle-handle (4677.X1) from Space 172, no flint sickles were recognized in (the remnants of) Building 18. One recalls the number of sickles from the earlier middens of Space 181, suggesting that at certain times it might have been considered inappropriate to leave such implements in a building after it had been abandoned (a claim somewhat complicated by the data from Space 182, Building 17, Level IX). On a grander scale, one can note how little 'macro' material comes from the excavation of houses (tools and chunky debris), a reflection of the regular 'cleaning' events within the rhythm of a building's life and a result of the treatment of mobiliary material culture in the processes of abandoning the structure.

It seems quite clear that most complete chipped-stone tools were removed at this time, albeit with certain pieces being deliberately left behind as structured deposits, such as the perforators from the bin and oven fill in Building 18 (Fig. 11.12c:3 on CD). While this removal of whole implements could be rationalized in terms as 'curation', one is tempted to view such practices as aligned to the inhabitants' notions of 'cleanliness' as witnessed through the scouring of floor surfaces, the re-plastering events, plus the division of 'dirty' and 'clean' areas, as part of the overarching social constructs that regulated how a building was treated during life and how it was abandoned. Perhaps a more telling insight to this world-view comes through considering the ashy rake-out assemblages, where one can often discern the deliberate attempt to winnow out the larger pieces, as for example with (4540) where only one piece of obsidian, out of 167, exceeded 1 cm in length. While one can note these general patterns, there are exceptions, perhaps even instances of resistance to such practices, as for example with the clusters of knapping debris from Building 23 that were left *in situ* ((4987), (4989) & (5095)).

Level IX

Level IX is represented in the South Area by Buildings 2, 16, 17 and 22. Buildings 2 and 17 were almost entirely undisturbed and significant progress was made in their excavation during 1998–99. Conversely, much of Building 16 (Space 164) was excavated in 1963 as Mellaart's Shrine IX.8, with only a small area (*c.* 2.4 × 1.2 m) left untouched in its southeast corner; Building 22 had also been dug largely in the 1960s.

Building 2 was subdivided into two spaces, with the larger room (Space 117) to the west and the smaller (Space 116) to the east, the former having been excavated to floor level and containing a series of fire installations, platforms, bins and other features. Building 16 was denoted by a single space (Space 164) despite the evidence for an original east–west dividing wall; the southeast corner contained a sequence of four fire installations, a constructed raised area of uncertain function (F.438), remnants of 'dirty' and clean floors and two obsidian clusters ((4305) & (4317)). Building 17 comprised a large eastern room (Space 170) and a narrow western space (Space 182); the structure underwent many phases of re-modelling and produced an elaborate series of features, including fire installations, platforms, bins, basins, plastered floors and 'dirty areas'. Building 22 retained little archaeology of note and will not be discussed further in this section. The four buildings generated 11,476 pieces of chipped stone, 11,070 of obsidian (96.5 per cent) and 406 of flint (3.5 per cent), weighing 5056.199 g and 286.663 g respectively (Tables 11.1 & 11.4).

The obsidian (Fig. 11.16a–e on CD)

The discussion of the Level IX obsidian industries on the CD is based on a sample of 2974 pieces, representing all dry-sieve and >4-mm obsidian from Buildings 2 (*n* = 1725), 16 (*n* = 169) and 17 (*n* = 1080), i.e. not only the priority unit material. The Level IX obsidian assemblage is the largest studied thus far (Table 11.1), and is technologically and typologically comparable to that from Level X. As with the preceding phase the obsidian was dominated by material relating to the 'in-house' obsidian industry 1 manufacture of small blades from opposed platform nuclei. Similarly, there were a few 'edge blades' (obsidian industry 3), plus a number of non-local prismatic blades, mainly from unipolar cores (obsidian industry 5), though some opposed platform products were recorded (obsidian industry 4). Interestingly, Building 17 produced three large flake scrapers akin to those that defined obsidian industry 6, a tradition that seemed to disappear after Level Pre-XII.B (Fig. 11.16d:1–2, 4 on CD). In turn, large 'quarry flakes' (obsidian industry 7) were recovered from two of the Level IX buildings. Those from Building 2 came from a hoard buried in Space 117 (Fig. 11.13), while Building 17 produced a few individual pieces, including an interesting group of five conjoining fragments distributed between Spaces 170 and 182. The following analysis is based on a sample of 2182 pieces from the dry-sieve and >4-mm heavy residue, coming from Buildings 2 (*n* = 933), 16 (*n* = 169) and 17 (*n* = 1080).

The flint (Fig. 11.16f:9 on CD)

Of the 406 pieces of flint from Level IX, the discussion of the flint industries on the attached CD are based on a sample of 248 pieces, namely all dry-sieve and >4-mm material from Buildings 2 (n = 26), 16 (n = 15) and 17 (n = 207), i.e. not only that flint from the priority units. Level IX generated 406 pieces of flint, 3.5 per cent of the chipped-stone assemblage from this phase (5.4 per cent by weight, Tables 11.1 & 11.4), broadly comparable figures to those from Level X. Most of the flint comes from Building 17 (Tables 11.14 & 11.16–11.18), 76.1 per cent by number and 67.2 per cent by weight, mainly in the form of grey/brown/tan limnoquartzite shatter from the 'dirty area' in Space 170 ((5121) in particular). Of the 406 pieces of flint from Level IX, the study is based on a sample of 248 pieces.

Table 11.14. *Chipped stone from Level IX by building, count and weight by raw material.*

Building	Chipped stone count	Obsidian count	Obsidian weight (g)	'Flint' count	'Flint' weight (g)
2	4348	4273	3583.470	75	85.387
16	426	410	268.458	16	8.320
17	6618	6309	1161.880	309	192.536
22	82	78	40.389	6	0.420

Table 11.15. *Obsidian from Level IX by building, count, weight and mean weight.*

Building	Count	% of total	Weight (g)	% of total	Mean weight (g)
2	4348	39.02	3583.470	71.42	0.82
16	410	3.68	268.458	5.35	0.65
17	6309	56.62	1161.880	23.16	0.18
22	76	0.68	3.498	0.07	0.05

Table 11.16. *'Flint' from Level IX by building, Number, weight and mean weight.*

Building	Count	% of total	Weight (g)	% of total	Mean weight (g)
2	75	18.47	85.387	29.79	1.14
16	16	3.94	8.320	2.90	1.92
17	309	76.11	192.536	67.16	0.62
22	6	1.48	0.420	0.15	0.07

Table 11.17. *Relative proportions of obsidian to 'flint' within Level IX buildings by count.*

Building	Obsidian	% of total	'Flint'	% of total
2	4348	98.30	75	1.70
16	410	96.24	16	3.76
17	6309	95.33	309	4.67
22	76	92.68	6	7.32

Table 11.18. *Relative proportions of obsidian to 'flint' within Level IX buildings by weight.*

Building	Obsidian weight (g)	% of total	'Flint' weight (g)	% of total
2	3583.470	97.67	85.387	2.33
16	268.458	96.99	8.320	3.01
17	1161.880	85.78	192.536	14.22
22	3.498	89.28	0.420	10.72

Raw materials

As with the flint from Level X, the assemblage was dominated by various coloured limnoquartzites, 95.6 per cent of the total (n = 237), with the tan/brown/grey-brown/grey variety the most popular (226, 91.1 per cent), followed by small quantities of yellow, pink, pink-red, orange and milky-white variants. The remaining material constituted eleven pieces of radiolarite, of which eight were the red variant known from previous levels, plus single pieces of dark-brown, grey-brown and grey-green. The distribution of the flint amongst the buildings is proportionate to the overall quantity of chipped stone recovered from these structures (Tables 11.14–11.18), with each of the raw materials, including the radiolarite, represented in those assemblages studied in detail (Buildings 2, 16 & 17).

Technology

Technologically the Level IX assemblage is similar to that preceding it, with a quantity of non-local prismatic blades from unipolar and opposed platform traditions (flint industries 2 & 3), one or two microblades that may represent residual material from much earlier levels (flint industry 1), plus a number of the 'in-house', small blades/blade-like flakes (flint industry 5). The assemblage was dominated by flakes however (n = 207, 83.5 per cent), only four of which bore any remnant cortex (1.9 per cent). The majority were unused, with only two exceptions (Table 11.7), one having been notched (1821.A1), the other a scraper (5232.A1).

Notable pieces include a small, opposed platform prismatic blade-core of yellow limnoquartzite from Building 17's Space 182 (flint industry 2), an extremely rare piece (Fig. 11.16f:8 on CD), plus 36 blades and blade-like flakes of various technologies. Typically, most of the blades had been used (n = 22, 61.1 per cent), while a not dissimilar proportion had been retouched (n = 20, 55.6 per cent). The implements included six perforators, four backed blades, three glossed blades/sickles, two notched blades (one also

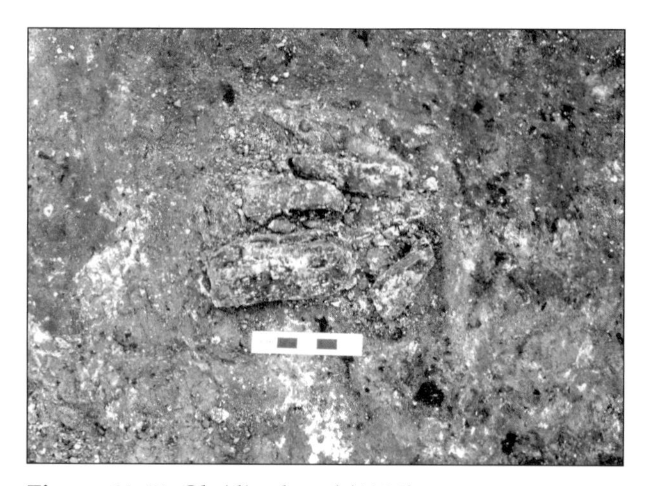

Figure 11.17. *Obsidian hoard (4138).*

backed), a backed double end-scraper and four with simple linear retouch.

The consumption of chipped stone in Level IX

The chipped-stone assemblages from Buildings 2, 16 and 17 included material relating to each of the various obsidian and flint industries documented in Level IX. This general equality in the distribution of local technical *savoir-faire* and access to non-local products, replicates what was seen in Level X. Furthermore, the Building 2, 16 and 17 assemblages also appear to include similar ranges of raw material, such as the various coloured limnoquartzites and the rarer red radiolarite. It would be a mistake, however, to take the above statement to indicate that the consumption of chipped stone in each of these buildings was the same; distinctions exist and these will be commented on below.

Consumption inside the buildings

That Buildings 2 and 17 produced the larger quantity of chipped stone out of the four Level IX structures is not surprising given the degree to which Building 16 had been truncated by the 1960s excavations and the fact that Building 22 has yet to be excavated (Tables 11.14–11.15). However, if one considers the ratio of obsidian to flint per structure, then they once again show great similarities, especially with regard to number (Table 11.17). There is some discrepancy when considering the ratios of raw materials on the basis of weight, with 98.3 per cent of the chipped stone from Building 2 being obsidian (Table 11.17). This can be explained by the fact that the structure produced three obsidian hoards ((4209), (4210), (4138)) and a cluster (4134). Building 16 has a similar imbalance (97.0 per cent) due to it having generated two assemblages containing large and heavy pieces of obsidian, (4317) a hoard and (4305) an obsidian cluster. The current absence of an obsidian hoard from Building 17 helps to deflate the figure for obsidian in Table 11.17, as does the number of quite large flint implements from Space 182 (including a 12 cm+ blade and a blade-core).

The analysis of the Level IX chipped stone focused on the material from Buildings 2, 16 and 17. In each case most of their obsidian came from the 'dirty' areas in proximity to fire installations. In Buildings 16 and 17, these were located in the southern part of these north–south structures, as for example represented by (4305), (4316), (4317) and (4318) in the former building, plus (5021) and (5041) in Space 170 of the latter structure. In Building 2, the foci of fire installations was also located in southern part of the structure in Space 117 (even though it had an east–west orientation), with an associated concentration of chipped stone, including three obsidian hoards ((4209), (4210), (4134)), a cluster (4138) and obsidian-rich ashy rake-outs (e.g. (4136) & (4137)).

The same pattern generally holds true for the distribution of flint in these structures, the most productive deposits invariably being obsidian-rich as well. Having said that, only Building 17 produced any notable (single unit) concentrations of flint. For instance, a number of the obsidian-rich heavy-residue samples taken from (5021) in the 'dirty area' of Building 17 (Space 170) also generated a lot of tan/grey-brown/brown limnoquartzite, with 27 pieces from heavy-residue Sample 5021.29 (>2-mm mesh, 24 litres), while Sample 5041.2 (another rich rake-out) produced 31 (>2-mm mesh, 14 litres). In contrast, the largest quantity of flint from a single unit in Building 2 was seven pieces from (3340) (1-mm mesh, one litre) and two cases of four pieces from (4304) and (4342) in Building 16 (>4-mm mesh, 35 and 26 litres respectively). Nine units in Building 17 (all Space 170) produced seven or more pieces of flint from single heavy-residue sample, while the infill deposit (4416) produced 15. The above statements are, of course, fairly general and there is a need for further investigation of how these generic raw materials were consumed within the structures, on an industry-by-industry basis.

The 'dirty areas'

As in Level X, each building produced clear evidence for the 'in-house' performance of obsidian industry 1, i.e. the manufacture of small blades/blade-like flakes. While the end products, cores and debris from this tradition were recovered throughout the structures, it seems that as with the preceding level, it was the 'dirty areas' that represent the foci for this industry. While we lack any *in situ* manufacturing debris akin to that from Level X's Building 23, the combination

Table 11.19. *Average number of pieces of obsidian per litre of water-sieved soil from the (5020) and (5021) floor deposits in Space 170, Building 17, Level IX.*

Fraction size	(5020) No. / L	(5020) flotation samples	(5021) No. / L	(5021) flotation samples
>1 mm	0.29	9	32.48	4
>2 mm	0.16	8	9.14	4
>4 mm	0.04	7	1.77	4

of assemblage size, structure and freshness combine to suggest that these small blades / blade-like flakes were knapped in the vicinity of the fire installations.

In Building 17, (5021) is the artefact-rich and ashy matrix associated with hearth F.536 that constitutes Space 170s Phase B 'dirty area', an extremely productive deposit in contrast to (5020) the floor immediately to the north of a white plaster ridge that separates the 'dirty' from the 'clean' areas (Table 11.19). The assemblage(s) from (5021) are dominated by tiny and unused non-cortical flakes and shatter, a high proportion of which was recovered complete and fresh (>68 per cent). Most, if not all of this material can be categorized as debris or end products from obsidian industry 1 (Fig. 11.16c:9 on CD). From a sample of 88 pieces of obsidian from the >4-mm mesh 87.5 per cent, were non-cortical flakes ($n = 77$), only one of which had been used and modified into a scraper (Fig. 11.16d:1 on CD). The remaining pieces included a small part-cortical flake, two small opposed-platform cores and eight unused and fragmentary blades / blade-like flakes. The end products are under-represented and little material shows signs of use, i.e. the implements once knapped were removed to be used elsewhere.

While the limited number of blades can be interpreted with reference to functional concerns (i.e. taken for use elsewhere), one might suggest that there was also a deliberate and repeated practice of 'winnowing out' the larger chunks of obsidian, as most of the (5021) assemblage is made up of very small pieces. Furthermore, we know that the 'dirty area' is an area of other craft / transformative activities, yet we do not find any discarded tools here, none of the notches, or the perforators that we found in Building 18 (Level X) just the one scraper (Fig. 11.16d:1 on CD). Once again one could invoke a 'common-sense' explanation whereby the sharp / dangerous chunks of obsidian were removed from an area where people worked and cooked, but we know from other structures that this was not always the case (e.g. the clusters of Buildings 23 and 2). Instead, one might suggest that this particularly careful treatment of 'waste' in Building 17 tied in more generally with the accentuated regular, cyclical cleaning of this structure.

Amongst the very few pieces over 2 cm in size ($n = 4$), is one of the aforementioned core fragments (Fig. 11.16b:1 on CD), 3.7 cm long, part-cortical and quite obviously made from one of the large 'quarry flakes' (obsidian industry 7) of the type seen in hoards from this and the preceding levels. Retouch along one edge suggests that the piece may have originally entered the site in the form of a side-scraper; such pieces have been recovered from the quarry / knapping areas at the Göllü Dağ-East, specifically the Bitlikeler workshop associated with the Kayırlı flow (Balkan-Atlı & Der Aprahamian 1998, 249–52 & fig. 10).

Assemblages from other Level IX rake-out contexts show much the same pattern, namely a dominance of fresh, primarily non-cortical and unused debris, plus the occasional exhausted nucleus from obsidian industry 1, and an under-representation of the actual blades / blade-like flakes. From Building 16 this included (4304), (4316), (4318) and (4342), with (4505) coming the closest to an *in situ* knapping deposit that had not been picked clean. Defined as an 'obsidian cluster' associated with rake-out (4304), it contained 60 pieces of obsidian from all samples, the diagnostic component clearly relating to the 'in-house' blade / blade-like flake tradition, obsidian industry 1 (Fig. 11.16g:5&8 on CD). It was distinct from the usual rake-out contexts owing to the larger size of many pieces, 12 blanks exceeding 2 cm in length.

In Building 2 we have much the same pattern with rake-out / trample assemblages in Space 117, as represented by (4137) and (4139). Both were extremely productive but also quite homogeneous, dominated by small, unused, fresh, non-cortical flakes, plus a few obsidian industry 1 cores and blades / blade-like flakes; once more the end products were under-represented. Associated with these rake-outs were two intact hoards ((4209) & (4210)) and a cluster of obsidian (4134) that may represent the remnants of a hoard that had been recovered and worked; it represents Building 2's best candidate for an *in situ* knapping deposit. (4209) was the larger of the two undisturbed hoards, a tightly-packed group of blanks (4209.X1–21 & X23–43) found together with part of a bone ring (4209.X22). The 42 pieces of obsidian appeared to have been deposited in an organic container. Some 25 cm southsouthwest of this hoard was another smaller cluster of chipped stone, eight pieces of obsidian and a single limnoquartzite blade (4210). The cluster of obsidian that defined unit (4134) comprised 69 pieces of obsidian found laying together in a shallow depression, with 18 / 24 pieces recovered complete (dry-sieve sample) despite the fact that much of the material was over 2 cm^2 and quite delicate. The distinction between the two types of unit, rake-out vs cluster, is one of the average size of the pieces and the assemblage's structure/form. It suggests that the assemblage was covered relatively quickly after it had been knapped, rather than undergoing the 'winnowing' process that one associates with rake-out material. The material was again made up of blade and blade-like flakes (e.g. 4134.A1), plus small opposed-platform cores from obsidian industry 1. Unfortunately there was no time to attempt refitting.

While obsidian industry 1 was obviously the primary knapping tradition performed in these 'dirty areas' (with the distinct possibility that the majority of its products were used elsewhere), it remains the case that, as in Level X, these material-rich areas should be considered more holistically and appreciated as zones of transformative processes, involving not only the reduction and modification of obsidian, but also food preparation, and a variety of other activities. Also, while I have been at pains throughout this chapter to avoid a reductionist approach with regard to 'chipped stone', it can be noted that the 'dirty areas' do produce evidence for the intersection of variant lithic traditions/*chaînes opératoires*. Nowhere else in a building does one have evidence for the comparable consumption of chipped-stone industries. By this I mean that in these zones of transformative processes, we have evidence for numerous obsidian and flint industries being performed in tandem, the one time that our siliceous media come together as a generic consumption of 'chipped stone'.

For instance, it is not uncommon for the larger rake-out/trample assemblages to also include fragmentary non-local prismatic obsidian blades, as for example with products from obsidian industry 5 in (4305) and (4134) (Building 16; Fig. 11.16g:3 on CD), though such material is notably absent from the large (5021) assemblage in Building 17 (a further indication of the rigorous 'cleansing' process this area cyclically underwent). These deposits also produce the occasional non-local flint blade, as for example in (4304) (Building 16), with a flint industry three retouched unipolar prismatic blade (Fig. 11.16g:1 on CD). There are also fragments of 'quarry flakes' from a number of these assemblages (e.g. Building 16's (4134) and Building 17's (5021)), employed as the cores of the 'in-house' obsidian industry 1 (Fig. 11.16b:1 on CD).

To summarize, in these 'dirty areas' we have evidence of multiple reduction sequences being enacted alongside each other, though it is important to acknowledge that not all of these industries are represented at the same stage of their *chaînes opératoires*. For example, for obsidian industry 1 these contexts essentially represent the point of departure, as it is here that the tradition's raw materials (obsidian industry 7's 'quarry flakes') are accessed and the manufacture of blades/blade-like flakes commences. Conversely, these zones represent the 'end of the line' for obsidian industry 7, the large flat scraper-flakes and bifaces that were produced up in the Göllü Dağ-East quarries. In turn, the fine non-local prismatic blades that comprise obsidian industries 4 and 5 arrive in the 'dirty areas' ready-made for use and modification, retouched into points, for example. Similarly, the fine non-local prismatic blades that comprise flint industries 2 and 3 also arrive ready-made, then transformed into sickles, perforators, backed pieces or end-scrapers. Finally, we have the occasional evidence for the introduction of a decorticated chunk of limnoquartzite, subsequently reduced in the manufacture of the small blades/blade-like flakes of flint industry 5.

While the above data have been used to emphasise structural and conceptual similarities between the 'dirty-area' assemblages of Level IX (and Level X), one must also acknowledge the variations between the material from these rake-out/trample contexts (the differences between the two hoards were noted above). Perhaps the clearest difference relates to the variant scale of these assemblages. While on average they are the most productive deposits in a building, they can range quite significantly in their relative densities. It is difficult to ascertain as to whether this is a reflection of time, or intensity of manufacture. Regarding time, the excavation process has elucidated quite clearly that these 'dirty areas' are comprised of a series of overlapping lenses, representing distinct horizons of deposition and accumulation in a relatively restricted area. However, it is exceedingly difficult, if not impossible, to gauge the temporal depth represented by each lens of ash/chipped-stone/bone-rich deposit. Does a particularly thick deposit represent a long-term accumulation of debris from craft working and cooking, or the remains of a short period of heightened activity? While one struggles to disentangle the time and effort embodied in these deposits, one can at least gain an insight to the practices that occurred in these areas during a building's history (even a sub-phase), their rhythms, their patterns, or lack thereof.

For example, one can query the relationship between the consumption of 'obsidian' and flint in these dirty areas. It has been noted already how the 'dirty' floor area of (5021) in Building 17's Space 170 produced significant quantities of both obsidian and flint debris, parallel evidence for their transformation in the same place, although representing quite distinct reduction stages within two distinct *chaînes opératoires*. While each of the heavy-residue samples taken from (5021) produced quantities of obsidian, the recovery of tan/brown/grey limnoquartzite was much more intermittent. For example, there were certain heavy-residue samples that produced virtually no flint, as for example Sample 5021.28 which generated obsidian from the >1-mm, >2-mm and >4-mm meshes (*n* = 12, 16 and 3) but no flint. Similarly, Sample 5021.30 produced considerable amounts of obsidian from the >1-mm, >2-mm and >4-mm meshes (*n* = 84, 66 and 16), but only two pieces of limnoquartzite from the >4-mm mesh. In contrast, Sample 5021.29 contained both obsidian and limnoquartzite in each of the three meshes, while Sample 5021.30 produced obsidian in three and limnoquartzite in two of the meshes (>2-mm and >4-mm). This suggests that while it was considered appropriate to work different raw materials in the same area the reduction of obsidian (mainly in the tradition of obsidian industry 1 and probably primarily in the form of Göllü Dağ-East material) was by far the more common, a recurrent (and part-defining) practice in these zones of transformative processes, while the working of limnoquartzite was far more episodic.

As to the technological significance of these (5021) flint assemblages, the material was remarkably homogeneous, all tiny (<1-mm^2) unused flakes of tan/brown/grey limnoquartzite, offering no obvious clue as to the manufacturing sequence that it was related to. Originally there was some discussion amongst the team members as to whether the debris resulted from chunks of limnoquartzite being used as a tinderlight to start the fire, rather than knapping. The homogeneity of the material argues against this theory, as one might have expected a more varied range of irregular chunks, chips and shatter from a strike-a-light. Instead it is thought that these tiny flakes are the residue from the modification of existing flint implements, i.e. the tiny retouch flakes from shaping a blade into a sickle, or a perforator.

It is within, or close to, the zones of transformative processes that we also find our evidence for at least one mechanism by which some of the 'raw material' entered the building. Hoards have been recovered from two of the Level IX buildings, one each from Buildings 2 and 16, though we are to be reminded that Buildings 17 and 22 have yet to be fully excavated. The Building 2 hoard (4138) was found laying in a shallow depression, located in the middle of the southern half of Space 117, sealed by the base of an oven F.412. The hoard comprised 16 large pieces of obsidian that were accorded X-find status (weighing 169.8 g), plus another 22 pieces from the dry sieve and 79 pieces from the heavy residue. The 'macro' components of the assemblage relate primarily to obsidian industry 4, with a complete opposed platform blade core (4138.X1), and two prismatic blades with bipolar dorsal scars (4138.X5 & X10), though one heavily-used prismatic blade appeared to be unipolar, obsidian industry 5 (4138.X2). There were also a number of blades whose technology was uncertain as their original dorsal surfaces had been obscured by retouch in the process of modifying them into point preforms (4138.X4 & X10–11). Among the remaining material were two large chunks/cores (4138.X8 & X15); it is difficult to tell if they were much reduced pieces relating to the blade industry, or parts of obsidian industry 7 'quarry flakes'. The hoard also included a 5.01-cm section of a prismatic blade of dark reddish-brown liminoquartzite (4138.X6), apparently from a unipolar core (flint industry 3); flint is extremely rare in hoard contexts. The Building 16 hoard, (4317) was less impressive in scale and related to a different industry. The main component were eight 'quarry flakes', or chunks thereof (obsidian industry 7), two part cortical and all quite small compared to the contents of other hoards.

Outside the 'zones of transformative processes'

In general one notes a significant fall-off in the consumption of chipped stone beyond the 'dirty areas', akin to the pattern documented in Level X, though Space 182 in Building 17 somewhat bucks the trend and will be returned to below. One can again witness a largely negative relationship between chipped stone and certain structural features, ovens and bins in particular. For instance, the series of make-up, floors and structural deposits related to Building 16's ovens (F.435, F.438, F.439 & F.457) produced little chipped stone. Similarly low quantities of material came from the majority of units associated with the Building 17 ovens (F.546, F.547 & F.555), with the exception of (5162), the base/lining of oven F.546 in the in south-west corner of Space 170, which produced 20 pieces of obsidian from the >4-mm heavy-residue sample. However, the assemblage (flakes and 'in-house' blades) appears to be residual from the underlying fill that had been disturbed in the excavation of a small hole for the oven's construction. A similar concentration of obsidian was recorded from debris (3673) relating to oven F.290 in Building 2 (Space 117), again interpreted as material in secondary context, a reflection of the structure's proximity to a 'dirty area', as opposed to representing a focus of consumption in itself. Nor does there appear to have been any strong association between the consumption of chipped stone and Building 17's basins (F. 569, 570, 577, 578, 586), clay ball pit (5154), or bins (F.547), features that tended to be equally unproductive in Level X.

Instances of make-up and construction

We currently lack many significant instances where 'interesting' implements were included, or deposited in make-up and construction contexts in Buildings 2, 16 and 17, akin to those discussed from Buildings 9 and 18 in Level X. Upon completing the excavation of our Level IX structures it will be possible to comment further as to whether similar practices can be documented.

Instances of destruction, demolition and abandonment

Level IX produces further evidence to suggest that in certain instances and in certain forms, chipped stone was employed deliberately in the acts performed during the remodelling and abandonment of a building. One act seems to have been particularly significant, that of placing a used projectile in the fill of a structure's pots-hole after the wooden post had been retrieved. This practice is documented in both Buildings 2 and 17, having already been documented in Level X (Building 23, Space 200, 5129.X1), and recorded again in later levels (see below). In Building 2, the middle section (in two pieces) of a finely-worked point (2048.A1) came from the post-retrieval fill associated with the post-hole located on the western wall of Space 117. The projectile was unifacially retouched, made on a long prismatic blade (5.32 cm long) from an opposed platform core technology (obsidian industry 4) and appears to have been used, with a snap scar towards the proximal end. In Building 17 (Space 170) a finely-worked, leaf-shaped point came from (4645), a unit recorded as the basal fill in the structure but possibly the upper part of the fill related to the post-retrieval pit in the central part of the northern wall. The projectile is different in form to that from Building 2, made on a non-local blade and with covering bifacial retouch; it was also recovered complete and had an unbroken and unused tip (Fig. 11.16a:8 on CD). Given how delicate the implement is, it seems most likely that the piece was deliberately placed here (in the top of the post-hole) and then covered by fill. While the fill associated with the post-hole on the west wall in Space 170 did not produce a point, one is tempted to associate the cluster (5183) with the upper part of the fill. The objects comprised a greenstone axe and two conjoining fragments of a large scraper/'quarry flake' (obsidian industry 7), 5183.X1 and X3.

One does not, however, see the same acts being performed with each episode of post-retrieval. Indeed, in many instances the fills of these features produced little or no chipped stone; for example (4656) and (5068) in Space 170, Building 17 contained none at all, while (2303) and (2726) in Space 117, Building 2 generated one tiny flake each. Perhaps in these instances other media were employed in the rites associated with the retrieval of the post and the subsequent backfilling of the pit. For example, a human skull was placed at the base of fill (5019) from the post-retrieval pit in the northwest corner of Space 170 (Building 17); heavy residue produced a relatively large amount of obsidian ($n = 18$), the most interesting of which was the medial section of a used non-local prismatic blade (Fig. 11.17a:5 on CD). The blade (obsidian industry 5) was not particularly striking, though these products were relatively rare in the building, so it might represent a piece that was deposited deliberately.

Some of these features are quite productive with regard to relatively undiagnostic shatter, though in certain instances this may simply reflect the fact that the soil used to fill the post-holes came from nearby obsidian rich 'dirty areas'. For example, in Building 17 fill (5036) produced four, five and eight pieces of obsidian from the >1-mm, >2-mm and >4-mm meshes, in marked contrast to the fills (4656) and (5068) which contained no chipped stone, while (4141) in Space 117 (Building 2) had on average three pieces per litre of soil, the third highest concentration of obsidian in the building after the (4137) and (4138) hoards. Similarly, (4302) in Building 16 generated a lot of shatter.

The final example of a particular chipped-stone implement being employed in abandonment rites comes from Building 17, involving the destruction of a large scraper, six conjoining fragments of which were discovered distributed within both Spaces 170 and 182, having been placed on the floor, or included in the very first fill dumped into the structure. The implement was an example of a large flake scraper, made on a 'quarry flake' (obsidian industry 7), albeit with much finer invasive retouch than is usually associated with such pieces. While it is the type of implement that one might associate with hoard contents, we have no way at present of knowing whether this piece did indeed originate from a buried hoard. The fact that it enjoyed a quite different form of consumption from other flake scrapers (which usually become cores for obsidian industry 1) might suggest that its mode of circulation within the site was distinct from that of other 'quarry flakes'. Its life as a scraper ended with the piece being knapped, or perhaps more truthfully, it being smashed, with the blow striking the centre of the implement, rather than its edge. Two of the (conjoining) fragments (5183.X3 & Fig. 11.16e:1 on CD) were then placed together with a small greenstone axe on the floor of Space 170 (5335), towards the centre of the western wall. There is a possibility that in fact they were placed in the upper fill of the post-hole once the wooden support

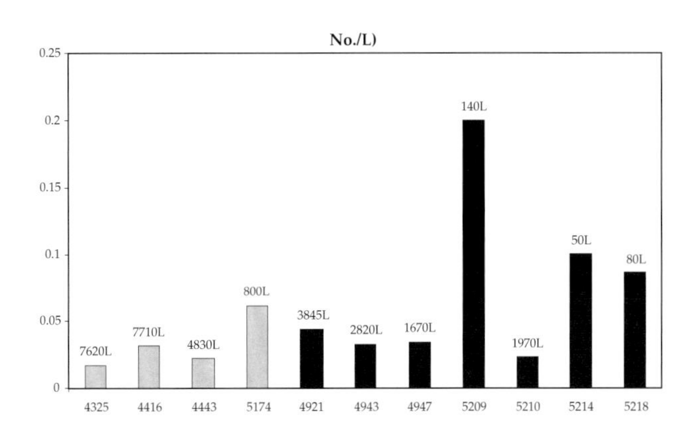

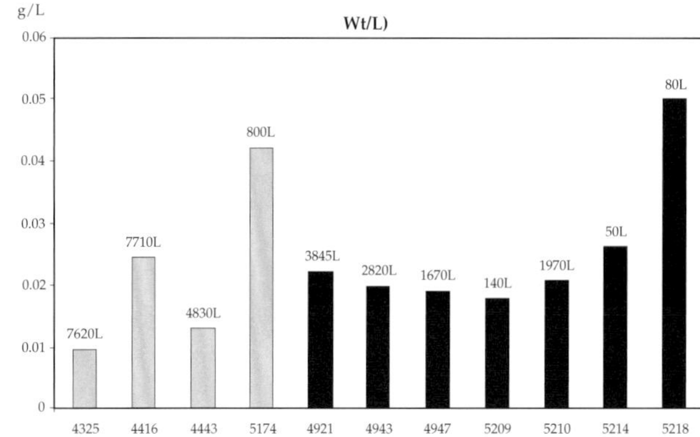

Figure 11.18. *Comparing the relative densities of obsidian from the infill of Spaces 170 and 182 — in black (dry sieve).*

had been removed (see above). The third piece from Space 170 was placed in the fill of the central northern post-retrieval pit (4647) (4647.A1), an analogous context to that of the (5183) material.

The other three fragments were then deposited next door in Space 182, with a large fragment from (5210) (Fig. 11.17e:2 on CD) interpreted as basal infill, though the distinction between infill and floor in this space was not particularly clear. The other two pieces came from (5215) (5215.A2) and (5221) (5221.A1) in the northeast corner of Space 182, i.e. once again just the other side of the crawl hole from the (4647) and (5183) deposits in Space 170. It is thought that these pieces may in fact be in secondary context having originally been placed somewhere in the northwest part of Space 170, then being cleaned up in the abandonment process and re-deposited into the narrow western room, Space 182. Specifically we have evidence that the white plaster floors in the northwest part of Space 170 had been scoured clean (to the extent of partial truncation?) with Farid (Volume 3, Part 2) claiming that the 'dirty' soil cleaned from this area, containing the three fragments of the 'quarry flake', was possibly thrown through the nearby crawl hole into Space 182. There is a similar fan of deposit radiating out from the smaller southern crawl hole into Space 182, suggesting a similar sequence of events in the southern half of the building. It is further worth noting that Space 182 also produced a number of fine flint implements made on non-local blades of an opposed platform technology (flint industry 2), plus the conjoining fragments of an imported pot (Chapter 5).

Comparing Spaces 170 and 182

One final issue worth commenting upon briefly is the relationship between Spaces 170 and 182 in Building 17 (Figs. 11.19 & 11.20). These two spaces are quite distinct with regard to their use and state at the time of abandonment. From an analysis of their respective floor deposits and basal fill (the latter excavated as 1 m^2 grids), it was concluded that Space 182 was on average a lot more productive, or 'dirtier' than Space 170. A number of questions stemmed from these data, namely whether this reflected the differential uses of these spaces (with Space 182 tentatively identified as a storage area, possibly containing even an animal or two), or the differential processes involved in the abandonment of these spaces. These two interpretations are not seen to be mutually exclusive.

The abandonment infill of Space 170 was excavated in quadrants, a northeast sector (4416), northwest sector (4325), southeast sector (4443), and southwest sector (4172), plus a strip of infill removed around the walls (5174), representing a large volume of dry-sieved soil containing a not insignificant amount of chipped stone. The fill was relatively homogeneous, suggesting that the soil had been processed carefully before being deposited in the structure. The infill of Space 182 was excavated quite differently to that of Space 170, a reflection of the different processes involved in its abandonment. The fill comprised a series of quite distinct tips/layers/lenses/fans, represented by a number of units: (4921), (4943), (4947), (5209), (5210), (5213), (5214), (5216), (5217) and (5218). Not all of these units were large enough to warrant dry sieving and were processed entirely by heavy-residue samples. The fact that the archaeology of this space required such a different excavation is perhaps the most obvious evidence we have for the fact that the infilling/abandonment processes of these respective spaces was quite distinct. The matrix in Space 182 was often seen to be much more 'blocky' with the occasional mud brick still distinguishable (there was also a scorched beam fragment) all of which suggested to the excavator (JAL) a much more rapid and 'less careful' process of infilling this side-room of Building 17.

The question that was asked of these data was whether the infilling deposits might reflect the 'less

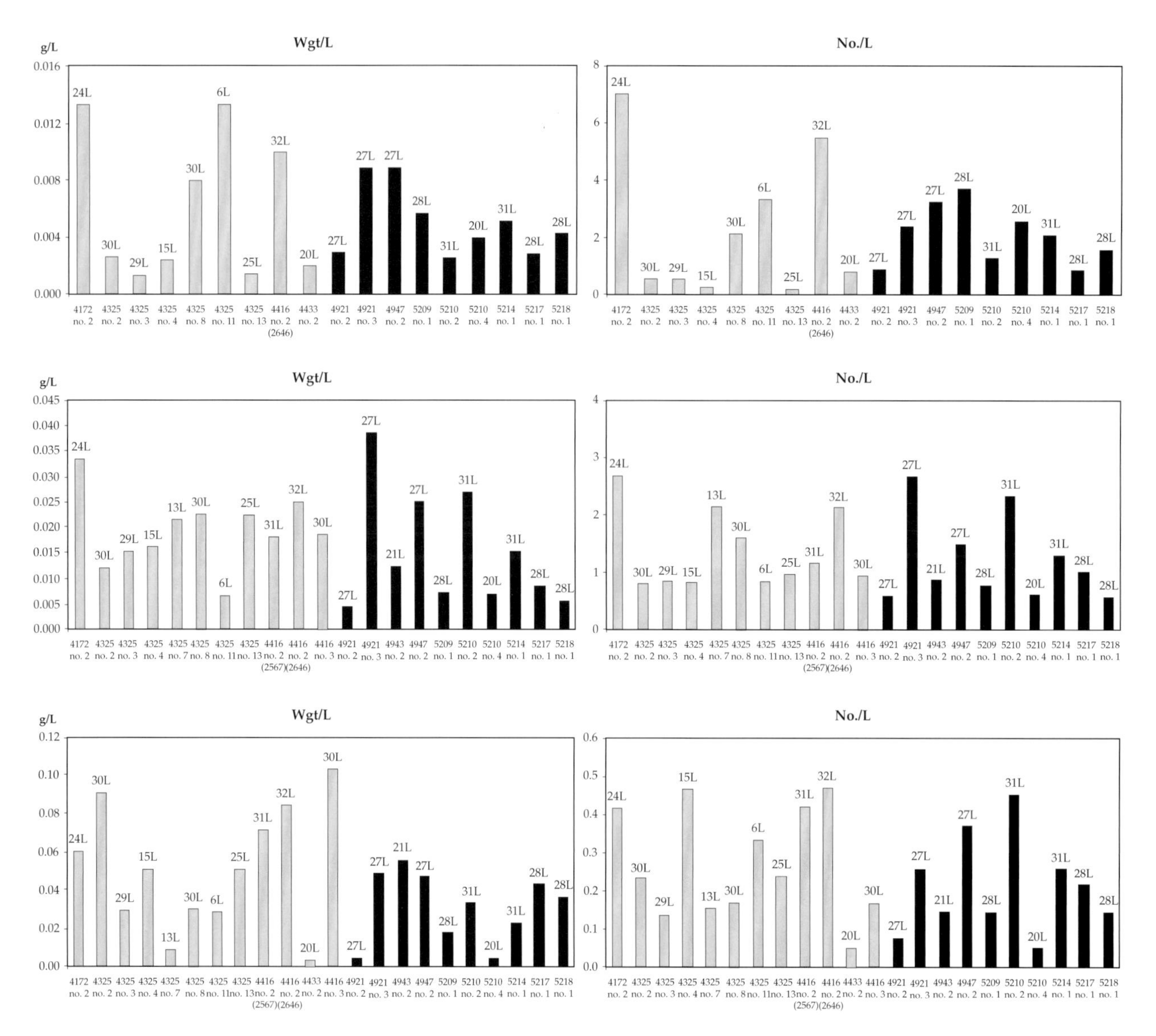

Figure 11.19. *Comparing the relative densities of obsidian from the infill of Spaces 170 and 182 shown in black, flotation >1 mm (upper), flotation > 2 mm (mid), flotation >4 mm (lower).*

careful/dirty' use of this space during the building's life? Space 170 seems to have been kept extremely clean during much of its use (as for example represented in the meticulous 'winnowing out' of the larger pieces of obsidian from the ashy rake-out deposits). At the point of its abandonment there was a general absence of macro-finds on its floors and evidence for the scouring of its white plaster surfaces. In contrast, Space 182 lacked the clearly-defined plaster floors, instead producing a series of overlapping lenses of deposits upon some of which were clearly-defined layers of phytolith that represented fodder or matting or some such surface/deposit that lay on an otherwise poorly-defined floor. Although the space has yet to be fully excavated, i.e. we are not sure as to whether it lacks the bin and hearth complexes seen in the structure above (Building 6, Space 173), it seems quite clear that the activities undertaken in this part of the building occurred in quite different surroundings. The room may have been much darker and was certainly accorded much less attention with respect to the preparation and maintenance of its floor surfaces in comparison to the plaster surfaces of Space 170 next door. Moreover, the basal fill/floor deposits of Space 182 produced a not insignificant quantity of complete chipped-stone implements, in stark contrast to Space 170 which had its mobiliary material culture removed prior to abandonment, with the exception of a few items deliberately placed into the upper fills of two post-retrieval pits ((4645), (4647) & (5183)).

The Space 182 chipped stone most notably included a 'group' of whole, or near whole flint implements, many of which were produced from bipolar technologies (flint industry 2): with an opposed platform prismatic blade-core of yellow limnoquartzite (Fig. 11.16e:2 on CD) plus a sickle made from a blade of the right scale and raw material to possibly be a product of the core (Fig. 11.16f:3 on CD), another sickle of red radiolarite sickle (Fig. 11.16f:4 on CD), a third sickle made on an extremely long blade of brown limnoquartzite (12.17 × 1.58 × 0.99 cm), later reworked as a perforator (Fig. 11.16f:1 on CD), plus a grey limnoquartzite double end-scraper made on a backed blade (Fig. 11.16f:2 on CD), and a retouched blade of dark-brown radiolarite (Fig. 11.16f:6 on CD). This sort of material is virtually unknown from Space 170, with only one retouched flint blade (a sickle) coming from the basal infill (5223.X1).

If the floor deposits and basal infill can be taken as some kind of indication as to the activities performed in these respective spaces (something which is not always entirely clear), then differences between the two 'rooms' are quite apparent. Space 170 is striking for its carefully defined 'dirty' and 'clean' areas, while Space 182 has a much less-focused consumption of chipped stone. There is also a significant difference with regard to the presence of flint in these two spaces, with Space 182 producing a far smaller flint component; in turn, this material all came from the >2-mm and >4-mm meshes, with no sample higher than three pieces. Thus Space 182 lacks both the tiny shatter and the concentrations of flint that one saw in Space 170, suggesting that the former context should be seen as the ultimate arena of consumption for the flint tools of Building 17, while Space 170 is perhaps where the blades entered the structure and the place where they were modified.

Levels VIII–VII

by Ana Spasojević

This section details the analysis and interpretation of chipped-stone assemblages from 62 priority units from Levels VIII and VII in the South Area, of which 45 came from Level VIII and 17 from Level VII. The assemblages' morphological and technological characteristics are documented level by level with a general integrated discussion at the end of the section, focusing on trends and differences between the levels. The wider chronological and technological implications of this assemblage will be evaluated here on the basis of analyses conducted on previously excavated material at Çatalhöyük by Bialor (1962), Mellaart (1964a) and Conolly (1996; 1999a).

An objective of this analysis is to understand contextual patterning with regards to the previously-acknowledged technological complexity of the assemblage (cf. Conolly 1999a) and to explore variations through time. The first thing to state, is that the Level VIII and VII assemblages continue to show the trends of having multiple contemporary industries and a dominance of obsidian over flint (Table 11.1).

Level VIII

Level VIII consists of four structures: Building 4 (Spaces 150 & 151); Building 6 (Spaces 163 & 173); Building 7 (Space 176) and Building 21 (Space 174), plus two infill deposits, Spaces 161 and 162, plus an external space: 115. Priority units analyzed in Building 4 came from infill and foundation deposits in Space 151 and bin backfill in Space 150. In Building 6 chipped stone was studied from a number of different features, including: oven structure, rake-out, pit, clay ball cluster, infill and a burial fill. A total of 15 units from Space 115 were studied in detail and in Space 162 a total of 4 units were analyzed. The study sample that constitutes the basis of this report does not include material from Buildings 7 and 21 as no priority units were assigned to these structures. Nor were units from the infill Space 161 designated as priorities.

Building 4 was divided into Space 150, a small room in the southeast corner and a larger room, Space 151; the spaces were connected by an access hole. The excavation of this building has not been concluded and the current phasing is therefore provisional. The phasing consists of two occupation phases and several sub-phases. Only 37 pieces were analyzed from this building (1.7 per cent), of which four came from Space 150 and 33 from Space 151 (a total of 4 units).

Building 6 comprised Space 163, a large room to the east and Space 173, a narrow room to the west. Most of Space 163 had been excavated in the 1960s as Shrine 10 (Volume 3, Part 2). The central floor area had been excavated during Mellaart's excavations; all that remained were fragments of some features against the north and south walls. Space 173 had not been excavated in the 1960s to the same level as Space 163 and thus produced a complete sequence. The building has two occupation phases based on internal alteration. The two phases in Space 163 and 173 cannot be correlated. The structure produced 5018 pieces of chipped stone, of which 300 pieces were analyzed, a six per cent sample of the assemblage. 205 stone tools were studied from Space 163 and 95 from Space 173 (a total of 24 units).

Space 115 was an external space, apparently employed primarily as a midden, as defined by fine accumulative deposits of domestic debris. Instead of isolating discreet deposits it was found to be more effective to consider midden surfaces as activity

Table 11.20. *Sample size of analyzed chipped stone from Levels VIII and VII.*

Level	Units analyzed	Obsidian count	'Flint' count
VIII	45	1131	36
VII	17	453	11

horizons. The total number of chipped stone from this space is 18,373, of which 792 pieces were analyzed, a 4.3 per cent sample of the assemblage (a total of 13 units). Space 162 produced 112 pieces, of which 38 pieces were analyzed (34 per cent) from four priority units.

Level VIII generated a total of 25,142 pieces of chipped stone (Table 11.1), comprising 24,835 of obsidian (98.8 per cent) and 307 of flint (1.2 per cent). Of this total a sample of 1167 (4.7 per cent) pieces of chipped stone were analyzed for this report (Table 11.20), of which obsidian was represented by 1131 pieces (4.6 per cent) and flint by 36 pieces (0.2 per cent). The obsidian industries in Level VIII are described on the CD.

The Level VIII chipped stone in context

Conolly's analyses of chipped-stone material from Mellaart's excavations of Level VIII show that the assemblage overall was well distributed throughout both houses and what were termed by Mellaart 'shrines' (Connolly 1999a, 82). Points were found in all analyzed houses and 'shrines' but not in the 'courtyards'. In Level VIII obsidian continues as the dominant raw material, comprising 97.0 per cent of the chipped-stone assemblage (Table 11.1). Seventy-two cores have been identified of which 69 were made on obsidian and only three were made on flint (Table 11.21). It is interesting to note that cores represent a higher proportion of the flint assemblage (8.3 per cent), than they do in obsidian (6.1 per cent). However, given the range of raw materials subsumed by the term flint, it remains the case that flint was primarily consumed by the inhabitants of the South Area in Level VII in the form of non-local products, mainly blades that enjoyed a particularly intensive exploitation (modification and use). There is limited evidence for the working of flint on site, as represented by the small core (Fig. 11.20f:5 on CD) and conjoining flake from the midden area of Space 115, a relatively simple technology (flint industry 5), that mirrors the long-term tradition of obsidian working (obsidian industry 1).

In total Space 115 produced six flint cores (12.0 per cent of the flint from this level) and the greatest concentration of obsidian cores and preparatory pieces. While quantities of this material may be in secondary context having been cleaned out of the surrounding structures, the aforementioned conjoining flint core and flake (found closely together) suggest that some of this material may be roughly *in situ*. Previous analyses of the obsidian microdebitage from some of the surfaces defined in Space 115 further offer evidence that this external space acted as both an area for working as well as discard (Conolly 1998; Underbjerg 1998). In turn, analysis of the faunal remains has denoted assemblages suggestive of single-event feasting and production activity (Volume 4, Chapter 2). No doubt some of the chipped stone from Space 115 was utilized in such episodes for butchery, food preparation and other such activities.

It is also possible to denote activity areas in the southeast rake-out part of Space 173, in Building 6, with concentrations of fresh knapping debris, including two cores and preparatory pieces. On the other hand there is a suggestion of some knapping activity in the northeast part of the same space, with a group of obsidian associated with the base of bin F.488. In the same building a core was found at the base of fire installation F.433 in the northeast of Space 163, while the associated lining of this feature (4288) also produced a small borer and a flake. One wonders if these pieces had simply been missed in the process of cleaning the oven, or whether they had been deliberately placed in the structural lining. The fill of the oven (4288) had by far the greater amount of material per litre than was recovered from the base of the oven (4279) (Fig. 11.21), suggesting further that knapping activity occurred in the vicinity during the oven's use-life. The obsidian from this assemblage is characterized by fresh, unused knapping debris.

Of further significance is the location near the oven of obsidian hoard (4276), consisting of three large bifacially-modified 'quarry flakes', likely projectile preforms (Fig. 11.20e:1–3 on CD) and 36 pieces of smaller debitage. One of the bifaces had traces of use-wear (4276.X1) and could be conjoined with another piece (4276.X2), their breakage considered on taphonomic bases to have occurred prior to their deposition. The deposit also included three *pièces esquillées*, one a blade fragment, the second a thick flake, the third more akin to an exhausted core.

Level VII

Mellaart's excavation areas known as Houses 2, 12 and 16, plus Courtyard 15 were re-defined in the 1995–99 excavations as Spaces 105, 106, 107 and 108 (Volume 3, Part 2). His shrines 1, 8 and 10 were redefined as Buildings 8, 20 and 24. Much of this area was dug during the 1960s so that most of the archaeology investigated by the new excavations was in the form of heavily-truncated deposits. Level VII generated 5870 pieces of chipped stone (Tables 11.1 & 11.20), of which 5793 were obsidian (98.7 per cent) and 77 flint (1.3 per cent). This report is based on a sample of 453 pieces of obsidian and 11 pieces of flint that came from the priority units assigned to this level (Tables 11.20 & 11.22).

Building 8 (Mellaart's Shrine 1) produced only 167 pieces of chipped stone, but only an ashy infill from between the walls of was prioritized for analysis, a sample of 32 pieces (22 per cent). Building 24 comprised Space 159, a small narrow room to the west connected to a larger room, Space 180, via an access hole. Space 180 was excavated during Mellaart's campaign in the 1960s as an antechamber to Shrine 10. Most of the sequence in Space 159 had been excavated in the 1960s but some floors remained. The structure generated 198 pieces of chipped stone; only one of the three prioritized units from this building contained chipped stone, thus the total sample from this building is represented by a single piece (0.5 per cent).

Space 105 produced 1194 pieces of chipped stone, 1181 of obsidian and 13 of flint; some 235 pieces were analyzed from five priority units. Space 108 had a total of 337 pieces of chipped stone, 335 of obsidian and 2 of flint. From this space only one unit was prioritized, a series of floors and make-up layers producing three pieces of chipped stone (0.9 per cent). Space 109 had also been excavated mainly in the 1960s and much of the floor deposits had been scoured; nonetheless it produced 473 pieces of chipped stone, of which 23 were analyzed from a single unit (4.9 per cent).

Space 112 was excavated largely by Mellaart as Shrine 9, leaving only heavily-worn patches of floor deposits and a few isolated features. The recent excavation generated 1464 pieces of chipped stone, comprising 1428 pieces of obsidian and 36 of flint. Of these, 17 pieces of obsidian were analyzed from a single priority unit (1.2 per cent). Most of the floors associated with Space 113 had similarly been excavated in the 1960s, leaving sporadic patches of floor deposits, mainly up against the walls. The total number of chipped stone from this structure was 558 pieces, 553 of obsidian and 5 of flint. The priority units assigned to this space relate to a pit, which was interpreted as some form of retrieval event. This pit is represented by four units that contained 134 pieces of chipped stone, 133 of obsidian and 1 of flint.

The Level VII obsidian and flint industries are described on the CD.

Table 11.21. *Generic typological division of Level VIII chipped stone (based on study of priority unit sample).*

Obsidian flakes	Obsidian blades	Obsidian cores	'Flint' flakes	'Flint' blades	'Flint' cores
1006	50	72	21	12	3
88.95%	4.42%	6.36%	58.3%	33.3%	8.3%

Table 11.22. *Generic typological division of Level VII chipped stone (based on study of priority unit sample).*

Obsidian flakes	Obsidian blades	Obsidian cores	'Flint' flakes	'Flint' blades	'Flint' cores
424	8	21	9	1	1
93.6%	1.76%	4.64%	81.81%	9.1%	9.1%

Table 11.23. *Details relating to the use and taphonomy of Level VII assemblages of note from Space 105.*

Unit	Retouched	Used	Cortex	Whole	Broken	Secondary use	Total
1511	5	9	12	26	35	1	61
1506	4	5	0	5	33	0	38
1092	30	41	14	25	51	1	76
1091	5	6	0	3	5	2	7

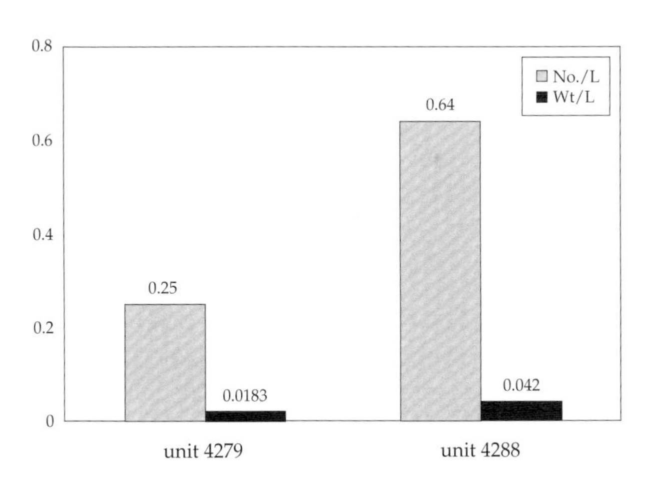

Figure 11.21. *Comparing the relative densities of chipped stone from oven F.433 fill (4288) and base (4279); sample from flotation.*

The Level VII chipped stone in context

Associated with a bone cluster, interpreted as feasting remains, (1092) generated a quantity of obsidian, with the highest ratio of used and retouched pieces (Fig. 11.23:6–10, 13 on CD). It is tempting to relate this material to the events surrounding the preparation and consumption of the various animals represented in the faunal assemblage, indeed a number of the bones

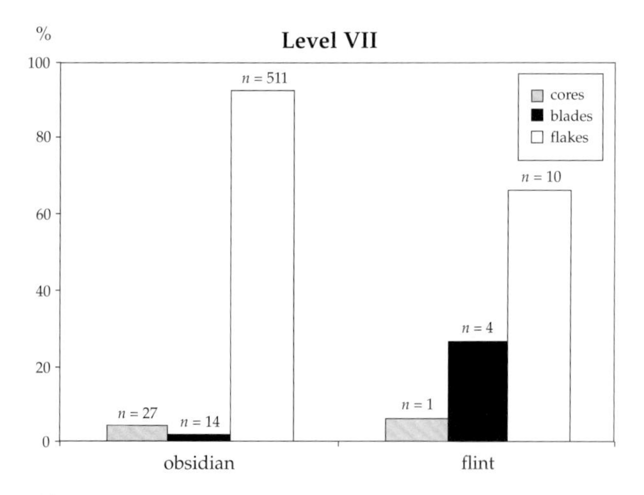

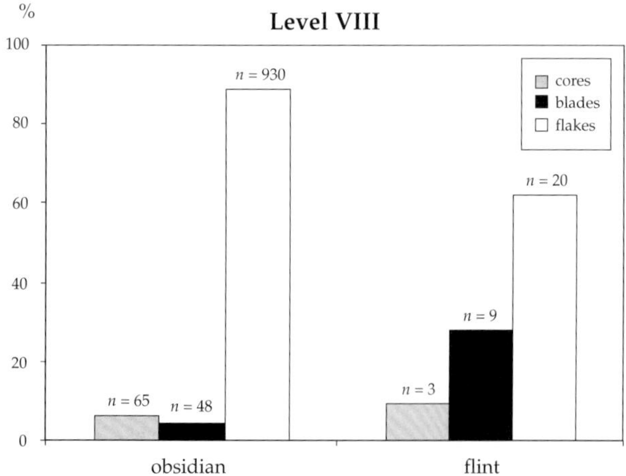

Figure 11.24. *Comparison of Levels VIII and VII chipped stone assemblages by generic type.*

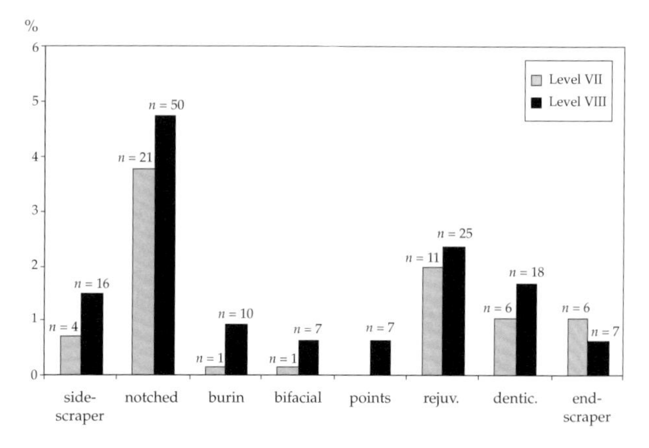

Figure 11.25. *Comparison of Levels VIII and VII obsidian by generic type.*

displayed cut-marks (Volume 4, Chapter 2). It is worth commenting further on the (1092) assemblage, as 20 per cent of its component blanks had part-cortical surfaces (Table 11.23), yet the obsidian from the nearby deposit (1091) had none. A similar pattern is noted with regard to two other juxtaposed units from the same space, (1506) and (1511), with the former having no cortical material while 20 per cent of the latter assemblage was part cortical (as with (1092)). A similar concentration of obsidian bearing cortex was recorded from (1043) a basal deposit in Space 105.

The Space 105 assemblage containing the feasting deposit also contained several pieces of obsidian with notable patination (Table 11.23) suggesting that a proportion the of soil had come from earlier levels. The aforementioned retouched and used obsidian from these units were, however, quite fresh and can be considered with some confidence as relating to the feasting activities.

Finally, little can be said as to how the Level VII material from the new excavations compares to that from the 1960s, as neither Bialor (1962), nor Mellaart (1964a) make any specific reference to the chipped stone of Level VII, despite the fact that their assemblages spanned Level IX to Level II.

Comparing the Level VIII and VII obsidian and flint industries

Raw materials

Obsidian was easily the dominant raw material in both levels, at 98.8 per cent and 98.7 per cent of their respective chipped-stone assemblages (Table 11.1). A selection of the obsidian from both levels was sent for trace-elemental characterization at CNRS and Aberystwyth (see Chapter 12), with 16 samples from Level VIII and 15 from Level VII. The material chosen for analysis was primarily in the form of non-cortical debitage, with most of the diagnostic samples comprising blades, blade-like flakes and cores/*pièces esquillées* from obsidian industry 1. The results indicate that all the obsidian has a south Cappadocian origin, with the majority of the samples, from both levels, having a chemical signature that correlates with the Göllü Dağ-East source, 15 from Level VIII (93.8 per cent) and 13 from Level VII (86.7 per cent). The remaining three pieces were characterized as coming from Nenezi Dağ.

The flint component of the Level VIII and Level VII assemblages can be divided into two separate groups, limnoquartzites and radiolariates. Within the two samples only one piece of green radiolariate was documented (Fig. 11.20f:1 on CD), a scraper on a blade from the Space 115 midden in Level VIII (3740.A59). The rest of the flint component belongs to the limnoquartzite group, predominantly tan/grey-brown/brown and orange-brown in colour. One variant is worthy of further comment, a translucent milky-white with macroscopic black plant fossils ('white planty') limnoquartzite, that is known, albeit in very small quantities and intermittently, from Level Pre-XII.D onwards.

Technology and typology

Starting with cores, in each level they tend to be exhausted on recovery and small in size; their mean measurements for Level VIII are: length 2 cm long, 1.6 cm wide and 0.66 cm thick, while those from Level VII are: 1.5 cm long, 1.4 cm wide and 0.58 cm thick. There thus appears to be a slight trend of core length diminishing over time; whether this is a reflection of more intensive reduction strategies (changing modes of consumption / procurement), or a result of sample size is unknown at present. Turning to flint cores, while so very few are found it remains possible to talk of a limited amount of on-site tool manufacture (flint industry 5). When compared these levels seem not to show any changes in number of cores, flakes and blades per litre (Fig. 11.24). The small blades and blade-like flake tradition of obsidian industry 1 dominate in both levels.

It remains the case, however, that the fine, long prismatic blades of unipolar and opposed platform traditions, both flint and obsidian, came from non-local industries with only the end-products circulating at Çatalhöyük where they enjoyed particularly intensive lives (initial use, re-sharpening and / or modification and re-use). Further distinctions can be made, however, when considering retouched tools, though it is to be stressed that these are often generic classes of modified implements (e.g. 'scrapers', or 'perforators') and that as Conolly (1999a, 34) has argued previously, the Çatalhöyük obsidian assemblage displays notable 'morphological variability' with regard to its tool types, with little standardization.

Focusing on the obsidian, it can be noted that there was a proportional decrease in retouched tool types from Level VIII to VII, in some cases by as much as 50 per cent, with the exception of end-scrapers which show a slight increase (Figs. 11.25–11.26 & Table 11.24). Points completely disappear in Level VII, though this is almost certainly a product of sample size / type, given their occurrence in post-Level VIII contexts at Çatalhöyük from the 1960s excavation (cf. Bialor 1962, 77, 82 & 86 *inter alia*; Mellaart 1964a, 103 & pl. XXVI.a).

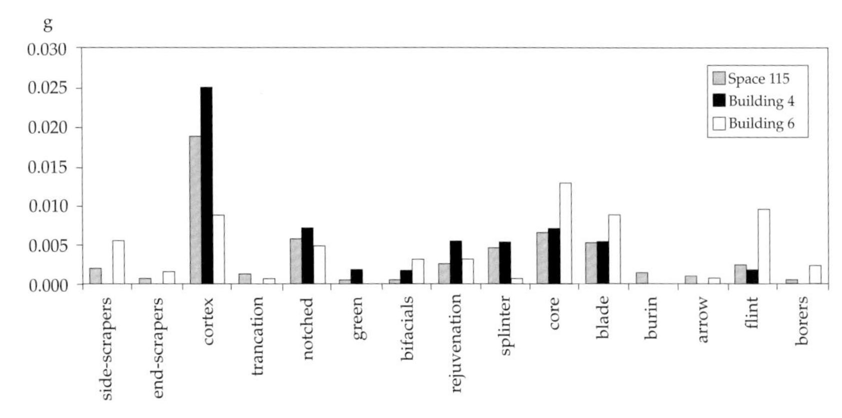

Figure 11.26. *Distribution of tool types within the three major contexts of Level VIII.*

Table 11.24. *Scraper types through Levels VIII and VII.*

Level	'Flint' end-scrapers	Obsidian end-scrapers	'Flint' side-scrapers	Obsidian side-scrapers
VIII	5	16	1	7
VII	1	3	0	5

The distribution of stone-tool types in Levels VIII and VII

A contextual analysis of the chipped stone from Levels VIII and VII allows one to suggest some statements concerning the patterns and distinctions in chipped stone consumption during these 'periods'. For instance, in Level VIII the majority of obsidian cortical and rejuvenation pieces came from Building 4, while the lion's share of cores was found in Building 6 (Fig. 11.27). One can also compare the consumption of specific tool types and implements on a level-by-level basis.

A total of eight bifacially-modified 'quarry flakes' (obsidian industry 7) were found in Level VIII, three of which were part of an obsidian hoard found in Building 6 (Fig. 11.20e:1–3 on CD). A broken tip of a bifacially-worked piece was found in the oven of Building 6 (Fig. 11.22:15 on CD) while the rest were found in the midden, without clear context. A small bifacially-retouched piece, used as a core (obsidian industry 3) was found in Space 150 of Level VIII in a bin fill (Fig. 11.20c:10 on CD), while Conolly (1999a, 84) reported eight bifacially-retouched points from Level VII; unfortunately none were from the priority units analyzed. Finally, only one piece of flint had bifacial modification (Fig. 11.20f:9 on CD).

A total of 37 scrapers came from Levels VIII and VII, implements that were divided into end-scrapers (n = 25) and side-scrapers (n = 12), depending on where they had been modified. Twenty-five end-scrapers were recorded in total (Figs. 11.20b:3&8;

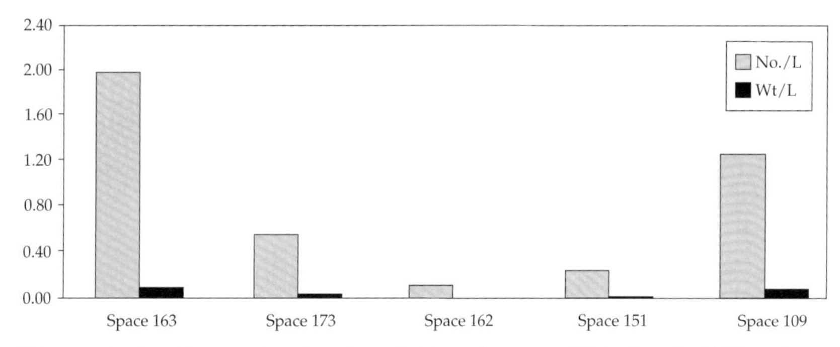

Figure 11.27. *Comparing density of chipped stone within Levels VIII and VII infill deposits (heavy-residue sample).*

11.22:8 on CD), and it seems that there is a decrease in scrapers through time (Table 11.24). There appears to be little pattern in the deposition of end-scrapers except in Space 115, where four pieces were recorded from (1668). Most of the side-scrapers came from Level VIII, with only four from Level VII, most of which came from midden deposits in Space 105. In Level VIII there is a similar midden-oriented deposition of side-scrapers, with only one coming from a secure primary context, a rake-out in Space 173, Building 6 (Figs. 11.20a:9; 11.20b:7 & 11.20c:3 on CD).

A total of nine burins were recorded, of which eight came from Level VIII and two from Level VII (Figs. 11.20b:6 & 11.22:6&14 on CD). Burins in both levels were found in midden contexts (Spaces 105 & 115) except for one piece that was found in a rake-out on Space 173, Building 6 (4898) and one from the infill of Space 162, Level VIII (2897). The Space 115 middens of Level VIII produced a concentration of burins ((3314) & (3740)), though one is aware that this may well be a reflection of the soil-sample size. Finally, a total of 12 perforators/borers were identified, with seven in Level VIII and five in Level VII (Figs. 11.20a:4&8; 11.20b:1; 11.20c:9; 11.20d:6; 11.20f:2 & 11.22:13 on CD), but none from a secure context.

The consumption of chipped stone in Levels VIII and VII by feature type

Bins

Further thoughts can be offered by turning our attention to the relationship between specific archaeological contexts and chipped stone. Starting with bins, F.488 in Building 6, Space 163 contained not only a number of clay balls, but also a flint and an obsidian core (4181) and three pieces of flint in total, of which two were of the same raw material, perhaps even from the same core. Both the cores had been reduced from opposing platforms, with resultant bipolar crushing at both ends, i.e. they could also be classified as *pièces esquillées*. It is conceivable that their final use was not as cores, but as small wedging implements, perhaps for splitting wood, or bone (Ataman 1988, 208–10; Conolly 1999a, 43). Indeed, analysis of the bones from this feature discovered cut marks. One of the other pieces of flint also had a notch on a broken end; as did a piece of obsidian from the bin. The bin was situated close to an oven, presumably for the storage of the unused clay balls (Chapter 6). Given that two of the pieces of flint were of such similar raw material and freshness and given the typological and functional correlations within the assemblage, it is tempting to see the chipped stone as having also been placed deliberately into the feature for later use. However, there is also a quantity of microdebitage from the heavy-residue sample (>1-mm, >2-mm and >4-mm samples) from the bin and similar quantities of material from surrounding (basal infill) contexts, so it might be safer to interpret the assemblage as primary infill, as opposed to seeing the implements as stored alongside the clay balls. Having said that, the assemblage does retain a certain coherence, whereby one might consider it as a structured deposition of material as part of the process of abandoning the building. Similar instances have been claimed for earlier levels, as for example an ochre-covered flint perforator placed in a bin in Building 18, Level X (see above).

The priority units analyzed from Space 151 in Building 4 were all from the bin F.91 located at the southeast of this space. (2028) shows the highest density of material from this feature; notably 31 per cent of the obsidian from this unit was part cortical but not a single core was found. Stylistically, the chipped-stone assemblage from (2036) in bin F.91 appears to be the product of one knapper. The debitage all has characteristically trimmed surfaces to control the platform angle.

Fills

Figures 11.28–11.29 show that the process of house abandonment (and preparation for the next structure above) may have involved some sort of sieving of the soil prior to infilling. Chipped stone was not particularly abundant in the infill of buildings in Level VIII Building 6 (Space 173 & 163), Building 4 (Space 151) and Space 162 when compared to the infill in Space 109 (Level VII). Maybe what we are seeing here are some different practices in sealing/burying/infilling houses. Even though Space 163 shows more quantity in the heavy-residue sample it still seems that some larger pieces (>4 mm) were possibly hand-picked out of the matrix.

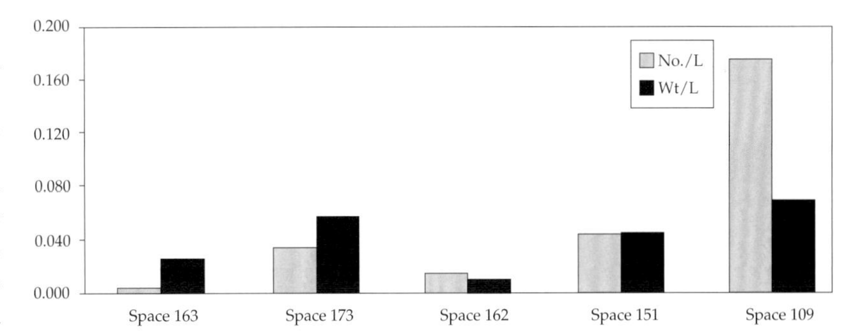

Figure 11.28. *Comparing density of chipped stone within Levels VIII and VII infill deposits (dry sieve sample).*

Middens

The external midden deposits, such as those that make up Space 115, comprised a series of fine layers and interdigitated lenses of ash, charcoal, clay and deposits identified as 'organic' matter, either food debris or coprolite. These deposits appear to be multiple individual events of dumping domestic/occupation debris, such as hearth or oven rake-out material. On the whole they appear to have accumulated in fairly quick succession, as there was no visible surface disturbance that would result when loose, fine ashy layers are exposed to the elements or human or animal activity.

The highest density among priority units analyzed from Space 115 was (3314). 16 per cent of the chipped stones within the assemblage were cortical pieces of which three were 'primary flakes', i.e. the first ones removed from the core. One of these was used as a burin, a not particularly common implement at Çatalhöyük (cf. Conolly 1999a, 56). One flake has very polished edges that seem to be from use. The scars on these edges indicate transversal motions, on a hard material. One flake has been burned but this piece was either intrusive or comes from an adjacent area.

Table 11.25. *Building 5 debitage categories.*

Category	Obsidian count	Obsidian percentage	'Flint' count	'Flint' percentage
Flakes	94	85.5	2	66.7
Prismatic blades	1	0.9	1	33.3
Non-prismatic blades	5	4.5	0	0.0
Crested blades	0	0.0	0	0.0
Core platform flakes	0	0.0	0	0.0
Blade cores	0	0.0	0	0.0
Flake cores	0	0.0	0	0.0
Shatter	4	3.6	0	0.0
Chips	1	0.9	0	0.0
Indeterminable	5	4.5	0	0.0
Total	110	99.9	3	100.0

A refit of two flint pieces from this assemblage was identified (Figs. 11.20d:10 & 11.20f:5 on CD), and it provides further evidence that some of the deposits in these external spaces represent activity-surfaces, albeit possibly short-lived ones. Associated faunal data provide corroborative evidence (Volume 4, Chapter 2). In turn, the assemblage from (3740) contained a significant proportion with remnant cortex (28 per cent), material that one would associate with knapping activity, though 'primary flakes' were absent.

Infill between walls

Two pieces of obsidian that conjoined came from Space 113/115, underneath the wall F.266 and between the walls F.52 and F.75. They were both found in the same context that was described as a mixed deposit that accumulated gradually *in situ*. On the basis of the quantity of animal bones, it has been suggested that this might represent the debris from a 'feasting' event deposited between the walls. It is most likely that the core was used in this 'feasting' activity, broken in the process (deliberately or accidentally) and eventually discarded. Another two cores belonging to this unit were also used.

Rake-outs

Analysis of the chipped stone from Levels VIII and VII allows us to conclude that the storage and working of obsidian is connected closely with hearths and the southern 'dirty' area of Buildings 6 and 4 (Fig. 11.29). The quantity of obsidian generated by rake-out (4808) (F.502) is notably higher than that generated from other features in Space 173, specifically the bins in the northern third of the room: F.488 ((4793) & (4794)), F.518 ((4618) & (4724)–(4730)) and F.520 ((4795) & (4796)). This interpretation is based solely on data generated by heavy-residue samples.

Levels VII–IV, North Area

by James Conolly

Conolly produced this report on the basis of studies undertaken during 1995–99. Its structure is different to that employed by Carter and Spasojević owing to changes made in the system of analysis after Conolly had passed the responsibility of the Çatalhöyük over to Carter. Wherever possible, references to the obsidian and flint industries, as defined at the beginning of this chapter, have been inserted.

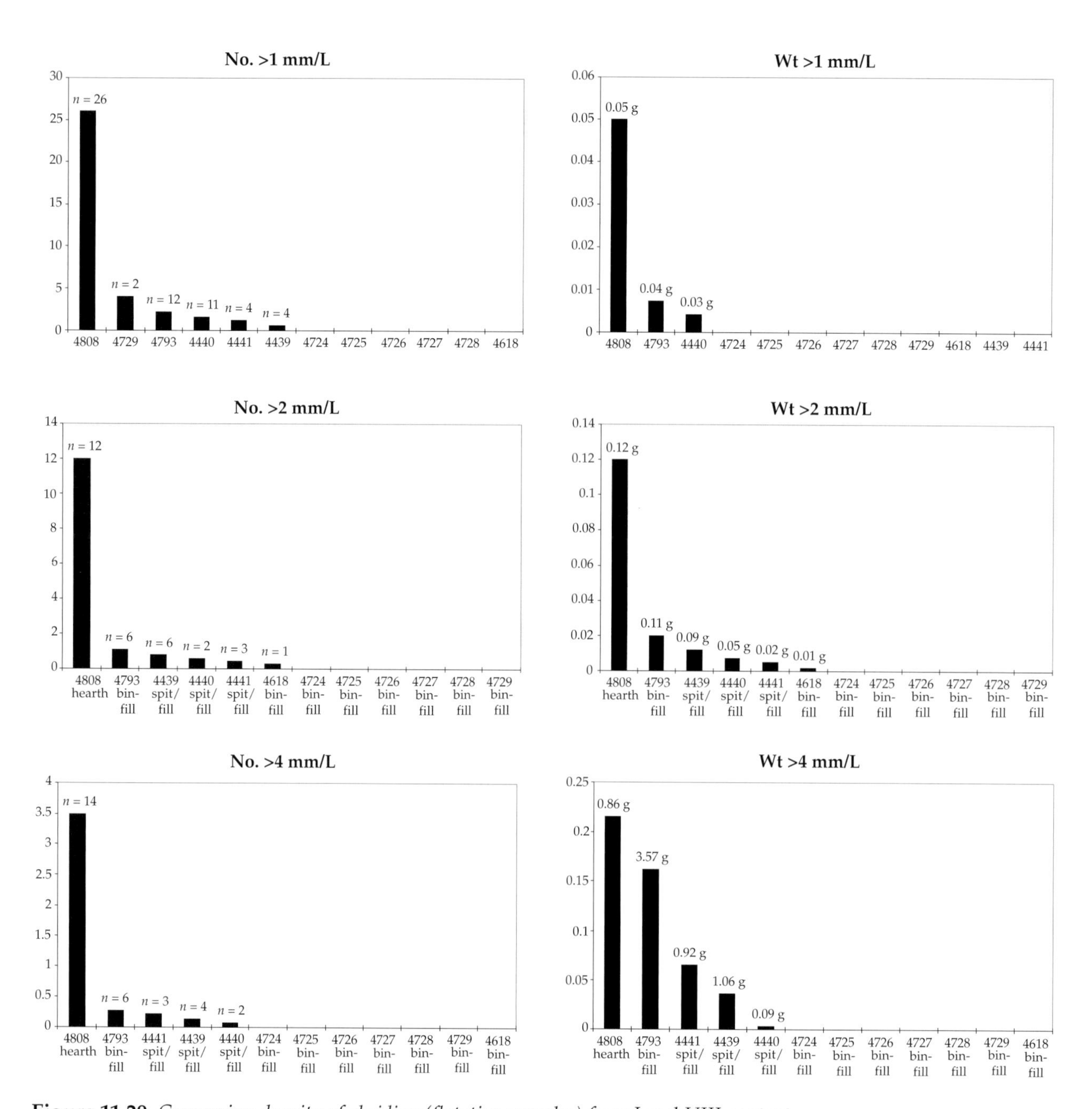

Figure 11.29. *Comparing density of obsidian (flotation samples) from Level VIII contexts.*

Building 5, assemblage size and raw material

A total of 113 pieces of flint and obsidian (102.8 g) have been examined from Building 5 (Table 11.25). Flint artefacts (n = 3, 2.7 per cent) are limited to two flakes and a yellow, likely tabular, blade. There do not appear to be any differences between Building 1 and 5 in terms of the character of the obsidian, or the proportion of blades in the assemblage (Building, 1 7.0 per cent; Building 5, 5.4 per cent).

Reduction strategies

Most of the Building 5 assemblage consists of small obsidian flakes, and their sizes are equivalent to the Building 1 sample (mean = 1.73 × 1.37 × 0.29 cm). Unlike Building 1, however, most of the Building 5 obsidian flakes are intact (53.6 per cent), which might relate to a greater proportion deriving from core reduction and biface thinning (Sullivan & Rosen 1985). There are too few flint flakes to extrapolate anything from their characteristics; both flint flakes are similar in size to the Building 1 sample. The obsidian prismatic blades also share identical characteristics to those from Building 1. Interestingly, there is also a very regular, prismatic, flint blade (2.92 × 1.12 × 0.4 cm) that may have been produced using pressure methods, although with only a single example this is too difficult to tell with any degree of certainty (flint industry 2 or 3). Very little production debris and only one possible core (Fig. 11.31a:4) were recovered from the excavated parts of Building 5, preventing any further interpretation of reduction strategies related to this context.

Blank selection and tools

There are very few retouched pieces from Building 5 ($n = 20$), although the proportion is roughly equivalent to that in Building 1 (17.7 per cent). These consist of ten expediently retouched flakes (one of which is flint), a retouched obsidian blade, three *pièces esquillées*, three projectile points (3298.X1, 3266.D2 & 3256.A1: Fig. 11.31a:2) and a biface (4014.X1). They are very much similar in style to the Building 1 examples (the latter tanged and shouldered, the former only tanged).

Summary by phase and space

Of the material that can be phased from Building 5 (Table 11.26), the single largest collection comes from Space 155 in Phase B5.A (although Space 154 and 155 in the latest phases B1.1A also have large collections). Earlier on in the history of Spaces 154 and 155 (Phases B5.B & B5.C), there are far fewer pieces. Indeed, there are few pieces in general from the earlier phases of Building 5 than later on in its occupation.

Feature summary

There are eight features that possess chipped stone from Building 5 (Table 11.27), of which post-retrieval pit F.240 and blocking F.249 are the most interesting. As it is large in volume F.240 has a relatively low density, but it is nevertheless unusual. It contains one of the two complete projectiles from Building 5, and two other flake tools (a flake scraper and a flake cutting tool); it cannot therefore be seen as a random collection of chipped-stone objects, as tools are relatively rare in Building 5. The blocking is interesting only because of its apparently high density (paralleled by the high density of chipped stone in the fill of the crawl-hole in Building 1 (1190), F.374), which likely is a product of general debris in the source of fill used (charcoal is present in (3863), hinting at the probable relationship discussed earlier between knapping debris and fire installations). The remaining features have very low numbers of chipped stone, all of which are small, unretouched flakes.

Analysis by unit category

The majority of the few lithic objects in Building 5 are found in units classified as construction/make-up/packing (Table 11.28). Together with those pieces found in fill deposits, they are also the largest, although only still only average at a gram each (see the following section for descriptions of the significantly larger objects).

Table 11.26. *Building 5 debitage categories by phase and space. PB = prismatic blade; Non-PB = non-prismatic blade; Ind. = indeterminate.*

Phase	Space	Total count	Total weight	Flakes	PB	Non-PB	Shatter	Chips	Ind.
B1.1A	154	25	22.8	21	0	0	2	1	1
B1.1A	155	20	21.1	18	0	0	0	0	2
B1.1A	156	3	1.9	3	0	0	0	0	0
B5.A	154	4	11.6	3	1	0	0	0	0
B5.A	155	30	33.1	27	0	2	0	0	1
B5.A	157	9	6.5	8	1	0	0	0	0
B5.B	154	1	1.6	0	0	1	0	0	1
B5.B	156	11	2.7	10	0	1	0	0	0
B5.B	156/157	4	1.5	2	0	0	2	0	0
B5.C	155	2	0	0	0	1	0	0	1
Total		109	102.7	92	2	5	4	1	6

Table 11.27. *Building 5 debitage categories by phase and space.*

Count	Feature	Feature type	Dry-sieve volume (L)	Density (per 100 L)
5	240	Pit	376	1.3
4	249	Blocking	67	6
3	244	Ladder emplacement	510	0.6
2	235	Bin		
1	241	Pit	120	0.8
1	227	Wall		
1	231	Wall	50	2

Table 11.28. *Building 5 Count and density of lithic material by unit category.*

Unit category	Dry-sieve volume (l)	Count	Weight (g)	Mean weight (g)	Density (g/100 L)
Arbitrary	45	5	1.15	0.2	2.6
Construction/make-up/packing	1100	35	34.72	1.0	3.2
Fill	4703.5	45	51.46	1.1	1.1
Floors (use)	225	4	0.94	0.2	0.4

Description of significant objects / contexts

There are five objects and contexts of particular interest: (i) 4014.X1; (ii) 3808.X1; (iii) 3819.X1–2; (iv) 3810.X4; and (v) 3266.D1. 4014.X1 is a large complete biface (obsidian industry 7), possibly a projectile preform (8.4 × 3.4 × 1.2 cm) apparently deliberately placed in a general dump of material in Space 155. 3808.X1 is a small (2.36 × 2.44 × 1.02 cm) tabular flint scraper manufactured on a flake, deliberately placed in the collapsed building debris of Space 155. 3819.X1–2 are two pieces of a broken blade utilized as a *pièce esquillée*; apparently deliberately placed in the infilling of Space 155. 3810.X4 is an unretouched flake fragment, possibly deliberately placed in amongst other artefacts, including clay balls and sheep horn-cores. 3266.D1 is a very finely made projectile point and part of a small collection of tools found in F.240, discussed above.

Building 1, assemblage size and raw material

This report on the chipped stone from Building 1 is based on a sample of over fifteen hundred pieces of obsidian and flint from the dry sieve and >4-mm heavy-residue mesh (n = 1543, 1735.3 g), the vast majority of which is obsidian of a generally grey-opaque and / or a banded black / grey variety (n = 1517, 98.3 per cent). Trace-elemental analysis of 80 pieces of obsidian from Building 1 (see Chapter 12) indicates that the inhabitants exploited two southern Cappadocian sources: Göllü Dağ-East and Nenezi Dağ. The flint, most of which can be categorized as limnoquartzite, comprises only 26 pieces, 100.8 g or 5.8 per cent by weight. The raw material varies in colour from yellow, light to dark brown fine-grained, and possibly tabular, to coarser varieties that appear to be struck from small cobbles, which range from browns to red-browns to brown-greys. Unmodified surfaces on obsidian are extremely rare (0.6 per cent of the sample possess cortex), and when cortex is present it never exceeds 2/3 of the dorsal surface. The flint also displays a low frequency of remnant cortex (4.8 per cent), indicating that as with the obsidian, these raw materials entered the structure already decorticated. Some pieces are an extremely fine-grained stone, akin to the tabular limnoquartzites used for dagger manufacture (cf. Conolly 1999a, 41–2), raw materials that were probably imported from considerable distance, and with more preparatory work than the coarser-grained and smaller cobble-flint nodules that are available from alluvial deposits closer to the settlement.

Cores and core-related products

There are only two definite cores from Building 1: a small obsidian flake-core fragment (1243.A2; 2.39 × 3.00 × 1.99 cm) from obsidian industry 1 (Fig. 11.30a:4 on CD), and a larger obsidian flake-core fragment (1279.X1; 6.61 × 5.19 × 3.03 cm). The latter is interesting as it retains some scars suggestive of a previous life as a blade core (?obsidian industry 4), subsequently reworked for flake production (Fig. 11.30a:3 on CD). Both of these are best described as multi-sequence / multi-platform flake cores (i.e. neither show any evidence of pre-planned debitage). Four other pieces of obsidian may also have functioned as cores. They are similar in morphology to the enigmatic *pièce esquillée*, but are slightly larger and may be related to obsidian industry 1 (Fig. 11.30a:5–7 on CD). Finally, there is a further small fragmentary piece of cobble-flint that might possibly have some use as a core (1436.A13; 3.3 × 1.1 × 0.8 cm), although the coarseness of the grain makes absolute identification of intentional removal difficult, and it might be more accurately classed as a piece of shatter (?flint industry 4 or 5).

Three possible crested-blades (1108.A2, 1335.A4 & 2505.A1) and a blade core platform rejuvenation flake (1236.X1) attest to blade core reduction activities (obsidian industry 4 or 5), although no blade cores were actually recovered from the North Area excavations.

Obsidian

Small obsidian flakes, blade-like flakes and flake fragments dominate the Building 1 assemblage (77.6 per cent: Table 11.29). Although a small percentage (9.3 per cent of all obsidian flakes) display evidence of retouched and / or macroscopic damage attributed to use (described in more detail, below, under the headings 'Blank Selection' and 'Tools and Retouched Pieces'), the majority are small, irregular, and are likely the waste by-products of core reduction rather than blanks for tool use. While these flakes may well have been potentially useful for any number of tasks that may have required a small, sharp, cutting edge, their overall shape and size (and the fact that they typically do not display evidence of use) suggests that they are the waste products of core reduction. In addition, the large number of pieces of obsidian shatter lends weight to the argument that, with some notable exceptions, the bulk of the Building 1 assemblage is waste produced during core reduction (obsidian industry 1).

Examination of these flakes' technological attributes helps to refine this interpretation. Obsidian flakes from Building 1 are typically fragmentary, under 2 cm in length (mean dimensions are 1.82 × 1.46 × 0.35 cm), and where it can be determined, have two to four remnant dorsal scars usually originating from the proximal end. Some 26 per cent of the flakes are complete, with a further 20 per cent possessing only proximal ends. Where it is possible to estimate accurately, most platform angles are close to 90° (53 per cent), 17 per cent are around 45°, and 30 per cent are significantly less than 45°. Some researchers have suggested that low platform angles (less than 45°), convex profiles, and expanding edges are the characteristics encountered preferentially on 'thinning' flakes, those flakes produced during the process of 'thinning-out' bifaces, such as projectile points (Newcomer & Karlin 1987; Whittaker 1994, 194–201). Although there are a small number of low-angled flakes in the Building 1 assemblage, only thirteen of these possess the full range of characteristics associated with biface thinning. Obsidian biface thinning therefore appears to have taken place, but such a small number only hints at this type of knapping activity and it is not a major source of the waste found in this building.

There is a tiny but significant obsidian blade component (n = 96, 7.0 per cent of obsidian assemblage). There is a suggested bias in the use of obsidian from each source in terms of blade and flake core reduction, with Nenezi Dağ material used preferentially in the manufacture of blade products, and Göllü Dağ-East used for the less standardized blades and blade-like flakes (see Chapter 12). Most of the blades from Building 1 are extremely fine and straight and the majority possess three unipolar dorsal scars (Fig. 11.30b:1–6 on CD), all of which indicate relatively standardized production on single platform cores (obsidian industry 5). Several of these cores were recorded in the 1960s excavations (cf. Conolly 1999a, 21). These characteristics define the 63 'prismatic' blades in Table 11.29, which have a mean length of 27.5 mm (although none were actually complete, and the majority show evidence of intentional truncation at both ends), width of 1.2 cm, and thickness of 0.29 cm. In the small sample selected for more detailed attribute analysis from Building 1 (n = 51), 27 per cent of the prismatic blades retained their remnant striking platforms, all of which are punctiform with detachment angles at or very near 90°. In all cases the upper dorsal surface near the platform shows many small facets, demonstrating that the core lip was prepared prior to the detachment of each blade. On the basis of their regularity, thinness and the morphology of the proximal end, these blades appear to have been produced by pressure debitage techniques (obsidian industry 5). Details of this sophisticated method are outlined systematically in Inizan *et al.* (1999), Tixier (1984) and Pelegrin (1988), and the blades from Building 1 have attributes that are consistent with this technique.

The technical attributes of the remaining blades (n = 33) suggest non-pressure, percussive (probably indirect) techniques and are described as 'non-prismatic'. They are on average twice as large as the regular, prismatic blades (6.21 × 1.91 × 0.66 cm), and have a more varied dorsal scar pattern, showing both unipolar and bipolar production techniques (obsidian industry 4 & 5) (e.g. Fig. 11.30b:7–11 on CD). There appear to be at least two separate production methods in operation for percussive blades: roughly a third (n = 12) are the products of a method that appears to be similar to the naviform method seen in the Levantine PPNB (Nishiaki 2000). These obsidian industry 4 blades are very much larger than those found elsewhere in Building 1 (9.8 × 2.79 × 0.87 cm vs. 2.61 × 1.09 × 0.33 cm), although this can partly be explained by the fact that most of the hoarded blades were recovered intact, whereas the non-hoarded blades are typically truncated at the

Table 11.29. *Building 1 debitage categories (not including 138 artefacts recorded by count and weight only).*

Debitage category	Obsidian count	Obsidian count %	Flint count	Flint count %
Flakes	1070	77.6	18	69.2
Prismatic blades	63	4.6	0	0
Non-prismatic blades	33	2.4	6	23.1
Crested blades	3	0.2	0	0
Core platform tables	1	0.1	0	0
Blade cores	0	0	0	0
Flake cores	2	0.1	0	0
Shatter	132	9.6	0	0
Chips	39	2.8	0	0
Indeterminable	36	2.6	2	7.7
Total	1379	100	26	100

Table 11.35. *Phase B1.1 debitage categories (abbreviations for Tables 11.35–11.39: PB = prismatic blade; Non-PB = non-prismatic blade; CB = crested blade; C-T = core tablet; Fl. Core = flake core Ind. = indeterminate).*

Phase	Space	No.	Weight (g)	Flakes	PB	Non-PB	CB	Shatter	Chips	Ind.
B1.1A	155/186	10	7.9	10	0	0	0	0	0	0
B1.1B	186	10	9.6	9	0	0	0	0	0	1
B1.1B	186/187	49	32.6	37	1	1	0	6	0	4
B1.1B	187	32	25.0	23	1	2	0	2	0	4
B1.1B	69/186/187	5	3.7	3	0	0	0	1	0	1
B1.1B	71	156	188	129	2	5	1	12	0	7
B1.1B	71/152/186	15	13.4	1	2	1	0	0	1	1
B1.1B	71/153/187	14	12.8	14	0	0	0	0	0	0
B1.1B	71/186/187	24	23.4	19	0	0	0	1	0	4
B1.1B	71/73	11	7.3	1	0	0	0	0	0	1
Total	-	326	327	264	6	9	1	22	1	23

proximal and/or distal ends (Fig. 11.31c:1–12 on CD). In any event, non-prismatic and non-hoarded blades represent a less standardized method of production than the prismatic blade manufacture, as their cross-sections are less-standardized (varying between triangular and trapezoidal), and their scar patterns show some bipolar reduction strategies (4.12 × 1.42 × 0.54 cm). It is possible that these blades are themselves products of the same reduction sequence used for prismatic blades but are derived from earlier, preparatory, stages in core reduction. On the other hand, as percussive blade strategies were employed prior to pressure techniques, these blades are likely products of an altogether separate reduction process unrelated to prismatic blade production.

Flint

There are only 18 flint flakes from Building 1, which limits the discussion to a few descriptive details. Flint flakes are on average a few millimetres larger than their obsidian counterparts (2.55 × 1.85 × 0.53 cm) and, as noted above, one retains a residual cortical surface; none retain their proximal end. Examination of the dorsal surface shows that most have more than three dorsal

Table 11.36. *Phase B1.2 debitage categories.*

Phase	Space	No.	Weight (g)	Flakes	PB	Non-PB	Shatter	Chips	Ind.
B1.2A	186	28	28.6	24	1	0	2	0	1
B1.2A	186/187	4	2.6	2	1	1	0	0	0
B1.2A	187	3	0.3	3	0	0	0	0	0
B1.2A	71	27	40.5	24	1	0	1	0	1
B1.2B	186	22	24.7	19	1	0	1	0	1
B1.2B	186/187	2	0.7	2	0	0	0	0	0
B1.2B	187	3	0.5	3	0	0	0	0	0
B1.2B	71	82	272.6	59	1	12	6	3	1
B1.2C	186	22	24.7	19	1	0	1	0	1
B1.2C	187	2	12.3	1	0	1	0	0	0
B1.2C	71	51	57.6	46	0	0	4	1	0
Total	-	246	465	202	6	14	15	4	5

Table 11.37. *Phase B1.3 debitage categories.*

Phase	Space	No.	Weight (g)	Flakes	PB	Non-PB	Shatter	Chips	Ind.
B1.3	110	15	9.8	13	2	0	0	0	0
B1.3	183	1	0.1	0	0	0	1	0	0
B1.3	186	10	6.6	8	0	0	2	0	0
B1.3	186/187	2	1.9	0	1	1	0	0	0
B1.3	187	44	194.5	38	2	1	2	1	0
B1.3	188	92	90.5	65	12	1	11	0	3
B1.3	71	8	20.8	4	1	0	3	0	0
Total	-	172	324.2	128	18	3	19	1	3

Table 11.38. *Phase B1.4 debitage categories.*

Phase	Space	No.	Weight (g)	Flakes	PB	Non-PB	Fl. Core	Shatter	Chips	Ind.
B1.4	110	15	10.5	12	3	0	0	0	0	0
B1.4	111	9	7.7	9	0	0	0	0	0	0
B1.4	183	82	36.4	72	5	1	0	3	0	1
B1.4	186	18	12.2	9	3	1	0	3	2	0
B1.4	187	27	34.0	19	3	1	1	1	1	1
B1.4	71	2	0.3	2	0	0	0	0	0	0
B1.4	71/110	1	9.4	1	0	0	0	0	0	0
Total	-	154	110.4	124	14	3	1	7	3	2

Table 11.39. *Phase B1.5 debitage categories.*

Phase	Space	No.	Weight (g)	Flakes	PB	Non-PB	CB	C-T	Fl. Core	Shatter	Chips	Ind.
B1.5A	110	34	147.5	24	2	1	0	0	1	5	0	1
B1.5A	110/183	5	0.9	4	0	0	0	0	0	1	0	0
B1.5A	111	11	4.6	10	0	0	0	0	0	0	1	0
B1.5A	183	66	40.5	45	5	0	1	0	0	12	2	1
B1.5A	184/187	18	12.4	15	0	0	0	0	0	1	2	0
B1.5A	185	8	4.1	5	1	0	0	0	0	1	1	0
B1.5A	186	84	40.7	70	0	0	0	0	0	11	2	1
B1.5A	186/187	8	12.2	8	0	0	0	0	0	0	0	0
B1.5A	187	73	112.1	51	2	4	0	0	0	8	6	2
B1.5A	71	22	21.1	11	1	0	0	0	0	9	1	0
B1.5A	71/187	5	3.5	5	0	0	0	0	0	0	0	0
B1.5B	183	10	7.2	5	0	0	0	0	0	4	1	0
B1.5B	184	35	33.5	17	1	1	1	1	0	5	9	0
B1.5B	185	150	127.9	118	6	5	0	0	0	15	5	1
B1.5B	188	8	6.3	5	2	0	0	0	0	1	0	0
B1.5C	184	21	14	14	3	0	0	0	0	3	1	0
B1.5C	184/187	18	12.4	15	0	0	0	0	0	1	2	0
B1.5C	185	5	1.4	5	0	0	0	0	0	0	0	0
B1.5C	72/185	2	0.5	2	0	0	0	0	0	0	0	0
Total	-	583	602.8	429	23	11	2	1	1	77	33	6

scars, which taken with their small size, is suggestive of intensive core reduction.

The flint blades are equivalent to the non-prismatic obsidian blades described above, but are on average slightly larger (4.54 × 2.0 × 0.6 cm; note again that none of these blades are complete lengthwise). They are unipolar and have triangular or trapezoidal cross-sections (flint industry 3), and are produced via percussive methods (Fig. 11.30b:9–11 on CD). No blade cores or debris that could be related to flint blade reduction were recovered from Building 1.

The obsidian and flint industries from Building 1 are described on the attached CD.

Summary by phase and space

A breakdown of the chipped stone by phase and space shows that, by count, Building 1's Phase B1.5 has the largest quantity of material associated with it (n = 580), followed by Phases B1.1, B1.2, B1.3 and B1.4, the latter of which has more than four times less material than Phase B1.5 (n = 154) (Tables 11.35–11.39). Proportions of debitage are relatively consistent between the phases. In the long-term technological history of Çatalhöyük, blade-making techniques undergo massive changes. Building 1 straddles the dividing line between flake and blade techniques, but phase differences are chronologically too subtle to pick up any changes in debitage techniques (e.g. blade proportions change from 4.6, 8.1, 12.2, 11.0, to 5.8 from Phases B1.1–5, respectively).

With regard to the changing use of space, examination of the percentage of 'waste' per phase, here calculated as the sum of unretouched flakes, shatter and chips divided by the total count, shows too that there are few differences between the five phases, all having upwards of 75 per cent waste in their composite assemblages (Table 11.40).

In summary, there are few notable differences in the character of the material between the phases

Table 11.40. *Amount of waste per phase.*

Phase	Waste	Total count	Percentage waste
B1.1A	10	10	100
B1.1B	243	316	76.9
B1.2A	52	62	83.9
B1.2B	86	109	78.9
B1.2C	64	75	85.3
B1.3	134	172	77.9
B1.4	125	154	81.2
B1.5A	285	334	85.3
B1.5B	171	203	84.2
B1.5C	41	46	89.1

Table 11.41. *Building 1 count and weight of material by unit type (dry-sieved samples only).*

Unit category	Dry-sieve volume	Number	Weight (g)	Mean weight (g)	Density (g/100 L)
Arbitrary	677	35	44.7	1.3	6.6
Cluster	0	12	13.0	1.1	na
Construction/make-up/packing	9164	88	128.5	1.5	1.4
Construction/make-up	110	3	0.4	0.1	0.3
Fill	51984	715	1195.0	1.7	2.3
Floors (use)	1701	89	159.7	1.8	9.4
Skeleton	0	6	7.5	1.2	na

Table 11.42. *Building 1 weight and density of artefacts by fill type (dry-sieved samples only).*

Fill type	Dry-sieve volume	Number	Weight (g)	Mean weight (g)	Density (g/100 L)
Building	49,487	529	829.1	1.6	1.7
Bin	210	5	3.8	0.8	1.8
Burial	778	30	24.5	0.8	3.1
Gully	15	2	0.5	0.3	3.4
Pit	1299	106	122.2	1.2	9.4
Posthole	0	1	1.4	1.4	na
Scoop	195	42	213.5	5.1	109.5

Table 11.43. *Building 1 count, weight and density of lithic artefacts by floor type (dry-sieved samples only).*

Floor type	Dry-sieve volume	Number	Weight (g)	Mean weight (g)	Density (g/100 L)
Basin	15	3	1.13	0.4	7.5
Bin	120	3	4.05	1.4	3.4
General	1323	69	129.62	1.9	9.8
Hearth	40	4	3.95	1.0	9.9
Oven	0	2	12.15	6.1	na
Raised area (platform)	203	8	8.83	1.1	4.3

Table 11.44. *Lithic counts and densities by Building 1 features.*

Count	Feature	Feature type	Dry-sieve volume (L)	Density (per 100 L)
120	17	Pit	975	12.3
55	369	Fire installation	0	na
41	362	Pit	424	9.7
35	11	Fire installation	40	87.5
20	34	Basin	0	na
20	361	Fire installation	52	38.5
17	5	Wall	2190	0.8
16	6	Wall	2205	0.7
15	1	Wall	2190	0.7
15	4	Wall	2180	0.7
15	7	Wall	1010	1.5
13	364	Pillar	0	na
12	384	Burial	50	24
11	38	Burial	0	na
9	381	Wall feature	360	2.5
8	32	Platform	90	8.9
8	359	Fire installation	0	na
8	374	Crawl-hole	15	53.3
7	2	Wall	850	0.8
7	39	Fire installation	360	1.9
7	363	Linear	95	7.4
6	13	Platform	155	3.9
6	29	Burial	330	1.8
5	3	Wall	1580	0.3
5	31	Burial	0	na
5	37	Platform	57	8.8
5	40	Burial	0	na
5	215	Bin	0	na
4	28	Burial	400	1
4	30	Burial	0	na
4	42	Burial	0	na
4	204	Burial	0	na
4	209	Burial	23	17.4
3	27	Basin	15	20
3	213	Burial	0	na
2	8	Wall	0	na
2	10	Wall	25	8
2	15	Wall	210	1
2	20	Wall	45	4.4
2	47	Burial	0	na
2	48	Wall relief	0	na
2	360	Fire installation	60	3.3
1	14	Fire installation	0	na
1	36	Burial	0	na
1	200	Burial	30	3.3
1	202	Burial	0	na
1	205	Burial	0	na
1	206	Burial	0	na
1	208	Burial	0	na
1	212	Burial	30	3.3
1	366	Ladder	20	5.0
1	372	Post	0	na
1	376	Burial	0	na

of Building 1, and the differences in the quantity of material in each of the spaces can be attributed to the different volumes of soil excavated. In the most general terms, each phase is basically composed of many small, unretouched flakes and chips and shatter (upwards of 75 per cent) primarily from obsidian industry 1, with smaller amounts of blades and retouched flakes. Phase B1.5 contains the only (phased) evidence for core-reduction activity (with two crested blades, a core-tablet, and a flake core), but little evidence exists in any phase for *in situ* knapping, with one possible exception, discussed below.

Analysis of unit density

Analysis of density by unit category for the whole of Building 1 shows that, unsurprisingly, most debitage comes from fill deposits (Table 11.41), although the highest density of material is associated with the floor category. The average size of pieces (i.e. as calculated by g/n) is also highest for floor deposits.

Breakdown of fill deposits into further categories perhaps provides a more useful comparison (Table 11.42). Here, it can be seen that 'scoop' deposits have the highest density, with 'pit' fills following well behind. The high density and size of objects found in the former is largely driven by F.362 (see below), which contained a large amount of debitage and some large tools.

Floor deposits can be examined in a similar manner (Table 11.43). If one ignores 'hearth' floors with their low frequency of objects (n = 4), the highest densities are related to non-specific (i.e. 'general') floor categories. This density value compares with pit deposits, as does the average weight of objects ('pits' = 1.2, 'general floors' = 1.9). The majority of these objects are small unretouched flakes and shatter, with very few (n = 15) showing evidence of retouch. Of these, seven are *pièces esquillées*, with the remainder consisting only of marginally-retouched flakes and blade fragments. Pit deposits are largely similar in composition (i.e. mostly consisting of debitage, *pièces esquillées*, and a few marginally-retouched blades and flakes), with the notable exception of (1334), where a tip of a biface was recovered from a deposit that also included bone tools.

Feature summary

Examination of the quantity of material in the 53 features with chipped stone shows that, with a few exceptions, densities are relatively low (Table 11.44). In general terms, it is extremely difficult to relate most of the chipped stone found in Building 1 to activities that may have taken place there during the use-life of the structure. Floors were for the most part kept clear of artefacts and the fill of buildings is also relatively 'clean'. Of the 53 defined features in Building 1 with chipped stone, five deserve special mention as they provide evidence for activities during the use of the building: (i) fire installation F.11; (ii) pit F.362; (iii) fire installation F.361; (iv) pit F.17; and (v) basin F.34. They are different from other features largely because of the

Table 11.45. *North Area external spaces debitage categories.*

Phase	Space	Count	Weight (g)	Flakes	Prismatic blades	Non-prismatic blades	Shatter	Chips	Ind.
B1.E1	73	16	7.7	13	0	0	1	2	0
B1.E1	73/77	2	1.2	1	0	0	0	0	1
B1.E2	153	16	8.3	6	0	1	0	7	2
B1.E2	69	17	9.7	14	1	1	0	0	1
B1.E2	73	129	47.1	77	2	0	12	5	1
B1.E3	72/185	2	0.5	2	0	0	0	0	0
Total	-	182	74.5	113	3	2	13	14	5

quantity of material found within them, and are interesting for the clues they provide to help make sense of the depositional process of chipped stone.

F.11 is a fire installation in the southwest corner of Space 184/187, and contains a total of 35 lithic artefacts (>4 mm), mostly consisting of small unretouched flakes. Note that F.11 is the latest phase of a long-lived fire-installation; the earlier two phases being F.359 and F.360. The latter two features have fewer artefacts ($n = 8$ and 2 respectively). (1108) consists of ashy fill as part of this F.11, containing small unretouched flakes and one of the very small possible biface fragments (?obsidian industry 1). Interestingly, the sample also contains a small fragment of what might be a crested-blade (1108.A16), and six pieces of what look to be biface fragments (obsidian industry 7). These pieces do not refit, and therefore might be from a number of different bifaces. As this sample also contained large amounts of <4-mm debris, my interpretation is that it contains production waste from knapping activities.

F.362 is a scoop at the southern end of Space 184/185, although it includes deposits described as mixed. It produced a large amount of debitage but only three retouched pieces: two blades and a *pièce esquillée* (obsidian industry 1). The excavators note that it might be a post-occupation event related to F.11. There is nothing in this assemblage that could be used to argue against that interpretation. Indeed, the density of material matches that of the fire-installation.

There is some ambiguity surrounding F.361, insofar as it is not clear to the excavators whether it is actually a hearth, or for that matter, a feature. However, on the basis of the amount and character of chipped stone in the fill (predominantly on the eastern half of the feature: (1121) and (1122) contain most of the material), it appears to be hearth-like, in that it has a high density of debitage, mostly unretouched flakes, a small blade fragment, and a *pièce esquillée* (obsidian industry 1).

F.17 is a pit cut into Building 1 after its abandonment, possibly to retrieve wall mouldings (F.48) on wall F.3. It is worth noting for the quantity of material recovered, although as its excavated soil volume is correspondingly high, this is not in itself unusual. However, as the pit is post-abandonment, the character of the chipped-stone assemblage might be able to shed some light on the relative time between abandonment of Building 1, and the filling of the pit. In fact, the character of the pit assemblage seems very much a representative sample of the material found in Building 1. The percentage of blades is relatively low ($n = 6$; 5.0 per cent), which suggests that the chipped-stone assemblage is relatively close in time to the abandonment of the building (as later assemblages have upwards of 50 per cent blades). (1334) consists of fill within this feature, with a number ($n = 29$) of mainly unretouched flakes, although a possible biface fragment (1334.X5), a flint drill/piercer (1334.A1), a retouched flint blade (1334.X3) and an obsidian *pièce esquillée* are also part of the unit. The relatively high number of tools and the fact that they are found in conjunction with a number of bone points, suggests that some of these objects were intentionally selected and specially placed in the base of the pit.

F.34 is a basin in Space 187, adjacent to wall F.3. It is unusual because it has a large amount of lithic material (largely unretouched flakes) in the fill ($n = 20$), the majority of which came from the heavy-residue sample. While the pit fill is not particularly ashy, debitage was included when the pit was filled (and the floors above constructed?).

These five features stand apart from the other features that contain chipped stone largely because of the quantity of debris that they contain, or in the case of F.17, the number of tools and type of deposit. However, the fact that it is mostly debris gives us an important clue to how knapping waste may have been managed in buildings where people lived. Given that the highest densities of debris are found in the ashy deposits of fire-installations (or suspected fire-installations), it appears that hearths were important intermediary places where waste was placed. This goes some way to explaining the wider phenomenon of higher densities of debitage being associated with ashy deposits outside buildings, as the discard process for knapping debris seems to begin with its deposition in fire-installations within houses. This also lends weight to arguments that knapping activity took place within households.

Description of significant units

There are a number of other individual units from Building 1 that are worth drawing attention to, either because of their notable context, or because they contain particularly interesting objects. (1461) an obsidian hoard (n = 12, 217 g) is arguably the most important chipped-stone assemblage from Building 1. It is a remarkable collection of blades struck from a large opposed-platform core (obsidian industry 4). Six of the blades are from one end of the core, and six from the other (Fig. 11.31c:1–12 on CD); the latter group are what have been referred to as 'upsilon' blades (Ataman 1988). The former group possess extremely sharp pointed edges that require only modification of the proximal end to form one of Çatalhöyük's more characteristic projectile types (cf. Bialor 1962, 69–70 & fig. 3.8–3.11 *inter alia*; Mellaart 1964a, 103 & pl. XXVI,a). The hoard was located in the southern end of Space 71 underneath a grinding area (F.27) with an upturned quern that appears to have been positioned deliberately as part of the abandonment process of this part of Building 1 (Volume 3, Part 3). Fragments of two of the blades were analyzed at CNRS, their trace-elemental signatures correlating with the Nenezi Dağ source (Chapter 12).

(1471) is noted as a possible retrieved hoard (Volume 3, Part 3), although it only contained a single chipped stone artefact when excavated, a heavily-used *pièce esquillée*.

(1387) and (1388), part of F.364, contain a total of thirteen objects, with ten small unretouched obsidian flakes, one unretouched prismatic blade fragment, and a possible biface fragment (obsidian industry 7). There is nothing remarkable about the assemblage; it appears to be a random assortment of debitage, but it is likely that the material was deliberately placed at the base of the moulded wall feature and might therefore have some symbolic meaning.

(1392) is the fill of a stake hole, which is part of F.369, discussed above, where all of the chipped stone (n = 55) was recovered. The artefacts are small flakes and debris, and appear to have been intentionally placed. (1108) is an ashy fill that is part of F.11, discussed above. The artefacts consist of small, unretouched flakes and a small possible biface fragment (obsidian industry 7).

Spaces external to Building 1

A small amount of chipped stone (n = 182) was recovered in the spaces external to Building 1 (Table 11.45), the majority of which are small unretouched flakes. No cores were recovered. There were twelve retouched pieces, all of which are obsidian. They consist of a set of possibly four very small fragments of one or more bifaces (three from (1306) and one from (1396)), four *pièces esquillées* ((1320), (3021) & (3206)), three small and irregularly-retouched flakes ((1346), (1381) & (3020)), and a small bilaterally-retouched blade from (1351). No significant deposits of knapped stone were otherwise located outside Building 1.

The 1999 KOPAL Area

by Tristan Carter

Of the 89 units excavated in the 1999 KOPAL Area, 43 produced chipped stone (48.3 per cent), with a total of 304 pieces (Table 11.1). The assemblage comprised 289 pieces of obsidian (95.1 per cent) and 15 of flint, weighing 127.995 g and 90.73 g respectively (Table 11.46). The data display marked discrepancies with regard to the obsidian and flint assemblages in terms of their recovery and mean weights (Table 11.4). Virtually all the flint came from the dry sieve with only two pieces generated by the numerous heavy-residue samples, indicating that these non-local resources were not being worked on this part of the site, but instead were introduced as ready-made blanks. Conversely, the heavy-residue sample produced the greater number of obsidian (Table 11.4), albeit in the form of lightweight 'shatter', indicating that some knapping occurred in the KOPAL Area, though again one has the impression that obsidian implements were manufactured primarily elsewhere and brought to the site. When the data are contextualized, the KOPAL Area produced a very low density of material compared to the broadly contemporary deposits excavated on Çatalhöyük East in Space 181 (Fig. 11.31).

The KOPAL Area chipped-stone assemblage came from two distinct chronological horizons, namely above and below the backswamp clay, or 'Lower Alluvium' (Volume 3, Part 4), with the majority of the chipped stone coming from the earlier deposits (Table 11.46). The flint and obsidian industries from the KOPAL Area are described on the attached CD.

Consumption and chronology

An important issue relating to the KOPAL Area lowest material, is its functional and temporal relationship with Çatalhöyük East. With regard to the activities represented, one can immediately note that far less material was consumed in this off-site area compared to those (midden and dumps) from the South Area in the Level Pre-XII sequence (Fig. 11.31). Furthermore, in contrast with the open spaces of Space 181, the lower KOPAL Area assemblage is dominated by end products. In turn, the relative quantity of utilized dry-sieved obsidian from the lower KOPAL Area deposits is slightly higher than that from Level Pre-XII.A–B assemblages but slightly lower than those

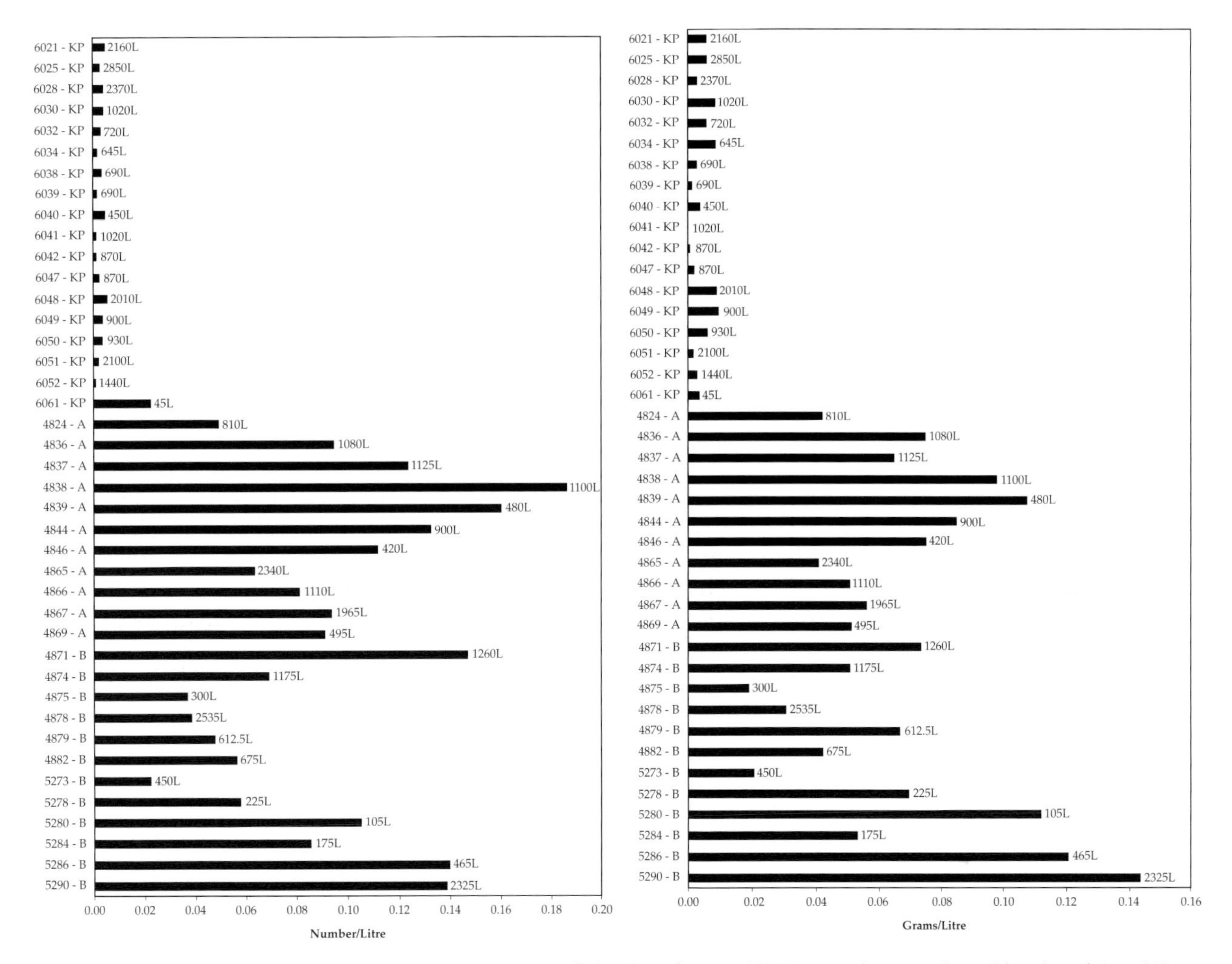

Figure 11.31. *(Right) Comparing relative quantities of obsidian from KOPAL Area lower cultural level and Level Pre-XII.A–B in Space 181 (dry sieve – number/litre and grams/litre). (Left) Comparing relative quantities of obsidian from KOPAL Area lower cultural level and Level Pre-XII.A–B in Space 181 (dry sieve – grams/litre).*

Table 11.46. *Chipped stone from KOPAL Area: number and weight by level.*

Context	Chipped stone count	Obsidian count	Obsidian weight (g)	'Flint' count	'Flint' weight (g)
Above backswamp clay	12	11	9.88	1	9.19
Below backswamp clay	294	280	121.545	14	81.54

from Level Pre-XII.C–D. The relative quantity of utilized dry-sieved flint from all of these early contexts appears to be much the same (Fig. 11.34).

With post Level XI domestic contexts appearing to be the primary locus for chipped-stone production at Çatalhöyük, then the structure of the KOPAL Area assemblage might perhaps be as expected. As to the particulars of how this material was consumed, there appears to be no specific pattern suggesting one function above any other. While crop processing seems to have been a major concern in the KOPAL Area, none of the chipped stone can be clearly linked to any such activities, with no sickle elements or any other blanks bearing 'gloss'; such pieces are, however, known from Level Pre-XII off-site deposits in the South Area.

The faunal record includes significant amounts of wild resources akin to what is seen in the Level Pre-XII deposits of the South Area (see Volume 4, Chapter 2), yet the KOPAL Area assemblage only produced what appears to be a single fragmentary projectile (Fig. 11.32b:14 on CD), in contrast to the Level Pre-XII.A–D assemblages that generated a not insubstantial quantity of points. With regard to the alleged working of skins, our assemblage does provide two scrapers (Fig. 11.32c:3–4 on CD), though this hardly represents a notable concentration.

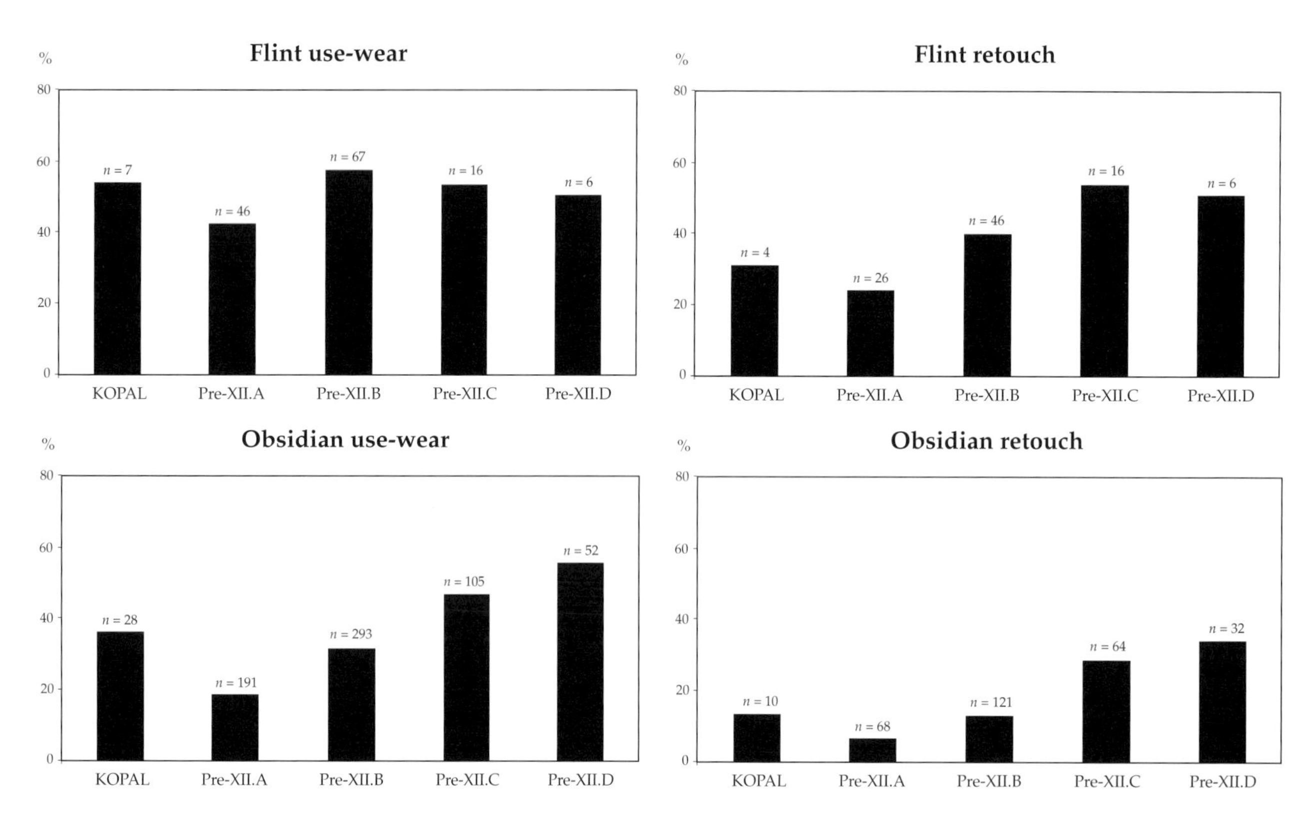

Figure 11.34. *(Left) Comparing the relative quantity of chipped stone with use-wear from KOPAL Area lower deposits with assemblages from Level Pre-XII.A–D contexts (sample = dry sieve). (Right) Comparing the relative quantity of chipped stone with retouched modification from KOPAL lower deposits with assemblages from Pre-Level XII.A–D contexts (sample = dry sieve).*

Concerning the assemblage's date, there are a few strands of evidence that can be used to suggest that the lower KOPAL Area material should equate roughly with Level Pre-XII.B (Space 181, South Area), i.e. in general accordance with the recent radiocarbon dates from the site (Cessford 2001, 723). That the site should fall somewhere within the Aceramic period of Çatalhöyük's [pre]history is well attested (see Chapters 4 & 5 and Volume 3, Part 4). The lower KOPAL Area chipped-stone assemblage indeed contains a quantity of the small percussive obsidian blade industry and opposed platform cores that form the technological/typological mainstay of the Level Pre-XII assemblages. Moreover, the lower KOPAL Area assemblage contains a few large unipolar and bipolar obsidian blades that are paralleled in the Level Pre-XII.B–D sequence (obsidian industries 4 & 5); however, it lacks the distinctive components associated with the earliest material from the South Area, specifically the Aşıklı Höyük-like features we have from Level Pre-XII.C–D, such as the naviform obsidian 'big-blade' technology (including projectiles and end-scrapers) and large flake-scrapers. The KOPAL Area did produce microblade cores (Fig. 11.32a:4–7 on CD, obsidian industry 2), though none of the associated microblades, or modified microliths, suggesting differential consumption and depositional habits to those of the Level Pre-XII.B–D off-site deposits in the South Area.

Perhaps the most significant piece of evidence that should chronologically link the KOPAL Area with Level Pre-XII.B is a backed core-tablet of light-brown limnoquartzite (Fig. 11.32c:1 on CD) that has an almost identical parallel from Space 181, Level Pre-XII.B (Fig. 11.6e:5 on CD). Both pieces are highly distinctive, share the same raw material, technology and typology and are the only examples so far documented from the new excavations. Further evidence to link KOPAL Area and the Level Pre-XII.B sequence is provided by the relative quantity of implements knapped from red radiolarite in their respective assemblages (Fig. 11.35). Finally, the KOPAL Area assemblage also included what appears to be the basal end of an obsidian unifacially-retouched point made on a prismatic blade (Fig. 11.32b:14 on CD); such projectiles, also known as Canhasan points (Ataman 1988, 117–19), are known primarily from Level Pre-XII.B contexts at Çatalhöyük.

Discussion

by Tristan Carter

The contextual analysis of the chipped stone from the 1995–99 excavations allows us to consider numerous issues and generate questions anew. This end of chapter discussion cannot hope to do justice to them all but instead focuses on a few that seem to relate most closely to the material produced by the recent work at Çatalhöyük.

Raw materials

Obsidian represents the primary raw material employed for chipped-stone technology throughout the Aceramic and Early Neolithic periods, usually in excess of 95 per cent of a level's assemblage (Fig. 11.37; Tables 11.1–11.2). A detailed consideration of the Çatalhöyük obsidians and their origin, in the light of a new characterization study, is presented in Chapter 12. The flint component is represented by a number of raw materials through the Level Pre-XII.D–Level V–IV sequence, mainly in the form of various coloured limnoquartzites, followed by red, then green radiolarites, plus small amounts of flint, chert, jasper and quartzite. The greatest consumption of flint (Fig. 11.36; Tables 11.1–11.2) and the widest variety of 'flints' (a claim based on visual inspection alone) is to be found during the earliest deposits at Çatalhöyük, namely Level Pre-XII.A–D (see below). Tan/brown/grey-brown limnoquartzite seems to be the staple flint worked at the site after Level Pre-XII.B, with most of the remaining material present in the form of finished implements. We unfortunately have little idea as to how many sources might be represented by our different raw materials, or indeed the significance of the varying colours within a 'single' resource such as limnoquartzite (including grey/brown/orange/red/pink and white), or radiolarite (green and red). Nor do we have any clear idea as to the location of these sources. Thus we unfortunately add little to Mellaart's claims of the 1960s, namely that the Taurus Mountains and southeast Anatolia represent some of the likeliest sources of our flint (Mellaart 1963, 103; 1967, 213); these issues are discussed further in Volume 6.

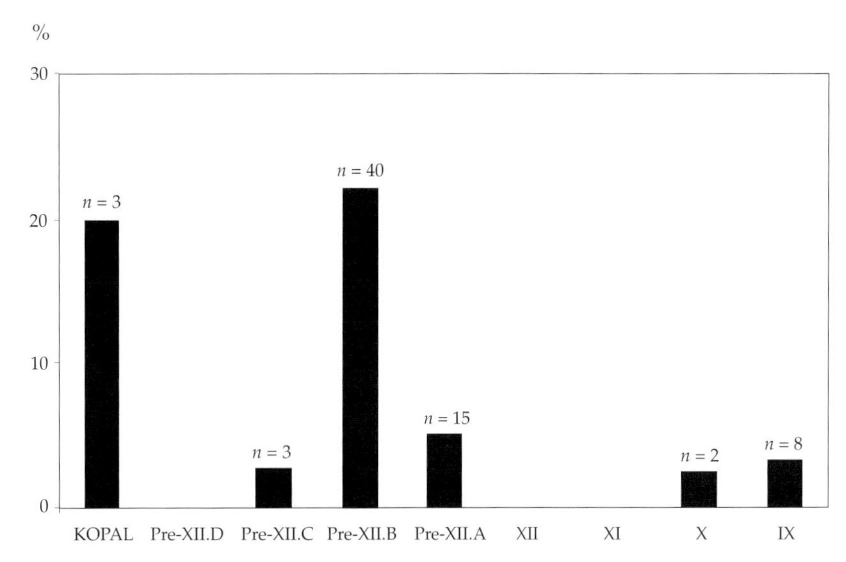

Figure 11.35. *Comparing the relative quantity of red radiolarite in flint assemblages from KOPAL lower deposits with assemblages from the South Area, Space 181.*

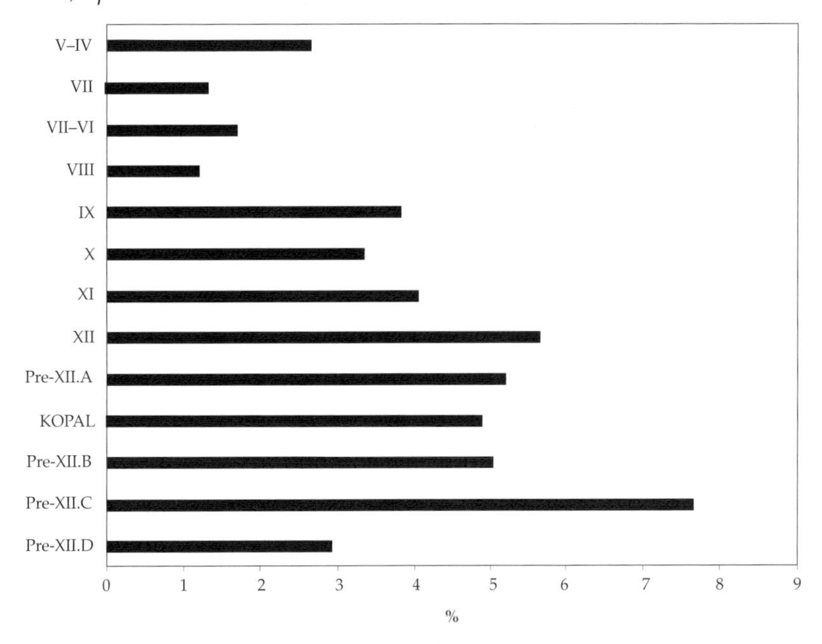

Figure 11.36. *Relative quantity of flint by level.*

Chipped-stone technologies at Çatalhöyük: diachronic and chrono-cultural perspectives

Throughout the Neolithic sequence the chipped-stone assemblages of Çatalhöyük embody multiple technologies and a variety of raw materials, the consumption of which undoubtedly involved the community drawing upon and experiencing a wide range of people, places, histories and knowledge. The nature of production changes through time, but the evidence for multiple *chaînes opératoires* is a recurrent feature from the earliest levels onward (Tables 11.47–11.48). The one tradition that continues throughout Level Pre-XII.D to Level V–IV is obsidian industry 1, a relatively unskilled technology using a percussive technique to manufacture small blades/blade-like flakes, the cores worked intensively until they resembled small splintered lumps of obsidian, or *pièces esquillées*. While this industry was performed locally and represents the mainstay mode of production at Çatalhöyük, it is not a tradition in isolation. The same industry is seemingly also attested at Canhasan III, Musular and Yellibellen during the Aceramic Neolithic (cf. Ataman 1988, 68–9; Balkan-Atlı 1998, 85; Özbaşaran 1999, 152), forming part of a broader suite of shared technologies and practices that define a sphere of interaction linking these central Anatolian communities.

From the outset it would appear that obsidian industry 1 was performed on site, employing a particular form of raw material as its point of departure, namely the large 'quarry flakes' that define our obsidian industry 7. These thick flakes were largely decorticated and had often received further modification in the form of rough, invasive, bifacial flaking, or the retouch of an edge, transforming the piece into a side-scraper. The preparation/manufacture of these blanks is documented at two locations on the mountain of Göllü Dağ in southern Cappadocia, at Bitlikeler (bifaces and scrapers) and Kaletepe (bifaces), situated atop the obsidian flows of Kayırlı and Kömürcü of the Göllü Dağ-East 'source' (Balkan-Atlı & Der Aprahamian 1998, 249–55).

From Level X onwards we have a fairly clear idea that these 'quarry flakes' were being accessed on a building-by-building basis. Having procured these blocks of raw material it seems that the inhabitants of each structure may then have deposited a significant proportion, if not all of them into specially-prepared pits located within their building's 'zone of transformative processes' ('dirty area'), usually in the southeast corner close to a hearth, or oven (cf. Mellaart 1963, 103). In certain instances these hoarding events may have been an end unto themselves, i.e. an act of burial, never to be retrieved, as is suggested by the hoard (1461) in Building 1. In other cases, however, the hoards were retrieved eventually, their burial having served to store a precious resource, or 'capital' (Mellaart 1963, 103), or perhaps as a process of 'domesticating' the 'wild' obsidian, transforming it into cultural objects and making it safe before it was worked by the inhabitants (Conolly 2003). Upon retrieval these large 'quarry flakes' (obsidian industry 7) served as the raw material/cores for obsidian industry 1. The resultant debris from the performance of obsidian industry 1 became the backbone of the obsidian clusters and rake-out assemblages that comprise the 'dirty area' assemblages. Level X's Building 23 (Space 178) provides us with the clearest evidence for the relationship between the two obsidian industries (1 and 7) with blades and blade-like flakes conjoining a core made from a large 'quarry flake', while chunks of other reworked bifaces and flake scrapers have been found in numerous other rake-out contexts. There is also good evidence to suggest that this *chaîne opératoire* was in existence from the beginning of the settlement, with an obsidian industry 1 core made on fragmentary flake scraper recovered from one of the midden deposits in Level Pre-XII.D (Fig. 11.4b:15 on CD).

Obsidian industry 1 is also the tradition that Conolly (1999a, 65–6; 1999b) described as the Çatalhöyük 'flake industry' (his obsidian strategy IV), the dominant mode of obsidian working from the earliest levels until Level VI.B when there was a radical shift to a prismatic blade-based technology. This author (Carter) takes issue with the definition of the 'flake industry' as it has been employed and stresses that the history of chipped-stone technology at Çatalhöyük is far more complex than an 'early : flake industry/late : blade-industry' dichotomy. It can be agreed that the bulk of the blanks produced within this tradition can typologically be classified as 'flakes', but it is the blades/blade-like flakes that were chosen primarily for use and/or modification, hence its conceptualization as a 'blade/blade-like flake' industry. Indeed, as Conolly (see above) himself reports, although a small percentage of the flakes had use-wear and/or retouch, the majority are small, irregular, and are likely the waste by-products of core reduction rather than blanks for tool use.

From a formalist perspective, obsidian industry 1 could be seen as eminently 'wasteful', an expedient technology involving a somewhat *ad hoc* reduction strategy and the discard of a large proportion of the core's mass as unused 'waste'. However, one might suggest an alternative interpretation focusing on how the debris from this tradition became part of each building's fabric, the daily experience of its black, shiny, jagged and crunchy texture being a habituated part of the structure's space, light, feeling and sound. In turn, the carefully-structured and repetitive practices of generating debris, followed by the cleansing of the 'dirty area', may have come to encapsulate a certain period, or cycle of 'domestic time', akin to the acts of plastering the walls and floors. One might further wonder if the relationship between the fire installations and obsidian brought some cosmological order, or temporality to place and practice? Might we see the fires that provided the occupants' heat, light and media of transformation, as embodying the lightening and flames of the surrounding mountains/volcanoes, the 'producer' of the Cappadocian obsidian. The interpretation could be pushed further by considering whether the flames, obsidian, flint, bone, plants and other fixed and mobiliary features of the house represented (embodied) the outside world 'writ small', whereby the Çatalhöyük buildings were mud-brick encapsulations of the cosmos, replete with traces of all that their inhabitants knew and belonged to, albeit in domesticated, controlled and reassuring form. As such, one might further posit that the carpet of obsidian in the 'dirty area' came to represent a necessary component of the building, analogous to the suggested structural role of the 'art' at Çatalhöyük (Last 1998). One should be wary, however, of focusing solely on the material, and remind ourselves of the characters, movement and activities represented in the palimpsests of black glass, to try and envision the performances and sounds played out in these buildings, the click/clack/crunch/shatter/spray that helped form the rhythms of the peoples' lives.

The highly-distinctive microblades and modified microliths that define obsidian industry 2 and its flint counterpart (flint industry 1) form a technology restricted to the earliest levels thus far excavated at Çatalhöyük, specifically Level Pre-XII.B–D. The recent excavations produced a not insignificant number of microliths from wet sieving, their quantity, freshness, state and occasional associated core serving to indicate that they are clearly products of this period, and not residual material from an earlier occupation as suggested recently by Baird (2002, 143). This industry links the early community with an Epipalaeolithic tradition known from the Konya plain and the Mediterranean coast. These fine, tiny asymmetric triangular tools (under 2 cm long) have parallels from the nearby site of Pinabarşı A dating to the ninth millennium cal BC, and from a series of earlier cave sites on the Mediterranean, including Öküzini, Belbaşi and Beldibi (Bostancı 1962, 261, pl. V; 1965; Léotard *et al.* 1998, 515–18; Otte *et al.* 1998, 536–7).

In the 1960s excavation reports Mellaart describes a microlithic component in Çatalhöyük's obsidian assemblage, including a hoard from Level II, and argues that many of the simpler blade and flake tools 'perpetuate (or seem to perpetuate) an earlier tradition', which ultimately 'derives from the Upper Palaeolithic' (Mellaart 1963, 105, fig. 47). A much later report claims that microliths were recovered from Level Pre-XII contexts in the 1960s deep sounding (Mellaart 1998, 40) but no examples were ever illustrated. In his study Mortensen (quoted in Conolly 1999a, 6) stated that, 'genuine microliths have not been found', yet Balkan-Atlı (1994b, 128) claimed subsequently that microliths comprised seven per cent of the retouched artefacts at Çatalhöyük. Given the attention to the discovery of such pieces in 1999, and the fact that virtually all came from water sieving (a mode of recovery not employed in the 1960s excavations) the author is confident that 'true' modified, geometric microliths are only a feature of Level Pre-XII.B and earlier. Unfortunately all our examples come from midden/dump contexts, thus limiting what we can say with regard to their context(s) of production and use. It should also be noted that not entirely dissimilar microblades are documented from the roughly contemporary Aceramic Neolithic sites of Canhasan III in the Konya plain and Aciyer in south Cappadocia (Ataman 1988, 112–13; Balkan-Atlı 1998, 82).

The 'edge blades'/burinated blades of obsidian industry 3 represent a minority component of the earliest assemblages: Level Pre-XII.A–D, thereafter present as only a handful of examples. One also wonders if the significance of this 'industry' lies not so much in the manufacture of 'edge blades', but in the transformation of the large non-local implements that served as their cores; these need not necessarily be mutually-exclusive concerns. The on-site transformation of exotic pieces can be witnessed in a number of traditions at Çatalhöyük, not least the aforementioned use of 'quarry flakes' (obsidian industry 7) as the raw material for obsidian industry 1, plus the modification of ready made flint blades (flint industries 2 and 3) into sickles and perforators. Perhaps in this tradition, however, there is a greater symbolic potential, with the new products embodying depths of meaning, drawn from the use and history of their cores, namely the large projectiles and scrapers of obsidian industries 4, 5 and 6. Certainly we have good evidence from throughout the Çatalhöyük sequence that points (both arrow and spear heads) represented highly-significant forms of material culture, as evidenced through their modes of production, curation and consumption.

Throughout the earlier part of the Neolithic sequence, i.e. Level Pre-XII.D–VII there is little evidence to suggest that the long prismatic blades of obsidian industries 4 and 5 were part of a local tradition. For both industries we have the occasional rejuvenation flake relating to the maintenance of the core's platform and face (fewer of obsidian industry 5), suggesting that some of these blades may have been knapped on site, but we lack both the nuclei and preparatory material. These absences are significant because they indicate that the technical *savoir faire* responsible for the shaping of the core and the initiation of blade manufacture, were non-local forms of knowledge. Experimental work has shown clearly that in the manufacture of long, regular prismatic blades (by pressure-flaking or skilled percussive techniques), the most important and skilled part of the knapping process is not the end-removal of blanks, albeit a 'difficult, and demanding practice, that requires an extensive knowledge of rock-flaking properties as well as good neuro-muscular coordination' (Perlès 1989, 11–13), but the careful shaping and preparation of the nucleus itself (Crabtree 1968, 451; J. Pelegrin pers. comm.). Thus these blades embodied exotic knowledge, their procurement perhaps bringing with them tales of the specific knapper responsible for their production and the place, time and portents associated with the craftsperson's performance.

While these blade-based projectiles were rare and carefully handled implements, whose bodies may have come to be known by length, form, curvature, retouch and break, their distribution suggests that their powers and spirits were shared amongst the community. Certainly for the earlier part of the site's history (pre Level VI.B) each building seems to produce a handful of these pieces. While some projectiles were discarded broken and used amongst the obsidian-rich deposits that constitute the 'dirty areas', other intricately-modified examples were placed carefully into postholes, or lain on floors in the process (theatre) of abandoning the structure. Though projectiles are common to every building thus far excavated, this is not to say that these implements did not enjoy some element of exclusivity in their consumption. It remains that only a handful of points are known from each of the structures investigated between 1996–99, suggesting that their possession and use were restricted amongst the inhabitants, most likely along lines of age and/or gender. These forms of restriction may have become accentuated later in the community's life. The Building 1 (Level VI–V) hoard of beautiful, razor sharp naviform blades (1461) provides us with a hint that eventually these exotica were manipulated through preferential access and modes of consumption, as potent forms of social currency and means of distinction.

Though obsidian industries 4 and 5, as currently defined, appear to be represented throughout Levels Pre-XII.D-V–IV, one can in fact distinguish facets of these 'two' traditions that have chrono-cultural implications. For example, it has often been quite apparent that the use of a simple bipolar versus unipolar dichotomy does not do justice to the material in hand. However, given the absence of associated manufacturing debris and the small number of blades involved, we have been wary of defining new industries on the basis of one, or two 'aberrant' pieces. The author has no doubt that in due course, with larger samples, we can distinguish further traditions that are, at present, subsumed into the two defined currently. One possible future distinction might be with regard to elucidating a 'big-blade' tradition amongst the opposed platform products (obsidian industry 4), i.e. the large naviform blades employed for the manufacture of projectiles, an industry that we first witness in the earliest deposits at Çatalhöyük (Level Pre-XII.B–D), as represented by our few stemmed/Byblos points, diagnostics of an Aceramic Neolithic date (PPNB in southeast Anatolian, Cypriot and Levantine terms). These pieces genuinely seem to disappear after Level Pre-XII.B (as do other 'big blade' tools, such as end-scrapers and pointed implements), yet other non-local blade products of opposed platform technologies continue to circulate at the site, albeit of smaller size and in different retouched forms. Interestingly, these naviform blade projectiles 'reappear' much later in the early Neolithic sequence, as represented by the Level VI–V hoard from Building 1 (1461), and other hoards of bifacially-worked spearheads that Mellaart refers to from post-Level VI.B contexts.

While many of the early Çatalhöyük chipped-stone industries closely resemble those from Canhasan III and the south Cappadocian Aceramic Neolithic sites, in particular obsidian industries 4 and 5, one can also point to subtle but important distinctions. For instance, some of the projectiles made on large opposed platform blades had their tips fashioned on the proximal end, in contrast to those from Aşıklı Höyük that use the distal ends. Similarly, when one considers those points that more closely resemble the Canhasan III types (i.e. those made on slightly narrower and shorter blades), then one notes that the Çatalhöyük versions use unipolar blades rather than bipolar (Ataman 1988, 129) and employ the proximal end for the tip, rather than the distal. These discrepancies suggest that while members of the Çatalhöyük community were aware of performing certain widespread technologies and practices, namely the ways of hunting/killing embodied in the 'Big Arrowhead Industries' of the Levant, Anatolia and Cyprus (Kozlowski 1999), the ultimate fashioning and use of these implements was a largely local affair. The data imply that people from Çatalhöyük were responsible for making at least a proportion of their projectiles and not only receiving finished projectiles from Canhasan III, or elsewhere. It is likely that the prismatic blades used to make the points were procured ready made, then perhaps buried in a hoard inside a building (akin to what we see in Building 1, Unit (1461)), followed by their modification by one of the inhabitants next to the fire installation, in the 'dirty area'.

Much of what has just been discussed concerning obsidian industries 3 and 4 applies similarly to their flint counterparts, flint industries 2 and 3. Both traditions are represented almost entirely by their end products until Level IX when we have a limnoquartzite opposed platform core from Building 17 (Space 182) in association with at least one blade that may have been knapped from it (Fig. 11.16f:8 on CD). Once again, it is almost certain that each of the 'two' industries subsumes different *chaînes opératoires*, given the variance in raw materials (different coloured limnoquartzites, red and green radiolarites *inter alia*) and the size of the blades, though we have little idea as to how many sources, workshops and distinct traditions these differences relate to. These implements quite possibly represent long distance imports, perhaps from southeast Anatolia where there is a tradition of blade manufacture using flint, in contrast to the obsidian-rich assemblages of central Anatolia.

Technologically there are close parallels between the obsidian and flint large prismatic blade industries, indeed they essentially replicate each other, but in different media (as did the microblade traditions of obsidian industry 2 and flint industry 1). Yet the origins of the obsidian blade industries are almost certainly to be located somewhere in Cappadocia near the raw-material sources, a region where we conversely have little evidence for the working of flint. Excavations at the Kaletepe (Kömürcü) workshop on Göllü Dağ-East have shown that that large naviform blades and slightly shorter unipolar blades (our obsidian industries 4 and 5) were being produced in tandem in the late ninth/early eighth millennia BC (Balkan-Atlı & Der Aprahamian 1998; Balkan-Atlı *et al.* 1999). Survey has attested a similar combination of unipolar and bipolar blade production at Bitlikeler and Ekinlik (Kayırlı/Göllü Dağ-East), at a unipolar blade workshop at İlbiz (Bozköy/Göllü Dağ-East), and at yet another workshop a few miles to the north at Nenezi Dağ, where the surface assemblages are dominated by unipolar cores and a lesser quantity of bipolar material, including shorter naviform nuclei (Balkan-Atlı *et al.* 1999). The survey material is less well dated, though a proportion is thought to be Aceramic Neolithic given its similarities to the Kaletepe material and that from nearby excavations.

Prismatic blade production was not restricted to the quarry workshops, with most of the naviform reduction sequence documented at Aşıklı Höyük, and to a lesser extent at Musular (Abbès *et al.* 1999; Balkan-Atlı 1994b; Özbaşaran 2000). Cores, manufacturing debris and end products are further recorded from surface investigations at the nearby sites of Sirçan Tepe, Yellibellen and Aycier, while small quantities are known from Canhasan III (Ataman 1988; Balkan-Atlı 1998). Çatalhöyük seems to be on the edge of this world, dependent either upon the workshops, or the aforementioned communities for access to the products of these skilled techniques. Once one enters the early ceramic Neolithic then we have a less clear idea as to where these traditions were being performed, with most of the Aceramic Neolithic Cappadocian settlements having been abandoned. At the sources, workshop activity continues at Kaletepe (Kömürcü/Göllü Dağ-East) throughout the seventh–fifth millennia BC, into the Middle Chalcolithic (Thissen 2002b, 325), while our own obsidian characterization studies have clearly documented a correlation between Level VI–IV prismatic blade industries (obsidian industries 4 and 5) and the use of Nenezi Dağ obsidian (Chapter 12), so that we might consider that some of the surface material at the mountain may relate to a blade workshop that is partly contemporary with Çatalhöyük Level VI.B onward.

Returning to the origins of the flint prismatic blade traditions, at none of the above sites do we have evidence for the parallel working of both flint and obsidian. A single unipolar, conical prismatic blade core with remnant crest was found at Sirçan Tepe, but was described as different from what is known in the region and a probable import (Balkan-Atlı 1998, 83, fig. 4:11). It is suggested that workshops near the Taurus mountains, or in southeast Anatolia represent some of the likeliest origins of the Çatalhöyük flint blades, with these regions having a long heritage of blade-based industries exploiting local siliceous resources. For example, blade working is attested at the ninth/eighth millennium BC Aceramic Neolithic (PPNB) sites of Çayönü, Nevalı Çori and Mezraa-Teleilat *inter alia* (Caneva *et al.* 1996, 390–98; Coşkunsu 2001, 182; Schmidt 1996, 366), while in the early Neolithic flint-blade manufacture is documented at Çayönü (mainly unipolar, occasional opposed platform) and Akarçay Tepe (Arimura *et al.* 2000; Özdoğan 1994, 271).

While clear technological parallels exist between the non-local obsidian and flint prismatic blade industries, one can distinguish clear differences in their consumption and by extension, their conceptualization. For example, we know that a proportion of the large obsidian blades were included in the process of hoarding, perhaps as a means of introducing the material from the *agrios* into the *domus*: a transformation of the wild 'raw' to the domestic 'cooked' (cf. Hodder 1990), as for example in Level X's Building 9 (4210), Level IX's Building 2 (4138) and the hoard of naviform blades from Level VII–VI's Building 1 (1461). Conversely, flint blades are notably absent from hoards at Çatalhöyük, the exception that proves the rule being the proximal section of a red radiolarite prismatic blade (flint industry 3) from a Level X hoard in Building 9

(4210.X5). Indeed, flint in any form is notable by its absence from hoards. In contrast, our characterization studies indicate that the products of more than one obsidian source are represented amongst the Çatalhöyük hoards. So it can be argued that this was an appropriate means of consuming 'obsidian' generically (the hoard contents also include a variety of industries), but an inappropriate context for flint.

One can distinguish other mutually-exclusive modes of consumption between these prismatic blades, perhaps most notably with regard to weaponry. The 1995–99 excavations generated numerous points yet only two of the projectiles are made of flint, including the distal section of one possible example made of dirty-grey limnoquartzite from a fire spot in Level Pre-XII.A (Fig. 11.8b:15 on CD). Blades from obsidian industries 4 and 5 were employed as the mainstay blanks for point production from Level Pre-XII.D onwards, retouched into a wide variety of forms (cf. Conolly 1999a, 39–41, figs. 4.1–4.2). Yet despite this use of a range of different projectiles, often at the same time, the one variable that was not experimented with was raw material beyond 'obsidian'. This is quite striking given that flint was the primary raw material employed for the manufacture of points in southeast Anatolia and the Levant in the PPNB and early Neolithic, i.e. those regions from where many of our flint prismatic blades may have originated (cf. Coşkunsu 2001, 183, figs. 1–2; Gopher 1994; Özdoğan 1994, 271, fig. 1; Schmidt 1994, 242–50, figs. 6–11; 1996, 366, figs. 3–4). It thus seems that it was the 'raw' blades that moved and not the modified implements. Nor do we seem to have any evidence that the meanings and notions of appropriate consumption associated with the traditions / raw materials in their homelands were respected, or accessible to those who consumed these blades at far-off Çatalhöyük.

Obsidian industry 6, the large round and flat scrapers, has parallels from sites in central Anatolia and beyond (PPNB southeast Anatolia and Levant). These implements are closely linked to the 'big-blade' tradition (obsidian industry 4), with regard to their arenas of production and consumption. Firstly, while these scrapers have been accorded industry status, many of them appear to be modified rejuvenation flakes knapped from the face of large bipolar prismatic blade cores. Secondly, these implements are contemporary with the large projectiles and disappear about the same time, i.e. post Level Pre-XII.B, suggesting that these scrapers may have been used to work the skins of the animals slain by the 'big-blade' spear and arrowheads.

As with some of the preceding traditions obsidian industry 7 presently subsumes more than one reduction sequence, referring to all large part modified flakes imported from the quarries. On procuring these large 'quarry flakes', one recurrent mode of consumption was to bury the material inside a small circular pit, usually in a building's main room, beside a fire installation (the 'dirty area'). How long these objects would have been in circulation prior to their burial is uncertain, however most of these pieces have clear traces of use-wear, often in the form of heavy percussive damage along one margin, perhaps related to butchery or wood-cutting activities. Suffice to say for present, that when (if) a hoard was subsequently retrieved, the contents were then usually knapped in the immediate locale. In the case of the bifacial projectile preforms we assume that the point's shaping was completed, while the large unmodified flakes and side-scrapers were reduced as cores, in the tradition of obsidian industry 1.

The 1995–99 excavations produced a number of obsidian hoards; Mellaart (1963, 103) similarly reported that hoards were 'frequently found'. Most of our examples were dominated by large bifaces and flake scrapers, indicating that the blade component of Çatalhöyük's hoards, as with the Building 1 example (1461), represents a later version of the phenomenon, perhaps primarily post-VIB, as with many other changes at the site (cf. Conolly 1999b). A more detailed discussion of hoards and their significance is presented elsewhere (Conolly 2003), however it is worth repeating the fact that at present these buried hoards appear to be peculiar to Çatalhöyük.

The remaining flint industries have essentially been discussed already, through reference to their obsidian counterparts. It remains to say that we neither have flint hoards, nor by extension any large flake scrapers or biface preforms. In turn, we also lack a parallel to the round flake scrapers of obsidian industry 6, despite the fact that we have contemporary opposed platform flint blade industries (that could have provided the rejuvenation flakes as blanks). This absence is arguably analogous to our lack of flint projectiles, suggesting that there was a taboo with regard to the use of flint in the hunting of animals and the preparation of their skins, though one might note the number of perforators which could have been used to pierce leather. Finally, one might also note that while obsidian industry 1 and flint industry 5 are essentially the same tradition performed on different media, they have a slightly different heritage, with the former present from the earliest deposits onward (Level Pre-XII.D) while latter makes its first appearance in Level Pre-XII.B. Until that moment the community appears to have been employing flint almost entirely in the form of ready made implements, with the possible exception of the microblades of flint industry 1.

Documenting change: the world and ways of living before and after Level Pre-XII.B

Çatalhöyük's Level Pre-XII.B–D chipped-stone assemblages (in particular Pre-XII.C–D) can be seen to form part of a central Anatolian Aceramic Neolithic technological and typological *koine*. Much of the material has direct parallels from sites in southern Cappadocia, as well as Canhasan III in the Konya Plain and Suberde in the Lake District. This *koine* is, however, comprised of various components, or traditions, not all of which share a common heritage. A proportion of the industries, including the opposed platform and unipolar prismatic blades, plus large flake-scrapers, relate ultimately to the PPNB interaction sphere of southeast Anatolia, the Levant and Cyprus. In contrast, the microblade/microlith tradition known from Çatalhöyük Level Pre-XII.B–D, Canhasan III and some of the south Cappadocian sites, can be seen to originate in a central/south-central Anatolian Epipalaeolithic tradition, as represented by the assemblages from Pinarbaşı A and the Mediterranean cave sites of Öküzini, Belbaşı and Beldibi. The one tradition that may appear to be a genuinely local central Anatolian Aceramic Neolithic phenomenon, is that of the small percussive blade/blade-like flake industry, obsidian industry 1 here at Çatalhöyük. The following section discusses these relationships in more detail and focuses upon what appears to be a significant disjuncture in the nature of the chipped stone before and after Level Pre-XII.B.

Our studies have thus demonstrated that the early Çatalhöyük material (Level Pre-XII.C–D) contains a significant quantity of material that has direct parallels at Aşıklı Höyük (cf. Balkan-Atlı 1994b). This includes the stemmed (Byblos) points and other 'big-blade' projectiles, end-scrapers, burins, pointed blades and a variety of retouched forms (obsidian industries 4 and 5), plus the large round scrapers (obsidian industry 6). Conversely, it seems that Aşıklı Höyük has generated only a few microliths (our obsidian industry 2). Aşıklı Höyük also lacks our small obliquely-truncated and backed blades. It is uncertain as to whether these absences are due to recovery bias, or a reflection in the difference in date.

It would be incorrect, however, to correlate directly the Aşıklı Höyük assemblage with that of Çatalhöyük Level Pre-XII.C–D, as most, if not all of the aforementioned material (including microliths in certain instances) is also documented at Musular and some of the other Aceramic Neolithic Cappadocian sites, Canhasan III and Suberde (Ataman 1988; Balkan-Atlı 1998). Indeed, recent radiocarbon dates indicate that these may be more pertinent assemblages for comparison, as the early occupation of Çatalhöyük is contemporary with Musular, Canhasan III and Suberde (Cessford 2001, 723–4; Thissen 2002b, 324). Recent work by Balkan-Atlı and her students has further begun to demonstrate the differences between the obsidian assemblages of Aşıklı Höyük and its near neighbours, Musular, Aycier, Sirçan Tepe and Yellibellen, and their likely chronological ramifications, as for example the dwindling of the naviform technology over time and the apparent shift from one- to two-shouldered points (Balkan-Atlı 1994b; 1998; Kayacan 2000; in press; Yıldırım 1999). Such work holds great hope for the future, but at present our sample from the early levels at Çatalhöyük precludes making any confident assertions as to where exactly our Level Pre-XII.D–C material falls within this south Cappadocian sequence.

One can, however, highlight the two inscribed pieces of obsidian from the Level Pre-XII sequence, the first to be found at Çatalhöyük and some of only a handful of examples that have been found outside Canhasan III, the two others coming from Musular and Kaletepe (N. Balkan-Atlı & D. Binder pers.comm.). The first example was a genuine Canhasan type point, recovered from a Level Pre-XII.C context (Fig. 11.5b:12 on CD), the second from Level Pre-XII.A (Fig. 11.9:1 on CD), identified tentatively as a fragment of a much reworked point. The decortication of neither example's decoration finds an exact parallel from Canhasan III, though they share design elements (triangles), and, as Ataman commented, these pieces' modification seems to have been deliberately idiosyncratic (1988, 266).

While the chipped stone from the earliest deposits of Space 181 exhibits technical and typological continuity, there is clear evidence for a disjuncture at Çatalhöyük in social, economic and technical practices after Level Pre-XII.B (see Volume 4, Chapters 2, 8 & 10). The chipped stone from the earliest deposits, Level Pre-XII.D–B, can be distinguished from the Level Pre-XII.A and later material on a number of counts. In many respects the Çatalhöyuk chipped-stone industries becoming more 'localized' in their nature, with the cessation of certain technologies and implement types that had previously linked its inhabitants to a sphere of knowledge and practice that encompassed communities in central Anatolia and beyond. In short, it can be argued that Çatalhöyük's world shrinks.

Technologically and typologically the chipped-stone industries from Level Pre-XII.D–B clearly relate to a larger central Anatolian world; they do not exist in isolation (*contra* Gérard 2002, 107). Nor has it appeared from nowhere; a heritage can be traced for each of the industries represented. The heritage is a mixed one, however, with clear links to earlier traditions in the Konya plain and the Mediterranean, plus southeast Anatolia and the Levant via Cappadocia. Most of Çatalhöyük's early obsidian industries (1, 4, 5, 6, 7) derive from the knapping traditions of Aceramic Neolithic communities in southern Cappadocia (i.e. Aşıklı Höyük and Musular *inter alia*, via Canhasan III), some of which, specifically the opposed platform and unipolar prismatic blades, plus large flake scrapers, ultimately relate to the technocomplexes of the Levantine PPN (cf. Bar-Yosef & Belfer-Cohen 1989; Kozlowski 1999). Conversely, our microblade / microlithic component (obsidian industry 2 / flint industry 1) can be viewed safely as having its roots in the Epipalaeolithic traditions of south central Anatolia (nearby Pinarbaşı A) and the Mediterranean coast (the cave sites of Öküzini, Belbaşı and Beldibi). Obsidian industry 3, the burinated 'edge blades' may be a local tradition, though not entirely dissimilar pieces are known from Aşıklı Höyük (Balkan-Atlı 1994b, 211, fig. 8, 10). What does appear to be unique to Çatalhöyük are certain modes of consumption, not least the burial of obsidian hoards in small under floor pits (though admittedly we have none from Level Pre-XII contexts), a practice that is currently unknown from Aşıklı Höyük, Musular and Canhasan III.

The mixed heritage of Çatalhöyük's Level Pre-XII.B–D industries arguably provides us with an indication as to the composition of the early community. In a recent discussion on the origins of Çatalhöyük, Asouti & Fairbairn (2002, 189–90) suggested that the archaeobotanical evidence would support the thesis that the early community represents a merging of two traditions, one 'local' and one 'foreign'. Prior to Çatalhöyük's establishment, sometime in the eighth-millennium BC, we know that mobile hunting groups were occupying seasonal camps at Pinarbaşı A and elsewhere in the Konya plain (Baird 2002, 142, fig. 4; Watkins 1996). Such people may have been related to the populations of the earlier Mediterranean cave sites. It seems likely that early Çatalhöyük simply represents another such seasonally occupied habitation. Survey in the nearby Konya Plain has produced evidence of another early small-scale settlement at Sancak (Baird 2002, 143–4; in press), its chipped stone seemingly contemporary with our Level Pre-XII.B–D material. Here we either have a small group of neighbours, or perhaps one of a number of impermanent campsites occupied by the people who eventually settled on the location we today refer to as Çatalhöyük

Given that Çatalhöyük was founded on a low lying alluvial delta / floodplain, with annual flooding of the surrounding soils (Roberts *et al.* 1996; Roberts *et al.* 1999) it seems reasonable to assume that hunting and gathering were important economic concerns of the earliest population (Asouti & Fairbairn 2002, 188–90). However, we know that the earliest community was exploiting fully domesticated cereals / pulses and sheep / goats (Martin *et al.* 2002), innovations that cannot be seen to have emerged within those peoples exploiting the Konya plain in the preceding period. Çatalhöyük's crop assemblages (and those of Aşıklı Höyük) 'indicate clear links with the southeast Anatolian Neolithic complex', their introduction conceivably in part due to the new presence of 'a 'foreign' element' (Martin *et al.* 2002, 189–90).

Çatalhöyük's earliest chipped-stone industries similarly invlude 'local' and 'foreign' components. The microlithic component of the Level Pre-XII.B–D assemblages relates to a 'local' Konya plain / Mediterranean coast mobile hunter / gatherer tradition, the implements perhaps serving partly as composite barbs in projectiles. In contrast, most of Çatalhöyük's other early industries derive from south Cappadocian traditions, as best represented at Aşıklı Höyük and Musular. Ultimately, however, many of these traditions are in fact 'foreign', i.e. their heritage can be traced back to the PPN Levant, via southeast Anatolia and perhaps to a lesser extent, Cyprus. Pivotal to this transmission of technical know-how were the people exploiting the south Cappadocian obsidian sources. Excavation at the site of Kaletepe atop the Kömürcü source (Göllü Dağ-East) has revealed a blade workshop and associated seasonal camp, occupied by highly-skilled knappers, whose products were consumed throughout the Levant (Balkan-Atlı & Der Aprahamian 1998; Binder 2002). Various strands of evidence have led many to believe that the workshop and quarrying were undertaken by specialist groups from the Near East during the summer months, visits that may have eventually contributed to the permanent peopling of the region (Binder 2002). In turn, these contacts served to influence the nature of chipped-stone production amongst the region's first Aceramic Neolithic communities, and those a little further to the southwest, specifically Canhasan III and ultimately, Çatalhöyük.

It may be unwise, however, to place too much weight upon the relative impact of the 'two' chipped-stone traditions that I have just outlined, i.e. the apparent predominant influence of the south Cappadocian / Levantine at the expense of a 'local' heritage; further work at Pinarbaşı A and a fuller publication of the extant chipped stone are necessary before such judgements can be passed with any conviction.

In my discussion of Çatalhöyük's Level Pre-XII.B–D chipped-stone industries, I have until this moment focused almost entirely on the obsidian. The flint has a great deal further to offer. As was mentioned at the start of this section, it is within the earliest deposits that we find the greatest quantity and variety of flint (Fig. 11.36; Tables 11.1–11.2). Flint, on average, represents 3.8 per cent of Çatalhöyük's chipped-stone assemblage, based on a sample from the 1996-99 excavations in the South and North areas and 1999 KOPAL trench. However, all of the Pre-XII assemblages (with the exception of the small sample from Level Pre-XII.D) exceed this figure, with the flint component of the Level Pre-XII.C assemblage comprising 7.7 per cent (Fig. 11.36; Tables 11.1–11.2). Arguably it is not so much the quantity, but the variety of raw materials in the early assemblages that are of the greatest significance. As in every period, the earliest material is dominated by various coloured limnoquartzites, however, it also contains the preponderance of the red and green radiolarites, resources that appear only sporadically after Level Pre-XII (Fig. 11.35). The Level Pre-XII assemblages also include small quantities of red chert, red-brown chert, dark-orange chert, black-brown flint, grey-brown flint, grey-blue flint, red jasper and mahogany radiolarite (the latter possibly from the Syrian-Iraqi border). Moreover, the Level Pre-XII limnoquartzites display a wider range of colours (grey / brown / orange / red / pink and white) than those from later contexts, where the tan / brown / grey-brown variant(s) predominate. We thus have clear evidence for the decrease in the number of raw materials being exploited through time. While we remain ignorant of the actual sources of these various siliceous resources, it seems reasonable to suggest that the data indicates that Çatalhöyük's world had shrunk and / or been reoriented. One might interpret the evidence as indicating the collapse of various socio-economic networks.

If the form and structure of the Level Pre-XII.B chipped-stone assemblages suggest the early community included, for want of a better term, a 'dual heritage' of Konya plain / Mediterranean coast and south Cappadocian / Levantine origin, one is beholden to consider how Çatalhöyük came into being. It has recently been suggested that seasonal expeditions by Levantine groups to the Cappadocian obsidian quarries were partly responsible for the settlement of central Anatolia in the second half of the ninth millennium BC (Binder 2002, 83; Cauvin 2000, 91–5 & 219). At the same time, we know that small quantities of obsidian were being exploited by mobile hunter-gatherer groups of southern central Anatolia, namely Pinarbaşı A, so that the Konya plain represents a possible 'theatre' for the interaction between the two groups (Binder 2002, 83). Moreover, one should also consider the possibility that the consumption of small quantities of obsidian (presumably Cappadocian) in the Konya plain at this time may have been embedded within much larger exchange networks, for it is during the ninth millennium BC that Göllü Dağ-East obsidian first appears in Cyprus, at Khirokitia, Kalavassos-Tenta and Parekklisha Shillourokambos *inter alia* (Chataigner 1998, fig. 7a; Gomez *et al.* 1995). With the earliest Neolithic on Cyprus displaying cultural links with the PPNB Levant, one might argue for the obsidian arriving from the east, however it is worth bearing in mind the possibility that some of the blade products from southern Cappadocia may have travelled via the Cilician Gates, a route that somewhat later the community of Canhasan III may have benefited from.

The nature of Çatalhöyük's early chipped-stone industries is a reflection of the community's mixed heritage and its contemporary spheres of interaction. During the Level Pre-XII occupation we can be relatively certain that members of the community would have been interacting with contemporaries nearby at Canhasan III (as most vividly represented by our two inscribed points) and those living close to the obsidian quarries in Cappadocia, such as Musular (for dates see Cessford 2001; Thissen 2002b). Indeed, it is quite likely that these communities lay on the route to and from Çatalhöyük to the south Cappadocian obsidian quarries, given that the direct route would have involved traversing the dry and exposed Konya plain, a far more risky and unattractive journey than that offered by the more circuitous route around the southern edge of the plain at the base of the Taurus Mountains with its springs and river mouths (cf. Kuzucuoğlu 2002, 41–3). The sites of Suberde, Pinarbaşı and Canhasan III all share such locations (Kuzucuoğlu 2002, 43, fig. 3). While the dissemination of specialized, non-local prismatic blade products (obsidian industries 4 and 5, flint industries 2 and 3) may have been articulated through exchange networks / trade partnerships and / or specialized expeditions to the obsidian quarries, such mechanisms of inter-community contact may be seen as insufficient to underwrite the emergence of regional pools of common technical knowledge and practice. The aforementioned differences in how non-local prismatic blades were modified into projectiles at Çatalhöyük and Canhasan III might be posited as examples of how regional emblemic styles were generated (interpreted) locally. However, there are other industries that appear to be performed quite similarly over large distances, most notably Çatalhöyük's mainstay industry (obsidian industry 1), a phenomenon that might only be explicable with reference to a more intense form of community interrelationships, i.e. population movement and intermarriage. In a recent discussion of how ceramic (Beaker) technology moved in Chalcolithic / Neolithic central Europe, Brodie (1997, 307) argues that in 'situations of short term face to face interaction only discursive representations would be properly suitable for verbal communication', whereas 'practices and technologies would be "stickier" in that they would be less suitable for rapid communication and assimilation', i.e. technologies are more likely to have moved with their practitioners. While we are presently ignorant of the size of Level Pre-XII Çatalhöyük, it seems reasonable to assume that initially (if Pinarbaşı and Sancak are anything to go on) the population was small enough for exogamy to have been necessary (Wobst 1974; 1976), as well as potentially socially beneficial to certain members of the community (cf. Irwin 1983, 47; Spriggs 1986, 13).

Finally, with the dissolution of the Aceramic Neolithic communities in Cappadocia (Aşıklı Höyük, Musular and related sites) and Canhasan III, Çatalhöyük may have gained some population from elsewhere, a process that would further help to explain the mixed heritage of its earliest chipped-stone industries. Gérard (2002, 107) has recently argued against any direct relationship between the abandonment of Aşıklı Höyük and the beginning of Çatalhöyük on the basis of three lines of evidence. Firstly, it is noted that it is not necessary to invoke Aşıklı Höyük / Cappadocia as a potential source of Çatalhöyük's earliest population, given that Pinarbaşı A and Canhasan III act as local precursors. Secondly, it is argued that the Çatalhöyük 'assemblages demonstrate a local origin' and thirdly, the site's 'impressive use of symbolism and imagery' stands in stark contrast to what was witnessed at Aşıklı Höyük (Gérard 2002, 107). Taking each of these arguments in turn, the first point is well received and would serve equally to produce the mixed heritage of Çatalhöyük's earliest chipped stone, though it does not necessarily negate the influx of a Cappadocian population. The second and third points are more problematic, for as I have argued above, while some forms of consumption may be viewed as idiosyncratic, the earliest chipped stone at Çatalhöyük is technologically and typologically derived largely from the Aceramic Neolithic traditions of south Cappadocia / the Levant. In turn, it would be extremely unwise to assume that the quite remarkable architecture and symbolism that we know from later periods represents the nature of the Level Pre-XII settlement. Indeed the presence of fine red-plaster fragments (Volume 3, Part 2) suggests that some of the early structures may have had more than a passing resemblance to those from Aşıklı Höyük and Musular. To be fair to Gérard, my ripostes are based largely on the hitherto unpublished data that forms the basis of this volume.

While we can claim that the earliest occupants of Çatalhöyük were located within regional *koines* of technical and social practice (e.g. ways of killing / hunting), underwritten by various socio-economic networks of trade partnerships and intermarriage, the world after Level Pre-XII.B is more difficult to fathom. With the ending of the Cappadocian sites and the dispersal of their populations (Aşıklı Höyük, Musular *et al.*) Canhasan III and Suberde, there have been claims that Çatalhöyük was left in 'splendid isolation' (Gérard 2002, 107), though this is to overlook the fact that at various times the communities of Erbaba, Pinarbaşı B and Mersin, amongst others, were all contemporaries.

From Space 181 to the settlement

It has been argued that Çatalhöyük was a somewhat different place before and after Level Pre-XII.B. It thus seems pertinent to comment next upon the chipped-stone assemblages from Level Pre-XII.A up to and including the North Area's Building 5. It is to be noted that the discussion of this material is somewhat introspective compared to the preceding section, i.e. focusing almost entirely on Çatalhöyük. Such an isolationist perspective is unfortunately somewhat forced upon us, not so much due to the community's absence of contemporaries (cf. Gérard 2002, 107), though there appear to be few close by, but as a reflection of so few well-published assemblages with which to compare our material.

While we have the aforementioned cessation of certain lithic traditions at the site / in the region, specifically the microblade / microlith industries, the 'big-blade' opposed platform blades and large scrapers (Tables 11.47–11.48), one can also note a significant degree of continuity in the chipped-stone assemblages pre / post Level Pre-XII.B. For instance, our 'in house' tradition of small percussive blades (obsidian industry 1) continues as the mainstay mode of consuming obsidian during this period, a technology that comes into clear focus once one enters the archaeology of settlement at Çatalhöyük. This is, of course, one of the major distinctions that has to be borne in mind when undertaking a diachronic appraisal of the chipped stone from the 1995–99 seasons. The Space 181 Level Pre-XII.A–D material comes from what appear to be predominantly (secondary) midden / dump contexts that lay outside the area of occupation, while the Level XII–XI material derives from open spaces within the settlement. It is not until Level X that we are dealing with deposits related to true structural / interior settlement archaeology.

Despite the contextual distinctions between Level Pre-XII.A, Level XII–XI and Level X–VI / V, one can argue for a significant degree of similarity in their respective chipped stone industries, certainly with regard to which traditions are represented at any one time (Tables 11.47–11.48). In terms of specific modes of consumption the earliest levels provide only a limited insight as to how chipped stone was in circulation and use at the site. Level Pre-XII.A did, however, provide one of the few potential candidates in Space 181 for an *in situ* deposit, with two complete obsidian points that had been placed next to each other on the ground, a surface that subsequently appears to have been set on fire (Fig. 11.8a:5 on CD). The archaeology of Level XII–XI is arguably only of interest in that it might suggest a largely negative relationship between on-site animal penning and the production and consumption of chipped stone, aside from the occasional sickle that may have been used to cut fodder (cf. Fig.11.9b:4 on CD). Contextually, it is the archaeology of Level X–VI/V that represents the most interesting context for our material.

The structure, form, location and size of the chipped-stone assemblages from the inside of those buildings excavated between 1995–99, offers a tantalizing insight to the hugely-significant roles that (what we define as) chipped stone played for the people of Çatalhöyük. Obviously there are what one might perceive as the everyday functional roles for our implements of obsidian and other siliceous resources, namely the cutting of plant materials and animal products in the preparation of foodstuffs for human consumption. Vast quantities of our material, albeit often in the form of small-scale debris and broken tools, are to be found in proximity to those areas where food was both prepared and cooked, in each of the buildings investigated. Functional analyses (edge-wear and residue) may elucidate further whether certain tool types enjoyed task/media specific roles (such as 'feasting events', as with Level VII's (1092)), however with the wealth of botanical and faunal data there is much information already to hand as to the likely uses of our implements in these parts of the structures. In turn, it is possible to recognize more specialized roles for our chipped stone, restricted to select buildings, modes of consumption that might traditionally be referred to as 'craft' activities. For example, in Level X's Building 18 there is evidence for the manufacture of both bone and stone beads, for which we have a number of related perforators made on non-local obsidian and flint blades. The increase in scrapers from Level VIII–VII (Figs. 11.25–11.26 & Table 11.24) may also eventually translate into building-specific activities such as leather-, or wood-working (though most it should be noted were actually found in external midden contexts), the latter a craft that Conolly indicates as a likely major consumer of obsidian at this time. There are also interesting accumulations of tool types that are more difficult to interpret within such an economic, task-related framework, such as the notable quantity of projectile points from Level V–IV's Building 1.

I wish here to make a departure from considering the use of chipped stone within buildings from a utilitarian standpoint, though this is not to negate the everyday 'functional' uses that much of this material would have enjoyed, i.e. to cut, scrape, pierce and work the food, skins, bones and wood that served to feed, cloth and furnish Çatalhöyük's inhabitants. It is the notion of the 'everyday' that I wish to examine, returning to some of those issues developed within the main part of the chapter. The first point to make is that each 'household', or whatever social group is embodied within these structures, seems to have enjoyed a relative equality of access to both obsidian and flint and in much the same form. This certainly appears to hold true for Level Pre-XII.A–VI\V, though it has been contested in late levels (Conolly 1999b). Despite the distances involved (see Chapter 12), it appears that not inconsiderable quantities of chipped stone was being both worked and used in these buildings and one cannot help but think that the sights and sounds associated with its consumption was an everyday, familiar occurrence. This is not to suggest that one cannot elicit distinctions between the buildings' assemblages in terms of quantity and form (see below), however it remains that each of our structures has produced a lot of obsidian and flint. It is not just the amount that is significant, but also the remarkably consistency with regard to the manner and context of the materials' consumption. The concept of a 'dirty' and 'clean' area, defined in part via the presence or absence of chipped stone, is a remarkably repetitive one, building-by-building, level-by-level. In turn, these areas are located in much the same place and are comprised of much the same structural and material components. Thus one can note a recurrent association between (those areas where one recovers) chipped stone and fire installations (ovens/hearths), often in the southern part of the structure. It also seems that this area of angular, crunchy stone would have been located in close proximity to where one descended from the roof into the structure at the base of the ladder, i.e. with preferential access to natural light. One can thus argue that the 'dirty area' was in fact a focus of brightness, from the leap of the hearth's flame, the glow of the oven and the glitter of sunlight on obsidian. It further appears quite convincing, on the basis of form/structure and history/ taphonomy of the assemblages, that it was in the 'dirty areas' that obsidian was primarily being worked and used in this luminous zone of transformative processes. Good examples of *in situ*, or near *in situ* knapping deposits include Building 23 ((4987), (4989) & (4990)), unit (4134) in Building 2, the dirty area of Building 17 (5021) and the southeast rake-outs of Building 6 (Space 173). On analysis it seems that one can link these rich 'dirty- area' deposits on many levels, through reference to their composition of parallel industries, the form and scale of the material and other attributes discussed above. It is argued that the layout and composition of our buildings' chipped-stone assemblages are highly regulated, generated by repetitive practices that were structured by (and served to help structure/maintain) more general social attitudes of 'how things should be'.

The patterning that we see within buildings extends to negative relationships, i.e. loci, or features where we recurrently find far less, or no chipped stone. Perhaps most notably, most of the floor spaces are devoid of obsidian and flint, beyond small quantities derived from the >1-mm and >2-mm heavy-residue sample (cf. Fig. 11.14). In part this absence of chipped stone, or any other media, is considered to be a reflection of the fact that these surfaces were covered with mats and/or swept clean on a regular basis up to an including the process of abandoning the structure. Interpreting the small quantities of material that we do find is problematic; in certain instances, Building 1 in particular, it can be argued strongly that these scraps of obsidian were largely introduced as part of the plaster (see Chapter 3). However in other instances, Building 17 for example, it is our opinion that some of the microdebitage may represent shatter that has sprayed onto the 'clean' area from the knapping areas to the south. Aside from the central floors, one can note further negative correlations between chipped stone and spaces/features, including basins, bins, clay-ball pits, and many of the platforms (particularly those located to the north of the building/opposite the 'dirty area'), though some of these contexts, bins in particular, became foci for special deposits of chipped stone during a structure's abandonment.

There are distinctions between building assemblages, both with regard to the amount of chipped stone in a structure and the nature of its consumption. These distinctions can largely be viewed within the patterns, rather than a divergence from them. Thus one can note differences in the form, structure and scale of our buildings' 'dirty-area' assemblages, such as the meticulous cleansing practices reflected in the Building 17 rake-out material. One can also consider the differences between the obsidian hoards. While these hoards for the most part have a common location (the 'dirty area' in proximity to fire installations, aside from two buried in external Space 113 (2038) and (2039)), the amount and form of obsidian interred is variable (see Conolly 2003). For instance Building 2 has least three hoards ((4209), (4210) & (4134)), while Building 23 has traces of two, while Building 6 only has one (4276).

Finally, we return to the exterior spaces, defined primarily as middens. For the most part it seems that the chipped stone is in secondary context, having been introduced as 'rubbish' in the process of cleaning and emptying buildings during their lives and at the point of their abandonment/'death'. As such, it seems that the Level Pre-XII.A–VI/V middens may share much in common with those from the earlier part of the Space 181 sequence. This includes the point that these deposits are comprised of soil/artefacts that have derived from more than one context (be that multiple buildings and/or off-site loci), as for example indicated by the variable condition of the chipped stone recovered from them (dulling/patination and breakage). These midden assemblages cannot all be interpreted as the product of secondary deposition. Level VIII's Space 115 was a massive deposit whose careful excavation revealed numerous different episodes of deposition, within which were recognized a few event horizons, i.e. instances of (short-term) activity on the exterior surface, as opposed to episodes of dumping artefact-rich soil. Spasojević has denoted one obsidian knapping scatter (3740) that was associated with faunal material, perhaps the remnants of a butchery, or related, event. This assemblage is interesting due to its high-proportion of cortical debris (most obsidian seems to have entered the site, throughout its history, in a decorticated state) and for the fact that it may indicate that certain forms of food preparation were intended as spectacles, located outside the building, perhaps so as to be viewed by more people than would have shared in its consumption.

A final comment can be made on the nature of chipped-stone consumption from Level Pre-XII. A–VI/V, specifically with regard to the material from the archaeology of settlement (Levels X–VI/V) and the theme of 'transition and performance'. We have numerous instances from our buildings, perhaps most overtly in the form of hoards, of structured deposits of chipped stone; many of these deposits it has been claimed one might link to episodes of transition, specifically instances of construction, transformation and abandonment. These include the deliberate deposition of individual (more rarely groups of) pieces of obsidian, or flint — more often than not non-local products such as blades, or points. In Building 18 we had a fine limnoquartzite perforator (Fig. 11.9b:4 on CD) placed in a bin and covered with ochre prior to the bin's destruction and the building's infilling, while another bin (F.488) in Building 6 produced a small cache of flint implements, including another perforator (4181). There are numerous other examples of oven and bin construction/destruction, or the relaying of floors, where 'special' pieces were interred as part of the event. Perhaps the most striking example of this relates to the abandonment of a structure and the removal of its wooden posts. We now have at least four examples (Buildings 5, 2, 17 & 23), and recorded again in later levels (see below) where the central post on the western wall, having been removed, had a used obsidian projectile placed into the now empty post-hole, before the structure was in-filled. The practice appears quite deliberate and warrants further searches for related phenomena involving other contexts and media.

Çatalhöyük post Level VI

Only a brief comment is offered here on the nature of change around Level VI. Significant changes have been documented with regard to the obsidian industry at this time, with an alleged shift from a dominance of the rather low-skilled percussive blade-like flake/blade tradition (obsidian industry 1) to a new emphasis on unipolar pressure-flaked blade production (obsidian industry 5). This argument has been presented in detail previously by Conolly (1999b) and receives further review in the text above; it serves little purpose to repeat the claims here. While change undoubtedly occurs, our combined analyses suggest that the transformation in technical practice is almost certainly more complex than was originally credited. The changes occur in a world where we have numerous parallel industries in obsidian and flint. Moreover, our recent characterization work has further complicated matters, indicating that shifts in the modes of knapping obsidian seem to correlate directly with an increased exploitation of the Nenezi Dağ source, at the expense of the Göllü Dağ-East outcrops (Chapter 12).

Future directions

As we have stressed during this chapter, our work on the chipped stone of Çatalhöyük continues, both with respect to studying material from newly-excavated deposits and the re-evaluation of the (theory-laden) data and interpretations offered in this text. More certainly remains to be done concerning the deconstruction of our various industries (in particular the non-local prismatic blade traditions) and further attempts to elucidate the temporal/contextual correlates of specific technologies and tool types, such as projectiles for which we seem to have a great array, both synchronically and diachronically. Thematically points seem to be a particularly interesting set of data, their range of forms, loci of recovery and histories (the vast majority were recovered with impact damage from use) indicating that they enjoyed roles of some significance for the community. One might further expand one's consideration of the projectiles to a study of the consumption of non-local products (obsidian and flint) more generally.

It is fair to say that throughout the Neolithic sequence non-local implements experienced a far higher rate of use than the contemporary 'in-house' products (cf. Fig. 11.34), with many of the large prismatic blades, scrapers and points being reworked and modified. While such behaviour may in part reflect the deliberate practice of 'curation', i.e. the intensive consumption of exotica as a response to distance/effort of procurement, it might be unwise to view these acts in purely economic terms. The fact that these implements enjoyed a longer time in circulation means that they had the potential to have been associated with a number of different events, people and places. Such a potential for their storage, transmission and manipulation of social information (cf. Gero 1989; Larrick 1991; Taçon 1991) may indeed have been realized given these tools' far more idiosyncratic nature, a result/reflection of their stylistic and technological input/complexity, both in terms of embodied technical *savoir faire* and the number of stages involved in their manufacture.

There are many such issues and sets of data that are deserving of our attention, as well as casting a critical eye over what we have presented thus far in this volume. In turn, we look forward to greater collaboration and interaction with those who elsewhere in Anatolia and beyond seek to elicit 'stories from stone' that we might tell of the inhabitants of Çatalhöyük and its contemporaries.

Acknowledgements

Tristan Carter acknowledges gratefully the feedback and practical assistance that he received from his co-authors, the members of the Çatalhöyük Research Project (in particular Craig Cessford, Shahina Farid, Ian Hodder and John G.H. Swogger), plus Nur Balkan-Atlı, Douglas Baird, Didier Binder, Marie-Claire Cauvin, Güner Coşkunsu, Sarah Delerue, Nurcan Kayacan, Henry Wright and Semra Yıldırım; all mistakes remain those of the author.

Ana Spasojević would like to thank very much to Ian Hodder for his patience and support. Tristan Carter offered invaluable discussion and very helpful comments on earlier versions of my work. I wish to thank Mirjana Stevanović and Ruth Tringham for inviting me to Çatalhöyük. Shahina Farid for making everything possible and Serap Ozdol. Special thanks goes to Dr Erdoğan Erol, Muammer Koyuncu and Gülseren Karakap from Konya Museum, plus the archaeological representatives of the Turkish Ministry of Culture at Çatalhöyük and the Archaeological Museum at Konya for allowing me to export chipped-stone material for further analyses. And Marin for all his love.

Chapter 12

From Chemistry to Consumption: Towards a History of Obsidian Use at Çatalhöyük through a Programme of Inter-laboratory Trace-elemental Characterization

Tristan Carter, Gérard Poupeau, Céline Bressy & Nicholas J.G. Pearce

Introduction
by Tristan Carter

Çatalhöyük is located in a particularly poor region with regard to local supplies of workable stone, yet it has produced a rich and varied chipped-stone industry. While the mountain of Karadağ, *c.* 35 km to the southeast, provided some of the volcanic tuffs and andesite for the ground-stone implements (Chapters 13 & 17), there is virtually nothing from the vicinity with a conchoidal fracture habit suitable for making chipped-stone tools. The chipped-stone industry is thus comprised almost entirely of exotic resources, many of which had to be procured from sources far beyond the Konya plain. Throughout the Neolithic the predominant raw material exploited at Çatalhöyük was obsidian, despite the fact that the nearest sources of this volcanic glass lay some 200 km away (as the crow flies) in Cappadocia (Fig. 12.1). From its earliest occupation onward over 90 per cent of the chipped-stone tools were made of obsidian (see Chapter 11), with the remaining raw materials comprising various coloured limnoquartzites, radiolarites, flint and jasper, whose origins continue to be debated, with the Taurus Mountains, southeast Turkey and the northern Levant all considered potential sources (Balkan-Atlı 1994a, 37; Conolly 1999a, 70; Mellaart 1963, 103; 1967, 213).

While the issue of 'flint' sourcing continues to frustrate archaeologists, not only those working in Anatolia, the characterization of obsidian has arguably been one of *the* success stories in archaeometry (cf. Henderson 2000, 297–323; Renfrew 1998a; Shackley 1998). Moreover, a recent multidisciplinary project has produced major advances in the location, mapping and characterization (geochemical and geochronological) of Anatolia's numerous obsidian sources, providing a context for new provenance studies of archaeological obsidian and the related issues of prehistoric trade, exchange and other forms of cultural interaction (Cauvin *et al.* 1998). This work has acted as an inspiration for the new Çatalhöyük project.

In 1999 a major programme of obsidian characterization was initiated to investigate the long-term history of procurement, exchange, transformation and use of obsidian at Çatalhöyük. This is an ongoing project, involving a number of international laboratories and a variety of analytical techniques (Carter 2000; Carter *et al.* 2001); this chapter represents the product of our first stage of our work, detailing the results from a trace-elemental analysis of 135 pieces of worked obsidian. These artefacts were produced by the 1996–99 excavations, coming primarily from Neolithic Çatalhöyük East (n = 128), together with a further seven from Early Chalcolithic contexts on Çatalhöyük West (Table 12.1). The analyses were undertaken at two laboratories in France and Britain, employing three analytical techniques, namely: the Groupe de Géophysique Nucléaire, UMR 5025 of the *Centre National de la Recherche Scientifique* (CNRS), Université Joseph Fourier, Grenoble, employing solution nebulization Inductively Coupled Plasma-Mass Spectroscopy (ICP-MS) and Inductively Coupled Plasma-Atomic Emission Spectroscopy (ICP-AES), plus the Institute of Geography and Earth Sciences, University of Wales, Aberystwyth, employing Laser Ablation Inductively Coupled Plasma Mass-Spectroscopy (LA-ICP-MS).

Our work at Çatalhöyük forms part of a post-1980s 'new wave' of archaeometric studies dedicated to characterizing archaeological obsidian in the Mediterranean, Anatolia and Near East (cf. Abbès *et al.* 2001; Chataigner *et al.* 1998; Gomez *et al.* 1995; Gratuze *et al.*

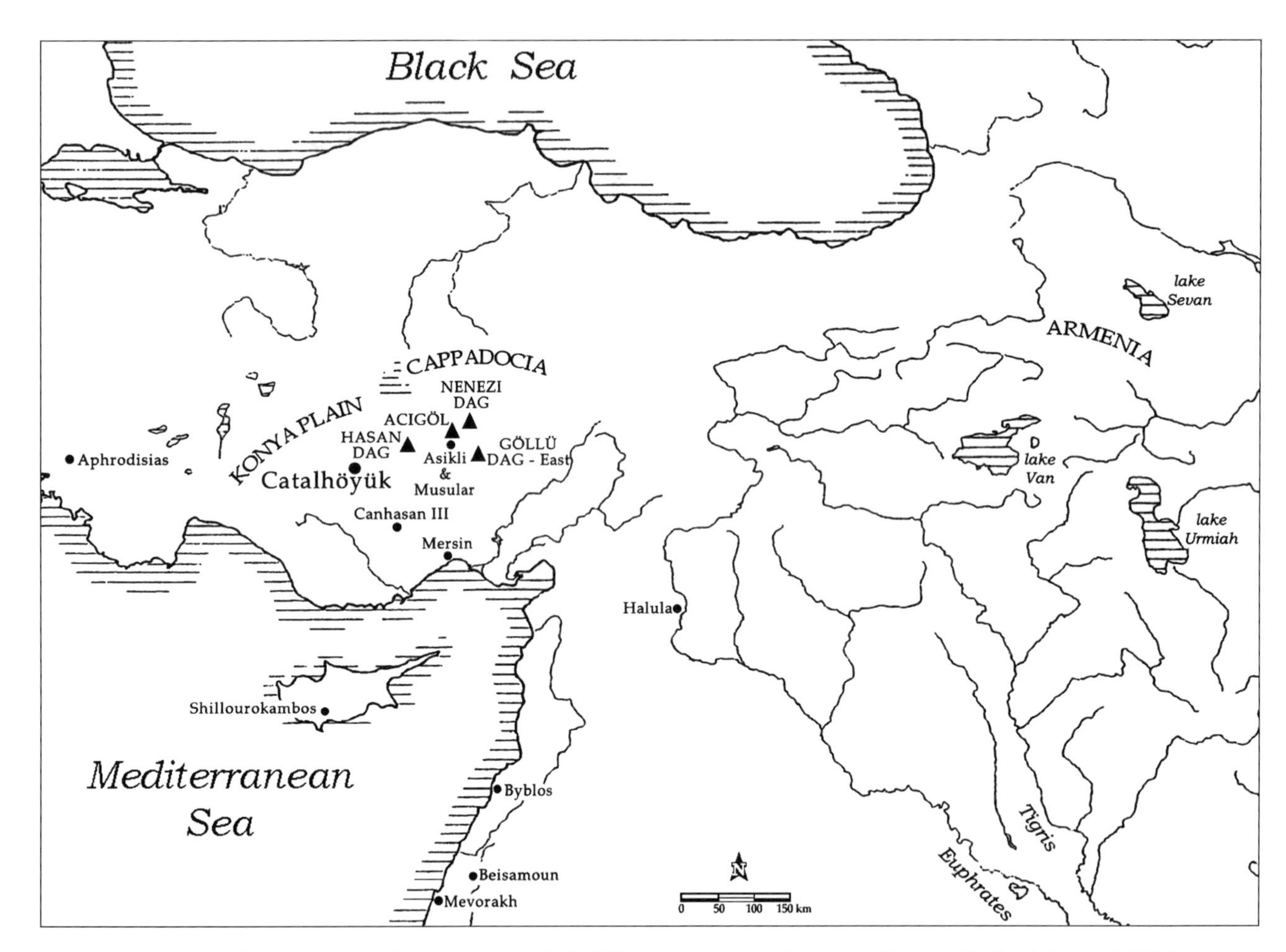

Figure 12.1. *Map showing main sites, regions and obsidian sources mentioned in Chapter 12 (by Marina Milić).*

Table 12.1. *Temporal distribution of the 135 artefacts analyzed by CNRS and Aberystwyth.*

Mound	Level	All samples	CNRS	Aberystwyth	Area	Building	Spaces
West	E. Chalcolithic	7	7	-	-	-	-
East	III	2	2	-	Summit	10	
East	N.VI–V	4	3	1	North	1	71/88, 185, 188
East	VIB	1	1	-	South	-	160
East	N.VII–VI	73	59	14	North	1	69–71, 73, 88, 110–11, 153, 186–7
East	N.VIII–VII	11	5	6	North	5/1, 5	154–7, 186
East	VII	15	15	-	South	-	105–9, 112–13
East	VIII?	2	2	-	South		114
East	VIII	14	-	14	South		115, 150
East	IX	5	5	-	South	2	

1994; Kilikoglou *et al.* 1997; Tykot 1996). Those of us working in Anatolia are extremely fortunate to have the aforementioned recent publication *L'Obsidienne au Proche et Moyen Orient: Du Volcan a l'Outil* (Cauvin *et al.* 1998), that provides a wealth of data on Turkey's obsidian sources. This collaborative, inter-disciplinary work, produced by teams of primarily French and Turkish geologists, geochemists (including G. Poupeau), geochronologists and archaeologists, represents a benchmark in archaeometric studies.

Background

This is not the first provenance study involving obsidian from Çatalhöyük, with 20 artefacts characterized in the past 35 years by three different projects (Table 12.2). Four blades were analyzed in Renfrew's seminal study of the mid 1960s (Renfrew *et al.* 1966), three of which fell within his 'Group 1e–f', associated with the north Cappadocian source of Acıgöl. The fourth artefact was sourced to Armenia ('Group 2b'), a result considered

Table 12.2. *Obsidian from Çatalhöyük sourced prior to 1999 (OES = Optical Emission Spectroscopy; XRF = X-Ray Fluorescence).*

Sample	Level	Mound	Object	Source	Method	Analysts
41	Neolithic	East	blade	Armenia (Group 2b)	OES	Renfrew *et al.* 1966
42	Neolithic	East	blade	Acigöl (Group 1e–f)	OES	Renfrew *et al.* 1966
43	Neolithic	East	blade	Acigöl (Group 1e–f)	OES	Renfrew *et al.* 1966
280	Neolithic	East	blade	Acigöl (Group 1e–f)	OES	Renfrew *et al.* 1966
643	Chalcolithic	West	?	Acigöl (Group 1e–f)	OES	Wright 1969
644	Chalcolithic	West	?	Acigöl (Group 1e–f)	OES	Wright 1969
645	Chalcolithic	West	?	Acigöl (Group 1e–f)	OES	Wright 1969
646	Neolithic	East	?	Çiftlik (Group 2b?)	OES	Wright 1969
647	Neolithic	East	?	Acigöl (Group 1e–f)	OES	Wright 1969
648	Neolithic	East	?	Çiftlik (Group 2b?)	OES	Wright 1969
6 pieces	?	?	?	Nenezi Dağ	XRF	Keller & Seifried 1990
4 pieces	?	?	?	Göllüdağ-Kömürcü	XRF	Keller & Seifried 1990

to be counter intuitive and treated with caution by the analysts, who thought that it might 'conceivably be an anomalous and exceptional product of a nearer source' (Renfrew *et al.* 1966, 33). Wright (1969) analyzed three pieces of worked obsidian from Çatalhöyük East and three from Çatalhöyük West; he used Optical Emission Spectroscopy, the same technique as Renfrew. Four artefacts, including all the Chalcolithic material, were allegedly made of obsidian from Acıgöl, but the raw material employed for the manufacture of two of the East mound blanks was claimed to be from the Çiftlik source in south Cappadocia. Lastly, Keller & Seifried (1990) characterized ten artefacts from Çatalhöyük (contexts unknown), the obsidian purportedly coming from the Çiftlik region. More specifically, their technique of X-ray Fluorescence allowed them to determine that six were made of obsidian from the mountain of Nenezi Dağ, while four originated from nearby 'Göllüdağ-Kömürcü' (Fig. 12.1).

With our new programme of obsidian characterization we are essentially starting afresh due to the problematic nature of the old data. For instance, Chataigner (1998, 285) has argued that Renfrew and Wright's technique of chemical discrimination (using ratios of Barium and Zirconium) means that the six artefacts that they attributed to the north Cappadocian source of Acıgöl could in fact be from Nenezi Dağ in south Cappadocia, as both sources fell within their Group 1e–f. Moreover, even if the raw material had originated from 'Acıgöl', the statement is problematic, as the term subsumes 50 obsidian outcrops that can be divided geologically into three groups, two of which can be distinguished chemically (Chataigner 1998, 277–85; Poidevin 1998, 110–15). Furthermore, the earlier studies provided little, if any, technological and typological descriptions of their samples, nor a great deal of contextual information (Table 12.2).

Traditionally obsidian sourcing has been employed to gain a clearer image of cultural interaction and as a means of investigating socio-economic complexity in the archaeological record (cf. Renfrew 1975, 38–51; Renfrew *et al.* 1968; Wright 1969). Yet more often than not, interpretations have been forwarded on the basis of a handful of analyses, whose descriptions rarely extend beyond a sample number, with little, if any, information as to the specific context of the material being characterized. Moreover, there is little discussion with regard to the conceptualization of 'obsidian' itself.

To talk about the trade or consumption of 'obsidian' is difficult since 'obsidian' is the geological name accorded a volcanic glass formed under certain conditions and embodying certain physical properties. As archaeologists working away from the sources we are not dealing with obsidian as a geological phenomenon, but as a cultural one (and this is to ignore for the moment the possibility that for these people there may have been no 'natural':'cultural' distinction: cf. Taçon 1991). The 'obsidian' that we are dealing with was exchanged, transformed, used, discarded, conceptualized and valued in a multitude of different ways. We might envisage (and recover at our archaeological sites) obsidian as a 'raw material', i.e. blocks of glass that would be transformed into different products, the worker drawing upon its mechanical and/or metaphysical properties: its fracture mechanics, sharpness, ancestral or totemic powers, colour, or brilliance (cf. Aufrère 1991; Decourt 1998; Saunders 2001; Taçon 1991). Alternatively, obsidian may have been displaced in the shape of 'preforms', such as part decorticated nodules, or prepared cores, as indeed we witness at Çatalhöyük with the 'quarry flakes' of obsidian industry 7 (Chapter 11). Finally, and this is perhaps a rather unimaginative technology-led tripartite division, we can also speak of obsidian circulating as end products, i.e. finished implements such as our non-local prismatic blades (obsidian industries 4 and 5).

One recent set of studies has started to bring some of these issues together in a most informative way, specifically the combined work of archaeologists and archaeometrists at the Kaletepe blade workshop (Aceramic Neolithic) located atop the Kömürcü obsidian outcrop of the Göllü Dağ-East 'source' (Balkan-Atlı & Der Aprahamian 1998; Cauvin & Balkan-Atlı 1996). Research at the site has included a techno-typological characterization of the workshop's industries (naviform and unipolar prismatic blades) and the geochemical signature of the source material. When one combines these data with trace-elemental analysis of obsidian artefacts from such Levantine PPNB sites as Mureybet and Cheikh Hasan, it is possible to start discussing trade of large black, shiny, razor-sharp projectiles, rather than talking simply of the exchange and movement of Göllü Dağ-East 'obsidian' (Abbès *et al.* 2001; Balkan-Atlı & Der Aprahamian 1998, 244, fig. 6; Chataigner 1998, 288–9).

Aims of the project and sampling strategy

The aims of the new programme are manifold. They include documenting Çatalhöyük's relationship with different sources through time, an investigation of the relationship between the variant industries and specific outcrops of obsidian and the potential for visually discriminating between the obsidians. For this reason, each artefact chosen for analysis has been described in detail and illustrated for publication alongside the results, an unfortunately all too rare occurrence in provenance studies. We also wish to know whether a building, or groups of buildings, synchronically had the same relationship with an obsidian source; for instance, one might envisage rights of access to an outcrop being based on kinship affiliations, or membership of some other social group (cf. Hampton 1999, 227–8; Torrence 1986, 52–7). Such a broad range of questions necessarily involves taking numerous samples, and we acknowledge the Çatalhöyük Research Project's support of this venture. Indeed, the number of artefacts submitted for analysis is significantly larger than usual for a single site study, following recent trends elsewhere, as for example with the *c.* 400 pieces from the La Mana Pre-Hispanic site in Ecuador (Pereira 2000; Pereira *et al.* 2001) and the thousands from the Lower Ulua Valley and the site of Puerto Escondido in Honduras (S. Shackley pers. comm.).

The Çatalhöyük East material that forms the basis of this chapter comes from the North, South and Summit Areas, spanning Levels IX–III, a period of approximately 500 years (Cessford 2001). A significant proportion of this data set comes from the Level VII–VI Building 1 in the North Area ($n = 78$), as we wished to make an intensive analysis of the consumption of obsidian(s) from one structure.

The samples were selected to examine a number of variables relating to raw material, time, space and modes of consumption. These included attempting to elucidate a relationship between source and what we perceived to be visual distinctions amongst the obsidian on the basis of its colour, banding, translucency, inclusions and texture. We also wished to analyze a representative selection of the various industries in the Çatalhöyük assemblages (see Chapter 11), to see if correlations existed between specific technologies and obsidian sources and to investigate these relationships through time (level by level) and space (building by building). 85 of the samples were selected by Tom Cawdron in 1998 (half of the CNRS material and all of the Aberystwyth samples), while Tristan Carter chose a further 50 pieces for CNRS in 1999.

It should be noted that not all of the obsidian industries from these levels have been sampled. The majority of pieces selected for analysis were unmodified knapping debris, irregular blades and blade-like flakes (obsidian industry 1), a limited number of prismatic blades (obsidian industries 4 and 5), plus a few fragmentary 'quarry flakes' (obsidian industry 7). None of the projectiles, or the majority of other finely-retouched pieces of non-local manufacture were selected for analysis, a sampling bias imposed largely by current archaeological bureaucracy; the extent to which such concerns structure our analytical agenda should not be underestimated. It is to this end that we are investigating the possibility of on-site conservators taking sub-samples from objects and other avenues of research, specifically non-destructive techniques, with particular reference to portable technologies (cf. Aloupi *et al.* 2000; Ferrence *et al* 2000; Moioli & Seccaroni 2000), so that eventually we may source the mirrors, spearheads, long blades, beads and other 'museum pieces'.

ICP-MS and ICP-AES analysis of 100 samples at CNRS

by Gérard Poupeau & Céline Bressy

The samples

Of the 100 pieces of archaeological obsidian sent to CNRS, seven came from Çatalhöyük West, while the remainder came from Çatalhöyük East, the material being selected from the North, South and Summit Areas (Table 12.1). The Neolithic artefacts comprised five pieces from Level IX (Building 2), two from Level VIII (Space 114), five from Level VIII–VII (Building 5, Building 5/1), fifteen from Level VII (Spaces 105–9, 112–13), fifty-nine from Level VII–VI (Building 1), one from Level VIB (Space 160) and six from Level V–III (Building 1, Building 10). With regard to the industries represented, the samples included a significant quantity of material relating to the long-term 'in-house' small percussive blade and blade-like flake industry (obsidian industry 1) from Levels IX, VII–VI and VII. In turn, we included fragments of large bipolar/naviform blades (obsidian industry 4) from the hoard in Building 1 (Level VII–VI), some regular prismatic blades from unipolar cores (obsidian industry 5) from Building 1 (Levels VII–VI & VI–V), Building 10 (Level III) and Çatalhöyük West (Early Chalcolithic), plus a few pieces related to 'quarry flakes' and biface preforms (obsidian industry 7).

Table 12.3. *Source of Çatalhöyük obsidian by level.*

Level	Samples	Göllü Dağ-east	Nenezi Dağ	Unknown
E. Chalcolithic	7	3	4	0
III	2	0	2	0
VI–V	7	0	7	0
VIB	1	1	0	0
VII–VI	73	37	35	1
VII	15	13	2	0
VIII–VII	11	9	2	0
VIII	16	15	1	0
IX	5	5	-	0
Total	**135**	**83 (61.5%)**	**51 (37.8%)**	**1 (0.7%)**

Table 12.4. *Source of Çatalhöyük obsidian by industry and level. Source of Çatalhöyük obsidian by industry and level (● = Göllü Dağ-east; ☆ = Nenezi Dağ; ns = not sampled). NB. Industry 2 not represented in these levels).*

Level	1	3	4	5	6	7
Early Chalcolithic	?	?		● ☆	?	?
III				☆		
VI–V	☆			☆		
VII–VI	● ☆		● ☆	● ☆		● ☆?
VIB	●?					
VIII–VII	●					●
VII	●		☆?	☆?		●
VIII	●		●	☆		●
IX	●	ns	ns	ns	ns	●

Analytical procedure

The 100 artefacts were analyzed at the Groupe de Géophysique Nucléaire, UMR 5025 of CNRS, Université Joseph Fourier, Grenoble, France, following the protocols described in Bellot-Gurlet (1998) and Bellot-Gurlet *et al.* (1999). Small slices were taken from each piece using either a thin diamond saw or a diamond wire saw. To minimize eventual surface contamination/alteration biases in analyses, each slice was crushed between thick books of paper sheets in order to obtain internal fragments. To ensure a representative sample was taken, about 100 mg of such millimetre-sized chips were carefully selected under a stereomicroscope, checking the freshness of their surfaces. In order to obtain a mother solution they were then dissolved in Teflon beakers with high-purity hydrofluoric acid under controlled atmosphere conditions.

For ICP-AES analyses of Al, Fe, Mn, Mg, Ca, Na, K, Ti and P, daughter solutions with different degrees of dilution were prepared. Four solutions of appropriate dilutions were prepared from pure element solutions for calibration purposes. 27 trace elements: Co, Rb, Sr, Y, Zr, Nb, Cs, Ba, La, Ce, Pr, Nd, Sm, Eu, Gd, Tb, Dy, Ho, Er, Tm, Yb, Lu, Hf, Ta, Pb, Th, U, were measured by ICP-MS from a single diluted daughter solution. Several solutions of geochemical standard reference materials (RGM-1, BIR-1, BHVO-1, SRM-278) were prepared in the same way. All these solutions were spiked with a thulium reference solution (Barrat *et al.* 1996). In order to take into account interferences in the REE, pure solutions of Sm→Tb, Pr+Nd, Ce and Ba were also analyzed. Finally, to compensate for instrumental drift, one unspiked standard (BHVO-1) was analyzed after each set of four samples. Element contents are then calculated following Bellot-Gurlet *et al.* (1999).

For provenance determination the data generated from the artefacts was compared with those previously obtained in the laboratory from obsidian samples of various geological sources. The trace-element data are presented conventionally in diagrams of normalized element abundances (cf. Chataigner *et al.* 1998; Poidevin 1998); the norm selected is the composition of the upper continental crust as given by Sun & McDonagh (1989).

Data

The trace-element normalized abundances of the 100 artefacts are presented in Figure 12.2. It is clear that two compositional groups are present comprising 55 and 45 samples respectively. In Figure 12.2a, the compositions of the 55 artefacts defining the largest group are reported along with geological obsidians from the 'Göllü Dağ-East' region (four and five samples from the Kömürcü and Kayırlı-East outcrops respectively); the artefacts show a clear affinity with the 'Göllü Dağ-East' type compositional group of Cauvin *et al.* (1986; 1991). The major element contents of the artefacts (Table 12.5 on CD) are also in agreement with that of the Göllü Dağ-East obsidians. As it is not possible from the 36 element contents to discriminate obsidians of the Kömürcü outcrops from those of Kayırlı-East, we attribute a Göllü Dağ-East origin to the 55 artefacts analyzed. In Figure 12.2b, the compositions of the 45 artefacts with another composition are compared to that of one geological sample from the Nenezi Dağ volcano. As above, from both the similarity of trace (Fig. 12.2) and major elemental (Table 12.6 on CD) contents of these obsidians with that measured from Nenezi Dağ (see also Cauvin *et al.* 1998), we assign them an origin from this volcano.

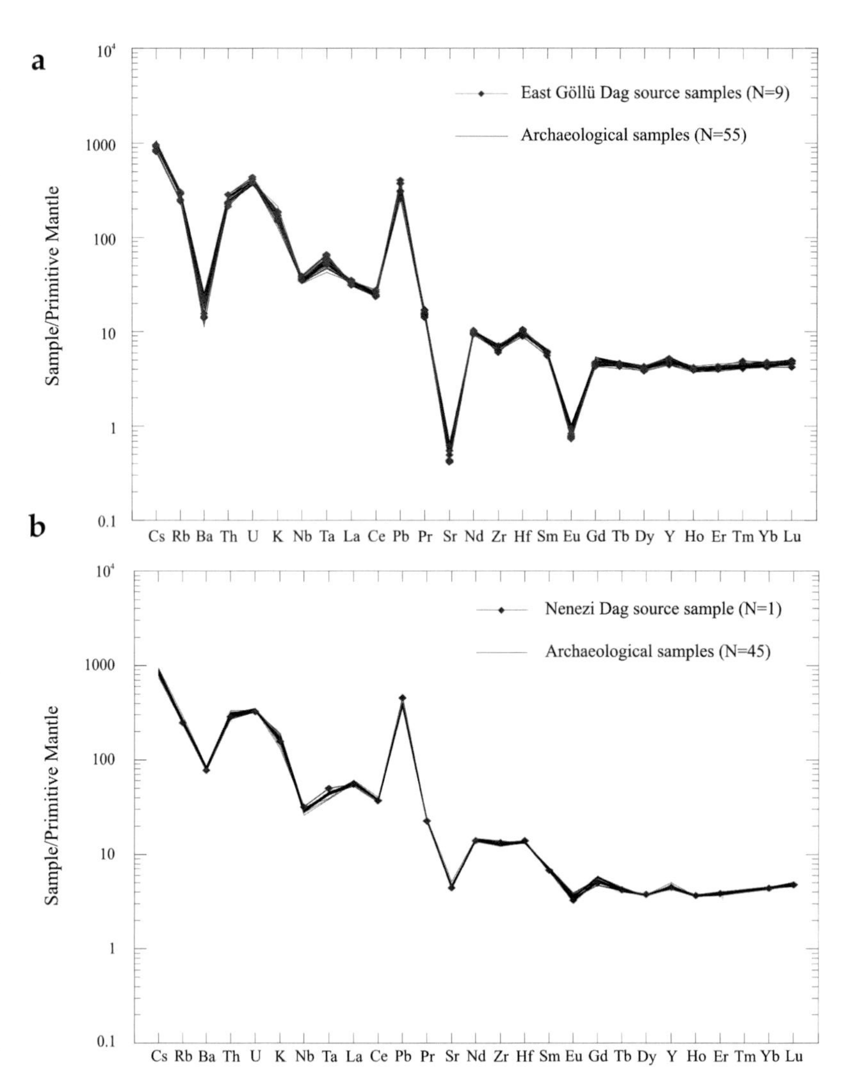

Figure 12.2. *Relative trace-element abundances for 100 artefacts analyzed at CNRS: a) relative trace-element abundances for artefacts with a Göllü Dağ-east composition; b) relative trace-element abundances for artefacts with a Nenezi Dağ composition.*

LA-ICP-MS analysis of 35 samples at Aberystwyth

by Nicholas J.G. Pearce

The samples

Thirty-five obsidian artefacts were analyzed at the Institute of Geography and Earth Sciences, University of Wales, Aberystwyth. This material came from the Early Neolithic East Mound, with twenty-one pieces from the North Area and fourteen from the South Area (Table 12.1). The twenty-one North Area samples came from Building 1, or Building 5/1 (Levels VI–IV), while the South Area material all related to Level VIII contexts, with a single piece from Building 4 (Space 150) and thirteen from external Space 115.

Analytical procedure

All analyses were performed by laser ablation (LA)-ICP-MS at Aberystwyth. Each flake of obsidian had five separate spectra acquired from it for forty separate elements (Table 12.7). Spectra are acquired by burning a small volume of material from the sample ('ablating') using a high-intensity ultra-violet pulsed laser beam and analyzing the vaporized material in the ICP-MS. The resulting ablation craters are typically 25 μm in diameter and about 50 μm deep, and are virtually invisible to the naked eye. The analyses were calibrated against the NIST 610 'Trace elements in Glass' reference material using concentrations taken from Pearce *et al.* (1997). To produce quantitative trace element analyses, LA-ICP-MS requires the knowledge of at least one element in the unknown to act as an internal standard. As no concentrations were known for any elements in the glass a value of 69.895 per cent was assumed for SiO_2 (the same concentration as in the NIST 610 reference material) to give approximate concentrations. The reported concentrations cannot be used directly for comparison (as they relate to an assumed value of the internal standard, not a true concentration), however ratios of one element to another (e.g. Zr/Y, Zr/Nb or any other element pair) are quantitative and correct, thus these can be used in identifying groups within the data (Fig. 12.2). Similarly triangular discrimination plots of the data ratio three elements, and thus can also be used in provenance/correlation studies (Fig. 12.3). The analysis of each sample requires no preparation with the flakes of obsidian being placed directly into the ablation chamber of the laser ablation system. The analysis of each flake takes approximately five minutes.

The spread of data in the LA-ICP-MS analyses of an individual flake is almost certainly real variation within the obsidian (Table 12.7). Large variations exist in the chemistry of rhyolitic glasses on a small scale as

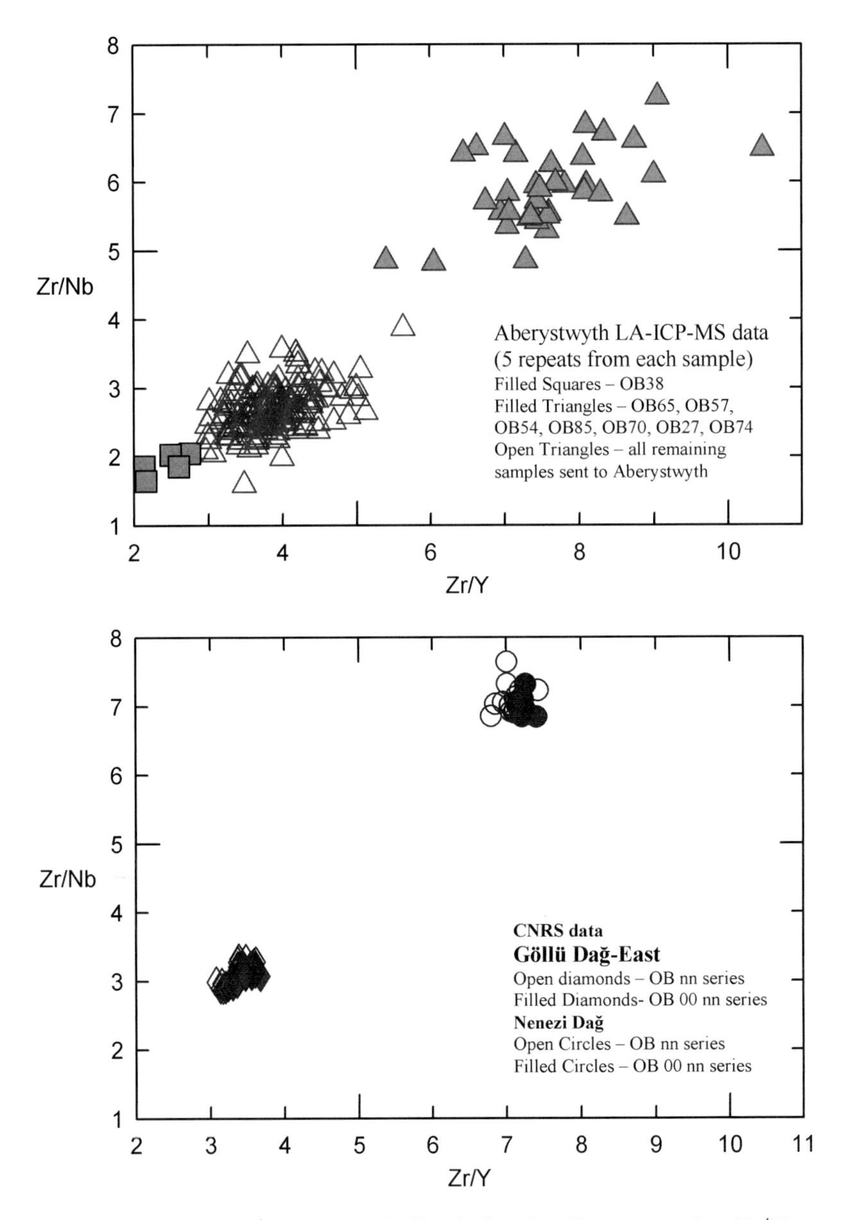

Figure 12.3. *Element/element ratio discrimination diagrams using Zr/Y vs Zr/Nb determined by LA-ICP-MS at Aberystwyth.*

a result of their viscous nature as a magma and this has recently been shown in the analyses of glass shards from the Minoan eruption of Santorini, where a two- to three-fold variation in many trace elements (e.g. REE, Zr, Y, Nb) has been observed between individual glass shards (Pearce *et al.* 2002).

LA-ICP-MS offers one advantage over solution analytical methods in that it is easy to identify analyses that have ablated into phenocryst phases (such as feldspars) within the obsidian. These analyses can be removed form the data sets so that only the glassy component of the obsidian is considered in the comparisons (see Pearce *et al.* 2002 for discussion of this application to tephra studies).

Data

Two clearly-distinct groups can be observed in the data, representing the south Cappadocian sources of Nenezi Dağ (n = 6) and Göllü Dağ-East (n = 28), while a third, as yet unidentified chemical type is represented by one sample alone (Figs. 12.3–12.4). The first group comprises six samples that form a clear grouping with high Zr/Nb and high Zr/Y ratios (Fig. 12.3), and correlate directly with the Nenezi Dağ group as identified at CNRS by Poupeau and Bressy: OB27, OB54, OB57, OB65, OB70, OB74. The second group of samples form the main cluster of analyses with 28 samples, and correlate with the Göllü Dağ-East analyses of CNRS: OB2, OB3, OB4, OB5, OB21, OB22, OB24, OB25, OB26, OB28, OB29, OB42, OB43, OB50, OB52, OB53, OB55, OB56, OB58, OB61, OB62, OB63, OB64, OB66, OB68, OB69, OB71, OB90.

There are some minor subdivisions evident in this second group that may merit further investigations, for example OB71, OB87 and OB4 often cluster together on many of the discriminant diagrams, having relatively low Ba. These variations form the cluster at the low Ba end of the main group of samples in Figure 12.4. These may be subtle variations on the main groupings, but at present with only a few of each group present it is hard to be precise in defining these groups, if indeed they are real. These sub groups are clearly related geochemically (similar trace-element ratios etc.) and are likely to have originated form a very similar source, such as a series of lava flows from the same volcano, and may thus be a reflection of subtle compositional differences between such flows. Without comparative material from individual sources though it is not possible to be certain about the causes of this variation.

Finally, sample OB38 stands alone in having the lowest Zr/Y and Zr/Nb ratios (Fig. 12.2), and having high Rb and extremely low Ba (Fig. 12.3). It is clearly distinct from all other samples analyzed by LA-ICP-MS and does not correlate with the Nenezi Dağ or Göllü Dağ-East sources. The source of this sample is unclear and this sample was not included in those analyzed at CNRS sets. It is hoped that future analyses (not least involving a greater range of Anatolian source standards) will be able to correlate the chemical signature of this piece to that of a known volcano.

Discussion
by Tristan Carter

Perhaps invariably, the data generated by our analyses have spawned more questions than they answered. Focusing for the time being on what we have learnt, it can be stated that all of the samples thus far analyzed have a chemical signature congruent with a Cappadocian source (Table 12.3; Figs. 12.2–12.4). At present, the trace-elemental characterization of 135 pieces of obsidian from Çatalhöyük allows us assign them with some confidence to 'two' sources, namely Göllü Dağ-East (*n* = 83) and Nenezi Dağ (*n* = 51), plus one currently unknown (OB38 defined by LA-ICP-MS analyses at Aberystwyth). We refer to 'two' sources, but the Göllü Dağ-East signature in fact represents three separate obsidian flows (Kayırlı-East, Kömürcü and Bozköy-East) that at present cannot be geochemically discriminated by the participant laboratories employing the analytical techniques described above (though see Gratuze 1999).

These new data thus seem to corroborate the work of Keller & Seified (1990) who had asserted previously that Çatalhöyük was procuring obsidian from these 'two' sources. Furthermore, the parallel exploitation of Göllü Dağ-East and Nenezi Dağ obsidian is now similarly claimed at a number of other Aceramic and Early Neolithic settlements in central Anatolia and beyond. These include Canhasan III (Konya plain), Aşıklı Höyük and Musular (southern Cappadocia), Mersin (Cilicia), Shillourokambos (Cyprus), Byblos and Halula (coastal and desert Syria), Beisamoun (southern Jordan) and Mevorakh (coastal Israel) (Ataman 1988, 43–52; Cauvin 1998, 261; Chataigner 1998, 285–92, figs. 5a–b, 7a–b; Gratuze *et al.* 1994; Renfrew *et al.* 1966, 63). For the (Late) Chalcolithic, the site of Aphrodisias in southwest Turkey has produced obsidian whose chemical signatures correlate with those of the Göllü Dağ-East and Nenezi Dağ sources (Blackman 1989).

Çatalhöyük has still to produce evidence for any obsidian from its closest source, Hasan Dağ (Fig. 12.1), the mountain occasionally visible from the site, its double-peaks allegedly represented in the wall painting from Shrine VII, 14 (Mellaart 1967, 176–7, pl. 59–60). Mellaart claimed that the mountain's depiction symbolized the significance accorded the source of Çatalhöyük's obsidian, 'from which the site probably derived much of its wealth' (Mellaart 1967, 177). It has since become clear, however, that the obsidian at Hasan Dağ is difficult to access and possesses a poor conchoidal fracture habit; moreover, analyses have failed to link any archaeological obsidian to this mountain, suggesting that it may never have been exploited in prehistory (Cauvin & Balkan-Atlı 1996, 252; Chataigner 1998, 292–3). Nor has the latest suite of analyses provided any corroborative evidence for Renfrew's alleged piece of obsidian from Armenia, though conceptually we have little problem with the idea that such material might be recovered at Çatalhöyük. In turn, we have still to analyze any obsidian whose signature matches that of the Acıgöl outcrops, supporting further Chataigner's claim

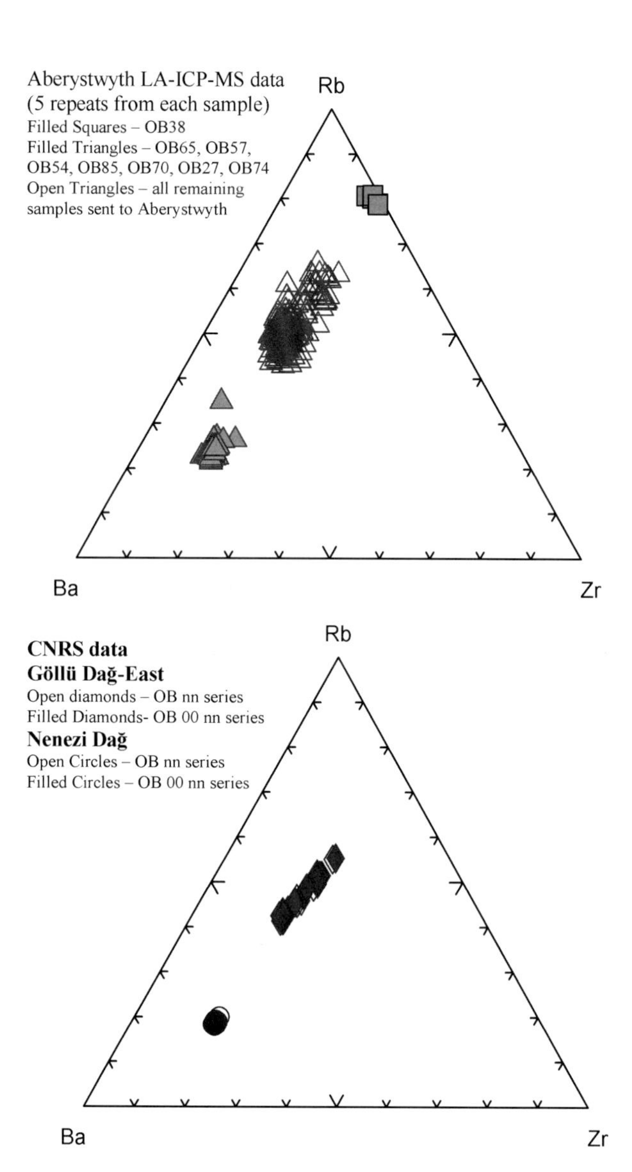

Figure 12.4. *Trace-element discrimination diagram for obsidian flakes using Rb, Zr and Ba determined by LA-ICP-MS at Aberystwyth.*

that the artefacts characterized by Renfrew and Wright were in fact made of Nenezi Dağ obsidian (Chataigner 1998, 285). It is also noteworthy that Renfrew and Wright's alleged Acıgöl obsidian was described as being in the form of blades, implements that we now know were often made of Nenezi Dağ obsidian at Çatalhöyük.

The nature of consumption through time

The above statements offer only the simplest appraisal of our new data, for there are far more nuanced patterns that one can observe in Çatalhöyük's consumption of the Göllü Dağ-East and Nenezi Dağ obsidian when one considers the artefacts' date, form and context. Our results suggest that there are significant differences in the history of Çatalhöyük's exploitation of these southern Cappadocian raw materials, both temporally and technologically. The Göllü Dağ-East obsidian appears to have enjoyed a long-term history of use at Neolithic Çatalhöyük, seemingly the primary raw material worked in each household from at least Level IX, whereas the Nenezi Dağ obsidian only makes a significant impact from Level VII–VI (Table 12.3). Moreover, there appears to be a technological component to this pattern, because the marked increase in the consumption of Nenezi Dağ obsidian correlates directly with unipolar pressure-flaked blade technology becoming the mainstay industry at Çatalhöyük (obsidian industry 5: Table 12.4).

Level IX

Five artefacts from Level IX were analyzed by CNRS, all from Building 2 (two from Space 116, three from Space 117: Table 12.1); the chemical signature of each piece correlated with that of the Göllü Dağ-East source (Fig. 12.5a on CD). The material comprised two retouched irregular blades/blade-like flakes (OB 33, OB34 - CNRS1) and a *pièce esquillée* on a thick flake/core (OB31) from obsidian industry 1. There was also a retouched flake (OB32) and a large, non-cortical blade-like flake that may be a thinning flake from a biface preform (obsidian industry 7).

Level VIII

A total of 16 artefacts were characterized from Level VIII, 14 at Aberystwyth and two at CNRS (Table 12.1), the samples coming from the external spaces 114 (n = 2), and 115 (n = 13) and a single piece from Building 4, Space 150 (Fig. 12.5a on CD). All except one of the artefacts was made from obsidian attributed a Göllü Dağ-East origin (n = 15, 93.8 per cent), with one piece made of Nenezi Dağ obsidian. The former raw material was represented in the form of two prismatic blades from an opposed platform technology (obsidian industry 4), one a centre blade (*plein débitage*) or just beyond (OB26 - Aber), plus one from the secondary series of removals with remnant cresting scars (OB2 - Aber). There was also what appeared to be a blade and core-fragment from the less regular and 'in-house' tradition (obsidian industry 1, OB21, OB3 - Aber; OB23 - CNRS 1), plus a variety of non-cortical flakes and *pièces esquillées* (OB20 - CNRS 1; OB90, OB24 - Aber) that may relate to the same industry. Less certain are two non-cortical thin blanks with multi-directional/bipolar dorsal scars, that might be thinning flakes from biface preforms (obsidian industry 7, OB4, OB58 - Aber). The one artefact made of obsidian from Nenezi Dağ (OB27 - Aber) seems to be a rejuvenation flake from the face of a unipolar prismatic blade core (obsidian industry 5).

Level VIII–VII

Eleven pieces of obsidian from the North Area comprise the Level VIII–VII sample (Building 5/1), six of which were analyzed at Aberystwyth, the remainder at CNRS (Fig. 12.5b on CD). Nine of the artefacts' trace-elemental signatures correlated with that of the Göllü Dağ-East source, while two were characterized as being made from Nenezi Dağ obsidian. The former material included a core from obsidian industry 1 (OB71 - Aber), plus a thinning flake from an obsidian industry 7 biface (OB66 - Aber). The Nenezi Dağ sample included a *pièce esquillée* on a flake (OB65 - Aber).

Level VII

Fifteen artefacts from Level VII were analyzed at CNRS (Fig. 12.5b on CD), the material coming from external spaces 105 (n = 2), 106 (n = 2), 107 (n = 2), 108, 109, 112 (n = 5) and 113 (n = 2). Thirteen pieces were made from obsidian characterized as coming from Göllü Dağ-East (86.7 per cent), while two had a signature that correlated with the Nenezi Dağ source (14.3 per cent). The Göllü Dağ-East material was represented by a small group of pieces that might be the remnants of flat 'quarry flakes' (obsidian industry 7, OB11, OB19), including some with cortical material (OB89, OB13). From the 'in-house' tradition (obsidian industry 1) there are a few end products (OB16), exhausted cores/*pièces esquillées* (OB6, OB10) and rejuvenation pieces, some of which had been retouched (OB14, OB7, OB9). Unfortunately, neither of the two non-cortical flakes made of Nenezi Dağ obsidian are particularly diagnostic (OB15, OB17), though one might be from the face of a blade core (OB15).

Level VII–VI

The Level VII–VI sample, all from Building 1, comprises the largest single group of artefacts sent for analysis from Çatalhöyük, with 73 pieces (Figs. 12.5c–12.5e on CD); 59 were characterized at CNRS and 14 at Aberystwyth (Table 12.1). Just over half the obsidian was assigned a Göllü Dağ-East source ($n = 37$, 50.7 per cent), with 35 pieces characterized as coming from Nenezi Dağ (47.9 per cent). The signature of one piece analyzed at Aberystwyth correlated with neither of these sources (OB38 - Aber); this sample will be reanalyzed in the near future to try and assign it to a known obsidian outcrop.

A number of different knapping traditions are represented amongst the artefacts made of Göllü Dağ-East obsidian, including fragments of prismatic blades from opposed platform technologies (obsidian industry 4, OB36 - CNRS1; OB20 - CNRS2) (Fig. 12.5c on CD), plus other prismatic blades of varying dimensions from unipolar cores (obsidian industry 5, OB29, OB3, OB5 - CNRS2) (Fig. 12.5c on CD). One relatively large flake seems to be a rejuvenation piece removing the back and edge (with remnant cresting scars) of a prismatic blade core (OB63 - Aber). There are also a number of less regular blades and blade-like flakes associated with obsidian industry 1 (OB5, OB8, OB45, OB42 *inter alia*) (Fig. 12.5c on CD), and fragmentary cores (OB56 - Aber) (Fig. 12.5d on CD). There are also a few thick flakes, both cortical and non-cortical, that likely represent much reduced 'quarry flakes' (obsidian industry 7, OB10, OB40, OB35) (Fig. 12.5c on CD) plus some fine flakes with multi-directional/bipolar dorsal scars that relate to the thinning of biface preforms (obsidian industry 7, OB64 - Aber) (Fig. 12.5c on CD). It is difficult to assign many of the remaining non-cortical flakes to any particular tradition, though most probably relate to the transformation of 'quarry' flakes in the manufacture of blades and blade-like flakes; some are used and a few retouched.

The artefacts made from Nenezi Dağ obsidian include a much higher proportion of regular prismatic blades ($n = 15$, 35.7 per cent), mainly unipolar (obsidian industry 5), of varying widths but many with their lips distinctively removed (OB47, OB28, OB23, OB31 *inter alia*) (Fig. 12.5e on CD). Many of these pieces displayed use wear and a number had been modified. There were also blades from opposed platform cores (obsidian industry 4, OB25 - CNRS2), including two of the very fine, large naviform blades that came from the (1461) hoard in Space 71 (OB15 - CNRS2; OB44, OB49 - CNRS1) (Fig. 12.5e on CD); due to an oversight in the sampling procedure, two pieces were analyzed from the same blade (OB15, OB44).

The Nenezi Dağ sample also included what appeared to be two much-reduced cores of the 'in house' percussive tradition (obsidian industry 1, OB37, OB38 - CNRS2) (Fig. 12.5e on CD), plus a variety of less regular blades and blade-like flakes that should also be associated with this industry. The remaining material includes some large and chunky flakes that may have come from 'quarry flakes' (obsidian industry 7, OB35, OB33, OB49 - CNRS2), plus a number of *pièces esquillées* (OB59 - CNRS1) and non-cortical flakes (Fig. 12.5f on CD). One piece of obsidian from Space 160, in the form of a *pièce esquillée* on a non-cortical flake, was analyzed by CNRS (OB1 - CNRS1); it possibly relates to the 'in-house' obsidian industry 1. It was assigned a Göllü Dağ-East source.

Level VI–V

Seven artefacts from Level VI–V were analyzed from the latest contexts in the North Area's Building 1; all except one piece was characterized at CNRS. Each piece's chemical signatures were consistent with that of the Nenezi Dağ source. The sample included a unipolar prismatic blade (obsidian industry 5, OB46), a *pièce esquillée*/exhausted blade core of obsidian industry 1 (OB57 - Aber) and a part-cortical flake (OB33) (Figs. 12.5e–f on CD).

Level III

A unipolar centre blade and a non-cortical flake from Building 10 (Summit Area) were characterized by CNRS (Fig. 12.5g on CD); both were sourced to Nenezi Dağ.

Early Chalcolithic

Seven pieces of worked obsidian from the excavations of the Early Chalcolithic West Mound were selected for chemical characterization at CNRS, with four assigned a Nenezi Dağ source and three a Göllü Dağ-East source (Fig. 12.5g on CD). The former raw material was represented by a non-cortical flake (OB83 - CNRS1), and three prismatic blades from a unipolar technology (obsidian industry 5). One blade had been truncated and had its lip removed by flaking (OB77 - CNRS1), while another was heavily retouched along both margins (OB79 - CNRS1). Interestingly, the implements made from Göllü Dağ-East obsidian also included a prismatic blade from a unipolar technology (obsidian industry 5), again with its lip removed by flaking; it also had and elongated notches on both edges (OB81 - CNRS1). The remaining two pieces were in the form of non-cortical flakes, one of which could also be classified as a *pièce esquillée* (OB78 - CNRS1).

The relationship between technology, time and source

Even allowing for the fact that our sample of 135 artefacts by no means represents all the industries thus far defined at Çatalhöyük East (Levels IX–III) or those from Early Chalcolithic Çatalhöyük West, we can still offer a number of comments on the history of obsidian consumption at Çatalhöyük. The first point is that we seem to have a temporal distinction with regard to the community's exploitation of the Göllü Dağ-East and Nenezi Dağ obsidians. The former raw material(s) are dominant in the earlier part of the sequence, with a shift during Level VII–VI, as represented by the Building 1 assemblage (Table 12.3 & Figs. 12.2–12.4). Indeed, of the 47 artefacts analyzed from Levels IX to VII–VI, just under 90 per cent were assigned a Göllü Dağ-East provenance (*n* = 42, 89.4 per cent), yet this figure drops to under 50 per cent when considering the sample from Levels VI–V and later (*n* = 41, 46.6 per cent). Significantly, the increase in the consumption of Nenezi Dağ obsidian correlates with a number of other changes witnessed at Çatalhöyük after the widespread burning event of Level VIB, including shifts in chipped stone, ceramic and building technologies (Conolly 1999b; Mellaart 1966a, 172; Matthews & Farid 1996, 295-6; Volume 4, Chapters 3 & 21). While future analyses will no doubt modify this picture, we are confident that the change in consumption patterns is genuine enough, as our sampling strategy throughout each level focused on the most common debris and products (it is the minority traditions, or 'exotica' that are under-represented).

Level IX to VII–VI

During Levels IX to VII–VI the Göllü Dağ-East obsidian(s) are represented by a number of distinct *chaînes opératoires*, i.e. the raw material was entering the site in different forms and being consumed in different ways. It appears that the dominant *chaîne opératoire* commenced with the knapping of large, flat flakes up at the quarries (obsidian industry 7), some modified as side-scrapers, that were then carried to Çatalhöyük in bulk, probably in small sacks, with a minimal amount of protective wrapping. Close parallels for these large flakes / scrapers have been collected from the surface of the Kayırlı-East and Kömürcü outcrops (Cauvin & Balkan-Atlı 1996, 257–64, figs. 7 & 12). As well as representing a form of raw material for the inhabitants of Çatalhöyük, these 'quarry flakes' often bear clear traces of use-wear. Some were employed as scrapers (indeed a few are modified as such), while others have accentuated step scars from a percussive use, such as butchery or chopping wood. It is uncertain as to where these pieces were used, at the quarries, en route to the site, or perhaps at Çatalhöyük itself (maybe edge of site butchery zones, see Volume 4, Chapter 2) prior to their distribution amongst the various buildings. When the large flakes were finally taken inside a structure, a proportion were then buried in hoards close to fire installations (Chapter 11), a number seemingly interred in their organic containers, the associated tiny obsidian shatter representing the residue from transport damage. To be clear, it must be stated that none of our analyzed material of obsidian industry 7 actually comes from hoard contexts. However, we feel quite confident that future characterization work will show that most of the 'quarry flakes' from caches (at least prior to Level VIB) are made of Göllü Dağ-East obsidian. This belief is based partly on visual discrimination, particularly with regard to white spherulitic inclusions, a feature that correlates strongly with this source (Table 12.8 on CD). At some unknown time later, these 'quarry flakes' were retrieved from their under-floor caches and then knapped to produce the small blades and blade-like flakes that define the dominant 'in house' tradition before Level VIB at Çatalhöyük (obsidian industry 1). Quantities of these irregular products, exhausted cores and a few rejuvenation pieces were included in our characterization study from Levels IX to VII–VI, with the great majority shown to have been manufactured from Göllü Dağ-East obsidian.

While obsidian industry 1 seems to be the dominant mode of consuming Göllü Dağ-East obsidian(s) during this time, we also have evidence for other industries exploiting this raw material. For example, the Level VIII artefacts analyzed included two fragmentary prismatic blades from an opposed platform technology (obsidian industry 4). We have no manufacturing debris that can be associated with this tradition, suggesting that the blades were brought to the site ready-made, having perhaps been knapped at one of the quarry workshops (Chapter 11). Up at the Göllü Dağ-East sources bipolar prismatic blade cores have been recorded by surface surveys at Bitlikeler, a seemingly long-lived workshop (based on the variety of products documented) atop the Kayırlı-East outcrop, while opposed platform blade technologies are known from the Aceramic Neolithic workshop of Kaletepe (Balkan-Atlı *et al.* 1999, 136–8, fig. 12). Finally, the Level IX artefacts characterized as having been made from Göllü Dağ-East obsidian also included examples of thinning flakes knapped from biface preforms. These preforms represent the other component of our obsidian industry 7 alongside the 'quarry flakes'; they too were manufactured at the quarries, then transported to the site and buried in hoards. Such bifaces have been found amongst the workshop debris at both Bitlikeler (Kayırlı-East) and Kömürcü (Balkan-Atlı *et al.* 1999, 136–8, figs. 14 & 17).

The only diagnostic piece from Levels IX to VII–VI characterized as being made from Nenezi Dağ obsidian, is a rejuvenation flake from the face of an opposed platform prismatic blade core, from Level VIII (OB27

- Aber) (Fig. 12.5a on CD). While quantities of knapped debris litter the slopes of Nenezi Dağ in association with the obsidian outcrop, excavations have yet to be conducted at the site. The Çatalhöyük characterization thus takes on another significance at this juncture, as we can indirectly start to describe the nature of production at the quarry, offering information as to what was being manufactured and when. Surface surveys have recorded the presence of bipolar blade cores at the quarry (Balkan-Atlı *et al.* 1999, 135–6, fig. 4.1), some of which it now seems can be related to Level VIII at Çatalhöyük.

Level VII–VI to Early Chalcolithic

We turn now to the major changes in obsidian procurement after Level VII (as represented by the Building 1 assemblage), specifically the major increase in Çatalhöyük's exploitation of the Nenezi Dağ source. Amongst the Level IX to VII–VI artefacts analyzed, only 10.6 per cent (n = 5) were characterized as being made of Nenezi Dağ obsidian, a figure that leaps to just under 50 per cent of the artefacts from Level IX–VII samples (Table 12.3). It is not only a change in the habits of raw material exploitation that we witness at this time, because Level VIB (which Building 1 immediately post-dates) has been highlighted as a watershed in the traditions of chipped-stone technology at Çatalhöyük East (Conolly 1999b). It is contended that these changes in procurement and production are related integrally.

New perspectives on technical change

Conolly (1999b, 791) discussed recently a 'profound change' in how obsidian was consumed at Çatalhöyük after Level VIB, with a shift from flake- to blade-based assemblages, with a concurrent transformation in blade technology from percussion to pressure-flaking, together with evidence that production became a more restricted affair. It was argued that these developments related to contemporary changes in subsistence practices and the organization of production. Our programme of obsidian sourcing has produced data that require a reappraisal of these arguments. The results of the characterization studies indicate that the alleged technical change correlates with, and was based upon, an increased exploitation of the Nenezi Dağ source, and / or a greater interaction with those people working at the sources.

Fine prismatic blades, some potentially of pressure-flaked technology, are not entirely unknown during the earlier part of Çatalhöyük's occupation (i.e. some of the obsidian industry 4 and 5 material), but they are extremely rare and present only as end products. Conolly (1999b, 796–8) argues that between Levels VIB and VIA this changed radically, with pressure-flaked blade production becoming dominant. In turn, we have the first evidence for their *in situ* manufacture, albeit restricted to a few structures, whose inhabitants were no doubt responsible for supplying the rest of the community. Pressure-flaked blade manufacture became the primary mode of consuming obsidian from this point onward, up to and including the Early Chalcolithic, as represented by the Çatalhöyük West material.

Drawing on a study of the material from Mellaart's 1960s excavation, plus the new Building 1 assemblage, Conolly claimed that the shift to pressure-flaked blade production was due to two factors. The first related to agricultural intensification and the necessary development of a more appropriate toolkit, while secondly, it was argued that the new mode of blade production represented a medium for the creation of social distinction within the community. The latter argument drew on a wealth of literature that has documented the highly-skilled nature of this technology (cf. Clark 1982; Crabtree 1968; Inizan 1984; Tixier 1984; *inter alia*) and the potential social ramifications for the adoption of a craft that patently lends itself to specialization (cf. Carter 1994, 137–8; Clark 1987; Perlès 1990;). It is contended that the 'pressure-flaking : specialization : socially significant act' set of correlates has been overstated, for as Pelegrin (1988) has shown, there are a number of different techniques within this mode of production, involving variant toolkits, stance, gesture, motor-habits, levels of technical *savoir faire* and visual impact. These critiques aside, it is now apparent from our new programme of characterization studies that Conolly's arguments must be further appraised with reference to the correlations between technologies and raw materials.

Raw material and technical change: non-functional considerations

It has long been acknowledged that people

> sometimes made exceptional efforts to obtain isotropic stone for purposes or reasons that had more to do with their sacred life than with more mundane considerations such as flaking or edge holding properties (Gould 1980, 141, quoted in Davidson 1988, 24).

At Çatalhöyük Mellaart argued that obsidian's value would have transcended purely functional considerations, highlighting sensual and aesthetic properties. Its 'transparency, reflective power and its jet black appearance', and how obsidian's volcanic and ultimately chthonic origin would have linked it to the underworld, the place of the dead a 'true gift of mother earth, and therefore imbued with magical potency'

(Mellaart 1967, 177). Though one might take issue with some of the specifics, there are recurrent cross-cultural references to the medico-magical properties, totemic and cosmological associations of stone. These range from small-scale to state societies, from Arnhem Land and Irian Jaya (Hampton 1999; Taçon 1991), to Pharaonic Egypt and the Aztecs (Aufrère 1991), via Theophrastus (*D.L.*) and Pliny (*N.H.*). Obsidian itself enjoys a wide range of meanings relating to fertility, virility, astral origins and body parts, both human and animal (Aufrère 1991, 563–9; Coqueugniot 1998; Decourt 1998; Saunders 2001).

To modern eyes the form, colour and texture of the exotic limnoquartzite, radiolarite and chert implements at Çatalhöyük offer a far greater potential for encoding and conveying a variety of information and stories relating to places, peoples, time, knowledge, experience and myth (cf. Gero 1989; Aufrère 1991; Taçon 1991; Sagona & Webb 1994; Gage *et al.* 1999; Jones & MacGregor 2002). It would be a mistake, however, to assume by extension that the ever present south Cappadocian obsidians were considered mundane. Indeed, there is good evidence to suggest that the consumption of these obsidians was in part structured by social and symbolic concerns. By interrelating detailed technological analyses and characterization studies within a broader temporal and spatial context, we can start to discern some highly-specific modes of consuming obsidian in the Neolithic of central Anatolia (and beyond). These may have little relationship to those issues that have traditionally concerned the archaeologist, such as fracture mechanics, strength, sharpness or source location. For instance, the Göllü Dağ-East and Nenezi Dağ obsidians share essentially the same physical properties, and for someone coming from Çatalhöyük, involve no great difference in the distances involved, or their ease of access. Yet, more often than not they appear to have been employed for quite different purposes, exploited by quite distinct knapping traditions through time. The data indeed hint that at certain periods specific industries were performed using specific obsidians; this will no doubt become clearer when we are able to discriminate the three separate obsidian outcrops that comprise currently the Göllü Dağ-East 'source'. Disentangling these data and offering intellectually-sound and stimulating arguments to interpret them remains a scintillating future challenge. However, it remains possible to consider the idea that Çatalhöyük's relationship to the obsidian sources in Cappadocia, and the people(s) that worked them, involved strong concepts of (non-mechanical) appropriateness and taboo that structured the procurement, transformation and consumption of their raw materials. What price the mirrors, spearheads and beads being made with obsidian from different outcrops? This is not to negate the significance of these raw materials' physical properties, it is simply that the literature suggests that what an archaeologist has traditionally deemed important, may be subsumed in quite different concerns by those who actually made and used these implements (cf. McKenzie 1983).

The underlying tenet of our argument is that all choices are cultural choices, including the sources chosen for quarrying, the technologies employed to transform the obsidian and the manner in which the finished implements were consumed. While this discussion has maybe privileged the agency of 'natural' resources and material culture in people's choices, we should not forget the people themselves, specifically those working at the quarries and how they related to the inhabitants of Çatalhöyük and their contemporaries. Do we assume that for each quarry, workshop or technology we equate a distinct group of people, who relocated to different parts of Anatolia and the Near East during the seasons when the obsidian sources were snow bound? While a 'special relationship' may have existed between particular people, sources and technologies, it is doubtful that these inter-relationships were entirely discrete. For example, we know from the Aceramic Neolithic (PPNB, early-late in Levantine terms) that Kaletepe acted both as a base camp, as well as a workshop, with obsidians from other sources (including Nenezi Dağ) brought to the site to be worked alongside, and in the same manner as, the local obsidian (Binder 2002, 80). At the same time, there is a suggestion that there was little contact between those working at Kaletepe (possibly Levantine knappers) and the 'locals' from nearby Aşıklı Höyük (Binder 2002, 80).

While we are wary of assuming that this was how things were from the Aceramic Neolithic until the Chalcolithic, it remains distinctly possible that different groups continued to work the volcanoes of south Cappadocia. By extension, it seems highly likely that the sources, quarries and workshops formed a web of symbolically-potent places, people and knowledge, offering prowess to those who were able to safely interact within it and return to Çatalhöyük laden with their sacks of clattering rocks, gleaming projectiles and carefully-wrapped caches of blades, plus all the exotic tales that others could only begin to imagine (cf. Helms 1988; 1993).

The consumption of obsidian in Building 1

Finally we turn to an appraisal of the Building 1 data, a sample of 78 artefacts, the material selected from contexts that represented each of the structure's phases and spaces (Tables 12.1 & 12.8 on CD). The chemical

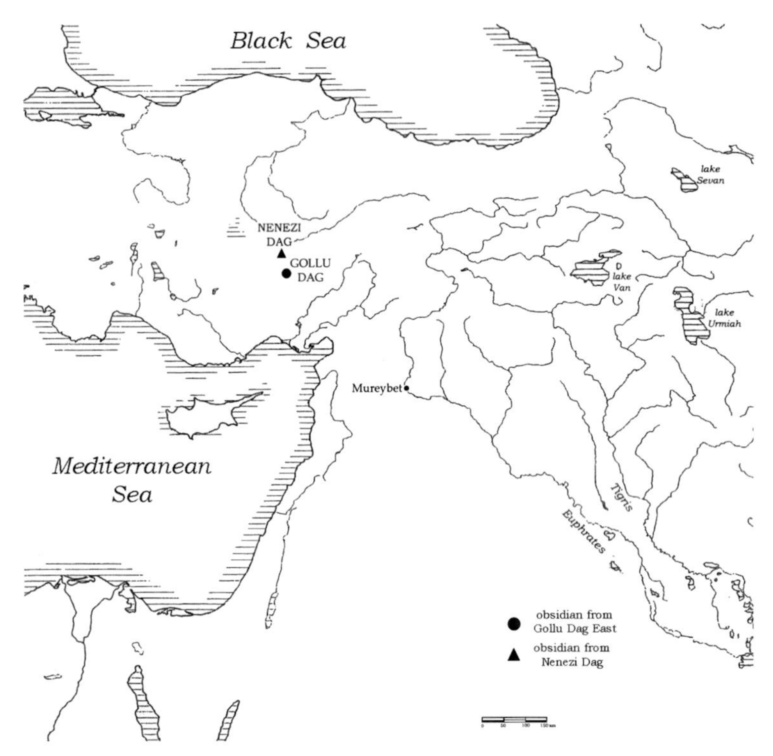

Figure 12.6a. *Distribution of obsidian from the Göllü Dağ-East and Nenezi Dağ sources during the Epi-Palaeolithic - Period 1/Early Central Anatolian I (12,000–10,000 BC).*

signature of 37 pieces correlated with that of the Göllü Dağ-East source (47.4 per cent), and 40 with Nenezi Dağ (51.3 per cent: Tables 12.3 & 12.8 on CD); the source of one sample from the Aberystwyth data set is currently unclear (OB38). While overall the relative proportions of these south Cappadocian raw materials seems quite even, this is not always the case when one considers how these obsidians were consumed inside the building. For example, only four of the 21 artefacts from Space 187 were characterized as Göllü Dağ-East obsidian, while 16 were sourced to Nenezi Dağ and the other sample (OB38 – Aber) being from an unknown provenance. In turn, the six pieces from Spaces 185 and 188 were all made of Nenezi Dağ obsidian; conversely the three from Space 111 were each characterized as coming from Göllü Dağ-East.

A history of the south Cappadocian obsidian sources in relationship to Çatalhöyük

The procurement of obsidians from Göllü Dağ-East and Nenezi Dağ by the inhabitants of Çatalhöyük represents just a short period within these south Cappadocian sources' long history of use. The earliest evidence for these mountains' exploitation comes from Kömürcü East (Göllü Dağ-East), where obsidian artefacts of Middle Palaeolithic date have recently been discovered, including a biface and Levallois flakes (Cauvin & Balkan-Atlı 1996, 257, fig. 6). It is during the Neolithic and Chalcolithic, however, that these sources enjoyed their greatest intensity of quarrying and the maximum dissemination of their obsidian (Fig. 12.6a–g). The following section reviews the procurement of Göllü Dağ-East and Nenezi Dağ obsidians through time, offering a broader context within which to locate the new characterization data from Çatalhöyük. It employs chronological terminology and period divisions including the Maison de l'Orient system (Hours *et al.* 1994; calibrated using the Oxcal programme), as well as the recently-suggested central Anatolian chronology (Özbaşaran & Buitenhuis 2002).

The Epi-Palaeolithic - Period 1/Early Central Anatolian I (12,000–10,000 BC)

It is during the Epi-Palaeolithic that we have the first evidence for the south Cappadocian sources being exploited from afar (Fig. 12.6a). Small quantities of obsidian sourced to Göllü Dağ-East have been recovered from a Natufian assemblage at Mureybet (period IA) in the Syrian Desert (Cauvin & Chataigner 1998, 330–31; Chataigner 1998, 292, figs. 7a–b).

Pre-Pottery Neolithic A - Period 2/Early Central Anatolian I (10,000–8300 BC)

The same source was exploited by an increased number of Levantine communities during Pre-Pottery Neolithic A (PPNA) (Fig. 12.6b). These include Mureybet IB, Aswad I, Jerf el-Ahmat, and Cheikh Hasan in the Middle Euphrates and as far south as Netiv Hagdud and Jericho (Abbès *et al.* 2001; Cauvin & Chataigner 1998, 332–3; Chataigner 1998, 292, figs. 7a–b). Recent studies of the Cheikh Hasan and Mureybet obsidian suggests that while there is a distinction between the two assemblages in terms of the technical quality of their respective blades (the latter being the more sophisticated), the distribution of the material at each site seems rather similar (Binder 2002, 79). It is suggested that south Cappadocian obsidian could have circulated in the Levant at this time through 'a local distribution organized by the mediation of itinerant hawkers, moving from village to village and knapping for consumers' demand' (Binder 2002, 79).

Pre-Pottery Neolithic B, early and middle - Period 3/Early Central Anatolian II (8700–7500 BC)

The above pattern develops further in the tenth–eighth millennia BC (Fig. 12.6c) with a greater number of sites in Jordan, the Syrian desert and southern Levant generating obsidian characterized as coming from Göllü Dağ-East (Cauvin & Chataigner 1998, 334–7; Chataigner 1998, 292, figs. 7a–b). It is at this time that we finally have direct evidence for human activity in southern Cappadocia. An obsidian workshop was established at Kaletepe (sector P-3.2) atop the Kömürcü outcrop on Göllü Dağ-East during the second half of the ninth millennium BC (Balkan-Atlı *et al.* 1999; Binder 2002). A little later we have the nearby settlement of Aşıklı Höyük *c.* 30 km to the west (Esin & Harmankaya 1999). These two sites provide us with our first clear indication as to some of the modes by which Göllü Dağ-East obsidian was exploited and put into circulation. The image we have is one of a complex and occasionally overlapping series of relationships between various groups of people and the obsidian outcrops. Recent excavations at Kaletepe (sector P) have produced evidence for a blade workshop, a seasonal camp occupied during those few summer months when the source was snow free and accessible. New radiocarbon dates from Kaletepe sector P-3.2 place the workshop between 8300 and 8200 cal BC, the earliest dates for any central Anatolian site (Binder 2002, 81, fig. 1). This correlates with a small set of dates for the Early and Middle PPNB of the Middle Euphrates and the second stage of the PPN of the Upper Euphrates (Binder 2002, 81, fig. 1).

At the workshop a group of highly-skilled knappers performed two blade traditions, a bipolar, or naviform technology, plus a unipolar prismatic blade industry (Balkan-Atlı & Der Aprahamian 1998). Of great interest is the fact that the workshop was also used as a base for expeditions to collect obsidian from other sources, including nearby Kayırlı-Eriklidere (Göllü Dağ) and Nenezi Dağ, some 15 km to the north-west. The obsidian was brought back to the Kaletepe workshop as preformed naviform cores before being knapped in the same ways as the Kömürcü material (Binder 2002, 80). The naviform tradition involved the manufacture of highly standardized blades that were used to make points. These were then displaced over very long distances (up to 900 km), some of which involved maritime routes. Large blades / points of the

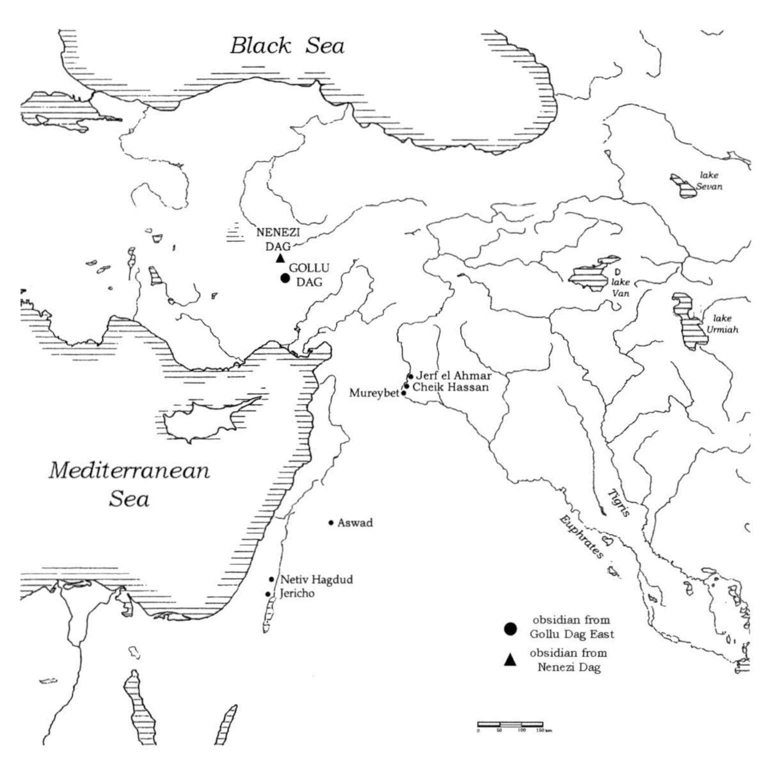

Figure 12.6b. *Distribution of obsidian from the Göllü Dağ-East and Nenezi Dağ sources during the Pre-Pottery Neolithic A - Period 2/Early Central Anatolian I (10,000–8300 BC).*

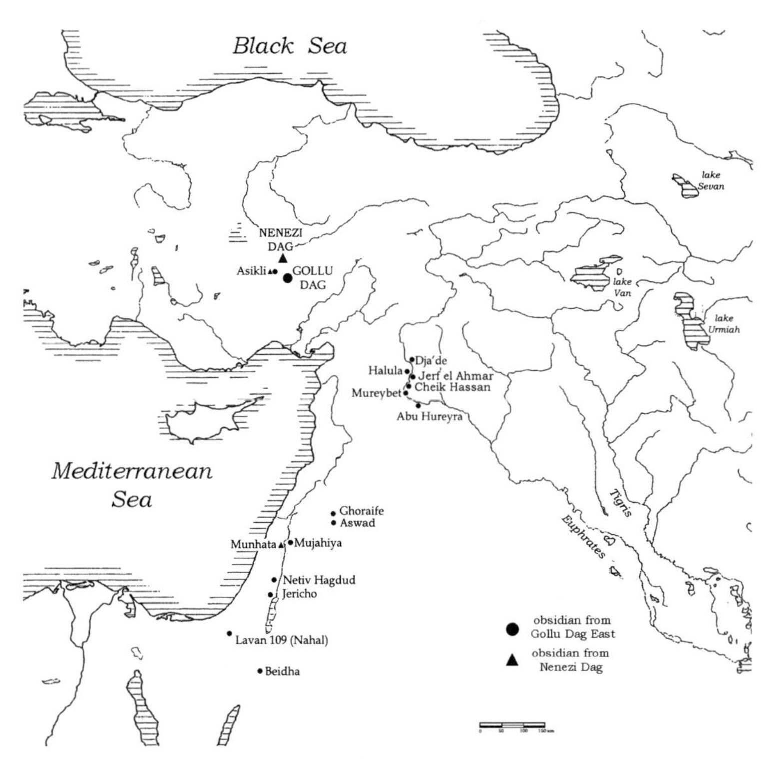

Figure 12.6c. *Distribution of obsidian from the Göllü Dağ-East and Nenezi Dağ sources during the Pre-Pottery Neolithic B, early and middle - Period 3/Early Central Anatolian II (8700–7500 BC).*

same technology and characterized as relating to the Kömürcü / Göllü Dağ-East source have been recovered from Beidha and Nahal Lavan in the southern Levant, Mureybet 4 in the Syrian desert and Shillourokambos on Cyprus (Balkan-Atlı & Der Aprahamian 1998, 248; Briois *et al.* 1997; Binder 2002, 80; Cauvin & Chataigner 1998, 334–7).

At nearby Aşıklı Höyük excavations have revealed a large Aceramic Neolithic community (corresponding to a late-middle PPNB horizon in Levantine terminology, or Early Central Anatolian II), part contemporary with the Kaletepe workshop (sector East: Binder 2002, 83). Perhaps a little surprisingly, the evidence suggests that the workshop was not supplying Aşıklı Höyük with its products. Instead the community seems to have been responsible for procuring its own raw material (as blocks and tablets) and manufacturing most of their tools on site, including opposed platform blades from naviform cores, of a similar tradition to that witnessed at Kaletepe (Abbès *et al.* 1999; Balkan-Atlı 1994b). Furthermore, the inhabitants of Aşıklı Höyük did not exploit the Kömürcü outcrops at Kaletepe, but instead collected their raw materials from the nearby Kayırlı-Eriklidere source (Göllü Dağ-East) and Nenezi Dağ (Binder 2002, 83).

Binder (2002, 83) has argued recently that the data suggest at least two different and coexisting groups were working amongst the south Cappadocian sources. With Kaletepe apparently established prior to any perennial settlement in the region and the fact that its products have been recovered from a number of Levantine sites, Binder (2002, 81–3) claims that the workshop was established and organized by people from the Levant, the result of specialized seasonal expeditions. The second group of people is represented by Aşıklı Höyük and a number of other smaller communities, including Acıyer and Sirçan Tepe, part of the recently-defined 'Aşıklı culture' (Balkan-Atlı 1998; Esin *et al.* 1991). These sites provide us with the earliest evidence for local, central Anatolian exploitation of south Cappadocian obsidian, having been settled a little while after the establishment of the Kaletepe workshop. With the chipped stone assemblages from these settlements including a distinctive microlithic component, it is clear that that the origins of the 'Aşıklı culture' relate partly to the Epi-Palaeolithic traditions of central Anatolia's Mediterranean coast (the Beldibi, Belbaşı and Öküzini cave sites), and the Konya plain (Pinarbaşı A), albeit with an assimilation of blade technologies that originated in the PPN Levant. Future characterization of obsidian from Pinarbaşı A, a site that we know to be partly contemporary with the Kaletepe workshop (Binder 2002, 83), should be most informative with regard to investigating these variant histories of interaction amongst the obsidian sources of southern Cappadocia.

This period also provides our first evidence for the exploitation of the Nenezi Dağ obsidian, albeit on a smaller scale than the Göllü Dağ-East source(s). Nor did its products travel as far. It was noted above that this source was used by the knappers based at the Kaletepe workshop / camp and those resident at Aşıklı Höyük (Binder 2002; G. Poupeau pers. comm.). One could thus argue that this source represents one of the arenas where these two (or more) groups of people may have interacted. We know that the knappers from Kaletepe roughed out naviform cores at Nenezi Dağ, but we unfortunately currently have little information as to how this obsidian was being worked at Aşıklı Höyük. Farther afield, obsidian characterized as having originated from the Nenezi Dağ source is reported from Munhata in the southern Levant and Cheikh Hasan in Syria (Chataigner 1998, 285, fig. 5a–b; Abbès *et al.* 2001). Once again, these characterization studies have included little comment about the form of the artefacts made from this obsidian. At Cheikh Hasan we know that some of the Göllü Dağ-East obsidian at the site was present in the form of prismatic blades and projectiles made on large naviform blades (Abbès *et al.* 2001, 5).

Pre-Pottery Neolithic B, late - Period 4/Early Central Anatolian II (7500–7000 BC)

In the following period the evidence indicates the continued local and long-distance consumption of obsidians from Göllü Dağ-East and Nenezi Dağ (Fig. 12.6d). In central Anatolia we are informed that Aşıklı Höyük continued to exploit both sources, as did its slightly later neighbour Musular, plus Canhasan III in the Konya Plain (G. Poupeau pers. comm.; Ataman 1988, 50–52). Once again, we have little indication as to which lithic traditions employed these raw materials. We now know that the earliest occupation at Çatalhöyük (Level Pre-XII.C–D) corresponds to this period (Cessford 2001; Binder 2002, fig. 1; Thissen 2002b). Our characterization programme has yet to select obsidian artefacts from these levels for analysis to see whether the community was also exploiting these 'two' sources, as it was later on (see below).

The Göllü Dağ-East sources remain the most significant with regard to long-distance procurement and use. Its products are represented at a number of sites in Cyprus, the Levantine coast, Jordan and Middle Euphrates, while the Nenezi Dağ material is recorded from Beisamoun in the southern Levant (Chataigner 1998, 285–92, fig. 7a–b; Cauvin & Chataigner 1998, 336–8). Aşıklı Höyük also had one artefact characterized whose signature correlated with that of the Acıgöl

East ante-caldera source, while another was sourced to Göllü Dağ-West (Chataigner 1998, 283, 292, fig. 4a). Evidence for the use of these obsidians remains exceedingly rare at this time.

Early Neolithic - Period 5/Early Central Anatolian IIIA (7000–6300 BC)

By the Early Neolithic we have evidence for a further increase in the number of sites, in Anatolia and beyond, procuring obsidian from Göllü Dağ-East and Nenezi Dağ (Fig. 12.6e). Obsidian characterized as coming from Göllü Dağ-East is recorded here at Çatalhöyük in the Konya plain, Ilicapinar a little further to the north, Mersin on the Cilician coast, plus a number of Cypriot sites (Khirokitia, Kalavassos, Kalepini-Troulli), and a series of settlements along the Levantine littoral, southern Levant and Middle Euphrates (Chataigner 1998, 285–92, fig. 7a–b). The distribution of Nenezi Dağ obsidian continues to be less well-attested, recorded from only a small proportion of the aforementioned sites. These include Çatalhöyük, Byblos on the Levantine coast, Mevrokah in the southern Levant and Halula in the Middle Euphrates; it is also the one obsidian source currently represented at Tarsus in Cilicia (Chataigner 1998, 285–92, fig. 7a–b). The literature does not permit us to say much about how these two sources were used by these communities. At the sources we only have a workshop radiocarbon dated to this period at Kaletepe (Kömürcü); we presently have no detailed report on the associated industries (Balkan-Atlı *et al.* 1999; Thissen 2002b, 307 & 324). The new Çatalhöyük data can indirectly make a significant contribution to this issue.

Çatalhöyük also offers a more fine-tuned diachronic perspective with regard to how the Göllü Dağ-East and Nenezi Dağ obsidians were being exploited by a single community. Stratigraphically, the period from Level Pre-XII.B–A to Level II at the site falls within the period under discussion (Period 5, Early Central Anatolian III), a sequence that can be further subdivided into Early Central Anatolian (ECA) IIIA (Level Pre-XII.B–A to Level VIB) and ECAIIIB (Levels VIA–II) following Özbaşaran & Buitenhuis (2002). The earliest artefacts characterized in this programme of analyses came from Level IX.

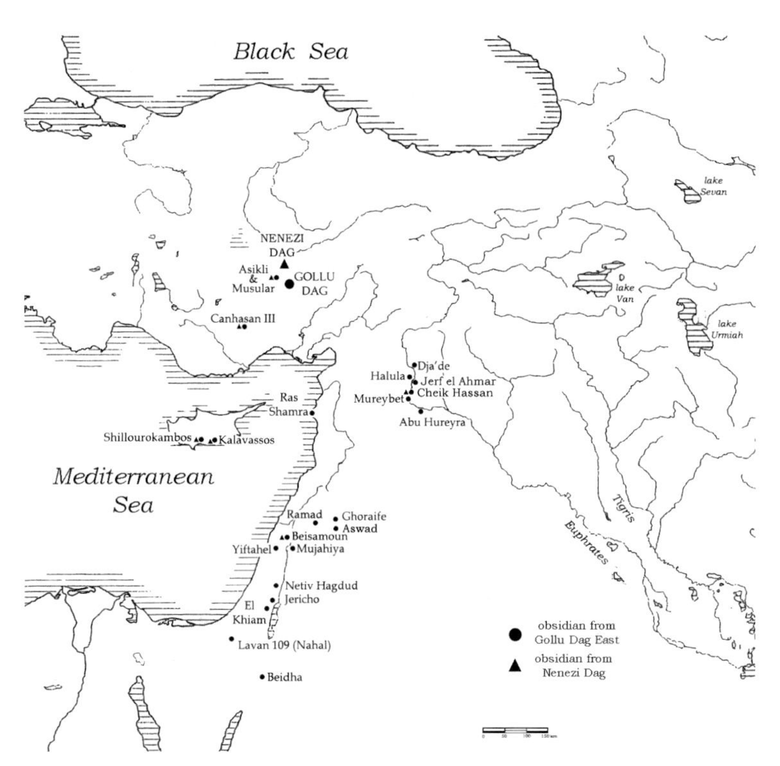

Figure 12.6d. *Distribution of obsidian from the Göllü Dağ-East and Nenezi Dağ sources during the Pre-Pottery Neolithic B, late - Period 4/Early Central Anatolian II (7500–7000 BC).*

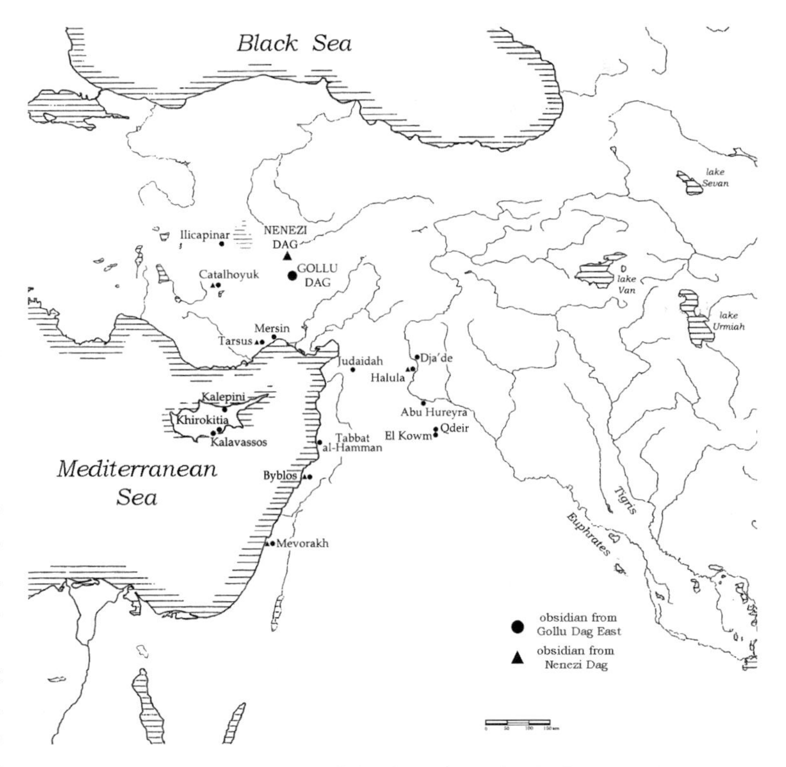

Figure 12.6e. *Distribution of obsidian from the Göllü Dağ-East and Nenezi Dağ sources during the Early Neolithic - Period 5/Early Central Anatolian IIIA (7000–6300 BC).*

From Level IX to VII–VI contexts we have a total of 47 artefacts analyzed (Tables 12.1 & 12.7 on CD), 42 of which were assigned a Göllü Dağ-East source, while only five pieces were characterized as Nenezi Dağ obsidian. Of those artefacts that could be assigned with confidence to one of the Çatalhöyük industries, many related to obsidian industry 1, our 'in-house' irregular blade and blade-like flake tradition, while a few others related to obsidian industries 4 and 7. It is these latter two traditions that are perhaps most significant here because in neither instance do we have evidence for the on-site manufacture of this material, whereby we might consider these blanks' origin to be the quarry workshops. Obsidian industry 4, regular prismatic blades from opposed platform cores, is represented by only two samples from Level VIII, a centre blade (OB26 - Aber), plus a secondary series blade (OB2 - Aber). We would suggest that these two pieces represent some of the implements being produced at the Göllü Dağ-East workshops at this time. At Kaletepe we know of opposed platform blade manufacture in Period 3 (ECII/PPNB, early and middle), but we are unaware as to the industry's duration at this locale. We also note that a range of opposed platform cores have been recovered from the surface at Kayırlı-East (Bitlikeler, in Cauvin & Balkan-Atlı 1996, 257–8, figs. 8–9), not only the 'Kaletepe type' that should presumably be of an Aceramic Neolithic date. It is tempting to suggest that some of the other nuclei may be of Period 5, and relate to the manufacture of the Çatalhöyük opposed platform blades.

Further evidence for a link between Çatalhöyük and the Bitlikeler workshop at Kayırlı-East is provided by some of the obsidian industry 7 artefacts assigned a Göllü Dağ-East source. 'Quarry flakes' modified into large side-scrapers, have been collected from the surface at Bitlikeler/Kayırlı-East (Cauvin & Balkan-Atlı 1996, 262, fig. 12). At Çatalhöyük 'quarry flakes' also occur in the form of biface preforms. Excavation at Kömürcü-East, at a short distance from the Kaletepe workshop, has revealed an area apparently dedicated to the manufacture of these distinctive blanks (Cauvin & Balkan-Atlı 1996, 257, fig. 7:1; Balkan-Atlı & Binder pers. comm.). Cauvin & Balkan-Atlı (1996, 257) have argued previously that this represents the workshop supplying Çatalhöyük; our new data clearly strengthen the case for a connection between the two sites.

Of the five artefacts from Level IX to VII–VI characterized as being made of Nenezi Dağ obsidian, only one was technologically diagnostic (OB27-Aber), a rejuvenation flake struck from the face of a unipolar prismatic blade industry. This is all the information that we can currently provide as to the knapping traditions being performed at Nenezi Dağ during this period (ECAIIIA). The data from Level VIB–II (ECAIIIB) analyses suggest a significant change in Çatalhöyük's relationship with the south Cappadocian sources and the people working there. Most notably we witness an increase in the consumption of Nenezi Dağ obsidian, from 10.6 per cent (n = 5) in the IX to VII–VI sample, to 52.3 per cent (n = 46) in the VI–V to Early Chalcolithic sample. Of the artefacts sourced to Göllü Dağ-East, most relate to the 'in-house' obsidian industry 1, but there are also a small number of regular prismatic blades from both opposed platform and unipolar technologies (obsidian industries 4 and 5), plus fragments of the obsidian industry 7 'quarry flakes'. The evidence indicates that bi- and unipolar prismatic blades continued to be manufactured at Kayırlı-East and/or Kömürcü, as were the large scrapers, thick flakes and biface preforms of obsidian industry 7. We see a further continuity in terms of how the 'quarry flakes' were consumed at Çatalhöyük, as they remained regular components of obsidian hoards, subsequently serving as the raw material for the manufacture of small irregular blades and large projectiles.

It is the relationship between Çatalhöyük and the Nenezi Dağ source that bears witness to the greatest change within this period (between ECAIIIA and ECAIIIB), with the marked increase in its consumption. The characterization data suggest that Çatalhöyük was procuring obsidian from Göllü Dağ-East and Nenezi Dağ in roughly equal proportions (46.6 per cent and 52.3 per cent respectively in the Level VIB to Early Chalcolithic sample). There are, however, distinctions in how their raw materials were used, with the latter source seemingly exploited in a far more restricted manner. While Göllü Dağ-East obsidian was employed in a number of traditions (obsidian industries 1, 4, 5 and 7), the great majority of the artefacts assigned a Nenezi Dağ source derived from a non-local prismatic blade traditions (primarily obsidian industry 5), together with only a very few pieces related to the 'in-house' obsidian industry 1, plus a single possible 'quarry flake' fragment (obsidian industry 7). It is worth adding a cautionary note to this impression we currently have of Göllü Dağ-East's varied forms of exploitation during this ECAIIIB period. Perhaps when we are able to discriminate chemically this source's three outcrops (Kayırlı-East, Kömürcü and Bozköy-East) we will discover that the above impression is incorrect, and that specific outcrops/workshops were responsible for specific industries.

While we know that the Nenezi Dağ workshop was not responsible for manufacturing all the regular prismatic blades in circulation at Çatalhöyük at this time, it certainly seems to have been the major producer. In turn, it appears that the fine naviform blades from Building 1, not least the cache from Space 71 unit (1461), were manufactured using Nenezi Dağ obsidian. Surface investigations at the source have recovered unipolar and opposed platform blade cores (Cauvin & Balkan-Atlı 1996, 266–7, fig. 14); our analyses provide us with a range of dates to which these industries might belong.

Late Neolithic to Early Chalcolithic - Period 6 (6300–5600 BC*)*

During the Late Neolithic and Early Chalcolithic the south Cappadocian sources of Göllü Dağ-East and Nenezi Dağ continued to be exploited, though the distribution of their obsidians is more restricted than in previous periods (Fig. 12.6f). Obsidian sourced to Göllü Dağ-East is recorded from Mersin in Cilicia, Tabbar-el-Hammam and Byblos on the Levantine coast, plus El Kowm in the Syrian Desert (Cauvin & Chataigner 1998, 345; Chataigner 1998, fig. 7a). In an apparently new development, we now witness the dissemination of obsidian from this source to sites in northwest Anatolia, including Pendik and Ilıpınar (Bigazzi *et al.* 1998, 82–6). Obsidian from the Nenezi Dağ source continued to be consumed by a few communities in Cilicia (Mersin, Tarsus) and the Levant (Byblos), as well as Hacılar in the Lake District of west central Anatolia (Chataigner 1998, fig. 7a). Hacılar also produced evidence for a small amount of obsidian from the Aegean source of Melos entering Anatolia at this time (Renfrew *et al.* 1965, 235–9). Recent radiocarbon dates taken from a core sample from near the base of the Çatalhöyük West suggest that the early deposits of the Early Chalcolithic site (Early Chalcolithic I) fall towards the end of the Maison de l'Orient Period 6 (C. Cessford pers. comm.). Four of the obsidian artefacts sourced derived from Early Chalcolithic I contexts at Çatalhöyük West (C. Gibson pers. comm.), with three assigned to the Nenezi Dağ source, specifically two prismatic blades (from unipolar cores) and a non-cortical flake (CNRS 1 OB 79, OB82 & OB83), plus another prismatic blade characterized as having been made from obsidian of Göllü Dağ-East (CNRS 1 OB81). In the late 1960s Wright (1969) analyzed three artefacts from Çatalhöyük West, each of which was allegedly made of obsidian from the Acıgöl sources in north Cappadocia. Chataigner (1998, 285) has since argued that the technique employed meant that in fact the obsidian could equally have come from Nenezi Dağ.

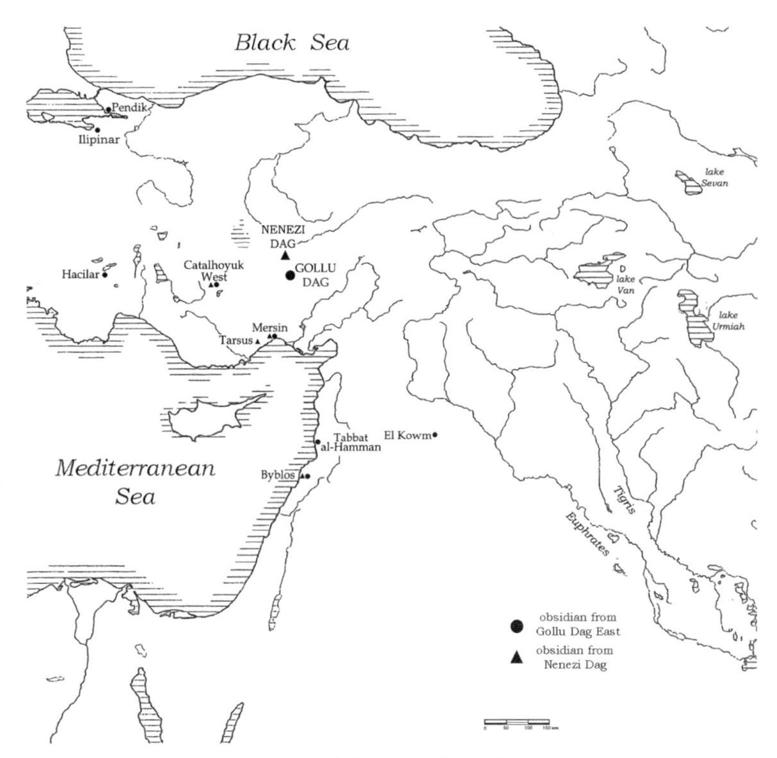

Figure 12.6f. *Distribution of obsidian from the Göllü Dağ-East and Nenezi Dağ sources during the Late Neolithic to Early Chalcolithic - Period 6 (6300–5600* BC*).*

Chataigner's case seems strengthened on the basis of our new analyses, given that all of our samples were sourced to south Cappadocia, with two of the blades made from Nenezi Dağ obsidian. This is also our first evidence for Çatalhöyük's exploitation of Göllü Dağ-East during the Early Chalcolithic period.

Early Chalcolithic - Period 7 (5800–5500 BC*)*

Only a very few artefacts from Early Chalcolithic II contexts have currently been analyzed. Thus it is difficult to ascertain a clear impression of how the south Cappadocian sources were exploited at this time (Fig. 12.6g) though huge deposits of knapped debris dating to the Chalcolithic have been partly investigated at the Kömürcü outcrop at Göllü Dağ-East (D. Binder pers. comm.). Obsidian assigned chemically to this source is again recorded from the north and south Levantine coast (Ras Shamra, Givat Ha Parsa), plus the site of Halula in the Syrian desert (Chataigner 1998, fig. 7a). It also continues to have been consumed in northwest Anatolia, at Ilıpınar (Chataigner 1998, fig. 7a; Bigazzi *et al.* 1998).

Radiocarbon dates and ceramic analysis suggest that much of the occupation at Çatalhöyük West should be considered Early Chalcolithic II, which falls into Period 7 (C. Cessford pers. comm.). Of the seven pieces of obsidian selected for analysis from

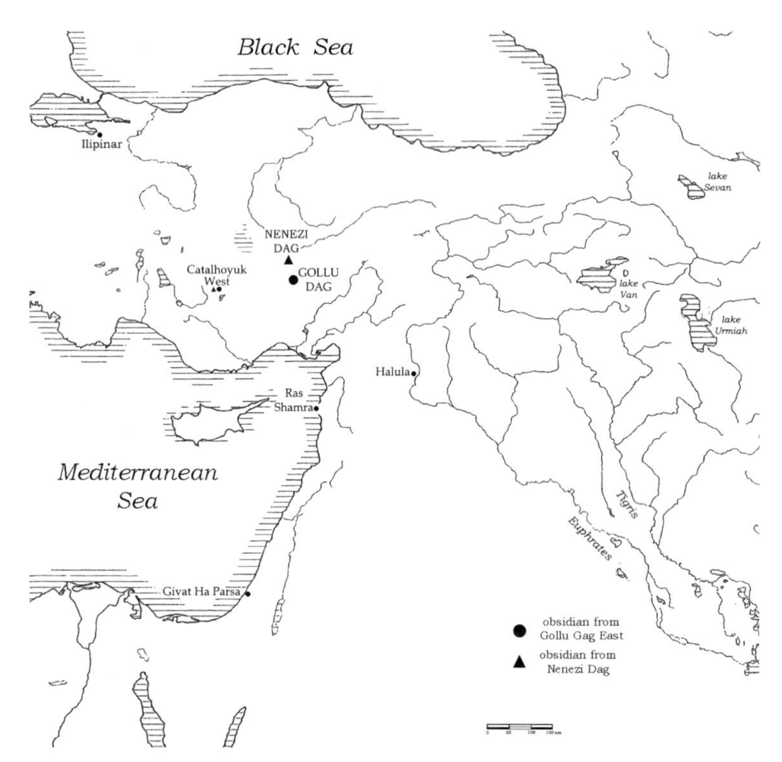

Figure 12.6g. *Distribution of obsidian from the Göllü Dağ-East and Nenezi Dağ sources during the Early Chalcolithic - Period 7 (5800–5500* BC*).*

the Çatalhöyük West (Fig. 12.5g on CD), three could be assigned an Early Chalcolithic II date, of which one sample comprised a pressure-flaked blade from a unipolar core characterized as having been made of Nenezi Dağ obsidian (CNRS 1 OB77), together with two non-cortical flakes assigned a Göllü Dağ-East source (CNRS 1 OB78 and OB80).

Conclusions

by Tristan Carter, Nicholas J.G. Pearce & Gérard Poupeau

While one of this obsidian sourcing project's undoubted strengths is its sample size, there remains room for improvement with regard to the sampling strategy itself. Some of these issues can be rectified relatively easily, for instance filling the chronological lacunae in our current data, not least the absence of samples from Level Pre-XII.D to Level X. In turn, one might wish to have a more even distribution of material amongst the various buildings and/or spaces on a level-by-level basis. Alternatively we could have selected obsidian from the 355 units chosen as study priorities for the current series of publications (Volume 4, Chapter 1). It is argued, however, that all of these are minor considerations in the context of what we claim should be the structuring principle of a meaningful sampling strategy. Namely that it is only after one has undertaken a full 'traditional' technological and typological analysis and gained an in-depth understanding of an assemblage, that one is justified in selecting samples for sourcing.

There has been a tradition in obsidian provenance studies of selecting relatively insignificant knapping debris for export to laboratories, based largely on limits on the export of museum-quality finds. We essentially followed this tradition in choosing the obsidian to be sent to CNRS and Aberystwyth, setting aside a group of samples dominated by relatively inconspicuous, small and broken flakes. These flakes were selected carefully on the basis of their date, context and physical characteristics (colour, banding, translucency, inclusions, texture). However, it remains the case that aside from some attention to the presence of cortex (in part a further attempt to discriminate raw material), many of these pieces are technologically undiagnostic and one would be hard pressed to assign each blank to a specific industry. With hindsight, we appreciate that such an approach is flawed and that a better approach would be to target samples that can be related directly to the various industries outlined in the preceding chapter (Chapter 11). The amount of time and money spent undertaking a sourcing project is not insignificant, from the selection of the obsidian, its recording and illustration, via the paperwork associated with exporting the material, the time expended in sample preparation (dissolution etc.), the running costs of the instrumentation, to the analysis and presentation of the data. As such the archaeologist shoulders a great responsibility in making sure that the intellectual return on this investment is maximized.

It was stressed at the beginning of this chapter that this report represents the end of the first stage of analyses; much work remains. Indeed, we have commenced already the next stage of Çatalhöyük's obsidian characterization studies, with artefacts from a range of new contexts and involving new laboratories and analytical techniques. Fifty artefacts from Levels X–VIII (Çatalhöyük East) are currently being analyzed by Inductively Coupled Plasma-Optical Emission Spectroscopy (ICP-OES) at the Chemistry Department, Middle Eastern Technical University (METU) in Ankara, while 42 are being characterized from Building 3 (located in the BACH Area and of comparable date to Building 1) at the Berkeley Archaeological XRF lab, using an Energy Dispersive X-Ray Fluorescence Spectrometer

(ED-XRF). A further 50 samples from the recent excavations of Early Chalcolithic Çatalhöyük West have also been selected for trace-elemental analysis at Stanford University employing Inductively Coupled Plasma-Atomic Emission Spectroscopy (ICP-AES).

The ramifications for an interlaboratory approach and the use of more than one analytical technique, are issues that will be explored more fully in specialist archaeometric publications elsewhere. However, Pearce comments that the application of LA-ICP-MS to these samples provides a novel and essentially non-destructive method for our analyses. Whilst LA-ICP-MS cannot produce quantitative trace element concentrations in the absence of an internal standard, accurate trace element data can be produced to give accurate element/element ratios for sourcing and discrimination. Trace element rations determined by LA-ICP-MS at Aberystwyth are indistinguishable from the solution ICP-MS analyses generated at CNRS. LA-ICP-MS is a rapid technique (the analysis of each flake takes about five minutes) and requires no sample preparation (grinding, acid digestion, dilution etc.) and thus has great value in archaeological studies where material is precious. Indeed, Laser ablation ICP-MS analyses may become increasingly valuable in this context, as these are essentially a non-destructive means of determining chemical characteristics of the piece, leaving behind only a series of minute craters on each sample as the legacy of the determination. These analyses can easily be concealed on the reverse, edges, corners or cracks within a sample, thus retaining its aesthetic and archaeological value. Thus, with permission to export samples, we might be able to characterize some of the larger and more aesthetic pieces, in particular the big 'quarry flakes' and biface preforms from hoard contexts (obsidian industry 7), plus the projectiles and naviform blades (obsidian industries 4 and 5), large scrapers (obsidian industry 6), microliths (obsidian industry 2) and those modified implements that served as cores for the manufacture of the 'burin blades' (obsidian industry 3). Until such inclusive analyses have been undertaken, the reader should be aware of the biases in the data presented in this chapter.

Acknowledgements

Tristan Carter thanks his co-authors in this project, in particular Gérard Poupeau for sharing standards and data with the other laboratories. For valuable feedback and practical assistance I am also grateful to Nur Balkan-Atlı, Didier Binder, Marie-Claire Cauvin, Tom Cawdron, Craig Cessford, Sarah Delerue, Shahina Farid, Catriona Gibson, Ian Hodder, Vassilis Kilikoglou, Wendy Matthews plus the archaeological representatives of the Turkish Ministry of Culture at Çatalhöyük and the Archaeological Museum at Konya. John G.H. Swogger, Gérard Der Aprahamian and Marina Milić drew the illustrations, while Marina Milić prepared the maps.

Chapter 13

Cooking, Crafts and Curation: Ground-stone Artefacts from Çatalhöyük

Adnan Baysal & Katherine I. Wright

This chapter is an interim report on ground stone and related artefacts from the 1995–99 excavations at Çatalhöyük. The artefacts come from the 355 priority contexts. To these we have added a few more contexts, the better to convey the range of variation. These additional contexts are marked in tables (see CD) with an asterisk. Not included here are relevant artefacts from flotation residues (e.g. micro-artefacts and debitage from ground-stone manufacture). Also not included are hundreds of additional artefacts, from non-priority contexts in the Cambridge excavations and from the excavations of Mellaart, the BACH team, the Poznań team and Çatalhöyük West. These will be presented in a future report.

Aims

The Çatalhöyük ground-stone analysis has several long-term, closely-related aims:

To explore the role of ground-stone artefacts in food preparation and craft production

Ground-stone assemblages consist of any artefacts in which abrasion played a central role in manufacture. As such, they encompass a wide range of types, such as grinding tools, vessels, maceheads, incised pebbles, figurines and beads. Such items proliferated in the Neolithic across western Asia. One of our goals is to explore the use of ground-stone artefacts in food preparation (e.g. milling), by investigating contextual relationships between the ground stone and other finds bearing on food (e.g. botanical and faunal remains, organic residues, ovens, hearths). A parallel aim is to investigate the use of ground-stone technology in craft activities: ochre grinding, plaster polishing, and the making of pottery, figurines, beads and other items (cf. Wright 2000; in prep. a; Wright & Garrard 2003).

To investigate what these artefacts can tell us about social relationships within and between households

A second aim is to explore the social organization of food processing and craft production involving ground-stone tools, by means of spatial and contextual analysis. Did individual houses have similar 'toolkits' or did some houses possess more of these tools than others? Where could milling or other activities involving ground stone have taken place? Were individual households self-sufficient in food preparation and craft production, or do we see evidence for the use of the tools in communal spaces (Baysal 2001)? A key issue concerns gender. Many archaeologists see milling in particular as an activity associated with adult women (e.g. Molleson 2000; Peterson 1997; 2002). What can the ground-stone analysis contribute to this debate?

To establish a detailed typology and sequence of ground-stone artefacts for Çatalhöyük

Final reports on ground-stone artefacts from Neolithic sites in western Asia are not as common as they should be. Early studies were of assemblages in Zagros sites (e.g. Hole *et al.* 1969). There are detailed reports on ground stone from Khirokitia in Cyprus (Cluzan 1984; Mouton 1984); from Jericho in Palestine (Dorrell 1983); from Netiv Hagdud and Munhata in Israel (Gopher 1997; Gopher & Orrelle 1995); and from sites in Jordan (Wright passim). There are detailed accounts for some sites in eastern Turkey and northern Mesopotamia, e.g. Çayönü (Davis 1982), Mureybet and Cheikh Hassan (Nierlé 1983), and Bouqras (Roodenberg 1986). For central Anatolia, the only extensive study so far is an unpublished PhD dissertation, by Hersh (1981), on ground stone from Suberde and Erbaba. Extensive assemblages have been recovered from other sites, but there is so far no published chronotypological sequence of ground-stone artefacts from any well-stratified Neolithic village in central Anatolia. One of our aims is to establish such a sequence for Çatalhöyük.

To establish the lithic technology of ground-stone tool production

Like chipped stone, ground-stone artefacts are the product of lithic-reduction sequences and *chaînes opératoires*. Some researchers have addressed this issue (e.g. Gopher & Orrelle 1995) but the study of ground-stone technology is still in its infancy. Static typologies of formal, 'finished' tools are not sufficient for ground stone. Debitage from ground-stone manufacture can and should be collected; ground-stone toolmaking often entailed flaking, whilst stone particles detached by grinding may be identifiable by micromorphology (Volume 4, Chapter 19). On-site manufacture has been identified in Neolithic sites, in the form of unfinished artefacts, cores, primary flakes, debitage and micro-debris found in flotation residues (e.g. Wright 1992a; 1992b; 1993; in prep. a–d; Wright, in Garrard *et al.* 1994; Wright & Garrard 2003). One of our goals is to reconstruct the lithic technology of the Çatalhöyük ground stone by adopting these fine-scale methods of recovery and analysis.

To determine the sources of raw materials used for making these artefacts

Source analysis of ground stone via petrography and other methods can inform on patterns of landscape use and exchange (Baysal 1998; 2004; Türkmenoğlu *et al.* 2001a,b; Philip & Williams-Thorpe 1993; Weinstein-Evron *et al.* 2001). For the people of Çatalhöyük, stone suitable for ground-stone tools would have been rather valuable, because the Konya plain is essentially alluvial and lacks substantial rock outcrops. Apart from soft marls and chalks, the only stones available in the immediate vicinity of Çatalhöyük are small, water-rolled pebbles in the Çarşamba Çay. These would have been useful for small items, but anything larger would have required quarrying in foothills and mountain ranges several dozen kilometres away, e.g. Karadağ, Bozdağ, and the Taurus mountains. Ground-stone quarry and manufacturing sites have been identified in the eastern Mediterranean (e.g. Roubet 1989; Rosen & Schneider 2001), and we hope to look for such sites in hilly areas surrounding the plain. We have already begun a programme of petrographic analysis (see below). We are especially interested in exploring variations in raw materials from house to house, and comparing raw material acquisition and exchange patterns to those of other artefacts (obsidian, etc.).

To document the life histories of ground-stone artefacts, from quarry to final abandonment

Analysis of the life histories of ground-stone artefacts — from quarry to manufacture, use, recycling and final abandonment — is essential for understanding how ground-stone assemblages form (Baysel in prep.; Wright 1992a). For Çatalhöyük, this is especially important since: 1) there is so much evidence for abandonment behaviour, refuse disposal, and caching; and 2) the artefacts appear to have been heavily curated and recycled. Ethnoarchaeological studies show that in a number of village societies, some milling tools had very long use-lives and were passed from generation to generation (Baysal 2001; Ertuğ-Yaraş 1997; 1998; Hayden 1987; Hayden & Cannon 1984; Kramer 1982). We are keen to identify stylistic and functional patterns as individual houses evolved and were rebuilt.

To conduct experimental and ethnoarchaeological studies in order to understand the lithic technology and the uses (practical and social) of ground-stone artefacts

Relatively little ethnoarchaeological and experimental work has been done on manufacture and use of ground-stone tools. One of the best ethnographic studies is Hayden's (1987) description of a specialist in Guatemala who uses chipped-stone tools to make grinding slabs. We have already begun experiments in replicating ground-stone artefacts and this work is continuing. There is a small literature on experiments in the productivity of food processing with ground-stone tools (Wright 1994 and references there).

Residue studies, widely applied to ceramics, have considerable potential for ground-stone artefacts. Analysis of inorganic residues is particularly promising. Materials such as ochre, plaster and carbon have been found adhering to the surfaces of ground-stone artefacts at Çatalhöyük and these have been sampled for purposes of identifying chemical composition. Several attempts at identifying organic residues on ground stone have been made. The results have been rather limited so far, but some successes have been reported (Procopiou & Treuil 2002).

Microwear analysis has been attempted on ground-stone tools (Adams 1988; Dubreuil 2002). As with microwear studies of chipped stone, there are uncertainties about how the wear patterns and polishes form, and what they really mean. The most detailed work is by Dubreuil (2002) and centres on fine-grained basalt grinding tools. We do not yet know to what degree such methods may be possible for the relatively coarse-grained andesite and andesitic basalt commonly used at Çatalhöyük, but some of the Çatalhöyük artefacts are quite fine-grained. Consequently, we plan to explore the potential of microwear along the lines suggested by Dubreuil, but adapted to the local materials. By combining microwear and residue studies together, it may be possible to ascertain something of the specific functions of ground-stone artefacts, subject to the caveat that these tools were probably multi-purpose.

Methods of field collection and conservation

To address these issues, we adopted certain procedures of artefact recovery, storage and analysis (see also Baysal 1998; 1999; 2000; Baysal & Wright 2002). In the field, all ground-stone artefacts were excavated and collected in consultation with a ground-stone specialist present on site. All artefacts potentially related to ground stone were collected, and many were recorded three-dimensionally. This applied to both worked and unworked stones.

We adopted a policy that no ground-stone artefacts should be washed until we have consulted other specialists, e.g. conservators, micromorphologists, and organic chemists. Some artefacts have visible residues on them (e.g. ochre, plaster), and invisible residues may also be present (e.g. organic compounds). We advised excavators to try not to touch the use surfaces but to handle artefacts from the edges where possible; in some cases, cotton gloves were used. Soil samples were taken from a 30 cm radius around *in situ* ground-stone artefacts, as a control, in order to check whether any residues on the tools could have been simply derived from the surrounding matrix. The artefacts were also photographed and drawn in the unwashed state. Closer examination of wear patterns — or any analysis that requires the artefact to be completely cleaned — should be the last step in analysis, not the first.

Each artefact was double-bagged (with the original field bags inside). Plastic bags were used initially, but in future, for artefacts that seem especially promising for residue studies, we will be using paper bags (polythene can interfere with chemical-residue signals). Individually bagged artefacts from the same context were placed in larger bags and stored in numbered crates.

Presentation

In this report, we present the artefacts according to the contexts in which they were found. We also decided to present complete lists of inventories for all contexts (see discussion and tables on CD), instead of summarizing by artefact type or some other grouping. We felt that with this approach, variations between houses and between individual contexts would be easier for readers to see.

In part, these decisions were pragmatic, the pace of excavation at Çatalhöyük is sedate, but we also felt that context-by-context analysis was an essential prerequisite for understanding the ground-stone technologies and artefact types in the first place. The contexts of final abandonment shed important light on how the artefacts were made and used, and how they acquired their final forms. Many occurrences of reuse and recycling of artefacts, the final 'types' discovered in excavation, could not have been understood without considering context in the first instance. Thus, as excavation and analysis proceed, new artefact types will be encountered and the overall Çatalhöyük typology will be constantly updated.

Recording and classification

The recording system is governed by the research issues listed above. Table 13.3 (on CD) shows the kinds of variables being developed for addressing these questions. The overriding purposes behind our classification scheme are to understand the technology and general functions of the artefacts.

Concerning technology, the diverse raw materials involved mean that there are a considerable number of technologies (plural) in any ground-stone assemblage. Table 13.4 (on CD) shows those we have encountered so far. Numerically, volcanic rocks, especially andesite and basalt, dominate the artefacts, with sandstone, limestone, marble, schist and greenstone making up much of the rest. These materials were brought into the site from a number of sources. At this stage we are not yet ready to present any in-depth discussion of reduction sequences or *chaînes opératoires* involved in manufacture of artefacts from these materials. However, this work is in progress. Further discussion of raw materials and technology can be found below.

Concerning typology, rock type is so fundamental to artefact production, use and final form, that we seriously considered incorporating raw material into the formal type names. After wrestling with this problem we decided not to do so. Instead, we settled on a four-part approach to classification, in which each artefact was assigned to: 1) a Material Group (andesite, basalt, schist, etc.); 2) an Artefact Class broadly reflecting very general functional categories (e.g. Vessel, Mortar, Pestle, etc.); 3) an Artefact Type based on somewhat more specific functions and traces of use; and 4) Subtypes 1 and 2 to account for specific variations relating to shape, use-life (e.g. number of use surfaces; degree of fragmentation) and other variables. For the moment, we are treating the presence of decoration as an attribute of function, but eventually it will be necessary to incorporate style variations. Most artefacts in our sample are utilitarian and undecorated. However, some broken fragments (notably of grinding slabs) display evidence that the original artefact had been extensively shaped into distinctive and elegant forms (e.g. corners of rectangular, flat-based grinding slabs with walls at 90 degrees to the base).

Table 13.5 (on CD) presents the definitions of the types so far encountered. Terminology merits some discussion. Ground-stone artefact types have been called by disparate names, some of which are widely used (e.g. handstone, *mano*), and some of which are idiosyncratic to specific scholars (e.g. processor). In general, we tried to adhere to widely-used terms, whilst stating as explicitly as we could what we mean by them.

We adopted certain conventions for the sake of conveying the nature of artefact use. For example, in the case of handstones, we decided to emphasize whether such items could be easily picked up and manipulated with one hand, or required two hands to operate effectively. Borrowing the term *mano* from New World archaeology, we settled on a distinction between one-hand and two-hand *manos*. This difference turns out to be an important one for understanding the spatial organization, and possibly the physical effects, of using ground-stone tools.

Another important distinction is between heavy-duty grinding tools (typically made of andesite or basalt) and artefacts apparently used for finer abrading activities (items made of finer-grained stones such as fine sandstone, marble, schist). The Çatalhöyük artefacts display a wide diversity of small tools clearly aimed at finer abrasion at different grades of coarseness (like sandpaper). These include both passive and active tools such as abrading slabs and abraders (of medium-grained sandstone); sanding slabs and sanders (made of fine-grained sandstone); and polishing slabs and polishing pebbles (made of limestone or marble).

Detailed building by building descriptions of the archaeological contexts of the ground stones are provided on the accompanying CD. These descriptions cover the North, South and KOPAL Areas.

Ground stone at Çatalhöyük: curated technologies

On the whole the Çatalhöyük ground-stone artefacts were highly curated, in the sense used by Binford (1977). That is, these artefacts were produced and maintained in anticipation of future use, with a heavy emphasis on reuse, recycling and adaptation of older tools to new forms and purposes (Binford 1979, 269–70).

Highly-curated ground-stone assemblages have been observed in some seasonally-occupied Neolithic sites located far from the sources of stone used for grinding tools. By contrast, other Neolithic sites, located close to suitable stone sources, display much more expedient organization of ground-stone tools (Wright 1993; 1998; in prep. b–d; Wright, in Garrard *et al.* 1994; Wright, in Gebel & Bienert 1997).

However, at Çatalhöyük there are variations in the degree of curation, according to specific rock types and the origins thereof. With this in mind, it seems best to discuss the artefacts in terms of possible stages of production and use, from acquisition of raw materials to final abandonment.

Properties, sources, transport and use of rock types

Volcanic rocks

Ethnoarchaeological studies suggest that materials for grinding tools are chosen on the basis of availability, transport 'costs', durability, surface roughness, and the degree to which surface particles detached during grinding interfere with the product being processed (that is, a compromise has to be made between enduring roughness and the ease with which grits will be detached, corrupting the ground material) (Baysal 2001). Among tools used for heavy-duty grinding, surface texture was clearly a central consideration. These considerations probably explain the very widespread use of volcanic rocks (especially basalt) in many societies, ancient and modern, for heavy millstones or grinding slabs, even when other rock types are available in abundance (Wright 1992b).

Of the 359 Çatalhöyük artefacts presented here, 289 (80.5 per cent) are made of volcanic rocks, chiefly andesite and basalt, with a few occurrences of pumice and gabbro (Türkmenoğlu *et al.* 2001a,b). The nearest *in situ* volcanic outcrops to Çatalhöyük are those of Pleistocene age at Karadağ, some 40 kilometres distant. Other possible sources are Karacadağ (with andesites of Pliocene age) and Karapınar (rich in Pleistocene basalts). (All information on local geology, stone sources and petrography is from Chapter 17 on the accompanying CD.)

Substantial supplies of andesite and basalt would have had to be quarried directly from these sources, although sporadic occurrences of volcanic rocks, transported by streams or slopewash into the plain, could have been exploited as well. Andesite and basalt would have been the most demanding rock types in terms of transport to Çatalhöyük. Not only are the sources quite distant, but the largest and heaviest artefacts (namely, grinding slabs) were made of these materials.

The vast majority of artefacts made from volcanic stones are fragments of grinding slabs and/or handstones (milling tools). Mellaart's reports likewise emphasize the prevalence of volcanic rocks amongst the heavy-milling tools. Mellaart's illustrations show a few unbroken grinding slabs found *in situ* (Mellaart 1962a, pl. 4b). From these, and from our own (as yet brief) examination of complete slabs from his excavations, we can see that the original artefacts from which the slab fragments came varied from simple saddle-shaped slabs to more complex forms with flat bases and sides rising at 90 degrees from the base.

In our sample, the artefacts made from volcanic rocks are very heavily curated and extensively recycled, which is not surprising in light of these observations. More research will be needed to investigate: 1) the probable sizes of blocks transported to Çatalhöyük; 2) the frequency of procurement trips to the sources; and 3) whether procurement trips changed through time.

Nearly half of the 359 artefacts are made of andesite (n = 170, 47.3 per cent). Some andesite artefacts from Çatalhöyük were examined petrographically and were composed of hornblende-andesite and hornblende-biotite andesite. They match samples from Karadağ-Kaletepe. Other artefacts were of dacitic andesite, matching samples from Karadağ-Kızıltepe.

Coarse and naturally rough in texture, andesite is by far the most common material used for robust grinding slabs (of which we have only fragments) and handstones (for definitions of artefact types see Table 13.5 on CD) (e.g. Figs. 13.1:1, 4, 5 & 13.2:9). Andesite is somewhat less dense than massive basalt and therefore potentially easier to transport. Depending on texture, the andesite at Çatalhöyük was capable of being flaked, albeit often only very roughly. Ground surfaces tend to retain considerable roughness, whilst not producing large quantities of grit during grinding, no doubt a key reason for choosing this material for heavy-duty grinding stones. However, some of the andesite artefacts we examined were rather friable once burnt.

An additional 30.9 per cent (n = 111) of all artefacts were made of basalt, sometimes with a rich component of andesite. Artefacts of this material were examined petrographically and were found to be composed of pyroxene basalts, matching samples from Karadağ. With only one or two exceptions, all of these basalts were massive, lacking vesicles characteristic of (for example) scoria. Massive basalt is eminently suited for shaping by flaking, having a conchoidal fracture. It is also dense, heavy, and resistant to breakage. The size and angularity of the inclusions vary greatly, affecting surface texture. In our sample, massive basalt was used for handstones, grinding slabs and robust pounding tools such as pestles and hammers (Figs. 13.2:11 & 13.5:7).

Closely similar in its properties to massive basalt, gabbro was found in only small numbers (n = 6). Of six artefacts made of gabbro, three are axes; one is a pestle-hammer, one is a mano, and one is a miniature vessel fragment.

Lightweight, highly-vesicular pumice is rare in our samples (n = 2), and was used for small hand-held abrading tools (Fig. 13.4:6).

Sedimentary rocks

Sedimentary marls and chalks are the only rocks abundantly available *in situ* in the Konya plain. Massive outcrops of limestone occur at Bozdağ and around the southern edges of the Plain. However, the Çarşamba Çay streambed gravels contain rocks transported from surrounding areas, and relatively small stones of sedimentary origin would have been available here. Generally speaking, the artefacts made from these materials seem to display somewhat less evidence for storage, recycling and curation. Fewer of the tools made of these materials were broken, compared to items made of volcanic rocks.

Only 9.5 per cent (n = 34) of the artefacts in our sample were made from sedimentary rocks. About half of these were made of sandstone (n = 18), of which the *in situ* origin is so far unknown, but which occurs in the Çarşamba Çay gravels. Sandstones of widely varying roughness were used for small hand-held abrading tools and rather petite abrading slabs, such as those found in Building 1 (Figs. 13.1:3, 6, 7 & 13.2:8).

Artefacts made of limestone (n = 13), chalk (n = 2) and conglomerate (n = 1) account for only 4.5 per cent of the artefacts in our sample. These include polishing slabs and hand-held polishing pebbles; one vessel rim; an incised stone; and a bead (e.g. Figs. 13.3:13 & 13.5:2).

In the 1960s excavations, stone bowls were rare, according to Mellaart. Those that are reported are fine and well made (as in the fragments we have seen) and a number are said to be made of limestone. Limestone vessels include flat 'plates' (of which we have a probable fragment) (Mellaart 1962b, fig. 17) (Fig. 13.3:13). We have not yet examined any stone figurines, but Mellaart reports a number that are made of limestone and chalk (cf. Mellaart 1962a, pl. VIIIc; 1963, pls. XXc, XXIa–b; 1964a, pls. XVIb, XVIIa; 1967, pls. 65, 69). Some limestone figurines appear to be unfinished, and the forms suggest that several were made from river pebbles, a possibility that needs further study (Mellaart 1963, pl. 19). Mellaart also reports the use of limestone for grooved polishers (cf. 'shaft straighteners'), maceheads (of 'blue' limestone), beads and 'marbles' (Mellaart 1962a, 55 & pl. 4b–c). Of maceheads, Mellaart reports that they are 'extremely common in all layers' (1963, 101), but they did not appear in our sample although they have been recovered by the current excavations

(Volume 3, Part 3). Mellaart reports other bowls that were made of sandstone (of which we found no examples in our sample). Some of these are small, shallow and have spouts (Mellaart 1967, pl. 112).

Metamorphic rocks

In situ outcrops of metamorphic rocks do not occur in the Konya plain, but the Çarşamba Çay could have been a source of small transported stones of these materials (Türkmenoğlu *et al.* 2001a,b). Only 30 artefacts (8.4 per cent) in our sample were made from metamorphic rocks (marble and schist). Of the 18 artefacts made of marble (recrystallized limestone), the vast majority were small polishing slabs and hand-held polishing pebbles (Figs. 13.3:14, 16 & 13.4:1, 7). In our sample, we encountered schist mainly in the form of small, rather flat rectangular palettes with one or two oval use surfaces; one or two of them had been fashioned into other items such as cutting or chopping tools (Figs. 13.2:10 & 13.5:3–4).

Mellaart reports that marble was used for making fine bowls. One of these, found with a burial, is shallow, with two perforations close to each other (1964a, pl. XVIIIa). Marble was also used for figurines (Mellaart 1963, pls. XXa,b & d, XXIc & XXII). Some figurines are reported as alabaster (Mellaart 1962a, pl. 9; 1964a, pl. XVIa,c & d). Mellaart also found a flat plaque with carved figures, made of what he variously described as 'greenish slate' (1963, fig. 27) and 'grey-green schist' (1967, pl. 83), possibly the same material as used to make small flat palettes.

Other rocks

We have not yet identified firmly the composition of the 'greenstone' that appears only as axes in our sample (Fig. 13.5:5). Possibilities include serpentine and green apatitic limestone, but further investigation is needed. Mellaart reports artefacts made of apatite, such as beads (1963, pl. XXVIIb) as well as a number of other materials, including calcite and unspecified 'black stones', which were used for figurines (1964a, pl. XVIIb–d).

Evidence for manufacture of ground-stone artefacts

Workshops for initial reduction of heavy grinding tools have been found near sources of suitable stones, in ancient Israel and Egypt, and in latter-day Guatemala (Hayden 1987; Rosen & Schneider 2001; Roubet 1989). Such workshops characteristically have large numbers of half-finished ground-stone 'blanks', in which artisans use flaking to produce roughouts that are more manageable and easier to transport. Unfinished blanks sometimes find their way to habitation sites for further refinement into tools (e.g. Wright 1992a; 1993; 2000; in prep. d).

The source areas for bulky non-local materials used for ground stone at Çatalhöyük have not been systematically surveyed (yet) for the presence of archaeological sites. So we do not know whether quarries or workshops existed there. We do have some evidence for on-site manufacture of ground-stone items at Çatalhöyük. That evidence is still sparse and so far there are no spatially-discrete production areas, with two possible exceptions (see below).

In the 1995–99 sample, there is debitage from ground-stone artefacts. In every case so far, these are flakes with at least one ground surface, indicating refashioning of an older tool rather than primary manufacture (e.g. Figs. 13.4:4 & 13.5:6). No cores, blanks or half-finished artefacts appeared in our sample, although such artefacts are easy to identify. However, discerning manufacture and manufacturing areas will require not only larger samples but also examination of unworked stones (which were collected) and microdebris from flotation residues (cf. Wright & Garrard 2003).

Mellaart reports two possible instances of ground-stone artefact production from his excavations. One is house A.III.2, which 'produced a large number of stone tools as well as raw material and might have been a stoneworker's shop' (Mellaart 1962a, 55). Another possible stoneworking area is Mellaart's 'Second Shrine', House E.VI.10. Here, 13 stone figurines of limestone and marble were found on the floor. Mellaart interpreted variations in these in terms of styles (from 'schematic' to more representational) (Mellaart 1963, 82–3). However, the photographs indicate that some of the 'schematic' figurines are actually unfinished (partly-worked). We see these finds as the remains of figurine-making activities, which is supported by the discovery of unworked limestone near the figurine group and the presence of mending holes in one figurine (Mellaart 1963, pls. XIX–XXI).

In situ activity areas and contexts of use

Most ground-stone artefacts in our sample came from discard contexts (e.g. external fills & middens) (Tables 13.1–13.2). Of all the priority contexts (including a few that we added), only 16.4 per cent of all contexts from floors and features contained any ground stone (Table 13.2). Of the 359 artefacts in our sample, only 88 (24.5 per cent) were found in association with house floors and specific features inside houses (Table 13.1). Within this group, the largest samples of ground stone came from fill above floor ($n = 30$); from general floor deposits ($n = 16$, including a grinding feature); from contexts

Table 13.1. *Ground-stone artefacts by context type: the 355 priority contexts.*

Context type	Description	Number of ground-stone artefacts	Percentage of all ground-stone artefacts
Floors and features			
Bin		10	2.8
Burial		1	0.3
Fill above floor		30	8.4
Floor		6	1.7
Grinding feature on floor		10	2.8
Oven	fill	9	2.5
Oven	floor interface - oven use	2	0.6
Oven	floor rake-out	1	0.3
Pit	fill	12	3.3
Platform	floor	3	0.8
Fire spot		1	0.3
Wall		3	0.8
Total - floors and features		*88*	*24.5*
Fills and middens associated with buildings			
Fill	building fill	5	1.4
Fill	infill - access	1	0.3
Fill	infill - building fill	12	3.3
Fill	infill - foundation/levelling	3	0.8
Fill	room fill	6	1.7
Midden	construction cut fill	4	1.1
Midden	foundation cut dump	27	7.5
Midden	in abandoned building	25	7.0
Midden	room fill dump	1	0.3
Midden	with collapse	1	0.3
Total - fills and middens associated with buildings		*85*	*23.7*
Fills and middens associated with external areas			
Alluvium and fill	external deposit	27	7.5
Cut	2	0.6	
Fill	between walls	37	10.3
Gully	2	0.6	
Midden	animal pen dump	2	0.6
Midden	demolition	1	0.3
Midden	exterior	115	32.0
Total - fills and middens associated with external areas		*186*	*51.8*
Grand total		**359**	**100.0**

associated with ovens (n = 12); from pits (n = 12); and from bins (n = 10). Most of the items are fragments. As noted, some fragments were themselves used as grinding tools, whilst others may have been used for purposes such as providing heating elements or supports in ovens.

Some artefacts found in these contexts may have been discarded rather than used or cached there, as in the case of fills of bins or ovens that had already gone out of use. Much of the evidence for *in situ* activity areas involving ground-stone artefacts is somewhat ambiguous. The grinding feature F.27 (1423) in Building 1 is one of the most conspicuous candidates, but even here, there are nuances. The small cluster of grinding slab and fragmentary handstones is directly associated with diverse plant remains, but two of these artefacts have visible residues of ochre on them, testifying to the probable use of these artefacts for both food processing and paintmaking. However, the slab itself was found lying on its use surface and this seems to have been deliberately placed in this way.

Finds of 'working toolkits', such as paired slabs and handstones deposited together, are few, but these rare examples are informative. The collection of tools from the Building 1 grinding feature shows that complete abrading slabs and *ad hoc* handstones recycled from older broken tools were probably used together. A similar pairing appeared in the contemporary Phase B1.2 'lentil bin' nearby (which also held a complete slab and a similar *ad hoc* handstone). Thus, Phase B1.2 in Building 1 revealed two complete kits for grinding activities. Some of Mellaart's finds may suggest that pairs of grinding slabs (and associated handstones) were sometimes abandoned together within houses (see below). In early village sites in the Levant, caches of two toolkits are sometimes seen (Wright 2000). Such habits could suggest a need for backup tool sets, or that more than one person might be using grinding tools at one time (see discussion of house variations, below).

Mellaart's reports suggest possible *in situ* activity areas, especially in later levels (Levels V–I) where the locations of ground-stone tools are recorded more often on the plans. (We do not know whether this reflects a true change from earlier levels or whether Mellaart simply recorded ground-stone artefacts less often in the plans of the lower levels: cf. Mellaart 1962a; 1966a).

Mellaart found complete grinding slabs and associated tools in diverse places inside houses. In house E.VI.2, a grinding slab and a handstone were found in a room corner on a bench against a wall, with another grinding slab at the edge of the adjacent platform (Mellaart 1962a, pl.IVb). In Levels I–III, a grinding slab (apparently complete) was found in a storeroom adjacent to house B1, and next to an oven on the south side of house A1 (Mellaart 1962a, fig. 3). In Level IV, two querns are shown in the storeroom on the south side of

Table 13.2. *Presence/absence of ground-stone artefacts by context type: includes several contexts added to the 355 in the priority list.*

Context type	Description	Number of contexts with ground stone present	Number of contexts with ground stone absent	Total number of contexts	Percentage with ground stone
Floors and features					
Bin	base	1	2	3	33.3
Bin	bin fill	4	13	17	23.5
Burial	fill	1	7	8	12.5
Fill above floor	general	10	31	41	24.4
Fill above floor	collapsed plaster	0	1	1	0.0
Floor	general	1	37	38	2.6
Floor	artefact clusters	1	6	7	14.3
Floor	ashy spreads/rake-outs/dirty areas	1	11	12	8.3
Floor	exterior surface	2	2	4	50.0
Hearth	fill	0	8	8	0.0
Hearth	feature use	0	2	2	0.0
Hearth	rake-out	0	1	1	0.0
Ladder	-	0	1	1	0.0
Oven	base	1	9	10	10.0
Oven	fill	2	4	6	33.3
Oven	interior deposits	0	4	4	0.0
Oven	floor rake-outs	1	3	4	25.0
Oven	superstructure	0	3	3	0.0
Oven	demolition - backfill	0	1	1	0.0
Pit	fill	7	11	18	38.9
Platform	fill - make-up/packing - basal building infill	0	1	1	0.0
Platform	floor	3	9	12	25.0
Posthole/Stakehole		0	12	12	0.0
Total		*35*	*179*	*214*	*16.4*
Fills and middens associated with buildings					
Building fill	arbitrary layer - basal building infill	0	5	5	0.0
Building fill	fill	2	0	2	100.0
Fill between walls	fill	3	0	3	100.0
Fill between walls	general	6	4	10	60.0
Fill between walls	ground-stone cluster	1	0	1	100.0
Foundation	-	0	1	1	0.0
Infill	artefact cluster - obsidian cache	0	2	2	0.0
Infill	building fill	5	3	8	62.5
Infill	building fill between walls	0	4	4	0.0
Infill	foundation	1	0	1	100.0
Infill	general	1	0	1	100.0
Infill	general	0	2	2	0.0
Infill	levelling	1	0	1	100.0
Midden	artefact cluster - bones	0	2	2	0.0
Midden	construction cut fill - dump	1	0	1	100.0
Midden	cut fill	0	1	1	0.0
Midden	demolition	1	0	1	100.0
Midden	foundation cut - dump	4	0	4	100.0
Midden	in abandoned building	7	1	8	87.5
Midden	room-fill dump	1	0	1	100.0
Midden	with collapse	1	0	1	100.0
Room fill	burnt collapse	0	1	1	0.0
Room fill	fill	4	11	15	26.7
Wall	-	2	8	10	20.0
Total		*41*	*45*	*86*	*47.7*
Fills and middens associated with external areas					
Alluvium and fill	external deposit	4	0	4	100.0
Cut	fill	1	2	3	33.3
Fire spot	exterior dump (burnt)	1	0	1	100.0
Firespot	lime-burning area	0	2	2	0.0
Firespot	lime-burning area	0	3	3	0.0
Firespot	scorched area	0	1	1	0.0
Gully	fill	1	0	1	100.0
Midden	animal pen - dump	2	0	2	100.0
Midden	animal pen - dump; stabling deposit	0	6	6	0.0
Midden	exterior	18	5	23	78.3
Midden	exterior - construction/make-up/packing	1	0	1	100.0
Midden	exterior alluvium	4	0	4	100.0
Midden	exterior dump	5	3	8	62.5
Total		*37*	*22*	*59*	*62.7*

house E4, with a third on the north side of the adjacent large room, next to a platform and a bench. In house E9, a slab was discovered next to a hearth in the larger room (Mellaart 1962a, fig. 4). No slabs are illustrated in the plan of Level V (Mellaart 1962a, fig. 5), but in the combined plan of Levels VI–IX (Mellaart 1962a, fig. 6), a slab lies on a platform near a bench in House E2 and in the centre of the main room of House E4.

It is possible that these occurrences represent deliberate, structured abandonment, rather than places of use. On the other hand, Mellaart's reports seem to indicate that the slabs were often found firmly set in place, with use surfaces facing upward. If we assume (for the sake of argument) that these are places where these slabs were routinely used, obviously depending on season or occasion, the diversity of locations tends to militate somewhat against the idea that there was a strict dichotomy between areas of 'domestic' activities and areas involving 'ritual' activities. That is, ground-stone items occur not only in 'kitchen' and storage areas but in the largest rooms; on platforms, in room centres, and against northern walls. The co-occurrence of grinding stones with both plant remains and ochre grinding in the same context (Building 1) likewise tends to militate against such a strict division. There is also the fact that domestic activities are inherently also 'rituals', and important ones at that (Bourdieu 1977; Wright 2000). But more data and further analysis are needed to clarify these issues.

Matthews (Volume 4, Chapter 19) suggests that some grinding activities may have been occurring on house roofs (e.g. Buildings 5 and 3), since oven remains and particles (possibly detached from grinding stones) appeared in roof collapse. We ourselves have not yet seen ground-stone artefacts from roof collapse contexts. However, certainly it would have been possible to conduct milling activities on rooftops. In contrast to the very heavy grinding tools (weighing as much as 50 kilograms) from some Neolithic villages (Wright 2000), the complete slabs we have seen so far from Neolithic Çatalhöyük are eminently portable tools, and could have been carried to rooftops without difficulty. We would not be surprised to discover grinding tools having fallen in from rooftops, although large clusters of heavy slabs on a single house roof might be somewhat unexpected, even given the strength of the original roofing. Again, contexts of ground-stone use undoubtedly varied seasonally and according to specific occasions.

Storage

It can be difficult to disentangle storage for later use from deliberate, structured abandonment. But the available data suggest that storing ground-stone artefacts, even fragments, was a habit at Çatalhöyük.

In our sample, ground-stone artefacts were found in four bins; in one case, we see a working toolkit cached in a bin fill (Building 1). Ground-stone artefacts also occur on the floors of small storerooms, where they may have been kept, rather than used. Ground-stone fragments occasionally appear inside ovens. In some cases, these are in fills deposited after an oven went out of use, but it is a possibility that broken items were used inside ovens, to distribute heat or support cooked items, a habit that is well-documented ethnographically. Similar fragments appear in pits and bins along with remains of wood (fuel?) and clay balls (pot-boilers?), possibly suggesting storage of supplies related to cooking (e.g. Buildings 2 & 6).

Refashioning and recycling

The vast majority of artefacts in our sample are either broken or display evidence of refashioning and recycling, even unto exhaustion. Flakes from previous ground-stone tools are often seen. The number of complete items is exceedingly low, and even these often display evidence for rejuvenation or transformation into new tools (e.g. Fig. 13.1:2). We also investigated all contexts for possible refits of fragments. On rare occasions we were successful (e.g. Fig. 13.3:12), but in many cases we were looking at clusters of artefacts from different originals.

Several observations hint at different approaches to the use and maintenance of finer abrading tools relative to andesite-basalt grinding tools. Building 1 illustrates this phenomenon quite well. Here as elsewhere, the great majority of andesite and basalt tools are fragments. Some of these were clearly reused as handstones. Such fragments were found directly associated with sandstone abrading slabs, in burnt bin fill above lentils (1344) (Fig. 13.1:4, 7), and in the grinding feature (1423) (Figs. 13.1:5 & 13.2:8). Some fragments were left in oven fills, perhaps for aiding in the dissemination of heat or for use as supports for grilling. And many were thrown away outside the house.

By contrast, the finer abrading tools occur more often as complete items. In addition, the use surfaces of the abrading slabs are shallow. There is no evidence for recycling of sandstone abrading tools, whilst there is much evidence suggesting recycling of andesite and basalt grinding-slab fragments into other uses. In the case of the grinding feature F.27, (1423), someone made a final use of a sandstone abrading slab (for ochre processing) and then carefully turned the slab over onto its face. Scattered around the slab were several grinding-slab fragments, one with ochre on its ground use surface.

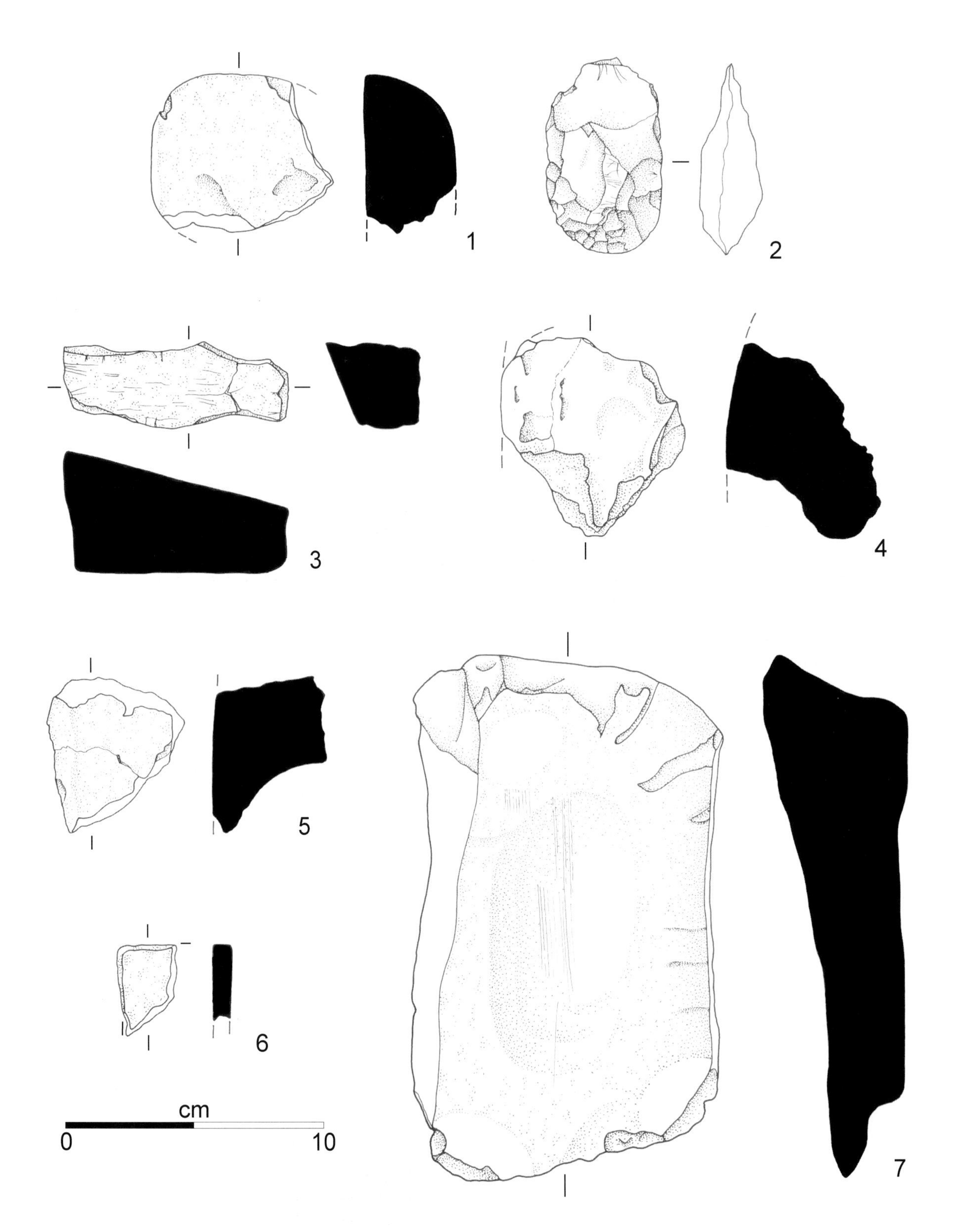

Figure 13.1. *Ground-stone artefacts from Building 1, North Area: 1) andesite mano (2165); 2) gabbro axe (2165); 3) sandstone sander (1488); 4) andesite grinding slab or handstone fragment (1344); 5) andesite grinding slab fragment re-used as a handstone (1423); 6) sandstone abrader (1423); 7) sandstone abrading slab (1344). For further details see Table 13.6. (Drawn by Graham Reed.)*

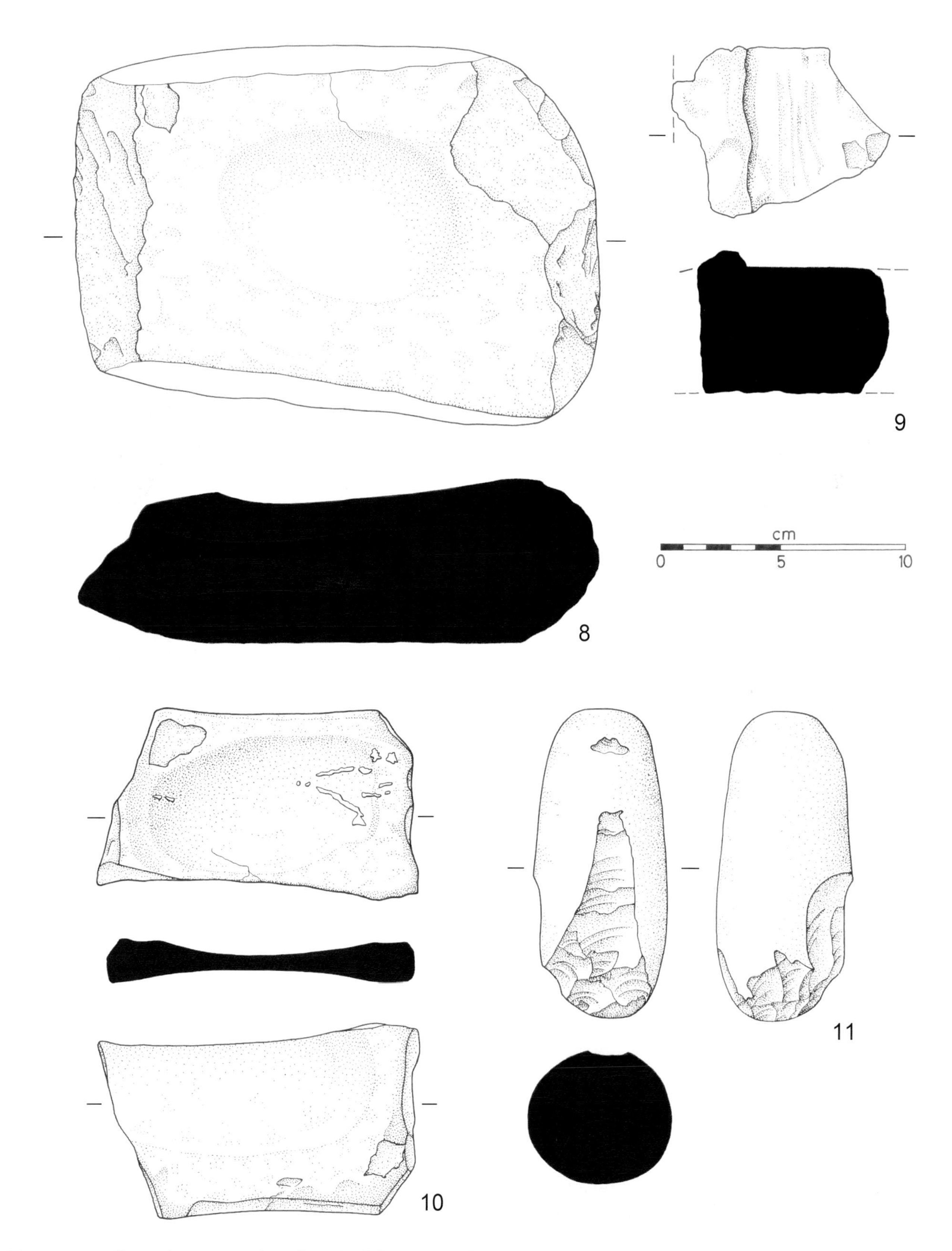

Figure 13.2. *Ground-stone artefacts from Building 1, North Area: 8) sandstone abrading slab (1423); 9) basalt grinding slab fragment (1188); 10) schist palette (1192); 11) gabbro pestle-hammer (1267). For further details see Table 13.6. (Drawn by Graham Reed.)*

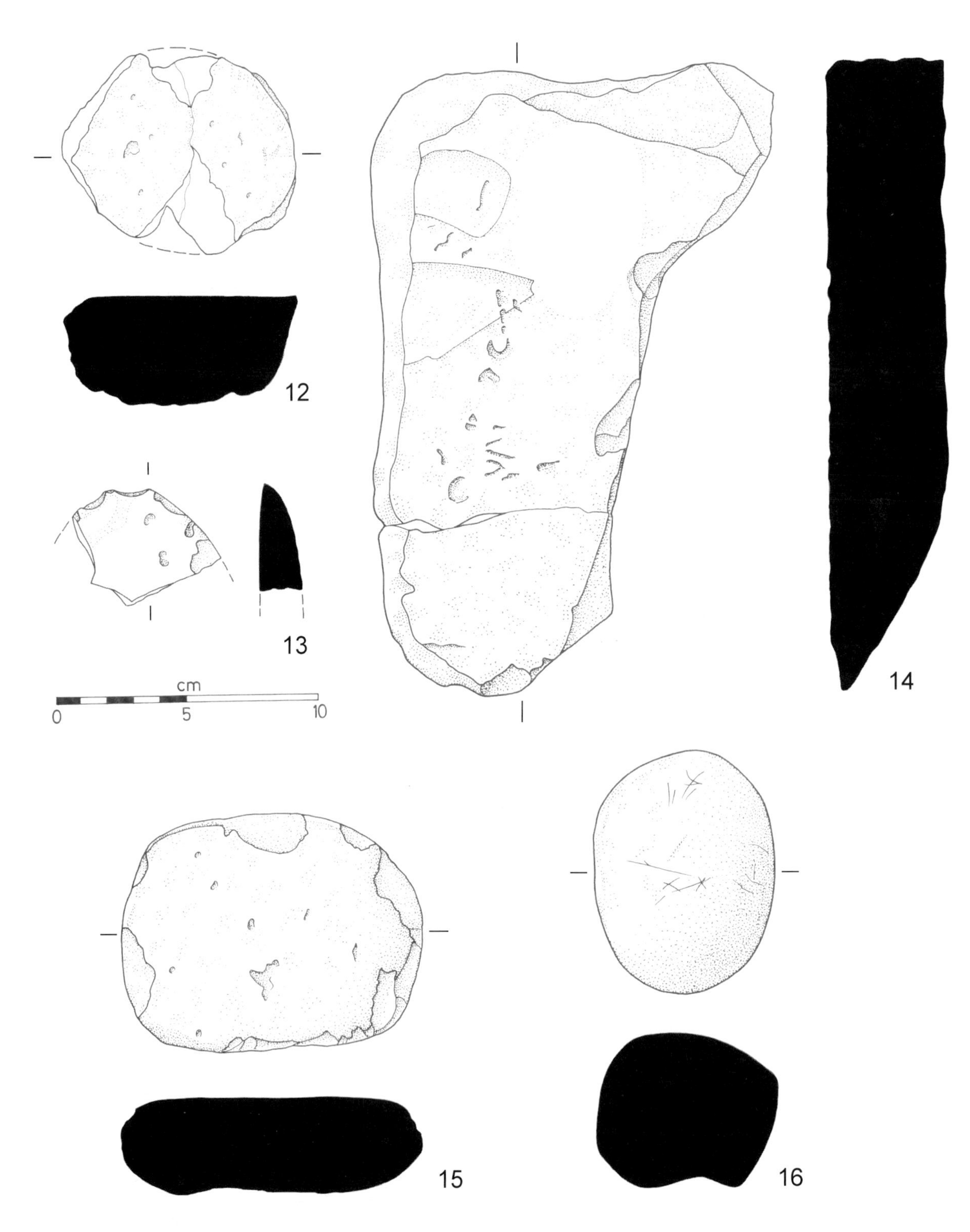

Figure 13.3. *Ground-stone artefacts from Building 1, North Area: 12) andesite mano (1267); 13) limestone vessel rim (1126); 14) marble polishing slab (2525); 15) Basalt mano (3044); 16) marble polishing pebble (3044). For further details see Table 13.6. (Drawn by Graham Reed.)*

The complete artefacts recovered so far suggest that activities involving ground-stone tools were conducted on a small scale. That is, the abrading slabs are very small and shallow, implying use with a one-hand mano or small abrader (the only complete handstones and hand-held abraders found are all petite, usable

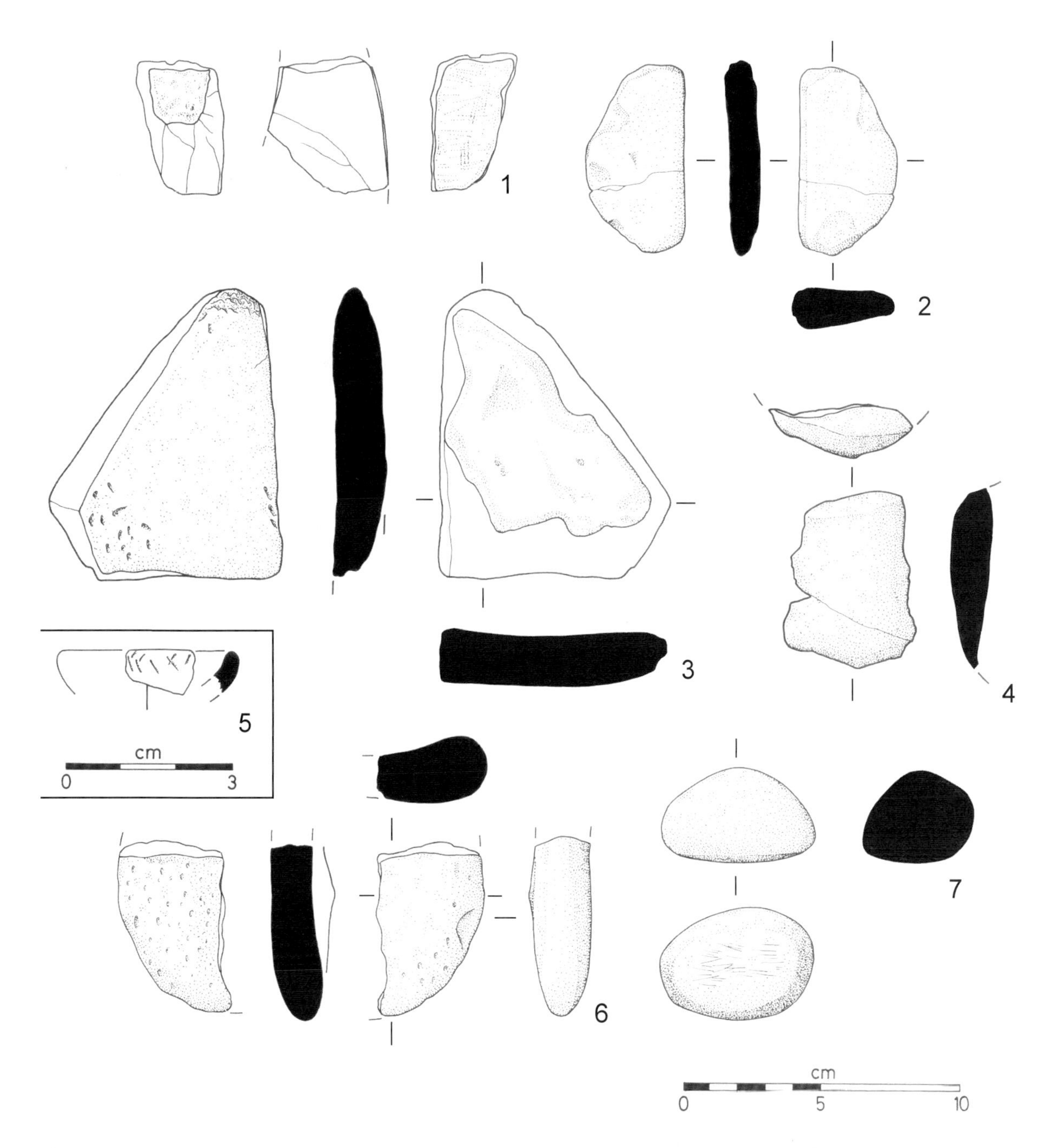

Figure 13.4. *Ground-stone artefacts from Space 181, South Area: 1) marble polishing slab fragment (5326); 2) sandstone abrader (5315); 3) sandstone abrading slab (5290); 4) andesite flake (4874); 5) gabbro vessel rim fragment (4837); 6) pumice abrader (4836); 7) marble polishing pebble (4837). For further details see Table 13.7. (Drawn by Graham Reed.)*

with one hand). To produce large quantities of processed material on these rather petite artefacts would have required quite a bit of time (we plan to conduct experiments to investigate productivity). In addition, the complete slabs are amenable to being picked up and moved around without difficulty (for a contrasting situation see Wright 2000).

These observations imply the multiple purposes of the grinding-slab fragments re-used as handstones and the abrading slabs found with them: ochre processing, certainly (e.g. (1423); and food processing, probably (1344)). Other artefacts deposited together also hint at activities such as polishing of small items (perhaps bone tools, beads and others), e.g. the palette

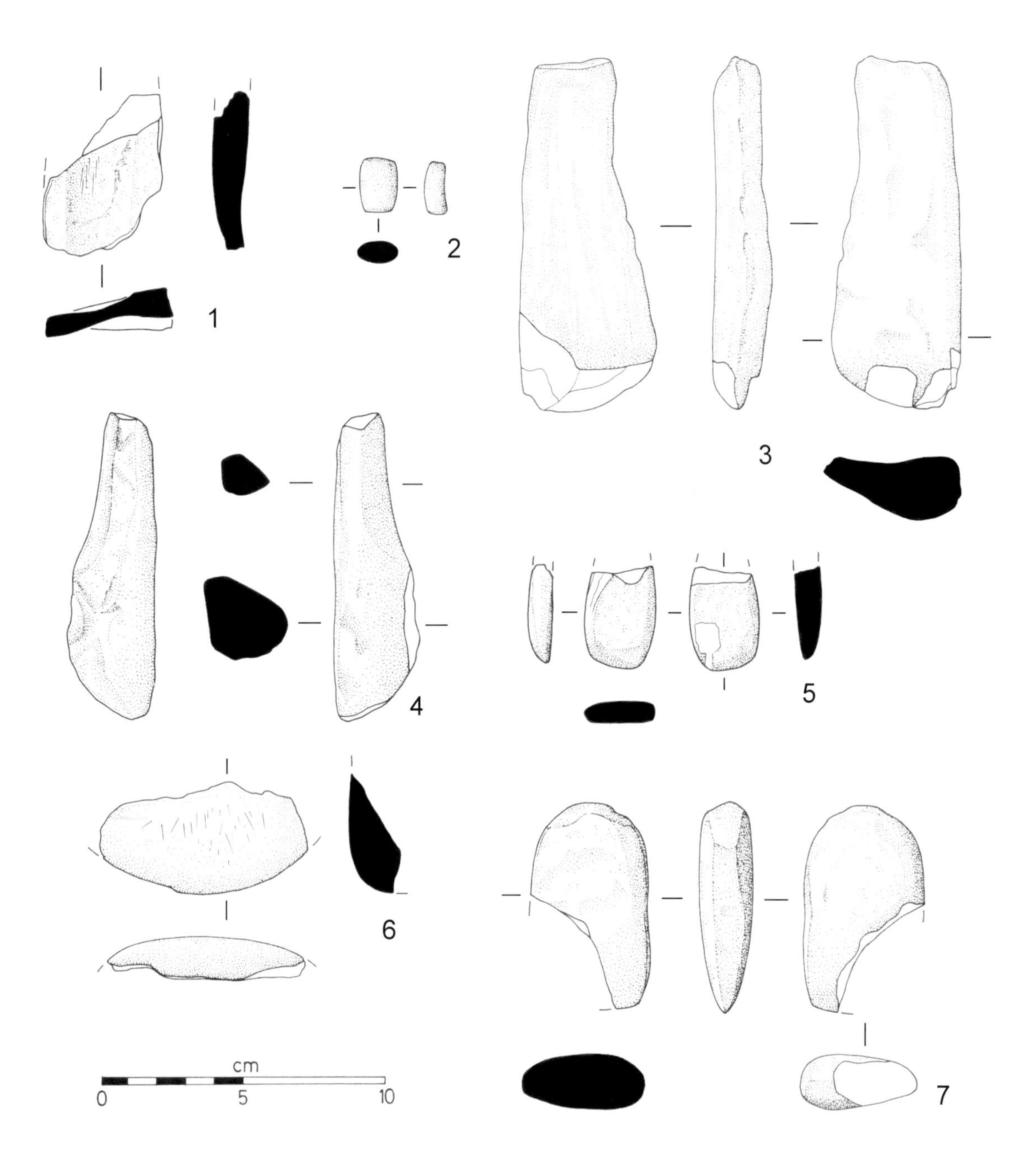

Figure 13.5. *Ground-stone artefacts from the South Area: 1) sandstone abrading slab fragment (4518); 2) limestone bead blank (4921); 3) schist chopper made from palette (5053); 4) schist abrader (4102); 5) greenstone axe (1895); 6) limestone flake from ground-stone tool (1505); 7) gabbro axe (1668). For further details see Tables 13.8, 13.10 & 13.12. (Drawn by Graham Reed.)*

and abrader found in (1192); and polishing of walls, floors or small items (e.g. the polishing slab and pebble in (2525)).

In all, the ground-stone artefacts from the selected contexts fit well with Martin & Russell's (2000) impression that materials were arriving on the site and not leaving it. Assuming that the selected contexts are fully representative of the building as a whole, andesite, basalt and gabbro seem to have arrived and been intensively recycled. Sandstone and a few other materials (schist, marble) seem to have arrived in some houses (e.g. Building 1), been used for a relatively brief period without recycling, and then carefully and deliberately abandoned.

We do not yet know how the extensive recycling and refashioning of ground-stone tools relates to changes through time in the availability of rock types or frequency of procurement trips. Equally, our samples are too small yet to determine whether there was a tendency for ground-stone tools to be 'recycled upward', with older artefacts passing into the hands of later occupants, who used, recycled and then discarded them.

This is, however, a question that has to be considered. A number of ethnographies of village societies indicate that carefully made ground-stone artefacts, particularly grinding slabs, typically have very long use-lives. In addition to practical considerations such as breakage, social factors such as inheritance can play a role in the history of such artefacts. For example, in a number of village societies, daughters inherit milling tools from their mothers (e.g. Hayden 1987; Hayden & Cannon 1984; Kramer 1982; Horne 1990; Watson 1979; Wright 1992b). Matrilineal inheritance of stone milling tools can be documented in Akkadian documents from second-millennium Mesopotamia (Wright 2000). In third-millennium Mesopotamia, legal texts used the expression 'to transfer the pestle' (in this case made of wood) to indicate the transfer of property (land, gardens, slaves) from person A to person B (Goetze 1966, 126–7; gis.ganna, obverse, line 4). Whilst it is obviously impossible to assume automatically that cultural practices of precisely this kind existed at Çatalhöyük, the ethnographic literature does suggest that we should be aware of the cultural as well as practical elements of artefact life-histories.

Discard

Of all priority contexts selected for analysis, most contexts that contained ground-stone artefacts were middens and fills (Table 13.2). Almost half (47.7 per cent) of all middens and fills associated with buildings had some ground stone. Of fill and midden contexts from outdoor areas, 62.7 per cent had some ground stone in them. Of the 359 artefacts in our sample, 75.5 per cent come from middens and fills (Table 13.1). About half (51.8 per cent) of all artefacts derive from exterior fills, dumps and middens outside of houses. A full 42.3 per cent of the total came from generalized exterior midden deposits (32.0 per cent) and fills between house walls (10.3 per cent). A further 23.7 per cent of all artefacts were found in dumps and fills in abandoned buildings or in other fills inside buildings.

Most of what was thrown away consisted of broken artefacts, but complete items (notably polishing tools and slabs) were also discarded. Ground stone appears to have been discarded with many other materials and items, often including plant remains. Some of the middens containing both grinding stones and plant remains may have been burnt *in situ* and could reflect processing (Volume 4, Chapter 8). In most cases the botanical material in contexts is probably residual and we cannot assume a direct link between it and the ground-stone artefacts. For some archaeologists, the throwing away of unwanted items is seen as governed mainly by practical, utilitarian considerations such as the effort involved, physical hindrances, and reuse value (Hayden & Cannon 1983; Schiffer 1976). On the other hand, rubbish can be discarded as part of ritual or symbolic acts, and discard may be closely related to culturally-specific ideas about cleanliness (Hill 1995; 1996; Hodder 1987; Richards & Thomas 1984; cf. Douglas 1966).

Martin & Russell (2000) showed that there were different ways of disposing rubbish at Çatalhöyük, probably depending on a mix of practical and social concerns. Some outdoor middens displayed high densities of debris suggesting rubbish from household activities; other disposal episodes involved rapid filling of abandoned houses with prepared material; yet other rubbish deposits, notably (1873) in Building 2, may represent remains of feasting.

Our own data do not display any clear patterns in the nature of rubbish discarded in the specific contexts discussed by Martin & Russell. The ranges of artefacts and their states of preservation are approximately similar in exterior middens and rubbish thrown into abandoned buildings, and we see no unusual evidence that sheds additional light on the 'feasting' interpretation of (1873). Still, one possible exception to the general homogeneity of ground-stone rubbish may be in the exterior areas of Building 1, where several complete polishing tools were thrown away (this would support Martin & Russell's interpretation of these middens as household debris). However, further analysis of more contexts may change this picture.

Given the general absence of complete andesite and basalt grinding and pounding tools in middens and dumps, we have to consider whether such tools were deliberately broken before being thrown away. We cannot resolve this question, but there are some hints that deliberate breakage may have been practised. Chiefly, we suspect this because so many of the fragments are similar in size, mostly small and between 5 and 15 cm in diameter (Tables 13.6–13.14). However, we have no occurrences of conjoinable fragments from a single tool from any of the middens, so this question is still open.

Variations through time

For the moment, we do not see any clear variations in materials or types of artefacts from the early levels to later ones. However, the range of types in our sample is rather narrow, so nuances about chronological change really must await additional study.

Variations within and between structures

In our sample, there are marked variations between structures, in the quantities of ground-stone artefacts and the circumstances of abandonment. Thus, some structures have substantial clusters whilst some buildings have extremely few. Tentatively, we can say that this picture is reinforced by Mellaart's reports, which indicate that some houses were rich in ground-stone artefacts and others were not. But any clear picture of house-to-house variation must await further study.

In some Neolithic villages, there are relatively standard household 'toolkits' of ground stone (cf. Wright 2000; in prep. d). So far it is not yet possible to speak of household toolkits at Çatalhöyük. However, some houses display sets of two to three unbroken grinding or abrading slabs (e.g. see Building 1 and finds discussed above from Mellaart 1962a). Our work on this issue is still in progress, but meanwhile, ethnographic data suggest some lines of research that we are pursuing (Esin 1991; Davis 1982; Duru 1998; Wright 2000; in prep. a–d).

In Hopi villages, each household tended to contain sets of two or three grinding slabs (Bartlett 1933, 14). In an ethnoarchaeological study of a Maya village, Hayden & Cannon found that the number of grinding slabs in a given house correlated with: 1) the number of economically-active women; 2) craft-specialist households (especially potters); and 3) lineage heads (1984, 68–74). Ethnographic data also show that household toolkits also vary according to whether specialized milling has been introduced. When grain is sent to be processed elsewhere, the association of handmills with each household unit is not nearly as close. This is the situation documented by Kramer and Watson in Iranian villages; grain was sent to specialist millers and handmills were relatively rare and somewhat prized. Rotary querns were few and were widely shared (Kramer 1982, 33f; Watson 1979, 168). Further research on house to house variations may shed light on household production activities, social organization and specialization.

Cooking and culture at Çatalhöyük

Evidence for nutcracking with stone tools first appears in the Lower Palaeolithic, and cooking dates from the Middle Palaeolithic if not earlier. However, a great wave of expansion in food-preparation technologies took place with the beginnings of farming in the Middle East. This expansion can be understood as intensification in production of prepared foods (Wright 1991; 1994, cf. Stahl 1989). From the very beginnings of this expansion, we can see very clear evidence for cultural variations between regions, in aesthetic choices surrounding food preparation and in customs of consumption (dining). By the time Çatalhöyük was occupied, the initial Neolithic technologies for cooking and dining, developed between 12,650 and 7550 cal BC, were undergoing rapid change all across the Middle East (Wright 2000; in prep. a).

These changes began just before the main phases of the 'secondary products revolution' (Sherratt 1981), but anticipated that revolution in a number of respects. Among these changes were the development of more complex cooking facilities (e.g. elaborate closed ovens), technological changes in ground-stone processing tools, elaborations in vessel-production technologies (e.g. stone, plaster, ceramics), development of diverse forms of storage, and early stages in domestication of new species of animals (sheep, goat, cattle) and plants (olive, vine, dates, figs). Collectively, archaeological data from the period between 7550 and 4350 cal BC in western Asia point to entirely new approaches to food preparation, including the use of special food preparation procedures in emerging hierarchies (Wright in prep. a).

The role of food preparation in social change has been discussed from a number of perspectives. Gender has been one concern (Hastorf 1991; 1998; Sherratt 1981; Wright 2000). A second issue centres on the degree to which feasting affected the initial beginnings of farming (Bender 1978; Hayden 2001). A third issue concerns the use of food preparation in negotiating political relations (the politics of gastronomy or commensal politics: Appadurai 1981; Dietler 1996; 2001; cf. Douglas 1972a; 1972b; 1984). Finally, questions have been raised about about the role of 'haute cuisines' in the emergence of socio-political hierarchies, and vice versa (Goody 1982; Joffe 1998; Wiessner & Schiefenhövel 1996).

Detailed discussion of these issues in relation to the wealth of Near Eastern data can be found in Wright (in prep. a). For the most part, it is too soon to address in depth how Çatalhöyük sheds light on these issues. Our evidence for the use of the ground-stone tools in food preparation is still only very preliminary, pending residue studies, other analyses, and larger samples. However, we can make a few general, and very provisional, observations.

1) Grinding and pounding of foodstuffs can serve

a number of basic purposes in food preparation, of both plants and animals. Detailed discussion of these purposes can be found elsewhere and will not be repeated here (Hillman 1984; Hillman *et al.* 1989; Stahl 1989; Wright 1994).

In our sample, grinding and abrading tools were found in the same contexts as plant remains, in a number of cases. The plant remains found in association with ground-stone artefacts are very diverse. They include cereals, acorns, lentils, tubers and hackberries. The contexts of these associations include bins and floors (e.g. Building 1) and midden deposits, some of which have evidence of *in situ* burning. Dietary diversity is also indicated by stable-isotope studies (Volume 4, Chapter 15).

Our own view is that the grinding and pounding tools associated with diverse plant species (not to mention animal bones) at Çatalhöyük could have been used to process any and all of these species, although such processing was not required for any of them (Hillman 1984; Stahl 1989; Wright 1994). It is essential to assume, in the absence of clear evidence to the contrary, that individual grinding / pounding artefacts or types were unspecialized and multi-functional. Ethnographic and archaeological data overwhelmingly support this assumption (Wright 1991; 1992b; 1994). In prehistoric societies in the Near East, there is no clear link between grinding / pounding tools and particular plant foods (such as cereals), although in later, complex societies based on intensive grain cultivation, breadmaking is a central function of certain types of tools (e.g. rotary querns). Likewise, there is nothing to prevent a tool used for food processing being used also for craft making.

2) Contextual evidence suggests that sandstone artefacts as well as those of andesite and basalt were probably used in connection with food preparation. The heavy use of andesite and basalt conforms to the expectations of material choices as documented in ethnography; that is, these materials combine surface roughness and durability, with low rates of particle detachment that would introduce grits into prepared foods.

However, the use of sandstone abrading slabs in food processing raises several conundrums. Sandstone, even relatively fine and dense sandstone, wears down heavily to very concave surfaces under conditions of extensive use over a long period (compare, for example, sandstone grinding slabs from PPNB Beidha, Jordan: Wright 1993; 2000). But the complete (Building 1) sandstone slabs are very shallow, as if not used over a long period. Sandstone also typically produces high rates of particle detachment under conditions of heavy grinding. One might therefore expect sandstone to have produced grits in prepared food that should show up as heavy wear in the human dentition.

But dental-wear patterns from the Çatalhöyük skeletons seemingly do not indicate high levels of abrasion (Volume 4, Chapters 12 & 24). More research on relationships between food preparation and dentition is clearly needed. Meanwhile, dental and other evidence (see below) suggest that grinding and pounding of foodstuffs did not play quite the same role in food preparation at Çatalhöyük as it did in other Neolithic villages.

3) Ground-stone artefacts from across the Neolithic Near East display distinctive regional styles, cultural practices and attitudes concerning food preparation and consumption. The material from Çatalhöyük fits this general picture of diversity. Although we have yet to compare this material to other Neolithic sites in central Anatolia, differences between this assemblage and those of contemporary sites in the Levant are very marked. They include (but are not limited to) the use of grinding slabs that were very carefully fashioned with flat bases and upright walls; and the use of stone vessels that have spouts (a feature extremely rare to absent in most Neolithic stone-vessel assemblages). Such vessels may suggest consumption of liquids and anticipate changes that attended the secondary products revolution (Wright in prep. a; cf. Sherratt 1981).

4) It is not at all clear that grinding tools played the same role in food preparation here as in other sites, for example, broadly coeval sites in the Levant (Wright 2000; in prep. a). At some Neolithic villages in western Asia, usually those situated next to a good source of grinding stones, grinding tools are large and heavy. At such sites, one sees essentially immovable grinding slabs (weighing up to 50 kilograms), with large use surfaces; and large manos demanding two hands to operate. These items testify to heavy-duty milling and suggest arduous work (as discussed in Wright 1993; 1994; 2000). At some sites, this pattern can be attributed to close proximity to sources of suitable stones. But some of these same sites also lack ovens (e.g. Beidha: Wright in prep. a).

The Çatalhöyük grinding tools are very different, with small grinding slabs and one-hand manos overwhelmingly dominating the heavier grinding equipment (so far). The Çatalhöyük grinding slabs are mostly small, light, and easily portable. (At least so far, very large slabs seem to come from later contexts: Çatalhöyük West and the Team Poznań area, where a very large slab was recovered along with loom weights and bone tools, in what appears to be a Chalcolithic context, (6948): Czerniak *et al.* 2001.) Undoubtedly this is a result, in part, of the fact that these artefacts were transported from as far away as Karadağ, some 40 km from Çatalhöyük. It may also relate to the fact that closed ovens are so common at Çatalhöyük.

These slabs could have been used in a wide variety of positions; sitting, holding the slab in the lap, moving slabs from place to place, etc. This raises questions about whether food processing at Çatalhöyük would have resulted in particular functional stresses that would show up in skeletons, adult females in particular (see Molleson 2000; Volume 4, Chapter 12). An osteological analysis of some 100 Natufian and Neolithic skeletons in the southern Levant, where many ground-stone assemblages are consistent with very arduous milling, showed that sexual dimorphism was actually greater in the Natufian than in the Neolithic, when both sexes displayed indications of heavier workloads (Peterson 1997; 2002).

5) In general, the contextual evidence suggests small-scale, household-based units of food preparation. As previously discussed, for the moment we do not see evidence (one way or another) for the use of ground-stone tools in feasting activities. There are no clusters suggesting large-scale group production of prepared food, and no indications of unusually large numbers of ground-stone artefacts discarded together. Nor do we see rare stone bowls associated with discard contexts that otherwise might suggest special consumption events. However, these observations are tentative and await further work.

Craft production

The Neolithic in western Asia involved an explosion in diversity of crafts produced in sedentary villages and this expansion is also part of the reason for the proliferation of ground stone in this period. Ground-stone artefacts clearly played a central role in the development of Neolithic craftsmanship. In addition to such items as stone bowls, figurines, and axes, all of which proliferated as the Neolithic began, ground-stone items were important in the rapid expansion of stone beadmaking at the beginning of the Aceramic Neolithic (Wright & Garrard 2003), whilst dressed masonry at some PPNB sites was obviously produced with robust hammers and axes. Ground-stone artefacts are central to the production of ceramics and other technologies (such as metalwork) that emerged later.

It is clear that the inhabitants of Çatalhöyük used ground-stone artefacts for production of diverse crafts. Direct evidence for ochre processing comes from the fine sandstone slab and fragmentary handstones recovered from the grinding feature in Building 1. Ochre milling can be related to a number of craft activities. One, of course, is paint making. We suspect that Çatalhöyük's painters sought out very fine-grained sandstone in order to pulverize ochre and other coloured minerals to the finest possible degree. We are in the process of exploring the role of ground-stone technology in painting and residues from ochre smeared tools have been removed for scientific analysis and comparison with paints found on walls. However, ochre also has other uses. It is commonly used in treating and preserving hides, and manos and other ground-stone tools also figure in hideworking, as documented in ethnographies and in experiments (e.g. Adams 1988).

Other artefacts that undoubtedly figured in craftmaking were various sandstone abraders; the fine marble and limestone polishing tools (e.g. for buffing plaster floors and walls); and the schist palettes (purpose unknown). That beads were being manufactured on site is evident from the occurrence of unfinished bead blanks. Neolithic stone-bead workshops in Jordan, dated to the same time range as Çatalhöyük, reveal that sandstone abraders and other small tools were an integral part of bead making (Wright & Garrard 2003). In addition, some of the fine bone tools were partly made by fine abrasion (Chapter 17) and we strongly suspect that small stone abraders are implicated here, too. For the most part, it is still too early to discuss the details of these technologies, but this work is in progress.

Conclusions

The Çatalhöyük ground-stone assemblage is a case of a highly-curated technology. Compared to ground-stone artefacts that we have studied from other Neolithic sites (both in Turkey and in the Levant), the assemblage from Çatalhöyük is an unusual one. The analysis of these artefacts is still at an early stage, so many questions are still being explored and cannot be resolved yet.

Acknowledgements

Adnan Baysal and Katherine Wright are grateful to Asuman Türkmenoğlu, Vedat Toprak and Cemal Göncüoğlu for their advice and assistance in understanding the raw materials. We also thank Graham Reed for inking the illustrations and preparing the figures. For useful discussions and general help, we are grateful to Ian Hodder, Shahina Farid, Craig Cessford, Douglas Baird, Louise Martin, Nerissa Russell, Wendy Matthews and Andrew Fairbairn.

Chapter 14

The Beads

Naomi Hamilton

This chapter will look at a range of topics concerning the beads from Çatalhöyük. These include frequency of occurrence, typology, material, colour, context, uses and manufacture. I have not carried out a technical study of the beads. A note on the mineralogy of a sample of almost 1000 of the beads excavated by the current team is reported in Chapter 18.

Beads occur in all types of context on site because of their small size, which has resulted in their being mixed into structural materials or dropped without hope of retrieval. Our intensive sampling system means that we have found them in such unlikely deposits as bricks and oven structures, where they would not usually be sought. In such contexts they are almost certainly accidental inclusions brought in with soil from external areas which has been used for the dumping of domestic refuse or for a variety of outdoor activities. The only clearly deliberate place of deposition, and the context in which the majority of beads are found, is burials. Although beads are found infrequently with burials, they can occur in large numbers. Occasional finds of groups of beads have also been made on the floors of buildings, and in external deposits. Unfortunately the larger groups found in external deposits came from Space 181, in very difficult excavation conditions in which recognition of tiny stone beads was unlikely, and therefore they were generally retrieved from flotation. This means that it is not possible to say whether they were deposited as a single string of beads, or were scattered. A number of unfinished beads from building floors are important for understanding both place and method of manufacture.

Recording of the beads needs a brief explanation. Altogether 1617 bead entries have been made on the data base for the East Mound excavations, but this includes 29 that are multiples forming the whole or part of groups regarded as necklaces or bracelets, reducing the number of individual entries to 1588. The fifteen 'necklace' groups are made up of a further 2750 beads, making a total of 4338 beads. Recording of bead groups offered some challenges within the finds system. An individual find recorded in the field should receive an 'X' number, but sometimes this number was given to a bead group. The possibility of recording necklaces as 'clusters' was considered, but this would have necessitated giving each bead in the group an individual number in the field, which could be very time consuming. In addition, many beads are black or dark brown and extremely small, and therefore they were frequently not observed in the field and were found in flotation, even in some cases when beads were known to be present in a burial. Therefore consistent recording was not practicable. The result has been a mixture of recording in groups and individually both in the field and in the laboratory. Where groups were found in burials or were definitely found together they have been given an additional 'N' number in a separate table of the data base. Where large numbers of beads came from flotation from units in Space 181 they were recorded individually, as it is not known whether or not they were found together although it is likely that they often were.

Almost all beads not deriving from burials were found in flotation samples, and as most are smaller than the 4-mm mesh used for dry sieving the remaining soil, it is likely that many more have not been retrieved.

Typology

The typology used in recording the beads was initially constructed as a method for re-examining the beads from Mellaart's excavation, a reassessment I carried out over two weeks in 1995 (Hamilton 1996, 246–8). Therefore a few types are completely absent from the current records but exist in Mellaart's material. Owing to time constraints, the original typology was fairly rough and ready, and contained a couple of catch all types: type 7, used for unusual shapes which only occurred once and seemed not to merit individual typing, often double-pierced or irregularly-shaped beads; and type 16, used for pendants, by which is meant items suspended from a piercing at one end or corner. However, type 16 was not used for deer teeth, real or imitation, although they could also be counted as pendants. Because of the specific nature of this group, and its importance in considering other issues such as economy, hunting, status and landscape use, deer teeth were given their own category, type 4. Similarly, a group of pendants made from *Unio* shell (mussel) and generally found with infant burials was later separated as type 27 because of the unity within the group and difference from other pendants. Type 16 covers all other pendants, including a range of shapes and materials. This is not entirely satisfactory, but explanatory (and subjective) notes are generally attached in the data base. The typology is shown in Table 14.1 (the suffix a indicates an unfinished bead).

The vast majority of beads belong to type 1. This is a simple circular bead with straight edges, often highly polished, that usually appears to have been sliced from a prepared cylinder of stone and then drilled from both sides (but see 'manufacture' below) although they are also made of bone and *Dentalium* shell. A type 1 bead has a diameter of less than 5 mm, and is usually around 1 mm thick although some are paper thin laminates of schist (the most common stone used for this type) and a number are considerably thicker. Beads of this type that exceed 5 mm in diameter are classed as type 21, but in all other respects the two groups are identical. Of the 4338 beads found on the East mound so far 3594 are type 1, and a further 208 are type 21, making 3802 altogether or 87.65 per cent of the total bead complement. All other types occur rarely, as is shown in Table 14.1.

Material

Beads are made from a range of materials. By far the most common are schist and limestones or impure marbles. Exotic stones such as serpentine, apatite and carnelian occur rarely. (For the sources of stone found at the site see Chapters 13 & 17.) The main shell in use is *Dentalium*, but *Unio* (freshwater mussel) is used for pendants and occurs in quantity on the site as food waste. Other marine shells including *arcularia*, *columbella*, *cowrie* and two types of *murex* are found occasionally (see Volume 4, Chapter 6). Clay is also used for beads, mainly restricted to a couple of types. Bone is not common (for a discussion of the bone beads see Chapter 16). Rare materials include lead and copper, obsidian, mica and red-deer incisors. (For evidence of copper use in central Anatolia at the earlier site of Aşikli Höyük see Esin 1995.)

Most of these materials are not readily available at the site. Mellaart noted that most come from

Table 14.1. *Typology and number of each type of bead found on the East Mound.*

Bead type	Description	Current excavation	Mellaart excavation
1	Slices with straight edges	3594	20,800+
2	Cylinders with straight edges	27 plus 7 possible	327+
3	Round flattish blobs with curved edges	3	107
4	Teeth	29	156+
5	Uncut shells	14	31
6	Cylinders, similar to type 2 but as long as they are wide	19	82
7	Miscellaneous shapes, e.g. birds, oddments		39+
8	Flat, square pierced cylinder	0	65
9	Squashed, pierced cylinder with straight edges	2	8
10	Cylinder with curved long edges	26	15
11	Very thin discs	1	3
12	Rectangular or square ellipse	1	131
13	Round 'button' with two holes that do not go through the whole bead	0	4
14	Oval 'button with two holes that do not go through the whole bead	0	9
15	Rounded cylinder, longer than wide	0	2
16	Pendant	22	38
17	Toggle	1	92
18	Double axe with slight flange	1	23
19	Squashed cylinder with curved edges	8	18
20	Sliced shells, except *Dentalium*	8	25
21	Large example of type 1	208	192+
22	Spherical	39	5
23	Squashed sphere	14	0
24	Rectangular, pierced widthways with irregular or trapezoidal section	16	0
25	Rectangular, pierced widthways with triangular section	1	0
26	Biconical	3	0
27	Unio pendant, often double pierced	11	8+

sources involving at least several day's travel (1964a, 97) yet the supply seems to be plentiful, suggesting regular long-distance travel or contacts. Clay and bone would be easily to hand, yet these are not the favoured materials from which to make beads despite the ease of working clay, and the fact that bones can often be strung without the need for piercing. Of the 4338 beads found during the current excavations, only 71 were of bone and 110 of clay. A number of the bone items are imitation deer teeth, and many of the clay ones were found in one unit, (3021), are unfired and frequently therefore broken spherical beads in a collection of unfired clay objects apparently thrown from a roof (see below). They seem to have been made as transitory items, perhaps playthings for a child, or made and used for a ceremony or event that did not require them to be either beautifully made, or retained afterwards. Their discovery does suggest that clay may have been utilized far more frequently, but not fired. This group of objects was partly preserved by the burning of Building 1, to which they lay adjacent. Beads of clay made to last seem to be rare.

Many of the beads are similar to those found in other sites of central Anatolia, at both slightly earlier sites such as Aşıklı Höyük (Esin 1991) where they are scarce, and later sites as at Hacılar (Mellaart 1970), Canhasan (French 1962, 169–72) and Köşk Höyük (Silistreli 1984; 1986; 1988) where they are not rare. However, the type 1 beads of Çatalhöyük stand out for their fineness, high quality and variety of colour and stone variety.

Material by level

Schist and the various coloured marbles and limestones used for type 1 and type 21 beads occur in all levels of the site, from Level Pre-XII.D onwards, and were presumably widely available. Schist is the most common stone in use for bead making, and being generally black, dark brown or a dark greenish-grey, these colours dominate the assemblage.

Dentalium shell beads occur almost exclusively in Levels VI and V of the site. Odd finds have been made as early as Level Pre-XII.B, which produced a single bead. This pattern is roughly the same for the Mellaart assemblage as for the current excavation, only one necklace before Level VI has more than one *Dentalium* shell bead and that is in Level VII. Presumably this relates to the availability of the material, which comes from the Mediterranean, and therefore is of relevance to issues of trade, exchange, and use of the landscape. *Dentalium* shells are almost always sliced up into type 1/21 beads, although they also occur as type 2 and type 6, i.e. short and longer cylinders. Finds of complete *Dentalium* shells are very unusual, and they were not used complete on necklaces in the way they were in surrounding areas such as the Levant and Cyprus (see for instance Belfer-Cohen 1995, 11–14; Dikaios 1953, 303–4, pl. xcix).

A dark green/blue/grey mottled serpentine is used mainly in Levels VIII and VII, for a restricted group of shapes, with very few later occurrences. Black serpentine is used for a wider range of types, and occurs as early as Level Pre-XII, but it is extremely rare at the site. The turquoise-coloured stone, probably apatite, used for various unusual bead shapes is found only in Levels VI–IV. Again, this is of interest in terms of material acquisition. How far away is the source of the stone, and was it collected directly by people living at Çatalhöyük or was it traded? The nearest source of apatite is not known. Carnelian is also present as a rarity. A number of carnelian beads were found in Levels VIII, V and IV in Mellaart's material, and several probable carnelian beads have been found in the early levels by the current team.

Types by material

Because the typology relates mainly to form, it is possible for the same type of bead to be made from a range of materials. In a few cases this is not so, for instance type 27 is defined as being made of *Unio*. Some shapes seem to be made particularly, if not exclusively, of certain types of stone, although the reason for this is not clear. For instance, type 12 and type 24 beads seem to be made almost exclusively of two types of stone, a white crystalline marble and a blue/green/grey veined serpentine, although a handful of type 12 beads are made of a turquoise stone, probably apatite, as is the single type 15, a variant of type 24. This colour of serpentine is rare, and hardly occurs among other types. Similarly, while white marble is common, this particular type is not, although a number of type 2 and type 6 beads are made from it. Type 12 and type 24 beads occur only in the early middle period of the site, with the serpentine beads in Levels VIII and VII and two white marble ones in Level IX. Other serpentine beads occur occasionally also in Levels VI and V in different types, and five black and a single blue-grey type 1 were found in Space 181 Level Pre-XII.

A turquoise-coloured stone, probably apatite rather than real turquoise, tends to be used for unusual shapes assigned to type 7 (see Hamilton 1996, 248 and tables) with just a handful of type 1s. In particular, types 18 and 19 are generally made of this stone, although a few are of serpentine and coal.

Type 1/21 beads occur in a number of materials, but predominantly in stones identified by Brian

Jackson (Chapter 18) as schist and a form of marble in many colours (often impure and appearing more as limestone, although this group also probably includes those identified for Mellaart as fossil coral). Schist does not seem to have been used for any other type of bead. Its laminating character accounts for the paper-thin beads found. This form of marble, often with a matt finish, is also used almost exclusively for type 1/21 beads, although a crystalline white form is used for type 12 and type 24 beads. *Dentalium* shell is also used commonly for type 1/21 beads. Type 2 beads are not made of any particular material, but can occur in *Dentalium*, marble, serpentine, copper and clay. Type 22 beads are always made of clay with a single exception in turquoise-coloured stone in Mellaart's material, and type 23 beads are generally of clay, with a few in turquoise-coloured stone.

Types by level

The most common types, 1 and 21, occur in all levels of the site (Table 14.2). However, they seem to be most common in the earlier levels. This is difficult to assess from the current excavations, because little has been dug above Level VI, and the volume of excavation at each level has been heavily skewed by working on a number of buildings that Mellaart had already largely removed. Only a tiny number of type 1/21 beads has been recovered from Levels XI (6) and XII (14) but far larger numbers were found in Space 181. Level Pre-XII.A has 145 and Level Pre-XII.B has 180, while the earlier levels had fewer. Levels IX (164) and VIII (167) are consistent with the upper levels of Space 181. However, most of these beads were individual finds, while the burials from the North Area produced large numbers of type 1 beads from a small number of contexts. Mellaart's material also shows a predominance of type 1/21 beads in the early middle levels of the site, with only a few occurrences in the upper levels and a concentration in Levels VIII–VI. While these are the most extensively-excavated areas, which could skew the data again, the necklaces with large numbers of beads come from these three levels, especially Level VIII. It is noticeable that most of these are made of stone; *Dentalium* shell beads occur very rarely, and usually as singles, before Level VI.

Table 14.2. *Beads by level, excluding necklaces.*

Level	No. of beads
N.V–IV	17
N.VI–V	172
N.VII–VI	16
VI.B	2
VII	84
VIII	192
IX	173
X	103
XI	17
XII	20
Pre-XII.A	178
Pre-XII.B	191
Pre-XII.C	80
Pre-XII.D	38
KOPAL	4

Deer-teeth beads/pendants are unusual, but of special interest. They are the incisors of adult male red deer, and have to be removed from the animal as they are not shed. Each animal has only two. Deer teeth are found mainly in the early levels of the site, particularly Levels VIII and VII, and it is in these levels that large numbers are found together. For instance Mellaart found a necklace of 32 teeth with the burial of a child in Level VIII, while another Level VIII necklace had 14. A Level VII necklace had ten and another had seven. This would necessitate killing a considerable number of deer. One Level IX necklace had six teeth but otherwise prior to Level VIII they occur singly. After Level VII real deer teeth are rare and occur singly again. However, bone imitations are also found, indicating that the genuine article was not only desirable but also hard to come by. An infant buried in Level VIII (4406) was wearing anklets of imitation deer teeth, and an elderly female (5169) was buried with a group of what seem to be unpierced imitation teeth or preforms. An earlier imitation comes from Level IX, but on the whole this is a later development, with imitations occurring mainly from Level VI onwards, at a time when genuine deer teeth become very rare. It is interesting that, where burial data can be linked to them, they have been found with infants/juveniles ((4406); VIII.31 child) and with adult females ((5169); IX.1; VIII.25?). Perhaps this is not surprising, as the majority of necklaces seem to have been found with females and juveniles, but it presents questions regarding the acquisition of bead materials, particularly when hunting is involved.

Manufacture

Bead manufacture seems to have taken place on site, within buildings (and possibly outside buildings as well). A number of unfinished beads have been found in Buildings 17 and 18 (Volume 3, Chapter 2). A larger number of unfinished beads has been found in Space 181 in external deposits. The only evidence of methods of bead making is tool marks and unfinished items. This evidence is extremely rare. The vast majority of type 1 and type 21 stone beads appear to have been made from prepared cylinders, polished on the outer edges in such as way as sometimes to leave facetted surfaces all the way round. These cylinders were then probably sliced up using obsidian blades, and the discs of stone were then pierced from each side, again probably using obsidian points. However, this is based on general observations and assumptions, as unpierced discs of stone that could be bead preforms are very rare (e.g. 814.H1, a surface find). A few recent discoveries in the early levels of the site suggest that this may be incorrect, or at least incorrect for some beads at that time. A number of unfinished beads have been found which suggest that thin slabs of stone were roughly shaped, then pierced, and then the outside edges polished down to the desired size and roundness. These unfinished beads are marked as type 1a or type 21a in the data base. In almost all cases they have broken in half during piercing, and have thus been abandoned. Bone beads seem to have been roughed out with blades and then worn down and polished with sandstone.

Examples of unfinished stone beads are found in Building 17, Level IX. In Space 182, the subsidiary room, four unfinished type 1 beads were found in deposits on or just above the floor of Phase B (5229.H2–3 in floor use deposits, and 5221.H1–2 in the immediately overlying packing layer), alongside a number of complete type 1 beads (5229.H1, 5221.H2, 5222.H1, 5223.H1, 5224.H1–2, 5225.H1, 5226.H1 & 5228.H1, these units all being equivalent to (5221), which was divided into squares for excavation). All these beads were made of a reddish-brown marble rather than the blackish schist, which is most common. The finished beads are all standard type 1 and type 21 and would normally have been interpreted as 'lost' beads that had fallen from a necklace and accidentally been trampled into debris on a floor. The presence of incompletely-shaped examples that have broken through the piercing suggests that they were being made here, and that some complete examples were swept up with the manufacturing debris. Fourteen more beads, all finished, were found in the overlying room infill, several of which were of schist, the remainder of reddish-brown marble. Thus although we have a number of unfinished beads in Space 182, all in deposits overlying the floor, no unfinished beads were found on the floor, nor were unfinished examples found in the higher infill deposits which did contain a number of complete beads but all in low density (one or two beads per unit). This suggests that manufacture was taking place in the room, but the debris was not *in situ*. However, the evidence is inconclusive, in part because of the low numbers involved.

In Space 170, the main room of Building 17, nine type 1 beads of black schist were found in floor-use deposit (5021), on the final floor around the hearth in the southeast corner. Given the presence of bead-making debris in the adjoining room at the same level, it is possible that this too represents evidence of bead manufacturing, although all are complete. Three flotation samples were taken from (5021), the first only 10 l and with no beads, the second 30 l with one bead, and the third 30 l, taken when lifting a scapula. This sample contained eight beads, showing a concentration of beads in one area. Very few beads were found elsewhere in Building 17, just ten, each found alone. Of these, two were on floors, one in rake-out, one in floor make-up, and the rest in fill. This is the type of density most common on the site, highlighting the unusual nature of the groups discussed above.

A similar situation is seen in Building 18, Level X, where a number of unfinished bone and stone beads were found amongst a collection of complete ones, largely in ashy occupation deposits around hearths or ovens at the southern edge of Space 171. Beads occur occasionally in many of these deposits, but clusters were found in the later phases consisting of some complete and some unfinished but broken beads of stone, as well as unfinished bone beads. Thus (4530), the latest ashy occupation or rake-out deposit from over F.473, contained eleven beads, nine of them stone of which all but one were schist, and one of these was broken during manufacture. The other two were of bone, one of them unfinished. The previous rake-out in the same place, (4533), contained five complete stone beads, three of them black schist, one reddish-brown marble, one white marble. Rake-out or occupation relating to the underlying oven F.477 also had a number of beads in it, (4539) the latest unit, had four stone beads of different colours and a bone pendant. The deposit below it (4540) contained six beads, four of them of schist and three of these unfinished due to breakage. These are all from Phase 2 occupation, but unfinished bone beads were found in occupation or rake-out from two ovens of Phase 1, a roughed out 'teardrop'/deer tooth imitation bead/pendant from (4587), associated with oven F.501, and another from (4578), associated with oven F.499. A single complete stone bead was found in each of these deposits. A third unfinished imitation deer tooth was found in Space 172 in probable floor-use deposit (4680), along with a single complete stone bead. (Only five beads were found altogether in this space.) Again, the presence of some broken unfinished beads among completed ones suggests manufacturing in the building, with debris swept into the ash, whereas without the unfinished ones, the other beads would have been regarded as losses during use rather than production. Whether manufacture actually took place at the fireside, to take advantage of the added light, is uncertain but seems likely.

Space 181 also contained a number of unfinished beads. Their contexts are varied. (4838), a large unit (1100 l of dry-sieved soil) contained 33 beads in the three 30 l flotation samples taken, most of them of a reddish or light brown shiny marble, but some of black or greenish schist. Of these, seven were broken during manufacture and not finished, all of them made of marble rather than schist. The distribution of the beads was very even, with nine in Sample 4838.2 (east), of which three were unfinished; eleven from Sample 4838.3 (centre), four of them unfinished; and thirteen from Sample 4838.4 (west), three unfinished. This suggests that bead production was taking place either *in situ* or nearby, with debris being deposited in this midden unit. (4839) was rather smaller (480 l of dry-sieved soil) and produced 15 beads from two 30 l flotation samples, all but one (of shell) made of a brown marble, and four of them unfinished and broken. Again, the distribution was even, with eight beads in Sample 4839.2, three of them unfinished; and six in Sample 4839.3, one unfinished. (4865), a huge unit (2340 l of dry sieve) had six beads in it, three of them shell, one schist, and two brown marble, of which one was unfinished. However, the distribution was very different. Of the three 30l flotation samples taken, the east and west ones contained no beads, while Sample 4865.4 (north) had four, one of them unfinished, and the remaining two were shell beads found in the dry sieve. Although there is an unfinished bead here, the density is extremely low. (4866), another large unit (1110 l) had 13 beads, of which one was bone, three shell, and the remainder stones of various colours. A single brown marble one was unfinished. Again, three flotation samples were taken, with Sample 4866.2 (east) containing six beads, one of them unfinished; Sample 4866.3 (west) containing five beads, one unfinished; and Sample 4866.4 (north) with no beads. The remaining two were shell beads found in the dry sieve. The context of each of these units is midden, from Level Pre-XII.A, so it is unclear how the beads arrived there. The different densities of beads within units that all contained unfinished beads suggest that they were not all deposited in the same way. (4838) and (4839) might have evidence of *in situ* production, while (4865) and (4866) may contain debris from production elsewhere.

(4842) is a pit fill from Level Pre-XII.A, and contained twelve beads in a small unit (only 60 l of dry-sieved soil), one of them made of shell, one possible imitation deer tooth of bone and most of the others brown marble. Six of these were unfinished, including the bone one. Two 30 l flotation samples were taken, a general one and a basal one. All eleven beads were found in the general sample, indicating that they are all part of the later fill. The high percentage of unfinished beads in this group indicates production debris, but it is apparently not *in situ*. (4868) is a fire spot (390l of dry sieved soil) in Level Pre-XII.A containing seven beads, one of them shell, the rest various colours of marble, of which one in the typical reddish-brown was unfinished. Three 30 l flotation samples were taken, with Sample 4868.2 (east) containing one bead; Sample 4868.3 (west) containing two beads, one unfinished; and Sample 4868.4 (north) containing four beads. Although this is an 'activity spot', the density of bead material is very low and not suggestive of *in situ* production, despite the presence of an unfinished bead.

In Level Pre-XII.B two units contained unfinished, broken beads, both in midden contexts. (5283) is a very small unit (30 l dry sieve) but eight beads were recovered from the single 30l flotation sample, four of grey schist, four of brown marble, one of which was unfinished. (5290) is a huge unit (2325 l dry sieve) which contained 43 beads, three of them shell pendants, the rest a mixture of schist and marble with a single serpentine bead. One white marble bead was unfinished. These came from seven unequal flotation units taken for different reasons: Sample 5290.6, a 2l sample from an ashy patch, had one bead; Sample 5290.11, a 5 l sample from an ashy spread, had two beads; and Sample 5290.5, a 30 l sample from a distinctive mixed patch, western upper area, had three. The large general samples had greater numbers of beads, but at a lower average density; twelve in Sample 5290.4 (upper central), one unfinished; six in Sample 5290.7 (lower central); seven in Sample 5290.10 (eastern) and nine in Sample 5290.12 (lower western). A single unfinished bead in such a large unit tells us little, but it is interesting that most beads came from the general midden rather than from the ashy spreads, given the discovery of bead production debris in ashy spreads within buildings.

An interesting point regarding bead production is that the majority of unfinished beads are made on a particular hard and shiny reddish or light brown marble, rather than the black, dark grey, dark brown or greenish schist which is more commonly used for beads. This marble is not an easy stone to work, and it does not occur widely later on at the site, perhaps for this reason. This may explain the number of beads of this material broken during manufacture compared to the very few unfinished schist beads. Schist is present in the earliest levels alongside this marble, but later becomes dominant, while other, softer limestones and marbles in a range of colours but especially reds and pinks are also used. Schist laminates, and would thus be easy to divide into slices ready for piercing, while piercing would also be fairly straightforward owing to the formation of the rock, particularly the presence of mica. The few unfinished schist beads seem in all but one instance to be laminates that broke away from larger beads and were abandoned, although in one case this was before shaping had been completed.

4530.H3 is unusual here, in that it had not been shaped much before two attempts at piercing had been made, one on each side but not opposite each other. They seem to show two different types of drill in use, one a simple drill the other a tubular drill. Given that this is more a small slab of stone than a bead preform, it may have been a practice piece. It is too small to have acted as an anvil. Wright & Garrard (2003, 279–81), in their study of bead production in Neolithic Jordan, also found that the majority of unfinished beads were made of a particular type of stone. In this case they suggest surplus production and stockpiling of one variety of bead while consuming other types, presumably manufactured elsewhere. That is, they suggest specialized production such as seen by large-scale producers in an ethnographic study of bead making in India (Kenoyer *et al.* 1991). In the case of Çatalhöyük, however, the quantities are too low and fit the model of household production. It is most likely that one type of stone proved particularly difficult to work although its shiny qualities made it worth the effort.

Other evidence of on-site production has been found in burial F.563 in Building 17. Here, an elderly female (5169) was buried with a cluster of twelve bone objects that appear to be imitation deer teeth in the process of manufacture. None has been pierced, and none is finished, the shaping is still rough, and they are not polished. Whether or not these were destined to be pierced and hung on a necklace, rather than being carried in a bag (which they may have been buried in, from the close clustering found), there is no way of telling. However, their manufacture was incomplete, and may well have been carried out in Building 17, perhaps by the person with whom they were buried.

Shell ornaments were also probably made on site. The pendants found generally with infant burials are made on freshwater mussel shells, which are found in large quantities throughout the site and are presumably food waste. 4518.H15 may be an unfinished shell pendant. Shaped into an oblong it has not been pierced but may have been intended as a pendant, although it could have been used for other decorative purposes.

Use

Beads are clearly ornaments. We know from their position in burials that they were worn as necklaces and bracelets. It is also possible that some were attached to fabric. Whether the use of bead ornaments was indicative of status of some sort is unclear. Mellaart believed he found most necklaces with adult females and with juveniles, and that adult males were sometimes buried with necklaces of just a few beads or pendants rather than the large numbers of tiny beads. However, they were not common finds, although they were the most commonly found grave goods. (Grave goods of any kind are rare at Çatalhöyük.) The experience of the current team is that grave goods are very rare, but that beads are found in a variety of contexts. While most of these are post-depositional and probably accidental, a group of beads (2798.X1) was found on the floor near the southern oven of Building 2, Space 117. This shows that bead necklaces and bracelets were unlikely to be purely funerary items, and the large numbers of beads found occasionally in midden contexts support this. As discussed above, the majority of beads are made of imported materials, and bead production of this quality and quantity required a major investment of time and effort. Although no studies on bead production have yet been carried out by the project, it is clear that the tiny stone beads were time-consuming to make, and Kenoyer's study offers ample evidence of this (Kenoyer *et al.* 1991). They are not, therefore, everyday items easily available to everyone in the form in which we find them. There are necklaces of sometimes thousands and often hundreds of tiny beads made from various stones, or there are just handfuls of beads made of rare and beautiful stones or minerals carved and polished into unusual shapes. They should probably be regarded as exotica to some extent, yet they were also suitable for burial and therefore disposable as well. Wright & Garrard suggest plausibly that sedentism brought with it different needs as regards social identification and that the sudden increase in body adornment in the form of beads as sedentism took hold in Jordan might well have played a part in that (Wright & Garrard 2003, 277–8). The materials used are not so rare that burial can be seen as removing valuable items from circulation. Sometimes they were even bone or clay, yet they must be seen as valued items. The bracelets and anklets found on skeleton (4406) seem very large for a baby of that age to have worn, and may have been supplied solely for burial.

However, this may be an incomplete picture. (3021) contained a large number of roughly spherical beads of unbaked clay alongside fragments of unbaked clay figurines. Many of the beads were broken, and both they and the figurines had largely been preserved by the burning of Building 1, beside which they lay. They were placed in an inter-building space that is probably not extensive (although the southern extent of Space 153 is not known). Unfortunately, it was not until the soil had been removed that the excavator decided, looking at the unexcavated section, that (3021) actually comprised four different layers of deposit, retrospectively numbered (3053), (3054), (3055) and

Table 14.3. *Beads by context type, excluding necklaces.*

Context	No. of beads
Activity	44
Cluster	9
Construction	110
Fill	350
Floors	216
Midden	525
Natural	2

(3056). It was not possible to retrospectively assign the finds to these different units, which were all retrieved from a 70 l flotation sample. A second, 36 l, sample contained no beads, suggesting that they were genuinely concentrated in one part of the unit. They appear to have fallen, or been thrown, from the roof of an adjacent building. Their crude manufacture, and unbaked condition, suggest that they were not made to last. Perhaps they were children's playthings, or perhaps they were made and used for a transitory occasion, a game, ritual or ceremony of some kind. The presence of figurines alongside the beads, a mixture of animal and humanoid figurines, points perhaps to some form of ritual, although the use and purpose of figurines is not clear and is addressed in Chapter 9. What *is* clear, however, is that these beads were preserved fortuitously rather than by design, and therefore it is possible, perhaps likely, that clay was actually used frequently for beads intended for everyday and casual wear. This both suggests that the incidence of beads utilizing this common and easily-available material was far higher than has been thought, and that the carefully-produced beads made to last that we find predominantly in burials were indeed used largely for special occasions or purposes (such as burial), or were regarded as items of significant value. Whether this can then be used to infer special status for those buried with necklaces is difficult to assess, particularly when considering the possibility of ascribed versus achieved status. Given that necklaces are found most commonly with juveniles, and particularly with infants, who cannot have either achieved status yet nor made the necklaces themselves, it is perhaps most likely that they represent the value attached to the dead child, in a society in which high infant mortality was a matter of serious concern.

Conclusion

Beads are rare finds at Çatalhöyük. They occur is small numbers in a range of contexts (Table 14.3), but seem to be deposited deliberately only in burials where necklaces of hundreds of beads are occasionally found. They are made of a variety of materials, mainly stones imported from unknown sources, as well as shells from the Mediterranean, indicating long distance trade or travel. Easily-available materials such as clay and bone are little used, but there is some evidence to suggest that clay may have been used more widely for beads (and other body decoration, see Chapter 9) but left unbaked, and therefore they have not normally survived. Beads seem to have been made at the site, probably on a household basis, but manufacturing evidence is too scarce at present to say whether every household produced beads or only a few specialists. The exotic nature of some beads, the level of work required for their manufacture, and the possibility that clay beads were common for everyday wear, suggests that the beads in burials may have been items of some value, but there is no evidence that they denote structural social status. There is scope for more detailed analysis of bead materials, their sources, and production methods in future years, and hopefully further excavation will also provide fuller contextual information for interpreting beads.

Chapter 15

Çatalhöyük Basketry

Willeke Wendrich

Preservation

Basketry at Çatalhöyük is preserved as phytolith remains, impressions in the soil and impressions on other objects, mostly clay balls and platters. Extant phytolith basketry remains occur mostly in relation to burials, where the burial pits were closed off with a dense clay layer. Non-funerary uses of basketry are mostly found immediately on top or in between clayey floor layers. During excavation these basketry and matting remains are usually discovered when the adhering upper soil layer is peeled back, thus resulting in a 'split' basket with a fragmentary top layer and an almost complete bottom layer. When a substantial amount of phytolith remains are present, this basket is split in equal halves and appears as a white, spirally shaped deposit of phytoliths. Often, however, one or both layers appears as an impression in the soil with some phytolith remains adhering to it. The layers form a 'negative' of the original basket where the phytolith remains have collapsed into the soil impression that came into existence after the object was deposited. Coiled basketry thus appears either as concentric depressions with protruding soil ridges, which indicate the indents where the coils of the basket were sewn together, or as white coloured spirals with soil lines visible in between (Fig. 15.1). Plaited matting appears mostly as impressions and soil colourations on clayey floors. A curved patch of phytolith remains indicates that the basket was damaged before deposition. When the 'winder', the sewing strip that connects the bundles, has worn off, the bundle material is not held together and forms an ongoing patch of plant fibres (Fig. 15.2).

The source of the impressions on the clay objects (mostly balls, but there are some fragments of platters),

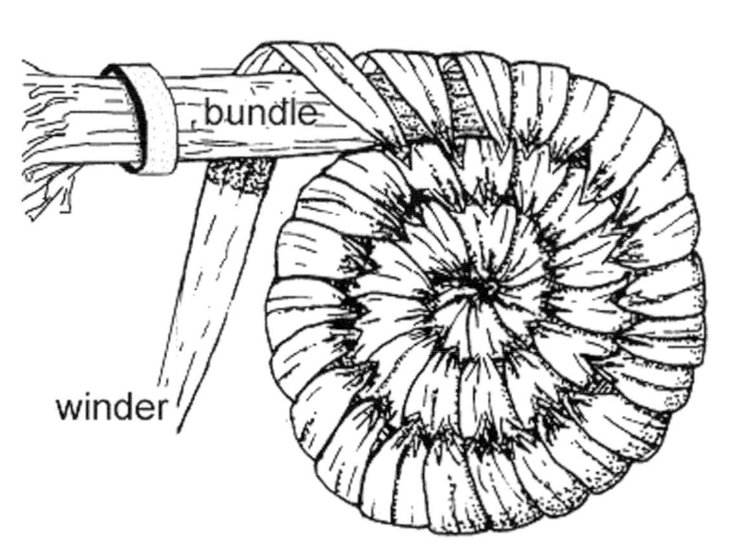

Figure 15.1. *Coiling (left) and the appearance of phytolith coiled basketry remains at Çatalhöyük (3228.X2, CD catalogue number 003, right). The drawing shows a ring of bone used during production as a gauge for the consistency of the bundle width, although such use at Çatalhöyük has not been attested with certainty.*

merits some discussion. One of the theories of the function of the clay balls is that they were used for cooking: after heating in the fire they were perhaps put in baskets to bring the contents to the boil (see below). The impressions on the clay balls, however, are not likely to have originated from this procedure. The impressions were clearly made when the clay was still soft, while the use of these clay balls in water-filled baskets would have resulted in different traces because of the hardening of the clay during heating. Furthermore, the impressions in the clay objects not only reflect coiled basketry, but also plaited matting (Fig. 15.3). Irrespective of their function it, therefore, seems more likely that the clay balls were put into baskets or on mats immediately after they were shaped, so they would stay clean during the drying period.

Figure 15.2. *Indication of pre-depositional damage (wear) on a coiled basket: the winders have worn away and the bundle material of several bundles appear as an ongoing patch of phytolith fibre remains (4931.S2, CD catalogue number 019). (Photograph by Michael Ashley.)*

Techniques and tools

As shown in Figure 15.3, at least two distinct techniques occur at Çatalhöyük: coiling and plaiting. The occurrence of patches of phytoliths over some of the skeletons could be interpreted as a layers of plant leaves and stems. Alternatively, these seemingly unconnected phytolith remains may indicate other matting techniques such as widely spaced twining or pierced matting (Fig. 15.4). The traces are too unclear, however, to be certain and, moreover, could only be studied from photographs. Both twined and pierced matting techniques require simple horizontal looms, for which there is at present no indication at Çatalhöyük. In contrast, coiling and plaiting do not require any fixed structures. The only implements are simple pointed bone or wooden tools such as awls or needles. Coiling is a versatile technique used for the production of baskets and, possibly, coaster-like mats. A bundle of plant material (often grass or straw) is fastened in a coil by winding a single leaf strip ('winder') around the bundle and fastening it with a stitch through the previous bundle of the spiral (cf. Fig. 15.1). Coiling can be used to produce baskets with very different properties: from very fine, thin walled, watertight containers to large coarse and sturdy storage baskets. Intricate decorative patterns can be produced by using

Figure 15.3. *Impressions of coiled basketry on a fragment of a platter (4298.X2, left) and of twill plaited matting on a clay ball (1063.S178, right). (Photographs by Michael Ashley.)*

winders with different colours, or by making stitched patterns over several bundles (Wendrich 1999, 217–25; 2000). The coiling technique can be used to produce an enormous variety of shapes, including footed baskets, baskets with inner rims to rest a lid on, bottle-shaped baskets, and straight-sided rectangular baskets. Since there is hardly any technical constraint, the skill of the producer and local tradition is the limit.

The centres of the Çatalhöyük coiled baskets were all slightly elongated. The basket was started with a straight bundle of approximately 25 mm. The elongated shape of the centre was gradually compensated for and finally the mat, or basket base, was rounded. One basket had a foot underneath with a height of one coil. No rims survived.

Tools used for the production of coiled basketry are few. The bundles have to be pierced to pass the winder through. This can be done with a needle or awl. Bird or large fish bones, for instance, are eminently suitable as basket making tools. Bone rings could have been employed as tools to guard the consistency of the bundle width, by feeding new bundle material through the ring (Fig. 15.1). Probably the bone rings found at Çatalhöyük were not used as such, however, since none of them are completely round and they vary in maximum diameter between 10.7 and 19.3 mm, which seems to be too coarse in comparison with the basketry. The inner diameter of a bone ring found near basketry remains in Space 156 is 10.7 mm, while the bundle diameter of the basket is only 5.1 mm.

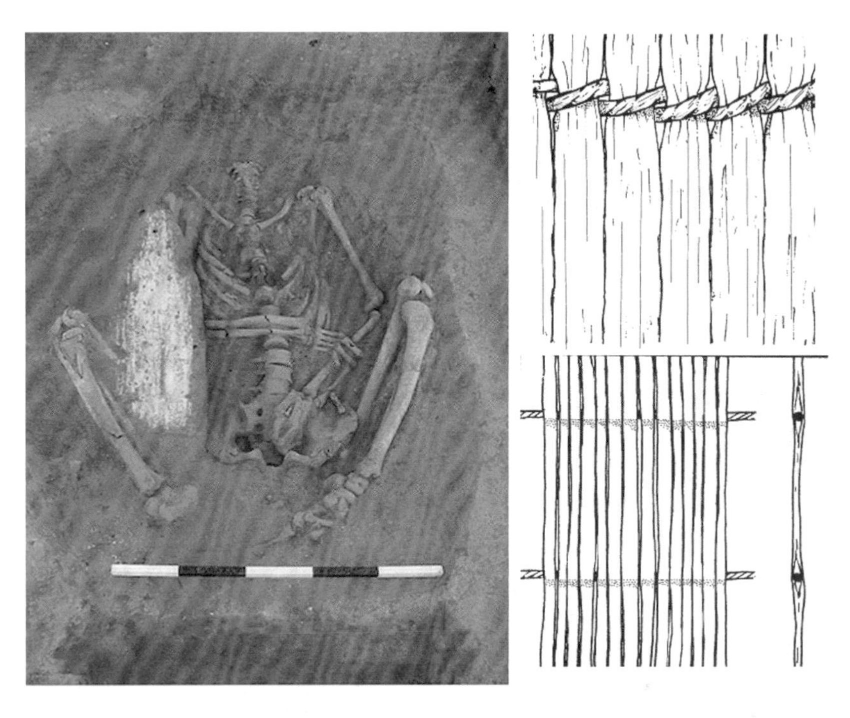

Figure 15.4. *Widely-spaced twined matting (upper right) and pierced matting (lower right). These techniques could explain the patches of seemingly unconnected plant materials covering some of the bodies such as burial F.492 (left), but have not been attested with certainty.*

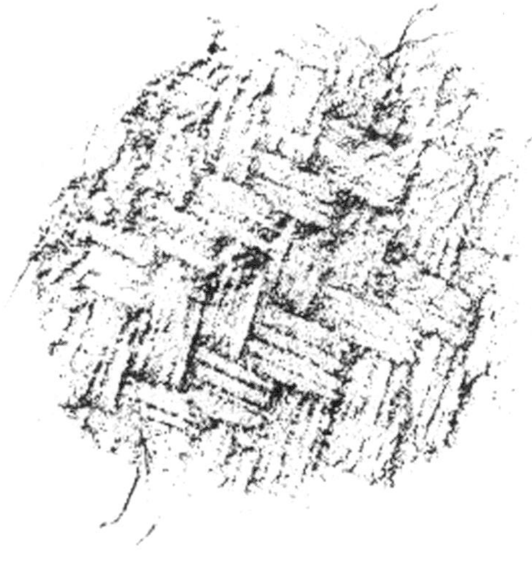

Figure 15.5. *Burial F.460 with remains of twill plaited matting and drawing of impression of twill plaited matting (from 1889.X48).*

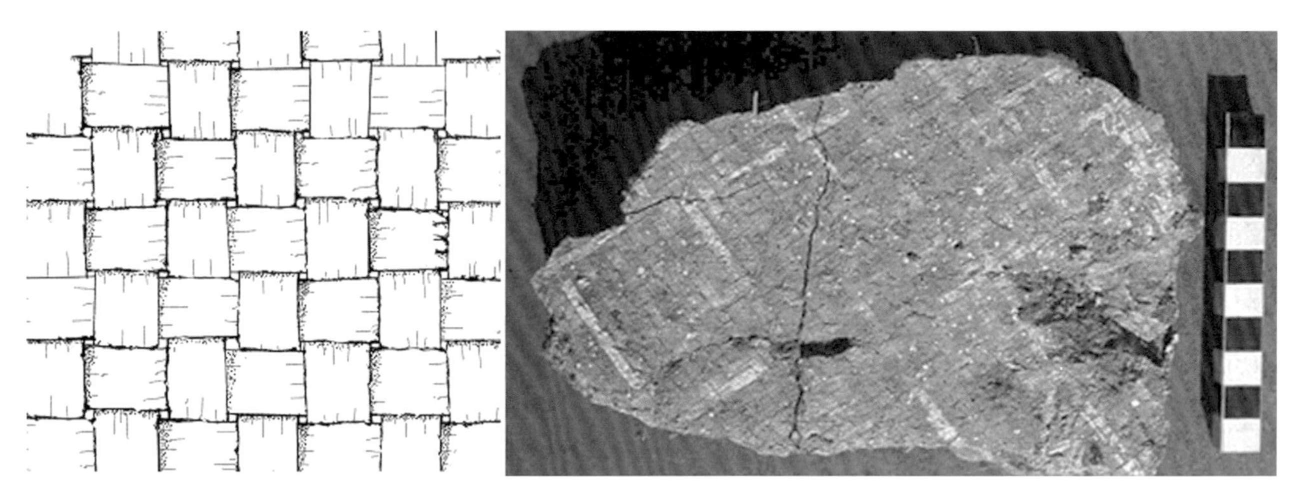

Figure 15.6. *Drawing of tabby plaited matting and tabby floor matting from Mellaart's excavation. (Photograph by Ian Todd.)*

Plaiting is a technique that requires even less in the way of tools. A knife to cut off excess material is sufficient. Indications of plaited floor matting in a twill pattern have been found on clay balls and as phytolith remains in the North Area (3860). Traces of similar matting were found on top of a skeleton (Fig. 15.5). Photographs of the Mellaart excavations show that during excavations in the 1960s several large patches of tabby plaited matting were uncovered (Fig. 15.6).

Materials

Analysis of some of the phytolith basketry remains has been performed by Dr A. Rosen (Volume 4, Chapter 9). The materials used were sedges and grasses. Exact identification of phytolith remains is extremely difficult, but the identifications given for various coiled basketry were *Cyperus* species, wild panicoid grass leaves, *Agropyron* inflorescence and stem as well as cereal straw.

The bundle and winders of coiled basketry are usually made of two different raw materials. The surviving phytolith remains are those of the bundle material, while the winders have mostly not been preserved and thus the material that determined the basket's appearance is not known. From the impressions on clay balls it seems that both grass leaves and strips of the epiderm of *Cyperus* stems could have been used. The material used for the plaited matting has not been determined, but the strongly-veined appearance of the twill impressions, compared to the smooth appearance of the tabby plaited matting indicate that the selection of raw materials was purposeful and linked to a specific application and technique.

Sizes, strength, flexibility and uses

The two basketry techniques that have been identified with certainty in Çatalhöyük, probably had quite distinct uses. Plaiting (both tabby and twill) is generally used for the production of matting that covers large areas. Plaiting demands much less material and effort to produce the considerable square footage necessary for floor matting. The few traces of plaiting show that the mats are made of strips of unidentified plant material with a width ranging from 10–20 mm.

As has been mentioned above, coiling is a versatile technique. By varying the ratio between the size of the bundle and the winders in relation to the shape and size of the basket, coiling can produce flexible to rigid mats or containers. Since the time and amount of material involved in producing coiled basketry is considerable, coiling is in general used for containers rather than mats. Containers require a certain rigidity of the fabric which is provided by a greater thickness of the bundles in relation to the size of the object.

The most likely uses for basketry are cooking, storage and transport (of dry and wet goods). In order to render baskets water tight both bundle and winder have to be quite fine and the plant material used has to be able to expand through the absorption of moisture. As will be discussed below, the Çatalhöyük basketry certainly had these properties and, therefore, could have been used for holding fluids, such as water or milk, and even for cooking.

Coiled basketry is less suitable as a means of transport. Compared to plaiting, twining or weaving techniques, coiling uses up a large quantity of material in order to build up the same space to contain goods. This is not a problem for stationary storage baskets, but to carry goods in coiled basketry means carrying a great deal of extra weight.

In areas of the world where there is not an abundance of wood, but reeds and grasses are readily available, coiled basketry is a preferred container for short- and long-term storage of goods. It often has the function of cupboard, chest, silo and even furniture. To make large sturdy storage baskets, the bundle size usually ranges between 10 and 20 mm, while the winder size is often half the bundle size.

The coiled basketry from Çatalhöyük has a bundle size which ranges from 3 to 8 mm, with a concentration between 5 and 6 mm (Fig. 15.7). This is not a particularly limited distribution in comparison with other archaeological assemblages, but it does represent quite a fine size (cf. Wendrich 1999, 184 & 221). There is little information on the size of the winders (Fig. 15.8). Only in one basket (4429) remains of winders could be traced. These were only 2.5 mm wide, and with a bundle width of 5.5 mm this would have resulted in quite elongated stitches and a very fine appearance of the coiled fabric. Other information on the relation between bundle diameter and width of the winders can only be gleaned from the impressions on clay balls and other clay objects, such as the disk fragment depicted in Figure 15.2. The coiling impressions are in general very regular and fine. This would be in keeping with the interpretation as baskets for cooking. The finely-coiled basketry from Çatalhöyük would have been watertight and it is certainly possible that they were used for cooking food, by using heated clay balls to cook the contents.

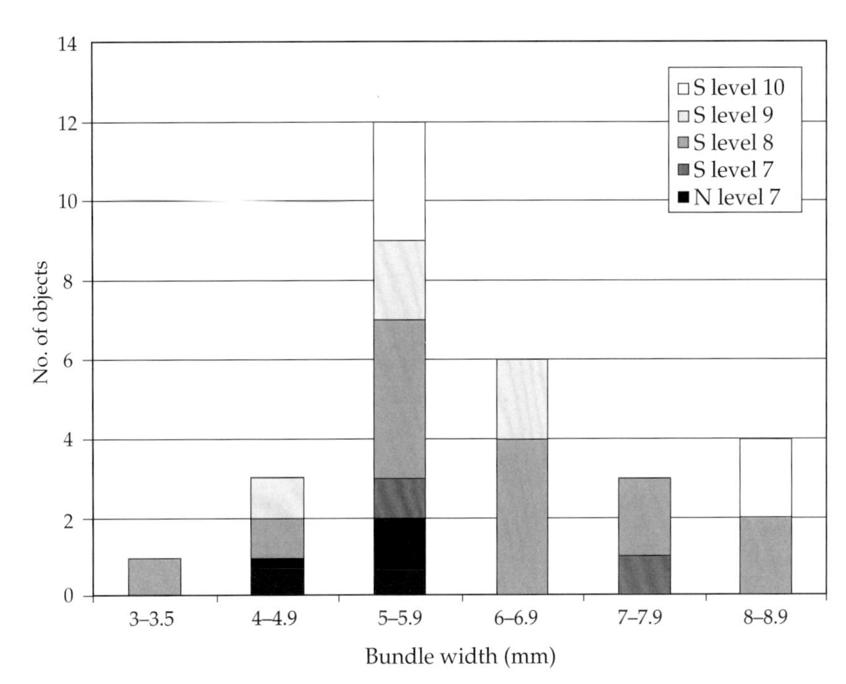

Figure 15.7. *Bundle size of coiled basketry in the North and South Areas at different levels. In general the size of the winders could not be retrieved.*

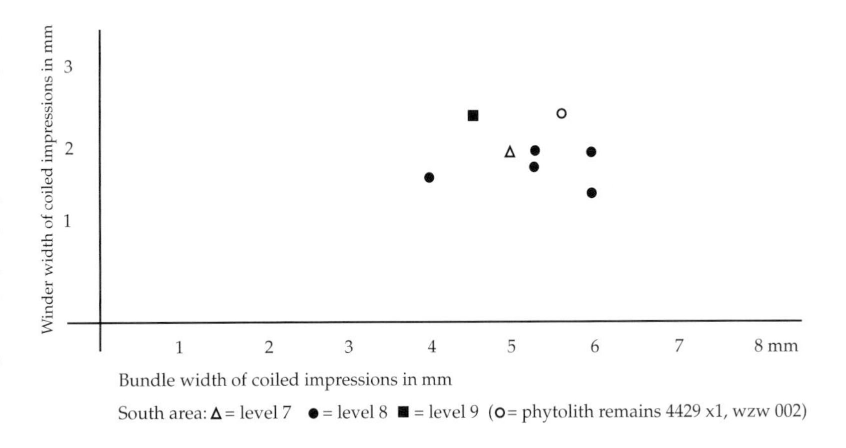

Figure 15.8. *Diagram of the relation between bundle and winder size in basketry impressions on clay balls and discs found in the South Area. Only one phytolith basket remain yielded information on winder size.*

Discussion of basketry from the North and South Areas

Although the coiled basketry found in the North Area is consistently fine, with bundle sizes between 4.5 and 5.2 mm (CD catalogue numbers 003, 010, 011, 012 & 020) there is a problem with interpreting these remains as cooking baskets. All phytolith traces found in Building 5 Space 156 seem to represent mats with a diameter of 200 mm, rather than baskets. Mats of that size would certainly not have been floor mats, but they may have been used as coasters or plates. Their use may have even been more symbolic than practical: they separate certain goods (e.g. foodstuffs) from the floor. Although we are completely in the realm of hypothesis, this seems to be a similar consideration as seen in the production of the clay balls. They too, were separated from the floor or earth, by putting them in baskets or on top of mats. The alternative, to consider the traces as remains of the bases of baskets, suggests that the sides of the baskets have disappeared without leaving a recognizable trace. We have to consider this possibility, because most phytolith basketry remains were preserved in contact with a clayey surface. It is possible that the clay composition of the floors provides better preservation than the infill layers, which would account for the survival of the bases (mostly an impression in the clay with phytolith remains attached, rather than extant remains), but not of any part of the superstructure. A third explanation would be that the finely coiled basketry is used as household and possibly cooking basketry, but is reused as coasters when the sides are damaged or when the basket is no longer watertight.

One of the questions at Çatalhöyük is if basketry would have been used as storage containers for bulk goods, such as cereals. Since the household coiled basketry found in Çatalhöyük is all quite fine, it is unlikely that large containers would have been very sturdy and rigid. Large coiled baskets could have been used as semi-flexible containers, however, if the contents would keep the baskets straight (very much like stuffed sacking).

The context of the basketry found in the North Area is very different from that in the South Area, where most basketry was found under floors and platforms in relation to burials. Infants were regularly buried in lidded coiled baskets. At least one of these baskets was footed (CD catalogue number 002). Still the bundle size as recorded from the phytolith remains shows a similar fineness of fabric as the North Area basketry. An important question is if the burial baskets were different from the household (and possibly cooking) baskets. Since we do not have complete baskets from household contexts it is impossible to assess if the burial baskets were distinguished by a different shape, size or material. It seems likely, however, that the burial baskets were not new, since at least some of them seem to show traces of wear (cf. Fig. 15.2).

Because funerary customs vary greatly, we can think of several scenarios in preparation of the burial. Perhaps the Çatalhöyük deceased were allowed to stay among the living, until a burial basket was finished. It takes a present-day basket maker approximately one week full time (80 hours) to produce a finely-coiled basket and lid. Perhaps, on the other hand, a person had to be buried as soon as possible after death and burial baskets were either prepared beforehand, or a suitable basket was taken from the household stock and used as a coffin. Even though mostly neonates and young children were buried in baskets, the possible high rate of perinatal death may have warranted the production of burial baskets during pregnancy, but such a pessimistic scenario does not seem likely, considering the probable wear traces on some of the burial baskets. Many of the older skeletons that were not buried in baskets were wrapped in matting or perhaps just covered with neatly-arranged grasses or other plant materials (cf. Fig. 15.4).

Conclusion

The Çatalhöyük basketry leaves us with a great deal of additional questions. We do not now who gathered the raw materials, who produced the baskets, who used the baskets and what they were used for (although at least some were probably associated with grain storage, see Volume 4, Chapter 9). We do not know what their full economic and social role in society were. Yet phytolith evidence suggests that adult burials are associated with mats made from sedge; whereas neonatal burial uses baskets made from a distinctive wild grass (Volume 4, Chapter 9). The basketry fabric could have been decorated with colourful patterns, carrying elaborate messages for those who understood the meaning. The context in which the basketry was found does give us some indication that the inhabitants of Çatalhöyük were possibly concerned with separation from the soil: basketry (re-)used as coasters, clay balls that were not put to dry in the sand, but on matting or in baskets and a burial ritual that involved a careful covering of the deceased, a separation of dust from dust.

Chapter 16

Çatalhöyük Worked Bone

Nerissa Russell

I report here on 565 bone tools excavated from the North, South and KOPAL Areas between 1995 and 1999. This includes all tools recognized in the field, and those found with the unworked animal bones that have been analyzed. It is likely that additional worked bone will come to light as the remainder of the animal bone is studied. Comparison of bone-tool densities from faunally-studied and unstudied units suggests that only about one-third of the bone tools are noticed in the field. This holds even for points, which are common and well known to excavators. Thus the distribution of tool types is probably not seriously biased. 'Bone' is interpreted broadly here to include objects made of any vertebrate skeletal material: bone, antler, tooth, or turtle shell. Shell artefacts are reported on elsewhere (Volume 4, Chapter 6). The remains of a crane wing with cut marks that suggest its use as part of a costume are described in the bird bone report (Volume 4, Chapter 3). While only the bone remains, the artefact itself consisted of a wing complete with skin and feathers, and hence is not really worked bone. Bone tools from the surface have been published earlier (Martin & Russell 1996, 210–13). The usual faunal information was recorded for each of the tools (although modification often makes identification difficult by removing diagnostic characters), as well as morphological and microwear (using a binocular light microscope at 25–40×) information about their manufacture and use.

Almost half the bone tools (43 per cent) are points and nearly one-quarter (22 per cent) can be described as ornaments (rings, beads, pendants, and others). There are no dramatic changes in the bone-tool assemblage through time in the levels considered here. Some changes within types are discussed below. While most variation in the frequency of tool types seems more related to context than to temporal trends, Level IX marks the point where some minor types are first found (see Table 16.4), and the first appearance of worked boar's tusk, mainly in the form of fishhooks. I can find no record of worked boar's tusk earlier than Level IX from Mellaart's excavations (Mellaart 1962; 1963; 1964a; 1966a; 1967).

The analysis of the worked bone from the surface noted a spatial distinction between the northern and southern eminences of the tell (Martin & Russell 1996, 213). Ground astragali were largely limited to the southern area (and the West Mound), and points with abraded bases were also more common there, while splitting was less common. At that time it was unclear whether the distinction reflected a chronological difference or functionally different areas of the site. In light of the material reported here, and informal observations of material from the upper layers of the southern part of the East Mound and the Chalcolithic West Mound (to be published at a later date), it is now clear that the distinction is largely temporal. The knucklebones and abraded points almost surely derive from Chalcolithic and latest Neolithic deposits in this area of the East Mound. Thus while temporal change within the Neolithic is minimal, the Chalcolithic assemblages have a different character.

Tool types

I have divided the tools into types based on form and evidence of function from microwear. In cases where a tool has been reworked from one type to another, I have classified it according to its final use.

Points

As in most Neolithic assemblages, by far the most common bone-tool type is the point (any tool with a sharp point and no perforation, including what are often referred to as awls, pins, perforators, and so on). The vast majority of the points are made on sheep/goat metapodials (see Tables 16.1–16.2, Fig. 16.1); most of the 'medium mammals' are probably also sheep and goat, and many of the points only identifiable as 'long bone' are likely on metapodials. Metacarpals and metatarsals are used in roughly equal quantities, but there is a preference for the distal end (61 per cent). Beyond the strong tendency to use sheep/goat metapodials, there is little standardization in the form of the points. They do not sort clearly into subtypes, but vary widely in shape, tip angle, and so on.

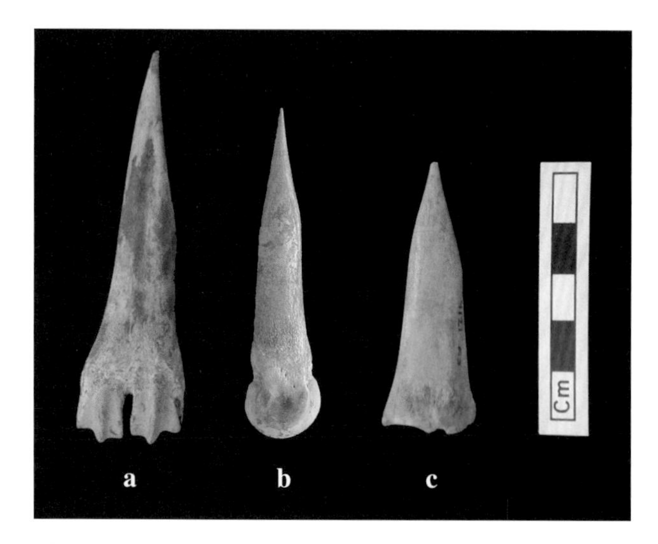

Figure 16.1. *a) Point on unsplit distal metapodial 4183.D1; b) point on split distal metapodial 1520.X2; c) point on split proximal metapodial 4121.F3.*

Unlike some (usually later) bone-tool assemblages (e.g. Choyke 1984; Russell 1995), the points at Çatalhöyük do not separate into expedient as opposed to formal tools, but rather form a continuum. Moreover, there is no indication from tip angle or microwear that the uses of the more expedient points were in any way different from those of the more formal ones. The most expedient points are simply utilized bone splinters. With only slightly more effort, the toolmaker can snap a long bone and grind a sharp tip on the broken end (Fig. 16.1a). More labour can be invested in splitting the long bone (which permits the manufacture of two or even four points from a single long bone), carefully grinding the edges and forming the tip symmetrically, and shaping the base (Fig. 16.1b–c). Beyond sharpening the tip, none of this is necessary for the functioning of the point for most purposes. Splitting may be an attempt to extend the raw material, and modification of the base may in some cases be designed to facilitate hafting. To a large extent, though, it reflects the degree of identification of the craftsperson with her/his tool: how much pride does the maker take in producing a beautiful tool that feels right in the hand? As Pétrequin (1993, 65) observes,

Table 16.1. *Tool types by taxon, with column percentages.*

	Point	Rounded point	Needle	Pick	Chisel/Gouge	Scraper	Burnisher	Pottery polisher	Plaster tool	Spoon/Spatula	Bowl/Cup	Handle	Ornament	Pendant	Bead	Ring	Belt hook or eye	Fishhook	Harpoon	Pressure flaker	Hammer/Mallet	Punch	Preform/Waste	Indeterminate	Total
Indeterminate								1					1												2
								25.0					*11.1*												*0.4*
Hare-size mammal	1														7								2		10
	0.4														*20.0*								*3.4*		*1.8*
Medium-sized mammal	63	1	34		1		1	2		1					4	58							11	12	188
	25.7	*25.0*	*69.4*		*33.3*		*25.0*	*50.0*		*33.3*					*11.4*	*93.5*							*19.0*	*30.8*	*33.3*
Large mammal	4	1	15				1	1	1				5	7	11	4	1			1		1	26	17	96
	1.6	*25.0*	*30.6*				*25.0*	*25.0*	*10.0*				*55.6*	*41.2*	*31.4*	*6.5*	*100*			*50.0*		*100*	*44.8*	*43.6*	*17.0*
Sheep/Goat	170	1			2	1	2		1														5	2	184
	69.4	*25.0*			*66.7*	*100*	*50.0*		*10.0*														*8.6*	*5.1*	*32.6*
Cattle									8					2					1				3		14
									80.0					*11.8*					*100*				*5.2*		*2.5*
Red/fallow deer	2	1		1						2		1	1	4	1					1	7		4	7	32
	0.8	*25.0*		*100*						*66.7*		*100*	*11.1*	*23.5*	*2.9*					*50.0*	*100*		*6.9*	*17.9*	*5.7*
Roe deer	1																								1
	0.4																								*0.2*
Pig													2	4				6					3	1	16
													22.2	*23.5*				*100*					*5.2*	*2.6*	*2.8*
Equid	3																						1		4
	1.2																						*1.7*		*0.7*
Fox															1								1		2
															2.9								*1.7*		*0.4*
Hare																							1		1
																							1.7		*0.2*
Bird	1														11								1		13
	0.4														*31.4*								*1.7*		*2.3*
Turtle											2														2
											100														*0.4*
Total	**245**	**4**	**49**	**1**	**3**	**1**	**4**	**4**	**10**	**3**	**2**	**1**	**9**	**17**	**35**	**62**	**1**	**6**	**1**	**2**	**7**	**1**	**58**	**39**	**565**
%	***43.4***	***0.7***	***8.7***	***0.2***	***0.5***	***0.2***	***0.7***	***0.7***	***1.8***	***0.5***	***0.4***	***0.2***	***1.6***	***3.0***	***6.2***	***11.0***	***0.2***	***1.1***	***0.2***	***0.4***	***1.2***	***0.2***	***10.3***	***6.9***	

'a bone point made from any handy splinter can be produced in 5 minutes and will be as effective as one knapped on a long bone rod sawn from a metapodial, which takes from 1 to 3 hours'.

At Çatalhöyük, most of the points fall into a middle range: moderately well finished, but not elaborately worked. The high percentage of splitting (90 per cent) in bone-point manufacture suggests that suitable raw material may not have been perceived as plentiful. Sheep/goat metapodials seem to have been the point material of choice; 94 per cent of the sheep/goat metapodial points are split (and 93 per cent of all metapodial points). Splitting is generally high on other elements: 100 per cent for antler and ulna, 75 per cent for the radius, and 67 per cent for ribs. The exception is the tibia, with only 50 per cent split. About half (44 per cent) of the tibia points may be described as casually-made, expedient tools, so this probably reflects a generally low value on tibiae as a raw material for points. Expedient points are rarely made on the preferred sheep/goat metapodials (about 14 per cent may be described as relatively expedient, but most of these were split); these were usually treated with care.

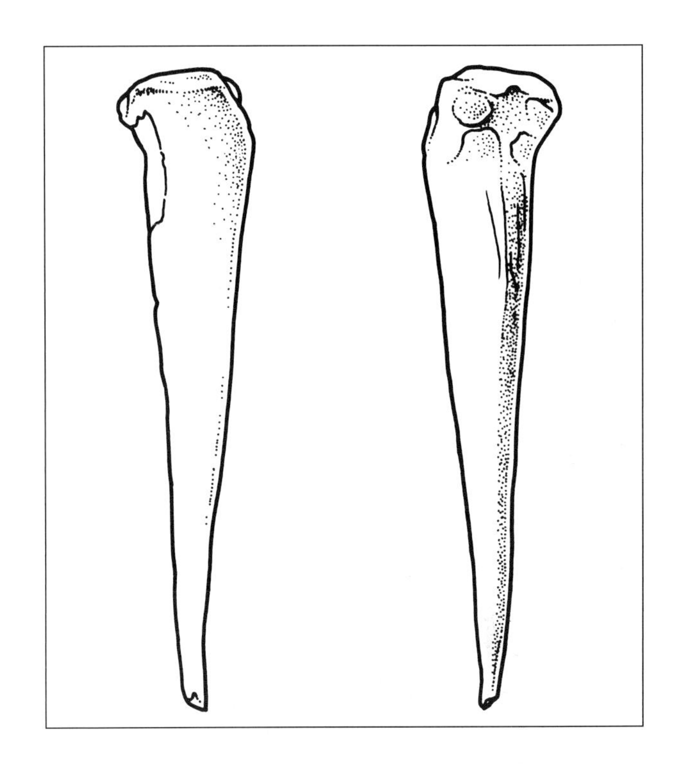

Figure 16.2. *Point on equid metapodial 3107.X1.*

Table 16.2. *Tool types by body part, with column percentages.*

	Point	Rounded point	Needle	Pick	Chisel/Gouge	Scraper	Burnisher	Pottery polisher	Plaster tool	Spoon/Spatula	Bowl/Cup	Handle	Ornament	Pendant	Bead	Ring	Belt hook or eye	Fishhook	Harpoon	Pressure flaker	Hammer/Mallet	Punch	Preform/Waste	Indeterminate	Total
Tooth													2	5	1			6					4	1	19
													22.2	*29.4*	*2.9*			*100*					*6.9*	*2.6*	*3.4*
Mandible														1										2	3
														5.9										*5.1*	*0.5*
Antler	2	1		1						2		1	1	4						1	7		4	7	31
	0.8	*25*		*100*						*66.7*		*100*	*11.1*	*23.5*						*50.0*	*100*		*6.9*	*17.9*	*5.5*
Vertebra																								1	1
																								2.6	*0.2*
Rib	3	1	49					4						2	3								12	15	89
	1.2	*25*	*100*					*100*						*11.8*	*8.6*								*20.7*	*38.5*	*15.8*
Scapula							2		10															2	14
							50.0		*100*															*5.1*	*2.5*
Humerus															1								1		2
															2.9								*1.7*		*0.4*
Radius	4																						2		6
	1.6																						*3.4*		*1.1*
Ulna	1																								1
	0.4																								*0.2*
Femur																25							4	1	30
																40.3							*6.9*	*2.6*	*5.3*
Tibia	17				2										1								5		25
	6.9				*66.7*										*2.9*								*8.6*		*4.4*
Metapodial	161	1				1								1	1				1				2	2	170
	65.7	*25.0*				*100*								*5.9*	*2.9*				*100*				*3.4*	*5.1*	*30.1*
Long bone	57	1			1		2			1			5	4	28	37	1			1		1	24	7	170
	23.3	*25.0*			*33.3*		*50.0*			*33.3*			*55.6*	*23.5*	*80.0*	*59.7*	*100*			*50.0*		*100*	*41.4*	*17.9*	*30.1*
Indeterminate													1											1	2
													11.1											*2.6*	*0.4*
Turtle shell											2														2
											100														*0.4*
Total	**245**	**4**	**49**	**1**	**3**	**1**	**4**	**4**	**10**	**3**	**2**	**1**	**9**	**17**	**35**	**62**	**1**	**6**	**1**	**2**	**7**	**1**	**58**	**39**	**565**

Other clues to the value of bone points at Çatalhöyük include the degree of curation (Russell 1985). The most expedient points are usually discarded after only slight use; they are probably made casually as needed and discarded as soon as the task is completed. Most points, though, even occasionally the expedient kind, are resharpened (79 per cent), often repeatedly, and continue in use for some time. Some were clearly highly prized. One point (5291.F374) was made on the split proximal end of a quite large, hence perhaps wild, sheep/goat metatarsal. Perhaps the wild bone gave it special value, for it was resharpened down to the nub, and finally abandoned after an unsuccessful attempt to put one more tip on it (Fig. 16.3b).

On the whole, little effort is devoted to modification of the bases of bone points at Çatalhöyük. Only 37 per cent of the points have any modification of the base beyond splitting. Only 10 per cent may be said to have extensive modification of the base; the rest show only slight smoothing, rounding, or flattening.

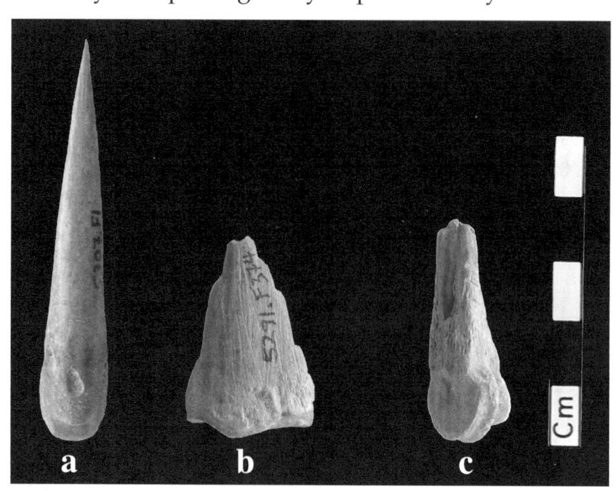

Figure 16.3. *a) Abraded point on split distal metapodial 5307.F1; b) heavily-reused point 5291.F374; c) point fragment with transverse cuts on the shaft 4871.F698.*

Some manufacturing choices may also be related to the value of the raw material. In many Neolithic assemblages, splitting, especially of metapodials, is accomplished with a groove-and-split technique. A burin, truncated blade, or other stone tool is used to score a deep longitudinal groove down the anterior and posterior faces of the long bone. On a ruminant metapodial, this follows a natural groove, especially on the anterior. Sometimes, particularly on the bones of larger animals such as red deer, grooves are cut down the medial and lateral sides as well to obtain four splinters. Chisels or wedges are then used to split the bone along the groove. This technique requires more labour than just fracturing the bone to obtain a suitable splinter, but increases the chance of getting one or more usable blanks from a long bone. Çatalhöyük bone toolmakers were familiar with this technique, but almost never used it. Of the 245 points considered here, only two exhibit clear traces of groove-and-split, with two more showing possible groove-and-split remnants. In addition, there is only a single piece of groove-and-split waste (Fig. 16.21). While later stages of manufacture and use would be expected to obliterate the groove marks on many points, this is a very low rate of visible traces. Moreover, many of the points were clearly not split by grooving, but rather by unassisted fracture. It is hard to tell exactly how the fracture was achieved; it is possible that the bones were split by exposing them to fire, causing them to crack longitudinally (Campana 1989, 25). A few do show traces of slight contact with fire. This further indicates a moderate value on sheep/goat metapodials as a raw material: valuable enough to split, not worth expending a lot of care in splitting well.

A still more labour-intensive method of point manufacture is to abrade the anterior and posterior surfaces (sometimes the medial and lateral as well) flat all the way along the bone splinter. Particularly when applied to a distal metapodial, the sectioning of the epiphysis thus achieved produces an aesthetically-pleasing effect (to modern eyes, at least). This technique has been applied to only four of the points reported here. One is actually a very crude example that is not particularly beautiful (4838.F764),

Table 16.3. *Density, splitting, reuse and use-wear of points by period.*

	Density		Splitting		Reuse		Rounded vs Battered wear	
Period	N	(no./litre)	N	%	N	%	N	% Battered
N.V–IV	4	.0020	4	100	3	100	3	33
N.VI–V	26	.0006	20	95	17	76	14	57
N.VII–VI	9	.0002	6	83	4	100	3	33
VI.B	1	.0004	1	100	1	100	1	0
VII	13	.0003	12	83	11	82	7	57
VIII	93	.0012	74	88	72	88	49	41
IX	27	.0004	25	76	22	64	12	58
X	7	.0003	4	100	5	100	5	20
XI	2	.0009	1	100	1	100	1	0
XII	2	.0003	2	100	2	0	1	0
Pre-XII.A	12	.0009	11	100	12	75	9	33
Pre-XII.B	18	.0013	14	100	13	69	7	57
Pre-XII.C	9	.0014	9	100	8	63	4	50
Pre-XII.D	8	.0016	7	100	7	86	4	50

Table 16.4. *Tool types by period, with row percentages.*

	Point	Rounded Point	Needle	Pick	Chisel/Gouge	Scraper	Burnisher	Pottery Polisher	Plaster Tool	Spoon/Spatula	Bowl/Cup	Handle	Ornament	Pendant	Bead	Ring	Fishhook	Harpoon	Pressure Flaker	Hammer/Mallet	Punch	Preform/Waste	Indeterminate	Total
N.V–IV	4															1								5
	80.0															*20.0*								
N.VI–V	26	1	2						4	1				5	5	11	2			2		3	6	68
	38.2	*1.5*	*2.9*						*5.9*	*1.5*				*7.4*	*7.4*	*16.2*	*2.9*			*2.9*		*4.4*	*8.8*	
N.VII–VI	9	1	2						2						1	3	1			1			1	21
	42.9	*4.8*	*9.5*						*9.5*						*4.8*	*14.3*	*4.8*			*4.8*			*4.8*	
VI.B	1																							1
	100																							
VII	13	1	4						1	1					2	6		1	1	1		4	1	36
	36.1	*2.8*	*11.1*						*2.8*	*2.8*					*5.6*	*16.7*		*2.8*	*2.8*	*2.8*		*11.1*	*2.8*	
VIII	93		21				4	1	2	1	1		2	6	6	27	2			1		9	10	186
	50.0		*11.3*				*2.2*	*0.5*	*1.1*	*0.5*	*0.5*		*1.1*	*3.2*	*3.2*	*14.5*	*1.1*			*0.5*		*4.8*	*5.4*	
IX	27		3		2			1					3	2	4	4	1		1	1		20	4	73
	37.0		*4.1*		*2.7*			*1.4*					*4.1*	*2.7*	*5.5*	*5.5*	*1.4*		*1.4*	*1.4*		*27.4*	*5.5*	
X	7											1			4	2						11	2	27
	25.9											*3.7*			*14.8*	*7.4*						*40.7*	*7.4*	
XI	2								1															3
	66.7								*33.3*															
XII	2														1									3
	66.7														*33.3*									
Pre-XII.A	12		5					2					1	1	7	5					1	1	3	38
	31.6		*13.2*					*5.7*					*2.6*	*2.6*	*18.4*	*13.2*					*2.6*	*2.6*	*7.9*	
Pre-XII.B	16		11		1	1							1	1	1							5	9	46
	34.8		*23.9*		*2.2*	*2.2*							*2.2*	*2.2*	*2.2*							*10.9*	*19.6*	
Pre-XII.C	9	1									1			1	1							1	1	15
	60.0	*6.7*									*6.7*			*6.7*	*6.7*							*6.7*	*6.7*	
Pre-XII.D	8		1										1									2	1	13
	61.5		*7.7*										*7.7*									*15.4*	*7.7*	
KOPAL	2			1																		1		4
	50.0			*25.0*																		*25.0*		
Total	**231**	**4**	**49**	**1**	**3**	**1**	**4**	**4**	**10**	**3**	**2**	**1**	**8**	**16**	**32**	**59**	**6**	**1**	**2**	**6**	**1**	**57**	**38**	**539**

while the others are carefully made (Fig. 16.3a). Rather more elaborate and thoroughly abraded versions are known from Canhasan III (French 1972).

After obtaining a suitable roughly pointed splinter of bone, the toolmaker must then shape the point into its finished form. Minimally, this involves forming a sharp tip. Usually, the edges are also smoothed and the base may be shaped to varying degrees. There are two main techniques used to accomplish these tasks at Neolithic sites: abrasion on a rough material such as sandstone, and scraping with chipped stone tools. While abrasion is a little faster and more easily produces symmetrical tools, there is little difference in labour input between the two techniques and the choice seems to be mainly one of personal or cultural preference (Campana 1989). At Çatalhöyük, both techniques are used, usually in combination. Most often, the main shaping is accomplished with abrasion, and scraping is used to form the tip; occasionally it is the other way around, or only one technique is used. Resharpening is almost always by scraping. One can imagine a standard toolkit consisting of a bone point and a chipped-stone scraper for resharpening as needed; perhaps abraders were not routinely kept with finished points, but only retrieved for manufacture.

The wear on the base of the points suggests that most (75 per cent) were hafted rather than simply held in the hand. Polish usually appears only on a few high spots, with the rest untouched. Since there is little modification of the base, and therefore most were quite irregular, the hafting may have been wrappings of sinew, fibre, or other material rather than wooden or other handles.

Function

The points were clearly used to pierce soft organic materials, but the microwear studies were unable to establish the specific materials on which they were used. There do seem to be at least two distinct materials or functions, however, which produce rounding (55 per cent) as opposed to battering (45 per cent) in the microscale use-wear on the tip. Presumably the battering is produced by use on a tougher material. While there is much overlap, points with rounding are generally more slender than those with battering, as measured by the breadth 1 cm from the tip (Fig. 16.4).

A few points hold other clues to their uses. Six (1012.F1, 1862.F3, 2321.X1, 3026.F1, 4711.F43 & 5324.F148) have very fine, faint striations perpendicular to the long axis near the tip that may result from using

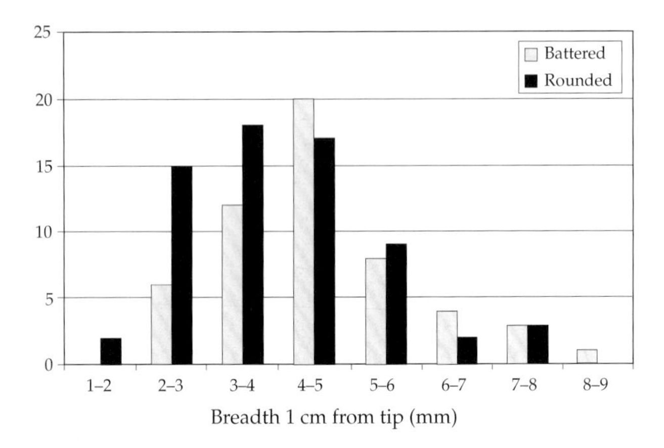

Figure 16.4. *Breadth of battered and rounded point tips.*

a drilling motion in basketry (Griffitts 2001; see also Chapter 15). Three points (2845.F1, 2899.X6 & 4246.F1) are more than merely battered at a micro-scale, with heavy chipping on the tip and battering on the base that suggests they were used as gouges on something firm such as soft wood. 2899.X6 seems a bit too delicate for such a use, and the battering is less extreme, so it may have been used on a different material, perhaps pounded through something relatively tough such as leather. Finally, an expedient point (5294.F1) has been used in some way that produces battering and rounding simultaneously.

More enigmatically, 14 points have one or more sets of rather deep transverse cuts on the shaft (Fig. 16.3c). These seem to have occurred in use; they post-date manufacture and are worn from use. In some cases, the different sets of cuts were made at various points during the use life of the point, as shown by varying degrees of wear. Most are too irregular, shallow, and narrow to have aided in tying on a fibre. My best guess is that they result from cutting something against the point, perhaps a fibre while sewing. Only four have sufficiently well-preserved tips to assess the microwear; of these, three are rounded and one is battered.

Change through time

Comparisons of periods are complicated by differing sample sizes, and by the differing balances of context types excavated for each period. There is no clear trend in the number of bone points recovered through time, when corrected for the volume excavated (Table 16.3). The variation is most likely primarily related to the kinds of contexts excavated in each period, with the tools tending to come primarily from middens and fills. There is no real change in choice of taxa or body parts for the raw material for bone points through time, although possibly there is some significance in that all the (rare) points on equid (Fig. 16.2) and deer bone, and on antler, radii, and ulnae come from Levels IX–VII. Partly this is a result of the larger sample sizes in Levels IX (n = 27) and VIII (n = 93), but this would not explain their appearance in Level VII (n = 13). For some reason, the toolmakers selected a wider range of raw materials at this time midway through the sequence, although sheep/goat metapodials still predominate.

Splitting declines through time, although it remains high. Not a single unsplit point has been recorded before Level IX; from Level IX up only the smallest samples have no unsplit points (see Table 16.3). There is no clear trend within these later periods, and much of the variation within them may be due to sample size. The decline in splitting might suggest a decreasing value of bone (or metapodials) as a raw material, perhaps because it is more available as the sheep flocks increase through the occupation. However, reuse (mostly resharpening, with occasional repair or reworking), which reflects the value of the tool rather than simply the raw material, if anything increases through time (see Table 16.3). Hafting shows no temporal trends. If rounded versus battered use microwear indicate two different tasks, they were clearly both practised throughout the sequence (see Table 16.3). There does not seem to be much variation in the balance between these two tasks, except perhaps in Levels IX and North VI–V, where, with modest samples, battering is more frequent than elsewhere. In sum, aside from a reduction in splitting, the bone points show few clear trends through time. While the patterning is not clear, Level IX does seem to be a point where some things change, at least in small ways.

Rounded points

'Rounded points' refers to pointed objects with rounded rather than sharp tips. They are certainly not used for the perforating tasks that the points perform, but may serve a variety of functions. One (2562.F1) from the fill of Building 1 in the North Area resembles a 'hairpin'. It is very carefully finished but shows no signs of use in piercing, and is probably ornamental. It is small (51 mm long), made on a sheep/goat long bone (metapodial?) shaft, and is circular in cross section except at the base, where it flattens as it flares out to a rounded diamond shape. Another rounded point (2181.F2), also from Building 1 (Level North VI–V) but in the fill of a burial, seems to be a rather different tool. It is even smaller (43 mm long), with a shape reminiscent of a sturdy modern-day needle, but without the perforation (Fig. 16.5a). The shape and size suggest it may have been part of a composite tool. Wear at the tip end clearly indicates extensive use on soft material; the base end shows considerable use, but is less rounded and very slightly battered, as though pushed against a haft or struck occasionally with a hard object. Possibly it was a weaving or basketry tool, passed through loose strands, as the tip is too dull for use as an awl. A third rounded point (5323.F249), from a dump layer in Space 181 in the South Area (Level Pre-XII.C) is made on a strip of antler extracted by the groove-and-splinter technique (Clark & Thompson 1954). The base is missing and no microwear is preserved, so the function is uncertain. It is very carefully made, symmetrical, and has a round cross-section. A final example (1511.F381), from foundation cut fill in the South Area (Space 105, Level VII) is a tip fragment of a tool made on split rib. The tip is small and rounded, quite dull, and shows some battering, suggesting use on relatively tough materials.

Needles

What I have termed needles at Çatalhöyük are not used for sewing, but rather are large, broad, flat tools with a perforation at one end and a flat rounded tip at the other. Mellaart (1967, 215) refers to them as bodkins, and elsewhere as weaving needles (e.g. Mellaart 1962, 56). They are likely to have been used in weaving, mat-making, or netting. Similar objects are known from the Natufian (Campana 1989) and from Beidha (Kirkbride 1966). There is one exception (4121.F10) that, while fragmentary, appears to be thinning to a real point and may have more closely resembled a sewing needle (Fig. 16.5b).

These artefacts are made on split ribs, mostly of sheep-size mammals, but some on larger ribs that have been ground considerably to thin them (Fig. 16.5c). Since they are made on long segments of ribs, the shafts are somewhat curved. The only complete example is 10 cm long, but some were clearly considerably longer. They are generally ground quite thin, making them fragile. As a result, almost all our examples are fragmentary. They were particularly prone to breaking through the perforations, which are rather large (1.6–9.0 mm in diameter, with a mean diameter of 4.2 mm) and thus leave only very thin walls of bone on the sides. Of the 20 with base ends preserved, five have been repaired by redrilling the perforation a little further up after such a break; an additional eight have unrepaired old breaks through the perforation that ended their use lives. 1862.F1 from Level VIII in the South Area is a particularly interesting instance of attempted repair. This needle apparently broke through the original perforation in the course of manufacture, while the sides were still unshaped. Instead of moving the perforation up, the maker made a new hole at the other end of the tool. The maker then started to shape

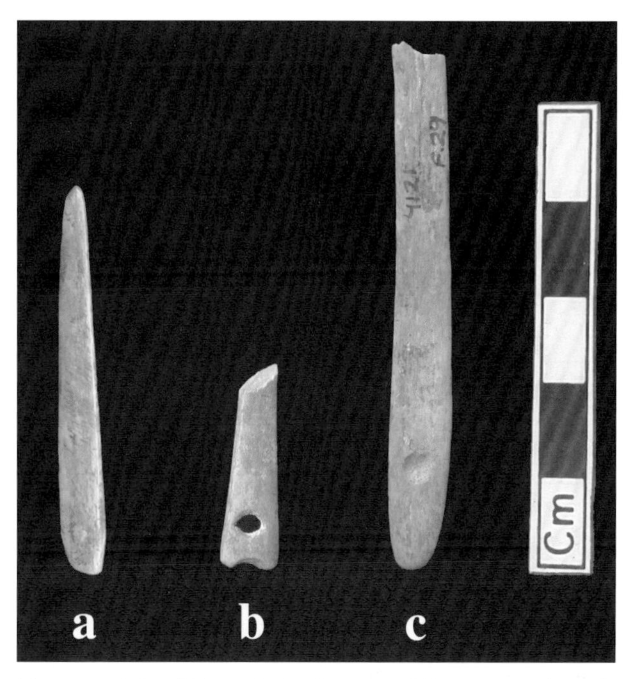

Figure 16.5. *a) Rounded point resembling an unpierced needle 2181.F2; b) 'real' needle, broken and reperforated, first perforation drilled, later one cut 4121.F10; c) unfinished needle 4121.F29.*

the edges at the broken perforation, but abandoned it without finishing the shaping of the tip. Two finished needles also preserve traces of hesitation in manufacture. They have false starts to drilled perforations, then completed perforations a little further up. Perhaps the maker realized the original perforation would be too close to the end.

The characteristics of these artefacts indicate some of the parameters of their use. It was important that they be quite flat and reasonably smooth with a flat rounded tip. The hole needs to be large, even at the cost of risking breakage. Indeed, the base sometimes flares to accommodate a larger perforation. Thus, they must have pulled rather large fibres through large spaces. They are often highly polished from use, with wear that suggests passing through a soft material. While they were evidently required in considerably lesser quantities than the points, they are still relatively common compared to most bone-tool types.

There is weak evidence for a temporal change in manufacturing technique for the needles. In those needles with the base preserved ($n = 19$), most perforations are drilled biconically, but a few are cut. Three of the four cut perforations are from Level Pre-XII.A, with the fourth from Level VIII. Two exhibit a combination of drilling and cutting: an initial drilling then enlarged by cutting. These are from Levels IX and VIII. All 13 of the purely-drilled perforations come from Levels IX and

Figure 16.6. *Antler pick 6029.F104.*

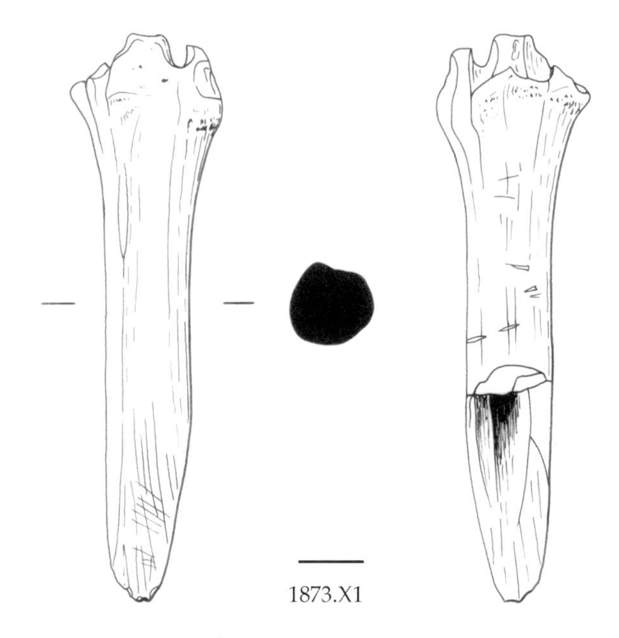

Figure 16.7. *Chisel/gouge 1873.X1.*

above. With so small a sample, it is not clear whether the perforation technique changed through time, whether this is a preference of individual toolmakers with no temporal association (two are from a single unit (4838) in Space 181 of Level Pre-XII.A, and thus may derive from a single episode of use), or whether it is a matter of what kind of stone tool is handy at the moment. When broken needles are repaired by reperforation, the same technique is consistently used, with the partial exception of 4121.F10, where the second perforation has been widened by cutting subsequent to drilling, while the original one seems to have been simply drilled (Fig. 16.5b). If the toolmaker is also the tool user, this suggests that individuals consistently use one technique or the other.

Picks

Only one artefact (6029.F104) falls into this category, and even then it is somewhat different from the antler picks that are rather common in Neolithic Europe. It is fragmentary, with only the tip end preserved, which consists of a small, sharp, slightly curved bevelled edge on a piece of antler beam or large tine (Fig. 16.6). If it resembles the usually larger European antler picks, it would have had a shaft hole through the base end for mounting on a wooden handle. It is highly polished from use, with striations that indicate a striking motion. The striations appear to result from contact with fine inorganic materials such as rock-free, fine-grained soil or untempered ceramics. The striations do not show the usual pattern resulting from digging in the soil, however, which includes random striations of irregular size and considerable damage to the edge. The tip also seems too small and delicate for digging. It could conceivably be used in house construction or destruction, but it was found in the off-tell KOPAL Area.

Chisel/gouges

I have characterized one complete and two fragmentary tools as chisels or more likely gouges. Where the species and element can be identified, they are made on unsplit sheep/goat distal tibiae. The complete example, from Level IX in the South Area (1873.X1), is made on an unsplit distal sheep tibia, with a heavy bevelled end (Fig. 16.7). The wear on the base suggests hafting. There are large chips off the bevelled tip, which has been resharpened, indicating use on a relatively hard material. The microwear does not support use in the soil, but it is consistent with use as a gouge to make the boxes and bowls of fir and other soft woods recovered by Mellaart (1967, 215). A tip fragment from Level Pre-XII.B (5286.F290) seems to show similar wear, but the edge has been shattered in excavation, so it is hard to be sure. Another fragmentary specimen from Level IX (1889.F20) is perhaps more chisel-like, with heavy damage but little polish to the tip. Wood working still seems the most likely use for this tool, but with greater percussive force. It is not suited for use in working chipped stone, nor does the wear support use in soil.

This artefact type is not found after Level IX in the assemblage considered here. However, the sample size is small, and there is a chisel/gouge of this same sort from the Summit Area, so this lack in later periods is probably not meaningful. Moreover, Mellaart (1964a, fig. 42) illustrates what appear to be examples of this artefact type from Levels III and IV.

Scrapers

One fragmentary tool (5286.F289, Level Pre-XII.B) formally resembles the chisel/gouges, although it is made on a metapodial rather than a tibia. The tip is only partially preserved, but seems to have been scraped to form a fairly delicate rounded bevel, like an apple corer. It appears too delicate for woodworking, and while it has considerable polish from use, there is too little edge damage for use on a material as hard as wood. The edge is very thin and has been somewhat rounded from wear. A good deal of use polish with fine striations running in various directions occurs on the back (flat, not bevelled side) of the tip area, suggesting a scraping or burnishing motion. Thus it was probably used to scrape out something relatively soft. Probably too small and delicate for use on hides, it may have been used for something like scraping the pith out of reeds.

Burnishers

Four artefacts have been used to burnish materials other than plaster and ceramics. Interestingly, all are from middens in Space 115 from Level VIII. One (1505.F321) started life as a sturdy point. The tip broke off obliquely, leaving a small bevel that was used extensively without reshaping on a soft material such as hide, so that this broken end has become quite rounded and polished. Two sheep/goat scapulae (4121.F496 & 4121.F529) were used expediently as burnishers on soft materials on their edges. The articulations and in one case the spine have been broken off, but they are otherwise unmodified. A fragment of sheep-sized long-bone shaft shows polish and faint striations indicating use on soft materials (4121.F1831). However, old breaks that postdate use have removed all of the original edges, so it is not possible to determine the original shape.

Pottery polishers

As is perhaps to be expected at a site with so little pottery, there are very few pottery polishers among the bone tools. While those reported here all derive from Levels VIII and earlier, they also occur in the BACH Area, so are not restricted to the early levels. All are made on split ribs of various sizes. None are particularly heavily used, and they may not all be pottery polishers in a strict sense, although they show striations typical of use on fine- or untempered ceramics. All are fragmentary.

4845.F25 from Level Pre-XII.A in the South Area is the most convincing as a pottery polisher, although only slightly used. Ironically, pottery has not been found in the Level Pre-XII deposits (Chapter 5). Both the inner and the outer surfaces have been thoroughly scraped to remove the spongy cancellous bone and render this segment of the tool nearly flat. The tip is rounded and fairly flat, but not really bevelled. It is highly polished by the transverse fine ceramic striations, especially at tip, but the manufacturing scrapes are still quite fresh. 4838.F357, also from Pre-XII.A, has likewise been formed into a flat, oblique but not bevelled tip. It has been scraped flat on both sides. The tip shows no sign of use, but both flat surfaces and both edges have striations resulting from contact with fine-tempered ceramic material. It could have been used on something other than pots, perhaps figurines or clay balls. 1889.X1 from Level IX has been similarly flattened and also has pottery striations on the flat sides and edges of the shaft rather than the (base?) end. It may really be a multi-purpose tool, as it also has some polish in areas without ceramic striations. A shaft fragment of a slightly used pottery polisher (4121.F3058) was found in a large midden in Level IX. Thus ceramic burnishing appears to be an occasional and not very intensive use of bone tools.

Plaster tools

Ten tools made on (mostly cattle) scapulae I have tentatively labelled as plastering tools. They take somewhat varied forms, but most have a bevelled edge running lengthwise down the blade of the scapula fragment. Except for one unused, but bevelled, example, they all bear use striations and polish leading back from the bevels (where present) that resemble wear from contact with fine- or untempered pottery. However, the form is not suited to pottery polishing, and the orientation suggests more of a slicing motion with the edge than a burnishing motion. They would not be suitable for applying wall plaster, which is very fine and thin and was apparently brushed or swabbed on, but make sense as tools to shape the coarser plaster features such as pillars and benches, or perhaps to form mud bricks.

3819.X4, from Building 5 in the North Area, is a particularly elaborate version of the bevelled form of this tool type. The caudal side of the neck of the scapula has been chopped and flaked to make a hand-hold. The wear indicates it was indeed held in this manner, by a left-handed person. It was found together with 3819.X3 (Volume 3, Part 3), which is one of the non-bevelled examples. Rather, it has been used mainly on the flat surfaces to smooth and shape, but not to slice.

Figure 16.8. *Rod-shaped plaster tool 4183.F19.*

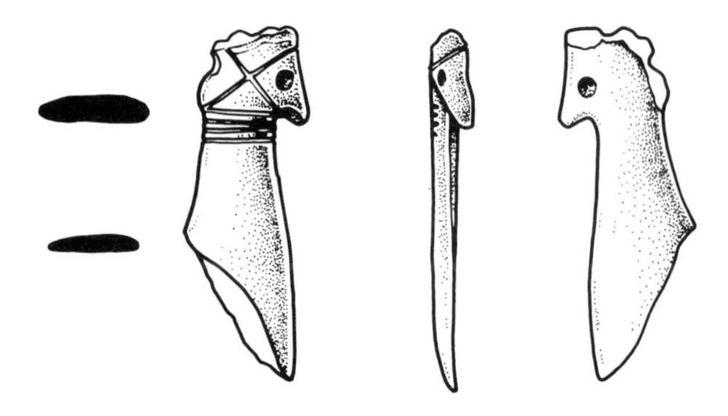

Figure 16.9. *Spoon fragment 1659.X1.*

The two of them may have formed a plaster-working toolkit. Another non-bevelled plaster tool (4183.F19) comes from the make-up layer in a platform in Level VIII in the South Area. A large, robust cattle scapula has been flaked along the juncture of the spine and the blade to make a long, heavy, crude rod (Fig. 16.8). There is no bevel and the only flat surface is less used than the rest. From the form, one could imagine it stuck in the wall and then used to stretch hides or other materials. However, the microwear matches that of other plaster tools and would not have been produced by use on a soft material such as hide, and it extends all the way to both ends and all around the bone. It is puzzling that this has been made on a scapula. This shape could more easily have been obtained by using an unsplit long bone shaft, and it must have been difficult to work a scapula into this shape. Apparently it was unthinkable to make a plaster tool from anything other than a scapula.

These tools first appear in Level XI, and then carry on through the sequence, becoming particularly frequent in the North Area. They tend to be found in houses, but this is not invariably the case. Their appearance coincides with a change in plaster technology from lime to clay plaster (Volume 3, Part 2).

Spoons and spatulas

Two spoons are made of large cervid antler, probably red deer. A fragmentary example (1659.X1) comes from a Level VIII midden in the South Area (Fig. 16.9). Both the base and the end of the blade are missing. The base is embellished with carved rounded barbs, three perforations, and incised lines, all on the outer surface. The blade is slightly concave on the inner side, and comes to quite a thin edge. There is little sign of use on the portion of the blade present. A complete spoon (1965.X1) was found in a burial in Building 1 in the North Area. This is a much simpler artefact, made on split antler beam. This artefact does not have a separate handle marked off from the blade, but consists of a thin, concave blade with slight use. The walls are thin (*c.* 3 mm) and rather concave but becoming flatter near the tip. The tip end is a rounded bevel, quite dull.

These spoons could be for eating or for preparing soft substances. The elaboration of one and the placement of the other in a burial, along with their rarity, suggest that they are not daily-eating implements, but used for special purposes or special occasions. It is also notable that neither has much use-wear.

Spatula is the term I apply to the delicate and often ornamented spreaders that Mellaart (1967, 214–15) termed 'cosmetics tools'. A fragmentary tool that is probably the base of a spatula (4225.F80) comes from a between-wall deposit in Level VII of the South Area. It is a delicate, carefully-worked artefact, with the base brought to a dull, plump bevel. The shaft has been ground thoroughly on all sides to achieve a regular, rounded rectangular cross-section, flaring slightly toward the missing tip end as well as toward the base.

Bowls/cups

There is little turtle shell at Çatalhöyük, and it is possible that it was all collected for use as containers rather than to eat the turtles. However, only two fragments (4321.F7, Level VIII; 5310.F190, Level Pre-XII.C) have scraping, abrasion, and polish on the inner sides, indicating that they were cleaned out and probably used as bowls or cups.

Handles

An antler sickle handle (4677.X1), without the sickle blades, was found stuck loosely into the wall of a bin in Building 18 in the South Area, Level X. Thus it was evidently curated without the blades in it. It is made on an antler tine that bears a deep groove along its length (Fig. 16.10). There are signs of use, so the blades must have fallen out or been removed before it was carefully stored in the bin wall. Mellaart (1967, 215) found an example of such a handle complete with obsidian blades.

Ornaments

This is a general class for items that seem to fill a decorative rather than utilitarian function (to the extent that this is a valid distinction), but cannot be assigned to a more specific type such as ring or pendant. Some are simply too fragmentary to classify, while others do not fit into other types. Nine specimens fall into this category.

An antler toggle (2308.F1) from a Level IX midden in the South Area is made on a split antler beam or possibly a large tine, sliced to shape the edges and flatten out the inner spongy bone a little. The rough outer surface of the antler has been only slightly flattened, and in general it seems rather crudely made. It is roughly rectangular, tapering slightly toward the ends, with a large perforation in the centre. There is some use-wear both within the perforation and on the ends. It is likely that this artefact functioned as a button on clothing, although other uses are possible.

A fragmentary carved boar's tusk collar (4416.F485) from fill in Building 16 (Level IX) is similar to one found by Mellaart (1967, 209 & pl. 98) in a Level VII burial (Fig. 16.11). The tusk has been split, and the dentine side smoothed to flatten the piece, while still leaving traces of the pulp cavity. Presumably it was worn with the enamel side out. On this side there are remnants of three sets of transverse incised lines. The only complete set consists of six lines, with the longest extending halfway across the face from the lower edge and the rest becoming gradually become shorter. The longest line is met by another coming from the upper edge, the beginning of a similar set of lines extending down from the upper edge and grading off in the other direction. Another set begins from the upper edge in mirror image, above the short end of the full set. Diagonal incisions cross the tops of each set of lines, marking the slope. These lines are about 1 mm wide, and range from 5 to 18 mm long. In addition, two perforations have been drilled along the lower edge, at the small end of the sloping lines. The most obvious way to wear this as a collar would be with the concave side of the curve up (while the holes are on the convex side), and would not involve using these perforations for suspension. There would likely have been holes for this purpose at the missing ends. These

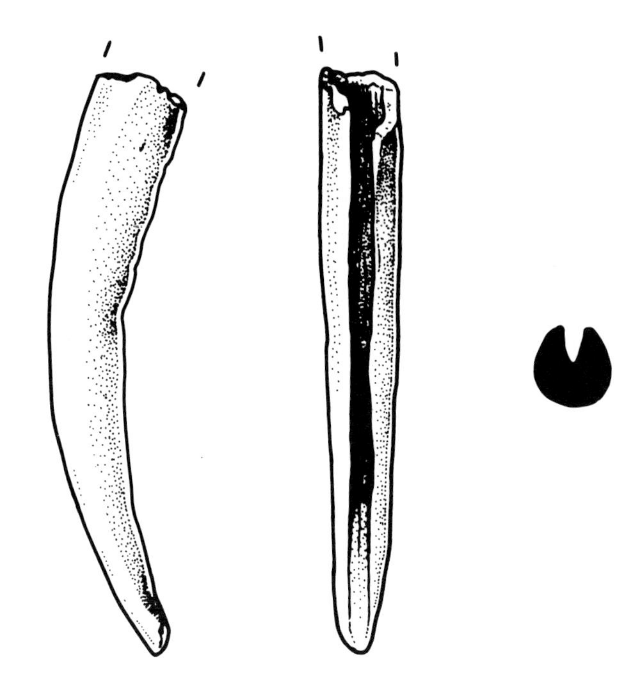

Figure 16.10. *Antler sickle handle 4677.X1.*

Figure 16.11. *Fragment of boar's tusk collar, 4416.F485.*

holes are worn, though, so either it was worn differently or other things were suspended from them.

Three enigmatic artefacts (5328.F434 from Level Pre-XII.D, 4943.F1 from Level IX & 4121.F28 from Level VIII) might be fragments of belt hooks and eyes (Fig. 16.12). All are carved from the thick cortex of large mammal long bones. 5328.F434 and 4943.F1 are likely to be fragments of eyes. They seem to form part of a hollow oval shape. 5328.F434 is thick and very regular and carefully worked, with a flat facet on the inside and the other surfaces rounded. 4943.F1 is very similar, with a concentrated area of polish in one small area of the inner edge of the curve. This could result from wear from the hook, although it seems too restricted; I would expect more movement of hook against eye. 4121.F28, on the other hand, might be part of a belt hook, preserving a straight and slightly flaring

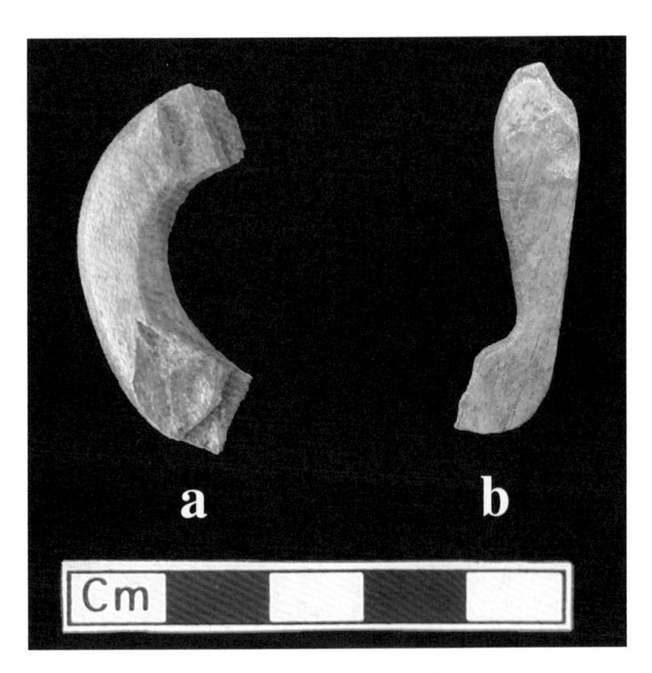

Figure 16.12. *a) Fragment of possible belt eye 4943.F1; b) fragment of possible belt hook 4121.F28.*

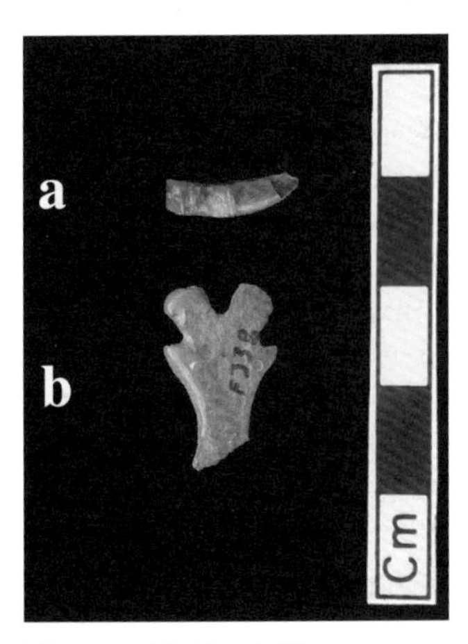

Figure 16.13. *a) Horn-shaped ornament 3979.F1; b) ornamented spatula (?) base 4844.F338.*

shank and the beginning of the hook. However, it seems too small for a belt hook and too thick and heavy for a fishhook. Moreover, it shows no wear on the edges, especially the inner curve as one would expect for a belt hook, but considerable wear on both flat surfaces, suggesting possible use as pendant.

2732.F1 from a Level VIII midden started life as a triangular pendant made of split boar's tusk. The pendant broke longitudinally through the perforation. It was then repaired by grinding the broken edge, but was not re-perforated, so it can no longer be considered a pendant. It was apparently of sufficient value to keep and perhaps carry as an amulet.

3979.F1, from unstratified deposits in the South Area, is a tiny enigmatic artefact on a burnt piece of probable long bone with old breaks at either end (Fig. 16.13a). It does not look as though it could continue much further. The entire surface is abraded and heavily modified. It is curved, and seems to taper toward one end like a horn. There are two offset notches on each side of the wider end (i.e., four in total); it is broken through one of these. These kinds of notches occur on the shanks of fishhooks and rings with pillars, but this artefact is too curved to be either of these.

4844.F338 from Level Pre-XII.A in the South Area is a piece of long bone carved into a four-lobed shape that could be seen as a stylized flower, hand or body (Fig. 16.13b). Four partial, apparently decorative perforations are placed irregularly on it. These seem to have been made in a two-step process, beginning with a cylinder drill and then using a regular chipped-stone drill. It is very small and delicate, highly polished and carefully worked. It is missing one end, and could be the base of a spatula, or part of a pendant or other ornament.

4871.F700 from Level Pre-XII.B in the South Area is a tiny fragment of bone with incised lines across the surface. The surface of the fragment is nearly covered by five longitudinal lines, crossed by two diagonal lines, one of them partial. They are relatively evenly spaced, from 0.7 to 1.1 mm apart. It is so fragmentary that it is impossible to tell what type of artefact it is, but it does appear to be decorated.

Pendants

The distinction between pendants and beads is difficult to draw. I have included as pendants objects that appear to be worn suspended and probably alone or as the centrepiece of a necklace, while designating suspended objects that form part of a composite necklace, bracelet, etc., as beads. While some general types recur, the forms of the pendants are quite variable and individual. There are 17 pendants, in addition to the one that was repaired into an unsuspended ornament (see above).

The most common sub-type of pendants, with four examples, is a long narrow, roughly-rectangular form made of antler. They are generally rather thick and often seem crude and poorly finished. One (4121.F7) has a groove, apparently the remnant of an unsuccessful attempt at the groove-and-splinter technique, running diagonally across it (Fig. 16.14a). Possibly these were not actually worn as pendants, but used for some other purpose that requires suspension, such as weights or possibly whirled around on a cord as bull-roarers (suggested by Dr Werner Bachmann, see Cohen 1973; Harding 1973). One artefact (5310.F262) that I include here, however, seems more likely to be a genuine pendant. It is smaller and more carefully shaped, with the unpierced end formed to a very blunt rounded point. These rough antler pendants are found throughout the sequence, from Level Pre-XII.C to VI–V in the North Area. All are from midden contexts; they have never been found in burials or *in situ* in houses.

Three pendants, while each unique in shape, can perhaps be grouped into a sub-type: notched and incised. In fact two of these were originally a single pendant that broke. The overall shape can be described as a rounded rectangle, with grooves and notches on the edges giving a waisted effect. A small pendant from the South Area (2798.X1), found as part of a necklace of stone and shell beads at the base of an occupation layer in fill in Building 2, has two incised grooves across the front becoming notches on the sides that create this waisted look. Two pendants (1921.X1 & 1921.H6) found in an older man's burial (not a child as previously stated in Russell 2001) in Building 1 are repaired pieces from a single pendant that broke longitudinally through the perforation (Volume 3, Part 3). The original was a rather elaborate pendant, perhaps a stylized human representation. The perforation was near the top, there was a raised knob in the centre surrounded by an oval incision, two horizontal incisions define a 'waist', and the base is marked by diagonal incisions. It was burnt to a deep even black that I suspect was deliberate; certainly it was not burnt after deposition in the burial, and both halves exhibit it to the same degree. The repair has made it difficult to assess the wear in the original perforation, but the general high level of wear that predates the repair suggests it may have been worn quite a bit. It then broke both lengthwise and crosswise through the perforation and was repaired to form two new pendants. 1921.H6 was re-perforated a little further down and abraded on the broken edge, the bottom and the back to reshape it slightly. The broken edge on 1921.X1 was only partially ground smooth, and there is also some grinding on the other surfaces as part of the reworking. It has been thinned in the upper area so that it somewhat resembles an imitation red deer canine bead (see Beads below). In both cases, the repair is not as carefully worked or polished as the original manufacture. 1921.H6 shows slight wear in the new perforation; it was recovered from flotation, so we do not know where it lay in the grave. 1921.X1 shows little if any suspension wear in the new perforation, but it was found at the neck of the skeleton along with a stone pendant, and so was probably worn in the grave. It is notable that the pendant was worth repairing, and striking that both pieces were kept together, at least in death. There is always the possibility that the pendant was deliberately broken, although there is nothing to indicate this. It would seem, though, that intentional breakage would most likely occur either because the two pieces were to be divided between two people, or as a symbolic killing or ending prior to discard, neither of which applies in this case.

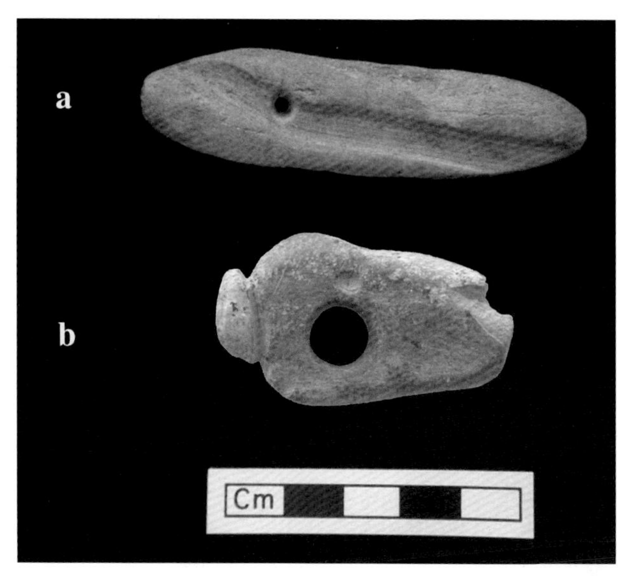

Figure 16.14. *a) Bull-roarer type pendant, with incised groove 4121.F7; b) pendant in shape of equid (?) head 5380.F1.*

Boar's tusk is most often worked into pendants shaped like rounded triangles, with the perforation at the wide end. There are two such from the fill of Building 1 (Level VI–V) in the North Area, 1208.F35 and 1239.H1, as well as the repaired pendant 2732.F1 described with the ornaments above. 4121.F26 from a Level VIII midden in the South Area is similar but more elongated.

Two pendants are simply perforated teeth. 4401.X8 is a very large and robust cattle incisor that has been drilled through the root. Both sides of the root were first scraped down to thin them, apparently to ease drilling. There is clear suspension wear in the perforation. It was part of a cluster of stone and bone in a pit in Building 6 that may have been contained in a bag. 2382.F1 is an extremely worn lower pig incisor. The natural wear has created a wedge-like rectangular shape that someone evidently found pleasing. The crown has been ground very slightly to even it up, and the root has been perforated and shows considerable use. It derives from a levelling layer of reused brick and mortar below a wall in Level VIII.

The remaining pendants do not seem to group in any way. 5177.X1, from a burial of an infant in a basket in Building 17, is the most elaborate of all the pendants, although it might conceivably be some type of fastener (Fig. 16.15). Mellaart (1964a, 100) refers to similar objects as eyes for belt hooks, but this one was not accompanied by a hook. It was found at the child's chin, although given how contracted the skeleton was in the basket it is not clear that it was worn around the neck. It is carved from the cortex of a thick, straight long bone, probably a large cattle metapodial. It forms

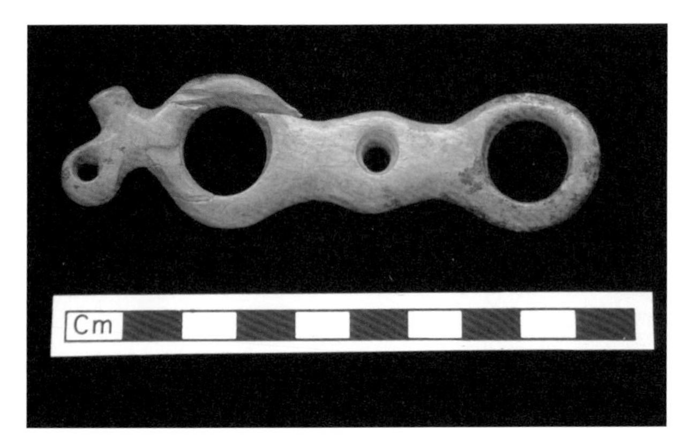

Figure 16.15. *Elaborate pendant/belt eye 5177.X1.*

Figure 16.16. *Pendant reworked from ring with pillar 5281.D1.*

an elaborate hourglass or figure-of-eight shape. There are two large (16–17 mm) circular perforations with a small (5 mm) one in between. The outer edge is carved to follow the shape of the perforations, and in addition one end flares into a forked form with a small (4 mm) perforation in one fork. The other fork was probably originally the same. It has broken off and been repaired by grinding the broken surface flat; considerable use wear postdates the repair. The small perforations have no use-wear and are apparently purely decorative. There is greater polish in the large perforation at the opposite end from the fork, especially in the far end. This indicates that it was suspended from this end if it was worn as a pendant. Alternatively, it may have been tied around the forks with a cord or piece of fabric looped through the perforation. At nearly 10 cm in length, it seems out of proportion for an infant to wear in any fashion. Someone else who wore it in life may therefore have placed it in the grave.

3999.X1 comes from a layer of backfill from Mellaart's excavations in Building 6. While its exact provenance is therefore unknown, it is likely to derive from Level VIII. It is an odd pendant made

Table 16.5. *Repair by tool type.*

Tool type	Number repaired	Percentage repaired
Points	3	1
Needles	5	10
Plaster tools	1	10
Pendants	4	24
Beads	2	6
Fishhooks	1	17

on a piece of split mandible, which has been ground to an irregular shape, smoothed somewhat on both surfaces, and perforated near the narrow end. It seems quite crude and there is no sign of use, so it may be unfinished. However, it has been worked all the way around the edges, which suggests that the shape is deliberate.

4845.F23 comes from an area of *in situ* burning in the dump deposits in Space 181, Level Pre-XII.A, and is itself burnt, most likely postdepositionally. It may also be unfinished, as it shows no sign of use. It may be something other than a pendant, but it is hard to imagine what. An unsplit large mammal rib has been perforated toward the proximal end, the 'base' end near the perforation has been ground to an oblique surface, and it has been thoroughly scraped all over the surface. The 'tip' end is missing, but it must have been at least 10 cm long.

5281.D1 (Fig. 16.16) is a pendant that has been reworked from a ring with pillar (see below). It comes from a lime burning deposit in Space 181, but is unburnt. The original ring had a tall, straight pillar that swells slightly in the centre, topped by a perforated circle. The ring portion broke after considerable wear, and was ground off to form a small plinth-like base. It was then worn as a pendant suspended from the perforation. The effect is quite phallic, although the perforation in the head of the phallus could be seen as female imagery, hence combining male and female. The knob and pillar are nearly 3.5 cm long; it would have been quite impressive worn as a ring, but less so as a pendant. It is carefully made and well polished, although the repair is not quite so painstaking.

Finally, 5380.F1 is an impressive pendant carved from the split rib of a very large animal, complete except for a couple of modern chips missing (see Fig. 16.14b). It is a surface find from Mellaart's backfill in the South Area. Although it has a large perforation, there is no indication of suspension wear or other use in it. Rather it appears to have been suspended from a strangulated area created at one end by a groove that runs around three sides. There are also two smaller partial perforations, one on the outer side of the rib that appears decorative and may even have had something set into it, and one on the inner side that looks

Table 16.6. *Bead types by level.*

Level	Simple tubular	Tall ring	Barrel-shaped	Red deer canine	Fake red deer canine	Stylized red deer canine	Double-ended	Total
N.VI–V	1				2	1	1	5
N.VII–VI							1	1
VII		1				1		2
VIII	3	2				1		6
IX	2	1				1		4
X	2		1			1		4
XII	1							1
Pre-XII.A	2	3				2		7
Pre-XII.B		1						1
Pre-XII.C				1				1
Total	**11**	**8**	**1**	**1**	**2**	**7**	**2**	**32**

more like a false start for the big perforation. The inner side has more wear polish and is less finished, hence it was probably worn against the body. The shape suggests an animal head, probably an equid but conceivably a boar, when set on its side. There are a few small scratches that could be stray marks, or could be decorative, indicating fur or perhaps the mane. The large perforation is presumably decorative, and is off-centre; it could be read as indicating the cheek on an equid. A somewhat similar artefact, also tentatively identified as representing an equid head, was found at PPNB Tell Ramad II in Syria (Stordeur 1982b, 18 & fig. 7). A belt hook that appears to be carved in the shape of an equid head was found in a Level VIA burial in Mellaart's excavations (Todd 1976, 89 & fig. 43).

Manufacture

Most of the perforations on the Çatalhöyük pendants are drilled from both sides with a pointed object of chipped stone. This creates a biconical profile, which occasionally is then enlarged and straightened by scraping. At least one and possibly two pendants appear to have been perforated with a cylinder drill, leaving a straight, tubular hole. One, a partial perforation on 5380.F1, has a rounded bottom that suggests a rod used with grit rather than a pointed drill. It is possible that such a drill produced the cylindrical perforations. While some of the needles have perforations that are cut rather than drilled, this is not seen on the pendants.

Context

The most elaborate pendants are found in burials or in one case on a complete necklace placed or lost in building fill. In general, pendants seem to be underrepresented in middens and fills (see Table 16.7). The combination of their relatively frequent placement in burials and the care taken to maintain them (see Table 16.5) suggests that at least some of the pendants were linked to identity. The variability in form might indicate that it is personal identity rather than membership in some group that is involved, although the two may not be mutually exclusive. The complete necklace and the pierced tooth that may have been in a bag of stone items suggest that at least some may have been deliberately placed in fills. In this case, however, they have been separated from the individual, and possibly linked to the house. These tend to be the less elaborate kinds of pendants. Are these more closely linked to household, family, or lineage identity? Do they belong to the house rather than the individual who wears them? Can we speak of abandoned and filled houses as graves in themselves, in addition to the burials that many of them contain?

Beads

Unlike the pendants, the beads (see also Chapter 14) sort fairly clearly into three major types, two of which subdivide further to produce a total of seven varieties (see Table 16.6). The major types are tubular beads, which use the natural hollow of a bone for stringing; red deer canine variants, which are perforated for suspension; and double-ended beads, which have no hole but rather a constricted area in the centre to permit them to be tied to a string.

Tubular

All the tubular beads are made from segments of small long bone shafts. Within them we can distinguish simple tubular beads, which are made by grooving around the shaft and then breaking at the groove, with relatively little further modification. The cut and broken edges may be ground smooth, and sometimes the outer side is polished. I have labelled another variety 'tall rings', because the manufacturing process is similar to that for rings, although usually slightly less elaborate, often leaving the inner side completely untouched. A third, more elaborate variety is barrel-shaped, with substantial shaping of the outer surface.

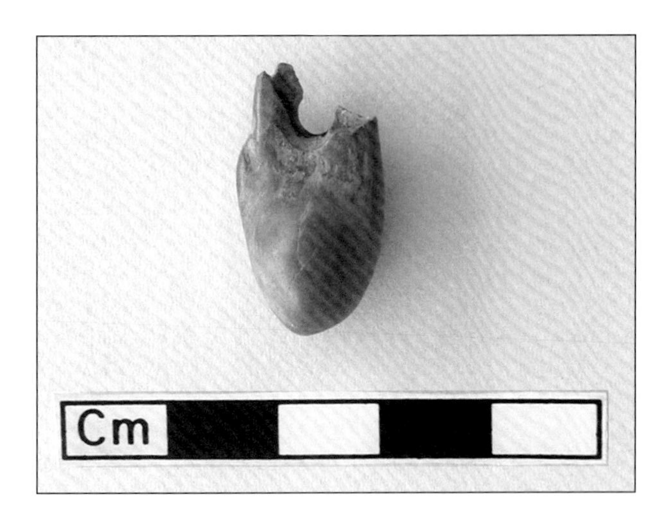

Figure 16.17. *Genuine red deer canine bead 5313.F1.*

Simple tubular
The simple tubular beads are the most common type of bone bead. They are made on segments of long bones of birds and of mammals of roughly hare-fox size in equal proportions. They have been found in a variety of contexts, including fills, middens, and sweepings in houses. Many of them are so simply, even crudely made, with the rough edges left unsmoothed, that it seems possible that they were made by children. I am not aware that they have ever been found in burials, suggesting that they have less symbolic significance than some of the other beads.

Tall rings
The tall ring beads are the next most common type, and to a certain extent they grade into the simple tubular beads. As well as having a more elaborate manufacturing process with more grinding and scraping, and perhaps deliberate polishing, they also tend to be shorter than the simple tubular beads. They are made on the same materials, but ranging up to the occasional medium mammal (sheep-size) long bone. They are found mostly in midden and floor units.

Barrel-shaped
This variety is represented by a single example, 5087.H3, from floor deposits in Building 23, Level X. This tiny bead (4 mm long) started out like a very small simple tubular bead, created by cut-and-break on a hare-size long bone. It was then shaped to slope down from the centre to each end. It may have been deliberately smoothed and rounded, and is certainly polished from use.

Red deer canine variants
This group of bead types is pierced rather than being tubular, and they seem to have a stylistic relationship to each other. It subdivides into three varieties:

Table 16.7. *Tool types by context type, with column percentages.*

	Point	Rounded point	Needle	Pick	Chisel/Gouge	Scraper	Burnisher	Pottery polisher	Plaster tool	Spoon/Spatula	Bowl/Cup	Handle	Ornament	Pendant	Bead	Ring	Belt hook or eye	Fishhook	Harpoon	Pressure flaker	Hammer/Mallet	Punch	Preform/Waste	Indeterminate	Total
Midden	134	1	36		2	1	4	3	1	1	1		6	6	12	30		1			1	1	18	24	283
	47.3	*0.4*	*12.7*		*0.7*	*0.4*	*1.4*	*1.1*	*0.4*	*0.4*	*0.4*		*2.1*	*2.1*	*4.2*	*10.6*		*0.4*			*0.4*	*0.4*	*6.4*	*8.5*	
Fill	42	3	5		1			1	6		1		2	2	9	8		3	1	1	3		12	8	108
	38.9	*2.8*	*4.6*		*0.9*			*0.9*	*5.6*		*0.9*		*1.9*	*1.9*	*8.3*	*7.4*		*2.8*	*0.9*	*0.9*	*2.8*		*11.1*	*7.6*	
Pit fill	8		1												1								1	2	13
	61.5		*7.7*												*7.7*								*7.7*	*15.4*	
Between-wall fill	6		2							1						3					1		1	3	17
	35.3		*11.8*							*5.9*						*17.6*					*5.9*		*5.9*	*17.6*	
Burials										1				3		5							12		21
										4.8				*14.3*		*23.8*							*57.1*		
Floor	14		2						1					1	5	5		2					1	1	32
	43.8		*6.3*						*3.1*					*3.1*	*15.6*	*15.6*		*6.3*					*3.1*	*3.1*	
Sweepings	3		1												2								11		17
	17.6		*5.9*												*11.8*								*64.7*		
Cluster	1													1	1	3					1				7
	14.3													*14.3*	*14.3*	*42.9*					*14.3*				
Construction material	6		1						1			1		1		3				1					14
	42.9		*7.1*						*7.1*			*7.1*		*7.1*		*21.4*				*7.1*					
Penning	3								1																4
	75.0								*25.0*																
Backswamp dump	2			1																			1		4
	50.0			*25.0*																			*25.0*		
Mixed	26		1										1	3	5	5	1				1		1	1	
	57.8		*2.2*										*2.2*	*6.7*	*11.1*	*11.1*	*2.2*				*2.2*		*2.2*	*2.2*	45
Total	**245**	**4**	**49**	**1**	**3**	**1**	**4**	**4**	**10**	**3**	**2**	**1**	**9**	**17**	**35**	**62**	**1**	**6**	**1**	**2**	**7**	**1**	**58**	**39**	**565**

real red deer canines that have been perforated; fake red deer canines, where the form has been imitated reasonably faithfully in carved bone; and stylized red deer canines, where the form evokes but does not directly imitate real red deer canines, being flattened and sometimes squared off.

Real red deer canines
Red deer have vestigial upper canines with an unusual shape that lends itself well to use as beads. These teeth have no enamel but are composed only of dentine, and have a smooth, globular shape with a flattened root that can easily be pierced. No doubt due both to their unusual and appealing form and to their relative rarity (only males produce canines large enough to use; only two per stag), they have been enthusiastically used as beads wherever red deer or their American elk equivalent occur (Choyke 2001; d'Errico & Vanhaeren 2002; McCabe 1982; Roussot-Larroque 1985; Sidéra 2001; Ursachi 1990; Voruz 1985a,b).

There is only one genuine red deer canine bead in the assemblage described here, which is also the earliest bead of all, from Level Pre-XII.C (Fig. 16.17). There are no unworked red deer canines. This might fit well with the pattern in the general fauna, in which the whole body of deer seems to be brought to the site only through Level Pre-XII.B, and after that only the antler. However, it should be noted that there is another red deer canine bead from the BACH Area (*c.* Level VI).

Fake red deer canines
Just as genuine red deer canines have been highly prized in many times and places, so they have been widely imitated (e.g. Choyke 2001; Phillips *et al.* 1998, Roussot-Larroque 1985; Russell 1990; Sidéra 2001). Indeed one can still buy imitations of North American elk canines made of bone, resin, or porcelain. It is not clear whether the prehistoric examples should be seen as deliberate counterfeits, or as simply evoking the shape and meaning of the real ones. Some of them are quite convincing imitations. At Çatalhöyük, the fake red deer canines are more common than the real ones. They are made out of chips of large mammal long bone, carved and polished to shape, and then drilled (see Preforms and Waste below). These occur throughout the sequence, from before Level X (mixed material from cleaning) through to Level VI–V in the North Area, in both indoor and outdoor contexts. In addition to those reported here, a large number of fake red deer canine beads were found in a child burial in a basket (Level VIII, Building 6) that was lifted and taken to the Konya Museum in block, so that the beads were unavailable for study.

Stylized red deer canines
While some imitation red deer canine beads are quite realistic, others do not attempt to pass for the real thing. These have a flattened teardrop shape. They are fairly clearly derived from the fake red deer canine beads, because there is a continuum from fully realistic to highly stylized. I have somewhat arbitrarily divided them, counting any that are not reasonably plausible facsimiles as stylized rather than fakes. These are even more common than the fakes, and occur over an even wider time span, from Level Pre-XII.A to North Level VI–V, again in a range of indoor and outdoor contexts. It is thus not clear that there was any differentiation between the fake and stylized beads in the eyes of the ancient inhabitants.

Double-ended
The final bead type is not even certainly a bead. They are shaped like elongated diamonds with two sharp, slender tips. The centre of the bead is notched and grooved, so that a string could be tied around it. The two examples in this assemblage are made on split large and medium mammal ribs; a third specimen from the BACH Area is made on bird long bone. The two examples in this assemblage are both just over 2 cm long and 2–3 mm wide; the BACH Area specimen is slightly larger. If they are not beads, they might be toggle-type buttons, although they seem small and sharp for this purpose. They would work quite well as fishing gorges that one baits like a hook and then jerks to set in the fish's throat (Campana 1989, 39; 1991; Craig 1967). However, the apparent lack of fish large enough to catch in this way argues against such an interpretation.

Change through time
The various bead sub-types show some temporal trends, although the sample sizes are small (see Table 16.6). The red deer canine variants are present throughout, but genuine teeth are not found after Level Pre-XII.C, until the specimen from the BACH Area. The tubular beads are found throughout the sequence in the South Area, but only one occurs in the North Area. On the other hand, the double-ended beads are found only in the North and BACH Areas.

Rings
After the points, rings are the most common bone-tool type at Çatalhöyük. The rings vary from rather rough to quite carefully finished. They also vary in size: some are so small that only children could have worn them, others would fit adults. Those intact enough to measure the internal diameter range from 10.7–19.3 mm. Rings occur from Level Pre-XII.A throughout the

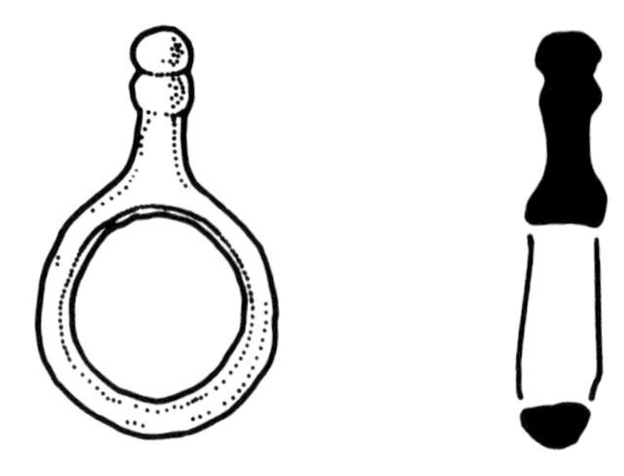

Figure 16.18. *Ring with pillar 1520.X1.*

sequence. Given how common they are in general, it is a little surprising that they do not occur earlier in the sequence. It may be that they are closely tied to activities in the vicinity of houses, as Space 181 (the only area with Level Pre-XII exposures) may have been further from houses prior to Level Pre-XII.A). With one notable exception (see below), the rings have not been found in burials. They occur in a variety of contexts, but especially in middens.

The single occurrence of rings as grave goods is in (2119) in the North Area. This adolescent skeleton was buried with five bone rings: one was in place on the thumb, the others seemed to have slipped in two pairs from the index and middle fingers (Volume 3, Part 3). All five were cut in sequence from a single femur, with internal diameters ranging from 16.8–19.3 mm. Two of them had been worn on the same finger extensively in life (this could be seen by matching wear and staining, and by the edges wearing into each other); these were not, however, on the same finger of the skeleton. The others had less wear. Thus they had been rearranged on the dead body for the burial. Indeed, it would be very difficult to do anything wearing five bone rings, so they were probably rarely worn all at the same time in life. It is striking that they were kept together as a unit nevertheless. One can imagine a person having their own ring bone, from which they cut off and form rings at intervals, perhaps to mark certain life events. Mellaart (1964a, 95) refers to a child burial with eleven bone rings on all its fingers from Level VI of the earlier excavations, as well as other burials with one or two bone rings.

Manufacture

Rings are made according to a very standardized method of manufacture that begins with cutting segments from a sheep-size long-bone shaft (usually or always a femur). Femora are well suited to this use, having a fairly straight, round shaft. The outside and edges are then smoothed slightly with sandstone, and the inside scraped quite heavily around the circumference with a chipped-stone tool to thin and smooth it. The ring is then probably deliberately polished, as well as acquiring still more gloss from use.

This *chaîne opératoire* is so rigidly adhered to that the only exceptions stand out like sore thumbs, and no doubt did to the ancient inhabitants of Çatalhöyük as well. 4836.F59 is a fragment of a bone ring made by somebody who did not know how. The edges are ground with sandstone in the approved manner, but the inner side is ground with sandstone parallel to the long axis of the bone (opposite to the usual direction of the chipped-stone scrapes), and the outer side is very crudely ground with sandstone into facets. There is some use wear, much heavier on the edges. Thus, given that it is relatively tall, it may have been a bead rather than a ring (it would have had to be strung with other beads of a similar size to achieve this wear pattern), but this kind of bead (tall ring) usually follows the ring-manufacturing technique, too. It may therefore have been a child's or novice's first attempt. On the other hand, it might reflect a slightly greater variability in manufacturing techniques early in the occupation. It comes from a Level Pre-XII.A midden in Space 181 in the South Area. Another ring from the same midden, 4867.F1, is also rather crude and lacks scraping on the inner surface. However the two remaining rings from this midden (4837.F244 & 4837.F373) follow the usual method. Together, these four rings are the earliest as yet recovered from the site. Later, in Level VIII, 3146.F1 is also ground on the interior with sandstone instead of scraped, but is otherwise normal and well-finished.

Rings with pillars

The vast majority of the Çatalhöyük rings are of the type described above. A few form a separate class and are necessarily made quite differently. Four rings have a tall pillar projecting from the circular portion, topped with some form of knob. This form may be temporally restricted to the earlier part of the occupation. Three are from Level VIII middens and one from an obsidian cache in the fill of Building 9 (Level X). Only one is complete, but it is from a midden. There is also an example of such a ring repaired into a pendant (see above) from the lime burning in Level Pre-XII.B. Indeed, there is some evidence that these rings were sometimes worn as pendants even when complete. Mellaart does not mention or illustrate this kind of ring in any of his publications. One apparently found in a Çatalhöyük burial is shown in a popular account of the site, where the pillar, which is shorter than any from the renewed excavations, is incorrectly described as 'a natural bone excrescence' (Hamblin 1973, 52). I have not been able to find any mention of comparable objects elsewhere.

The only complete ring with pillar is 1520.X1 (Fig. 16.18). The pillar is surmounted by a knob that is circled by a sharp groove. It is burnt a deep, even black all over and all the way through the bone. This burning is almost surely deliberate, as with the pendants from (1921). The use wear raises the possibility that it was actually worn as a pendant, as it is more polished on one face than the other, and there is virtually no use polish on the inside of the ring portion. However, other rings with pillars were clearly worn as rings, so this may have been as well, but not very much.

A fragmentary ring (2739.X2) from another Level VIII midden in the same space is similar, but has a simple knob (Fig. 16.19a). The pillar is *c.* 9 mm long and 3–4 mm across; the knob and pillar would project fully 2 cm from the finger. 4209.X22, from the obsidian cache, has a knob in the shape of a flat, rounded diamond. It is set off from the pillar on which it sits by an encircling groove, giving a strangulated effect. Below this, the pillar has three notches on one side and four on the other, with the last one at the juncture of pillar and ring. There is a further notch on each side of the pillar on the outer surface of the ring. It has broken through one of these predepositionally.

4121.F25, again from a Level VIII midden, is a fragment of an extreme version of this type (Fig. 16.19b). The pillar is extraordinarily tall, so that the knob stands more than 3 cm above the finger. The pillar itself is a simple rod. The knob consists of two small balls side by side, set off by grooves below them. Held upside down, it is quite phallic; right side up, they could be breasts, much like the Dolní Věstonice carvings (Nelson 1990). Thus one could see it as deliberately combining male and female imagery, as in some of the figurines. In any case, it must have been very impressive when worn. It is highly polished, and shows signs of considerable wear. Although the interior of the ring portion is worn, supporting use as a ring, one outer side of the entire artefact is more worn than the other, which could indicate use as a pendant. Perhaps it was worn both ways?

The shape of these rings requires an entirely different manufacturing process from the standard rings. Rather than cutting them crosswise from a long-bone shaft, the entire form must be carved from the thick cortex of a large mammal long bone, very likely a cattle metapodial, in a lengthwise orientation. They are carved out with chipped-stone tools, and then notches and details may be either carved or formed with sandstone abrasion. The rings are then deliberately polished with a soft material. This process would require much more skill and effort than the standard rings. They are carefully finished and clearly exhibit pride of craftsmanship.

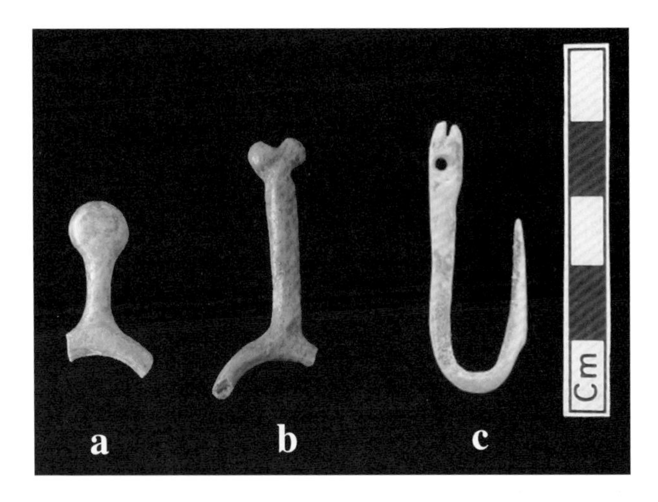

Figure 16.19. *a) Ring with pillar 2739.X2; b) ring with pillar 4121.F25; c) fishhook 4416.D1.*

While the standard rings are all very similar, with some variation in size and height, like the pendants every one of the rings with pillars is different. They all follow the basic formula of knob on pillar, but the details of both knob and pillar are unique. As with the pendants, then, they may be linked to the identity of individuals. Unlike the pendants, though, they do not remain with the person in death (with the apparent exception of the ring with pillar from Mellaart's excavations), but are generally discarded or placed in middens. As they extend 2–3 cm from the finger, they would have been quite striking when worn. They would have made a brass knuckle effect, and it is hard to imagine using the hands very much while wearing one. Thus their use was probably limited to special occasions. Given that there are not very many of them, they may have been worn by people who were special in some way.

Fishhooks

All six fishhooks from the site are made of split boar's tusk. This material is also used for fishhooks in Neolithic Europe (Choyke & Bartosiewicz 1994; Clark 1952, 86) and the Natufian (Campana 1989, 41). They are rather puzzling artefacts. It is clear that they are meant to be fishhooks (as opposed to belt hooks, for instance), since they have sharp tips and some have barbs. They are also too small and delicate to be belt hooks. However, the fish remains from the site are all from minnows; there is no sign of fish large enough to be caught by these hooks. If they were used in fishing, it must have been elsewhere, and the fish themselves were not brought back to the site although the hooks were. The wear also does not occur where one would expect from use in fishing. Some show more polish on one face than the other, though, suggesting they were actually worn as pendants. Perhaps, like the Maori fishhook pendants (Harsant 1987, 133), they were only meant to evoke fishhooks rather than to function as hooks.

As with most of the pendants and the rings with pillars, there are general similarities, but every fishhook has a unique form. They all have straight shanks and some means of fastening to a cord at the top: sometimes notches, sometimes perforations. The perforations are found on two of the earlier hooks, from Levels IX and VIII. The other Level VIII hook is notched, as are the later ones. Some have barbs, and these are variably placed. One (4416.D1) seems to have been repaired. It broke through the original perforation, which was cut, and was reperforated by drilling. The broken edges were ground down to a forked bevel. Given the substantial subsequent wear, however, it may be that this was all part of the original manufacturing process; that is they were cutting a notch in the end rather than a perforation in the shaft.

So far, fishhooks do not occur before Level IX, and they tend to cluster. Except for one from a Level VIII midden (4121.D6), the fishhooks are all built into floors or building / foundation fills, and are associated with two sequences of houses. In the South Area, 4416. D1 (Fig. 16.19c) comes from the fill of Building 17 (along with two fishhook preforms), while 4252.X1 is from the floors of Building 6 directly above it. In the North Area, 3047.F1 comes from the foundation fill separating Building 5 and Building 1 (Subphase B1.1A), 2166. F1 comes the foundation fill of Building 1 (Subphase B1.1B), and 1415.X1 is built into the floor of the lentil bin (Subphase B1.2B). There is thus the hint of an association with particular buildings, and specifically with building construction or the transition from one building to the next. The single fishhook recovered by Mellaart was from shrine E.IX.1 (our Building 22), two buildings to the west of Building 17 in Level IX (Mellaart 1964a, 163 & fig. 43).

Manufacture

The manufacturing sequence begins with splitting the lower boar canine to obtain a flat piece. This is ground into a flat oval or elongated trapezoid. Two adjacent large holes are then drilled in the centre, sometimes intersecting each other (Fig. 16.24b). It is then snapped through the holes and carved into shape. This is similar to the process used for Hawaiian shell fishhooks (Craig 1967) and Natufian boar's tusk and bone hooks (Campana 1989, 41), and slightly different from that used on boar's tusk in Neolithic Hungary, where a series of small perforations are drilled to outline the hook shape (Choyke & Bartosiewicz 1994).

Harpoons

Only one object can be described as a harpoon. 4351.F26 is a barbed tool carved on the back of a large cattle metatarsal, using a natural indentation on one side of the artefact and carving the other side to match it. The tip end is beautifully symmetrical and the base asymmetrical. The wear indicates that this was for hafting onto a wooden shaft. Back from the tip there is a single large, carved barb with a somewhat blunt tip. The manufacturing wear in this region is very fresh, arguing against use as a hook in a snare, a grappling hook, or a belt hook. In addition to the hafting wear on the base, wear is concentrated in the tip area. It is hard to see what the original shape of the tip was, as a number of large flakes have occurred in use, with use continuing after most of them. These clearly indicate a high impact use, such as a javelin head. It is puzzling, though, that the tip is now quite blunt, and was for some time while it was still used. This makes hunting or fishing with it hard to imagine. Perhaps in its later life, at least, it was just used for target practice. This is the only bone artefact that is plausible as a weapon.

Pressure flakers

Pressure flakers are typically made of antler, which is softer than bone and thus preserves microwear less well. As a result, it can be difficult to identify them, and they may have been more common than they appear. 1683.X1 is a possible pressure flaker on an antler tine with the tip cut or worn off to form a broad, dull bevel. There appear to be faint gouges from the stone leading away from the bevel. This artefact was evidently built into a wall in Building 20 in Level VII of the South Area.

4325.F12 (from the fill of Building 17 in the South Area, Level IX) is a more certain pressure flaker, but started life as a different tool. It was pointed and perforated, perhaps a weaving or netting tool, but quite different from the usual 'needles'. Made on a thick, heavy piece of large mammal long-bone cortex, it would have been shaped like an elongated diamond, with the shoulders just above the perforation. The tip broke off in use with a fairly clean, slightly-hinged fracture, leaving a flattish blunt tip that was reused (without reworking) as a pressure flaker, causing battering and scratching.

Hammers/mallets

One of the principal uses of antler at Çatalhöyük is as mallets, probably in woodworking. The shapes of the working surfaces are wrong for soft hammers used to work stone. Rather, they most likely struck obsidian chisels (Fig. 16.20). These artefacts range from rather carefully-shaped hammers to unmodified chunks of antler. Even these should perhaps not be regarded as expedient tools, however, since it is likely that the antler was brought to the site for tool use. Postcranial deer remains are virtually absent after the earliest levels.

The most formal example (3037.F8) is made on the base of a probably shed antler, using the first tine as a handle. It was found in what is interpreted as a deposit of feasting remains outside the south wall of Building 1 in the North Area. The beam has been removed and this cut surface ground to round it off to form the hammering area. On this surface are stray marks from a hard material, some probably flint/obsidian. It may also have been used to strike bone chisel/gouges, as not all of the marks are clearly made by stone tools. Its presence in a feasting deposit is intriguing. Was it used to produce wooden serving vessels for the meal? 1014.F1 (from Mellaart's backfill in the South Area) is an antler tine that has been shaped to produce a flat striking surface along one side. It fits conveniently in the hand and is likely to have been used for finer, more controlled work than some of the larger mallets.

Four additional antler tines and one chunk of beam, from Levels IX, VIII, VII, and North VII–VI and North VI–V, have scars and battering that indicate use as mallets. Some have minimal shaping, others none at all. Although the numbers are small, it is interesting that these artefacts are not found before Level IX, possibly indicating an increase in woodworking or a change in technology. Bone chisels do not appear after Level IX in the assemblage reported here, although there is a later example (see Chisels/Gouges above).

Punches

4838.F461, from a Level Pre-XII.A midden, may be a punch used in working chipped stone. A splinter of large mammal long bone has been shaped into a rough cylinder. Both ends are rounded, blunt, and fairly flat. They seem battered but lack clear microwear, at least partly as a result of heavy manganese deposits. Some scars on the underside could be from pressure flaking, and the battering suggests use as a punch.

Preforms and waste

Unfinished tools and discarded pieces of bone and antler removed during working provide evidence for bone-tool manufacture. It is sometimes difficult to distinguish between preforms and waste, or between unfinished and finished but unused tools. In some cases, it is clear what kind of tool is being made, in others this cannot be determined. The presence of substantial amounts of preforms and waste from bone-tool manufacture in the South Area shows that Mellaart (1967, 71 & 211) was incorrect in asserting that no craft activities took place in the part of the tell that he excavated. The distribution of this manufacturing debris suggests household level rather than specialized production. There are some indications, however, that there may have been limited, part-time specialization. People who were particularly skilled at a certain craft may have supplied their neighbours.

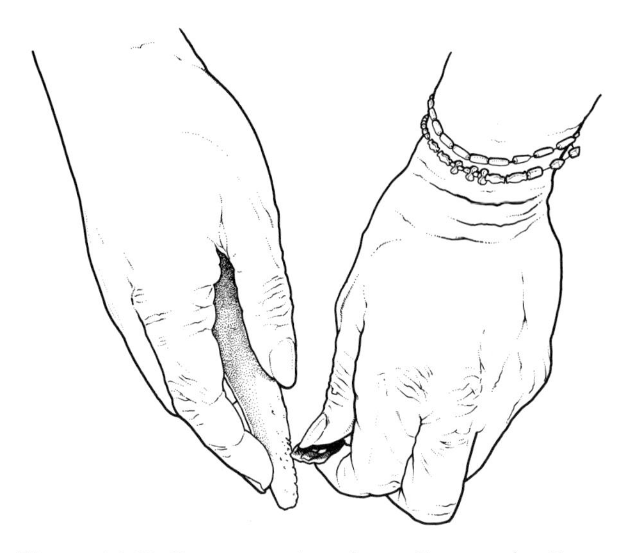

Figure 16.20. *Reconstruction of use of hammer/mallet with obsidian chisel.*

Point preforms

While at many Neolithic sites preforms for points are commonly found, they are very rare at Çatalhöyük. This is probably a result of the manufacturing techniques used here, where points are overwhelmingly roughed out with simple fracture rather than abrasion or groove-and-split. While groove-and-split in particular tends to leave considerable recognizable waste and abandoned rough-outs, long bones broken into a rough shape are indistinguishable from those broken for marrow.

Only four unfinished points and one piece of apparent waste have been identified. The waste piece, 4871.F699, is a rare example of groove-and-split technology from a Level Pre-XII.B midden (Fig. 16.21). It seems to be the remains of a bad split on a distal metatarsal that was not worked further, although it is possible that a usable piece was obtained from the proximal end.

One unfinished tip fragment (1001.F2, from Mellaart's backfill in the South Area) illustrates the sequence of point manufacture. The edges have already been ground carefully, but scraping to form the tip has only begun. This preform may have broken in progress. 1092.F816, from Level VII foundation cut fill, is also in the process of being scraped to form a tip, but in this case a modern break has removed the shaft so that

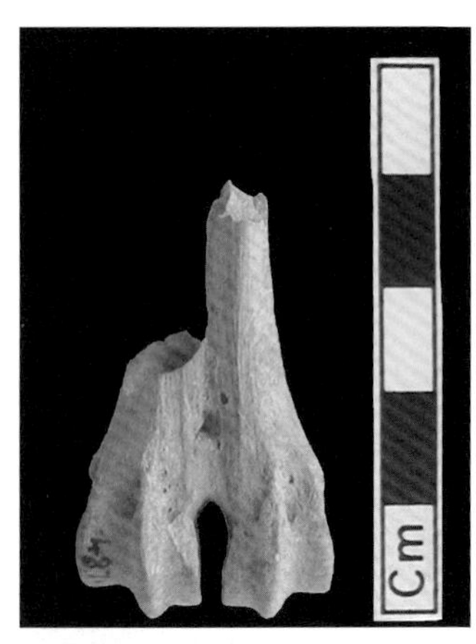

Figure 16.21. *Groove-and-split waste 4871.F699.*

we cannot assess the state of the edges. 4121.F1830, from a Level VIII midden, is a base fragment at an earlier stage, exhibiting an unusual and laborious manufacturing technique. The distal shaft of a sheep/goat metapodial has been heavily scraped (abrasion would be more usual for this technique, which is rare at Çatalhöyük) to form two flat surfaces. They have not broken through to the marrow cavity, but may have influenced a longitudinal fracture. Indeed, this fracture may be deliberate splitting after thinning the cortex. The tip end is missing through a modern break, but there is no sign of further working or smoothing of the broken edges. It seems odd to abandon it after so much work, and obtaining an apparently usable preform. Perhaps a better piece was created on the other end or other side of the bone.

1889.X81, from Building 2 in Level IX, is made in the more usual way, in this case rather expediently. A broken, unsplit tibia has received some longitudinal scraping at the end to form a tip. An old break at the tip end may have occurred during the making of the point, terminating manufacture. There are no indications of use on what remains, but since the tip is missing it is possible that it was in fact finished and only used very slightly. Other similarly-broken but unworked tibiae were recovered in this unit. They may be early preforms, or the tibia for the preform may have been picked out from consumption debris. There are also a number of metapodial splinters that could be preforms. There may be little distinction between the remnants of marrow fracture and preforms for points. Rather than setting out to make a point from an intact bone, the makers may simply sort through consumption remains for suitable pieces.

Needle preforms

Needle preforms are somewhat more plentiful (six, and one piece of waste), especially in comparison to the number of finished artefacts. All derive from midden contexts in Space 181 (Level Pre-XII.B–D) and Space 115 (Level VIII). From these pieces, which were abandoned at various stages, it is possible to reconstruct what appears to be a fairly consistent sequence of needle manufacture, although with some variation.

The earliest stage, splitting the rib and roughing out the form, is not attested and would probably be hard to recognize. The undulating edges of 4121.F33 suggest that this may have been accomplished by flaking along the edges and prying the two plates of cortical bone apart (Fig. 16.22a). The next step is to abrade or scrape the inner and outer surfaces thoroughly. This first flattens and eventually totally removes the cancellous (spongy) bone from the inner surface, and at least when using a large mammal rib (as in three out of these seven cases) substantially thins the cortex. Thus the thinness of the needles, which renders them quite fragile, is a deliberate choice and must be necessary for their function (or at least to conform to the notion of a proper needle). The edges are also scraped at this point, smoothing and straightening them. Then the base and tip are formed, using a cut-and-break technique to remove any excess bone (5308.F152 & 5328.F435), followed by scraping or abrading to form the ends (5290.F1830). The final step is the perforation. 4121.F29 is the only one of the preforms carried through to this last stage. It was apparently abandoned because the two sides of the biconically-drilled hole did not line up. One side shows an attempt at correction, or else indicates that the drill started in the right place but then slipped. It is surprising that the maker gave up on it, since needles that break through the perforation are often repaired. Alternatively, the needle may be perforated before grinding the base and final scraping to refine the shape and thin the shaft, as seen in 3740.F488.

Pendant preforms

Four artefacts appear to be unfinished pendants. 4871.F162 (Space 181 midden, Level Pre-XII.B) is an unfinished antler pendant of the bull-roarer type. It seems fully shaped except that the perforation is unfinished, having been drilled from only one side. There is no obvious reason to abandon it. A roughed-out plaque of a very thick piece of split large mammal rib (4875.F243, from the same area) seems most likely destined to be a pendant, although there is no perforation and not much clue to the final shape (currently roughly rectangular). A roughly-triangular fragment of large mammal proximal tibia shaft (4256.X2, from the fill of Building 6, Level VIII) has two partial perforations and just a bit of grinding on one surface; the edges are untouched (Fig. 16.22b). These perforations are unusual, as they are not drilled biconically. Rather a drill with a rounded, blunt tip was used with grit to make one perforation and start the other. Using the small hole (6.8 mm diameter) as a guide, a larger tubular drill has also been used with grit to start a larger hole (10.6 mm). 3107.F75 (Level VIII fill) is another fragment of large mammal tibia shaft with a large perforation in the centre and the beginning of grinding on one edge; there is no working on the rather rough surfaces. It has broken through the perforation, perhaps while in process. This one might possibly be a rough-out for a ring with pillar rather than a pendant. All in all, these preforms suggest that with the exception of the 'bull-roarer' pendants the perforation is made early in the manufacturing process, before most of the shaping.

Bead preforms

The most common kind of preform is for beads: 24 unfinished beads and two pieces of waste. While finished beads are a relatively common artefact type, they are less frequent than needles or rings, both of which have reasonably recognizable preforms. On the face of it, this would suggest that beads are for some reason very often not finished; indeed there are almost as many unfinished as finished beads. However, this is probably at least partially skewed by two particular contexts: a burial with a set of bead preforms and a building that seems to have been a centre of bead-making activity. Only four preforms and one piece of waste derive from contexts other than these two.

Four preforms and two pieces of waste are derived from the manufacture of simple tubular beads. One of these preforms has broken longitudinally, which may have aborted the manufacture, although it is not certain whether this happened during working or later. The others are simply unfinished for unknown reasons. They need only a bit of grinding to smooth the ends.

The most frequent kind of bead preform is for some variant of the imitation red deer canine bead type. Some are already flattened enough to indicate that they will belong to the stylized variety; others are too early in the process to tell. The manufacturing sequence varies somewhat. Usually suitable chips of long bone cortex are first shaped by grinding, and then pierced at the end of the process. In two cases, however, the perforation occurred at the beginning. It may depend in part on whether the raw chip has an area thin enough to pierce without grinding. Usually these beads are made on large mammal long bones, but one preform (4842.F76, from the fill of a Level Pre-XII.A pit) is made on medium mammal (sheep-size) long bone. As a result it is quite thin even though it remains very rough; finishing it might have made it too thin and may be the reason it was abandoned. This poor choice of material suggests a novice bead maker. An unusual preform (4540.F31, from the bead-making deposits in Building 18) may also belong in this category. Rather than long-bone shaft, it is made on a large tooth fragment, probably an equid incisor. Part of

Figure 16.22. *a) Needle preform 4121.F33; b) pendant preform 4256.X2.*

the occlusal surface is preserved without modification, and has a beautiful polish from occlusion. The sides and bottom of the piece have been extensively ground to form a little bar, roughly the shape of the stylized red deer canine beads. There is no perforation. This experiment with an unusual material was abandoned, although it looks as though it would work.

A particularly interesting group of bead preforms is 5169.X2-13, from grave F.563 in Building 17. These twelve preforms for imitation red deer canine beads (roughed out but not perforated and lacking final shaping) were found in a cluster between the arms of the elderly female skeleton, perhaps originally in a bag. One possible scenario is that the woman buried was working on them at the time of her death, suggesting that at least some bead makers were female. Another is that the beads were being made by someone else for a necklace to offer as grave goods, but for some reason could not be finished in time for the funeral and so were offered as is. A later infant burial in the house above (Building 6) included many such finished beads, but was sent in block to the Konya Museum and so the beads are not included in this study. This seems to show a continuing use of these beads as grave goods in this household, if we imagine such an entity connecting one level of a house to the next. Two buildings to the east in Level IX, (IX.31, actually apparently interred in the process of filling this building to construct Shrine VIII.31) Mellaart (1966a, 182) excavated a burial with a composite necklace of stone beads and twelve pierced deer teeth, as well as other more unusual grave goods. The illustration shows considerably more than twelve red deer canine beads, at least some of which are almost surely imitations. If twelve is actually the correct number, it is an

Figure 16.23. *Boar's tusk bead perform, 4121.F23.*

interesting repetition.

One building to the west of Building 17 and a level earlier (Level X), Building 18 contains evidence of *in situ* bead-making through several of its phases (Russell 2001, 243). Both preforms and finished beads are present, including both tubular and imitation red deer canine types. This combination suggests that the ancient bead maker had a concept of 'bead' similar to mine. Neither Building 18 nor its successor, Building 16, contained burials. Thus it is within the realm of possibility that burial 563 contains the B. 18 bead-maker, still working on beads at the end of her long life.

One apparent bead preform does not correspond to a known type of bead. 4121.F23, from a Level VIII midden, is a piece of boar's tusk that seems to have been worked by someone with little understanding of this raw material (Fig. 16.23). Male lower canines tend to split into flat segments, a property that is often exploited in tool manufacture. In this case, the toolmaker tried to use it unsplit, apparently for beads resembling the tall ring type, but triangular rather than round due to the shape of the tusk, and requiring a more elaborate manufacturing sequence. First the tusk was ground with sandstone to round it slightly and to round off the pointed tip. Then a perforation was drilled through this rounded end to meet the central cavity and thus form a continuous hole through the centre. Five transverse grooves were then marked out at roughly 1-cm intervals (there may have been more originally, as the piece probably started out larger). These seem to be the beginnings of a cut-and-break technique, like that used to make rings. The tooth probably split in the course of cutting these grooves. Tubular beads were now impossible, but an abortive attempt at reworking is evident. Part of the broken edge has been ground to smooth it, perhaps trying to make it into a pendant. However, the grooves would have been very difficult to disguise, so evidently the maker gave up on the idea and discarded the piece. This must have been a painful learning experience, as boar's tusk was probably a relatively highly-valued material. Certainly it, and pig bones in general, are quite rare at the site, and it may have been brought from a certain distance. This very rarity may have contributed to the lack of knowledge of its properties.

Ring preforms

Five ring preforms cover various points in the manufacturing process. They also show that while the operations in ring manufacture were highly standardized (see Rings above), the sequence could vary somewhat. Three of these preforms are femur shafts at some stage of the cut-and-break process to detach ring blanks. 2557.F1 (between-wall fill in the North Area) is earliest in the process. The distal end has been removed by cut-and-break, and a second groove circles the bone at this end, ready to detach a blank. Two grooves similarly circle the proximal shaft, but the proximal articulation is still attached, although some of it was knocked off by simple percussion. The rest of the shaft is ungrooved. There is a little grinding with a coarse sandstone-type material in the vicinity of the grooves. This does not really seem to be shaping, perhaps periosteum removal to facilitate the cuts. 4416.F42 (from the fill of Building 17) is at a slightly later stage (Fig. 16.24a). Both ends, and possibly some rings (judging from the length) have been removed by cut-and-break, but there are no further grooves marking out rings on this segment. Most of the outer surface has been abraded with fine sandstone; in contrast to 2557.F1, this seems to be aimed at smoothing the outer surface of the rings to be. While the previous two artefacts seem to be quite usable, so that their abandonment is puzzling, 3370.X3 (from the fill of Building 24) broke longitudinally in the process of removing a ring blank, ruining the preform. It has six grooves circling the shaft, which still retains the distal end. Thus one approach is to mark out all the rings while one articulation, at least, is still attached. Another is to remove both ends at the start, in the process of removing a ring blank from each end of the shaft. Perhaps subsequent rings were grooved and removed one at a time.

1033.F1 (from a Level VIII midden in the South Area) is a blank without further working, although it shows slight abrasion on the outer surface similar to 2557.F1. 1073.F438 (from a Level VII foundation cut fill in the South Area) is at a later stage. It suggests that the scraping and grinding to finish the ring, at least in this case, do not form discrete steps, but are carried out in alternation. The outer surface has been substantially abraded with coarse sandstone and awaits smoothing; the cut-and-break edges have been only slightly smoothed. The inner surface has been scraped a little but remains very uneven and clearly needs more work. Grinding the edges smooth will leave a rather low ring, and smoothing the inner and outer surfaces will leave very thin walls. Thus there may have been some miscalculations in creating the blank, which might account for its abandonment.

Fishhook preforms
Fishhook manufacture has been described above (see Fishhooks). Both preforms so far discovered (Fig. 16.24b) derive from the fill of Building 17 (Level IX), which also contained a finished fishhook and a boar's tusk collar.

Split rib preforms
Three pieces of split rib have been discarded before completion of unknown tool types, and one piece seems to be waste removed from the end of a preform. None of these is identifiably a needle preform, and some are clearly not. They evidence at least two splitting methods: percussion to knock off the margin of the rib, or scraping to remove it. With the edges removed, the two pieces of cortex must then have been separated by prying or wedging them apart through the spongy cancellous bone, although this step is not directly attested.

Antler preforms
A strip of antler (2165.F117, from the fill of Building 1) extracted by the groove-and-splinter technique (Clark & Thompson 1954) and further shaped by cutting seems to be a blank for a pointed object. Two pieces of cut antler beam, both from the fill of Building 2 (Level IX), are likely waste from the manufacture of antler tools.

Miscellaneous preforms
4205.F73, from the fill of Building 9 (Level X), seems to be an unfinished blank for some tool. It is a roughly-rectangular bar of bone from a very robust cattle proximal tibia shaft, with a natural foramen running through it. It has been abraded so that one end is flat, the other bevelled. The surfaces have been ground only slightly to begin to smooth them out. At 48 mm long and 17 mm wide, it is unclear what it was destined to be; it seems too short for a spatula and too small for a belt hook or eye, for instance. A fragment of the distal shaft of a cattle radius from the KOPAL Area (6029.F60) preserves traces of cut-and-break on one end. The other end is heavily gnawed by carnivores, and it has been broken; however, it seems to be waste rather than a preform. It

Figure 16.24. *a) Ring perform 4416.F42; b) possible fishhook preform 4921.F209.*

was probably detached in the process of producing a chunk of long-bone cortex for carving.

Indeterminate
This is a residual category for pieces of worked bone that are not easily classified, usually because they are small fragments, but sometimes because they are simply enigmatic. Among those that are enigmatic, some may be preforms. Five strips of worked antler may be preforms, perhaps for 'bull-roarer' type pendants. 1889.X119 (from the fill of a bin in Building 2, Level IX) is a mysterious flat object carved in the shape of a bow tie: a rectangle with indentations on the two long sides, 95 mm long by 35 mm wide (Fig. 16.25). The manufacturing wear is very fresh, and there is no sign of wear from use, so it may not be finished. It might be a blank for a toggle, pendant, or belt hook/eye, for instance. 4205.F39, from the fill of Building 9 (Level X), may also be a preform for a pendant or other flat tool (Fig. 16.26a). It is a piece of split sheep-size mandible that has been heavily scraped on the outer surface. A series of holes were drilled from the inner side along one edge, and the bone broken along this line of holes, probably as a deliberate step in extracting a blank. The broken edges between the perforations have been ground smooth and seem worn, but the rest of the fragment is not. While this has produced a denticulated effect along one edge, the placement of the wear does not support use as a comb. It is conceivably a musical rasp, but the notches seem overly deep and too irregularly spaced for this purpose, and I would

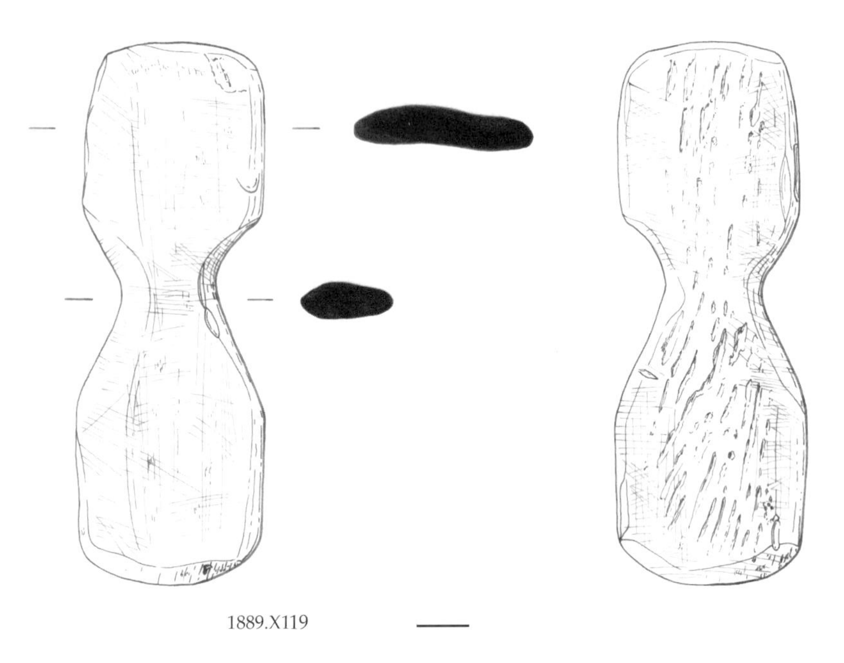

Figure 16.25. *Carved bone object 1889.X119.*

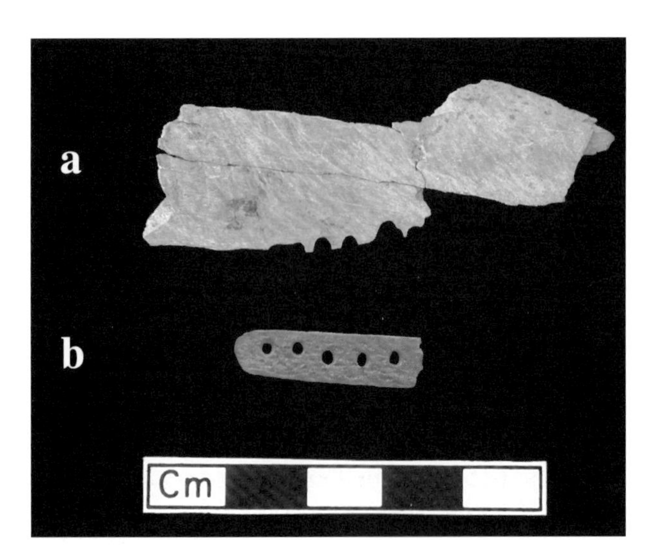

Figure 16.26. *a) Fragment broken along drilled holes 4205.F39; b) perforated rib 5323.F250.*

expect the wear to extend some way into the gaps. There are certainly easier ways to make a rasp.

Some tools look like preforms, but show signs of use. 5290.F1842 (from a Level Pre-XII.B midden) is a splinter of long bone with a pointy end as a result of fracture. There is a small amount of abrasion on the shaft that has not affected the tip or accomplished much shaping, but looks like just the beginning of shaping. On the other hand, the tip seems to have been used unmodified. Perhaps this was an expedient point that the user started to work into a more formal tool, then changed her/his mind. 4121.F1712 (from a Level VIII midden) is the base end of a split-rib tool that looks like a thickish needle without a perforation, but shows use wear from handling. 4121.F3061 is quite similar, but has been removed from the rest of the tool with the cut-and-break technique, for reasons that are unclear. Perhaps the other end was damaged. It was then used in some fashion, perhaps for burnishing a soft material, although it lacks the high polish that would come from extensive use of this kind. A split piece from the heel and alveolar areas of a large mammal mandible (1057.F156) has been extensively ground to flatten it and create a bevelled edge all around, originally forming a large oval. While the shape suggests a preform for a pendant or other ornament, it is worn from use. The most obvious functions from the shape would be some kind of burnisher or scraper, but both of these would be likely to produce more polish.

3039.F1 is a fragment of carved bone from near the base of the handle of something like a 'hairpin' or spatula (Fig. 16.27). It is made on a section of thick long-bone cortex, carved into a distinctive shape, not all of it present. It could be a representation of a human or a bird, among other things. One end is cylindrical, heading toward the tip. It is very carefully worked and polished, but appears to have little actual use. 5323.F250, from a Level Pre-XII.C midden, is an odd little artefact on split rib (Fig. 16.26b). As preserved, it is 2.5 cm long by 6.7 mm wide and 1.1 mm deep. The surviving end has been ground into a truncated triangle, and a series of six small (1.7-mm) perforations have been drilled in a row down the centre. The holes have been scraped out slightly to make the sides less biconical. The artefact has broken through one of these perforations. It is carefully made and could be an ornament, or possibly something like a rigid heddle, but there is little sign of use. 4205.F72 (Building 9 fill, Level X) is the spinous process from a large mammal thoracic vertebra, which has been scraped extensively on both sides for no apparent reason. Is this idle whittling, or a child playing at making bone tools?

The value of worked bone

The Çatalhöyük worked-bone objects form a continuum from expedient to formal and elaborate artefacts. I would argue that it is wrong to view them in terms of utilitarian vs symbolic/ornamental, as there is no sign of such a division. Rather the ancient inhabitants seem to have felt varying degrees and varying kinds of attachment to these objects. I have discussed much of this in the context of the particular types, and here offer some observations at a larger scale.

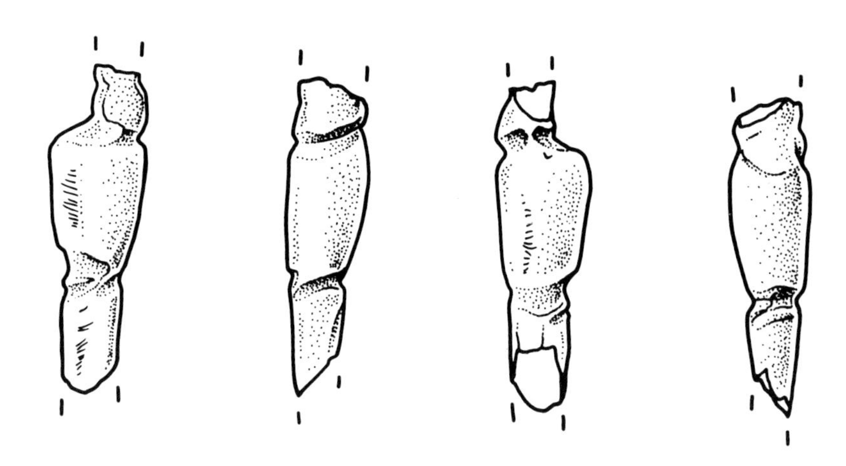

Figure 16.27. *Carved bone object 3039.F1.*

Raw material

As discussed above, the technological choices made in point manufacture indicate that some value was placed on sheep/goat metapodials as a raw material. The morphology and physical properties of these bones are particularly well-suited to the manufacture of points, but there may also have arisen an association of 'real' points with metapodials. Similarly, the exclusive use of cattle scapulae for plaster tools is based only partly on their shape and size. A scapula was still used when a different shape was needed, and it is clear that scapulae held special meaning beyond their utility as raw material (Volume 4, Chapter 2).

Other materials such as antler and boar's tusk are likely to have held special value owing to their rarity and perhaps difficulty of acquisition. They may also have gained significance through their derivation from wild animals. Antler is used virtually throughout the sequence in small quantities, from Level Pre-XII.C to North Level VI–V. It is likely that after Level Pre-XII.B most or all of the antler was brought specially to the site rather than acquired incidentally through hunting (Volume 4, Chapter 2). It was thus valuable enough to collect, transport, and perhaps trade for. Worked boar's tusk (male lower canines) is found only from Level IX and later. There are three fragments of unworked boar's tusk from the Pre-XII levels, a time when boars seem to have been hunted near the site in small numbers. Like the deer, later usually only selected body parts, mostly heads and feet, are brought to the site. From Level IX on, there is only a single piece of unworked boar's tusk in the areas reported on here: an originally complete tusk from the floor of Building 1 that shattered when it burned. Thus boar's tusk became a raw material after it was no longer locally available. It is used for fishhooks and ornaments; as discussed above, the fishhooks may themselves have been ornamental. Much of the display value may have derived from the importation of the raw material. In Neolithic Europe, boar's tusk and red deer canines become more common in burials at a time when hunting declines; the wild takes on greater symbolic strength as it becomes more separate from daily life (Choyke 2001; Sidéra 2000a). Possibly we see a similar process at Çatalhöyük.

Colour

Most of the worked bone would have been white when first manufactured, gradually ageing to an ivory tone. In some cases, though, the colour has been deliberately modified. Some pieces are an even ebony black that is almost surely the result of burning in a reducing atmosphere, probably buried in sand or other soil. Of course, some have burnt post-depositionally when a fire nearby scorched the sediments that contained them. But others come from unburnt sediments in primary contexts, and must have been burnt deliberately (Phillips *et al.* 1998; Sidéra 2000b). One simple tubular bead from a necklace (4845.F142) that is otherwise unburnt and two pendants (originally a single pendant that broke, 1921.H6 & 1921.X1) are heat treated in this fashion. Additionally, a ring with pillar (1520.X1) shows this same even burning, but the context does not preclude accidental burning elsewhere.

Another colour variation is striking in the archaeological specimens, but it is less clear what it would have looked like when fresh and whether it results from deliberate treatment. Fifteen of the rings (25 per cent) are white as though the bone were still fresh, in contrast to the varying shades of brown that characterize most of the bone objects as a result of age and soil staining. I do not know what causes this colour difference. It is not a matter of particularly thorough polish, as the amount of polish is quite variable on the white rings as well as the ordinary ones. Possibly it indicates the use of uncooked bone, or perhaps there was some special chemical treatment. The only other pieces of worked bone that exhibit this colour are a 'tall ring' type bead (4709.F2), which conceivably might be a ring, and a stylized red deer canine bead (1360.H1). These are found in a variety of context types (midden, floor, fill, etc.) and throughout the levels in which rings are found. Some of the unworked bone from the penning deposits shows a similar light colour, as do occasional fragments from other contexts.

Repair

I have discussed the resharpening of points above. Table 16.5 summarizes the repair of broken bone tools. In part, the distribution of repairs reflects the tendency of perforated objects to break through the weak point created by the perforation. It also indicates that the object was valuable enough to repair. It is notable that nearly a quarter of the pendants have been repaired. If we exclude the 'bull-roarer' type, which may not actually be pendants, nearly a third are repaired. In addition, a shell pendant (2105.F1) has been repaired in the same way (grinding and reperforation), and 2732.F1, a boar's tusk pendant, was 'repaired' without a new perforation so that it is no longer a pendant. Pendants must have been not only valuable but also worn frequently, and perhaps during vigorous activities (dances? sacrifices?) that exposed them to impacts.

Bone objects and identity

Many bone objects, such as carefully worked and maintained points (Spector 1991), may have been linked to the identity of their owners through pride in craftsmanship and the activities associated with them. Some objects, however, seem to be primarily about identity of various kinds.

The more elaborate pendants seem related to personal identity. Along with beads, they are the kind of worked bone most frequently found in burials, although most come from other contexts, and most burials lack them. While to some extent they sort into types, each one is unique. They have been found with both infants and adults, thus do not relate to achieved status. Not only do they stay with a person in death (if we can assume that this same person wore them in life), but in one case when a pendant broke and was repaired into two pendants (1921.X1 & 1921.H6), both stayed with the same individual. The rings with pillars also form a related set, with each one unique. So far, though, none have been found in burials; most are from middens and one fragmentary example from an obsidian cache. Thus while they are individualized and ostentatious, they do not stay with the person, and perhaps mark a status or position rather than an individual. Fishhooks, which may be worn as pendants and likewise are variable in their design, also do not appear in graves and seem to be tied more to particular houses than to people. Thus they may denote household or lineage identity. The same is perhaps true of some of the simpler pendants, for instance 1208.F35 and 1239.H1, both from the fill of Building 1 and both, like the fishhooks, made of boar's tusk.

Worked bone in context

At a gross level, some bone-tool types are more common in certain context types than others (see Table 16.7). In total, half of the bone tools come from midden contexts. While midden accounts for only about a quarter of the volume excavated, it is defined in part by its high density of material, so this is not surprising. About half the excavated volume is some variety of fill. These deposits are generally sparser in artefact content, and more mixed, often with substantial amounts of building material. In general the pattern of bone-tool types found in fills is not very different from that found in middens. However, needles are relatively scarce in fills, and also in floor and sweepings contexts. (I term 'sweepings' contexts characterized as ashy occupation or rake-outs or trample, which seem to contain the swept-up remnants of indoor activities.) Together with their occurrence in concentrations in particular middens, this suggests that needles were used primarily outside houses, either in the open midden areas or perhaps on the roofs whence they fell or were swept into middens. This might account for their comparatively high representation (although based on a small sample) in between-wall fills. Needle preforms also occur only in middens. If these are indeed weaving tools, the implication is that weaving happened outdoors.

On the other hand, bone-tool manufacture seems to have occurred primarily inside. The proportion of preforms and waste is higher in fill than in midden, and very high in sweepings (largely as the result of bead-making in Building 18). Their high level in burials is entirely attributable to the find of a dozen bead preforms in a single burial (see above). Beads and rings also occur more frequently in indoor contexts. There is a particularly high occurrence of rings in obsidian clusters in comparison to other bone artefacts, although this accounts for only three of 25 obsidian clusters. A fourth obsidian cluster contains a complete simple tubular bead; the remaining clusters with bone tools are composed of feasting remains or more mixed materials. All the rings from clusters are fragmentary. Two are ordinary rings, one a ring with pillar. Two of these obsidian clusters consist of debitage, two of cached blanks. Thus bone rings may in some way be linked to obsidian working, although the nature of the connection is not obvious. Broken rings seem unlikely to be 'cached' in anticipation of recovery. Conceivably the rings are part of the exchange relationships through which the obsidian was obtained, in which case their fragmentation may not be accidental (Chapman 2000).

While Mellaart (1967, 209) mentions a somewhat wider range of bone objects as grave goods (including belt hooks and eyes, a small fork, a boar's tusk collar, a carved dagger handle, antler toggles, and points), only a few tool types are securely associated with skeletons in the excavations reported here. These are all ornaments or preforms for ornaments rather than tools, except for a spoon. The absence of the otherwise ubiquitous points is striking, and suggests that these tools are not associated with an aspect of identity that needs to be indicated in burial.

Conclusion

The worked bone forms a relatively minor part of the Çatalhöyük artefact assemblage, but some, such as points and needles, were probably essential for performing the tasks of daily life. Others contributed to the construction of individual and group identity. Technological analysis of the worked bone indicates that there were strong ideas about how certain tool types should be made, and general notions of the form of some types, but room for individual expression in the specific form. While the bone-tool industry is quite stable through the occupation of the site, there seem to be some minor changes around Level IX. These include the use of a somewhat wider range of taxa and elements and a slight decline in splitting in the points; a change from cut to drilled perforations in the needles; and the appearance of worked boar's tusk and some minor tool types, many of them associated with woodworking.

Chapter 17

Ground-stone Raw Material from Çatalhöyük

Asuman G. Türkmenoğlu, Adnan Baysal,
Vedat Toprak & M. Cemal Göncüoğlu

The surroundings of the Çatalhöyük site are drained by the Çarşamba River and its tributaries. The river forms meandering channels in the widespread alluvial deposits in the Konya plain leaving some small remnant hills. The mountain slopes rise slowly at long distances away from the site. The Çatalhöyük site is divided into East and West Mounds, which are easily recognizable from a distance since they rise from a low-lying topographic surface. During the excavations a lot of stone material and artefacts were found. So, one of the major concerns is to find the geological sources of the stone materials. This study aims to investigate the provenance of the Çatalhöyük ground stones. Their petrographic properties are compared with the rock samples collected from the area surrounding the site in order to find the possible sources.

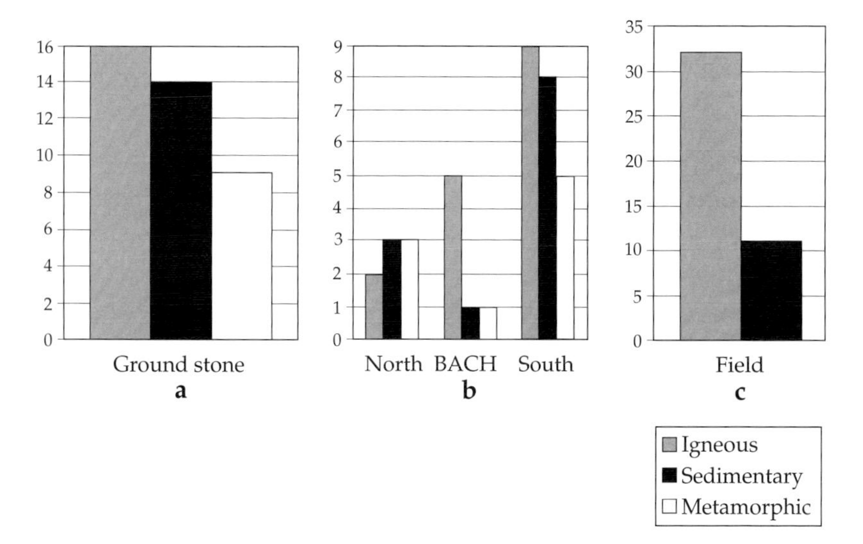

Figure 17.1. *a) Petrographic abundances of the all ground stones studied; b) abundances of ground-stone types from North, BACH and South areas; c) abundances of the field samples.*

Geological framework

The Konya basin is a closed lacustrine basin surrounded by high mountains to the west, south and east. It is separated from the Lake Tuz drainage area by a pass only 50 m high to the north. The basin has a tectonic origin and appeared during Miocene times during the uplift of the Taurus mountains which form the southern drainage area of the basin. Rivers like the Çarşamba originate from lakes and flow downslope towards the Konya plain. The sediment fill of the Konya plain is lime-rich marls, enriched in clastic material imported by rivers from the Taurus mountains, and by slope processes from the limestone and volcanic reliefs. At present, the Konya plain is a flat-lying palaeolake bottom, with an altitude of around 1000 m. Surrounding heights reach up to 1500 m like Bozdağ (a limestone palaeorelief). Two stratovolcanoes, Karadağ and Karacadağ, are higher than 2000 m.

The oldest rocks in the area are slightly recrystallized limestones of Mesozoic age and ophiolithic rocks structurally overlying them. Calcalcaline volcanic rocks of differing compositions and ages are more common and some of them are erosional remnants of volcanic necks. The Karadağ volcano of Pleistocene age is the major volcanic feature close to the Çatalhöyük site. The Karacadağ volcano is of Pliocene age and is mainly andesitic. Near Karapınar, Upper Pleistocene strombolian basaltic cones and maar form a plateau. Most of the area is covered by limestones of Miocene age that expose at the

Table 17.1. *Analyzed field samples from Konya plain: V = volcanic, S = sedimentary.*

Sample	Sample no.	Location	Rock type
Arab.Tomek 51			V: Ho-andesite
Arab.Tomek 53			S: Conglomerate
Kara Tomek 23			V: Px-basalt
K/Necktepe 1			S: Limestone
K/Necktepe 2			V: Dacitic andesite
K/Necktepe 3			V: Dacitic andesite
K/Necktepe 4			V: Dacitic andesite
K/Necktepe 5			V: Dacitic andesite
K/Necktepe 6			V: Dacitic andesite
K/Necktepe 7			S: Limestone
K.Dağ/Kaletepe1			V: Ho-andesite,Ho-Bi-andesite
K.Dağ/Kaletepe2			V: Ho-andesite,Ho-Bi-andesite
K.Dağ/Kaletepe3			V: Ho-andesite,Ho-Bi-andesite
K.Dağ/Kaletepe4			V: Ho-andesite,Ho-Bi-andesite
K.Dağ/Kaletepe5			V: Ho-andesite,Ho-Bi-andesite
Dineksaray 1			S: Silttaşı
Dineksaray 2			S: Chert
Dineksaray 3			S: Conglomerate
K.T. Mahalli 1			S: Limestone
K.T.Mahalli 2			S: Limestone
Belkuyu 1			S: Chert
Belkuyu 2			
K/Necktepe 8			
CK1	1	Karadağ	
CK2	2	Karadağ	V:
CK3	3	Karadağ	V:
CK4	4	Karadağ	V:
CK5	5	Karadağ	
CK6	6	Karadağ	V:
CK7	7	Karadağ	V:
CK8	8	Karadağ	V:
CK9	9	Karadağ	V:
CK10	10	Karadağ	V:
Ck11	11	Karadağ	V:
CK12	12	Karadağ	V:
CK13	13	Karadağ	V:
CK14	14	Karadağ	V:
CK15	15	Karadağ	V:
CK16	16	Karadağ	
CK17	17	Karadağ	V:
CK18	18	Karadağ	V:
CK19	19	Karadağ	V:
CK20	20	Karadağ	V:
CK21	21	Karadağ	S:
CK22	22	Karadağ	V:
CK23	23	Karadağ	V:

Table 17.2. *Analyzed stone samples from Çatalhöyük: V = volcanic, S = sedimentary, M = metamorphic.*

Unit	Sample no.	Area	Rock type
3049	Stn/S3	North	V: Ho-andesite, Ho-Bi-andesite
2525	Stn/S1	North	
2518	Stn/S3	North	M:
2525	Stn/S2	North	
1242	Stn/S3	North	V: Ho-andesite, Ho-Bi-andesite
1344	Stn/18	North	M: Meta-sandstone
2519	Stn/S3	North	M:
3243	Stn/S4	North	
1214	Stn/S4	North	
3401	Stn/	BACH	
3501	Stn/	BACH	V: Ho-andesite, Ho-Bi-andesite
2289	Stn/	BACH	V: Ho-andesite (highly altered)
3506	Stn/	BACH	V:Px-basalt
3501x5	Stn/	BACH	V: Px-basalt
6129	7	BACH	V:
F160	9	BACH	S: Marl
2910	Stn/S22	West Mound	V: Px-basalt
2910	Stn/S21	West Mound	
2910	Stn/S23	West Mound	
1020	Stn/S1	South	
3115.1	Stn/S8	South	S: Siltstone
3115.2	Stn/S8	South	S: Limestone
3743	Stn/S1	South	M: Meta-sandstone
1092.1	Stn/S4	South	S: Chert
1092.2	Stn/S4	South	
3314	Stn/S8	South	S: Limestone
1074	Stn/S1	South	
1015	Stn/S1	South	M:
4340	1	South	V: Scoria
4121	2	South	S: Quartz-sandstone(with Fe-oxide)
4796	4	South	V:
4246	5	South	V:
4321	6	South	V:
4186	11	South	M: Quartz-mica schist
4796	12	South	S: Quartz-sandstone(with Fe-oxide)
4246	13	South	M: Quartz-mica schist
4246	14	South	V:
4196	24	South	V:
4196	25	South	M: Metadiabase
5304	26	South	V:
5290	27	South	
5308	28	South	S: Oolitic limestone
4871	29	South	S:
5232	32	South	V:
6010	16	KOPAL	
6010	17	KOPAL	S: Limestone (recrystallized)
6010	18	KOPAL	S: Radiolarian Chert

northern slope of the Taurus mountains forming the southern boundary of the Konya plain (Karabıyıkoğlu & Kuzucuoğlu 1998).

Methods of study

Geological investigations were carried out during September 1997, in a wide area around the Çatalhöyük site in order to collect samples from possible source rocks. Samples were collected from igneous rocks including a volcanic neck in the Karadağ area and from the limestone outcrops at Kanal Taksim location. The Çarşamba river gravels were also sampled from exposures of river deposits such as alluvial fans, stream terraces and channel beds in order to detect the possible varieties of rock types transported by the river from far distances. The list of 46 field samples analyzed are given in Table 17.1. In addition to field samples, 47 ground stones from the excavation site were selected for petrographic investigations in order to compare their petrographic characteristics (Table 17.2). The thin sections of all samples were prepared and examined with a polarizing microscope to study their mineralogical compositions, textures and alteration products.

Results

The ground stones from the site can be classified into volcanic, sedimentary and metamorphic rock types

Table 17.3. *Provenance analysis of ground stones.*

Field outcrop	Rock type	Matching material from Çatalhöyük
Volcanic sources/Pleistocene age		
Karadağ / Kaletepe	HO-andesite, Ho-Bi-andesite	3049, 3501, 1242
Karadağ	Px-basalt	2910, 3501.X5, 3506
Karadağ / Necktepe	Dacitic andesite	No match
Sedimentary sources/possible geological formation-age		
Kaletepe / Necktepe7,K.T.Mahalli	Lake limestone-marl / Karahisarlı Lst-Neogene	3115.2, 3314, 5308, F160
Dineksaray, Belkuyu	Radiolarian Chert / Ophiolithic melange-Cretaceous age	1091.1, 6010
Dineksaray	Conglomerate, Sandstone, Siltstone / alluvial deposits of Çarşamba River / Quaternary	3315.1, 4121, 4796
Metamorphic sources/possible geologic formation-age		
No match	Recrstallized limestone / Taurus Belt–Permian age	6010
No match	Metadiabase / Hatip Melange at the south of Konya plain	4194
No match	Quartz-mica schist / metagranite of basement rocks-Precambrian age	4186, 4246, 2518, 1015
No match	Meta-sandstone / ?	1344, 3743

based on petrographic analysis. Among the volcanic varieties three subgroups are recognized:

1. hornblende-andesite and hornblende-biotite andesite;
2. pyroxene basalt;
3. dacite and dacitic andesite.

The ground stones of the first subgroup can be correlated with the field samples collected from the Karadağ-Kaletepe location (Table 17.3). They exhibit porphyritic texture with hornblende and plagioclase as the common phenocrysts. Hornblende crystals show brown and green pleochroism and they have opaque rims. Plagioclase crystals show zoning and twinning. In the groundmass plagioclase microliths are common and may be aligned. Calcitization and argillization are detected in plagioclase phenocrysts. The ground stones of the second subgroup include pyroxene and are defined as basalt or basaltic andesite. They have porphyritic texture with plagioclase and pyroxene phenocrysts. These minerals are also abundant in the groundmass as microliths. They are correlated with the field samples collected from the Karadağ location. In the third subgroup there is only one ground stone which is petrographically similar to those field samples obtained from Karadağ-Necktepe location at the faulted contact of volcanics with limestone. The volcanic rock is defined as dacitic andesite with quartz, hornblende and plagioclase phenocrysts. It is intensely altered to clay, hematite and calcite which is also typical for a ground stone (2289) belonging petrographically to the first subgroup.

Ground stones from sedimentary raw material are also present at the Çatalhöyük site. They are white-coloured, massive-looking micritic lake limestones which have similar petrographic features to the field samples collected at two locations. Chert is another variety of sedimentary ground stones. In the field, at two locations in the alluvial plain chert was collected which correlates with the ground stone. In the sediments of the Çarşamba river, gravels of siltstone, sandstone and conglomerate are also present and match with a few of the ground-stone petrographies (Table 17.3).

Very few of the ground-stone samples belong to the metamorphic group. The raw material is low grade metamorphic rocks which contain metadiabase, mica-schist / metagranites and metasandstone and recrystallized limestone (marble). No exposures of metamorphic rocks are present in close vicinity of the site. These types of ground stones are most probably collected from river sediments. In Figure 17.1 histograms show the frequencies of rock types both for ground stones and field samples.

Conclusions

The ground stones from the Çatalhöyük Neolithic site mainly have volcanic sources of andesitic-basaltic nature. They may be collected from nearby outcrops. Sedimentary types are also present and can be correlated with close geological sources and river deposits. Metamorphic varieties are less common, and it is suggested that these sources were collected from the fluvial deposits of the Çarşamba river. They are probably transported from distant outcrops of metamorphic rocks belonging to the Taurus Belt, Hatip melange and Paleozoic basement rocks located to south, by the river.

Chapter 18

Report on Bead Material Identification

Brian Jackson

A total of 989 beads were examined (Table 18.1). They were grouped into seven major categories that were further divided into 26 sub-categories.

Method

All specimens were examined using a microscope. Other techniques used included inspection under both long- and short-wave ultraviolet light, specific gravity, refractive index, micro-hardness tests and micro-chemical tests.

Marbles

The marble (*sensu stricto*) beads fell into two broad colour types; white and brownish-red of varying hues. These could additionally be differentiated on the basis of their fluorescence. The white marbles exhibited a cream-colour fluorescence (LWUV) whilst the brownish-red marbles exhibited a dull red fluorescence (LWUV). The differing fluorescent effects arise from different activators thus suggesting a different geologic event. This does not necessarily indicate a different source as lithologies can vary within short distances within a single geological province. The grain size varied even within the different colour groups and therefore did not assist provenance differentiation.

Other brownish-red marbles of varying hues were designated as impure based on insoluble residue remaining after micro-chemical tests. These marbles exhibited no fluorescence effects and this was the principle method of identification. As with the marbles described above the same criteria apply to provenancing.

Although difficult to assess, some marbles, rarely and mainly those of the type designated as impure, appeared to have a reconstituted structure. These would need further examination to confirm the assessment. One specimen (1803.H2) did exhibit prominent breccia features that were assessed as evidence of reconstruction.

Thirteen specimens were very fine grained and were thought to be limestone rather than marble. Two specimens (2271.H1 & 3076.H1) showed features consistent with a travertine origin.

Clays

These fine-grained greyish-brown beads were subdivided into seven categories.

1) Carbonaceous clay

On the basis of micro-chemical test these specimens showed evidence of a substantial carbonate content. There are two major possibilities. Many specimens, mostly non-clay beads, had secondary carbonate encrustation. This is evidence of circulating carbonated ground waters. Clay with voids would act as a trap for secondary carbonate deposition from ground water. The other alternative is that powdered marble was added to the clay during the manufacturing process. The evidence indicates an exceptionally fine-grained intimate mixture of clay and carbonate and therefore the latter possibility seems the most likely.

2) Carbonaceous clay with marble fragments

Microscope examination revealed tiny angular marble fragments imbedded in the clay. As with the above there are two major possibilities. First, the unconsolidated sedimentary source material may have been a mixture of fine-grained clay and coarser marble. Although poor sorting is possible this incongruity seems highly unlikely especially as the marble fragments show no evidence of rounding. The second possibility, and the most likely, is that poorly-ground marble fragments were added during the manufacturing process.

3) Carbonaceous clay with quartz fragments

Microscope examination revealed tiny angular quartz fragments imbedded in carbonaceous clay. Microchemical testing indicated that the clay had a signifi-

Table 18.1. *Bead material types.*

Type	Total
Marble	531
Clay	79
Schist	264
Serpentine	31
Shell	45
Others	19
Unidentified	20
Sub-type	
Marble	427
Impure marble	88
Reconstructed marble	1
Limestone	13
Travertine	2
Carbonaceous clay	19
Carbonaceous clay with visible quartz	19
Clay with marble fragments aggregate	25
Carbonaceous siltstone	3
Chalky clay with quartz fragments	8
Micaceous siltstone	3
Siltstone	2
Schist	264
Serpentine	31
Shell	45
Common opal	1
Pyroxenite/amphibolite	1
Quartz variety carnelian	3
Quartz granular	1
Sandstone	1
Apatite	1
Barite	1
Basalt/dolerite	1
Bone	8
Gypsum	1
Unidentified	20

cant carbonate content (see 1 above). As with 2 above poor sorting seems an improbable conclusion given that the quartz fragments are angular. The conclusion is that quartz fragments were added to the carbonaceous clay during the manufacturing process.

4) Chalky clay with quartz fragments
These are essentially the same as 3 above but with a greater carbonate content. The conclusion is that they are an aggregated construction.

5) Carbonaceous siltstone
These are similar to 1 above but the source material is more siliceous and coarser. The conclusion is similar to 1 above.

6) Siltstone
These specimens exhibited no evidence of a carbonate content, the source material being a more siliceous and coarser clay. This is probably primary source material.

7) Micaceous siltstone
These specimens exhibited no evidence of a carbonate content, the source material being a more siliceous and coarser clay with visible mica content. This is probably primary source material.

Schist

These beads were varying shades of grey and black. Microscopic examination showed a mineral content consistent with mica schist although one specimen (4530.H3) had the appearance of a very fine-layered semi-pelitic schist. Laminated schistosity was visible in many specimens. This was clearly evident where beads had split along the lamination.

Serpentine

These beads were variegated in colour, mottled dark green/grey/black to olive yellow-green-brownish. They had a characteristic waxy lustre and were translucent. Some specimens (e.g. 5325.H3 & 5316.H12) had inclusions of black octahedral crystals of probably magnetite or chromite. All specimens were inert under ultraviolet light. These beads often showed evidence of tooling suggesting a low hardness. Specific gravity was recorded as 2.65, which, although 0.05 above the upper limit for this species, can be accounted for by the heavy inclusions. There was no reaction to micro-chemical testing with acid.

Shell/Bone

A number of beads already identified as bone and shell beads were examined (see Chapter 17 & Volume 4, Chapter 6) and, based on fluorescence, micro-chemical tests and structure, the previous identification was confirmed.

Other materials

A small number of beads were identified as common opal, apatite, barite, gypsum, pyroxenite or possibly amphibolite, quartz variety carnelian, basalt/dolerite, quartz and sandstone.

Common opal (2235.D2) was identificatied based upon lustre and specific gravity. Apatite (1591.H2) identification was based upon previous x-ray diffraction. Several other turquoise-blue-coloured beads were examined. Their appearance has much in common with the gem material odontolite, a blue-green form of fossilized teeth. This material is identical to apatite and can be identified by the organic structures seen under very high magnification. Literature on odontolite is not extensive and the cause of colour is not fully understood. However there is a link with heating. Experimental heating work on bone has produced a blue colour and one specimen of 'blue bone' found at Catalhoyuk exhibited identical colouration to that of the beads. Further work needs to be done to identify the origins of this material.

- Barite (913.H1); identification of this beige bead is based on the specific gravity (4.0: literature value 4.5), two cleavages, low hardness and lack of reaction to micro-chemical acid testing.
- Gypsum (1432.X1); identification of this white bead with saccharoidal texture was based on low hardness and a specific gravity less than 2.64.
- Pyroxenite or possibly amphibolite (0858.H1); identification of this dark grey bead was on the basis of interlocking acicular crystal structure.
- Quartz variety carnelian (5221.H2, 4930.H1 and 1375.X21); three red chalcedonic beads identified visually.
- Basalt/Dolerite (1630.H1); a fine-grained dark rock with igneous texture, identified visually.
- Quartz (granular) (4511.H1); a white bead with granular structure, identified visually and resistance to micro-hardness test.
- Sandstone (5153.H1); identification based on visual characteristics, fine-grained granular appearance.

Production

Many beads exhibited offset drill holes the apertures narrowing towards the centre of the bead. This is consistent with the specimen having been drilled from opposite ends rather than a single hole drilled from one direction.

Conclusion

Examination of the beads from Çatalhöyük has revealed that these were made of various types of clay, shell, bone and various stones, particularly marble, schist and serpentine with a wide range of other materials occurring occasionally.

References

Abbès, F., N. Balkan-Atlı, D. Binder & M.-C. Cauvin, 1999. Gestion de la matière première et économie du débitage. Rapport préliminaire sur l'industrie d'Asikli. *Tüba-Ar* 2, 117–37.

Abbès, F., L. Bellot-Gurlet, C. Bressy, M.-C., Cauvin, B. Gratzue & G. Poupeau, 2001. Nouvelles recherches sur l'obsidienne de Cheikh Hasan (Vallée de l'Euphrate, Syrie) au Néolithique PPNA et PPNB. *Syria* 78, 1–13.

Adams, J., 1988. Use-wear analysis on manos and hide-processing stones. *Journal of Field Archaeology* 15, 307–15.

Aitken, M.J., 1985. *Thermoluminescence Dating*. London: Academic Press.

Aitken, M.J., 1990. *Science-based Dating in Archaeology*. London: Longman.

Aitken, M.J., 1998. *An Introduction to Optical Dating*. Oxford: Oxford University Press.

Aloupi E., A.G. Karydas & T. Paradellis, 2000. Pigment analysis of wall paintings and ceramics from Greece and Cyprus: the optimal use of X-ray spectrometry on specific archaeological issues. *X-Ray Spectrometry* 29, 18–24.

Angel, L.J., 1971. Early Neolithic skeletons from Çatal Huyuk: demography and pathology. *Anatolian Studies* 21, 77–98.

Appadurai, A., 1981. Gastropolitics in Hindu South Asia. *American Ethnologist* 8, 494–511.

Arimura, M., N. Balkan-Atlı, F. Borell, W. Cruells, G. Duru, A. Erım-Özdoğan, J.J. Ibáñez, O. Maede, Y. Miyake, M. Molist & M. Özbaşaran, 2000. A new Neolithic settlement in the Urfa region: Akarçay Tepe, 1999. *Anatolia Antiqua* VIII, 227–55.

Arnold, D.E., 1985. *Ceramic Theory and Cultural Process*. Cambridge: Cambridge University Press.

Ashmore, P.J., 1999. Radiocarbon dating: avoiding errors by avoiding mixed samples. *Antiquity* 73, 124–30.

Asouti, E. & A. Fairbairn, A., 2002. Subsistence economy in Central Anatolia during the Neolithic: the archaeobotanical evidence, in *The Neolithic of Central Anatolia: Internal Developments and External Relations During the 9th–6th Millennia cal* BC, eds. F. Gérard & L. Thissen. Istanbul: Eye Yayinlari, 181–92.

Asouti, E. & A. Fairbairn, forthcoming. Animal dung versus firewood: a history of fuel exploitation at the Neolithic site of Çatalhöyük.

Atalay, S., 2000. Clay balls and objects. *Çatalhöyük 2000 Archive Report*. http://catal.arch.cam.ac.uk/catal/Archive_rep00/atalay00.html.

Atalay, S., 2001. BACH Area clay balls, mini balls and geometric objects. *Çatalhöyük 2001 Archive Report*. http://catal.arch.cam.ac.uk/catal/Archive_rep01/atalay01.html.

Atalay, S., 2003. Domesticating Clay in the Public Eye: Clay Balls from Neolithic Çatalhöyük and Public Archaeology for Indigenous Communities. Unpublished PhD Dissertation, University of California, Berkeley.

Ataman, K., 1988. The Chipped Stone Assemblage from Can Hasan III: a Study in Typology, Technology and Function. Unpublished PhD thesis, Institute of Archaeology, University College London.

Aufrère, S., 1991. *L'Univers minéral dans la pensée Egyptienne*. Cairo: Institut Francais d'Archeologie Orientale.

Aurenche, O., J. Evin & F. Hours (eds.), 1987. *Chronologies in the Near East*. (British Archaeological Reports, International Series 379.) Oxford: BAR.

Aurenche, O., P. Galet, E. Régagnon-Carolie & J. Evin, 2001. Proto-Neolithic and Neolithic cultures in the Middle East — the birth of agriculture, livestock raising and ceramics: a calibrated 14C chronology, 12,500–5500 calBC. *Radiocarbon* 43, 1191–202.

Baillie, M.G.L., 1990. Checking back on an assemblage of published radiocarbon dates. *Radiocarbon* 32, 361–6.

Baird, D., 1991. Independent variables? A flexible classification of Late Neolithic and Chalcolithic pottery, in *Cypriot Ceramics: Reading the Prehistoric Record*, eds. J.A. Barlow, D. Bolger & B. Kling. (University Museum Monograph 74.) Philadelphia (PA): University of Pennsylvania: University Museum, 21–7.

Baird, D., 1996. The Konya Plain survey: aims and methods, in *On the Surface: Çatalhöyük 1993–95*, ed. I. Hodder. (McDonald Institute Monographs; BIAA Monograph 22.) Cambridge: McDonald Institute for Archaeological Research; London: British Institute of Archaeology at Ankara, 41–6.

Baird, D., 2000. The chipped stone, in *Excavations at Pinarbaŝı, Near Çatalhöyük in Central Turkey*. http://www.arcl.ed.ac.uk/arch/pinarbasi/lithics.htm.

Baird, D., 2002. Early Holocene settlement in Central Anatolia: problems and prospects as seen from the Konya Plain, in *The Neolithic of Central Anatolia: Internal Developments and External Relations during the 9th–6th Millennia cal* BC, eds. F. Gérard & L. Thissen. Istanbul: Ege Yayınları, 139–52.

Baird, D., in press. A Neolithic assemblage from the neighbourhood of Çatalhöyük, in *4th Workshop on PPN Chipped Lithic Industries*, eds. N. Balkan-Atlı & D. Binder. Berlin: Ex Oriente.

Balkan-Atlı, N., 1991. Part III: The chipped stone industry of Aşıklı Höyük: a general presentation. *Anatolica* 17, 145–9.

Balkan-Atlı, N., 1994a. *La Neolithisation de l'Anatolie*. Paris: De Boccard.

Balkan-Atlı, N., 1994b. The typological characteristics of the Aşıklı Höyük chipped stone, in *Neolithic Chipped Stone Industries of the Fertile Crescent. Proceedings of the First Workshop on PPN Chipped Lithic Industries*, eds.

H.G. Gebel & S.K. Kozlowski. (Studies in Early Near Eastern Production, Subsistence, and Environment 1.) Berlin: *Ex Oriente*, 209–21.

Balkan-Atlı, N., 1998. The aceramic Neolithic of Central Anatolia: recent finds in the chipped stone industry, in *Light on Top of the Black Hill. Studies Presented to Halet Çambel*, eds. G. Arsebük, M.J. Mellink & W. Schirmer. Istanbul: Ege Yayınları, 81–94.

Balkan-Atlı, N. & G. Der Aprahamian, 1998. Les nucléus de Kaletepe et deux ateliers de taille en Cappadoce, in *L'Obsidienne au Proche et Moyen Orient: Du Volcan à l'Outil*, eds. M.-C. Cauvin, A. Gourgaud, A. Gratuze, N. Arnaud, G. Poupeau, J.-L. Poidevin & C. Chataigner. (British Archaeological Reports, International Series 738.) Oxford: Maison de l'Orient Méditerranéen/BAR, 241–57.

Balkan-Atlı, N., D. Binder & M.-C. Cauvin, 1999. Obsidian: sources, workshops and trade in Central Anatolia, in *Neolithic in Turkey: the Cradle of Civilization. New Discoveries*, eds. M. Özdoğan & N. Başgelen. Istanbul: Arkeoloji ve Sanat Yayınları, 133–45.

Bar-Yosef, O. & A. Belfer-Cohen, 1989. The Levantine 'PPNB' interaction sphere, in *People and Culture in Change: Proceedings of the Second Symposium on Upper Palaeolithic, Mesolithic and Neolithic Populations of Europe and the Mediterranean Basin*, ed. I. Hershkovitz. (British Archaeological Reports, International Series 508.) Oxford: BAR, 59–72.

Barrat, J.A., F. Keller, J. Amosse, R.N. Taylor, R.W. Nesbitt & T. Hirata, 1996. Determination of rare earth elements in sixteen silicate reference by ICP-MS after Tm addition and ion exchange separation. *Geostandards Newsletter* 20, 133–9.

Bartlett, K., 1933. *Pueblo Milling Stones of the Flagstaff Region and their Relation to Others in the Southwest: a Study in Progressive Efficiency*. (Bulletin 3.) Flagstaff (AZ): Museum of Northern Arizona.

Baxter, M.J., 1994. *Exploratory Multivariate Analysis in Archaeology*. Edinburgh: Edinburgh University Press.

Baysal, A., 1998. Provisional report on geological surveys in relation to ground stone study: Çatalhöyük 1998. *Çatalhöyük 1998 Archive Report*. http: / / catal.arch.cam.ac.uk / catal / Archive_rep98 / baysalstone98.html.

Baysal, A., 1999. Ground stones. *Çatalhöyük 1999 Archive Report*. http: / / catal.arch.cam.ac.uk / catal / Archive_rep99 / baysal99.html.

Baysal, A., 2000. Ground stones. *Çatalhöyük 2000 Archive Report*. http: / / catal.arch.cam.ac.uk / catal / Archive_rep00 / baysal00.html

Baysal, A., 2001. Arkeolojide Öğütme Tasları ve Tasın Sosyal ve Kültürel Önemi Açısından Bir Değerlendirme. I. *Uluslararasi 'Çatalhöyükten Günümüze Çumra' Kongresi, Çumra, 2001*. Çumra Belediyesi: Damla Ofse, 245–52.

Baysal, A., 2004, Çatalhöyük ground stone report, 2004, Çatalhöyük Archive Report 2004. http: / / catal.arch.cam.ac.uk / catal / Archive_rep04 / baysal04.html.

Baysal, A., in prep. Life Histories of Ground Stone Artefacts: a Case Study from Çatalhöyük. Unpublished PhD dissertation, Department of Archaeology, University of Liverpool.

Baysal, A. & K. Wright, 2002. Analysis of ground stone artefacts from the excavations of 1995–1999. *Çatalhöyük 2002 Archive Report*, http: / / catal.arch.cam.ac.uk / catal / Archive_rep02 / a10.html.

Belfer-Cohen, A., 1995. Rethinking social stratification in the Natufian culture: the evidence from burials, in *The Archaeology of Death in the Ancient Near East*, eds. S. Campbell & A. Green. (Oxbow Monograph 51.) Oxford: Oxbow, 9–16.

Belfer-Cohen, A. & O. Bar-Yosef, 2000. Early sedentism in the Near East: a bumpy ride to village life, in *Life in Neolithic Farming Communities: Social Organization, identity, and Differentiation*, ed. I. Kuijt. New York (NY): Kluwer Academic/Plenum Publishers, 19–38.

Bell, G.H., 1973. Solubilities of normal aliphatic acids, alcohols and alkanes in water. *Chemistry and Physics of Lipids* 10, 1–10.

Bellot-Gurlet, L., 1998. Caractérisation par Analyse Élémentaire (PIXE et ICP-MS / -AES) d'un Verre Naturel: L'Obsidienne. Application à l'Étude de Provenance d'Objets Archéologiques. Unpublished PhD thesis, Université Joseph Fourier, Grenoble.

Bellot-Gurlet, L., F. Keller & G. Poupeau, 1999. Description of the procedures for ICP-AES and ICP-MS analysis at Grenoble, France, in An inter-laboratory comparison of element compositions for two obsidian sources, by M.D. Glascock. *International Association for Obsidian Studies Bulletin* 23, 13–25.

Bender, B., 1978. Gatherer-hunter to farmer: a social perspective. *World Archaeology* 10, 204–22.

Benjamin, W., 1969. *Illuminations*. New York (NY): Schocken.

Bialor, P., 1962. The chipped stone industry of Çatal Hüyük. *Anatolian Studies* 12, 67–110.

Biçakçi, E., 1998. An essay on the chronology of the Pre-pottery Neolithic settlements of the East-Taurus region (Turkey), in *Light on Top of the Black Hill: Studies Presented to Halet Çambel*, eds. G. Arsebük, M. Mellink & W. Schrimer. Istanbul; Ege Yayıları, 137–50.

Bigazzi, G., G. Poupeau, L. Bellot-Gurlet & Z. Yezingili, 1998. Provenance studies of obsidian artefacts in Anatolia using the fission-track dating method: an overview, in *L'Obsidienne au Proche et Moyen Orient: Du Volcan à l'Outil*, eds. M.-C. Cauvin, A. Gourgaud, A. Gratuze, N. Arnaud, G. Poupeau, J.-L. Poidevin & C. Chataigner. 1998. (British Archaeological Reports, International Series 738.) Oxford: Maison de l'Orient Méditerranéen/BAR, 69–89.

Binder, D., 2002. Stones making sense: what obsidian could tell us about the origins of the Central Anatolian Neolithic, in *The Neolithic of Central Anatolia: Internal Developments and External Relations During the 9th–6th Millennia Cal BC*, eds. F. Gérard & L. Thissen. Istanbul: Eye Yayinlari, 79–90.

Binford, L., 1977. Forty-seven trips: a case study in the character of archaeological formation processes, in *Stone Tools as Cultural Markers*, ed. R. Wright. Canberra: Australian Institute of Aboriginal Studies, 24–36.

Binford, L., 1979. Organization and formation processes: looking at curated technologies. *Journal of Anthropo-*

logical Research 35, 255–73.

Blackman, M.J., 1989. The provenience of obsidian artifacts from Late Chalcolithic levels at Aphrodisias, in *Prehistoric Aphrodisias: an Account of the Excavations and Artifact Studies*, ed. M. Joukowsky. (Archaeologia Transatlantica III.) Providence (RI): Brown University Centre for Old World Archaeology and Art; Louvain-la-Neuve: Institute Supérieur d'Archéologie et d'Histoire de l'Art, College Erasmus, 279–85.

Bordaz, J., 1969. The Suberde excavations, southwestern Turkey. An interim report. *Turk Arkeoloji Dergisi* 17, 43–71.

Bordaz, J., 1970. *Tools of the Old and New Stone Age*. New York (NY): Natural History Press.

Bordaz, J., 1973. Current research in the Neolithic of South central Turkey: Suberde, Erbaba and the chronological implications. *American Journal of Archaeology* 77, 282–8.

Bordaz, J. & L. Bordaz, 1976. Erbaba excavations 1974. *Türk Arkeoloji Dergisi* 23, 39–44.

Bostancı, E.Y., 1962. A new Upper Palaeolithic and Mesolithic facies at Belbaşı rock shelter on the Mediterranean Coast of Anatolia. *Belleten* 26, 252–92.

Bostancı, E.Y., 1965. The Mesolithic facies of Beldibi and Belbaşı and the relation with the other findings in Anatolia. *Antropoloji* 3, 55–91.

Bourdieu, P., 1977. *Outline of a Theory of Practice*. Cambridge: Cambridge University Press.

Bourdieu, P., 1990. *The Logic of Practice*. Cambridge: Polity Press.

Bourgeois, J.-L., C. Pelos & B. Davidson, 1989. *Spectacular Vernacular: the Adobe Tradition*. New York (NY): Aperture Foundation.

Bowman, S., 1990. *Radiocarbon Dating*. London: British Museum Publications.

Boyd, R., 1999. *Indians, Fire, and the Land in the Pacific Northwest*. Corvallis (OR): Oregon State University Press.

Bray, W. & D. Trump, 1982. *The Dictionary of Archaeology*. Middlesex: Penguin Books.

Breunig, P., 1987. *14C-Chronologie des vorderasiarischen, sudost- und mitteleuropaischen Neolithikums*. Cologne / Vienna: Bohlau-Verlag.

Brigham, W.T., 1902. Stone implements and stone work of the Ancient Hawaiians, in *Memoirs of the Bernice Pauahi Bishop Museum of Polynesian Ethnology and Natural History*, vol. I, no. 4. Honololu (HI): Bishop Museum Press, 333–435.

Briois, F., B. Gratuze & J. Guilaine, 1997. Obsidiennes du site néolithique préceramique de Shillourokambos. *Paléorient* 23, 95–112.

Brodie, N., 1997. New perspectives on the Bell-Beaker culture. *Oxford Journal of Archaeology* 16, 297–314.

Broman, V.L., 1958. Jarmo Figurines. Unpublished MA Degree Thesis, Department of Anthropology, Radcliffe College.

Broman, V.L., 1983. Jarmo figurines and other clay objects, in *Prehistoric Archaeology along the Zagros Flanks*, ed. L. Braidwood. Chicago (IL): Oriental Institute, 369–424.

Broman-Morales, V.L., 1990. *Figurines and Other Clay Objects from Sarab and Çayönü*. (Oriental Institute Communications 25.) Chicago (IL): University of Chicago.

Bronk Ramsey, C., 2000. OxCal 3.5. http://info.ox.ac.uk/departments/rlaha/orau/index.htm.

Bronk Ramsey, C. & R.E.M. Hedges, 1999. Hybrid ion sources: radiocarbon measurements from microgram to milligram. *Nuclear Instruments and Methods in Physics Research* B 123, 539–45.

Bronk Ramsey, C., P.B. Pettitt, R.E.M. Hedges, G.W.L. Hodgins & D.C. Owen, 2000. Radiocarbon dates from the Oxford AMS system: Archaeometry datelist 30. *Archaeometry* 42, 459–79.

Bruins, H.J. & J. van der Plicht, 1998. Early Bronze Jericho: high-precision 14C sates of short-lived palaeobotanic remains. *Radiocarbon* 40, 621–8.

Bucha, V. & J. Mellaart, 1967. Archaeomagnetic intensity measurements of some Neolithic samples from Çatal Hüyük (Anatolia). *Archaeometry* 10, 23–6.

Buck, C.E., J.B. Kenworthy, C.D. Litton & A.F.M. Smith, 1991. Combining archaeological and radiocarbon information: a Bayesian approach to calibration. *Antiquity* 65, 808–21.

Buck, C.E., C.D. Litton & A.F.M. Smith, 1992. Calibration of radiocarbon results pertaining to related archaeological events. *Journal of Archaeological Science* 19, 497–512.

Buck, C.E., J.A. Christen, J.B. Kenworthy & C.D. Litton, 1994a. Estimating the duration of archaeological activity using C14 determinations. *Oxford Journal of Archaeology* 13, 229–40.

Buck, C.E., C.D. Litton & E.M. Scott, 1994b. Making the most of radiocarbon dating: some statistical considerations. *Antiquity* 68, 252–63.

Buck, C.E., J.A. Christen & G.N. James, 1999. BCal: an online Bayesian radiocarbon calibration tool. *Internet Archaeology* 7. http://intarch.ac.uk/journal/issue7/buck_toc.html.

Bullock, P.E.A., N. Fedoroff, A. Jongerius, G. Stoops & T. Tursina, 1984. *Handbook for Soil Thin Section Description*. Wolverhampton: Waine Research.

Busch, H. & B. Silver, 1994, *Why Cats Paint*. Berkeley (CA): Ten Speed Press.

Cameron, C.M. & S.A. Tomka (eds.), 1993. *Abandonment of Settlements and Regions: Ethnoarchaeological and Archaeological Approaches*. Cambridge: Cambridge University Press.

Campana, D.V., 1989. *Natufian and Protoneolithic Bone Tools*. (British Archaeological Reports, International Series 494.) Oxford: BAR.

Campana, D.V., 1991. Bone implements from Hayonim Cave: some relevant issues, in *The Natufian Culture in the Levant*, eds. O. Bar-Yosef & F.R. Valla. (International Monographs in Prehistory 1.) Ann Arbor (MI): International Monographs in Prehistory, 459–66.

Caneva, I., 1999. Early farmers on the Cilician coast: Yumuktepe in the 7th millennium BC, in *Neolithic in Turkey: the Cradle of Civilisation. New Discoveries*, eds. M. Özdogan & N. Basgelen. Istanbul: Arkeoloji ve Sanat Yayınları, 105–14.

Caneva, I., C. Lemorini & D. Zampetti, 1996. Lithic technology and functionality through time and space at Çayönü, in *Neolithic Chipped Stone Industries of the Fertile Crescent, and their Contemporaries in Adjacent Regions: Proceedings of the Second Workshop on PPN Chipped Lithic Industries*, eds. S.K. Kozlowski & H.G. Gebel. (Studies in Early Near Eastern Production, Subsistence, and Environment 3.) Berlin: Ex Oriente, 385–402.

Caneva, I., C. Lemorini & D. Zampetti, D., 1998. Chipped stones at Aceramic Çayönü: technology, activities, traditions, innovations. in *Light on Top of the Black Hill: Studies Presented to Halet Çambel*, eds. G. Arsebük, M.J. Mellink & W. Schirmer. Istanbul: Ege Yayınları, 199–206.

Carr, C., 1984. The nature of organization of intrasite archaeological records and spatial analytic approaches to their investigation. *Advances in Archaeological Method and Theory* 7, 103–222.

Carter, S., 1998. Ancient Reflections / Mirrors. Unpublished text.

Carter, T., 1994. Southern Aegean fashion victims: an overlooked aspect of Early Bronze Age burial practices, in *Stories in Stone*, eds. N. Ashton & A. David. (Occasional Paper 4.) London: Lithics Society, 127–44.

Carter, T., 2000. Chipped stone report. *Çatalhöyük 2000 Archive Report*. http: / / catal.arch.cam.ac.uk / catal / Archive_rep00 / carter00.html.

Carter, T., C. Bressy & G. Poupeau, 2001. People and place: new information on technical change at Çatalhöyük. *American Journal of Archaeology* 105, 280.

Casteel, R.W., 1972. Some biases in the recovery of archaeological faunal remains. *Proceedings of the Prehistoric Society* 38, 382–8.

Cauvin, J., 1994. *Naissance des divinités, Naissance de l'agriculture*. Paris: CNRS.

Cauvin, J., 2000. *The Birth of the Gods and the Origins of Agriculture*, trans. T. Watkins. Cambridge: Cambridge University Press.

Cauvin, J., O. Aurenche, M.-C. Cauvin & N. Balkan-Atlı, 1999. The Pre-Pottery site of Cafer Höyük, in *Neolithic in Turkey: the Cradle of Civilization. New Discoveries*, M. Özdoğan & N. Başgelen. Istanbul: Arkeoloji ve Sanat Yayınları, 87–103.

Cauvin, M.-C., 1998. L'obsidienne: données recéntes provenant de sites-habitats Néolithiques, in *L'Obsidienne au Proche et Moyen Orient: Du Volcan à l'Outil*, eds. M.-C. Cauvin, A. Gourgaud, B. Gratauze, N. Arnaud, G. Poupeau, J.-L. Poidevin & C. Chataigner. (British Archaeological Reports, International Series 738.) Oxford: Maison de l'Orient Méditerranéen / BAR, 259–71.

Cauvin, M.-C. & N. Balkan-Atlı, 1996. Rapport sur les recherches sur l'obsidienne en Cappadoce, 1993–1995. *Anatolica Antiqua* 4, 249–71.

Cauvin, M.-C. & C. Chataigner, 1998. Distribution de l'obsidienne dans les sites archéologiques du Proche et Moyen Orient, in *L'Obsidienne au Proche et Moyen Orient: du Volcan à l'Outil*, eds. M.-C. Cauvin, A. Gourgaud, B. Gratauze, N. Arnaud, G. Poupeau, J.-L. Poidevin & C. Chataigner. (British Archaeological Reports, International Series 738.) Oxford: Maison de l'Orient Méditerranéen / BAR, 325–50.

Cauvin M.-C., N. Balkan, Y. Besnus & F. Saroglu, 1986. Origine de l'obsidienne de Cafer Höyük (Turquie): Premiers résultats. *Paléorient* 12, 87–97.

Cauvin M.-C., Y. Besnus, J. Tripier & R. Montigny, 1991. Nouvelles analyses d'obsidiennes du Proche-Orient: Modèle de géochimie des magmas utilisé pour la recherche archéologique. *Paléorient* 17, 5–19.

Cauvin, M.-C., A. Gourgaud, B. Gratauze, N. Arnaud, P. Poupeau, J.-L. Poidevin & C. Chataigner, 1998. *L'Obsidienne au Proche et Moyen Orient: Du Volcan à l'Outil*. (British Archaeological Reports, International Series 738.) Oxford: Maison de l'Orient Méditerranéen / BAR.

Cessford, C., 2001. A new dating sequence for Çatalhöyük. *Antiquity* 75, 717–25.

Cessford, C., 2002. Bayesian statistics and the dating of Çatalhöyük East, in *The Neolithic of Central Anatolia, Internal Developments and External Relations during the 9th–6th Millennia cal BC*, eds. F. Gérard & L. Thissen. Istanbul: Ege Yayınları, 27–31.

Cessford, C., 2003. Microartefactual floor patterning: the case at Çatalhöyük. *Assemblage* 7. http: / / www.shef.ac.uk / assem / issue7 / cessford.html.

Cessford, C. & T. Carter, forthcoming. Quantifying the consumption of obsidian at Çatalhöyük. *Journal of Field Archaeology*.

Chapman, J., 2000. *Fragmentation in Archaeology: People, Places and Broken Objects in the Prehistory of Southeast Europe*. London: Routledge.

Charters, S., R.P. Evershed, A. Quye, P.W. Blinkhorn & V. Reeves, 1997. Simulation experiments for determining the use of ancient pottery vessels: the behaviour of epicuticular leaf wax during boiling of a leafy vegetable. *Journal of Archaeological Science* 24, 1–7.

Chataigner, C., 1998. Sources des artefacts néolithiques, in *L'Obsidienne au Proche et Moyen Orient: Du Volcan à l'Outil*, eds. M.-C. Cauvin, A. Gourgaud, B. Gratauze, N. Arnaud, G. Poupeau, J.-L. Poidevin & C. Chataigner. (British Archaeological Reports, International Series 738.) Oxford: Maison de l'Orient Méditerranéen / BAR, 273–324.

Chataigner C., J.-L. Poidevin & N.O. Arnaud, 1998. Turkish occurrences of obsidian and use by prehistoric peoples in the Near-East from 14,000 to 6000 BP. *Journal of Volcanology and Geothermal Research* 85, 517–37.

Chikalenko, L., 1953. The origin of the Palaeolithic meander. *The Annals of the Ukrainian Academy of Arts and Sciences in the US* 3, 518–34.

Childe, V.G., 1939. *Man Makes Himself*. Oxford: Oxford University Press.

Choyke, A.M., 1984. An analysis of bone, antler and tooth tools from Bronze Age Hungary. *Mitteilungen des Archäologischen Instituts der Ungarischen Akademie der Wissenschaften* 12 / 13, 13–57.

Choyke, A.M., 2001. Late Neolithic red deer canine beads and their imitations, in *Crafting Bone: Skeletal Technologies through Time and Space*, eds. A.M. Choyke & L. Bartosiewicz. (British Archaeological Reports, International Series 937.) Oxford: BAR, 251–66.

Choyke, A.M. & L. Bartosiewicz, 1994. Angling with bones, in *Fish Exploitation in the Past*, ed. W. Van Neer. (Annales du Musée Royal de l'Afrique Centrale, Sciences Zoologiques 274.) Tervuren: Musée Royal de l'Afrique Centrale, 177–82.

Clark, J.E., 1982. Manufacture of Mesoamerican prismatic blades, an alternative technique. *American Antiquity* 47, 355–76.

Clark, J.E., 1987. Politics, prismatic blades, and Mesoamerican civilisation, in *The Organisation of Core Technology*, eds. J.K. Johnson & C.A. Morrow. Boulder (CO): Westview Press, 259–84.

Clark, J.G.D., 1952. *Prehistoric Europe: the Economic Basis*. London: Methuen.

Clark, J.G.D. & M.W. Thompson, 1954. The groove and splinter technique of working antler in Upper Palaeolithic and Mesolithic Europe, with special reference to the material from Star Carr. *Proceedings of the Prehistoric Society* 19, 158–60.

Cluzan, S., 1984. L'outillage et les petits objets en Pierre, in *Fouilles Récentes à Khirokitia (Chypre), 1977–1981*, ed. A. LeBrun. Paris: Éditions Recherche sur les Civilisations, 111–44.

Cohen, S., 1973. The bullroarer. *El Palacio* 78.4, 29–33.

Colomeda, L. & L. Anne, 1999. *Keepers of the Central Fire: Issues in Ecology for Indigenous Peoples*. Boston (MA): Jones & Bartlett.

Conolly, J., 1996. The knapped stone, in *On the Surface: Çatalhöyük 1993–95*, ed. I. Hodder. (McDonald Institute Monographs; BIAA Monograph 22.) Cambridge: McDonald Institute for Archaeological Research; London: British Institute of Archaeology at Ankara, 173–98.

Conolly, J., 1998. Çatalhöyük 1998 lithic report. *Çatalhöyük 1998 Archive Report*. http://catal.arch.cam.ac.uk/catal/Archive_rep98/conolly98.html.

Conolly, J., 1999a. *The Çatalhöyük Flint and Obsidian Industry. Technology and Typology in Context*. (British Archaeological Reports, International Series 787.) Oxford: BAR.

Conolly, J., 1999b. Technical strategies and technical change at Neolithic Çatalhöyük, Turkey. *Antiquity* 73, 791–800.

Conolly, J., 2003. The Çatalhöyük obsidian hoards: a contextual analysis of technology, in *Lithic Studies for the New Millennium*, eds. N. Moloney & M. Shott. London: Archtype Books, 55–78.

Contenson, H.D., 1992. *Préhistoire de Ras Shamra, Les Sondages Stratigraphiques de 1955 à 1976 (I-Texte)*. Paris: Éditions Recherche sur les Civilizations.

Cook, G.T., C. Bonsall, R.E.M. Hedges, K. McSweeney, V. Boroneant, L. Bartosiewicz & P.B. Pettitt, 2002. Problems of dating human bones from the Iron Gates. *Antiquity* 76, 77–85.

Copley, M.S., 2002. Chemical Investigations of Pottery Vessels and Palaeoenvironmental Material from Qasr Ibrim, Egypt. Unpublished PhD Thesis, Bristol University.

Copley, M.S., R. Berstan, S.N. Dudd, G. Docherty, A.J. Mukherjee, V. Straker, S. Payne & R.P. Evershed, 2001. Processing palm fruits in the Nile Valley — biomolecular evidence from Qasr Ibrim. *Antiquity* 75, 538–42.

Copley, M.S., P.J. Rose, A. Clapham, D.N. Edwards, M.C. Horton & R.P. Evershed, 2003. Direct chemical evidence for widespread dairying in prehistoric Britain. *Proceedings of the National Academy of Sciences of the USA* 100, 1524–9.

Copley, M.S., H.A. Bland, P. Rose, M. Horton & R.P. Evershed, 2005a. Gas chromatographic, mass spectrometric and stable carbon isotopic investigations of organic residues of plant oils and animal fats employed as illuminants in archaeological lamps from Egypt. *Analyst* 130, 860–71.

Copley, M.S., R. Berstan, A.J. Mukherjee, S.N. Dudd, V. Straker, S. Payne & R.P. Evershed, 2005b. Dairying in antiquity. III. Evidence from absorbed lipid residues dating to the British Neolithic. *Journal of Archaeological Science* 32, 523–46.

Coqueugniot, É., 1998. L'obsidienne en Méditerranée orientale aux époques post-néolithiques, in *L'Obsidienne au Proche et Moyen Orient: Du Volcan à l'Outil*, eds. M.-C. Cauvin, A. Gourgaud, B. Gratauze, N. Arnaud, G. Poupeau, J.-L. Poidevin & C. Chataigner. (British Archaeological Reports, International Series 738.) Oxford: Maison de l'Orient Méditerranéen/BAR, 351–61.

Coşkunsu, G., 2001. Chipped stone finds from Mezraa-Teleilat 1999: preliminary report, in *Salvage Project of the Archaeological Heritage of the Ilısu and Carcamish Dam Reservoirs Activities in 1999*, eds. N. Tuna, J. Öztürk & J. Velibeyoğlu. Ankara: Middle East Technical University, METU Centre for Research and Assessment of the Historic Environment (TAÇDAM), 175–86.

Courty, M.A., P. Goldberg & R. Macphail, 1989. *Soils and Micromorphology in Archaeology*. Cambridge: Cambridge University Press.

Courty, G.M.-A., W. Matthews & J. Wattez, 1993. Sedimentary formation processes of occupation surfaces, in *Formation Processes in Archaeological Context*, eds. P. Goldberg, D.T. Nash & M.D. Petraglia. (Monographs in World Archaeology 17.) Madison (WI): Prehistory Press, 149–63.

Cowan, M.R., M.L. Gabel, H.A. Jahren & L.L. Tieszen, 1996. Growth and biomineralization of *Celtis occidentalis* (Ulmaceae) Pericarps. *The American Midland Naturalist* 137, 266–73.

Crabtree, D.E., 1968. Mesoamerican polyhedral cores and prismatic blades. *American Antiquity* 33, 446–78.

Crabtree, P.J., 1982. A summary of current approaches to recovery of a reliable record of ancient plant remains. *Museum Applied Science Center of Archaeology Journal* 2, 91–5.

Craig, A.K., 1967. Some observations on the manufacture and utilization of fishhooks among Indians of North America. *The Florida Anthropologist* 20, 79–88.

Crown, P. & W.H. Wills, 1995. Economic intensification and the origins of ceramic containers in the American Southwest, in *The Emergence of Pottery: Technology and Innovation in Ancient Societies*, eds. W.K. Barnett & J.W. Hoopes. Washington (DC): Smithsonian Institution Press, 241–54.

Cucchiari, S., 1981. The gender revolution and the transition from bisexual horde to patrilocal band: the origins of gender hierarchy, in *Sexual Meanings: the Cultural Construction of Gender and Sexuality*, eds. S.B. Ortner & H. Whitehead. Cambridge: Cambridge University Press, 31–79.

Czerniak, L., M. Kwiatkowska, A. Marciniak & J. Pyzel, 2001. The excavations of the TP (Team Poznań) area in the 2001 season. *Çatalhöyük 2001 Archive Report*, http://catal.arch.cam.ac.uk/catal/Archive_rep01/czerniak01.html.

Davidson, I., 1988. The naming of parts: ethnography and the interpretation of Australian prehistory, in *Archaeology with Ethnography: an Australian Perspective*, eds. B. Meehen & R. Jones. Canberra: Highland Press, 17–32.

Davis, M., 1982. The Çayönü ground stone, in *Prehistoric Village Archaeology in Turkey*, eds. L. Braidwood & R. Braidwood. (British Archaeological Reports, International Series 138.) Oxford: BAR, 73–174.

de Vries, K., P.I. Kuniholm, G.K. Sams & M.M. Voigt, 2003. New dates for Iron Age Gordion. *Antiquity*. http://antiquity.ac.uk/ProjGall/devries/devries.html.

Deal, M., 1985. Household pottery disposal in the Maya Highlands: an ethnoarchaeological interpretation. *Journal of Anthropological Archaeology* 4, 243–91.

Decourt, J.-C., 1998. L'obsidienne dans les sources anciennes: notes sur l'histoire due mot et l'utilisation de la roche dans l'Antiquité, in *L'Obsidienne au Proche et Moyen Orient: Du Volcan à l'Outil*, eds. M.-C. Cauvin, A. Gourgaud, B. Gratauze, N. Arnaud, G. Poupeau, J.-L. Poidevin & C. Chataigner. (British Archaeological Reports, International Series 738.) Oxford: Maison de l'Orient Méditerranéen/BAR, 363–77.

DeMarrais, E., J.L. Castillo & T. Earle, 1996. Ideology, materialization and power strategies. *Current Anthropology* 37, 15–31.

d'Errico, F. & M. Vanhaeren, 2002. Criteria for identifying red deer (*Cervus elaphus*) age and sex from their canines. Application to the study of Upper Palaeolithic and Mesolithic ornaments. *Journal of Archaeological Science* 29, 211–32.

Dietler, M., 1996. Feasts and commensal politics in the political economy: food, power and status in prehistoric Europe, in *Food and the Status Quest*, eds. P. Wiessner & W. Schiefenhovel. Providence (RI): Berghahn Books, 87–126.

Dietler, M., 2001. Theorizing the feast: rituals of consumption, commensal politics and power in African contexts, in *Feasts: Archaeological and Ethnographic Perspectives on Food, Politics and Power*, eds. M. Dietler & B. Hayden. Washington (DC): Smithsonian Institution Press, 65–113.

Dietler, M. & B. Hayden (eds.), 2001. *Feasts: Archaeological and Ethnographic Perspectives on Food, Politics, and Power.* Washington (DC): Smithsonian Institution Press.

Dikaios, P., 1953. *Khirokitia*. Oxford: Oxford University Press.

Dithier, J., 1982. *Down to Earth. Adobe Architecture: an Old Idea, a New Future*. New York (NY): Facts on File.

Dobres, M.-A., 2000. *Technology as Social Agency*. Oxford: Blackwell.

Donadoni, S., 1969. *Egyptian Museum, Cairo*. New York (NY): Newsweek & Arnoldo Mondadori Editore.

Donald, M., 1991. *Origins of the Modern Mind*. Cambridge (MA): Harvard University Press.

Dorrell, P., 1983. Appendix A: Stone vessels, tools and objects, in *Jericho V*, eds. K. Kenyon & T. Holland. London: British School of Archaeology in Jerusalem, 485–575.

Douglas, M., 1966. *Purity and Danger*. London: Routledge & Kegan Paul.

Douglas, M., 1972a. Deciphering a meal. *Daedalus* 1972, 61–81.

Douglas, M., 1972b. Symbolic orders in the use of domestic space, *in Man, Settlement and Urbanism*, eds. P. Ucko, R. Tringham & G. Dimbleby. London: Duckworth, 63–73.

Douglas, M., 1984. *Food in the Social Order*. New York (NY): Russell Sage Foundation.

Driver, H.E. & W.C. Massey, 1957. *Comparative Studies of North American Indians*. (Transactions 47, pt 2.) Philadelphia (PA): American Philosophical Society.

Dubreuil, L., 2002. Étude fonctionelle des outils de broyage natoufiens: nouvelles perspectives sur l'émergence de l'agriculture au proche-orient. Unpublished PhD Thesis, University of Bordeaux.

Dudd, S.N. & R.P. Evershed, 1998. Direct demonstration of milk as an element of archaeological economies. *Science* 282, 1478–81.

Dudd, S.N., M. Regert & R.P. Evershed, 1998. Assessing microbial lipid contributions during laboratory degradations of fats and oils and pure triacylglycerols absorbed in ceramic potsherds. *Organic Geochemistry* 29, 1345–54.

Dunnell, R.C. & J.K. Stein, 1989. Theoretical issues in the interpretation of microartifacts. *Geoarchaeology* 4, 31–41.

Düring, B.S., 2001. Social dimensions in the architecture of Neolithic Çatalhöyük. *Anatolian Studies* 51, 1–18.

Durkheim, É., 1893. *De la division du travail social: étude sur l'organisation des sociétés supérieures*. Paris: Alcan.

Duru, R., 1989. Were the earliest cultures at Hacılar really Aceramic, in *Anatolia and the Near East: Studies in Honour of Tahsin Özgüç*, eds. K. Emre & B. Hrouda. Ankara: Türk Tarih Kurumu Basimevi, 94–104.

Duru, R., 1992. Höyücek kazıları 1989. *Belleten* 216.LVI, 551–6.

Duru, R., 1995. Höyücek Kazilari 1991/92. *Belleten* 59, 447–90.

Duru, R., 1998. Bademağacı Kazıları, 1995 ve 1996 Yılları Çalışma Raporu. *Belleten* 61, 709–30.

Duru, R., 1999. The Neolithic of the Lake District, in *Neolithic in Turkey: the Cradle of Civilisation. New Discoveries*, eds. M. Özdogan & N. Basgelen. Istanbul: Arkeoloji ve Sanat Yayınları, 165–91.

Eriç, M., 1980. *Kerpic eski eserlerin onarimi ve korunmasinda bir arastirma*. Third International Symposium on Mud Brick (Adobe), Ankara.

Ertuğ-Yaraş, F., 1997. An Ethnoarchaeological Study of

Subsistence and Plant Gathering in Central Anatolia. Unpublished PhD Dissertation, Department of Anthropology. St Louis, Missouri, Washington University.

Ertuğ-Yaraş, F., 1998. Orta anadolu'da bir etnoarkeoloji ve Etnobotanik Çalışması, in *Light on Top of the Black Hill*, eds. G. Arsebük, M.J. Mellink & W. Schirmer. İstanbul: Ege Yayınları, 325–38.

Esin, U., 1991. Aşikli Höyük Kazisi 1990. *Kazi Sonuçlari Toplantisi* XIII, 131–53.

Esin, U., 1995. Early copper metallurgy at the Pre-Pottery site of Asikli, in *Light on Top of the Black Hill: Studies Presented to Halet Çambel*, eds. G. Arsebük, M.J. Mellinik & W. Schrimer. Istanbul: Eye Yayınları, 61–77.

Esin, U., 1999. The Neolithic in Turkey: a general review, in *Neolithic in Turkey: the Cradle of Civilisation. New Discoveries*, eds. M Özdoğan & N. Basgelen. Istanbul: Arkeoloji ve Sanat Yayınları, 13–23.

Esin, U. & S. Harmankaya, 1999. Aşıklı, in *Neolithic in Turkey: the Cradle of Civilization. New Discoveries*, eds. M. Özdoğan & N. Başgelen. Istanbul: Arkeoloji ve Sanat Yayınları, 115–32.

Esin, U., M. Özbaşaran, E. Biçkaçı, N. Balkan-Atlı, D. Berker, I. Yağmur & A. Korkut Atlı, 1991. Salvage excavations at the Pre-Pottery site of Aşıklı Höyük in Central Anatolia. *Anatolica* 17, 123–74.

Evershed, R.P., C. Heron & L.J. Goad, 1990. Analysis of organic residues of archaeological origin by high-temperature gas-chromatography and gas-chromatography mass-spectrometry. *Analyst* 115, 1339–42.

Evershed, R.P., C. Heron & L.J. Goad, 1991. Epicuticular wax components preserved in potsherds as chemical indicators of leafy vegetables in ancient diets. *Antiquity* 65, 540–44.

Evershed, R.P., C. Heron, S. Charters & L.J. Goad, 1992. The survival of food residues: new methods of analysis, interpretation and application, in *New Developments in Archaeological Science*, ed. A.M. Pollard. Oxford: Oxford University Press, 187–208.

Evershed, R.P., K.I. Arnot, J. Collister, G. Eglinton & S. Charters, S., 1994. Application of isotope ratio monitoring gas-chromatography mass-spectrometry to the analysis of organic residues of archaeological origin. *Analyst* 119, 909–14.

Evershed, R.P., A.W. Stott, A. Raven, S.N. Dudd & A. Leyden, 1995. Formation of long-chain ketones in ancient pottery vessels by pyrolysis of acyl lipids. *Tetrahedron Letters* 36, 8875–8.

Evershed, R.P., H.R. Mottram, S.N. Dudd, S. Charters, A.W. Stott, G.J. Lawrence, A.M. Gibson, A. Conner, P.W. Blinkhorn & V. Reeves, 1997a. New criteria for the identification of animal fats preserved in archaeological pottery. *Naturwissenschaften* 84, 402–6.

Evershed, R.P., S.J. Vaughan, S.N. Dudd & J.S. Soles, 1997b. Fuel for thought? Beeswax in lamps and conical cups from the late Minoan Crete. *Antiquity* 71, 979–85.

Evershed, R.P., S.N. Dudd, S. Charters, H. Mottram, A.W. Stott, A. Raven, P.F. van Bergen & H.A. Bland, 1999. Lipids as carriers of anthropogenic signals from prehistory. *Philosophical Transactions of the Royal Society of London Series B-Biological Sciences* 354, 19–31.

Evershed, R.P., S.N. Dudd, V.R. Anderson-Stojanovic & E.R. Gebhard, 2003. New chemical evidence for the use of combed ware pottery vessels as beehives in ancient Greece. *Journal of Archaeological Science* 30, 1–12.

Evin, J., 1995. Possibilité et nécessité de la calibration des datations C-14 de l'archéologie du Proche-Orient. *Paléorient* 21, 5–16.

Fairbairn, A., E. Asouti, J. Near & D. Martinoli, 2002. Macro-botanical evidence for plant use at Neolithic Çatalhöyük, south-central Anatolia, Turkey. *Vegetation History and Archaeobotany* 11, 41–54.

Ferrence, S., K. Melesanaki, T. Stratoudaki, D. Stambouli, D. Anglos & P. Betancourt, 2000. Analysis of archaeological materials using laser-induced breakdown spectroscopy, in *Physics in Culture I*, ed. K.M. Paraskevopoulos. Thessaloniki: University Studio Press, 186–93.

Fischer, A., P.V. Hansen & P. Rasmussen, 1984. Macro and micro wear traces on lithic projectile points. *Journal of Danish Archaeology* 3, 19–46.

FitzPatrick, D.G. & J. Kimbuna, 1983. *Bundi: the Culture of a Papua New Guinea People*. Nerang, Qld: Ryebuck.

Fladmark, K.R., 1982. Microdebitage analysis: initial considerations. *Journal of Archaeological Science* 92, 205–20.

Forbes, R.J., 1954. Chemical, culinary, and cosmetic arts, in *A History of Technology*, vol. 1, eds. C. Singer, E.J. Holmyard & A. Hall. London: Oxford University Press, 238–98.

Ford, J.A. & C.H. Webb, 1956. *Poverty Point, a Late Archaic Site in Louisiana*. (Anthropological Papers of the American Museum of Natural History 46.1.) New York (NY): American Museum of Natural History.

French, D.H., 1962. Excavations at Can Hasan: third preliminary report. *Anatolian Studies* 14, 27–40.

French, D.H., 1967. Excavations at Can Hasan 1966: sixth preliminary report. *Anatolian Studies* 17, 165–77.

French, D.H., 1972. Excavations at Can Hasan III 1969–1970, in *Papers in Economic Prehistory: Studies by Members and Associates of the British Academy Major Research Project in the Early History of Agriculture*, ed. E.S. Higgs. Cambridge: Cambridge University Press, 181–90.

Friedli, H., H. Lotscher, H. Oeschger, U. Siegenthaler & B. Stauffer, 1986. Ice-core record of the 13C/12C ratio of atmospheric CO2 in the past two centuries. *Nature* 324, 237–8.

Friedman, J. & M. Rowlands (eds.), 1977. *The Evolution of Social Systems*. London: Academic Press.

Gage, J., A. Jones, R. Bradley, K. Spence, E.J.W. Barber & P.S.C. Taçon, 1999. Viewpoint: what meaning had colour in early societies? *Cambridge Archaeological Journal* 9(1), 109–26.

Garrard, A., D. Baird, S. Colledge, L. Martin & K. Wright, 1994. Prehistoric environment and settlement in the Azraq Basin: an interim report on the 1987 and 1988 excavation seasons. *Levant* 26, 73–109.

Garstang, J., 1953. *Prehistoric Mersin: Yümük Tepe in South Turkey*. Oxford: Clarendon Press.

Gebel, H. & H. Bienert, 1997. Ba'ja hidden in the Petra Mountains, in *The Prehistory of Jordan II*, eds. H. Gebel, Z. Kafafi & G. Rollefson. Berlin: Ex Oriente, 247–9.

Gell, A., 1998. *Art and Agency*. Oxford: Clarendon.
Gérard, F., 2002. Transformation and societies in the Neolithic of Central Anatolia, in *The Neolithic of Central Anatolia, Internal Developments and External Relations during the 9th–6th millennia cal BC*, eds. F. Gérard & L. Thissen. Istanbul: Ege Yayınları, 105–17.
Gero, J.M., 1989. Assessing social information in material objects: how well do lithics measure up?, in *Time, Energy and Stone Tools*, ed. R. Torrence. Cambridge: Cambridge University Press, 92–105.
Gibson, A. & A. Woods, 1990. *Prehistoric Pottery for the Archaeologist*. Leicester: Leicester University Press.
Godfrey-Smith, D.I., D.J. Huntley & W.H. Chen, 1988. Optical dating studies of quartz and feldspar sediment extracts. *Quaternary Science Reviews* 7, 373–80.
Goetze, A., 1966. An archaic legal document. *Journal of Cuneiform Studies* 20, 126–7.
Göktürk, E.H., D.J. Hillegonds, M.E. Lipschutz & I. Hodder, 2002. Accelerator mass spectrometry dating at Çatalhöyük. *Radiochimica Acta* 90, 407–10.
Goldberg, P., 1979. The micromorphology of Pech-de-l'Azé II Sediments. *Journal of Archaeological Science* 6, 17–47.
Goldman, H., 1956. *Excavations at Gözlü Kule, Tarsus*, vol. II: *From the Neolithic through the Bronze Age*. Princeton (NJ): Princeton University Press.
Gomez, B., M.D. Glascock, J. Blackman & I.A. Todd, 1995. Neutron activation analysis of obsidian from Kalavasos-Teneta. *Journal of Field Archaeology* 22, 503–8.
Goodman, M., 1999. Micromorphology of depositional sequences from Montículo and Santiago excavations, in *Early Settlement at Chiripa, Bolivia: Research of the Taraco Archaeological Project*, ed. C. Hastorf. Berkeley (CA): Contributions to the University of California, ARF, 130–32.
Goody, J., 1982. *Cooking, Cuisine and Class*. Cambridge: Cambridge University Press.
Gopher, A., 1994. *Arrowheads of the Neolithic Levant: a Seriation Analysis*. (American Schools of Oriental Research, Dissertation Series 10.) Winona Lake (IN): Eisenbrauns.
Gopher, A., 1997. Ground stone tools and other stone objects from Netiv Hagdud, in *An Early Neolithic Village in the Jordan Valley*, eds. O. Bar-Yosef & A. Gopher. Cambridge (MA): American School of Prehistoric Research, 151–76.
Gopher, A. & E. Orrelle, 1995. *The Ground Stone Assemblages of Munhata, a Neolithic Site in the Jordan Valley, Israel: a Report*. Paris: Cahiers des Missions Archéologiques Françaises en Israel, Association Paléorient.
Gould, R.A., 1980. *Living Archaeology*. Cambridge: Cambridge University Press.
Grace, R., 1989. *Interpreting the Function of Stone Tools: the Quantification and Computerisation of Microwear Analysis*. (British Archaeological Reports, International Series 474.) Oxford: BAR.
Grace, R., 1990. The use-wear analysis of drill bits from Kumartepe. *Anatolica* 16, 145–55.
Gratuze, B., 1999. Obsidian characterization by Laser Ablation ICP-MS and its application to prehistoric trade in the Mediterranean and the Near East: sources and distribution of obsidian with the Aegean and Anatolia. *Journal of Archaeological Science* 26, 869–81.
Gratuze, B., J.N. Barrandon, K. Al Isa & M.-C. Cauvin, 1994. Non-destructive analysis of obsidian artefacts using nuclear techniques: Investigations of provenance of Near Eastern artefacts. *Archaeometry* 35, 1–11.
Griffin, G.M., 1971. Interpretation of x-ray diffraction data, in *Procedures in Sedimentary Petrology*, ed R.E. Carver. New York (NY): John Wiley & Sons, 541–69.
Griffitts, J., 2001. Bone tools from Los Pozos, in *Crafting Bone: Skeletal Technologies through Time and Space*, eds. A.M. Choyke & L. Bartosiewicz. (British Archaeological Reports, International Series 937.) Oxford: BAR, 185–95.
Guilaine, J. & F. Briois, 2001. Parekklisha Shillourokambos: an Early Neolithic site in Cyprus, in *The Earliest Prehistory of Cyprus: from Colonization to Exploitation*, ed. S. Swiny. (CAARI Monograph Series.) Boston (MA): American Schools of Oriental Research Archaeological Reports, 37–53.
Hamblin, D.J., 1973. *The First Cities*. New York (NY): Time-Life Books.
Hamilton, N., 1996. Figurines, clay balls, small finds and burials, in *On the Surface: Çatalhöyük 1993–95*, ed. I. Hodder. (McDonald Institute Monographs; BIAA Monograph 22.) Cambridge: McDonald Institute for Archaeological Research; London: British Institute of Archaeology at Ankara, 215–63.
Hamilton, N., 2000. Ungendering archaeology: sex and gender in figurine studies, in *Representations of Gender from Prehistory to the Present. Proceedings of the conference 'Gender and Material Culture from Prehistory to the Present', held at Exeter University, July 1994*, eds. L. Hurcombe & M. Donald. London & New York (NY): Macmillan, 17–30.
Hamilton, N., 2001. Gender and Social Structure in Prehistory: the Uses and Abuses of Material Culture. A Case Study of the Neolithic Site of Çatalhöyük, Çumra (Turkey). Unpublished PhD thesis, Edinburgh University.
Hampton, O.W., 1999. *Culture of Stone: Sacred and Profane Use of Stone Among the Dani*. Austin (TX): Texas A&M University Press.
Hansel, F.A., M.S. Copley, L.A.S. Madureira & R.P. Evershed, 2004. Thermally produced ω-(o-alkylphenyl)alkanoic acids provide evidence for the processing of marine products in archaeological pottery vessels. *Tetrahedron Letters* 45, 2999–3002.
Harding, J.R., 1973. The bull-roarer in history and in antiquity. *African Music* 5, 40–42.
Harsant, W., 1987. The beauty of taonga: arts of the Maori, in *From the Beginning: the Archaeology of the Maori*, ed. J. Wilson. Auckland: Penguin, 125–39.
Hartley, L.P., 1974. *The Go-between*. London: H. Hamilton.
Hassan, F.A., 1978. Sediments in archaeology: methods and applications for paleoenvironmental and cultural analysis. *Journal of Field Archaeology* 5, 197–213.
Hastorf, C., 1991. Gender, space and food in prehistory, in *Engendering Archaeology*, eds. J. Gero & M. Conkey. Oxford: Blackwell, 132–62.
Hastorf, C., 1998. The cultural life of domestic plant use.

Antiquity 72, 773–82.

Hauptmann, H., 1988. Nevali Çori. Arkitektur. *Anatolica* 15, 99–110.

Hauptmann, H., 1999. The Urfa region, in *Neolithic in Turkey: the Cradle of Civilization. New Discoveries*, eds. M. Özdoğan & N. Başgelen. Istanbul: Arkeoloji ve Sanat Yayınları, 65–86.

Hauptmann, J., 1993. Ein Kultgebäude in Nevali Çori, in *Between the Rivers and Over the Mountains*, eds. M. Frangipane, H. Hauptmann, M. Liverani, P. Matthai & M. Mellink. Rome: Universiti di Roma La Sapienza, 37–69.

Hayden, B., 1987. Traditional metate manufacturing in Guatemala using chipped stone tools, in *Lithic Studies Among the Contemporary Highland Maya*, ed. B. Hayden. Tucson (AZ): University of Arizona Press, 8–119.

Hayden, B., 1990. Nimrods, piscators, pluckers, and planters: the emergence of food production. *Journal of Anthropological Archaeology* 9, 31–69.

Hayden, B., 1995. The emergence of prestige technologies and pottery, in *The Emergence of Pottery: Technology and Innovation in Ancient Societies*, eds. W.K. Barnett & J.W. Hoopes. Washington (DC): Smithsonian Institution Press, 257–65.

Hayden, B., 2001. Fabulous feasts: a prolegemon to the importance of feasting, in *Feasts: Archaeological and Ethnographic Perspectives on Food, Politics and Power*, eds. M. Dietler & B. Hayden. Washington (DC): Smithsonian Institution Press, 23–63.

Hayden, B. & A. Cannon, 1983. Where the garbage goes: refuse disposal in the Maya highlands. *Journal of Anthropological Archaeology* 2, 117–63.

Hayden, B. & A. Cannon, 1984. *The Structure of Material Systems: Ethnoarchaeology in the Maya Highlands.* (Society of American Archaeology Papers 3.) Washington (DC): Society of American Archaeology.

Heidegger, M., 1927. *Sein und Zeit.* Tübingen: Neomarius Verlag.

Helbaek, H., 1964. First impressions of the Çatal Hüyük plant husbandry. *Anatolian Studies* 14, 121–3.

Helms, M.W., 1988. *Ulysses Sail: an Ethnographic Odyssey of Power, Knowledge, and Geographical Distance.* Princeton (NJ): Princeton University Press.

Helms, M.W., 1993. *Craft and the Kingly Ideal: Art, Trade and Power*. Austin (TX): University of Texas Press.

Helms, M.W., 2003 (2004). Tangible materiality and cosmological others in the development of sedentism, in *Rethinking Materiality: the Engagement of Mind with the Material World*, eds. E. DeMarrais, C. Gosden & C. Renfrew. (McDonald Institute Monographs.) Cambridge: McDonald Institute for Archaeological Research.

Henderson, J., 2000. *The Science and Archaeology of Materials.* London: Routledge.

Hersh, T., 1981. Grinding Stones and Food Processing Techniques of the Neolithic Societies of Turkey and Greece. Unpublished PhD dissertation, Department of Anthropology, Columbia University.

Higham, T.F.G., 1994. Radiocarbon dating New Zealand prehistory with moa eggshell: some preliminary results. *Quaternary Geochronology* (*Quaternary Science Reviews*) 13, 163–9.

Hill, J.D., 1995. *Ritual and Rubbish in the Iron Age of Wessex.* (British Archaeological Reports, British Series 424.) Oxford: BAR, 95–101.

Hill, J.D., 1996. The identification of ritual deposits of animal bones, in *Ritual Treatment of Human and Animal Remains*, eds. S. Anderson & K. Boyle. Oxford: Oxbow, 17–32.

Hiller, S., 2001. Unverzierte und Ritzverzierte 'Tonpolster' aus Karanovo (Südbulgarien). *Archaeologia Bulgarica* 3, 1–7.

Hiller, S. & V. Nikolov, 1997. *Tell Karanovo 1996–1997.* Salzburg: Vorläufiger Bericht. Schriftenrihe des Instituts für Klassische Archäologie der Universität Salzburg.

Hillman, G., 1984. Traditional husbandry and processing of archaic cereals in recent times. *Bulletin on Sumerian Agriculture* 1, 114–52.

Hillman, G., E. Madeyska & J. Hather, 1989. Wild plant foods and diet at Late Palaeolithic Wadi Kubbaniya: Evidence from charred remains, in *The Prehistory of Wadi Kubbaniya*, vol. 2, eds. F. Wendorf, R. Schild & A. Close. Dallas (TX): Southern Methodist University Press, 162–242.

Hodder, I., 1982. *Symbols in Action: Ethnoarchaeological Studies of Material Culture.* Cambridge: Cambridge University Press.

Hodder, I., 1987. The meaning of discard: ash and domestic space in Baringo, in *Method and Theory for Activity Area Research: an Ethnoarchaeological Approach*, ed. S. Kent. New York (NY): Columbia University Press, 424–48.

Hodder, I., 1990. *The Domestication of Europe: Structure and Contingency in Neolithic Societies.* Oxford: Blackwell.

Hodder, I. (ed.), 1996. *On the Surface Çatalhöyük 1993–95.* (McDonald Institute Monographs; BIAA Monograph 22.) Cambridge: McDonald Institute for Archaeological Research; London: British Institute of Archaeology at Ankara.

Hodder, I., 1999a. Renewed work at Çatalhöyük, in *Neolithic in Turkey: the Cradle of Civilization*, eds. M. Özdoğan & N. Başgelen. Ankara: Arkeoloji ve Sanat Yayınları, 157–64.

Hodder, I., 1999b. *The Archaeological Process: an Introduction.* Oxford: Blackwell.

Hodder, I. (ed.), 2000. *Towards Reflexive Method in Archaeology: the Example at Çatalhöyük.* (McDonald Institute Monographs; BIAA Monograph 28.) Cambridge: McDonald Institute for Archaeological Research; London: British Institute of Archaeology at Ankara.

Hodder, I., 2001. Çatalhöyük 2001. *Anatolian Archaeology* 7, 2-3.

Hodder, I. & C. Cessford, 2004. Daily practice and social memory at Çatalhöyük. *American Antiquity* 69, 17–40.

Hole, F., K. Flannery & J. Neeley, 1969. *Prehistory and Human Ecology of the Deh Luran Plain.* (Memoirs of the Museum of Anthropology 1.) Ann Arbor (MI): Museum of Anthropology.

Horne, L., 1990. *Village Spaces, Settlement and Society in Iran.* Washington (DC): Smithsonian Institution Press.

Horne, L., 1994. *Village Spaces: Settlement and Society in*

Northeastern Iran. Washington (DC): Smithsonian Institution Press.

Hours, F., O. Aurenche, J. Cauvin, M.-C. Cauvin, L. Copeland & P. Sanlaville, 1994. *Atlas des Sites du Proche Orient (14,000–5700 BP)*. Lyon: Travaux de la Maison de l'Orient.

Hudson, T. & T.C. Blackburn, 1982. *The Material Culture of the Chumash Interaction Sphere*. Santa Barbara (CA): Ballena.

Inizan, M.-L., 1984. Débitage par pression et standardisation des supports: un exemple Caspien au Relilaï (Algerie). *Préhistoire de la Pierre Taillée 2: Économie du Débitage Laminaire: Technologie et Éxpérimentation*. Meudon: Cercle de Recherches et d' Études Préhistoriques, 85–92.

Inizan, M.-L., H. Roche & J. Tixier, 1999. *Technology of Knapped Stone*. 2nd edition. Meudon: Cercle de Recherches et d' Études Préhistoriques.

Irwin, G.J,. 1983. Chieftainship, kula and trade in Massim prehistory, in *The Kula: New Perspectives on Massim Exchange*, eds. J.W. Leach & E. Leach. Cambridge: Cambridge University Press, 29-72.

Jahren, H.A., M.L. Gabel & R. Amundson, 1998. Biomineralization in seeds: developmental trends in isotopic signatures of hackberry. *Palaeogeography, Palaeoclimatology, Palaeoecology* 138, 259–69.

Jahren, H.A., R. Amundson, C. Kendall & P. Wigand, 2001. Paleoclimatic Reconstruction Using the Correlation in δ18O of Hackberry Carbonate and Environmental Water, North America. *Quaternary Research* 56, 252–63.

James, P. & N. Thorpe, 1995. *Ancient Inventions*. New York (NY): Ballantine.

Jarman, H.N., H.J. Legge & J.A. Charles, 1972. Retrieval of plant remains from archaeological sites by froth flotation, in *Papers in Economic Prehistory: Studies by Members and Associates of the British Academy Major Research Project in the Early History of Agriculture*, ed. E.S. Higgs. Cambridge: Cambridge University Press, 39–48.

Joffe, A., 1998. Alcohol and social complexity in ancient western Asia. *Current Anthropology* 39, 297–322.

Jones, A. & G. MacGregor (eds.), 2002. *Colouring the Past: the Significance of Colour in Archaeological Research*. Oxford: Berg.

Joyce, R.A., 2000. Heirlooms and houses: materiality and social memory, in *Beyond Kinship: Social and Material Reproduction in House Societies*, eds. R.A. Joyce & S.D. Gillespie. Philadelphia (PA): University of Pennsylvania Press, 189–212.

Kalsbeek, J., 1969. A systematic approach to the study of the Iron Age pottery, in *Excavations at Tell Deir 'All'a*, ed. H.J. Franken. Leiden: Brill, 73–80.

Kamminga, J., 1979. The nature of use-polish and abrasive smoothing on stone tools, in *Lithic Use-Wear Analysis*, ed. B. Hayden. New York (NY): Academic Press, 143–57.

Karabıyıkoğlu, M. & C. Kuzucuoğlu, 1998. *Late Quaternary Chronology, Environmental Evolution and Climatic Change of the Konya Basin*. MTA-TÜBİTAK (Turkey)/URA 141-CNRS.

Karageorghis, J., 1977. *La Grande Déesse de Chypre et Son Culte*. Lyons: Maison de L'Orient.

Karageorghis, V., 1990. *Cyprus from the Stone Age to the Romans*. London: Thames & Hudson.

Kayacan, N., 2000. Yüzey Obsidien Buluntularının Tekno-Kültürel Açıdan Deûerlendirilmesi: Neolitik Musular Yerleûmesi Örneûi. Unpublished MA thesis, İstanbul Üniversitesi Sosyal Bilimler Enstitüsü Edebiyat Fakültesi Prehistorya Anabilim Dalı.

Kayacan, N., in press. Preliminary results of the technological analyses of Musular obsidian, central Anatolia, in *Proceedings of the 4th Workshop on PPN Chipped Stone Industries*, eds. N. Balkan-Atlı & D. Binder. Berlin: Ex Oriente.

Keller, J. & C. Seifried, 1990. The present state of obsidian source identification in Anatolia and the Near East, in *Volcanologie et Archéologie*, eds. C. Albore Livadie & F. Wideman. (PACT 25.) Strasbourg; Conseil de l'Europe, 58–87.

Kemp, B., 2000. Soil (including mud-brick architecture), in *Ancient Egyptian Materials and Technology*, ed. P.T.N.I. Shaw. Cambridge: Cambridge University Press, 78–103.

Kenoyer, J., M. Vidale & K. Bahn, 1991. Contemporary stone bead-making in Khambar, India. *World Archaeology* 23, 44–63.

Kenward, H.K., A.R. Hall & A.K.G. Jones, 1980. A tested set of techniques for the extraction of plant and animal macrofossils from waterlogged archaeological deposits. *Science and Archaeology* 22, 3–15.

Kenyon, K., 1957. *Digging Jericho*. London: E. Benn.

Kilikoglou, V., Y. Bassiakos, R.C. Doonan & J. Stratis, 1997. NAA and ICP analysis of obsidian from Central Europe and the Aegean: source characterisation and provenance determination. *Journal of Radioanalytical and Nuclear Chemistry, Articles* 216, 87–93.

Kingery, W.D., 1960. *Introduction to Ceramics*. New York (NY): Wiley.

Kirkbride, D., 1966. Five seasons at the Pre-Pottery Neolithic village of Beidha in Jordan. *Palestine Exploration Quarterly* 98, 8–72.

Korfmann, M., 1972. *Schleuder und Bogen in Sèudwestasien; von den frèuhesten Belegen bis zum Beginn der historischen Stadtstaaten*. (Antiquitas. Reihe 3, Abhandlungen zur Vor- und Frèuhgeschichte, zur klassischen und provinzial-rèomischen Archèaologie und zur Geschichte des Altertums Bd. 13.) Bonn: R. Habelt.

Kozlowski, S.K., 1999. The big arrowhead industries: BAI in the Near East. *Neo-Lithics* 2, 8–10.

Kramer, C., 1982. *Village Ethnoarchaeology: Rural Iran in Archaeological Perspective*. New York (NY): Academic Press.

Kromer, B., S.W. Manning, P.I. Kuniholm, M.W. Newton, M. Spurk & I. Levin, 2001. Regional 14CO2 offsets in the troposphere: magnitude, mechanisms, and consequences. *Science* 294, 2529–32.

Kuniholm, P.I. & M.W. Newton, 1996. Interim dendrochronological progress report 1995/6, in *On the Surface: Çatalhöyük 1993–95*, ed. I. Hodder. (McDonald Institute Monographs; BIAA Monograph 22.) Cambridge: McDonald Institute for Archaeological Research; London:

British Institute of Archaeology at Ankara, 345–7.

Kuniholm, P.I. & M.W. Newton, 2002. Radiocarbon and dendrochronology, in *The Neolithic of Central Anatolia. Internal Developments and External Relations during the 9th–6th Millennia cal* BC, eds. F. Gérard & L. Thissen. Istanbul: Eye Yayınları, 275–7.

Kuzucuoğlu, C., 2002. The environmental frame in Central Anatolia from the 9th to 6th millennia cal BC, in *The Neolithic of Central Anatolia: Internal Developments and External Relations during the 9th–6th millennia cal* BC, eds. F. Gérard & L. Thissen. Istanbul: Ege Yayınları, 33–58.

Lamberg-Karlovsky, C. & R.H. Meadows, 1970. A unique female figurine: the Neolithic at Tepe Yahya. *Archaeology* 23, 12–17.

LaMotla, V.M. & M.B. Schiffer, 1999. Formation processes of house floor assemblages, in *The Archaeology of Household Activities*, ed. P.M. Allison. London: Routledge, 19–29.

Larting, J.N. & J. van der Plicht, 1994. 14C AMS: pros and cons for archaeology. *Palaeohistoria* 35/36, 1–12.

Larting, J.N. & J. van der Plicht, 1998. Reservoir effects and apparent ages. *Journal of Irish Archaeology* 9, 151–65.

Larrick, R., 1991. Warriors and blacksmiths: mediating ethnicity in East African spears. *Journal of Anthropological Archaeology* 10, 299–331.

Lass, E.H.E., 1994. Quantitiative studies in flotation at Ashkelon, 1986 to 1988. *Bulletin of the American Schools of Oriental Research* 294, 23–30.

Last, J., 1996. Surface pottery at Çatalhöyük, in *On the Surface: Çatalhöyük 1993–95*, ed. I. Hodder. (McDonald Institute Monographs; BIAA Monograph 22.) Cambridge: McDonald Institute for Archaeological Research; London: British Institute of Archaeology at Ankara, 115–71.

Last, J., 1998. A design for life: interpreting the art of Çatalhöyük. *Journal of Material Culture* 3, 355–78.

Latour, B., 1996 *Aramis, or, the Love of Technology*. Cambridge (MA): Harvard University Press.

Leach, E.R., 1954. Primitive time reckoning, in *A History of Technology*, vol. 1, eds. C. Singer, E.J. Holmyard & A.R. Hall. London: Oxford University Press, 110–27.

Lemonnier, P. (ed.), 1993. *Technological Choices: Transformation in Material Culture since the Neolithic*. London: Routledge.

Léotard, J.-M., I. López Bayón & M. Kartal, 1998. La grotte d'Öküzini: evolution technologique et cynegetique, in *Préhistoire d'Anatolie, Genèse de Deux Mondes*, ed. M. Otte. Liège: ERAUL, 509–29.

Limp, W.F., 1974. Water separation and flotation processes. *Journal of Field Archaeology* 1, 337–42.

Lucas, G., 1997. Forgetting the past. *Anthropology Today* 13, 8–14.

Makkay, J., 1984. *Early Stamp Seals in South-East Europe*. Budapest: Akadémiai Kiado.

Manning, S.W., B. Kromer, P.I. Kuniholm & M.W. Newton, 2001. Anatolian tree rings and a new chronology for the eastern Mediterranean Bronze–Iron Ages. *Science* 294, 2532–5.

Marinval, P., 1986. Recherches experimentales sur l'acquisition des données en paléocarpologi. *Revue Archéometrie* 10, 57–68.

Marshack, A., 1972. *The Roots of Civilization: the Cognitive Beginnings of Man's First Art, Symbol and Notation*. London: Weidenfeld & Nicolson.

Marshack, A., 1985. On the dangers of serpents in the mind. *Current Anthropology* 26, 139–45.

Marshall, L., 1976. *The !Kung of Nyae Nayae*. Cambridge (MA): Harvard University Press.

Martin, L. & N. Russell, 1996. Surface material: animal bone and worked bone, in *On the Surface: Çatalhöyük 1993–95*, ed. I. Hodder. (McDonald Institute Monographs; BIAA Monograph 22.) Cambridge: McDonald Institute for Archaeological Research; London: British Institute of Archaeology at Ankara, 199–214.

Martin, L. & N. Russell, 2000. Trashing rubbish, in *Towards Reflexive Method in Archaeology: the Example of Çatalhöyük*, ed. I. Hodder. (McDonald Institute Monographs; BIAA Monograph 28.) Cambridge: McDonald Institute for Archaeological Research; London: British Institute of Archaeology at Ankara, 57–70.

Martin, L., N. Russell & D. Carruthers, 2002. Animal remains from the Central Anatolian Neolithic, in *The Neolithic of Central Anatolia: Internal Developments and External Relations during the 9th–6th millennia cal* BC, eds. F. Gérard & L. Thissen. Istanbul: Ege Yayınları, 193–204.

Matthews, W. & S. Farid, 1996. Exploring the 1960s surface-the stratigraphy of Çatalhöyük, in *On the Surface: Çatalhöyük 1993–95*, ed. I. Hodder. (McDonald Institute Monographs; BIAA Monograph 22.) Cambridge: McDonald Institute for Archaeological Research; London: British Institute of Archaeology at Ankara, 271–300.

Matthews, W., C.A.I. French, T. Lawrence & D.F. Cutler, 1996. Multiple surfaces: the micromorphology, in *On the Surface: Çatalhöyük 1993–95*, ed. I. Hodder. (McDonald Institute Monographs; BIAA Monograph 22.) Cambridge: McDonald Institute for Archaeological Research; London: British Institute of Archaeology at Ankara, 301–42.

McCabe, R.E., 1982. Elk and Indian: historical values and perspectives, in *Elk of North America: Ecology and Management*, eds. J.W. Thomas & D.E. Toweill. Harrisburg (PA): Stackpole, 61–123.

McCartney, C., 1999. Opposed platform core technology and the Cypriot Aceramic Neolithic. *Neo-Lithics* 1, 7–10.

McHenry, P.G., 1984. *Adobe and Rammed Earth Buildings*. New York (NY): John Wiley & Sons.

McKenzie, R., 1983. *The Spear in the Stone*. (Film). Canberra: Australian Institute of Aboriginal and Torres Islander Studies.

Mellaart, J., 1960. Anatolia and the Balkans. *Antiquity* 34, 270–78.

Mellaart, J., 1962. Excavations at Çatal Höyük, 1961: first preliminary report. *Anatolian Studies* 12, 41–65.

Mellaart, J., 1963. Excavations at Çatal Hüyük, 1962: second preliminary report. *Anatolian Studies* 13, 43–103.

Mellaart, J., 1964a. Excavations at Çatal Höyük, 1963: third preliminary report. *Anatolian Studies* 14, 39–119.

Mellaart, J., 1964b. A Neolithic city in Turkey. *Scientific American* 210, 94–104.

Mellaart, J., 1965a. *Earliest Civilizations of the Near East*. New York (NY): McGraw-Hill.

Mellaart, J., 1965b. Çatal Hüyük, a Neolithic city in Anatolia. *Proceedings of the British Academy* 51, 201–13.

Mellaart, J., 1966a. Excavations at Çatal Hüyük: fourth preliminary report, 1965. *Anatolian Studies* 16, 165–91.

Mellaart, J., 1966b. Excavations at Çatal Hüyük 1965. *Archäologisher Anzeiger*, 1–15.

Mellaart, J., 1967. *Çatal Hüyük: a Neolithic Town in Anatolia*. London: Thames & Hudson.

Mellaart, J., 1970. *Excavations at Hacılar*. (Occasional Publications of the British Institute of Archaeology at Ankara 9.) Edinburgh: Edinburgh University Press.

Mellaart, J., 1975. *The Neolithic of the Near East*. London: Thames & Hudson.

Mellaart, J., 1989. Neolithic chronology at Çatal Hüyük?, in *Anatolia and the Ancient Near East: Studies in Honor of Tahsin Ozguc*, eds. K. Emre, M. Mellink, B. Hrouda, & N. Ozguc. Ankara: Türk Tarih Kurumu Basimevi, 315–18.

Mellaart, J., 1990. The earliest representations of the goddess of Anatolia and her entourage, in *Anatolische Kelims: (Symposium Basel), Die Vorträge*, ed. J. Rageth. Basel: Galerie Rageth, 27–46.

Mellaart, J., 1998. Çatal Hüyük: the 1960's seasons, in *Ancient Anatolia: Fifty Years Work by the British Institute of Archaeology at Ankara*, ed. R. Matthews. London: British Institute of Archaeology at Ankara, 35–41.

Mellink, M.J., 1956. Neolithic and Chalcolithic pottery, in *Excavations at Gözlü Kule, Tarsus II: from the Neolithic through the Bronze Age*, ed. H. Goldman. Princeton (NJ): Princeton University Press, 65–91.

Mellink, M.J. & R.S. Young, 1966. *Art Treasures of Turkey*. Washington (DC): Smithsonian Institution.

Merleau-Ponty, M., 1962. *Phenomenology of Perception*. London: Routledge.

Meskell, L., forthcoming. *Material Biographies: Object Worlds from Ancient Egypt and Beyond*. Oxford: Berg.

Miksicek, C.H., 1987. Formation processes of the archaeobotanical record. *Advances in Archaeological Method and Theory* 10, 211–47.

Miller, D., 1985. *Artefacts as Categories: a Study of Ceramic Variability in Central India*. Cambridge: Cambridge University Press.

Miller, D., 1987. *Material Culture and Mass Consumption*. Oxford: Blackwell.

Miller, D. (ed.), 1998. *Material Cultures*. Chicago (IL): University of Chicago Press.

Miller-Rosen, A., 1989. Ancient town and city sites: a view from the microscope. *American Antiquity* 54, 564–78.

Miller-Rosen, A., 1993. Microartifacts as a reflection of cultural factors in site formation, in *Formation Processes in Archaeological Context*, eds. P. Goldberg, D.T. Nash & M.D. Petraglia. (Monographs in World Archaeology 17.) Madison (WI): Prehistory Press, 141–8.

Mithen, S., 1996. *The Prehistory of the Mind*. London: Thames & Hudson.

Moioli, P. & C. Seccaroni, 2000. Analysis of art objects using a portable x-ray fluorescence spectrometer. *X-Ray Spectrometry* 29, 48–52.

Molleson, T., 2000. The people of Abu Hureyra, in *Village on the Euphrates: from Foraging to Farming at Abu Hureyra*, eds. A.M.T. Moore, G.C. Hillman & A.L. Legge. Oxford: Oxford University Press, 321–6.

Molleson, T., G. Cressey, G. Jones & J. Ambers, forthcoming. Trace Elements in Sickness and Health at Çatalhöyük. Paper at Archaeological Science 2003 conference.

Moore, A.M.T., 1995. The inception of potting in Western Asia and its impact on economy and society, in *The Emergence of Pottery: Technology and Innovation in Ancient Societies*, eds. W.K. Barnett, & J.W. Hoopes. Washington (DC): Smithsonian Institution Press, 39–53.

Morris, D., 1985. *The Art of Ancient Cyprus*. London: Phaidon.

Mortenson, P., 1964. Notes on Obsidian and Flint from Çatal Hüyük 1961–1963. Unpublished manuscript.

Mottram, H.R., S.N. Dudd, G.J. Lawrence, A.W. Stott & R.P. Evershed, 1999. New chromatographic, mass spectrometric and stable isotope approaches to the classification of degraded animal fats preserved in archaeological pottery. *Journal of Chromatography* A 833, 209–21.

Mouton, M., 1984. La vaisselle en pierre, in *Fouilles Récentes à Khirokitia (Chypre), 1977–1981*, ed. A. LeBrun. Paris: Éditions Recherche sur les Civilisations, 97–116.

Naveh, D., 2003. PPNA Jericho: a socio-political perspective. *Cambridge Archaeological Journal* 13(1), 83–96.

Nelson, S.M., 1990. Diversity of the Upper Paleolithic 'Venus' figurines and archeological mythology, in *Powers of Observation: Alternative Views in Archeology*, eds. S.M. Nelson & A.B. Kehoe. (Archeological Papers of the American Anthropological Association 2.) Washington (DC): American Anthropological Association, 11–22.

Newcomer, M., 1975. 'Punch technique' and Upper Palaeolithic blades, in *Lithic Technology, Making and Using Stone Tools*, ed. E. Swanson. The Hague & Paris: Mouton, 97–102.

Newcomer, M. & C. Karlin, 1987. Flint chips from Pincevent, in *The Human Uses of Flint and Chert*, eds. G. Sieveking & M. Newcomer. Cambridge: Cambridge University Press, 33–6.

Newton, M.W. & P.I. Kuniholm, 1999. Wiggles worth watching — making radiocarbon work: the case of Çatal Höyük, in *Meletemata. Studies in Aegean Archaeology presented to Malcolm H. Wiener as he enters his 65th year*, eds. P.P. Betancourt, V. Karageorghis, R. Laffineur & W.-D. Niemeier. (Aegaeum 20.) Liège: Université de Liège, 527–37.

Nierlé, M.-C., 1983. Mureybet et Cheikh Hassan (Syrie): Outillage de mouture et de broyage. *Cahiers de l'Euphrate* 3, 177–216.

Nishiaki, Y., 2000. *Lithic Technology of Neolithic Syria*. (British Archaeological Reports, International Series 840.) Oxford: BAR.

Norton, J., 1997. *Building With Earth: a Handbook*. London: Intermediate Technology.

O'Connor, S.M., M. Spriggs & P. Veth, in press. *The Archaeology of the Aru Islands*. Rotterdam: Balkema.

Oates, D., 1990. Innovations in mud-brick: decorative and structural techniques in ancient Mesopotamia. *World*

Archaeology 21, 388–406.
Oates, J., 1996. A prehistoric communication revolution. *Cambridge Archaeological Journal* 6(1), 165–76.
Onassoglou, A., 1996. Seals, in *Neolithic Culture in Greece*, ed. G. Papathanasopoulos. Athens: N.P. Goulandris Foundation, 163–4.
Ortiz, B., 1991. *It Will Live Forever: Traditional Yosemite Indian Acorn Preparation*. Berkeley (CA): Heyday.
Otte, M., I. Yalçinkaya, J.-M. Léotard, I. López Bayón, O. Bar-Yosef & M. Kartal, 1998. Öküzini: un site de chasseurs Epipaléolithiques en Anatolie, in *Préhistoire d'Anatolie, Genèse de Deux Mondes*, ed. M. Otte. Liège: ERAUL, 531–49.
Oyuela-Caycedo, A., 1995. Rock versus clay: the evolution of pottery technology in the Case of San Jacinto 1, Columbia, in *The Emergence of Pottery: Technology and Innovation in Ancient Societies*, eds. W.K. Barnett & J.W. Hoopes. Washington (DC): Smithsonian Institution Press, 133–44.
Özbal, R., 2000. Microartifact analysis – 1999, in The Kurdu excavation 1999, by K.A. Yener, C. Edens, J. Casana, B. Diebald, H. Ekstrom, M. Loyet & R. Özbal. *Anatolica* 26, 49–55.
Özbaşaran, M., 1998. The heart of a house: the hearth. Aşıklı Höyük, a Pre-Pottery Neolithic site in Central Anatolia, in *Light on Top of the Black Hill: Studies Presented to Halet Cambel*, ed. G. Arsebuk, M.J. Mellink & W. Schirmer. Istanbul: Ege Yayinlari, 555–66.
Özbaşaran, M., 1999. Musular: a general assessment on a new Neolithic site in Central Anatolia, in *Neolithic in Turkey: the Cradle of Civilization. New Discoveries*, eds. M. Özdoğan & N. Başgelen. Istanbul: Arkeoloji ve Sanat Yayınları, 147–55.
Özbaşaran, M., 2000. The Neolithic site of Musular - Central Anatolia. *Anatolica* 26, 129–52.
Özbaşaran, M. & H. Buitenhuis, 2002. Proposal for a regional terminology for Central Anatolia, in *The Neolithic of Central Anatolia: Internal Developments and External Relations During the 9th–6th Millennia cal* BC, eds. F. Gérard & L. Thissen. Istanbul: Eye Yayınları, 67–77.
Özdoğan A., 1999. Çayönü, in *Neolithic in Turkey: the Cradle of Civilization. New Discoveries*, eds. M. Özdoğan & N. Başgelen. Istanbul: Arkeoloji ve Sanat Yayınları, 35–63.
Özdoğan, M., 1994. Çayönü: the chipped stone industry of the Pottery Neolithic layers, in *Neolithic Chipped Stone Industries of the Fertile Crescent. Proceedings of the First Workshop on PPN Chipped Lithic Industries*, eds. H.G. Gebel & S.K. Kozlowski. (Studies in Early Near Eastern Production, Subsistence and Environment 1.) Berlin: Ex Oriente, 267–77.
Özdoğan, M., 1997. The beginnings of Neolithic economies in Southeastern Europe: an Anatolian perspective. *Journal of European Archeology* 5, 1–33.
Özdoğan, M., 1999. Northwestern Turkey: Neolithic Cultures in between the Balkans and Anatolia, in *Neolithic in Turkey: the Cradle of Civilisation. New Discoveries*, eds. M. Özdoğan & N. Başgelen. Istanbul: Arkeoloji ve Sanat Yayınları, 203–24.
Özdoğan, M., 1999. Preface, in *Neolithic in Turkey: the Cradle of Civilisation. New Discoveries*, eds. M. Özdoğan & N. Başgelen. Istanbul: Arkeoloji ve Sanat Yayinlari, 9–12.
Özdoğan, M., 2002. Defining the Neolithic of Central Anatolia, in *The Neolithic of Central Anatolia: Internal Developments and External Relations during the 9th–6th millennia cal* BC, eds. F. Gérard & L. Thissen. Istanbul: Ege Yayınları, 253–61.
Özdoğan, M. & N. Başgelen, 1999. *Neolithic in Turkey: the Cradle of Civilization. New Discoveries*. Istanbul: Arkeoloji ve Sanat Yayinlari.
Özkan, S., 2001. Köşk Höyük Seals. *Anatolica* 27, 15–22.
Papadopoulos, J.K., J.F. Vedder & T. Schreiber, 1998. Drawing circles: experimental archaeology and the pivoted multiple brush. *American Journal of Archaeology* 102, 507–29.
Parish, R., 1996. Luminescence dating of mud brick from Çatalhöyük, in *On the Surface: Çatalhöyük 1993–95*, ed. I. Hodder. (McDonald Institute Monographs; BIAA Monograph 22.) Cambridge: McDonald Institute for Archaeological Research; London: British Institute of Archaeology at Ankara, 343–4.
Pearce, N.J.G., W.T. Perkins, J.A. Westgate, M.P. Gorton, S.E. Jackson, C.R. Neal & S.P. Chenery, 1997. A compilation of new and published major and trace element data for NIST SRM 610 and NIST SRM 612 glass reference materials. *Geostandards Newsletter* 21, 115–44.
Pearce, N.J.G., W.J. Eastwood, J.A. Westgate & W.T. Perkins, 2002. Trace-element composition of single glass shards in distal Minoan tephra from SW Turkey. *Journal of the Geological Society* 159, 545–56.
Pearsall, D.M., 1989. *Paleoethnobotany: a Handbook of Procedures*. San Diego (CA): Academic Press.
Pearson, K. & P. Connor, 1968. *The Dorak Affair*. New York (NY): Athenaeum.
Pedley, J.G., 1993. *Greek Art and Archaeology*. New York (NY): H.N. Abrams.
Pelegrin, J., 1988. Débitage expérimental par pression «Du plus petit au plus grand», *Technologie Préhistorique. Notes et Monographies Techniques* 25, ed. J. Tixier. Paris: Éditions du CNRS, 37–53.
Peltenburg, E., 1991. Towards definition of the Late Chalcolithic in Cyprus: the monochrome pottery debate, in *Cypriot Ceramics: Reading the Prehistoric Record*, eds. J.A. Barlow, D. Bolger & B. Kling. (University Museum Monograph 74.) Philadelphia (PA): University of Pennsylvania: University Museum, 9–20.
Peltenburg, E., P. Croft, A. Jackson, C. McCartney & M.A. Murray, 2001a. Well-established colonists: Mylouthkia 1 and the Cypro-Pre-Pottery Neolithic B, in *The Earliest Prehistory of Cyprus: From Colonization to Exploitation*, ed. S. Swiny. (CAARI Monograph Series.) Boston (MA): American Schools of Oriental Research Archaeological Reports, 61–93.
Peltenburg, E., S. Colledge, P. Croft, A. Jackson, C. McCartney & A. Murray, 2001b. Neolithic dispersals from the Levantine Corridor: a Mediterranean perspective. *Levant* 33, 35–64.
Pendleton, M.W., 1983. A comment concerning 'testing flotation recovery rates'. *American Antiquity* 48, 615–16.

Pennington, C.W., 1963. *The Tarahumar of Mexico: their Environment and Material Culture.* Salt Lake City (UT): University of Utah Press.

Pereira, C.E de B., 2000. Otimização de Metodologias Para a Análise Multiementar de Obsidianas por ICP-MS com Amostragem por Ablação a Laser e Aplicações em Estudos de Proveniência de Artefactos Arqueológicos. Unpublished PhD thesis, PUC-Rio.

Pereira, C.E de B., N. Miekeley, G. Poupeau & I.L. Küchler, 2001. Determination of minor and trace elements in obsidian rock samples and archaeological artefacts by laser ablation inductively coupled plasma mass spectrometry using synthetic obsidian standards. *Spectrochimica Acta* Part B 56, 1927–40.

Perlès, C., 1989. From Stone Procurement to Neolithic Society in Greece. David Skomp distinguished lectures in Anthropology, February 1989.

Perlès, C., 1990. L'outillage de pierre taillée Néolithique en Grèce: Approvisionnement et exploitation des matières premières. *Bulletin de Correspondance Hellénique* 114, 1–42.

Perlès, C., 2001. *The Early Neolithic in Greece: the First Farming Communities in Europe.* Cambridge: Cambridge University Press.

Peterson, J., 1997. Tracking activity patterns through skeletal remains: a case study from Jordan and Palestine, in *The Prehistory of Jordan II: Perspectives From 1997*, eds. H.G. Gebel, Z. Kafafi & G. Rollefson. Berlin: Ex Oriente, 475–92.

Peterson, J., 2002. *Sexual Revolutions: Gender and Labor at the Dawn of Agriculture.* Walnut Creek (CA): Altamira.

Pétrequin, P., 1993. North wind, south wind: Neolithic technical choices in the Jura Mountains, 3700–2400 BC, in *Technological Choices: Transformation in Material Cultures Since the Neolithic*, ed. P. Lemonnier. London: Routledge, 36–76.

Philip, G. & O. Williams-Thorpe, 1993. A provenance study of Jordanian basalt vessels of the Chalcolithic and Early Bronze Age I periods. *Paléorient* 19, 51–63.

Phillips, J.L., A. Belfer-Cohen & I.N. Saca, 1998. A collection of Natufian bone artefacts from old excavations at Kebara and El-Wad. *Palestine Exploration Quarterly* 130, 145–53.

Pliny *N.H. Historia Naturalis.* Translated by C. Mayhoff (1892–1905). Leipzig: Teubner Series.

Poidevin, J.-L., 1998. Les gisements d'obsidienne de Turquie et de Transcaucasie: géologie, géochemie et chronométrie, in *L'Obsidienne au Proche et Moyen Orient: Du Volcan à l'Outil*, eds. M.-C. Cauvin, A. Gourgaud, B. Gratuze, N. Arnaud, G. Poupeau, J.-L. Poidevin & C. Chataigner. (British Archaeological Reports, International Series 738.) Oxford: Maison de l'Orient Méditerranéen / BAR, 105–203.

Pollard, T., C. Shell & D.R. Twigg, 1996. Topographic survey of the Çatalhöyük mounds, in *On the Surface: Çatalhöyük 1993–95*, ed. I. Hodder. (McDonald Institute Monorgraphs; BIAA Monograph 22.) McDonald Institute for Archaeological Research / British Institute of Archaeology at Ankara Monograph 22, 59–72.

Prehistoric Ceramics Research Group (PCRG), 1995. *The Study of Later Prehistoric Pottery: General Policies and Guidelines for Analysis and Publication.* Occasional Papers Nos. 1 & 2.

Prendergast, D.M., 2000. The problems raised by small charcoal samples for radiocarbon analysis. *Journal of Field Archaeology* 27, 237–9.

Preston, R.J., 1976. *North American trees (Exclusive of Mexico and Tropical United States).* 3rd edition. Boise (IA): Iowa State University Press.

Procopiou, H. & R. Treuil, 2002. *Moudre et Broyer. L'interpretation Fonctionnelle de l'outillage de Mouture et de Broyage dans la Préhistoire et L'antiquité. I: Méthodes. II: Archéologie.* Paris: CTHS.

Puche, M.C.S., 1994. Objetos de Obsidiana y Otros Cristales en el Mexico Antiguo, in *Cristales Y Obsidiana Prehispanicos*, eds. M.C.S. Puche & F.S. Olguin. Mexico City: Delegación Coyoacán, 73–215.

Rainville, L., 2000. Microdebris analysis in Early Bronze Age Mesopotamian households. *Antiquity* 74, 291.

Raven, A.M., P.F. van Bergen, A.W. Stott, S.N. Dudd & R.P. Evershed, 1997. Formation of long-chain ketones in archaeological pottery vessels by pyrolysis of acyl lipids. *Journal of Analytical and Applied Pyrolysis* 40, 267–85.

Reber, E.A., S.N. Dudd, N.J. van der Merwe & R.P. Evershed, 2004. Direct detection of maize in pottery residues via compound specific stable carbon isotope analysis. *Antiquity* 78, 682–91.

Rees-Jones, J. & M.S. Tite, 1997. Optical dating result for British archaeological sediments. *Archaeometry* 39, 177–88.

Renfrew, C., 1975. Trade as action at a distance: questions of integration and communication, in *Ancient Civilisation and Trade*, eds. J.A. Sabloff & C.C. Lamberg-Karlovsky. Albuquerque (NM): University of New Mexico Press, 3–60.

Renfrew, C., 1998a. Foreword, in *L'Obsidienne au Proche et Moyen Orient: Du Volcan à l'Outil*, eds. M.-C. Cauvin, A. Gourgaud, B. Gratauze, N. Arnaud, G. Poupeau, J.-L. Poidevin & C. Chataigner. (British Archaeological Reports, International Series 738.) Oxford: Maison de l'Orient Méditerranéen / BAR, 5–6.

Renfrew, C., 1998b. Mind and matter: cognitive archaeology and external symbolic storage, in *Cognition and Material Culture: the Archaeology of Symbolic Storage*, eds. C. Renfrew & C. Scarre. (McDonald Institute Monographs.) Cambridge: McDonald Institute for Archaeological Research, 1–6.

Renfrew, C., 2001. Symbol before concept. Material engagement and the early development of society, in *Archaeological Theory Today*, ed. I. Hodder. Cambridge: Polity Press, 122–40.

Renfrew, C., 2003. Towards a theory of material engagement. Paper presented at conference *Rethinking materiality*. McDonald Institute for Archaeological Research, Cambridge. [Published as Renfrew, C., 2004. Towards a theory of material engagement, in *Rethinking Materiality: the Engagement of Mind with the Material World*, eds. E. DeMarrais, C. Gosden & C. Renfrew. (McDonald Institute Monographs.) Cambridge: McDonald Institute for Archaeological Research, 23–31.]

Renfrew, C., J.R. Cann & J.E. Dixon, 1965. Obsidian in the Aegean. *Annual of the British School at Athens* 60, 225–47.

Renfrew, C., J.E. Dixon & J.R. Cann, 1966. Obsidian and early culture contact in the Near East. *Proceedings of the Prehistoric Society* 32, 30–72.

Renfrew, C., J.E. Dixon & J.R. Cann, 1968. Further analysis of Near Eastern obsidians. *Proceedings of the Prehistoric Society* 34, 319–31.

Renfrew, J.M., M. Monk & P. Murphy, 1976. *First Aid for Seeds*. Hertford: Rescue.

Rice, P.M., 1987. *Pottery Analysis : a Sourcebook*. Chicago (IL): University of Chicago Press.

Richards, C. & J. Thomas, 1984. Ritual activity and structured deposition in later Neolithic Wessex, in *Neolithic Studies: a Review of Some Current Research*, eds. R. Bradley & J. Gardiner. (British Archaeological Reports, British Series 133.) Oxford: BAR, 189–218.

Roberts, N., P. Boyer & R. Parish, 1996. Preliminary results of geoarchaeological investigations at Çatalhöyük, in *On the Surface: Çatalhöyük 1993–95*, ed. I. Hodder. (McDonald Institute Monographs; BIAA Monograph 22.) Cambridge: McDonald Institute for Archaeological Research; London: British Institute of Archaeology at Ankara, 19–39.

Roberts, N., S. Black, P. Boyer, W.J. Eastwood, H.I. Griffiths, H.F. Lamb, M.J. Leng, R. Parish, J.M. Reed, D. Twigg & H. Yiðitbaþioðlu, 1999. Chronology and stratigraphy of Late Quaternary sediments in the Konya Basin, Turkey: results from the KOPAL Project. *Quaternary Science Reviews* 18, 611–30.

Rodden, R.J., 1964. A European link with Catal Höyük: uncovering a 7th millennium settlement in Macedonia, Part I: Site & pottery. *Illustrated London News, April 11th*, 564–8.

Roodenberg, J., 1986. *Le Mobilier en Pierre de Bouqras*. Leiden: Nederlands Institut Voor het Nabije Oosten.

Rosen, A., 1986. *Cities of Clay: the Geoarchaeology of Tells*. Chicago (IL): The University of Chicago Press.

Rosen, S. & J. Schneider, 2001. Early Bronze Age milling stone production and exchange in the Negev: preliminary conclusions. *Mitekufat Haeven, Journal of the Israel Prehistoric Society* 31, 201–12.

Roubet, C., 1989. Report on site E-82-1, in *The Prehistory of Wadi Kubbaniya*, vol. 3, eds. F. Wendorf, R. Schild & A. Close. Dallas (TX): Southern Methodist University Press, 588–610.

Roussot-Larroque, J., 1985. Objets anciformes et pendeloques en quille des allées couvertes d'Aquitaine, in *Industrie de l'Os Néolithique et de l'Age des Métaux 3*, ed. H. Camps-Fabrer. Paris: Éditions du Centre National de la Recherche Scientifique, 90–111.

Rowling, J.K., 1999. *Harry Potter and the Sorcerer's Stone*. New York (NY): Scholastic.

Russell, N., 1985. Le traitement de l'os comme matiére premiére: aperçus de Yougoslavie et du Pakistan, in *Industrie de l'Os Néolithique et de l'Age des Métaux 3*, ed. H. Camps-Fabrer. Paris: Éditions du Centre National de la Recherche Scientifique, 25–32.

Russell, N., 1990. The Selevac bone tools, in *Selevac: a Neolithic Village in Yugoslavia*, eds. R.E. Tringham & D. Krstić. Los Angeles (CA): UCLA Institute of Archaeology, 521–48.

Russell, N., 1995. The bone tool industry at Mehrgarh and Sibri, in *Mehrgarh: Field Reports 1974–1985. From Neolithic Times to the Indus Civilization*, eds. C. Jarrige, J.-F. Jarrige, R.H. Meadow & G. Quivron. Karachi: Department of Culture and Tourism, Government of Sindh, Pakistan, 583–613.

Russell, N., 2001. The social life of bone: a preliminary assessment of bone tool manufacture and discard at Çatalhöyük, in *Crafting Bone: Skeletal Technologies through Time and Space*, eds. A.M. Choyke & L. Bartosiewicz. (British Archaeological Reports, International Series 937.) Oxford: BAR, 241–9.

Rye, O., 1981. *Pottery Technology: Principles and Reconstruction*. Washington (DC): Taraxacum.

Sagona, A. & J.A. Webb, 1994. Toolumbunner in perspective, in *Bruising the Red Earth: Ochre Mining and Ritual in Aboriginal Tasmania*, ed. A. Sagona. Melbourne: Melbourne University Press, 137–42.

Sassaman, K.E., 1995. The social contradictions of traditional cooking technologies in the prehistoric American southeast, in *The Emergence of Pottery: Technology and Innovation in Ancient Societies*, eds. W.K. Barnett & J.W. Hoopes. Washington (DC): Smithsonian Institution Press, 223–40.

Saunders, N., 2001. A dark light: reflections on obsidian in Mesoamerica. *World Archaeology* 33, 220–36.

Schaaf, J.M., 1981. A method for reliable and quantifiable subsampling of archaeological features for flotation. *Mid-Continental Journal of Archaeology* 6, 219–48.

Schiffer, M.B., 1976. *Behavioral Archeology*. New York (NY): Academic Press.

Schiffer, M.B., 1987. *Formation Processes of the Archaeological Record*. Albuquerque (NM): University of New Mexico Press.

Schiffer, M.B., 1990. The influence of surface treatment on heating effectiveness of ceramic vessels. *Journal of Archaeological Science* 17, 373–81.

Schmandt-Besserat, D., 1977. The earliest uses of clay in Anatolia. *Anatolian Studies* 27, 133–50.

Schmandt-Besserat, D., 1992. *Before Writing: from Counting to Cuneiform*. Austin (TX): University of Texas Press.

Schmandt-Besserat, D., 1997. Accounting before writing in the Near East. *Porocilo o razisko vanju paleolitika, neolitika in eneolitika v Slovenj* 24, 1–11.

Schmidt, K., 1994. The Nevalli Çori industry: status of research. Preliminary results, in *Neolithic Chipped Stone Industries of the Fertile Crescent. Proceedings of the First Workshop on PPN Chipped Lithic Industries*, eds. H.G. Gebel & S.K. Kozlowski. (Studies in Early Near Eastern Production, Subsistence, and Environment 1.) Berlin: Ex Oriente, 239–51.

Schmidt, K., 1996. Nevali Çori: chronology and intrasite distribution of lithic tool classes. Preliminary results, in *Neolithic Chipped Stone Industries of the Fertile Crescent, and their Contemporaries in Adjacent Regions. Proceedings of the Second Workshop on PPN Chipped Lithic Industries*, eds. S.K. Kozlowski & H.G. Gebel. (Studies in Early

Near Eastern Production, Subsistence, and Environment 3.) Berlin: Ex Oriente, 363–76.
Schmidt, K., 2001. Göbekli Tepe, southeastern Turkey: a preliminary report on the 1995–1999 excavations. *Paléorient* 26, 45–54.
Schoop, U.-D., 2002. Frühneolithikum im südwestanatolischen Seengebiet? Eine kritische Betrachtung, in *Mauerschau: Festschrift für Manfred Korfmann*, vol. 1, eds. R. Aslan, S. Blum, G. Kastl, F. Schweizer & D. Thumm. Remshalden-Grunbach: Verlag Bernhard Albert Greiner, 421–36.
Schweig, B., 1941. Mirrors. *Antiquity* 15, 257–68.
Shackley, M.S., 1998. *Archaeological Obsidian Studies: Methods and Theory*. New York (NY): Plenum Press.
Shennan, S., 1988. *Quantifying Archaeology*. Edinburgh: Edinburgh University Press.
Shennan, S., 1997. *Quantifying Archaeology*. 2nd edition. Edinburgh: Edinburgh University Press.
Sherratt, A., 1981. Plough and pastoralism: aspects of the secondary products revolution, in *Pattern of the Past*, eds. I. Hodder, G. Isaac & N. Hammond. Cambridge: Cambridge University Press, 261–305.
Sherwood, S.C. & S.D. Osley, 1995. Quantifying microartifacts using a personal computer. *Geoarchaeology* 10, 423–8.
Sherwood, S.C., J.F. Simek & R.R. Polhemus, 1995. Artifact size and spatial process: macro- and microartifacts in a Mississipian house. *Geoarchaeology* 10, 429–55.
Sidéra, I., 2000a. Animaux doméstiques, bêtes sauvages et objets en matières animales du Rubané au Michelsberg: de l'économie aux symboles, des techniques à la culture. *Gallia Préhistoire* 42, 107–94.
Sidéra, I., 2000b. Feu et industrie osseuse: Un marqueur d'identité culturelle. *Paléorient* 26, 51–9.
Sidéra, I., 2001. Domestic and funerary bone, antler and tooth objects in the Neolithic of western Europe: a comparison, in *Crafting Bone: Skeletal Technologies through Time and Space*, eds. A.M. Choyke & L. Bartosiewicz. (British Archaeological Reports, International Series 937.) Oxford: BAR, 221–9.
Silistreli, U., 1984. Köşk Höyük 1983. *Kazi Sonuçlari Toplantisi* VI, 31–6.
Silistreli, U., 1986. Köşk Höyük 1985. *Kazi Sonuçlari Toplantisi* VIII, 173–9.
Silistreli, U., 1988. Köşk Höyük 1987. *Kazi Sonuçlari Toplantisi* X, 61–6.
Silverblatt, I., 1988. Women in states. *Annual Review of Anthropology* 17, 427–60.
Skibo, J.M., M.B. Schiffer & K.C. Reid, 1989. Organic-tempered pottery: an experimental study. *American Antiquity* 54, 122–46.
Skibo, J.M., T.C. Butts & M.B. Schiffer, 1997. Ceramic surface treatment and abrasion resistance: an experimental study. *Journal of Archaeological Science* 24, 311–17.
Spector, J.D., 1991. What this awl means: toward a feminist archaeology, in *Engendering Archaeology: Women and Prehistory*, eds. J.M. Gero & M.W. Conkey. Oxford: Blackwell, 388–406.
Spencer, B., 1928. *Wanderings in Wild Australia*, vol. II. London: Macmillan & Co.
Sperl, G., 1988. Montangeschichte des Erzberggebietes nach archäologischen und schriftlichen Dokumenten. *Habilitationsschrift; Geisteswissenschaftliche Fakultät der Universität Wien*, 230–32.
Spooner, N.A., M.J. Aitken, B.W. Smith, M. Franks & C. McElroy, 1990. Archaeological dating by infrared stimulated luminescence using a diode array. *Radiation Protection Dosimetry* 34, 83–6.
Spriggs, M., 1986. Landscape, land use and political transformation in southern Melanesia, in *Island Societies: Archaeological Approaches to Evolution and Transformation*, ed. P.V. Kirch. Cambridge: Cambridge University Press, 6–19.
Stahl, A., 1989. Plant-food processing: implications for dietary quality, in *Foraging and Farming*, eds. D. Harris & G.C. Hillman. London: Unwin Hyman, 171–94.
Stein, J.K. & P.A. Telset, 1989. Size distributions of artifact classes: combining macro and micro-fractions. *Geoarchaeology* 4, 1–30.
Stevanović, M., 1997. The age of clay: the social dynamics of house destruction. *Journal of Anthropological Archaeology* 16, 334–95.
Stevanović, M. & R. Tringham, 1998. The BACH 1 Area, *Çatalhöyük 1998 Archive Report*. http://catal.arch.cam.ac.uk/catal/Archive_rep98/tringham98.html.
Stevanović, M. & R. Tringham, 2001. The excavations of the BACH Area. *Çatalhöyük 2001 Archive Report*. http://catal.arch.cam.ac.uk/catal/Archive_rep01/stevanotring/01.html.
Stoops, G., 2003. *Guidelines for Analysis and Description of Soil and Regolith Thin Sections*. Madison (WI): Soil Science Society of America.
Stordeur, D., 1982a. El Kowm 2- Caracol, Campagnes 1978, 1979, et 1980. Stratigraphie et architectures, in *Cahiers de l'Euphrate 3*, ed. J. Cauvin. Paris: Edition Recherché sur les Civilizations, 33–49.
Stordeur, D., 1982b. L'industrie osseuse de la Damascène du VIIIe au VIe Millénaire, in *Industrie de l'Os Néolithique et de l'Âge des Métaux* 2, ed. H. Camps-Fabrer. Paris: Éditions du Centre National de la Recherche Scientifique, 9–25.
Stordeur, D., M. Benet, G. der Aprahamian & J.-C. Roux, 2000. Les bâtiments communautaires de Jerf el Ahmar et Mureybet Horizon PPNA (Syrie). *Paléorient* 26, 29–44.
Stott, A.W., R.P. Evershed, R.E.M. Hedges, C. Bronk Ramsey & M.J. Humm, 2002. Radiocarbon dating of single compounds isolated from pottery cooking vessel residues. *Radiocarbon* 43, 191–7.
Stuckenrath, R. & B. Lawn, 1969. University of Pennsylvania radiocarbon dates XI. *Radiocarbon* 11, 1150–62.
Stuckenrath, R. & E.K. Ralph, 1965. University of Pennsylvania radiocarbon dates VIII. *Radiocarbon* 7, 187–99.
Stuiver M., P.J. Reimer, E. Bard, J.W. Beck, G.S. Burr, K.A. Hughen, B. Kromer, G. McCormac, J. van der Plicht & M. Spurk, 1998. INTCAL98 Radiocarbon age calibration, 24000–0 cal BP. *Radiocarbon* 40, 1041–83.
Sullivan, A.P. & K.C. Rosen, 1985. Debitage analysis and archaeological interpretation. *American Antiquity* 50, 755–79.

Sun, S.S. & W.F. McDonagh, 1989. Chemical and isotopic systematics of oceanic basalts: implications for mantle composition and processes, in *Magmatism in the Ocean Basins*, eds. A.D. Saunders & M.J. Norry. (Special Publication 42.) London: Geological Society, 313–45.

Suponcic, S., 1998. Clay ball archive report. *Çatalhöyük 1998 Archive Report*. http://catal.arch.cam.ac.uk/catal/Archive_rep98/suponcic98.html.

Suponcic, S., 1999. Clays, clay balls & other clay objects, *Çatalhöyük 1999 Archive Report*. http://catal.arch.cam.ac.uk/catal/Archive_rep99/suponcic99.html.

Swiny, H. & S. Swiny, 1983. An anthropomorphic figurine from the Sotira area. *Report of the Department of Antiquities, Cyprus*, 56–9.

Swogger, J.G.H., 2001. *Çatalhöyük Online Image Archive*, http://catal.arch.cam.ac.uk/illustration.

Taçon, P.S.C., 1991. The power of stone: symbolic aspects of stone use and tool development in Western Arnhem Land, Australia. *Antiquity* 65, 192–207.

Talalay, L.E., 1987. Rethinking the function of clay figurine legs from Neolithic Greece: an argument by analogy. *American Journal of Archaeology* 91, 161–9.

Tanaka, J., 1980. *The San Hunter-gatherers of the Kalahari*. Tokyo: University of Tokyo Press.

Teit, J.A., 1930. Ethnobotany of the Thompson Indians of British Columbia, in *44th Annual Report of the Bureau of American Ethnology, 1927–1928*, ed. E.V. Steedman. Washington (DC): Smithsonian Institution, 441–522.

Testart, A., 1982. *Les chasseurs-cueilleurs ou l origine des inégalités*. Paris: Klincksieck.

Theophrastus *D.L. De Lapidibus*. Translation and commentary by D.F. Eichholz 1965. Oxford: Oxford University Press.

Thissen, L., 2002a. Time trajectories for the Neolithic of Central Anatolia, in *The Neolithic of Central Anatolia: Internal Developments and External Relations during the 9th–6th millennia cal* BC, eds. F. Gérard & L. Thissen. Istanbul: Eye Yayınları, 13–26.

Thissen, L., 2002b. Appendix I. The CANeW 14C databases. Anatolia, 10,000–5000 cal BC, in *The Neolithic of Central Anatolia: Internal Developments and External Relations during the 9th–6th millennia cal* BC, eds. F. Gérard & L. Thissen. Istanbul: Eye Yayınları, 299–337.

Thomas, J., 1996. *Time, Culture and Identity*. Cambridge: Cambridge University Press.

Thomas, N., 1991. *Entangled Objects: Exchange, Material Culture, and Colonisation in the Pacific*. Cambridge (MA): Harvard University Press.

Tilley, C., 1996. *An Ethnography of the Neolithic: Early Prehistoric Societies in Southern Scandinavia*. Cambridge: Cambridge University Press.

Tilley, C., 1999. *Metaphor and Material Culture*. Oxford: Blackwell.

Tixier, J., 1984. Le débitage par pression, in *Préhistoire de la Pierre Taillée 2: Économie du Débitage Laminaire: Technologie et Éxpérimentation. IIIe Table Ronde de Technologie Lithique Meudon-Bellevue, Octobre 1982*. Paris: Cercle de Recherches et d' Études Préhistoriques, 57–70.

Todd, I.A., 1966. Aşıklı Höyük: a Protoneolithic site in Central Anatolia. *Anatolian Studies* 16, 139–63.

Todd, I.A., 1976. *Çatal Hüyük in Perspective*. Menlo Park (CA): Cummings.

Todd, I.A., 1980. *The Prehistory of Central Anatolia I: the Neolithic Period*. (Studies in Mediterranean Archaeology 50.) Göteborg: Paul Åstroms Förlag.

Torraca, G., G. Chiari & G. Gullini, 1972. Report on mud brick preservation. *Mesopotamia* 7, 259–86.

Torrence, R., 1986. *Production and Exchange of Stone Tools*. Cambridge: Cambridge University Press.

Tringham, R. & M. Stevanović, 1990. Clay materials, in *Selevac: a Prehistoric Village in Yugoslavia*, ed. R. Tringham & D. Krstic. Los Angeles (CA): UCLA Institute of Archaeology Press, 323–68.

Tringham, R., B. Bruckner & B. Voytek, 1985. The Opovo Project: a study of socio-economic change in the Balkan Neolithic. *Journal of Field Archaeology* 12, 425–44.

Türe, F., 1999. *Auf Der Suche Nach Verschwundenen Zeiten: Die Ausgrabunen Des Deutschen Archäologischen Instituts in der Türkei*. Istanbul: Yapi Kredi Kültür Sanat Yayincilik.

Türkmenoğlu, A., A. Baysal, V. Toprak & C. Göncüoğlu, 2001a. Raw Material Types of Ground Stone from Çatalhöyük Neolithic Site in Turkey. Symposium on 'Raw Materials of Neolithic/Aneolithic Polished Stone Artefacts: Their Migration Paths in Europe', Geneva.

Türkmenoğlu, A., A. Baysal, V. Toprak & C. Göncüoğlu, 2001b. Raw material types of groundstones from Çatalhöyük Neolithic site in Turkey. *Slovak Geological Magazine* 7/4, 409–11.

Turner, V., 1969. *The Ritual Process: Structure and Anti-structure*. London: Routledge & Kegan Paul.

Tykot, R.H., 1996. Obsidian procurement and distribution in the central and western Mediterranean. *Journal of Mediterranean Archaeology* 9, 39–82.

Ucko, P.J., 1968. *Anthropomorphic Figurines of Predynastic Egypt and Neolithic Crete with Comparative Material from the Prehistoric Near East and Mainland Greece*. (Royal Anthropological Institute Occasional Paper 24.) London: Szmidla.

Umurtak, G., 2000. Neolitik ve Erken Kalkolitik Çağlar'da Burdur – Antalya Bölgesi Mühürcülüğü Üzerine Bazı Gözlemler. *Adalya* IV, 1–20.

Underbjerg, H., 1998. Obsidian microdebitage at Çatalhöyük. *Çatalhöyük 1998 Archive Report*. http://catal.arch.cam.ac.uk/catal/Archive_rep98/underbjerg98.html

Underbjerg, H., 1999. Knapping Technology and Microdebitage in the Neolithic Context. Unpublished Bachelors thesis, Carsten Niebuhr Institute, Copenhagen

Ursachi, V., 1990. Le dépôt d'objets de parure énéolithiques de Brad, Com. Negri, Dép. de Bacău, in *Le Paléolithique et le Néolithique de la Roumanie en Contexte Européen*, eds. V. Chirica & D. Monah. Iaşi: Institut d'Archéologie-Iacœi, 335–86.

van der Plicht, J. & H.J. Bruins, 2001. Radiocarbon dating in Near-Eastern contexts: confusion and quality control. *Radiocarbon* 43, 1155–66.

van Zeist, W. & G.J. de Roller, 1995. Plant remains from Aşıklı Höyük, a pre-pottery Neolithic site in central Anatolia. *Vegetation History and Archaeobotany* 4, 179–85.

Vandiver, P.B., 1987. Sequential slab construction: a conservative southwest Asiatic ceramic tradition, *c.* 7000–3000 BC. *Paléorient* 13, 9–35.

Vedder, J.F., 1996. Tools of the trade. *Cyprus American Archaeological Research Institute News* 12, 6–7.

Vedder, J.F., 2001. Grinding it out. Making a mirror the old fashioned way. *Archaeology Online News* April 2. http://www.archaeology.org/online/news/mirrors.html.

Vitelli, K.D., 1984. Greek Neolithic pottery by experiment, in *Pots and Potters: Current Approaches in Ceramic Archaeology*, ed. P. Rice. (Monograph 24.) Los Angeles (CA): UCLA Institute of Archaeology, 113–31.

Vitelli, K.D., 1993. *Franchthi Neolithic Pottery*. (Excavations at Franchthi Cave, Greece. Fascicule 8.) Bloomington (IN): Indiana University Press.

Vitelli, K.D., 1995. Pots, potters and the shaping of Greek Neolithic society, in *The Emergence of Pottery: Technology and Innovation in Ancient Societies,* eds. W.K. Barnett & J.W. Hoopes. Washington (DC): Smithsonian Institution Press, 55–64.

Voigt, M.M., 2000. Çatalhöyük in context: ritual at Early Neolithic sites in Central and Eastern Turkey, in *Life in Neolithic Farming Communities: Social Organization, Identity, and Differentiation,* ed. I. Kuijt. New York (NY): Kluwer Academic/Plenum, 253–93.

von Wickede, A., 1990. *Praehistorische Stempelglyptik in Vorderasien. MVS VI.* München: Profil Verlag.

Voruz, J.-L., 1985a. Des pendeloques néolithiques particulières: Les os longs perforés, in *Industrie de l'Os Néolithique et de l'Age des Métaux 3*, ed. H. Camps-Fabrer. Paris: Éditions du Centre National de la Recherche Scientifique, 123–62.

Voruz, J.-L., 1985b. Outillage osseux et dynamisme industriel dans le Néolithique jurassien, in *Industrie de l'Os Néolithique et de l'Age des Métaux 3*, ed. H. Camps-Fabrer. Paris: Éditions du Centre National de la Recherche Scientifique, 83–9.

Wagner, G.E., 1982. Testing flotation recovery rates. *American Antiquity* 47, 127–32.

Wandsnider, L., 1997. The roasted and the boiled: food composition and heat treatment with special emphasis on pit-hearth cooking. *Journal of Anthropological Archaeology* 16, 1–48.

Wang, Y., A.H. Jahren & R. Amundson, 1997. Biogenic carbonate in Hackberry (*Celtis*) endocarps: potential for 14C dating. *Quaternary Research* 47, 337–43.

Waterbolk, H.T., 1971. Working with radiocarbon dates. *Proceedings of the Prehistoric Society* 37, 15–33.

Waterbolk, H.T., 1987. Working with radiocarbon dates in SouthWest Asia, in *Chronologies in the Near East,* eds. O. Aurenche, J. Evin & F. Hours. (British Archaeological Reports, British Series 379.) Oxford: BAR, 39–59.

Watkins, T., 1996. Excavations at Pınarbaşı: the early stages, in *On the Surface: Çatalhöyük 1993–95*, ed. I. Hodder. (McDonald Institute Monographs; BIAA Monograph 22.) Cambridge: McDonald Institute for Archaeological Research; London: British Institute of Archaeology at Ankara, 47–57.

Watkins, T., 2003. The beginnings of architecture in southwest Asia: preliminaries. Paper presented at conference *Rethinking materiality*. McDonald Institute for Archaeological Research, Cambridge. [Published as Watkins, T., 2004. Architecture and 'theatres of memory' in the Neolithic of Southwest Asia, in *Rethinking Materiality: the Engagement of Mind with the Material World*, eds. E. DeMarrais, C. Gosden & C Renfrew. (McDonald Institute Monographs.) Cambridge: McDonald Institute for Archaeological Research, 97–106.]

Watson, P.J., 1979. *Archaeological Ethnography in Western Iran.* Tuscon (AZ): University of Arizona Press for the Wenner-Gren Foundation for Anthropological Research.

Weiner, A., 1992. *Inalienable Possessions: the Paradox of Keeping-While-Giving*. Berkeley (CA): University of California Press.

Weinstein-Evron, M., D. Kaufman & N. Bird-David, 2001. Rolling stones: basalt implements as evidence for trade/exchange in the Levantine Epipalaeolithic. *Mitekufat Haeven, Journal of the Israel Prehistoric Society* 31, 25–42.

Wendrich, W.Z., 1999. *The World According to Basketry: an Ethnoarchaeological Interpretation of Basketry Production in Egypt.* (CNWS Publication Series 83.) Leiden: CNWS.

Wendrich, W.Z., 2000. Basketry, in *Ancient Egyptian Materials and Technology*, ed. P.T. Nicholson & I. Shaw. Cambridge: Cambridge University Press, 254–67.

Wescott, D. (ed.), 1999. *Primitive Technology: a Book of Earth Skills from the Society of Primitive Technology*. Salt Lake City (UT): Gibbs-Smith.

Whittaker, J.C., 1994. *Flintknapping: Making and Understanding Stone Tools*. Austin (TX): University of Texas Press.

Wiessner, P. & W. Schiefenhövel, 1996. *Food and the Status Quest: an Interdisciplinary Perspective*. Oxford: Berghahn.

Wilke, P.J. & L.A. Quintero, 1994. Naviform core-and-blade technology: assemblage character as determined by replicative experiments, in *Neolithic Chipped Stone Industries of the Fertile Crescent. Proceedings of the First Workshop on PPN Chipped Lithic Industries,* eds. H.G. Gebel & S.K. Kozlowski. (Studies in Early Near Eastern Production, Subsistence, and Environment 1.) Berlin: Ex Oriente, 33–60.

Wilkinson, C.F., 1999. *Fire on the Plateau: Conflict and Endurance in the American Southwest*. Washington (DC): Island Press/Shearwater.

Winnicott, D.W., 1958. *Collected Papers*. London: Tavistock Publications.

Wobst, H., 1974. Boundary conditions for Paleolithic social systems. *American Antiquity* 39, 147–78.

Wobst, H., 1976. Locational relationships in Paleolithic society. *Journal of Human Evolution* 5, 49–58.

Woldring, H. & R. Cappers, 2001. The origin of the 'wild orchards' of Central Anatolia. *Turkish Journal of Botany* 25, 1–9.

Woodburn, J., 1980. Hunters and gatherers today and reconstruction of the past, in *Soviet and Western Anthropology*, ed. E. Gellner. London: Duckworth, 95–117.

Wright, G.A., 1969. *Obsidian Analyses and Prehistoric Near Eastern Trade: 7500 to 3500* BC. (Anthropological Papers 37.) Ann Arbor (MI): Museum of Anthropology, University of Michigan.

Wright, K., 1991. The origins and development of ground stone assemblages in late Pleistocene southwest Asia. *Paléorient* 17, 19–45.

Wright, K., 1992a. A classification system for ground stone tools from the prehistoric Levant. *Paléorient* 18, 53–81.

Wright, K., 1992b. Ground Stone Assemblage Variations and Subsistence Strategies in the Levant, 22,000 to 5500 BP. Unpublished PhD Dissertation, Yale University, Department of Anthropology.

Wright, K., 1993. Early Holocene ground stone assemblages in the Levant. *Levant* 25, 93–111.

Wright, K., 1994. Ground stone tools and hunter-gatherer subsistence in southwest Asia: implications for the transition to farming. *American Antiquity* 59, 238–63.

Wright, K., 1998. Dhuweila: Ground stone, in *The Harra and the Hamad: Excavations and Surveys in Eastern Jordan*, vol, 1, ed. A.V.G. Betts. (Sheffield Archaeological Monographs 9.) Sheffield: Sheffield Academic Press, 121–34.

Wright, K., 2000. The social origins of cooking and dining in early villages of western Asia. *Proceedings of the Prehistoric Society* 66, 89–121.

Wright, K., in prep. a. *The Origins of Cooking, Dining and Cuisine in the Middle East.* Oxford: Oxford University Press.

Wright, K., in prep. b. Ground-stone technology and Late Palaeolithic adaptations in the eastern Jordanian desert, in *Beyond the Fertile Crescent: Epipalaeolithic and Neolithic Communities of the Azraq Basin,* ed. A. Garrard. (Monograph Series.) London: British Academy.

Wright, K., in prep. c. Neolithic ground stone assemblages from the Azraq Basin and their implications, in *Beyond the Fertile Crescent: Epipalaeolithic and Neolithic Communities of the Azraq Basin,* ed. A. Garrard. (Monograph Series.) London: British Academy.

Wright, K., in prep. d. The Beidha ground stone assemblage: Technologies, space and activities, in *The Neolithic Village of Beidha: Architecture, Occupation History and Spatial Organization,* ed. B. Byrd. (Monograph Series.) Oxford: British Academy.

Wright, K. & A. Garrard, 2003. Social identities and the expansion of stone bead-making in Neolithic Western Asia: new evidence from Jordan. *Antiquity* 77, 267–84.

Wright, K., N. Qadi, K. Ibrahim, & H. Mustafa, in prep. Ground stone tools and vessels from Abu Hamid, in *Fouilles à Abou Hamid (Jordanie),* eds. G. Dollfus & Z. Kafafi. Paris: Éditions Recherche sur les Civilisations.

Yakar, J., 1991. *Prehistoric Anatolia: the Neolithic Transformation and the Early Chalcolithic Period.* (Monograph Series 9.) Tel Aviv: Institute of Archaeology Tel Aviv University.

Yakar, J., 1994. *Prehistoric Anatolia: the Neolithic Transformation and the early Chalcolithic period. Supplement No. 1.* (Monograph Series 9a.) Tel Aviv: Institute of Archaeology Tel Aviv University.

Yıldırım, S., 1999. *Çanak Çömlezsiz Neolitik Dönemde ok ve Mizrak Uçlarinin Gelişimi Aşıklı Höyük Örneği.* Yüksek Lisans Tezi, T.C. İstanbul Üniversitesi Sosyal Bilimler Enstitüsü Edebiyat Fakültesi Prehistorya Anabilim Dalı.